MODERN COMMUNICATIONS LAW

MODERN COMMUNICATIONS LAW

Donald E. Lively

PRAEGER

New York
Westport, Connecticut
London

Library of Congress Cataloging-in-Publication Data

Lively, Donald E., 1947–
    Modern communications law / Donald E. Lively.
      p. cm.
    Includes index.
    ISBN 0–275–93735–6 (lib. bdg. : alk. paper)
    1. Mass media—Law and legislation—United States—Cases.
  2. Press law—United States—Cases. 3. Telecommunication—Law and
legislation—United States—Cases. I. Title.
KF2750.A7L58   1991
343.7309′9—dc20
[347.30399]   90–7504

Library of Congress Catalog Card Number: 90–7504
ISBN: 0–275–93735–6

First published in 1991

Praeger Publishers, One Madison Avenue, New York, NY 10010
An imprint of Greenwood Publishing Group, Inc.

Printed in the United States of America

The paper used in this book complies with the
Permanent Paper Standard issued by the National
Information Standards Organization (Z39.48–1984).

10 9 8 7 6 5 4 3 2 1

To my wife Pam and to Rico with love

CONTENTS

PREFACE

Communications law like the communications industry has evolved at an exponential pace over the course of this century. Media that were nonexistent one hundred years ago, much less when the First Amendment was drafted, not only have surfaced but have become dominant sources of information for the public. Official response to the expansion, concentration, and electronification of the press and the merging capabilities of all media have been resounding and often confounding. As modern media continue to emerge and the capabilities of existing media develop even further, the law has become increasingly detailed, complex, and unwieldy. Many textbooks continue to approach the subject from a perspective that, although timely a decade or two ago, is for practical purposes light-years removed from the modern communication universe. A central aim of this book, therefore, is to consider media law in the broadest and timeliest sense. Telephone communications, which implicate virtually the entire citizenry as both information sources and recipients, are accorded the attention they deserve but have been denied in other textbooks. New media, especially cable, are afforded substantial attention. More established media, including print and broadcasting, are given their due but with the freshest possible gloss.

The book incorporates several unique features designed to enhance teaching and learning efficiency. The selection of cases and other primary materials, which are reproduced in edited form, reflects a judgment of the subject matter which lends itself best to classroom discussion. Although narrative is tightly edited, extensive annotations provide direction to sources that afford more detailed examination of particular subjects. Pinpoint citations are intended to enhance the book's utility for research and reference purposes. A final innovation is the incorporation of case summaries preceding major court opinions. The synopses are not included as a substitute for or shortcut around the cases. Rather, they are offered as a means of affording first-time readers a general framework and opportunity for familiarization which should make study of the cases themselves more fruitful and enhance the quality of class discussion.

Special thanks are owed to Nancy Bedard, Ernest Bollinger, Charles Butler, Tammy

Johns, Grant Keune, Karen McCrudden, Denise McNulty, Frank Simmons, Dave Webster, and Greg Weinman for their valuable research assistance. Extra special thanks go to Fran Molnar, who facilitated the smooth production of the project and kept her humor even at times when she would have been justified in losing it. John Harney and Lynn Flint, as acquisitions editor and production editor, have contributed immeasurably to this book's quality. As consistent sources of encouragement, facilitation and support, they have been truly indispensable parties. Finally, I am grateful to the faculty at the University of Toledo College of Law who continue to maintain an enviable climate refreshingly untouched by the pretensions of academia but nonetheless graced by persons of eminence and excellence.

MODERN COMMUNICATIONS LAW

INTRODUCTION: MEDIA AND COMMUNICATIONS POLICY PAST, PRESENT AND FUTURE

A dominant characteristic of modern communications is the media's penchant for continuous self-redefinition. Law in general has a dynamic quality insofar as it is subject to adaption, extension, and revision. Fluidity is doubly evinced by communications law, given the constantly and rapidly expanding perimeters of the field it governs. Each century in the nation's experience has ended with media forms, structure, and capabilities unanticipated at the outset. Although the terms of the First Amendment have remained fixed, the multiplication of new realities and consequential concerns with their nature and effect have accounted for a particularly active competition between regulatory premises and constitutional principles.

For the communications universe, invention of the printing press was the functional equivalent of the big bang. The capacity to reproduce the printed word voluminously and efficiently was the crucial facilitator of the first mass medium. Modern technology has engendered new communications methodologies which disseminate information to mass audiences not just in print but by image and sound. The emergence of electronic media has vastly expanded the communications galaxy. In enlarging and reconstituting the shape of the press generally, new instrumentalities of communication have begotten media-specific regulation[1] and significant constitutional variances.[2] As newer methodologies have appeared, the tendency of the law has been to identify structural differences as a predicate for creating media-specific rules. With capabilities increasingly merging and distinctions becoming more blurred, however, it is the functional characteristic of propagating information that yet may emerge as the dominant trait shared by all media.

Modern media bear scant resemblance to the press which existed at the time of the republic's founding. Newspapers had begun to emerge as a significant force during the first half of the eighteenth century.[3] The press's emergence owed much to commercial and business interests, which sought effective vehicles for promoting their goods and services. It was the political turmoil that eventually led to the American Revolution, however, that secured the newspaper's position as an enduring and significant institution. Because partisanship was the primary force behind publication, rumor, fabrication, and outright prevarication tended to be norms rather than exceptions. Opinion merged with fact, as advocacy and persuasion rather than objectivity were operative standards.

Despite the press's central role in securing American independence and the prominent position of freedom of the press in the Bill of Rights,[4] the historical record provides scant evidence with respect to the original purpose of the First Amendment. The notes of James Madison, who is credited for the nature and shape of the First Amendment, suggest that precious little time was devoted to discussing press liberty. Such disregard, however, may be less an indication of deprecation than a presumption that freedom of the press was adequately secured. What eventually became a First Amendment right already had been set forth in the constitutions of most states.[5] Although many framers originally seemed to find no need for constitutionally protecting the freedom of expression, a faction of the convention insisted upon a specific guarantee and managed to swing public opinion to its side. The First Amendment, along with the remaining Bill of Rights, thus was added to the document as a concession calculated to ensure the charter's ratification.

Freedom of the press was a general concept which was passed on from Great Britain to the colonies. It was the constitutionalization of the principle that represented a distinctive American twist. Press freedom in Great Britain even today is a function of the common law and Acts of Parliament. The importance of the press for the nation's future was graphically demonstrated by its central role in effectuating the constitution as basic law. Ratification of the document was anything but a foregone conclusion. What proved critical to the ultimate investment of thirteen fractious states in a unifying charter and strong central government was a series of newspaper articles that later

would be assembled and denominated generally as *The Federalist*.[6] The Federalist case trumpeted by partisan publications proved persuasive enough to secure the constitution. The experience was an early example of the mass media's actual and potential influence.

The press, as it existed at the time of the First Amendment's drafting, was infant in structure and capability compared with modern media. Although new communications methodologies have expanded the media universe beyond what existed when the constitution was framed, the principle of press freedom has not traveled coextensively. As electronic dissemination of information increasingly has become dominant, the functional breadth of the First Amendment as originally applied has become correspondingly narrower. For older media relying on the printed word, maximum constitutional freedom consistently has been afforded. Subsequently developed media, including motion pictures, radio, television, and cable may have become more pervasive and dominant than their predecessors, but their liberty consciously has been qualified.[7] Undifferentiated security of the press which existed two centuries ago thus has devolved into a circumstantially variable guarantee. Because the media universe has expanded, but maximum constitutional protection is afforded only the print media, the ambit of freedom of the press has narrowed relative to the media's development and expansion.

Changes in and additions to the ways in which information is disseminated have been a function of technological progress. Through most of the nation's first century, mass communication was the product of small enterprises built around the printing press. During the past century, electronic media have proliferated, and concentrated ownership has become a characteristic of all media.[8] As control over public discourse has passed from the individual to increasingly remote editorial decision makers and as the media have become major economic powers, it is not entirely surprising that regulation rather than freedom has become a dominant governing impulse. Responsive concerns in assessing the desirability of official intervention include whether it can promote the ends of expressive pluralism as effectively as unqualified press freedom and whether it is responsive to the even newer or pending realities of decentralization and audience fragmentation that may characterize future media. Given the prominence of newer media in contemporary society, it is no exaggeration to assert that the formulation of policy toward them is as critical now as the standards for their antecedents were two centuries ago.

NOTES _____

1. *See* Chapter 2 of this book.
2. *See* Chapters 8–11 of this book.
3. *See* E. EMERY, THE PRESS AND AMERICA 13 (1971).
4. *See* U.S. CONST., amend. I.
5. *See* E. EMERY, THE PRESS AND AMERICA 55–56.
6. *The Federalist* articles originally were published in a New York newspaper and reprinted throughout the country prior to the constitution's ratification.
7. *See, e.g.,* Red Lion Broadcasting Co. v. Federal Communications Commission, 395 U.S. 367, 386–87 (1969); Joseph Burstyn, Inc. v. Wilson, 343 U.S. 495, 503 (1952).
8. *See* Miami Herald Publishing Co. v. Tornillo, 418 U.S. 241, 248–51 (1974).

Part One

THE PROPERTIES AND CONTEXT OF MEDIA

Chapter 1

GENERAL CONSTITUTIONAL CONSIDERATIONS

I. DEFINING THE PRESS

Charting the contours of press freedom is a process that is complicated by the difficulty of establishing a satisfactory definition of the institution itself. Efforts to define the press have traveled three basic avenues. The press has been described respectively in institutional, functional, and registry terms. None of those approaches, however, is without significant problems.

An institutional definition, advanced by Justice Stewart, essentially would regard the press as the industry whose business it is to publish. Stewart suggested that

> the Free Press guarantee is, in essence, a *structural* provision of the constitution. Most of the other provisions in the Bill of Rights protect specific liberties or specific rights of individuals: freedom of speech, freedom of worship, the right to counsel, the privilege against compulsory self-incrimination, to name a few. In contrast, the Free Press Clause extends protection to an institution. The publishing business is, in short, the only organized private business that is given explicit constitutional protection.[1]

Stewart's depiction of the press in a structural sense, at least in part, avoids concep-

tualization of freedom of the press synonymously with freedom of expression. Although publishers like all other persons are guaranteed the latter pursuant to the free speech clause, Stewart maintained that interpretation of freedom of speech and of the press as coextensive would be a constitutional redundancy.[2] The institutional definition of the press clearly identifies speech and media as distinct notions and predicates constitutional protection of the media upon a discrete footing. However, the focus upon structure has been criticized as dangerously narrow. Excluded from the purview of an institutional press may be the artist, scientist, and novelist. Even the individual pamphleteer whose partisan works may have fit squarely within the ambit of the press, at the time the constitution was framed, might not qualify for institutional standing. Especially insofar as classification of the press may determine special rights of access[3] or privilege,[4] the constitutional status of an individual or entity is of considerable threshold significance. Distinguishing speech and press thus may have more than merely semantical import.

An alternative view of the press regards it as any methodology for communicating information or opinion to the public. Largely in response to the institutional definition's potential for "conferring special [constitutional] status on a limited group,"[5] former Chief Justice Burger found that there was "no difference between the right of those who seek to disseminate ideas by way of a newspaper and those who give lectures or speeches and seek to enlarge the audience by publication and wide dissemination.... [T]he First Amendment does not "belong" to any definable category of persons or entities: It belongs to all who exercise its freedoms."[6]

Not surprisingly, given Burger's adoption of a functional definition of the press, he was hostile toward recognition of any special freedom or rights of the institutional media. Oddly, however, it was Justice Stewart who supported opinions denying the press a right of access to prisons[7] and Chief Justice Burger who afforded the press access rights that were special in effect if not letter.[8] Unlike the institutional definition, which is criticized for its narrowness, the focus upon function is objected to for its expansiveness.[9] Because of its breadth, the functional definition of the press may be indistinguishable from speech. By thus making the freedom of speech and press clauses redundant, it tends to effectuate what the institutional concept endeavors to avoid.

The difficulty if not impossibility of satisfactorily identifying the common character and associative traits of the press may enhance the appeal of merely itemizing the media which constitute the press. In discussing liberty of the press, some years ago, the Court described the press itself in terms of newspapers, periodicals, pamphlets, and leaflets.[10] Although presenting its characterization in a sweeping rather than restrictive tone,[11] the rendition demonstrated the significant dangers inherent in what amounts to a registry definition. Conspicuously missing from the Court's list were motion pictures, which effectively had been denied press status at the time,[12] and radio and television, whose status for constitutional purposes was then largely uncertain.[13] The problem with composing a definition akin to a laundry list, therefore, is the absence of any standard for determining qualification and consequent risk of subjectivity.

Justice Brennan, in an extrajudicial commentary, has suggested that both structural and functional conceptualizations are relevant but that the utility of either depends upon circumstances. Insofar as the press operates in a "public spokesman" role, Brennan would find that it "readily lends itself to the rhetoric of absolutism."[14] He cautions against exclusive reliance upon a spokesperson model, however, because it creates the mistaken impression that the First Amendment is merely concerned with speech and protects only self-expression.[15] Brennan suggests that the constitution "also protects the structure of communications necessary for the existence of our democracy."[16] As a consequence, it is necessary to protect the press not only when it speaks out but also when it performs the associated tasks of collecting and disseminating news.[17] Unlike a focus upon the public spokesperson function, analysis of the structural role would require balancing of functional inhibitions against competing societal interests.[18] Whether the press can be regulated because of what it says or with respect to its newsgathering role requires two distinct forms of review, Brennan counsels, with the former tending toward absolutism and the latter always requiring balancing.[19]

No matter how the press is defined, exclusion from any official denomination of it has profound consequences. The original depiction of motion pictures as "a business pure and simple,...not to be regarded... as part of the press,"[20] effectively left the medium without any First Amendment protection. The further failure of the Court to recognize a constitutional interest in film as a medium is a forceful example of the free press clause's independent significance, as well as an illustration of definitional importance. Government as a consequence was free to regulate the medium in ways that would be intolerable if the same expression was communicated by print.[21] Censorship boards in the South, for instance, capitalized upon the constitutional void to ban any film at odds with law and custom that did not countenance scenes of racial mixing or suggesting equality.[22]

More recently the question of what the press comprises arose in the context of whether an investment newsletter constituted a "bona fide" publication that would be immune from regulation by the federal securities laws.[23] Such a publication conceivably fits within the bounds of the institutional, functional, and registry models. To the extent an investment newsletter is the output of a publishing business, it falls within the institutional definition. Its role in informing the public also satisfies the criteria of the functional definition. Determination of bona fide status, however, represents a subjectivity problem akin to that associated with whether any medium falls within a registry definition of the press. Uncertainty of standards and unpredictability of results suggest that the analytical process remains capable of treacherous consequences.

II. ORIGINS AND NATURE OF REGULATORY CONCERN

The transformation of the press from an essentially print medium run by individual entrepreneurs to a concentrated and diversified information industry has profoundly affected public perceptions of the press and consequent policy toward it. Early concern with the role and influence of mass media was articulated in the late nineteenth century by Louis Brandeis. If the print media's

technological capabilities had been more developed at the time of the constitution's drafting, they too conceivably might have been subject to official attitudes now reserved for newer media. The advent of photojournalism drastically altered the performance and perceptions of the media by the beginning of the twentieth century, as newspapers and magazines increasingly became regarded as instrumentalities of intrusion, impropriety, and indecency.[24] For Brandeis, the media which in 1789 were primarily vehicles for partisan debate had become purveyors of idle gossip catering to prurient tastes.[25] He thus expressed revulsion over increasing journalistic commitment to sensationalism and entertainment.[26] Such emphasis troubled Brandeis because, by displacing space that otherwise could be afforded "matters of genuine community concerns," it inverted public priorities.[27] His advancement of a right of privacy in significant part constituted a proposed regulatory solution for controlling perceived media excesses.

Brandeis' concern over the functioning of the press has proved to be anything but unique. Reduced to its essentials, it seems to reflect primarily a reaction based upon personal taste. To enforce the preferences and to protect the sensibilities with which he identified, Brandeis' right of privacy would have operated to place certain subject matter off limits.[28] Although declaring gossip to be the primary target of his enmity, the constitutional problems in effectuating official control of it are manifest. Gossip as a category of expression probably is impossible to define without encountering problems of vagueness and overbreadth. Reports of a married politician's extramarital sexual liaisons, for instance, might qualify both as intrusive gossip that titillates and political speech that facilitates informed voting. Still, the type of qualitative concerns expressed by Brandeis have been a consistent source of regulatory rationales and even jurisprudence supporting official control calculated to civilize the level of public discourse.[29] The proposal of a right of privacy thus may be regarded as one of the first important responses to changes in the nature, focus, and influence of the mass media.

Less than half a century after Brandeis articulated his distress over the modern media's coursing, Congress enacted a broad regulatory scheme for radio and television that required broadcasters to operate in the public interest. The concept of broadcasters as public trustees might be viewed in part as an extension and formalization of Brandeis' notion that the media should focus upon matters of "genuine community concern." In subsequent years, a chairman of the Federal Communications Commission characterized television as "a vast wasteland" and defined the public interest in terms of promoting the "character, citizenship and intellectual capacity of the people."[30] More recently, the broadcast of indecent and offensive language has been subject to less charitable constitutional review than would be the norm for other media or speech.[31] Contemporary depictions of programming as being akin to allowing "a pig in the parlor"[32] or characterizations to the effect it is "disgusting" or "garbage"[33] suggest too an effort to elevate the quality of or sanitize public discourse. Such an objective, no matter how well intentioned, invites criticism that it is elitist and insensitive to the realities and imperatives of cultural pluralism. Public interest can be defined synonymously with popularity or tolerance as easily as it can be tied to notions of what is healthy or educational. It is the subjective spin of Brandeis or his philosophical progeny that enables a concept such as the public interest to operate as an intrusive regulatory predicate. For

critics, a gloss of that nature may call to mind Alexis de Tocqueville's warning that the greatest threat to democratic institutions is well-intentioned policies with poorly foreseeable consequences.[34]

Even before the emergence of broadcasting as a dominant mass medium, the sentiments expressed by Brandeis had seeped into communications jurisprudence. In *Mutual Film Corp. v. Industrial Commission of Ohio*,[35] the Supreme Court considered a challenge to a state law providing for censorship of motion pictures.[36] Although the motion picture company alleged only violations of state speech and publication guarantees,[37] the Court's observations and opinion applied logically to First Amendment interests as well. Despite recognizing the role of film as a means for expressing opinion, disseminating information, and educating,[38] the Court determined that motion pictures offered a "mere representation of events, of ideas and sentiments published and known."[39] Disregarding the fact that publishers were protected by freedom of the press, the Court focused instead upon what it characterized as the medium's power to promote evil—a capability enhanced by its "attractiveness and manner of exhibition."[40] For the first time, therefore, an interest was identified that would permit content regulation of the media. Freedom of the press interests were avoided only in a technical or legalistic sense, as the Court excluded motion pictures from the purview of the press.[41] Not until the middle of the century was the *Mutual Film* decision overturned[42] and motion pictures "included in the press whose freedom is guaranteed by the First Amendment."[43] Even then, concerns with a particular medium's effect if no longer a basis for constitutional deprivation remained a predicate for constitutional dilution.[44]

Mutual Film Corp. v. Industrial Commission of Ohio, 236 U.S. 230 (1915)

An appeal was brought for an interlocutory injunction that would bar enforcement of a state law creating a board of censors for motion picture films.

The business of the complainant and the description, use, object and effect of motion pictures and other films contained in the bill, stated narratively, are as follows: Complainant is engaged in the business of purchasing, selling and leasing films, the films being produced in other States than Ohio, and in European and other foreign countries. The film consists of a series of instantaneous photographs or positive prints of action upon the stage or in the open. By being projected upon a screen with great rapidity there appears to the eye an illusion of motion. They depict dramatizations of standard novels, exhibiting many subjects of scientific interest, the properties of matter, the growth of the various forms of animal and plant life, and explorations and travels; also events of historical and current interest—the same events which are described in words and by photographs in newspapers, weekly periodicals, magazines and other publications, of which photographs are promptly secured a few days after the events which they depict happen; thus regularly furnishing and publishing news through the medium of motion pictures under the name of "Mutual Weekly." Nothing is depicted of a harmful or immoral character....

The board has demanded of complainant that it submit its films to censorship and threatens, unless complainant complies with the demand, to arrest any and all persons who seek to place on exhibition any film not so censored or approved by the censor congress on and after November 4, 1913, the date to which the act was extended. It is physically impossible to comply with such demand and physically impossible for the board to censor the films with such rapidity as to enable complainant to proceed with its business, and the delay consequent upon such examination would cause great and irreparable injury to such business and would involve a multiplicity of suits....

Mr. Justice McKenna, after stating the case as above, delivered the opinion of the court.

The ... contention is that the statute violates the freedom of speech and publication guaranteed by the Ohio constitution. In its discussion counsel have gone into a very elaborate description of moving picture exhibitions and their many useful purposes as graphic expressions of opinion and sentiments, as exponents of policies, as teachers of science and history, as useful, interesting, amusing, educational and moral. And a list of the "campaigns," as counsel call them, which may be carried on is given. We may concede the praise. It is not questioned by the Ohio statute and under its comprehensive description, "campaigns" of an infinite variety may be conducted. Films of a "moral, educational or amusing and harmless character shall be passed and approved" are the words of the statute. No exhibition, therefore, or "campaign" of complainant will be prevented if its pictures have those qualities. Therefore, however missionary of opinion films are or may become, however educational or entertaining, there is no impediment to their value or effect in the Ohio statute. But they may be used for evil, and against that possibility the statute was enacted. The power of amusement and, it may be, education, the audiences they assemble, not of women alone nor of men alone, but together, not of adults only, but of children, make them the more insidious in corruption by a pretense of worthy purpose or if they should degenerate from worthy purpose. Indeed, we may go beyond that possibility. They take their attraction from the general interest, eager and wholesome it may be, in their subjects, but a prurient interest may be excited and appealed to. Besides, there are some things which should not have pictorial representation in public places and to all audiences. And not only the State of Ohio but other States have considered it to be in the interest of the public morals and welfare to supervise moving picture exhibitions. We would have to shut our eyes to the facts of the world to regard the precaution unreasonable or the legislation to effect it a mere wanton interference with personal liberty.

We do not understand that a possibility of an evil employment of films is denied, but a freedom from the censorship of the law and a precedent right of exhibition are asserted, subsequent responsibility only, it is contended, being incurred for abuse. In other words, as we have seen, the constitution of Ohio is invoked and an exhibition of films is assimilated to the freedom of speech, writing and publication assured by that instrument and for the abuse of which only is there responsibility, and, it is insisted, that as no law may be passed "to restrain the liberty of speech or of the press," no law may be passed to subject moving pictures to censorship before their exhibition.

We need not pause to dilate upon the freedom of opinion and its expression, and whether by speech, writing or printing. They are too certain to need discussion—of such conceded value as to need no supporting praise. Nor can there be any doubt of their breadth nor that their underlying safeguard is, to use the words of another, "that opinion is free and that conduct alone is amenable to the law."

Are moving pictures within the principle, as it is contended they are? They, indeed, may be mediums of thought, but so are many things. So is the theatre, the circus, and all other shows and spectacles, and their performances may be thus brought by the like reasoning under the same immunity from repression or supervision as the public press,—made the same agencies of civil liberty.

Counsel have not shrunk from this extension of their contention and cite a case in this court where the title of drama was accorded to pantomime; and such and other spectacles are said by counsel to be publications of ideas, satisfying the definition of the dictionaries,—that is, and we quote counsel, a means of making or announcing publicly something that otherwise might have remained private or unknown,—and this being peculiarly the purpose and effect of moving pictures they come directly, it is contended, under the protection of the Ohio constitution.

The first impulse of the mind is to reject the contention. We immediately feel that the argument is wrong or strained which extends the guaranties of free opinion and speech to the multitudinous shows which are advertised on the billboards of our cities and towns and which regards them as emblems of public safety, to use the words of Lord Camden, quoted by counsel, and which seeks to bring motion pictures and other spectacles into practical and legal similitude to a free press and liberty of opinion.

The judicial sense supporting the common sense of the country is against the contention. As pointed out by the District Court, the police power is familiarly exercised in granting or withholding licenses for theatrical performances as a means of their regulation. The court cited the following cases: *Marmet v. State,* 45 Ohio, 63, 72, 73; *Baker v. Cincinnati,* 11 Ohio St. 534; *Commonwealth v. McGann,* 213 Massachusetts, 213, 215; *People v. Steele,* 231 Illinois, 340, 344, 345.

The exercise of the power upon moving picture exhibitions has been sustained. *Greenberg v. Western Turf Ass'n,* 148 California, 126; *Laurelle v. Bush,* 17 Cal. App. 409; *State v. Loden,* 117 Maryland, 373; *Block v. Chicago,* 239 Illinois, 251; *Higgins v. Lacroix,* 119 Minnesota, 145. See also *State v. Morris,* 76 Atl. Rep. 479; *People v. Gaynor,* 137 N. Y. S. 196, 199; *McKenzie v. McClellan,* 116 N. Y. S. 645, 646.

It seems not to have occurred to anybody in the cited cases that freedom of opinion was repressed in the exertion of the power which was illustrated. The rights of property were only considered as involved. It cannot be put out of view that the exhibition of moving pictures is a business pure and simple, originated and conducted for profit, like other spectacles, not to be regarded, nor intended to be regarded by the Ohio constitution, we think, as part of the press of the country or as organs of public opinion. They are mere representations of events, of ideas and sentiments published and known, vivid, useful and entertaining no doubt, but, as we have said, capable of evil, having power for it, the greater because of their attractiveness and manner of exhibition. It was this capability and power, and it may be in experience of them, that induced the State of Ohio, in addition to prescribing penalties for immoral exhibitions, as it does in its Criminal Code, to require censorship before exhibition, as it does by the act under review. We cannot regard this as beyond the power of government.

It does not militate against the strength of these considerations that motion pictures may be used to amuse and instruct in other places than theatres—in churches, for instance, and in Sunday schools and public schools. Nor are we called upon to say on this record whether such exceptions would be within the provisions of the statute nor to anticipate that it will be so declared by the state courts or so enforced by the state officers.

Like many well-intentioned ideas subject to close scrutiny, notions that the media should address matters of genuine community concern or otherwise function in the public interest have a dangerous potential. What may be advanced as culturally uplifting by Brandeis may, from a competing perspective, rate as culturally imperialistic. Brandeis' displeasure with and expectations of the media in large part translate into an expression of subjective preference.[15] Such claims to the public interest, however, are no more or less legitimate than a definition attuned to competing cultural values or synonymous with raw popularity. Pursuant to any such standard of subjectivity, interests of diversity and pluralism may be endangered. Whether denominated as gossip, sensationalism, or indecency, classification of expression as a prelude to regulation implicates vagueness and overbreadth problems. Standards for elevating or purifying public discourse, no less than facially restrictive regulation, necessitate an enforcement mechanism. To the extent that perimeters of acceptability are officially set, and regardless of regulatory motive, editorial autonomy is put at risk.

III. STATE ACTION

All media are governed by one of three distinct regulatory models. The press which existed at the time the First Amendment was drafted receives the fullest measure of constitutional protection. Freedom of the press is closest to absolute, therefore, for the print media.[46] At the opposite pole, common carriage is subject to policies that facilitate universal service on equal terms. Nondiscriminatory access, rather then editorial autonomy, is the focus of common carrier regulation.[47] Between the extremes of maximum and nonexistent editorial autonomy exists the regulatory structure for what is now the dominant medium. Governance of broadcasting, as well as of cable casting, borrows from both the print and common carrier models. Although broadcasters may be obligated to serve the public interest, and thus to satisfy an array of subsidiary requirements as a condition for licensing, they also maintain a measure of editorial freedom.[48] Cable casters too may be required, as part of their franchising agreement, to fulfill obligations that legally could not be impressed upon the print media.[49]

All newer media are subject to regulatory schemes that insinuate the government into the editorial function. Some also are subject to official technical, financial, character and other structural standards. Given the pervasive nature of such regulation, the argument exists that such media "are instrumentalities of the Government for First Amendment purposes."[50] Acceptance of the notion that broadcasting or cable casting constitutes state action would have significant consequences for even the qualified editorial freedom that currently exists for those media. The First Amendment is a restraint not on private persons but on government.[51] As the Court has observed, were it to find government action, "few licensee decisions on the content of broadcasts or the process of editorial evaluation would escape constitutional scrutiny."[52] Because government is prohibited from discriminating on the basis of content, a finding of state action might require media operators to afford the public access to facilities and transmission. Since equal access is a hallmark of common carriage,[53] state action is a less significant issue with respect to telephone or telegraph service. Precisely because such a requirement would reduce cable to the status of a common carrier, the Court invalidated regulations that would have effectuated access terms.[54] A general finding of state action nonetheless might set as a constitutional requirement what is mostly impermissible now as a regulatory objective.

In *Columbia Broadcasting System, Inc. v. Democratic National Committee,*[55] the Court considered the notion that editorial decisions of broadcasters constitute state action. The court of appeals had determined that broadcasters were instrumentalities of the government because they are awarded use of the public domain and are regulated as "proxies" or "fiduciaries of the people."[56] Although recognizing the significant government controls upon broadcasting, a plurality opinion authored by Chief Justice Burger rejected the state action argument and expressed serious concern with the implications of a contrary finding. The Burger plurality noted broadcasting's emergence as "a vital [and dominant] part of our system of communications."[57] It also intimated reluctance to undermine further the qualified First Amendment freedom of broadcasters, given Congress' adoption of a regulatory scheme reflecting "a desire to maintain for licensees, so far as consistent with necessary regulation, a traditional journalistic role."[58] The opinion identified mixed responsibilities that officially charged broadcasters with public trustee obligations for fairly and objectively informing the public and delegated to government the function of " 'overseer' and ultimate arbiter and guardian of the public interest."[59] It nonetheless refused to equate the association with a partnership, symbiotic relationship, or any other tie that would rise to the level of state action.[60]

Justice Brennan, in contrast, adverted to prior determinations that "[c]onduct that is formally 'private' may become so entwined with government policies or so impregnated with a government character as to become subject to the constitutional limitations placed upon [governmental] actions."[61] In pressing the case for state action, Brennan emphasized "the public nature of the airwaves, the governmentally created preferred status of broadcast licensees, the pervasive federal regulation of broadcast programming, and the [Federal Communications] Commission's specific approval of the challenged broadcaster policy."[62] More particularly, he noted that ownership and ultimate control of the electromagnetic spectrum is vested in the public[63] and that consequent regulatory power is an established denotation of governmental involvement.[64] The centrality of the government's role was further evinced, from Brennan's perspective, by the dependence of licensees upon an official grant of broadcasting rights and privileges.[65] Although recognizing that regulation of an industry by itself had never been sufficient to establish state action,[66] he noted the "elaborate," "automatic," "continuing," and "pervasive" nature of broadcast controls. He also reiterated the court of appeals' observation that "[a]lmost no other regulated private business—is so intimately bound by government."[67]

Although a majority was not formed in support of or in opposition to the principle that broadcasting constituted state action, Justice Douglas identified the consequences that would follow if it were found to exist. Douglas noted that public broadcasting in particular is a creature of Congress, managed by a directorate chosen by the president and Senate, and thus comparable to having "the United States own[ing] and manag[ing] a prestigious newspaper like the *New York Times, Washington Post,* or *Sacramento Bee.*"[68] Acknowledging rejection of his position in earlier cases that rejected licensing as a premise for state action,[69] he maintained that public broadcasters at least had no "free[dom] to pick and choose news items as [they] desired,"[70] were obligated to provide access to the public,[71] and could let "(p)olitics, ideolog[y]..., rightist or leftist tendencies...play no part in [their] design of programs."[72]

Douglas's position even with respect to public broadcasting never has been embraced by a majority. The trend in constitutional law in recent years appears to be against finding state action. The concept in fact is malleable and manipulable insofar as its discernment depends upon the "sifting [of] the facts and weighting [of] the circumstances."[73] Given the opportunity to analyze the issue on a case-by-case basis and the draconian consequences if state action actually was discerned, the likelihood seems slim that broadcasting will be designated the functional equivalent of official action.

Even more improbable is the possibility that cable casting would be denominated as state action. Cable operators are subject to a bifurcated system of regulation. Under the Cable Communications Policy Act of 1984,[74] local government may award cable franchises although various functions are subject to federal control.[75] A cable system thus seems analogous, for state action purposes, to a public utility which provides gas or electricity. In *Jackson v. Metropolitan Edison Co.,*[76] the Court determined that a utility's termination of customer service did not constitute state action.[77] Although licensing and regulation evinced a relationship between the utility and government, the connection was not considered significant enough to establish a symbiotic relationship or joint venture.[78] The Court also rejected the notion that the utility's services themselves constituted a public function.[79] It left open the possibility, however, that a practice commanded, encouraged, or sanctioned by government might amount to state action.[80]

Although specifically finding that discontinuance of electric service was not so ordained,[81] the language of *Jackson* suggests that a specific practice dictated by government could have constitutional implications. It is difficult to conclude with certainty what activity might qualify on such grounds. Presumably, given the recent disinclination to find state action, a claim would have to make a strong showing that the action in question was a function of official prescription and not private discretion. It seems unlikely that compliance with general regulatory policy or provisions alone would qualify as state action.[82]

Extensive regulation of an industry does not appear to translate into state action. A state action theory might be tied to the contention that government commands or encourages a broadcaster's action. It could be argued, therefore, that a broadcaster's decision not to allow the public to speak for itself on radio or television is the result of a specific federally prescribed fiduciary function for licensees. In measuring such a claim against the Court's recent trends in the area of state action, it would seem necessary to establish (1) the deprivation of a constitutional right by a state-created rule of conduct and (2) a function that may fairly be denominated a state action because the otherwise private party has acted together with or has been significantly aided by state officials or conduct otherwise attributable to the state.[83] Satisfying the first prong of the test would appear to be easier than meeting the second. Because the Court has established in broadcasting a First Amendment right of the public to receive access to diverse views and voices,[84] it is arguable that an official policy which disserves diversity interests constitutes a deprivation chargeable to the state. Ample evidence in fact exists that fairness regulation has undercut the diversity aims[85] underlying the public's First Amendment rights. Still, the second prong appears to require a showing of a partnership, symbiotic relationship, or other entwining of function and roles which the modern Court seems less inclined to recognize. Finally, it is questionable as a matter of sheer policy and practical consequence, given the role of broadcasting in modern society, whether the Court would craft a decision that might entirely remove the most dominant contemporary medium from the First Amendment's protective ambit.

IV. MEDIA-SPECIFIC FIRST AMENDMENT STANDARDS

For constitutional purposes, not all media are the same. It may be argued that all elements of the press, regardless of how individually labeled, have the overarching purpose of disseminating information and thus should be treated the same under the First Amendment. The Court has focused upon structural differences among media, however, and has thereby created varying degrees of constitutional protection for the media that did not exist when the First Amendment was drafted.

Media-specific analysis for newer forms of communication became entrenched at the same time the Court determined that motion pictures had First Amendment status. In *Joseph Burstyn, Inc. v. Wilson*,[86] the Court rejected its earlier determination to the contrary[87] and concluded that "expression by means of motion pictures is included within the ... guaranty of the First and Fourteenth Amendments."[88] Although the *Wilson* case generally was hailed as a major First Amendment victory for new media,[89] it actually constitutionalized their qualified standing within a press hierarchy. While it expanded the reach of the First Amendment, the Court also affirmed a scheme of constitutional relativity.

An accommodation which afforded First Amendment status at the price of regulation has proved to be the model for defining the constitutional protection for all new media. As the Court observed in *Wilson*, First Amendment recognition "is not the end of [the] problem" but the beginning.[90] No uniform criteria determine the scope and contours of a medium's freedom. Rather, the Court favors individualized evaluation and standards pursuant to the premise that "each tends to present its own peculiar problems."[91] Such analysis borrows substantially and substantively from Justice Jackson's concurring opinion, in *Kovacs v. Cooper*,[92] which supported an ordinance banning loud and raucous sound trucks from public streets.[93] Jackson observed that approval of the regulation did not necessarily obligate the Court to allow like controls of other communications methodologies. Rather, he concluded, "(t)he moving picture screen, the radio, the newspaper, the handbill, the sound truck and the street orator have differing natures, values, abuses, and dangers. Each, in my view, is a law unto itself."[94]

Applying Jackson's media-specific formula to motion pictures, the Court initially rejected rationales which it earlier had relied upon to deny film First Amendment status. It thus acknowledged that motion pictures were "a significant medium for the communication of ideas ... [that] may affect public attitudes and behavior in a variety of ways, ranging from direct espousal of a political or social doctrine to the subtle shaping of thought which characterizes all artistic expression."[95] The Court abandoned any distinction upon the grounds that film may entertain more than inform, noting that the line between information and entertainment is too elusive.[96] An earlier notation that motion pictures represented a mere business product also was dropped because that reality did not truly set them apart from the print media which likewise produce and sell their output for profit.[97] The medium's potential for evil, especially in connection with children, was not recognized in *Wilson* as a basis for denying First Amendment protection altogether,[98] as previously had been the case.[99] The Court nonetheless found that "capacity for evil...may be relevant in determining the permissible scope of community control."[100] Consistent with the concerns recognized in the *Wilson* decision, censorship boards could continue to function provided their focus was calibrated to considerations acknowledged by the Court and valid and proper administrative procedures were followed.[101]

Rationales for content regulation of radio and television have been diverse and problematical. Some measure of government control generally has been conceded as necessary because technical factors require administration to prevent interference between or among signals. Arguments to regulate the electronic media more tightly than the print media surfaced in *Banzhaf v. Federal Communications Commission*.[102] The court of appeals in that case suggested that broadcasting is distinguishable from a written press characterized by "a rich variety of outlets for expression and persuasion,... which are available to those without technical skills or deep pockets."[103] It also found a difference on the grounds that "(w)ritten messages are not communicated unless...read, and reading requires an affirmative act. Broadcast messages, in contrast, are 'in the air'."[104] Because the electronic media were pervasive and their effect was difficult to calculate, the Court found it reasonable to conclude that their impact was greater.[105]

Both the multiplicity and magnitude of effect rationales, however, are problematical. In reality, dissemination of information to a mass audience may be prohibitively costly regardless of the medium chosen. For practical purposes, the opportunity to own or operate any mass medium is primarily a function of capital. Most persons would be denied an opportunity to become a broadcaster primarily because of inadequate resources and thus would never even reach the point of being considered for a license. Nor is a medium's relative impact a persuasive basis for differentiating its First Amendment status. As recognized in freedom of speech cases, relative influence is an impermissible basis for regulation.[106] If it were, the First Amendment would protect only ineffective or inconsequential expression.[107]

The Supreme Court subsequently advanced the concept of spectrum security as a basis for requiring broadcasters to comply with special content controls upon their programming.[108] In *Red Lion Broadcasting Co. v. Federal Communications Commission*[109] the Court observed that "only a tiny fraction of [the public] can hope to communicate if intelligible communication is to be had, even if the entire radio spectrum is utilized in the present state of commercially acceptable technology."[110] The scarcity premise, as discussed in Part III of this book, has been widely criticized, abandoned by broadcasting's primary regulator, and is the subject of increasing judicial criticism. Among other things, it does not account for competition among the media as opposed to within a medium itself, and it ignores the reality that the primary barrier to broadcasting like any other mass medium is financial. It also fails to distinguish broadcasting meaningfully from a newspaper industry which suffers from even a more obvious scarcity problem in terms of raw numbers.[111]

Shortly after the *Red Lion* decision, Chief Justice Burger suggested that it was proper "to take into account the reality that in a very real sense listeners and viewers constitute a 'captive audience'."[112] Burger's opinion further developed the pervasiveness theory advanced in the *Banzhaf* decision and tied it to early regulatory concerns with the advent of radio.[113] Thereafter, the pervasiveness concern was combined with privacy interests and worries about the presence of children in the audience to justify particularized controls upon indecent and offensive programming. In addition to the scarcity rationale, media-specific regulation of broadcasting was grounded upon (1) broadcasting's "uniquely pervasive presence in the lives of all Americans, ... (2) the privacy of the home, where the individual's right to be left alone plainly outweighs the First Amendment rights of an intruder, ... [and] (3) the ease with which children may obtain access to broadcast material."[114]

Pursuant to those concerns, it is broadcasting that has been afforded the most limited First Amendment protection of any medium.[115] The rationales for diminished constitutional status are not unassailable. It is not clear, for instance, why children must be protected from broadcasting but not from the same content in other media or other surroundings. Although broadcast transmission to the home is subject to official control, to weed out indecent expression, common carriage, cable transmission, or the electronic playback of recordings on the same audio or viewing system is not. Equally problematical is why an expletive is any less objectionable when it is printed and publicly displayed than when it is communicated electronically. The same vulgarity, constitutionally protected when expressed publicly,[116] is regulable when broadcast.[117]

Another troubling point is why the special privacy interest of the home cuts in favor of instead of against regulation. Just as an indecent or offensive guest can be ordered to leave the home, so too can a radio or television be switched to a different channel or turned off.[118] Traditional concepts of privacy, and particularly privacy that translates into personal autonomy, arguably are more affronted by governance which determines what individuals can see and hear in their homes.[119] It also remains to be explained why the interests of offended persons require depriving the rest of the public of what

it might choose if it were free to make autonomous selections. Consent to the risk of being offended might be presumed from the decision to place a radio or television in the home. The option also exists for viewers and listeners to obtain knowledge of available programming and avoid it.[120] Problems of exposure are not unique to a given medium. Each has the potential for presenting material to which the reader, viewer, or listener objects. None is so powerful or pervasive, however, as to operate beyond the ultimate control of the individual.

From a viewer's perspective, it is unlikely that cable and broadcasting are significantly distinguishable.[121] Because the obligation exists to identify the differences in the characteristics of new media, courts nonetheless have endeavored to identify differentiating traits. In so doing, they have divided over whether cable is more akin to the medium of print or broadcasting. Some courts have focused upon cable's capacity to carry a multitude of channels and have consequently distinguished it from broadcasting which is able to transmit only a limited number of signals.[122] They also have noted that cable, unlike broadcasting, is not saddled with the problem of "physical interference and scarcity requiring an umpiring role of the government."[123] A competing determination holds that constraints upon competition in the cable industry create scarcity analogous to that identified in broadcasting.[124] Monopoly status for many cable operators exists as a consequence of franchising and capital costs.[125] Yet the scarcity theory also has been discounted with reference to the Supreme Court's observation that economic scarcity does not justify "intrusions into First Amendment rights."[126]

It may be that the problems of equating cable satisfactorily with newspapers or radio and television emphasize the deficiencies of media-specific analysis. If so, casual public perceptions that would fit more neatly with media-comprehensive than media-specific assessments may prove more sensible than distinctions that are increasingly technical or legalistic. Cable, like broadcasting and the print media, provides information, disseminates original or retransmitted data, and has an interest in editorial discretion. If cable were afforded freedom comparable to the print medium's, denying such liberty to broadcasters would seem even more difficult to justify. At least with respect to the portion of a broadcaster's programming that is identical to a cable caster's, imposition of content restrictions on one but not the other would seem anomalous. Alternatively, regulation of cable by a scheme akin to what governs broadcasting actually might endanger broader freedoms of the print medium. Subjecting the electronic but not the printed edition of a newspaper to content regulation might engender more than a problem of inconsistency. Insofar as cable was equated with broadcasting for purposes of control, but the analogy between cable and print was apt, a predicate would exist for conditioning the liberty of all media. A focus on functional similarity rather than structural difference would favor uniformity rather than disparity of standards. Even then, it would be necessary to decide whether media should be governed by constitutional standards governing old or new media. Especially as the capabilities of traditional and evolving media merge and because qualified constitutional protection for media is well established, any such choice between regulatory models seems destined to be the function of a highly competitive process.

V. PRIOR RESTRAINT

A. DIRECT RESTRAINT

Restraint of expression prior to its articulation or publication generally is considered to be at serious odds with the First Amendment.[127] Until 1694, publishing in England was subject to the approval of the church and state. Following the demise of the licensing system, assurance against prior restraint became regarded as a central feature of press freedom. Blackstone thus observed that

> (t)he liberty of the press ... consists in laying no previous restraints upon publication. ... To subject the press to the restrictive power of a licenser ... is to subject all freedom of sentiment to the prejudices of one man, and to make him the arbitrary and infallible judge of all controverted points in learning, religion and government.[128]

A prior restraint in simplest terms is an official restraint upon expression prior to its dissemination. It is possible to identify several variants of such a restriction. A prior restraint exists, for instance, when government forbids expression without approval or a permit.[129] Censorship boards, park and street permits, and even a radio or television license, which precludes broadcasting by an unsuccessful applicant, exemplify such official prohibition. Prior restraint also may be effectuated by the judiciary if it prohibits publication by means of an injunction.[130] Media subject to official action calculated to silence criticism[131] or to block the release of government information have relied upon the First Amendment for relief.[132] Statutes or regulations requiring compliance with specific legal standards or demands also constitute a variant of prior restraint.[133]

Prior restraints, regardless of the form they take, traditionally have been regarded with special concern and as a particularly grave threat to First Amendment interests. It has been observed that "the most significant feature of systems of prior restraint is that they contain within themselves forces which drive irresistibly toward unintelligent, overzealous, and usually absurd administration."[134] Because the function of any censor is to censor,[135] the perceived problem is that institutional impulses and First Amendment interests cannot harmoniously coexist.[136] It is the fundamental mission of the Securities and Exchange Commission, for instance, to protect investors and the integrity of the investment marketplace.[137] Registration materials including promotional information for dissemination to the public are edited by attorneys who function as official censors. Assuming they identify with agency goals and have normal interests in career advancement, they are more likely than not to perform their tasks energetically.[138] It is improbable that a staff attorney who edited sparsely out of concern for freedom of expression, rather than full disclosure, would be rewarded for having effectively served agency goals. Pursuant to career and institutional objectives, the common tendency would be to maximize challenges and revisions.[139] Under such circumstances, it would seem that the incentive exists to censor more rather than less.[140]

Prior restraint also tends to be considered especially worrisome because, unlike a system of subsequent punishment, suppression is thought to be more effective.[141] Although harsh criminal sanctions seemingly could operate as forcefully and effectively as prior restraint, postpublication punishment is not a certainty. Although the government sought to restrain publication of the Pentagon Papers[142] and an article on how to make a hydrogen bomb,[143] subsequent punishment did not follow despite arguments that pertinent laws had been violated.[144] At least in theory, prior restraint is considered categorically more serious than subsequent punishment because a greater possibility exists under the latter scheme that ideas or expression will reach the public. Such a distinction may be overrated to the extent that knowledge of likely punishment operates as a significant deterrent.

Near v. Minnesota[145] represents the seminal case on prior restraint. In *Near*, the Court examined a public nuisance statute which enabled the state to secure an injunction barring publication of any "malicious, scandalous and defamatory newspaper, magazine or other periodical."[146] The statute was directed toward a weekly newspaper, the *Saturday Press*, which had an unapologetically anti-Semitic bias.[147] At the same time, the publication was responsible for identifying persons controlling vice activities in Minneapolis and linking the police chief and other city officials to organized crime.[148] Even if identifiable as malicious, scandalous, and defamatory, therefore, the *Saturday Press* performed an important role in exposing serious corruption among local officials. Suppression thus was the consequence of published allegations of official misconduct.[149] If such reporting was declared a nuisance, and future publication enjoined, the publisher would have been vulnerable to contempt for any subsequent allegation of public corruption or misdeed.[150] Such a result would have been unfortunate, the Court observed, because the increasing complexity of government and multiplying opportunities for corruption and malfeasance necessitate "a vigilant and courageous press."[151] From the Court's perspective, that imperative was not diminished by the possibility or even the reality that liberty of the press may be abused.[152] Because the statute afforded excessive protection to officials who otherwise could sue for defamation,[153] and suppression would ensue unless the publisher proved truth, good motive, and justifiable ends, the Court found that the law facilitated a system of censorship.[154]

In declaring the nuisance statute unconstitutional, the Court concluded that "it has been generally, if not universally, considered that it is the chief purpose of [freedom of the press] to prevent previous restraints upon publication."[155] Adverting to Blackstone's commentary upon the liberty of the press, the Court further observed that "(e)very freeman has an undoubted right to lay what sentiments he pleases before the public; to forbid this is to destroy the freedom of the press; but if he publishes what is improper, mischievous or illegal, he must take the consequence of his own temerity."[156] Even if the First Amendment did not countenance prior restraint, at least under the circumstances, the possibility of subsequent punishment was not foreclosed. A libel action might be available, for instance, to those who claimed they had been defamed by the newspaper.[157]

Although it refused to restrain publication of the *Saturday Press*, the Court observed that the guarantee against censorship is not absolute.[158] It further noted that any exception to the rule must be justified by extraordinary interests. The Court mentioned several exceptional cases that would justify prior restraint:

> government [during wartime] might prevent actual obstruction to its recruiting service or the publication of the sailing dates of transports or the number and location of troops. On similar grounds, the primary requirements of decency may be enforced against obscene publications. The security of the community life may be protected against incitements to acts of violence and the overthrow by force of orderly government. The constitution [] does not 'protect a man from an injunction against uttering words that may have all the effect of force' [citation omitted].[159]

Near v. Minnesota, 283 U.S. 697 (1931)

A Minnesota statute declared anyone "in the business of regularly or customarily producing, publishing, or circulating . . . a malicious, scandalous and defamatory newspaper, magazine or other periodical," is guilty of a nuisance, and authorized suits, in the name of the State, by which such periodicals may be abated and their publishers

enjoined from future violations. Malice was presumed from the fact of publication, and the only defense was truth, good motive, and justifiable ends. Justice Butler's dissenting opinion reproduced pertinent stories printed by *The Saturday Press,* whose publisher was enjoined by the lower court.

FACTS NOT THEORIES

'I am a bosom friend of Mr. Olson,' snorted a gentleman of Yiddish blood, 'and I want to protest against your article,' and blah, blah, blah, ad infinitum, ad infinitum, ad nauseam.

I am not taking orders from men of Barnett faith, at least right now. There have been too many men in this city and especially those in official life, who HAVE been taking orders and suggestions from JEW GANGSTERS, therefore we HAVE Jew Gangsters, practically ruling Minneapolis.

It was buzzards of the Barnett stripe who shot down my buddy. It was Barnett gunmen who staged the assault on Samuel Shapiro. It is Jew thugs who have "pulled" practically every robbery in this city. It was a member of the Barnett gang who shot down George Rubenstein (Ruby) while he stood in the shelter of Mose Barnett's ham-cavern on Hennepin avenue. It was Mose Barnett himself who shot down Roy Rogers on Hennepin avenue. It was at Mose Barnett's place of "business" that the "13 dollar Jew" found a refuge while the police of New York were combing the country for him. It was a gang of Jew gunmen who boasted that for five hundred dollars they would kill any man in the city. It was Mose Barnett, a Jew, who boasted that he held the chief of police of Minneapolis in his hand—had bought and paid for him.

It is Jewish men and women—pliant tools of the Jew gangster, Mose Barnett, who stand charged with having falsified the election records and returns in the Third ward. And it is Mose Barnett himself, who, indicted for his part in the Shapiro assault, is a fugitive from justice today.

Practically every vendor of vile hooch, every owner of a moonshine still, every snake-faced gangster and embryonic yegg in the Twin Cities is a JEW.

Having these examples before me, I feel that

I am justified in my refusal to take orders from a Jew who boasts that he is a "bosom friend" of Mr. Olson.

I find in the mail at least twice per week, letters from gentlemen of Jewish faith who advise me against "launching an attack on the Jewish people." These gentlemen have the cart before the horse. I am launching, nor is Mr. Guilford, no attack against any race, BUT:

When I find men of a certain race banding themselves together for the purpose of preying upon Gentile or Jew; gunmen, KILLERS, roaming our streets shooting down men against whom they have no personal grudge (or happen to have); defying OUR laws; corrupting OUR officials; assaulting business men; beating up unarmed citizens; spreading a reign of terror through every walk of life, then I say to you in all sincerity, that I refuse to back up a single step from that "issue"—if they choose to make it so.

If the people of Jewish faith in Minneapolis wish to avoid criticism of these vermin whom I rightfully call "Jews" they can easily do so BY THEMSELVES CLEANING HOUSE.

I'm not out to cleanse Israel of the filth that clings to Israel's skirts. I'm out to "hew to the line, let the chips fly where they may."

I simply state a fact when I say that ninety per cent of the crimes committed against society in this city are committed by Jew gangsters.

It was a Jew who employed JEWS to shoot down Mr. Guilford. It was a Jew who employed a Jew to intimidate Mr. Shapiro and a Jew who employed JEWS to assault that gentleman when he refused to yield to their threats. It was a JEW who wheedled or employed Jews to manipulate the election records and returns in the Third ward in flagrant violation of law. It was a Jew who left two hundred dollars with another JEW to pay to our chief of police just before the last municipal election, and:

It is Jew, Jew, Jew, as long as one cares to comb over the records.

I am launching no attack against the Jewish people AS A RACE. I am merely calling attention to a FACT. And if the people of that race and faith wish to rid themselves of the odium and stigma THE RODENTS OF THEIR OWN RACE HAVE BROUGHT UPON THEM, they need only to step to the front and help the decent citizens of Minneapolis rid the city of these criminal Jews.

Either Mr. Guilford or myself stand ready to do battle for a MAN, regardless of his race, color or creed, but neither of us will step one inch out of our chosen path to avoid a fight IF the Jews want to battle.

Both of us have some mighty loyal friends among the Jewish people but not one of them comes whining to ask that we "lay off" criticism of Jewish gangsters and none of them who comes carping to us of their "bosom friendship" for any public official now under our journalistic guns.

GIL'S [Guilford's] CHATTERBOX

I headed into the city on September 26th, ran across three Jews in a Chevrolet; stopped a lot of lead and won a bed for myself in St. Barnabas Hospital for six weeks....

Whereupon I have withdrawn all allegiance to anything with a hook nose that eats herring. I have adopted the sparrow as my national bird until Davis' law enforcement league or the K. K. K. hammers the eagle's beak out straight. So if I seem to act crazy as I ankle down the street, bear in mind that I am merely saluting MY national emblem.

All of which has nothing to do with the present whereabouts of Big Mose Barnett. Methinks he headed the local delegation to the new Palestine-for-Jews-only. He went ahead of the boys so he could do a little fixing with the Yiddish chief of police and get his twenty-five per cent of the gambling rake-off. Boys will be boys and "ganefs" will be ganefs.

GRAND JURIES AND DITTO

There are grand juries, and there are grand juries. The last one was a real grand jury. It acted. The present one is like the scion who is labelled "Junior." That means not so good. There are a few mighty good folks on it—there are some who smell bad. One petty peanut politician whose graft was almost pitiful in its size when he was a public official, has already shot his mouth off in several places. He is establishing his alibi in advance for what he intends to keep from taking place.

But George, we won't bother you. [Meaning a grand juror.] We are aware that the gambling syndicate was waiting for your body to convene before the big crap game opened again. The Yids had your dimensions, apparently, and we always go by the judgment of a dog in appraising people.

We will call for a special grand jury and a special prosecutor within a short time, as soon as half of the staff can navigate to advantage, and then we'll show you what a real grand jury can do. Up to the present we have been merely tapping on the window. Very soon we shall start smashing glass.

Mr. Chief Justice Hughes delivered the opinion of the Court.

The object of the statute is not punishment, in the ordinary sense, but suppression of the offending newspaper or periodical. The reason for the enactment, as the state court has said, is that prosecutions to enforce penal statutes for libel do not result in "efficient repression or suppression of the evils of scandal." Describing the business of publication as a public nuisance, does not obscure the substance of the proceeding which the statute authorizes. It is the continued publication of scandalous and defamatory matter that constitutes the business and the declared nuisance. In the case of public officers, it is the reiteration of charges of official misconduct, and the fact that the newspaper or periodical is principally devoted to that purpose, that exposes it to suppression. In the present instance, the proof was that nine editions of the newspaper or periodical in question were published on successive dates, and that they were chiefly devoted to charges against public officers and in relation to the prevalence and protection of crime. In such a case, these officers are not left to their ordinary remedy in a suit for libel, or the authorities to a prosecution for criminal libel. Under this statute, a publisher of a newspaper or periodical, undertaking to conduct a campaign to expose and to censure official derelictions, and devoting his publication principally to that purpose, must face not simply the possibility of a verdict against him in a suit or prosecution for libel, but a determination that his newspaper or periodical is a public nuisance to be abated, and that this abatement and suppression will follow unless he is prepared with legal

evidence to prove the truth of the charges and also to satisfy the court that, in addition to being true, the matter was published with good motives and for justifiable ends.

This suppression is accomplished by enjoining publication and that restraint is the object and effect of the statute....

The statute not only operates to suppress the offending newspaper or periodical but to put the publisher under an effective censorship. When a newspaper or periodical is found to be "malicious, scandalous and defamatory," and is suppressed as such, resumption of publication is punishable as a contempt of court by fine or imprisonment. Thus, where a newspaper or periodical has been suppressed because of the circulation of charges against public officers of official misconduct, it would seem to be clear that the renewal of the publication of such charges would constitute a contempt and that the judgment would lay a permanent restraint upon the publisher, to escape which he must satisfy the court as to the character of a new publication. Whether he would be permitted again to publish matter deemed to be derogatory to the same or other public officers would depend upon the court's ruling. In the present instance the judgment restrained the defendants from "publishing, circulating, having in their possession, selling or giving away any publication whatsoever which is a malicious, scandalous or defamatory newspaper, as defined by law." The law gives no definition except that covered by the words "scandalous and defamatory," and publications charging official misconduct are of that class. While the court, answering the objection that the judgement was too broad, saw no reason for construing it as restraining the defendants "from operating a newspaper in harmony with the public welfare to which all must yield," and said that the defendants had not indicated "any desire to conduct their business in the usual and legitimate manner," the manifest inference is that, at least with respect to a new publication directed against official misconduct, the defendant would be held, under penalty of punishment for contempt as provided in the statute, to a manner of publication which the court considered to be "usual and legitimate" and consistent with the public welfare.

If we cut through mere details of procedure,

the operation and effect of the statute in substance is that public authorities may bring the owner or publisher of a newspaper or periodical before a judge upon a charge of conducting a business of publishing scandalous and defamatory matter—in particular that the matter consists of charges against public officers of official dereliction—and unless the owner or publisher is able and disposed to bring competent evidence to satisfy the judge that the charges are true and are published with good motives and for justifiable ends, his newspaper or periodical is suppressed and further publication is made punishable as a contempt. This is of the essence of censorship.

The question is whether a statute authorizing such proceedings in restraint of publication is consistent with the conception of the liberty of the press as historically conceived and guaranteed. In determining the extent of the constitutional protection, it has been generally, if not universally, considered that it is the chief purpose of the guaranty to prevent previous restraints upon publication. The struggle in England, directed against the legislative power of the licenser, resulted in renunciation of the censorship of the press. The liberty deemed to be established was thus described by Blackstone: "The liberty of the press is indeed essential to the nature of a free state; but this consists in laying no *previous* restraints upon publications, and not in freedom from censure for criminal matter when published. Every freeman has an undoubted right to lay what sentiments he pleases before the public; to forbid this, is to destroy the freedom of the press; but if he publishes what is improper, mischievous or illegal, he must take the consequence of his own temerity." 4 Bl. Com. 151, 152; see Story on the Constitution, §§ 1884, 1889. The distinction was early pointed out between the extent of the freedom with respect to censorship under our constitutional system and that enjoyed in England. Here, as Madison said, "the great and essential rights of the people are secured against legislative as well as against executive ambition. They are secured, not by laws paramount to prerogative, but by constitutions paramount to laws. This security of the freedom of the press requires that it should be exempt not only from previous restraint by the Executive, as in Great Britain, but

from legislative restraint also." Report on the Virginia Resolutions, Madison's Works, vol. IV, p. 543. This Court said, in *Patterson v. Colorado,* 205 U.S. 454, 462: "In the first place, the main purpose of such constitutional provisions is 'to prevent all such *previous restraints* upon publications as had been practiced by other governments,' and they do not prevent the subsequent punishment of such as may be deemed contrary to the public welfare. *Commonwealth v. Blanding,* 3 Pick. 304, 313, 314; *Republica v. Oswald,* I Dallas, 319, 325. The preliminary freedom extends as well to the false as to the true; the subsequent punishment may extend as well to the true as to the false. This was the law of criminal libel apart from statute in most cases, if not in all. *Commonwealth v. Blanding, ubi sup.;* 4 Bl. Com. 150."

The criticism upon Blackstone's statement has not been because immunity from previous restraint upon publication has not been regarded as deserving of special emphasis, but chiefly because that immunity cannot be deemed to exhaust the conception of the liberty guaranteed by state and federal constitutions. The point of criticism has been "that the mere exemption from previous restraints cannot be all that is secured by the constitutional provisions"; and that "the liberty of the press might be rendered a mockery and a delusion, and the phrase itself a by-word, if, while every man was at liberty to publish what he pleased, the public authorities might nevertheless punish him for harmless publications." 2 Cooley, Const. Lim., 8th ed., p. 885. But it is recognized that punishment for the abuse of the liberty accorded to the press is essential to the protection of the public, and that the common law rules that subject the libeler to responsibility for the public offense, as well as for the private injury, are not abolished by the protection extended in our constitutions. *id.* pp. 883, 884. The law of criminal libel rests upon that secure foundation. There is also the conceded authority of courts to punish for contempt when publications directly tend to prevent the proper discharge of judicial functions. *Patterson v. Colorado, supra; Toledo Newspaper Co. v. United States,* 247 U.S. 402, 419. In the present case, we have no occasion to inquire as to the permissible scope of subsequent punishment. For whatever wrong the appellant has committed or may commit, by his publications, the State appropriately affords both public and private redress by its libel laws. As has been noted, the statute in question does not deal with punishments; it provides for no punishment, except in case of contempt for violation of the court's order, but for suppression and injunction, that is, for restraint upon publication.

The objection has also been made that the principle as to immunity from previous restraint is stated too broadly, if every such restraint is deemed to be prohibited. That is undoubtedly true; the protection even as to previous restraint is not absolutely unlimited. But the limitation has been recognized only in exceptional cases: "When a nation is at war many things that might be said in time of peace are such a hindrance to its effort that their utterance will not be endured so long as men fight and that no Court could regard them as protected by any constitutional right." *Schenck v. United States,* 249 U.S. 47, 52. No one would question but that a government might prevent actual obstruction to its recruiting service or the publication of the sailing dates of transports or the number and location of troops. On similar grounds, the primary requirements of decency may be enforced against obscene publications. The security of the community life may be protected against incitements to acts of violence and the overthrow by force of orderly government. The constitutional guaranty of free speech does not "protect a man from an injunction against uttering words that may have all the effect of force. *Gompers v. Buck Stove & Range Co.,* 221 U.S. 418. 439." *Schenck v. United States, supra.* These limitations are not applicable here. Nor are we now concerned with questions as to the extent of authority to prevent publications in order to protect private rights according to the principles governing the exercise of the jurisdiction of courts of equity.

The exceptional nature of its limitations places in a strong light the general conception that liberty of the press, historically considered and taken up by the Federal Constitution, has meant, principally although not exclusively, immunity from previous restraints or censorship. The conception of the liberty of the press in this country had broadened with the exigencies of the colonial period and with the efforts to secure freedom from oppressive administration. That liberty was especially cherished for the immunity it afforded from previous restraint of the publication of censure of public officers and charges of official misconduct. As was said by Chief Justice Parker, in *Commonwealth v. Blanding,* 3 Pick. 304, 313, with respect to the constitution of Massachusetts: "Besides, it is well understood, and received as a commentary on this provision for the liberty of the press, that it was intended to prevent all such *previous restraints* upon publications as had been practiced by other governments, and in early times here, to stifle the efforts of patriots towards enlightening their fellow subjects upon their rights and the duties of rulers. The liberty of the press was to be unrestrained, but he who used it was to be responsible in case of its abuse." In the letter sent by the Continental Congress (October 26, 1774) to the Inhabitants of Quebec, referring to the "five great rights" it was said: "The last right we shall mention, regards the freedom of the press. The importance of this consists, besides the advancement of truth, science, morality, and arts in general; in its diffusion of liberal sentiments on the administration of Government, its ready communication of thoughts between subjects, and its consequential promotion of union among them, whereby oppressive officers are shamed or intimated, into more honourable and just modes of conducting affairs." Madison, who was the leading spirit in the preparation of the First Amendment of the Federal Constitution, thus described the practice and sentiment which led to the guaranties of liberty of the press in state constitutions:

In every State, probably, in the Union, the press has exerted a freedom in canvassing the merits and measures of public men of every description which has not been confined to the strict limits of the common law. On this footing the freedom of the press has stood; on this footing it yet stands.... Some degree of abuse is inseparable from the proper use of everything, and in no instance is this more true than in that of the press. It has accordingly been decided by the practice of the States, that it is better to leave a few of its noxious branches to their luxuriant growth, than, by pruning them away, to injure the vigour of those yielding the proper fruits. And can the wisdom of this policy be doubted by any who reflect that to the press alone, chequered as it is with abuses, the world is indebted for all the triumphs which have been gained by reason and humanity over error and oppression; who reflect that to the same beneficent source the United States owe much of the lights which conducted them to the ranks of a free and independent nation, and which have improved their political system into a shape so auspicious to their happiness? Had "Sedition Acts," forbidding every publication that might bring the constituted agents into contempt or disrepute, or that might excite the hatred of the people against the authors of unjust or pernicious measures, been uniformly enforced against the press, might not the United States have been languishing at this day under the infirmities of a sickly Confederation? Might they not, possibly, be miserable colonies, groaning under a foreign yoke?

The fact that for approximately one hundred and fifty years there has been almost an entire absence of attempts to impose previous restraints upon publications relating to the malfeasance of public officers is significant of the deep-seated conviction that such restraints would violate constitutional right. Public officers, whose character and conduct remain open to debate and free discussion in the press, find their remedies for false accusations in actions under libel laws providing for redress and punishment, and not in proceedings to restrain the publication of newspapers and periodicals. The general principle that the constitutional guaranty of the liberty of the press gives immunity from previous restraints has been approved in many decisions under the provisions of state constitutions.

The importance of this immunity has not lessened. While reckless assaults upon public men, and efforts to bring obloquy upon those who are endeavoring faithfully to discharge official duties, exert a baleful influence and deserve the severest condemnation in public opinion, it cannot be said that this abuse is greater, and it is believed to be less, than that which characterized the period in which our institutions took shape. Meanwhile, the administration of government has become more complex, the opportunities for malfeasance and corruption have multiplied, crime has grown to most serious proportions, and the danger of its protection by unfaithful officials and of the impairment of the fundamental security of life and property by criminal alliances and official neglect, emphasizes the primary need of a vigilant and courageous press, especially in great cities. The fact that the liberty of the press may be abused by miscreant purveyors of scandal does not make any the less necessary the immunity of the press from previous restraint in dealing with official misconduct. Subsequent punishment for such abuses as may exist is the appropriate remedy, consistent with constitutional privilege.

From the *Near* Court's first limitation upon the rule against prior restraint, an exception based upon national security may be logically inferred and amplified. Four decades later, such a reservation was further developed. In *New York Times Co. v. United States*,[160] the Court determined that the *Washington Post* and the *New York Times* should not be restrained from publishing a classified report on American policy-making in Vietnam eventually known as the Pentagon Papers.[161] In a per curiam opinion, the Court determined that "(a)ny system of prior restraint . . . bear[s] a heavy presumption against its constitutionality," and the "Government . . . carries a heavy burden of showing justification for the prior restraint."[162] Although it dismissed temporary restraining orders entered by a lower court,[163] the Court's contributions to the law of prior restraint were scattered among nine opinions. Justices Black and Douglas, who asserted prior restraint was categorically impermissible,[164] effectively combined with Justices Brennan, Stewart, White, and Marshall to deny an injunction against publication of the Pentagon Papers.[165] However, Justices Burger, Harlan, and Blackmun's determination that an injunction against the newspapers was appropriate under the circumstances,[166] combined with Justices Stewart, White, and Marshall's suggestion that prior restraint was permissible when statutorily authorized,[167] would have led to a different outcome under altered circumstances. Although affirming the First Amendment's antagonism toward prior restraint, the elements of the Pentagon Papers decision may have helped enlarge the category of exceptions to the rule against prior restraint[168] and represented a retreat from the fullest implications of the *Near* decision.[169]

In seeking the injunction, President Nixon had claimed an inherent power to protect national security against harm.[170] Justices Black and Douglas not only rejected the chief executive's argument but staked out a position even more absolutist than the *Near* Court's. Black characterized the government's case as a request "to hold that the First Amendment does not mean what it says, but rather means that the Government can halt the publication of current news of vital importance to the people in this country."[171] Thus, Black regarded the president's claim of inherent power as "a threat that would wipe out the First Amendment,"[172] which he saw as having been conceived primarily to outlaw "injunctions like those sought here."[173] Finally, he warned that national security is a vague term capable of being manipulated and misused at the expense of basic freedoms and informed representative government.[174]

Justice Douglas expressed his preference for resolving the issue pursuant to the literal terminology of the First Amendment. From his perspective, the guarantee that " 'Congress shall make no law ... abridging the freedom ... of the press,' ... [left] no room for governmental restraint of the press."[175] He noted, moreover, that no relevant statute barred publication of the official study.[176] Douglas also emphasized that the presidential claim of inherent powers to obtain an injunction had been repudiated by *Near*[177] and that governmental secrecy in the end was antidemocratic.[178]

Justice Brennan found error in the granting of injunctive relief under the circumstances.[179] Unlike Black and Douglas, however, Brennan concluded that judicial restraints on the press might be permissible in certain instances. The primary flaw in the government's case, from his viewpoint, was its predication "upon surmise or conjecture that untoward consequences may result."[180] Adverting to a primary exception to the rule against prior restraint cited by the *Near* Court, Brennan concluded that "only governmental allegation and proof that publication must inevitably, directly and immediately cause the occurrence of an event kindred to imperiling the safety of a transport already at sea can support even the issuance of an interim restraining order."[181] In effect, Brennan engrafted the modern clear and present danger test[182] upon the categorical exclusion identified in *Near*. Pursuant to his analysis, it would be enough for the government not merely to assert the exception but to demonstrate significant, direct, and imminent harm.[183]

Justice Stewart, although concurring that an injunction was inappropriate under the circumstances, observed that the president nonetheless had plenary power to conduct foreign affairs and maintain national defense.[184] Thus, he maintained that the president also had a "largely unshared duty to determine and preserve the degree of internal security to exercise that power successfully."[185] Stewart had no doubt that confidentiality and secrecy were essential at times for successful diplomacy and effective defense.[186] He emphasized that truly effective security is characterized by maximum possible disclosure, however, because secrecy works only when credibility is maintained. Stewart noted both the executive and congressional power respectively to promulgate rules and enact legislation to protect confidentiality, but he found no such provision applicable to the case.[187] Although he believed the president was correct about the consequences flowing from publication of some of the documents,[188] Stewart like Brennan could not conclude that disclosure would "surely result in direct, immediate, and irreparable damage to our Nation or its people."[189]

Both Justices White and Marshall concurred in the judgment but might have decided otherwise if Congress had authorized a prior restraint of the materials at issue.[190] Justice White, like Stewart, was confident that "revelation of these documents will do substantial damage to public interests."[191] Because he determined that the government had not met its heavy burden for restraint and Congress had not enacted pertinent authorizing legislation, he too refused to ban publication.[192] White's denial of the requested relief was grudging, however, and apparently reached only because of the infrequency of prior restraint cases and his sense that security already had been breached and damage done if the information was available for publication.[193]

Chief Justice Burger and Justices Harlan and Blackmun dissented from the judgment. Burger favored at least temporary relief because the Court did not really know all the facts, and he thought that the issue was being resolved "in unseemly haste."[194] He thus chastised the newspaper, which had spent from three to four months studying purloined documents, for pressing the Court for a decision in a matter of hours.[195] For Black and Douglas, each moment that a prior restraint operated constituted offense to the First Amendment.[196] Burger, however, would have factored in the interests of "the effective functioning of a complex modern government and specifically the effective exercise of certain constitutional powers of the Executive."[197] He thus would have allowed whatever time was necessary for "deliberate and reasonable judicial treatment."[198]

Justice Harlan also complained about a rush to judgment, suggesting "that the

Court ha[d] been almost irresponsibly feverish."[199] Harlan's concern was that the quick decision required bypassing several pertinent issues including whether (1) the Justice Department could bring the suits in the name of the United States, (2) the First Amendment allows injunctions against a publication that endangers national security, (3) national security would be harmed regardless of the documents' context, (4) unauthorized disclosure would impair national security, (5) the newspapers could use stolen documents, and (6) national security interests should prevail despite First Amendment policy and the possibility that security had already been compromised.[200] Beyond his sense that the case required more deliberation, Harlan dissented from the judgment on grounds that judicial review of executive power in the field of foreign affairs was "very narrowly restricted."[201] Thus, he would have permitted judicial inquiry only to determine whether the subject matter fell within the president's power and a finding of irreparable harm to national security had been made by the head of the relevant executive department.[202]

Justice Blackmun criticized the judgment as paying too high a tribute to the First Amendment, which he characterized "after all, [as] only one part of an entire Constitution."[203] What Blackmun found missing was a balancing, pursuant to properly developed standards, "of the broad right of the press to print and of the very narrow right of the Government to prevent."[204] Like Burger and Harlan, Blackmun would have favored more extensive deliberation before passing judgment.[205] Extensive personnel changes since the opinions were rendered leave open the possibility that, if faced with a similar issue, the Court's review would be at least more protracted.

New York Times Co. v. United States, 403 U.S. 713 (1971)

Per Curiam.

We granted certiorari in these cases in which the United States seeks to enjoin the *New York Times* and the *Washington Post* from publishing the contents of a classified study entitled "History of U.S. Decision-Making Process on Viet Nam Policy." *Post,* pp. 942, 943.

"Any system of prior restraints of expression comes to this Court bearing a heavy presumption against its constitutional validity." *Bantam Books, Inc. v. Sullivan,* 372 U.S. 58, 70 (1963); see also *Near v. Minnesota,* 283 U.S. 697 (1931). The Government "thus carries a heavy burden of showing justification for the imposition of such a restraint." *Organization for a Better Austin v. Keefe,* 402 U.S. 415, 419 (1971). The District Court for the Southern District of New York in the *New York Times* case and the District Court for the District of Columbia and the Court of Appeals for the District of Columbia Circuit in the *Washington Post* case held that the Government had not met that burden. We agree.

The judgment of the Court of Appeals for the District of Columbia Circuit is therefore affirmed. The order of the Court of Appeals for the Second Circuit is reversed and the case is remanded with directions to enter a judgment affirming the judgment of the District Court for the Southern District of New York. The stays entered June 25, 1971, by the Court are vacated. The judgments shall issue forthwith.

So ordered.

Mr. Justice Black, with whom Mr. Justice Douglas joins, concurring.

I adhere to the view that the Government's case against the *Washington Post* should have been dismissed and that the injunction against the *New York Times* should have been vacated without oral argument when the cases were first presented to this Court. I believe that every moment's continuance of the injunctions against these newspapers amounts to a flagrant, indefensible, and continuing violation of the First Amendment. Furthermore, after oral argument, I agree completely that we must affirm the judgment of the Court of Appeals for the District of Columbia Circuit and reverse the judgment of the Court of Appeals for the Second Circuit for the reasons stated by my Brothers Douglas and Brennan. In my view it is unfortunate that some of my Brethren are apparently willing to hold that the publication of news may sometimes be enjoined. Such a holding would make a shambles of the First Amendment.

Our Government was launched in 1789 with the adoption of the Constitution. The Bill of Rights, including the First Amendment, followed in 1791. Now, for the first time in the 182 years since the founding of the Republic, the federal courts are asked to hold that the First Amendment does not mean what it says, but rather means that the Government can halt the publication of current news of vital importance to the people of this country.

In the First Amendment the Founding Fathers gave the free press the protection it must have to fulfill its essential role in our democracy. The press was to serve the governed, not the governors. The Government's power to censor the press was abolished so that the press would remain forever free to censure the Government. The press was protected so that it could bare the secrets of government and inform the people. Only a free and unrestrained press can effectively expose deception in government. And paramount among the responsibilities of a free press is the duty to prevent any part of the government from deceiving the people and sending them off to distant lands to die of foreign fevers and foreign shot and shell. In my view, far from deserving condemnation for their courageous reporting, the *New York Times*, the *Washington Post*, and other newspapers should be commended for serving the purpose that the Founding Fathers saw so clearly. In revealing the workings of government that led to the Vietnam war, the newspapers nobly did precisely that which the Founders hoped and trusted they would do....

To find that the President has "inherent power" to halt the publication of news by resort to the courts would wipe out the First Amendment and destroy the fundamental liberty and security of the very people the Government hopes to make "secure." No one can read the history of the adoption of the First Amendment without being convinced beyond any doubt that it was injunctions like those sought here that Madison and his collaborators intended to outlaw in this Nation for all time.

The word "security" is a broad, vague generality whose contours should not be invoked to abrogate the fundamental law embodied in the First Amendment. The guarding of military and diplomatic secrets at the expense of informed representative government provides no real security for our Republic. The Framers of the First Amendment, fully aware of both the need to defend a new nation and the abuses of the English and Colonial governments, sought to give this new society strength and security by providing that freedom of speech, press, religion, and assembly should not be abridged....

Mr. Justice Douglas, with whom Mr. Justice Black joins, concurring.

While I join the opinion of the Court I believe it necessary to express my views more fully.

It should be noted at the outset that the First Amendment provides that "Congress shall make no law . . . abridging the freedom of speech, or of the press." That leaves, in my view, no room for governmental restraint on the press.

There is, moreover, no statute barring the publication by the press of the material which the *Times* and the *Post* seek to use. Title 18 U.S.C. § 793(e) provides that "[w]hoever having unauthorized possession of, access to, or control over any document, writing . . . or information relating to the national defense which information the possessor has reason to believe could be used to the injury of the United States or to the advantage of any foreign nation, willfully communicates . . . the same to any person not entitled to receive it . . . [s]hall be fined not more than $10,000 or imprisoned not more than ten years, or both."

The Government suggests that the word "communicates" is broad enough to encompass publication.

There are eight sections in the chapter on espionage and censorship, §§ 792–799. In three of those eight "publish" is specifically mentioned: § 794(b) applies to "Whoever, in time of war, with intent that the same shall be communicated to the enemy, collects, records, *publishes,* or communicates . . . [the disposition of armed forces]."

Section 797 applies to whoever "reproduces, *publishes,* sells, or gives away" photographs of defense installations.

Section 798 relating to cryptography applies to whoever: "communicates, furnishes, transmits, or otherwise makes available . . . *or publishes*" the described material. (Emphasis added.)

Thus it is apparent that Congress was capable of and did distinguish between publishing and communication in the various sections of the Espionage Act.

The Government says that it has inherent powers to go into court and obtain an injunction to protect the national interest, which in this case is alleged to be national security.

Near v. Minnesota, 283 U.S. 697, repudiated that expansive doctrine in no uncertain terms.

Secrecy in government is fundamentally antidemocratic, perpetuating bureaucratic errors. Open debate and discussion of public issues are vital to our national health. On public questions there should be "uninhibited, robust, and wideopen" debate. *New York Times Co. v. Sullivan,* 376 U.S. 254, 269–270.

The stays in these cases that have been in effect for more than a week constitute a flouting of the principles of the First Amendment as interpreted in *Near v. Minnesota.*

Mr. Justice Brennan, concurring.

The error that has pervaded these cases from the outset was the granting of any injunctive relief whatsoever, interim or otherwise. The entire thrust of the Government's claim throughout these cases has been that publication of the material sought to be enjoined "could," or "might," or "may" prejudice the national interest in various ways. But the First Amendment tolerates absolutely no prior judicial restraints of the press predicated upon surmise or conjecture that untoward consequences may result. Our cases, it is true, have indicated that there is a single, extremely narrow class of cases in which the First Amendment's ban on prior judicial restraint may be overridden. Our cases have thus far indicated that such cases may arise only when the Nation "is at war," *Schenck v. United States,* 249 U.S. 47, 52 (1919), during which times "[n]o one would question but that a government might prevent actual obstruction to its recruiting service or the publication of the sailing dates of transports or the number and location of troops." *Near v. Minnesota,* 283 U.S. 697, 716 (1931). Even if the present world situation were assumed to be tantamount to a time of war, or if the power of presently available armaments would justify even in peacetime the suppression of information that would set in motion a nuclear holocaust, in neither of these actions has the Government presented or even alleged that publication of items from or based upon the material at issue would cause the happening of an event of that nature. "[T]he chief purpose of [the First Amendment's] guaranty [is] to prevent previous restraints upon publication." *Near v. Minnesota, supra,* at 713. Thus, only governmental allegation and proof that publication must inevitably, directly, and immediately cause the occurrence of an event kindred to imperiling the safety of a transport already at sea can support even the issuance of an interim restraining order. In no event may mere conclusions be sufficient: for if the Executive Branch seeks judicial aid in preventing publication, it must inevitably submit the basis upon which that aid is sought to scrutiny by the judiciary. And therefore, every restraint issued in this case, whatever its form, has violated the First Amendment—and not less so because that restraint was justified as necessary to afford the courts an opportunity to examine the claim more thoroughly. Unless and until the Government has clearly made out its case, the First Amendment commands that no injunction may issue.

Mr. Justice Stewart, with whom Mr. Justice White joins, concurring.

In the governmental structure created by our Constitution, the Executive is endowed with enormous power in the two related areas of national defense and international relations. This power, largely unchecked by the Legislative and Judicial branches, has been pressed to the very hilt since the advent of the nuclear missile age. For better or for worse, the simple fact is that a President of the United States possesses vastly greater constitutional independence in these two vital areas of power than does, say, a prime minister of a country with a parliamentary form of government.

In the absence of the governmental checks and balances present in other areas of our national life, the only effective restraint upon executive policy and power in the areas of national defense and international affairs may lie in an enlightened citizenry — in an informed and critical public opinion which alone can here protect the values of democratic government. For this reason, it is perhaps here that a press that is alert, aware, and free most vitally serves the basic purpose of the First Amendment. For without an informed and free press there cannot be an enlightened people.

Yet it is elementary that the successful conduct of international diplomacy and the maintenance of an effective national defense require both confidentiality and secrecy. Other nations can hardly deal with this Nation in an atmosphere of mutual trust unless they can be assured that their confidences will be kept. And within our own executive departments, the development of considered and intelligent international policies would be impossible if those charged with their formulation could not communicate with each other freely, frankly, and in confidence. In the area of basic national defense the frequent need for absolute secrecy is, of course, self-evident.

I think there can be but one answer to this dilemma, if dilemma it be. The responsibility must be where the power is. If the Constitution gives the Executive a large degree of unshared power in the conduct of foreign affairs and the maintenance of our national defense, then under the Constitution the Executive must have the largely unshared duty to determine and preserve the degree of internal security necessary to exercise that power successfully. It is an awesome responsibility, requiring judgment and wisdom of a high order. I should suppose that moral, political, and practical considerations would dictate that a very first principle of that wisdom would be an insistence upon avoiding secrecy for its own sake. For when everything is classified, then nothing is classified, and the system becomes one to be disregarded by the cynical or the careless, and to be manipulated by those intent on self-protection or self-promotion. I should suppose, in short, that the hallmark of a truly effective internal security system would be the maximum possible disclosure, recognizing that secrecy can best be preserved only when credibility is truly maintained. But be that as it may, it is clear to me that it is the constitutional duty of the Executive—as a matter of sovereign prerogative and not as a matter of law as the courts know law—through the promulgation and enforcement of executive regulations, to protect the confidentiality necessary to carry out its responsibilities in the fields of international relations and national defense.

This is not to say that Congress and the courts have no role to play. Undoubtedly Congress has the power to enact specific and appropriate criminal laws to protect government property and preserve government secrets. Congress has passed such laws, and several of them are of very colorable relevance to the apparent circumstances of these cases. And if a criminal prosecution is instituted, it will be the responsibility of the courts to decide the applicability of the criminal law under which the charge is brought. Moreover, if Congress should pass a specific law authorizing civil proceedings in this field, the courts would likewise have the duty to decide the constitutionality of such a law as well as its applicability to the facts proved.

But in the cases before us we are asked neither to construe specific regulations nor to apply specific laws. We are asked, instead, to perform a function that the Constitution gave to the Executive, not the Judiciary. We are asked, quite simply, to prevent the publication by two newspapers of material that the Executive Branch insists should not, in the national interest, be published. I am convinced that the Executive is correct with respect to some of the documents involved. But I cannot say that disclosure of any of them will surely result in direct, immediate, and irreparable damage to our Nation or its people. That being so, there can under the First Amendment be but one judicial resolution of the issues before us. I join the judgments of the Court.

Mr. Justice White, with whom Mr. Justice Stewart joins, concurring.

I concur in today's judgments, but only because of the concededly extraordinary protection against prior restraints enjoyed by the press under our constitutional system. I do not say that in no circumstances would the First Amendment permit an injunction against publishing infor-

mation about government plans or operations. Nor, after examining the materials the Government characterizes as the most sensitive and destructive, can I deny that revelation of these documents will do substantial damage to public interests. Indeed, I am confident that their disclosure will have that result. But I nevertheless agree that the United States has not satisfied the very heavy burden that it must meet to warrant an injunction against publication in these cases, at least in the absence of express and appropriately limited congressional authorization for prior restraints in circumstances such as these.

At least in the absence of legislation by Congress, based on its own investigations and findings, I am quite unable to agree that the inherent powers of the Executive and the courts reach so far as to authorize remedies having such sweeping potential for inhibiting publications by the press. Much of the difficulty inheres in the "grave and irreparable danger" standard suggested by the United States. If the United States were to have judgment under such a standard in these cases, our decision would be of little guidance to other courts in other cases, for the material at issue here would not be available from the Court's opinion or from public records nor would it be published by the press. Indeed, even today where we hold that the United States has not met its burden, the material remains sealed in court records and it is properly not discussed in today's opinions. Moreover, because the material poses substantial dangers to national interests and because of the hazards of criminal sanctions, a responsible press may choose never to publish the more sensitive materials. To sustain the Government in these cases would start the courts down a long and hazardous road that I am not willing to travel, at least without congressional guidance and direction.

It is not easy to reject the proposition urged by the United States and to deny relief on its good-faith claims in these cases that publication will work serious damage to the country. But that discomfiture is considerably dispelled by the infrequency of prior-restraint cases. Normally, publication will occur and the damage be done before the Government has either opportunity or grounds for suppression. So here, publication has already begun and a substantial part of the threatened damage has already occurred. The fact of a massive breakdown in security is known, access to the documents by many unauthorized people is undeniable, and the efficacy of equitable relief against these or other newspapers to avert anticipated damage is doubtful at best.

What is more, terminating the ban on publication of the relatively few sensitive documents the Government now seeks to suppress does not mean that the law either requires or invites newspapers or others to publish them or that they will be immune from criminal action if they do. Prior restraints require an unusually heavy justification under the First Amendment; but failure by the Government to justify prior restraints does not measure its constitutional entitlement to a conviction for criminal publication. That the Government mistakenly chose to proceed by injunction does not mean that it could not successfully proceed in another way.

Mr. Justice Marshall, concurring.

The problem here is whether in these particular cases the Executive Branch has authority to invoke the equity jurisdiction of the courts to protect what it believes to be the national interest. See *In re Debs*, 158 U.S. 564, 584 (1895). The Government argues that in addition to the inherent power of any government to protect itself, the President's power to conduct foreign affairs and his position as Commander in Chief give him authority to impose censorship on the press to protect his ability to deal effectively with foreign nations and to conduct the military affairs of the country. Of course, it is beyond cavil that the President has broad powers by virtue of his primary responsibility for the conduct of our foreign affairs and his position as Commander in Chief. *Chicago & Southern Air Lines v. Waterman S.S. Corp.*, 333 U.S. 103 (1948); *Hirabayashi v. United States*, 320 U.S. 81, 93 (1943); *United States v. Curtiss-Wright Corp.*, 299 U.S. 304 (1936). And in some situations it may be that under whatever inherent powers the Government may have, as well as the implicit authority derived from the President's mandate to conduct foreign affairs and to act as Commander in Chief, there is a basis for the invocation of the equity jurisdiction of this Court as an aid to prevent the publication of ma-

terial damaging to "national security," however that term may be defined.

It would, however, be utterly inconsistent with the concept of separation of powers for this Court to use its power of contempt to prevent behavior that Congress has specifically declined to prohibit. There would be a similar damage to the basic concept of these co-equal branches of Government if when the Executive Branch has adequate authority granted by Congress to protect "national security" it can choose instead to invoke the contempt power of a court to enjoin the threatened conduct. The Constitution provides that Congress shall make laws, the President execute laws, and courts interpret laws. *Youngstown Sheet & Tube Co. v. Sawyer*, 343 U.S. 579 (1952). It did not provide for government by injunction in which the courts and the Executive Branch can "make law" without regard to the action of Congress. It may be more convenient for the Executive Branch if it need only convince a judge to prohibit conduct rather than ask the Congress to pass a law, and it may be more convenient to enforce a contempt order than to seek a criminal conviction in a jury trial. Moreover, it may be considered politically wise to get a court to share the responsibility for arresting those who the Executive Branch has probable cause to believe are violating the law. But convenience and political considerations of the moment do not justify a basic departure from the principles of our system of government.

Mr. Chief Justice Burger, dissenting.

So clear are the constitutional limitations on prior restraint against expression, that from the time of *Near v. Minnesota*, 283 U.S. 697 (1931), until recently in *Organization for a Better Austin v. Keefe*, 402 U.S. 415 (1971), we have had little occasion to be concerned with cases involving prior restraints against news reporting on matters of public interest. There is, therefore, little variation among the members of the Court in terms of resistance to prior restraints against publication. Adherence to this basic constitutional principle, however, does not make these cases simple. In these cases, the imperative of a free and unfettered press comes into collision with another imperative, the effective functioning of a complex modern government and specifically the effective exercise of certain constitutional powers of the Executive. Only those who view the First Amendment as an absolute in all circumstances—a view I respect, but reject—can find such cases as these to be simple or easy.

These cases are not simple for another and more immediate reason. We do not know the facts of the cases. No District Judge knew all the facts. No Court of Appeals judge knew all the facts. No member of this Court knows all the facts.

Why are we in this posture, in which only those judges to whom the First Amendment is absolute and permits of no restraint in any circumstances or for any reason, are really in a position to act?

I suggest we are in this posture because these cases have been conducted in unseemly haste. Mr. Justice Harlan covers the chronology of events demonstrating the hectic pressures under which these cases have been processed and I need not restate them. The prompt setting of these cases reflects our universal abhorrence of prior restraint. But prompt judicial action does not mean unjudicial haste.

Here, moreover, the frenetic haste is due in large part to the manner in which the *Times* proceeded from the date it obtained the purloined documents. It seems reasonably clear now that the haste precluded reasonable and deliberate judicial treatment of these cases and was not warranted. The precipitate action of this Court aborting trials not yet completed is not the kind of judicial conduct that ought to attend the disposition of a great issue.

The newspapers make a derivative claim under the First Amendment; they denominate this right as the public "right to know"; by implication, the *Times* asserts a sole trusteeship of that right by virtue of its journalistic "scoop." The right is asserted as an absolute. Of course, the First Amendment right itself is not an absolute, as Justice Holmes so long ago pointed out in his aphorism concerning the right to shout "fire" in a crowded theater if there was no fire. There are other exceptions, some of which Chief Justice Hughes mentioned by way of example in *Near v. Minnesota*. There are no doubt other exceptions no one has had occasion to describe or discuss. Conceivably such exceptions may be lurking in these cases

and would have been flushed had they been properly considered in the trial courts, free from unwarranted deadlines and frenetic pressures. An issue of this importance should be tried and heard in a judicial atmosphere conducive to thoughtful, reflective deliberation, especially when haste, in terms of hours, is unwarranted in light of the long period the *Times,* by its own choice, deferred publication.

It is not disputed that the *Times* has had unauthorized possession of the documents for three to four months, during which it has had its expert analysts studying them, presumably digesting them and preparing the material for publication. During all of this time, the *Times,* presumably in its capacity as trustee of the public's "right to know," has held up publication for purposes it considered proper and thus public knowledge was delayed. No doubt this was for a good reason; the analysis of 7,000 pages of complex material drawn from a vastly greater volume of material would inevitably take time and the writing of good news stories takes time. But why should the United States Government, from whom this information was illegally acquired by someone, along with all the counsel, trial judges, and appellate judges be placed under needless pressure? After these months of deferral, the alleged "right to know" has somehow and suddenly become a right that must be vindicated instanter.

Would it have been unreasonable, since the newspaper could anticipate the Government's objections to release of secret material, to give the Government an opportunity to review the entire collection and determine whether agreement could be reached on publication? Stolen or not, if security was not in fact jeopardized, much of the material could no doubt have been declassified, since it spans a period ending in 1968. With such an approach—one that great newspapers have in the past practiced and stated editorially to be the duty of an honorable press—the newspapers and Government might well have narrowed the area of disagreement as to what was and was not publishable, leaving the remainder to be resolved in orderly litigation, if necessary. To me it is hardly believable that a newspaper long regarded as a great institution in American life would fail to perform one of the basic and simple duties of every citizen with respect to the discovery or possession of stolen property or secret government documents. That duty, I had thought—perhaps naively—was to report forthwith, to responsible public officers. This duty rests on taxi drivers, Justices, and the *New York Times*. The course followed by the *Times*, whether so calculated or not, removed any possibility of orderly litigation of the issues. If the action of the judges up to now has been correct, that result is sheer happenstance.

Our grant of the writ of certiorari before final judgment in the *Times* case aborted the trial in the District Court before it had made a complete record pursuant to the mandate of the Court of Appeals for the Second Circuit.

The consequence of all this melancholy series of events is that we literally do not know what we are acting on. As I see it, we have been forced to deal with litigation concerning rights of great magnitude without an adequate record, and surely without time for adequate treatment either in the prior proceedings or in this Court. It is interesting to note that counsel on both sides, in oral argument before this Court, were frequently unable to respond to questions on factual points. Not surprisingly they pointed out that they had been working literally "around the clock" and simply were unable to review the documents that give rise to these cases and were not familiar with them. This Court is in no better posture. I agree generally with Mr. Justice Harlan and Mr. Justice Blackmun but I am not prepared to reach the merits.

I would affirm the Court of Appeals for the Second Circuit and allow the District Court to complete the trial aborted by our grant of certiorari, meanwhile preserving the status quo in the *Post* case. I would direct that the District Court on remand give priority to the *Times* case to the exclusion of all other business of that court but I would not set arbitrary deadlines.

I should add that I am in general agreement with much of what Mr. Justice White has expressed with respect to penal sanctions concerning communication or retention of documents or information relating to the national defense.

We all crave speedier judicial processes but

when judges are pressured as in these cases the result is a parody of the judicial function.

Mr. Justice Harlan, with whom the Chief Justice and Mr. Justice Blackmun join, dissenting.

These cases forcefully call to mind the wise admonition of Mr. Justice Holmes, dissenting in *Northern Securities Co. v. United States,* 193 U.S. 197, 400–401 (1904):

> Great cases like hard cases make bad law. For great cases are called great, not by reason of their real importance in shaping the law of the future, but because of some accident of immediate overwhelming interest which appeals to the feelings and distorts the judgment. These immediate interests exercise a kind of hydraulic pressure which makes what previously was clear seem doubtful, and before which even well settled principles of law will bend.

With all respect, I consider that the Court has been almost irresponsibly feverish in dealing with these cases.

Both the Court of Appeals for the Second Circuit and the Court of Appeals for the District of Columbia Circuit rendered judgment on June 23. The *New York Times'* petition for certiorari, its motion for accelerated consideration thereof, and its application for interim relief were filed in this Court on June 24 at about 11 a.m. The application of the United States for interim relief in the *Post* case was also filed here on June 24 at about 7:15 p.m. This Court's order setting a hearing before us on June 26 at 11 a.m., a course which I joined only to avoid the possibility of even more peremptory action by the Court, was issued less than 24 hours before. The record in the *Post* case was filed with the Clerk shortly before 1 p.m. on June 25; the record in the *Times* case did not arrive until 7 or 8 o'clock that same night. The briefs of the parties were received less than two hours before argument on June 26.

This frenzied train of events took place in the name of the presumption against prior restraints created by the First Amendment. Due regard for the extraordinarily important and difficult questions involved in these litigations should have led the Court to shun such a precipitate timetable. In order to decide the merits of these cases properly, some or all of the following questions should have been faced:

1. Whether the Attorney General is authorized to bring these suits in the name of the United States. Compare *In re Debs,* 158 U.S. 564 (1895), with *Youngstown Sheet & Tube Co. v. Sawyer,* 343 U.S. 579 (1952). This question involves as well the construction and validity of a singularly opaque statute—the Espionage Act, 18 U.S.C. § 793 (e).

2. Whether the First Amendment permits the federal courts to enjoin publication of stories which would present a serious threat to national security. See *Near v. Minnesota,* 283 U.S. 697, 716 (1931) (dictum).

3. Whether the threat to publish highly secret documents is of itself a sufficient implication of national security to justify an injunction on the theory that regardless of the contents of the documents harm enough results simply from the demonstration of such a breach of secrecy.

4. Whether the unauthorized disclosure of any of these particular documents would seriously impair the national security.

5. What weight should be given to the opinion of high officers in the Executive Branch of the Government with respect to questions 3 and 4.

6. Whether the newspapers are entitled to retain and use the documents notwithstanding the seemingly uncontested facts that the documents, or the originals of which they are duplicates, were purloined from the Government's possession and that the newspapers received them with knowledge that they had been feloniously acquired. Cf. *Liberty Lobby, Inc. v. Pearson,* 129 U.S. App. D.C. 74, 390 F. 2d 489 (1967, amended 1968).

7. Whether the threatened harm to the national security or the Government's possessory interest in the documents justifies the issuance of an injunction against publication in light of—

a. The strong First Amendment policy against prior restraints on publication;

b. The doctrine against enjoining conduct in violation of criminal statutes; and

c. The extent to which the materials at issue have apparently already been otherwise disseminated.

These are difficult questions of fact, of law, and of judgment; the potential consequences of erroneous decision are enormous. The time which has been available to us, to the lower courts, and to the parties has been wholly inadequate for giving these cases the kind of consideration they deserve. It is a reflection on the stability of the judicial process that these great issues—as important as any that have arisen during my time on the Court—should have been decided under the pressures engendered by the torrent of publicity that has attended these litigations from their inception.

Forced as I am to reach the merits of these cases, I dissent from the opinion and judgments of the Court. Within the severe limitations imposed by the time constraints under which I have been required to operate, I can only state my reasons in telescoped form, even though in different circumstances I would have felt constrained to deal with the cases in the fuller sweep indicated above.

It is a sufficient basis for affirming the Court of Appeals for the Second Circuit in the *Times* litigation to observe that its order must rest on the conclusion that because of the time elements the Government had not been given an adequate opportunity to present its case to the District Court. At the least this conclusion was not an abuse of discretion....

But I think there is another and more fundamental reason why this judgment cannot stand—a reason which also furnishes an additional ground for not reinstating the judgment of the District Court in the *Times* litigation, set aside by the Court of Appeals. It is plain to me that the scope of the judicial function in passing upon the activities of the Executive Branch of the Government in the field of foreign affairs is very narrowly restricted. This view is, I think, dictated by the concept of separation of powers upon which our constitutional system rests.

The power to evaluate the "pernicious influence" of premature disclosure is not, however, lodged in the Executive alone. I agree that, in performance of its duty to protect the values of the First Amendment against political pressures, the judiciary must review the initial Executive determination to the point of satisfying itself that the subject matter of the dispute does lie within the proper compass of the President's foreign relations power. Constitutional considerations forbid "a complete abandonment of judicial control." Cf. *United States v. Reynolds,* 345 U.S. 1, 8 (1953). Moreover, the judiciary may properly insist that the determination that disclosure of the subject matter would irreparably impair the national security be made by the head of the Executive Department concerned—here the Secretary of State or the Secretary of Defense—after actual personal consideration by that officer. This safeguard is required in the analogous area of executive claims of privilege for secrets of state. See *id.,* at 8 and n. 20; *Duncan v. Cammell, Laird & Co.,* [1942] A. C. 624, 638 (House of Lords).

But in my judgment the judiciary may not properly go beyond these two inquiries and re-determine for itself the probable impact of disclosure on the national security.

Mr. Justice Blackmun, dissenting.

The First Amendment, after all, is only one part of an entire Constitution. Article II of the great document vests in the Executive Branch primary power over the conduct of foreign affairs and places in that branch the responsibility for the Nation's safety. Each provision of the Constitution is important, and I cannot subscribe to a doctrine of unlimited absolutism for the First Amendment at the cost of downgrading other provisions. First Amendment absolutism has never commanded a majority of this Court. See, for example, *Near v. Minnesota,* 283 U.S. 697, 708 (1931), and *Schenck v. United States,* 249 U.S. 47, 52 (1919). What is needed here is a weighing, upon properly developed standards, of the broad right of the press to print and of the very narrow right of the Government to prevent. Such standards are not yet developed. The parties here are in disagreement as to what those standards should be. But even the newspapers concede that there are situations where restraint is in order and is constitutional. Mr. Justice Holmes gave us a suggestion when he said in *Schenck,* "It is a question of proximity and degree. When a nation is at war many things that might be said in time of peace are such a hindrance to its effort that their utterance will not be endured so long as men fight and that no Court could regard them as protected by any constitutional right" 249 U.S., at 52.

I therefore would remand these cases to be developed expeditiously, of course, but on a schedule permitting the orderly presentation of evidence from both sides, with the use of discovery, if necessary, as authorized by the rules, and

with the preparation of briefs, oral argument, and court opinions of a quality better than has been seen to this point. In making this last statement, I criticize no lawyer or judge. I know from past personal experience the agony of time pressure in the preparation of litigation. But these cases and the issues involved and the courts, including this one, deserve better than has been produced thus far.

Despite the highly fragmented nature of the Pentagon Papers decision, several important principles emerge clearly from the case. The Court generally embraced the general notions that prior restraints have a presumption of unconstitutionality and that government carries a heavy burden in justifying them.[206] Majority support also exists for the propositions that the president does not possess inherent power to secure a prior restraint on national security grounds and that, even if publication is not enjoined, subsequent criminal prosecution may be appropriate. Finally, when the three dissenting opinions are added to Justice White, Stewart, and Marshall's concurrences, support seemingly would have existed for a contrary result if Congress had enacted legislation specifically authorizing restraint under the circumstances.

The presence of a pertinent statute seems to have been critical to a lower court's decision to restrain publication of an article explaining how to construct a hydrogen bomb. In *United States v. The Progressive, Inc.,*[207] a federal district court determined that national security outweighed competing First Amendment interests. Although acknowledging the heavy presumption against the constitutionality of a prior restraint,[208] it was convinced that the government had demonstrated that publication would gravely, directly, immediately, and irreparably injure the national interest.[209] The trial court found unpersuasive arguments that, because the article contained material available in the public domain, dissemination could not violate a statutory prohibition against disclosing restricted data. Rather, it concluded that the article could facilitate development of a weapon more efficiently by less developed notions and enable them to bypass what otherwise might be blind alleys.[210] The district court proceeded to distinguish the case from the Pentagon Papers decision on three basic grounds. First, it noted that the documents at issue in the *New York Times* case were historical documents.[211] Second, government had offered no cogent reason to block publication except that it might embarrass the United States.[212] Third, a precise statute prohibited communication, including publication, of restricted data concerning the production of nuclear weapons.[213]

The trial court portrayed the essential question as "a basic confrontation between the First Amendment right to freedom of the press and national security."[214] The interests it actually balanced, however, were "the right to continued life and the right to freedom of the press."[215] Because freedom of the press can be reconstructed even if lost, while life cannot, the district court determined that the disparity of risk to the important interests at stake favored restraint.[216] Noting that "the right to publish becomes moot . . . [if] our right to life is extinguished,"[217] it found publication at least equivalent to publication of troop movements during wartime and thereby within the exceptions to the rule against prior restraint recognized in *Near*.[218]

Although alluding to a test of "immediate, direct and irreparable harm" to justify a prior restraint, akin to Justice Brennan's formula in the Pentagon Papers case,[219] it is evident that the trial court's application of the standard varied from its precise terms. The decision to restrain publication essentially was grounded in the magnitude of possible harm rather than any proof of actual or imminent damage. Thus, a restraint of publication was premised upon speculation rather than certainty of consequence. The case ultimately actuated Justice White's earlier observation that, once security is breached at its origin, prior restraint generally is an ineffective response. While the issue was on appeal, other newspapers published the article which *The Progressive* had been enjoined from disseminating. Thereafter, the case was dismissed.[220]

United States v. The Progressive, Inc., 467 F. Supp. 990 (W.D. Wis.), *appeal dismissed,* 610 F.2d 819 (7th Cir. 1979).

Warren, District Judge.

On March 9, 1979, this Court, at the request of the government, but after hearing from both parties, issued a temporary restraining order enjoining defendants, their employees, and agents from publishing or otherwise communicating or disclosing in any manner any restricted data contained in the article: "The H-Bomb Secret: How We Got It, Why We're Telling It."

In keeping with the Court's order that the temporary restraining order should be in effect for the shortest time possible, a preliminary injunction hearing was scheduled for one week later, on March 16, 1979. At the request of the parties and with the Court's acquiescence, the preliminary injunction hearing was rescheduled for 10:00 a.m. today in order that both sides might have additional time to file affidavits and arguments. The Court continued the temporary restraining order until 5:00 p.m. today.

Under the facts here alleged, the question before this Court involves a clash between allegedly vital security interests of the United States and the competing constitutional doctrine against prior restraint in publication.

In its argument and briefs, plaintiff relies on national security, as enunciated by Congress in The Atomic Energy Act of 1954, as the basis for classification of certain documents. Plaintiff contends that, in certain areas, national preservation and self-interest permit the retention and classification of government secrets. The government argues that its national security interest also permits it to impress classification and censorship upon information originating in the public domain, if when drawn together, synthesized and collated, such information acquires the character of presenting immediate, direct and irreparable harm to the interests of the United States.

Defendants argue that freedom of expression as embodied in the First Amendment is so central to the heart of liberty that prior restraint in any form becomes anathema. They contend that this is particularly true when a nation is not at war and where the prior restraint is based on surmise or conjecture. While acknowledging that freedom of the press is not absolute, they maintain that the publication of the projected article does not rise to the level of immediate, direct and irreparable harm which could justify incursion into First Amendment freedoms....

From the founding days of this nation, the rights to freedom of speech and of the press have held an honored place in our constitutional scheme. The establishment and nurturing of these rights is one of the true achievements of our form of government.

Because of the importance of these rights, any prior restraint on publication comes into court under a heavy presumption against its constitutional validity. *New York Times v. United States,* 403 U.S. 713, 91 S.Ct. 2140, 29 L.Ed.2d 822 (1971).

However, First Amendment rights are not absolute. They are not boundless....

Thus, it is clear that few things, save grave national security concerns, are sufficient to override First Amendment interests. A court is well admonished to approach any requested prior restraint with a great deal of skepticism.

Juxtaposed against the right to freedom of expression is the government's contention that the national security of this country could be jeopardized by publication of the article.

The Court is convinced that the government has a right to classify certain sensitive documents to protect its national security. The problem is with the scope of the classification system.

Defendants contend that the projected article merely contains data already in the public domain and readily available to any diligent seeker. They say other nations already have the same information or the opportunity to obtain it. How then, they argue, can they be in violation of 42 U.S.C. §§ 2274(b) and 2280 which purport to authorize injunctive relief against one who would disclose restricted data "with reason to believe such data will be utilized to injure the United States or to secure an advantage to any foreign nation . . ."?

Even if some of the information is in the public domain, due recognition must be given to the human skills and expertise involved in writing this article. The author needed sufficient expertise to recognize relevant, as opposed to irrelevant, information and to assimilate the information obtained. The right questions had to be asked or the correct educated guesses had to be made.

The ability of G. I. Taylor to calculate the yield of the first nuclear explosion from a *Life* magazine photo demonstrates that certain individuals with some knowledge, ability to reason and extraordinary perseverance may acquire additional knowledge without access to classified information, even though the information thus acquired may not be obvious to others not so equipped or motivated. All of this must be considered in resolving the issues before the Court.

Does the article provide a "do-it yourself" guide for the hydrogen bomb? Probably not. A number of affidavits make quite clear that a *sine qua non* to thermonuclear capability is a large, sophisticated industrial capability coupled with a coterie of imaginative, resourceful scientists and technicians. One does not build a hydrogen bomb in the basement. However, the article could possibly provide sufficient information to allow a medium size nation to move faster in developing a hydrogen weapon. It could provide a ticket to by-pass blind alleys.

The Morland piece could accelerate the membership of a candidate nation in the thermonuclear club. Pursuit of blind alleys or failure to grasp seemingly basic concepts have been the cause of many inventive failures. . . .

The point has also been made that it is only a question of time before other countries will have the hydrogen bomb. That may be true. However, there are times in the course of human history when time itself may be very important. This time factor becomes critical when considering mass annihilation weaponry—witness the failure of Hitler to get his V-1 and V-2 bombs operational quickly enough to materially affect the outcome of World War II.

Defendants have stated that publication of the article will alert the people of this country to the false illusion of security created by the government's futile efforts at secrecy. They believe publication will provide the people with needed information to make informed decisions on an urgent issue of public concern.

However, this Court can find no plausible reason why the public needs to know the technical details about hydrogen bomb construction to carry on an informed debate on this issue. Furthermore, the Court believes that the defendants' position in favor of nuclear non-proliferation would be harmed, not aided, by the publication of this article.

The defendants have also relied on the decision in the *New York Times* case. In that case, the Supreme Court refused to enjoin the *New York Times* and the *Washington Post* from publishing the contents of a classified historical study of United States decision-making in Viet Nam, the so-called "Pentagon Papers."

This case is different in several important respects. In the first place, the study involved in the *New York Times* case contained historical data relating to events that occurred some three to twenty years previously. Secondly, the Supreme Court agreed with the lower court that no cogent reasons were advanced by the government as to why the article affected national security except that publication might cause some embarrassment to the United States.

A final and most vital difference between these two cases is the fact that a specific statute is involved here. Section 2274 of The Atomic Energy Act prohibits anyone from communicating, transmitting or disclosing any restricted data to any person "with reason to believe such data will be utilized to injure the United States or to secure an advantage to any foreign nation."

Section 2014 of the Act defines restricted data. " 'Restricted Data' means all data concerning 1) design, manufacture, or utilization of atomic weapons; 2) the production of special nuclear material; or 3) the use of special nuclear material in the production of energy, but shall not include data declassified or removed from the Restricted Data category pursuant to section 2162 of this title."

As applied to this case, the Court finds that the statute in question is not vague or overbroad. The Court is convinced that the terms used in the statute—"communicates, transmits or discloses"—include publishing in a magazine.

The Court is of the opinion that the government has shown that the defendants had reason to believe that the data in the article, if published, would injure the United States or give an advantage to a foreign nation. Extensive reading and studying of the documents on file lead to the conclusion that not all the data is available in the public realm in the same fashion, if it is available at all.

What is involved here is information dealing with the most destructive weapon in the history of mankind, information of sufficient destructive potential to nullify the right to free speech and to endanger the right to life itself.

Stripped to its essence then, the question before the Court is a basic confrontation between the First Amendment right to freedom of the press and national security.

The Court believes that each of us is born seized of a panoply of basic rights, that we institute governments to secure these rights and that there is a hierarchy of values attached to these rights which is helpful in deciding the clash now before us.

Certain of these rights have an aspect of imperativeness or centrality that make them transcend other rights. Somehow it does not seem that the right to life and the right to not have soldiers quartered in your home can be of equal import in the grand scheme of things. While it may be true in the long-run, as Patrick Henry instructs us, that one would prefer death to life without liberty, nonetheless, in the short-run, one cannot enjoy freedom of speech, freedom to worship or freedom of the press unless one first enjoys the freedom to live.

Faced with a stark choice between upholding the right to continued life and the right to freedom of the press, most jurists would have no difficulty in opting for the chance to continue to breathe and function as they work to achieve perfect freedom of expression.

Is the choice here so stark? Only time can give us a definitive answer. But considering another aspect of this panoply of rights we all have is helpful in answering the question now before us. This aspect is the disparity of the risk involved.

The destruction of various human rights can come about in differing ways and at varying speeds. Freedom of the press can be obliterated overnight by some dictator's imposition of censorship or by the slow nibbling away at a free press through successive bits of repressive legislation enacted by a nation's lawmakers. Yet, even in the most drastic of such situations, it is always possible for a dictator to be overthrown, for a bad law to be repealed or for a judge's error to be subsequently rectified. Only when human life is at stake are such corrections impossible.

The Court is faced with the difficult task of weighing and resolving these divergent views.

A mistake in ruling against *The Progressive* will seriously infringe cherished First Amendment rights. If a preliminary injunction is issued, it will constitute the first instance of prior restraint against a publication in this fashion in the history of this country, to this Court's knowledge. Such notoriety is not to be sought. It will curtail defendants' First Amendment rights in a drastic and substantial fashion. It will infringe upon our right to know and to be informed as well.

A mistake in ruling against the United States could pave the way for thermonuclear annihilation for us all. In that event, our right to life is extinguished and the right to publish becomes moot.

In the *Near* case, the Supreme Court recognized that publication of troop movements in time of war would threaten national security and could therefore be restrained. Times have changed significantly since 1931 when *Near* was decided. Now war by foot soldiers has been replaced in large part by war by machines and bombs. No longer need there be any advance warning or any preparation time before a nuclear war could be commenced.

In light of these factors, this Court concludes that publication of the technical information on the hydrogen bomb contained in the article is analogous to publication of troop movements or locations in time of war and falls within the extremely narrow exception to the rule against prior restraint.

Because of this "disparity of risk," because the government has met its heavy burden of showing justification for the imposition of a prior restraint on publication of the objected-to technical portions of the Morland article, and because the Court is unconvinced that suppression of the objected-to technical portions of the Morland article would in any plausible fashion impede the defendants in their laudable crusade to stimulate public knowledge of nuclear armament and bring about enlightened debate on national policy questions, the Court finds that the objected-to portions of the article fall within the narrow area recognized by the Court in *Near v. Minnesota* in which a prior restraint on publication is appropriate.

The government has met its burden under section 2274 of The Atomic Energy Act. In the Court's opinion, it has also met the test enunciated by two Justices in the *New York Times* case, namely grave, direct, immediate and irreparable harm to the United States.

The Court has just determined that if necessary it will at this time assume the awesome responsibility of issuing a preliminary injunction against *The Progressive*'s use of the Morland article in its current form.

However, the Court is acutely aware of the old legal adage that "bad cases make bad law." This case in its present posture will undoubtedly go to the Supreme Court because it does present so starkly the clash between freedom of press and national security. Does it go there with the blessing of the entire press? The Court thinks not. Many elements of the press see grave risk of permanent damage to First Amendment freedoms if this case goes forward. They feel appellate courts will find, as this Court has, that the risk is simply too great to permit publication.

Furthermore, if there is any one inescapable conclusion that one arrives at after wading through all these experts' affidavits, it is that many wise, intelligent, patriotic individuals can hold diametrically opposite opinions on the issues before us.

Recognizing that both sides at the moment may seem adamant, the Court nonetheless was greatly impressed by the arguments in the *amicus* brief submitted by the Federation of American Scientists through its director, Dr. Jeremy J. Stone.

This group, with half of America's Nobel laureates in its ranks, urged *The Progressive* to recognize the damage the article could do to both nuclear non-proliferation policies and First Amendment rights....

NOW THEREFORE, acting on this suggestion, the Court herewith poses to the parties a final choice:

We will now adjourn until 2:00 p.m. At that time the case will be recalled. In the interim, each party is to consider whether it would be willing to meet with a panel of five mediators appointed by the Court to attempt to resolve the parties' differences.

The Progressive case was dismissed in 610 F.2d 819 (7th Cir. 1979) after the article appeared in other publications.

Chief Justice Burger, who had dissented from the judgment in the Pentagon Papers case, authored the Court's opinion in *Nebraska Press Association v. Stuart,* which vindicated First Amendment interests. The decision[221] lifted a gag order entered by a state court restraining publication of a defendant's statements before a criminal trial. The trial court had entered the restraining order pursuant to its determination of "a clear and present danger that pre-trial publicity could impinge upon the defendant's right to a fair trial."[222] The lower court obviously had departed from the modern requirements for finding a clear and present danger, as evidenced by its conclusion that harm could rather than would likely result. Although noting that the restraining order would have postponed rather than prohibited publication, as in the *New York Times* case,[223] Burger determined that officially imposed delay was intolerable because prompt reporting of criminal proceedings was more imperative.[224]

The Court identified three pertinent factors for determining whether a gag order was appropriate. It considered "(a) the nature and extent of pretrial news coverage; (b) whether other measures would be likely to mitigate the effects of unrestrained pretrial publicity; and (c) how effectively a restraining order would operate to prevent the threatened danger."[225] Although recognizing that the trial judge reasonably could have concluded that pretrial publicity would be pervasive and intensive and might impair the right to a fair trial, the Court found error in his speculation of harm.[226] In emphasizing an obligation to consider less restrictive alternatives, the Court noted that possibilities included change of venue, postponement of trial, searching voir dire of prospective jurors, emphatic and clear jury instructions to consider only the evidence, and sequestration.[227] Finally, the Court doubted the efficacy of a restraining order under the particular circumstances, given the limited territorial jurisdiction of the Court and a small town in which information traveled swiftly by word of mouth anyway.[228]

The *Nebraska Press Association* decision is not without problems both on fair trial and First Amendment grounds. Each of the less restrictive alternatives identified by the Court may burden a defendant. Given the pervasiveness of modern media and expansion of markets effectuated by the emergence of cable and satellites, venues not exposed to publicity may be difficult to locate. Postponement to let public sentiment abate may create speedy trial problems. Extensive questioning of jurors may expose the jury to negative information for the first time or condition it against the defendant. Individuals also may be unlikely to recognize or acknowledge prejudice. Even clear jury instructions may not overcome the natural difficulty of compartmentalizing information, and sequestration may foster juror resentment. The ruling in favor of First Amendment interests, despite those problems, also contains some language that is potentially incongruous with freedom of the press. The Court observed that "(t)he extraordinary protections afforded by the First Amendment carry with them something in the nature of a fiduciary duty to exercise the protected rights responsibly."[229] Although not amplified, beyond an announced expectation that the press would exercise some effort to protect rights of the accused to a fair trial, the declaration of a fiduciary duty is reminiscent of the public trustee standard used to impose special content obligations upon broadcasters.[230] It is a philosophical predicate, whether developed or not, for a fair rather than free press.[231]

Although concurring in the Court's judgment, Justice Brennan would have gone farther in advancing First Amendment interests. Brennan would have held that prior restraint is never a permissible means of securing the right to a fair trial.[232] Furthermore, he would have found that deprivation of the Sixth Amendment right to an impartial jury never could rise to the level of harm required for prior restraint. Because a defendant always has a right to appeal, Brennan maintained that harm could never be irreparable.[233]

Nebraska Press Association v. Stuart, 427 U.S. 539 (1976)

Mr. Chief Justice Burger delivered the opinion of the Court.

The respondent State District Judge entered an order restraining the petitioners from publishing or broadcasting accounts of confessions or admissions made by the accused or facts "strongly implicative" of the accused in a widely reported murder of six persons. We granted certiorari to decide whether the entry of such an order on the showing made before the state court violated the constitutional guarantee of freedom of the press.

On the evening of October 18, 1975, local police found the six members of the Henry Kellie family murdered in their home in Sutherland, Neb., a town of about 850 people. Police released the description of a suspect, Erwin Charles Simants, to the reporters who had hastened to the scene of the crime. Simants was arrested and arraigned in Lincoln County Court the following morning, ending a tense night for this small rural community.

The crime immediately attracted widespread news coverage, by local, regional, and national newspapers, radio and television stations. Three days after the crime, the County Attorney and Simants' attorney joined in asking the County Court to enter a restrictive order relating to "matters that may or may not be publicly reported or disclosed to the public," because of the "mass coverage by news media" and the "reasonable likelihood of prejudicial news which would make difficult, if not impossible, the impaneling of an impartial jury and tend to prevent a fair trial." The County Court heard oral argument but took no evidence; no attorney for members of the press appeared at this stage. The County Court granted the prosecutor's motion for a restrictive order and entered it the next day, October 22. The order prohibited everyone in attendance from "releas[ing] or authoriz[ing] the release for public dissemination in any form or manner whatsoever any testimony given or evidence adduced"; the order also required members of the press to observe the Nebraska Bar-Press Guidelines.

Simants' preliminary hearing was held the same day, open to the public but subject to the order. The County Court bound over the defendant for trial to the State District Court. The charges, as amended to reflect the autopsy findings, were that Simants had committed the murders in the course of a sexual assault.

Petitioners—several press and broadcast associations, publishers, and individual reporters—moved on October 23 for leave to intervene in the District Court, asking that the restrictive order imposed by the County Court be vacated. The District Court conducted a hearing, at which the County Judge testified and newspaper articles about the *Simants* case were admitted in evidence. The District Judge granted petitioners' motion to intervene and, on October 27, entered his own restrictive order. The judge found "because of the nature of the crimes charged in the complaint that there is a clear and present danger that pretrial publicity could impinge upon the defendant's right to a fair trial." The order applied only until the jury was impaneled, and specifically prohibited petitioners from reporting five subjects: (1) the existence or contents of a confession Simants had made to law enforcement officers, which had been introduced in open court at arraignment; (2) the fact or nature of statements Simants had made to other persons; (3) the contents of a note he had written the night of the crime; (4) certain aspects of the medical testimony at the preliminary hearing; and (5) the identity of the victims of the alleged sexual assault and the nature of the assault. It also prohibited reporting the exact nature of the restrictive order itself. Like the County Court's order, this order incorporated the Nebraska Bar-Press Guidelines. Finally, the order set out a plan for attendance, seating, and courthouse traffic control during the trial.

The problems presented by this case are almost as old as the Republic. Neither in the Constitution nor in contemporaneous writings do we find that the conflict between these two important rights was anticipated, yet it is inconceivable that the authors of the Constitution were unaware of the potential conflicts between the right to an unbiased jury and the guarantee of freedom of the press. . . .

The thread running through [earlier] cases is that prior restraints on speech and publication are the most serious and the least tolerable infringement on First Amendment rights. A criminal penalty or a judgment in a defamation case is subject to the whole panoply of protections afforded by deferring the impact of the judgment until all avenues of appellate review have been exhausted. Only after judgment has become final, correct or otherwise, does the law's sanction become fully operative.

A prior restraint, by contrast and by definition, has an immediate and irreversible sanction. If it can be said that a threat of criminal or civil sanctions after publication "chills" speech, prior restraint "freezes" it at least for the time.

The damage can be particularly great when the prior restraint falls upon the communication of news and commentary on current events. Truthful reports of public judicial proceedings have been afforded special protection against subsequent punishment. See *Cox Broadcasting Corp. v. Cohn,* 420 U.S. 469, 492–493 (1975); see also, *Craig v. Harney,* 331 U.S. 367, 374 (1947). For the same reasons the protection against prior restraint should have particular force as applied to reporting of criminal proceedings, whether the crime in question is a single isolated act or a pattern of criminal conduct.

> A responsible press has always been regarded as the handmaiden of effective judicial administration, especially in the criminal field. Its function in this regard is documented by an impressive record of service over several centuries. The press does not simply publish information about trials but guards against the miscarriage of justice by subjecting the police, prosecutors, and judicial processes to extensive public scrutiny and criticism." *Sheppard v. Maxwell,* 384 U.S., at 350.

The extraordinary protections afforded by the First Amendment carry with them something in the nature of a fiduciary duty to exercise the protected rights responsibly—a duty widely acknowledged but not always observed by editors and publishers. It is not asking too much to suggest that those who exercise First Amendment rights in newspapers or broadcasting enterprises direct some effort to protect the rights of an accused to a fair trial by unbiased jurors.

Of course, the order at issue—like the order requested in *New York Times*—does not prohibit but only postpones publication. Some news can be delayed and most commentary can even more readily be delayed without serious injury, and there often is a self-imposed delay when responsible editors call for verification of information. But such delays are normally slight and they are self-imposed. Delays imposed by governmental authority are a different matter.

> We have learned, and continue to learn, from what we view as the unhappy experiences of other nations where government has been allowed to meddle in the internal editorial affairs of newspapers. Regardless of how beneficent-sounding the purposes of controlling the press might be, we . . . remain intensely skeptical about those measures that would allow government to insinuate itself into the edito-

rial rooms of this Nation's press." *Miami Herald Publishing Co. v. Tornillo*, 418 U.S. 241, 259 (1974) (White, J., concurring).

See also *Columbia Broadcasting v. Democratic Comm.*, 412 U.S. 94 (1973). As a practical matter, moreover, the element of time is not unimportant if press coverage is to fulfill its traditional function of bringing news to the public promptly.

We turn now to the record in this case to determine whether, as Learned Hand put it, "the gravity of the 'evil,' discounted by its improbability, justifies such invasion of free speech as is necessary to avoid the danger." *United States v. Dennis*, 183 F. 2d 201, 212 (CA2 1950), aff'd, 341 U.S. 494 (1951); see also L. Hand, The Bill of Rights 58–61 (1958). To do so, we must examine the evidence before the trial judge when the order was entered to determine (a) the nature and extent of pretrial news coverage; (b) whether other measures would be likely to mitigate the effects of unrestrained pretrial publicity; and (c) how effectively a restraining order would operate to prevent the threatened danger. The precise terms of the restraining order are also important. We must then consider whether the record supports the entry of a prior restraint on publication, one of the most extraordinary remedies known to our jurisprudence....

Our review of the pretrial record persuades us that the trial judge was justified in concluding that there would be intense and pervasive pretrial publicity concerning this case. He could also reasonably conclude, based on common human experience, that publicity might impair the defendant's right to a fair trial. He did not purport to say more, for he found only "a clear and present danger that pre-trial publicity *could* impinge upon the defendant's right to a fair trial." (Emphasis added.) His conclusion as to the impact of such publicity on prospective jurors was of necessity speculative, dealing as he was with factors unknown and unknowable.

We find little in the record that goes to another aspect of our task, determining whether measures short of an order restraining all publication would have insured the defendant a fair trial. Although the entry of the order might be read as a judicial determination that other measures would not suffice, the trial court made no express findings to that effect; the Nebraska Supreme Court referred to the issue only by implication. See 194 Neb., at 797–798, 236 N. W. 2d, at 803.

Most of the alternatives to prior restraint of publication in these circumstances were discussed with obvious approval in *Sheppard v. Maxwell*, 384 U.S., at 357–362: (a) change of trial venue to a place less exposed to the intense publicity that seemed imminent in Lincoln County; (b) postponement of the trial to allow public attention to subside; (c) searching questioning of prospective jurors, as Mr. Chief Justice Marshall used in the *Burr* case, to screen out those with fixed opinions as to guilt or innocence; (d) the use of emphatic and clear instructions on the sworn duty of each juror to decide the issues only on evidence presented in open court. Sequestration of jurors is, of course, always available. Although that measure insulates jurors only after they are sworn, it also enhances the likelihood of dissipating the impact of pretrial publicity and emphasizes the elements of the jurors' oaths....

We must also assess the probable efficacy of prior restraint on publication as a workable method of protecting Simants' right to a fair trial, and we cannot ignore the reality of the problems of managing and enforcing pretrial restraining orders. The territorial jurisdiction of the issuing court is limited by concepts of sovereignty, see, e.g., *Hanson v. Denckla*, 357 U.S. 235 (1958); *Pennoyer v. Neff*, 95 U.S. 714 (1878). The need for *in personam* jurisdiction also presents an obstacle to a restraining order that applies to publication at large as distinguished from restraining publication within a given jurisdiction....

Finally, we note that the events disclosed by the record took place in a community of 850 people. It is reasonable to assume that, without any news accounts being printed or broadcast, rumors would travel swiftly by word of mouth. One can only speculate on the accuracy of such reports, given the generative propensities of rumors; they could well be more damaging than reasonably accurate news accounts. But plainly a whole community cannot be restrained from discussing a subject intimately affecting life within it.

Given these practical problems, it is far from clear that prior restraint on publication would have protected Simants' rights....

Mr. Justice Brennan, with whom Mr. Justice Stewart and Mr. Justice Marshall join, concurring in the judgment.

The question presented in this case is whether, consistently with the First Amendment, a court may enjoin the press, in advance of publication, from reporting or commenting on information acquired from public court proceedings, public court records, or other sources about pending judicial proceedings. The Nebraska Supreme Court upheld such a direct prior restraint on the press, issued by the judge presiding over a sensational state murder trial, on the ground that there existed a "clear and present danger that pretrial publicity could substantially impair the right of the defendant [in the murder trial] to a trial by an impartial jury unless restraints were imposed." *State v. Simants*, 194 Neb. 783, 794, 236 N. W. 2d 794, 802 (1975). The right to a fair trial by a jury of one's peers is unquestionably one of the most precious and sacred safeguards enshrined in the Bill of Rights. I would hold, however, that resort to prior restraints on the freedom of the press is a constitutionally impermissible method for enforcing that right; judges have at their disposal a broad spectrum of devices for ensuring that fundamental fairness is accorded the accused without necessitating so drastic an incursion on the equally fundamental and salutary constitutional mandate that discussion of public affairs in a free society cannot depend on the preliminary grace of judicial censors. . . .

I would reject the contention that speculative deprivation of an accused's Sixth Amendment right to an impartial jury is comparable to the damage to the Nation or its people that *Near* and *New York Times* would have found sufficient to justify a prior restraint on reporting. Damage to that Sixth Amendment right could never be considered so direct, immediate and irreparable, and based on such proof rather than speculation, that prior restraints on the press could be justified on this basis.

In *Lowe v. Securities and Exchange Commission*[234] the Court confronted the issue of whether the Commission could obtain an injunction restraining an investment adviser from publishing and selling newsletters. The court of appeals had upheld the agency's authority to bar publication as a permissible remedy against an investment adviser who had violated the federal securities laws.[235] A dissenting judge noted the First Amendment dangers of the regulatory scheme, however, since the newsletters contained expression on political, economic, and social issues that "could appear in our favorite local newspaper."[236] He thus observed that the prohibition against publishing was akin to the English licensing system abandoned in 1694.[237] Although the Supreme Court reversed the appeals court decision,[238] only Justice White, joined by Chief Justice Burger and Justice Rehnquist, confronted the constitutional issue. In a concurring opinion, they concluded that "to prevent petitioner from publishing at all is inconsistent with the First Amendment."[239]

The Court refused to review a temporary order barring the airing of telephone conversations between a criminal defendant and his attorneys. In *Cable News Network, Inc. v. Noriega*,[240] it thus allowed a prior restraint to operate at least until the district court evaluated the tapes and determined whether it was necessary to protect the right to a fair trial. Justices Marshall and O'Connor dissented on grounds the Court's denial of review deviated from precedent and allowed suppression to operate minus any threshold showing of impairment to fair trial interests or consideration of other means for averting harm. The district court, having satisfied itself that airing the tapes would not compromise a fair trial, lifted the ban several days later. The procedure, coupled with the Court's refusal to intervene, suggests the possibility that judges sometimes may impose short-term restraints free of normal presumptions of invalidity. Even allowing for a relaxation of normative criteria, it would be reasonable to expect that any temporary restraint should operate no longer than necessary for a court to ascertain whether dissemination would cause intolerable harm.

When the media themselves are a party to litigation, proscriptions against prior restraint may abate. A gag order against a media defendant in a defamation action thus was upheld in *Seattle Times Co. v. Rinehart*.[241] A protective order against disclosing information, obtained in the course of discovery, was upheld on grounds it was supported by "good cause."[242] The Court observed that liberal pretrial discovery practice presents significant potential for abuse and is not a traditional public source of information. In *Butterworth v. Smith*,[243] the Court invalidated a state law prohibiting grand jury witnesses from revealing their testimony. A reporter had challenged the statute pursuant to his appearance before a grand jury. The Court discerned a constitutional right to relate truthful information he possessed and otherwise could communicate freely.[244]

The presumption against prior restraints either is less strong in relationship to newer media, or the justifications for them are more easily accepted. Licensing of radio and television stations, for instance, is based upon past experience when unrestrained competition resulted in chaos, confusion, and massive signal interference.[245] Less convincing is the Court's rationale for allowing censorship boards to review films and to determine whether they are suitable for public viewing.[246] Although consistent with the notion that each medium presents unique problems,[247] arguments that motion pictures have a special capacity for evil never have been subjected to rigorous examination. Even if usable as a basis for other regulatory action, the rationale does not seem to comport with the heavy burden of actually proving the need for a prior restraint. Despite the diminished protection afforded motion pictures, the Court has insisted upon procedural safeguards for any censorship system. Thus, administrative review must be

prompt, the burden of proof is upon the censor to demonstrate that the expression is unprotected, and an opportunity must exist for speedy judicial review.[248]

The special concern that the Court has evinced toward prior restraint rests in large part upon a perception that they impose "an immediate and irreversible sanction."[249] While recognizing that subsequent punishment may chill expression, the Court has observed that prior restraint freezes it.[250] The bifurcated regard of prior restraint and subsequent punishment has been criticized, however, for a failure to explain why an injunction justifies special constitutional disfavor.[251] Despite a dominant sense that prior restraint is peculiarly intolerable when timeliness of information is a pertinent factor,[252] one commentator has suggested that jurisprudence is a function of "a remote and usually unarticulated premise underlying a broad and uncritical acceptance of the conventional rhetoric of prior restraint."[253] In so doing, he notes that the doctrine of prior restraint too often focuses on an inconsequential form that diverts attention from critical substantive issues of First Amendment coverage.[254] The *Near* decision, which could have rested on grounds the statute at issue was vague, overbroad, and inconsistent with basic First Amendment principles of robust and open debate,[255] thus is regarded as having elevated form or substance in a way that may deny government a sometimes proper means for vindicating valid interests.[256] Even if principles operating against prior restraint may divert attention from substantive First Amendment and competing interests, categorical rejection of the doctrine dismisses the danger especially in national security cases that judges may overpredict harm if allowed merely to balance harms.[257] Perhaps that danger is offset by the prospect that, when confidentiality is breached, the flow of information cannot effectively be controlled anyway.

B. INDIRECT RESTRAINT

Criticism of the doctrine of prior restraint, to the effect that it is overly inclusive, is not pertinent to the Court's analysis of official clearance procedures for employee publications. In *Snepp v. United States,*[258] the Court disregarded how an employment contract, requiring a former CIA agent to submit a book to the agency for prepublication approval, had at least the same functional effect as a prior restraint.[259] Per curiam, it found that the employee violated not only his contract with the government but also his fiduciary duty even though the book at issue contained no classified information.[260] Given a breach of the employment agreement, the Court ordered the channeling of profits from the book into a constructive trust.[261]

The Court thus upheld an official preclearance procedure as a legitimate means for the government to determine whether publication would be harmful to the intelligence interests and the safety of agents.[262] Justice Stevens, in dissent, criticized the Court for "enforc[ing] a species of prior restraint on a citizen's right to criticize his government."[263] In part, the decision rested upon analysis tied to the law of contracts. The Court, however, did not address the possibility that the contract at issue might be unconscionable. Although some contracts are void because they violate public policy, the Court also did not appear to consider whether the employment agreement might be invalid as a contravention of First Amendment policy.

C. COMPULSORY PROPAGATION

When government commands rather than prohibits publication, the Court has recognized a form of restraint that does "not fall into familiar or traditional patterns."[264] In *Miami Herald Publishing Co. v. Tornillo,*[265] the Court declared unconstitutional a statutory right for political candidates to obtain equal space in response to newspaper criticisms of their records.[266] Such compulsion, it observed, exacted a penalty "in terms of the cost in printing and composing time and materials and in taking up space that could be devoted to other material the newspaper may have preferred to print."[267] The practical effect of the law thus was considered identical to a forthright restraint. Because the choice of what is to be published and decisions concerning newspaper size and content are at the heart of editorial control and judgment, the Court concluded that regulation of that process was inconsistent with free press guarantees.[268]

Similarly, a federal appeals court found regulations requiring cable operators to carry the signals of local broadcasters inconsistent with the First Amendment.[269] Adverting to the *Tornillo* decision, it concluded that "(f)orcing an editor to print that which he otherwise would not ... was a restraint the First Amendment would not tolerate."[270] Nor would it make any difference from the appeals court's standpoint if the intrusion into editorial autonomy was not extensive.[271] A contrary result was reached when the Supreme Court examined personal attack and political editorial rules and the fairness doctrine as they applied to broadcasting. Rejecting any suggestion that such restraints were inconsistent with the First Amendment, the Court in *Red Lion Broadcasting Co. v. Federal Communications Commission*[272] found that the regulations were justified by the medium's scarce nature.[273] Because "there are substantially more individuals who want to broadcast than there are frequencies to allocate, [the Court found it] idle to posit an unabridgeable First Amendment right to broadcast comparable to the right ... to ... publish."[274] The continuing viability of that distinction is dubious, given the

Court's indication that it is prepared to re-evaluate the scarcity principle[275] and the Federal Communications Commission's abandonment of the fairness doctrine[276] and expressed intention to accord broadcasters the same constitutional status as publishers.[277] In any event, the operation of systems of prior restraint as a norm in some settings evinces that the constitutional barrier against them is semipermeable rather than entirely impenetrable.

NOTES

1. Stewart, *Or of the Press,* 26 HASTINGS L.J. 631, 633–34 (1975).

2. *Id.*

3. Arguments have been made, albeit unsuccessfully so far, that the press as a proxy of the public should have a special right of access to public facilities and information. *See* Pell v. Procunier, 417 U.S. 817 (1974). Saxbe v. Washington Post Co., 117 U.S. 843 (1974).

4. Some courts, for instance, have extended a qualified journalistic privilege against testifying or providing evidence in civil proceedings. *See, e.g.,* Baker v. F&F Investment, 470 F.2d 778 (2d Cir. 1972); Democratic National Committee v. McCord, 356 F. Supp. 1394 (D.D.C. 1973). Despite an opinion of the Court to the effect that reporters are not immune from a grand jury subpoena in the criminal context, Justice Powell's concurring opinion and the views of four dissenters can be combined to support a qualified journalistic privilege subjecting a subpoena to good faith and need. Branzburg v. Hayes, 408 U.S. 665 (1972). Media or nonmedia status also may be pertinent in determining whether the actual malice standard will defeat a defamation action by a private person. *See* Prosser & Keeton on The Law of Torts, Ch. 19, § 113, at 807–08, (5th ed. 1984).

5. First National Bank of Boston v. Bellotti, 435 U.S. 765, 801–02 (1978) (Burger, C.J., concurring).

6. *Id.* at 802.

7. *See, e.g.,* Houchins v. KQED, Inc., 438 U.S. 1, 16 (1978) (Stewart, J., concurring). Stewart nonetheless would have recognized and "accommodated the practical distinctions between the press and the general public." *Id.*

8. In acknowledging a general right of access to public trials, the Court's decision had the primary effect of facilitating media coverage of such proceedings. Richmond Newspapers, Inc. v. Virginia, 448 U.S. 555 (1980).

9. *See, e.g.,* Nimmer, *Introduction—Is Freedom of the Press a Redundancy? What Does It Add to Freedom of Speech?,* 26 HASTINGS L.J. 639, 651–52 (1975).

10. Lovell v. City of Griffin, 303 U.S. 444, 452 (1938).

11. *Id.*

12. *See* Mutual Film Corp. v. Industrial Commission of Ohio, 236 U.S. 230 (1915).

13. A few years later, the Court found broadcasting properly susceptible to content regulation. National Broadcasting Co. v. United States, 319 U.S. 190, 226 (1943).

14. Brennan, *Address,* 32 RUTGERS L. REV. 173 (1979).

15. *Id.* at 176.

16. *Id.*

17. *Id.* at 177.

18. *Id.* at 176–177.

19. *Id.* For a more detailed accounting of problems in and implications of defining the press, *see* Lange, *The Speech and Press Clauses,* 23 U.C.L.A. L.Rev. 77 (1975).

20. Mutual Film Corp. v. Industrial Commission of Ohio, 236 U.S. at 244.

21. *See* Lively, *Fear and the Media: A First Amendment Horror Show,* 69 MINN. L.REV. 1071, 1078 (1985).

22. United Artists Corp. v. Board of Censors, 189 Tenn. 397, 401, 225 S.W.2d 550, 551–52 (1949).

23. *See* Lowe v. Securities and Exchange Commission, 472 U.S. 181, 208 (1985).

24. Brandeis & Warren, *The Right to Privacy,* 4 HARV. L.REV. 193, 195 (1890).

25. *Id.*

26. *Id.*

27. *Id.*

28. *Id.*

29. *See* Federal Communications Commission v. Pacifica Foundation, 438 U.S. 726, 750–51 (1978); Cohen v. California, 403 U.S. 15, 25 (1971).

30. Address of Federal Communications Commission Chairman Newton Minow to the National Association of Broadcasters (May 9, 1961).

31. *See* Federal Communications Commission v. Pacifica Foundation, 438 U.S. at 748–49.

32. *Id.* at 750.

33. Pacifica Station WBAI, 56 F.C.C. 2d 94, 103 (1975) (Comm'r. Quello concurring).

34. *See* A. de TOCQUEVILLE, DEMOCRACY IN AMERICA 303 (1835) (R. Heffner ed. 1956).

35. 236 U.S. 230.

36. *Id.* at 239–41.

37. *Id.* at 239.

38. *Id.* at 241.

39. *Id.* at 244.

40. *Id.*

41. *Id.*

42. Joseph Burstyn, Inc. v. Wilson, 343 U.S. 495 (1952).

43. United States v. Paramount Pictures, Inc., 334 U.S. 131, 166 (1948).

44. As the Court observed in overturning the Mutual Film decision, "First Amendment recognition is not the end of [the] problem." Joseph Burstyn, Inc. v. Wilson, 343 U.S. at 502. Instead of having a common constitutional footing, media would be evaluated individually because "each tends to present its own peculiar problems." *Id.* at 503.

45. The Court has noted, in the freedom of speech context, that "one man's vulgarity is another's lyric." Cohen v. California, 403 U.S. at 25.

46. *See* Miami Herald Publishing Co. v. Tornillo, 418 U.S. 241 (1974).

47. *See* Federal Communications Commission v. Midwest Video Corporation, 440 U.S. 689, 701–02 (1979).

48. Columbia Broadcasting System, Inc. v. Democratic National Committee, 412 U.S. 94, 103–14 (1973).

49. *See, e.g.,* Berkshire Cablevision of Rhode Island, Inc. v. Burke, 571 F. Supp. 976, 985–88 (D.R.I. 1983).

50. Columbia Broadcasting System, Inc. v. Democratic National Committee, 412 U.S. at 115.

51. *Id.* at 114.

52. *Id.* at 120.

53. *See* Federal Communications Commission v. Midwest Video Corp., 440 U.S. at 702.

54. *Id.* at 700.

55. 412 U.S. 94.

56. Business Executives for Vietnam Peace v. Federal Communications Commission, 450 U.S. 642, 652 (D.C.Cir. 1971).

57. Columbia Broadcasting System, Inc. v. Democratic National Committee, 412 U.S. at 116 (Burger, C.J., joined by Rehnquist and Stewart, J.J.).

58. *Id.*

59. *Id.* at 117.

60. *Id.* at 119.

61. *Id.* at 172 (Brennan, J., dissenting), *citing* Evans v. Newton, 382 U.S. 296, 299 (1966).

62. *Id.* at 173 (Brennan, J., dissenting).

63. *Id.* at 173–74 (Brennan, J., dissenting).

64. *Id.* at 175 (Brennan, J., dissenting).

65. *Id.* at 175 (Brennan, J., dissenting).

66. *Id.* at 176 (Brennan, J., dissenting), *citing* Moose Lodge No. 107 v. Irvis, 407 U.S. 163, 173 (1972).

67. *Id.* at 177 (Brennan, J., dissenting).

68. *Id.* at 149 (Douglas, J., concurring).

69. *See, e.g.,* Moose Lodge No. 107 v. Irvis, 407 U.S. at 179 (Douglas, J., dissenting).

70. Columbia Broadcasting System, Inc. v. Democratic National Committee, 418 U.S. at 149 (Douglas, J., concurring).

71. *Id.* at 150 (Douglas, J., concurring).

72. *Id.* at 149 (Douglas, J., concurring). For a competing notion that government still would have an editorial function, *see* Yudof, *When Governments Speak: Toward a Theory of Government Expression and the First Amendment,* 57 TEX. L. REV. 563 (1979).

73. Burton v. Wilmington Parking Authority, 365 U.S. 715, 722 (1961).

74. 47 U.S.C. § 151 *et seq.*

75. *Id.,* §§ 521–59.

76. 419 U.S. 345 (1974).

77. *Id.* at 358–59.

78. *Id.* at 357–58.

79. *Id.* at 352–53.

80. *Id.* at 356–57. The Court distinguished between the utility's exercise of choice under state law and obligatory functions initiated and mandated by the state. *Id., citing* Public Utilities Commission v. Pollak, 343 U.S. 451 (1952).

81. *Id.* at 357.

82. *See, e.g.,* Flagg Brothers, Inc. v. Brooks, 436 U.S. 149 (1978). For a sophisticated explication of how state action concepts may influence the perimeters of constitutional freedom, *see* Marshall, *Diluting Constitutional Rights: Rethinking "Rethinking State Action,"* 80 NW. U. L.Rev. 558 (1985).

83. *See, e.g.,* Lugar v. Edmundson Oil Co., Inc. 457 U.S. 922, 937 (1982).

84. Red Lion Broadcasting Co. v. Federal Communications Commission, 395 U.S. 367, 390 (1969).

85. *See,* Syracuse Peace Council, 2 F.C.C. Rec. 5043, 5055–57 (1987); Inquiry into § 73.1910 of the Commission's Rules and Regulations Concerning the General Fairness Doctrine Obligations of Broadcast Licensees, 58 R.R.2d 1137, 1196–98 (1985).

86. 343 U.S. 495 (1952).

87. *See* Mutual Film Corp. v. Industrial Commission of Ohio, 236 U.S. 230 (1915).

88. Joseph Burstyn, Inc. v. Wilson, 343 U.S. at 502.

89. *See, e.g., The Supreme Court, 1951 Term,* 66 HARV. L. REV. 99, 115 (1952).

90. Joseph Burstyn, Inc. v. Wilson, 343 U.S. at 502.

91. *Id.* at 503.

92. 336 U.S. 77 (1949).

93. See *id.* at 78.

94. *Id.* at 97 (Jackson, J., concurring).

95. Joseph Burstyn, Inc. v. Wilson, 343 U.S. at 501.

96. *Id.*

97. *Id.* at 500.

98. *Id.* at 502.

99. Mutual Film Corp. v. Industrial Commission of Ohio, 236 U.S. at 244.

100. Joseph Burstyn, Inc. v. Wilson, 343 U.S. at 502.

101. *See* Freedman v. Maryland, 380 U.S. 51 (1965).

102. 405 F.2d 1082 (D.C.Cir. 1968), *cert. denied,* 396 U.S. 842 (1969).

103. *Id.* at 1100.

104. *Id.*

105. *Id.* at 1100–01.

106. *See, e.g.,* First National Bank of Boston v. Bellotti, 435 U.S. 765, 790–91 (1978); Telecommunications Research and Action Center v. Federal Communications Commission, 801 F.2d 501, 508 (D.C.Cir. 1986) *cert. denied,* 482 U.S. 919 (1987).

107. 435 U.S. at 790.

108. Red Lion Broadcasting Co. v. Federal Communications Commission, 395 U.S. at 388–89.

109. 395 U.S. 367.

110. *Id.* at 388.

111. In 1987, 8,943 commercial radio stations, 1,290 television stations operated in the United States. STATISTICAL ABSTRACT OF THE UNITED STATES 1989, No. 900, at 544. A total of 1,646 daily, 6,750 weekly and 510 semiweekly newspapers published during the same year. *Id.,* No. 913, at 549.

112. Columbia Broadcasting System, Inc. v. Democratic National Committee, 412 U.S., at 127.

113. Burger referred to then Commerce Secretary Herbert Hoover's remark that "the radio listener does not have the same option that the reader of a publication has—to ignore [that] in which he is not interested—and he may resent its invasion on his set. *Id.* at 128.

114. Federal Communications Commission v. Pacifica Foundation, 438 U.S. at 748–50.

115. *Id.* at 748.

116. Cohen v. California, 403 U.S. 15, 22–23 (1971).

117. Federal Communications Commission v. Pacifica Foundation, 438 U.S. at 750–51. The Court has observed that "because broadcasting involves unique considerations, our cases have not followed precisely the same approach that we have applied to other media and have never gone so far as to demand that such regulation serve 'compelling' interests." FCC v. League of Women Voters, 468 U.S. 364, 376 (1984). Although review is not strict in the most exacting sense, it also is not entirely deferential. Rather, a regulation will be analyzed to determine if it is supported by a substantial state interest and is narrowly tailored. *Id.* at 380. The analytical process in large part seems reducible to balancing, "in light of the particular circumstances," the constitutional and regulatory interests. *Id.* at 381.

118. *See* Lively, Fear and the Media: A First Amendment Horror Show, MINN. L.REV. 1071, 1089–90 (1985).

119. *Id.*

120. *Id.*

121. Quincy Cable TV, Inc., v. Federal Communications Commission, 768 F.2d 1434 (D.C.Cir. 1985), *cert. denied,* 476 U.S. 1169 (1986).

122. *Id.* at 1448.

123. *Id.* at 1449.

124. Berkshire Cablevision of Rhode Island Inc. v. Burke, 571 F.Supp. at 985–88; Omega Satellite Product Co. v. City of Indianapolis, 694 F.2d 119, 126 (7th Cir. 1982).

125. *See* Community Communications Company, Inc. v. City of Boulder, Colorado, 660 F.2d 1370, 1379 (10th Cir. 1981), *cert. dismissed,* 456 U.S. 1001 (1982).

126. Quincy Cable TV, Inc. v. Federal Communications Commission, 768 F.2d at 1450, *citing* Miami Herald Publishing Co. v. Tornillo, 418 U.S. 241, (1974).

127. A prior restraint thus has a heavy presumption against its constitutionality, and government has a heavy burden of demonstrating its justification. New York Times Co. v. United States, 403 U.S. 713, 713 (1971) (per curiam).

128. 4 W. BLACKSTONE, COMMENTARIES ON THE LAWS OF ENGLAND 151–52 (2d ed. 1872).

129. Emerson, *The Doctrine of Prior Restraint,* 20 L. & CONTEMP. PROBS. 648, 655 (1955).

130. *Id.* at 655–56

131. United States v. The Progressive, Inc., 467 U.S. 990 (W.D.Wis. 1979).

132. *See* New York Times Co. v. United States, 403 U.S. 713.

133. Emerson, *The Doctrine of Prior Restraint,* 20 L. & CONTEMP. PROBS. at 656. Federal securities law, for instance, prohibits dissemination of a prospectus unless official disclosure standards are satisfied. *See* 15 U.S.C. § 77e.

134. 20 L. & CONTEMP. PROBS, at 658.

135. Freedman v. Maryland, 380 U.S. 51, 57 (1965); Times Film Corporation v. City of Chicago, 365 U.S. 43, 67–68 (Warren, C.J., dissenting).

136. Emerson, *The Doctrine of Prior Restraint,* 20 L. & CONTEMP. PROBS. At 658–659.

137. Securities and Exchange Commission v. Capital Gains Research Bureau, Inc., 375 U.S. 180, 186 (1963); Securities and Exchange Commission v. Ralston Purina Co., 346 U.S. 119, 124 (1953).

138. *See* R. KARMEL, REGULATION BY PROSECUTION 27 (1982).

139. *See* Posner, *The Federal Trade Commission,* 37 U. CHI. L.REV. 47, 84–86 (1969).

140. *See* Times Film Corp. v. City of Chicago, 365 U.S. at 67–68 (Warren, C.J., dissenting).

141. Emerson, *The Doctrine of Prior Restraint*, 20 L. & CONTEMP. PROBS. At 659.

142. New York Times Co. v. United States, 403 U.S. 713.

143. United States v. The Progressive, Inc., 467 U.S. 990.

144. Although charges were filed to punish those responsible for leaking the Pentagon Papers, the case was dismissed on grounds of government misconduct.

145. 283 U.S. 697 (1931).

146. *Id.* at 701–02.

147. *See* F. FRIENDLY, MINNESOTA RAG 40–54 (1981).

148. *Id.* at 55–59. *See* Near v. Minnesota, 283 U.S. at 704.

149. 283 U.S. at 711.

150. *Id.* at 712.

151. *Id.* at 719–20.

152. *Id.*

153. *Id.* at 718–19.

154. *Id.* at 721.

155. *Id.* at 713.

156. *Id.* at 713–14.

157. *Id.* at 715.

158. *Id.* at 716.

159. *Id.*

160. 403 U.S. 713 (1971).

161. *Id.*

162. *Id.*

163. *Id.*

164. *Id.* at 714–17 (Black, J., concurring); *id.* at 720 (Douglas, J., concurring).

165. *Id.* at 727 (Brennan, J., concurring); *id.* at 730 (Stewart, J., concurring); *id.* at 731 (White, J., concurring); *id.* at 747 (Marshall, J., concurring).

166. *Id.* at 751–52 (Burger, J., dissenting); *id.* at 753–59 (Harlan, J., dissenting); *id.* at 759–62 (Blackmun, J., dissenting).

167. *Id.* at 731–32 (White, J., Stewart, J. concurring); *id.* at 742–47. (Marshall, J., concurring).

168. *Id.*

169. In evaluating a statute, albeit outside the national security context, the *Near* Court was not swayed by the existence of legislative authorization.

170. New York Times Co. v. United States, 403 U.S. at 723 (Douglas, J., concurring).

171. *Id.* at 715 (Black, J., concurring).

172. *Id.* at 719 (Black, J., concurring).

173. *Id.* (Black, J., concurring).

174. *Id.* (Black, J., concurring).

175. *Id.* at 720 (Douglas, J., concurring).

176. Although acknowledging that Congress had barred "communication" of information relating to na-
tional defense, Douglas noted that the term did not include "publication" which was used in parts of the statute when considered pertinent. *Id.* at 720–22 (Douglas, J., concurring), *citing* 18 U.S.C. §§ 793(e), 794(b), 797 and 798.

177. *Id.* at 723 (Douglas, J., concurring).

178. *Id.* at 724 (Douglas, J., concurring).

179. *Id.* at 725–26 (Brennan, J., concurring).

180. *Id.* (Brennan, J., concurring).

181. *Id.* at 726–27 (Brennan, J., concurring).

182. *Id.* (Brennan, J., concurring).

183. *Id.* (Brennan, J., concurring).

184. *Id.* at 727 (Stewart, J., concurring).

185. *Id.* at 729 (Stewart, J., concurring).

186. *Id.* at 728 (Stewart, J., concurring).

187. *Id.* at 729–30 (Stewart, J., concurring).

188. *Id.* at 730 (Stewart, J., concurring).

189. *Id.* (Stewart, J., concurring).

190. *Id.* at 732 (White, J., concurring), *id.* at 742–47 (Marshall, J., concurring).

191. *Id.* at 731 (White, J., concurring).

192. *Id.* at 732 (White, J., concurring).

193. *Id.* at 733 (White, J., concurring). *See also* Linde, *Courts and Censorship*, 66 MINN. L.REV. 171, 196 (1981).

194. New York Times Co. v. United States, 403 U.S. at 749 (Burger, C.J., dissenting).

195. *Id.* (Burger, C.J., dissenting).

196. *Id.* at 714–15 (Black, J. and Douglas, J., concurring).

197. *Id.* at 748 (Burger, J., dissenting).

198. *Id.* at 749 (Burger, J., dissenting).

199. *Id.* at 753 (Harlan, J., dissenting).

200. *Id.* at 753–55 (Harlan, J., dissenting).

201. *Id.* at 756 (Harlan, J., dissenting).

202. *Id.* at 757 (Harlan, J., dissenting).

203. *Id.* at 761 (Blackmun, J., dissenting).

204. *Id.* (Blackmun, J., dissenting).

205. *Id.* at 761–62 (Blackmun, J., dissenting).

206. *Id.* at 713.

207. 467 F.Supp. 990 (W.D.Wis. 1979), *appeal dismissed*, 610 F.2d 819 (7th Cir. 1979).

208. *Id.* at 992.

209. *Id.* at 996.

210. *Id.* at 993–94.

211. *Id.* at 994.

212. *Id.*

213. *Id.*

214. *Id.* at 995.

215. *Id.*

216. *Id.*

217. *Id.* at 996.

218. *Id.*

219. *See* New York Times Co. v. United States, 403 U.S. at 726–27 (Brennan, J., concurring). For criticism

to the effect that the district court employed a standard of review less demanding than what was required by the *New York Times* case, *see* Entin, *United States v. Progressive, Inc., The Faustian Bargain and the First Amendment,* 75 Nw. U. L.REV. 538 (1980).

220. 610 F.2d 819 (7th Cir. 1979).

221. 427 U.S. 539 (1976).

222. *Id.* at 543.

223. *See* New York Times Co. v. United States, 403 U.S. 713.

224. Nebraska Press Association v. Stuart, 427 U.S. at 560.

225. *Id.* at 562.

226. *Id.* at 562–63.

227. *Id.* at 563–64.

228. *Id.* at 567.

229. *Id.* at 560.

230. *See* Red Lion Broadcasting Co. v. Federal Communications Commission, 395 U.S. at 389.

231. *See* Lively, *Old Media, New Dogma,* 30 ARIZ. L.REV. 257, 262 (1988).

232. Nebraska Press Association v. Stuart, 427 U.S. at 572 (Brennan, J., concurring).

233. *Id.* at 603–04 (Brennan, J., concurring).

234. 472 U.S. 181.

235. Securities and Exchange Commission v. Lowe, 725 F.2d 892 (D.C.Cir. 1984) *aff'd,* 472 U.S. 181 (1985).

236. *Id.* at 908 (Breiant, J., dissenting).

237. *Id.* (Breiant, J., dissenting).

238. 472 U.S. 181.

239. *Id.* at 211 (White, J., dissenting).

240. 111 S. Ct. (1990).

241. 467 U.S. 20 (1984).

242. *Id.* at 37.

243. 110 S. Ct 1376 (1990).

244. *Id.* at 1383.

245. National Broadcasting Co. v. United States, 319 U.S. 190, 210–12.

246. Times Film Corp. v. City of Chicago, 365 U.S. 43.

247. Joseph Burstyn, Inc. v. Wilson, 343 U.S. at 503.

248. Freedman v. Maryland, 380 U.S. 51.

249. Nebraska Press Association v. Stuart, 427 U.S. at 559.

250. *Id.*

251. *See* Jeffries, *Rethinking Prior Restraint,* 92 YALE L.J. 409, 420 (1983).

252. It is noted that an effective penal sanction actually may suppress information permanently. *Id* at 429–30.

253. *Id.* at 433.

254. *Id.* at 433–34.

255. *Id.* at 416.

256. *Id.* at 434.

257. When national security interests are at stake, it may be argued that courts have incentive to overpredict harm. A decision against restraining information leaves the Court responsible for any harm, while suppression minimizes such risks and thereby shelters the judiciary from criticism for any adverse consequences. *See* Blasi, *Toward a Theory of Prior Restraint: The Central Linkage,* 66 MINN. L.REV. 11, 51–54. (1981).

258. 444 U.S. 507 (1980).

259. *See id.* at 526 (Stevens, J., dissenting).

260. *Id.* at 510–11.

261. *Id.* at 515–16.

262. *Id.* at 512–13.

263. *Id.* at 526 (Stevens, J., dissenting).

264. Miami Herald Publishing Co. v. Tornillo, 418 U.S. at 256.

265. 418 U.S. 241.

266. *Id.* at 258.

267. *Id.* at 256.

268. *Id.* at 258.

269. Quincy Cable TV, Inc. v. Federal Communications Commission, 768 F.2d at 1463.

270. *Id.* at 1453.

271. *Id.*

272. 395 U.S. 367.

273. *Id.* at 388–90.

274. *Id.* at 388.

275. Federal Communications Commission v. League of Women Voters of California, 468 U.S. 364, 376–77 n. 11, 13 (1984).

276. Syracuse Peace Council, 2 F.C.C. Rcd. at 5057.

277. *Id.* at 5055–57.

Chapter 2

FREEDOM OF THE PRESS AND COMPETING INTERESTS

The First Amendment, like other constitutional provisions, does not operate as an absolute.[1] Despite Justice Black's theory that the framers performed "all the 'balancing' that was to be done in this field,"[2] the Court has rejected the notion that the guarantee must prevail in all instances or be construed literally.[3] When freedom of the press collides with competing constitutional provision, statute, or policy, therefore, the question is which interest must give way or how the con flicting concerns can be accommodated. Prominent rival constitutional interests implicate the Fourth, Fifth, Sixth, and Fourteenth Amendments. Nonconstitutional concerns that may delimit press freedom include defamation, privacy, public morals, and copyright.

I. CONSTITUTIONAL CONCERNS

A. FOURTH AMENDMENT: SEARCH AND SEIZURE

The Supreme Court for the most part has refused to confer upon the press any special privilege in or immunity from the criminal justice process.[4] In *Zurcher v. Stanford Daily*,[5] the Court upheld the seizure of evidence from a newsroom pursuant to a valid search warrant.[6] The search had been judicially authorized upon probable cause that the newspaper possessed photographs revealing the identities of persons who allegedly had assaulted police officers during a demonstration. The Court found the procedure constitutional even though the newspaper was not suspected of a crime.[7] It rejected an argument that First Amendment interests require, when practicable, use of a subpoena duces tecum.[8] For the Court, the critical element of a reasonable search was not that the owner or holder of property is suspected of a crime but that reasonable cause exists to believe that evidence of a crime is located upon the premises.[9] Rather than create any special rule for obtaining evidence from the press, the Court observed that the standards for a search warrant must be applied with particular exactitude when First Amendment interests are implicated.[10] Any unique consideration for the press with respect to searches and seizures thus appears limited to urgings of special caution to ensure that the medium's ability to gather, analyze, and disseminate news is not compromised.

The Court's decision at least coincides

with some practical realities. Most prosecutors, as elected officials, are unlikely to risk unnecessarily antagonizing the media. Although a subpoena may be less intrusive than a search warrant, it also may be less effective if evidence disappears.[11] Justice Stewart in dissent noted that the procedure upheld by the Court would enable police to ransack news files and thus chill sources and the flow of information.[12] Whether or not his worries would have proved well founded, Congress enacted legislation restricting the ability of federal and state police to obtain evidence from the news media by means of search warrants.[13]

Subchapter I—First Amendment Privacy Protection, 42 U.S.C. § 2000aa *et seq.*

PART A—UNLAWFUL ACTS

§ 2000aa. Searches and seizures by government officers and employees in connection with investigation or prosecution of criminal offenses

(a) Work Product Materials

Notwithstanding any other law, it shall be unlawful for a government officer or employee, in connection with the investigation or prosecution of a criminal offense, to search for or seize any work product materials possessed by a person reasonably believed to have a purpose to disseminate to the public a newspaper, book, broadcast, or other similar form of public communication, in or affecting interstate or foreign commerce; but this provision shall not impair or affect the ability of any government officer or employee, pursuant to otherwise applicable law, to search for or seize such materials, if—

(1) there is probable cause to believe that the person possessing such materials has committed or is committing the criminal offense to which the materials relate: *Provided, however,* That a government officer or employee may not search for or seize such materials under the provisions of this paragraph if the offense to which the materials relate consists of the receipt, possession, communication, or withholding of such materials or the information contained therein (but such a search or seizure may be conducted under the provisions of this paragraph if the offense consists of the receipt, possession, or communication of information relating to the national defense, classified information, or restricted data under the provisions of section 793, 794, 797, or 798 of title 18, or section 2274, 2275, or 2277 of this title, or section 783 of title 50; or

(2) there is reason to believe that the immediate seizure of such materials is necessary to prevent the death of, or serious bodily injury to, a human being.

(b) Other Documents

Notwithstanding any other law, it shall be unlawful for a government officer or employee, in connection with the investigation or prosecution of a criminal offense, to search for or seize documentary materials, other than work product materials, possessed by a person in connection with a purpose to disseminate to the public a newspaper, book, broadcast, or other similar form of public communication, in or affecting interstate or foreign commerce: but this provision shall not impair or affect the ability of any government officer or employee, pursuant to otherwise applicable law, to search for or seize such materials, if—

(1) there is probable cause to believe that the person possessing such materials has committed or is committing the criminal offense to which the materials relate: *Provided, however,* That a government officer or employee may not search for or seize such materials under the provisions of this paragraph if the offense to which the materials relate consists of the receipt, possession, communication, or withholding of such materials or the information contained therein (but such a search or seizure may be conducted under the provisions of this paragraph if the offense consists of the receipt, possession, or communication of information relating to the national defense, classified information, or restricted data under the provisions of section 793, 794, 797, or 798 of title 18, or section 2274, 2275, or 2277 of this title, or section 783 of title 50;

(2) there is reason to believe that the immediate seizure of such materials is necessary

to prevent the death of, or serious bodily injury to, a human being;

(3) there is reason to believe that the giving of notice pursuant to a subpena duces tecum would result in the destruction, alteration, or concealment of such materials; or

(4) such materials have not been produced in response to a court order directing compliance with a subpena duces tecum, and—

(A) all appellate remedies have been exhausted; or

(B) there is reason to believe that the delay in an investigation or trial occasioned by further proceedings relating to the subpena would threaten the interests of justice.

(c) Objections to court ordered subpoenas: affidavits

In the event a search warrant is sought pursuant to paragraph (4)(B) of subsection (b) of this section, the person possessing the materials shall be afforded adequate opportunity to submit an affidavit setting forth the basis for any contention that the materials sought are not subject to seizure.

PART B—REMEDIES, EXCEPTIONS, AND DEFINITIONS

§ *2000aa–5. Border and customs searches*

This chapter shall not impair or affect the ability of a government officer or employee, pursuant to otherwise applicable law, to conduct searches and seizures at the borders of, or at international points of, entry into the United States in order to enforce the customs laws of the United States.

§ *2000aa–6. Civil actions by aggrieved persons*

(a) Right of action

A person aggrieved by a search for or seizure of materials in violation of this chapter shall have a civil cause of action for damages for such search or seizure—

(1) against the United States, against a State which has waived its sovereign immunity under the Constitution to a claim for damages resulting from a violation of this chapter, or against any other governmental unit, all of which shall be liable for violations of this chapter by their officers or employees while acting within the scope or under color of their office or employment; and

(2) against an officer or employee of a State who has violated this chapter while acting within the scope or under color of his office or employment, if such State has not waived its sovereign immunity as provided in paragraph (1).

(b) Good faith defense

It shall be a complete defense to a civil action brought under paragraph (2) of subsection (a) of this section that the officer or employee had a reasonable good faith belief in the lawfulness of his conduct.

(c) Official immunity

The United States, a State, or any other governmental unit liable for violations of this chapter under subsection (a)(1) of this section, may not assert as a defense to a claim arising under this chapter the immunity of the officer or employee whose violation is complained of or his reasonable good faith belief in the lawfulness of his conduct, except that such a defense may be asserted if the violation complained of is that of a judicial officer.

(d) Exclusive nature of remedy

The remedy provided by subsection (a)(1) of this section against the United States, a State, or any other governmental unit is exclusive of any other civil action or proceeding for conduct constituting a violation of this chapter, against the officer, or employee whose violation gave rise to the claim, or against the estate of such officer or employee.

(e) Admissibility of evidence

Evidence otherwise admissible in a proceeding shall not be excluded on the basis of a violation of this chapter.

(f) Damages; costs and attorney's fees

A person having a cause of action under this section shall be entitled to recover actual damages but not less than liquidated damages of $1,000, and such reasonable attorneys' fees and other litigation costs reasonably incurred as the court, in its discretion, may award: *Provided, however,* That the United States, a State, or any other governmental unit shall not be liable for interest prior to judgment.

(g) Attorney General; claims settlement; regulations

The Attorney General may settle a claim for damages brought against the United States under this section, and shall promulgate regulations to provide for the commencement of an administrative inquiry following a determination of a violation of this chapter by an officer or employee of the United States and for the imposition of administrative sanctions against such officer or employee, if warranted.

(h) Jurisdiction

The district courts shall have original jurisdiction of all civil actions arising under this section.

§ 2000aa–7. *Definitions*

(a)"Documentary materials," as used in this chapter, means materials upon which information is recorded, and includes, but is not limited to, written or printed materials, photographs, motion picture films, negatives, video tapes, audio tapes, and other mechanically, magnetically or electronically recorded cards, tapes, or discs, but does not include contraband or the fruits of a crime or things otherwise criminally possessed, or property designed or intended for use, or which is or has been used as, the means of committing a criminal offense.

(b) "Work product materials," as used in this chapter, means materials, other than contraband or the fruits of a crime or things otherwise criminally possessed, or property designed or intended for use, or which is or has been used, as the means of committing a criminal offense, and—

(1) in anticipation of communicating such materials to the public, are prepared, produced, authored, or created, whether by the person in possession of the materials or by any other person;

(2) are possessed for the purposes of communicating such materials to the public; and

(3) include mental impressions, conclusions, opinions, or theories of the person who prepared, produced, authored, or created such material.

(c) "Any other governmental unit," as used in this chapter, includes the District of Columbia, the Commonwealth of Puerto Rico, any territory or possession of the United States, and any local government, unit of local government, or any unit of State government.

Subchapter II—Attorney General Guidelines

§ 2000aa–11. *Guidelines for Federal officers and employees*

(a) Procedures to obtain documentary evidence; protection of certain privacy interests

The Attorney General shall, within six months of October 13, 1980, issue guidelines for the procedures to be employed by any Federal officer or employee, in connection with the investigation or prosecution of an offense, to obtain documentary materials in the private possession of a person when the person is not reasonably believed to be a suspect in such offense or related by blood or marriage to such a suspect, and when the materials sought are not contraband or the fruits or instrumentalities of an offense. The Attorney General shall incorporate in such guidelines—

(1) a recognition of the personal privacy interests of the person in possession of such documentary materials;

(2) a requirement that the least intrusive method or means of obtaining such materials be used which do not substantially jeopardize the availability or usefulness of the materials sought to be obtained:

(3) a recognition of special concern for privacy interests in cases in which a search or seizure for such documents would intrude upon a known confidential relationship such as that which may exist between clergyman and parishioner; lawyer and client; or doctor and patient; and

(4) a requirement that an application for a warrant to conduct a search governed by this subchapter be approved by an attorney for the government, except that in an emergency situation the application may be approved by another appropriate supervisory official if within 24 hours of such emergency the appropriate United States Attorney is notified.

(b) Use of search warrants; reports to Congress

The Attorney General shall collect and compile information on, and report annually to the Committees on the Judiciary of the Senate and the House of Representatives on the use of search warrants by Federal officers and employees for documentary materials described in subsection (a)(3) of this section.

§ 2000aa–12. *Binding nature of guidelines; disciplinary actions for violations; legal proceedings for non-compliance prohibited*

Guidelines issued by the Attorney General under this subchapter shall have the full force and effect of Department of Justice regulations and any violation of these guidelines shall make the employee or officer involved subject to appropriate administrative disciplinary action. However, an issue relating to the compliance, or the failure to comply, with guidelines issued pursuant to this subchapter may not be litigated, and a court may not entertain such an issue as the basis for the suppression or exclusion of evidence.

B. FIFTH AMENDMENT: GRAND JURY

Consistent with the determination that the First Amendment confers no special immunity from the needs of the criminal justice system, the Court has concluded that it also creates no privilege against testifying in a grand jury proceeding.[14] The Court, in *Branzburg v. Hayes,*[15] rejected the argument that the First Amendment authorized a reporter's refusal to identify confidential sources.[16] It responded at least partially to the concern, however, that confidentiality requires protection if the flow of information to the public is not to be impaired. Thus, the Court observed that "(o)nly where news sources themselves are implicated in crime or possess information relevant to the grand jury's task need they or the reporter be concerned about grand jury subpoenas."[17] Such a standard may be construed as imposing a relevancy requirement that does not otherwise attach to grand jury requests for information.[18] Still, the Court evinced a reluctance to single out the media for special treatment, noting that it was not immune from the general principle that the criminal justice system is entitled to receive "every man's evidence."[19]

The *Branzburg* decision is problematical on more than one count. Although only a qualified privilege was sought, the Court depicted the claim as "virtually impenetrable" in nature.[20] In dismissing the First Amendment argument as an imposition on the criminal justice system and even of a criminal defendant's rights,[21] the Court failed to mention that several interests of a nonconstitutional order justify a like burden. Attorney-client, physician-patient, accountant-client, and other privileges are allowed to encumber the rights of the accused because they are perceived as advancing significant policy interests. Intentionally or not, the *Branzburg* decision suggests that First Amendment interests are less important than those other concerns.

Despite its firm language, the *Branzburg* decision's dismissal of a First Amendment privilege may not be as complete as it appears. In a concurring opinion, Justice Powell observed that if "a newsman believes that the grand jury investigation is not being conducted in good faith he is not without remedy."[22] Essentially, Powell would have assessed a grand jury subpoena against a standard of good faith, relevancy, and need.[23] The implication of such a test is that a grand jury may not seek information from the media unless it first exhausts other alternatives.[24] Powell's criteria combined with the dissenting opinions, therefore, actually may provide support for a qualified privilege.[25]

The *Branzburg* decision by its terms was limited to the criminal justice context. Left unanswered was whether and to what extent a First Amendment privilege may exist in other settings. Some courts have found the holding inapplicable in the civil arena on the grounds that the interest at stake there is less compelling. Relevance and need as a result have helped determine whether discovery should be permitted against the media.[26] Pertinent too has been whether the press was a party or witness.[27]

Branzburg v. Hayes, 408 U.S. 665 (1972)

Opinion of the Court by Mr. Justice White, announced by the Chief Justice.

The issue in these cases is whether requiring newsmen to appear and testify before state or federal grand juries abridges the freedom of speech and press guaranteed by the First Amendment. We hold that it does not. . . .

Petitioners Branzburg and Pappas and respondent Caldwell press First Amendment claims that may be simply put: that to gather news it is often necessary to agree either not to identify the source of information published or to publish only part of the facts revealed, or both; that if the reporter is nevertheless forced to reveal these confidences to a grand jury, the source so identified and other confidential sources of other reporters will be measurably deterred from furnishing publishable information, all to the detriment of the free flow of information protected by the First Amendment. Although the newsmen in these cases do not claim an absolute privilege against official interrogation in all circumstances, they assert that the reporter should not be forced either to appear or to testify before a grand jury or at trial until and unless sufficient grounds are shown for believing that the reporter possesses information relevant to a crime the grand jury is investigating, that the information the reporter has is unavailable from other sources, and that the need for the information is sufficiently compelling to override the claimed invasion of First Amendment interests occasioned by the disclosure. Principally relied upon are prior cases emphasizing the importance of the First Amendment guarantees to individual development and to our system of representative government, decisions requiring that official action with adverse impact on First Amendment rights be justified by a public interest that is "compelling" or "paramount," and those precedents establishing the principle that justifiable governmental goals may not be achieved by unduly broad means having an unnecessary impact on protected rights of speech, press, or association. The heart of the claim is that the burden on news gathering resulting from compelling reporters to disclose confidential information outweighs any public interest in obtaining the information.

We do not question the significance of free speech, press, or assembly to the country's welfare. Nor is it suggested that news gathering does not qualify for First Amendment protection; without some protection for seeking out the news, freedom of the press could be eviscerated. But these cases involve no intrusions upon speech or assembly, no prior restraint or restriction on what the press may publish, and no express or implied command that the press publish what it prefers to withhold. No exaction or tax for the privilege of publishing, and no penalty, civil or criminal, related to the content of published material is at issue here. The use of confidential sources by the press is not forbidden or restricted; reporters remain free to seek news from any source by means within the law. No attempt is made to require the press to publish its sources of information or indiscriminately to disclose them on request.

The sole issue before us is the obligation of reporters to respond to grand jury subpoenas as other citizens do and to answer questions relevant to an investigation into the commission of crime. Citizens generally are not constitutionally immune from grand jury subpoenas; and neither the First Amendment nor any other constitutional provision protects the average citizen from disclosing to a grand jury information that he has received in confidence. The claim is, however, that reporters are exempt from these obligations because if forced to respond to subpoenas and identify their sources or disclose other confidences, their informants will refuse or be reluctant to furnish newsworthy information in the future. This asserted burden on news gathering is said to make compelled testimony from newsmen constitutionally suspect and to require a privileged position for them. . . .

The prevailing constitutional view of the newsman's privilege is very much rooted in the ancient role of the grand jury that has the dual function of determining if there is probable cause to believe that a crime has been committed and of protecting citizens against unfounded criminal prosecutions. Grand jury proceedings are constitutionally mandated for the institution of federal criminal prosecutions for capital or other serious crimes, and "its constitutional prerogatives are rooted in long centuries of Anglo-American history." *Hannah v. Larche,* 363 U.S. 420, 489–490 (1960) (Frankfurter, J., concurring in result). The Fifth Amendment provides that "[n]o person shall be held to answer for a capital, or otherwise infamous crime, unless on a presentment or indictment of a Grand Jury." The adoption of the grand jury "in our Constitution as the sole method for preferring charges in serious criminal cases shows the high place it held as an instrument of justice." *Costello v. United States,* 350 U.S. 359, 362 (1956). Although state systems of criminal procedure differ greatly among themselves, the grand jury is similarly guaranteed by many state constitutions and plays an important role in fair and effective law enforcement in the overwhelming majority of the States. Because its task is to inquire into the existence of possible criminal conduct and to return only well-founded indictments, its investigative powers are necessarily broad. "It is a grand inquest, a body with powers of investigation and inquisition, the scope of whose inquiries is not to be limited narrowly by questions of propriety or forecasts of the probable result of the investigation, or by doubts whether any particular individual will be found properly subject to an accusation of crime." *Blair v. United States,* 250 U.S. 273, 282 (1919). Hence, the grand jury's authority to subpoena witnesses is not only historic, *id.,* at 279–281, but essential to its task. Although the powers of the grand jury are not unlimited and are subject to the supervision of a judge, the longstanding principle that "the public . . . has a right to every man's evidence," except for those persons protected by a constitutional, common-law, or statutory privilege, *United States v. Bryan,* 339 U.S., at 331; *Blackmer v. United States,* 284 U.S. 421, 438 (1932); 8 J. Wigmore, Evidence § 2192 (McNaughton rev. 1961), is particularly applicable to grand jury proceedings.

A number of States have provided newsmen a statutory privilege of varying breadth, but the majority have not done so, and none has been provided by federal statute. Until now the only testimonial privilege for unofficial witnesses that is rooted in the Federal Constitution is the Fifth Amendment privilege against compelled self-incrimination. We are asked to create another by interpreting the First Amendment to grant newsmen a testimonial privilege that other citizens do not enjoy. This we decline to do. Fair and effective law enforcement aimed at providing security for the person and property of the individual is a fundamental function of government, and the grand jury plays an important, constitutionally mandated role in this process. On the records now before us, we perceive no basis for holding that the public interest in law enforcement and in ensuring effective grand jury proceedings is insufficient to override the consequential, but uncertain, burden on news gathering that is said to result from insisting that reporters, like other citizens, respond to relevant questions put to them in the course of a valid grand jury investigation or criminal trial.

This conclusion itself involves no restraint on what newspapers may publish or on the type or quality of information reporters may seek to acquire, nor does it threaten the vast bulk of confidential relationships between reporters and their sources. Grand juries address themselves to the issues of whether crimes have been committed and who committed them. Only where news sources themselves are implicated in crime or possess information relevant to the grand jury's task need they or the reporter be concerned about grand jury subpoenas. Nothing before us indicates that a large number or percentage of *all* confidential news sources falls into either category and would in any way be deterred by our holding that the Constitution does not, as it never has, exempt the newsman from performing the citizen's normal duty of appearing and furnishing information relevant to the grand jury's task.

The preference for anonymity of those confidential informants involved in actual criminal conduct is presumably a product of their desire to escape criminal prosecution, and this preference, while understandable, is hardly deserving of constitutional protection. It would be frivolous to assert—and no one does in these cases—that the First Amendment, in the interest of securing news or otherwise, confers a license on either the reporter or his news sources to violate valid criminal laws. Although stealing documents or private wiretapping could provide newsworthy information, neither reporter nor source is immune from conviction for such conduct, whatever the impact on the flow of news. Neither is immune, on First Amendment grounds, from testifying against the other, before the grand jury or at a criminal trial. The Amendment does not reach so far as to override the interest of the public in ensuring that neither reporter nor source is invading the rights of other citizens through reprehensible conduct forbidden to all other persons. To assert the contrary proposition

> is to answer it, since it involves in its very statement the contention that the freedom of the press is the freedom to do wrong with impunity and implies the right to frustrate and defeat the discharge of those governmental duties upon the performance of which the freedom of all, including that of the press, depends. . . . It suffices to say that, however complete is the right of the press to state public things and discuss them, that right, as every other right enjoyed in human society, is subject to the restraints which separate right from wrong-doing. *Toledo Newspaper Co. v. United States,* 247 U.S. 402, 419–420 (1918).

Thus, we cannot seriously entertain the notion that the First Amendment protects a newsman's agreement to conceal the criminal conduct of his source, or evidence thereof, on the theory that it is better to write about crime than to do something about it. Insofar as any reporter in these cases undertook not to reveal or testify about the crime he witnessed, his claim of privilege under the First Amendment presents no substantial question. The crimes of news sources are no less reprehensible and threatening to the public interest when witnessed by a reporter than when they are not.

There remain those situations where a source is not engaged in criminal conduct but has information suggesting illegal conduct by others. Newsmen frequently receive information from such sources pursuant to a tacit or express agreement to withhold the source's name and suppress any information that the source wishes not published. Such informants presumably desire anonymity in order to avoid being entangled as a witness in a criminal trial or grand jury investigation. They

may fear that disclosure will threaten their job security or personal safety or that it will simply result in dishonor or embarrassment.

The argument that the flow of news will be diminished by compelling reporters to aid the grand jury in a criminal investigation is not irrational, nor are the records before us silent on the matter. But we remain unclear how often and to what extent informers are actually deterred from furnishing information when newsmen are forced to testify before a grand jury. The available data indicate that some newsmen rely a great deal on confidential sources and that some informants are particularly sensitive to the threat of exposure and may be silenced if it is held by this Court that, ordinarily, newsmen must testify pursuant to subpoenas, but the evidence fails to demonstrate that there would be a significant constriction of the flow of news to the public if this Court reaffirms the prior common-law and constitutional rule regarding the testimonial obligations of newsmen. Estimates of the inhibiting effect of such subpoenas on the willingness of informants to make disclosures to newsmen are widely divergent and to a great extent speculative. It would be difficult to canvass the views of the informants themselves; surveys of reporters on this topic are chiefly opinions of predicted informant behavior and must be viewed in the light of the professional self-interest of the interviewees. Reliance by the press on confidential informants does not mean that all such sources will in fact dry up because of the later possible appearance of the newsman before a grand jury. The reporter may never be called and if he objects to testifying, the prosecution may not insist. Also, the relationship of many informants to the press is a symbiotic one which is unlikely to be greatly inhibited by the threat of subpoena: quite often, such informants are members of a minority political or cultural group that relies heavily on the media to propagate its views, publicize its aims, and magnify its exposure to the public. Moreover, grand juries characteristically conduct secret proceedings, and law enforcement officers are themselves experienced in dealing with informers, and have their own methods for protecting them without interference with the effective administration of justice. There is little before us indicating that informants whose interest in avoiding exposure is that it may threaten job security, personal safety, or peace of mind, would in fact be in a worse position, or would think they would be, if they risked placing their trust in public officials as well as reporters. We doubt if the informer who prefers anonymity but is sincerely interested in furnishing evidence of crime will always or very often be deterred by the prospect of dealing with those public authorities characteristically charged with the duty to protect the public interest as well as his.

Accepting the fact, however, that an undetermined number of informants not themselves implicated in crime will nevertheless, for whatever reason, refuse to talk to newsmen if they fear identification by a reporter in an official investigation, we cannot accept the argument that the public interest in possible future news about crime from undisclosed, unverified sources must take precedence over the public interest in pursuing and prosecuting those crimes reported to the press by informants and in thus deterring the commission of such crimes in the future.…

We are admonished that refusal to provide a First Amendment reporter's privilege will undermine the freedom of the press to collect and disseminate news. But this is not the lesson history teaches us. As noted previously, the common law recognized no such privilege, and the constitutional argument was not even asserted until 1958. From the beginning of our country the press has operated without constitutional protection for press informants, and the press has flourished. The existing constitutional rules have not been a serious obstacle to either the development or retention of confidential news sources by the press.

It is said that currently press subpoenas have multiplied, that mutual distrust and tension between press and officialdom have increased, that reporting styles have changed, and that there is now more need for confidential sources, particularly where the press seeks news about minority cultural and political groups or dissident organizations suspicious of the law and public officials. These developments, even if true, are treacherous grounds for a far-reaching interpretation of the First Amendment fastening a nationwide rule on courts, grand juries, and prosecuting officials everywhere. The obligation to testify in response to grand jury subpoenas will not threaten these

sources not involved with criminal conduct and without information relevant to grand jury investigations, and we cannot hold that the Constitution places the sources in these two categories either above the law or beyond its reach.…

The privilege claimed here is conditional, not absolute; given the suggested preliminary showings and compelling need, the reporter would be required to testify. Presumably, such a rule would reduce the instances in which reporters could be required to appear, but predicting in advance when and in what circumstances they could be compelled to do so would be difficult. Such a rule would also have implications for the issuance of compulsory process to reporters at civil and criminal trials and at legislative hearings. If newsmen's confidential sources are as sensitive as they are claimed to be, the prospect of being unmasked whenever a judge determines the situation justifies it is hardly a satisfactory solution to the problem. For them, it would appear that only an absolute privilege would suffice.

We are unwilling to embark the judiciary on a long and difficult journey to such an uncertain destination.…

At the federal level, Congress has freedom to determine whether a statutory newsman's privilege is necessary and desirable and to fashion standards and rules as narrow or broad as deemed necessary to deal with the evil discerned and, equally important, to refashion those rules as experience from time to time may dictate. There is also merit in leaving state legislatures free, within First Amendment limits, to fashion their own standards in light of the conditions and problems with respect to the relations between law enforcement officials and press in their own areas. It goes without saying, of course, that we are powerless to bar state courts from responding in their own way and construing their own constitutions so as to recognize a newsman's privilege, either qualified or absolute.

In addition, there is much force in the pragmatic view that the press has at its disposal powerful mechanisms of communication and is far from helpless to protect itself from harassment or substantial harm. Furthermore, if what the newsmen urged in these cases is true—that law enforcement cannot hope to gain and may suffer from subpoenaing newsmen before grand juries—prosecutors will be loath to risk so much for so little. Thus, at the federal level the Attorney General has already fashioned a set of rules for federal officials in connection with subpoenaing members of the press to testify before grand juries or at criminal trials. These rules are a major step in the direction the reporters herein desire to move. They may prove wholly sufficient to resolve the bulk of disagreements and controversies between press and federal officials.

Finally, as we have earlier indicated, news gathering is not without its First Amendment protections, and grand jury investigations if instituted or conducted other than in good faith, would pose wholly different issues for resolution under the First Amendment. Official harassment of the press undertaken not for purposes of law enforcement but to disrupt a reporter's relationship with his news sources would have no justification. Grand juries are subject to judicial control and subpoenas to motions to quash. We do not expect courts will forget that grand juries must operate within the limits of the First Amendment as well as the Fifth. . . .

Mr. Justice Powell, concurring.

I add this brief statement to emphasize what seems to me to be the limited nature of the Court's holding. The Court does not hold that newsmen, subpoenaed to testify before a grand jury, are without constitutional rights with respect to the gathering of news or in safeguarding their sources. Certainly, we do not hold, as suggested in Mr. Justice Stewart's dissenting opinion, that state and federal authorities are free to "annex" the news media as "an investigative arm of government." The solicitude repeatedly shown by this Court for First Amendment freedoms should be sufficient assurance against any such effort, even if one seriously believed that the media—properly free and untrammeled in the fullest sense of these terms—were not able to protect themselves.

As indicated in the concluding portion of the opinion, the Court states that no harassment of newsmen will be tolerated. If a newsman believes that the grand jury investigation is not being conducted in good faith he is not without remedy. Indeed, if the newsman is called upon to give information bearing only a remote and tenuous relationship to the subject of the investigation, or if he has some other reason to believe that his testi-

mony implicates confidential source relationships without a legitimate need of law enforcement, he will have access to the court on a motion to quash and an appropriate protective order may be entered. The asserted claim to privilege should be judged on its facts by the striking of a proper balance between freedom of the press and the obligation of all citizens to give relevant testimony with respect to criminal conduct. The balance of these vital constitutional and societal interests on a case-by-case basis accords with the tried and traditional way of adjudicating such questions.

In short, the courts will be available to newsmen under circumstances where legitimate First Amendment interests require protection.

Mr. Justice Douglas, dissenting in No. 70–57, *United States v. Caldwell.*

Today's decision will impede the wide-open and robust dissemination of ideas and counterthought which a free press both fosters and protects and which is essential to the success of intelligent self-government. Forcing a reporter before a grand jury will have two retarding effects upon the ear and the pen of the press. Fear of exposure will cause dissidents to communicate less openly to trusted reporters. And, fear of accountability will cause editors and critics to write with more restrained pens.

I see no way of making mandatory the disclosure of a reporter's confidential source of the information on which he bases his news story.

The press has a preferred position in our constitutional scheme, not to enable it to make money, not to set newsmen apart as a favored class, but to bring fulfillment to the public's right to know. The right to know is crucial to the governing powers of the people, to paraphrase Alexander Meiklejohn. Knowledge is essential to informed decisions.

As Mr. Justice Black said in *New York Times Co. v. United States,* 403 U.S. 713, 717 (concurring opinion), "The press was to serve the governed, not the governors. . . . The press was protected so that it could bare the secrets of government and inform the people."

Government has an interest in law and order; and history shows that the trend of rulers—the bureaucracy and the police—is to suppress the radical and his ideas and to arrest him rather than the hostile audience. See *Feiner v. New York,* 340 U.S. 315. Yet, as held in *Terminiello v. Chicago,* 337 U.S. 1, 4, one "function of free speech under our system of government is to invite dispute." We went on to say, "It may indeed best serve its high purpose when it induces a condition of unrest, creates dissatisfaction with conditions as they are, or even stirs people to anger. Speech is often provocative and challenging. It may strike at prejudices and preconceptions and have profound unsettling effects as it presses for acceptance of an idea."

The people who govern are often far removed from the cabals that threaten the regime; the people are often remote from the sources of truth even though they live in the city where the forces that would undermine society operate. The function of the press is to explore and investigate events, inform the people what is going on, and to expose the harmful as well as the good influences at work. There is no higher function performed under our constitutional regime. Its performance means that the press is often engaged in projects that bring anxiety or even fear to the bureaucracies, departments, or officials of government. The whole weight of government is therefore often brought to bear against a paper or a reporter.

A reporter is no better than his source of information. Unless he has a privilege to withhold the identity of his source, he will be the victim of governmental intrigue or aggression. If he can be summoned to testify in secret before a grand jury, his sources will dry up and the attempted exposure, the effort to enlighten the public, will be ended. If what the Court sanctions today becomes settled law, then the reporter's main function in American society will be to pass on to the public the press releases which the various departments of government issue.

It is no answer to reply that the risk that a newsman will divulge one's secrets to the grand jury is no greater than the threat that he will in any event inform to the police. Even the most trustworthy reporter may not be able to withstand relentless badgering before a grand jury. . . .

Today's decision is more than a clog upon news gathering. It is a signal to publishers and editors that they should exercise caution in how they use whatever information they can obtain. Without immunity they may be summoned to account for their criticism. Entrenched officers have been quick to crash their powers down upon unfriendly commentators. E.g., *New York Times Co. v. Sullivan,* 376 U.S. 254; *Garrison v. Louisiana,* 379 U.S. 64; *Pickering v. Board of Education,* 391 U.S. 563; *Gravel v. United States, ante,* p. 606.

The intrusion of government into this domain is symptomatic of the disease of this society. As the years pass the power of government becomes more and more pervasive. It is a power to suffocate both people and causes. Those in power, whatever their politics, want only to perpetuate it. Now that the fences of the law and the tradition that has protected the press are broken down, the people are the victims. The First Amendment, as I read it, was designed precisely to prevent that tragedy.

Mr. Justice Stewart, with whom Mr. Justice Brennan and Mr. Justice Marshall join, dissenting.

The Court's crabbed view of the First Amendment reflects a disturbing insensitivity to the critical role of an independent press in our society. The question whether a reporter has a constitutional right to a confidential relationship with his source is of first impression here, but the principles that should guide our decision are as basic as any to be found in the Constitution. While Mr. Justice Powell's enigmatic concurring opinion gives some hope of a more flexible view in the future, the Court in these cases holds that a newsman has no First Amendment right to protect his sources when called before a grand jury. The Court thus invites state and federal authorities to undermine the historic independence of the press by attempting to annex the journalistic profession as an investigative arm of government. Not only will this decision impair performance of the press' constitutionally protected functions, but it will, I am convinced, in the long run harm rather than help the administration of justice.

I respectfully dissent. . . .

A corollary of the right to publish must be the right to gather news. The full flow of information to the public protected by the free-press guarantee would be severely curtailed if no protection whatever were afforded to the process by which news is assembled and disseminated. We have, therefore, recognized that there is a right to publish without prior governmental approval, *Near v. Minnesota,* 283 U.S. 697; *New York Times Co. v.*

United States, 403 U.S. 713, a right to distribute information, see, e.g., *Lovell v. Griffin,* 303 U.S. 444, 452; *Marsh v. Alabama,* 326 U.S. 501; *Martin v. City of Struthers,* 319 U.S. 141; *Grosjean, supra,* and a right to receive printed matter, *Lamont v. Postmaster General,* 381 U.S. 301.

No less important to the news dissemination process is the gathering of information. News must not be unnecessarily cut off at its source, for without freedom to acquire information the right to publish would be impermissibly compromised. Accordingly, a right to gather news, of some dimensions, must exist. *Zemel v. Rusk,* 381 U.S. 1. Note, The Right of the Press to Gather Information, 71 Col. L. Rev. 838 (1971). As Madison wrote: "A popular Government, without popular information, or the means of acquiring it, is but a Prologue to a Farce or a Tragedy; or, perhaps both." 9 Writings of James Madison 103 (G. Hunt ed. 1910).

The right to gather news implies, in turn, a right to a confidential relationship between a reporter and his source. This proposition follows as a matter of simple logic once three factual predicates are recognized: (1) newsmen require informants to gather news; (2) confidentiality—the promise or understanding that names or certain aspects of communications will be kept off the record—is essential to the creation and maintenance of a news-gathering relationship with informants; and (3) an unbridled subpoena power—the absence of a constitutional right protecting, in *any* way, a confidential relationship from compulsory process—will either deter sources from divulging information or deter reporters from gathering and publishing information.

It is obvious that informants are necessary to the news-gathering process as we know it today. If it is to perform its constitutional mission, the press must do far more than merely print public statements or publish prepared handouts. Familiarity with the people and circumstances involved in the myriad background activities that result in the final product called "news" is vital to complete and responsible journalism, unless the press is to be a captive mouthpiece of "newsmakers."

It is equally obvious that the promise of confidentiality may be a necessary prerequisite to a productive relationship between a newsman and his informants. An officeholder may fear his su-

perior; a member of the bureaucracy, his associates; a dissident, the scorn of majority opinion. All may have information valuable to the public discourse, yet each may be willing to relate that information only in confidence to a reporter whom he trusts, either because of excessive caution or because of a reasonable fear of reprisals or censure for unorthodox views. The First Amendment concern must not be with the motives of any particular news source, but rather with the conditions in which informants of all shades of the spectrum may make information available through the press to the public. Cf. *Talley v. California,* 362 U.S. 60, 65; *Bates v. Little Rock,* 361 U.S. 516; *NAACP v. Alabama,* 357 U.S. 449....

Finally, and most important, when governmental officials possess an unchecked power to compel newsmen to disclose information received in confidence, sources will clearly be deterred from giving information, and reporters will clearly be deterred from publishing it, because uncertainty about exercise of the power will lead to "self-censorship." *Smith v. California,* 361 U.S. 147, 149–154; *New York Times Co. v. Sullivan,* 376 U.S., at 279. The uncertainty arises, of course, because the judiciary has traditionally imposed virtually no limitations on the grand jury's broad investigatory powers. See Antell, The Modern Grand Jury: Benighted Supergovernment, 51 A. B. A. J. 153 (1965). See also Part II, *infra.*

After today's decision, the potential informant can never be sure that his identity or off-the-record communications will not subsequently be revealed through the compelled testimony of a newsman. A public-spirited person inside government, who is not implicated in any crime, will now be fearful of revealing corruption or other governmental wrongdoing, because he will now know he can subsequently be identified by use of compulsory process. The potential source must, therefore, choose between risking exposure by giving information or avoiding the risk by remaining silent.

The reporter must speculate about whether contact with a controversial source or publication of controversial material will lead to a subpoena. In the event of a subpoena, under today's decision the newsman will know that he must choose between being punished for contempt if he refuses to testify, or violating his profession's ethics and impairing his resourcefulness as a reporter if he discloses confidential information.

In the wake of *Branzburg,* several states passed shield laws designed to create a statutory privilege for news reporters. Such enactments are consistent with the Court's observation that Congress and the states may create press immunity laws that are absolute or qualified.[28] Regardless of how framed, such measures do not necessarily constitute an impregnable defense. Some courts have balanced statutory privileges against both federal and state constitutional guarantees. Despite the presence of an unequivocal shield law, in *Matter of Farber,*[29] the state supreme court assessed a privilege claim pursuant to a relevancy, less intrusive means, and need test.

C. Fifth, Sixth, and Fourteenth Amendments: Fair Trial and Related Rights

1. Access to Judicial Proceedings

Fair trial and free press interests most frequently come into conflict in connection with the issue of prejudicial publicity.[30] News coverage of a crime, pretrial proceedings or of a trial itself has presented demonstrable problems of fairness in the adjudicative process. The media's role, when combined with the poor judgment of prosecutors or judges, may facilitate something less than an impartial criminal justice system. Reporting also may undermine the fairness of a trial by influencing jurors to the point that guilt is decided on grounds other than the evidence presented. If so, not only the guarantee to a fair trial but also the Sixth Amendment right to an impartial jury is compromised.

Prejudice to the rights of the accused may result from reporting of information concerning a case or from the media's presence at an adjudicative event. In *Nebraska Press Association v. Stuart,*[31] the trial court attempted to minimize the danger of pretrial publicity by enjoining the media from publishing certain information.[32] As noted previously,[33] such a restraint is an impermissible intrusion of the freedom of the press, at least absent exhaustion of less restrictive avenues for securing a defendant's fair trial rights.[34] Equally if not more suppressive in its effect would be a judicial decision to close a proceeding entirely to the press and public. Despite consequences that are practicably indistinguishable from a prior restraint, and a procedure arguably more burdensome to First Amendment interests, the Court in *Gannett Company, Inc. v. DePasquale*[35] upheld closure of a pretrial hearing.[36] The decision rested primarily upon the Sixth Amendment guarantee of a public trial, which the Court identified as a right of the defendant's and not assertable by the press or public.[37] Closure also was tied to the mutual assent of the prosecutor, judge, and defendant.[38] In denying a right of access on Sixth Amendment grounds, the Court noted that interests associated with open proceedings were not being sacrificed. After the danger of prejudice had abated, a transcript of the proceeding had been available to the press.[39]

The *Gannett* decision invited criticism on multiple grounds. Although the facts of the case concerned a suppression hearing, the language of the decision mixed references to pretrial proceedings and trials.[40] Contrary to the strict conditions imposed on issuance of a gag order, moreover, the Court determined that a trial judge might close a pretrial proceeding despite the availability of other options.[41] Support for closure was premised upon the consequences of freedom afforded the press to publish information legally acquired.[42]

A year later, in *Richmond Newspapers, Inc., v. Virginia,*[43] the Court determined that the First Amendment established a right to attend trials.[44] Emphasizing the traditional openness of trials to the public, and the risk of abuse including collusion and misconduct if such proceedings are conducted in secret,[45] the Court narrowed the power of a trial judge to order closure.[46] Although the opinions were splintered, a majority supported a right of access premised upon the First Amendment.[47] Soon thereafter, the Court reinforced the notion that the press and public had a right of access to criminal trials not only because they historically have been open but "to ensure [the] constitutionally protected 'discussion of governmental affairs' is an informed one."[48] In *Globe Newspaper Company v. Superior Court*,[49] a state law requiring exclusion of the press and public from the courtroom during a young sex offense victim's testimony was invalidated.[50] The key flaw in the statute was its mandatory nature. Although intended to protect victims from further injury and embarrassment and to encourage testimony,[51] the Court concluded that an absolute requirement was too demanding and that a trial judge should factor in age, maturity, family desires, nature of the crime, and whether testimony could be elicited without closure.[52] A denial of access thus must rest upon demonstration of "a compelling governmental interest . . . narrowly tailored to serve that interest."[53] Although child sex abuse cases may present special problems with respect to further traumatizing of victims, they also may have the potential for overzealousness and misconduct by prosecutors more interested in headlines than justice. Consequently, the Court's insistence upon examination of less restrictive alternatives and its refusal to exclude a category of cases entirely from public view seem to strike a more sensitive balance among the competing interests. The *Gannett* decision as a consequence was effectively narrowed to reach only pretrial proceedings. Since the Court in *Gannett* found no evidence supporting the notion that the public historically had a right to attend pretrial proceedings as opposed to trials,[54] a basis for

distinguishing the two circumstances persisted. Pursuant to a post-*Globe Newspaper* decision discussed later, it appears that the Court now will forego such a distinction.

Globe Newspaper Co. v. Superior Court, 457 U.S. 596 (1982)

Justice Brennan delivered the opinion of the Court.

Section 16A of Chapter 278 of the Massachusetts General Laws, as construed by the Massachusetts Supreme Judicial Court, requires trial judges, at trials for specified sexual offenses involving a victim under the age of 18, to exclude the press and general public from the courtroom during the testimony of that victim. The question presented is whether the statute thus construed violates the First Amendment as applied to the States through the Fourteenth Amendment.

The Court's recent decision in *Richmond Newspapers* firmly established for the first time that the press and general public have a constitutional right of access to criminal trials. Although there was no opinion of the Court in that case, seven Justices recognized that this right of access is embodied in the First Amendment, and applied to the States through the Fourteenth Amendment. 448 U.S., at 558–581 (plurality opinion); *id.*, at 584–598 (Brennan, J., concurring in judgment); *id.*, at 598–601 (Stewart, J., concurring in judgment); *id.*, at 601–604 (Blackmun, J., concurring in judgment).

Of course, this right of access to criminal trials is not explicitly mentioned in terms in the First Amendment. But we have long eschewed any "narrow, literal conception" of the Amendment's terms, *NAACP v. Button*, 371 U.S. 415, 430 (1963), for the Framers were concerned with broad principles, and wrote against a background of shared values and practices. The First Amendment is thus broad enough to encompass those rights that, while not unambiguously enumerated in the very terms of the Amendment, are nonetheless necessary to the enjoyment of other First Amendment rights. *Richmond Newspapers, Inc. v. Virginia*, 448 U.S., at 579–580, and n. 16 (plurality opinion) (citing cases); *id.*, at 587–588, and n. 4 (Brennan, J., concurring in judgment). Underlying the First Amendment right of access to criminal trials is the common understanding that "a major purpose of that Amendment was to protect the free discussion of governmental affairs," *Mills v. Alabama*, 384 U.S. 214, 218 (1966). By offering such protection, the First Amendment serves to ensure that the individual citizen can effectively participate in and contribute to our republican system of self-government. See *Thornhill v. Alabama*, 310 U.S. 88, 95 (1940); *Richmond Newspapers, Inc. v. Virginia*, 448 U.S., at 587–588 (Brennan, J., concurring in judgment). See also *id.*, at 575 (plurality opinion) (the "expressly guaranteed freedoms" of the First Amendment "share a common core purpose of assuring freedom of communication on matters relating to the functioning of government"). Thus to the extent that the First Amendment embraces a right of access to criminal trials, it is to ensure that this constitutionally protected "discussion of governmental affairs" is an informed one.

Two features of the criminal justice system, emphasized in the various opinions in *Richmond Newspapers*, together serve to explain why a right of access to *criminal trials* in particular is properly afforded protection by the First Amendment. First, the criminal trial historically has been open to the press and general public. "[A]t the time when our organic laws were adopted, criminal trials both here and in England had long been presumptively open." *Richmond Newspapers, Inc. v. Virginia, supra*, at 569 (plurality opinion). And since that time, the presumption of openness has remained secure. Indeed, at the time of this Court's decision in *In re Oliver*, 333 U.S. 257 (1948), the presumption was so solidly grounded that the Court was "unable to find a single instance of a criminal trial conducted in camera in any federal, state, or municipal court during the history of this country." *Id.*, at 266 (footnote omitted). This uniform rule of openness has been viewed as significant in constitutional terms not only "because the Constitution carries the gloss of history," but also because "a tradition of accessibility implies the favorable judgment of experience." *Richmond Newspapers, Inc. v. Virginia, supra*, at 589 (Brennan, J., concurring in judgment).

Second, the right of access to criminal trials plays a particularly significant role in the functioning of the judicial process and the government as a whole. Public scrutiny of a criminal trial enhances the quality and safeguards the integrity of the factfinding process, with benefits to both the defendant and to society as a whole. Moreover, public access to the criminal trial fosters an appearance of fairness, thereby heightening public respect for the judicial process. And in the broadest terms, public access to criminal trials permits the public to participate in and serve as a check upon the judicial process—an essential component in our structure of self-government. In sum, the institutional value of the open criminal trial is recognized in both logic and experience.

B

Although the right of access to criminal trials is of constitutional stature, it is not absolute. See *Richmond Newspapers, Inc. v. Virginia, supra*, at 581, n. 18 (plurality opinion); *Nebraska Press Assn. v. Stuart*, 427 U.S., at 570. But the circumstances under which the press and public can be barred from a criminal trial are limited; the State's justification in denying access must be a weighty one. Where, as in the present case, the State attempts to deny the right of access in order to inhibit the disclosure of sensitive information, it must be shown that the denial is necessitated by a compelling governmental interest, and is narrowly tailored to serve that interest. See, e.g., *Brown v. Hartlage*, 456 U.S. 45, 53–54 (1982); *Smith v. Daily Mail Publishing Co.*, 443 U.S. 97, 101–103 (1979); *NAACP v. Button*, 371 U.S., at 438. We now consider the state interests advanced to support Massachusetts' mandatory rule barring press and public access to criminal sex-offense trials during the testimony of minor victims.

IV

The state interests asserted to support § 16A, though articulated in various ways, are reducible to two: the protection of minor victims of sex crimes from further trauma and embarrassment; and the encouragement of such victims to come forward and testify in a truthful and credible manner. We consider these interests in turn.

We agree with appellee that the first interest—safeguarding the physical and psychological well-being of a minor—is a compelling one. But as compelling as that interest is, it does not justify a *mandatory* closure rule, for it is clear that the circumstances of the particular case may affect the significance of the interest. A trial court can determine on a case-by-case basis whether closure is necessary to protect the welfare of a minor victim. Among the factors to be weighed are the minor victim's age, psychological maturity and understanding, the nature of the crime, the desires of the victim, and the interests of parents and relatives. Section 16A, in contrast, requires closure even if the victim does not seek the exclusion of the press and general public, and would not suffer injury by their presence. In the case before us, for example, the names of the minor victims were already in the public record, and the record indicates that the victims may have been willing to testify despite the presence of the press. If the trial court had been permitted to exercise its discretion, closure might well have been deemed unnecessary. In short, § 16A cannot be viewed as a narrowly tailored means of accommodating the State's asserted interest: That interest could be served just as well by requiring the trial court to determine on a case-by-case basis whether the State's legitimate concern for the well-being of the minor victim necessitates closure. Such an approach ensures that the constitutional right of the press and public to gain access to criminal trials will not be restricted except where necessary to protect the State's interest.

Nor can § 16A be justified on the basis of the Commonwealth's second asserted interest—the encouragement of minor victims of sex crimes to come forward and provide accurate testimony. The Commonwealth has offered no empirical support for the claim that the rule of automatic closure contained in § 16A will lead to an increase in the number of minor sex victims coming forward and cooperating with state authorities. Not only is the claim speculative in empirical terms, but it is also open to serious question as a matter of logic and common sense. Although § 16A bars the press and general public from the courtroom during the testimony of minor sex victims, the press is not denied access to the transcript, court personnel, or any other possible source that could provide an account of the minor victim's testimony. Thus § 16A cannot prevent the press from

publicizing the substance of a minor victim's testimony, as well as his or her identity. If the Commonwealth's interest in encouraging minor victims to come forward depends on keeping such matters secret, § 16A hardly advances that interest in an effective manner. And even if § 16A effectively advanced the State's interest, it is doubtful that the interest would be sufficient to overcome the constitutional attack, for that same interest could be relied on to support an array of mandatory closure rules designed to encourage victims to come forward: Surely it cannot be suggested that minor victims of sex crimes are the *only* crime victims who, because of publicity attendant to criminal trials, are reluctant to come forward and testify. The State's argument based on this interest therefore proves too much, and runs contrary to the very foundation of the right of access recognized in *Richmond Newspapers:* namely, "that a presumption of openness inheres in the very nature of a criminal trial under our system of justice." 448 U.S., at 573 (plurality opinion).

V

For the foregoing reasons, we hold that § 16A, as construed by the Massachusetts Supreme Judicial Court, violates the First Amendment to the Constitution. Accordingly, the judgment of the Massachusetts Supreme Judicial Court is

Reversed.

Chief Justice Burger, with whom Justice Rehnquist joins, dissenting.

Historically our society has gone to great lengths to protect minors *charged* with crime, particularly by prohibiting the release of the names of offenders, barring the press and public from juvenile proceedings, and sealing the records of those proceedings. Yet today the Court holds unconstitutional a state statute designed to protect not the *accused,* but the minor *victims* of sex crimes. In doing so, it advances a disturbing paradox. Although states are permitted, for example, to mandate the closure of all proceedings in order to protect a 17-year-old charged with rape, they are not permitted to require the closing of part of criminal proceedings in order to protect an innocent child who has been raped or otherwise sexually abused.

The Court has tried to make its holding a narrow one by not disturbing the authority of state legislatures to enact more narrowly drawn statutes giving trial judges the discretion to exclude the public and the press from the courtroom during the minor victim's testimony. *Ante*, at 611, n. 27. I also do not read the Court's opinion as foreclosing a state statute which mandates closure except in cases where the victim agrees to testify in open court. But the Court's decision is nevertheless a gross invasion of state authority and a state's duty to protect its citizens—in this case minor victims of crime. I cannot agree with the Court's expansive interpretation of our decision in *Richmond Newspapers, Inc. v. Virginia*, 448 U.S. 555 (1980), or its cavalier rejection of the serious interests supporting Massachusetts' mandatory closure rule. Accordingly, I dissent.

In *Press-Enterprise Co. v. Superior Court*,[55] the Court found that a First Amendment right of access to a preliminary hearing exists.[56] In addition to recognizing a traditional practice of openness in the particular jurisdiction, the Court emphasized the widespread preference of modern practice for open proceedings.[57] It also accounted for a reality that seemed to have been disregarded or discounted in *Gannett*. Although the Court in *Richmond Newspapers* had stressed the importance of openness in a critical proceeding such as a trial, pretrial proceedings for many defendants are the dispositive event in the criminal justice system. Because the vast majority of cases result in pleas without a trial, the pretrial phase for practical purposes may be the most crucial. If public access is to operate as a check upon the process's abuse, therefore, its extension to the pretrial context is well justified.

The *Press-Enterprise* decision responded to the preliminary hearing context but refers generally to criminal proceedings.[58] Although concern was expressed that the determination might apply also to grand juries,[59] it is unlikely that the Court would extend its logic that far. The opinion itself,

which suggested that the grand jury's investigative function requires secrecy and confidentiality, is supported by a long history of such practice.[60] Closure also remains a possibility for pretrial proceedings if the appropriate standard is satisfied. Thus, when the right to a fair trial is asserted, exclusion of the press and public is permissible "if specific findings are made that first, there is a substantial probability that the defendant's right to a fair trial will be prejudiced by publicity that closure would prevent and second, reasonable alternatives to closure cannot adequately protect the defendant's free trial rights."[61] Although enunciated in the context of a preliminary hearing, the standard presumably would be relevant for other proceedings including a trial.[62] Even if the showing necessary for closure is made, it would seem that a transcript must be made available as soon as the threat of prejudicial publicity abates.[63]

Press-Enterprise Co. v. Superior Court, 478 U.S. 1 (1986)

The right to an open public trial is a shared right of the accused and the public, the common concern being the assurance of fairness. Only recently, in *Waller v. Georgia*, 467 U.S. 39 (1984), for example, we considered whether the defendant's Sixth Amendment right to an open trial prevented the closure of a suppression hearing over the defendant's objection. We noted that the First Amendment right of access would in most instances attach to such proceedings and that "the explicit Sixth Amendment right of the accused is no less protective of a public trial than the implicit First Amendment right of the press and public." *Id.*, at 46. When the defendant objects to the closure of a suppression hearing, therefore, the hearing must be open unless the party seeking to close the hearing advances an overriding interest that is likely to be prejudiced. *Id.*, at 47.

Here, unlike *Waller*, the right asserted is not the defendant's Sixth Amendment right to a public trial since the defendant requested a *closed* preliminary hearing. Instead, the right asserted here is that of the public under the First Amendment. See *Gannett, supra*, at 397 (Powell, J., concurring). The California Supreme Court concluded that the First Amendment was not implicated because the proceeding was not a criminal trial, but a preliminary hearing. However, the First Amendment question cannot be resolved solely on the label we give the event, i.e., "trial" or otherwise, particularly where the preliminary hearing functions much like a full-scale trial. . . . *Newspapers, Globe,* and *Press-Enterprise I* that public access to criminal trials and the selection of jurors is essential to the proper functioning of the criminal justice system. California preliminary hearings are sufficiently like a trial to justify the same conclusion.

In California, to bring a felon to trial, the prosecutor has a choice of securing a grand jury indictment or a finding of probable cause following a preliminary hearing. Even when the accused has been indicted by a grand jury, however, he has an absolute right to an elaborate preliminary hearing before a neutral magistrate. *Hawkins v. Superior Court*, 22 Cal. 3d 584, 586 P. 2d 918 (1978). The accused has the right to personally appear at the hearing, to be represented by counsel, to cross-examine hostile witnesses, to present exculpatory evidence, and to exclude illegally obtained evidence. Cal. Penal Code Ann. §§ 859–866 (West 1985), § 1538.5 (West Supp. 1986). If the magistrate determines that probable cause exists, the accused is bound over for trial; such a finding leads to a guilty plea in the majority of cases.

It is true that unlike a criminal trial, the California preliminary hearing cannot result in the conviction of the accused and the adjudication is before a magistrate or other judicial officer without a jury. But these features, standing alone, do not make public access any less essential to the proper functioning of the proceedings in the overall criminal justice process. Because of its extensive scope, the preliminary hearing is often the final and most important step in the criminal proceeding. See *Waller v. Georgia*, 467 U.S., at 46–47. As the California Supreme Court stated in *San Jose Mercury-News v. Municipal Court*, 30 Cal. 3d 498, 511, 638 P. 2d 655, 663 (1982), the preliminary hearing in many cases provides "the sole occasion for public observation of the criminal justice system." See also *Richmond Newspapers*, 448 U.S., at 572.

Similarly, the absence of a jury, long recognized as "an inestimable safeguard against the corrupt or overzealous prosecutor and against the compliant, biased, or eccentric judge," *Duncan v. Louisiana*, 391 U.S. 145, 156 (1968), makes the importance of public access to a preliminary hearing even more significant. "People in an open society do not demand infallibility from their institutions, but it is difficult for them to accept what they are prohibited from observing." *Richmond Newspapers*, 448 U.S., at 572.

Denying the transcript of a 41-day preliminary hearing would frustrate what we have characterized as the "community therapeutic value" of openness. *Id.*, at 570. Criminal acts, especially certain violent crimes, provoke public concern, outrage, and hostility. "When the public is aware that the law is being enforced and the criminal justice system is functioning, an outlet is provided for these understandable reactions and emotions." *Press-Enterprise I*, 464 U.S., at 509. See also H. Weihofen, The Urge to Punish 130–131 (1956); T. Reik, The Compulsion to Confess (1959). In sum:

> The value of openness lies in the fact that people not actually attending trials can have confidence that standards of fairness are being observed; the sure knowledge that *anyone* is free to attend gives assurance that established procedures are being followed and that deviations will become known. Openness thus enhances both the basic fairness of the criminal trial and the appearance of fairness so essential to public confidence in the system. *Press-Enterprise I, supra,* at 508 (emphasis in original).

We therefore conclude that the qualified First Amendment right of access to criminal proceedings applies to preliminary hearings as they are conducted in California.

2. Cameras in the Courtroom

Prejudice to a defendant's right of a fair trial and associated guarantees may be attributed to consequences of the media's general function of disseminating information or to specific difficulties created by its presence at a judicial proceeding. Of particular concern to the Court has been the influence of broadcasting upon the fairness of the criminal justice system. From 1937 until fairly recently, the American Bar Association Canons of Judicial Ethics provided that a judge should prohibit cameras from the courtroom because they detracted from the dignity of the proceeding.[64] When first confronted with the effect of television coverage, it reversed a murder conviction on the grounds that pretrial publicity had contributed to the jury's verdict.[65] Thereafter, it found a due process violation attributable to the broadcast of a defendant's confession prior to trial.[66] Given what it characterized as the public's pervasive exposure to a spectacle, moreover, the Court assumed a constitutional deprivation instead of requiring proof the jury actually was prejudiced.[67] The mere presence of cameras in the courtroom, over the defendant's objection, convinced a plurality of the Court[68] that due process was denied. In *Estes v. Texas,* it was observed that the presence of the electronic media involves "such a probability of prejudice that it is deemed inherently lacking in due process."[69] The Court's fears about the effect of television were based upon possibilities that jurors might be distracted; parties, witnesses, counsel, and judges might have their attention diverted; and the quality of legal representation might be undermined.[70]

Only Justice Harlan's concurring opinion precluded the *Estes* decision from operating as a constitutional prohibition of the electronic media from the courtroom.[71] Harlan expressed serious concerns about the constitutional compatibility of cameras in the courtroom, especially in connection with cases attracting widespread interest, but he noted that technological advances ultimately might make the media's presence less of a threat to the imperatives of a fair criminal justice system.[72]

As television acquired the capacity to cover events in a less intrusive fashion, working with available light, minimal cable, and miniaturized equipment, some states became more willing to accommodate electronic coverage of court proceedings. In *Chandler v. Florida,*[73] the Court upheld a state law permitting broadcast coverage of a criminal proceeding even if the defendant objected.[74] The unanimous decision found no satisfactory evidence that the presence of cameras in the courtroom inherently denies due process.[75] Critical to the determination eappears to have been the presence of guidelines obligating judges to safeguard the rights of the accused.[76] A defendant still may assert that media coverage may adversely affect any of the trial participants to the point that due process is compromised.[77] A satisfactory showing requires a particularized demonstration of prejudice in the given case, however, rather than a mere showing of "juror awareness" of the media's presence and interest.[78]

Although conclusively abandoning previous intimations that the presence of the electronic media amounted to a per se constitutional violation, the Court emphasized that its decision did not establish a right of access to broadcast court proceedings.[79] Such a determination in practical terms arguably puts broadcasters at a constitutional disadvantage, given recognition of a right of access to trials for the press and public.[80] Although justifiable on legalistic grounds, insofar as radio and television have been regarded as the least protected media, such a result does not conform especially well with the holding that cameras in the courtroom do not inherently compromise due process. The Judicial Conference of the United States has planned a three year experiment through 1994 with television and radio access to federal district and circuit courts. Considerable movement toward accommodating the electronic media already has been evidenced at the state level, where most jurisdictions with the endorsement of the American Bar Association have revised their laws to permit cameras in the courtroom. Typically, such statutes permit electronic coverage provided it is unobtrusive and subject to guidelines that help avoid interference with the defendant's rights. Pursuant to *Chandler,* the only issue concerning admission of cameras into the courtroom is whether, under the particular circumstances of a given case, their presence and operation cause a due process deprivation.

Chandler v. Florida, 449 U.S. 560 (1981)

Chief Justice Burger delivered the opinion of the Court.

The question presented on this appeal is whether, consistent with constitutional guarantees, a state may provide for radio, television, and still photographic coverage of a criminal trial for public broadcast, notwithstanding the objection of the accused.

I

A

Background. Over the past 50 years, some criminal cases characterized as "sensational" have been subjected to extensive coverage by news media, sometimes seriously interfering with the conduct of the proceedings and creating a setting wholly inappropriate for the administration of justice. Judges, lawyers, and others soon became concerned, and in 1937, after study, the American Bar Association House of Delegates adopted Judicial Canon 35, declaring that all photographic and broadcast coverage of courtroom proceedings should be prohibited. In 1952, the House of Delegates amended Canon 35 to proscribe television coverage as well. 77 A.B.A. Rep. 610–611 (1952). The Canon's proscription was reaffirmed in 1972 when the Code of Judicial Conduct replaced the Canons of Judicial Ethics and Canon 3A (7) superseded Canon 35. E. Thode, Reporter's Notes to Code of Judicial Conduct 56–59 (1973). Cf. Fed. Rule Crim. Proc. 53. A majority of the states, including Florida, adopted the substance of the ABA provision and its amendments. In Florida, the rule was embodied in Canon 3A (7) of the Florida Code of Judicial Conduct.

In February 1978, the American Bar Associa-

tion Committee on Fair Trial-Free Press proposed revised standards. These included a provision permitting courtroom coverage by the electronic media under conditions to be established by local rule and under the control of the trial judge, but only if such coverage was carried out unobtrusively and without affecting the conduct of the trial. The revision was endorsed by the ABA's Standing Committee on Standards for Criminal Justice and by its Committee on Criminal Justice and the Media, but it was rejected by the House of Delegates on February 12, 1979. 65 A.B.A.J. 304 (1979).

In 1978, based upon its own study of the matter, the Conference of State Chief Justices, by a vote of 44 to 1, approved a resolution to allow the highest court of each state to promulgate standards and guidelines regulating radio, television, and other photographic coverage of court proceedings....

Following its review of this material, the Florida Supreme Court concluded "that on balance there [was] more to be gained than lost by permitting electronic media coverage of judicial proceedings subject to standards for such coverage." *In re Petition of Post-Newsweek Stations, Florida, Inc.,* 370 So. 2d 764, 780 (1979). The Florida court was of the view that because of the significant effect of the courts on the day-to-day lives of the citizenry, it was essential that the people have confidence in the process. It felt that broadcast coverage of trials would contribute to wider public acceptance and understanding of decisions. *Ibid.* Consequently, after revising the 1977 guidelines to reflect its evaluation of the pilot program, the Florida Supreme Court promulgated a revised Canon 3A (7). *Id.,* at 781. The Canon provides:

> Subject at all times to the authority of the presiding judge to (i) control the conduct of proceedings before the court, (ii) ensure decorum and prevent distractions, and (iii) ensure the fair administration of justice in the pending cause, electronic media and still photography coverage of public judicial proceedings in the appellate and trial courts of this state shall be allowed in accordance with standards of conduct and technology promulgated by the Supreme Court of Florida. *Ibid.*

The implementing guidelines specify in detail the kind of electronic equipment to be used and the manner of its use. *Id.,* at 778–779, 783–784.

For example, no more than one television camera and only one camera technician are allowed. Existing recording systems used by court reporters are used by broadcasters for audio pickup. Where more than one broadcast news organization seeks to cover a trial, the media must pool coverage. No artificial lighting is allowed. The equipment is positioned in a fixed location, and it may not be moved during trial. Videotaping equipment must be remote from the courtroom. Film, videotape, and lenses may not be changed while the court is in session. No audio recording of conferences between lawyers, between parties and counsel, or at the bench is permitted. The judge has sole and plenary discretion to exclude coverage of certain witnesses, and the jury may not be filmed. The judge has discretionary power to forbid coverage whenever satisfied that coverage may have a deleterious effect on the paramount right of the defendant to a fair trial. The Florida Supreme Court has the right to revise these rules as experience dictates, or indeed to bar all broadcast coverage or photography in courtrooms.

Appellants rely chiefly on *Estes v. Texas*, 381 U.S. 532 (1965), and Chief Justice Warren's separate concurring opinion in that case. They argue that the televising of criminal trials is inherently a denial of due process, and they read *Estes* as announcing a *per se* constitutional rule to that effect.

Chief Justice Warren's concurring opinion, in which he was joined by Justices Douglas and Goldberg, indeed provides some support for the appellants' position:

> While I join the Court's opinion and agree that the televising of criminal trials is inherently a denial of due process, I desire to express additional views on why this is so. In doing this, I wish to emphasize that our condemnation of televised criminal trials is not based on generalities or abstract fears. The record in this case presents a vivid illustration of the inherent prejudice of televised criminal trials and supports our conclusion that this is the appropriate time to make a definitive appraisal of television in the courtroom. *Id.*, at 552.

If appellants' reading of *Estes* were correct, we would be obliged to apply that holding and reverse the judgment under review....

Parsing the six opinions in *Estes*, one is left with a sense of doubt as to precisely how much of

Justice Clark's opinion was joined in, and supported by, Justice Harlan. In an area charged with constitutional nuances, perhaps more should not be expected. Nonetheless, it is fair to say that Justice Harlan viewed the holding as limited to the proposition that "*what was done in this case* infringed the fundamental right to a fair trial assured by the Due Process Clause of the Fourteenth Amendment," *id.*, 587 (emphasis added), he went on:

> At the present juncture I can only conclude that televised trials, *at least in cases like this one,* possess such capabilities for interfering with the even course of the judicial process that they are constitutionally banned. *Id.*, at 596 (emphasis added).

Justice Harlan's opinion, upon which analysis of the constitutional holding of *Estes* turns, must be read as defining the scope of that holding; we conclude that *Estes* is not to be read as announcing a constitutional rule barring still photographic, radio, and television coverage in all cases and under all circumstances. It does not stand as an absolute ban on state experimentation with an evolving technology, which, in terms of modes of mass communication, was in its relative infancy in 1964, and is, even now, in a state of continuing change.

IV

Since we are satisfied that *Estes* did not announce a constitutional rule that all photographic or broadcast coverage of criminal trials is inherently a denial of due process, we turn to consideration, as a matter of first impression, of the appellants' suggestion that we now promulgate such a *per se* rule....

Not unimportant to the position asserted by Florida and other states is the change in television technology since 1962, when Estes was tried. It is urged, and some empirical data are presented, that many of the negative factors found in *Estes*—cumbersome equipment, cables, distracting lighting, numerous camera technicians—are less substantial factors today than they were at that time.

It is also significant that safeguards have been built into the experimental programs in state courts, and into the Florida program, to avoid some of the most egregious problems envisioned by the six opinions in the *Estes* case. Florida admonishes its courts to take special pains to protect certain witnesses—for example, children, victims of sex crimes, some informants, and even the very timid witness or party—from the glare of publicity and the tensions of being "on camera." *In re Petition of Post-Newsweek Stations, Florida, Inc.,* 370 So.2d, at 779.

The Florida guidelines place on trial judges positive obligations to be on guard to protect the fundamental right of the accused to a fair trial. The Florida Canon, being one of the few permitting broadcast coverage of criminal trials over the objection of the accused, raises problems not present in the rules of other states. Inherent in electronic coverage of a trial is the risk that the very awareness by the accused of the coverage and the contemplated broadcast may adversely affect the conduct of the participants and the fairness of the trial, yet leave no evidence of how the conduct or the trial's fairness was affected. Given this danger, it is significant that Florida requires that objections of the accused to coverage be heard and considered on the record by the trial court. See e.g., *Green v. State,* 377 So. 2d 193, 201 (Fla. App. 1979). In addition to providing a record for appellate review, a pretrial hearing enables a defendant to advance the basis of his objection to broadcast coverage and allows the trial court to define the steps necessary to minimize or eliminate the risks of prejudice to the accused. Experiments such as the one presented here may well increase the number of appeals by adding a new basis for claims to reverse, but this is a risk Florida has chosen to take after preliminary experimentation. Here, the record does not indicate that appellants requested an evidentiary hearing to show adverse impact or injury. Nor does the record reveal anything more than generalized allegations of prejudice....

To say that the appellants have not demonstrated that broadcast coverage is inherently a denial of due process is not to say that the appellants were in fact accorded all of the protections of due process in their trial. As noted earlier, a defendant has the right on review to show that the media's coverage of his case—printed or broadcast—compromised the ability of the jury to judge him fairly. Alternatively, a defendant might show that broadcast coverage of his particular case had an adverse impact on the trial participants sufficient to

constitute a denial of due process. Neither showing was made in this case.

To demonstrate prejudice in a specific case a defendant must show something more than juror awareness that the trial is such as to attract the attention of broadcasters. *Murphy v. Florida,* 421 U.S. 794, 800 (1975). No doubt the very presence of a camera in the courtroom made the jurors aware that the trial was thought to be of sufficient interest to the public to warrant coverage. Jurors, forbidden to watch all broadcasts, would have had no way of knowing that only fleeting seconds of the proceeding would be reproduced. But the appellants have not attempted to show with any specificity that the presence of cameras impaired the ability of the jurors to decide the case on only the evidence before them or that their trial was affected adversely by the impact on any of the participants of the presence of cameras and the prospect of broadcast.

Although not essential to our holding, we note that at *voir dire,* the jurors were asked if the presence of the camera would in any way compromise their ability to consider the case. Each answered that the camera would not prevent him or her from considering the case solely on the merits. App. 8–12. The trial court instructed the jurors not to watch television accounts of the trial, *id.,* at 13–14, and the appellants do not contend that any juror violated this instruction. The appellants have offered no evidence that any participant in this case was affected by the presence of cameras. In short, there is no showing that the trial was compromised by television coverage, as was the case in *Estes.*

3. Prejudicial Influences

The press, apart from any problems attributable to a particular medium, is generally capable of upsetting fair trial guarantees. In *Sheppard v. Maxwell,*[81] the Court found a denial of due process resulting from the combined effect of massive pretrial publicity and disruptive conduct by all elements of the press.[82] Prior to the trial, a newspaper had printed numerous inflammatory and erroneous articles about the defendant.[83] It also published the identities of the jurors, thereby conferring celebrity status upon and making them susceptible to public pressure.[84] The ingredients for a circus atmosphere were compounded by the fact that the presiding judge was in the midst of a reelection campaign.[85] At the trial itself, reporters dominated the courtroom, walked freely in the bar area, examined and handled evidence, and at times made it difficult for witnesses and counsel to be heard and for the defendant and his attorney to communicate with each other.[86]

While noting the significance of First Amendment interests, the Court emphasized that freedom of discussion must be coordinated with the fair and orderly administration of justice.[87] Paramount in the weighing of those interests was ensuring the resolution of cases based solely on evidence adduced in open court.[88] In striking a proper balance between competing constitutional concerns, the Court suggested several avenues of recourse: rules governing the media's behavior and numbers in the courtroom, judge-directed voir dire to ensure juror impartiality has not been compromised by pretrial publicity, sequestration to maintain such objectivity, change of venue or postponement, and orders prohibiting parties, witnesses, police, judicial employees, and counsel from divulging information that might be prejudicial.[89] The Court also observed that "there is nothing that proscribes the press from reporting events that transpire in the courtroom." Not surprisingly, given its emphasis upon the trial judge's duty to take steps necessary to protect the adjudicative process from prejudice,[90] restraining orders barring the media from publishing certain information became increasingly common. Eventually, such orders became subject to the strong presumption against a prior restraint's constitutionality and requirement that they could not be entered unless alternatives, less burdensome to First Amendment interests, were exhausted.[91]

Sheppard v. Maxwell, 384 U.S. 333 (1966)

Petitioner's wife was bludgeoned to death July 4, 1954. From the outset officials focused suspicion on petitioner, who was arrested on a murder charge July 30 and indicted August 17. His trial began October 18 and terminated with his conviction December 21, 1954. During the entire pretrial period virulent and incriminating publicity about petitioner and the murder made the case notorious, and the news media frequently aired charges and countercharges besides those for which petitioner was tried. Three months before trial he was examined for more than five hours without counsel in a televised three-day inquest conducted before an audience of several hundred spectators in a gymnasium. Over three weeks before trial the newspapers published the names and addresses of prospective jurors causing them to receive letters and telephone calls about the case. The trial began two weeks before a hotly contested election at which the chief prosecutor and the trial judge were candidates for judgeships. Newsmen were allowed to take over almost the entire small courtroom, hounding petitioner, and most of the participants. Twenty reporters were assigned seats by the court within the bar and in close proximity to the jury and counsel, precluding privacy between petitioner and his counsel. The movement of the reporters in the courtroom caused frequent confusion and disrupted the trial; and in the corridors and elsewhere in and around the courthouse they were allowed free rein by the trial judge. A broadcasting station was assigned space next to the jury room. Before the jurors began deliberations they were not sequestered and had access to all news media though the court made "suggestions" and "requests" that the jurors not expose themselves to comment about the case. Though they were sequestered during the five days and four nights of their deliberations, the jurors were allowed to make inadequately supervised telephone calls during that period. Pervasive publicity was given to the case throughout the trial, much of it involving incriminating matter not introduced at the trial, and the jurors were thrust into the role of celebrities. At least some of the publicity deluge reached the jurors. At the very inception of the proceedings and later, the trial judge announced that neither he nor anyone else could restrict the prejudicial news accounts. Despite his awareness of the excessive pretrial publicity, the trial judge failed to take effective measures against the massive publicity which continued throughout the trial or to take adequate steps to control the conduct of the trial. The petitioner filed a habeas corpus petition contending that he did not receive a fair trial. The District Court granted the writ. The Court of Appeals reversed.

The principle that justice cannot survive behind walls of silence has long been reflected in the "Anglo-American distrust for secret trials." *In re Oliver,* 333 U.S. 257, 268 (1948). A responsible press has always been regarded as the handmaiden of effective judicial administration, especially in the criminal field. Its function in this regard is documented by an impressive record of service over several centuries. The press does not simply publish information about trials but guards against the miscarriage of justice by subjecting the police, prosecutors, and judicial processes to extensive public scrutiny and criticism. This Court has, therefore, been unwilling to place any direct limitations on the freedom traditionally exercised by the news media for "[w]hat transpires in the court room is public property." *Craig v. Harney,* 331 U.S. 367, 374 (1947). The "unqualified prohibitions laid down by the framers were intended to give to liberty of the press...the broadest scope that could be countenanced in an orderly society." *Bridges v. California,* 314 U.S. 252, 265 (1941). And where there was "no threat or menace to the integrity of the trial," *Craig v. Harney, supra,* at 377, we have consistently required that the press have a free hand, even though we sometimes deplored its sensationalism.

But the Court has also pointed out that "[l]egal trials are not like elections, to be won through the use of the meeting-hall, the radio, and the newspaper." *Bridges v. California, supra,* at 271. And the Court has insisted that no one be punished for a crime without "a charge fairly made and fairly tried in a public tribunal free of prejudice, passion, excitement, and tyrannical power." *Chambers v. Florida,* 309 U.S. 227, 236–237 (1940). "Freedom of discussion should be given the widest range compatible with the es-

sential requirement of the fair and orderly administration of justice." *Pennekamp v. Florida,* 328 U.S. 331, 347 (1946). But it must not be allowed to divert the trial from the "very purpose of a court system...to adjudicate controversies, both criminal and civil, in the calmness and solemnity of the courtroom according to legal procedures." *Cox v. Louisiana,* 379 U.S. 559, 583 (1965) (Black, J., dissenting). Among these "legal procedures" is the requirement that the jury's verdict be based on evidence received in open court, not from outside sources. Thus, in *Marshall v. United States,* 360 U.S. 310 (1959), we set aside a federal conviction where the jurors were exposed "through news accounts" to information that was not admitted at trial. We held that the prejudice from such material "may indeed be greater" than when it is part of the prosecution's evidence "for it is then not tempered by protective procedures." At 313. At the same time, we did not consider dispositive the statement of each juror "that he would not be influenced by the news articles, that he could decide the case only on the evidence of record, and that he felt no prejudice against petitioner as a result of the articles." At 312. Likewise, in *Irvin v. Dowd,* 366 U.S. 717 (1961), even though each juror indicated that he could render an impartial verdict despite exposure to prejudicial newspaper articles, we set aside the conviction holding:

> With his life at stake, it is not requiring too much that petitioner be tried in an atmosphere undisturbed by so huge a wave of public passion....At 728.

The undeviating rule of this Court was expressed by Mr. Justice Holmes over half a century ago in *Patterson v. Colorado,* 205 U.S. 454, 462 (1907):

> The theory of our system is that the conclusions to be reached in a case will be induced only by evidence and argument in open court, and not by any outside influence, whether of private talk or public print.

Moreover, "the burden of showing essential unfairness...as a demonstrable reality," *Adams v. United States ex rel. McCann,* 317 U.S. 269, 281 (1942), need not be undertaken when television has exposed the community "repeatedly and in depth to the spectacle of [the accused] personally confessing in detail to the crimes with which he was later to be charged." *Rideau v. Louisiana,* 373 U.S. 723, 726 (1963). In *Turner v. Louisiana,* 379 U.S. 466 (1965), two key witnesses were deputy sheriffs who doubled as jury shepherds during the trial. The deputies swore that they had not talked to the jurors about the case, but the Court nonetheless held that,

> even if it could be assumed that the deputies never did discuss the case directly with any members of the jury, it would be blinking reality not to recognize the extreme prejudice inherent in this continual association.... At 473.

Only last Term in *Estes v. Texas,* 381 U.S. 532 (1965), we set aside a conviction despite the absence of any showing of prejudice. We said there:

> It is true that in most cases involving claims of due process deprivations we require a showing of identifiable prejudice to the accused. Nevertheless, at times a procedure employed by the State involves such a probability that prejudice will result that it is deemed inherently lacking in due process. At 542–543.

And we cited with approval the language of Mr. Justice Black for the Court in *In re Murchison,* 349 U.S. 133, 136 (1955), that "our system of law has always endeavored to prevent even the probability of unfairness."

It is clear that the totality of circumstances in this case also warrants such an approach. Unlike Estes, Sheppard was not granted a change of venue to a locale away from where the publicity originated; nor was his jury sequestered. The Estes jury saw none of the television broadcasts from the courtroom. On the contrary, the Sheppard jurors were subjected to newspaper, radio and television coverage of the trial while not taking part in the proceedings. They were allowed to go their separate ways outside of the courtroom, without adequate directions not to read or listen to anything concerning the case. The judge's "admonitions" at the beginning of the trial are representative:

> I would suggest to you and caution you that you do not read any newspapers during the progress of this trial, that you do not listen to radio comments nor watch or listen to television comments, insofar as this case is concerned. You will feel very much better as the trial proceeds.... I am sure that we shall all feel very much better if we do not indulge in any

newspaper reading or listening to any comments whatever about the matter while the case is in progress. After it is all over, you can read it all to your heart's content....

At intervals during the trial, the judge simply repeated his "suggestions" and "requests" that the jurors not expose themselves to comment upon the case. Moreover, the jurors were thrust into the role of celebrities by the judge's failure to insulate them from reporters and photographers. See *Estes v. Texas, supra,* at 545–546. The numerous pictures of the jurors, with their addresses, which appeared in the newspapers before and during the trial itself exposed them to expressions of opinion from both cranks and friends. The fact that anonymous letters had been received by prospective jurors should have made the judge aware that this publicity seriously threatened the jurors' privacy.

The press coverage of the Estes trial was not nearly as massive and pervasive as the attention given by the Cleveland newspapers and broadcasting stations to Sheppard's prosecution. Sheppard stood indicted for the murder of his wife; the State was demanding the death penalty. For months the virulent publicity about Sheppard and the murder had made the case notorious. Charges and countercharges were aired in the news media besides those for which Sheppard was called to trial. In addition, only three months before trial, Sheppard was examined for more than five hours without counsel during a three-day inquest which ended in a public brawl. The inquest was televised live from a high school gymnasium seating hundreds of people. Furthermore, the trial began two weeks before a hotly contested election at which both Chief Prosecutor Mahon and Judge Blythin were candidates for judgeships.

While we cannot say that Sheppard was denied due process by the judge's refusal to take precautions against the influence of pretrial publicity alone, the court's later rulings must be considered against the setting in which the trial was held. In light of this background, we believe that the arrangements made by the judge with the news media caused Sheppard to be deprived of that "judicial serenity and calm to which [he] was entitled." *Estes v. Texas, supra,* at 536. The fact is that bedlam reigned at the courthouse during the trial and newsmen took over practically the entire courtroom, hounding most of the participants in the trial, especially Sheppard. At a temporary table within a few feet of the jury box and counsel table sat some 20 reporters staring at Sheppard and taking notes. The erection of a press table for reporters inside the bar is unprecedented. The bar of the court is reserved for counsel, providing them a safe place in which to keep papers and exhibits, and to confer privately with client and co-counsel. It is designed to protect the witness and the jury from any distractions, intrusions or influences, and to permit bench discussions of the judge's rulings away from the hearing of the public and the jury. Having assigned almost all of the available seats in the courtroom to the news media the judge lost his ability to supervise that environment. The movement of the reporters in and out of the courtroom caused frequent confusion and disruption of the trial. And the record reveals constant commotion within the bar. Moreover, the judge gave the throng of newsmen gathered in the corridors of the courthouse absolute free rein. Participants in the trial, including the jury, were forced to run a gantlet of reporters and photographers each time they entered or left the courtroom. The total lack of consideration for the privacy of the jury was demonstrated by the assignment to a broadcasting station of space next to the jury room on the floor above the courtroom, as well as the fact that jurors were allowed to make telephone calls during their five-day deliberation.

There can be no question about the nature of the publicity which surrounded Sheppard's trial. We agree, as did the Court of Appeals, with the findings in Judge Bell's opinion for the Ohio Supreme Court:

> Murder and mystery, society, sex and suspense were combined in this case in such a manner as to intrigue and captivate the public fancy to a degree perhaps unparalleled in recent annals. Throughout the preindictment investigation, the subsequent legal skirmishes and the nine-week trial, circulationcons-cious editors catered to the insatiable interest of the American public in the bizarre.... In this atmosphere of a "Roman holiday" for the news media, Sam Sheppard stood trial for his life. 165 Ohio St., at 294; 135 N. E. 2d, at 342.

Indeed, every court that has considered this case, save the court that tried it, has deplored the man-

ner in which the news media inflamed and prejudiced the public.

Much of the material printed or broadcast during the trial was never heard from the witness stand, such as the charges that Sheppard had purposely impeded the murder investigation and must be guilty since he had hired a prominent criminal lawyer; that Sheppard was a perjurer; that he had sexual relations with numerous women; that his slain wife had characterized him as a "Jekyll-Hyde"; that he was "a bare-faced liar" because of his testimony as to police treatment; and, finally, that a woman convict claimed Sheppard to be the father of her illegitimate child. As the trial progressed, the newspapers summarized and interpreted the evidence, devoting particular attention to the material that incriminated Sheppard, and often drew unwarranted inferences from testimony. At one point, a front-page picture of Mrs. Sheppard's blood-stained pillow was published after being "doctored" to show more clearly an alleged imprint of a surgical instrument.

Nor is there doubt that this deluge of publicity reached at least some of the jury. One the only occasion that the jury was queried, two jurors admitted in open court to hearing the highly inflammatory charge that a prison inmate claimed Sheppard as the father of her illegitimate child. Despite the extent and nature of the publicity to which the jury was exposed during trial, the judge refused defense counsel's other requests that the jurors be asked whether they had read or heard specific prejudicial comment about the case, including the incidents we have previously summarized. In these circumstances, we can assume that some of this material reached members of the jury. See *Commonwealth v. Crehan*, 345 Mass. 609, 188 N. E. 2d 923 (1963).

The court's fundamental error is compounded by the holding that it lacked power to control the publicity about the trial. From the very inception of the proceedings the judge announced that neither he nor anyone else could restrict prejudicial news accounts. And he reiterated this view on numerous occasions. Since he viewed the news media as his target, the judge never considered other means that are often utilized to reduce the appearance of prejudicial material and to protect the jury from outside influence. We conclude that these procedures would have been sufficient to guarantee Sheppard a fair trial and so do not consider what sanctions might be available against a recalcitrant press nor the charges of bias now made against the state trial judge.

The carnival atmosphere at trial could easily have been avoided since the courtroom and courthouse premises are subject to the control of the court. As we stressed in *Estes,* the presence of the press at judicial proceedings must be limited when it is apparent that the accused might otherwise be prejudiced or disadvantaged. Bearing in mind the massive pretrial publicity, the judge should have adopted stricter rules governing the use of the courtroom by newsmen, as Sheppard's counsel requested. The number of reporters in the courtroom itself could have been limited at the first sign that their presence would disrupt the trial. They certainly should not have been placed inside the bar. Furthermore, the judge should have more closely regulated the conduct of newsmen in the courtroom. For instance, the judge belatedly asked them not to handle and photograph trial exhibits lying on the counsel table during recess.

Secondly, the court should have insulated the witnesses. All of the newspapers and radio stations apparently interviewed prospective witnesses at will, and in many instances disclosed their testimony. A typical example was the publication of numerous statements by Susan Hayes, before her appearance in court, regarding her love affair with Sheppard. Although the witnesses were barred from the courtroom during the trial the full verbatim testimony was available to them in the press. This completely nullified the judge's imposition of the rule. See *Estes v. Texas, supra,* at 547.

Thirdly, the court should have made some effort to control the release of leads, information, and gossip to the press by police officers, witnesses, and the counsel for both sides. Much of the information thus disclosed was inaccurate, leading to groundless rumors and confusion....

The fact that many of the prejudicial news items can be traced to the prosecution, as well as the defense, aggravates the judge's failure to take any action. See *Stroble v. California,* 343 U.S. 181, 201 (1952) (Frankfurter, J., dissenting). Effective control of these sources—concededly within the court's power—might well have prevented the divulgence of inaccurate information, rumors, and accusations that made up much of the inflammatory publicity, at least after Sheppard's indictment.

More specifically, the trial court might well have proscribed extrajudicial statements by any lawyer, party, witness, or court official which divulged prejudicial matters, such as the refusal of Sheppard to submit to interrogation or take any lie detector tests; any statement made by Sheppard to officials; the identity of prospective witnesses or their probable testimony; any belief in guilt or innocence; or like statements concerning the merits of the case. See *State v. Van Duyne,* 43 N. J. 369, 389, 204 A. 2d 841, 852 (1964), in which the court interpreted Canon 20 of the American Bar Association's Canons of Professional Ethics to prohibit such statements. Being advised of the great public interest in the case, the mass coverage of the press, and the potential prejudicial impact of publicity, the court could also have requested the appropriate city and county officials to promulgate a regulation with respect to dissemination of information about the case by their employees. In addition, reporters who wrote or broadcast prejudicial stories, could have been warned as to the impropriety of publishing material not introduced in the proceedings. The judge was put on notice of such events by defense counsel's complaint about the WHK broadcast on the second day of trial. See p. 346, *supra.* In this manner, Sheppard's right to a trial free from outside interference would have been given added protection without corresponding curtailment of the news media. Had the judge, the other officers of the court, and the police placed the interest of justice first, the news media would have soon learned to be content with the task of reporting the case as it unfolded in the courtroom—not pieced together from extrajudicial statements.

From the cases coming here we note that unfair and prejudicial news comment on pending trials has become increasingly prevalent. Due process requires that the accused receive a trial by an impartial jury free from outside influences. Given the pervasiveness of modern communications and the difficulty of effacing prejudicial publicity from the minds of the jurors, the trial courts must take strong measures to ensure that the balance is never weighed against the accused. And appellate tribunals have the duty to make an independent evaluation of the circumstances. Of course, there is nothing that proscribes the press from reporting events that transpire in the courtroom. But where there is a reasonable likelihood that prejudicial news prior to trial will prevent a fair trial, the judge should continue the case until the threat abates, or transfer it to another county not so permeated with publicity. In addition, sequestration of the jury was something the judge should have raised *sua sponte* with counsel. If publicity during the proceedings threatens the fairness of the trial, a new trial should be ordered. But we must remember that reversals are but palliatives; the cure lies in those remedial measures that will prevent the prejudice at its inception. The courts must take such steps by rule and regulation that will protect their processes from prejudicial outside interferences. Neither prosecutors, counsel for defense, the accused, witnesses, court staff nor enforcement officers coming under the jurisdiction of the court should be permitted to frustrate its function. Collaboration between counsel and the press as to information affecting the fairness of a criminal trial is not only subject to regulation, but is highly censurable and worthy of disciplinary measures.

Since the state trial judge did not fulfill his duty to protect Sheppard from the inherently prejudicial publicity which saturated the community and to control disruptive influences in the courtroom, we must reverse the denial of the habeas petition. The case is remanded to the District Court with instructions to issue the writ and order that Sheppard be released from custody unless the State puts him to its charges again within a reasonable time.

II. NONCONSTITUTIONAL CONCERNS

A policy interest need not be of a constitutional order to prevail over the First Amendment. Defamation, privacy, obscenity, and copyright laws operate either because the expression they regulate is constitutionally unprotected or the harm they address is considered significant enough to require control of speech and press.

A. DEFAMATION

Until fairly recently, defamation was a category of expression that like obscenity was considered to be outside the First Amendment's protective ambit. Defamation comprises libel and slander, which traditionally implicated injury to reputation respectively by the written and spoken word. Given the merged characteristics of modern media, and unless contrary to peculiar circumstantial requirements, simplicity and accuracy are served by using the term defamation when considering harm to reputational interests caused by the press.

In *Beauharnais v. Illinois*,[92] the Court upheld a criminal statute designed to prohibit and punish group libel. Essentially, the state law criminalized any publication portraying "depravity, criminality, unchastity, or lack of virtue of a class of citizens, of any race, color, creed or religion [subjecting a group] to contempt, derision, obloquy or which is productive of breach of the peace or of riots."[93] Pursuant to that statute, a person disseminating leaflets warning of "the need to prevent the mongrelization of the white race" was convicted.[94]

In affirming the conviction, the Court determined that "(l)ibelous utterances [are not] within the area of constitutionally protected speech" and thus may be proscribed.[95] Only if regulation represented a deliberate and irrational restraint unrelated to the peace and well-being of the community would the Court have found a constitutional issue. The Court in *Beauharnais* thus recognized that speech promoting racial tension and strife is subject to official control. Because the decision never has been expressly overruled, it conceivably might still be relevant for contemporary institutional policymaking that attempts to factor racial and religious sensitivity into standards of acceptable conduct and discourse.[96] Justice Black, in dissent, identified significant risks that in-

PRESERVE and PROTECT WHITE NEIGHBORHOODS!

FROM THE CONSTANT AND CONTINUOUS INVASION, HARASSMENT AND ENCROACHMENT BY THE NEGROES

(WE WANT TWO MILLION SIGNATURES OF WHITE MEN AND WOMEN)

PETITION
To The Honorable Martin H. Kennelly
and City Council of the City of Chicago.

WHEREAS, the white population of the City of Chicago, particularly on the South Side of said city, are seething, nervous and agitated because of the constant and continuous invasion, harassment and encroachment by the Negroes upon them, their property and neighborhoods and —

WHEREAS, there have been disastrous incidents within the past year, all of which are fraught with grave consequences and great danger to the Peace and Security of the people, and

WHEREAS, there is great danger to the Government from communism which is rife among the Negroes, and
WHEREAS, we are not against the negro; we are for the white people and the white people are entitled to protection: —

We, the undersigned white citizens of the City of Chicago and the State of Illinois, hereby petition the Honorable Martin H. Kennelly, Mayor of the City of Chicago and the Alderman of the City of Chicago, to halt the further encroachment, harassment and invasion of white people, their property, neighborhoods and persons, by the Negro — through the exercise of the Police Power; of the Office of the Mayor of the City of Chicago, and the City Council.

WANTED

ONE MILLION SELF RESPECTING WHITE PEOPLE IN CHICAGO TO UNITE UNDER THE BANNER OF THE WHITE CIRCLE LEAGUE OF AMERICA to oppose the National Campaign now on and supported by TRUMAN'S INFAMOUS CIVIL RIGHTS PROGRAM and many Pro Negro Organizations to amalgamate the black and white races with the object of mongrelizing the white race!

THE WHITE CIRCLE LEAGUE OF AMERICA is the only articulate white voice in America being raised in protest against negro agressions and infiltrations into all white neighborhoods. The white people of Chicago MUST take advantage of this opportunity to become UNITED. If persuasion and the need to prevent the white race from becoming mongrelized by the negro will not unite us, then the aggressions . . . rapes, robberies, knives, guns and marijuana of the negro, SURELY WILL.

The Negro has many national organizations working to push him into the midst of the white people on many fronts. The white race does not have a single organization to work on a NATIONAL SCALE to make its wishes articulate and to assert its natural rights to self-preservation. THE WHITE CIRCLE LEAGUE OF AMERICA proposes to do the job.
WE ARE NOT AGAINST THE NEGRO! WE ARE FOR THE WHITE PEOPLE!
We must awaken and protect our white families and neighborhoods before it is too late. Let us work unceasingly to conserve the white man's dignity and rights in America.

THE WHITE CIRCLE LEAGUE OF AMERICA, INC. - Joseph Beauharnais, Pres. - FR 2-8533, Suite 808, 82 W. Washington St.
VOLUNTEERS NEEDED TO GET 26 SIGNATURES ON PETITION! COME TO HEADQUARTERS!

I wish to be enrolled as a member in THE WHITE CIRCLE LEAGUE OF AMERICA and I will do my best to secure ten (10) or more members.

THE FIRST LOYALTY OF EVERY WHITE PERSON IS TO HIS RACE. ALL THE COMBINED PRO NEGRO FORCES HAVE HURLED THEIR ULTIMATUM INTO THE FACES OF THE WHITE PEOPLE. WE ACCEPT THEIR CHALLENGE.

THEY CANNOT WIN!

IT WILL BE EASIER TO REVERSE THE CURRENT OF THE ATLANTIC OCEAN THAN TO DEGRADE THE WHITE RACE AND ITS NATURAL LAWS BY FORCED MONGRELIZATION.

THE HOUR HAS STRUCK FOR ALL NORMAL WHITE PEOPLE TO STAND UP AND FIGHT FOR OUR RIGHTS TO LIFE, LIBERTY AND THE PURSUIT OF HAPPINESS.

JOSEPH BEAUHARNAIS.

APPLICATION FOR 1950 MEMBERSHIP
THE WHITE CIRCLE LEAGUE OF AMERICA, INC.
(Not For Profit)

Mail To —

THE WHITE CIRCLE
LEAGUE OF AMERICA
Inc.
82 W. Washington St.
Chicago 2, Illinois
Tel. FR 2-8533

DATE_____19____

☐ Membership _____$1.00

☐ Subscripton to Monthly Magazine (WHITE
CIRCLE NEWS) per year _____$3.00

☐ Voluntary Contribution $_____

☐ I can volunteer some of my time to aid the
WHITE CIRCLE in getting under way.

(SIGNED) (Print Name) _____

NAME _____

ADDRESS _____ PHONE_____

CITY _____ STATE_____

(Note: Tear Off and Mail to Headquarters with Your Remittance)

here in such a regulatory approach. Black not only found the group libel statute at direct odds with the terms of the First Amendment[97] but also noted the vulnerability created for the media in general and special danger presented to minority interests. When used by the majority against a minority, such a regulation has particularly oppressive potential. Thus, Black observed that, if "there be any minority groups who hail this holding as their victory, they might consider the possible relevancy of this ancient remark: 'Another such victory and I am undone.' "[98]

Black's worries became fully realized a decade later when the police commissioner of Montgomery, Alabama, sued civil rights activists and the *New York Times* in response to an advertisement criticizing the way in which police handled a civil rights demonstration. The advertisement did not mention the plaintiff by name.[99] It also contained some minor inaccuracies, although none pertained to the plaintiff's character. Nonetheless, a state court awarded half a million dollars in damages pursuant to a jury's finding that the advertisement was false and pertained to the plaintiff.[100] The damage amount was based not upon any proof of actual loss but upon the state's doctrine of presumed damages.[101]

In *New York Times Co. v. Sullivan*,[102] the Court reversed the Alabama decision.[103] and significantly recontoured defamation law. For the first time, the Court declared that even defamatory expression implicated First Amendment interests.[104] Regulation of it, moreover, was to be measured against "the profound national commitment to the principle that debate on public issues should be uninhibited, robust, and wide-open, and that it may well include vehement, caustic, and sometimes unpleasantly sharp attacks on government and public officials."[105] Given the competing concerns presented, namely the reputational interests of public

officials and expressive freedom, the Court recognized a need to create a breathing space that would countenance even vilification and falsehood.[106] Such a result reflects an investment in the theory that expression relating to self-government deserves maximum constitutional security.[107] It also afforded symmetry within the law. Government officials, who had been accorded a privilege to make defamatory statements within the scope of their official duties,[108] became partially disabled from suing on grounds they had been falsely criticized.

Prior to the *New York Times* decision, the primary defense against a defamation claim was truth. To better accommodate First Amendment interests, the Court formulated a standard that afforded broader latitude for erroneous criticism of public officials. Liability does not exist, therefore, unless a defamatory statement directly relates to the public official, who has the burden of proving it was false and made with "actual malice."[109] The actual malice standard operates as a term of art rather than in a literal sense. Although translating for general purposes into spite or ill will, actual malice for purposes of a defamation action means "knowledge that [the statement] was false or . . . reckless disregard of whether it was false or not."[110] As subsequent application of the standard has revealed, liability cannot be based upon a showing of negligence or pursuant to any traditional criterion of strict liability.[111] The Court has observed that although the notion of reckless disregard "cannot be fully encompassed in one infallible definition . . . we have made clear that the defendant must have made the false publication with a 'high degree of awareness of probable falsity . . .' or must have 'entertained serious doubts as to the truth of his publication.' "[112] Proof of actual malice also has to be established by "clear and convincing" evidence.[113] The same clear and convincing standard operates independently to guide appellate review which is delimited, however, to examination of evidence that was undisputed or not rejected by the trier of fact.[114]

The practical consequences of the *New York Times* decision have placed a significant crimp in the actionability of allegedly defamatory expression concerning public officials. Litigation immediately focused upon pertinent terms, such as "official conduct" and "public official" itself, which the Court did not fully define. Allegations of criminality, regardless of whether they directly relate to service in office, have been protected by the actual malice standard.[115] It would appear, therefore, that the relevant scope of "official conduct" is to be regarded broadly rather than narrowly to include any comment pertaining to official qualification. The term "public official" so far has included an array of persons possessing the common trait of having significant responsibility or discretion for the transaction of official affairs.[116] It has been read to include candidates for public office.[117] The term also applies retroactively to protect comments upon past official action by a former public servant.[118] Beyond litigation concerning those terminological issues, the *New York Times* decision has tended to minimize disputes over material facts and facilitated resolution pursuant to summary judgment motions.

New York Times Co. v. Sullivan, 376 U.S. 254 (1964)

Mr. Justice Brennan delivered the opinion of the Court.

We are required in this case to determine for the first time the extent to which the constitutional protections for speech and press limit a State's power to award damages in a libel action brought by a public official against critics of his official conduct.

Respondent L. B. Sullivan is one of the three elected Commissioners of the City of Montgomery, Alabama. He testified that he was "Commissioner of Public Affairs and the duties are supervision of the Police Department, Fire Department, Department of Cemetery and Department of Scales." He brought this civil libel action against the four individual petitioners, who are Negroes and Alabama clergymen, and against petitioner the New York Times Company, a New York Corporation which publishes the *New York Times,* a daily newspaper. A jury in the Circuit Court of Montgomery County awarded him damages of $500,000, the full amount claimed, against all the petitioners, and the Supreme Court of Alabama affirmed. 273 Ala. 656, 144 So. 2d 25.

Respondent's complaint alleged that he had been libeled by statements in a full-page advertisement that was carried in the *New York Times* on March 29, 1960. Entitled "Heed Their Rising Voices," the advertisement began by stating that "As the whole world knows by now, thousands of Southern Negro students are engaged in widespread non-violent demonstrations in positive affirmation of the right to live in human dignity as guaranteed by the U. S. Constitution and the Bill of Rights." It went on to charge that "in their efforts to uphold these guarantees, they are being met by an unprecedented wave of terror by those who would deny and negate that document which the whole world looks upon as setting the pattern for modern freedom...." Succeeding paragraphs purported to illustrate the "wave of terror" by describing certain alleged events. The text concluded with an appeal for funds for three purposes: support of the student movement, "the struggle for the right-to-vote," and the legal defense of Dr. Martin Luther King, Jr., leader of the movement, against a perjury indictment then pending in Montgomery.

The text appeared over the names of 64 persons, many widely known for their activities in public affairs, religion, trade unions, and the performing arts. Below these names, and under a line reading "We in the south who are struggling daily for dignity and freedom warmly endorse this appeal," appeared the names of the four individual petitioners and of 16 other persons, all but two of whom were identified as clergymen in various Southern cities. The advertisement was

Heed Their Rising Voices

"The growing movement of peaceful mass demonstrations by Negroes is something new in the South, something understandable....

Let Congress heed their rising voices, for they will be heard."

—*New York Times editorial*
Saturday, March 19, 1960

As the whole world knows by now, thousands of Southern Negro students are engaged in wide-spread non-violent demonstrations in positive affirmation of the right to live in human dignity as guaranteed by the U. S. Constitution and the Bill of Rights. In their efforts to uphold these guarantees, they are being met by an unprecedented wave of terror by those who would deny and negate that document which the whole world looks upon as setting the pattern for modern freedom....

In Orangeburg, South Carolina, when 400 students peacefully sought to buy doughnuts and coffee at lunch counters in the business district, they were forcibly ejected, tear-gassed, soaked to the skin in freezing weather with fire hoses, arrested en masse and herded into an open barbed-wire stockade to stand for hours in the bitter cold.

In Montgomery, Alabama, after students sang "My Country, 'Tis of Thee" on the State Capitol steps, their leaders were expelled from school, and truck-loads of police armed with shotguns and tear-gas ringed the Alabama State College Campus. When the entire student body protested to state authorities by refusing to re-register, their dining hall was padlocked in an attempt to starve them into submission.

In Tallahassee, Atlanta, Nashville, Savannah, Greensboro, Memphis, Richmond, Charlotte, and a host of other cities in the South, young American teen-agers, in face of the entire weight of official state appa-ratus and police power, have boldly stepped forth as protagonists of democracy. Their courage and amaz-ing restraint have inspired millions and given a new dignity to the cause of freedom.

Small wonder that the Southern violators of the Constitution fear this new, non-violent brand of freedom fighter . . . even as they fear the upswelling right-to-vote movement. Small wonder that they are determined to destroy the one man who, more than any other, symbolizes the new spirit now sweeping the South—the Rev. Dr. Martin Luther King, Jr., world-famous leader of the Montgomery Bus Protest. For it is his doctrine of non-violence which has inspired and guided the students in their widening wave of sit-ins; and it this same Dr. King who founded and is president of the Southern Christian Leadership Con-ference—the organization which is spearheading the surging right-to-vote movement. Under Dr. King's direction the Leadership Conference conducts Stu-dent Workshops and Seminars in the philosophy and technique of non-violent resistance.

Again and again the Southern violators have answered Dr. King's peaceful protests with intimida-tion and violence. They have bombed his home almost killing his wife and child. They have assaulted his person. They have arrested him seven times—for "speeding," "loitering" and similar "offenses." And now they have charged him with "perjury"—a *felony* under which they could imprison him for *ten years*. Obviously, their real purpose is to remove him physi-cally as the leader to whom the students and millions of others—look *all* leaders who may rise in the South. Their strategy is to behead this affirmative movement, and thus to demoralize Negro Americans and weaken their will to struggle. The defense of Martin Luther King, spiritual leader of the student sit-in movement, clearly, therefore, *is* an integral part of the total struggle for freedom in the South.

Decent-minded Americans cannot help but applaud the creative daring of the students and the quiet heroism of Dr. King. But this is one of those moments in the stormy history of Freedom when men and women of good will must do more than applaud the rising-to-glory of others. The America whose good name hangs in the balance before a watchful world, the America whose heritage of Liberty these Southern Upholders of the Constitution are defending, is *our* America as well as theirs . . .

We must heed their rising voices—yes—but we must add our own.

We must extend ourselves above and beyond moral support and render the material help so urgently needed by those who are taking the risks, facing jail, and even death in a glorious re-affirmation of our Constitution and its Bill of Rights.

We urge you to join hands with our fellow Amer-icans in the South by supporting, with your dollars, this Combined Appeal for all three needs—the defense of Martin Luther King—the support of the embattled students—and the struggle for the right-to-vote.

Your Help Is Urgently Needed . . . NOW!!

Stella Adler
Raymond Pace Alexander
Harry Van Arsdale
Julie Belafonte
Dr. Algernon Black
Marc Blitzstein
William Branch
Marlon Brando
Mrs. Ralph Bunche
Diahann Carroll

Dr. Alan Knight Chalmers
Richard Coe
Nat King Cole
Cheryl Crawford
Dorothy Dandridge
Ossie Davis
Sammy Davis, Jr.
Ruby Dee
Dr. Philip Elliott
Dr. Harry Emerson Fosdick

Anthony Franciosa
Lorraine Hansberry
Rev. Donald Harrington
Nat Hentoff
James Hicks
Mary Hinkson
Van Heflin
Langston Hughes
Morris Iushewitz
Mahalia Jackson
Mordecai Johnson

John Killens
Eartha Kitt
Rabbi Edward Klein
Hope Lange
John Lewis
Viveca Lindfors
Carl Murphy
Don Murray
John Murray
A. J. Muste
Frederick O'Neal

L. Joseph Overton
Clarence Pickett
Shad Polier
Sidney Poitier
A. Philip Randolph
John Raitt
Elmer Rice
Jackie Robinson
Mrs. Eleanor Roosevelt
Bayard Rustin
Robert Ryan

Maureen Stapleton
Frank Silvera
Hope Stevens
George Tabori
Rev. Gardner C. Taylor
Norman Thomas
Kenneth Tynan
Charles White
Shelley Winters
Max Youngstein

We in the south who are struggling daily for dignity and freedom warmly endorse this appeal

Rev. Ralph D. Abernathy
(Montgomery, Ala.)

Rev. Fred L. Shuttlesworth
(Birmingham, Ala.)

Rev. Kelley Miller Smith
(Nashville, Tenn.)

Rev. W. A. Dennis
(Chattanooga, Tenn.)

Rev. C. K. Steele
(Tallahassee, Fla.)

Rev. Matthew D.
McCollom
(Orangeburg, S.C.)

Rev. William Holmes
Borders
(Atlanta, Ga.)

Rev. Douglas Moore
(Durham, N.C.)

Rev. Wyatt Tee Walker
(Petersburg, Va.)

Rev. Walter L. Hamilton
(Norfolk, Va.)

I. S. Levy
(Columbia, S.C.)

Rev. Martin Luther King, Sr.
(Atlanta, Ga.)

Rev. Henry C. Bunton
(Memphis, Tenn.)

Rev. S. S. Seay, Sr.
(Montgomery, Ala.)

Rev. Samuel W. Williams
(Atlanta, Ga.)

Rev. A. L. Davis
(New Orleans, La.)

Mrs. Katie E. Whickham
(New Orleans, La.)

Rev. W. H. Hall
(Hattiesburg, Miss.)

Rev. J. E. Lowery
(Mobile, Ala.)

Rev. T. J. Jemison
(Baton Rouge, La.)

COMMITTEE TO DEFEND MARTIN LUTHER KING AND THE STRUGGLE FOR FREEDOM IN THE SOUTH

312 West 125th Street, New York 27, N. Y. UNiversity 6-1700

Chairmen: A. Philip Randolph, Dr. Gardner C. Taylor; *Chairman of Cultural Division:* Harry Belafonte, Sidney Poitier; *Treasurer:* Nat King Cole; *Executive Director:* Bayard Rustin; *Chairmen of Church Division:* Father George B. Ford, Rev. Harry Emerson Fosdick, Rev. Thomas Kilgore, Jr., Rabbi Edward E. Klein; *Chairman of Labor Division:* Morris Iushewitz

Please mail this coupon TODAY!

Committee To Defend Martin Luther King
and
The Struggle For Freedom In The South

312 West 125th Street, New York 27, N. Y.
UNiversity 6-1700

I am enclosing my contribution of $_____
for the work of the Committee.

Name _____ (PLEASE PRINT)

Address _____

City _____ Zone ____ State ____

I want to help [ ]   Please send further information [ ]

Please make checks payable to:

Committee To Defend Martin Luther King

87

signed at the bottom of the page by the "Committee to Defend Martin Luther King and the Struggle for Freedom in the South," and the officers of the Committee were listed.

Of the 10 paragraphs of text in the advertisement, the third and a portion of the sixth were the basis of respondent's claim of libel. They read as follows:

Third paragraph:

> In Montgomery, Alabama, after students sang "My Country, 'Tis of Thee" on the State Capitol steps, their leaders were expelled from school, and truckloads of police armed with shotguns and tear-gas ringed the Alabama State College Campus. When the entire student body protested to state authorities by refusing to re-register, their dining hall was padlocked in an attempt to starve them into submission.

Sixth paragraph:

> Again and again the Southern violators have answered Dr. King's peaceful protests with intimidation and violence. They have bombed his home almost killing his wife and child. They have assaulted his person. They have arrested him seven times—for "speeding," "loitering" and similar "offenses." And now they have charged him with "perjury"—a *felony* under which they could imprison him for *ten years*. . . .

Although neither of these statements mentions respondent by name, he contended that the world "police" in the third paragraph referred to him as the Montgomery Commissioner who supervised the Police Department, so that he was being accused of "ringing" the campus with police. He further claimed that the paragraph would be read as imputing to the police, and hence to him, the padlocking of the dining hall in order to starve the students into submission. As to the sixth paragraph, he contended that since arrests are ordinarily made by the police, the statement "They have arrested [Dr. King] seven times" would be read as referring to him; he further contended that the "They" who did the arresting would be equated with the "They" who committed the other described acts and with the "Southern violators." Thus, he argued, the paragraph would be read as accusing the Montgomery police, and hence him, of answering Dr. King's protests with "intimidation and violence," bombing his home, assaulting his person, and charging him with perjury. Respondent and six

other Montgomery residents testified that they read some or all of the statements as referring to him in his capacity as Commissioner.

It is uncontroverted that some of the statements contained in the two paragraphs were not accurate descriptions of events which occurred in Montgomery. Although Negro students staged a demonstration on the State Capitol steps, they sang the National Anthem and not "My Country, 'Tis of Thee." Although nine students were expelled by the State Board of Education, this was not for leading the demonstration at the Capitol, but for demanding service at a lunch counter in the Montgomery County Courthouse on another day. Not the entire student body, but most of it, had protested the expulsion, not by refusing to register, but by boycotting classes on a single day; virtually all the students did register for the ensuing semester. The campus dining hall was not padlocked on any occasion, and the only students who may have been barred from eating there were the few who had neither signed a preregistration application nor requested temporary meal tickets. Although the police were deployed near the campus in large numbers on three occasions, they did not at any time "ring" the campus, and they were not called to the campus in connection with the demonstration on the State Capitol steps, as the third paragraph implied. Dr. King had not been arrested seven times, but only four; and although he claimed to have been assaulted some years earlier in connection with his arrest for loitering outside a courtroom, one of the officers who made the arrest denied that there was such an assault.

On the premise that the charges in the sixth paragraph could be read as referring to him, respondent was allowed to prove that he had not participated in the events described. Although Dr. King's home had in fact been bombed twice when his wife and child were there, both of these occasions antedated respondent's tenure as Commissioner, and the police were not only not implicated in the bombings, but had made every effort to apprehend those who were. Three of Dr. King's four arrests took place before respondent became Commissioner. Although Dr. King had in fact been indicted (he was subsequently acquitted) on two counts of perjury, each of which carried a possible five-year sentence, respondent had nothing to do with procuring the indictment.

Respondent made no effort to prove that he suffered actual pecuniary loss as a result of the alleged libel.[a] One of his witnesses, a former employer, testified that if he had believed the statements, he doubted whether he "would want to be associated with anybody who would be a party to such things that are stated in that ad," and that he would not re-employ respondent if he believed "that he allowed the Police Department to do the things that the paper say he did." But neither this witness nor any of the others testified that he had actually believed the statements in their supposed reference to respondent.

The cost of the advertisement was approximately $4800, and it was published by the Times upon an order from a New York advertising agency acting for the signatory Committee. The agency submitted the advertisement with a letter from A. Philip Randolph, Chairman of the Committee, certifying that the persons whose names appeared on the advertisement had given their permission. Mr. Randolph was known to the Times' Advertising Acceptability Department as a responsible person, and in accepting the letter as sufficient proof of authorization it followed its established practice. There was testimony that the copy of the advertisement which accompanied the letter listed only the 64 names appearing under the text, and that the statement, "We in the south . . . warmly endorse this appeal," and the list of names thereunder, which included those of the individual petitioners, were subsequently added when the first proof of the advertisement was received. Each of the individual petitioners testified that he had not authorized the use of his name, and that he had been unaware of its use until receipt of respondent's demand for a retraction. The manager of the Advertising Acceptability Department testified that he had approved the advertisement for publication because he knew nothing to cause him to believe that anything in it was false, and because it bore the endorsement of "a number of people who are well known and whose reputation" he "had no reason to question." Neither he nor anyone

else at the Times made an effort to confirm the accuracy of the advertisement, either by checking it against recent *Times* news stories relating to some of the described events or by any other means.

Alabama law denies a public officer recovery of punitive damages in a libel action brought on account of a publication concerning his official conduct unless he first makes a written demand for a public retraction and the defendant fails or refuses to comply. Alabama Code, Tit. 7, § 914. Respondent served such a demand upon each of the petitioners. None of the individual petitioners responded to the demand, primarily because each took the position that he had not authorized the use of his name on the advertisement and therefore had not published the statements that respondent alleged had libeled him. The Times did not publish a retraction in response to the demand, but wrote respondent a letter stating, among other things, that "we . . . are somewhat puzzled as to how you think the statements in any way reflect on you," and "you might, if you desire, let us know in what respect you claim that the statements in the advertisement reflect on you." Respondent filed this suit a few days later without answering the letter. The Times did, however, subsequently publish a retraction of the advertisement upon the demand of Governor John Patterson of Alabama, who asserted that the publication charged him with "grave misconduct and . . . improper actions and omissions as Governor of Alabama and Ex-Officio Chairman of the State Board of Education of Alabama." When asked to explain why there had been a retraction for the Governor but not for respondent, the Secretary of the Times testified: "We did that because we didn't want anything that was published by The Times to be a reflection on the State of Alabama and the Governor was, as far as we could see, the embodiment of the State of Alabama and the proper representative of the State and, furthermore, we had by that time learned more of the actual facts which the ad purported to recite and, finally, the ad did refer to the action of the State authorities and the Board of Education presumably of which the Governor is the ex-officio chairman. . . . " On the other hand, he testified that he did not think that "any of the language in there referred to Mr. Sullivan."

The trial judge submitted the case to the jury

---

a. Approximately 394 copies of the edition of the *Times* containing the advertisement were circulated in Alabama. Of these, about 35 copies were distributed in Montgomery County. The total circulation of the *Times* for that day was approximately 650,000 copies.

under instructions that the statements in the advertisement were "libelous per se" and were not privileged, so that petitioners might be held liable if the jury found that they had published the advertisement and that the statements were made "of and concerning" respondent. The jury was instructed that, because the statements were libelous *per se,* "the law . . . implies legal injury from the bare fact of publication itself," "falsity and malice are presumed," "general damages need not be alleged or proved but are presumed," and "punitive damages may be awarded by the jury even though the amount of actual damages is neither found nor shown." An award of punitive damages—as distinguished from "general" damages, which are compensatory in nature—apparently requires proof of actual malice under Alabama law, and the judge charged that "mere negligence or carelessness is not evidence of actual malice or malice in fact, and does not justify an award of exemplary or punitive damages." He refused to charge, however, that the jury must be "convinced" of malice, in the sense of "actual intent" to harm or "gross negligence and recklessness," to make such an award, and he also refused to require that a verdict for respondent differentiate between compensatory and punitive damages. The judge rejected petitioners' contention that his rulings abridged the freedoms of speech and of the press that are guaranteed by the First and Fourteenth Amendments.

In affirming the judgment, the Supreme Court of Alabama sustained the trial judge's rulings and instructions in all respects. 273 Ala. 656, 144 So. 2d 25. It held that "where the words published tend to injure a person libeled by them in his reputation, profession, trade or business, or charge him with an indictable offense, or tend to bring the individual into public contempt," they are "libelous per se"; that "the matter complained of is, under the above doctrine, libelous per se, if it was published of and concerning the plaintiff"; and that it was actionable without "proof of pecuniary injury . . . , such injury being implied." *Id.,* at 673, 676, 144 So. 2d, at 37, 41. It approved the trial court's ruling that the jury could find the statements to have been made "of and concerning" respondent, stating: "We think it common knowledge that the average person knows that municipal agents, such as police and firemen, and

others, are under the control and direction of the city governing body, and more particularly under the direction and control of a single commissioner. In measuring the performance or deficiencies of such groups, praise or criticism is usually attached to the official in complete control of the body." *Id.,* at 674–675, 144 So. 2d, at 39. In sustaining the trial court's determination that the verdict was not excessive, the court said that malice could be inferred from the Times' "irresponsibility" in printing the advertisement while "the Times in its own files had articles already published which would have demonstrated the falsity of the allegations in the advertisement"; from the Times' failure to retract for respondent while retracting for the Governor, whereas the falsity of some of the allegations was then known to the Times and "the matter contained in the advertisement was equally false as to both parties"; and from the testimony of the Times' Secretary that, apart from the statement that the dining hall was padlocked, he thought the two paragraphs were "substantially correct." *Id.,* at 686–687, 144 So. 2d, at 50–51. The court reaffirmed a statement in an earlier opinion that "There is no legal measure of damages in cases of this character." *Id.,* at 686, 144 So. 2d, at 50. It rejected petitioners' constitutional contentions with the brief statements that "The First Amendment of the U.S. Constitution does not protect libelous publications" and "The Fourteenth Amendment is directed against State action and not private action." *Id.,* at 676, 144 So. 2d, at 40.

Because of the importance of the constitutional issues involved, we granted the separate petitions for certiorari of the individual petitioners and of the Times. 371 U.S. 946. We reverse the judgment. We hold that the rule of law applied by the Alabama courts is constitutionally deficient for failure to provide the safeguards for freedom of speech and of the press that are required by the First and Fourteenth Amendments in a libel action brought by a public official against critics of his official conduct. We further hold that under the proper safeguards the evidence presented in this case is constitutionally insufficient to support the judgment for respondent. . . .

The general proposition that freedom of expression upon public questions is secured by the First Amendment has long been settled by our decisions. The constitutional safeguard, we have said, "was fashioned to assure unfettered interchange of ideas for the bringing about of political and social changes desired by the people." *Roth v. United States*, 354 U.S. 476, 484. "The maintenance of the opportunity for free political discussion to the end that government may be responsive to the will of the people and that changes may be obtained by lawful means, an opportunity essential to the security of the Republic, is a fundamental principle of our constitutional system." *Stromberg v. California*, 283 U.S. 359, 369. "[I]t is a prized American privilege to speak one's mind, although not always with perfect good taste, on all public institutions," *Bridges v. California*, 314 U.S. 252, 270, and this opportunity is to be afforded for "vigorous advocacy" no less than "abstract discussion." *N.A.A.C.P. v. Button*, 371 U.S. 415, 429. The First Amendment, said Judge Learned Hand, "presupposes that right conclusions are more likely to be gathered out of a multitude of tongues, than through any kind of authoritative selection. To many this is, and always will be, folly; but we have staked upon it our all." *United States v. Associated Press*, 52 F. Supp. 362, 372 (D. C. S. D. N. Y. 1943). Mr. Justice Brandeis, in his concurring opinion in *Whitney v. California*, 274 U.S. 357, 375–376, gave the principle its classic formulation:

> Those who won our independence believed . . . that public discussion is a political duty; and that this should be a fundamental principle of the American government. They recognized the risks to which all human institutions are subject. But they knew that order cannot be secured merely through fear of punishment for its infraction; that it is hazardous to discourage thought, hope and imagination; that fear breeds repression; that repression breeds hate; that hate menaces stable government; that the path of safety lies in the opportunity to discuss freely supposed grievances and proposed remedies; and that the fitting remedy for evil counsels is good ones. Believing in the power of reason as applied through public discussion, they eschewed silence coerced by law—the argument of force in its worst form. Recognizing the occasional tyrannies of governing majorities, they amended the Constitution so that free speech and assembly should be guaranteed.

Thus we consider this case against the background of a profound national commitment to the principle that debate on public issues should be uninhibited, robust, and wide-open, and that it may well include vehement, caustic, and sometimes unpleasantly sharp attacks on government and public officials. See *Terminiello v. Chicago*, 337 U.S. 1, 4; *De Jonge v. Oregon*, 299 U.S. 353, 365. The present advertisement, as an expression of grievance and protest on one of the major public issues of our time, would seem clearly to qualify for the constitutional protection. The question is whether it forfeits that protection by the falsity of some of its factual statements and by its alleged defamation of respondent.

Authoritative interpretations of the First Amendment guarantees have consistently refused to recognize an exception for any test of truth—whether administered by judges, juries, or administrative officials—and especially one that puts the burden of proving truth on the speaker. Cf. *Speiser v. Randall*, 357 U.S. 513, 525–526. The constitutional protection does not turn upon "the truth, popularity, or social utility of the ideas and beliefs which are offered." *N. A. A. C. P. v. Button*, 371 U.S. 415, 445. As Madison said, "Some degree of abuse is inseparable from the proper use of every thing; and in no instance is this more true than in that of the press." 4 Elliot's Debates on the Federal Constitution (1876), p. 571. In *Cantwell v. Connecticut*, 310 U.S. 296, 310, the Court declared:

> In the realm of religious faith, and in that of political belief, sharp differences arise. In both fields the tenets of one man may seem the rankest error to his neighbor. To persuade others to his own point of view, the pleader, as we know, at times, resorts to exaggeration, to vilification of men who have been, or are, prominent in church or state, and even to false statement. But the people of this nation have ordained in the light of history, that, in spite of the probability of excesses and abuses, these liberties are, in the long view, essential to enlightened opinion and right conduct on the part of the citizens of a democracy.

That erroneous statement is inevitable in free debate, and that it must be protected if the freedoms of expression are to have the "breathing space" that they "need . . . to survive," *N.A.A.C.P. v. Button*, 371 U.S. 415, 433, was also recognized by the Court of Appeals for the District of Columbia Circuit in *Sweeney v. Patterson*, 76 U.S. App. D. C. 23, 24, 128 F. 2d 457, 458 (1942), cert. denied, 317 U.S. 678. Judge Edgerton spoke for a unanimous court which affirmed the dismissal of a Congressman's libel suit based upon a newspaper article charging him with anti-Semitism in opposing a judicial appointment. He said:

> Cases which impose liability for erroneous reports of the political conduct of officials reflect the obsolete doctrine that the governed must not criticize their governors.... The interest of the public here outweighs the interest of appellant or any other individual. The protection of the public requires not merely discussion, but information. Political conduct and views which some respectable people approve, and others condemn, are constantly imputed to Congressmen. Errors of fact, particularly in regard to a man's mental states and processes, are inevitable.... Whatever is added to the field of libel is taken from the field of free debate.

Injury to official reputation affords no more warrant for repressing speech that would otherwise be free than does factual error. Where judicial officers are involved, this Court has held that concern for the dignity and reputation of the courts does not justify the punishment as criminal contempt of criticism of the judge or his decision. *Bridges v. California,* 314 U.S. 252. This is true even though the utterance contains "half-truths" and "misinformation." *Pennekamp v. Florida,* 328 U.S. 331, 342, 343, n. 5, 345. Such repression can be justified, if at all, only by a clear and present danger of the obstruction of justice. See also *Craig v. Harney,* 331 U.S. 367; *Wood v. Georgia,* 370 U.S. 375. If judges are to be treated as "men of fortitude, able to thrive in a hardy climate," *Craig v. Harney, supra,* 331 U.S., at 376, surely the same must be true of other government officials, such as elected city commissioners. Criticism of their official conduct does not lose its constitutional protection merely because it is effective criticism and hence diminishes their official reputations....

What a State may not constitutionally bring about by means of a criminal statute is likewise beyond the reach of its civil law of libel. The fear of damage awards under a rule such as that invoked by the Alabama courts here may be markedly more inhibiting than the fear of prosecution under a criminal statute. See *City of Chicago v. Tribune Co.,* 307 Ill. 595, 607, 139 N. E. 86, 90 (1923). Alabama, for example, has a criminal libel law which subjects to prosecution "any person who speaks, writes, or prints of and concerning another any accusation falsely and maliciously importing the commission by such person of a felony, or any other indictable offense involving moral turpitude," and which allows as punishment upon conviction a fine not exceeding $500 and a prison sentence of six months. Alabama Code, Tit. 14, § 350. Presumably a person charged with violation of this statute enjoys ordinary criminal-law safeguards such as the requirements of an indictment and of proof beyond a reasonable doubt. These safeguards are not available to the defendant in a civil action. The judgment awarded in this case—without the need for any proof of actual pecuniary loss—was one thousand times greater than the maximum fine provided by the Alabama criminal statute, and one hundred times greater than that provided by the Sedition Act. And since there is no double-jeopardy limitation applicable to civil lawsuits, this is not the only judgment that may be awarded against petitioners for the same publication. Whether or not a newspaper can survive a succession of such judgments, the pall of fear and timidity imposed upon those who would give voice to public criticism is an atmosphere in which the First Amendment freedoms cannot survive. Plainly the Alabama law of civil libel is "a form of regulation that creates hazards to protected freedoms markedly greater than those that attend reliance upon the criminal law." *Bantam Books, Inc., v. Sullivan,* 372 U.S. 58, 70....

A rule compelling the critic of official conduct to guarantee the truth of all his factual assertions—and to do so on pain of libel judgments virtually unlimited in amount—leads to a comparable "self-censorship." Allowance of the defense of truth, with the burden of proving it on the defendant, does not mean that only false speech will be deterred. Even courts accepting this defense as an adequate safeguard have recognized the difficulties of adducing legal proofs that the alleged libel was true in all its factual particulars. See, e.g., *Post Publishing Co. v. Hallam,* 59 F. 530, 540 (C. A. 6th Cir. 1893); see also Noel, Defamation of Public Officers and Candidates, 49 Col. L. Rev. 875, 892 (1949). Under such a rule, would-be critics of official conduct may be deterred from voicing their criticism, even though it is believed to be true and even though it is in fact true, because of doubt whether it can be proved in court or fear of the expense of having to do so. They tend to make only statements which "steer far wider of the unlawful zone." *Speiser v. Randall, supra,* 357 U.S., at 526. The rule thus dampens the vigor and limits the variety of public debate. It is inconsistent with the First and Fourteenth Amendments.

The constitutional guarantees require, we think, a federal rule that prohibits a public official from recovering damages for a defamatory falsehood relating to his official conduct unless he proves that the statement was made with "actual malice"—that is, with knowledge that it was false or with reckless disregard of whether it was false or not.

Such a privilege for criticism of official conduct is appropriately analogous to the protection accorded a public official when *he* is sued for libel by a private citizen. In *Barr v. Matteo,* 360 U.S. 564, 575, this Court held the utterance of a federal official to be absolutely privileged if made "within the outer perimeter" of his duties. The States accord the same immunity to statements of their highest officers, although some differentiate their lesser officials and qualify the privilege they enjoy. But all hold that all officials are protected unless actual malice can be proved. The reason for the official privilege is said to be that the threat of damage suits would otherwise "inhibit the fearless, vigorous, and effective administration of policies of government" and "dampen the ardor of all but the most resolute, or the most irresponsible, in the unflinching discharge of their duties." *Barr v. Matteo, supra,* 360 U.S., at 571. Analogous considerations support the privilege for the citizen-critic of government. It is as much his duty to criticize as it is the official's duty to administer. See *Whitney v. California,* 274 U.S. 357, 375 (concurring opinion of Mr. Justice Brandeis), quoted *supra,* p. 270. As Madison said, see *supra,* p. 275, "the censorial power is in the people over the Government, and not in the Government over the people." It would give public servants an unjustified preference over the public they serve, if critics of official conduct did not have a fair equivalent of the immunity granted to the officials themselves.

We conclude that such a privilege is required by the First and Fourteenth Amendments.

We hold today that the Constitution delimits a State's power to award damages for libel in actions brought by public officials against critics of their official conduct. Since this is such an action, the rule requiring proof of actual malice is applicable. While Alabama law apparently requires proof of actual malice for an award of punitive damages, where general damages are concerned malice is "presumed." Such a presumption is inconsistent with the federal rule. "The power to create presumptions is not a means of escape from constitutional restrictions," *Bailey v. Alabama,* 219 U.S. 219, 239; "the showing of malice required for the forfeiture of the privilege is not presumed but is a matter for proof by the plaintiff.... " *Lawrence v. Fox,* 357 Mich. 134, 146, 97 N. W. 2d 719, 725 (1959). Since the trial judge did not instruct the jury to differentiate between general and punitive damages, it may be that the verdict was wholly an award of one or the other. But it is impossible to know, in view of the general verdict returned. Because of this uncertainty, the judgment must be reversed and the case remanded. *Stromberg v. California,* 283 U.S. 359, 367–368; *Williams v. North Carolina,* 317 U.S. 287, 291–292; see *Yates v. United States,* 354 U.S. 298, 311–312; *Cramer v. United States,* 325 U.S. 1, 36, n. 45.

Mr. Justice Black, with whom Mr. Justice Douglas joins, concurring.

I concur in reversing this half-million-dollar judgment against the New York Times Company and the four individual defendants. In reversing the Court holds that "the Constitution delimits a State's power to award damages for libel in actions brought by public officials against critics of their official conduct." *Ante,* p. 283. I base my vote to reverse on the belief that the First and Fourteenth Amendments not merely "delimit" a State's power to award damages to "public officials against critics of their official conduct" but completely prohibit a State from exercising such a power. The Court goes on to hold that a State can subject such critics to damages if "actual malice" can be proved against them. "Malice," even as defined by the Court, is an elusive, abstract concept, hard to prove and hard to disprove. The requirement that malice be proved provides at best an evanescent protection for the right critically to discuss public affairs and certainly does not measure up to the sturdy safeguard embodied in the First Amendment. Unlike the Court, therefore, I vote to reverse exclusively on the ground that the Times and the individual defendants had an absolute, unconditional constitutional right to publish in the Times advertisement their criticisms of the Montgomery agencies and officials. I do not base my vote to reverse on any failure to prove that these individual defendants signed the advertisement or that their criticism of the Police Department was aimed at the plaintiff Sullivan, who was then the Montgomery City Commissioner having supervision of the city's police; for present purposes I assume these things were proved. Nor is my reason for reversal the size of the half-million-dollar judgment, large as it is. If Alabama has constitutional power to use its civil libel law to impose damages on the press for criticizing the way public officials perform or fail to perform their duties, I know of no provision in the Federal Constitution which either expressly or impliedly bars the State from fixing the amount of damages.

The half-million-dollar verdict does give dramatic proof, however, that state libel laws threaten the very existence of an American press virile enough to publish unpopular views on public affairs and bold enough to criticize the conduct of public officials. The factual background of this case emphasizes the imminence and enormity of that threat. One of the acute and highly emotional issues in this country arises out of efforts of many people, even including some public officials, to continue state-commanded segregation of races in the public schools and other public places, despite our several holdings that such a state practice is forbidden by the Fourteenth Amendment. Montgomery is one of the localities in which widespread hostility to desegregation has been manifested. This hostility has sometimes extended itself to persons who favor desegregation, particularly to so-called "outside agitators," a term which can be made to fit papers like the *Times,* which is published in New York. The scarcity of testimony to show that Commissioner Sullivan suffered any actual damages at all suggests that these feelings of hostility had at least as much to do with rendition of this half-million-dollar verdict as did an appraisal of damages. Viewed realistically, this record lends support to an inference that instead of being damaged Commissioner Sullivan's political, social, and financial prestige has likely been enhanced by the *Times'*

publication. Moreover, a second half-million-dollar libel verdict against the *Times* based on the same advertisement has already been awarded to another Commissioner. There a jury again gave the full amount claimed. There is no reason to believe that there are not more such huge verdicts lurking just around the corner for the *Times* or any other newspaper or broadcaster which might dare to criticize public officials. In fact, briefs before us show that in Alabama there are now pending eleven libel suits by local and state officials against the *Times* seeking $5,600,000, and five such suits against the Columbia Broadcasting System seeking $1,700,000. Moreover, this technique for harassing and punishing a free press—now that it has been shown to be possible—is by no means limited to cases with racial overtones; it can be used in other fields where public feelings may make local as well as out-of-state newspapers easy prey for libel verdict seekers.

In my opinion the Federal Constitution has dealt with this deadly danger to the press in the only way possible without leaving the free press open to destruction—by granting the press an absolute immunity for criticism of the way public officials do their public duty. Compare *Barr v. Matteo,* 360 U.S. 564. Stopgap measures like those the Court adopts are in my judgment not enough. This record certainly does not indicate that any different verdict would have been rendered here whatever the Court had charged the jury about "malice," "truth," "good motives," "justifiable ends," or any other legal formulas which in theory would protect the press. Nor does the record indicate that any of these legalistic words would have caused the courts below to set aside or to reduce the half-million-dollar verdict in any amount. . . .

We would, I think, more faithfully interpret the First Amendment by holding that at the very least it leaves the people and the press free to criticize officials and discuss public affairs with impunity. This Nation of ours elects many of its important officials; so do the States, the municipalities, the counties, and even many precincts. These officials are responsible to the people for the way they perform their duties. While our Court has held that some kinds of speech and writings, such as "obscenity," *Roth v. United States,* 354 U.S. 476, and "fighting words," *Chaplinsky v.*

New Hampshire, 315 U.S. 568, are not expression within the protection of the First Amendment, freedom to discuss public affairs and public officials is unquestionably, as the Court today holds, the kind of speech the First Amendment was primarily designed to keep within the area of free discussion. To punish the exercise of this right to discuss public affairs or to penalize it through libel judgments is to abridge or shut off discussion of the very kind most needed. This Nation, I suspect, can live in peace without libel suits based on public discussions of public affairs and public officials. But I doubt that a country can live in freedom where its people can be made to suffer physically or financially for criticizing their government, its actions, or its officials. "For a representative democracy ceases to exist the moment that the public functionaries are by any means absolved from their responsibility to their constituents; and this happens whenever the constituent can be restrained in any manner from speaking, writing, or publishing his opinions upon any public measure, or upon the conduct of those who may advise or execute it." An unconditional right to say what one pleases about public affairs is what I consider to be the minimum guarantee of the First Amendment.

I regret that the Court has stopped short of this holding indispensable to preserve our free press from destruction.

Mr. Justice Goldberg, with whom Mr. Justice Douglas joins, concurring in the result.

The conclusion that the Constitution affords the citizen and the press an absolute privilege for criticism of official conduct does not leave the public official without defenses against unsubstantiated opinions or deliberate misstatements. "Under our system of government, counterargument and education are the weapons available to expose these matters, not abridgment...of free speech...." *Wood v. Georgia*, 370 U.S. 375, 389. The public official certainly has equal if not greater access than most private citizens to media of communication. In any event, despite the possibility that some excesses and abuses may go unremedied, we must recognize that "the people of this nation have ordained in the light of history, that, in spite of the probability of excesses and abuses, [certain] liberties are, in the long view,

essential to enlightened opinion and right conduct on the part of the citizens of a democracy." *Cantwell v. Connecticut*, 310 U.S. 296, 310. As Mr. Justice Brandeis correctly observed, "sunlight is the most powerful of all disinfectants."

For these reasons, I strongly believe that the Constitution accords citizens and press an unconditional freedom to criticize official conduct. It necessarily follows that in a case such as this, where all agree that the allegedly defamatory statements related to official conduct, the judgments for libel cannot constitutionally be sustained.

For a decade after the *New York Times* decision, the Court worked upon expanding the actual malice test beyond public officials. Chief Justice Warren, noting that speech concerning self-government transcends the acts of public officials, initially advanced the notion that public influence and prominence should be regarded akin to official status.[119] Warren thus created the concept of public figures, which he defined as persons "intimately involved in the resolution of important public questions or [who], by reason of their fame, shape events in areas of concern to society at large."[120] Thereafter, a plurality, in *Rosenbloom v. Metromedia, Inc.*,[121] supported the furthest logical extension of theory emphasizing the value of speech pertaining to self-government. It thus declared that the actual malice standard should govern any allegedly defamatory statement concerning a matter of public interest.[122] Justice Black's insistence upon an unconditioned liberty to express oneself freely[123] helped preclude emergence of a standard protecting "statements concerning matter[s] of general or public interest."[124]

The Court eventually abandoned development of a public interest standard on the grounds that it unreasonably interfered with legitimate state interests in protecting private reputation.[125] It also expressed concern with committing to judges responsibility to decide on an *ad hoc* basis what does and does not implicate the general or public interest.[126] Although expressing legitimate concern with the manipulability of such terms and their susceptibility to subjective delineation, the Court has not been hesitant to draw lines in other First Amendment areas possessing equally treacherous potential.[127] Incongruously, Justice Powell, who rejected the *Metromedia* standard, later reintroduced the concept of public concern as a standard for determining the availability of damages.[128]

In *Gertz v. Robert Welch, Inc.,*[129] the Court limited the actual malice standard to defamation actions brought by public officials and figures.[130] The relevant inquiry for determining the standard's operability is the status of the plaintiff rather than the nature of the controversy. Arguably, a focus upon the qualitative aspects of the expression instead of the defendant's denomination would be more pertinent to "the profound national commitment to . . . uninhibited, robust and wide-open debate" on public issues predicate set forth in the *New York Times* decision.[131] Instead, the Court expanded the actual malice standard less radically to include public figures respectively for general and limited purposes.[132] It made clear that public figure status could result not just from widespread fame[133] but also from injection of oneself into a particular public controversy for purposes of influencing the outcome.[134] Diminished protection for public figures was justified on the grounds that they invited public comment and commanded greater access to the media.[135] An arguable counterpoint, however, may be that any such advantage is offset by a greater potential for reputation damage or loss. The rationale also invites criticism, along the lines expressed by Justice Brennan in dissent, that no evidence supports the notion of disparate access. A competitive medium actually may be quick to identify flaws in a rival's characterization of events.

Given the criteria for a public figure, it may have been reasonable for the Court to determine that Gertz fit them. He was an attorney who had brought a wrongful death action on behalf of the family of a young man who had been shot by a police officer.[136] Gertz had been described in a publication of the John Birch Society as the "architect [of a] communist frame-up," a "Communist-fronter," and the possessor of a criminal record.[137] The Court determined that he had not advanced himself into the public eye beyond serving as an attorney and, although also active in community affairs, was not a general or a limited public figure in the context of the case.[138] Conceivably, as a member of various government commissions and boards and as an officer of the court, Gertz also could have been denominated a public official. Such a determination, however, would have removed an entire profession from the normal protection of defamation laws. In Gertz's case, moreover, the falsehoods did not pertain to his official extralegal positions.

Having determined that Gertz's status was that of a private person,[139] the Court refused to extend the actual malice standard to that category of plaintiffs.[140] Rather, it concluded that "so long as they do not impose liability without fault, the States may define for themselves the appropriate standard of liability for a publisher or broadcaster of defamatory falsehood injurious to a private individual."[141] The Court thus did not announce a uniform standard for scienter that must be established in a defamation action by a private person. Provided that strict liability is not the operative criterion, states have latitude to choose the relevant standard. As a consequence, the law among the states varies from actual malice to negligence sometimes coupled with the public interest standard rejected as a constitutional requirement in *Gertz*.[142] The consequent disparity of standards for liability may be of special concern to any medium disseminating information across state lines, including broadcasters whose signals may be picked up by satellite or cable and carried outside their immediate markets.

Actual malice also remains pertinent in defamation actions brought by private persons insofar as punitive or presumed damages are sought.[143] Recoverable damages otherwise are limited to "actual damages," which the Court depicted as "not only out-of-pocket loss [but]...impairment of reputation and standing in the community, personal humiliation, and mental anguish and suffering."[144] Such a rule appears to have been designed to protect the media from the prospect of bankrupting judgments but has elicited criticism for its potential to convert defamation into an action for mental distress.[145]

Concern that the concept of damages delineated by *Gertz* might invite claims for mere emotional distress may be less trenchant given the decision in *Hustler Magazine v. Falwell*.[146] The Court determined "that public figures and public officials may not recover for the tort of intentional infliction of emotional distress by reason of publication such as the one at issue without showing in addition that the publication contains a false statement of fact which was made with 'actual malice'."[147] At issue was a characterization of the plaintiff, a well-known evangelist, in a parody of liquor advertisements in which celebrities describe their "first time."[148] The mock advertisement, accompanied by a disclaimer and notice not to take it seriously, featured an interview in which "he states that his 'first time' was during a drunken incestuous rendezvous with his mother in an outhouse."[149] Given its sense that the law does not generally favor the tort of intentional distress, the Court found that the operation of such claims presented unacceptable risks to First Amendment interests.[150] The consequences were considered particularly undesirable "in the world of debate about public affairs, [where] many things are done with motives that are less admirable and protected by the First Amendment."[151] Voicing its concern with the risks that otherwise would be presented to satire, parody, and other well-established forms of social criticism, the Court resolved that the constitution prohibits reference to bad motive in charting the perimeters of debate about public officials and public figures.[152] The decision, however, does not discuss whether the interests underlying the disfavored tort would be more competitive against First Amendment concerns minus the presence of public interest.

Justice White criticized the *Gertz* decision for reasons that were polar opposite to concerns with the dangerous potential of an emotional distress claim. From his perspective, the modern press was vigorous and robust enough to accept responsibility for defamation of private citizens even on terms of strict liability.[153] Protection of the media from chilling libel judgments, in White's view, was facilitated satisfactorily by the Court's restrictions on punitive and presumed damages.[154] Given Justice Brennan's competing criticism that the decision promotes self-censorship on matters of public interest concerning persons not clearly within the public official category,[155] the *Gertz* decision has been denounced both on grounds that it respectively is overly sympathetic and too insensitive to First Amendment needs.[156]

Gertz v. Robert Welch, Inc., 418 U.S. 323 (1974)

Mr. Justice Powell delivered the opinion of the Court.

This Court has struggled for nearly a decade to define the proper accommodation between the law of defamation and the freedoms of speech and press protected by the First Amendment. With this decision we return to that effort. We granted certiorari to reconsider the extent of a publisher's constitutional privilege against liability for defamation of a private citizen. 410 U.S. 925 (1973).

I

In 1968 a Chicago policeman named Nuccio shot and killed a youth named Nelson. The state authorities prosecuted Nuccio for the homicide and ultimately obtained a conviction for murder in the second degree. The Nelson family retained petitioner Elmer Gertz, a reputable attorney, to represent them in civil litigation against Nuccio.

Respondent publishes *American Opinion,* a monthly outlet for the views of the John Birch Society. Early in the 1960's the magazine began to warn of a nationwide conspiracy to discredit local law enforcement agencies and create in their stead a national police force capable of supporting a Communist dictatorship. As part of the continuing effort to alert the public to this assumed danger, the managing editor of *American Opinion* commissioned an article on the murder trial of Officer Nuccio. For this purpose he engaged a regular contributor to the magazine. In March 1969 respondent published the resulting article under the title "FRAME-UP: Richard Nuccio and the War on Police." The article purports to demonstrate that the testimony against Nuccio at his criminal trial was false and that his prosecution was part of the Communist campaign against the police.

In his capacity as counsel for the Nelson family in the civil litigation, petitioner attended the coroner's inquest into the boy's death and initiated actions for damages, but he neither discussed Officer Nuccio with the press nor played any part in the criminal proceeding. Notwithstanding petitioner's remote connection with the prosecution of Nuccio, respondent's magazine portrayed him as an architect of the "frame-up." According to the article, the police file on petitioner took "a big, Irish cop to lift." The article stated that petitioner had been an official of the "Marxist League for Industrial Democracy, originally known as the Intercollegiate Socialist Society, which has advocated the violent seizure of our

government." It labeled Gertz a "Leninist" and a "Communist-fronter." It also stated that Gertz had been an officer of the National Lawyers Guild, described as a Communist organization that "probably did more than any other outfit to plan the Communist attack on the Chicago police during the 1968 Democratic Convention."

These statements contained serious inaccuracies. The implication that petitioner had a criminal record was false. Petitioner had been a member and officer of the National Lawyers Guild some 15 years earlier, but there was no evidence that he or that organization had taken any part in planning the 1968 demonstrations in Chicago. There was also no basis for the charge that petitioner was a "Leninist" or a "Communist-fronter." And he had never been a member of the "Marxist League for Industrial Democracy" or the "Intercollegiate Socialist Society."

The managing editor of *American Opinion* made no effort to verify or substantiate the charges against petitioner. Instead, he appended an editorial introduction stating that the author had "conducted extensive research into the Richard Nuccio Case." And he included in the article a photograph of petitioner and wrote the caption that appeared under it: "Elmer Gertz of Red Guild harrasses Nuccio." Respondent placed the issue of *American Opinion* containing the article on sale at newsstands throughout the country and distributed reprints of the article on the streets of Chicago. . . .

The principal issue in this case is whether a newspaper or broadcaster that publishes defamatory falsehoods about an individual who is neither a public official nor a public figure may claim a constitutional privilege against liability for the injury inflicted by those statements. . . .

In affirming the trial court's judgment in the instant case, the Court of Appeals relied on Mr. Justice Brennan's conclusion for the *Rosenbloom* plurality that "all discussion and communication involving matters of public or general concern," 403 U.S., at 44, warrant the protection from liability for defamation accorded by the rule originally enunciated in *New York Times Co. v. Sullivan,* 376 U.S. 254 (1964). . . .

We begin with the common ground. Under the First Amendment there is no such thing as a false idea. However pernicious an opinion may seem, we depend for its correction not on the conscience of judges and juries but on the competition of other ideas. But there is no constitutional value in false statements of fact. Neither the intentional lie nor the careless error materially advances society's interest in "uninhibited, robust, and wide-open" debate on public issues. *New York Times Co. v. Sullivan,* 376 U.S., at 270. They belong to that category of utterances which "are no essential part of any exposition of ideas, and are of such slight social value as a step to truth that any benefit that may be derived from them is clearly outweighed by the social interest in order and morality." *Chaplinsky v. New Hampshire,* 315 U.S. 568, 572 (1942).

Although the erroneous statement of fact is not worthy of constitutional protection, it is nevertheless inevitable in free debate. As James Madison pointed out in the Report on the Virginia Resolutions of 1798: "Some degree of abuse is inseparable from the proper use of every thing; and in no instance is this more true than in that of the press." 4 J. Elliot, Debates on the Federal Constitution of 1787, p. 571 (1876). And punishment of error runs the risk of inducing a cautious and restrictive exercise of the constitutionally guaranteed freedoms of speech and press. Our decisions recognize that a rule of strict liability that compels a publisher or broadcaster to guarantee the accuracy of his factual assertions may lead to intolerable self-censorship. Allowing the media to avoid liability only by proving the truth of all injurious statements does not accord adequate protection to First Amendment liberties. As the Court stated in *New York Times Co. v. Sullivan, supra,* at 279: "Allowance of the defense of truth, with the burden of proving it on the defendant, does not mean that only false speech will be deterred." The First Amendment requires that we protect some falsehood in order to protect speech that matters.

The need to avoid self-censorship by the news media is, however, not the only societal value at issue. If it were, this Court would have embraced long ago the view that publishers and broadcasters enjoy an unconditional and indefeasible immunity from liability for defamation. See *New York Times Co. v. Sullivan, supra,* at 293 (Black, J., concurring); *Garrison v. Louisiana,* 379 U.S., at 80 (Douglas, J., concurring); *Curtis Publishing Co. v.*

Butts, 388 U.S., at 170 (opinion of Black, J.). Such a rule would, indeed, obviate the fear that the prospect of civil liability for injurious falsehood might dissuade a timorous press from the effective exercise of First Amendment freedoms. Yet absolute protection for the communications media requires a total sacrifice of the competing value served by the law of defamation.

The legitimate state interest underlying the law of libel is the compensation of individuals for the harm inflicted on them by defamatory falsehood. We would not lightly require the State to abandon this purpose, for, as Mr. Justice Stewart has reminded us, the individual's right to the protection of his own good name

> reflects no more than our basic concept of the essential dignity and worth of every human being—a concept at the root of any decent system of ordered liberty. The protection of private personality, like the protection of life itself, is left primarily to the individual States under the Ninth and Tenth Amendments. But this does not mean that the right is entitled to any less recognition by this Court as a basic of our constitutional system. *Rosenblatt v. Baer,* 383 U.S. 75, 92 (1966) (concurring opinion).

Some tension necessarily exists between the need for a vigorous and uninhibited press and the legitimate interest in redressing wrongful injury. As Mr. Justice Harlan stated, "some antithesis between freedom of speech and press and libel actions persists, for libel remains premised on the content of speech and limits the freedom of the publisher to express certain sentiments, at least without guaranteeing legal proof of their substantial accuracy." *Curtis Publishing Co. v. Butts, supra,* at 152. In our continuing effort to define the proper accommodation between these competing concerns, we have been especially anxious to assure to the freedoms of speech and press that "breathing space" essential to their fruitful exercise. *NAACP v. Button,* 371 U.S. 415, 433 (1963). To that end this Court has extended a measure of strategic protection to defamatory falsehood.

The *New York Times* standard defines the level of constitutional protection appropriate to the context of defamation of a public person. Those who, by reason of the notoriety of their achievements or the vigor and success with which they seek the public's attention, are properly classed as public figures and those who hold governmental office may recover for injury to reputation only on clear and convincing proof that the defamatory falsehood was made with knowledge of its falsity or with reckless disregard for the truth. This standard administers an extremely powerful antidote to the inducement to media self-censorship of the common-law rule of strict liability for libel and slander. And it exacts a correspondingly high price from the victims of defamatory falsehood. Plainly many deserving plaintiffs, including some intentionally subjected to injury, will be unable to surmount the barrier of the *New York Times* test. Despite this substantial abridgment of the state law right to compensation for wrongful hurt to one's reputation, the Court has concluded that the protection of the *New York Times* privilege should be available to publishers and broadcasters of defamatory falsehood concerning public officials and public figures. *New York Times Co. v. Sullivan, supra; Curtis Publishing Co. v. Butts, supra.* We think that these decisions are correct, but we do not find their holdings justified solely by reference to the interest of the press and broadcast media in immunity from liability. Rather, we believe that the *New York Times* rule states an accommodation between this concern and the limited state interest present in the context of libel actions brought by public persons. For the reasons stated below, we conclude that the state interest in compensating injury to the reputation of private individuals requires that a different rule should obtain with respect to them....

[W]e have no difficulty in distinguishing among defamation plaintiffs. The first remedy of any victim of defamation is self-help—using available opportunities to contradict the lie or correct the error and thereby to minimize its adverse impact on reputation. Public officials and public figures usually enjoy significantly greater access to the channels of effective communication and hence have a more realistic opportunity to counteract false statements than private individuals normally enjoy. Private individuals are therefore more vulnerable to injury, and the state interest in protecting them is correspondingly greater.

More important than the likelihood that private individuals will lack effective opportunities for rebuttal, there is a compelling normative consideration underlying the distinction between public and private defamation plaintiffs. An individual who decides to seek governmental office must accept certain necessary consequences of that involvement in public affairs. He runs the risk of closer public scrutiny than might otherwise be the case. And society's interest in the officers of government is not strictly limited to the formal discharge of official duties. As the Court pointed out in *Garrison v. Louisiana,* 379 U.S., at 77, the public's interest extends to "anything which might touch on an official's fitness for office.... Few personal attributes are more germane to fitness for office than dishonesty, malfeasance, or improper motivation, even though these characteristics may also affect the official's private character."

Those classed as public figures stand in a similar position. Hypothetically, it may be possible for someone to become a public figure through no purposeful action of his own, but the instances of truly involuntary public figures must be exceedingly rare. For the most part those who attain this status have assumed roles of especial prominence in the affairs of society. Some occupy positions of such persuasive power and influence that they are deemed public figures for all purposes. More commonly, those classed as public figures have thrust themselves to the forefront of particular public controversies in order to influence the resolution of the issues involved. In either event, they invite attention and comment.

Even if the foregoing generalities do not obtain in every instance, the communications media are entitled to act on the assumption that public officials and public figures have voluntarily exposed themselves to increased risk of injury from defamatory falsehood concerning them. No such assumption is justified with respect to a private individual. He has not accepted public office or assumed an "influential role in ordering society." *Curtis Publishing Co. v. Butts,* 388 U.S., at 164 (Warren, C. J., concurring in result). He has relinquished no part of his interest in the protection of his own good name, and consequently he has a more compelling call on the courts for redress of injury inflicted by defamatory falsehood. Thus, private individuals are not only more vulnerable to injury than public officials and public figures; they are also more deserving of recovery.

For these reasons we conclude that the States should retain substantial latitude in their efforts to enforce a legal remedy for defamatory false-hood injurious to the reputation of a private individual. The extension of the *New York Times* test proposed by the *Rosenbloom* plurality would abridge this legitimate state interest to a degree that we find unacceptable. And it would occasion the additional difficulty of forcing state and federal judges to decide on an *ad hoc* basis which publications address issues of "general or public interest" and which do not—to determine, in the words of Mr. Justice Marshall, "what information is relevant to self-government." *Rosenbloom v. Metromedia, Inc.*, 403 U.S., at 79. We doubt the wisdom of committing this task to the conscience of judges. Nor does the Constitution require us to draw so thin a line between the drastic alternatives of the *New York Times* privilege and the common law of strict liability for defamatory error. The "public or general interest" test for determining the applicability of the *New York Times* standard to private defamation actions inadequately serves both of the competing values at stake. On the one hand, a private individual whose reputation is injured by defamatory falsehood that does concern an issue of public or general interest has no recourse unless he can meet the rigorous requirements of *New York Times*. This is true despite the factors that distinguish the state interest in compensating private individuals from the analogous interest involved in the context of public persons. On the other hand, a publisher or broadcaster of a defamatory error which a court deems unrelated to an issue of public or general interest may be held liable in damages even if it took every reasonable precaution to ensure the accuracy of its assertions. And liability may far exceed compensation for any actual injury to the plaintiff, for the jury may be permitted to presume damages without proof of loss and even to award punitive damages.

We hold that, so long as they do not impose liability without fault, the States may define for themselves the appropriate standard of liability for a publisher or broadcaster of defamatory falsehood injurious to a private individual. This approach provides a more equitable boundary between the competing concerns involved here. It recognizes the strength of the legitimate state interest in compensating private individuals for wrongful injury to reputation, yet shields the press and broadcast media from the rigors of strict liability for defamation. At least this conclusion obtains where, as here, the substance of the defamatory statement "makes substantial danger to reputation apparent." This phrase places in perspective the conclusion we announce today. Our inquiry would involve considerations somewhat different from those discussed above if a State purported to condition civil liability on a factual misstatement whose content did not warn a reasonably prudent editor or broadcaster of its defamatory potential. Cf. *Time, Inc. v. Hill*, 385 U.S. 374 (1967). Such a case is not now before us, and we intimate no view as to its proper resolution.

IV

Our accommodation of the competing values at stake in defamation suits by private individuals allows the States to impose liability on the publisher or broadcaster of defamatory falsehood on a less demanding showing than that required by *New York Times*. This conclusion is not based on a belief that the considerations which prompted the adoption of the *New York Times* privilege for defamation of public officials and its extension to public figures are wholly inapplicable to the context of private individuals. Rather, we endorse this approach in recognition of the strong and legitimate state interest in compensating private individuals for injury to reputation. But this countervailing state interest extends no further than compensation for actual injury. For the reasons stated below, we hold that the States may not permit recovery of presumed or punitive damages, at least when liability is not based on a showing of knowledge of falsity or reckless disregard for the truth.

The common law of defamation is an oddity of tort law, for it allows recovery of purportedly compensatory damages without evidence of actual loss. Under the traditional rules pertaining to actions for libel, the existence of injury is presumed from the fact of publication. Juries may award substantial sums as compensation for supposed damage to reputation without any proof that such harm actually occurred. The largely uncontrolled discretion of juries to award damages where there is no loss unnecessarily compounds the potential of any system of liability for defamatory falsehood to inhibit the vigorous exercise of First Amendment freedoms. Additionally, the doctrine of presumed damages invites juries to punish unpopular opinion rather than to compensate individuals for injury sustained by the publication of a false fact. More to the point, the States have no substantial interest in securing for plaintiffs such as this petitioner gratuitous awards of money damages far in excess of any actual injury.

We would not, of course, invalidate state law simply because we doubt its wisdom, but here we are attempting to reconcile state law with a competing interest grounded in the constitutional command of the First Amendment. It is therefore appropriate to require that state remedies for defamatory falsehood reach no farther than is necessary to protect the legitimate interest involved. It is necessary to restrict defamation plaintiffs who do not prove knowledge of falsity or reckless disregard for the truth to compensation for actual injury. We need not define "actual injury," as trial courts have wide experience in framing appropriate jury instructions in tort actions. Suffice it to say that actual injury is not limited to out-of-pocket loss. Indeed, the more customary types of actual harm inflicted by defamatory falsehood include impairment of reputation and standing in the community, personal humiliation, and mental anguish and suffering. Of course, juries must be limited by appropriate instructions, and all awards must be supported by competent evidence concerning the injury, although there need be no evidence which assigns an actual dollar value to the injury.

We also find no justification for allowing awards of punitive damages against publishers and broadcasters held liable under state-defined standards of liability for defamation. In most jurisdictions jury discretion over the amounts awarded is limited only by the gentle rule that they not be excessive. Consequently, juries assess punitive damages in wholly unpredictable amounts bearing no necessary relation to the actual harm caused. And they remain free to use their discretion selectively to punish expressions of unpopular views. Like the doctrine of presumed damages, jury discretion to award punitive damages unnecessarily exacerbates the danger of

media self-censorship, but, unlike the former rule, punitive damages are wholly irrelevant to the state interest that justifies a negligence standard for private defamation actions. They are not compensation for injury. Instead, they are private fines levied by civil juries to punish reprehensible conduct and to deter its future occurrence. In short, the private defamation plaintiff who establishes liability under a less demanding standard than that stated by *New York Times* may recover only such damages as are sufficient to compensate him for actual injury.

Notwithstanding our refusal to extend the *New York Times* privilege to defamation of private individuals, respondent contends that we should affirm the judgment below on the ground that petitioner is either a public official or a public figure. There is little basis for the former assertion. Several years prior to the present incident, petitioner had served briefly on housing committees appointed by the mayor of Chicago, but at the time of publication he had never held any remunerative governmental position. Respondent admits this but argues that petitioner's appearance at the coroner's inquest rendered him a "de facto public official." Our cases recognize no such concept. Respondent's suggestion would sweep all lawyers under the *New York Times* rule as officers of the court and distort the plain meaning of the "public official" category beyond all recognition. We decline to follow it.

Respondent's characterization of petitioner as a public figure raises a different question. That designation may rest on either of two alternative bases. In some instances an individual may achieve such pervasive fame or notoriety that he becomes a public figure for all purposes and in all contexts. More commonly, an individual voluntarily injects himself or is drawn into a particular public controversy and thereby becomes a public figure for a limited range of issues. In either case such persons assume special prominence in the resolution of public questions.

Petitioner has long been active in community and professional affairs. He has served as an officer of local civic groups and of various professional organizations, and he has published several books and articles on legal subjects. Although petitioner was consequently well known in some circles, he had achieved no general fame or notoriety in the community. None of the prospective jurors called at the trial had ever heard of petitioner prior to this litigation, and respondent offered no proof that this response was atypical of the local population. We would not lightly assume that a citizen's participation in community and professional affairs rendered him a public figure for all purposes. Absent clear evidence of general fame or notoriety in the community, and pervasive involvement in the affairs of society, an individual should not be deemed a public personality for all aspects of his life. It is preferable to reduce the public-figure question to a more meaningful context by looking to the nature and extent of an individual's participation in the particular controversy giving rise to the defamation.

In this context it is plain that petitioner was not a public figure. He played a minimal role at the coroner's inquest, and his participation related solely to his representation of a private client. He took no part in the criminal prosecution of Officer Nuccio. Moreover, he never discussed either the criminal or civil litigation with the press and was never quoted as having done so. He plainly did not thrust himself into the vortex of this public issue, nor did he engage the public's attention in an attempt to influence its outcome. We are persuaded that the trial court did not err in refusing to characterize petitioner as a public figure for the purpose of this litigation.

We therefore conclude that the *New York Times* standard is inapplicable to this case and that the trial court erred in entering judgment for respondent. Because the jury was allowed to impose liability without fault and was permitted to presume damages without proof of injury, a new trial is necessary. We reverse and remand for further proceedings in accord with this opinion.

Mr. Chief Justice Burger, dissenting.

Agreement or disagreement with the law as it has evolved to this time does not alter the fact that it has been orderly development with a consistent basic rationale. In today's opinion the Court abandons the traditional thread so far as the ordinary private citizen is concerned and introduces the concept that the media will be liable for negligence in publishing defamatory statements with respect to such persons. Although I agree with much of what Mr. Justice White states,

I do not read the Court's new doctrinal approach in quite the way he does. I am frank to say I do not know the parameters of a "negligence" doctrine as applied to the news media. Conceivably this new doctrine could inhibit some editors, as the dissents of Mr. Justice Douglas and Mr. Justice Brennan suggest. But I would prefer to allow this area of law to continue to evolve as it has up to now with respect to private citizens rather than embark on a new doctrinal theory which has no jurisprudential ancestry.

The petitioner here was performing a professional representative role as an advocate in the highest tradition of the law, and under that tradition the advocate is not to be invidiously identified with his client. The important public policy which underlies this tradition—the right to counsel—would be gravely jeopardized if every lawyer who takes an "unpopular" case, civil or criminal, would automatically become fair game for irresponsible reporters and editors who might, for example, describe the lawyer as a "mob mouthpiece" for representing a client with a serious prior criminal record, or as an "ambulance chaser" for representing a claimant in a personal injury action.

I would reverse the judgment of the Court of Appeals and remand for reinstatement of the verdict of the jury and the entry of an appropriate judgment on that verdict.

Mr. Justice Douglas, dissenting.

The Court describes this case as a return to the struggle of "defin[ing] the proper accommodation between the law of defamation and the freedoms of speech and press protected by the First Amendment." It is indeed a struggle, once described by Mr. Justice Black as "the same quagmire" in which the Court "is now helplessly struggling in the field of obscenity." *Curtis Publishing Co. v. Butts,* 388 U.S. 130, 171 (concurring opinion). I would suggest that the struggle is a quite hopeless one, for, in light of the command of the First Amendment, no "accommodation" of its freedoms can be "proper" except those made by the Framers themselves.

Unlike the right of privacy which, by the terms of the Fourth Amendment, must be accommodated with reasonable searches and seizures and warrants issued by magistrates, the rights of free speech and of a free press were protected by the Framers in verbiage whose proscription seems clear. I have stated before my view that the First Amendment would bar Congress from passing any libel law. This was the view held by Thomas Jefferson and it is one Congress has never challenged through enactment of a civil libel statute. The sole congressional attempt at this variety of First Amendment muzzle was in the Sedition Act of 1798—a criminal libel act never tested in this Court and one which expired by its terms three years after enactment. As President, Thomas Jefferson pardoned those who were convicted under the Act, and fines levied in its prosecution were repaid by Act of Congress. The general consensus was that the Act constituted a regrettable legislative exercise plainly in violation of the First Amendment.

With the First Amendment made applicable to the States through the Fourteenth, I do not see how States have any more ability to "accommodate" freedoms of speech or of the press than does Congress. This is true whether the form of the accommodation is civil or criminal since "[w]hat a State may not constitutionally bring about by means of a criminal statute is likewise beyond the reach of its civil law of libel." *New York Times Co. v. Sullivan,* 376 U.S. 254, 277. Like Congress, States are without power "to use a civil libel law or any other law to impose damages for merely discussing public affairs." *Id.,* at 295 (Black, J., concurring).

Mr. Justice Brennan, dissenting.

I agree with the conclusion, expressed in Part V of the Court's opinion, that, at the time of publication of respondent's article, petitioner could not properly have been viewed as either a "public official" or "public figure"; instead, respondent's article, dealing with an alleged conspiracy to discredit local police forces, concerned petitioner's purported involvement in "an event of public or general interest." *Rosenbloom v. Metromedia, Inc.,* 403 U.S. 29, 31–32 (1971); see *ante,* at 331–332, n. 4. I cannot agree, however, that free and robust debate—so essential to the proper functioning of our system of government—is permitted adequate "breathing space," *NAACP v. Button,* 371 U.S. 415, 433 (1963), when, as the Court holds, the States may impose all but strict liability for

defamation if the defamed party is a private person and "the substance of the defamatory statement 'makes substantial danger to reputation apparent.' " *Ante,* at 348. I adhere to my view expressed in *Rosenbloom v. Metromedia, Inc., supra,* that we strike the proper accommodation between avoidance of media self-censorship and protection of individual reputations only when we require States to apply the *New York Times Co. v. Sullivan,* 376 U.S. 254 (1964), knowing-or-reckless-falsity standard in civil libel actions concerning media reports of the involvement of private individuals in events of public or general interest. . . .

Although acknowledging that First Amendment values are of no less significance when media reports concern private persons' involvement in matters of public concern, the Court refuses to provide, in such cases, the same level of constitutional protection that has been afforded the media in the context of defamation of public persons. The accommodation that this Court has established between free speech and libel laws in cases involving public officials and public figures—that defamatory falsehood be shown by clear and convincing evidence to have been published with knowledge of falsity or with reckless disregard of truth—is not apt, the Court holds, because the private individual does not have the same degree of access to the media to rebut defamatory comments as does the public person and he has not voluntarily exposed himself to public scrutiny.

While these arguments are forcefully and eloquently presented, I cannot accept them, for the reasons I stated in *Rosenbloom:*

> The *New York Times* standard was applied to libel of a public official or public figure to give effect to the [First] Amendment's function to encourage ventilation of public issues, not because the public official has any less interest in protecting his reputation than an individual in private life. While the argument that public figures need less protection because they can command media attention to counter criticism may be true for some very prominent people, even then it is the rare case where the denial overtakes the original charge. Denials, retractions, and corrections are not 'hot' news, and rarely receive the prominence of the original story. When the public official or public figure is a minor functionary, or has left the position that put him in the public eye

..., the argument loses all of its force. In the vast majority of libels involving public officials or public figures, the ability to respond through the media will depend on the same complex factor on which the ability of a private individual depends: the unpredictable event of the media's continuing interest in the story. Thus the unproved, and highly improbable, generalization that an as yet [not fully defined] class of "public figures" involved in matters of public concern will be better able to respond through the media than private individuals also involved in such matters seems too insubstantial a reed on which to rest a constitutional distinction. 403 U.S., at 46–47.

Moreover, the argument that private persons should not be required to prove *New York Times* knowing-or-reckless falsity because they do not assume the risk of defamation by freely entering the public arena "bears little relationship either to the values protected by the First Amendment or to the nature of our society." *Id.*, at 47. Social interaction exposes all of us to some degree of public view. This Court has observed that "[t]he risk of this exposure is an essential incident of life in a society which places a primary value on freedom of speech and of press." *Time, Inc. v. Hill,* 385 U.S., at 388. Therefore,

> [v]oluntarily or not, we are all "public" men to some degree. Conversely, some aspects of the lives of even the most public men fall outside the area of matters of public or general concern. See . . . *Griswold v. Connecticut,* 381 U.S. 479 (1965). Thus, the idea that certain "public" figures have voluntarily exposed their entire lives to public inspection, while private individuals have kept theirs carefully shrouded from public view is, at best, a legal fiction. In any event, such a distinction could easily produce the paradoxical result of dampening discussion of issues of public or general concern because they happen to involve private citizens while extending constitutional encouragement to discussion of aspects of the lives of "public figures" that are not in the area of public or general concern. *Rosenbloom, supra,* at 48 (footnote omitted).

We recognized in *New York Times Co. v. Sullivan, supra,* at 279, that a rule requiring a critic of official conduct to guarantee the truth of all of his factual contentions would inevitably lead to self-censorship when publishers, fearful of being unable to prove truth or unable to bear the expense of attempting to do so, simply eschewed printing controversial articles. Adoption, by many States, of a reasonable-care standard in cases where private individuals are involved in matters of public interest—the probable result of today's decision—will likewise lead to self-censorship since publishers will be required carefully to weigh a myriad of uncertain factors before publication. The reasonable-care standard is "elusive," *Time, Inc. v. Hill, supra,* at 389; it saddles the press with "the intolerable burden of guessing how a jury might assess the reasonableness of steps taken by it to verify the accuracy of every reference to a name, picture or portrait." *Ibid.* Under a reasonable-care regime, publishers and broadcasters will have to make pre-publication judgments about juror assessment of such diverse considerations as the size, operating procedures, and financial condition of the newsgathering system, as well as the relative costs and benefits of instituting less frequent and more costly reporting at a higher level of accuracy. See The Supreme Court, 1970 Term, 85 *Harv. L. Rev.* 3, 228 (1971). Moreover, in contrast to proof by clear and convincing evidence required under the *New York Times* test, the burden of proof for reasonable care will doubtless be the preponderance of the evidence. . . .

The Court does not discount altogether the danger that jurors will punish for the expression of unpopular opinions. This probability accounts for the Court's limitation that "the States may not permit recovery of presumed or punitive damages, at least when liability is not based on a showing of knowledge of falsity or reckless disregard for the truth." *Ante,* at 349. But plainly a jury's latitude to impose liability for want of due care poses a far greater threat of suppressing unpopular views than does a possible recovery of presumed or punitive damages. Moreover, the Court's broad-ranging examples of "actual injury," including impairment of reputation and standing in the community, as well as personal humiliation, and mental anguish and suffering, inevitably allow a jury bent on punishing expression of unpopular views a formidable weapon for doing so. Finally, even a limitation of recovery to "actual injury"—however much it reduces the size or frequency of recoveries—will not provide the necessary elbowroom for First Amendment expression.

It is not simply the possibility of a judgment for damages that results in self-censorship. The very possibility of having to engage in litigation, an expensive and protracted process, is threat enough to cause discussion and debate to "steer far wider of the unlawful zone" thereby keeping protected discussion from public cognizance.... Too, a small newspaper suffers equally from a substantial damage award, whether the label of the award be "actual" or "punitive." *Rosenbloom, supra,* at 52–53.

On the other hand, the uncertainties which the media face under today's decision are largely avoided by the *New York Times* standard. I reject the argument that my *Rosenbloom* view improperly commits to judges the task of determining what is and what is not an issue of "general or public interest." I noted in *Rosenbloom* that performance of this task would not always be easy. *Id.,* at 49 n. 17. But surely the courts, the ultimate arbiters of all disputes concerning clashes of constitutional values, would only be performing one of their traditional functions in undertaking this duty. Also, the difficulty of this task has been substantially lessened by that "sizable body of cases, decided both before and after *Rosenbloom,* that have employed the concept of a matter of public concern to reach decisions in ... cases dealing with an alleged libel of a private individual that employed a public interest standard ... and ... cases that applied *Butts* to the alleged libel of a public figure." Comment, The Expanding Constitutional Protection for the News Media from Liability for Defamation: Predictability and the New Synthesis, 70 *Mich. L. Rev.* 1547, 1560 (1972). The public interest is necessarily broad; any residual self-censorship that may result from the uncertain contours of the "general or public interest" concept should be of far less concern to publishers and broadcasters than that occasioned by state laws imposing liability for negligent falsehood.

Mr. Justice White, dissenting.

For some 200 years—from the very founding of the Nation—the law of defamation and right of the ordinary citizen to recover for false publication injurious to his reputation have been almost exclusively the business of state courts and legislatures. Under typical state defamation law, the defamed private citizen had to prove only a false publication that would subject him to hatred, contempt, or ridicule. Given such publication, general damage to reputation was presumed, while punitive damages required proof of additional facts. The law governing the defamation of private citizens remained untouched by the First Amendment because until relatively recently, the consistent view of the Court was that libelous words constitute a class of speech wholly unprotected by the First Amendment, subject only to limited exceptions carved out since 1964.

But now, using that Amendment as the chosen instrument, the Court, in a few printed pages, has federalized major aspects of libel law by declaring unconstitutional in important respects the prevailing defamation law in all or most of the 50 States. That result is accomplished by requiring the plaintiff in each and every defamation action to prove not only the defendant's culpability beyond his act of publishing defamatory material but also actual damage to reputation resulting from the publication. Moreover, punitive damages may not be recovered by showing malice in the traditional sense of ill will; knowing falsehood or reckless disregard of the truth will now be required.

I assume these sweeping changes will be popular with the press, but this is not the road to salvation for a court of law. As I see it, there are wholly insufficient grounds for scuttling the libel laws of the States in such wholesale fashion, to say nothing of deprecating the reputation interest of ordinary citizens and rendering them powerless to protect themselves. I do not suggest that the decision is illegitimate or beyond the bounds of judicial review, but it is an ill-considered exercise of the power, entrusted to this Court, particularly when the Court has not had the benefit of briefs and argument addressed to most of the major issues which the Court now decides. I respectfully dissent....

The impact of today's decision on the traditional law of libel is immediately obvious and indisputable. No longer will the plaintiff be able to rest his case with proof of a libel defamatory on its face or proof of a slander historically actionable *per se.* In addition, he must prove some further degree of culpable conduct on the part of the publisher, such as intentional or reckless falsehood or negligence. And if he succeeds in this respect, he faces still another obstacle: recovery for loss of reputation will be conditioned upon "competent" proof of actual injury to his standing in the community. This will be true regardless of the nature of the defamation and even though it is one of those particularly reprehensible statements that have traditionally made slanderous words actionable without proof of fault by the publisher or of the damaging impact of his publication. The Court rejects the judgment of experience that some publications are so inherently capable of injury, and actual injury so difficult to prove, that the risk of falsehood should be borne by the publisher, not the victim. Plainly, with the additional burden on the plaintiff of proving negligence or other fault, it will be exceedingly difficult, perhaps impossible, for him to vindicate his reputation interest by securing a judgment for nominal damages, the practical effect of such a judgment being a judicial declaration that the publication was indeed false. Under the new rule the plaintiff can lose, not because the statement is true, but because it was not negligently made. . . .

III

The Court concedes that the dangers of self-censorship are insufficient to override the state interest in protecting the reputation of private individuals who are both more helpless and more deserving of state concern than public persons with more access to the media to defend themselves. It therefore refuses to condition the private plaintiff's recovery on a showing of intentional or reckless falsehood as required by *New York Times*. But the Court nevertheless extends the reach of the First Amendment to all defamation actions by requiring that the ordinary citizen, when libeled by a publication defamatory on its face, must prove some degree of culpability on the part of the publisher beyond the circulation to the public of a damaging falsehood. . . . Furthermore, if this major hurdle to establish liability is surmounted, the Court requires proof of actual injury to reputation before any damages for such injury may be awarded. . . .

The Court evinces a deep-seated antipathy to "liability without fault." But this catch-phrase has no talismanic significance and is almost meaningless in this context where the Court appears to be addressing those libels and slanders that are defamatory on their face and where the publisher is no doubt aware from the nature of the material that it would be inherently damaging to reputation. He publishes notwithstanding, knowing that he will inflict injury. With this knowledge, he must intend to inflict that injury, his excuse being that he is privileged to do so—that he has published the truth. But as it turns out, what he has circulated to the public is a very damaging falsehood. Is he nevertheless "faultless"? Perhaps it can be said that the mistake about his defense was made in good faith, but the fact remains that it is he who launched the publication knowing that it could ruin a reputation.

In these circumstances, the law has heretofore put the risk of falsehood on the publisher where the victim is a private citizen and no grounds of special privilege are invoked. The Court would now shift this risk to the victim, even though he has done nothing to invite the calumny, is wholly innocent of fault, and is helpless to avoid his injury. I doubt that jurisprudential resistance to liability without fault is sufficient ground for employing the First Amendment to revolutionize the law of libel, and in my view, that body of legal rules poses no realistic threat to the press and its service to the public. The press today is vigorous and robust. To me, it is quite incredible to suggest that threats of libel suits from private citizens are causing the press to refrain from publishing the truth. I know of no hard facts to support that proposition, and the Court furnishes none.

The communications industry has increasingly become concentrated in a few powerful hands operating very lucrative businesses reaching across the Nation and into almost every home. Neither the industry as a whole nor its individual components are easily intimidated, and we are fortunate that they are not. Requiring them to pay for the occasional damage they do to private reputation will play no substantial part in their future performance or their existence.

In any event, if the Court's principal concern is to protect the communications industry from large libel judgments, it would appear that its new requirements with respect to general and punitive damages would be ample protection. Why it also feels compelled to escalate the threshold standard of liability I cannot fathom, particularly when this will eliminate in many instances the plaintiff's possibility of securing a judicial determination that the damaging publication was indeed false, whether or not he is entitled to recover money damages. Under the Court's new rules, the plaintiff must prove not only the defamatory statement but also some degree of fault accompanying it. The publication may be wholly false and the wrong to him unjustified, but his case will nevertheless be dismissed for failure to prove negligence or other fault on the part of the publisher. I find it unacceptable to distribute the risk in this manner and force the wholly innocent victim to bear the injury; for, as between the two, the defamer is the only culpable party. It is he who circulated a falsehood that he was not required to publish.

It is difficult for me to understand why the ordinary citizen should himself carry the risk of damage and suffer the injury in order to vindicate First Amendment values by protecting the press and others from liability for circulating false information. This is particularly true because such statements serve no purpose whatsoever in furthering the public interest or the search for truth but, on the contrary, may frustrate that search and at the same time inflict great injury on the defenseless individual. The owners of the press and the stockholders of the communications enterprises can much better bear the burden. And if they cannot, the public at large should somehow pay for what is essentially a public benefit derived at private expense.

The Court is clearly right when at one point it states that "the law of defamation is rooted in our experience that the truth rarely catches up with a lie." *Ante,* at 344 n. 9. But it ignores what that experience teaches, *viz.,* that damage to reputation is recurringly difficult to prove and that requiring actual proof would repeatedly destroy any chance for adequate compensation. Eminent authority has warned that

> it is clear that proof of actual damage will be impossible in a great many cases where, from the character of the defamatory words and the circumstances of publication, it is all but certain that serious harm has resulted in fact. W. Prosser, Law of Torts § 112, p. 765 (4th ed. 1971).

The Court fears uncontrolled awards of damages by juries, but that not only denigrates the good sense of most jurors—it fails to consider the role of trial and appellate courts in limiting excessive jury verdicts where no reasonable relationship exists between the amount awarded and the injury sustained. Available information tends to confirm that American courts have ably discharged this responsibility.

The new rule with respect to general damages appears to apply to all libels or slanders, whether defamatory on their face or not, except, I gather, when the plaintiff proves intentional falsehood or reckless disregard. Although the impact of the publication on the victim is the same, in such circumstances the injury to reputation may apparently be presumed in accordance with the traditional rule. Why a defamatory statement is more apt to cause injury if the lie is intentional than when it is only negligent, I fail to understand. I suggest that judges and juries who must live by these rules will find them equally incomprehensible. . . .

In disagreeing with the Court on the First Amendment's reach in the area of state libel laws protecting nonpublic persons, I do not repudiate the principle that the First Amendment "rests on the assumption that the widest possible dissemination of information from diverse and antagonistic sources is essential to the welfare of the public, that a free press is a condition of a free society." *Associated Press v. United States,* 326 U.S. 1, 20 (1945); see also *Miami Herald Publishing Co. v. Tornillo, ante,* at 260 (White, J., concurring). I continue to subscribe to the *New York Times* decision and those decisions extending its protection to defamatory falsehoods about public persons. My quarrel with the Court stems from its willingness "to sacrifice good sense to a syllogism"—to find in the *New York Times* doctrine an infinite elasticity. Unfortunately, this expansion is the latest manifestation of the destructive potential of any good idea carried out to its logical extreme.

Recovery under common-law standards for defamatory falsehoods about a private individual, who enjoys no "general fame or notoriety in the community," who is not "pervasive[ly] involve[d] in the affairs of society," and who does not "thrust himself into the vortex of [a given] public issue . . . in an attempt to influence its outcome," is simply not forbidden by the First Amendment. A distinguished private study group put it this way:

> Accountability, like subjection to law, is not necessarily a net subtraction from liberty. The First Amendment was intended to guarantee free expression, not to create a privileged industry. Commission on Freedom of the Press, A Free and Responsible Press 130, 81 (1947).

I fail to see how the quality or quantity of public debate will be promoted by further emasculation of state libel laws for the benefit of the news media. If anything, this trend may provoke a new and radical imbalance in the communications process. Cf. Barron, Access to the Press—A New First Amendment Right, 80 *Harv. L. Rev.* 1641, 1657 (1967). It is not at all inconceivable that virtually unrestrained defamatory remarks about private citizens will discourage them from speaking out and concerning themselves with social problems. This would turn the First Amendment on its head. Note, The Scope of First Amendment Protection for Good-Faith Defamatory Error, 75 *Yale L. J.* 642, 649 (1966); Merin, 11 *Wm. & Mary L. Rev.*, at 418. David Riesman, writing in the midst of World War II on the fascists' effective use of defamatory attacks on their opponents, commented: "Thus it is that the law of libel, with its ecclesiastic background and domestic character, its aura of heart-balm suits and crusading nineteenth-century editors, becomes suddenly important for modern democratic survival." Democracy and Defamation: Fair Game and Fair Comment I, 42 *Col. L. Rev.* 1085, 1088 (1942).

This case ultimately comes down to the importance the Court attaches to society's "pervasive and strong interest in preventing and redressing attacks upon reputation." *Rosenblatt v. Baer, 383 U.S.,* at 86. From all that I have seen, the Court has miscalculated and denigrates that interest at a time when escalating assaults on individuality and personal dignity counsel otherwise.

If the Court by adopting a public figure criterion had sought to avoid the fine and potentially subjective exercises which made the public interest standard unacceptable, it soon became evident that the definition of a public figure would be an equally treacherous process. In *Time, Inc. v. Firestone,*[157] the Court applied the public figure test in a narrow fashion. The plaintiff was not held to the actual malice standard governing a public figure, despite being a prominent Palm Beach socialite, employing a press agent, maintaining a news clipping service, and conducting news conferences in the course of a divorce proceeding which was the subject of the defamatory article.[158] The magazine had erred by stating a divorce was granted on the grounds of extreme cruelty and adultery, when in fact the actual basis had not been set forth explicitly in the judge's order.[159] The Court found that she did not have special prominence in the resolution of public questions and had not voluntarily injected herself into "the forefront of any particular public controversy in order to influence the resolution of the issues involved in it."[160] It also emphasized that the plaintiff, to obtain a divorce, had no choice but to avail herself of a public process.[161]

The Court discounted the significance of the plaintiff's press conferences pursuant to its sense that they were not calculated to influence the outcome of the legal dispute.[162] Such a characterization may be criticized as too narrow, legalistic, and perhaps reflective of an instinctual rather than well-reasoned reaction to the subject matter and focus of the article. It arguably disregards or discounts acts that may have been designed to influence perceptions in the court of public opinion. The observation that a divorce proceeding was not the type of public controversy meriting special constitutional attention[163] may reveal precisely the type of subjectivism which worried the Court when it chose governing standards in *Gertz.* At a minimum, the result demonstrates the divergence of outcomes possible pursuant to public figure or public interest criteria.

Further limiting the definition of a public figure was the Court's determination, in *Wolston v. Reader's Digest Association, Inc.*[164] that characterization of the plaintiff as a Soviet agent was not protected by the actual malice standard.[165] Sixteen years prior to publication of the actionable statement, the plaintiff, claiming illness, had failed to respond to a grand jury subpoena and was cited for contempt.[166] Although his refusal to appear had been extensively reported at the time, the plaintiff since had not been in the public eye.[167] Thus, the Court concluded that failure to respond to the subpoena could not represent a voluntary injection of himself into a controversy over foreign espionage unless it was calculated to protect the investigation and influence public opinion.[168] The *Wolston* decision reiterates the principle, set forth in *Firestone*, that qualification as a public figure requires affirmative entry into a public controversy with intent to shape public sentiment on a precise issue. Status as a limited public figure in one context will not suffice to establish such standing in an unrelated setting. As the Court has noted, moreover, the category of involuntary figures is an extremely limited one.[169] The concept in fact has yet to be fleshed out in a meaningful way. Nor is it a likely classification for development, since recognition of involuntary public figures could reach so far as potentially to create a *de facto* public interest standard.

Further shrinkage of the public figure category seems to have occurred in *Hutchinson v. Proxmire*.[170] The plaintiff had been named in connection with a United States senator's dubious "Golden Fleece of the Month" award for a government research award on animal behavior.[171] Although the trial court considered the recipient of the research grant a public figure, because of his long record of publicly funded research, the local media coverage of his work, and public interest in government spending, the Court reversed.[172] It found instead that mere receipt of a public grant does not result in public figure standing.[173] More important, a person's access to the media, which was a key

attribute in *Gertz* of such status,[174] must be regular and continuing to qualify him as a public figure.[175] Since such access is limited to very few persons, and perhaps none that could not qualify as general purpose public figures, a possible basis exists for reading limited purpose public figures out of existence for practical purposes.

Because the *Gertz* decision applies directly to media defendants, the possibility remains that a different standard may apply for non-media defendants. Arguments have been advanced that the operation of the actual malice standard against media defendants presumes the presence of some minimal public concern that is not necessarily present in private communications.[176] Creation of a different standard for media and nonmedia defendants, however, would elevate the press above the public for constitutional purposes contrary to the Court's general reluctance to accord it any special status.[177] The possibility of such a result also has elicited criticism to the effect that it would afford maximum protection to those capable of causing the most damage.[178]

Despite the Court's inclination to set standards on the basis of a plaintiff's status rather than on the nature of the pertinent expression, it appears that the public concern standard rejected in *Gertz* has not been buried entirely. In *Dun & Bradstreet, Inc. v. Greenmoss Builders, Inc.*,[179] Justice Powell, who authored the *Gertz* opinion, found it significant that the defamatory statement at issue was a "purely private" rather than "public concern."[180] Because an erroneous credit report was a private rather than a public matter, Powell with Justices O'Connor and Rehnquist concluded that reputational interests supported the availability of presumed and punitive damages even absent actual malice.[181] He left undetermined whether such damages might be available without proof of fault. Also unclear is whether he would allow a public official or figure to collect presumed or punitive damages when a defamation was not tied to a matter of public concern.

Resurrection of a public concern standard would invite the risks of subjectivity and ad hoc judgment which worried the Court in *Gertz*. Possible hostility to the press's interest in the *Firestone* divorce proceeding and subsequent delimitation of the public figure standard suggest the pertinence of those anxieties. A public interest standard is highly malleable and risks significant judicial meddling in the editorial process. So too is a public figure determination, however, which dismisses the relevance of public concern entirely if the plaintiff is identified as a private person. Concern with the impact of multimillion dollar damage awards has prompted arguments that they cross not only First Amendment concerns but the Eighth Amendment guarantee against "excessive fines." In *Browning-Ferris Industries of Vermont, Inc., v. Kelso Disposal Inc.*,[182] the Court found that a six million dollar punitive damage award did not violate the Eighth Amendment. Left open was the possibility, however, that the size of a punitive damages award may be at odds with due process guaranteed by the Fourteenth Amendment.

The evolution of constitutional standards reveals a significant rethinking on the part of the Court in its valuation of false expression. In *New York Times Co. v. Sullivan*, the Court proclaimed the merits of false speech without regard to whether it constituted fact or idea.[183] Within a decade, it observed in *Gertz* that "there is no such thing as a false idea . . . , but there is no constitutional value in false statements of facts."[184] A decade later, in *Keeton v. Hustler Magazine, Inc.*,[185] the Court noted that false statements not only injure a specific victim but also harm the public.[186] Consistent with that determination, Justice White, who joined in formulating the actual malice standard, now urges its abandonment.[187] His concern is that false expression

misinforms the public, creates misleading impressions, and pollutes the flow of information.[188] Thus, he has asserted that "the Court struck an improvident balance in the *New York Times* case between the public's interest in being informed about public officials and public affairs and the competing interests of those who have been defamed in vindicating their reputation."[189] White complains that the actual malice standard lets "the lie" stand and the public remain misinformed about public matters.[190] His preferred methodology, for protecting reputation from defamation and the press from intimidation, would be to retain common law standards of negligence and strict liability but limit the amount of damages available.[191]

Dun & Bradstreet, Inc. v. Greenmoss Builders, Inc., 472 U.S. 749 (1985)

Justice White, concurring in the judgment.

I joined the judgment and opinion in *New York Times*. I also joined later decisions extending the *New York Times* standard to other situations. But I came to have increasing doubts about the soundness of the Court's approach and about some of the assumptions underlying it. I could not join the plurality opinion in *Rosenbloom*, and I dissented in *Gertz*, asserting that the common-law remedies should be retained for private plaintiffs. I remain convinced that *Gertz* was erroneously decided. I have also become convinced that the Court struck an improvident balance in the *New York Times* case between the public's interest in being fully informed about public officials and public affairs and the competing interest of those who have been defamed in vindicating their reputation.

In a country like ours, where the people purport to be able to govern themselves through their elected representatives, adequate information about their government is of transcendent importance. That flow of intelligence deserves full First Amendment protection. Criticism and assessment of the performance of public officials and of government in general are not subject to penalties imposed by law. But these First Amendment values are not at all served by circulating false statements of fact about public officials. On the contrary, erroneous information frustrates these values. They are even more disserved when the statements falsely impugn the honesty of those men and women and hence lessen the confidence in government. As the Court said in *Gertz:* "[T]here is no constitutional value in false statements of fact. Neither the intentional lie nor the careless error materially advances society's interest in 'uninhibited, robust, and wide-open' debate on public issues." 418 U.S., at 340. Yet in *New York Times* cases, the public official's complaint will be dismissed unless he alleges and makes out a jury case of a knowing or reckless falsehood. Absent such proof, there will be no jury verdict or judgment of any kind in his favor, even if the challenged publication is admittedly false. The lie will stand, and the public continue to be misinformed about public matters. This will recurringly happen because the putative plaintiff's burden is so exceedingly difficult to satisfy and can be discharged only by expensive litigation. Even if the plaintiff sues, he frequently loses on summary judgment or never gets to the jury because of insufficient proof of malice. If he wins before the jury, verdicts are often overturned by appellate courts for failure to prove malice. Furthermore, when the plaintiff loses, the jury will likely return a general verdict and there will be no judgment that the publication was false, even though it was without foundation in reality. The public is left to conclude that the challenged statement was true after all. Their only chance of being accurately informed is measured by the public official's ability himself to counter the lie, unaided by the courts. That is a decidedly weak reed to depend on for the vindication of First Amendment interests—"it is the rare case where the denial overtakes the original charge. Denials, retractions, and corrections are not 'hot' news, and rarely receive the prominence of the original story." *Rosenbloom,* 403 U.S., at 46–47 (opinion of Brennan, J.); *Gertz, supra,* at 363–364 (Brennan, J., dissenting).

Also, by leaving the lie uncorrected, the *New York Times* rule plainly leaves the public official without a remedy for the damage to his reputa-tion. Yet the Court has observed that the individual's right to the protection of his own good name is a basic consideration of our constitutional system, reflecting " 'our basic concept of the essential dignity and worth of every human being— a concept at the root of any decent system of ordered liberty.' " *Gertz, supra,* at 341, quoting *Rosenblatt v. Baer,* 383 U.S. 75, 92 (1966) (Stewart, J., concurring). The upshot is that the public official must suffer the injury, often cannot get a judgment identifying the lie for what it is, and has very little, if any, chance of countering that lie in the public press.

The *New York Times* rule thus countenances two evils: first, the stream of information about public officials and public affairs is polluted and often remains polluted by false information; and second, the reputation and professional life of the defeated plaintiff may be destroyed by falsehoods that might have been avoided with a reasonable effort to investigate the facts. In terms of the First Amendment and reputational interests at stake, these seem grossly perverse results.

Of course, the Court in *New York Times* could not have been unaware of these realities. Despite our ringing endorsement of "wide-open" and "uninhibited" debate, which taken literally would protect falsehoods of all kinds, we cannot fairly be accused of giving constitutional protection to false information as such, for we went on to find competing and overriding constitutional justification for our decision. The constitutional interest in the flow of information about public affairs was thought to be very strong, and discovering the truth in this area very difficult, even with the best of efforts. These considerations weighed so heavily that those who write and speak about public affairs were thought to require some breathing room—that is, they should be permitted to err and misinform the public as long as they act unknowingly and without recklessness. If the press could be faced with possibly sizable damages for every mistaken publication injurious to reputation, the result would be an unacceptable degree of self-censorship, which might prevent the occasional mistaken libel, but would also often prevent the timely flow of information that is thought to be true but cannot be readily verified. The press must therefore be privileged to spread false information, even though that information has negative First Amendment value and is severely damaging to reputation, in order to encourage the full flow of the truth, which otherwise might be withheld.

Gertz is subject to similar observations. Although rejecting the *New York Times* malice standard where the plaintiff is neither a public official nor a public figure, there the Court nevertheless deprived the private plaintiff of his common-law remedies, making recovery more difficult in order to provide a margin for error. In doing so, the Court ruled that without proof of at least negligence, a plaintiff damaged by the most outrageous falsehoods would be remediless, and the lie very likely would go uncorrected. And even if fault were proved, actual damage to reputation would have to be shown, a burden traditional libel law considered difficult, if not impossible, to discharge. For this reason Justice Powell would not impose on the plaintiff the burden of proving damages in the case now before us....

We are not talking in these cases about mere criticism or opinion, but about misstatements of fact that seriously harm the reputation of another, by lowering him in the estimation of the community or to deter third persons from associating or dealing with him. Restatement of Torts § 559 (1938). The necessary breathing room for speakers can be ensured by limitations on recoverable damages; it does not also require depriving many public figures of any room to vindicate their reputations sullied by false statements of fact. It could be suggested that even without the threat of large presumed and punitive damages awards, press defendants' communication will be unduly chilled by having to pay for the actual damages caused to those they defame. But other commercial enterprises in this country not in the business of disseminating information must pay for the damage they cause as a cost of doing business, and it is difficult to argue that the United States did not have a free and vigorous press before the rule in *New York Times* was announced. In any event, the *New York Times* standard was formulated to protect the press from the chilling danger of numerous large damages awards. Nothing in the central rationale behind *New York Times* demands an absolute im-

munity from suits to establish the falsity of a defamatory misstatement about a public figure where the plaintiff cannot make out a jury case of actual malice. . . .

As I have said, I dissented in *Gertz*, and I doubt that the decision in that case has made any measurable contribution to First Amendment or reputational values since its announcement. Nor am I sure that it has saved the press a great deal of money. Like the *New York Times* decision, the burden that plaintiffs must meet invites long and complicated discovery involving detailed investigation of the workings of the press, how a news story is developed, and the state of mind of the reporter and publisher. See *Herbert v. Lando,* 441 U.S. 153 (1979). That kind of litigation is very expensive. I suspect that the press would be no worse off financially if the common-law rules were to apply and if the judiciary was careful to insist that damages awards be kept within bounds. A legislative solution to the damages problem would also be appropriate. Moreover, since libel plaintiffs are very likely more interested in clearing their names than in damages, I doubt that limiting recoveries would deter or be unfair to them. In any event, I cannot assume that the press, as successful and powerful as it is, will be intimidated into withholding news that by decent journalistic standards it believes to be true.

Given such revisionist thought, combined with the uncertain operation of a public concern standard and unknown sentiments of recent Court appointees, the constitutional law of defamation has the potential for considerable instability.[192]

B. PRIVACY

Facts and circumstances supporting a defamation action also may support a privacy claim. The claims tend to be comparable except for the type of injury suffered. In a defamation case, the harm asserted is reputational damage. Injury in a privacy action is the actual breach of privacy itself. In examining the law of privacy, it is imperative to recognize that significant disparity may exist between the law as it appears to exist and as it likely would be applied today. That reality owes to developments in privacy law, prior to *Gertz,* which coursed along a public concern rather than a public figure track. Especially in false light privacy cases, which mirror defamation actions except with respect to the actual injury claimed, it is essential to understand the law as it was enunciated earlier but recognize that subsequent developments in defamation law likely would be relevant to any future privacy jurisprudence.

The right of privacy exists pursuant to state statute or common law. Essentially four subcategories of actionability exist including a right of publicity, unreasonable intrusion into a person's privacy, unreasonable publicity of a person's private life, and false light privacy.[193]

1. Right of Publicity

A right of publicity establishes a person's interest in the availability and exploitation of name, likeness, and image.[194] Thus, a person may seek to enjoin unauthorized profiting from such qualities of self or require compensation as a condition for such usage. Actions based on appropriation are a rarity at least so far as the media are concerned. Even so, the Supreme Court has emphasized that unauthorized use of an entertainer's performance impairs a protectible proprietary interest.[195] In *Zacchini v. Scripps-Howard Broadcasting Co.,*[196] the Court determined that a television news presentation of the plaintiff's performance as a human cannonball at a county fair appropriated his entire act.[197] It is questionable, as Justice Powell noted, whether the fifteen-second clip minus prelude and fanfare truly constituted the whole act.[198] Also uncertain is whether a different result would be reached if a lesser part of an act were appropriated. If type of use and significance of the presentation are

critical, review amounts to both a qualitative and quantitative appraisal. Even if liability is established, damages may be difficult to calculate and perhaps nonexistent if publicity results in larger crowds for and enhanced profits from future performances. In any event, the Court concluded that laws protecting publicity interests, like copyright statutes, protect creative activity and thus do not offend the First Amendment.[199]

Zacchini v. Scripps-Howard Broadcasting Co., 433 U.S. 562 (1977)

Mr. Justice White delivered the opinion of the Court.

Petitioner, Hugo Zacchini, is an entertainer. He performs a "human cannonball" act in which he is shot from a cannon into a net some 200 feet away. Each performance occupies some 15 seconds. In August and September 1972, petitioner was engaged to perform his act on a regular basis at the Geauga County Fair in Burton, Ohio. He performed in a fenced area, surrounded by grandstands, at the fair grounds. Members of the public attending the fair were not charged a separate admission fee to observe his act.

On August 30, a freelance reporter for Scripps-Howard Broadcasting Co., the operator of a television broadcasting station and respondent in this case, attended the fair. He carried a small movie camera. Petitioner noticed the reporter and asked him not to film the performance. The reporter did not do so on that day; but on the instructions of the producer of respondent's daily newscast, he returned the following day and videotaped the entire act. This film clip, approximately 15 seconds in length, was shown on the 11 o'clock news program that night, together with favorable commentary.

Petitioner then brought this action for damages, alleging that he is "engaged in the entertainment business," that the act he performs is one "invented by his father and . . . performed only by his family for the last fifty years," that respondent "showed and commercialized the film of his act without his consent," and that such conduct was an "unlawful appropriation of plaintiff's professional property"....

Like the concurring judge in the Court of Appeals, the Supreme Court of Ohio rested petitioner's cause of action under state law on his "right to publicity value of his performance." 47 Ohio St. 2d 224, 351 N. E. 2d 454, 455 (1976). The opinion syllabus, to which we are to look for the rule of law used to decide the case, declared first that one may not use for his own benefit the name or likeness of another, whether or not the use or benefit is a commercial one, and second that respondent would be liable for the appropriation, over petitioner's objection and in the absence of license or privilege, of petitioner's right to the publicity value of his performance. *Ibid.* The court nevertheless gave judgment for respondent because, in the words of the syllabus:

> A TV station has a privilege to report in its newscasts matters of legitimate public interest which would otherwise be protected by an individual's right of publicity, unless the actual intent of the TV station was to appropriate the benefit of the publicity for some non-privileged private use, or unless the actual intent was to injure the individual. *Ibid.*

We granted certiorari, 429 U.S. 1037 (1977), to consider an issue unresolved by this Court: whether the First and Fourteenth Amendments immunized respondent from damages for its alleged infringement of petitioner's state-law "right of publicity." Pet. for Cert. 2. Insofar as the Ohio Supreme Court held that the First and Fourteenth Amendments of the United States Constitution required judgment for respondent, we reverse the judgment of that court.

The broadcast of a film of petitioner's entire act poses a substantial threat to the economic value of that performance. As the Ohio court recognized, this act is the product of petitioner's own talents and energy, the end result of much time, effort, and expense. Much of its economic value lies in the "right of exclusive control over the publicity given to his performance"; if the public can see the act free on television, it will be less willing to pay to see it at the fair. The effect of a public broadcast of the performance is similar to preventing petitioner from charging an admission fee. "The rationale for [protecting the right of publicity] is the straightforward one of preventing unjust enrichment by the theft of good will. No social purpose is served by having the defendant get free some aspect of the plaintiff that would have market value and for which he would normally pay." Kalven, Privacy in Tort Law—Were Warren and Brandeis Wrong?, 31 *Law & Contemp. Prob.* 326, 331 (1966). Moreover, the broadcast of petitioner's entire performance, unlike the unauthorized use of another's name for purposes of trade or the incidental use of a name or picture by the press, goes to the heart of petitioner's ability to earn a living as an entertainer. Thus, in this case, Ohio has recognized what may be the strongest case for a "right of publicity"—involving, not the appropriation of an entertainer's reputation to enhance the attractiveness of a commercial product, but the appropriation of the very activity by which the entertainer acquired his reputation in the first place.

Of course, Ohio's decision to protect petitioner's right of publicity here rests on more than a desire to compensate the performer for the time and effort invested in his act; the protection provides an economic incentive for him to make the investment required to produce a performance of interest to the public. This same consideration underlies the patent and copyright laws long enforced by this Court. As the Court stated in *Mazer v. Stein*, 347 U.S. 201, 219 (1954):

> The economic philosophy behind the clause empowering Congress to grant patents and copyrights is the conviction that encouragement of individual effort by personal gain is the best way to advance public welfare through the talents of authors and inventors in "Science and useful Arts." Sacrificial days devoted to such creative activities deserve rewards commensurate with the services rendered.

These laws perhaps regard the "reward to the owner [as] a secondary consideration," *United States v. Paramount Pictures*, 334 U.S. 131, 158 (1948), but they were "intended definitely to grant valuable, enforceable rights" in order to afford greater encouragement to the production of works of benefit to the public. *Washingtonian Publishing Co. v. Pearson*, 306 U.S. 30, 36 (1939). The Constitution does not prevent Ohio from making a similar choice here in deciding to protect the entertainer's incentive in order to encourage the production of this type of work. Cf.

Goldstein v. California, 412 U.S. 546 (1973); *Kewanee Oil Co. v. Bicron Corp.*, 416 U.S. 470 (1974).

There is no doubt that entertainment, as well as news, enjoys First Amendment protection. It is also true that entertainment itself can be important news. *Time, Inc. v. Hill.* But it is important to note that neither the public nor respondent will be deprived of the benefit of petitioner's performance as long as his commercial stake in his act is appropriately recognized. Petitioner does not seek to enjoin the broadcast of his performance; he simply wants to be paid for it. Nor do we think that a state-law damages remedy against respondent would represent a species of liability without fault contrary to the letter or spirit of *Gertz v. Robert Welch, Inc.*, 418 U.S. 323 (1974). Respondent knew that petitioner objected to televising his act but nevertheless displayed the entire film.

We conclude that although the State of Ohio may as a matter of its own law privilege the press in the circumstances of this case, the First and Fourteenth Amendments do not require it to do so.

Reversed.

Mr. Justice Powell, with whom Mr. Justice Brennan and Mr. Justice Marshall join, dissenting.

Disclaiming any attempt to do more than decide the narrow case before us, the Court reverses the decision of the Supreme Court of Ohio based on repeated incantation of a single formula: "a performer's entire act." The holding today is summed up in one sentence:

> Wherever the line in particular situations is to be drawn between media reports that are protected and those that are not, we are quite sure that the First and Fourteenth Amendments do not immunize the media when they broadcast a performer's entire act without his consent. *Ante,* at 574–575.

I doubt that this formula provides a standard clear enough even for resolution of this case. In any event, I am not persuaded that the Court's opinion is appropriately sensitive to the First Amendment values at stake, and I therefore dissent.

Although the Court would draw no distinction, *ante,* at 575, I do not view respondent's action as comparable to unauthorized commercial broadcasts of sporting events, theatrical performances,

and the like where the broadcaster keeps the profits. There is no suggestion here that respondent made any such use of the film. Instead, it simply reported on what petitioner concedes to be a newsworthy event, in a way hardly surprising for a television station—by means of film coverage. The report was part of an ordinary daily news program, consuming a total of 15 seconds. It is a routine example of the press' fulfilling the informing function so vital to our system.

The Court's holding that the station's ordinary news report may give rise to substantial liability has disturbing implications, for the decision could lead to a degree of media self-censorship. Cf. *Smith v. California*, 361 U.S. 147, 150–154 (1959). Hereafter, whenever a television news editor is unsure whether certain film footage received from a camera crew might be held to portray an "entire act," he may decline coverage—even of clearly newsworthy events—or confine the broadcast to watered-down verbal reporting, perhaps with an occasional still picture. The public is then the loser. This is hardly the kind of news reportage that the First Amendment is meant to foster. See generally *Miami Herald Publishing Co. v. Tornillo*, 418 U.S. 241, 257–258 (1974); *Time, Inc. v. Hill*, 385 U.S. 374, 389 (1967); *New York Times Co. v. Sullivan*, 376 U.S. 254, 270–272, 279 (1964).

In my view the First Amendment commands a different analytical starting point from the one selected by the Court. Rather than begin with a quantitative analysis of the performer's behavior—is this or is this not his entire act?—we should direct initial attention to the actions of the news media: what use did the station make of the film footage? When a film is used, as here, for a routine portion of a regular news program, I would hold that the First Amendment protects the station from a "right of publicity" or "appropriation" suit, absent a strong showing by the plaintiff that the news broadcast was a subterfuge or cover for private or commercial exploitation.

I emphasize that this is a "reappropriation" suit, rather than one of the other varieties of "right of privacy" tort suits identified by Dean Prosser in his classic article. Prosser, Privacy, 48 *Calif. L. Rev.* 383 (1960). In those other causes of action the competing interests are considerably different. The plaintiff generally seeks to avoid any sort of public exposure, and the existence of constitutional privilege is therefore less likely to turn on whether the publication occurred in a news broadcast or in some other fashion. In a suit like the one before us, however, the plaintiff does not complain about the fact of exposure to the public, but rather about its timing or manner. He welcomes some publicity, but seeks to retain control over means and manner as a way to maximize for himself the monetary benefits that flow from such publication. But having made the matter public—having chosen, in essence, to make it newsworthy—he cannot, consistent with the First Amendment, complain of routine news reportage. Cf. *Gertz v. Robert Welch, Inc.,* 418 U.S. 323, 339–348, 351–352 (1974) (clarifying the different liability standards appropriate in defamation suits, depending on whether or not the plaintiff is a public figure).

Since the film clip here was undeniably treated as news and since there is no claim that the use was subterfuge, respondent's actions were constitutionally privileged. I would affirm.

2. Intrusion

Actions asserting invasion of a legally protected zone of privacy, such as a home or office, also are infrequent. Typical defendants in instances when they do occur, however, are the media. Actionable intrusion may result from the use of video or audio technology enabling a reporter to snoop into private space and obtain information that otherwise would be confidential.[200] Unlike other actions for privacy, the intrusion itself is sufficient to complete the wrong and no publication is required.[201] Nor is newsworthiness necessarily a defense against such a claim. In *Dietemann v. Time, Inc.,*[202] reporters from a magazine used false representations to obtain entry into the plaintiff's home.[203] With use of a hidden camera and recording equipment, they elicited information demonstrating that the plaintiff was a medical quack.[204] Nonetheless, the plaintiff prevailed on his privacy claim because the First Amendment afforded no protection against liability that might arise in the course of news gathering.[205] The wrong was not the publi-

cation of the story but the intrusion effectuated by false pretenses.[206] Investigative journalists, and undercover reporters should be especially alert that intrusion as a consequence of misrepresentation is hazardous. A mitigating reality may be that if wrongdoing is revealed but the public interest is advanced by the actionable procedure, sympathy for the ends may factor into a jury's damage award punishing the means.

The use of purloined documents or leaked information may present ethical questions, but it does not necessarily create a legal problem at least for the media.[207] Those who steal or reveal information, however, may be subject to criminal or civil liability themselves.

3. Disclosure of Intimate Details

Publication of accurate facts that are damaging do not give rise to a defamation action, since truth is a defense, but still may support a privacy claim. In *Cox Broadcasting Corp. v. Cohn,*[208] the Court determined that the media could not be held liable by statute or common law for publishing damaging or embarrassing information contained in records open to the public.[209] The plaintiff had sued the television station for identifying his deceased daughter as a murder-rape victim.[210] Although the Court curtailed the reach of the tort, it did not eliminate the availability of an action altogether. Left open is the possibility that a privacy claim based on truthful but damaging statements can be asserted when information was not obtained from a public record. If the Court is not willing to provide comprehensive protection for the media, it becomes necessary to determine how far a newsworthiness defense or privilege might reach and whether liability should vary, as in a defamation action, according to the plaintiff's status.

The Court refused an opportunity to clarify the ambit of First Amendment interest in such instances when it denied review in *Virgil v. Time, Inc.*[211] The case concerned a story about a surfer who was interviewed but revoked his consent upon learning that the article would address some of his bizarre personal ways as well as his surfing.[212] The court of appeals refused to accept the argument that truth affords complete defense against a privacy claim premised on true but harmful facts.[213] Such a holding prevents the First Amendment from swallowing an entire category of tort. At the same time, the determination that a defense requires a showing that the story is newsworthy, and not just an appeal to the public's idle curiosity, complicates the process of achieving principled results. Separating the public's idle curiosity from the public interest implicates the same exercises that plagued early suggestions to have the media focus upon matters of "genuine community concern"[214] and early decisions suggesting a constitutional line between information and entertainment.[215] As eventually became manifest, "the line between the informing and the entertaining is too elusive for the protection of that basic right [a free press]. . . . What is one man's amusement, teaches another's doctrine."[216] Nonetheless, it is the type of line, evidenced by the Court's observation that a divorce proceeding was not the type of controversy it had in mind when setting the qualifications of a public figure,[217] that it still seems inclined to draw albeit subjectively and unpredictably.

The *Cohn* decision and its aftermath did not determine the general question of whether publication of truthful information ever could be punished consistent with the First Amendment. Nor was the more specific issue resolved of whether truthful publication ever could give rise to criminal or civil liability for invading a zone of privacy. Although recently afforded the opportunity to consider either proposition, the Court again declined to issue a comprehensive statement. In *The Florida Star v. B.J.F.*,[218] it concluded "that the sensitivity and significance

of the interests presented in clashes between the First Amendment and privacy rights counsel relying on limited principles that sweep no more broadly than the appropriate context of the [immediate] case."[219] The Court thus determined that a newspaper could not be held liable for publication of a rape victim's identity when it obtained her name from a publicly released police report.[220]

The state in the *Florida Star* case had made it unlawful only for an "instrument of mass communication" to disclose the name of a sex offense victim.[221] The statute was premised upon the interests of securing the privacy of victims, protecting them from retaliation, and encouraging reporting of crimes without fear of exposure.[222] The Court observed, however, that publication of lawfully obtained information concerning "a matter of public significance" could not be punished "absent a need to further a state interest of the highest order."[223] Because the information was contained in a government news release (indicating the government had failed to police itself), truthful speech was punished without a scienter requirement, and the statute was underinclusive insofar as it reached only the mass media, the Court found a failure to further an "interest of the highest order."[224]

The Florida Star v. B.J.F., 109 S.Ct. 2603 (1989)

Appellant, *The Florida Star*, is a newspaper which publishes a "Police Reports" section containing brief articles describing local criminal incidents under police investigation. After appellee B.J.F. reported to the Sheriff's Department that she had been robbed and sexually assaulted, the Department prepared a report, which identified B.J.F. by her full name, and placed it in the Department's press room. The Department does not restrict access to the room or to the reports available there. A *Star* reporter-trainee sent to the press room copied the police report verbatim, including B.J.F.'s full name. Consequently, her name was included in a "Police Reports" story in the paper, in violation of the *Star*'s internal policy. Florida Stat. § 794.03 makes it unlawful to "print, publish, or broadcast...in any instrument of mass communication" the name of the victim of a sexual offense. B.J.F. filed suit in a Florida court alleging, *inter alia*, that the *Star* had negligently violated § 794.03. The trial court denied the *Star*'s motion to dismiss, which claimed, among other things, that imposing civil sanctions on the newspaper pursuant to § 794.03 violated the First Amendment. However, it granted B.J.F.'s motion for a directed verdict on the issue of negligence, finding the *Star per se* negligent based on its violation of § 794.03. The jury then awarded B.J.F. both compensatory and punitive damages. The verdict was upheld on appeal.

Justice Marshall delivered the opinion of the Court.

The tension between the right which the First Amendment accords to a free press, on the one hand, and the protections which various statutes and common-law doctrines accord to personal privacy against the publication of truthful information, on the other, is a subject we have addressed several times in recent years. Our decisions in cases involving government attempts to sanction the accurate dissemination of information as invasive of privacy, have not, however, exhaustively considered this conflict. On the contrary, although our decisions have without exception upheld the press' right to publish, we have emphasized each time that we were resolving this conflict only as it arose in a discrete factual context.

We conclude that imposing damages on appellant for publishing B.J.F.'s name violates the First Amendment, although not for either of the reasons appellant urges. Despite the strong resemblance this case bears to *Cox Broadcasting*, that case cannot fairly be read as controlling here. The name of the rape victim in that case was obtained from courthouse records that were open to public inspection, a fact which Justice White's opinion for the Court repeatedly noted. 420 U.S., at 492, 95 S.Ct., at 1044–45 (noting "special protected nature of accurate reports of *judicial* proceed-

ings") (emphasis added); see also *id.*, at 493, 496, 95 S.Ct., at 1045, 1046–47. Significantly, one of the reasons we gave in *Cox Broadcasting* for invalidating the challenged damages award was the important role the press plays in subjecting trials to public scrutiny and thereby helping guarantee their fairness. *Id.*, at 492–493, 95 S.Ct., at 1044–1045. That role is not directly compromised where, as here, the information in question comes from a police report prepared and disseminated at a time at which not only had no adversarial criminal proceedings begun, but no suspect had been identified.

Nor need we accept appellant's invitation to hold broadly that truthful publication may never be punished consistent with the First Amendment. Our cases have carefully eschewed reaching this ultimate question, mindful that the future may bring scenarios which prudence counsels our not resolving anticipatorily. See, e.g., *Near v. Minnesota ex rel. Olson*, 283 U.S. 697, 716, (1931) (hypothesizing "publication of the sailing dates of transports or the number and location of troops"); see also *Garrison v. Louisiana*, 379 U.S. 64, 72, n. 8, 74 (1964) (endorsing absolute defense of truth "where discussion of public affairs is concerned," but leaving unsettled the constitutional implications of truthfulness "in the discrete area of purely private libels"); *Landmark Communications, Inc. v. Virginia*, 435 U.S. 829, 838 (1978); *Time, Inc. v. Hill*, 385 U.S. 374, 383, n. 7 (1967). Indeed, in *Cox Broadcasting*, we pointedly refused to answer even the less sweeping question "whether truthful publications may ever be subjected to civil or criminal liability" for invading "an area of privacy" defined by the State. 420 U.S., at 491. Respecting the fact that press freedom and privacy rights are both "plainly rooted in the traditions and significant concerns of our society," we instead focused on the less sweeping issue of "whether the State may impose sanctions on the accurate publication of the name of a rape victim obtained from public records—more specifically, from judicial records which are maintained in connection with a public prosecution and which themselves are open to public inspection." *Ibid.* We continue to believe that the sensitivity and significance of the interests presented in clashes between First Amendment and privacy rights counsel relying on limited principles that sweep no more broadly than the appropriate context of the instant case.

The first inquiry is whether the newspaper "lawfully obtain[ed] truthful information about a matter of public significance." 443 U.S., at 103, 99 S.Ct., at 2671. It is undisputed that the news article describing the assault on B.J.F. was accurate. In addition, appellant lawfully obtained B.J.F.'s name. Appellee's argument to the contrary is based on the fact that under Florida law, police reports which reveal the identity of the victim of a sexual offense are not among the matters of "public record" which the public, by law, is entitled to inspect. Brief for Appellee 17–18, citing Fla.Stat. § 119.07(3)(h) (1983). But the fact that state officials are not required to disclose such reports does not make it unlawful for a newspaper to receive them when furnished by the government. Nor does the fact that the Department apparently failed to fulfill its obligation under § 794.03 not to "cause or allow to be... published" the name of a sexual offense victim make the newspaper's ensuing receipt of this information unlawful. Even assuming the Constitution permitted a State to proscribe *receipt* of information, Florida has not taken this step. It is, clear, furthermore, that the news article concerned "a matter of public significance," 443 U.S., at 103, in the sense in which the *Daily Mail* synthesis of prior cases used that term. That is, the article generally, as opposed to the specific identity contained within it, involved a matter of paramount public import: the commission, and investigation, of a violent crime which had been reported to authorities. See *Cox Broadcasting, supra* (article identifying victim of rape-murder); *Oklahoma Publishing Co. v. District Court,* 430 U.S. 308 (1977) (article identifying juvenile alleged to have committed murder); *Daily Mail, supra* (same); cf. *Landmark Communications, Inc. v. Virginia,* 435 U.S. 829 (1978) (article identifying judges whose conduct was being investigated).

The second inquiry is whether imposing liability on appellant pursuant to § 794.03 serves "a need to further a state interest of the highest order." *Daily Mail,* 443 U.S., at 103, 99 S.Ct., at 2671. Appellee argues that a rule punishing publication furthers three closely related interests: the privacy of victims of sexual offenses; the phys-

ical safety of such victims, who may be targeted for retaliation if their names become known to their assailants; and the goal of encouraging victims of such crimes to report these offenses without fear of exposure. Brief for Appellee 29–30.

At a time in which we are daily reminded of the tragic reality of rape, it is undeniable that these are highly significant interests, a fact underscored by the Florida Legislature's explicit attempt to protect these interests by enacting a criminal statute prohibiting much dissemination of victim identities. We accordingly do not rule out the possibility that, in a proper case, imposing civil sanctions for publication of the name of a rape victim might be so overwhelmingly necessary to advance these interests as to satisfy the *Daily Mail* standard. For three independent reasons, however, imposing liability for publication under the circumstances of this case is too precipitous a means of advancing these interests to convince us that there is a "need" within the meaning of the *Daily Mail* formulation for Florida to take this extreme step. Cf. *Landmark Communications, supra* (invalidating penalty on publication despite State's expressed interest in nondissemination, reflected in statue prohibiting unauthorized divulging of names of judges under investigation).

First is the manner in which appellant obtained the identifying information in question. As we have noted, where the government itself provides information to the media, it is most appropriate to assume that the government had, but failed to utilize, far more limited means of guarding against dissemination than the extreme step of punishing truthful speech. That assumption is richly borne out in this case. B.J.F.'s identity would never have come to light were it not for the erroneous, if inadvertent, inclusion by the Department of her full name in an incident report made available in a press room open to the public. Florida's policy against disclosure of rape victims' identities, reflected in § 794.03, was undercut by the Department's failure to abide by this policy. Where, as here, the government has failed to police itself in disseminating information, it is clear under *Cox Broadcasting, Oklahoma Publishing,* and *Landmark Communications* that the imposition of damages against the press for its subsequent publication can hardly be said to be a narrowly tailored means of safeguarding anonymity. See *supra,* at 2609. Once the government has placed such information in the public domain, "reliance must rest upon the judgment of those who decide what to publish or broadcast," *Cox Broadcasting,* 420 U.S., at 496, and hopes for restitution must rest upon the willingness of the government to compensate victims for their loss of privacy, and to protect them from the other consequences of its mishandling of the information which these victims provided in confidence.

That appellant gained access to the information in question through a government news release makes it especially likely that, if liability were to be imposed, self-censorship would result. Reliance on a news release is a paradigmatically "routine newspaper reporting techniqu[e]." *Daily Mail,* 443 U.S., at 103. The government's issuance of such a release, without qualification, can only convey to recipients that the government considered dissemination lawful, and indeed expected the recipients to disseminate the information further. Had appellant merely reproduced the news release prepared and released by the Department, imposing civil damages would surely violate the First Amendment. The fact that appellant converted the police report into a news story by adding the linguistic connecting tissue necessary to transform the report's facts into full sentences cannot change this result.

A second problem with Florida's imposition of liability for publication is the broad sweep of the negligence *per se* standard applied under the civil cause of action implied from § 794.03. Unlike claims based on the common law tort of invasion of privacy, see Restatement (Second) of Torts § 652D (1977), civil actions based on § 794.03 require no case-by-case findings that the disclosure of a fact about a person's private life was one that a reasonable person would find highly offensive. On the contrary, under the *per se* theory of negligence adopted by the courts below, liability follows automatically from publication. This is so regardless of whether the identity of the victim is already known throughout the community; whether the victim has voluntarily called public attention to the offense; or whether the identity

of the victim has otherwise become a reasonable subject of public concern—. . . .

Third, and finally, the facial underinclusiveness of § 794.03 raises serious doubts about whether Florida is, in fact, serving, with this statute, the significant interests which appellee invokes in support of affirmance. [It] prohibits the publication of identifying information only if this information appears in an "instrument of mass communication" . . . and does not prohibit the spread by any other means of the identities of victims of sexual offenses. . . .

When a State attempts the extraordinary measure of punishing truthful publication in the name of privacy, it must demonstrate its commitment to advancing this interest by applying its prohibition evenhandedly, to the smalltime disseminator as well as the media giant. Where important First Amendment interests are at stake, the mass scope of disclosure is not an acceptable surrogate for injury. A ban on disclosures effected by "instrument[s] of mass communication" simply cannot be defended on the ground that partial prohibitions may effect partial relief. See *Daily Mail,* 443 U.S., at 104–105, (statute is insufficiently tailored to interest in protecting anonymity where it restricted only newspapers, not the electronic media or other forms of publication, from identifying juvenile defendants); *id.,* at 110, (Rehnquist, J., concurring in judgment) (same); cf. *Arkansas Writers' Project, Inc. v. Ragland,* 481 U.S. 221, 229, 107 S.Ct. 1722, 1727, 95 L.Ed.2d 209 (1987); *Minneapolis Star & Tribune Co. v. Minnesota Comm'r of Revenue,* 460 U.S. 575, 585 (1983). Without more careful and inclusive precautions against alternative forms of dissemination, we cannot conclude that Florida's selective ban on publication by the mass media satisfactorily accomplishes its stated purpose.

Our holding today is limited. We do not hold that truthful publication is automatically constitutionally protected, or that there is no zone of personal privacy within which the State may protect the individual from intrusion by the press, or even that a State may never punish publication of the name of a victim of a sexual offense. We hold only that where a newspaper publishes truthful information which it has lawfully obtained, punishment may lawfully be imposed, if at all, only when narrowly tailored to a state interest of the highest order, and that no such interest is satisfactorily served by imposing liability under § 794.03 to appellant under the facts of this case. The decision below is therefore

Reversed.

Justice White, with whom the Chief Justice and Justice O'Connor join, dissenting.

"Short of homicide, [rape] is the 'ultimate violation of self.' " *Coker v. Georgia,* 433 U.S. 584, 597 (1977) (opinion of White, J.). For B.J.F., however, the violation she suffered at a rapist's knifepoint marked only the beginning of her ordeal. A week later, while her assailant was still at large, an account of this assault—identifying by name B.J.F. as the victim—was published by *The Florida Star.* As a result, B.J.F. received harassing phone calls, required mental health counseling, was forced to move from her home, and was even threatened with being raped again. Yet today, the Court holds that a jury award of $75,000 to compensate B.J.F. for the harm she suffered due to the *Star*'s negligence is at odds with the First Amendment. I do not accept this result. . . .

We are left, then, to wonder whether the three "independent reasons" the Court cites for reversing the judgment for B.J.F. support its result. See *Ante.* . . .

The first of these reasons relied on by the Court is the fact "appellant gained access to [B.J.F.'s name] through a government news release." *Ante,* . . . "The government's issuance of such a release, without qualification, can only convey to recipients that the government considered dissemination lawful," the Court suggests. *Ibid.* So described, this case begins to look like the situation in *Oklahoma Publishing,* where a judge invited reporters into his courtroom, but then tried to forbid them from reporting on the proceedings they observed. But this case is profoundly different. Here, the "release" of information provided by the government was not, as the Court says, "without qualification." As the *Star*'s own reporter conceded at trial, the crime incident report that inadvertently included B.J.F.'s name was posted in a room that contained signs making it clear that the names of rape victims were not matters of public record, and were not to be published. See 2 Record 113, 115, 117. The *Star*'s

reporter indicated that she understood that she "[was not] allowed to take down that information" (*i.e.,* B.J.F.'s name) and that she "[was] not supposed to take the information from the police department." *Id.,* at 117. Thus, by her own admission the posting of the incident report did not convey to the *Star*'s reporter the idea that "the government considered dissemination lawful"; the Court's suggestion to the contrary is inapt.

Instead, Florida has done precisely what we suggested, in *Cox Broadcasting,* that States wishing to protect the privacy rights of rape victims might do: "respond [to the challenge] by means which *avoid* public documentation or other exposure of private information." *Cox Broadcasting,* 420 U.S., at 496 (emphasis added). By amending its public records statute to exempt rape victims names from disclosure, Fla. Stat. § 119.07(3)(h) (1983), and forbidding its officials from releasing such information, Fla. Stat. § 794.03 (1983), the State has taken virtually every step imaginable to prevent what happened here. This case presents a far cry, then, from *Cox Broadcasting* or *Oklahoma Publishing,* where the State asked the news media not to publish information it had made generally available to the public: here, the State is not asking the media to do the State's job in the first instance. Unfortunately, as this case illustrates, mistakes happen: even when States take measures to "avoid" disclosure, sometimes rape victims' names are found out. As I see it, it is not too much to ask the press, in instances such as this, to respect simple standards of decency and refrain from publishing a victim's name, address, and/or phone number.

Second, the Court complains that appellant was judged here under too strict a liability standard. The Court contends that a newspaper might be found liable under the Florida courts' negligence *per se* theory without regard to a newspaper's scienter or degree of fault. *Ante,* . . . . The short answer to this complaint is that whatever merit the Court's argument might have, it is wholly inapposite here, where the jury found that appellant acted with "reckless indifference towards the rights of others," 2 Record 170, a standard far higher than the *Gertz* standard the Court urges as a constitutional minimum today. *Ante,* . . . . B.J.F. proved the *Star*'s negligence at trial—and, actually, far more than simple negligence; the

Court's concerns about damages resting on a strict liability or mere causation basis are irrelevant to the validity of the judgment for appellee.

But even taking the Court's concerns in the abstract, they miss the mark. Permitting liability under a negligence *per se* theory does not mean that defendants will be held liable without a showing of negligence, but rather, that the standard of care has been set by the legislature, instead of the courts. The Court says that negligence *per se* permits a plaintiff to hold a defendant liable without a showing that the disclosure was "of a fact about a person's private life... that a reasonable person would find highly offensive." *Ibid.* But the point here is that the legislature—reflecting popular sentiment—has determined that disclosure of the fact that a person was raped is categorically a revelation that reasonable people find offensive. And as for the Court's suggestion that the Florida courts' theory permits liability without regard for whether the victim's identity is already known, or whether she herself has made it known—these are facts that would surely enter into the calculation of damages in such a case. In any event, none of these mitigating factors was present here; whatever the force of these arguments generally, they do not justify the Court's ruling against B.J.F. in this case.

Third, the Court faults the Florida criminal statute for being underinclusive: § 794.03 covers disclosure of rape victims' names in "instrument[s] of mass communication," but not other means of distribution, the Court observes. *Ante,.* ...But our cases which have struck down laws that limit or burden the press due to their underinclusiveness have involved situations where a legislature has singled out one segment of the news media or press for adverse treatment, see, *e.g., Daily Mail* (restricting newspapers and not radio or television), or singled out the press for adverse treatment when compared to other similarly situated enterprises, see, *e.g., Minneapolis Star & Tribune Co. v. Minnesota Comm'r of Revenue,* 460 U.S. 575, 578 (1983). Here, the Florida law evenhandedly covers all "instrument[s] of mass communication" no matter their form, media, content, nature or purpose. It excludes neighborhood gossips, cf. *ante,* at 2612–2613, because presumably the Florida Legislature has determined that neighborhood gossips do not pose the

danger and intrusion to rape victims that "instrument[s] of mass communication" do. Simply put: Florida wanted to prevent the widespread distribution of rape victims' names, and therefore enacted a statute tailored almost as precisely as possible to achieving that end.

Moreover, the Court's "underinclusiveness" analysis itself is "underinclusive." After all, the lawsuit against the *Star* which is at issue here is not an action for violating the statute which the Court deems underinclusive, but is, more accurately, for the negligent publication of appellee's name. See App. to Juris. Statement A10. The scheme which the Court should review, then, is not only § 794.03 (which, as noted above, merely provided the standard of care in this litigation), but rather, the whole of Florida privacy tort law. As to the latter, Florida does recognize a tort of publication of private facts. Thus, it is quite possible that the neighborhood gossip whom the Court so fears being left scot-free to spread news of a rape victim's identity would be subjected to the same (or similar) liability regime under which appellant was taxed. The Court's myopic focus on § 794.03 ignores the probability that Florida law is more comprehensive than the Court gives it credit for being.

Consequently, neither the State's "dissemination" of B.J.F.'s name, nor the standard of liability imposed here, nor the underinclusiveness of Florida tort law require setting aside the verdict for B.J.F. And as noted above, such a result is not compelled by our cases. I turn, therefore, to the more general principles at issue here to see if they recommend the Court's result.

III

At issue in this case is whether there is any information about people, which—though true—may not be published in the press. By holding that only "a state interest of the highest order" permits the State to penalize the publication of truthful information, and by holding that protecting a rape victim's right to privacy is not among those state interests of the highest order, the Court accepts appellant's invitation, see Tr. of Oral Arg. 10–11, to obliterate one of the most note-worthy legal inventions of the 20th-Century: the tort of the publication of private facts. W. Prosser, J. Wade, & V. Schwartz, Torts 951–952 (8th ed. 1988). Even if the Court's opinion does not say as much today, such obliteration will follow inevitably from the Court's conclusion here. If the First Amendment prohibits its wholly private persons (such as B.J.F.) from recovering for the publication of the fact that she was raped, I doubt that there remain any "private facts" which persons may assume will not be published in the newspapers, or broadcast on television.

Of course, the right to privacy is not absolute. Even the article widely relied upon in cases vindicating privacy rights, Warren & Brandeis, The Right to Privacy, 4 *Harv. L. Rev.*, at 193, recognized that this right inevitably conflicts with the public's right to know about matters of general concern—and that sometimes, the latter must trump the former. *Id.*, at 214–215. Resolving this conflict is a difficult matter, and I do not fault the Court for attempting to strike an appropriate balance between the two, but rather, for according too little weight to B.J.F.'s side of equation, and too much on the other.

I would strike the balance rather differently. Writing for the Ninth Circuit, Judge Merrill put this view eloquently:

Does the spirit of the Bill of Rights require that individuals be free to pry into the unnewsworthy private affairs of their fellowmen? In our view it does not. In our view, fairly defined areas of privacy must have the protection of law if the quality of life is to continue to be reasonably acceptable. The public's right to know is, then, subject to reasonable limitations so far as concerns the private facts of its individual members. *Virgil v. Time, Inc.*, 527 F.2d 1122, 1128 (1975), cert. denied, 425 U.S. 998 (1976).

Ironically, this Court, too, had occasion to consider this same balance just a few weeks ago, in *United States Department of Justice v. Reporters Committee for Freedom of the Press*, 489 U.S. _____ (1989). There, we were faced with a press request, under the Freedom of Information Act, for a "rap sheet" on a person accused of bribing a Congressman—presumably, a person whose privacy rights would be far less than B.J.F.'s. Yet this Court rejected the media's request for disclosure of the "rap sheet," saying:

The privacy interest in maintaining the practical obscurity of rap-sheet information will always be high.

When the subject of such a rap sheet is a private citizen and when the information is in the Government's control as a compilation, rather than as a record of "what the government is up to," the privacy interest . . . is . . . at its apex while the . . . public interest in disclosure is at its nadir. *Id.*, at _____ , 109 S.Ct., at 1485.

The Court went on to conclude that disclosure of rap sheets "categorical[ly]" constitutes an "unwarranted" invasion of privacy. *Id.*, at _____ . The same surely must be true—indeed, much more so—for the disclosure of a rape victim's name.

I do not suggest that the Court's decision today is radical departure from a previously charted course. The Court's ruling has been foreshadowed. In *Time, Inc. v. Hill*, 385 U.S. 374, 383–384, n. 7 (1967), we observed that—after a brief period early in this century where Brandeis' view was ascendant—the trend in "modern" jurisprudence has been to eclipse an individual's right to maintain private any truthful information that the press wished to publish. More recently, in *Cox Broadcasting*, 420 U.S. at 491, we acknowledged the possibility that the First Amendment may prevent a State from ever subjecting the publication of truthful but private information to civil liability. Today, we hit the bottom of the slippery slope.

I would find a place to draw the line higher on the hillside: a spot high enough to protect B.J.F.'s desire for privacy and peace-of-mind in the wake of a horrible personal tragedy. There is no public interest in publishing the names, addresses, and phone numbers of persons who are the victims of crime—and no public interest in immunizing the press from liability in the rare cases where a State's efforts to protect a victim's privacy have failed. Consequently, I respectfully dissent.

Despite its holding, the Court emphasized that it did not find truthful publication categorically and automatically protected, or that publication of a sex offense victim's name never could be punished.[225] It also disregarded the warning in *Gertz*, unheeded also in *Dun & Bradstreet*, against drawing lines pursuant to such subjective standards as public concern or public significance.

4. False Light Privacy

A false light privacy action is most evocative of and may be intertwined with a defamation claim. Liability arises insofar as a false portrayal of a person may invade privacy regardless of whether the falsehood is actionable as defamation. In *Time, Inc. v. Hill*,[226] the plaintiff had stated a false light privacy claim on the grounds that the magazine had inaccurately depicted what had occurred to him and his family when they had been taken captive by a group of escaped convicts.[227] In real life, they had been held hostage but never harmed.[228] The magazine's reporting of a play, showing similar circumstances but including violence and verbal abuse, presented photographs of actors reenacting events at the plaintiff's home and purporting to recount the incident there.[229]

Although state law did not provide a newsworthiness defense, the Court introduced a standard of that ilk. It held that liability could not be established if (1) the plaintiffs were implicated in a matter of public interest[230] and (2) the article was published with knowledge of its falsity or with reckless disregard of the truth.[231] The determination essentially transferred the actual malice standard from the defamation context to the related false light privacy setting and extended its reach beyond public officials and public figures. For false light privacy purposes, the Court embraced a standard that subsequently would not command a majority in the defamation setting. The Court in the latter instance, as noted previously, has veered away from similarly assessing persons who voluntarily or involuntarily became objects of public interest.[232]

The rerouting of defamation law from a public interest to a public figure focus suggests that a false light privacy claim today would be analyzed pursuant to the standards of *Gertz* rather than *Hill*. In *Cantrell v. Forest City Publishing Co.*,[233] the Court affirmed liability on a false light privacy theory for the publication of an article mischaracterizing a family's living conditions, and causing mental distress and humiliation.[234] Jury instructions were framed in terms of having to prove actual malice,[235] and reckless disregard was established. The Court thus considered it inapt to determine whether, in an action by a private figure, a lesser showing of scienter could have sufficed.[236] Given the identical nature of defamation and false light privacy actions in all aspects but the technical nature of the injury, it would be surprising if the standards for scienter were to be as asymmetrical as established case law otherwise might suggest.

C. PUBLIC MORALS

1. Obscenity

Unlike defamation, expression denominated as obscene has not been welcomed into the protective fold of the First Amendment. Obscenity is a form of expression which the Court consistently has found to have "no essential part of any exposition of ideas, and [is] of such slight social value as a step to the truth that any benefit derived from [it] is clearly outweighed by the social interest in morality."[237] Even before any formal pronouncement, the Court appears to have assumed that obscenity was not safeguarded by the First Amendment. In *Near v. Minnesota*,[238] the Court noted that the state's interest in regulating obscenity constituted one of the few exceptions justifying departure from the normal rule against prior restraint.[239] Because any definition of obscenity is unlikely to be consensual, much of the Supreme Court's energy has been devoted to constructing standards that will be broadly subscribed to and workable. The effort itself has largely succeeded in demonstrating how invariably subjective the concept is. Nonetheless, criteria persist both for identifying obscenity and punishing its dissemination.

Despite multiple allusions in dicta to the unprotected nature of obscenity, it was not until 1957 that the Court made that status official. In *Roth v. United States*,[240] the Court found "implicit in the history of the first amendment... rejection of obscenity as utterly without redeeming social importance."[241] Noting that ideas with even the slightest social importance have full First Amendment security, the Court added that "obscenity is not within the area of constitutionally protected speech or press."[242]

Having carved out a special category of expression immune from constitutional norms, the Court turned to the still daunting task of defining it. In *Roth*, the Court depicted obscenity as "material which deals with sex in a manner appealing to prurient interest."[243] The term prurient is at best imprecise and was not particularly well fleshed out, as the Court's dictionary references to "(i)tching; longing; uneasy with desire or longing [and so on]" suggest.[244] Given a concept that did not lend itself to a clearly articulable and objectifiable definition, the Court provided for individualized assessments of whether "to the average person, applying contemporary standards, the dominant theme of the material taken as a whole appeals to prurient interest."[245]

Although largely formalizing what previously had been assumed with respect to obscenity and the constitution, the *Roth* decision had significant and enduring implications. Without any First Amendment status, expression denominated as obscene can be freely regulated. As the Court noted, it is unnecessary in a particular instance to identify a competing interest or even prove harm as a basis for regulation.[246] The *Roth* case disclosed both extremes in the spectrum of philosophies and attitudes that continues to characterize the debate over obscenity. Contrary to the Court's notion that such expression is categorically unprotected, Justices Douglas and Black argued that obscenity could be suppressed only if "so closely brigaded with illegal action as to be an inseparable part of it."[247] Their dissent raised questions and concerns that largely have been avoided by analysis consisting of categorical exclusion and consequent deference to regulatory supposition. As Douglas and Black observed, it was an assumption rather than provable fact that "the arousing of sexual thoughts and desires [which] happens every day in normal life in dozens of ways"[248] is worthless. Nonetheless, the Court has never seriously or openly questioned the press and even has gone out of its way to dismiss any need for requiring a causal connection between obscenity and illegality or harm. Some years later, the Court would point out that "(f)rom the beginning of civilized societies, legislators and judges have acted on various unprovable assumptions."[249] Such an observation contrasts with its demands for compelling reasons for official occlusion of a constitutional interest and strong proof that the regulatory action taken truly advances the legitimate and pressing governmental concern. The Roth Court, however, was untroubled by the absence of conclusive proof of linkage between obscene material and antisocial behavior and willing to countenance presumption of such a connection.[250]

Roth v. United States, 354 U.S. 476 (1957)

Mr. Justice Brennan delivered the opinion of the Court.

The dispositive question is whether obscenity is utterance within the area of protected speech and press. Although this is the first time the question has been squarely presented to this Court, either under the First Amendment or under the Fourteenth Amendment, expressions found in numerous opinions indicate that this Court has always assumed that obscenity is not protected by the freedoms of speech and press. . . .

The guaranties of freedom of expression in effect in 10 of the 14 States which by 1792 had ratified the Constitution, gave no absolute protection for every utterance. Thirteen of the 14 States provided for the prosecution of libel, and all of those States made either blasphemy or profanity, or both, statutory crimes. As early as 1712, Massachusetts made it criminal to publish "any filthy, obscene, or profane song, pamphlet, libel or mock sermon" in imitation or mimicking of religious services. Acts and Laws of the Province of Mass. Bay, c. CV, § 8 (1712), Mass. Bay Colony Charters & Laws 399 (1814). Thus, profanity and obscenity were related offenses.

In light of this history, it is apparent that the unconditional phrasing of the First Amendment was not intended to protect every utterance. This phrasing did not prevent this Court from concluding that libelous utterances are not within the area of constitutionally protected speech. *Beauharnais v. Illinois,* 343 U.S. 250, 266. At the time of the adoption of the First Amendment, obscenity law was not as fully developed as libel law, but there is sufficiently contemporaneous evidence to show that obscenity, too, was outside the protection intended for speech and press.

The protection given speech and press was fashioned to assure unfettered interchange of ideas for the bringing about of political and social changes desired by the people. This objective was made explicit as early as 1774 in a letter of the Continental Congress to the inhabitants of Quebec:

> The last right we shall mention, regards the freedom of the press. The importance of this consists, besides the advancement of truth, science, morality, and arts in general, in its diffusion of liberal sentiments on the administration of Government, its ready communication of thoughts between subjects, and its consequential promotion of union among them, whereby oppressive officers are shamed or intimidated, into more honourable and just modes of conducting affairs. 1 Journals of the Continental Congress 108 (1774).

All ideas having even the slightest redeeming social importance—unorthodox ideas, controversial ideas, even ideas hateful to the prevailing climate of opinion—have the full protection of the guaranties, unless excludable because they encroach upon the limited area of more important interests. But implicit in the history of the First Amendment is the rejection of obscenity as utterly without redeeming social importance. This rejection for that reason is mirrored in the universal judgment that obscenity should be restrained, reflected in the international agreement of over 50 nations, in the obscenity laws of all of the 48 States, and in the 20 obscenity laws enacted by the Congress from 1842 to 1956. This is the same judgment expressed by this Court in *Chaplinsky v. New Hampshire,* 315 U.S. 568, 571–572:

> There are certain well-defined and narrowly limited classes of speech, the prevention and punishment of which have never been thought to raise any Constitutional problem. *These include the lewd and obscene. . . . It has been well observed that such utterances are no essential part of any exposition of ideas, and are of such slight social value as a step to truth that any benefit that may be derived from them is clearly outweighed by the social interest in order and morality.* . . . (Emphasis added.)

We hold that obscenity is not within the area of constitutionally protected speech or press.

It is strenuously urged that these obscenity statutes offend the constitutional guaranties because they punish incitation to impure sexual *thoughts,* not shown to be related to any overt antisocial conduct which is or may be incited in the persons stimulated to such *thoughts.* In *Roth,* the trial judge instructed the jury: "The words 'obscene, lewd and lascivious' as used in the law, signify that form of immorality which has relation to sexual impurity and has a tendency to excite lustful *thoughts.*" (Emphasis added.) In *Alberts,* the trial judge applied the test laid down in *People v. Wepplo,* 78 Cal. App. 2d Supp. 959, 178 P. 2d 853, namely, whether the material has "a substantial tendency to deprave or corrupt its readers by inciting lascivious *thoughts* or arousing lustful desires." (Emphasis added.) It is insisted that the constitutional guaranties are violated because convictions may be had without proof either that obscene material will perceptibly create a clear and present danger of antisocial conduct, or will probably induce its recipients to such conduct. But, in light of our holding that obscenity is not protected speech, the complete answer to this argument is in the holding of this Court in *Beauharnais v. Illinois, supra,* at 266:

Libelous utterances not being within the area of constitutionally protected speech, it is unnecessary, either for us or for the State courts, to consider the issues behind the phrase "clear and present danger." Certainly no one would contend that obscene speech, for example, may be punished only upon a showing of such circumstances. Libel, as we have seen, is in the same class."

However, sex and obscenity are not synonymous. Obscene material is material which deals with sex in a manner appealing to prurient interest. The portrayal of sex, e.g., in art, literature and scientific works, is not itself sufficient reason to deny material the constitutional protection of freedom of speech and press. Sex, a great and mysterious motive force in human life, has indisputably been a subject of absorbing interest to mankind through the ages; it is one of the vital problems of human interest and public concern. As to all such problems, this Court said in *Thornhill v. Alabama,* 310 U.S. 88, 101–102:

I.e., material having a tendency to excite lustful thoughts. Webster's New International Dictionary (Unabridged, 2d ed., 1949) defines *prurient,* in pertinent part, as follows:

"... Itching; longing; uneasy with desire or longing; of persons, having itching, morbid, or lascivious longings; of desire, curiosity, or propensity, lewd...."

Pruriency is defined, in pertinent part, as follows:
"... Quality of being prurient; lascivious desire or thought...."

See also *Mutual Film Corp. v. Industrial Comm'n,* 236 U.S. 230, 242, where this Court said as to motion pictures: "... They take their attraction from the general interest, eager and wholesome it may be, in their subjects, but a *prurient interest may be excited and appealed to....*" (Emphasis added.)

We perceive no significant difference between the meaning of obscenity developed in the case law and the definition of the A.L.I., Model Penal Code, § 207.10 (2) (Tent. Draft No. 6, 1957), *viz.:*

"... A thing is obscene if, considered as a whole, its predominant appeal is to prurient interest, i.e., a shameful or morbid interest in nudity, sex, or excretion, and if it goes substantially beyond customary limits of candor in description or representation of such matters...." See Comment, *id.,* at 10, and the discussion at page 29 *et seq.*

The freedom of speech and of the press guaranteed by the Constitution embraces at the least the liberty to discuss publicly and truthfully *all matters of public concern* without previous restraint or fear of subsequent pun-ishment. The exigencies of the colonial period and the efforts to secure freedom from oppressive administration developed a broadened conception of these liberties as adequate to supply the public need for *information and education with respect to the significant issues of the times....* Freedom of discussion, if it would fulfill its historic function in this nation, must embrace *all issues about which information is needed or appropriate to enable the members of society to cope with the exigencies of their period.* (Emphasis added.)

It is argued that the statutes do not provide reasonably ascertainable standards of guilt and therefore violate the constitutional requirements of due process. *Winters v. New York,* 333 U.S. 507. The federal obscenity statute makes punishable the mailing of material that is "obscene, lewd, lascivious, or filthy ... or other publication of an indecent character." The California statute makes punishable, *inter alia,* the keeping for sale or advertising material that is "obscene or indecent." The thrust of the argument is that these words are not sufficiently precise because they do not mean the same thing to all people, all the time, everywhere.

Many decisions have recognized that these terms of obscenity statutes are not precise. This Court, however, has consistently held that lack of precision is not itself offensive to the requirements of due process. "... [T]he Constitution does not require impossible standards"; all that is required is that the language "conveys sufficiently definite warning as to the proscribed conduct when measured by common understanding and practices...." *United States v. Petrillo,* 332 U.S. 1, 7–8. These words, applied according to the proper standard for judging obscenity, already discussed, give adequate warning of the conduct proscribed and mark "... boundaries sufficiently distinct for judges and juries fairly to administer the law.... That there may be marginal cases in which it is difficult to determine the side of the line on which a particular fact situation falls is no sufficient reason to hold the language too ambiguous to define a criminal offense...." *Id.,* at 7. See also *United States v. Harriss,* 347 U.S. 612, 624, n. 15; *Boyce Motor Lines, Inc. v. United States,* 342 U.S. 337, 340; *United States v. Ragen,* 314 U.S. 513, 523–524; *United States v. Wurzbach,* 280 U.S. 396; *Hygrade Provision Co. v. Sherman,* 266 U.S. 497; *Fox v. Washington,* 236 U.S. 273; *Nash v. United States,* 229 U.S. 373.

In summary, then, we hold that these statutes, applied according to the proper standard for judging obscenity, do not offend constitutional safeguards against convictions based upon protected material, or fail to give men in acting adequate notice of what is prohibited.

Mr. Justice Harlan, concurring in the result in No. 61, and dissenting in No. 582.

I regret not to be able to join the Court's opinion. I cannot do so because I find lurking beneath its disarming generalizations a number of problems which not only leave me with serious misgivings as to the future effect of today's decisions, but which also, in my view, call for different results in these two cases.

I.

My basic difficulties with the Court's opinion are threefold. First, the opinion paints with such a broad brush that I fear it may result in a loosening of the tight reins which state and federal courts should hold upon the enforcement of obscenity statutes. Second, the Court fails to discriminate between the different factors which, in my opinion, are involved in the constitutional adjudication of state and federal obscenity cases. Third, relevant distinctions between the two obscenity statutes here involved, and the Court's own definition of "obscenity," are ignored.

In final analysis, the problem presented by these cases is how far, and on what terms, the state and federal governments have power to punish individuals for disseminating books considered to be undesirable because of their nature or supposed deleterious effect upon human conduct. Proceeding from the premise that "no issue is presented in either case, concerning the obscenity of the material involved," the Court finds the "dispositive question" to be "whether obscenity is utterance within the area of protected speech and press," and then holds that "obscenity" is not so protected because it is "utterly without redeeming social importance." This sweeping formula appears to me to beg the very question before us. The Court seems to assume that "obscenity" is a peculiar *genus* of "speech and press," which is as distinct, recognizable, and classifiable as poison ivy is among other plants. On this basis

the *constitutional* question before us simply becomes, as the Court says, whether "obscenity," as an abstraction, is protected by the First and Fourteenth Amendments, and the question whether a *particular* book may be suppressed becomes a mere matter of classification, of "fact," to be entrusted to a fact-finder and insulated from independent constitutional judgment. But surely the problem cannot be solved in such a generalized fashion. Every communication has an individuality and "value" of its own. The suppression of a particular writing or other tangible form of expression is, therefore, an *individual* matter, and in the nature of things every such suppression raises an individual constitutional problem, in which a reviewing court must determine for *itself* whether the attacked expression is suppressable within constitutional standards. Since those standards do not readily lend themselves to generalized definitions, the constitutional problem in the last analysis becomes one of particularized judgments which appellate courts must make for themselves.

I do not think that reviewing courts can escape this responsibility by saying that the trier of the facts, be it a jury or a judge, has labeled the questioned matter as "obscene," for, if "obscenity" is to be suppressed, the question whether a particular work is of that character involves not really an issue of fact but a question of constitutional *judgment* of the most sensitive and delicate kind. Many juries might find that Joyce's *Ulysses* or Bocaccio's *Decameron* was obscene, and yet the conviction of a defendant for selling either book would raise, for me, the gravest constitutional problems, for no such verdict could convince me, without more, that these books are "utterly without redeeming social importance." In short, I do not understand how the Court can resolve the constitutional problems now before it without making its own independent judgment upon the character of the material upon which these convictions were based. I am very much afraid that the broad manner in which the Court has decided these cases will tend to obscure the peculiar responsibilities resting on state and federal courts in this field and encourage them to rely on easy labeling and jury verdicts as a substitute for facing up to the tough individual problems of constitutional judgment involved in every obscenity case.

Mr. Justice Douglas, with whom Mr. Justice Black concurs, dissenting.

When we sustain these convictions, we make the legality of a publication turn on the purity of thought which a book or tract instills in the mind of the reader. I do not think we can approve that standard and be faithful to the command of the First Amendment, which by its terms is a restraint on Congress and which by the Fourteenth is a restraint on the States.

In the *Roth* case the trial judge charged the jury that the statutory words "obscene, lewd and lascivious" describe "that form of immorality which has relation to sexual impurity and has a tendency to excite lustful thoughts." He stated that the term "filthy" in the statute pertains "to that sort of treatment of sexual matters in such a vulgar and indecent way, so that it tends to arouse a feeling of disgust and revulsion." He went on to say that the material "must be calculated to corrupt and debauch the minds and morals" of "the average person in the community," not those of any particular class. "You judge the circulars, pictures and publications which have been put in evidence by present-day standards of the community. You may ask yourselves does it offend the common conscience of the community by present-day standards."

The trial judge who, sitting without a jury, heard the *Alberts* case and the appellate court that sustained the judgment of conviction, took California's definition of "obscenity" from *People v. Wepplo,* 78 Cal. App. 2d Supp. 959, 961, 178 P. 2d 853, 855. That case held that a book is obscene "if it has a substantial tendency to deprave or corrupt its readers by inciting lascivious thoughts or arousing lustful desire."

By these standards punishment is inflicted for thoughts provoked, not for overt acts nor antisocial conduct. This test cannot be squared with our decisions under the First Amendment. Even the ill-starred *Dennis* case conceded that speech to be punishable must have some relation to action which could be penalized by government. *Dennis v. United States,* 341 U.S. 494, 502–511. Cf. Chafee, The Blessings of Liberty (1956), p. 69. This issue cannot be avoided by saying that obscenity is not protected by the First Amendment.

The question remains, what is the constitutional test of obscenity?

The tests by which these convictions were obtained require only the arousing of sexual thoughts. Yet the arousing of sexual thoughts and desires happens every day in normal life in dozens of ways. Nearly 30 years ago a questionnaire sent to college and normal school women graduates asked what things were most stimulating sexually. Of 409 replies, 9 said "music"; 18 said "pictures"; 29 said "dancing"; 40 said "drama"; 95 said "books"; and 218 said "man." Alpert, Judicial Censorship of Obscene Literature, 52 *Harv. L. Rev.* 40, 73.

The test of obscenity the Court endorses today gives the censor free range over a vast domain. To allow the State to step in and punish mere speech or publication that the judge or the jury thinks has an *undesirable* impact on thoughts but that is not shown to be a part of unlawful action is drastically to curtail the First Amendment. As recently stated by two of our outstanding authorities on obscenity, "The danger of influencing a change in the current moral standards of the community, or of shocking or offending readers, or of stimulating sex thoughts or desires apart from objective conduct, can never justify the losses to society that result from interference with literary freedom." Lockhart & McClure, Literature, The Law of Obscenity, and the Constitution, 38 *Minn. L. Rev.* 295, 387....

The absence of dependable information on the effect of obscene literature on human conduct should make us wary. It should put us on the side of protecting society's interest in literature, except and unless it can be said that the particular publication has an impact on action that the government can control.

As noted, the trial judge in the *Roth* case charged the jury in the alternative that the federal obscenity statute outlaws literature dealing with sex which offends "the common conscience of the community." That standard is, in my view, more inimical still to freedom of expression.

The standard of what offends "the common conscience of the community" conflicts, in my judgment, with the command of the First Amendment that "Congress shall make no law ... abridging the freedom of speech, or of the press." Certainly that standard would not be an acceptable one if religion, economics, politics or philosophy were involved. How does it become a constitutional standard when literature treating with sex is concerned?

Any test that turns on what is offensive to the community's standards is too loose, too capricious, too destructive of freedom of expression to be squared with the First Amendment. Under that test, juries can censor, suppress, and punish what they don't like, provided the matter relates to "sexual impurity" or has a tendency "to excite lustful thoughts." This is community censorship in one of its worst forms. It creates a regime where in the battle between the literati and the Philistines, the Philistines are certain to win. If experience in this field teaches anything, it is that "censorship of obscenity has almost always been both irrational and indiscriminate." Lockhart & McClure, *op. cit. supra,* at 371. The test adopted here accentuates that trend.

I assume there is nothing in the Constitution which forbids Congress from using its power over the mails to proscribe *conduct* on the grounds of good morals. No one would suggest that the First Amendment permits nudity in public places, adultery, and other phases of sexual misconduct.

I can understand (and at times even sympathize) with programs of civic groups and church groups to protect and defend the existing moral standards of the community. I can understand the motives of the Anthony Comstocks who would impose Victorian standards on the community. When speech alone is involved, I do not think that government, consistently with the First Amendment, can become the sponsor of any of these movements. I do not think that government, consistently with the First Amendment, can throw its weight behind one school or another. Government should be concerned with antisocial conduct, not with utterances. Thus, if the First Amendment guarantee of freedom of speech and press is to mean anything in this field, it must allow protests even against the moral code that the standard of the day sets for the community. In other words, literature should not be suppressed merely because it offends the moral code of the censor.

The legality of a publication in this country should never be allowed to turn either on the purity of thought which it instills in the mind of the reader or on the degree to which it offends the community conscience. By either test the role of the censor is exalted, and society's values in literary freedom are sacrificed. . . .

I do not think that the problem can be resolved by the Court's statement that "obscenity is not expression protected by the First Amendment." With the exception of *Beauharnais v. Illinois,* 343 U.S. 250, none of our cases has resolved problems of free speech and free press by placing any form of expression beyond the pale of the absolute prohibition of the First Amendment. Unlike the law of libel, wrongfully relied on in *Beauharnais,* there is no special historical evidence that literature dealing with sex was intended to be treated in a special manner by those who drafted the First Amendment. In fact, the first reported court decision in this country involving obscene literature was in 1821. Lockhart & McClure, *op. cit. supra,* at 324, n. 200. I reject too the implication that problems of freedom of speech and of the press are to be resolved by weighing against the values of free expression, the judgment of the Court that a particular form of that expression has "no redeeming social importance." The First Amendment, its prohibition in terms absolute, was designed to preclude courts as well as legislatures from weighing the values of speech against silence. The First Amendment puts free speech in the preferred position.

Freedom of expression can be suppressed if, and to the extent that, it is so closely brigaded with illegal action as to be an inseparable part of it. *Giboney v. Empire Storage Co.,* 336 U.S. 490, 498; *Labor Board v. Virginia Power Co.,* 314 U.S. 469, 477–478. As a people, we cannot afford to relax that standard. For the test that suppresses a cheap tract today can suppress a literary gem tomorrow. All it need do is to incite a lascivious thought or arouse a lustful desire. The list of books that judges or juries can place in that category is endless.

I would give the broad sweep of the First Amendment full support. I have the same confidence in the ability of our people to reject noxious literature as I have in their capacity to sort out the true from the false in theology, economics, politics, or any other field.

Since *Roth,* the Court has evinced little interest in examining any empirical uncertainties or considering any alternatives to obscenity's entirely unprotected status.[251] The law of obscenity thus has evolved as a function of the Court's conscious inclination to assume rather than establish that such expression has no value and so does not implicate constitutional concern. Such broad assumptions preclude even the possibility of considering whether, in a given instance, prurient materials might be valuable because they afford pleasure or release, contribute to formation of sexual identity, or safeguard against imposition of "politically correct sex."[252] The categorical exclusion of obscenity diverges from traditional libertarian wisdom that favors decision making by rather than for individuals and does not lightly brook interference with personal thoughts and beliefs.[253] The analysis ultimately assumes that official definition of acceptable expression is less dangerous than the exercise of individual judgment. Critics would argue that, if the individual cannot be trusted to make decisions regarding one type of expression, especially when lack of value is presumed rather than proved, it may be difficult to establish meaningful limiting principles against the expansion or transferability of such thinking.

Jurisprudence satisfied with assumption rather than proof has relegated to a level of marginal relevance official or scholarly efforts to discern harm attributable to obscenity. President Nixon appointed a special commission to identify any linkage between obscenity and antisocial behavior. It found no evidence that exposure to explicit sexual materials caused delinquent or criminal conduct.[254] A subsequent study, commissioned by President Reagan, concluded that a relationship exists between exposure to sexually degrading material and aggression toward women.[255] Insofar as the law concerning obscenity continues to rest on assumptions, the findings of either report have no real constitutional influence. The contin-

uing debate, however, presents an interest in jurisprudence that at least has the appearance of being informed rather than presumptive. Even if evidence shows a causal connection between obscenity and a definable harm, the question likely will remain as to whether the problem should be solved by policies of official control or individual autonomy.

Roth and its progeny have supported Justice Harlan's observation that obscenity is an elusive concept.[256] Justice Stewart eventually would depict classification efforts as "trying to define what may be indefinable" and concede that he could do no better than "know it when I see it."[257] Justice Brennan, who authored the *Roth* opinion, later would maintain that formulation of a viable description was impossible and a threat to First Amendment values.[258] Nonetheless, the Court has pressed forward in a largely frustrating and confounding effort to distill the essence of obscenity and to uphold governmental power to regulate it. Following a lower court determination that the book *Fanny Hill* was obscene,[259] a fragmented Court reversed.[260] A plurality of three led by Justice Brennan concluded that the work was not *"utterly* without redeeming social value" and accordingly not beyond the First Amendment's purview.[261] The *Roth* decision had emphasized prurience and assumed that obscenity was utterly without redeeming social importance. The Brennan plurality depicted the latter reference point as an independent standard that must be affirmatively satisfied and demanded a showing that the subject matter must offend contemporary community standards.[262] The tripartite criteria focusing upon speech appealing to prurient interests, offending contemporary community standards, and entirely lacking redeeming social value obligated prosecutors to satisfy not just any but each of the standards.[263]

Proof that material was without redeeming social value whatsoever constituted an exacting standard. It became evident, however, that it would not operate as a consistent bar to successful prosecution. In *Ginzburg v. United States*,[264] the Court concluded that forthright pandering to prurient interests was sufficient to support an obscenity conviction.[265] The defendant overtly had marketed his publication in a way that emphasized its sexually provocative nature and manifested an intent to capitalize upon "an unrestricted license allowed by law in the expression of sex and sexual matters."[266] By itself, a conscious and forthright appeal to prurient interests proved to be adequate grounds for conviction regardless of whether the materials themselves might have had redeeming social value.[267] The latter question was preempted by the former determination.

Until 1973, a majority of the Court was unable to coalesce behind a unifying set of principles for analyzing obscenity issues. As a consequence, the Court for several years followed a rather unusual practice of reversing per curiam whenever five or more justices considered materials less than obscene.[268] Eventually, in *Miller v. California*,[269] a majority fashioned a formula to the effect that obscenity is to be discerned according to:

> (a) whether 'the average person, applying contemporary community standards' would find that the work, taken as a whole, appeals to the prurient interest, (b) whether the work depicts or describes, in a patently offensive way, sexual conduct specifically defined by the applicable state law, and (c) whether the work taken as a whole, lacks serious literary, artistic, political, or scientific value.[270]

Although the *Miller* opinion emphasized that the First Amendment's meaning "does not vary from community to community,"[271] the decision to measure prurient interest and patent offensiveness created the possibility that reality would diverge from theory. Even if the consequences might be rationa-

lized on grounds that a finding of obscenity eliminates the First Amendment as a pertinent concern, the variability of results pursuant to disparate community standards would transform the guarantee into a relative rather than consistent safeguard. Reliance on community standards not only extended an invitation for prosecutorial forum shopping but, as was soon evidenced, presented a problem for actuating rights transcending a given community. In *Jenkins v. Georgia*,[272] the Court reversed a jury determination that the relatively mainstream film, "Carnal Knowledge," was obscene.[273] Although its assignment of the prurient interest and patent offensiveness questions to juries probably reflected to a considerable extent its own frustration with an "intractable . . . problem,"[274] the *Jenkins* decision demonstrates that local community standards will not be allowed to operate unchecked.[275] Because the Court has not rescinded its assignment to the trier of fact, however, future oversight for practical purposes may be a function of its own subjective predilections.

The *Miller* decision itself concerned jury instructions denominating the relevant community as the state.[276] It has become evident, however, that a trial judge would not necessarily err by using a community standard without any geographically qualifying reference point.[277] An exception arguably might arise in the event a national standard was prescribed when a local standard would be more tolerant. The Court's adoption of the community standard approach was to recognize "that the people of Maine or Mississippi [need] not accept public depiction of conduct found tolerable in Las Vegas or New York City."[278] Arguably, the converse would be true with respect to allowing local norms to operate unimpaired by less tolerant outside standards.

Patent offensiveness, as the second part of the *Miller* test, also must be measured against contemporary community standards.[279]

Whatever is punishable as patently offensive, however, must depict or describe sexual conduct that the law specifically defines.[280] Examples of statutory definitions satisfying the *Miller* criteria include

> (a) Patently offensive representation or descriptions of ultimate sexual acts, normal or perverted, actual or simulated. (b) Patently offensive representations or descriptions of masturbation, excretory functions and lewd exhibition of the genitals.[281]

As the Court subsequently emphasized, those recitations were examples rather than exhaustive guidelines.[282] The models themselves do not afford clear notice of what is proscribed, and the Court effectively has acceded to inevitable imprecision by noting that the "specifically defined" requirement can be satisfied by a regulation "as written or authoritatively construed."[283] Given the nature of the subject, and the invariable need to rely upon such subjective terms as "normal," "perverted," and "lewd," any expectations of precise guidelines probably would have been misplaced. Constitutional safety for expression relating to what the Court might consider normal or healthy sexual desires[284] suggests that the dividing line between "materials depict[ing], or describ[ing] patently offensive 'hard core' sexual conduct"[285] and protected characterizations at bottom is subjective. That likelihood in itself creates strong incentive for media in general to exercise caution in the selection and presentation of sexually oriented materials.

The final component of the *Miller* test, obligating prosecutors to demonstrate that material "lacks serious literary, artistic, political, or scientific value,"[286] altered preceding terminology that "a work must be 'utterly without redeeming social value.' "[287] It is doubtful whether the modification has profound significance, although the Court has intimated that it is a distinguishing characteristic of the *Miller* test.[288] It also has held

that determinations of literary, artistic, political, or scientific value are to be made pursuant to a reasonable person rather than the community standard.[289] Such attempted objectification is premised upon the notion that value is not a function of local popularity or acceptability.[290] The amplified standard has the potential for neutralizing the influence of community standards operating in connection with the first two parts of the test. Notwithstanding its operation, the standard does not entirely eliminate the problem of subjectivity insofar as all reasonable persons do not subscribe to like values or have the same sensitivities.[291]

Miller v. California, 413 U.S. 15 (1973)

Mr. Chief Justice Burger delivered the opinion of the Court.

This is one of a group of "obscenity-pornography" cases being reviewed by the Court in a re-examination of standards enunciated in earlier cases involving what Mr. Justice Harlan called "the intractable obscenity problem." *Interstate Circuit, Inc. v. Dallas,* 390 U.S. 676, 704 (1968) (concurring and dissenting).

Appellant conducted a mass mailing campaign to advertise the sale of illustrated books, euphemistically called "adult" material. After a jury trial, he was convicted of violating California Penal Code § 311.2 (a), a misdemeanor, by knowingly distributing obscene matter, and the Appellate Department, Superior Court of California, County of Orange, summarily affirmed the judgment without opinion. Appellant's conviction was specifically based on his conduct in causing five unsolicited advertising brochures to be sent through the mail in an envelope addressed to a restaurant in Newport Beach, California. The envelope was opened by the manager of the restaurant and his mother. They had not requested the brochures; they complained to the police.

The brochures advertise four books entitled *Intercourse, Man-Woman, Sex Orgies Illustrated,* and *An Illustrated History of Pornography,* and a film entitled *Marital Intercourse.* While the brochures contain some descriptive printed material, primarily they consist of pictures and drawings very explicitly depicting men and women in groups of two or more engaging in a variety of sexual activities, with genitals often prominently displayed.

I

This case involves the application of a State's criminal obscenity statute to a situation in which sexually explicit materials have been thrust by aggressive sales action upon unwilling recipients who had in no way indicated any desire to receive such materials. This Court has recognized that the States have a legitimate interest in prohibiting dissemination or exhibition of obscene material when the mode of dissemination carries with it a significant danger of offending the sensibilities of unwilling recipients or of exposure to juveniles. *Stanley v. Georgia*, 394 U.S. 557, 567 (1969); *Ginsberg v. New York*, 390 U.S. 629, 637–643 (1968); *Interstate Circuit, Inc. v. Dallas, supra*, at 690; *Redrup v. New York*, 386 U.S. 767, 769 (1967); *Jacobellis v. Ohio*, 378 U.S. 184, 195 (1964). See *Rabe v. Washington*, 405 U.S. 313, 317 (1972) (Burger, C. J., concurring); *United States v. Reidel*, 402 U.S. 351, 360–362 (1971) (opinion of Marshall, J.); *Joseph Burstyn, Inc. v. Wilson*, 343 U.S. 495, 502 (1952); *Breard v. Alexandria*, 341 U.S. 622, 644–645 (1951); *Kovacs v. Cooper*, 336 U.S. 77, 88–89 (1949); *Prince v. Massachusetts*, 321 U.S. 158, 169–170 (1944). Cf. *Butler v. Michigan*, 352 U.S. 380, 382–383 (1957); *Public Utilities Comm'n v. Pollak*, 343 U.S. 451, 464–465 (1952). It is in this context that we are called on to define the standards which must be used to identify obscene material that a State may regulate without infringing on the First Amendment as applicable to the States through the Fourteenth Amendment....

While *Roth* presumed "obscenity" to be "utterly without redeeming social importance," *Memoirs* required that to prove obscenity it must be affirmatively established that the material is "*utterly* without redeeming social value." Thus, even as they repeated the words of *Roth*, the *Memoirs* plurality produced a drastically altered test that called on the prosecution to prove a negative, i.e., that the material was "*utterly* without redeeming social value"—a burden virtually impossible to discharge under our criminal standards of proof.

Such considerations caused Mr. Justice Harlan to wonder if the "*utterly* without redeeming social value" test had any meaning at all. See *Memoirs v. Massachusetts, id.,* at 459 (Harlan, J., dissenting). See also *id.,* at 461 (White, J., dissenting); *United States v. Groner,* 479 F. 2d 577, 579–581 (CA5 1973)....

This much has been categorically settled by the Court, that obscene material is unprotected by the First Amendment. *Kois v. Wisconsin,* 408 U.S. 229 (1972); *United States v. Reidel,* 402 U.S., at 354; *Roth v. United States, supra,* at 485. "The First and Fourteenth Amendments have never been treated as absolutes [footnote omitted]." *Breard v. Alexandria,* 341 U.S., at 642, and cases cited. See *Times Film Corp. v. Chicago,* 365 U.S. 43, 47–50 (1961); *Joseph Burstyn, Inc. v. Wilson,* 343 U.S., at 502. We acknowledge, however, the inherent dangers of undertaking to regulate any form of expression. State statutes designed to regulate obscene materials must be carefully limited. See *Interstate Circuit, Inc. v. Dallas, supra,* at 682–685. As a result, we now confine the permissible scope of such regulation to works which depict or describe sexual conduct. That conduct must be specifically defined by the applicable state law, as written or authoritatively construed. A state offense must also be limited to works which, taken as a whole, appeal to the prurient interest in sex, which portray sexual conduct in a patently offensive way, and which, taken as a whole, do not have serious literary, artistic, political, or scientific value.

The basic guidelines for the trier of fact must be: (a) whether "the average person, applying contemporary community standards" would find that the work, taken as a whole, appeals to the prurient interest, *Kois v. Wisconsin, supra,* at 230, quoting *Roth v. United States, supra,* at 489; (b) whether the work depicts or describes, in a patently offensive way, sexual conduct specifically defined by the applicable state law; and (c) whether the work, taken as a whole, lacks serious literary, artistic, political, or scientific value. We do not adopt as a constitutional standard the "*utterly* without redeeming social value" test of *Memoirs v. Massachusetts,* 383 U.S., at 419; that concept has never commanded the adherence of more than three Justices at one time.[a] See *supra,* at 21.

---

a. "A quotation from Voltaire in the flyleaf of a book

If a state law that regulates obscene material is thus limited, as written or construed, the First Amendment values applicable to the States through the Fourteenth Amendment are adequately protected by the ultimate power of appellate courts to conduct an independent review of constitutional claims when necessary. See *Kois v. Wisconsin, supra,* at 232; *Memoirs v. Massachusetts, supra,* at 459–460 (Harlan, J., dissenting); *Jacobellis v. Ohio,* 378 U.S., at 204 (Harlan, J., dissenting); *New York Times Co. v. Sullivan,* 376 U.S. 254, 284–285 (1964); *Roth v. United States, supra,* at 497–498 (Harlan, J., concurring and dissenting).

We emphasize that it is not our function to propose regulatory schemes for the States. That must await their concrete legislative efforts. It is possible, however, to give a few plain examples of what a state statute could define for regulation under part (b) of the standard announced in this opinion, *supra*:

(a) Patently offensive representations or descriptions of ultimate sexual acts, normal or perverted, actual or simulated.

(b) Patently offensive representations or descriptions of masturbation, excretory functions, and lewd exhibition of the genitals.

Sex and nudity may not be exploited without limit by films or pictures exhibited or sold in places of public accommodation any more than live sex and nudity can be exhibited or sold without limit in such public places. At a minimum, prurient, patently offensive depiction or description or sexual conduct must have serious literary, artistic, political, or scientific value to merit First Amendment protection. See *Kois v. Wisconsin, supra,* at 230–232; *Roth v. United States, supra,* at 487; *Thornhill v. Alabama,* 310 U.S. 88, 101–102 (1940). For example, medical books for the education of physicians and related personnel necessarily use graphic illustrations and descriptions of human anatomy. In resolving the inevitably sensitive questions of fact and law, we must continue to rely on the jury system, accompanied by the safeguards that judges, rules of evidence, presumption of innocence, and other protective features provide, as we do with rape, murder, and a host of other offenses against society and its individual members.

Mr. Justice Brennan, author of the opinions of the Court, or the plurality opinions, in *Roth v. United States, supra*; *Jacobellis v. Ohio, supra*; *Ginzburg v. United States,* 383 U.S. 463 (1966); *Mishkin v. New York,* 383 U.S. 502 (1966); and *Memoirs v. Massachusetts, supra,* has abandoned his former position and now maintains that no formulation of this Court, the Congress, or the States can adequately distinguish obscene material unprotected by the First Amendment from protected expression, *Paris Adult Theatre I v. Slaton, post,* p. 73 (Brennan, J., dissenting). Paradoxically, Mr. Justice Brennan indicates that suppression of unprotected obscene material is permissible to avoid exposure to unconsenting adults, as in this case, and to juveniles, although he gives no indication of how the division between protected and nonprotected materials may be drawn with greater precision for these purposes than for regulation of commercial exposure to consenting adults only. Nor does he indicate where in the Constitution he finds the authority to distinguish between a willing "adult" one month past the state law age of majority and a willing "juvenile" one month younger.

Under the holdings announced today, no one will be subject to prosecution for the sale or exposure of obscene materials unless these materials depict or describe patently offensive "hard core" sexual conduct specifically defined by the regulating state law, as written or construed. We are satisfied that these specific prerequisites will provide fair notice to a dealer in such materials that his public and commercial activities may bring prosecution. See *Roth v. United States, supra,* at 491–492. Cf. *Ginsberg v. New York,* 390 U.S., at 643. If the inability to define regulated materials with ultimate, god-like precision altogether removes the power of the States or the Congress to regulate, then "hard core" pornography may be exposed without limit to the juvenile, the passerby, and the consenting adult alike, as, indeed, Mr. Justice Douglas contends. As to Mr. Justice Douglas' position, see *United States v. Thirty-seven Photographs,* 402 U.S. 363, 379–380 (1971) (Black,

---

will not constitutionally redeem an otherwise obscene publication...." *Kois v. Wisconsin,* 408 U.S. 229, 231 (1972). See *Memoirs v. Massachusetts,* 383 U.S. 413, 461 (1966) (White, J., dissenting). We also reject, as a constitutional standard, the ambiguous concept of "social importance." See *id.,* at 462 (White, J., dissenting).

J., joined by Douglas, J., dissenting); *Ginzburg v. United States, supra,* at 476, 491–492 (Black, J., and Douglas, J., dissenting); *Jacobellis v. Ohio, supra,* at 196 (Black, J., joined by Douglas, J., concurring); *Roth, supra,* at 508–514 (Douglas, J., dissenting). In this belief, however, Mr. Justice Douglas now stands alone.

Mr. Justice Brennan also emphasizes "institutional stress" in justification of his change of view. Noting that "[t]he number of obscenity cases on our docket gives ample testimony to the burden that has been placed upon this Court," he quite rightly remarks that the examination of contested materials "is hardly a source of edification to the members of this Court." *Paris Adult Theatre I v. Slaton, post,* at 92, 93. He also notes, and we agree, that "uncertainty of the standards creates a continuing source of tension between state and federal courts...." "The problem is...that one cannot say with certainty that material is obscene until at least five members of this Court, applying inevitably obscure standards, have pronounced it so." *Id.,* at 93, 92.

It is certainly true that the absence, since *Roth,* of a single majority view of this Court as to proper standards for testing obscenity has placed a strain on both state and federal courts. But today, for the first time since *Roth* was decided in 1957, a majority of this Court has agreed on concrete guidelines to isolate "hard core" pornography from expression protected by the First Amendment. Now we may abandon the casual practice of *Redrup v. New York,* 386 U.S. 767 (1967), and attempt to provide positive guidance to federal and state courts alike.

This may not be an easy road, free from difficulty. But no amount of "fatigue" should lead us to adopt a convenient "institutional" rationale—an absolutist, "anything goes" view of the First Amendment—because it will lighten our burdens. "Such an abnegation of judicial supervision in this field would be inconsistent with our duty to uphold the constitutional guarantees." *Jacobellis v. Ohio, supra,* at 187–188 (opinion of Brennan, J.). Nor should we remedy "tension between state and federal courts" by arbitrarily depriving the States of a power reserved to them under the Constitution, a power which they have enjoyed and exercised continuously from before the adoption of the First Amendment to this day. See

Roth v. United States, supra, at 482–485. "Our duty admits of no 'substitute for facing up to the tough individual problems of constitutional judgment involved in every obscenity case.' [*Roth v. United States, supra,* at 498]; see *Manual Enterprises, Inc. v. Day,* 370 U.S. 478, 488 (opinion of Harlan, J.) [footnote omitted]." *Jacobellis v. Ohio, supra,* at 188 (opinion of Brennan, J.).

III

Under a National Constitution, fundamental First Amendment limitations on the powers of the States do not vary from community to community, but this does not mean that there are, or should or can be, fixed, uniform national standards of precisely what appeals to the "prurient interest" or is "patently offensive." These are essentially questions of fact, and our Nation is simply too big and too diverse for this Court to reasonably expect that such standards could be articulated for all 50 States in a single formulation, even assuming the prerequisite consensus exists. When triers of fact are asked to decide whether "the average person, applying contemporary community standards" would consider certain materials "prurient," it would be unrealistic to require that the answer be based on some abstract formulation. The adversary system, with lay jurors as the usual ultimate factfinders in criminal prosecutions, has historically permitted triers of fact to draw on the standards of their community, guided always by limiting instructions on the law. To require a State to structure obscenity proceedings around evidence of a *national* "community standard" would be an exercise in futility....

We conclude that neither the State's alleged failure to offer evidence of "national standards," nor the trial court's charge that the jury consider state community standards, were constitutional errors. Nothing in the First Amendment requires that a jury must consider hypothetical and unascertainable "national standards" when attempting to determine whether certain materials are obscene as a matter of fact. Mr. Chief Justice Warren pointedly commented in his dissent in *Jacobellis v. Ohio, supra,* at 200:

It is my belief that when the Court said in *Roth* that obscenity is to be defined by reference to "community standards," it meant community standards—not a national standard, as is sometimes argued. I believe that there is no provable "national standard". . . . At all events, this Court has not been able to enunciate one, and it would be unreasonable to expect local courts to divine one.

It is neither realistic nor constitutionally sound to read the First Amendment as requiring that the people of Maine or Mississippi accept public depiction of conduct found tolerable in Las Vegas, or New York City. See *Hoyt v. Minnesota,* 399 U.S. 524–525 (1970) (Blackmun, J., dissenting); *Walker v. Ohio,* 398 U.S. 434 (1970) (Burger, C. J., dissenting); *id.,* at 434–435 (Harlan, J., dissenting); *Cain v. Kentucky,* 397 U.S. 319 (1970) (Burger, C. J., dissenting); *id.,* at 319–320 (Harlan, J., dissenting); *United States v. Groner,* 479 F. 2d, at 581–583; O'Meara & Shaffer, Obscenity in The Supreme Court: A Note on *Jacobellis v. Ohio,* 40 *Notre Dame Law.* 1, 6–7 (1964). See also *Memoirs v. Massachusetts,* 383 U.S., at 458 (Harlan, J., dissenting); *Jacobellis v. Ohio, supra,* at 203–204 (Harlan, J., dissenting); *Roth v. United States, supra,* at 505–506 (Harlan, J., concurring and dissenting). People in different States vary in their tastes and attitudes, and this diversity is not to be strangled by the absolutism of imposed uniformity. As the Court made clear in *Mishkin v. New York,* 383 U.S., at 508–509, the primary concern with requiring a jury to apply the standard of "the average person, applying contemporary community standards" is to be certain that, so far as material is not aimed at a deviant group, it will be judged by its impact on an average person, rather than a particularly susceptible or sensitive person—or indeed a totally insensitive one. See *Roth v. United States, supra,* at 489. Cf. the now discredited test in *Regina v. Hicklin,* [1868] L. R. 3 Q. B. 360. We hold that the requirement that the jury evaluate the materials with reference to "contemporary standards of the State of California" serves this protective purpose and is constitutionally adequate.

IV

The dissenting Justices sound the alarm of repression. But, in our view, to equate the free and robust exchange of ideas and political debate with commercial exploitation of obscene material

demeans the grand conception of the First Amendment and its high purposes in the historic struggle for freedom. It is a "misuse of the great guarantees of free speech and free press. . . ." *Breard v. Alexandria,* 341 U.S., at 645. The First Amendment protects works which, taken as a whole, have serious literary, artistic, political, or scientific value, regardless of whether the government or a majority of the people approve of the ideas these works represent. "The protection given speech and press was fashioned to assure unfettered interchange of *ideas* for the bringing about of political and social changes desired by the people," *Roth v. United States, supra,* at 484 (emphasis added). See *Kois v. Wisconsin,* 408 U.S., at 230–232; *Thornhill v. Alabama,* 310 U.S., at 101–102. But the public portrayal of hard-core sexual conduct for its own sake, and for the ensuing commercial gain, is a different matter.

There is no evidence, empirical or historical, that the stern 19th century American censorship of public distribution and display of material relating to sex, see *Roth v. United States, supra,* at 482–485, in any way limited or affected expression of serious literary, artistic, political, or scientific ideas. On the contrary, it is beyond any question that the era following Thomas Jefferson to Theodore Roosevelt was an "extraordinarily vigorous period," not just in economics and politics, but in *belles lettres* and in "the outlying fields of social and political philosophies." We do not see the harsh hand of censorship of ideas—good or bad, sound or unsound—and "repression" of political liberty lurking in every state regulation of commercial exploitation of human interest in sex.

Mr. Justice Brennan finds "it is hard to see how state-ordered regimentation of our minds can never be forestalled." *Paris Adult Theatre I v. Slaton, post,* at 110 (Brennan, J., dissenting). These doleful anticipations assume that courts cannot distinguish commerce in ideas, protected by the First Amendment, from commercial exploitation of obscene material. Moreover, state regulation of hard-core pornography so as to make it unavailable to nonadults, a regulation which Mr. Justice Brennan finds constitutionally permissible, has all the elements of "censorship" for adults; indeed even more rigid enforcement techniques may be called for with such dichotomy of regulation. See *Interstate Circuit, Inc. v. Dallas,* 390 U.S., at 690. One can concede that the "sexual revolution" of recent years may have had useful byproducts in striking layers of prudery from a subject long irrationally kept from needed ventilation. But it does not follow that no regulation of patently offensive "hard core" materials is needed or permissible; civilized people do not allow unregulated access to heroin because it is a derivative of medicinal morphine.

In sum, we (a) reaffirm the *Roth* holding that obscene material is not protected by the First Amendment; (b) hold that such material can be regulated by the States, subject to the specific safeguards enunciated above, without a showing that the material is *"utterly* without redeeming social value"; and (c) hold that obscenity is to be determined by applying "contemporary community standards," see *Kois v. Wisconsin, supra,* at 230, and *Roth v. United States, supra,* at 489, not "national standards." The judgment of the Appellate Department of the Superior Court, Orange County, California, is vacated and the case remanded to that court for further proceedings not inconsistent with the First Amendment standards established by this opinion. See *United States v. 12 200-ft. Reels of Film, post,* at 130 n. 7.

Vacated and remanded.

Mr. Justice Douglas, dissenting.

Today we would add a new three-pronged test: "(a) whether 'the average person, applying contemporary community standards' would find that the work, taken as a whole, appeals to the prurient interest, . . . (b) whether the work depicts or describes, in a patently offensive way, sexual conduct specifically defined by the applicable state law, and (c) whether the work, taken as a whole, lacks serious literary, artistic, political, or scientific value."

Those are the standards we ourselves have written into the Constitution. Yet how under these vague tests can we sustain convictions for the sale of an article prior to the time when some court has declared it to be obscene?

Today the Court retreats from the earlier formulations of the constitutional test and undertakes to make new definitions. This effort, like the earlier ones, is earnest and well intentioned. The difficulty is that we do not deal with consti-tutional terms, since "obscenity" is not mentioned in the Constitution or Bill of Rights. And the First Amendment makes no such exception from "the press" which it undertakes to protect nor, as I have said on other occasions, is an exception necessarily implied, for there was no recognized exception to the free press at the time the Bill of Rights was adopted which treated "obscene" publications differently from other types of papers, magazines, and books. So there are no constitutional guidelines for deciding what is and what is not "obscene." The Court is at large because we deal with tastes and standards of literature. What shocks me may be sustenance for my neighbor. What causes one person to boil up in rage over one pamphlet or movie may reflect only his neurosis, not shared by others. We deal here with a regime of censorship which, if adopted, should be done by constitutional amendment after full debate by the people.

Obscenity cases usually generate tremendous emotional outbursts. They have no business being in the courts. If a constitutional amendment authorized censorship, the censor would probably be an administrative agency. Then criminal prosecutions could follow as, if, and when publishers defied the censor and sold their literature. Under that regime a publisher would know when he was on dangerous ground. Under the present regime—whether the old standards or the new ones are used—the criminal law becomes a trap. A brand new test would put a publisher behind bars under a new law improvised by the courts after the publication. That was done in *Ginzburg* and has all the evils of an *ex post facto* law.

While the right to know is the corollary of the right to speak or publish, no one can be forced by government to listen to disclosure that he finds offensive. That was the basis of my dissent in *Public Utilities Comm'n v. Pollak,* 343 U.S. 451, 467, where I protested against making streetcar passengers a "captive" audience. There is no "captive audience" problem in these obscenity cases. No one is being compelled to look or to listen. Those who enter newsstands or bookstalls may be offended by what they see. But they are not compelled by the State to frequent those places; and it is only state or governmental action against which the First Amendment, applicable to the States by virtue of the Fourteenth, raises a ban.

The idea that the First Amendment permits government to ban publications that are "offensive" to some people puts an ominous gloss on freedom of the press. That test would make it possible to ban any paper or any journal or magazine in some benighted place. The First Amendment was designed "to invite dispute," to induce "a condition of unrest," to "create dissatisfaction with conditions as they are," and even to stir "people to anger." *Terminiello v. Chicago,* 337 U.S. 1, 4. The idea that the First Amendment permits punishment for ideas that are "offensive" to the particular judge or jury sitting in judgment is astounding. No greater leveler of speech or literature has ever been designed. To give the power to the censor, as we do today, is to make a sharp and radical break with the traditions of a free society. The First Amendment was not fashioned as a vehicle for dispensing tranquilizers to the people. Its prime function was to keep debate open to "offensive" as well as to "staid" people. The tendency throughout history has been to subdue the individual and to exalt the power of government. The use of the standard "offensive" gives authority to government that cuts the very vitals out of the First Amendment. As is intimated by the Court's opinion, the materials before us may be garbage. But so is much of what is said in political campaigns, in the daily press, on TV, or over the radio. By reason of the First Amendment—and solely because of it—speakers and publishers have not been threatened or subdued because their thoughts and ideas may be "offensive" to some. . . .

If there are to be restraints on what is obscene, then a constitutional amendment should be the way of achieving the end. There are societies where religion and mathematics are the only free segments. It would be a dark day for America if that were our destiny. But the people can make it such if they choose to write obscenity into the Constitution and define it.

We deal with highly emotional, not rational, questions. To many the Song of Solomon is obscene. I do not think we, the judges, were ever given the constitutional power to make definitions of obscenity. If it is to be defined, let the people debate and decide by a constitutional amendment what they want to ban as obscene and what standards they want the legislatures and the courts to apply. Perhaps the people will decide that the path towards a mature, integrated society requires that all ideas competing for acceptance must have no censor. Perhaps they will decide otherwise. Whatever the choice, the courts will have some guidelines. Now we have none except our own predilections.

The status of obscenity as unprotected expression has deterred if not preempted any serious inquiry into whether concerns underlying regulation could be effectuated in a fashion that is more deferential to individual autonomy. In *Stanley v. Georgia,*[292] the Court determined that a person could not be punished for mere possession of obscenity in the privacy of the home.[293] The possibility that the law of obscenity might be contoured along the lines of individual rather than authoritative selection, however, essentially has been aborted. The Court cut short potential jurisprudential development in that direction when, in *Paris Adult Theatre I v. Slaton,*[294] it ruled against a theater owner who posted signs warning about the nature of the films being exhibited and whose audience was limited to consenting adults.[295] Although finding state regulation of obscenity permissible, even pursuant to "unprovable assumptions,"[296] the Court identified several reasons for official control of the expression at issue. Such amplification, which technically was unnecessary given obscenity's unprotected status, nonetheless referred to states' interests in advancing neighborhood quality and aesthetics, improving the nature of commerce, and promoting public safety.[297] Even if claiming to be unbothered by any void in precise justification for regulating obscenity, the recital of rationales for control at least offered an accounting for the particular circumstances. So long as constitutional interests are not recognized, however, a rendition of that nature is optional.

While the Court delineated a virtually unbridled power to regulate obscenity, Justice Brennan used the *Paris Adult Theatre* decision as his point of departure from the jurisprudential course he had commenced in *Roth.* Although acknowledging significant regulatory interests, he concluded that problems in defining obscenity and applying vague standards "cannot justify the substantial damage to constitutional rights and to this Nation's judicial machinery."[298] Brennan thus argued for reading the First Amendment as a bar to categorical exclusion of sexually oriented materials except to protect juveniles and unconsenting adults.[299] Brennan's position thus would coalesce the implications of the *Stanley* decision[300] with *Ginsberg v. New York*[301] and make them the central body of obscenity law.[302] The Court in *Ginsberg* recognized a government's special interest in children, given their impressionability, and thus constructed an obscenity standard that is more encompassing when they are a concern.[303] So far, however, Brennan's urgings that the Court alter and narrow its focus have been officially unheeded.

Paris Adult Theatre I v. Slaton, 413 U.S. 49 (1973)

Mr. Chief Justice Burger delivered the opinion of the Court.

Petitioners are two Atlanta, Georgia, movie theaters and their owners and managers, operating in the style of "adult" theaters. On December 28, 1970, respondents, the local state district attorney and the solicitor for the local state trial court, filed civil complaints in that court alleging that petitioners were exhibiting to the public for paid admission two allegedly obscene films, contrary to Georgia Code Ann. § 26–2101.

After viewing the films, the Georgia Supreme Court held that their exhibition should have been enjoined, stating:

> The films in this case leave little to the imagination. It is plain what they purport to depict, that is, con-

duct of the most salacious character. We hold that these films are also hard core pornography, and the showing of such films should have been enjoined since their exhibition is not protected by the first amendment. *Id.,* at 347, 185 S. E. 2d, at 770.

We categorically disapprove the theory, apparently adopted by the trial judge, that obscene, pornographic films acquire constitutional immunity from state regulation simply because they are exhibited for consenting adults only. This holding was properly rejected by the Georgia Supreme Court. Although we have often pointedly recognized the high importance of the state interest in regulating the exposure of obscene materials to juveniles and unconsenting adults, see *Miller v. California, ante,* at 18–20; *Stanley v. Georgia,* 394 U.S., at 567; *Redrup v. New York,* 386 U.S. 767, 769 (1967), this Court has never declared these to be the only legitimate state interests permitting regulation of obscene material. The States have a long-recognized legitimate interest in regulating the use of obscene material in local commerce and in all places of public accommodation, as long as these regulations do not run afoul of specific constitutional prohibitions. See *United States v. Thirty-seven Photographs, supra,* at 376–377 (opinion of White, J.); *United States v. Reidel,* 402 U.S., at 354–356. Cf. *United States v. Thirty-seven Photographs, supra,* at 378 (Stewart, J., concurring). "In an unbroken series of cases extending over a long stretch of this Court's history, it has been accepted as a postulate that 'the primary requirements of decency may be enforced against obscene publications.' [*Near v. Minnesota,* 283 U.S. 697, 716 (1931)]." *Kingsley Books, Inc. v. Brown, supra,* at 440.

In particular, we hold that there are legitimate state interests at stake in stemming the tide of commercialized obscenity, even assuming it is feasible to enforce effective safeguards against exposure to juveniles and to passersby. Rights and interests "other than those of the advocates are involved." *Breard v. Alexandria,* 341 U.S. 622, 642 (1951). These include the interest of the public in the quality of life and the total community environment, the tone of commerce in the great city centers, and, possibly, the public safety itself. The Hill-Link Minority Report of the Commission on Obscenity and Pornography indicates that there is at least an arguable correlation between obscene material and crime. Quite apart from sex crimes, however, there remains one problem of large proportions aptly described by Professor Bickel:

It concerns the tone of the society, the mode, or to use terms that have perhaps greater currency, the style and quality of life, now and in the future. A man may be entitled to read an obscene book in his room, or expose himself indecently there.... We should protect his privacy. But if he demands a right to obtain the books and pictures he wants in the market, and to foregather in public places—discreet, if you will, but accessible to all—with others who share his tastes, *then to grant him his right is to affect the world about the rest of us, and to impinge on other privacies.* Even supposing that each of us can, if he wishes, effectively avert the eye and stop the ear (which, in truth, we cannot), what is commonly read and seen and heard and done intrudes upon us all, want it or not. 22 *The Public Interest* 25–26 (Winter 1971). (Emphasis added.)

As Mr. Chief Justice Warren stated, there is a "right of the Nation and of the States to maintain a decent society...," *Jacobellis v. Ohio*, 378 U.S. 184, 199 (1964) (dissenting opinion). See *Memoirs v. Massachusetts*, 383 U.S. 413, 457 (1966) (Harlan, J., dissenting); *Beauharnais v. Illinois*, 343 U.S. 250, 256–257 (1952); *Kovacs v. Cooper*, 336 U.S. 77, 86–88 (1949).

But, it is argued, there are no scientific data which conclusively demonstrate that exposure to obscene material adversely affects men and women or their society. It is urged on behalf of the petitioners that, absent such a demonstration, any kind of state regulation is "impermissible." We reject this argument. It is not for us to resolve empirical uncertainties underlying state legislation, save in the exceptional case where that legislation plainly impinges upon rights protected by the Constitution itself. Mr. Justice Brennan, speaking for the Court in *Ginsberg v. New York*, 390 U.S. 629, 642–643 (1968), said: "We do not demand of legislatures 'scientifically certain criteria of legislation.' *Noble State Bank v. Haskell*, 219 U.S. 104, 110." Although there is no conclusive proof of a connection between antisocial behavior and obscene material, the legislature of Georgia could quite reasonably determine that such a connection does or might exist. In deciding *Roth*, this Court implicitly accepted that a legislature could

legitimately act on such a conclusion to protect *"the social interest in order and morality." Roth v. United States*, 354 U.S., at 485, quoting *Chaplinsky v. New Hampshire*, 315 U.S. 568, 572 (1942) (emphasis added in *Roth*).

From the beginning of civilized societies, legislators and judges have acted on various unprovable assumptions. Such assumptions underlie much lawful state regulation of commercial and business affairs. See *Ferguson v. Skrupa*, 372 U.S. 726, 730 (1963); *Breard v. Alexandria*, 341 U.S., at 632–633, 641–645; *Lincoln Federal Labor Union v. Northwestern Iron & Metal Co.*, 335 U.S. 525, 536–537 (1949). The same is true of the federal securities and antitrust laws and a host of federal regulations. See *SEC v. Capital Gains Research Bureau, Inc.*, 375 U.S. 180, 186–195 (1963); *American Power & Light Co. v. SEC*, 329 U.S. 90, 99–103 (1946); *North American Co. v. SEC*, 327 U.S. 686, 705–707 (1946), and cases cited. See also *Brooks v. United States*, 267 U.S. 432, 436–437 (1925), and *Hoke v. United States*, 227 U.S. 308, 322 (1913). On the basis of these assumptions both Congress and state legislatures have, for example, drastically restricted associational rights by adopting antitrust laws, and have strictly regulated public expression by issuers of and dealers in securities, profit sharing "coupons," and "trading stamps," commanding what they must and must not publish and announce. See *Sugar Institute, Inc. v. United States*, 297 U.S. 553, 597–602 (1936); *Merrick v. N. W. Halsey & Co.*, 242 U.S. 568, 584–589 (1917); *Caldwell v. Sioux Falls Stock Yards Co.*, 242 U.S. 559, 567–568 (1917); *Hall v. Geiger-Jones Co.*, 242 U.S. 539, 548–552 (1917); *Tanner v. Little*, 240 U.S. 369, 383–386 (1916); *Rast v. Van Deman & Lewis Co.*, 240 U.S. 342, 363–368 (1916). Understandably those who entertain an absolutist view of the First Amendment find it uncomfortable to explain why rights of association, speech, and press should be severely restrained in the marketplace of goods and money, but not in the marketplace of pornography.

Likewise, when legislatures and administrators act to protect the physical environment from pollution and to preserve our resources of forests, streams, and parks, they must act on such imponderables as the impact of a new highway near or through an existing park or wilderness area. See *Citizens to Preserve Overton Park v. Volpe*, 401 U.S.

402, 417–420 (1971). Thus, § 18 (a) of the Federal-Aid Highway Act of 1968, 23 U.S.C. § 138, and the Department of Transportation Act of 1966, as amended, 82 Stat. 824, 49 U.S.C. § 1653 (f), have been described by Mr. Justice Black as "a solemn determination of the highest law-making body of this Nation that the beauty and health-giving facilities of our parks are not to be taken away for public roads without hearings, factfindings, and policy determinations under the supervision of a Cabinet officer.... " *Citizens to Preserve Overton Park, supra,* at 421 (separate opinion joined by Brennan, J.). The fact that a congressional directive reflects unprovable assumptions about what is good for the people, including imponderable aesthetic assumptions, is not a sufficient reason to find that statute unconstitutional.

If we accept the unprovable assumption that a complete education requires the reading of certain books, see *Board of Education v. Allen,* 392 U.S. 236, 245 (1968), and *Johnson v. New York State Education Dept.,* 449 F. 2d 871, 882–883 (CA2 1971) (dissenting opinion), vacated and remanded to consider mootness, 409 U.S. 75 (1972), *id.,* at 76–77 (Marshall, J., concurring), and the well nigh universal belief that good books, plays, and art lift the spirit, improve the mind, enrich the human personality, and develop character, can we then say that a state legislature may not act on the corollary assumption that commerce in obscene books, or public exhibitions focused on obscene conduct, have a tendency to exert a corrupting and debasing impact leading to antisocial behavior? "Many of these effects may be intangible and indistinct, but they are nonetheless real." *American Power & Light Co. v. SEC, supra,* at 103. Mr. Justice Cardozo said that all laws in Western civilization are "guided by a robust common sense...." *Steward Machine Co. v. Davis,* 301 U.S. 548, 590 (1937). The sum of experience, including that of the past two decades, affords an ample basis for legislatures to conclude that a sensitive, key relationship of human existence, central to family life, community welfare, and the development of human personality, can be debased and distorted by crass commercial exploitation of sex. Nothing in the Constitution prohibits a State from reaching such a conclusion and acting on it legislatively simply because there is no conclusive evidence or empirical data.

It is argued that individual "free will" must govern, even in activities beyond the protection of the First Amendment and other constitutional guarantees of privacy, and that government cannot legitimately impede an individual's desire to see or acquire obscene plays, movies, and books. We do indeed base our society on certain assumptions that people have the capacity for free choice. Most exercises of individual free choice—those in politics, religion, and expression of ideas—are explicitly protected by the Constitution. Totally unlimited play for free will, however, is not allowed in our or any other society. We have just noted, for example, that neither the First Amendment nor "free will" precludes States from having "blue sky" laws to regulate what sellers of securities may write or publish about their wares. See *supra,* at 61–62. Such laws are to protect the weak, the uninformed, the unsuspecting, and the gullible from the exercise of their own volition. Nor do modern societies leave disposal of garbage and sewage up to the individual "free will," but impose regulation to protect both public health and the appearance of public places. States are told by some that they must await a "laissez-faire" market solution to the obscenity-pornography problem, paradoxically "by people who have never otherwise had a kind word to say for laissez-faire," particularly in solving urban, commercial, and environmental pollution problems. See I. Kristol, On the Democratic Idea in America 37 (1972).

The States, of course, may follow such a "laissez-faire" policy and drop all controls on commercialized obscenity, if that is what they prefer, just as they can ignore consumer protection in the marketplace, but nothing in the Constitution *compels* the States to do so with regard to matters falling within state jurisdiction. See *United States v. Reidel,* 402 U.S., at *357; Memoirs v. Massachusetts,* 383 U.S., at 462 (White, J., dissenting). "We do not sit as a super-legislature to determine the wisdom, need, and propriety of laws that touch economic problems, business affairs, or social conditions." *Griswold v. Connecticut,* 381 U.S. 479, 482 (1956). See *Ferguson v. Skrupa,* 372 U.S., at 731; *Day-Brite Lighting, Inc. v. Missouri,* 342 U.S. 421, 423 (1952).

It is asserted, however, that standards for evaluating state commercial regulations are inapposite in the present context, as state regulation of access by consenting adults to obscene material violates the constitutionally protected right to privacy enjoyed by petitioners' customers. Even assuming that petitioners have vicarious standing to assert potential customers' rights, it is unavailing to compare a theater open to the public for a fee, with the private home of *Stanley v. Georgia*, 394 U.S., at 568, and the marital bedroom of *Griswold v. Connecticut, supra*, at 485–486. This Court, has, on numerous occasions, refused to hold that commercial ventures such as a motion-picture house are "private" for the purpose of civil rights litigation and civil rights statutes. See *Sullivan v. Little Hunting Park, Inc.*, 396 U.S. 229, 236 (1969); *Daniel v. Paul*, 395 U.S. 298, 305–308 (1969); *Blow v. North Carolina*, 379 U.S. 684, 685–686 (1965); *Hamm v. Rock Hill*, 379 U.S. 306, 307–308 (1964); *Heart of Atlanta Motel, Inc. v. United States*, 379 U.S. 241, 247, 260–261 (1964). The Civil Rights Act of 1964 specifically defines motion-picture houses and theaters as places of "public accommodation" covered by the Act as operations affecting commerce. 78 Stat. 243, 42 U.S.C. §§ 2000a (b)(3), (c).

Our prior decisions recognizing a right to privacy guaranteed by the Fourteenth Amendment included "only personal rights that can be deemed 'fundamental' or 'implicit in the concept of ordered liberty.' *Palko v. Connecticut*, 302 U.S. 319, 325 (1937)." *Roe v. Wade*, 410 U.S. 113, 152 (1973). This privacy right encompasses and protects the personal intimacies of the home, the family, marriage, motherhood, procreation, and child rearing. Cf. *Eisenstadt v. Baird*, 405 U.S. 438, 453–454 (1972); *id.*, at 460, 463–465 (White, J., concurring); *Stanley v. Georgia, supra*, at 568; *Loving v. Virginia*, 388 U.S. 1, 12 (1967); *Griswold v. Connecticut, supra*, at 486; *Prince v. Massachusetts*, 321 U.S. 158, 166 (1944); *Skinner v. Oklahoma*, 316 U.S. 535, 541 (1942); *Pierce v. Society of Sisters*, 268 U.S. 510, 535 (1925); *Meyer v. Nebraska*, 262 U.S. 390, 399 (1923). Nothing, however, in this Court's decisions intimates that there is any "fundamental" privacy right "implicit in the concept of ordered liberty" to watch obscene movies in places of public accommodation....

It is also argued that the State has no legitimate interest in "control [of] the moral content of a person's thoughts," *Stanley v. Georgia, supra*, at 565, and we need not quarrel with this. But we reject the claim that the State of Georgia is here attempting to control the minds or thoughts of those who patronize theaters. Preventing unlimited display or distribution of obscene material, which by definition lacks any serious literary, artistic, political, or scientific value as communication, *Miller v. California, ante*, at 24, 34, is distinct from a control of reason and the intellect. Cf. *Kois v. Wisconsin*, 408 U.S. 229 (1972); *Roth v. United States, supra*, at 485–487; *Thornhill v. Alabama*, 310 U.S. 88, 101–102 (1940); Finnis, "Reason and Passion": The Constitutional Dialectic of Free Speech and Obscenity, 116 *U. Pa. L. Rev.* 222, 229–230, 241–243 (1967). Where communication of ideas, protected by the First Amendment, is not involved, or the particular privacy of the home protected by *Stanley*, or any of the other "areas or zones" of constitutionally protected privacy, the mere fact that, as a consequence, some human "utterances" or "thoughts" may be incidentally affected does not bar the State from acting to protect legitimate state interests. Cf. *Roth v. United States, supra*, at 483, 485–487; *Beauharnais v. Illinois*, 343 U.S., at 256–257. The fantasies of a drug addict are his own and beyond the reach of government, but government regulation of drug sales is not prohibited by the Constitution. Cf. *United States v. Reidel, supra*, at 359–360 (Harlan, J., concurring).

Finally, petitioners argue that conduct which directly involves "consenting adults" only has, for that sole reason, a special claim to constitutional protection. Our Constitution establishes a broad range of conditions on the exercise of power by the States, but for us to say that our Constitution incorporates the proposition that conduct involving consenting adults only is always beyond state regulation, is a step we are unable to take. Commercial exploitation of depictions, descriptions, or exhibitions of obscene conduct on commercial premises open to the adult public falls within a State's broad power to regulate commerce and protect the public environment. The issue in this context goes beyond whether someone, or even the majority, considers the conduct depicted as "wrong" or "sinful." The States have the power to make a morally neutral judgment that public exhibition of obscene material, or commerce in such material, has a tendency to injure the community as a whole, to endanger the public safety, or to jeopardize, in Mr. Chief Justice Warren's words, the States' "right . . . to maintain a decent society." *Jacobellis v. Ohio,* 378 U.S. at 199.

Mr. Justice Brennan, with whom Mr. Justice Stewart and Mr. Justice Marshall join, dissenting.

This case requires the Court to confront once again the vexing problem of reconciling state efforts to suppress sexually oriented expression with the protections of the First Amendment, as applied to the States through the Fourteenth Amendment. No other aspect of the First Amendment has, in recent years, demanded so substantial a commitment of our time, generated such disharmony of views, and remained so resistant to the formulation of stable and manageable standards. I am convinced that the approach initiated 16 years ago in *Roth v. United States,* 354 U.S. 476 (1957), and culminating in the Court's decision today, cannot bring stability to this area of the law without jeopardizing fundamental First Amendment values, and I have concluded that the time has come to make a significant departure from that approach. . . .

In *Roth v. United States,* 354 U.S. 476 (1957), the Court held that obscenity, although expression, falls outside the area of speech or press constitutionally protected under the First and Fourteenth Amendments against state or federal infringement. But at the same time we emphasized in *Roth* that "sex and obscenity are not synonymous," *id.,* at 487, and that matter which is sexually oriented but not obscene is fully protected by the Constitution. For we recognized that "[s]ex, a great and mysterious motive force in human life, has indisputably been a subject of absorbing interest to mankind through the ages; it is one of the vital problems of human interest and public concern." *Ibid. Roth* rested, in other words, on what has been termed a two-level approach to the question of obscenity. While much criticized, that approach has been endorsed by all but two members of this Court who have addressed the question since *Roth.* Yet our efforts to implement that approach demonstrate that agreement on the existence of something called "obscenity" is still a long and painful step from agreement on a workable definition of the term. . . .

The problems of fair notice and chilling pro-

tected speech are very grave standing alone. But it does not detract from their importance to recognize that a vague statute in this area creates a third, although admittedly more subtle, set of problems. These problems concern the institutional stress that inevitably results where the line separating protected from unprotected speech is excessively vague. In *Roth* we conceded that "there may be marginal cases in which it is difficult to determine the side of the line on which a particular fact situation falls. . . ." 354 U.S., at 491–492. Our subsequent experience demonstrates that almost every case is "marginal." And since the "margin" marks the point of separation between protected and unprotected speech, we are left with a system in which almost every obscenity case presents a constitutional question of exceptional difficulty. "The suppression of a particular writing or other tangible form of expression is . . . an *individual* matter, and in the nature of things every such suppression raises an individual constitutional problem, in which a reviewing court must determine for *itself* whether the attacked expression is suppressable within constitutional standards." *Roth, supra.* at 497 (separate opinion of Harlan, J.). . . .

As a result of our failure to define standards with predictable application to any given piece of material, there is no probability of regularity in obscenity decisions by state and lower federal courts. That is not to say that these courts have performed badly in this area or paid insufficient attention to the principles we have established. The problem is, rather, that one cannot say with certainty that material is obscene until at least five members of this Court, applying inevitably obscure standards, have pronounced it so. The number of obscenity cases on our docket gives ample testimony to the burden that has been placed upon this Court. . . .

Our experience since *Roth* requires us not only to abandon the effort to pick out obscene materials on a case-by-case basis, but also to reconsider a fundamental postulate of *Roth:* that there exists a definable class of sexually oriented expression that may be totally suppressed by the Federal and State Governments. Assuming that such a class of expression does in fact exist, I am forced to conclude that the concept of "obscenity" cannot be defined with sufficient specificity and clarity to provide fair notice to persons who create and distribute sexually oriented materials, to prevent substantial erosion of protected speech as a by-product of the attempt to suppress unprotected speech, and to avoid very costly institutional harms. Given these inevitable side effects of state efforts to suppress what is assumed to be *unprotected* speech, we must scrutinize with care the state interest that is asserted to justify the suppression. For in the absence of some very substantial interest in suppressing such speech, we can hardly condone the ill effects that seem to flow inevitably from the effort.... Like the proscription of abortions, the effort to suppress obscenity is predicated on unprovable, although strongly held, assumptions about human behavior, morality, sex, and religion. The existence of these assumptions cannot validate a statute that substantially undermines the guarantees of the First Amendment, any more than the existence of similar assumptions on the issue of abortion can validate a statute that infringes the constitutionally protected privacy interests of a pregnant woman.

If, as the Court today assumes, "a state legislature may...act on the...assumption that commerce in obscene books, or public exhibitions focused on obscene conduct, have a tendency to exert a corrupting and debasing impact leading to antisocial behavior," *ante,* at 63, then it is hard to see how state-ordered regimentation of our minds can ever be forestalled. For if a State, in an effort to maintain or create a particular moral tone, may prescribe what its citizens cannot read or cannot see, then it would seem to follow that in pursuit of that same objective a State could decree that its citizens must read certain books or must view certain films. Cf. *United States v. Roth,* 237 F. 2d 796, 823 (CA2 1956) (Frank, J., concurring). However laudable its goal—and that is obviously a question on which reasonable minds may differ—the State cannot proceed by means that violate the Constitution.

Even a legitimate, sharply focused state concern for the morality of the community cannot, in other words, justify an assault on the protections of the First Amendment. Cf. *Griswold v. Connecticut,* 381 U.S. 479 (1965); *Eisenstadt v. Baird,* 405 U.S. 438 (1972); *Loving v. Virginia,* 388 U.S. 1 (1967). Where the state interest in regulation

of morality is vague and ill defined, interference with the guarantees of the First Amendment is even more difficult to justify.

In short, while I cannot say that the interests of the State—apart from the question of juveniles and unconsenting adults—are trivial or non-existent, I am compelled to conclude that these interests cannot justify the substantial damage to constitutional rights and to this Nation's judicial machinery that inevitably results from state efforts to bar the distribution even of unprotected material to consenting adults. *NAACP v. Alabama,* 377 U.S. 288, 307 (1964); *Cantwell v. Connecticut,* 310 U.S., at 304. I would hold, therefore, that at least in the absence of distribution to juveniles or obtrusive exposure to unconsenting adults, the First and Fourteenth Amendments prohibit the State and Federal Governments from attempting wholly to suppress sexually oriented materials on the basis of their allegedly "obscene" contents. Nothing in this approach precludes those governments from taking action to serve what may be strong and legitimate interests through regulation of the manner of distribution of sexually oriented material.

Jurisprudential and critical ferment suggested abiding concern with the *Miller* test, if not a consensus for a replacement standard. Consistent with Justice Brennan's sense that obscenity cannot be defined with sufficient precision, Justice Scalia has observed that:

> It is quite impossible to come to an objective assessment of (at least literary or artistic value, there being many accomplished people who have found literature in Dada and art in the replication of a soup can.... I think we would be better advised to adopt as a legal maxim what has long been the wisdom of mankind: *De gustibus non est disputandum.* Just as there is no use arguing about taste, there is no use litigating about it.[304]

Meanwhile, Justices Stevens, Marshall, and Blackmun have suggested that constitutional protection should be afforded if "*some reasonable people* would consider [the expression] as having serious literary, artistic, political, or scientific value."[305] Some theorists advocate moving jurisprudence beyond the notion that obscenity has no value to the more assertive premise that it harms women and reinforces their societal subordination. They would redefine obscenity to account for speech depicting women as sex objects, characterizing them in a diminished position or reinforcing harmful ways of thinking about women.[306] Although acknowledging the validity of such concerns, the court of appeals in *American Booksellers Association v. Hudnut*[307] found that freedom of speech assumes the risk that insidious expression may "influence the culture and shape our socialization." It further warned that "if a process of [social] conditioning were enough to permit governmental regulation, that would be the end of freedom of speech." Even if the future direction is uncertain, the potential at least exists for some movement beyond existing standards.

2. Indecency

The absence of any constitutional concern for sexually oriented expression characterized as obscene may have helped condition and facilitate less tolerant attitudes toward speech which, even if not obscene, is depicted as offensive or indecent. The consequences are particularly significant for broadcasting which, as the Court has observed, has the most limited First Amendment protection of all media.[308] In *Federal Communications Commission v. Pacifica-Foundation*[309] the Court concluded that civil and criminal liability could attach to the broadcast of indecent or profane language.[310] The First Amendment thereby was not violated by standards for sexually oriented expression that were less exacting than the *Miller* formula.[311]

The *Pacifica* decision referenced its holdings to what was described as radio and tele-vision's pervasive presence, intrusive nature, and unique accessibility to children. Permeating the opinions, however, was a subjective revulsion to the nature of the expression. Deprecating references to a satire upon attitudes toward several commonly used expletives[312] are reminiscent of obscenity-related review to the effect that they reflect a sense that "modern civilization does not leave disposal of garbage and sewage to free will."[313]

A majority of the Court has never formally endorsed the notion that indecent expression constitutes a distinct and less protected speech form.[314] For practical purposes, however, it is difficult not to recognize that a special speech classification exists subject to variable standards tied largely to taste. That sense is magnified by the observation, in *Young v. American Mini Theatres, Inc.,*[315] that "few of us would send our sons and daughters off to war to preserve the citizen's right to see [explicit sex portrayals] exhibited in the theaters of our choice."[316] Such commentary, in support of a zoning ordinance regulating the location of adult bookstores and movie houses, accurately may reflect the notion that many persons do not cherish or revere the subject expression. Even if the observation is accurate, a competing reality is that there are many people for whom political expression is so irrelevant that they might not consider it worth fighting for. A more pertinent argument may be that it is the full ambit and dynamics of a pluralistic system of free expression, rather than any segment of it, and the opportunity to select autonomously from a diverse menu of expression that evoke and merit defense. Conclusions that a particular form of expression is unworthy of protection not only endangers that variant of speech but also narrows the range of diversity and choice. The constitutional challenge, if devaluation is to be brooked in discrete instances, is to ensure that the process functions as an isolated and well-justified exception rather than a norm.

D. COMMERCIAL SPEECH

Commercial speech is a form of expression characterized by an unusually high degree of constitutional instability. Until the 1970s, the level of protection afforded commercial speech attracted little discussion because the Court had set it outside the First Amendment's purview. A challenge to a city's prohibition of for-hire advertising on trucks, therefore, elicited more equal protection than First Amendment interest.[317] Eventual recognition that commercial speech merited constitutional protection has been compounded by subsequent holdings and observations tending to diminish its First Amendment status. A key problem flowing from the determination that commercial expression is a protected speech variant, and the focus of litigation since, is the proper standard of review for regulation and the interests and concern justifying government control. Even more fundamental, and tracing back to commercial expression's preconstitutional status, is what such speech comprises.

Nearly half a century ago, in *Valentine v. Chrestensen,*[318] the Court held that the First Amendment did not preclude regulation of "purely commercial advertising."[319] Notwithstanding the unprotected nature of commercial speech at the time, the decision was problematical and revealed an analytical treachery that has endured. The Court in *Chrestensen* affirmed the conviction of an entrepreneur who violated a municipal ordinance by distributing a handbill advertising a commercial exhibition on one side and protesting the city's refusal to provide a show place for him on the other.[320] It classified the leaflet in singular terms as commercial speech,[321] although the content also had a political dimension.

The consequences of selective classification are significant, when expression may have multiple dimensions, because depiction determines relative constitutional status and consequent vulnerability to regulation. Even since determining that commercial expression falls within the First Amendment's ambit, the Court has tended to classify complex expression in singular terms. By focusing upon what is perceived to be the primary purpose of speech,[322] or merely denominating expression as commercial without further elaboration,[323] review essentially discounts or disregards what may be significant secondary attributes. Such analysis is reminiscent of the *Chrestensen* Court's inclination not to "indulge nice appraisal based on subtle distinctions."[324]

The evolution of commercial speech into a constitutionally protected variant of expression commenced during the early 1970s. In *Capital Broadcasting Company v. Mitchell,*[325] the Court upheld a federal law prohibiting cigarette advertising on radio and television.[326] Although the net result was indistinguishable from *Chrestensen,* the lower court decision affirmed without opinion suggested limits upon government's regulatory power. The observation that the state may restrict truthful advertising of lawful activities determined by the legislature to be harmful[327] intimated a qualifying predicate that would have been unnecessary if the expression at issue categorically was unprotected.

Shortly thereafter, in *Pittsburgh Press Company v. Pittsburgh Commission on Human Relations,*[328] the Court by its own words moved a step further toward altering the constitutional status of commercial speech. In upholding an ordinance that prohibited a newspaper's segregation of help-wanted advertisements by gender,[329] the Court determined that states may prohibit advertising of illegal activities.[330] A logical inference from the decision was that commercial expression concerning a lawful activity was entitled to some measure of constitutional protection.

The implication of the *Pittsburgh Press* decision was stated more affirmatively, in *Bigelow v. Virginia*,[331] when the Court held that the government may not prohibit touting of a lawful activity.[332] The *Bigelow* opinion was characterized by a rather vain effort to reconcile evolving commercial speech doctrine with the *Chrestensen* decision. The Court depicted its original ruling as affirming a reasonable time, place, and manner restriction rather than insulating all regulation of commercial speech from constitutional challenge.[333] Reconciliation of emerging principle with *Chrestensen*'s exclusion of commercial speech from the First Amendment soon was abandoned in favor of official discrediting. What emerged as a predicate for the newly recognized status of commercial speech was a candid recognition that the value of such expression for many was "as keen, if not keener by far, than [any] interest in the day's most urgent political debate."[334] In *Virginia State Board of Pharmacy v. Virginia Citizens Consumer Council*,[335] the Court thus recognized the public's interest in the flow of commercial expression and forthrightly conferred upon it First Amendment status.[336]

Virginia State Board of Pharmacy v. Virginia Citizens Consumer Council, 425 U.S. 748 (1976)

Mr. Justice Blackmun delivered the opinion of the Court.

The plaintiff-appellees in this case attack, as violative of the First and Fourteenth Amendments, that portion of § 54–524.35 of Va. Code Ann. (1974), which provides that a pharmacist licensed in Virginia is guilty of unprofessional conduct if he "(3) publishes, advertises or promotes, directly or indirectly, in any manner whatsoever, any amount, price, fee, premium,

discount, rebate or credit terms . . . for any drugs which may be dispensed only by prescription."

V

We begin with several propositions that already are settled or beyond serious dispute. It is clear, for example, that speech does not lose its First Amendment protection because money is spent to project it, as in a paid advertisement of one form or another. *Buckley v. Valeo*, 424 U.S. 1, 35–59 (1976); *Pittsburgh Press Co. v. Human Relations Comm'n*, 413 U.S., at 384; *New York Times Co. v. Sullivan*, 376 U.S., at 266. Speech likewise is protected even though it is carried in a form that is "sold" for profit, *Smith v. California*, 361 U.S. 147, 150 (1959) (books); *Joseph Burstyn, Inc. v. Wilson*, 343 U.S. 495, 501 (1952) (motion pictures); *Murdock v. Pennsylvania*, 319 U.S., at 111 (religious literature), and even though it may involve a solicitation to purchase or otherwise pay or contribute money. *New York Times Co. v. Sullivan, supra*; *NAACP v. Button*, 371 U.S. 415, 429 (1963); *Jamison v. Texas*, 318 U.S., at 417; *Cantwell v. Connecticut*, 310 U.S. 296, 306–307 (1940).

If there is a kind of commercial speech that lacks all First Amendment protection, therefore, it must be distinguished by its content. Yet the speech whose content deprives it of protection cannot simply be speech on a commercial subject. No one would contend that our pharmacist may be prevented from being heard on the subject of whether, in general, pharmaceutical prices should be regulated, or their advertisement forbidden. Nor can it be dispositive that a commercial advertisement is noneditorial, and merely reports a fact. Purely factual matter of public interest may claim protection. *Bigelow v. Virginia*, 421 U.S., at 822; *Thornhill v. Alabama*, 310 U.S. 88, 102 (1940).

Our question is whether speech which does "no more than propose a commercial transaction," *Pittsburgh Press Co. v. Human Relations Comm'n*, 413 U.S., at 385, is so removed from any "exposition of ideas," *Chaplinsky v. New Hampshire*, 315 U.S. 568, 572 (1942), and from " 'truth, science, morality, and arts in general, in its diffusion of liberal sentiments on the administration of Government,' " *Roth v. United States*, 354 U.S. 476,

484 (1957), that it lacks all protection. Our answer is that it is not. . . .

Generalizing, society also may have a strong interest in the free flow of commercial information. Even an individual advertisement, though entirely "commercial," may be of general public interest. The facts of decided cases furnish illustrations: advertisements stating that referral services for legal abortions are available, *Bigelow v. Virginia, supra*; that a manufacturer of artificial furs promotes his product as an alternative to the extinction by his competitors of fur-bearing mammals, see *Fur Information & Fashion Council, Inc. v. E. F. Timme & Son*, 364 F. Supp. 16 (SDNY 1973); and that a domestic producer advertises his product as an alternative to imports that tend to deprive American residents of their jobs, cf. *Chicago Joint Board v. Chicago Tribune Co.*, 435 F. 2d 470 (CA7 1970), cert. denied, 402 U.S. 973 (1971). Obviously, not all commercial messages contain the same or even a very great public interest element. There are few to which such an element, however, could not be added. Our pharmacist, for example, could cast himself as a commentator on store-to-store disparities in drug prices, giving his own and those of a competitor as proof. We see little point in requiring him to do so, and little difference if he does not.

Moreover, there is another consideration that suggests that no line between publicly "interesting" or "important" commercial advertising and the opposite kind could ever be drawn. Advertising, however tasteless and excessive it sometimes may seem, is nonetheless dissemination of information as to who is producing and selling what product, for what reason, and at what price. So long as we preserve a predominantly free enterprise economy, the allocation of our resources in large measure will be made through numerous private economic decisions. It is a matter of public interest that those decisions, in the aggregate, be intelligent and well informed. To this end, the free flow of commercial information is indispensable. See *Dun & Bradstreet, Inc. v. Grove*, 404 U.S. 898, 904–906 (1971) (Douglas, J., dissenting from denial of certiorari). See also *FTC v. Procter & Gamble Co.*, 386 U.S. 568, 603–604 (1967) (Harlan, J., concurring). And if it is indispensable to the proper allocation of resources in a free enterprise system, it is also indispensable to the for-mation of intelligent opinions as to how that system ought to be regulated or altered. Therefore, even if the First Amendment were thought to be primarily an instrument to enlighten public decisionmaking in a democracy, we could not say that the free flow of information does not serve that goal. . . .

VI

In concluding that commercial speech, like other varieties, is protected, we of course do not hold that it can never be regulated in any way. Some forms of commercial speech regulation are surely permissible. We mention a few only to make clear that they are not before us and therefore are not foreclosed by this case.

There is no claim, for example, that the prohibition on prescription drug price advertising is a mere time, place, and manner restriction. We have often approved restrictions of that kind provided that they are justified without reference to the content of the regulated speech, that they serve a significant governmental interest, and that in so doing they leave open ample alternative channels for communication of the information. Compare *Grayned v. City of Rockford*, 408 U.S. 104, 116 (1972); *United States v. O'Brien*, 391 U.S. 367, 377 (1968); and *Kovacs v. Cooper*, 336 U.S. 77, 85–87 (1949), with *Buckley v. Valeo*, 424 U.S. 1; *Erznoznik v. City of Jacksonville*, 422 U.S. 205, 209 (1975); *Cantwell v. Connecticut*, 310 U.S., at 304–308; and *Saia v. New York*, 334 U.S. 558, 562 (1948). Whatever may be the proper bounds of time, place, and manner restrictions on commercial speech, they are plainly exceeded by this Virginia statute, which singles out speech of a particular content and seeks to prevent its dissemination completely.

Nor is there any claim that prescription drug price advertisements are forbidden because they are false or misleading in any way. Untruthful speech, commercial or otherwise, has never been protected for its own sake. *Gertz v. Robert Welch, Inc.*, 418 U.S. 323, 340 (1974); *Konigsberg v. State Bar*, 366 U.S. 36, 49, and n. 10 (1961). Obviously, much commercial speech is not provably false, or even wholly false, but only deceptive or misleading. We foresee no obstacle to a State's dealing effectively with this problem.ᵃ The First Amendment, as we construe it today, does not prohibit the State from insuring that the stream of commercial information flow cleanly as well as freely. See, for example, Va. Code Ann. § 18.2–216 (1975).

---

a. In concluding that commercial speech enjoys First Amendment protection, we have not held that it is wholly undifferentiable from other forms. There are commonsense differences between speech that does "no more than propose a commercial transaction," *Pittsburgh Press Co. v. Human Relations Comm'n,* 413 U.S., at 385, and other varieties. Even if the differences do not justify the conclusion that commercial speech is valueless, and thus subject to complete suppression by the State, they nonetheless suggest that a different degree of protection is necessary to insure that the flow of truthful and legitimate commercial information is unimpaired. The truth of commercial speech, for example, may be more easily verifiable by its disseminator than, let us say, news reporting or political commentary, in that ordinarily the advertiser seeks to disseminate information about a specific product or service that he himself provides and presumably knows more about than anyone else. Also, commercial speech may be more durable than other kinds. Since advertising is the *sine qua non* of commercial profits, there is little likelihood of its being chilled by proper regulation and forgone entirely.

Attributes such as these, the greater objectivity and hardiness of commercial speech, may make it less necessary to tolerate inaccurate statements for fear of silencing the speaker. Compare *New York Times Co. v. Sullivan,* 376 U.S. 254 (1964), with *Dun & Bradstreet, Inc. v. Grove,* 404 U.S. 898 (1971). They may also make it appropriate to require that a commercial message appear in such a form, or include such additional information, warnings, and disclaimers, as are necessary to prevent its being deceptive. Compare *Miami Herald Publishing Co. v. Tornillo,* 418 U.S. 241 (1974), with *Banzhaf v. FCC,* 132 U.S. App. D.C. 14, 405 F. 2d 1082 (1968), cert. denied *sub nom. Tobacco Institute, Inc. v. FCC,* 396 U.S. 842 (1969). Cf. *United States v. 95 Barrels of Vinegar,* 265 U.S. 438, 443 (1924) ("It is not difficult to choose statements, designs and devices which will not deceive"). They may also make inapplicable the prohibition against prior restraints. Compare *New York Times Co. v. United States,* 403 U.S. 713 (1971), with *Donaldson v. Read Magazine,* 333 U.S. 178, 189–191 (1948); *FTC v. Standard Education Society,* 302 U.S. 112 (1937); *E.F. Drew & Co. v. FTC,* 235 F. 2d 735, 739–740 (CA2 1956), cert. denied, 352 U.S. 969 (1957).

Also, there is no claim that the transactions proposed in the forbidden advertisements are themselves illegal in any way. Cf. *Pittsburgh Press Co. v. Human Relations Comm'n,* 413 U.S. 376 (1973); *United States v. Hunter,* 459 F. 2d 205 (CA4), cert. denied, 409 U.S. 934 (1972). Finally, the special problems of the electronic broadcast media are likewise not in this case. Cf. *Capitol Broadcasting Co. v. Mitchell,* 333 F. Supp. 582 (DC 1971), aff'd *sub nom. Capitol Broadcasting Co. v. Acting Attorney General,* 405 U.S. 1000 (1972).

What is at issue is whether a State may completely suppress the dissemination of concededly truthful information about entirely lawful activity, fearful of that information's effect upon its disseminators and its recipients. Reserving other questions, we conclude that the answer to this one is in the negative.

Despite explicitly conferring constitutional status upon commercial speech, the Court stopped short of affording it unqualified protection. Rather, it sought to differentiate commercial from political expression and created a separate standard of review on the grounds that the former was hardier and "more easily verifiable by its disseminator."[337] Adverting to "common sense differences" between commercial and other forms of speech, the Court concluded "that a different degree of protection is necessary to insure that the flow of truthful and legitimate commercial information is unimpaired."[338] Given the nature and propensities attributed to commercial speech, it emphasized that government might legitimately require disclosure, disclaimers, or warnings.[339] Furthermore, the Court noted that traditional presumptions against the validity of prior restraint would not operate.[340]

Diminished constitutional status, at least to the extent predicated upon notions of hardiness and verifiability, is problematical. The conclusion that commercial expression is uniquely durable underestimates, for instance, the resiliency of political speech. Although the profit motive may be a powerful force that enhances commercial expression's immunity against official chilling influences, durability is not a unique categorical feature. A politician's interest in being elected, for instance, constitutes a motivating force at least as significant as the impulse to make money. If resiliency were to be given its full logical impact, an important form of political expression would merit diminished protection. Hardiness thus may be less than adequate as a point for distinguishing commercial and other variants of speech satisfactorily. Any inherent resiliency possessed by commercial expression may be immaterial, moreover, given the consequences of regulation. The obvious effect of systems of prior restraint or compulsory disclosure is the forced weakening of any expression's propagating tendencies. The offer and sale of securities and the marketing of tobacco products, for instance, are governed by regulatory schemes that previously restrain and define the terms of expression. Speech that does not meet the demands of official criteria thus may be irretrievably lost.[341]

The companion rationale that commercial speech is easier to verify also is troublesome. Deceptive commercial and political statements present potential problems that are essentially indistinguishable. Promotion of products, candidates, and ideas all can be a function of misrepresentation. To the extent that any expression shortchanges the truth, whether to obtain money or votes, the authentication problem is comparable.

Although not expressed in direct terms, the diminished constitutional status of commercial expression might be explicable as a matter of simple valuation that fits within a broader constitutional value system that affords less regard to economic rights and interests. Modern due process and equal protection analysis of regulation affecting commercial activity consists of a highly deferential standard of review, contrasted with the enhanced scrutiny for legislation touch-

ing various other individual rights.[342] Even that value-based explication, however, is imperfect. If carried to its logical extreme, the generally lesser constitutional concern afforded commercial interests would swallow the particularized recognition that commercial speech may have value equal to or surpassing political expression.

The process of distinguishing commercial speech for constitutional purposes might consider or account for relativities in the nature or cause of identified harms. Injury from a misleading commercial advertisement affecting a purchasing decision, for instance, is likely to be more direct than false political promises affecting a person's vote. Although a false pledge not to raise taxes if elected may translate into an identifiable harm, if relied upon, the injury is a result of combined voting preferences rather than entirely individual influence. Because the collective action of voting also is susceptible to diverse influences, many of which may respond to concerns unconnected to the false statement, the linkage between cause and harm may be more attenuated.

False political expression also may have relatively higher value in effectuating informed decision making. In propounding his developmental theory of democracy,[343] John Stuart Mill noted that competition among ideas, whether true or false, strengthened truth, compelled the continuous reevaluation of ideas, and promoted the evolution of ideas based upon reason rather than prejudice.[344] Although false political statements may connect with the broad philosophical underpinnings of a system of freedom of expression, the relationship for untrue commercial speech is less manifest.

Distinctions resting upon category would seem to assume that the type of speech at issue can be clearly identified. The Court has defined commercial speech as expression inviting a commercial transaction[345] or relating to the economic interest of the speaker and the audience.[346] Presumably, the latter definition subsumes the former and affords an overarching delineation. It also presents overbreadth problems, as even the most manifestly political expression may have underlying economic motivation. Even the authoring, promotion, and dissemination of anticapitalist polemics may be associated with profit making. The Court has observed that the presence of a profit motive is not necessarily dispositive toward determining whether expression should be labeled as commercial.[347] Evolving and increasingly fine labeling standards suggest that, like obscenity, commercial speech may lend itself better to being "known when seen" rather than being objectively defined. Speech categorization is a treacherous process, moreover, insofar as singular classification may dismiss the multidimensional nature of expression, and the chosen identification is outcome determinative of First Amendment status.

The mixed nature of much speech and consequent difficulties of drawing precise lines for the real world were evidenced in *Village of Schaumburg v. Citizens for a Better Environment.*[348] The Court in that case invalidated a regulation prohibiting door-to-door solicitation by certain charitable organizations.[349] In so doing, it attempted to distinguish such fund-raising from commercial speech on the grounds that the former "does more than inform private economic decision and is not primarily concerned with providing information about the characteristics and costs of goods and services."[350] Justice Rehnquist, in dissent, asserted that the activity was purely commercial in its nature and merited no special constitutional solicitude.[351] Greater acuity and sophistication might have been evinced in either instance by forthright recognition of the mixed character of the speech. Such a denomination need not have altered the outcome but would have avoided the procrustean appear-

ance if not nature of the analysis. Review nonetheless seems disposed to favor polar choices rather than finer distinctions and intermediary determinations accounting for degrees of political or commercial character.

The conferral of constitutional status upon commercial expression was not accompanied by a clear enunciation of standards for assessing the pertinence or influence of regulatory interests. Subsequently, the Court invalidated prohibitions on the display of residential for-sale signs,[352] promotion of contraceptives,[353] and attorney advertising.[354] In *Linmark Associates, Inc. v. Township of Willingboro,*[355] the Court emphasized the importance of free flowing information despite claims that the posting of for-sale signs encouraged white flight and undermined racial integration goals.[356] Official justifications for precluding contraceptive advertisement, on the grounds that they were offensive, were rejected as inadequate.[357] Implicit was a balancing of First Amendment interests and the importance of regulatory concerns.[358] The invalidation of restrictions upon attorney advertising further suggested a requirement that any official limitation upon commercial speech must be supported by a substantial state interest.[359] The protective reach of the First Amendment was explicitly delineated, however, to exclude false advertising.[360]

Critical to the invalidation of attorney advertising restraints was their operation against general publicity and not merely face-to-face solicitations which the Court considered more dangerous and subject to stricter control.[361] Interests in protecting unsophisticated or distressed individuals from vexation conduct thus were recognized as grounds for limiting the style of attorney solicitation.[362] Solicitation for private gain was distinguished, however, from the activities of nonprofit organizations which litigate for political purposes.[363] In-person solicitation may be proscribed when likely to result in deception or improper influence, but regulation may not "abridge unnecessarily the associational freedom of" politically-oriented legal organizations.[364]

Although the Court recognized the value of commercial expression for constitutional purposes, actual standards of review were not well articulated or connected. Eventually, in *Central Hudson Gas & Electric Co. v. Public Service Commission of New York*,[365] the Court formulated a comprehensive framework for analyzing commercial speech problems. At issue was a regulation prohibiting power companies from promoting the use of electricity.[366] The state had justified the ban on the grounds that the ban advanced energy conservation.[367] The Court invalidated the prohibition pursuant to a four-part test for determining the permissibility of official control.

Central Hudson Gas & Electric Co. v. Public Service Commission of New York, 447 U.S. 597 (1980)

The First Amendment's concern for commercial speech is based on the informational function of advertising. See *First National Bank of Boston v. Bellotti*, 435 U.S. 765, 783 (1978). Consequently, there can be no constitutional objection to the suppression of commercial messages that do not accurately inform the public about lawful activity. The government may ban forms of communication more likely to deceive the public than to inform it, *Friedman v. Rogers, supra*, at 13, 15–16; *Ohralik v. Ohio State Bar Assn., supra*, at 464–465, or commercial speech related to illegal activity, *Pittsburgh Press Co. v. Human Relations Comm'n*, 413 U.S. 376, 388 (1973).

If the communication is neither misleading nor related to unlawful activity, the government's power is more circumscribed. The State must assert a substantial interest to be achieved by restrictions on commercial speech. Moreover, the regulatory technique must be in proportion to that interest. The limitation on expression must be designed carefully to achieve the State's goal.

Compliance with this requirement may be measured by two criteria. First, the restriction must directly advance the state interest involved; the regulation may not be sustained if it provides only ineffective or remote support for the government's purpose. Second, if the governmental interest could be served as well by a more limited restriction on commercial speech, the excessive restrictions cannot survive.

Under the first criterion, the Court has declined to uphold regulations that only indirectly advance the state interest involved. In both *Bates* and *Virginia Pharmacy Board*, the Court concluded that an advertising ban could not be imposed to protect the ethical or performance standards of a profession. The Court noted in *Virginia Pharmacy Board* that "[t]he advertising ban does not directly affect professional standards one way or the other." 425 U.S., at 769. In *Bates*, the Court overturned an advertising prohibition that was designed to protect the "quality" of a lawyer's work. "Restraints on advertising ... are an ineffective way of deterring shoddy work." 433 U.S., at 378.

The second criterion recognizes that the First Amendment mandates that speech restrictions be "narrowly drawn." *In re Primus*, 436 U.S. 412, 438 (1978). The regulatory technique may extend only as far as the interest it serves. The State cannot regulate speech that poses no danger to the asserted state interest, see *First National Bank of Boston v. Bellotti, supra*, at 794–795, nor can it completely suppress information when narrower restrictions on expression would serve its interest as well. For example, in *Bates* the Court explicitly did not "foreclose the possibility that some limited supplementation, by way of warning or disclaimer or the like, might be required" in promotional materials. 433 U.S., at 384. See *Virginia Pharmacy Board, supra*, at 773. And in *Carey v. Population Services International*, 431 U.S. 678, 701–702 (1977), we held that the State's "arguments ... do not justify the total suppression of advertising concerning contraceptives." This holding left open the possibility that the State could implement more carefully drawn restrictions. See *id.*, at 712 (Powell, J., concurring in part and in judgment); *id.*, at 716–717 (Stevens, J., concurring in part and in judgment).

In commercial speech cases, then, a four-part analysis has developed. At the outset, we must determine whether the expression is protected by the First Amendment. For commercial speech to come within that provision, it at least must concern lawful activity and not be misleading. Next, we ask whether the asserted governmental interest is substantial. If both inquiries yield positive answers, we must determine whether the regulation directly advances the governmental interest asserted, and whether it is not more extensive than is necessary to serve that interest.

In applying the four-part test, the Court determined that a constitutional interest was present because the expression was not deceptive and did not promote unlawful activity.[368] It also recognized an important state interest in energy efficiency and acknowledged that the legislative methodology would effectuate that aim.[369] The regulatory means failed, however, because it reached too far and because less burdensome alternatives existed for facilitating the state's objectives. The Court noted that advertisements for energy-efficient products were ensnared by the broad prohibition, and thus a more narrowly drawn restriction or review process must be employed.[370]

Prior to *Central Hudson*, it was becoming evident that the Court might not hold firm to the *Virginia Board of Pharmacy* statement of principle disfavoring regulation unless expression is misleading or the underlying activity is illegal.[371] In *Friedman v. Rogers*,[372] the Court upheld a regulation prohibiting optometrists from using trade names.[373] The decision rested in part upon the predicate that trade names have "no intrinsic meaning," convey no real information, and may mislead the public.[374] In *Friedman*, the Court strained to justify the regulation within the contours of the falseness or deception allowance provided by *Virginia Board of Pharmacy*. More recently, the Court has expanded the focus on underlying illegality to include any activity that the state has the authority to control even if the regulatory power is not exercised.[375] In *Posadas de Puerto Rico Asso-*

ciates v. Tourism Co. of Puerto Rico,[376] it thus further relaxed the conditions that categorically preclude official regulation of commercial speech.

The *Posadas de Puerto Rico Associates* decision is reminiscent, in a critical sense, of the devaluation of commercial speech in *Valentine v. Chrestensen* and its early progeny. For the first time since the shelving of *Chrestensen*, the Court, in *Posadas de Puerto Rico Associates,* countenanced official restraint of truthful information regarding a lawful activity.[377] The Court held that a legislature may ban expression concerning an activity it considers harmful, even if not made illegal, because "the greater power to completely ban casino gambling necessarily includes the lesser power to ban advertising of casino gambling."[378]

By allowing restrictions on the promotion of a lawful activity,[379] the *Posadas* Court distinguished its holding from earlier decisions invalidating bans on contraceptive[380] and abortion[381] advertisements on the ground that those matters were constitutionally protected but gambling was not.[382] In making that distinction, however, it introduced the newly restrictive notion that the First Amendment precludes official abridgment of advertising only when the underlying activity is not constitutionally protected.[383] Few products, services, or activities are without potential for harm. Many are not constitutionally protected. Measuring First Amendment protection according to the constitutional status of the underlying activity, therefore, represents a check on legislative power that may prove illusory.[384] In any event, the Court has significantly departed from jurisprudence regarding commercial speech differently only to the extent necessary to facilitate an unimpaired flow of truthful and legitimate information.[385]

The *Posadas* Court also effectively diluted the standard for judicial scrutiny of commercial speech. The Court purported to employ an elevated standard of review, as set forth in *Central Hudson,* requiring that the regulation directly advance a substantial state interest and restrict speech no more than necessary.[386] Although referencing its analysis to those criteria, the Court concluded that the legislature could decide the regulatory alternative that would best serve its end.[387] Such a determination translates in practice into a deferential model of review.

In addition to using a standard resembling a rational basis test, the Court appeared to discount if not disregard less restrictive means of effectuating regulatory aims. Justice Brennan suggested that, if concerned with social harm from casino gambling, Puerto Rico could have monitored gambling operations to guard against infiltration by organized crime, aggressively enforced relevant criminal statutes, and promulgated competing speech calculated to discourage participation by residents.[388] The availability of less restrictive alternatives led the Court just a few years earlier to conclude that government could not completely suppress commercial speech even if acting to further "an imperative national goal."[389]

Posadas de Puerto Rico Associates v. Tourism Co. of Puerto Rico, 478 U.S. 328 (1986)

Justice Rehnquist delivered the opinion of the Court.

In this case we address the facial constitutionality of a Puerto Rico statute and regulations restricting advertising of casino gambling aimed at the residents of Puerto Rico. Appellant Posadas de Puerto Rico Associates, doing business in Puerto Rico as Condado Holiday Inn Hotel and Sands Casino, filed suit against appellee Tourism Company of Puerto Rico in the Superior Court of Puerto Rico, San Juan Section. Appellant sought a declaratory judgment that the statute and regulations, both facially and as applied by the Tourism Company, impermissibly sup-

pressed commercial speech in violation of the First Amendment and the equal protection and due process guarantees of the United States Constitution. The Superior Court held that the advertising restrictions had been unconstitutionally applied to appellant's past conduct. But the court adopted a narrowing construction of the statute and regulations and held that, based on such a construction, both were facially constitutional. The Supreme Court of Puerto Rico dismissed an appeal on the ground that it "d[id] not present a substantial constitutional question." We postponed consideration of the question of jurisdiction until the hearing on the merits. We now hold that we have jurisdiction to hear the appeal, and we affirm the decision of the Supreme Court of Puerto Rico with respect to the facial constitutionality of the advertising restrictions.

Appellant argues . . . that the challenged advertising restrictions are underinclusive because other kinds of gambling such as horse racing, cockfighting, and the lottery may be advertised to the residents of Puerto Rico. Appellant's argument is misplaced for two reasons. First, whether other kinds of gambling are advertised in Puerto Rico or not, the restrictions on advertising of casino gambling "directly advance" the legislature's interest in reducing demand for games of chance. See *id.,* at 511, (plurality opinion of White, J.) ("[W]hether onsite advertising is permitted or not, the prohibition of offsite advertising is directly related to the stated objectives of traffic safety and esthetics. This is not altered by the fact that the ordinance is underinclusive because it permits onsite advertising"). Second, the legislature's interest, as previously identified, is not necessarily to reduce demand for all games of chance, but to reduce demand for casino gambling. According to the Superior Court, horse racing, cockfighting, "picas," or small games of chance at fiestas, and the lottery "have been traditionally part of the Puerto Rican's roots," so that "the legislator could have been more flexible than in authorizing more sophisticated games which are not so widely sponsored by the people." In other words, the legislature felt that for Puerto Ricans the risks associated with casino gambling were significantly greater than those associated with the more traditional kinds of gambling in Puerto Rico. In our view, the legislature's separate classification of casino gambling, for purposes of the advertising ban, satisfies the third step of the *Central Hudson* analysis.

We also think it clear beyond peradventure that the challenged statute and regulations satisfy the fourth and last step of the *Central Hudson* analysis, namely, whether the restrictions on commercial speech are no more extensive than necessary to serve the government's interest. The narrowing constructions of the advertising restrictions announced by the Superior Court ensure that the restrictions will not affect advertising of casino gambling aimed at tourists, but will apply only to such advertising when aimed at the residents of Puerto Rico. See also n. 7, *infra*; cf. *Oklahoma Telecasters Assn. v. Crisp*, 699 F.2d 490, 501 (CA10 1983), rev'd on other grounds *sub nom. Capital Cities Cable, Inc. v. Crisp*, 467 U.S. 691 (1984). Appellant contends, however, that the First Amendment requires the Puerto Rico Legislature to reduce demand for casino gambling among the residents of Puerto Rico not by suppressing commercial speech that might *encourage* such gambling, but by promulgating additional speech designed to *discourage* it. We reject this contention. We think it is up to the legislature to decide whether or not such a "counterspeech" policy would be as effective in reducing the demand for casino gambling as a restriction on advertising. The legislature could conclude, as it apparently did here, that residents of Puerto Rico are already aware of the risks of casino gambling, yet would nevertheless be induced by widespread advertising to engage in such potentially harmful conduct. Cf. *Capital Broadcasting Co. v. Mitchell*, 333 F.Supp. 582, 585 (DC 1971) (three-judge court) ("Congress had convincing evidence that the Labeling Act of 1965 had not materially reduced the incidence of smoking"), aff'd, 405 U.S. 1000, 92 S.Ct. 1290, 31 L.Ed.2d 472 (1972); *Dunagin v. City of Oxford, Miss.*, 718 F.2d 738, 751 (CA5 1983) (en banc) ("We do not believe that a less restrictive time, place and manner restriction, such as a disclaimer warning of the dangers of alcohol, would be effective. The state's concern is not that the public is unaware of the dangers of alcohol.... The concern instead is that advertising will unduly promote alcohol consumption despite known dangers"), cert. denied, 467 U.S. 1259, 104 S.Ct. 3553, 82 L.Ed.2d 855 (1984).

In short, we conclude that the statute and regulations at issue in this case, as construed by the Superior Court, pass muster under each prong of the *Central Hudson* test. We therefore hold that the Supreme Court of Puerto Rico properly rejected appellant's First Amendment claim....

Appellant argues...that the challenged advertising restrictions are constitutionally defective...[on grounds] the underlying conduct was constitutionally protected and could not have been prohibited by the State. Here...the Puerto Rico legislature surely could have prohibited casino gambling by the Residents of Puerto Rico altogether. In our view, the greater power to completely ban casino gambling necessarily includes the lesser power to ban advertising of casino gambling....

Justice Brennan, with whom Justice Marshall and Justice Blackmun join, dissenting.

II

The Court, rather than applying strict scrutiny, evaluates Puerto Rico's advertising ban under the relaxed standards normally used to test government regulation of commercial speech. Even under these standards, however, I do not believe that Puerto Rico constitutionally may suppress all casino advertising directed to its residents. The Court correctly recognizes that "[t]he particular kind of commercial speech at issue here, namely, advertising of casino gambling aimed at the residents of Puerto Rico, concerns a lawful activity and is not misleading or fraudulent." *Ante,* at ____. Under our commercial speech precedents, Puerto Rico constitutionally may restrict truthful speech concerning lawful activity only if its interest in doing so is substantial, if the restrictions directly advance the Commonwealth's asserted interest, and if the restrictions are no more extensive than necessary to advance that interest. See *Zauderer,* 471 U.S., at ____, *In re R.M.J.,* 455 U.S. 191, 203, (1982); *Central Hudson,* 447 U.S., at 564. While tipping its hat to these standards, the Court does little more than defer to what it perceives to be the determination by Puerto Rico's legislature that a ban on casino advertising aimed at residents is reasonable. The Court totally ignores the fact that commercial speech is entitled to substantial First Amendment protection, giving the government unprecedented authority to eviscerate constitutionally protected expression.

The Court . . . sustains Puerto Rico's advertising ban because the legislature *could* have determined that casino gambling would seriously harm the health, safety, and welfare of the Puerto Rican citizens. *Ante,* at _____. This reasoning is contrary to this Court's long established First Amendment jurisprudence. When the government seeks to place restrictions upon commercial speech, a court may not, as the Court implies today, simply speculate about valid reasons that the government might have for enacting such restrictions. Rather, the government ultimately bears the burden of justifying the challenged regulation, and it is incumbent upon the government to *prove* that the interests it seeks to further are real and substantial. See *Zauderer,* 471 U.S., at _____. *In re R.M.J.,* 455 U.S., at 205–206.

The deference to legislative judgment apparent in *Posadas* suggested a spirit more akin to *Chrestensen* than to later decisions that discredited it. During the *Chrestensen* era, commercial speech was not constitutionally protected. Absent a fundamental constitutional interest, the Court normally applied a rational basis test that deferred to legislative judgment.[390] That approach contrasts with the elevated level of review used in later commercial speech cases in which the Court demanded proof of a substantial state interest.[391] In affirming the ban on casino gambling advertising, and particularly by concluding that Puerto Rico could have found the underlying activity harmful to the citizenry and thus prohibited it,[392] the *Posadas* Court seems to have retreated to a more deferential mode of review. Judicial speculation concerning what might constitute a proper and significant legislative purpose further denotes use of a rational basis test.[393] Reversion toward a more deferential posture also seems evidenced by a determination that regulation, although required to be no more extensive than necessary, need not be the least restrictive option available to advance government's interest.[394]

Commercial speech analysis appears to be drifting away from traditional notions that the First Amendment is designed to prevent "highly paternalistic" intrusions by the state which would limit the information available to the public.[395] Until *Posadas,* modern revised analysis seemed less inclined to tolerate regulation reflecting government concern that the public might act irrationally on truthful information concerning a lawful activity.[396] First Amendment jurisprudence traditionally holds the public responsible for evaluation of information[397] and for making decisions by means of autonomous rather than authoritative selection. *Virginia Pharmacy* integrated that principle to a considerable extent into subsequent commercial speech doctrine.[398] The Court later recognized that the First Amendment accepts the risk that the public might exercise poor judgment or even be deceived.[399] More recent jurisprudence, however, allows states to regulate commercial speech on essentially paternalistic grounds.

The Court has observed that the distinction between commercial and other forms of expression is a commonsense one.[400] It also acknowledged that the line "will not always be easy to draw."[401] The latter confession has proved to be more accurate then the former expectation. Definitional problems and uncertainty of how standards will be applied continue to be the primary treacheries of commercial speech analysis. It is evident that traditional risk assumption models premised upon opportunity for response in a self-regulating marketplace of information will not be relied upon exclusively to address concerns with the effects of commercial speech. Criteria settled in their articulation and application, however, await further development.[402]

E. COPYRIGHT

First Amendment rights and First Amendment values collide in the area of copyright. The constitution provides that "Congress shall have Power...To Promote the Progress of Science and useful Arts, by securing for limited Times to Authors and Inventors the exclusive Right to their respective Writings and Discoveries."[403] Copyright thus promotes First Amendment interests by "motivat[ing] the creative [process] by the provision of a special reward."[404] The consequent privilege, however, creates First Amendment problems insofar as it denies access to or restricts use of materials. Congress' delicate task pursuant to its constitutional charge, therefore, is to balance creative interests that are the source of expression against social interests in a free flow of information and ideas.[405] At the same time, copyright law must remain congruent with developing technology and advances in disseminating information.

Federal copyright law in its most basic form has been codified pursuant to congressional act which, since 1976, protects both published and unpublished works.[406] The Copyright Act of 1976,[407] responding to the emergence of new media that confounded its statutory antecedent, covers originally authored works "fixed in any tangible medium of expression, now known or later developed, from which they can be perceived, reproduced, or otherwise communicated either directly or with the aid of machine or device."[408] Still, problems arise in determining ambits of coverage. In *Sony Corp. of America v. Universal City Studios, Inc.*[409] the Supreme Court refused without congressional direction to include usage of videotape recorders as an act of infringement.[410] Noting the fluidity of technology and concerns, and the constitution's specific assignment of responsibility to the legislative branch, the Court emphasized that "(s)ound policy, as well as history supports our constant deference to Congress."[411] Excluded from the Copyright Act's protective ambit is "any idea, procedure, process, system, method of operation, concept, principle, or

discovery, regardless of the form in which it is described, explained, illustrated, or embodied in such work."[412] The 1976 Act preempts all state control, statutory or common law, of the field.[413]

The inherent tension that copyright law struggles with is protecting intellectual property but doing so in a fashion that does not impede the flow of information to the detriment of First Amendment values. Although the way in which news or history is packaged merits protection, therefore, raw information is not copyrighted.[414] Copyright protection of ideas, facts, and theory is afforded as an economic incentive designed to enlarge general knowledge.[415] It is not intended to confer exclusive rights to account for history or contemporary events, however, so actual protection only extends to the author's unique expression.[416] Copyright interests seldom will have such public significance that the author's interest will be subordinated to unfettered usage.[417]

As a general proposition, a copyright owner has the exclusive right to reproduce the subject work; to prepare derivative works from it; to market or distribute copies; and to perform or display literary, musical, dramatic, pantomime, film, pictorial graphic, sculpture, or other audiovisual work in public.[418] The right, which is segregable from the author in the event of a "work made for hire" or a subsequent transfer,[419] runs on one of two tracks. Pursuant to the present enactment, protection extends for fifty years beyond an author's death.[420] Under preceding law, which is still relevant to the extent that many works were copyrighted under it, an initial period of protection was available for twenty-eight years followed by an opportunity to renew for a second period of equal duration. Procedures for obtaining a valid copyright include proper notice upon all copies and filing with the Register of Copyrights.[421] Failure to do so may be curable, so long as the omission affected a small number of copies and reasonable efforts are made to correct the problem.[422] Probably the grayest and thus the most heavily litigated area of copyright law pertains to the doctrine of fair use. Federal statute provides that fair use is to be determined by:

> (1) the purpose and character of the use, including whether such use is of a commercial nature or is for nonprofit educational purpose;
>
> (2) the nature of the copyrighted work;
>
> (3) the amount and substantiality of the portion used in relation to the copyrighted work as a whole; and
>
> (4) the effect of the use upon the potential market for or value of the copyrighted work.[423]

The law thus requires the balancing of several competing interests to determine whether usage of a work constitutes infringement or fair use.

In *Harper & Row Publishers, Inc. v. Nation Enterprises,*[424] the Court considered a fair use argument by a magazine which excerpted segments concerning the pardon of Richard Nixon from President Ford's soon-to-be-published memoirs.[425] Publication of the article occurred before another magazine, which had contracted to publish like excerpts, went to press.[426] Although the information was newsworthy, the Court determined that the primary purpose of publication was commercial profit.[427] Neither the fact that the work was factual in nature or that a small fraction was used proved dispositive. The Court emphasized that the fair use defense had less pertinence to works that had not been published in their original form.[428] Because a crucial part of the book had been excerpted, moreover, actual quantity was considered less pertinent.[429] Finally, the actual loss of money suffered when the other magazine decided not to publish or pay convinced the Court that the unauthorized publication had hurt the book's marketability and had diminished

its value.[430] Although publication of the excerpts easily might be characterized as news, the *Harper & Row* decision demonstrates that a strong public interest alone will not prevent a finding of infringement. It evinces moreover a sensitivity of the Court to proprietary interests even in expression that otherwise qualifies as the most highly protected form of speech.[431]

Further illustrative of a restrictive fair use doctrine is a Second Circuit decision, in *Salinger v. Random House, Inc.,*[432] which enjoined the publication of a biography because it included small excerpts from letters which the subject of the book had copyrighted but had donated to libraries.[433] In examining the factors relevant to determining fair use, the court first, despite recognizing a valid purpose for usage, found that the biographer's needs could have been satisfied without using the actual contents of the letters.[434] Second, because the letters were unpublished, the scope of fair use was much narrower.[435] Third, although only small excerpts from many letters had been used, the court found that in sum they permeated a substantial portion of the biography.[436] Finally, because the letters constituted such a significant portion of the work, the court determined that the potential market for the copyrighted works would be impaired.[437] Despite the significant impact upon editorial discretion, neither the *Harper & Row* nor the *Salinger* case directly addressed First Amendment claims.

The Second Circuit revisited fair use in *New Era Publications International v. Carol Publishing Group,*[438] in which numerous passages from an author's published works were included in an unflattering biography. Although the district court had enjoined publication pending elimination of what it considered to be infringing excerpts,[439] the court of appeals found their incorporation to be fair use.[440] Notwithstanding publication of the book for profit, the appeals court distinguished the circumstances from *Harper & Row* on grounds they did not concern "underhanded" action calculated to realize "undeserved economic profit."[441] It also emphasized the factual and published nature of the copyrighted works and that the book at issue did not draw too heavily upon them.[442] Finally, the court determined that harm to the marketability of a forthcoming authorized biography, resulting from a "devastating critique," was not a concern of copyright law.[443]

Special copyright problems have arisen in the context of cable television. At a time when cable largely was a retransmission or siphoning medium, the Supreme Court held that its service was not a "performance for profit."[444] Consequently, it was not subject to copyright liability and could retransmit broadcast signals without obtaining permission of copyright owners whose works might be implicated.[445] Congress, however, since has required cable operators retransmitting copyrighted programming to pay a license fee.[446] The amount of the fee is set by the Copyright Royalty Tribunal, which also distributes monies collected pursuant to a complex formula intended to account for the interests of broadcasters and the producers and syndicators of programmers.[447] Despite claims by broadcasters that the fee distribution system grossly undervalues their interests, and by cable casters that it makes signal carriage in some instances prohibitive, the scheme has survived legal challenge.[448]

NOTES

1. Konigsberg v. State Bar of California, 366 U.S. 36, 49–51 (1961).

2. *Id.* at 60–61 (Black, J., dissenting).

3. *Id.* at 49.

4. *But see* interpretations of Branzburg v. Hayes, 408 U.S. 665 (1972), discussed in this chapter.

5. 436 U.S. 547 (1978).

6. *Id.* at 567–68.

7. *Id.* at 559.

8. *Id.*

9. *Id.*

10. *Id.* at 564.

11. The newspaper in fact had a policy of destroying photographs that might have aided in the prosecution of demonstrators. *Id.* at 568 n.1 (Powell, J., concurring).

12. *Id.* at 573 (Stewart, J., dissenting).

13. Pursuant to the Privacy Protection Act of 1980, federal or state officers may not seize the media's work product unless (1) probable cause exists that those in possession of it have committed or are committing a crime other than receiving the material, and (2) reason exists to believe that immediate seizure is necessary to prevent death or serious injury. Other documentary evidence cannot be seized except pursuant to the aforementioned exceptions or upon reason to believe that notice would result in loss of evidence or because materials have not been produced pursuant to subpoena. 42 U.S.C. § 2000aa–1 *et seq.*

14. Branzburg v. Hayes, 408 U.S. 665.

15. *Id.*

16. *Id.* at 688.

17. *Id.* at 691.

18. *See id.* at 710 (Powell, J., concurring).

19. Branzburg v. Hayes, 408 U.S. at 688.

20. *Id.* at 697. For an argument that an absolute privilege should operate, at least absent a competing constitutional claim, *see* Monk, *Evidentiary Privilege For Journalists' Source: Theory and Statutory Protection*, 51 MO. L.REV. 1 (1986).

21. *Id.* at 686–92, 698.

22. *Id.* at 710 (Powell, J., concurring).

23. *Id.* (Powell, J., concurring).

24. *Id.* (Powell, J., concurring).

25. *Id.* at 725 (Stewart, J., dissenting). *See* Silkwood v. Kerr-McGee Corporation, 563 F.2d 433, 437 (10th Cir. 1977).

26. *See, e.g.,* Baker v. F & F Investment, 470 F.2d 778 (2d Cir. 1972), *cert. denied,* 411 U.S. 966 (1973); Democratic National Committee v. McCord, 356 F.Supp. 1394 (D.D.C. 1973).

27. *See* Herbert v. Lando, 441 U.S. 153 (1979).

28. Branzburg v. Hayes, 408 U.S. at 706.

29. Matter of Farber, 78 N.J. 259, 394 A.2d 330, *cert. denied,* 439 U.S. 439 U.S. 997 (1978).

30. Prejudice linked to the media's coverage of the criminal justice system is discussed at I.C.2. and 3. of this chapter.

31. 427 U.S. 539 (1976).

32. *Id.* at 543–44.

33. *See* Chapter 2 of this book.

34. Nebraska Press Association v. Stuart, 427 U.S. at 563–64.

35. 443 U.S. 368 (1979).

36. *Id.* at 394.

37. *Id.* at 379–80.

38. *Id.* at 375, 383–84, 392–93.

39. *Id.* at 393.

40. *E.g., id.* at 380–83

41. *Id.* at 378–79, 393 n.25.

42. *Id.* at 378–79.

43. 448 U.S. 555 (1980).

44. Although the Court was divided with respect to its rationale, a majority supported the premise of a right of access. *Id.* at 580 (Burger, C. J., White and Stevens, J. J.); *id.* at 585 (Brennan and Marshall, J. J., concurring); *id.* at 599 (Stewart, J., concurring); *id.* at 604 (Blackmun, J., concurring).

45. *Id.* at 564–70.

46. *Id.* at 580–81. At minimum, the Court indicated a trial judge must make findings regarding the need for closure and consider whether less restrictive alternatives would be effective.

47. *Id.* at 580 (Burger, C. J., White and Stevens, J. J.); *id.* at 582 (White, J., concurring); *id.* at 584 (Stevens, J., concurring); *id.* at 585 (Brennan and Marshall, J. J., concurring); *id.* at 599 (Stewart, J., concurring); *id.* at 604 (Blackmun, J., concurring).

48. Globe Newspaper Co. v. Superior Court, 457 U.S. 596, 605 (1982).

49. 457 U.S. 596.

50. *Id.* at 610–11.

51. *Id.* at 607.

52. *Id.* at 608–09.

53. *Id.* at 607.

54. Gannett Co., Inc. v. DePasquale, 443 U.S. at 387–96.

55. 478 U.S. 1 (1986).

56. *Id.* at 15.

57. *Id.* at 10–11.

58. *Id.* at 15.

59. *Id.* at 26–27 (Stevens, J., dissenting).

60. *Id.* at 9. Special problems may arise in connection with contempt actions against grand jury witnesses. Although the proceedings may be judicial in nature, government may seek closure to protect grand jury secrecy. *See* Freedman, *Freedom of Information and the First Amendment in a Bureaucratic Age,* 49 BROOKLYN L.REV. 835 (1983).

61. *Id.* at 14.

62. Such was the standard advanced by the dissenters in Gannett Co., Inc. v. DePasquale, 443 U.S. at 441–42 (Blackmun, J., dissenting).

63. *See* Gannett Co., Inc. v. DePasquale, 443 U.S. at 393.

64. Judicial Canon 3A(7), preceded by ABA Canon of Judicial Ethics No. 35, was abandoned in 1982 and replaced with a guideline providing that judges might allow unobtrusive recording of judicial proceedings.

65. Irvin v. Dowd, 366 U.S. 717 (1961).

66. Rideau v. Louisiana, 373 U.S. 723 (1963).

67. *Id.* at 725–27.

68. Estes v. Texas, 381 U.S. 532 (1965).

69. *Id.* at 542–43.

70. *Id.* at 545–50.

71. *Id.* at 587 (Harlan, J., concurring). *See* Chandler v. Florida, 449 U.S. 560, 573–74 (1981).

72. Estes v. Texas, 381 U.S. at 590–96 (Harlan, J., concurring).

73. 449 U.S. 560.

74. *Id.* at 583.

75. *Id.* at 578–79.

76. *Id.* at 576–77.

77. *Id.* at 581–82.

78. *Id.* at 581.

79. *Id.* at 569.

80. *See* Globe Newspaper Co. v. Superior Court, 457 U.S. at 603.

81. 384 U.S. 333 (1966).

82. *Id.* at 363.

83. Details of the grossly sensational and inflammatory media crusade against the defendant are set forth at *Id.* at 335–49.

84. *Id.* at 344–45.

85. *Id.* at 342.

86. *Id.* at 342–45.

87. *Id.* at 350.

88. *Id.* at 351.

89. *Id.* at 358–63.

90. *Id.*

91. Nebraska Press Association v. Stuart, 427 U.S. at 563–64.

92. 343 U.S. 250 (1952).

93. *Id.* at 251.

94. *Id.* at 252.

95. *Id.* at 266.

96. For a contemporary examination of problems in protecting population subgroups from expression that is particularly derogatory or unsettling to them, *see* Berney, *When Academic Freedom and Freedom of Speech Confront Holocaust Denial and Group Libel,* 8 CARDOZO L. REV. 559 (1987).

97. *Id.* at 268 (Black, J., dissenting).

98. *Id.* at 275 (Black, J., dissenting).

99. New York Times Co., v. Sullivan, 376 U.S. 254, 258 (1964). A basic requirement for actionability is that an allegedly defamatory statement must concern the plaintiff. It is not necessary, however, that the victim of a falsehood be specifically identified by name. It is possible that a work of fiction can lead to a defamation action provided the "of and concerning" standard is satisfied with respect to an identifiable and actual person. *See, e.g.,* Pring v. Penthouse International Ltd., 7 Med. L.Rptr. (BNA) 1101 (D. Wyo. 1981), *rev'd* 695 F.2d 438 (10th Cir. 1982), *cert. denied,* 462 U.S. 1132

(1983). For a discussion of special problems presented by defamation actions arising from fictional works, *see* Rosen & Babcock, *Of and Concerning Real People and Writers of Fiction,* 7 COMM/ENT L.J. 221 (1985).

100. *Id.* at 256.

101. *Id.* at 262.

102. 376 U.S. 254.

103. *Id.* at 292.

104. *Id.* at 271–72.

105. *Id.* at 270.

106. *Id.* at 271–72.

107. *Id.* at 270. *See* A. Meiklejohn, *The First Amendment Is an Absolute,* 1961 SUP. CT. REV., 245, 255–57 (expression facilitating informed self-government is most valued).

108. Barr v. Matteo, 360 U.S. 564 (1959).

109. New York Times v. Sullivan, 376 U.S. at 279–80. Whether a genuine issue of fact exists with respect to actual malice must be determined under a "clear and convincing" standard. Minus clear and convincing evidence of actual malice, and even if the plaintiff asserts a jury might not believe the defendant, summary judgment is required. Anderson v. Liberty Lobby, Inc., 477 U.S. 242 (1986).

110. *Id.* at 280.

111. *See* St. Amant v. Thompson, 390 U.S. 727 (1968); Garrison v. Louisiana, 379 U.S. 64 (1964).

112. 390 U.S. at 730–32.

113. Hart-Hanks Communications, Inc. v. Connaughton, 109 S. CT. 2678, 2685–86 (1989).

114. *Id.* at 2697. Procedural aspects of a defamation action are discussed in Matheson, *Procedure in Public Defamation Cases: The Impact of The First Amendment,* 66 TEX. L. REV. 215 (1987).

115. Monitor Patriot Co. v. Roy, 401 U.S. 265, 277 (1971).

116. Rosenblatt v. Baer, 383 U.S. 75, 85 (1966).

117. Monitor Patriot Co. v. Roy, 401 U.S. at 271.

118. Rosenblatt v. Baer, 383 U.S. at 78.

119. Curtis Publishing Co. v. Butts, 388 U.S. 130, 162 (1967) (Warren, C.J. concurring).

120. *Id.* at 164.

121. 403 U.S. 29 (1971).

122. *Id.* at 43–44.

123. *Id.* at 57 (Black, J., concurring).

124. *Id.* at 43–44.

125. Gertz v. Robert Welch, Inc., 418 U.S. 323, 343–44 (1974).

126. *Id.* at 343.

127. The Court has not been daunted in drawing lines between commercial and political speech, for instance, even though the categories may overlap and the line thus is not "easy to draw." In re Primus, 436 U.S. 412, 438 n. 32 (1978). The treacherous nature of the undertaking was considered "no reason for avoiding the undertaking." *Id.*

128. Dun & Bradstreet, Inc. v. Greenmoss Builders, Inc., 472 U.S. 749, 758–59 (1985).

129. 418 U.S. 323.

130. *Id.* at 345–46.

131. New York Times v. Sullivan, 376 U.S. at 270.

132. Gertz v. Robert Welch, Inc., 418 U.S. at 351–52.

133. *Id.* at 345.

134. *Id.*

135. *Id.* at 344.

136. *Id.* at 325.

137. *Id.* at 326.

138. *Id.* at 351–52.

139. *Id.* at 352.

140. *Id.*

141. *Id.* at 347.

142. For a comparative evaluation of laws in selected jurisdictions governing defamation, in addition to privacy, access, shield laws and other matters discussed in this chapter, *see* Sylvester, *How the States Govern the News Media—A Survey of Selected Jurisdictions,* 16 Sw. U. L.REV. 723 (1986).

143. Gertz v. Robert Welch, Inc., 418 U.S. at 349.

144. *Id.* at 350.

145. *See* Ashdown, *Gertz and Firestone: A Study in Constitutional Policy-Making,* 61 MINN. L.REV. 645, 670–71 (1977).

146. 108 S.Ct. 876 (1988).

147. *Id.* at 882.

148. *Id.* at 878.

149. *Id.*

150. *Id.* at 880–81.

151. *Id.* at 880.

152. *Id.* at 881.

153. Gertz v. Robert Welch, Inc., 418 U.S. at 390 (White, J., dissenting).

154. *Id.* at 391 (White, J., dissenting).

155. For a detailed examination of the *Gertz* decision and its impact upon defamation law, *see* Watkins, *Gertz and the Common Law of Defamation,* 15 TEX TECH. L.REV. 823 (1984).

156. 418 U.S. at 355–60 (Douglas, J., dissenting) (too insensitive); *id.* at 361–69 (Brennan, J., dissenting) (too insensitive); *id.* at 369–404 (White, J., dissenting) (too sympathetic).

157. 424 U.S. 448 (1976).

158. *Id.* at 454–55; *id* at 485 (Marshall, J., dissenting).

159. *Id.* at 458.

160. *Id.* at 453.

161. *Id.* at 454.

162. *Id.* at 454 n.3.

163. *Id.* at 454.

164. 443 U.S. 157 (1979).

165. *Id.* at 161.

166. *Id.* at 162–63.

167. *Id.* at 165.

168. *Id.* at 166–67.

169. Gertz v. Robert Welch, Inc., 418 U.S. at 345.

170. 443 U.S. 111 (1979).

171. *Id.* at 114–17.

172. *Id.* at 134–36.

173. *Id.*

174. Gertz v. Robert Welch, Inc., 418 U.S. at 344.

175. Hutchinson v. Proxmire, 443 U.S. at 136.

176. *See* PROSSER & KEETON ON THE LAW OF TORTS, § 113, AT 807–08 (5th ed. 1984).

177. *See e.g.,* Pell v. Procunier, 417 U.S. 817, 826 (1974).

178. *See* J. NOWAK, R. ROTUNDA, J. YOUNG, CONSTITUTIONAL LAW, § 16.35, AT 935 n.11 (1986).

179. 472 U.S. 749.

180. *Id.* at 759. Whether speech relates to a public concern also is relevant to allocation of the burden of proof. If such a tie exists, a private plaintiff has the burden of proving falsehood by a media defendant. Philadelphia Newspapers Inc. v. Hepps, 475 U.S. 767 (1986).

181. *Id.* at 762.

182. 109 S. Ct. 2909 (1989).

183. New York Times Co. v. Sullivan, 376 U.S. at 271.

184. Gertz v. Robert Welch, Inc., 418 U.S. at 339–40. Despite the premise that "false ideas" do not exist for constitutional purposes, the Court has refused "to create a wholesale defamation exception for anything that might be labeled 'opinion.' " Milkovich v. Lorain Journal Co., 110 S.Ct. (1990). Inquiry thus does not terminate upon determining how expression is styled but proceeds to consider whether it "may . . . imply assertion of objective fact." Id.

185. 465 U.S. 770 (1984).

186. *Id.* at 776.

187. Dun & Bradstreet, Inc. v. Greenmoss Builders, Inc., 472 U.S. at 767 (White, J., dissenting).

188. *Id.* (White, J., dissenting).

189. *Id.* (White, J., dissenting).

190. *Id.* at 768 (White, J., dissenting).

191. *Id.* at 774 (White, J., dissenting).

192. Some of the issues that linger in the area of defamation are identified and examined in Diamond, *Unanswered Defamation Questions,* 10 COMM/ENT L.J. 125 (1987).

193. Zacchini v. Scripps-Howard Broadcasting Co., 433 U.S. 562 (1977).

194. *Id.* at 569–70. For a comprehensive rendition of the nature of the right to publicity, including an accounting of how the commercial interests underlying it help distinguish it from other privacy rights, *see* Halpern, *The Right of Publicity: Commercial Exploitation of the Associative Value of Personality,* 39 VAND. L.REV. 1199 (1986). *See also* Sims, *Right of Publicity: Survivability Reconsidered,* 49 FORDHAM L.REV. 453 (1981).

195. 433 U.S. at 573.

196. 433 U.S. 562.

197. *Id.* at 575.

198. *Id.* at 580–82 (Powell, J., dissenting).

199. *Id.* at 573.

200. PROSSER & KEETON ON THE LAW OF TORTS, § 117, at 854–56 (1985). For an examination of problems in balancing First Amendment and individual interests in physical security and control over intimate facts, *see* Linder, *When Names Are Not News They're Negligence: Media Liability for Injuries Resulting from the Publication of Accurate Information,* 52 U.M.K.C. L. REV. 421 (1984).

201. PROSSER & KEETON ON THE LAW OF TORTS, § 117 at 858.

202. 449 F.2d 245 (9th Cir. 1971).

203. *Id.* at 246.

204. *Id.* at 246.

205. *Id.* at 249.

206. *Id.* at 250.

207. *See* Pearson v. Dodd, 410 F.2d 701 (D.C.Cir. 1969). *See generally* New York Times Co. v. United States, 403 U.S. 713 (1971).

208. 420 U.S. 469 (1975).

209. *Id.* at 494–95. Insofar as the pertinent state law punished only disclosure by the media, rather than individuals, the Court's decision fits with a broader pattern of jurisprudence steering away from significant distinctions between speech and press that would prioritize or order the respective rights.

210. *Id.* at 471–74.

211. 527 F.2d 1122 (9th Cir. 1975), *cert. denied,* 425 U.S. 998 (1976).

212. *Id.* at 1124.

213. *Id.* at 1127–28.

214. *See* Brandeis & Warren, *The Right to Privacy,* 4 HARV. L.REV. 193, 193–95 (1890).

215. *See* Mutual Film Corp. v. Industrial Commission of Ohio, 236 U.S. 230, 244 (1915).

216. Joseph Burstyn, Inc. v. Wilson, 343 U.S. 495, 501 (1952).

217. *See* Time, Inc. v. Firestone, 424 U.S. 448, 454 (1976).

218. 109 S.Ct. 2603 (1989).

219. *Id.* at 2609.

220. *Id.* at 2610, 2613.

221. *Id.* at 2612.

222. *Id.* at 2611.

223. *Id.* at 2613.

224. *Id.* at 2612–13.

225. *Id.* at 2613.

226. 385 U.S. 374 (1967).

227. *Id.* at 378.

228. *Id.*

229. *Id.* at 377–78.

230. *Id.* at 388.

231. *Id.* at 387.

232. *See* Gertz v. Robert Welch, Inc., 418 U.S. at 343–44.

233. 419 U.S. 245 (1974).

234. *Id.* at 248.

235. *Id.* at 250.

236. *Id.*

237. Chaplinsky v. New Hampshire, 315 U.S. 568, 572 (1942).

238. 283 U.S. 697 (1931).

239. *Id.* at 716.

240. 354 U.S. 476 (1957).

241. *Id.* at 484–85.

242. *Id.* at 485.

243. *Id.* at 487.

244. *Id.* at 487 n.20.

245. *Id.* at 489.

246. *Id.* at 486–87.

247. *Id.* at 514 (Douglas, J., dissenting).

248. *Id.* at 509 (Douglas, J., dissenting).

249. Paris Adult Theatre I v. Slaton, 413 U.S. 49, 61 (1973).

250. *Id.* at 62–63.

251. The refusal to probe any such points reflects the sense that no constitutional interest is at stake. *Id.* at 62–64.

252. *See* Lively, *The Sometimes Relevant First Amendment,* 60 TEMPLE L.Q. 881, 885 (1987).

253. *See* Lockhart & McClure, *Literature, the Law of Obscenity and the Constitution,* 38 MINN. L.REV. 295, 380 (1954).

254. *See* THE REPORT OF THE U.S. COMMISSION ON OBSCENITY AND PORNOGRAPHY 27 (1970).

255. *See* REPORT OF THE ATTORNEY GENERAL'S COMMISSION ON PORNOGRAPHY, § 2.2 (1986).

256. Roth v. United States, 354 U.S. at 497 (Harlan, J., concurring and dissenting).

257. Jacobellis v. Ohio, 378 U.S. 184, 197 (1964) (Stewart, J., concurring).

258. Paris Adult Theatre I v. Slaton, 413 U.S. at 112–14 (Brennan, J., dissenting).

259. A Book Named "John Cleland's Memoirs of a Woman of Pleasure" v. Attorney General of Massachusetts, 383 U.S. 413 (1966).

260. *Id.* at 417.

261. *Id.* at 419.

262. *Id.* at 418.

263. *Id.*

264. 383 U.S. 463 (1966).

265. *Id.* at 470–71.

266. *Id.* at 468.

267. *Id.* at 470–71.

268. Paris Adult Theatre I v. Slaton, 413 U.S. at 82–83 (Brennan, J., dissenting).

269. 413 U.S. 15 (1973).

270. *Id.* at 24.

271. *Id.* at 30.

272. 418 U.S. 153 (1974).

273. *Id.* at 161.

274. Miller v. California, 413 U.S. at 16, *citing* Interstate Circuit, Inc. v. Dallas, 390 U.S. 676, 704 (1968) (Harlan, J., concurring and dissenting).

275. Jenkins v. Georgia, 418 U.S. at 160.

276. Miller v. California, 413 U.S. at 33.

277. Jenkins v. Georgia, 418 U.S. at 157.

278. Miller v. California, 413 U.S. at 32.

279. Pope v. Illinois, 107 S.Ct. 1918, 1920 (1987).

280. Miller v. California, 413 U.S. at 24.

281. *Id.* at 25.

282. *Id.*

283. *See* Ward v. Illinois, 431 U.S. 767, 773–74 (1977).

284. Brockett v. Spokane Arcades, Inc., 472 U.S. at 491, 505 (1985).

285. Miller v. California, 413 U.S. at 35.

286. *Id.* at 24.

287. A Book Named "John Cleland's Memoirs of a Women of Pleasure" v. Attorney General of Massachusetts, 383 U.S. at 418.

288. Pope v. Illinois, 107 S.Ct. at 1921.

289. *Id.*

290. *Id.*

291. *See id.* at 1926 (Stevens, J., dissenting).

292. 394 U.S. 557 (1969).

293. *Id.* at 568.

294. 413 U.S. 49 (1973).

295. *Id.* at 52.

296. *Id.* at 62.

297. *Id.* at 58.

298. *Id.* at 112 (Brennan, J., dissenting).

299. *Id.* at 112–13 (Brennan, J., dissenting).

300. 394 U.S. 557.

301. 390 U.S. 629 (1968).

302. *See* Paris Adult Theatre I v. Slaton, 413 U.S. at 112–13 (Brennan, J., dissenting). The operation of obscenity as a variable concept is not unique in its application to children. Majority support has existed for the principle that prurient aims of materials directed to a deviant sexual group are to be measured by the group's rather then a normal person's interests. Mishkin v. New York, 383 U.S. 502, 508 (1966). A total ban on materials not obscene for all purposes, because they might harm

children, would be impermissible. Butler v. Michigan, 352 U.S. 380 (1957). A contrary result would reduce standards governing adults to those applicable to children. *Id.* at 383.

303. Ginsberg v. New York, 390 U.S. at 641–43.

304. Pope v. Illinois, 107 S.Ct. at 1923 (Scalia, J., concurring).

305. *Id.* at 1927 (Stevens, J., dissenting).

306. *See e.g.*, MacKinnon, *Pornography, Civil Rights and Speech*, 20 HARV. C. R.-C.L. L.REV. 1 (1985).

307. 771 F. 2d 323 (7th Cir. 1985), *aff'd* 475 U.S. 1001 (1986).

308. Federal Communications Commission v. Pacifica Foundation, 438 U.S. 726, 748 (1978).

309. 438 U.S. 726.

310. *Id.* at 731–38.

311. *Id.* at 740–41; 748–51.

312. *Id.* at 749–50 (analogizing expression at issue to "a pig in the parlor instead of the barnyard").

313. Paris Adult Theatre I v. Slaton, 413 U.S. at 64.

314. Federal Communications Commission v. Pacifica Foundation, 438 U.S. at 761–62 (Powell, J., concurring); *id* at 762–63 (Brennan, J., dissenting).

315. 427 U.S. 50 (1976).

316. *Id.* at 70.

317. Railway Express Agency v. New York, 336 U.S. 106 (1949).

318. 316 U.S. 52 (1942).

319. *Id.* at 54.

320. *Id.* at 52–53.

321. *Id.* at 55.

322. The Court, for instance, has observed that advertising " 'link[ing] a product to a current public debate' is not thereby entitled to the constitutional protection afforded noncommercial speech." Board of Trustees of State University of New York v. Fox, 109 S.Ct. 3028, 3032 (1989), *citing* Central Hudson Gas & Electric Co. v. Public Service Commission of New York, 447 U.S. 557, 563 n.5 (1980).

323. *E.g.*, Central Hudson Gas & Electric Co. v. Public Service Commission of New York 447 U.S. 557 (advertisements promoting electricity); Bigelow v. Virginia, 421 U.S. 809 (1975) (advertisements regarding abortion).

324. Valentine v. Chrestensen, 316 U.S. at 55.

325. 333 F. Supp. 582 (D.D.C. 1971), *aff'd*, 405 U.S. 1000 (1972).

326. *Id.* at 584.

327. *Id.* at 585–86.

328. 413 U.S. 376 (1973).

329. *Id.* at 391.

330. *Id.* at 388–89.

331. 421 U.S. 809 (1975).

332. *Id.* at 822.

333. *Id.* at 819–20.

334. Virginia State Board of Pharmacy v. Virginia Citizens Consumer Council, 425 U.S. 748, 763 (1976).

335. 425 U.S. 748.

336. *Id.,* at 770.

337. *Id.* at 771 n.24.

338. *Id.*

339. *Id.*

340. *Id.*

341. If requirements of full disclosure and accuracy according to standards set by the Securities and Exchange Commission are unmet, for instance, promotional information may be restrained. *See* Securities Act of 1933, § 5(a) and (c), 15 U.S.C. § 77e(a) and (c).

342. *See, e.g.*, City of New Orleans v. Dukes, 427 U.S. 297, 303–04 (1976) (mere rationality standard for economic regulation); Roe v. Wade, 410 U.S. 113, 153 (1973) (strict scrutiny when fundamental right of privacy implicated).

343. *See* C. MacPherson, THE LIFE AND TIMES OF LIBERAL DEMOCRACY 51 (1977).

344. *See* J. S. Mill, ON LIBERTY 19–67 (C. Shields rev. ed. 1976) (1859).

345. Virginia State Board of Pharmacy v. Virginia Citizens Consumers Council, 425 U.S. at 762, *citing* Pittsburgh Press Co. v. Pittsburgh Commission on Human Relations, 413 U.S. 376, 385 (1973).

346. Central Hudson Gas & Electric Co. v. Public Service Commission of New York, 447 U.S. at 561.

347. Board of Trustees of State University of New York v. Fox, 109 S.Ct. at 3036.

348. 444 U.S. 620 (1980).

349. *Id.* at 636–38.

350. *Id* at 636.

351. *Id.* at 641–42 (Rehnquist, J., dissenting). For the view that Rehnquist's analysis fits a broader pattern of extreme deference to governmental interests present in various expressive contexts, *see* Lind, Jr., *Justice Rehnquist: First Amendment Speech in the Labor Context*, 8 HASTINGS CONST. L.Q. 93 (1980).

352. Linmark Associates, Inc. v. Township of Willingboro, 431 U.S. 85 (1977).

353. Carey v. Population Services International, 431 U.S. 678 (1977).

354. In re R.M.J., 455 U.S. 191 (1982); Bates v. State Bar of Arizona, 433 U.S. 350 (1977).

355. 431 U.S. 85.

356. *Id.* at 95–97.

357. Carey v. Population Services International, 431 U.S. at 701.

358. *See id.*

359. *See* In re R.M.J., 455 U.S. at 203–04.

360. *Id.* at 203.

361. Ohralik v. Ohio State Bar, 436 U.S. 447, 464–66 (1978).

362. *Id.*

363. In re Primus, 436 U.S. 412, 435 (1978).

364. *Id.* at 438–39.

365. 447 U.S. 557 (1980).

366. *Id.* at 559–60.

367. *Id.* at 568.

368. *Id.* at 566–68.

369. *Id.* at 568–69.

370. *Id.* at 570–71.

371. Virginia State Board of Pharmacy v. Virginia Citizens Consumer Council, 425 U.S. at 771–73.

372. 440 U.S. 1 (1979).

373. *Id.* at 19.

374. *Id.* at 12–13. Justice Blackmun countered, however, that a trade name may denote product or service quality and "deceive only if it is used in a misleading context." *Id.* 24 (Blackmun, J., concurring and dissenting in part).

375. Posadas de Puerto Rico Associates v. Tourism Co. of Puerto Rico 478 U.S. 328, 345–47 (1986).

376. 478 U.S. 328.

377. *Id.* at 351 (Brennan, J., dissenting).

378. *Id.* at 345–46.

379. *Id.*

380. Carey v. Population Services International 431 U.S. 678.

381. Bigelow v. Virginia, 421 U.S. 809.

382. 478 U.S. at 345.

383. *Id.*

384. Insofar as government has the power to reach a harmful underlying activity, arguably it might regulate advertising with political dimensions such as the promotion of nuclear power.

385. Virginia State Board of Pharmacy v. Virginia Citizens Consumer Council, 425 U.S. at 771 n.24.

386. Central Hudson Gas & Electric Co. v. Public Service Commission of New York, 447 U.S. at 566, 572.

387. Posadas de Puerto Rico Associates v. Tourism Co. of Puerto Rico, 478 U.S. at 344.

388. *Id.* at 356–57 (Brennan, J., dissenting).

389. Central Hudson Gas & Electric Co. v. Public Service Commission of New York, 447 U.S. at 571.

390. *E.g.,* Railway Express Agency v. New York, 336 U.S. 106.

391. *E.g.,* Zauderer v. Office of Disciplinary Council, 471 U.S. 626, 638 (1985).

392. Posadas de Puerto Rico Associates v. Tourism Co. of Puerto Rico, 478 U.S. at 345–46.

393. *Id.* at 354–55 (Brennan, J., dissenting). The Court's reliance upon its own conjecture and surmise was especially visible, since the legislature expressed no concern that the underlying activity would harm local citizens.

394. Board of Trustees of State University of New York v. Fox, 109 S.Ct. at 3035.

395. *See* First National Bank of Boston v. Bellotti, 435 U.S. 765, 791 n.31 (1978).

396. *Id.* at 791–92.

397. *Id.*

398. Virginia State Board of Pharmacy v. Virginia Citizens Consumer Council, 425 U.S. at 770.

399. First National Bank of Boston v. Bellotti, 435 U.S. at 792.

400. *E.g.,* Ohralik v. Ohio State Bar, 436 U.S. at 455–56.

401. In re Primus, 436 U.S. at 438 n.32.

402. For a nonetheless generally approving evaluation of the Court's modern direction with respect to commercial speech, *see* Cass, *Commercial Speech, Constitutionalism, Collective Choice,* 56 U. CIN. L.REV. 1317 (1988).

403. U.S. CONST., art. I. § 8.

404. Sony Corp. of America v. Universal City Studios, Inc., 464 U.S. 417, 429 (1984).

405. *Id.*

406. Copyright Act of 1976, 17 U.S.C. § 101, *et seq.*

407. *Id.*

408. *Id.,* § 102.

409. 464 U.S. 417.

410. *Id.* at 421. For a detailed examination of copyright problems presented by the emergence of video recorders, *see* Beard, *The Sale, Rental and Reproduction of Motion Picture Videocassettes: Piracy or Privilege,* 15 NEW ENGL. L.REV. 435 (1979–80).

411. 464 U.S. at 431.

412. 17 U.S.C. § 102.

413. *Id.,* § 301.

414. International News Service v. Associated Press, 248 U.S. 215, 234 (1918).

415. *See* Sony Corp. of America v. Universal City Studios, Inc. 464 U.S. 417, 419 (1984).

416. *See* Harper & Row Publishers, Inc. v. Nation Enterprises, 471 U.S. 539, 556–57 (1985).

417. *See id.* at 557–58, *quoting* Iowa State University Research Foundation, Inc., v. American Broadcasting Companies, Inc. 621 F.2d 57, 61 (2d Cir. 198d). *But see* Time, Inc., v. Bernard Geis Associates, 293 F.Supp. 130, 146 (S.D.N.Y. 1968).

418. 17 U.S.C. § 102.

419. *Id.,* § 101.

420. *Id.,* § 302(e).

421. *Id.,* § 408.

422. *Id.,* § 401.

423. *Id.,* § 107.

424. 471 U.S. 539 (1985).

425. *Id.* at 542.

426. *Id.* at 543.

427. *Id.* at 568.

428. *Id.* at 550.

429. *Id.* at 565–66.

430. *Id.* at 567.

431. Expression pertaining to self-government generally is afforded maximum First Amendment protection. Central Hudson Gas & Electric Co. v. Public Service Commission of New York, 447 U.S. at 562–63. *Id.* at 579–83 (Stevens, J., concurring); *id.* at 595–99 (Rehnquist, J., dissenting). For a critical evaluation of the *Harper & Row* decision, and warning that infringement cases will multiply to the detriment of First Amendment interests, *see* Francione, *Facing the Nation: The Standards For Copyright, Infringement and Fair Use of Factual Works,* 134 U. PA. L.REV. 519 (1985).

432. 818 F.2d 252 (2d Cir.), *cert. denied,* 108 S.Ct. 213 (1987). Although certiorari was denied, Second Circuit decisions have particular relevance to copyright law given the heavy concentration of publishers in the New York area.

433. *Id.* at 253.

434. *Id.*

435. *Id.*

436. *Id.* at 254.

437. *Id.* at 253.

438. 904 F. 2d 152 (2d Cir.), *cert. denied,* 111 S.Ct. — — (1990).

439. 729 F. Supp. 992, 100–02 (S.D. N.Y. 1990).

440. 904 F. 2d at 160–61.

441. *Id.* at 156.

442. *Id.* at 158–59.

443. *Id.* at 160.

444. Fortnightly Corp. v. United Artists Television, Inc., 392 U.S. 390, 401 (1968). For consideration of some of the issues raised by new technologies and copyright demands, *see* M. LEAFFER, UNDERSTANDING COPYRIGHT LAW, Ch. 9 (1989). *See also* Barnett, *From New Technology to Moral Rights: Passive Carriers, Teletext, and Deletion as Copyright Infringement,* 31 J. COPYRIGHT SOC'Y 427 (1984).

445. 392 U.S. at 393–95, 402.

446. 17 U.S.C. § 111 (c) and (d).

447. *Id.,* §§ 111 (f) (3)–(5), 801 (b) (3).

448. *See, e.g.,* National Cable Television Association v. Copyright Royalty Tribunal, 724 F.2d 176 (D.C. Cir. 1983).

Chapter 3

ECONOMIC REGULATION OF THE MEDIA INDUSTRY

Media regulation in its various forms usually reflects an exercise of the commerce power[1] at the federal level and police power at the state level.[2] Consistent with the constitutional regard in which they are held, the print and broadcast media, respectively, are subject to the least and most official governance. The most comprehensive regulatory scheme is the Communications Act of 1934,[3] which originally accounted for governance of radio, television, and common carriers. By its terms, the act applies to:

> all interstate and foreign communication by wire or radio and all interstate and foreign transmissions of energy by radio, which originates and/or is received within the United States, and to all persons engaged within the United States in such communication or such transmission of energy by radio and to the licensing and regulating of all radio stations.[4]

The Communications Act has been amended to include provisions applicable to cable service and the facilities of cable operators relating to such service.[5]

The general purpose of the act is to regulate "interstate and foreign commerce in communication by wire and radio so as to make available, so far as possible, to all the people of the United States a rapid, efficient, nationwide, and worldwide wire and radio communication service."[6] More specifically, it is calculated "to maintain the control of the United States over all the channels of interstate and foreign radio transmission; and to provide for the use of such channels, but not the ownership thereof, by persons for limited periods of time, under licenses granted by Federal authority."[7]

To effectuate the purposes of the act, the Federal Communications Commission (FCC) was established with the power, among other things, to classify radio stations; to determine the nature of the service to be provided by each class of station and the stations within each class; to assign bands of frequencies to each class of station and specific frequencies to individual stations; to determine the location of classes of and individual stations; to set technical operational standards; to encourage the larger and more effective use of radio in the public interest (a power which is the source of most content regulation); to establish areas to be served by any station; to make rules applicable to chain (or network) broadcasting; to set licensee record keeping requirements; to suspend licenses of broadcasters for violating the law or for transmitting obscene or profane language; to adopt rules relating to international agreements concerning radio; and to set standards for the broadcast equipment used in broadcast reception.[8]

I. FEDERAL PREEMPTION

Federal regulation of broadcasting is so pervasive that it raises immediately the question at the outset of whether such control occupies the entire field. The constitution provides that federal law is "the Supreme Law of the Land" to the point of preempting any concurrent state law.[9] To determine whether a federal enactment preempts state regulation, it is necessary first to ascertain whether a specific clause to that effect exists.[10] Because the Communications Act of 1934 contains no such provision, a supremacy inquiry requires consideration of three factors. Congressional intent may be evidenced by the pervasiveness of the regulatory scheme, the dominance of the federal interest and the need for national uniformity, and the danger of conflict in the administration , and enforcement of competing laws.[11]

For most purposes, given the pervasive nature of federal regulation, strong federal interest and a need for uniformity, and the dangers of conflicting governance, analysis leads to a determination of preemption. In *National Broadcasting Co. v. Board of Public Utility Commissioners of New Jersey*,[12] a broadcaster challenged a state law requiring approval for construction of a transmitter even after its erection had been authorized by the FCC.[13] Congress had empowered the FCC to grant such permits, but the state had a concurrent regulatory scheme that required broadcasters to obtain "a certificate of public convenience" and enabled the pertinent body to set conditions that would avoid "unreasonable blanketing or interference with radio transmission and reception."[14] Be-

cause the broadcaster was operating in the field of interstate commerce, state law was preempted by the federal scheme.[15] The district court refused to address the issue of whether purely intrastate transmissions might be concurrently regulated. Given the same set of facts, it is inconceivable that a modern court would not find that pervasiveness, dominance, uniformity, and potential for conflict concerns all favor federal preemption.

Special circumstances may exist, however, that would militate against preemption. In *Ross v. Hatfield*,[16] a federal court rejected the argument that a restrictive covenant barring satellite dishes from a landowner's property was preempted by federal law.[17] The claim was dismissed in part because of the absence of state action.[18] Presumably, however, state action would exist and a constitutional question would arise if the covenant were judicially enforced.[19] The issue also would be presented by a zoning ordinance or other state or local prohibition. As the district court noted, federal law would preempt zoning or other regulations differentiating "between satellite receiving antennae and other types of antennae."[20] The possibility at least exists that a nondiscriminatory ordinance, reflecting legitimate zoning or other concerns, might survive supremacy clause scrutiny.

By its terms, the Cable Communications Policy Act of 1984 confers upon state and local government partial regulatory responsibility for cable. The general purposes of the Cable Act include the establishment of a national policy concerning cable, the provision of franchise procedures and standards which encourage industry growth and ensure responsiveness to local needs, the facilitation of content diversity, the creation of a fair and orderly process for franchise renewal, and the promotion of industry competition and the minimization of economically burdensome regulation.[21] Although diminished in comparison to broadcasting, the federal interest in regulating cable nonetheless is strong. To the extent that federal dominance and pervasiveness are reduced, the consequence follows from explicit assignments of power to state and local power rather than intergovernmental competition. As one court has noted, the Cable Act "establishes a national framework and standards for regulating the cable television industry. It authorizes local governments to regulate cable television through the franchise process, but at the same time it restricts that regulatory power."[22]

The Supreme Court, in *Capital Cities Cable, Inc. v. Crisp*,[23] considered a preemption question that arose prior to the Cable Act's passage but which undoubtedly would lead to the same result now. At issue was a state law requiring cable operators to eliminate all liquor advertisements from out-of-state signals retransmitted to cable subscribers.[24] The Court determined that the FCC's power "plainly comprises authority to regulate the signals carried by cable television systems."[25] Consequently, the advertising ban was found to have exceeded the authority reserved to local government by F.C.C. rules and intruded upon an exclusive federal domain.[26] The Court noted that the ruling did not alter or diminish local authority to regulate the aspects of cable systems specifically assigned to it.[27] Absent express investment of authority, therefore, local governance risks running afoul of the supremacy clause.

Preemption also was found, albeit by a slimmer margin, in *City of New York v. Federal Communications Commission*.[28] The subject of the controversy was a commission rule predating the Cable Act of 1984 and barring local governments from imposing technical requirements on cable operators that were more stringent then federal standards.[29] Although the stricter criteria were set as a condition of awarding a franchise, the FCC argued that they imposed divergent and sometimes unworkable demands and subverted its objective of promoting efficient and innovative service.[30] The Court noted the Cable Act's division of responsibility between state and local franchising authority and the FCC's interest in the operational aspects of cable service itself.[31] It concluded that because legislation was enacted against the backdrop of the regulation, which was neither eliminated nor criticized in the process, Congress essentially had endorsed and affirmed the disputed provision.[32]

II. ECONOMIC CONTROL

Not all regulation of the press, at least as far as the Court is concerned, implicates First Amendment interests. Insofar as the media are engaged in business, they are subject to most laws governing general economic activity. The diverse requirements of antitrust, securities, and tax law thus impinge upon the media. Although subject to their demands, particular application of such enactments may create problems of a constitutional order.

A. ANTITRUST LAW

The Court consistently has found that antitrust provisions apply with the same force to the media industry as they do to other lines of business. It has noted, moreover, that enforcement of antitrust laws may promote the same interests underlying the First Amendment. In *Associated Press v. United States*,[33] the Court determined that the constitution provided no refuge from the prohibitions against combinations and conspiracies in restraint of trade.[34] As a news service, the Associated Press collected, assembled, and distributed news solely for and to members of its organization.[35] The Court found that such exclusivity was anticompetitive, monopolistic, and a legitimate regulatory concern.[36] In concluding that the Sherman Antitrust Act applied unequivocally to such circumstances, the Court rejected arguments that its operation constituted an abridgment of freedom of the press. It thus observed that

> (i)t would be strange indeed, . . . if the grave concern for freedom of the press which prompted the adoption of the First Amendment should be read as a command that the government was without power to protect that freedom. The First Amendment, far from providing an argument against application of the Sherman Act, here provides powerful reasons to the contrary. That Amendment rests on the assumption that the widest possible dissemination of information from diverse and antagonistic sources is essential to the welfare of the public, that a free press is a condition of a free society. Surely a command that the government itself shall not impede the free flow of ideas does not afford nongovernmental combinations a refuge if they impose restraints upon that constitutionally guaranteed freedom. Freedom to publish means freedom for all and not for some. Freedom to publish is guaranteed by the Constitution, but freedom to combine to keep others from publishing is not. Freedom of the press from governmental interference under the First Amendment does not sanction repression of that freedom by private interests. The First Amendment affords not the slightest support for the contention that a combination to restrain trade in news and views has any constitutional immunity.[37]

Although emphasizing the harmony of antitrust and First Amendment objectives, the Court's analysis may be subject to the criticism that it mistook constitutional values for constitutional rights. The First Amendment operates against government rather than state action, but the *Associated Press* decision at times blurs the distinction between constitutional and statutory freedoms to publish. The constitutional liberty was defined in terms of "a command that the govern-

ment itself shall not impede the free flow of ideas."[38] Freedom of the press as provided by the First Amendment safeguards editorial discretion generally which presumably includes autonomous judgment with respect to whether to publish at all and to whom information will be distributed. Statutory freedom, secured by antitrust laws, ensures opportunities to compete. Although multiplicity of competitors may promote diversity of information, restrictions on the use of information nonetheless implicate First Amendment interests of editorial discretion. The *Associated Press* decision might read better, therefore, if the actuality and pertinence of the constitutional concern had been clearly identified. First Amendment interests still might have been overridden by a determination that antitrust considerations presented a sufficiently compelling reason for displacing them.

The Court dismissed First Amendment concerns altogether in *Lorain Journal v. United States*,[39] when it determined that an order restraining a publisher from engaging in anticompetitive practices did not constitute a prior restraint. A newspaper had responded to the licensing of a radio station in its market area by adopting a policy that denied advertising space to persons and entities buying time from the broadcaster.[40] Contrary to the publisher's arguments, the Court found that the injunction against its practice constituted no restriction upon freedom of the press but merely applied to him "what the law applies to others."[41] Had the newspaper specifically or media generally been singled out for special regulatory attention, it then might have been possible to argue that the press was burdened in an unconstitutional fashion.[42]

A publisher's requirement that advertisers pay for space in both a morning and afternoon newspaper has survived an antitrust challenge. Despite the government's contention that such a condition constituted an illegal tying agreement, the Court, in *Times-Picayune Publishing Co. v. United States*,[43] determined that the challenged policy did not force an unwanted service upon advertisers.[44] In support of its conclusion, the Court found that the publishing company did not occupy a dominant position in the newspaper advertising market as required by the Sherman Act.[45] It further defined the relevant market as both morning and evening newspapers, described morning and evening readers as fungible, and found no discrimination against buyers of advertising in the third newspaper.[46] The Court thus found "no leverage in one market exclud[ing] sellers in the second, because for present purposes the products are identical and the market the same."[47]

A different result would have followed if the argument, that morning and afternoon markets are different, had been embraced. Under such circumstances, a unit pricing policy might be used to prop up a weak afternoon newspaper against its competition. The dissenters in the *Times-Picayune* case maintained that the publishing combine had used its monopoly on morning newspaper to restrain unreasonably the competition between its evening newspaper and its rival.[48] In regarding the morning and evening newspaper markets as distinct, the dissenters found advertising in the evening paper to be "an inescapable part of the price of access to the all-important columns of the single morning paper."[49]

Commentary regarding the desirability of anticompetitive regulation and its ultimate consonance with First Amendment interests is not undivided. One observer has characterized government intervention to remedy structural or institutional constraints upon freedom of expression through the media as a logical extension of the First Amendment.[50] The notion that private centers of power can be as much a threat to diversity of ideas and voices fits neatly with the sentiments expressed by the Court in the *Associated Press* case. Agglomerations of power in the media marketplace are described as more worrisome than concentration in the general economic marketplace. A high degree of discretionary power enables the person exercising it to restrain ideas. Rational economic behavior, insofar as it is tied to profit maximization, does not necessarily parallel the exercise of editorial judgment. Because media operators have money-making motives mixed with ideological impulses, however, it has been argued that a uniquely strong temptation exists to exclude ideas even at the cost of lost profits.[51] If it is assumed that competition in the marketplace of ideas facilitates political freedom, the argument is advanced that it is only a small step from condemnation of government monopoly to intolerance of private monopoly.[52]

At the opposite pole is the contention that information diversity is better advanced by relaxation of antitrust laws and their ilk. The concern underlying that argument is that competition can lead to negative results when resources are limited or scarce, so that the firm providing the cheapest and worst service survives. Reflective of such concern is modern broadcasting which maximizes profits by maximizing its audience—a formula that facilitates programming keyed to mainstream tastes or the lowest common denominator.[53] When resources are limited or divided, coaction typified by commercial broadcasting's contributions of support to public broadcasting or antitrust immunity afforded failing newspapers is suggested as an alternative preferable to competition.[54] Since antitrust laws work against cooperation, the argument is that a new plateau of enlightenment must be reached to strike a sensitive balance between "competitive and cooperative aspects of converging information services."[55]

For now, the line of antitrust cases concerning the media evidences that the First Amendment affords no immunity from laws applicable to industry and business practices in general. Exemption from the reach of antitrust regulation requires a statutory provision to that effect. The Newspaper Preservation Act,[56] discussed in Chapter 4, exemplifies precisely such an enactment. Short of such a congressionally conferred privilege, however, the courts have shown no inclination to limit the force of antitrust law.

B. SECURITIES REGULATION

The purpose of the federal securities laws is to protect investors and to maintain the integrity of the investment marketplace. In pursuing those objectives, securities regulation can implicate the First Amendment in two basic ways. Controls upon the content of what issuers and promoters of securities can disseminate to the public affect expressive freedom and ultimately the collective pool of information for public consumption. Restrictions upon or accountability for what is published in any medium with respect to investment implicate even broader First Amendment concerns.

The Supreme Court, in something less than the most flattering or elegant terms, has characterized the purpose of the federal securities laws as protecting "the weak, the uninformed, the unsuspecting, and the gullible from the exercise of their own volition."[57] Another court has singled out the securities industry for regulation that must respect constitutional rights but must be enforced against frauds that "take on more subtle and involved forms than those in which dishonesty manifests itself in cruder and less specialized activities."[58] To the extent that regulation promotes disclosure of material information, it might appear harmonious with the First Amendment values associated with expression from "a multitude of

tongues."[59] Insofar as content control makes government the head editor of information disseminated to investors, however, the model of governance is susceptible to depiction as "authoritative selection."[60] The Securities and Exchange Commission (SEC) is empowered, among other things, to review and approve the content of offering materials before they may be disseminated to the public.[61] As a condition to propagation, it may insist upon amplification, deletion, or alteration of content.[62] If necessary to enforce its content demands, the SEC may issue an order restraining dissemination of promotional materials to the public. The agency thus exercises censorship powers reminiscent of those associated with the long-abandoned English system of licensing.[63]

Survival of a system of editorial oversight and prior restraint, with minimal constitutional scrutiny, is largely attributable to an analytical process that calibrates First Amendment protection according to how expression is classified.[64] The promotion of investments and dissemination of investment advice, respectively, would seem to qualify as commercial speech which, until the mid–1970s, was unprotected.[65] Even now, the conferral of First Amendment status upon commercial speech has been conditioned by the observation that the general prohibition against prior restraint may be inapplicable.[66] Prior to recognizing that regulation of commercial expression implicated constitutional concerns, the Court observed its control could be premised upon "unprovable assumptions."[67] Given its constitutional standing now, even if limited, principled review would seem to require something more than the works of imagination or speculation as rationales.

Earlier cases deprecate any intimation of a First Amendment concern with respect to the promotion of securities. The SEC's position, that editorial freedom of securities issues, promoters, and advisers is outweighed by the potential harm to investors, has remained consistent despite commercial expression's evolution into a constitutionally protected speech form.[68] In *Carl M. Loeb, Rhoades & Co.*[69] the commission rejected arguments that a statutory bar against dissemination of offering materials should not be construed to prohibit news releases and other publicity concerning a future offering.[70] The SEC affirmed its intention to regard any publicity relevant to a marketing initiative as impermissible unless a registration statement was in effect.[71] In so doing, it distinguished the flow of normal corporate news unrelated to a selling effort as "natural, desirable and entirely consistent with the objective of disclosure to the public which underlines the federal securities' laws."[72] The commission expressed its special concern with sales-related publicity when an issue has "news value," since the potential for whipping up a "speculative frenzy" under such circumstances is enhanced.[73] It distinguished the dissemination of information by reporters neither offering nor selling securities, however, and noted that its "interpretation . . . in no way restricts the freedom of news media to seek out and publish financial news."[74]

The lines of distinction that determined regulatory interest were less easily drawn in another context. In *Lowe v. Securities and Exchange Commission,*[75] the Court examined the commission's enforcement of the Investment Advisers Act of 1940, which provides for the licensing and regulation of persons who provide investment counseling.[76] An investment adviser, for purposes of the act, is "any person who, for compensation, engages in the business of advising others, either directly or through publications or writings, as of the value of securities or as to the advisability of investing in [them] . . . or . . . as part of a regular business, issues or promulgates analyses or reports concerning

securities."[77] The definition at first blush could include many popular economic or financial publications or even daily general interest newspapers and magazines insofar as they maintain business sections.

Such commonly recognized publications never felt the direct impact of the regulation, since the SEC assumed they fit within an exclusion for "any bona fide newspaper, news magazine or business of financial publication of general and regular circulation."[78] The *Lowe* case resulted from the commission's effort to suppress newsletters which also discussed the investment marketplace and offered insight and comment that was as much political, social, and economic as commercial.[79] Its effort to restrain publication was not occasioned by proof of actual harm attributable to the newsletters' content,[80] or that they were false and misleading,[81] but on the grounds that the publisher had been convicted of various fraud-related crimes.[82] Publishing thus was regarded, at least by the SEC, as a further opportunity "for dishonesty and self-dealing."[83]

Instead of confronting the First Amendment issue directly, the Court substituted its own definition of "bona fide publication" which disabled the SEC from suppressing the investment newsletters at issue.[84] Specifically, it determined that a publication is "bona fide" and thereby excluded from the definition of an investment adviser if it provides impersonal or disinterested rather than intermittent or promotional advice to the subscriber.[85] It would appear, therefore, that the SEC retains broad powers to regulate the flow of investment information, including the authority to restrain it entirely, when generated by a party having an interest in the offer, sale, or purchase of a security.[86]

Even if responsible for a bona fide publication, the editorial process itself is not entirely immune from official oversight and control. In *United States v. Winans,*[87] the government successfully prosecuted a *Wall Street Journal* columnist for a scheme to trade in securities based on information misappropriated from the newspaper.[88] The plan, under which the defendant provided a broker advance notice of firms that would be discussed favorably in a widely read newspaper column,[89] was characterized as a scheme to defraud and a breach of fiduciary duty between employer and employee.[90] In convicting the defendant, the trial court rejected arguments that criminalization of that breach would create a threat to the freedom of the press generally.[91] The court concluded that the theory of liability created no new obligations but merely enforced preexisting ones.[92] Nor did it find an unconstitutional imposition of duties upon editors with respect to how they must respond under such circumstances.[93] Their freedom, in deciding whether to seek criminal penalties, take disciplinary action, or do nothing, was considered to be unaffected.[94] It remained a matter of editorial discretion, moreover, whether to run the tainted article.[95] The *Winans* case evinces nonetheless that the journalistic process itself can be adapted into a scheme to defraud and, to the extent converted toward such ends, is a basis for civil and criminal liability.

C. Taxation

The power to tax almost from the outset has been recognized as the power to destroy.[96] The media generally have the same obligations to pay taxes as any other individual or entity. When taxation authority is used selectively or punitively, however, the power becomes destructive of First Amendment rights and interests. Such concern accounted for the decision, in *Grosjean v. American Press Co., Inc.*,[97] that a gross receipts tax upon newspapers having a certain minimum circulation was unconstitutional.[98] The effect of the tax was to impose a discriminatory

burden upon major Louisiana newspapers which had become critical of the governor.[99] It was defined by its own terms as a "license tax for the privilege of engaging in such business."[100]

In determining the levy's unconstitutionality, the Supreme Court focused upon its operation as a prior restraint rather than discriminatory design. The Court adverted to the history behind the First Amendment, with pointed references to the elimination of licensed publishing and the use of taxes to deter colonial protest.[101] It characterized the American Revolution itself not as mere warfare against taxation but as a struggle to establish a right to full information regarding the operation of government.[102] A few years before the First Amendment was drafted, Massachusetts had levied taxes on magazines, newspapers, and advertising which precipitated angry opposition and swift repeal. Based upon that history, the Court concluded that the First Amendment had been adopted "to preclude the states, from adopting any form of previous restraint upon printed publications, or their circulation, including" by means of taxation.[103]

The Court noted that its decision did not exempt government from ordinary forms of taxation that provide support for government.[104] What it found constitutionally inimical was "a deliberate and calculated device in the guise of a tax to limit the circulation of information to which the public is entitled."[105] Even so, the sweeping appearance of the decision prompted arguments that the Court had created a general immunity from taxation. The following year, the Court demonstrated that its interpretation was not so broad. In *Giragi v. Moore*, it dismissed for lack of a federal question an appeal claiming that a general sales and income tax was unconstitutional as applied to the media.[106]

A year later, the Court rejected the argument that state and local taxes on gross receipts of advertising revenue imposed an unconstitutional burden on interstate commerce.[107] In *Western Live Stock v. Bureau of Revenue*,[108] the Court determined that levies did not unreasonably impair commerce.[109] A critical determinant in assessing the constitutionality of any state tax for an entity doing interstate business, however, remains whether the levy is fairly apportioned.

Nearly half a century after *Grosjean,* the Court confronted again the issue of a special tax uniquely directed at a discrete segment of the press. In *Minneapolis Star and Tribune Co. v. Minnesota Commissioner of Revenue*,[110] it declared unconstitutional a levy upon any publisher's annual paper and ink charges exceeding $100,000.[111] Pursuant to the revenue enactment, 11 out of 388 newspapers incurred a tax liability and one publisher's tax bill accounted for two-thirds of the total monies raised.[112] Although noting the applicability of general economic regulations including tax provisions to newspapers, the Court determined that a special or discriminatory tax could not stand unless supported by a compelling governmental interest.[113] It found differential taxation problematical because the political constraints preventing passage of crippling taxes of general application diminish when one group is singled out.[114] Especially when the special target is the press,[115] the threat of regulation can check critical comment and thus neutralize a key function of the press.[116] The interest asserted by the state in raising revenue was rejected as inadequate since alternative taxes of general application could be used.[117] The First Amendment thus was offended because the tax scheme singled out the press, targeted further a small group of newspapers, and was not adequately justified.[118]

A similar result was reached in *Arkansas Writers' Project, Inc. v. Ragland*,[119] when the court considered a state tax law exempting all newspapers and religious, professional, trade and sports journals.[120] Discrimination among magazines was found especially troublesome insofar as it constituted a content-based distinction.[121] Because constitutional offense was established by discrimination within a particular class of media, the Court declined an invitation to consider whether disparate taxation of different media presents a first Amendment problem.[122]

It appears, therefore, that taxes of general applicability, if challenged by the media, will be reviewed as mere economic regulations. Absent any cognizable First Amendment interest, judicial review will be executed pursuant to a deferential rational basis test. Selective taxation of the media, however, apparently will implicate First Amendment concerns automatically. In such an instance, the level of review will be elevated, and the state thereby will be required to justify the differential with a reason compelling enough to outweigh First Amendment interests.

NOTES _____

1. U.S. CONST., art. I, § 8(3). Regulation of a more discrete nature may be pursuant to the taxing power. *Id.,* art. I, § 8(1).

2. Although not specifically explicated by the constitution, states retain authority to protect their respective citizenries' health, safety and welfare subject to circumscription by properly exercised federal power.

3. 47 U.S.C. § 151 *et seq.*

4. *Id.,* § 152(a).

5. *Id.*

6. *Id.,* § 151.

7. *Id.,* § 301.

8. *Id.,* § 303.

9. U.S. CONST., art. VI[2].

10. *See* Pacific Gas & Electric Company v. State Energy Resources Conservation & Development Commission, 461 U.S. 190, 203 (1983).

11. *Id.* at 203–4.

12. 25 F.Supp. 761 (C.D.N.J. 1938).

13. *Id.* at 762.

14. *Id.* at 762.

15. *Id.* at 763.

16. 640 F.Supp. 708 (D.Kan. 1986).

17. *Id.* at 712.

18. *Id.* at 712.

19. *Id.* at 710.

20. *Id.* at 712.

21. 47 U.S.C. § 303.

22. Tribune-United Cable of Montgomery County v. Montgomery County, Maryland, 784 F.2d 1227, 1229 (4th Cir. 1986).

23. 467 U.S. 691 (1984).

24. *Id.* at 694.

25. *Id.* at 699.

26. *Id.* at 704.

27. *Id.* at 704.

28. 108 S.Ct. 1637 (1988).

29. *Id.* at 1639.

30. *Id.* at 1640.

31. *Id.* at 1640–41.

32. *Id.* at 1644.

33. 326 U.S. 1 (1945).

34. *Id.* at 19–20.

35. *Id.* at 9.

36. *Id.* at 12–13.

37. *Id.* at 20.

38. *Id.*

39. 342 U.S. 143 (1951).

40. *Id.* at 148.

41. *Id.* at 155–56.

42. Laws that have a discriminatory effect upon the press or some media subgroup have been invalidated. *See* Minneapolis Star and Tribune Co. v. Minnesota Commissioner of Revenue, 460 U.S. 575 (1983); Grosjean v. American Press Co. Inc., 297 U.S. 233 (1936).

43. 345 U.S. 594 (1953).

44. *Id.* at 614.

45. *Id.* at 611–13.

46. *Id.* at 627.

47. *Id.* at 614.

48. *Id.* at 628 (Burton, J., dissenting).

49. *Id.* at 628 (Burton, J., dissenting).

50. B. OWEN, ECONOMICS AND FREEDOM OF EXPRESSION 2 (1975).

51. *Id.* at 4.

52. *Id.* at 6.

53. H. INOSE & J. PIERCE, INFORMATION TECHNOLOGY AND CIVILIZATION 178 (1984).

54. *Id.* at 179.

55. *Id.*

56. 15 U.S.C. § 1801 *et seq.*

57. Paris Adult Theatre I v. Slaton, 413 U.S. 49, 64 (1973).

58. Archer v. Securities and Exchange Commission, 133 F.2d 795, 803 (8th Cir. 1943).

59. *See* United States v. Associated Press, 52 F.Supp. 362, 372 (1943), *aff'd*, 326 U.S. 1 (1945).

60. *See id.*

61. Prior to offering a security, an issuer must file informational and promotional materials with the SEC. *See* 15 U.S.C. §§ 77e, 77g, 77h, 77j, and 77aa. The offering materials include a registration statement, which must be editorially approved by the Commission before a prospectus may be disseminated. *See id.* A prospectus contains the same information as a registration statement, *see* 15 U.S.C. § 77j(a), but also may include any notice, circular, advertisement, letter, or communication, written or by radio or television, which offers a security for sale. *See* 15 U.S.C. § 77b(10). Absent an officially approved registration statement, dissemination of a prospectus may be restrained. *See* 15 U.S.C. § 77e.

62. *See* 15 U.S.C. § 77h(b).

63. Prior restraints are discussed in Chapter 1, V.

64. The Court classifies expression and assigns it a value, based upon perceived social utility, which determines the level of constitutional protection if any afforded. Central Hudson Gas & Electric Company v. Public Service Commission, 447 U.S. 557, 561–63; *id.* at 579–83 (Stevens, J., concurring); *id.* at 595–99 (Rehnquist, J., dissenting).

65. *See* Virginia Board of Pharmacy v. Virginia Citizens Consumer Council, 425 U.S. 748 (1976).

66. *Id.* at 771 n.24.

67. Paris Adult Theatre I v. Slaton, 413 U.S. at 61.

68. *See* Lowe v. Securities and Exchange Commission, 472 U.S. 181, 233 (1985) (White, J., concurring).

69. 38 S.E.C. 843 (1959).

70. *Id.* at 851.

71. *Id.*

72. *Id.* at 853.

73. *Id.*

74. *Id.* at 852 n.15.

75. 472 U.S. 181.

76. *See* Investment Advisers Act of 1940, 15 U.S.C. § 80b *et seq.*

77. *Id.,* § 80b–2(a)(11).

78. Lowe v. Securities and Exchange Commission, 472 U.S. at 208.

79. *Id.* at 210. *See* SEC v. Lowe, 725 F.2d 892, 906 (2d Cir. 1984) (Breiant, J., dissenting).

80. 472 U.S. at 209.

81. *Id.*

82. *Id.* at 183.

83. *Id.* at 184.

84. *Id.* at 211.

85. *Id.* at 206.

86. *Id.* at 210. For a discussion of problems in effectuating legitimate ethical controls and protecting free expression, and an argument that the *Lowe* decision is confounding rather than constructive, *see* Aman, Jr., *SEC v. Lowe: Professional Regulation and the First Amendment,* 1985 SUP. CT. REV. 93.

87. 612 F.Supp. 827 (S.D.N.Y. 1985).

88. *Id.* at 844.

89. *Id.* at 829–32.

90. *Id.* at 845.

91. *Id.* at 843 n.10.

92. *Id.*

93. *Id.*

94. *Id.*

95. *Id.*

96. *See* McCulloch v. Maryland, 17 U.S. (4 Wheat.) 316, 427 (1819).

97. 297 U.S. 233 (1936).

98. *Id.* at 241.

99. *Id.*

100. *Id.* at 244.

101. *Id.* at 245.

102. *Id.* at 247.

103. *Id.* at 249.

104. *Id.* at 250.

105. *Id.*

106. 301 U.S. 670 (1937).

107. Western Live Stock v. Bureau of Revenue, 303 U.S. 250, 254–55 (1938).

108. 303 U.S. 250.

109. *Id.* at 259.

110. 460 U.S. 575 (1983).

111. *Id.* at 591–93.

112. *Id.* at 578.

113. *Id.* at 585.

114. *Id.*

115. *Id.*

116. *Id.*

117. *Id.* at 586.

118. *Id.* at 592–93.

119. 481 U.S. 221 (1987).

120. *Id.* at 223–24.

121. *Id.* at 229.

122. *Id.* at 233.

Part Two

STRUCTURAL REGULATION OF THE MEDIA

A dominant concern with the media as they have evolved, especially over the course of the twentieth century, relates to the number of editorial voices actually accounted for by the press. By the early 1980s, approximately two-thirds of the nation's daily newspapers were group owned.[1] The Gannett chain, which is the nation's largest, by itself publishes daily newspapers in eighty-five cities and weekly or semiweekly newspapers in thirty-five communities.[2] Notwithstanding the increasing development of UHF channels, networks continue to dominate broadcast programming especially in prime time. Despite cable's promise of channel multiplicity and virtually unlimited diversity, the fact remains that programming in most communities is the function of a single franchisee's editorial decisions.

The nature of the media industry has prompted official reactions on two levels. Content regulation, calculated to enhance diversity, is the primary concern of Part Three of this volume. Structural controls, which are the focus of Part Two, interest themselves with the makeup and character of the various media. They too may be and have been used to promote diversity and First Amendment objectives. Invariably, therefore, they must be recognized as having content implications albeit perhaps in a more indirect or less proximate fashion than the concepts discussed in Part Three.

NOTES

1. Editor & Publisher, April 28, 1984, at 17.
2. Editor & Publisher International Yearbook 1989, at 272. Gannett also owns ten television and fifteen radio stations. *Id.*

Chapter 4

THE NEWSPAPER INDUSTRY

I. CONCENTRATION

The newspaper industry over the past several decades has been characterized not only by concentration but also by a steadily declining number of metropolitan dailies in large cities. In 1910, a total of 2,600 daily metropolitan newspapers were being published.[1] By 1988, the number had diminished to 1,745.[2] At the midpoint of this century, approximately 80 percent of the nation's cities with daily newspapers had but one publication, 10 percent had multiple newspapers controlled by a single publisher, and 10 percent had actual competition between or among publishers.[3] Two decades later, the Supreme Court observed that one-newspaper towns "have become the rule, with effective competition operating in only four percent of our large cities."[4] During those years of declining competition within established cities, mobility, freeways, modern mass transit systems, and social and economic forces have fostered a massive migration out of major cities.[5] Consistent with the outward flow of business and people from cities to new outlying communities, an economically healthy suburban press has evolved in response to those new realities.[6]

Demographic changes have thrust metropolitan dailies into competition with new publications which may serve discrete local interests more effectively. At the same time, the newspaper industry, which largely stood by itself as the daily press at the turn of this century, is but one of several media from which the public obtains its information.

At least one prominent commentator has criticized the failure of Congress and the judiciary to recognize concentrations of media power as political power and to account for it in a meaningful fashion.

B. Bagdikian, The Media Monopoly (1983)*

Controlled information has a morbid history. It is not morbid solely because it violates the ideology of democracy, though it does that. It is morbid because it is usually wrong. Unchallenged information is inherently flawed information. If it is in error to begin with, it is not open to correction. If it is correct at the time, it will soon be obsolete. If it changes without uninhibited response from the real world, it becomes detached from the real world. For a realistic picture of society there is no such thing as a central authority.

But the righteousness of power is irresistible. Every authority figure in the Western world once knew for certain that the world was flat and silenced anyone who pointed out the error. The authorities knew the earth was the center of the universe and constructed ill-fated philosophies based on the illusion. When the bubonic plague decimated the population of Europe, the authorities burned not guilty rats but guiltless "witches." For two thousand years the best doctors treated fevers by draining the patients' blood and kindly killed more human beings than the most murderous cannon.

The authorities were wrong. Their errors created intellectual sterility and immeasurable human misery. But they were not wrong because they were always unintelligent or evil. They were wrong and they remained wrong because their information, which they sincerely believed, was not effectively challenged by open and competitive ideas.

The Age of Enlightenment created a new kind of society. It rejected dictators and kings. It celebrated democracy and individual freedom. It acknowledged that the democratic consent of the governed is meaningless unless the consent is informed consent. Controlled information has survived in the twentieth century's grim parade of dictatorships, but these dictatorships have been the enemies of democracy and they have ultimately failed. The first amendment of the most sacred document in the quintessential democracy of the Enlightenment, the United States, guarantees freedom of expression. Diversity of expression was assumed to be the natural state of enduring liberty.

Modern technology and American economics have quietly created a new kind of central authority over information—the national and multinational corporation. By the 1980s, the majority of all major American media—newspapers, magazines, radio, television, books, and movies—were controlled by fifty giant corporations. These corporations were interlocked in common financial interest with other massive industries and with a few dominant international banks.

There are other media voices outside the control of the dominant fifty corporations. Most are small and localized, and many still disappear as they are acquired by the giants. The small voices, as always, are important, a saving remnant of diversity. But their diminutive sounds tend to be drowned by the controlled thunder of half the media power of a great society.

The United States has an impressive array of mass communications. There are 1,700 daily newspapers, 11,000 magazines, 9,000 radio and 1,000 television stations, 2,500 book publishers, and 7 movie studios. If each of these were operated by a different owner there would be 25,000 individual media voices in the country. Such a large number would almost guarantee a full spectrum of political and social ideas distributed to the population. It would limit the concentration of power since each owner would share influence over the national mind with 24,999 other owners. The division of the market into so many companies would mean firms would be smaller, which would make it easier for newcomers to enter the scene with new ideas.

But there are not 25,000 different owners. Today fifty corporations own most of the output of daily newspapers and most of the sales and audience in magazines, broadcasting, books, and movies. The fifty men and women who head these corporations would fit in a large room. They constitute a new Private Ministry of Information and Culture.

Modern technology and social organization have intensified the problems of centralized control of information. In an earlier age citizen talked to citizen about public policies that affected them. Each community could gather in a hall or church to decide its own fate. Deciding its fate was real because in older, agricultural societies each community came close to self-sufficiency and remote events had marginal meaning. That method of politics disappeared long ago. In place of the small towns are huge urban complexes where no citizen can know most other members of the community. No town hall or church could possibly hold all the voters. Each citizen's fate is shaped by powerful forces in distant places. The individual now depends on great machines of information and imagery that inform and instruct. The modern systems of news, information, and popular culture are not marginal artifacts of technology. They shape the consensus of society.

It is a truism among political scientists that while it is not possible for the media to tell the population what to think, they do tell the public what to think about. What is reported enters the public agenda. What is not reported may not be lost forever, but it may be lost at a time when it is most needed. More than any other single private source and often more than any governmental source, the fifty dominant media corporations can set the national agenda.

The size of the dominant media corporations makes them participants in the world of international finance. Most are traded on the stock market, under pressure to compete with the most speculative investments around the world. . . .

For the first time in the history of American journalism, news and public information have been integrated formally into the highest levels of financial and nonjournalistic corporate control. Conflicts of interest between the public's need for information and corporate desires for "positive" information have vastly increased. . . .

The last twenty-five years have not seen unrelieved degradation of the media. Much has improved. Journalism has experienced growth in its social perceptions, fresh creativity in drama and art, and ingenious applications of communication techniques, sometimes for social good. But these improvements have been paralleled and often overwhelmed by the effects of the control of large corporations.

The fifty corporations in control of most of our media differ in policies and practices. Their subsidiaries' products vary in quality, some excellent, many mediocre, some wretched. The corporations are led by men and women who differ in personality and values. In the massive output of the fifty corporations there is a wide variety of kinds of stories, ideas, and entertainments, including information that sometimes is critical of giant corporations.

The problem is not one of universal evil among the corporations or their leaders. Nor is it a general practice of constant suppression and close monitoring of the content of their media companies. There is, in the output of the dominant fifty, a rich mixture of news and ideas. But there are also limits, limits that do not exist in most other democratic countries with private enterprise media. The limits are felt on open discussion of the system that supports giantism in corporate life and of other values that have been enshrined under the inaccurate label "free enterprise."

Many of the corporations claim to permit great freedom to the journalists, producers, and writers they employ. Some do grant great freedom. But when their most sensitive economic interests are at stake, the parent corporations seldom refrain from using their power over public information.

Media power is political power. The formal American political system is designed as though in response to Lord Acton's aphorism that power corrupts and absolute power corrupts absolutely. Media power is no exception. When fifty men and women, chiefs of their corporations, control more than half the information and ideas that reach 220 million Americans, it is time for Americans to examine the institutions from which they receive their daily picture of the world.

II. NEWSPAPER PRESERVATION ACT

Although the Court has expressed concern with an increasingly concentrated mass media, which "places[s] in a few hands the power to inform the American people and shape public opinion",[7] it has refused to countenance promotion of diversity by means that overtly would impair editorial discretion. Congress, with the assent of the judiciary so far, has fashioned statutory privileges designed to insulate major daily newspapers from the effects of an otherwise inclement economic environment. The policy it has chosen, instead of encouraging new competition, actually attempts to reconcile diversity needs with the realities of concentration.

Responding to the changing circumstances in which they functioned, newspapers half a century ago began merging noneditorial operations to save costs and to maintain economic viability. The first joint operating agreement (JOA) was commenced in 1933 when three newspapers in

Albuquerque, New Mexico, combined their business and printing activities.[8] In 1966, twenty-two JOAs had been consummated.[9] By then, the Justice Department had initiated an investigation of such arrangements to determine whether they breached antitrust law and soon brought suit against two newspapers in Tucson, Arizona.[10]

In *Citizen Publishing Co. v. United States*,[11] the Supreme Court found that the JOA at issue constituted an antitrust violation.[12] The newspapers had argued that the scheme was justified because one of them was in serious economic jeopardy and thereby qualified for antitrust immunity under the "failing company" doctrine.[13] The principle, derived by common law, permits otherwise prohibited mergers pursuant to the assumption that competition cannot be impaired if the alternative is one company's failure and another's monopolization.[14]

The Court, however, construed the failing company doctrine so that it was unavailable unless three conditions were satisfied. Specifically, a purportedly failing company had to demonstrate that it was anticipating liquidation, so that a JOA essentially would be its last alternative for survival.[15] It also would have to show that the entity with which it merged was "the only available purchaser."[16] Exemption finally would not be awarded unless the possibility for reorganization under federal bankruptcy law was "dim or nonexistent."[17] The failure of the Tucson newspapers to satisfy the Court's stringent delineation of the failing company defense resulted in the determination that their merger was at odds with antitrust law.[18]

Congressional response to the *Citizen Publishing Company* decision was swift. One year after the judgment, Congress enacted the Newspaper Preservation Act (NPA).[19] For newspapers, the legislation essentially codified the failing company doctrine in terms that were friendlier to the effectuation of partial mergers. Special regard for the news-

paper industry, in the form of antitrust immunity, manifested a sense that "the economics of the newspaper industry make it more likely for newspapers to fail when faced with competition than other businesses."[20] Experience has demonstrated that when a newspaper obtains even a relatively slight edge in circulation, it may plunge into a downward and irreversible spiral as advertisers opt for the publication reaching the larger audience.[21] Unlike the strict test of *Citizen Publishing Company*, requiring contemplated liquidation and imminent bankruptcy, the NPA defines a newspaper as failing and thus eligible for a JOA when it is "in probable danger of financial failure."[22] An even less demanding standard governs JOAs entered into prior to the NPA's enactment. Those business combinations are legal if, when structured, only one of the publications was "likely to remain or become financially sound."[23] A valid JOA enables newspapers to merge their business operations, while maintaining independent editorial functions.[24]

The prerequisite to a JOA is a finding by the Attorney General that a newspaper is in probable danger of economic failure and that the merger would serve the NPA's "policy and purpose."[25] The overarching aim of the legislation, expressly identified by Congress, is to maintain "a newspaper press [that is] editorially independent and competitive."[26] The NPA assumes that such objectives, which tie in to the general interest in a diversified information marketplace, are served best by combinations that cooperate at least as much as they compete. A possibility exists that, although the NPA may preserve existing voices, the economic advantage acquired by the merged entity may deter future competition that would diversify the marketplace. A prospective publisher, for instance, might be unable to offer the favorable rate-to-circulation ratios available from newspapers publishing under a

JOA.[27] Experience demonstrates that both advertising display rates[28] and the cost of purchasing a newspaper escalates immediately after a JOA is consummated.[29] The earnings available under a partial merger, therefore, may be so attractive that newspapers not truly in danger of failing may consciously compound losses so that they can qualify for a JOA.[30] Such concerns have been responsible for legal challenges to JOAs and even divisions within the Justice Department which must consider any merger application. Since the NPA's enactment, five JOAs have been approved,[31] three have been contested,[32] but no challenge has been successful.[33]

The first post-NPA challenge to a JOA was couched largely in First Amendment terms. In *Bay Guardian Co. v. Chronicle Publishing Co.*,[34] a small monthly newspaper asserted that the merger of two daily San Francisco newspapers and the elimination of a third destroyed or weakened any potential competition.[35] The plaintiffs asserted that the cooperative features of the JOA, including profit sharing and joint advertising rates, created "a stranglehold on the San Francisco newspaper market."[36] They thus argued that, because the combine prevented or deterred the publication of others, the NPA itself breached the guarantee of freedom of the press.[37]

The district court refused to take the First Amendment argument seriously, noting that "(t)he simple answer to the plaintiffs' contention is that the Act does not authorize any conduct."[38] It characterized the NPA as "a selective repeal of the antitrust laws" for the purpose of rescuing newspapers in danger of failing.[39] Observing further that the legislation "was designed to preserve independent editorial voices,"[40] it concluded that the NPA, regardless of its underlying economic or social wisdom, was not at odds with the First Amendment.[41]

Nor was the court willing to regard the consequences of a JOA as having imposed a restraint upon the publication of other newspapers.[42] That disinclination was attributable to the court's conclusion that the NPA specifically prohibits merged publishers from engaging in predatory practices. It may be that the court skirted the issue of effect to some extent by characterizing the regulation at issue as essentially economic in nature.[43] To the extent that legislation is so classified, judicial review becomes deferential and does not seriously evaluate the wisdom upon which an enactment is predicated.[44]

Contentions that the NPA was inimical to competitive and constitutional interests surfaced again pursuant to the Attorney General's approval of a JOA for two Seattle, Washington, newspapers.[45] In *Committee for an Independent P-I v. Hearst Corp.*,[46] however, allegations also were considered that one of the newspapers was in danger of failing because of mismanagement rather than the economic realities of the industry.[47] The administrative law judge who conducted the hearing had determined that the purportedly failing newspaper probably could have been sold to a third party who would have maintained its independence, but that inquiries concerning a possible sale had been rebuffed.[48] Despite the Antitrust Division's objections, the Attorney General rejected the hearing examiner's finding regarding probable marketability as unsupported by the evidence and approved the JOA.[49]

First Amendment arguments that the antitrust exemption caused economic injury, which would affect "the 'breadth' of one's freedom of press," as in the *Bay Guardian* case, were dismissed as "lack[ing] substantial merit."[50] The court of appeals determined that the NPA did "not affect the content of speech of . . . smaller newspapers" claiming injury.[51] Rather, it was a mere "economic regulation which has the intent of promoting and aiding the press."[52] Although recognizing that the regulatory scheme might affect negatively "the number of 'readers' a newspaper has,"[53] the Court refused characterization of that consequence as an abridgment.[54] Consequently, it found an effect not unlike "any other economic regulation of the newspaper industry, . . . [no] First Amendment rights implicated" and grounds therefore for deferential rather than exacting review of legislative judgment.[55] Insofar as the NPA might be unwise, the court noted that it was the responsibility of Congress to alter or repeal it.[56]

The court also rejected the challenge that the JOA did not "effectuate the policy and purpose of the Act."[57] The gist of the claim was that potential injury to other newspapers had been disregarded, and merger terms had not been limited to the least anticompetitive terms possible.[58] In refusing to concern itself with the impact of a JOA upon other publications or to gloss the NPA with a least burdensome alternative requirement, the court concluded "that the Act itself is a policy determination that the preservation of editorial diversity through joint operating agreements outweighs any potentially anticompetitive effect this antitrust exemption might cause."[59] Thus, it found that Congress had performed all the balancing of competing interests required and accepted any harm to other publishing voices.[60] Such deference to legislative judgment again necessitated the assumption that no First Amendment interests were implicated.

Finally, the court determined that the failure to offer the newspaper for sale or to respond to inquiries about its availability did not merit disapproval of the JOA.[61] Rather, it identified as "(t)he critical question [whether] it was shown that the . . . financial condition was such that new management might be successful in reversing the P-I's difficulties."[62] Finding evidence of a downward spiral, management's competent and rea-

sonable efforts to restore profitability, the unworkability of the challengers' proposals for profitable operations, and no proof that new management could turn the newspaper around, the Court determined that "failure to consider purchase inquiries lost importance."[63]

If a newspaper is not obligated to consider sale as an alternative to merger, concern exists that publishers will be motivated to lose money so that they can attain effective market dominance and enhanced profitability afforded by a JOA. Such concern was central to objections to a JOA approved for Detroit, Michigan's, two daily newspapers.[64] Unlike any prior circumstance leading to antitrust exemption, neither newspaper had entered into a "downward spiral." The newspapers, at the time of the JOA approval, were owned respectively by Gannett and Knight-Ridder—the nation's two largest group owners.[65] Both publications had competed fiercely for many years, with the dominant newspaper maintaining a consistent 51-percent to 49-percent circulation edge and a 60-percent share of advertising linage.[66] Critical to the operating losses of both newspapers was a circulation price war that had dropped the purchase price to 20 cents for the dominant publication and 15 cents for its rival.[67] An administrative law judge observed that unit costs more in line with the price of newspapers elsewhere would have resulted in profitability for both newspapers.[68]

Testimony that the dominant newspaper would not raise its price[69] was followed by its competition's promise to shut down operations if not allowed to enter into a JOA.[70] Although neither newspaper had entered into a downward spiral or had acquired dominance, the Attorney General approved the merger on the grounds that continuing pricing practices would enable one newspaper to outlast the other. The determination was upheld on appeal in *Michigan*

Citizens for an Independent Press v. Thornburgh.[71] The Supreme Court, divided four to four, affirmed the judgment without opinion.[72]

The result has compounded concern that the availability of JOAs in an already concentrated newspaper industry creates a dangerous combination. Critics maintain that a partial merger, under circumstances as they existed in Detroit, "allow deep pocket newspaper owners to obtain a JOA almost at will."[73] Their concern is that large group owners, recognizing the economic advantage of a JOA, may be willing to purchase a newspaper, slash prices, absorb short-term losses, and then obtain a partial merger exempting them from antitrust law.[74] Critics of the Detroit outcome note that the willingness of the dominant newspaper to divide profits evenly under the JOA suggests that the other newspaper was not about to exit the market and that the merger was a calculated corporate objective.[75] The fundamental worry, therefore, is that the NPA, which was conceived to preserve editorial diversity where it otherwise could be lost, may operate as a means for "eliminating competitive newspapers even where both . . . would survive."[76] In the *Michigan Citizens* case, the Attorney General's determination that the record "did not present such a situation" was found "reasonable."[77] Thus, the court did "not consider the hypothetical situation where the initial and principal motivating factor behind a price was the prospect of a future JOA."[78] Any such perversion of the NPA's utility and purpose, at least for now, is a matter which the courts seem inclined to leave for congressional consideration. Such deference is manifested clearly by the Court's reiteration of the Attorney General's observation, in the *Michigan Citizens* case, that newspapers cannot be precluded from factoring a possible JOA into their business strategy or "faulted for considering and acting upon an alternative that Congress has created."[79]

Michigan Citizens for an Independent Press v. Thornburgh, 868 F.2d 1285 (D.C. Cir.), suggestion for rehearing en banc denied, 868 F.2d 1300, aff'd, 110 S.Ct. 229 (1989)

Silberman, Circuit Judge:

This case presents a challenge to a decision and order of the Attorney General, pursuant to the Newspaper Preservation Act ("NPA"), 15 U.S.C. §§ 1801–1804 (1982), approving a joint operating arrangement between the *Detroit Free Press* and *Detroit News* newspapers. Appellants, which include Michigan Citizens for an Independent Press, seven individuals, and the interest group Public Citizen, brought suit against the Attorney General and the two newspapers in the district court alleging that the Attorney General's decision violates the NPA and the Administrative Procedure Act, 5 U.S.C. § 706 (1982), because it is not based on substantial evidence, is arbitrary and capricious, and is otherwise in violation of law. The district court granted summary judgment in favor of defendants, 695 F.Supp. 1216, and plaintiffs appealed to this court. We conclude that the Attorney General's decision was based on a permissible construction of the statute, and that his application of the legal standard to the facts of this case was not arbitrary, capricious, or an abuse of discretion. We therefore affirm the judgment of the district court. . . .

The *Detroit Free Press* and the *Detroit News* are daily newspapers that compete in Detroit, which is the nation's fifth largest newspaper market. The papers are owned by the two largest news organizations in the United States; Knight-Ridder, Inc. owns the *Free Press,* and the Gannett Company has controlled the *News* since February 1986, when it purchased the paper from the Evening News Association. Over the past fifteen years, the papers have been engaged in fierce competition for absolute dominance of the Detroit market, which was motivated, at least initially, by the knowledge that many junior papers have been unable to survive as the second paper in metropolitan area competition.

This bitter fight has led to large operational losses by both papers. The *Free Press* has lost money every year since 1979, and it lost over $10 million per year from 1981 to 1986. The *News* has sustained operational losses since 1980, and it lost over $50 million between 1981 and 1986. A circulation price war has driven the daily prices in Detroit to twenty cents for the *News* and fifteen cents for the *Free Press*—probably the lowest daily prices in the United States. In recent years, the *News* has maintained a consistent circulation lead of approximately 51% to 49%. Perhaps more important, the *News* has continuously maintained more than a 60% share of total full-run advertising linage.

As a result of their losses, the papers began to consider the alternative of a JOA as early as 1980 when the chief executive officers of Knight-Ridder and the Evening News Association first discussed the possibility. Negotiations continued sporadically from January 1981 to January 1984, but no agreement was reached during that period. In August 1985, Gannett agreed in principle to purchase the *News* from the Evening News Association, and senior officials of Gannett and Knight-Ridder thereafter met 16 times between August 1985 and April 1986 to shape the final agreement. On April 11, 1986 the *News* and the *Free Press* executed the JOA.

The agreement, which has an initial term of 100 years, provides—as is typical—that the news and editorial staffs of the two papers are to remain independent and insulated from influence by the other party to the arrangement. The *Free Press* would publish a morning paper on Monday through Friday, and the *News* would print a corresponding afternoon edition. On Saturday and Sunday, the parties would publish only one paper, with each paper assuming separate editorial and news responsibilities.

During the first three years of the JOA, the *News* would receive 55% of the profits of the combined enterprise, while the *Free Press* would receive 45%. In the fourth and fifth years, the profit split would reduce to 53%/47% and 51%/49%, respectively. Beginning in the sixth year, the profits and losses would be shared equally by the *News* and the *Free Press*.

On May 9, 1986, the two papers applied for approval of the JOA by the Attorney General as required by the Act, and the application was referred to the Assistant Attorney General in charge of the Antitrust Division, pursuant to Justice Department regulations. See 28 C.F.R. § 48.7 (1988). The then Assistant Attorney General, Douglas H. Ginsburg (now Judge Ginsburg), issued a report on July 23, 1986, concluding that the applicants had "not yet sustained their burden of proof of showing that the *Detroit Free Press* is a 'failing newspaper' within the meaning of the Act and that approval of the application would effectuate the policy and purpose of the Act." However, he did not advise disapproval of the application; instead, he recommended that the Attorney General order that a hearing be held before an administrative law judge to resolve material issues of fact raised by the application. See 28 C.F.R. § 48.7(b)(2) (1988).

Attorney General Edwin Meese followed his Assistant Attorney General's advice and pursuant to the Justice Department's regulations, 28 C.F.R. § 48.10, an administrative law judge was appointed to conduct the hearing. On December 29, 1987, ten months later, the ALJ issued a decision, recommending that the application be denied. He concluded, *inter alia,* that the applicants had failed to prove that there exists in Detroit an irreversible market condition that will probably lead to the failure of the *Free Press*. According to the ALJ, the *Free Press* is not dominated by the *News* and the *Free Press* is not in a downward spiral toward failure. He instead attributed the losses incurred by the *Free Press* and the *News* to "their strategies of seeking market dominance and future profitability at any cost along with the expectation that failure to achieve these goals would result in favorable consideration of a JOA application."

The ALJ did not deny that the fiercely competitive strategies employed by both papers were perfectly rational, given the disastrous history of junior papers in the United States. But he believed that each paper had an eye on a potential JOA application in the event that it turned out to be the loser. They both saw the JOA as a safety net, in other words, and were thereby encouraged to engage in particularly risky competitive acrobatics.

Indisputably, the *News* was leading the *Free Press* in most of the circulation, revenue, and advertising linage figures used to measure the relative positions of rival newspapers. The ALJ maintained, however, that the *Free Press* was within "striking distance" of the total circulation lead, and that the *News'* advertising lead was "vulnerable" to a change in the circulation lead. Neither paper could achieve profitability as long as they both pursued the current price war, but he believed that the record did not support the conclusion that "reader and advertiser demand in Detroit is so inadequate that the market cannot sustain two profitable papers irrespective of changes in pricing policies." He hypothesized that Detroit could sustain two profitable papers if the *Free Press* and the *News* both raised circulation and advertising prices. Still, he recognized that since "neither the *Free Press* nor the *News* can raise circulation or advertising prices without regard to what the other paper does, there is no completely unilateral course of action which either paper can pursue which would return it to profitability."

The ALJ accepted the testimony of the Antitrust Division's expert, who calculated that the 50/50 profit split (after five years) represented a perception by Gannett that it could not achieve domination of the market for "at least seven years." He was, moreover, unpersuaded by Gannett officials' testimony that if the JOA were denied, they would *not* raise circulation prices, and he found "contemporaneous evidence" indicating that "absent a JOA Gannett may eventually initiate circulation price increases." He also assigned "little weight" to testimony from Knight-Ridder's CEO that he would close down the *Free Press* if the JOA application were denied. Essentially, the ALJ predicted that if the JOA were denied, the *News* would give the *Free Press* sorely needed relief by raising the *News'* circulation and advertising prices, thereby allowing the *Free Press* to follow suit.

Attorney General Meese, in his opinion of August 8, 1988, disagreed with the conclusions of the ALJ and granted approval of the JOA. The Attorney General "accepted as accurate the fact findings of the Administrative Law Judge," but differed with his "ultimate conclusion as to where those facts lead." Adopting the legal standard

enunciated by the Ninth Circuit in *Hearst* the Attorney General asked: "Is the newspaper suffering losses which more than likely cannot be reversed?" *Committee for an Independent P-I v. Hearst*, 704 F.2d 467, 478 (9th Cir.), *cert. denied*, 464 U.S. 892 (1983). The Attorney General decided that the answer was yes: the *Free Press* had met its burden of proof, because it had suffered persistent operating losses over nearly a decade and had no prospect of unilateral action to reverse those losses.

Central to the Attorney General's opinion was his disagreement with the ALJ's prediction of future behavior by the two papers in the event that the JOA is denied. He noted and accepted the ALJ's finding that the *News* was in a stronger competitive position according to all major economic indices. But he determined—or more accurately predicted—that if the *News* continues its current pricing practices, it "undoubtedly has the ability on such terms to outlast the *Free Press*." Given this premise, the Attorney General found persuasive Gannett's testimony that it would continue its current competitive policies (and not raise prices), which he said "hardly reflects unsound business judgment." Similarly, the Attorney General felt that the testimony of Knight-Ridder's CEO concerning a possible closure of the *Free Press* "cannot be wholly disregarded," because it would be "neither counterintuitive nor contradictory" for Knight-Ridder to discontinue the paper if it concluded that it could not outlast the *News* in a prolonged price war.

In response to the allegation that the papers had pursued their competitive strategies *because* of the potential of a JOA, the Attorney General read the record as showing that Knight-Ridder was not "*principally* pursuing any end other than market domination." (emphasis added). Moreover, he noted that "newspapers cannot be faulted for considering and acting upon an alternative that Congress had created."

II

Appellants allege that the Attorney General's determination is invalid both because it is based on an impermissible interpretation of the statute and is arbitrary or capricious. As is not unusual in appeals from agency actions, the claims are interrelated. At the core of appellants' case is the assertion that the Attorney General could not legally grant approval for a JOA because the *Detroit Free Press* was not in a tough enough spot to qualify as "in probable danger of financial failure." Whether the Attorney General legally decided that the Free Press did meet the statutory standard in turn depends to a large extent on whether his prediction of the newspapers' future course (if he did not approve the JOA) was reasonable. The Attorney General's interpretation of the probable danger of financial failure test draws content from the factual showing that he requires to meet that test. See *INS v. Cardoza-Fonseca,* 480 U.S. 421 (1987) (ambiguous statutory terms "can only be given concrete meaning through a process of case-by-case adjudication"). And there is no question in our mind that if the Attorney General's statutory interpretation is reasonable, it is entitled to deference under *Chevron U.S.A. Inc. v. NRDC,* 467 U.S. 837, 842–43 (1984), because we are certainly unable to discern a specific congressional intent governing this case.

Not surprisingly, the exact meaning of the linguistically imprecise phrase "probable danger of financial failure" is not apparent from the statute or the legislative history. The Senate bill, which differed slightly from the House version, "defined" a failing newspaper as one "in danger of probable failure." The Senate took this phrase—or at least the words "probable failure"—from the Bank Merger Act, 12 U.S.C. § 1828(c)(3) (1982), recognizing that the phrase was informed by the Supreme Court's decision in *United States v. Third National Bank,* 390 U.S. 171, (1968). S.Rep. No. 535, 91st Cong., 1st Sess. 2 (1969). The House version, which was eventually adopted, used the clause "probable danger of *financial* failure" as the standard for new JOAs (emphasis added). Despite its minor difference from the Senate version, the chief House sponsor of the bill explained that "[t]he term 'probable danger of financial failure' . . . comes out of the Bank Merger Act," and "is understood by the courts in the field." 116 Cong.Rec. 23,146 (1970) (statement of Rep. Kastenmeier). The Supreme Court had held in *Third National Bank* that where managerial deficiencies are responsible for a bank's financial problems, the banks, in order to prove "probable failure,"

must establish that improved management could not achieve profitability. 390 U.S. at 190. More generally, the parties seeking the merger must "reliably establish the unavailability of alternative solutions" to the financial woes of the failing bank. *Id.* Thus, strong evidence of probable failure was required.

To be sure, the Attorney General had not previously faced a case such as this. Prior approvals of JOAs had always involved at least one newspaper that had actually entered the downward spiral, whereas the *Detroit Free Press* could be said to be poised on the brink of the spiral, its future dependent on the competitive behavior of the *News.* Still, the only prior case reviewing an Attorney General's approval of a JOA—the pre-*Chevron* decision of the Ninth Circuit in *Hearst*—phrased the question before the Attorney General in broader terms than whether one of the newspapers had entered a downward spiral. The court asked: "Is the newspaper suffering losses which more than likely cannot be reversed?" This interpretation of the statutory language, which the court called a "commonsense construction," *id.* at 478, was explicitly adopted by the Attorney General in this case, and thus made his own interpretation entitled to *Chevron* deference. Only for cogent reasons would we reject as unreasonable an interpretation of a statute that a sister circuit had considered a commonsense construction.

The Ninth Circuit thought implicit in its inquiry was an examination of alternative forms of relief for the putatively failing newspaper. Was there, for example, a group of interested buyers or a potential for improved management? Congress' reference to the *Third National Bank* case in the legislative history of the statute suggested to the Ninth Circuit that Congress intended the Attorney General to consider alternatives to a JOA before approving an application. We quite agree, but so apparently did the Attorney General. He concluded that if no form of relief was within the control of the sick newspaper—its survival depended only on improbable behavior by its competitor—the statutory test was satisfied. Appellants artificially construe the Attorney General's decision to permit a JOA without regard to consideration of the competitors' behavior, but that is not what the Attorney General said. . . .

III

Even if the Attorney General is statutorily authorized to treat a newspaper as in probable danger of failing before it actually enters the downward spiral, appellants claim that the Attorney General's decision was arbitrary and capricious because not rationally connected to the facts before him. *Bowman Transp., Inc. v. Arkansas-Best Freight System, Inc.,* 419 U.S. 281, 285, (1974) (quoting *Burlington Truck Lines v. United States,* 371 U.S. 156, 168 (1962) (agency must articulate a "rational connection between the facts found and the choice made"). This, as we have noted, is in essence a challenge to the reasonableness of the Attorney General's determination that the *News* had the economic power to outlast the *Free Press* and was not likely to reduce competitive pressure by raising prices.

The only specific challenge, as far as we can determine, to the Attorney General's appraisal of the respective competitive strengths of the two newspapers is based on the different opinion of the ALJ (and the Antitrust Division's brief to the ALJ). It is true that the Attorney General's crucial conclusions that the *Free Press* "has no realistic prospect of outlasting the *News* given the latter's substantial advertising and persistent circulation lead" and that the *News* "undoubtedly has the ability . . . to outlast the *Free Press*" was predicated on the ALJ's findings recounting the *News'* lead in all major indices. It is also true that the ALJ went on to offer a somewhat different conclusion: that the *Free Press* was still within "striking distance" of the *News* and the latter's lead was "vulnerable." The Attorney General would not, however, be legally obliged to conform his judgment to that of a statutorily-required ALJ, much less this one, who was employed as a matter of discretion rather than law. See 28 C.F.R. § 48.8 (1988). Both men relied on the very same facts to make different evaluations of the competitive strength of the *Free Press*. But, it is only the Attorney General's conclusions that have legal significance, and we cannot say that his determination is unreasonable. It is undisputed, after all, that the *News* has maintained the lead for a long time and that the *Free Press* had suffered extensive losses. Debatable, the Attorney General's appraisal may well be, but hardly unreasonable.

Similarly, appellants rely on the ALJ's contrary prediction to dispute the Attorney General's conclusion that the *News* would *not* release the pressure on the *Free Press* by raising prices if the JOA were disapproved. Gannett officials testified that they had no intention of raising prices regardless of the Attorney General's decision. The ALJ refused to credit this testimony, not on account of the witnesses' demeanor, but because he, the ALJ, thought that course would only cause more losses for the *News* and was therefore irrational. Cf. *Universal Camera Corp. v. NLRB,* 340 U.S. 474, 494–95 (1951) ("The significance of [the ALJ's] report . . . depends largely on the importance of credibility in the particular case."). The Attorney General's judgment of the *News'* likely future behavior was premised on his determination, which we have already found reasonable, that the *News* had the competitive strength to outlast the *Free Press*.[a] The ALJ never squarely found otherwise, and if the *News* had such strength, we do not see how the Attorney General's projection can be deemed unreasonable. Under those circumstances, Gannett's refusal to raise prices, as the Attorney General said, "hardly reflects unsound business judgment."

Knight-Ridder seems to have thought that its competitor's strategy was rational, since its CEO

---

a. The Attorney General wrote:
The argument is made that both papers should raise prices and discontinue advertising discounts. But the *Free Press* is currently selling its daily copy at 5 cents above the *News* and it offers a smaller discount rate. There is thus no competitive advantage to be gained by Knight-Ridder from a unilateral increase in prices; that market move must be accompanied by parallel price increases (and discount reductions) at the *News* if the papers have any chance of becoming profitable.

Gannett has made clear that it has no intention of embarking on such a course, either unilaterally or in conjunction with Knight-Ridder. While the Administrative Law Judge questioned the testimony of Gannett officials to this effect, it hardly reflects unsound business judgment to retain awhile longer the *News'* current depressed pricing practices with so many indications that the *Free Press* and Knight-Ridder have abandoned all hope of market domination. (Citations omitted.)

testified that if the JOA were disapproved, the *Free Press* would close down. The ALJ again assigned "little weight" to that testimony, because "if a *Free Press* closure was imminent, it would have made no economic sense for [the *News*] to agree to share prospective JOA profits with [the *Free Press*]." Also, he stressed that an anti-trust division expert had testified that the terms of the profit split (reaching 50/50 after five years) suggested that Gannett thought the *Free Press* would remain in existence for seven to ten years. The difficulty with the ALJ's analysis is that he equated the parties' bargaining positions prior to submission of a proposed JOA with their strategies after a rejection by the Attorney General. Prior to agreement, the *Free Press* had every incentive to convince the *News* that it would compete fiercely, and indefinitely into the future: Damn the losses; full speed ahead. Only by emphasizing its potential longevity could the *Free Press* extract favorable terms in a JOA. Thus, the Attorney General described the situation as the parties entered into the JOA, as a "competitive stalemate" with market domination "no longer within the grasp of either paper." But, that the *News* was willing to negotiate peace terms (the JOA) does not belie the Attorney General's appraisal of its fundamental superior strength. After this proceeding, in which all cards are placed on the table, it is wholly unrealistic to assume that the parties will return to the game and play it as if this proceeding had never occurred. If a JOA were denied, the *News* would have every incentive to force the *Free Press* to the wall; even if it took seven years to win, at the end of that period the *News* would have a monopoly. And, if the *Free Press* were doomed to defeat in the long run, it was not only reasonable but optimal for the paper to close immediately.

The Attorney General had to consider which of the two papers would blink first in the event the JOA were *denied*. Gannett said that it would not, and Knight-Ridder said that it would. Appellants assert that it was unreasonable for the Attorney General to believe them, because the more likely event was the exact reverse: that if the JOA were denied, Gannett would raise prices and the *Free Press* would remain in business. The Attorney General, it would seem, did not want to play the high stakes regulatory game that his ALJ

proposed. He obviously was concerned that if he gambled on the ALJ's prediction that both newspaper were bluffing, Detroit would lose a newspaper. That is not to say that the Attorney General should put undue stress on self-serving declarations by newspaper executives seeking a JOA. But here, the statements that the Attorney General credited follow a long period of bitter competition. For the *News* to stay the course, as for the British and French in 1917, promised absolute victory.

It may well be, as appellants argue and the ALJ found, that under ideal circumstances, Detroit could support two newspapers. The same could also be true of many cities that have lost competing newspapers and are now one newspaper monopoly towns. It is not at all clear whether the newspaper business in some cities is a natural monopoly, and, if so, in cities of what size. This sort of speculation, it seems to us, as it did to the Attorney General, is hardly conclusive. That an omniscient Detroit newspaper czar could set circulation and advertising prices that would permit both papers to return to profitable status is not a useful observation in this context. The Attorney General is required to determine what will actually happen in Detroit if his approval is withheld. It would, moreover, be anomalous for those responsible for enforcing the antitrust laws to try to guide and calibrate the competitive zeal of the two newspapers so as to reach that level of competition at which both newspapers could be profitable....

The real difficulty with this case—the factor that quite plainly underlies the ALJ's discomfort as well as appellants' quarrel with the Attorney General's decision—is the effect that the prospect of a JOA has on the behavior of competing newspapers. See also dissent at 1299. It is feared that the statute authorizing a JOA creates a self-fulfilling prophecy. Newspapers in two-newspaper towns will compete recklessly because of a recognition that the loser will be assured a soft landing.

Appellants argue that the Attorney General inadequately considered whether or not "critical aspects of the newspapers' conduct were influenced by the prospect of obtaining a JOA." But his opinion addressed this "dual motive" concern at some length; he observed that this was not the classic case that had worried Congress, where a newspaper had "brought itself to the brink of financial failure through improper marketing practices or culpable management." Instead, the record of years of fierce competitive and consequent losses to both papers led the Attorney General reasonably to conclude that both papers were principally pursuing market domination and that their strategies had been followed before any mutual discussion of a JOA. Nevertheless, the Attorney General implicitly recognized that it would be impossible completely to preclude competing newspapers from factoring into their business strategy the prospect of a JOA. As he laconically put it, "newspapers cannot be faulted for considering and acting upon an alternative that Congress has created."[b]

We can envision a perfectly rational different policy, one that would require a showing that the weaker paper was more bloodied before approving a JOA and therefore *might* discourage the sort of competition we saw in Detroit. Congress, however, delegated to the Attorney General, not to us, the delicate and troubling responsibility of putting content into the ambiguous phrase "probable danger of financial failure." We cannot therefore say that his interpretation of that phrase as applied to this case, with all of its obvious policy implications, was unreasonable. The judgment of the district court therefore is

AFFIRMED.

Ruth Bader Ginsburg, Circuit Judge, dissenting:

As a condition to the consummation of a joint operating agreement (JOA), and receipt of the attendant antitrust exemption, Congress required the approval of the Attorney General, an approval intended to "act as a brake" upon premature resort to such devices. 116 CONG.REC. 2006 (1970) (statement of Sen. Hruska). In this important and unprecedented case, the Attorney General approved a JOA and, in so doing, rejected the contrary conclusions of the administrative law judge (ALJ) and the Justice Department's Antitrust Division, as elaborated in the post-hearing brief the Division presented to the ALJ. At issue is a large and attractive newspaper market, Detroit, one concededly capable of sustaining two profitable newspapers. I have grave doubts whether the Attorney General properly performed in this instance the braking function Congress envisioned for him. I would therefore remand the case for reconsideration and a fuller account of the standard of approval the Attorney General deems applicable.

I.

As the Antitrust Division emphasized before the ALJ, no prior JOA application "has presented a comparable situation." Post-Hearing Brief of the Antitrust Division, Docket No. 44–03–24–8 (Sept. 23, 1987) [hereafter, Antitrust Division Brief], at 2. The *Detroit Free Press* (a morning newspaper)–*Detroit News* (evening paper) application "involves the largest market and largest newspapers" in the nation "ever to be involved in a JOA." *Id.* Applicants concede that the *Free Press* is unlike any other newspaper thus far declared "failing." The typical case presents an applicant caught in a "downward spiral" in which the newspaper's "declining circulation and lessening advertising feed off one another, eventually forcing it to close." *Committee for an Independent P-I v. Hearst,* 704 F.2d 467, 471 (9th Cir.), *cert. denied,* 464 U.S. 892, (1983). The only Newspaper Preservation Act–JOA before this one to be examined in court, *Hearst,* fit that description.

Just as there is no dispute that the *Free Press* and the *News* have both incurred significant losses on an operating basis, so it is undisputed that neither paper has experienced any "downward spiral" effect. On the contrary, in the relevant time period, 1976 to 1986, the *Free Press* share of daily circulation was never less than 49%; its competitive position has remained essentially stable; the *News,* though retaining a "leading" edge, is not "dominant." Antitrust Division Brief at 7–11. In other words, the two papers, each now maintained by a "deep pocket," the *News* by Gannett, the *Free Press* by Knight-Ridder, have fought to a draw. Neither has achieved supremacy. The

---

b. We need not consider the hypothetical situation where the initial and principal motivating factor behind a price war is the prospect of a future JOA. The Attorney General was reasonable to conclude that this record did not present such a situation.

competition today "is as close, or closer, than it was a decade ago." *Id.* at 2.

Gannett, it is also conceded, acquired the *News* only after obtaining expression of Knight-Ridder's willingness to consider a JOA. *Id.* at 27–28. The nearly equal profit split for the *Free Press* under the JOA indicates the "standoff" that existed; it reflects "a recognition on Gannett's part that the *Free Press* was not likely to exit the market in the near future." *Id.* at 20–22. No "failing" paper in Newspaper Preservation Act history, it appears, has emerged so advantageously under an approved JOA. *Id.* at 22. In these circumstances, I believe it incumbent on the Attorney General to recall—as our sister court observed—the legislature's "primary" concern "to prevent newspapers from allowing or encouraging financial difficulties in the hope of reaping long-term financial gains through a JOA." *Hearst,* 704 F.2d at 478....

The Attorney General's readiness to say "Yes" to a JOA for *Free Press–Detroit News* now, despite the view of the Antitrust Division and the ALJ that such a judgment remains premature, seems to me problematic on two counts. First, the Decision affords no assurance that the Attorney General has found a "middle ground" firmer than the pliant "not likely to...become financially sound" ground Congress thought inadequate for new agreements. The Decision never suggests any separate content for the "probable danger" standard to distinguish it from the more accommodating one. Second, the demonstration that satisfied the Attorney General allows parties situated as Gannett and Knight-Ridder are artificially to generate and maintain the conditions that will yield them a passing JOA. I remain unpersuaded that, with passage of the Newspaper Preservation Act, Congress opened the door to this sort of self-serving, competition-quieting arrangement. Cf. Attorney General's Decision at 12 (maintaining that "Congress opened the door to just this sort of response with passage of the Newspaper Preservation Act").

It is accepted by the Attorney General that the *Free Press* and *News* have arrived at a "competitive stalemate," Attorney General's Decision at 5, and that market dominance is "no longer within the grasp of either paper." *Id.* at 13. It is also a "given" that "the Detroit market *could* sustain two prof-

itable newspapers *if* both circulation and advertising prices were increased." *Id.* at 9 n. 3 (emphasis in original). But "the unbroken pattern of annual operating losses" cannot be reversed by *Free Press* "unilateral actions," and that, in the Attorney General's judgment, makes "probable" if not "imminent" the "danger of financial failure." *Id.* at 7, 12.

Without the lure of a JOA, however, what reason is there to believe that the losses here "likely *cannot* be reversed"? Absent the Attorney General's promise of that large pot of gold, would the parties not have, as the Antitrust Division suggested, an effective "incentive to adopt strategies directed toward achieving profitability in a competitive marketplace"? Antitrust Division Brief at 27, 28.

The Attorney General does not disavow "the well-recognized rule that antitrust exemptions must be narrowly construed." *Hearst,* 704 F.2d at 478 (citing *Group Life & Health Ins. Co. v. Royal Drug Co.,* 440 U.S. 205, 231, (1979)). This accepted rule should be factored into an evaluation already weighted by (1) the concession that both newspapers, by their own projections, "could achieve profitability with price increases and the elimination of discounting," Attorney General's Decision at 5, and (2) the burden of proof which JOA applicants bear, 28 C.F.R. § 48.10(a)(4) (1988). A remand would give the Attorney General an opportunity to state more comprehensibly why the JOA-route is ripe for his approbation now, i.e., why that course should not be deferred for consideration "at some future time" when the results of the current competition afford a firmer basis for predicting whether the *Free Press,* profitably for itself, for readers, and for advertisers, can survive. See Antitrust Division Brief at 29.

CONCLUSION

Detroit, as the Attorney General said, "is a highly prized $300 million dollar market." Attorney General's Decision at 4. That market could sustain two profitable newspapers. *Id.* at 9 n. 3. Market dominance is now beyond the grasp of the *News* as well as the *Free Press. Id.* at 13. The Attorney General has not cogently explained why, on the facts thus far found, the proposed JOA has become "an available option." *Id.* Making the JOA an option now, in the situation artificially created and maintained by the *Free Press* and the *News,* moves boldly away from the "frame of reference [Congress] essentially embraced"— "the scenario of a strong newspaper poised to drive from the market a weaker competitor," a newspaper experiencing, "due to external market forces," a decline in revenues and circulation "that in all probability cannot be reversed." *Id.* at 6, 13–14. I therefore dissent from the majority's disposition approving instanter the giant stride the Attorney General has taken.

Concerns about the utility and ends of the NPA, which transcend its susceptibility to abuse as a profit-maximizing device, also endure. The need for it has been questioned, for instance, on the grounds that the measure is so narrowly focused that it loses sight of the broader realities of the modern media industry. Newspapers are not the only enterprises that have exited major cities in recent decades. Corporate investment has relocated into newer, mostly suburban communities rather than dried up altogether. Although intended to save an endangered species, the NPA actually operates not against a diminution but the redistribution of editorial outlets. Viewed from a macrocosmic perspective that includes new media forms, daily newspapers actually have more rivals now than ever. Competition as a whole thus may not have slipped as much as it has been reconfigured. The NPA in such a context nonetheless reflects a value judgment that a particular segment of the newspaper industry merits preservation in its existing form. Even if it confers a preferential advantage upon a class of publishers and impedes the emergence of competing voices, the NPA is destined to endure unless Congress revises its thinking or the judiciary becomes inclined to regard it as an abridgment of First Amendment interests rather than a mere economic regulation.

NOTES

1. Times-Picayune Publishing Co. v. United States, 345 U.S. 594, 603 (1953).

2. STATISTICAL ABSTRACT OF THE UNITED STATES 1989, No. 913 at 549. The number of weekly papers published in the same year totaled 7,438. *Id.*

3. Times-Picayune Publishing Co. v. United States, 345 U.S. at 603.

4. Miami Herald Publishing Co. v. Tornillo, 418 U.S. 241, 249 n.13, (1974), *quoting* Balk, Background Paper in TWENTIETH CENTURY FUND TASK FORCE REPORT FOR A NATIONAL NEWS COUNCIL: A FREE AND RESPONSIVE PRESS 18 (1973).

5. *See* Lively, *Old Media, New Dogma,* 30 ARIZ. L. REV. 257, 265 (1988).

6. *Id.*

7. Miami Herald Publishing Co. v. Tornillo, 418 U.S. at 250.

8. *See* Michigan Citizens for an Independent Press v. Thornburgh, 868 F.2d 1285, 1287 (D.C.Cir.), *aff'd,* 110 S.Ct. 229 (1989).

9. *See id.*

10. *See id.*

11. 394 U.S. 131 (1969).

12. *Id.* at 135.

13. *Id.* at 136–37.

14. *Id.* at 138.

15. *Id.* at 137–38.

16. *Id.* at 138.

17. *Id.*

18. *Id.* at 138–39.

19. 18 U.S.C. § 1801 *et seq.* (1970). The terms of the Newspaper Preservation Act are as follows:

§ 1801. Congressional declaration of policy

In the public interest of maintaining a newspaper press editorially and reportorially independent and competitive in all parts of the United States, it is hereby declared to be the public policy of the United States to preserve the publication of newspapers in any city, community, or metropolitan area where a joint operating arrangement has been heretofore entered into because of economic distress or is hereafter effected in accordance with the provisions of this Act [15 USCS §§ 1801 et seq.]. (July 24, 1970, P. L. 91–353, § 2, 84 Stat. 466.)

§ 1802. Definitions

As used in this Act [15 USCS §§ 1801 et seq.]—
(1) The term "antitrust law" means the Federal Trade Commission Act [15 USCS §§ 41 et seq.] and each statute defined by section 4 thereof (15 U.S.C. 44) [15 USCS § 44] as "Antitrust Acts"

and all amendments to such Act and such statutes and any other Acts in pari materia.

(2) The term "joint newspaper operating arrangement" means any contract, agreement, joint venture (whether or not incorporated), or other arrangement entered into by two or more newspaper owners for the publication of two or more newspaper publications, pursuant to which joint or common production facilities are established or operated and joint or unified action is taken or agreed to be taken with respect to any one or more of the following: printing; time, method, and field of publication; allocation of production facilities; distribution; advertising solicitation; circulation solicitation; business department; establishment of advertising rates; establishment of circulation rates and revenue distribution: Provided, That there is no merger, combination, or amalgamation of editorial or reportorial staffs, and that editorial policies be independently determined.

(3) The term "newspaper owner" means any person who owns or controls directly, or indirectly through separate or subsidiary corporations, one or more newspaper publications.

(4) The term "newspaper publication" means a publication produced on newsprint paper which is published in one or more issues weekly (including as one publication any daily newspaper and any Sunday newspaper published by the same owner in the same city, community, or metropolitan area), and in which a substantial portion of the content is devoted to the dissemination of news and editorial opinion.

(5) The term "failing newspaper" means a newspaper publication which, regardless of its ownership or affiliations, is in probable danger of financial failure.

(6) The term "person" means any individual, and any partnership, corporation, association, or other legal entity existing under or authorized by the law of the United States, any State or possession of the United States, the District of Columbia, the Commonwealth of Puerto Rico, or any foreign country.

(July 24, 1970, P. L. 91–353, § 3, 84 Stat. 466.)

§ 1803. Antitrust exemption

(a) Joint operating arrangements entered into prior to July 24, 1970. It shall not be unlawful under any antitrust law for any person to perform, enforce, renew, or amend any joint newspaper operating arrangement entered into prior to the effective date of this Act [enacted July 24, 1970], if at the time at which such arrangement was first entered into, re-

gardless of ownership or affiliations, not more than one of the newspaper publications involved in the performance of such arrangement was likely to remain or become a financially sound publication: Provided, That the terms of a renewal or amendment to a joint operating arrangement must be filed with the Department of Justice and that the amendment does not add a newspaper publication or newspaper publications to such arrangement.

(b) Written consent for future joint operating arrangements. It shall be unlawful for any person to enter into, perform, or enforce a joint operating arrangement, not already in effect, except with the prior written consent of the Attorney General of the United States. Prior to granting such approval, the Attorney General shall determine that not more than one of the newspaper publications involved in the arrangement is a publication other than a failing newspaper, and that approval of such arrangement would effectuate the policy and purpose of this Act [15 USCS §§ 1801 et seq.].

(c) Predatory practices not exempt. Nothing contained in the Act [15 USCS §§ 1801 et seq.] shall be construed to exempt from any antitrust law any predatory pricing, any predatory practice, or any other conduct in the otherwise lawful operations of a joint newspaper operating arrangement which would be unlawful under any antitrust law if engaged in by a single entity. Except as provided in this Act [15 USCS §§ 1801 et seq.], no joint newspaper operating arrangement or any party thereto shall be exempt from any antitrust law.

(July 24, 1970, P. L. 91–353, § 4, 84 Stat. 467.)

§ 1804. Reinstatement of joint operating arrangements previously adjudged unlawful under antitrust laws

(a) Notwithstanding any final judgment rendered in any action brought by the United States under which a joint operating arrangement has been held to be unlawful under any antitrust law, any party to such final judgment may reinstitute said joint newspaper operating arrangement to the extent permissible under section 4(a) hereof [15 USCS § 1803(a)].

(b) The provisions of section 4 [15 USCS § 1803] shall apply to the determination of any civil or criminal action pending in any district court of the United States on the date of enactment of this Act [enacted July 24, 1970] in which it is alleged that any such joint operating agreement is unlawful under any antitrust law.

(July 24, 1970, P. L. 91–353, § 5, 84 Stat. 467.)

20. S. Rep. No. 535, 91st Cong., 1st Sess. 4 (1969).
21. Michigan Citizens for an Independent Press v. Thornburgh, 868 F.2d at 1288.

22. 15 U.S.C. § 1802 (5).

23. *Id.,* § 1803 (a).

24. *Id.,* § 1801.

25. *Id.,* § 1803 (b).

26. *Id.,* § 1801.

27. *See* Times Picayune Publishing Co. v. United States, 345 U.S. at 604–05.

28. Advertising rates in Detroit Newspapers increased as much as to 35% a month after a JOA was approved. *See* Advertisers start to hear new newspaper rates, *Detroit Free Press,* December 7, 1989, § E, cols. 2–6, at 1.

29. Within a month of entering into a JOA, newspapers in Detroit increased their purchase prices by five cents. *See* Newsstand prices rising for Free Press, News, *Detroit Free Press,* December 6, 1989, § A, cols. 5–6, at 1.

30. The possibility is discussed further at *infra* notes 73–79 and accompanying text.

31. JOA's have been approved in Detroit, Michigan; Seattle, Washington; Chattanooga, Tennessee; Cincinnati, Ohio; and Anchorage, Alaska. *See* Michigan Citizens for an Independent Press v. Thornburgh, 868 F.2d at 1288 n.5, 1297.

32. *See id.;* Committee for an Independent P-I v. Hearst, 704 F.2d 467 (9th Cir. 1983); Bay Guardian Co. v. Chronicle Publishing Co., 344 F. Supp. 1155 (N.D. Cal. 1972).

33. Negotiations to save failing newspapers by means of a JOA have collapsed, and the weaker publication consequently has disappeared, in Washington, D.C.; Houston, Texas, Indianapolis, Indiana; and St. Louis (Sen. Fong) Missouri: *See* 116 CONG. REC. 1999 (1970) (Sen. Fong); St. Louis Blues, EDITOR AND PUBLISHER, Dec, 14, 1985, at 14–15.

34. 344 F.Supp. 1155.

35. *Id.* at 1157.

36. *Id.*

37. *Id.*

38. *Id.*

39. *Id.* at 1158.

40. *Id.*

41. *Id.*

42. *Id.* at 1159.

43. *Id.*

44. *Id.*

45. Committee for an Independent P-I v. Hearst, 704 F.2d at 471.

46. 704 F.2d 467.

47. *Id.* at 478–79.

48. *Id.* at 474–76.

49. *Id.* at 471.

50. *Id.* at 482–83.

51. *Id.*

52. *Id.*

53. *Id.*

54. *Id.*

55. *Id.*

56. *Id.*

57. *Id.* at 482.

58. *Id.* at 481.

59. *Id.*

60. *Id.*

61. *Id.* at 476.

62. *Id.* at 478.

63. *Id.* at 479.

64. *See* Michigan Citizens for an Independent Press v. Thornburgh, 868 F.2d at 1296–97; *id.* at 1299 (R.B. Ginsburg, J., dissenting).

65. *Id.* at 1288.

66. *Id.* at 1289.

67. *Id.*

68. *Id.* at 1290; *id.* at 1304 (rehearing denial) (Wald, C.J., dissenting).

69. *Id.* at 1294, 1295 n.11.

70. *Id.* at 1295.

71. 868 F.2d 1285.

72. Michigan Citizens for an Independent Press v. Thornburgh, 110 S.Ct. 229.

73. The possibility was emphasized in a dissent from the appeals court's denial of a suggestion for rehearing *en banc.* Michigan Citizens for an Independent Press v. Thornburgh, 868 F.2d at 1306 n.7 (rehearing denial) (Wald, C.J., dissenting).

74. *Id.* at 1306 n.7 (rehearing denial) (Wald, C.J., dissenting).

75. Michigan Citizens for an Independent Press v. Thornburgh, 868 F.2d at 1298 (R.J. Ginsburg, J., dissenting).

76. *Id.* (R.J. Ginsburg, J., dissenting).

77. *Id.* at 1297 n.13.

78. *Id.*

79. *Id.* at 1297.

Chapter 5

THE BROADCASTING INDUSTRY

Broadcasting generally has been structurally distinguishable from publishing on the grounds that it uses a public resource, the airwaves, for the radiation of electronic signals that become pictures or sound. Insofar as some publishers now use satellites to distribute information from editorial centers to a printing plant, in addition to public resources such as sidewalks and highways to disseminate their product, the distinction is less than perfect. The lines blur further to the extent that some broadcasters use satellites primarily to disseminate signals beyond their normal market and employ on-screen text to communicate.

I. THE NATURE OF BROADCASTING

Broadcasting over the course of this century has evolved from a virtually nonexistent state to being the most dominant and pervasive mass medium. In 1987, a total of 9,911 commercial radio and television stations were in operation.[1] Radio was in more than 99 percent of the nation's homes, with an average of 5.6 receivers per household.[2] Television was found in more than 98 per-

cent of the nation's homes, with an average of 1.90 sets per household.[3]

Prior to the twentieth century, radio was largely experimental and developmental. The first practical use of the medium in this country was for defense purposes when the U.S. Navy used it to broadcast orders to its fleet. After World War I, commercial development of radio commenced. Under license from the Department of Commerce, the first radio stations operated in Massachusetts and Pennsylvania. Network broadcasting, linking stations together and making simultaneous national programming possible, started in 1926. Radio broadcasting in 1940 expanded from the amplitude modulated (AM) to the frequency modulated (FM) band. AM service continued to be dominant until relatively recently, when the demand for FM licenses became so great that the FCC adopted rules permitting new stations to operate on the band provided they do not interfere with existing service.[4]

Experiments with electronic signals to carry impulses resulting in visual images as well as sound followed close behind those for radio. In 1927, an experimental television program was transmitted by wire between New York and Washington, D.C. The FCC began issuing licenses for commercial stations in 1941 and, by mid-century, color programming was available. Television, which originally was consigned to very high frequencies (VHF), proved so popular that its original channel allotment was expanded to include ultra high frequency (UHF) assignments. Following a decade, in which available channels were rapidly consumed, the FCC devised an allocation scheme calculated to provide nationwide television service and to ensure that every community was served by at least one television station.[5]

A. TECHNICAL ASPECTS OF BROADCASTING

The key characteristics of radio waves are frequency and wavelength, which vary inversely with one another. The former term refers to cycles per second, and the latter term relates to the distance between points in separate cycles. Mass media services mostly are located on medium frequencies, denominated in terms of kilohertz (previously kilocycles) and very high and ultrahigh frequencies, classified in terms of megahertz. AM service operates between 540 and 1705 kilohertz, and upon 107 frequencies at 10-kilohertz intervals. FM broadcasting is assigned frequencies from 88 to 108 megahertz, allowing 100 channels at intervals of 200 kilohertz. Television requires wider channels to accommodate picture and sound. Thus, VHF assignments are from 54 to 72 megahertz, 76 to 88 megahertz, and 174 to 216 megahertz (respectively, channels 2, 3, and 4; 5 and 6; and 7 through 13) at 6-megahertz intervals. UHF broadcasting occupies frequencies from 470 to 806 megahertz, which runs from channel 14 to channel 69.

Broadcasting essentially entails the conversion of vibrations from voice or other inputs into electrical signals, which vary accordingly in strength and frequency and are amplified as they are transmitted onto a carrier wave. AM and FM are terms that denote the means by which audio or video detail are impressed onto a carrier wave. AM refers to audio waves which vary in power and thus in length. With FM broadcasting, wave frequency varies, but amplitude is unchanged. Amplitude modulation is the methodology for AM radio service and the video aspect of television in the United States, and it is employed worldwide for shortwave service. Frequency modulation provides FM radio service and the audio dimension of television. Transmission of radio signals occurs at the speed of light along various routes, depending upon the nature of the signal. AM transmission, for instance, proceeds in waves that both follow the contour of the ground and move upward through the atmosphere. Sky waves are reflected back to the earth effectively at night, which can greatly enhance service range and interference potential. FM signals, like other VHF emissions, travel by line of sight and are subject to distortion or absorption by obstacles between transmitting and receiving points.

AM stations are divided into four general channel classifications providing clear channel (classes I and II), regional (class III), and local (class IV) service. Class I sets aside forty-seven clear channels which are allowed to provide service over a broad geographical area without significant interference from otherwise competing signals. Stations allowed to operate in class I may do so full time with from 10 to 50 kilowatts of power. Class II stations may operate on clear channels insofar as they do not create objectionable interference with class I stations and do not conflict with foreign service protected by international agreement. Such stations operate with from 250 watts to 50 kilowatts of power, but they must alter or terminate their signal to the extent that it would conflict with class I service. Thus, class II broadcasting may be subject not only to power restrictions but also to time restrictions to avoid interference with primary ground wave or secondary sky wave service of class I stations.

A total of forty-one regional channels are set aside for class III service. Stations operating in a class III category provide primary service to a major population center and surrounding areas. They operate at from 500 watts to 5 kilowatts. Service hours and area vary according to the potential for interference with other stations.

Class IV stations, which serve suburban and rural communities, are assigned to the remaining six channels. The maximum power for such stations is 1 kilowatt.

Rules governing FM service divide the country into three geographical zones and provide six classes of commercial stations based upon power ratings. Because transmission correlates to line of sight, antenna height is a critical factor and is regulated as specifically as power. The FCC has composed a table which sets aside FM channels for the various states and communities. From that table, approximately 3,000 assignments have been made to nearly 2,000 communities on the mainland. Television channels are allotted in a similar fashion.

Educational broadcasting, which now has reserved space on the FM band, originally operated on the AM spectrum. By the time the FCC emerged in 1934, most AM educational broadcasting had been replaced by commercial service. Early congressional proposals to set aside a percentage of service for educational programming did not materialize. The eventual opening up of the FM band to general broadcasting, however, led toward the eventual dedication of twenty FM channels between 88 and 92 megahertz for noncommercial stations. Subsequently, tele-vision channel allotments were revised so that they also set aside space for educational use.

Upward of 2,000 television channels, comprising seventy UHF positions and two VHF slots, have been assigned to 1,300 communities. Early use of the UHF band was impaired by the fact that most receivers were VHF only. Consequently, advertising revenue flowed primarily to VHF stations. Over the years, the problem has been ameliorated by FCC rules that require all televisions to receive both VHF and UHF signals[6] and to be fitted with comparable tuning mechanisms.[7] Slow development of UHF, although having accelerated in recent years due to the near universality of UHF-equipped receivers, improved tuning mechanisms and signal quality, and the growth of cable, nonetheless has resulted in reassignment of some frequencies for competing uses such as cellular telephones.

Broadcasting service over recent years has been augmented by technological developments that afford stereophonic service, multichannel sound in television, teletext service, closed-captioning FM subcarrier service, and subscription programming based on scrambling and decoding of signals. Awaiting final development and standardization is high definition television which is supposed to offer pictures of unprecedented quality and resolution. Further augmenting broadcast service are ground translators, which amplify and retransmit FM radio and television signals to expand service areas; satellite relays for overseas and remote transmissions; direct broadcast satellite service; and low-power television, which is designed to enhance programming diversity choices by means of origination or retransmission. Such methodologies or enhancements, like the basis of broadcast service, are subject to FCC regulation and pertinent international agreement.

B. REGULATORY HISTORY

1. Early Regulation

Regulation of broadcasting commenced well before the medium acquired its modern pervasive character. Federal regulation of radio commenced with the Wireless Ship Act in 1910,[8] which reflected the medium's primary utility in its early incarnation as a facilitator of marine safety.[9] Soon thereafter, Congress enacted legislation that required the presence of radios and radio operators on board oceangoing passenger vessels and assigned enforcement responsibility to the Secretary of Commerce and Labor.[10] Over the course of the next two decades, uses and usage of broadcasting multiplied at such a rate that service was unpredictable, chaotic, and largely beyond the ken of effective governance. Experience during that period of development, expansion, and conflict shaped the eventual model of regulation that has endured over the past half century.

National Broadcasting Co. v. United States, 319 U.S. 190 (1943)

Federal regulation of radio begins with the Wireless Ship Act of June 24, 1910, 36 Stat. 629, which forbade any steamer carrying or licensed to carry fifty or more persons to leave any American port unless equipped with efficient apparatus for radio communication, in charge of a skilled operator. The enforcement of this legislation was entrusted to the Secretary of Commerce and Labor, who was in charge of the administration of the marine navigation laws. But it was not until 1912, when the United States ratified the first international radio treaty, 37 Stat. 1565, that the need for general regulation of radio communication became urgent. In order to fulfill our obligations under the treaty, Congress enacted the Radio Act of August 13, 1912, 37 Stat. 302. This statute forbade the operation of radio apparatus without a license from the Secretary of Commerce and Labor; it also allocated certain frequencies for the use of the Government, and imposed restrictions upon the character of wave emissions, the transmission of distress signals, and the like.

The enforcement of the Radio Act of 1912 presented no serious problems prior to the World War. Questions of interference arose only rarely because there were more than enough frequencies for all the stations then in existence. The war accelerated the development of the art, however, and in 1921 the first standard broadcast stations were established. They grew rapidly in number, and by 1923 there were several hundred such stations throughout the country. The Act of 1912 had not set aside any particular frequencies for the use of private broadcast stations; consequently, the Secretary of Commerce selected two frequencies, 750 and 833 kilocycles, and licensed all stations to operate upon one or the other of these channels. The number of stations increased so rapidly, however, and the situation became so chaotic, that the Secretary, upon the recommendation of the National Radio Conferences which met in Washington in 1923 and 1924, established a policy of assigning specified frequencies to particular stations. The entire radio spectrum was divided into numerous bands, each allocated to a particular kind of service. The frequencies ranging from 550 to 1500 kilocycles (96 channels in all, since the channels were separated from each other by 10 kilocycles) were assigned to the standard broadcast stations. But the problems created by the enormously rapid development of radio were far from solved. The increase in the number of channels was not enough to take care of the constantly growing number of stations. Since there were more stations than available frequencies, the Secretary of Commerce attempted to find room for everybody by limiting the power and hours of operation of stations in order that several stations might use the same channel. The number of stations multiplied so rapidly, however, that by November, 1925, there were almost 600 stations in the country, and there were 175 applications for new stations. Every channel in the standard broadcast band was, by that time, already occupied by at least one station, and many by several. The new stations could be accommodated only by extending the standard broadcast band, at the expense of the other types of services, or by imposing still greater limitations upon time and power. The National Radio Conference which met in November, 1925, opposed both of these methods and called upon Congress to remedy the situation through legislation.

The Secretary of Commerce was powerless to deal with the situation. It had been held that he could not deny a license to an otherwise legally qualified applicant on the ground that the proposed station would interfere with existing private or Government stations. *Hoover v. Intercity Radio Co.*, 52 App. D.C. 339, 286 F. 1003. And on April 16, 1926, an Illinois district court held that the Secretary had no power to impose restrictions as to frequency, power, and hours of operation, and that a station's use of a frequency not assigned to it was not a violation of the Radio Act of 1912. *United States v. Zenith Radio Corp.*, 12 F.2d 614. This was followed on July 8, 1926, by an opinion of Acting Attorney General Donovan that the Secretary of Commerce had no power, under the Radio Act of 1912, to regulate the power, frequency or hours of operation of stations. 35 Ops. Atty. Gen. 126. The next day the Secretary of Commerce issued a statement abandoning all his efforts to regulate radio and urging that the stations undertake self-regulation.

But the plea of the Secretary went unheeded. From July, 1926, to February 23, 1927, when Congress enacted the Radio Act of 1927, 44 Stat. 1162, almost 200 new stations went on the air. These new stations used any frequencies they desired, regardless of the interference thereby caused to others. Existing stations changed to other frequencies and increased their power and hours of operation at will. The result was confusion and chaos. With everybody on the air, nobody could be heard. The situation became so intolerable that the President in his message of December 7, 1926, appealed to Congress to enact a comprehensive radio law:

"Due to the decisions of the courts, the authority of the department [of Commerce] under the law of 1912 has broken down; many more stations have been operating than can be accommodated within the limited number of wave lengths available; further stations are in course of construction; many stations have departed from the scheme of allocations set down by the department, and the whole service of this most important public function has drifted into such chaos as seems likely, if not remedied, to destroy its great value. I most urgently recommend that this legislation should be speedily enacted." (H. Doc. 483, 69th Cong., 2d Sess., p. 10.)

The plight into which radio fell prior to 1927 was attributable to certain basic facts about radio as a means of communication—its facilities are limited; they are not available to all who may wish to use them; the radio spectrum simply is not large enough to accommodate everybody. There is a fixed natural limitation upon the number of stations that can operate without interfering with one another. Regulation of radio was therefore as vital to its development as traffic control was to the development of the automobile. In enacting the Radio Act of 1927, the first comprehensive scheme of control over radio communication, Congress acted upon the knowledge that if the potentialities of radio were not to be wasted, regulation was essential.

The Radio Act of 1927 created the Federal Radio Commission, composed of five members, and endowed the Commission with wide licensing and regulatory powers. We do not pause here to enumerate the scope of the Radio Act of 1927 and of the authority entrusted to the Radio Commission, for the basic provisions of that Act are incorporated in the Communications Act of 1934, 48 Stat. 1064, 47 U.S.C. § 151 *et seq.*, the legislation immediately before us. As we noted in *Federal Communications Comm'n v. Pottsville Broadcasting Co.*, 309 U.S. 134, 137, "In its essentials the Communications Act of 1934 [so far as its provisions relating to radio are concerned] derives from the Federal Radio Act of 1927.... By this Act Congress, in order to protect the national interest involved in the new and far-reaching science of broadcasting, formulated a unified and comprehensive regulatory system for the industry. The common factors in the administration of the various statutes by which Congress had supervised the different modes of communication led to the creation, in the Act of 1934, of the Communications Commission. But the objectives of the legislation have remained substantially unaltered since 1927."

Section 1 of the Communications Act states its "purpose of regulating interstate and foreign commerce in communication by wire and radio so as to make available, so far as possible, to all the people of the United States a rapid, efficient, Nation-wide, and world-wide wire and radio communication service with adequate facilities at reasonable charges." Section 301 particularizes this general purpose with respect to radio: "It is the purpose of this Act, among other things, to maintain the control of the United States over all the channels of interstate and foreign radio transmission; and to provide for the use of such channels, but not the ownership thereof, by persons for limited periods of time, under licenses granted by Federal authority, and no such license shall be construed to create any right, beyond the terms, conditions, and periods of the license." To that end a Commission composed of seven members was created, with broad licensing and regulatory powers.

2. Modern Regulation

Contemporary regulation of broadcasting derives from the Communication Acts of 1934.[11] The 1934 act created the Federal Communications Commission, which was authorized to set and enforce standards for broadcasting. The FCC's general duties, as congressionally prescribed, are as follows:

> to make available, so far as possible, to all the people of the United States, rapid, efficient, Nationwide and worldwide wire and radio communication service with adequate facilities at reasonable charges for the purpose of promoting safety of life and property through the use of wire and radio communication.[12]

More specifically, the FCC is empowered to classify radio stations; prescribe the nature of service to be provided within each classification; assign bands of frequencies to classes of stations and establish frequency assignments, power usage, and operational times for individual stations; determine the location of stations; regulate and set standards for broadcasting equipment and signals; prevent interference between or among diverse transmissions; promote larger and more effective use of radio in the public interest; establish service areas for sta-

tions; regulate chain broadcasting; adopt and promulgate rules requiring licensees to keep records of programming and technical operations; suspend a license upon proof that the broadcaster violated a federal law, which the FCC may administer, or transmitted profanity or obscenity; and make rules and regulations not inconsistent with law as are lawful and necessary to carry out the act.[13] In exercising its power and responsibility, the commission is obligated to serve "the public interest, convenience or necessity."[14]

The public interest standard has been described as the "touchstone" criterion for federal regulation of broadcasting.[15] From the outset, its imprecision was recognized. An early observer characterized it as meaning "about as little as any phrase that the drafters of the Act could have used and still comply with the constitutional requirement that there be some standard to guide the administrative wisdom of the licensing authority."[16] In more charitable terms, the Supreme Court has found it "as concrete as complicated factors for judgment in such a field of delegated authority permit."[17] Delineation of the public interest in exact but comprehensive terms would be vain. At one time, the Court described it "as the interest of the listening public in the larger and more effective use of radio."[18] Such a definition, although broad, hardly begins to afford guidance with respect to what constitutes "effective use" of the medium and in the end merely refers back in a circular fashion to indefinite statutory language. Because the FCC's powers range so broadly, the public interest governs rules and policy pertaining to industry structure and practices, licensing qualifications, and programming. Given the broad territory that it covers, and the open-ended nature of the terminology, the public interest might be understood best as the function of values chosen to inspire it in those diverse settings.

FCC determinations of the public interest, within the scope of its authority, are subject to limited review.[19] As the Court has noted:

> [o]urs is not the duty of reviewing determinations of 'fact', in the narrow, colloquial scope of that concept. Congress has charged the courts with the responsibility of saying whether the Commission has fairly exercised its discretion within the vaguish, penumbral bounds expressed by the standard of "public interest." It is our responsibility to say whether the Commission has been guided by proper considerations in bringing the deposit of its experience, the disciplined feel of the expert, to bear on applications for licenses in the public interest.[20]

Judicial review may be more exacting insofar as constitutional considerations are present. The Court has determined that the 1934 act itself represents a valid exercise of Congress' commerce power[21] and the public interest standard by its mere existence does not contravene the First Amendment.[22] Still, regulation that touches editorial discretion and determines who is authorized to broadcast invariably implicates questions of editorial freedom and discretion. The licensing process and pertinent criteria affect both the content and structure of broadcasting. Given such consequences, differentiation between content and structural control may be somewhat illusory. For the sake of convenience, however, discussion of content regulation is reserved for Part Three of this volume.

II. LICENSING

Central to the Communications Act of 1934 is a scheme for licensing broadcasters.[23] Licensing was the primary methodology chosen for addressing the chaos and confusion of an unregulated electronic marketplace. The 1934 act, although setting some basic qualifications in terms of citizenship, character, and financial and technical capability,[24] left the formulation of detailed licensing criteria to the FCC. Pursuant to its legislative charge, the commission has contributed detailed general provisions by adopting and promulgating rules and standards. Because the number of broadcasting frequencies generally has been less than the number of potential broadcasters, the FCC also has set qualitative standards to determine which applicant for a particular frequency would best serve the public interest.

The process is reminiscent in part of the much condemned English practice of licensing publishers. The Supreme Court, in its first freedom of the press case,[25] observed that the fundamental purpose of the First Amendment is to safeguard against a system of prior restraint.[26] Licensing of broadcasters in practice and effect is a form of prior restraint. Yet, if measured against contemporary standards, it probably would survive. Although a prior restraint is presumptively invalid and imposes upon government a heavy burden of justification,[27] the consequences of an unregulated marketplace are evidenced by history and provide a compelling reason for licensing. Methodologies exist that would remove government from content-related assessments in the course of licensing.[28] Consistent with broadcasting's evolution as a medium with the least First Amendment status, however, analysis never has insisted upon licensing criteria and procedures that would have the least burdensome impact upon constitutional interests.

Considerations governing all license applications include whether basic citizenship, character, technical, and financial qualifications are satisfied[29] and whether limits would be exceeded upon the number of broadcast holdings an individual or entity may own. When more than one application is received for the same frequency or a renewal is contested, comparative criteria operate. Standing to participate in the licensing process may extend to other stations demonstrating technical interference[30] and to representatives of the public itself whose participation may be critical to determine whether a broadcaster has violated its fiduciary role. In *Office of Communication of United Church of Christ v. Federal Communications Commission*,[31] therefore, citizen groups were allowed to challenge a renewal on the grounds that the licensee consistently had underserved or disserved the interests of African-Americans.[32] License terms are five years for television and seven years for radio,[33] subject to revocation for certain violations of the law.[34]

A. Basic Qualifications

Congress has provided that "the Commission by regulation may prescribe as to the citizenship, character, and financial, technical and other qualifications of a broadcast licensee."[35] The Communications Act of 1934 by its own terms denies licenses to aliens[36] or persons whose licenses have been revoked by a federal court as a consequence of antitrust violations.[37] Beyond those two statutory proscriptions, it is the FCC's task to formulate basic qualification policies and other criteria for assessing license applications and renewals. Licensing standards by their nature narrow the class of potential broadcasters. Although basic in form, they are not entirely without controversy in substantive operation.

1. Citizenship

Alienage restrictions, which preclude noncitizens from obtaining a broadcasting license, may be regarded not only as a prior restraint but also as an equal protection issue. For Fourteenth Amendment purposes, however, federal law that classifies on the basis of alienage tends to be less closely scrutinized than distinctions by state and local government.[38] Thus, it would seem that the

1934 act's citizenship requirement is permissible so long as it is rationally related to a valid federal interest.[39] Such deference purports to recognize the federal government's dominant interest in foreign affairs and immigration and naturalization.[40] Even so, it might be asserted that, unless it is evident that the restrictions advance a clear foreign policy aim, they are essentially arbitrary.[41]

2. Character

Consistent perhaps with the notion of broadcasters as public trustees,[42] a licensee must satisfy official character requirements. The problem with such criteria, however, is identifying what if any concept of character is relevant and how it is to be measured. Over the years, character inquiries have been a source of regulatory inconsistency and problematical results.

Character qualifications until recently have factored in criminal convictions, anticompetitive practices, and general albeit usually undefined notions of morality. Such considerations would be entirely impermissible as a basis for determining whether a person may publish.[43] In broadcasting, however, character is an independent grounds for disqualification as well as a subsidiary factor in determining whether the public interest is served. In *Federal Communications Commission v. WOKO, Inc.*, the Court noted the potentially dispositive nature of a determination that a licensee's character was deficient.

> We cannot say that the Commission is required as a matter of law to grant a license on a deliberately false application even if the falsity were not of this duration and character, nor can we say the refusal to renew the license is arbitrary and capricious under such circumstances. It may very well be that this Station has established such a standard of public service that the Commission would be justified in

considering that its deception was not a matter that affected its qualifications to serve the public. But it is the Commission, not the courts, which must be satisfied that the public interest will be served by renewing the license. And the fact that we might not have made the same determination on the same facts does not warrant a substitution of judicial for administrative discretion since Congress has confided the problem to the latter. We agree that this is a hard case, but we cannot agree that it should be allowed to make bad law.[44]

The problem with a character standard is defining it so that it has some relevance. A court once identified "character" as embracing "all of an individual's qualities and deficiencies regarding traits of personality, behavior, integrity, temperament, consideration, sportsmanship, altruism, etc., which distinguish him as a human being from his fellow men."[45] Although such a standard would not necessarily predict quality service to the public, the FCC has not been reticent at times to assess character in similarly broad terms. Thus, it has observed that character should be appraised on the basis of "past observance of moral, ethical, legal and professional rules of conduct."[46]

Implicit in the standard's presence is the assumption that a nexus exists between good character and quality of service. Until recently, the FCC assumed that "[o]ne who has in the past led an exemplary life in and out of broadcasting has been presumed likely to serve the public interest as a broadcaster in the future."[47] As it eventually realized, however, moral character does not guarantee competent broadcast service.[48] Complications and inconsistency result, moreover, when the commission is faced with similar conduct in different cases, draws distinctions based upon degree, and produces apparently conflicting results.[49] License applicants who had violated federal regulation promulgated by other agencies, for instance,

have been subject to favorable and negative determinations of character.[50] Despite its refusal to consider a licensee's overall performance in circumstances leading to the aforementioned *WOKO, Inc.* decision,[51] the FCC determined that two other corporations found guilty of price fixing had provided consistent meritorious service.[52] Taking into account a broader picture, therefore, the commission renewed the licenses despite the criminal records.[53]

Consideration of character in the context of a licensee's overall service may have afforded a fairer assessment of a licensee's record, but it also conferred an advantage upon incumbent broadcasters. A new applicant, without any record of service in radio or television, could offer only future promises to convince the FCC that past misconduct would not be repeated. Given no option of placing any character deficiency in perspective with actual broadcast service, established licensees had a preferential edge under the standard.[54] Incumbent advantage in comparative proceedings as discussed later,[55] however, is not unique to the issue of character.

Problems also arose with respect to the effect of identified character defects upon licensees with multiple holdings. Insofar as moral character is portable, a logical implication is that a broadcaster's loss of one license for character shortcomings justifies denial or revocation of all licenses. Misrepresentation or deceit in a license application, for instance, is a character trait that transcends the particular proceeding. Adding to the confusion surrounding use of character, however, loss of a license for dishonesty did not always affect the status of a broadcaster's other holdings.[56]

Recognizing the potentially limitless reach of the character standard, its manipulability and the inconsistency of results it had engendered, the FCC commenced an inquiry designed to yield "a more coherent licensing policy" on character.[57] The commission itself acknowledges that

> use of "character" as a license qualification is in our opinion, extremely troublesome. The term's definition is unclear and its measurement imprecise. Also, it may not be, in its strictest application, a sure indicator of future broadcast service. Its uniform application to existing licenses and new applicants yields disparate results, moreover, the Commission's attempts to apply the standard to multiple-owner licensees have resulted in decisions which contain confusing reasoning. The character requirement forces the Commission to perform the exceedingly difficult exercise of attempting to demonstrate why behavior in one case did not evidence bad "character" even though similar behavior in another case did. While the Commission has often asserted that an applicant lacking character must be denied, in practice the Commission has treated character as but one factor for predicting future service in the public interest. The Commission's inquiry into character qualifications is but an intermediate step in the licensing process. The ultimate licensing question to be answered under the Communications Act is whether an applicant can be expected to serve the public interest as a broadcaster. 47 U.S.C. §§ 308, 319. Any character inquiry supposedly is conducted to assist the Commission in reaching that public interest determination. To the extent that the character examination obfuscates rather than facilitates that determination, it is necessary to inquire whether the Commission has allowed the process to gain dominance over its goals.[58]

Pursuant to its inquiry into the pertinence and utility of character, the FCC tightened its evaluative focus. Character inquiry focuses especially upon honesty with the Commission, disregard of the law governing broadcasting, and fraudulent acts or performance that negatively affect the public.[59] The FCC in its most recent character statement, however, has reenlarged the purview

of official concern. It thus has announced its sense that all felonies and mass-media related antitrust violations will be relevant to character assessment, subject to mitigating circumstances such as intent, extent and magnitude of the wrong.[60] Despite the narrowed concern, consistency of results is not assured as degrees of character deficiency are bound to exist even within discrete categories of interest. Nor does the continuing presence of character standards, even in a limited sense, render impertinent the overarching question of their pertinence and permissibility. It remains possible that a dishonest person, even one who has flouted FCC rules in a given instance, might serve the public's interest in receiving diverse and quality programming as well as or better than a "cleaner" individual. Notwithstanding recent FCC dicta to the effect that broadcasters and publishers should be on the same constitutional plane, a comparable requirement for the print media would be found contrary to the First Amendment. The continuing vitality of character requirements perhaps may be best understood as an extension or implication of the concept of broadcasters as public fiduciaries and the operation of a public interest standard that may override constitutional concerns.

3. Concentration

Concentrated ownership in the newspaper industry, as noted in Chapter 5, has evoked concern but no quantitative restrictions upon the total holdings of an individual or entity. Like a character requirement, limitations upon a publisher's entrepreneurial reach invariably would engender a constitutional challenge. Multiple ownership rules have evolved, however, which limit the number of broadcast holdings a single individual or entity may possess. The rules speak in terms of ownership which subsequent glosses have defined in terms of a 5-percent interest—except for investment concerns which may hold a 10-percent stake.[61] Such regulation reflects a commitment to promoting information diversification in the electronic marketplace as a function of ownership diversification. The restrictions in general seek to effectuate their aim, subject to waiver upon a specific showing that the public interest would be advanced,[62] by prohibiting multiple ownership in the same market, restricting the total number of licenses an individual or entity may hold and forbidding cross-ownership of television stations and newspaper or cable service in the same community.

A. LOCAL CONCENTRATION

1) *Cross-Ownership of Like Media.* Multiple ownership rules generally prohibit a single person or entity from owning more than one station providing the same type of service in the same community.[63] If a party owns or controls an AM station, it may not have another AM station in the same service area. The same would be true respectively for FM and television stations. Multiple ownership to the extent that it involves different types of service may be permissible depending upon the combination. AM and FM stations may be jointly owned pursuant to an early policy that recognized FM service as an underdeveloped resource and encouraged established AM station owners to acquire FM stations. Despite the dominance of FM radio in many markets, the allowance of joint ownership remains essentially unchanged. Further restrictions prohibit mutual ownership in the same community of a VHF television station and AM or FM station. Because of the slow development of UHF television, the FCC has chosen to evaluate applications resulting in multiple ownership on a case-by-case basis. Preexisting combinations were grandfathered in, subject to cross-ownership restrictions in the event of future sale. The

rule may be waived in the event of ownership in a top 25 market that has at least 30 other licensees.

2) *Cross-Ownership of Different Media.* The FCC also has endeavored to promote local diversification by rules that prohibit acquisition of a broadcasting license by a person who owns a newspaper in the same service area.[64] Like controls have been enacted by Congress to forbid cross-ownership of cable systems by television licensees and common carriers.[65] Such regulations reflect concern that cross-ownership of mass media in a given community diminish competition in both the economic and information marketplaces.[66] Although most established newspaper-broadcasting combinations were grandfathered in, the commission ordered divestiture in sixteen instances. Given the scope and nature of the rules, they affect not only the broadcasting but also the newspaper industry. Not surprisingly, they were challenged by both.

In *Federal Communications Commission v. National Citizens Committee for Broadcasting,*[67] the Supreme Court held that the cross-ownership restrictions neither exceeded the commission's regulatory authority nor violated the constitutional rights of publishers.[68] The Court cast its determination with past decisions recognizing "that the First Amendment and antitrust values underlying the Commission's diversification policy may properly be considered by the Commission in determining where the public interest lies."[69] One objection to the rules was that they departed from factors which previously had been used to evaluate license applications by newspaper publishers.[70] In fact, the FCC in early years of television had encouraged newspaper owners to acquire colocated broadcast stations because of a shortage of qualified license applicants.[71] Thereafter, the application pool swelled, the number of available channels diminished, and diversification became more imperative and feasible.[72] The Court thus found the policy change "a reasonable administrative response to changed circumstances in the broadcasting industry."[73]

Constitutional arguments were rejected, despite the rules' inclusion of newspaper publishers within their purview. The Court acknowledged that policies intended to enhance the extent and quality of coverage of public issues may be permissible in broadcasting "where similar efforts to regulate the print media would not be."[74] It resisted the invitation, however, to regard the cross-ownership rules as a regulation of newspapers. The Court concluded instead that "[r]equiring those who wish to obtain a broadcast license to demonstrate that such would serve the 'public interest' does not restrict the speech of those who are denied licensing, rather it preserves the interests of the 'people as a whole in free speech.' "[75] Insofar as the public interest supported denial of a broadcast license, therefore, the Court determined that First Amendment interests were not compromised.[76]

Equally unavailing as a constitutional argument was the claim that the regulations imposed a forfeiture upon publishers as a condition for receiving a license.[77] The Court dismissed that characterization because, even if not able to procure a license in the same community, a publisher could acquire one elsewhere.[78] The limited disqualification was distinguished from selection criteria that might operate on the basis of viewpoint.[79] While such content-related considerations would be constitutionally problematical, the Court found that the cross-ownership rules' "purpose and effect is to promote free speech, not restrict it."[80] Recognizing that the FCC must choose from multiple applicants, the Court observed that the policy had been "chosen on a 'sensible basis,' one designed to further, rather than

contravene, 'the system of freedom of expression.' "[81]

Because the FCC grandfathered in most existing combinations, but ordered divestiture in what was depicted as sixteen "egregious cases,"[82] the prospective aspect of the regulation was challenged as arbitrary and capricious.[83] The Court determined, however, that the FCC properly took into account the already declining number of colocated combinations.[84] Recognizing that widespread divestiture would disrupt the stability and continuity of meritorious service, cause economic dislocations that might impair program quality, and diminish local ownership, the Court noted that a more sweeping order might harm the public interest.[85]

Finally, the Court endorsed the standards that the FCC had used to determine which publishers would be required to divest.[86] The criteria assumed not that divestiture would be more harmful in the exempted markets but "that the need for diversification was especially great in cases of local monopoly."[87] Thus, the Court found it "hardly unreasonable for the Commission to confine divestiture to communities in which there is common ownership of the only daily newspaper and either the only television station or the only broadcast station of any kind encompassing the entire community with a clear signal."[88] Nor was it considered unreasonable, given the dominance of broadcasting and newspapers as information sources, of the FCC to disregard the presence of other media.[89]

Federal Communications Commission v. National Citizens Committee for Broadcasting, 436 U.S. 775 (1978)

Mr. Justice Marshall delivered the opinion of the Court.

I

A

In setting its licensing policies, the Commission has long acted on the theory that diversification of mass media ownership serves the public interest by promoting diversity of program and service viewpoints, as well as by preventing undue concentration of economic power. See, e.g., *Multiple Ownership of Standard, FM and Television Broadcast Stations,* 45 F.C.C. 1476, 1476–1477 (1964). This perception of the public interest has been implemented over the years by a series of regulations imposing increasingly stringent restrictions on multiple ownership of broadcast stations. In the early 1940's, the Commission promulgated rules prohibiting ownership or control of more than one station in the same broadcast service (AM radio, FM radio, or television) in the same community.... Diversification of ownership has not been the sole consideration thought relevant to the public interest, however. The Commission's other, and sometimes conflicting, goal has been to ensure "the best practicable service to the public...." Moreover, the Commission has given considerable weight to a policy of avoiding undue disruption of existing service. As a result, newspaper owners in many instances have been able to acquire broadcast licenses for stations serving the same communities as their newspapers, and the Commission has repeatedly renewed such licenses on findings that continuation of the service offered by the common owner would serve the public interest. See Order, at 1066–1067, 1074–1075.

B

The regulations at issue here were promulgated and explained in a lengthy report and order released by the Commission on January 31, 1975. The Commission concluded, first, that it had statutory authority to issue the regulations under the Communications Act, Order, at 1048, citing 47 U.S.C. §§ 2(a), 4(i), 4(j), 301, 303, 309(a), and that the regulations were valid under the First and Fifth Amendments to the Constitution, Order, at 1050–1051. It observed that "[t]he term public interest encompasses many factors including 'the widest possible dissemination of information from diverse and antagonistic sources.' " Order, at 1048, quoting *Associated Press v. United States,* 326 U.S. 1, 20 (1945), and that "ownership carries with it the power to select, to edit, and to choose the methods, manner and emphasis of presentation," Order, at 1050. The Order further explained that the prospective ban on creation of co-located newspaper-broadcast combinations was grounded primarily in First Amendment concerns, while the divestiture regulations were based on both First Amendment and antitrust policies. *Id.,* at 1049. In addition, the Commission rejected the suggestion that it lacked the power to order divestiture, reasoning that the statutory requirement of license renewal every three years necessarily implied authority to order divestiture over a five-year period. *Id.,* at 1052.

After reviewing the comments and studies submitted by the various parties during the course of the proceeding, the Commission then turned to an explanation of the regulations and the justifications for their adoption. The prospective rules, barring formation of new broadcast-newspaper combinations in the same market, as well as transfers of existing combinations to new owners, were adopted without change from the proposal set forth in the notice of rulemaking. While recognizing the pioneering contributions of newspaper owners to the broadcast industry, the Commission concluded that changed circumstances made it possible, and necessary, for all new licensing of broadcast stations to "be expected to add to local diversity." *Id.,* at 1075. In reaching this conclusion, the Commission did not find that existing co-located newspaper-broadcast combinations had not served the public interest, or that such combinations necessarily "spea[k] with one voice" or are harmful to competition. *Id.,* at 1085, 1089. In the Commission's view, the conflicting studies submitted by the parties concerning the effects of newspaper ownership on competition and station performance were inconclusive, and no pattern of specific abuses by existing cross-owners was demonstrated. See *id.,* at 1072–1073, 1085, 1089. The prospective rules were justified, instead, by reference to the Commission's policy of promoting diversification of ownership: Increases in diversification of ownership would possibly result in enhanced diversity of viewpoints, and, given the absence of persuasive countervailing considerations, "even a small gain in diversity" was "worth pursuing." *Id.*, at 1076, 1080 n. 30.

With respect to the proposed across-the-board divestiture requirement, however, the Commission concluded that "a mere hoped-for gain in diversity" was not a sufficient justification. *Id.*, at 1078. Characterizing the divestiture issues as "the most difficult" presented in the proceeding, the Order explained that the proposed rules, while correctly recognizing the central importance of diversity considerations, "may have given too little weight to the consequences which could be expected to attend a focus on the abstract goal alone." *Ibid.* Forced dissolution would promote diversity, but it would also cause "disruption for the industry and hardship for individual owners," "resulting in losses or diminution of service to the public." *Id.*, at 1078, 1080.

The Commission concluded that in light of these countervailing considerations divestiture was warranted only in "the most egregious cases," which it identified as those in which a newspaper-broadcast combination has an "effective monopoly" in the local "marketplace of ideas as well as economically." *Id.*, at 1080–1081. The Commission recognized that any standards for defining which combinations fell within that category would necessarily be arbitrary to some degree, but "[a] choice had to be made." *Id.*, at 1080. It thus decided to require divestiture only where there was common ownership of the sole daily newspaper published in a community and either (1) the sole broadcast station providing that entire community with a clear signal, or (2) the sole television station encompassing the entire community with a clear signal. *Id.*, at 1080–1084.

The Order identified 8 television-newspaper and 10 radio-newspaper combinations meeting the divestiture criteria. *Id.*, at 1085, 1098. Waivers of the divestiture requirement were granted *sua sponte* to 1 television and 1 radio combination, leaving a total of 16 stations subject to divestiture. The Commission explained that waiver requests would be entertained in the latter cases, but, absent waiver, either the newspaper or the broadcast station would have to be divested by January 1, 1980.

C

Various parties—including the National Citizens Committee for Broadcasting (NCCB), the National Association of Broadcasters (NAB), the American Newspaper Publishers Association (ANPA), and several broadcast licensees subject to the divestiture requirement—petitioned for review of the regulations in the United States Court of Appeals for the District of Columbia Circuit, pursuant to 47 U.S.C. § 402(a) and 28 U.S.C. §§ 2342 (1), 2343 (1970 ed. and Supp. V). Numerous other parties intervened, and the United States—represented by the Justice Department—was made a respondent pursuant to 28 U.S.C. §§ 2344, 2348. NAB, ANPA, and the broadcast licensees subject to divestiture argued that the regulations went too far in restricting cross-ownership of newspapers and broadcast stations; NCCB and the Justice Department contended that the regulations did not go far enough and that the Commission inadequately justified its decision not to order divestiture on a more widespread basis.

Agreeing substantially with NCCB and the Justice Department, the Court of Appeals affirmed the prospective ban on new licensing of co-located newspaper-broadcast combinations, but vacated the limited divestiture rules, and ordered the Commission to adopt regulations requiring dissolution of all existing combinations that did not qualify for a waiver under the procedure outlined in the Order. The court held, first, that the prospective ban was a reasonable means of furthering "the highly valued goal of diversity" in the mass media, 181 U.S. App. D.C., at 17, 555 F. 2d, at 954, and was therefore not without a rational basis. The court concluded further that, since the Commission "explained why it considers diversity to be a factor of exceptional importance," and since the Commission's goal of promoting diversification of mass media ownership was strongly supported by First Amendment and antitrust policies, it was not arbitrary for the prospective rules to be "based on [the diversity] factor to the exclusion of others customarily relied on by the Commission." *Id.*, at 13 n. 33, 555 F. 2d, at 950 n. 33; see *id.*, at 11–12, 555 F. 2d, at 948–949.

The court also held that the prospective rules did not exceed the Commission's authority under the Communications Act. The court reasoned that the public interest standard of the Act permitted, and indeed required, the Commission to consider diversification of mass media ownership in making its licensing decisions, and that the Commission's general rulemaking authority under 47 U.S.C. §§ 303(r) and 154(i) allowed the Commission to adopt reasonable license qualifications implementing the public-interest standard. 181 U.S. App. D.C., at 14–15, 555 F. 2d, at 951–952. The court concluded, moreover, that since the prospective ban was designed to "increas[e] the number of media voices in the community," and not to restrict or control the content of free speech, the ban would not violate the First Amendment rights of newspaper owners. *Id.*, at 16–17, 555 F. 2d, at 953 954.

After affirming the prospective rules, the Court of Appeals invalidated the limited divestiture requirement as arbitrary and capricious within the meaning of § 10(e) of the Administrative Procedure Act (APA), 5 U.S.C. § 706 (2) (A) (1976 ed.). The court's primary holding was that the Commission lacked a rational basis for "grandfathering" most existing combinations while banning all new combinations. The court reasoned that the Commission's own diversification policy, as reinforced by First Amendment policies and the Commission's statutory obligation to "encourage the larger and more effective use of radio in the public interest," 47 U.S.C. § 303(g), required the Commission to adopt a "presumption" that stations owned by co-located newspapers "do not serve the public interest," 181 U.S. App. D.C., at 25–26, 555 F. 2d, at 962–963. The court observed that, in the absence of countervailing policies, this "presumption" would have dictated adoption of an across-the-board divestiture requirement, subject only to waiver "in those cases where the evidence clearly discloses that cross-ownership is in the public interest." *Id.*, at 29, 555 F. 2d, at 966. The countervailing policies relied on by the Commission in its decision were, in the court's view, "lesser policies" which

had not been given as much weight in the past as its diversification policy. *Id.*, at 28, 555 F. 2d, at 965. And "the record [did] not disclose the extent to which divestiture would actually threaten these [other policies]." *Ibid.* The court concluded, therefore, that it was irrational for the Commission not to give controlling weight to its diversification policy and thus to extend the divestiture requirement to all existing combinations.

The Court of Appeals held further that, even assuming a difference in treatment between new and existing combinations was justifiable, the Commission lacked a rational basis for requiring divestiture in the 16 "egregious" cases while allowing the remainder of the existing combinations to continue in operation. The court suggested that "limiting divestiture to small markets of 'absolute monopoly' squanders the opportunity where divestiture might do the most good," since "[d]ivestiture . . . may be more useful in the larger markets." *Id.*, at 29, 555 F. 2d, at 966. The court further observed that the record "[did] not support the conclusion that divestiture would be more harmful in the grandfathered markets than in the 16 affected markets," nor did it demonstrate that the need for divestiture was stronger in those 16 markets. *Ibid.* On the latter point, the court noted that, "[a]lthough the affected markets contain fewer voices, the amount of diversity in communities with additional independent voices may in fact be no greater." *Ibid.*

The Commission, NAB, ANPA, and several cross-owners who had been intervenors below, and whose licenses had been grandfathered under the Commission's rules but were subject to divestiture under the Court of Appeals' decision, petitioned this Court for review. We granted certiorari, 434 U.S. 815 (1977), and we now affirm the judgment of the Court of Appeals insofar as it upholds the prospective ban and reverse the judgment insofar as it vacates the limited divestiture requirement.

II

Petitioners NAB and ANPA contend that the regulations promulgated by the Commission exceed its statutory rulemaking authority and violate the constitutional rights of newspaper owners. We turn first to the statutory, and then to the constitutional, issues.

A

(1)

Section 303(r) of the Communications Act, 47 U.S.C. § 303(r), provides that "the Commission from time to time, as public convenience, interest, or necessity requires, shall . . . [m]ake such rules and regulations and prescribe such restrictions and conditions, not inconsistent with law, as may be necessary to carry out the provisions of [the Act]." See also 47 U.S.C. § 154(i). As the Court of Appeals recognized, 181 U.S. App. D.C., at 14, 555 F. 2d, at 951, it is now well established that this general rulemaking authority supplies a statutory basis for the Commission to issue regulations codifying its view of the public-interest licensing standard, so long as that view is based on consideration of permissible factors and is otherwise reasonable. If a license applicant does not qualify under standards set forth in such regulations, and does not proffer sufficient grounds for waiver or change of those standards, the Commission may deny the application without further inquiry. See *United States v. Storer Broadcasting Co.,* 351 U.S. 192 (1956); *National Broadcasting Co. v. United States,* 319 U.S. 190 (1943).

This Court has specifically upheld this rulemaking authority in the context of regulations based on the Commission's policy of promoting diversification of ownership. In *United States v. Storer Broadcasting Co., supra,* we sustained the portion of the Commission's multiple-ownership rules placing limitations on the total number of stations in each broadcast service a person may own or control. See n. 2, *supra.* And in *National Broadcasting Co. v. United States, supra,* we affirmed regulations that, *inter alia,* prohibited broadcast networks from owning more than one AM radio station in the same community, and from owning " 'any standard broadcast station in any locality where the existing standard broadcast stations are so few or of such unequal desirability . . . that competition would be substantially restrained by such licensing.' " See 319 U.S., at 206–208; n. 1, *supra.*

Petitioner NAB attempts to distinguish these cases on the ground that they involved efforts to increase diversification within the boundaries of the broadcasting industry itself, whereas the instant regulations are concerned with diversification of ownership in the mass communications media as a whole. NAB contends that, since the Act confers jurisdiction on the Commission only to regulate "communication by wire or radio," 47 U.S.C. § 152(a), it is impermissible for the Commission to use its licensing authority with respect to broadcasting to promote diversity in an overall communications market which includes, but is not limited to, the broadcasting industry.

This argument undersells the Commission's power to regulate broadcasting in the "public interest." In making initial licensing decisions between competing applicants, the Commission has long given "primary significance" to "diversification of control of the media of mass communications," and has denied licenses to newspaper owners on the basis of this policy in appropriate cases. See *supra,* at 781, and n. 4. As we have discussed on several occasions, see, e.g., *National Broadcasting Co. v. United States, supra,* at 210–218; *Red Lion Broadcasting Co. v. FCC,* 395 U.S. 367, 375–377, 387–388 (1969), the physical scarcity of broadcast frequencies, as well as problems of interference between broadcast signals, led Congress to delegate broad authority to the Commission to allocate broadcast licenses in the "public interest." And "[t]he avowed aim of the Communications Act of 1934 was to secure the maximum benefits of radio to all the people of the United States." *National Broadcasting Co. v. United States, supra,* at 217. It was not inconsistent with the statutory scheme, therefore, for the Commission to conclude that the maximum benefit to the "public interest" would follow from allocation of broadcast licenses so as to promote diversification of the mass media as a whole.

Our past decisions have recognized, moreover, that the First Amendment and antitrust values underlying the Commission's diversification policy may properly be considered by the Commission in determining where the public interest lies. "[T]he 'public interest' standard necessarily invites reference to First Amendment principles," *Columbia Broadcasting System, Inc. v. Democratic National Committee,* 412 U.S. 94, 122 (1973), and, in particular, to the First Amendment goal of achieving "the widest possible dissemination of information from diverse and antagonistic sources," *Associated Press v. United States*, 326 U.S., at 20. See *Red Lion Broadcasting Co. v. FCC, supra,* at 385, 390. See also *United States v. Midwest Video Corp.,* 406 U.S. 649, 667–669, and n. 27 (1972) (plurality opinion). And, while the Commission does not have power to enforce the antitrust laws as such, it is permitted to take antitrust policies into account in making licensing decisions pursuant to the public-interest standard. See, e.g., *United States v. Radio Corp. of America*, 358 U.S. 334, 351 (1959); *National Broadcasting Co. v. United States, supra,* at 222–224. . . .

It is thus clear that the regulations at issue are based on permissible public-interest goals and, so long as the regulations are not an unreasonable means for seeking to achieve these goals, they fall within the general rulemaking authority recognized in the *Storer Broadcasting and National Broadcasting* cases. Petitioner ANPA contends that the prospective rules are unreasonable in two respects: first, the rulemaking record did not conclusively establish that prohibiting common ownership of co-located newspapers and broadcast stations would in fact lead to increases in the diversity of viewpoints among local communications media; and second, the regulations were based on the diversification factor to the exclusion of other service factors considered in the past by the Commission in making initial licensing decisions regarding newspaper owners, see *supra,* at 782. With respect to the first point, we agree with the Court of Appeals that, notwithstanding the inconclusiveness of the rulemaking record, the Commission acted rationally in finding that diversification of ownership would enhance the possibility of achieving greater diversity of viewpoints. As the Court of Appeals observed, "[d]iversity and its effects are . . . elusive concepts, not easily defined let alone measured without making qualitative judgments objectionable on both policy and First Amendment grounds." 181 U.S. App. D.C., at 24, 555 F. 2d, at 961. Moreover, evidence of specific abuses by common owners is difficult to compile; "the possible benefits of competition do not lend themselves to detailed forecast." *FCC v. RCA Communications, Inc.,* 346 U.S. 86, 96 (1953). In these circumstances, the Commission was entitled to rely on its judgment, based on experience, that "it is unrealistic to expect true diversity from a commonly owned station-newspaper combination. The divergency of their viewpoints cannot be expected to be the same as if they were antagonistically run." Order, at 1079–1080; see 181 U.S. App. D.C., at 25, 555 F. 2d, at 962.

As to the Commission's decision to give controlling weight to its diversification goal in shaping the prospective rules, the Order makes clear that this change in policy was a reasonable administrative response to changed circumstances in the broadcasting industry. Order, at 1074–1075; see *FCC v. Pottsville Broadcasting Co.,* 309 U.S. 134, 137–138 (1940). The Order explained that, although newspaper owners had previously been allowed, and even encouraged, to acquire licenses for co-located broadcast stations because of the shortage of qualified license applicants, a sufficient number of qualified and experienced applicants other than newspaper owners was now available. In addition, the number of channels open for new licensing had diminished substantially. It had thus become both feasible and more urgent for the Commission to take steps to increase diversification of ownership, and a change in the Commission's policy toward new licensing offered the possibility of increasing diversity without causing any disruption of existing service. In light of these considerations, the Commission clearly did not take an irrational view of the public interest when it decided to impose a prospective ban on new licensing of co-located newspaper-broadcast combinations.

B

Petitioners NAB and ANPA also argue that the regulations, though designed to further the First Amendment goal of achieving "the widest possible dissemination of information from diverse and antagonistic sources," *Associated Press v. United States,* 326 U.S., at 20, nevertheless violate the First Amendment rights of newspaper owners. We cannot agree, for this argument ignores the fundamental proposition that there is no "unabridgeable First Amendment right to broadcast comparable to the right of every individual to speak, write, or publish." *Red Lion Broadcasting Co. v. FCC*, 395 U.S., at 388.

The physical limitations of the broadcast spectrum are well known. Because of problems of interference between broadcast signals, a finite number of frequencies can be used productively; this number is far exceeded by the number of persons wishing to broadcast to the public. In light of this physical scarcity, Government allocation and regulation of broadcast frequencies are essential, as we have often recognized. *Id.*, at 375–377, 387–388; *National Broadcasting Co. v. United States*, 319 U.S., at 210–218; *Federal Radio Comm'n v. Nelson Bros. Bond & Mortgage Co.*, 289 U.S. 266, 282 (1933); see *supra*, at 795. No one here questions the need for such allocation and regulation, and, given that need, we see nothing in the First Amendment to prevent the Commission from allocating licenses so as to promote the "public interest" in diversification of the mass communications media.

NAB and ANPA contend, however, that it is inconsistent with the First Amendment to promote diversification by barring a newspaper owner from owning certain broadcasting stations. In support, they point to our statement in *Buckley v. Valeo*, 424 U.S. 1 (1976), to the effect that "government may [not] restrict the speech of some elements of our society in order to enhance the relative voice of others," *id.*, at 48–49. As *Buckley* also recognized, however, " 'the broadcast media pose unique and special problems not present in the traditional free speech case.' " *Id.*, at 50 n. 55, quoting *Columbia Broadcasting System v. Democratic National Committee*, 412 U.S., at 101. Thus efforts to " 'enhanc[e] the volume and quality of coverage' of public issues" through regulation of broadcasting may be permissible where similar efforts to regulate the print media would not be. 424 U.S., at 50–51, and n. 55, quoting *Red Lion Broadcasting Co. v. FCC, supra*, at 393; cf. *Miami Herald Publishing Co. v. Tornillo*, 418 U.S. 241 (1974). Requiring those who wish to obtain a broadcast license to demonstrate that such would serve the "public interest" does not restrict the speech of those who are denied licenses; rather, it preserves the interests of the "people as a whole . . . in free speech." *Red Lion Broadcasting Co., supra*, at 390. As we stated in *Red Lion*, "to deny a

station license because 'the public interest' requires it 'is not a denial of free speech.' " 395 U.S., at 389, quoting *National Broadcasting Co. v. United States, supra*, at 227. See also *Federal Radio Comm'n v. Nelson Bros. Bond & Mortgage Co., supra.*

Relying on cases such as *Speiser v. Randall*, 357 U.S. 513 (1958), and *Elrod v. Burns*, 427 U.S. 347 (1976), NAB and ANPA also argue that the regulations unconstitutionally condition receipt of a broadcast license upon forfeiture of the right to publish a newspaper. Under the regulations, however, a newspaper owner need not forfeit anything in order to acquire a license for a station located in another community. More importantly, in the cases relied on by those petitioners, unlike the instant case, denial of a benefit had the effect of abridging freedom of expression, since the denial was based solely on the content of constitutionally protected speech; in *Speiser* veterans were deprived of a special property-tax exemption if they declined to subscribe to a loyalty oath, while in *Elrod* certain public employees were discharged or threatened with discharge because of their political affiliation. As we wrote in *National Broadcasting, supra*, "the issue before us would be wholly different" if "the Commission [were] to choose among applicants upon the basis of their political, economic or social views." 319 U.S., at 226. Here the regulations are not content related; moreover, their purpose and effect is to promote free speech, not to restrict it.

Finally, NAB and ANPA argue that the Commission has unfairly "singled out" newspaper owners for more stringent treatment than other license applicants. But the regulations treat newspaper owners in essentially the same fashion as other owners of the major media of mass communications were already treated under the Commission's multiple-ownership rules, see *supra*, at 780–781, and nn. 1–3; owners of radio stations, television stations, and newspapers alike are now restricted in their ability to acquire licenses for co-located broadcast stations. *Grosjean v. American Press Co.*, 297 U.S. 233 (1936), in which this Court struck down a state tax imposed only on newspapers, is thus distinguishable in the degree to which newspapers were singled out for special treatment. In addition, the effect of the tax in *Grosjean* was "to limit the circulation of information to which the public is entitled," *id.,* at 250, an effect inconsistent with the protection conferred on the press by the First Amendment.

In the instant case, far from seeking to limit the flow of information, the Commission has acted, in the Court of Appeals' words, "to enhance the diversity of information heard by the public without on-going government surveillance of the content of speech." 181 U.S. App. D.C., at 17,555 F. 2d, at 954. The regulations are a reasonable means of promoting the public interest in diversified mass communications; thus they do not violate the First Amendment rights of those who will be denied broadcast licenses pursuant to them. Being forced to "choose among applicants for the same facilities," the Commission has chosen on a "sensible basis," one designed to further, rather than contravene, "the system of freedom of expression." T. Emerson, The System of Freedom of Expression 663 (1970).

III

After upholding the prospective aspect of the Commission's regulations, the Court of Appeals concluded that the Commission's decision to limit divestiture to 16 "egregious cases" of "effective monopoly" was arbitrary and capricious within the meaning of § 10(e) of the APA, 5 U.S.C. § 706(2)(A) (1976 ed.).[a] We agree with the Court of Appeals that regulations promulgated after informal rulemaking, while not subject to review under the "substantial evidence" test of the APA, 5 U.S.C. § 706(2)(E) (1976 ed.) ... may be invalidated by a reviewing court under the "arbitrary or capricious" standard if they are not rational and based on consideration of the relevant factors. *Citizens to Preserve Overton Park v. Volpe,* 401 U.S. 402, 413–416 (1971). Although this review "is to be searching and careful," "[t]he court is not empowered to substitute its judgment for that of the agency." *Id.,* at 416.

In the view of the Court of Appeals, the Commission lacked a rational basis, first, for treating existing newspaper-broadcast combinations more leniently than combinations that might seek licenses in the future; and, second, even assuming a distinction between existing and new combinations had been justified, for requiring divestiture in the "egregious cases" while allowing all other existing combinations to continue in operation. We believe that the limited divestiture requirement reflects a rational weighing of competing policies, and we therefore reinstate the portion of the Commission's order that was invalidated by the Court of Appeals.

A

(1)

The Commission was well aware that separating existing newspaper-broadcast combinations would promote diversification of ownership. It

---

a. The reasonableness of the regulations as a means of achieving diversification is underscored by the fact that waivers are potentially available from both the prospective and the divestiture rules in cases in which a broadcast station and a co-located daily newspaper cannot survive without common ownership.

The APA provides in relevant part:

"To the extent necessary to decision and when presented, the reviewing court shall decide all relevant questions of law, interpret constitutional and statutory provisions, and determine the meaning or applicability of the terms of an agency action. The reviewing court shall—

(2) hold unlawful and set aside agency action, findings, and conclusions found to be—

(A) arbitrary, capricious, an abuse of discretion, or otherwise not in accordance with law;

(B) contrary to constitutional right, power, privilege, or immunity;

(C) in excess of statutory jurisdiction, authority, or limitations, or short of statutory right;

(D) without observance of procedure required by law;

(E) unsupported by substantial evidence in a case subject to sections 556 and 557 of this title or otherwise reviewed on the record of an agency hearing provided by statute; or

(F) unwarranted by the facts to the extent that the facts are subject to trial de novo by the reviewing court.

"In making the foregoing determinations, the court shall review the whole record or those parts of it cited by a party, and due account shall be taken of the rule of prejudicial error." 5 U.S.C. § 706 (2) (1976 ed.).

concluded, however, that ordering widespread divestiture would not result in "the best practicable service to the American public," Order, at 1074, a goal that the Commission has always taken into account and that has been specifically approved by this Court, *FCC v. Sanders Bros. Radio Station,* 309 U.S. 470, 475 (1940); see *supra,* at 782. In particular, the Commission expressed concern that divestiture would cause "disruption for the industry" and "hardship for individual owners," both of which would result in harm to the public interest. Order, at 1078. Especially in light of the fact that the number of co-located newspaper-broadcast combinations was already on the decline as a result of natural market forces, and would decline further as a result of the prospective rules, the Commission decided that across-the-board divestiture was not warranted. See *id.,* at 1080 n. 29.

The Order identified several specific respects in which the public interest would or might be harmed if a sweeping divestiture requirement were imposed: the stability and continuity of meritorious service provided by the newspaper owners as a group would be lost; owners who had provided meritorious service would unfairly be denied the opportunity to continue in operation; "economic dislocations" might prevent new owners from obtaining sufficient working capital to maintain the quality of local programming; and local ownership of broadcast stations would probably decrease. *Id.,* at 1078. We cannot say that the Commission acted irrationally in concluding that these public-interest harms outweighed the potential gains that would follow from increasing diversification of ownership.

In the past, the Commission has consistently acted on the theory that preserving continuity of meritorious service furthers the public interest, both in its direct consequence of bringing proved broadcast service to the public, and in its indirect consequence of rewarding—and avoiding losses to—licensees who have invested the money and effort necessary to produce quality performance. Thus, although a broadcast license must be renewed every three years, and the licensee must satisfy the Commission that renewal will serve the public interest, both the Commission and the courts have recognized that a licensee who has given meritorious service has a "legitimate re-

newal expectanc[y]" that is "implicit in the structure of the Act" and should not be destroyed absent good cause. *Greater Boston Television Corp. v. FCC,* 143 U.S. App. D.C. 383, 396, 444 F. 2d 841, 854 (1970), cert. denied, 403 U.S. 923 (1971); see *Citizens Communications Center v. FCC,* 145 U.S. App. D.C. 32, 44, and n. 35, 447 F. 2d 1201, 1213, and n. 35 (1971); *In re Formulation of Policies Relating to the Broadcast Renewal Applicant, Stemming from the Comparative Hearing Process,* 66 F.C.C. 2d 419, 420 (1977); n. 5, *supra.* Accordingly, while diversification of ownership is a relevant factor in the context of license renewal as well as initial licensing, the Commission has long considered the past performance of the incumbent as the most important factor in deciding whether to grant license renewal and thereby to allow the existing owner to continue in operation. Even where an incumbent is challenged by a competing applicant who offers greater potential in terms of diversification, the Commission's general practice has been to go with the "proved product" and grant renewal if the incumbent has rendered meritorious service. See generally *In re Formulation of Policies Relating to the Broadcast Renewal Applicant, Stemming from the Comparative Hearing Process, supra;* n. 5, *supra.*

In the instant proceeding, the Commission specifically noted that the existing newspaper-broadcast cross-owners as a group had a "long record of service" in the public interest; many were pioneers in the broadcasting industry and had established and continued "[t]raditions of service" from the outset. Order, at 1078. Notwithstanding the Commission's diversification policy, all were granted initial licenses upon findings that the public interest would be served thereby, and those that had been in existence for more than three years had also had their licenses renewed on the ground that the public interest would be furthered. The Commission noted, moreover, that its own study of existing co-located newspaper-television combinations showed that in terms of percentage of time devoted to several categories of local programming, these stations had displayed "an undramatic but nonetheless statistically significant superiority" over other television stations. *Id.,* at 1078 n. 26. An across-the-board divestiture requirement would result in loss of the services of these superior licensees, and—whether divestiture caused actual losses to existing owners, or just denial of reasonably anticipated gains—the result would be that future licensees would be discouraged from investing the resources necessary to produce quality service.

At the same time, there was no guarantee that the licensees who replaced the existing cross-owners would be able to provide the same level of service or demonstrate the same long-term commitment to broadcasting. And even if the new owners were able in the long run to provide similar or better service, the Commission found that divestiture would cause serious disruption in the transition period. Thus, the Commission observed that new owners "would lack the long knowledge of the community and would have to begin raw," and—because of high interest rates—might not be able to obtain sufficient working capital to maintain the quality of local programming. *Id.*, at 1078; see n. 22, *supra*.

The Commission's fear that local ownership would decline was grounded in a rational prediction, based on its knowledge of the broadcasting industry and supported by comments in the record; see Order, at 1068–1069, that many of the existing newspaper-broadcast combinations owned by local interests would respond to the divestiture requirement by trading stations with out-of-town owners. It is undisputed that roughly 75% of the existing co-located newspaper-television combinations are locally owned, see 181 U.S. App. D.C., at 26–27, 555 F. 2d, at 963–964, and these owners' knowledge of their local communities and concern for local affairs, built over a period of years, would be lost if they were replaced with outside interests. Local ownership in and of itself has been recognized to be a factor of some—if relatively slight—significance even in the context of initial licensing decisions. See *Policy Statement on Comparative Broadcast Hearings*, 1 F.C.C. 2d, at 396. It was not unreasonable, therefore, for the Commission to consider it as one of several factors militating against divestiture of combinations that have been in existence for many years.

In light of these countervailing considerations, we cannot agree with the Court of Appeals that it was arbitrary and capricious for the Commission to "grandfather" most existing combinations,

and to leave opponents of these combinations to their remedies in individual renewal proceedings. In the latter connection we note that, while individual renewal proceedings are unlikely to accomplish any "overall restructuring" of the existing ownership patterns, the Order does make clear that existing combinations will be subject to challenge by competing applicants in renewal proceedings, to the same extent as they were prior to the instant rulemaking proceedings. Order, at 1087–1088 (emphasis omitted); see n. 12, *supra*. That is, diversification of ownership will be a relevant but somewhat secondary factor. And, even in the absence of a competing applicant, license renewal may be denied if, *inter alia*, a challenger can show that a common owner has engaged in specific economic or programming abuses. See nn. 12 and 13, *supra*.

(2)

In concluding that the Commission acted unreasonably in not extending its divestiture requirement across the board, the Court of Appeals apparently placed heavy reliance on a "presumption" that existing newspaper-broadcast combinations "do not serve the public interest." See *supra*, at 790–791. The court derived this presumption primarily from the Commission's own diversification policy, as "reaffirmed" by adoption of the prospective rules in this proceeding, and secondarily from "[t]he policies of the First Amendment," 181 U.S. App. D.C., at 26, 555 F. 2d, at 963, and the Commission's statutory duty to "encourage the larger and more effective use of radio in the public interest," 47 U.S.C. § 303(g). As explained in Part II above, we agree that diversification of ownership furthers statutory and constitutional policies, and, as the Commission recognized, separating existing newspaper-broadcast combinations would promote diversification. But the weighing of policies under the "public interest" standard is a task that Congress has delegated to the Commission in the first instance, and we are unable to find anything in the Communications Act, the First Amendment, or the Commission's past or present practices that would require the Commission to "presume" that its diversification policy should be given controlling weight in all circumstances.

Such a "presumption" would seem to be inconsistent with the Commission's longstanding and judicially approved practice of giving controlling weight in some circumstances to its more general goal of achieving "the best practicable service to the public." Certainly, as discussed in Part III-A(1) above, the Commission through its license renewal policy has made clear that it considers diversification of ownership to be a factor of less significance when deciding whether to allow an existing licensee to continue in operation than when evaluating applicants seeking initial licensing. Nothing in the language or the legislative history of § 303(g) indicates that Congress intended to foreclose all differences in treatment between new and existing licensees, and indeed, in amending § 307(d) of the Act in 1952, Congress appears to have lent its approval to the Commission's policy of evaluating existing licensees on a somewhat different basis from new applicants. Moreover, if enactment of the prospective rules in this proceeding itself were deemed to create a "presumption" in favor of divestiture, the Commission's ability to experiment with new policies would be severely hampered. One of the most significant advantages of the administrative process is its ability to adapt to new circumstances in a flexible manner, see *FCC v. Pottsville Broadcasting Co.,* 309 U.S., at 137–138, and we are unwilling to presume that the Commission acts unreasonably when it decides to try out a change in licensing policy primarily on a prospective basis.

The Court of Appeals also relied on its perception that the policies militating against divestiture were "lesser policies" to which the Commission had not given as much weight in the past as its diversification policy. See *supra,* at 791. This perception is subject to much the same criticism as the "presumption" that existing co-located newspaper-broadcasting combinations do not serve the public interest. The Commission's past concern with avoiding disruption of existing service is amply illustrated by its license renewal policies. In addition, it is worth noting that in the past when the Commission has changed its multiple-ownership rules it has almost invariably tailored the changes so as to operate wholly or primarily on a prospective basis. For example, the regulations adopted in 1970 prohibiting common

ownership of a VHF television station and a radio station serving the same market were made to apply only to new licensing decisions; no divestiture of existing combinations was required. See n. 3, *supra.* The limits set in 1953 on the total numbers of stations a person could own, upheld by this Court in *United States v. Storer Broadcasting Co.,* 351 U.S. 192 (1956), were intentionally set at levels that would not require extensive divestiture of existing combinations. See *Multiple Ownership of AM, FM and Television Broadcast Stations,* 18 F.C.C., at 292. And, while the rules adopted in the early 1940's prohibiting ownership or control of more than one station in the same broadcast service in the same community required divestiture of approximately 20 AM radio combinations, FCC Eleventh Annual Report 12 (1946), the Commission afforded an opportunity for case-by-case review, see Multiple Ownership of Standard Broadcast Stations, 8 Fed. Reg. 16065 (1943). Moreover, television and FM radio had not yet developed, so that application of the rules to these media was wholly prospective. See Rules and Regulations Governing Commercial Television Broadcast Stations, *supra,* n. 1: Rules Governing Standard and High Frequency Broadcast Stations, *supra,* n. 1.

The Court of Appeals apparently reasoned that the Commission's concerns with respect to disruption of existing service, economic dislocations, and decreases in local ownership necessarily could not be very weighty since the Commission has a practice of routinely approving voluntary transfers and assignments of licenses. See 181 U.S. App. D.C., at 26–28, 555 F. 2d, at 963–965. But the question of whether the Commission should compel proved licensees to divest their stations is a different question from whether the public interest is served by allowing transfers by licensees who no longer wish to continue in the business. As the Commission's brief explains:

> [I]f the Commission were to force broadcasters to stay in business against their will, the service provided under such circumstances, albeit continuous, might well not be worth preserving. Thus, the fact that the Commission approves assignments and transfers in no way undermines its decision to place a premium on the continuation of proven past service by those licensees who wish to remain in busi-

ness. Brief for Petitioner in No. 76–1471, p. 38 (footnote omitted).

The Court of Appeals' final basis for concluding that the Commission acted arbitrarily in not giving controlling weight to its divestiture policy was the Court's finding that the rulemaking record did not adequately "disclose the extent to which divestiture would actually threaten" the competing policies relied upon by the Commission. 181 U.S. App. D.C., at 28, 555 F. 2d, at 965. However, to the extent that factual determinations were involved in the Commission's decision to "grandfather" most existing combinations, they were primarily of a judgmental or predictive nature—e.g., whether a divestiture requirement would result in trading of stations with out-of-town owners; whether new owners would perform as well as existing crossowners, either in the short run or in the long run; whether losses to existing owners would result from forced sales; whether such losses would discourage future investment in quality programming; and whether new owners would have sufficient working capital to finance local programming. In such circumstances complete factual support in the record for the Commission's judgment or prediction is not possible or required; "a forecast of the direction in which future public interest lies necessarily involves deductions based on the expert knowledge of the agency," *FPC v. Transcontinental Gas Pipe Line Corp.,* 365 U.S. 1, 29 (1961); see *Industrial Union Dept., AFL-CIO v. Hodgson,* 162 U.S. App. D.C. 331, 338–339, 499 F. 2d 467, 474–475 (1974).

B

We also must conclude that the Court of Appeals erred in holding that it was arbitrary to order divestiture in the 16 "egregious cases" while allowing other existing combinations to continue in operation. The Commission's decision was based not—as the Court of Appeals may have believed, see *supra,* at 792—on a conclusion that divestiture would be more harmful in the "grandfathered" markets than in the 16 affected markets, but rather on a judgment that the need for diversification was especially great in cases of local monopoly. This policy judgment was certainly not irrational, see *United States v. Radio Corp. of*

America, 358 U.S., at 351–352, and indeed was founded on the very same assumption that underpinned the diversification policy itself and the prospective rules upheld by the Court of Appeals and now by this Court—that the greater the number of owners in a market, the greater the possibility of achieving diversity of program and service viewpoints.

As to the Commission's criteria for determining which existing newspaper-broadcast combinations have an "effective monopoly" in the "local marketplace of ideas as well as economically," we think the standards settled upon by the Commission reflect a rational legislative-type judgment. Some line had to be drawn, and it was hardly unreasonable for the Commission to confine divestiture to communities in which there is common ownership of the only daily newspaper and either the only television station or the only broadcast station of any kind encompassing the entire community with a clear signal. Cf. *United States v. Radio Corp. of America, supra,* at 351–352, quoted, *supra,* at 796. It was not irrational, moreover, for the Commission to disregard media sources other than newspapers and broadcast stations in setting its divestiture standards. The studies cited by the Commission in its notice of rulemaking unanimously concluded that newspapers and television are the two most widely utilized media sources for local news and discussion of public affairs; and, as the Commission noted in its Order, at 1081, "aside from the fact that [magazines and other periodicals] often had only a tiny fraction in the market, they were not given real weight since they often dealt exclusively with regional or national issues and ignored local issues." Moreover, the differences in treatment between radio and television stations, see n. 10, *supra,* were certainly justified in light of the far greater influence of television than radio as a source for local news. See Order, at 1083.

The judgment of the Court of Appeals is affirmed in part and reversed in part.

It is so ordered.

Mr. Justice Brennan took no part in the consideration or decision of these cases.

Temporary waivers from the cross-ownership rules may be available so that a publisher-broadcaster, who otherwise would violate the rules upon award or transfer of a license, has time to sell the newspaper property.[90] Two such waivers have been awarded, in each case to the same entity.[91] Congress attempted to prohibit their extension in each instance. Because the action singled out only one individual, an appeals court invalidated it on equal protection and First Amendment grounds.[92]

Paralleling the restrictions on newspaper-broadcaster combines are prohibitions of cross-owned television stations and cable systems in the same primary service area.[93] Telephone companies also are barred from owning cable systems within their service areas, unless the cable operation is in a rural area.[94] The exception is reminiscent of early encouragement of newspapers to acquire broadcast licenses in communities that otherwise would be slow in attaining the benefits of radio or television service. The cross-ownership rules concerning cable, unlike those governing broadcasting, are mandated by statute. Future modification if any, therefore, requires an act of Congress. The cable cross-ownership rules are discussed in Chapter 6.

B. NATIONAL CONCENTRATION

1) *Quantitative ceilings.* Another aspect of regulatory policy slanted toward diversification is a ceiling upon the total number of broadcast holdings a person or entity may have nationwide. In their present incarnation, FCC rules set a limit of twelve AM, twelve FM, and twelve television stations.[95] The restriction on television station ownership is further qualified by a restriction that limits total audience reach to 25 percent of the nation's population. Both the twelve-station and the audience reach limit may be relaxed if significant minority participation exists. In the event "that at least two of the stations in which they hold cognizable interests are minority controlled . . . , group owners of television and radio stations [may]

utilize a maximum numerical cap of 14 stations."[96] Moreover, a group owner may "reach a maximum of 30 percent of the national audience, provided that at least five percent of the aggregate reach of its audience is contributed by minority controlled stations."[97]

The elevation of ceilings and the expansion of audience reach are calculated to enhance minority ownership in broadcasting. Dissenting commissioners asserted that the evils of concentration are not diminished by the nature of an owner's race.[98] The rules also may elicit argument that they undermine their aims if predominantly white group owners buy out minority businesses and effectively minimize minority presence and influence. The provisions exist in a constitutional context increasingly hostile to racial preferences.[99] The Court, however, has upheld preferential policies to the extent they promote and are substantially related to achieving "the important governmental objective of broadcast diversity."[100] It also has noted Congress's support for minority ownership policies generally as a means of advancing program diversity[101] and announced a deferential level of review insofar as such programs are legislatively approved or mandated.[102]

Restrictions upon the total number of broadcast holdings have weathered judicial review. In *United States v. Storer Broadcasting Co.*,[103] the Court determined that the multiple ownership rules furthered Congress's regulatory aims.[104] The restrictions had been challenged on the grounds that they precluded a broadcaster from demonstrating in a hearing that the award of a license would further the public interest.[105] Although noting that a hearing might be required upon a sufficient showing that the public interest would benefit from a waiver,[106] the Court observed that:

> This commission, like other agencies, deals with the public interest. *Scripps-Howard Radio*

v. Federal Communications Comm'n, 316 U.S. 4, 14. Its authority covers new and rapidly developing fields. Congress sought to create regulation for public protection with careful provision to assure fair opportunity for open competition in the use of broadcasting facilities. Accordingly, we cannot interpret § 309(b) as barring rules that declare a present intent to limit the number of stations consistent with a permissible "concentration of control." It is but a rule that announces the Commission's attitude on public protection against such concentration. The Communications Act must be read as a whole and with appreciation of the responsibilities of the body charged with its fair and efficient operation. The growing complexity of our economy induced the Congress to place regulation of businesses like communication in specialized agencies with broad powers. Courts are slow to interfere with their conclusions when reconcilable with statutory directions. We think the Multiple Ownership Rules, as adopted, are reconcilable with the Communications Act as a whole. An applicant files his application with knowledge of the Commission's attitude toward concentration of control.[107]

c. Network Influence and Control

Also pertinent to the issue of national concentration is the question of network influence. Like any other group owner, networks are subject to rules that quantitatively limit broadcast holdings. Networks provide significant amounts of broadcast programming, however, including most of what is watched during prime time. Their reach is magnified, therefore, by the distribution of their service through affiliated stations. Network practices, although exceeding the ken of ownership rules, are subject to antitrust law.[108] Considerations of that nature may be factored into concepts of the public interest.[109]

Pursuant to an inquiry into network activities, the FCC in 1941 promulgated regulations governing network and affiliate relationships.[110] Among other things, the rules set limits on network programming time and ownership. Collectively, the restrictions were designed to curtail control over programming decisions at the local level. Although challenged by one of the networks, the Court in *National Broadcasting Co. v. United States*[111] found them within the purview of the public interest.[112] In sum, the Court rejected arguments that the FCC's power to regulate chain broadcasting was limited to technical and engineering aspects.[113] It noted too "(t)he Commission's duty under the Communications Act of 1934 is not only to see that the public receives the advantages and benefits of chain broadcasting, but also, so far as its powers enable it, to see that practices which adversely affect the ability of licensees to operate in the public interest are eliminated."[114]

Contemporary network broadcasting rules, which now pertain primarily to television, are given below.

§ 73.132 TERRITORIAL EXCLUSIVITY.

No licensee of an AM broadcast station shall have any arrangement with a network organization which prevents or hinders another station serving substantially the same area from broadcasting the network's programs not taken by the former station, or which prevents or hinders another station serving a substantially different area from broadcasting any program of the network organization: *Provided, however,* That this section does not prohibit arrangements under which the station is granted first call within its primary service area upon the network's programs. The term "network organization" means any organization originating program material, with or without commercial messages, and furnishing the same to stations interconnected so as to permit simultaneous broadcast by all or some of them. However, arrangements involving only stations under common ownership, or only the rebroadcast by one station or programming from another with no compensation other than a lump-sum payment by the station rebroadcasting, are not considered arrangements with a network organization. The term "arrangement" means any contract, arrangement or understanding, expressed or implied.

§ 73.232 TERRITORIAL EXCLUSIVITY.

No licensee of an FM broadcast station shall have any arrangement with a network organization which prevents or hinders another station serving substantially the same area from broadcasting the network's programs not taken by the former station, or which prevents or hinders another station serving a substantially different area from broadcasting any program of the network organization: *Provided, however,* that this section does not prohibit arrangements under which the station is granted first call within its primary service area upon the network's programs. The term "network organization" means any organization originating program material, with or without commercial messages, and furnishing the same to stations interconnected so as to permit simultaneous broadcast by all or some of them. However, arrangements involving only stations under common ownership, or only the rebroadcast by one station or programming from another with no compensation other than a lump-sum payment by the station rebroadcasting, are not considered arrangements with a network organization. The term "arrangement" means any contract, arrangement or understanding, express or implied.

FM broadcasting in a particular area and (a) which is not available for use by other FM broadcast station licensees; and (b) no other comparable site is available in the area; and (c) where the exclusive use of such site by the applicant or licensee would unduly limit the number of FM broadcast stations that can be authorized in a particular area or would unduly restrict competition among FM broadcast stations.

§ 73.658 AFFILIATION AGREEMENTS AND NETWORK PROGRAM PRACTICES; TERRITORIAL EXCLUSIVITY IN NON-NETWORK PROGRAM ARRANGEMENTS.

(a) *Exclusive affiliation of station.* No license shall be granted to a television broadcast station having any contract, arrangement, or understanding, express or implied, with a network organization un-

der which the station is prevented or hindered from, or penalized for, broadcasting the programs of any other network organization. (The term "network organization" as used in this section includes national and regional network organizations. See ch. VII, J, of Report on Chain Broadcasting.)

(b) *Territorial exclusively.* No license shall be granted to a television broadcast station having any contract, arrangement, or understanding, express or implied, with a network organization which prevents or hinders another broadcast station located in the same community from broadcasting the network's programs not taken by the former station, or which prevents or hinders another broadcast station located in a different community from broadcasting any program of the network organization. This section shall not be construed to prohibit any contract, arrangement, or understanding between a station and a network organization pursuant to which the station is granted the first call in its community upon the programs of the network organization. As employed in this paragraph, the term "community" is defined as the community specified in the instrument of authorization as the location of the station.

(c) *Term of affiliation.* No license shall be granted to a television broadcast station having any contract, arrangement, or understanding, express or implied, with a network organization which provides, by original terms, provisions for renewal, or otherwise for the affiliation of the station with the network organization for a period longer than 2 years: *Provided,* That a contract, arrangement, or understanding for a period up to 2 years may be entered into within 6 months prior to the commencement of such period.

(d) *Station commitment of broadcast time.* No license shall be granted to a television broadcast station having any contract, arrangement, or understanding, express or implied, with any network organization, which provides for optioning of the station's time to the network organization, or which has the same restraining effect as time optioning. As used in this section, time optioning is any contract, arrangement, or understanding, express or implied, between a station and a network organization which prevents or hinders the station from scheduling programs before the network agrees to utilize the time during which such programs are scheduled, or which requires the station to clear time already scheduled when the network organization seeks to utilize the time.

(e) *Right to reject programs.* No license shall be granted to a television broadcast station having any contract, arrangement, or understanding, express or implied, with a network organization which, with respect to programs offered or already contracted for pursuant to an affiliation contract, prevents or hinders the station from: (1) Rejecting or refusing network programs which the station reasonably believes to be unsatisfactory or unsuitable or contrary to the public interest, or (2) substituting a program which, in the station's opinion, is of greater local or national importance.

(f) *Network ownership of stations.* No license shall be granted to a network organization, or to any person directly or indirectly controlled by or under common control of a network organization for a television broadcast station in any locality where the existing television broadcast stations are so few or of such unequal desirability (in terms of coverage, power, frequency, or other related matters) that competition would be substantially restrained by such licensing. (The work "control" as used in this section, is not limited to full control but includes such a measure of control as would substantially affect the availability of the station to other networks.)

(g) *Dual network operation.* No license shall be issued to a television broadcast station affiliated with a network organization which maintains more than one network of television broadcast stations: *Provided,* That this section shall not be applicable if such networks are not operated simultaneously, or if there is no substantial overlap in the territory served by the group of stations comprising each such network.

(h) *Control by networks of station rates.* No license shall be granted to a television broadcast station having any contract, arrangement, or understanding, express or implied, with a network organization under which the station is prevented or hindered from, or penalized for, fixing or altering its rates for the sale of broadcast time for other than the network's programs.

(i) No license shall be granted to a television broadcast station which is represented for the sale of non-network time by a network organization or by an organization directly or indirectly controlled by or under common control with a network organization, if the station has any contract, arrangement or understanding, express or implied, which provides for the affiliation of the station with such network organization: *Provided, however,* That this rule shall not be applicable to stations licensed to a network organization or to a subsidiary of a network organization.

(j) *Network syndication and program practices.* (1) Except as provided in paragraph (j)(3) of this section, no television network shall:

(i) After June 1, 1973, sell, license, or distribute television programs to television station licensees within the United States for non-network television exhibition or otherwise engage in the business commonly known as "syndication" within the United States; or sell, license, or distribute television programs of which it is not the sole producer for exhibition outside the United States; or reserve any option or right to share in revenues or profits in connection with such domestic and/or foreign sale, license, or distribution; or

(ii) After August 1, 1972, acquire any financial or proprietary right or interest in the exhibition, distribution, or other commercial use of any television program produced wholly or in part by a person other than such television network, except the license or other exclusive right to network exhibition within the United States and on foreign stations regularly included within such television network: *Provided,* That if such network does not timely avail itself of such license or other exclusive right to network exhibition within the United States, the grantor of such license or right to network exhibition may, upon making a timely offer reasonably to compensate the network, reacquire such license or other exclusive right to exhibition of the program.

(2) Nothing contained in paragraphs (j)(1) and (2) of this section shall prevent any television network from selling or distributing programs of which it is the sole producer for television exhibition outside the United States, or from selling or otherwise disposing of any program rights not acquired from another person, including the right to distribute programs for non-network exhibition (as in syndication) within the United States as long as it does not itself engage in such

distribution within the United States or retain the right to share the revenues or profits therefrom.

(3) Nothing contained in this paragraph shall be construed to include any television network formed for the purpose of producing, distributing, or syndicating program materials for educational, noncommercial, or public broadcasting exhibition or uses.

(4) For the purposes of this paragraph and paragraph (k) of this section the term network means any person, entity, or corporation which offers an interconnected program service on a regular basis for 15 or more hours per week to at least 25 affiliated television licensees in 10 or more States; and/or any person, entity, or corporation controlling, controlled by, or under common control with such person, entity, or corporation.

(k) Effective September 8, 1975, commercial television stations owned by or affiliated with a national television network in the 50 largest television markets (see Note 1 to this paragraph) shall devote, during the four hours of prime time (7–11 p.m. e.t. and p.t., 6–10 p.m. c.t. and m.t.), no more than three hours to the presentation of programs from a national network, programs formerly on a national network (off-network programs) other than feature films, or, on Saturdays, feature films: *Provided, However,* That the following categories of programs need not be counted toward the three-hour limitation:

(1) On nights other than Saturdays, network or off-network programs designed for children, public affairs programs or documentary programs (see Note 2 to this paragraph for definitions).

(2) Special news programs dealing with fast-breaking news events, on-the-spot coverage of news events or other material related to such coverage, and political broadcasts by or on behalf of legally qualified candidates for public office.

(3) Regular network news broadcasts up to a half hour, when immediately adjacent to a full hour of continuous locally produced news or locally produced public affairs programing.

(4) Runovers of live network broadcasts of sporting events, where the event has been reasonably scheduled to conclude before prime time or occupy only a certain amount of prime time, but the event has gone beyond its expected duration due to circumstances not reasonably foreseeable by the networks or under their control. This exemption does not apply to post-game material.

(5) In the case of stations in the Mountain and Pacific time zones, on evenings when network prime-time programing consists of a sports event or other program broadcast live and simultaneously throughout the contiguous 48 states, such stations may assume that the network's schedule that evening occupies no more of prime time in these time zones than it does in the Eastern and Central time zones.

(6) Network broadcasts of an international sports event (such as the Olympic Games), New Year's Day college football games, or any other network programing of a special nature other than motion pictures or other sports events, when the network devotes all of its time on the same evening to the same programing, except brief incidental fill material.

Note 1: The top 50 markets to which this paragraph applies are the 50 largest markets in terms of average prime time audience for all stations in the market. For broadcast years before fall 1980, the 50 markets are the largest 50 as listed in the Arbitron publication "Television Markets and Rankings Guide," generally published in November, which will apply for the broadcast year starting the following fall, except that, for 1978–79, "Syracuse-Elmira" will not be included and the Salt Lake City market will be included. For broadcast years starting in the fall of 1980 and thereafter, the 50 largest markets to which this paragraph applies will be determined at 3-year intervals, on the basis of the average of two Arbitron February-March audience surveys occuring roughly 2½ years and roughly 3½ years before the start of the 3-year period. The 50 markets to which this paragraph will apply for 3 years from fall 1980 to fall 1983 will be determined by an average of the prime time audience figures (all market stations combined) contained in the reports of Arbitron February/March 1977 and February/March 1978 audience surveys. Shortly after the results of the 1978 survey are available the Commission will issue a list of the 50 largest markets to which this paragraph will apply from fall 1980 to fall 1983. The same procedure will take place, on the basis of February/March 1980 and 1981 surveys, for the 3-year period from fall 1983 to fall 1986.

Note 2: As used in this paragraph, the term "programs designed for children" means programs primarily designed for children aged 2 through 12. The term "documentary programs" means programs which are nonfictional and educational or informational, but not including programs where the information is used as part of a contest among participants in the program; and not including programs relating to the visual entertainment arts (stage, motion pictures or television) where more than 50% of the program is devoted to the presentation of entertainment material itself. The term "public affairs programs" means talks, commentaries, discussions, speeches, editorials, political programs, documentaries, forums, panels, roundtables, and similar programs primarily concerning local, national, and international public affairs.

(1) *Broadcast of the programs of more than one network.* The provisions of this paragraph govern and limit the extent to which, after October 1, 1971, commercial television stations in the 50 States of the United States, which are regular affiliates of one of the three national television networks, may broadcast programs of another network, in markets where there are two such affiliated stations and one or more operational VHF or UHF stations having reasonably comparable facilities which are not regular affiliates of any network. Whether or not the stations in a particular market come within the provisions of this paragraph is determined by whether, as of July 1 of each year with respect to programs beginning October 1, or as of January 1 of each year with respect to programs beginning April 1, there are in the market the stations specified in the last sentence.

(1) *Definitions.* As used in this paragraph, the following terms have the meanings given:

(i) "Station" means a commercial television station in the 50 States of the United States.

(ii) "Operational station" means a station authorized and operating as of June 10 (with respect to programs beginning October 1) or as of December 10 (with respect to programs beginning April 1), or a station authorized and which gives notice to the Commission by such June 10 or

December 10 date that it will be on the air by such October 1 or April 1 date (including request for program test authority if none has previously been given), and commits itself to remain on the air for 6 months after such October 1 or April 1 date. Such notice shall be received at the Commission by the June 10 or December 10 date mentioned, and shall show that copies thereof have been sent to the three national networks and to the licensees of all operating television stations in the market.

(iii) "Affiliated station" means a station having a regular affiliation with one of the three national television networks, under which it serves as that network's primary outlet for the presentation of its programs in a market. It includes any arrangement under which the network looks primarily to this station rather than other stations for the presentation of its programs and the station chiefly presents the programs of this network rather than another network.

(iv) "Unaffiliated station" means a station not having an affiliation arrangement as defined in this subparagraph with a national television network, even though it may have other types of agreements or per-program arrangements with it.

(v) "Network" means a national organization distributing programs for a substantial part of each broadcast day to television stations in all parts of the United States, generally via interconnection facilities.

(vi) "Unaffiliated network" means a network not having an affiliated station (as defined in this paragraph) in a particular market, even though it may have other types of agreements or per-program arrangements.

(vii) "Market" means the television markets of the United States, and the stations in them, as identified in the latest publication of American Research Bureau (ARB), together with any stations which have since become operational in the same communities.

(viii) "Evening programing" means programing (regular programs or "specials") starting and concluding on a network between the hours of 7:30 p.m. and 11 p.m. local time (except 6:30 p.m. and 10 p.m. in the Central time zone), plus all programs other than regular newscasts starting on the network between 7 and 7:30 p.m. local time (6 and 6:30 p.m. local time in the Central time zone). It does not include portions broadcast after 7 p.m. of programs starting earlier, or portions broadcast after 11 p.m. of programs starting earlier.

(ix) "Specials" means programs not carried on the network at least as often as once a week. It includes both programs scheduled well in advance and those scheduled very shortly before broadcast on the network.

(x) "Reasonably comparable facilities" means station transmitting facilities (effective radiated power and effective antenna height above average terrain) such that the station Grade B coverage area is at least two-thirds as large (in square kilometers) as the smallest of the market affiliated stations' Grade B coverage areas. Where one or both of the affiliates is licensed to a city different from that of the unaffiliated station, the term "reasonably comparable facilities" also includes the requirement that the unaffiliated station must put a predicted Grade A or better signal over all of the city of license of the other regular (non-satellite) station(s), except that where one of the affiliated stations is licensed to the same city as the unaffiliated station, and puts a Grade B but not a Grade A signal over the other city of license, the unaffiliated station will be considered as having reasonably comparable facilities if it too puts a predicted Grade B signal over all of the other city of license.

(2) *Taking programs from unaffiliated networks.* No affiliated station, in a market covered by this paragraph, shall take and broadcast, from an unaffiliated network, any programing of the times and types specified in this subparagraph, unless the conditions specified have first been met:

(i) Any evening programing (as defined in this paragraph), unless and until the entire schedule of such programs has been offered by the unaffiliated network to the unaffiliated station as provided in paragraph (1)(4) of this section, and the unaffiliated station has either accepted 15 hours per week of such programs, plus additional "special" hours when part of the "special" is included in the 15 hours, or has accepted a lesser amount and indicated that it does not wish to carry any more. Such acceptance shall be governed by the provisions of paragraph (1)(4) of this section.

(ii) Any programing beginning on the network between 12 noon and 7 p.m. on Saturdays, Sun-

days, and holidays, and consisting of sports events (including, without limitation, college football and basketball, professional football, baseball, ice hockey, golf, tennis, horseracing and autoracing), unless and until the program has first been offered to the unaffiliated station and that station has indicated that it does not wish to accept it.

(iii) Any programing broadcast after 11 p.m. local time (except 10 p.m. local time in the Central time zone) which is a continuation of programs starting earlier and carried by the unaffiliated station; or any material broadcast after 7 p.m. (6 p.m. in the Central time zone) which is a continuation of sports programs beginning earlier and carried by the unaffiliated station.

(iv) Any program presented in the same week by the unaffiliated station.

(3) *Carriage of programs of a network which has an affiliate.* No affiliated station in a market covered by this paragraph shall broadcast, from another network which has an affiliated station in the market, any evening programing or Saturday, Sunday, or holiday sports programing, unless such programing has first been offered to the unaffiliated station in the market and the latter has indicated that it does not wish to carry it.

(4) *Offer and acceptance.* (i) The "offer" by a network referred to in this paragraph means an offer to the unaffiliated station of the programs for broadcast. Programs so offered cannot be withdrawn by the network until the following April 1 or October 1, unless the station does not in fact broadcast the program as accepted, in which case the provisions of paragraph (1)(4)(ii) of this section shall apply, or unless the program is canceled on the network, in which case the replacement or substitute program shall be offered to the station as a new program under paragraphs (1)(2) or (3) of this section. If a program accepted by the unaffiliated station is shifted in time, the station may exercise its right of "first call" either with respect to the program at its new time, or the previous time segment, at its option.

(ii) The acceptance referred to in paragraphs (1) (2) and (3) of this section means that the unaffiliated station agrees to broadcast the program accepted, at its live network time or a delayed time acceptable to the network, unless in its judgment the program is not in the public interest or it wishes to substitute a local, or other live, program for it. The provisions of paragraph (a) of this section, prohibiting agreements which hinder the presentation of the programs of other networks, shall not apply to material covered by this paragraph. If a program is not presented in a particular week live or at a delayed time acceptable to the network, the network may place this particular broadcast of the program on another station; and if this occurs more than 4 times in any 13-week period the network may withdraw the program from the station without obligation to offer it any additional programing. The unaffiliated station is free to seek and obtain other terms of acceptance from the network; but the offer of programing by the network on the foregoing terms satisfies its obligations under this paragraph.

(iii) The offer by the network shall, to the extent possible, be up to and including August 2, 1971 with respect to programs beginning in the fall season, and by January 15 with respect to programs presented after April 1, or otherwise as soon as possible. The unaffiliated station's acceptance or indication of nonacceptance shall be within 2 weeks after the date of the offer; where any negotiations between the network and the station concerning particular programs are involved, programs not accepted within 30 days of the date of the offer shall be deemed not accepted.

Note 1: If there are in a particular market two affiliated stations and two (or more) operational unaffiliated stations with reasonably comparable facilities, the provisions of this paragraph (1) shall require an offer of programing to each; but the 15-hour-per-week "first call" provision applies to the total programing taken by all such stations.

Note 2: The provisions of this paragraph (1) do not apply to a market in which there are two VHF affiliated U.S. stations, and a foreign VHF station to which a national U.S. television network transmits programs pursuant to authority granted under section 325 of the Communications Act of 1934, as amended, and which serves as that network's primary affiliate in the market.

(m) *Territorial exclusivity in non-network arrangements.* (1) No television station shall enter into any contract, arrangement, or understanding, expressed or implied; with a non-network program producer, distributor, or supplier, or other person; which prevents or hinders another television station located in a community over 56.3 kilometers (35 miles) away, as determined by the reference points contained in § 76.53 of this chapter, (if reference points for a community are not listed in § 76.53, the location of the main post office will be used) from broadcasting any program purchased by the former station from such non-network program producer, distributor, supplier, or other person, except that a television station may secure exclusivity against a television station licensed to another designated community in a hyphenated market specified in the market listing as contained in § 76.51 of this chapter for those 100 markets listed, and for markets not listed in § 76.51 of this chapter, the listing as contained in the ARB Television Market Analysis for the most recent year at the time that the exclusivity contract, arrangement or understanding is complete under practices of the industry. As used in this paragraph, the term "community" is defined as the community specified in the instrument of authorization as the location of the station.

(2) Notwithstanding paragraph (m)(1) of this section, a television station may enter into a contract, arrangement, or understanding with a producer, supplier, or distributor of a non-network program if that contract, arrangement, or understanding provides that the broadcast station has exclusive national rights such that no other television station in the United States may broadcast the program.

1) *Prime Time Access Rule.* Network regulation, as the aforementioned rules evince, is largely effectuated by licensing policy. Directly responsive to concern with network influence is the Prime Time Access Rule.[116] Specifically, it provides that television stations in the top fifty markets owned by or affiliated with a network may offer network programming during only three of the four hours of prime time.[117] The central purpose of the rule was to encourage the development of independent programming.[118] The policy translated not just into a structural reform but also into an overt content restriction. Nonetheless, it was upheld, in *Mt. Mansfield Television, Inc. v. Federal Communications Commission*,[119] as a means for promoting First Amendment interests in

diversity.[120] Key to the outcome was the appeals court's determination that the unique scarcity of broadcasting defeated "an analogy between the . . . rule and an imaginary government edict prohibiting newspapers in the fifty largest cities from devoting more than a given portion of their news space to items taken from national news services."[121] Like other results predicated upon the concept of scarcity, the Prime Time Access Rule would seem vulnerable to the Supreme Court's possible reservations about that purportedly peculiar attribute[122] and FCC's divestment of it.[123]

Nonetheless, the Prime Time Access Rule continues to operate albeit in a version altered somewhat from its original form. In 1975, the FCC expanded the category of exemptions to include feature films and noted its expectation that licensees would use some of the time to address "needs or problems of [their] . . . communit[ies]."[124] The modified rule was upheld in *National Association of Independent Television Producers and Distributors v. FCC.*[125] In response to contentions that the rule was contrary to constitutional and statutory prohibitions against censorship, the Court made the following observations:

> The only way that broadcasters can operate in the "public interest" is by broadcasting programs that meet somebody's view of what is in the "public interest." That can scarcely be determined by the broadcaster himself, for he is in an obvious conflict of interest. "There is no sanctuary in the First Amendment for unlimited private censorship operating in a medium not open to all." *Red Lion, supra,* 395 U.S. at 392, 89 S.Ct. at 1808. "It is the right of the viewers and listeners, not the right of the broadcasters, which is paramount." *Id.* at 390, 89 S.Ct. at 1806.
>
> Since the public cannot through a million stifled yawns convey that their television fare, as a whole, is not in their interest, the Congress has made the F.C.C. the guardian of that pub-

lic interest. All that the Commission can do about it is to encourage competitive fare. If a large segment of the public prefers game shows to documentaries, the Commission can hardly do more than admit paradoxically that taste *is* a matter for dispute. The Commission surely cannot do its job, however, without interesting itself in general program format and the kinds of programs broadcast by licensees. *National Broadcasting Co. v. United States, supra.* Thus, as we have seen, the F.C.C. was sustained when it abrogated by regulation the chain broadcasting clauses which forced network programs on affiliated stations. *National Broadcasting Co. v. United States, supra.* It was also given a free hand to tell the subscription television people what types of programs they must *not* broadcast in order to qualify for a license. See *National Association of Theatre Owners v. F.C.C.,* 136 U.S.App.D.C. 352, 420 F.2d 194, 207–08 (1969), cert. denied, 397 U.S. 922, 90 S.Ct. 914, 25 L.Ed.2d 102 (1970).

> The Commission by this amendment of the rule is not ordering any program or even any type of program to be broadcast in access time. It has simply lifted a restriction on network programs if the licensee chooses to avail himself of such network programs in specified categories of programming.[126]

Results of the Prime Time Access Rule have been mixed at best and demonstrate certain practical realities to which the public interest is subject. With few exceptions local programming has not increased significantly, and syndicated game shows and the like have filled time that previously would have been devoted to network programming. Any expectation that program quality would improve, however, probably was misplaced. As the appeals court observed in upholding the modified rule, the commission may account for competition but not taste. Critical to a waiver of network rules that otherwise would apply to Fox Television's emergence as a fourth network was the condition that Fox would abide by terms of the Prime Time Access Rule.[127]

4. Programming

The FCC is barred from exercising "the power of censorship" or promulgating regulations which would "interfere with the right of free speech by means of radio communications."[128] Despite that prohibition, the commission has used its authority to influence programming in a variety of ways. Its capacity to do so in the licensing context was generally endorsed by the Supreme Court in *National Broadcasting Co. v. United States.*[129] The Court observed then that a public interest determination may require qualitative assessment of proposed or actual service.[130]

A certain amount of conflict exists between preclusion of official content control and the duty as it has evolved to regulate in the public interest. The FCC has avoided minimum programming requirements of any type on the grounds that they are equivalent to censorship.[131] Nonetheless, it has prohibited indecent or offensive expression that would be constitutionally protected if not broadcast.[132] Although no longer employed, various programming guidelines of a general nature have operated in the past.

An early policy noted that the FCC would give particular consideration in a licensing proceeding to service factors that included unsponsored programming, locally originated programming, public affairs programming, and the amount of time devoted to advertising in any given hour.[133] Later, it introduced a policy requiring applicants for a new commercial license or renewal to ascertain and report the programming needs of their communities.[134] Among other things, it was necessary to determine the demographic composition of the service area and meet with leaders of relevant community groups and representatives of the public. License applications had to contain specific program proposals that would meet ascertained community needs.[135] Failure to fulfill that obligation was grounds for de-

nying a license even in an instance when a community was deprived of what would have been its only FM service.[136]

Such formal guidelines largely have been eliminated pursuant to the FCC's recent philosophy that programming should be determined primarily by the marketplace. Ascertainment rules were lifted for radio in 1981[137] and for television in 1984.[138] Pertinent to their abandonment is the notion that administrative costs were too high and marketplace forces function toward effectuating the programming goals which originally prompted regulation.[139]

5. Employment Practices

Broadcasters are prohibited not only by general federal law[140] but also by FCC rule from discriminating on the basis of race.[141] License applicants, moreover, must file a form certifying that they do not discriminate against designated minorities and have an affirmative action program in place.[142] Evolving equal protection standards have proved increasingly hostile to preferential policies absent proven instances of discrimination.[143] Insofar as regulation may be tied to congressional directive and found "substantially related" to facilitating "the important governmental objective of broadcast diversity," however, it may survive constitutional scrutiny.[144]

Absent a challenge to a licensee's employment figures or allegations of discrimination, the only question is "whether the aggregate picture presented by [a licensee's] employment policies and practices ma[k]e a *prima facie* case for refusing to renew the station's license."[145] Generally, a mere statistical disparity between the percentage of minorities employed and in the service area will be "[in]sufficient to require evidentiary exploration."[146] The result may be different if the disparity is beyond a "zone of reasonableness."[147] Although not defined in precise terms, the perimeters of the zone may vary depending upon considerations such as whether a broadcaster is just commencing operations or is well established.[148] No license has ever been denied so far for failure to comply with employment standards.

B. COMPARATIVE REVIEW

Licensing is a relatively uncomplicated process when the FCC must consider only one application for a particular frequency. When competition exists for a new license or a renewal is subject to challenge, however, the commission must make a choice. The Supreme Court has determined that a comparative hearing is required whenever mutually exclusive applications are filed.[149] In an effort to maximize clarity of standards and consistency of results, the FCC has developed criteria that govern comparative proceedings in both an initial proceeding and a renewal context.

1. New Applications

Evaluation of competing applications for a new license, under the governing regulatory scheme, does not work as a precise science. The FCC has observed that relevant considerations "cannot be assigned absolute values, some factors may be present in some cases and not in others, and the difference between applicants with respect to each factor are almost infinitely variable."[150] Like any other administrative decision, moreover, continuity is affected by turnover of personnel and individual perceptions of a pertinent factor's relative significance.[151]

The FCC, in the interest of maximizing clarity and consistency, rendered a policy on comparative broadcast hearings that has generally informed the review process over the past quarter of a century.[152] The policy statement identifies two overarching objectives which are "first, the best practicable ser-

vice to the public, and, second, a maximum diffusion of control of the mass media."[153] Noting that "independence and individuality of approach are elements of rendering good program service," the FCC characterized "the primary goals of good service and diversification of control [as]...fully compatible."[154] Primary factors identified as critical in a comparative proceeding include diversification of media ownership and control, participation by ownership in station operations, proposed program service, past broadcast record, and efficient use of frequency.[155]

Policy Statement on Comparative Broadcast Hearings, 1 F.C.C.2d 393 (1965)

1. *Diversification of control of the media of mass communications.*—Diversification is a factor of primary significance since, as set forth above, it constitutes a primary objective in the licensing scheme.

As in the past, we will consider both common control and less than controlling interests in other broadcast stations and other media of mass communications. The less the degree of interest in other stations or media, the less will be the significance of the factor. Other interests in the principal community proposed to be served will normally be of most significance, followed by other interests in the remainder of the proposed service area and, finally, generally in the United States. However, control of large interests elsewhere in the same State or region may well be more significant than control of a small medium of expression (such as a weekly newspaper) in the same community. The number of other mass communication outlets of the same type in the community proposed to be served will also affect to some extent the importance of this factor in the general comparative scale.

It is not possible, of course, to spell out in advance the relationships between any significant number of the various factual situations which may be presented in actual hearings. It is possible, however, to set forth the elements which we believe significant. Without indicating any order of priority, we will consider interests in existing media of mass communications to be more significant in the degree that they:

(*a*) are larger, i.e., go towards complete ownership and control;

and to the degree that the existing media:

(*b*) are in, or close to, the community being applied for;

(*c*) are significant in terms of numbers and size, i.e., the area covered, circulation, size of audience, etc.;

(*d*) are significant in terms of regional or national coverage; and

(*e*) are significant with respect to other media in their respective localities.

2. *Full-time participation in station operation by owners.*—We consider this factor to be of substantial importance. It is inherently desirable that legal responsibility and day-to-day performance be closely associated. In addition, there is a likelihood of greater sensitivity to an area's changing needs, and of programing designed to serve these needs, to the extent that the station's proprietors actively participate in the day-to-day operation of the station. This factor is thus important in securing the best practicable service. It also frequently complements the objective of diversification, since concentrations of control are necessarily achieved at the expense of integrated ownership.

We are primarily interested in full-time participation. To the extent that the time spent moves away from full time, the credit given will drop sharply, and no credit will be given to the participation of any person who will not devote to the station substantial amounts of time on a daily basis. In assessing proposals, we will also look to the positions which the participating owners will occupy, in order to determine the extent of their policy functions and the likelihood of their playing important roles in management. We will accord particular weight to staff positions held by the owners, such as general manager, station manager, program director, business manager, director of news, sports, or public service broadcasting, and sales manager. Thus, although positions of less responsibility will be considered, especially if there will be full-time integration by those holding those positions, they cannot be

given the decisional significance attributed to the integration of stockholders exercising policy functions. Merely consultative positions will be given no weight.

Attributes of participating owners, such as their experience and local residence, will also be considered in weighing integration of ownership and management. While, for the reasons given above, integration of ownership and management is important per se, its value is increased if the participating owners are local residents and if they have experience in the field. Participation in station affairs on the basis described above by a local resident indicates a likelihood of continuing knowledge of changing local interests and needs. Previous broadcast experience, while not so significant as local residence, also has some value when put to use through integration of ownership and management.

Past participation in civic affairs will be considered as a part of a participating owner's local residence background, as will any other local activities indicating a knowledge of and interest in the welfare of the Community. Mere diversity of business interests will not be considered. Generally speaking, residence in the principal community to be served will be of primary importance, closely followed by residence outside the community, but within the proposed service area. Proposed future local residence (which is expected to accompany meaningful participation) will also be accorded less weight than present residence of several years' duration.

Previous broadcasting experience includes activity which would not qualify as a past broadcast record, i.e., where there was not ownership responsibility for a station's performance. Since emphasis upon this element could discourage qualified newcomers to broadcasting, and since experience generally confers only an initial advantage, it will be deemed of minor significance. It may be examined qualitatively, upon an offer of proof of particularly poor or good previous accomplishment.

The discussion above has assumed full-time, or almost full-time, participation in station operation by those with ownership interests. We recognize that station ownership by those who are local residents and, to a markedly lesser degree, by those who have broadcasting experience, may still be of some value even where there is not the substantial participation to which we will accord weight under this heading. Thus, local residence complements the statutory scheme and Commission allocation policy of licensing a large number of stations throughout the country, in order to provide for attention to local interests, and local ownership also generally accords with the goal of diversifying control of broadcast stations. Therefore, a slight credit will be given for the local residence of those persons with ownership interests who cannot be considered as actively participating in station affairs on a substantially full-time basis but who will devote some time to station affairs, and a very slight credit will similarly be given for experience not accompanied by full-time participation. Both of these factors, it should be emphasized, are of minor significance. No credit will be given either the local residence or experience of any person who will not put his knowledge of the community (or area) or experience to any use in the operation of the station.

3. *Proposed program service.*—The U.S. Court of Appeals for the District of Columbia Circuit has stated that, "in a comparative consideration, it is well recognized that comparative service to the listening public is the vital element, and programs are the essence of that service." *Johnston Broadcasting Co. v. Federal Communications Commission,* 85 U.S. App. D.C. 40, 48, 175 F. 2d 351, 359. The importance of program service is obvious. The feasibility of making a comparative evaluation is not so obvious. Hearings take considerable time and precisely formulated program plans may have to be changed not only in details but in substance, to take account of new conditions obtaining at the time a successful applicant commences operation. Thus, minor differences among applicants are apt to prove to be of no significance.

The basic elements of an adequate service have been set forth in our July 27, 1960 "Report and Statement of Policy Re: Commission en banc Programing Inquiry," 25 F.R. 7291, 20 Pike & Fischer, R.R. 1901, and need not be repeated here. And the applicant has the responsibility for a reasonable knowledge of the community and area, based on surveys or background, which will show that the program proposals are designed to meet the needs and interests of the public in that area. See *Henry v. Federal Communications Commission,* 112 U.S. App. D.C. 257, 302 F. 2d 191, *cert. den.* 371 U.S. 821. Contacts with local civic and other groups and individuals are also an important means of formulating proposals to meet an area's needs and interests. Failure to make them will be considered a serious deficiency, whether or not the applicant is familiar with the area.

Decisional significance will be accorded only to material and substantial differences between applicants' proposed program plans. See *Johnston Broadcasting Co. v. Federal Communications Commission,* 85 U.S. App. D.C. 40, 175 F. 2d 351. Minor differences in the proportions of time allocated to different types of programs will not be considered. Substantial differences will be considered to the extent that they go beyond ordinary differences in judgment and show a superior devotion to public service. For example, an unusual attention to local community matters for which there is a demonstrated need, may still be urged. We will not assume, however, that an unusually high percentage of time to be devoted to local or other particular types of programs is necessarily to be preferred. Staffing plans and other elements of planning will not be compared in the hearing process except where an inability to carry out proposals is indicated.

In light of the considerations set forth above, and our experience with the similarity of the program plans of competing applicants, taken with the desirability of keeping hearing records free of immaterial clutter, no comparative issue will ordinarily be designated on program plans and policies, or on staffing plans or other program planning elements, and evidence on these matters will not be taken under the standard issues. The Commission will designate an issue where examination of the applications and other information before it makes such action appropriate, and applicants who believe they can demonstrate significant differences upon which the reception of evidence will be useful may petition to amend the issues.

No independent factor of likelihood of effectuation of proposals will be utilized. The Commission expects every licensee to carry out its proposals, subject to factors beyond its control, and subject to reasonable judgment that the public's needs and interests require a departure from original plans. If there is a substantial indication that any party will not be able to carry out its proposals to a significant degree, the proposals themselves will be considered deficient.

4. *Past broadcast record.*—This factor includes past ownership interest and significant participation in a broadcast station by one with an ownership interest in the applicant. It is a factor of substantial importance upon the terms set forth below.

A past record within the bounds of average performance will be disregarded, since average future performance is expected. Thus, we are not interested in the fact of past ownership per se, and will not give a preference because one applicant has owned stations in the past and another has not.

We are interested in records which, because either unusually good or unusually poor, give some indication of unusual performance in the future. Thus, we shall consider past records to determine whether the record shows (i) unusual attention to the public's needs and interests, such as special sensitivity to an area's changing needs through flexibility of local programs designed to meet those needs, or (ii) either a failure to meet the public's needs and interests or a significant failure to carry out representations made to the Commission (the fact that such representations have been carried out, however, does not lead to an affirmative preference for the applicant, since it is expected, as a matter of course, that a licensee will carry out representations made to the Commission).

If a past record warrants consideration, the particular reasons, if any, which may have accounted for that record will be examined to determine whether they will be present in the proposed operation. For example, an extraordinary record compiled while the owner fully participated in operation of the station will not be accorded full credit where the party does not propose similar participation in the operation of the new station for which he is applying.

5. *Efficient use of frequency.*—In comparative cases where one of two or more competing applicants proposes an operation which, for one or more engineering reasons, would be more efficient, this fact can and should be considered in determining which of the applicants should be preferred. The nature of an efficient operation may depend upon the nature of the facilities applied for, i.e., whether they are in the television or FM bands where geographical allocations have been made, or in the standard broadcast (AM) band where there are no such fixed allocations. In addition, the possible variations of situations in comparative hearings are numerous. Therefore, it is not feasible here to delineate the outlines of this element, and we merely take this occasion to point out that the element will be considered where the facts warrant.

6. *Character.*—The Communications Act makes character a relevant consideration in the issuance of a license. See section 308(b), 47 U.S.C. 308(b). Significant character deficiencies may warrant disqualification, and an issue will be designated where appropriate. Since substantial demerits may be appropriate in some cases where disqualification is not warranted, petitions to add an issue on conduct relating to character will be entertained. In the absence of a designated issue, character evidence will not be taken....

7. *Other factors.*—As we stated at the outset, our interest in the consistency and clarity of decision and in expedition of the hearing process is not intended to preclude the full examination of any relevant and substantial factor. We will thus favorably consider petitions to add issues when, but only when, they demonstrate that significant evidence will be adduced.

As the FCC itself had observed, "a general statement cannot dispose of all problems or decide cases in advance."[156] Qualitative evaluations still must be made and, as experience has demonstrated, "[d]ifficult cases will remain difficult."[157] Determination of which applicant will provide the best practicable service may involve more than determining who is superior in the most categories. An applicant's edge in a particular category may range from slight to substantial,[158] so a qualitative and essentially subjective consideration would seem unavoidable.

Since announcing its policy on comparative evaluations, the FCC has flirted somewhat inconsistently with the use of race and gender as additional comparative factors. Its original position, that race was irrelevant, was rejected by the court of appeals which found minority ownership and participation grounds for a comparative preference.[159] A subsequent appeals court holding, that the Commission lacked statutory authority to award credit for female applicants,[160] was vacated and the case remanded so that the agency could reconsider its policy.[161] Congress then passed and the president signed a law prohibiting the FCC from eliminating or modifying provisions for enhancing minority ownership.[162] In *Metro Broadcasting, Inc. v. Federal Communications Commission*[163] the Supreme Court determined that comparative preferences on the basis of race were permissible because they serve the important objective of broadcast diversity... [and] are substantially related to the achievement of that objective."[164]

2. Renewal Proceedings

Equally if not more problematical than selecting from competing applicants for a new license is the task of choosing between an incumbent broadcaster and a challenger. Such circumstances present a dilemma. If performance is not rewarded, broadcasters may invest less in quality service, and the public interest as a consequence may suffer. Extensive turnover in licensees may have a disruptive effect not only upon the industry but more importantly upon the public interest. On the other hand, a system that favors incumbents may transform comparative review into an exercise that is more theoretical than real. To date, no television licensee has been denied a renewal, and nearly three decades have elapsed since a radio licensee was so denied.[165]

Standards governing comparative renewal proceedings have evolved from the FCC's determination, in *Hearst Radio, Inc. (WBAL)*,[166] that meritorious service in the

past was a dispositive factor.[167] Both applicants were found to be equally qualified, and the challenger had proposed programming emphasizing extensive community input and local orientation.[168] The commission regarded the incumbent's programming proposal as superior, however, based on its past service and concern that the challenger might be overpromising on its actual ability to perform.[169] The *Hearst* decision thus struck a balance in favor of a "high degree of probability of continuation of existing desirable performance [and] against paper proposals which... we are not convinced can be fulfilled."[170] Resultant policy was that "(e)xcellent performance as a licensee [would] be given favorable consideration where we find a reasonable likelihood that such performance will continue.... [A] record of poor service... will be given due weight in appraising the likelihood of effectuation of the licensee's proposals."[171]

The FCC and courts have wrestled with comparative renewal criteria since and, although the actual standards have been refined, the practical advantage to incumbents has remained constant. In *Greater Boston Television Corp. v. Federal Communications Commission*,[172] the court of appeals upheld the commission's decision to award a license to a challenger.[173] The *Greater Boston* case, however, was the result of extraordinary circumstances.[174] The original license had been tainted by ex parte contacts with the commission initiated by what proved to be the successful applicant.[175] Although the same entity was selected again, its wrongdoing was factored into an award of a short-term (four-month) license.[176] While hearings proceeded, the incumbent was allowed to operate under a temporary license but eventually was displaced in what amounted to a new rather than renewal proceeding.[177] The court of appeals observed that, absent the unusual conditions, a question would exist as to "whether the Commission had interfered with legitimate renewal expectancies implicit in the structure of the [Communications] Act."[178]

Just before the *Greater Boston* decision, the FCC announced new comparative renewal standards that largely would have reduced such hearings to a single issue. Central to the criteria was a provision awarding "a decisive preference for incumbents with a record of 'substantial' past performance without serious deficiencies."[179] In *Citizens Communications Center v. Federal Communications Commission*,[180] the court determined that the rule contravened requirements for a comparative hearing set forth by statute and precedent.[181] As the court noted, "(u)nless the renewal applicant's past performance is found to be insubstantial or marred by serious deficiencies, the competing applications get no hearing at all. The proposition that the [policy] violates Section 309(e), . . . is so obvious it need not be labored."[182] Surviving the decision nonetheless was the concept of a renewal expectancy fueled by the court's observation that "*superior* performance should be a plus of major significance in renewal proceedings."[183]

Subsequent litigation has been aimed at trying to ensure that the FCC does not as a practical matter give absolutely controlling preference to substantial past performance. In *Central Florida Enterprises, Inc. v. Federal Communications Commission*,[184] the court of appeals reversed a license renewal on the grounds that the commission (1) inadequately had assessed factors weighing against the incumbent and (2) its "handling of the facts [had made] embarrassingly clear that [it had] practically erected a presumption of renewal that is inconsistent with the full hearing requirement."[185] On remand, the FCC acknowledged that the challenger merited a clear preference on diversification and slight preference on integration grounds.[186] It also discounted a licensee misconduct issue associated with illegally moving the station's main studio from one city to another in the same service area.[187] Each of those factors nonetheless was outweighed, in the commission's mind, by substantial past service.[188] Diversification and integration factors in particular, the FCC observed, may have primary importance in a new license proceeding but should have lesser weight when performance has been tested and proved acceptable.[189]

In upholding the renewal decision, in *Central Florida Enterprises, Inc. v. Federal Communications Commission*,[190] the court of appeals observed how in the past the commission had "impermissibly raised renewal expectancy to an irrebuttable presumption in favor of the incumbent."[191] Upon remand, the FCC employed criteria in the nature of a sliding scale. Thus,

> the strength of the expectancy depends on the merit of the past record. Where, as in this case, the incumbent rendered substantial but not superior service, the expectancy takes the form of a comparative preference weighed against [the] other factors. . . . An incumbent performing in a superior manner would receive an even stronger preference. An incumbent rendering minimal service would receive no preference.[192]

Or, as the court described the formula in approving it, "*renewal expectancy is to be a factor weighed with all the other factors, and the better the past record, the greater the renewal expectancy weight.*"[193]

Despite its approval of the commission's findings, the court identified "an important caveat."[194] As a reminder that review should serve the interest of the public rather than the convenience of the broadcasting industry, the court emphasized that "doctrine is a means to this end, and it should not become more. If in a given case . . . denial of a license renewal would not undermine renewal expectancy *in a way harmful to the public interest*, then renewal expectancy should not be invoked."[195] Implicit is an expectancy that is not an automatic perquisite of incumbency or an administrative shortcut but a facilitator of the public interest insofar as it cuts against overpromising by challengers, encourages investment in quality service, and avoids haphazard restructuring of the broadcast industry.[196]

Somewhat ironically as it turned out, the court observed that it was "reassured by a recent FCC decision granting for the first time since 1961, on *comparative* grounds, the application of the challenger for a radio station license and denying the renewal application of the incumbent licensee."[197] Despite the incumbent's advantages on diversity and integration grounds, the commission in *Application of Simon Geller*[198] was more impressed by the challenger's plans to increase greatly total programming time and service of community interests and needs.[199] On review, the court of appeals vacated the decision on the grounds that the FCC had deviated from and discounted the usual significance it attached to the factors favoring the incumbent.[200]

The courts remain troubled by the fact that an incumbent television licensee has never been denied renewal in a comparative challenge.[201] As it noted:

> American television viewers will be reassured, although a trifle baffled, to learn that even the worst television stations—those which are, presumably, the ones picked out as vulnerable to a challenge—are so good that they never need replacing. We suspect that somewhere, sometime, somehow, some television *licensee* should fail in a comparative renewal challenge, but the FCC has never discovered such a licensee yet.[202]

A renewal has yet to be denied in the years since the court's observation.

A. SETTLEMENT
Comparative proceedings invite the possibility that a frivolous challenge will be mounted merely to extract a monetary payoff from the incumbent as the cost of voluntary dismissal.[203] Recognizing the potential for abuse, Congress originally prohibited cash settlements that included payments beyond actual litigation costs.[204] The policy, however, deterred serious challengers from considering settlement and thus magnified uncertainties that already existed. The bar eventually was relaxed,[205] but rules have since evolved that (1) prohibit payments other than to the incumbent prior to an initial renewal decision, and (2) permit settlements only to the extent they cover legitimate application expenses.[206]

B. FORMAT CHANGES
Although the public interest governs all licensing decisions, a community's general programming preferences must be dictated through the marketplace rather than by regulation. The issue of whether format changes are consonant with the public interest has arisen in both the renewal and transfer contexts. As a general rule, the FCC has attempted to distance itself from general programming as a licensing criterion. It has observed that significant programming differences are unusual, and it has expressed concern that applicants would overpromise and, once a license was obtained, underperform.[207] Also implicated is the statutory prohibition against functioning as a censor or interfering with freedom of expression.[208]

In 1976, the FCC adopted a policy to the effect: "that the marketplace is the best way to allocate entertainment formats in radio, whether the hoped for result is expressed in First Amendment terms...or economic terms."[209] The court of appeals rejected the FCC's position on grounds "the Commission must sometimes consider the loss of diversity" in determining whether licenses "are used in the public interest."[210] It also adverted to a previous ruling that "preservation of a format [that] would otherwise disappear, although economically and technically viable and preferred by a significant number of listeners, is generally in the public interest."[211]

In *Federal Communications Commission v. WNCN Listeners Guild,*[212] the Supreme Court reversed the appeals court's judgment and found the policy statement "not inconsistent with the [Communications] Act."[213] Noting that the public interest is not self-defining,[214] the Court found it reasonable for the commission to conclude that "reliance on the market is the best method of promoting diversity in entertainment formation."[215] The FCC had identified practical considerations that further supported its disinclination to regulate. Specifically, it complained about having to categorize past and subsequent formats to determine if a change had occurred, ascertain whether the prior programming was unique, and balance public harm from abandonment against public benefit from the change.[216] It then "emphasized the difficulty of evaluating the strength of listener preferences, of comparing the desire for diversity within a particular type of programming to the desire for a broader range of formats, and of assessing the financial feasibility of a unique format."[217] Because a decision in that regard would be largely subjective and "only approximately serve the public interest,"[218] the Court agreed "that the market, although imperfect, would serve the public interest as well or better by responding quickly to changing preference and by inviting experiments with new types of programming."[219]

Nor was the Court willing to regard format preservation as a logical extension of the public's paramount right in broadcasting "to receive suitable access to social, political, esthetic, moral, and other ideas and experiences."[220] Emphasizing that the right did not confer upon individual listeners power to have the FCC "review the abandonment of their favorite entertainment programs,"[221] the Court found the commission's reliance

upon marketplace forces to promote diversity and satisfy entertainment preferences consonant with the First Amendment.[222]

Justice Marshall dissented from the Court's decision on the grounds that the FCC foreclosed entirely any consideration of whether a format change might be inconsistent with the public interest.[223] He also criticized the selective exemption of entertainment programming from the commission's scope of concern[224] and suggested that the commission could assess the impact of a format change without enormous difficulty or subjectivity.[225] A subsequent appeals court decision noted that the FCC is responsible for the consequences of its policy and must remain ready to alter its rule if the public interest requires.[226]

Federal Communications Commission v. WNCN Listeners Guild, 450 U.S. 582 (1981)

Justice White delivered the opinion of the Court.

I

Beginning in 1970, in a series of cases involving license transfers, the Court of Appeals for the District of Columbia Circuit gradually developed a set of criteria for determining when the "public-interest" standard requires the Commission to hold a hearing to review proposed changes in entertainment formats. Noting that the aim of the Act is "to secure the maximum benefits of radio to all the people of the United States," *National Broadcasting Co. v. United States,* 319 U.S. 190, 217 (1943), the Court of Appeals ruled in 1974 that "preservation of a format [that] would otherwise disappear, although economically and technologically viable and preferred by a significant number of listeners, is generally in the public interest." *Citizens Committee to Save WEFM v. FCC,* 165 U.S. App. D.C. 185, 207, 506 F. 2d 246, 268 (en banc). It concluded that a change in format would not present "substantial and material questions of fact" requiring a hearing if (1) notice of the change had not precipitated "significant public grumbling"; (2) the segment of the population preferring the format was too small to be accommodated by available frequencies; (3) there was an adequate substitute in the service area for the format being abandoned[a] or (4) the format would be economically unfeasible even if the station were managed efficiently. The court rejected the Commission's position that the choice of entertainment formats should be left to the judgment of the licensee, stating that the Commission's interpretation of the public-interest standard was contrary to the Act.

In January 1976, the Commission responded to these decisions by undertaking an inquiry into its role in reviewing format changes. In particular, the Commission sought public comment on whether the public interest would be better served by Commission scrutiny of entertainment programming or by reliance on the competitive marketplace.

Following public notice and comment, the Commission issued a Policy Statement pursuant to its rulemaking authority under the Act. The Commission concluded in the Policy Statement that review of format changes was not compelled by the language or history of the Act, would not advance the welfare of the radio-listening public, would pose substantial administrative problems, and would deter innovation in radio programming. In support of its position, the Commission quoted from *FCC v. Sanders Brothers Radio Station,* 309 U.S. 470, 475 (1940): "Congress intended to leave competition in the business of broadcasting where it found it, to permit a licensee... to survive or succumb according to his ability to make his programs attractive to the public."[b] The Com-

mission also emphasized that a broadcaster is not a common carrier and therefore should not be subjected to a burden similar to the common carrier's obligation to continue to provide service if abandonment of that service would conflict with public convenience or necessity.

The Commission also concluded that practical considerations as well as statutory interpretation supported its reluctance to regulate changes in formats. Such regulation would require the Commission to categorize the formats of a station's prior and subsequent programming to determine whether a change in format had occurred; to determine whether the prior format was "unique"; and to weigh the public detriment resulting from the abandonment of a unique format against the public benefit resulting from that change. The Commission emphasized the difficulty of objectively evaluating the strength of listener preferences, of comparing the desire for diversity within a particular type of programming to the desire for a broader range of program formats and of assessing the financial feasibility of a unique format.

The Court of Appeals, sitting en banc, held that the Commission's policy was contrary to the Act as construed and applied in the court's prior format decisions. 197 U.S. App. D.C. 319, 610 F. 2d 838 (1979). The court questioned whether the Commission had rationally and impartially reexamined its position and particularly criticized the Commission's failure to disclose a staff study on the effectiveness of market allocation of formats before it issued the Policy Statement. The court

---

a. In *Citizens Committee to Save WEFM v. FCC,* for example, the court directed the Commission to consider whether a "fine arts" format was a reasonable substitute for a classical music format. 165 U.S. App. D.C., at 203–204, 506 F.2d, at 264–265. The court observed that 19th-century classical music and 20th-century classical music could be classified as different formats, since "the loss of either would unquestionably lessen diversity." *Id.,* at 204, n. 28, 506 F. 2d, at 265, n. 28.

b. The Commission observed that radio broadcasters naturally compete in the area of program formats, since there is virtually no other form of competition available. A staff study of program diversity in major markets

supported the Commission's view that competition is effective in promoting diversity in entertainment formats. *Policy Statement, supra,* at 861.

The *Notice of Inquiry* also explained the Commission's reasons for relying on competition to provide diverse entertainment formats:

"Our traditional view has been that the station's entertainment format is a matter best left to the discretion of the licensee or applicant, since he will tend to program to meet certain preferences of the area and fill significant voids which are left by the programming of other stations. The Commission's accumulated experience indicates that... [f]requently, when a station changes its format, other stations in the area adjust or change their formats in an effort to secure the listenership of the discontinued format." 57 F.C.C.2d, at 583.

then responded to the Commission's criticisms of the format doctrine. First, although conceding that market forces generally lead to diversification of formats, it concluded that the market only imperfectly reflects listener preferences and that the Commission is statutorily obligated to review format changes whenever there is "strong prima facie evidence that the market has in fact broken down." *Id.*, at 332, 610 F. 2d, at 851. Second, the court stated that the administrative problems posed by the format doctrine were not insurmountable. Hearings would only be required in a small number of cases, and the Commission could cope with problems such as classifying radio format by adopting "a rational classification schema." *Id.*, at 334, 610 F. 2d, at 853. Third, the court observed that the Commission had not demonstrated that the format doctrine would deter innovative programming. Finally, the court explained that it had not directed the Commission to engage in censorship or to impose common carrier obligations on licensees: *WEFM* did not authorize the Commission to interfere with licensee programming choices or to force retention of an existing format; it merely stated that the Commission had the power to consider a station's format in deciding whether license renewal or transfer would be consistent with the public interest. 197 U.S. App. D.C., at 332–333, 610 F. 2d, at 851–852.

Although conceding that it possessed neither the expertise nor the authority to make policy decisions in this area, the Court of Appeals asserted that the format doctrine was "law," not "policy," and was of the view that the Commission had not disproved the factual assumptions underlying the format doctrine. Accordingly, the court declared that the Policy Statement was "unavailing and of no force and effect." *Id.*, at 339, 610 F. 2d, at 858.

II

Rejecting the Commission's reliance on market forces to develop diversity in programming as an unreasonable interpretation of the Act's public-interest standard, the Court of Appeals held that in certain circumstances the Commission is required to regard a change in entertainment format as a substantial and material fact in deciding whether a license renewal or transfer is in the public interest. With all due respect, however, we are unconvinced that the Court of Appeals' format doctrine is compelled by the Act and that the Commission's interpretation of the public-interest standard must therefore be set aside.

It is common ground that the Act does not define the term "public interest, convenience, and necessity." The Court has characterized the public-interest standard of the Act as "a supple instrument for the exercise of discretion by the expert body which Congress has charged to carry out its legislative policy." *FCC v. Pottsville Broadcasting Co.*, 309 U.S. 134, 138 (1940). Although it was declared in *National Broadcasting Co. v. United States,* that the goal of the Act is "to secure the maximum benefits of radio to all the people of the United States," 319 U.S., at 217, it was also emphasized that Congress had granted the Commission broad discretion in determining how that goal could best be achieved. . . .

. . . . Furthermore, we recognized that the Commission's decisions must sometimes rest on judgment and prediction rather than pure factual determinations. In such cases complete factual support for the Commission's ultimate conclusions is not required since " 'a forecast of the direction in which future public interest lies necessarily involves deductions based on the expert knowledge of the agency.' "

The Commission has provided a rational explanation for its conclusion that reliance on the market is the best method of promoting diversity in entertainment formats. . . .

In making these judgments, the Commission has not forsaken its obligation to pursue the public interest. On the contrary, it has assessed the benefits and the harm likely to flow from Government review of entertainment programming, and on balance has concluded that its statutory duties are best fulfilled by not attempting to oversee format changes. This decision was in major part based on predictions as to the probable conduct of licensees and the functioning of the broadcasting market and on the Commission's assessment of its capacity to make the determinations required by the format doctrine. The Commission concluded that " '[e]ven after all relevant facts ha[d] been fully explored in an evidentiary hearing, [the Commission] would have no assurance that a decision finally reached by [the Commission] would contribute more to listener satisfaction than the result favored by station management.' " *Policy Statement,* 60 F.C.C. 2d 858, 865 (1976). It did not assert that reliance on the marketplace would achieve a perfect correlation between listener preferences and available entertainment programming. Rather, it recognized that a perfect correlation would never be achieved, and it concluded that the marketplace alone could best accommodate the varied and changing tastes of the listening public. These predictions are within the institutional competence of the Commission. . . .

III

It is contended that rather than carrying out its duty to make a particularized public-interest determination on every application that comes before it, the Commission, by invariably relying on market forces, merely assumes that the public interest will be served by changes in entertainment format. Surely, it is argued, there will be some format changes that will be so detrimental to the public interest that inflexible application of the Commission's Policy Statement would be inconsistent with the Commission's duties. But radio broadcasters are not required to seek permission to make format changes. The issue of past or contemplated entertainment format changes arises in the courses of renewal and transfer proceedings; if such an application is approved, the Commission does not merely assume but affirmatively determines that the requested renewal or transfer will serve the public interest.

Under its present policy, the Commission determines whether a renewal or transfer will serve the public interest without reviewing past or proposed changes in entertainment format. This policy is based on the Commission's judgment that market forces, although they operate imperfectly, not only will more reliably respond to listener preference than would format oversight by the Commission but also will serve the end of increasing diversity in entertainment programming. This Court has approved of the Commission's goal of promoting diversity in radio programming, *FCC v. Midwest Video Corp.,* 440 U.S. 689, 699 (1979), but the Commission is nevertheless vested with broad discretion in determining how much weight should be given to that goal and what policies should be pursued in promoting it. The Act itself, of course, does not specify how the Commission should make its public-interest determinations.

A major underpinning of its Policy Statement is the Commission's conviction, rooted in its experience, that renewal and transfer cases should not turn on the Commission's presuming to grasp, measure, and weigh the elusive and difficult factors involved in determining the acceptability of changes in entertainment format. To assess whether the elimination of a particular "unique" entertainment format would serve the public interest, the Commission would have to consider the benefit as well as the detriment that would result from the change. Necessarily, the Commission would take into consideration not only the number of listeners who favor the old and the new programming but also the intensity of their preferences. It would also consider the effect of the format change on diversity within formats as well as on diversity among formats. The Commission is convinced that its judgments in these respects would be subjective in large measure and would only approximately serve the public interest. It is also convinced that the market, although imperfect, would serve the public interest as well or better by responding quickly to changing preferences and by inviting experimentation with new types of programming. Those who would overturn the Commission's Policy Statement do not take adequate account of these considerations.

It is also contended that since the Commission has responded to listener complaints about nonentertainment programming, it should also review challenged changes in entertainment formats. But the difference between the Commission's treatment of nonentertainment programming and its treatment of entertainment programming is not as pronounced as it may seem. Even in the area of nonentertainment programming, the Commission has afforded licensees broad discretion in selecting programs. Thus, the Commission has stated that "a substantial and material question of fact [requiring an evidentiary hearing] is raised *only* when it appears that the licensee has abused its broad discretion by acting unreasonably or in bad faith." *Mississippi Authority for Educational TV*, 71 F.C.C. 2d 1296, 1308 (1979). Furthermore, we note that the Commission has recently reexamined its regulation of commercial radio broadcasting in light of changes in the structure of the radio industry. See *Notice of Inquiry and Proposed Rulemaking, In the Matter of Deregulation of Radio*, 73 F.C.C. 2d 457 (1979). As a result of that re-examination, it has eliminated rules requiring maintenance of comprehensive program logs, guidelines on the amount of nonentertainment programming radio stations must offer, formal requirements governing ascertainment of community needs, and guidelines limiting commercial time. See *Deregulation of Radio*, 46 Fed. Reg. 13888 (1981) (to be codified at 47 CFR Parts 0 and 73).

These cases do not require us to consider whether the Commission's present or past policies in the area of nonentertainment programming comply with the Act. We attach some weight to the fact that the Commission has consistently expressed a preference for promoting diversity in entertainment programming through market forces, but our decision ultimately rests on our conclusion that the Commission has provided a reasonable explanation for this preference in its Policy Statement.

We decline to overturn the Commission's Policy Statement, which prefers reliance on market forces to its own attempt to oversee format changes at the behest of disaffected listeners. Of course, the Commission should be alert to the consequences of its policies and should stand ready to alter its rule if necessary to serve the public interest more fully. As we stated in *National Broadcasting Co. v. United States:*

> If time and changing circumstances reveal that the "public interest" is not served by application of the Regulations, it must be assumed that the Commission will act in accordance with its statutory obligations. 319 U.S., at 225.

IV

Respondents contend that the Court of Appeals' judgment should be affirmed because, even if not violative of the Act, the Policy Statement conflicts with the First Amendment rights of listeners "to receive suitable access to social, political, esthetic, moral, and other ideas and experiences." *Red Lion Broadcasting Co. v. FCC*, 395 U.S. 367, 390 (1969). *Red Lion* held that the Commission's "fairness doctrine" was consistent with the public-interest standard of the Communications Act and did not violate the First Amendment, but rather enhanced First Amendment values by promoting "the presentation of vigorous debate of controversial issues of importance and concern to the public." *Id.*, at 385. Although observing that the interests of the people as a whole were promoted by debate of public issues on the radio, we did not imply that the First Amendment grants individual listeners the right to have the Commission review the abandonment of their favorite entertainment programs. The Commission seeks to further the interests of the listening public as a whole by relying on market forces to promote diversity in radio entertainment formats and to satisfy the entertainment preferences of radio listeners. This policy does not conflict with the First Amendment.

Contrary to the judgment of the Court of Appeals, the Commission's Policy Statement is not inconsistent with the Act. It is also a constitutionally permissible means of implementing the public-interest standard of the Act. Accordingly, the judgment of the Court of Appeals is reversed, and the case is remanded for further proceedings consistent with this opinion.

So ordered.

C. LICENSE TRANSFERS

Licenses are transferable subject to the FCC's determination that "the public interest, convenience and necessity will be served thereby."[227] A transfer proceeding operates under the same general standard, therefore, that governs new application or renewal proceedings. By law, however, the FCC only may consider whether the proposed purchaser rather then any other party would serve the public interest.[228]

Because the broadcasting industry has proved to be so profitable, and the number of available frequencies is limited, transfers are a common occurrence. Noting that excessive licensee turnover may be inimical to the public interest,[229] the FCC has imposed limits on how soon a broadcaster may transfer a license. Original rules that required a three-year waiting period absent a hardship waiver,[230] however, have been modified to a one-year holding period for licenses obtained through a comparative hearing.[231]

The transfer process has afforded the FCC an opportunity to promote minority ownership aims. Broadcasters whose licenses are designated for a revocation hearing or whose renewal applications are subject to hearing on basic qualification grounds are allowed "to transfer or assign licenses at a 'distress sale' price to applicants with a significant minority ownership interest, assuming the proposed assignee or transferee meets our other qualifications."[232] The policy promotes minority ownership by encouraging broadcasters, whose licenses are at risk on public interest grounds, to sell their facilities with an effective license factored into the price.[233] The preference has been limited to designated minorities, as the FCC explicitly has excluded women from its purview.[234] In *Metro Broadcasting, Inc. v. Federal Communications Commission,*[235] the Court rejected an equal protection challenge and upheld the policy on grounds it promoted and was substantially related to effectuating "the important governmental objective of broadcast diversity."[236]

In recent years, the FCC has had to consider transfers in the context of merging media conglomerates, friendly acquisitions, and even hostile takeovers. Issues have implicated not only questions of control, when corporate shareholders remain the same and a board of directors is changed, but also diversification policies. To satisfy cross-ownership requirements,[237] the Gannett Company in the late 1970s had to sell some of its broadcast properties when it merged with another major media company. Simi-

larly, when Capital Cities Communications acquired ABC a few years ago, it had to sell off television properties to bring its total audience reach under the 25-percent ceiling.[238] Transfer proceedings in such instances are a two-way proposition, requiring the FCC to make a public interest judgment on the acquisition of the merging or purchasing company and the necessary spin-off of previous holdings to another party.

D. LICENSE REVOCATION, DENIAL AND SHORT-TERM RENEWAL

More common than denial of a renewal application in a comparative proceeding is a nonrenewal decision or other sanction because the licensee's actions have been found to be inconsistent with the public interest. Official action of that nature ordinarily reflects a determination that a licensee either has defaulted on character or some "other" basic qualification that factors into the public interest.[239] Revocation[240] or nonrenewal is the functional equivalent of the death penalty for a licensee's broadcast operation. Short-term renewal[241] and monetary fines[242] enable the commission to reach conduct that may not justify loss of a license but nonetheless merits sanction. Fines may not exceed $25,000 per offense, although "[e]ach day of a continuing violation . . . constitute[s] a separate offense" provided the total amount does not exceed $250,000."[243] A short-term renewal essentially amounts to a probation period which, if satisfactorily completed, precedes renewal for a regular license term.

From 1970 to 1978, the FCC revoked or denied renewal of sixty-eight licenses.[244] Most of those decisions were based upon licensee conduct that intimated character shortcomings. Misrepresentations to the commission constituted the most frequent basis for denial.[245] Even when deceit was by an employee, who may have made false entries into station records or otherwise misled the commission, such wrongdoing has been imputed to a licensee who knew, or should have known of it, or failed to exercise adequate control and supervision expected from a public trustee.[246] Until recently, the FCC interested itself with nonbroadcast activities of a licensee including fraudulent billing practices, false advertising, inflated audience ratings, and the like. In some instances, renewal was denied on such grounds.[247] Activities covered by other federal laws or subject to state control since have been eliminated from the commission's purview.[248]

Loss of a license for content reasons creates tension with the statutory provision that explicitly prohibits censorship or "interfere[nce] with the right of free speech by means of radio communication."[249] The commission and judiciary, when afforded multiple bases for revoking a license or denying renewal, generally have grounded decisions exclusively on nonspeech grounds.[250] The FCC, however, has emphasized that it will not shy away from imposing the most extreme sanctions available in some instances when content is the only concern. A broadcaster who violates rules against indecent or offensive expression, as discussed in Chapter 9, does so at the risk of its license.[251] Failure to address the programming needs of a substantial part of the population in a licensee's service area also may result in the loss of a license. Findings that a state educational television system's programming policies discriminated on the basis of race and neglected the needs of black viewers led to a nonrenewal decision.[252] Content also was at the heart of a court of appeals decision that vacated a renewal on the grounds that a licensee had not served the public interest.[253] Nearly half of the population in the television station's service area was black, but the licensee, among other things, had a policy of eliminating any

programming that depicted blacks positively or was focused on racial concerns.[254]

Such results are the exception rather than the norm. Especially when controversy in the form of bigotry or prejudice has been the issue, the FCC and judiciary have preferred to rely on less restrictive regulatory mechanisms such as the fairness doctrine. For the most part, neither has been willing "to judge the merit, wisdom or accuracy of any broadcast discussion or commentary but has [sought] to insure that all viewpoints are given fair and equal opportunity for expression and that controverted allegations are balanced by the presentation of opposing viewpoints."[255] Although the fairness doctrine has been discontinued, present regulatory philosophy probably would contemplate that the interests of balance and opportunity are fulfilled by a marketplace occupied by multiple and diverse media rather than by a licensing decision that constituted suppression.[256]

E. Licensing Alternatives

Although well established, the licensing of broadcasters has evoked criticism both as a general concept and in the specific way it operates. The following comments suggest alternatives predicated upon market forces.

Coase, The Federal Communications Commission, 2 J.L. & Econ. 1 (1959)*

First of all, it must be observed that resources do not go, in the American economic system, to those with the most money but to those who are willing to pay the most for them. The result is that, in the struggle for particular resources, men who earn $5,000 per annum are every day outbidding those who earn $50,000 per annum. To be con-

---

*Reprinted by permission of the publisher from *Journal of Law and Economics*, vol. 1, pp 1–7, 35–40. Copyright 1959 by University of Chicago Press.

vinced that this is so, we need only imagine a situation occurring in which all those who earned $50,000 or more per annum arrived at the stores one morning and, at the prices quoted, were able to buy everything in stock, with nothing left over for those with lower incomes. Next day we may be sure that the prices quoted would be higher and that those with higher incomes would be forced to reduce their purchases—a process which would continue as long as those with lower incomes were unable to spend all they wanted. The same system which enables a man with $1 million to obtain $1 million's worth of resources enables a man with $1,000 to obtain a $1,000's worth of resources. Of course, the existence of a pricing system does not insure that the distribution of money between persons (or families) is satisfactory. But this is not a question we need to consider in dealing with broadcasting policy. Insofar as the ability to pay for frequencies or channels depends on the distribution of funds, it is the distribution not between persons but between firms which is relevant. And here the ethical problem does not arise. All that matters is whether the distribution of funds contributes to efficiency, and there is every reason to suppose that, broadly speaking, it does. Those firms which use funds profitably find it easy to get more; those which do not, find it difficult. The capital market does not work perfectly, but the general tendency is clear. In any case, it is doubtful whether the Federal Communications Commission has, in general, awarded frequencies to firms which are in a relatively unfavorable position from the point of view of raising capital. The inquiries which the Commission conducts into the financial qualifications of applicants must, in fact, tend in the opposite direction. And if we take as examples of "choice outlets in prime markets" network-affiliated television stations in the six largest metropolitan areas in the United States on the basis of population (New York, Chicago, Los Angeles, Philadelphia, Detroit, and San Francisco), we find that five stations are owned by American Broadcasting–Paramount Theatres, Inc., four by the National Broadcasting Company (a subsidiary of the Radio Corporation of America), four by the Columbia Broadcasting System, Inc., and one each by the Westinghouse Broadcasting Company (a subsidiary of the Westinghouse Electric

Corporation), the Storer Broadcasting Company, and three newspaper publishing concerns. It would be difficult to argue that these are firms which have been unduly handicapped in their growth by their inability to raise capital.

The Supreme Court appears to have assumed that it was impossible to use the pricing mechanism when dealing with a resource which was in limited supply. This is not true. Despite all the efforts of art dealers, the number of Rembrandts existing at a given time is limited; yet such paintings are commonly disposed of by auction. But the works of dead painters are not unique in being in fixed supply. If we take a broad enough view, the supply of all factors of production is seen to be fixed (the amount of land, the size of the population, etc.). Of course, this is not the way we think of the supply of land or labor. Since we are usually concerned with a particular problem, we think not in terms of the total supply but rather of the supply available for a particular use. Such a procedure is not only practically more useful; it also tells us more about the processes of adjustment at work in the market. Although the quantity of a resource may be limited in total, the quantity that can be made available to a particular use is variable. Producers in a particular industry can obtain more of any resource they require by buying it on the market, although they are unlikely to be able to obtain considerable additional quantities unless they bid up the price, thereby inducing firms in other industries to curtail their use of the resource. This is the mechanism which governs the allocation of factors of production in almost all industries. Notwithstanding the almost unanimous contrary view, there is nothing in the technology of the broadcasting industry which prevents the use of the same mechanism. Indeed, use of the pricing system is made particularly easy by a circumstance to which Professor Smythe draws our special attention, namely, that the broadcasting industry uses but a small proportion of "spectrum space." A broadcasting industry, forced to bid for frequencies, could draw them away from other industries by raising the price it was willing to pay. It is impossible to say whether the result of introducing the pricing system would be that the broadcasting industry would obtain more frequencies than are allocated to it by the Federal

Communications Commission. Not having had, in the past, a market for frequencies, we do not know what these various industries would pay for them. Similarly, we do not know for what frequencies the broadcasting industry would be willing to outbid these other industries. All we can say is that the broadcasting industry would be able to obtain all the existing frequencies it now uses (and more) if it were willing to pay a price equal to the contribution which they could make to production elsewhere. This is saying nothing more than that the broadcasting industry would be able to obtain frequencies on the same basis as it now obtains its labor, buildings, land, and equipment.

A thoroughgoing employment of the pricing mechanism for the allocation of radio frequencies would, of course, mean that the various governmental authorities, which are at present such heavy users of these frequencies, would also be required to pay for them. This may appear to be unnecessary, since payment would have to be made to some other government agency appointed to act as custodian of frequencies. What was paid out of one government pocket would simply go into another. It may also seem inappropriate that the allocation of resources for such purposes as national defense or the preservation of human life should be subjected to a monetary test. While it would be entirely possible to exclude from the pricing process all frequencies which government departments consider they need and to confine pricing to frequencies available for the private sector, there would seem to be compelling reasons for not doing so. A government department, in making up its mind whether or not to undertake a particular activity, should weigh against the benefits this would confer, the costs which are also involved: that is, the value of the production elsewhere which would otherwise be enjoyed. In the case of a government activity which is regarded as so essential as to justify any sacrifice, it is still desirable to minimize the cost of any particular project. If the use of a frequency which if used industrially would contribute goods worth $1 million could be avoided by the construction of a wire system or the purchase of reserve vehicles costing $100,000, it is better that the frequency should not be used, however essential the project. It is the merit of the pricing system that, in these circumstances, a government

department (unless very badly managed) would not use the frequency if made to pay for it. Some hesitation in accepting this argument may come from the thought that, though it might be better to provide government departments with the funds necessary to purchase the resources they need, it by no means follows that Congress will do this. Consequently, it might be better to accept the waste inherent in the present system rather than suffer the disadvantages which would come from government departments having inadequate funds to pay for frequencies. This, of course, assumes that government departments are, in general, denied adequate funds by Congress, but it is not clear that this is true, above all for the defense departments, which, at present, use the bulk of the frequencies. Furthermore, it has to be remembered that a pricing scheme for frequencies would not involve any budgetary strain, since all government payments would be exactly balanced by the receipts of the agency responsible for disposing of frequencies, and there would be a net gain from the payments by private firms. In any case, such considerations do not apply to the introduction of pricing in the private sector and, in particular, for the broadcasting industry.

The desire to preserve government ownership of radio frequencies coupled with an unwillingness to require any payment for the use of these frequencies has had one consequence which has caused some uneasiness. A station operator who is granted a license to use a particular frequency in a particular place may, in fact, be granted a very valuable right, one for which he would be willing to pay a large sum of money and which he would be forced to pay if others could bid for the frequency. This provision of a valuable resource without charge naturally raises the income of station operators above what it would have been in competitive conditions. It would require a very detailed investigation to determine the extent to which private operators of radio and television stations have been enriched as a result of this policy. But part of the extremely high return on the capital invested in certain radio and television stations has undoubtedly been due to this failure to charge for the use of the frequency. Occasionally, when a station is sold, it is possible to glimpse what is involved. Strictly, of course, all that can be sold is the station and its organization; the frequency is public property, and the grant of a license gives no rights of any sort in that frequency. Furthermore, transfers of the ownership of radio and television stations have to be approved by the Federal Communications Commission. However, the Commission almost always approves such negotiated transfers, and, when these take place, there can be little doubt that often a great part of the purchase price is in fact payment for obtaining the use of the frequency. Thus when WNEW in New York City was sold in 1957 for $5 million or WDTV in Pittsburgh in 1955 for $10 million or WCAV (AM, FM, and TV) in Philadelphia in 1958 for $20 million, it is possible to doubt that it would cost $5 million or $10 million or $20 million to duplicate the transmitter, studio equipment, furniture, and the organization, which nominally is what is being purchased. The result of sales at such prices is, of course, to reduce the return earned by the new owners to (or at any rate nearer to) the competitive level. When, as happened in the early days of radio regulation but less often since the Commission refused to sanction transfers at a price much more than the value of the physical assets and the organization being acquired, the effect was simply to distribute the benefits derived from this free use of public property more widely among the business community: to enable the new as well as the old owners to share in it. I do not wish to discuss whether such a redistribution of the gain is socially desirable. My point is different: there is no reason why there should be any gain to redistribute.

The extraordinary gain accruing to radio and television station operators as a result of the present system of allocating frequencies becomes apparent when stations are sold. Even before the 1927 Act was passed, it was recognized that stations were transferred from one owner to another at prices which implied that the right to a license was being sold. Occasionally, references to this problem are found in the literature, but the subject has not been discussed extensively. In part, I think this derives from the fact that the only solution to the problem of excessive profits was thought to be rate regulation or profit control. Such solutions were unlikely to gain support for a number of reasons. Although in the early

days of the broadcasting industry it was commonly thought that it would be treated as another public utility, this view was later largely abandoned. An attempt to make broadcasters common carriers failed. And broadcasting has come to be thought of, so far as its business operations are concerned, as an unregulated industry. As the Supreme Court has said: "...the field of broadcasting is one of free competition." In any case, the determination of the rates to be charged or the level of profits to be allowed would not seem an easy matter, although it has been claimed that "it should be possible for resource and tax economists to develop norms for levying such special franchise taxes." Furthermore, rate or profit regulation with the concomitant need for control of the quality of the programs is hardly an attractive prospect....

There is no reason why users of radio frequencies should not be in the same position as other businessmen. There would not appear, for example, to be any need to regulate the relations between users of the same frequency. Once the rights of potential users have been determined initially, the rearrangement of rights could be left to the market. The simplest way of doing this would undoubtedly be to dispose of the use of a frequency to the highest bidder, thus leaving the subdivision of the use of the frequency to subsequent market transactions. Nor is it clear that the relations between users of adjacent frequencies will necessarily call for special regulation. It may well be that several people would normally be involved in a single transaction if conflicts of interests between users of adjacent frequencies are to be settled through the market. But, though an increase in the number of people involved increases the cost of carrying out a transaction, we know from experience that it is quite practicable to have market transactions which involve a multiplicity of parties. Whether the number of parties normally involved in transactions involving users of adjacent frequencies would be unduly large and call for special regulation, only experience could show. *Some* special regulation would certainly be required. For example, some types of medical equipment can apparently be operated in such a way as to cause interference on many frequencies and over long distances. In such a case, a regulation limiting the power of the equipment and requiring shielding would probably be desirable. It is also true that the need for wide bands of frequencies for certain purposes may require the exercise of the power of eminent domain; but this does not raise a problem different from that encountered in other fields. It is easy to embrace the idea that the interconnections between the ways in which frequencies are used raise special problems not found elsewhere or, at least, not to the same degree. But this view is not likely to survive the study of a book on the law of torts or on the law of property in which will be found set out the many (and often extraordinary) ways in which one person's actions can affect the use which others can make of their property.

Fowler and Brenner, "A Marketplace Approach to Broadcast Regulation," 60 *Tex. L.Rev.* 207 (1982)*

Although a good way to have started in the 1920's, an auction would substantially disrupt current service and frustrate the expectations of those who have long held spectrum rights and of their customers. Another way to encourage optimum frequency use would be to allow licenses to be bought and sold freely after the initial grant, regardless of whether the initial grant is determined by auction, lottery, or under the old trusteeship approach. On resale, the seller, rather than the government, would capture the higher value of the frequency, but the allocation of resale profit would not prevent the frequency from reaching its highest use, thereby achieving the market objective.

To some, the major objection to free resale would be the windfall to incumbent licensees. The windfall, to the extent that it actually occurred, would consist of the increased value of a deregulated license created by its release from content and ownership restrictions and its new, freely transferable character. The problem presented by the windfall of free transferability is not entirely novel. Except for distressed prop-

erties or those that have never been transferred, the price paid to a transferor under existing assignment rules already reflects the steadily increasing value of the exclusivity. It is almost always greater than the value of the nonlicense assets being transferred. Restricted resales under section 310(d) of the 1934 Act have already occurred several times with respect to many licenses, so that the windfall has been captured.

More generally, the marketplace approach could be most expeditiously introduced to broadcasting by granting existing licensees "squatter's rights" to their frequencies. These rights embody the reasonable expectation of renewal that licensees presently enjoy for satisfactory past performance. The critical next step, from a market viewpoint, would be to deregulate fully the sale of licenses.

This approach to resale need not preclude the use of lotteries or auctions for new assignments to broadcasters or other spectrum users. Consider the Commission's handling of low-power television service. Announcement of this new service led to the submission of thousands of applications, many mutually exclusive, so that the Commission is faced with choosing among competing applicants. Although the Commission has approved a comparative process to license this new service, initial grants using either a lottery and resale or an auction could inject market incentives into the distribution of this service. Either technique would be likely to raise the frequency exclusivity to its highest use as a broadcast frequency.

Congress in recent years has authorized the FCC to use a lottery procedure that would randomly select licensees from a pool of applicants found to satisfy basic qualifications.[257] If it were to employ such a process in place of a comparative review procedure, the commission would be obligated, pending possible constitutional challenge, to extend a preference to applications of minority groups that would enhance the overall diversification of the media.[258] So far, however, the FCC has refrained from adopting random selection and persists with comparative review of broadcast license applicants.

NOTES

1. STATISTICAL ABSTRACT OF THE UNITED STATES 1989, No. 900, at 544.

2. *Id.*

3. *Id.*

4. *See* FM Broadcast Stations, 53 R.R.2d 1550 (1983).

5. For a critical appraisal of the FCC's overarching emphasis upon local service, *see* Collins, *The Local Service Concept in Broadcasting: An Evaluation and Recommendation for Change*, 65 IOWA L.REV. 553 (1980).

6. 47 C.F.R. § 15.117(b).

7. *Id.*, § 15.117(c).

8. National Broadcasting Co. v. United States, 319 U.S. 190, 210 (1943).

9. *Id.*

10. *Id.*

11. 48 Stat. 1064 (1934), as amended, 47 U.S.C. § 151 *et seq.*

12. *Id.*, § 151.

13. *Id.*, § 303.

14. *Id.*

15. National Broadcasting Co. v. United States, 319 U.S at 216.

16. Caldwell, *The Standard of Public Interest, Convenience or Necessity as Used in the Radio Act of 1927*, 1 AIR L.REV. 295, 296 (1930).

17. Federal Communications Commission v. Pottsville Broadcasting Co., 309 U.S. 134, 138 (1940).

18. National Broadcasting Co. v. United States, 319 U.S. at 216.

19. Most public interest renderings, at least insofar as they do not implicate constitutional interests, are assessed to determine whether they are supported by substantial evidence. *See* Administrative Procedure Act, 5 U.S.C. § 706(2) (e).

20. Federal Communications Commission v. RCA Communications, Inc. 346 U.S. 86, 91 (1953).

21. National Broadcasting Co. v. United States, 319 U.S at 227.

22. *Id.* at 226–27.

23. "It is the purpose of this [Act], among other things, to maintain the control of the United States over all the channels of interstate and foreign radio transmission; and to provide for the use of such channels, but not the ownership thereof, by persons for limited periods of time, under licenses granted by Federal authority...." 47 U.S.C. § 301.

24. *Id.*, § 308 (b).

25. Near v. Minnesota, 283 U.S. 697 (1931).

26. *Id.* at 713.

27. New York Times Co. v. United States, 403 U.S. 713 (1971).

28. *See* II.E. of this Chapter.

29. 47 U.S.C. § 308(b). A prospective licensee must have the financial capability to operate a station for three months without advertising revenue. Financial Qualifications 45 R.R.2d 925 (1979). Provided that requirement is satisfied, relative financial strength is not considered in a comparative license proceeding. Scripps-Howard Radio v. FCC, 189 F.2d 677, 681 (D.C.Cir. 1951). License applicants also are obligated to show they will meet technical requirements for operations and transmissions. Character and citizenship requirements raise more serious issues that are discussed in the text.

30. Federal Communications Commission v. National Broadcasting Co., Inc. (KOA), 319 U.S. 239, 247 (1943).

31. 359 F.2d 994 (D.C.Cir. 1966)

32. *See* Office of Communication of United Church of Christ v. Federal Communications Commission, 359 F.2d. at 1000–05.

33. 47 U.S.C. § 306(c)

34. *Id.*, § 312(a)

35. 47 U.S.C. § 308(b) 301(d).

36. *Id.*, § 310(b)

37. *Id.*, § 313(a).

38. Mathews v. Diaz, 426 U.S. 67, 84–87 (1976).

39. *See id.* at 82–83.

40. *Id.* at 81, 87.

41. *See* J. NOWAK, R. ROTUNDA, J. YOUNG, CONSTITUTIONAL LAW, § 14.12, at 633 (1986).

42. The public trustee concept and its implications are explicated in Red Lion Broadcasting Co. v. Federal Communications Commission, 395 U.S. 367, 389–94 (1969).

43. *Cf.* Miami Herald Publishing Co. v. Tornillo, 418 U.S. 241, 258 (1974).

44. Federal Communications Commission v. WOKO, Inc., 329 U.S. 223, 229 (1946).

45. Mester v. United States, 70 F.Supp. 118, 122 (E.D.N.Y.), *aff'd*, 372 U.S. 749 (1947).

46. WKAT, Inc., 29 F.C.C. 221, 237 (1958).

47. In the Matter of Policy Regarding Character Qualifications in Broadcast Licensing, 87 F.C.C.2d 836, 841 1981) (hereafter cited as "Character Qualifications").

48. *Id.*

49. *Id.* at 842.

50. *Id.*

51. 329 U.S. 223.

52. *See* General Electric Co., 2 R.R.2d 1038 (1964); Westinghouse Broadcasting Co., Inc., 22 R.R. 1023 (1962).

53. *Id.*

54. Character Qualifications, 87 F.C.C.2d at 842.

55. *See* II.B. of this Chapter.

56. Character Qualifications, 87 F.C.C.2d at 842.

57. *Id.* at 836; The notion that character is portable would suggest that all licenses would be affected by an identifiable deficiency.

58. *Id.* at 843–44.

59. Character Qualifications in Broadcast Licensing, 102 F.C.C.2d 1179 (1986) *affd*, National Association for Better Broadcasting v. Federal Communications Commission, F. 2d (D.C. Cir. 1987).

60. Character Qualifications Policy, 67 R.R. 2d 1107 (1990).

61. Multiple Ownership Rules, 55 R.R.2d 1465 (1984).

62. The FCC must consider whether, despite the ceiling, the public interest would be served by a waiver. *See* United States v. Storer Broadcasting Co., 351 U.S. 192, 205 (1956).

63. 47 C.F.R. § 73.3555(a)–(c).

64. 47 U.S.C. § 533(a) (television and cable) and § 533(b) (common carrier and cable).

65. Federal Communications Commission v. National Citizens Committee for Broadcasting, 436 U.S. 775, 780 (1978).

66. *Id.* at 786.

67. 436 U.S. 775.

68. *Id.* at 794–96, 802.

69. *Id.* at 795.

70. *Id.* at 797.

71. *Id.*

72. *Id.*

73. *Id.*

74. *Id.* at 800.

75. *Id. quoting* Red Lion Broadcasting Co. v. Federal Communications Commission, 395 U.S. at 390.

76. 436 U.S. at 800.

77. *Id.*

78. *Id.*

79. *Id.* at 800–801.

80. *Id.* at 801–2.

81. *Id.* at 802.

82. *Id.*

83. *Id.*

84. *Id.* at 804.

85. *Id.*

86. *Id.* at 804–8.

87. *Id.* at 814.

88. *Id.* at 814–15.

89. *Id.* at 815.

90. *See* Health and Medicine Policy Research Group v. Federal Communications Commission, 807 F.2d 1038, 1041 (D.C.Cir. 1986).

91. *Id.* at 1040; Twentieth Century Holdings Corp., 1 F.C.C. Rcd. 1201 (1986).

92. News America Publishing, Inc. v. Federal Communications Commission, 844 F.2d 800, 813–16 (D.C.Cir. 1988).

93. 47 U.S.C. § 533 (a).

94. *Id.,* § 533(b).

95. 47 C.F.R. § 73.5555(d).

96. Multiple Ownership Rules, 100 F.C.C.2d 17 (1984). Minority control is defined as "more than 50 percent controlled by one or more members of a minority group." 47 C.F.R. § 73.3555 (d) (3) (iii). Qualifying minorities include "Black, Hispanic, American Indian, Alaska Native, Asian and Pacific Islander." *Id.* §73.3555 (d) (3) (iv).

97. 47 C.F.R. § 73.3555 (d) (2).

98. Multiple Ownership Rules, 100 F.C.C.2d 17 (Comm'r Dawson dissenting); *id.* (Comm'r Patrick dissenting).

99. City of Richmond v. J.A. Croson Co., 109 S.Ct. 706, 721 (1989). The Court foreclosed race-conscious remediation as a methodology for redressing societal discrimination but left open the possibility of race-dependent means to account for provable instances of discrimination. *Id.* at 729.

100. Metro Broadcasting, Inc. v. Federal Communications Commission, 110 S.Ct. 2997, 3009 (1990). Approval of the preferences, concerning comparative renewal proceedings and distress sales, are discussed later in this chapter.

101. *Id.* at 3009–10.

102. Deference to Congress on an issue that otherwise would elicit close scrutiny was justified as "appropriate in light of Congress's institutional competence as the national legislature,... as well as powers under the Commerce Clause,... the Spending Clause,... and the Civil War Amendments." *Id.* at 3008.

103. 351 U.S. 192 (1956).

104. *Id.* at 205.

105. *Id.* at 195.

106. *Id.* at 201–2.

107. *Id.* at 203.

108. United States v. Radio Corp. of America, 358 U.S. 334, 351–52 (1959).

109. *Id.*

110. National Broadcasting Co. v. United States, 319 U.S. at 194–95.

111. 319 U.S. 190.

112. *Id.* at 217–19.

113. *Id.* at 217.

114. *Id.* at 198.

115. 47 C.F.R. § 73.132 (AM) § 73.232 (FM) and § 73.658 (television).

116. Amendment of Part 73 of the Commission's Rules and Regulations with Respect to Competition and Responsibility in Network Television Broadcasting, 23 F.C.C.2d 382 (1970).

117. *Id.* at 384. Exceptions were provided for news public affairs, children's and spill-over programming in the nature of athletic and special events. *Id.* at 385.

118. *Id.* at 384.

119. 442 F.2d 470 (2d Cir. 1970).

120. *Id.* at 477.

121. *Id.*

122. *See* Federal Communications Commission v. League of Women Voters of California, 468 U.S. 364, 376 n.11 (1984).

123. *See* Syracuse Peace Council, 2 F.C.C. Rcd. 5043, 5057–58 (1987).

124. Request for Waiver of the Prime Time Access Rule, 50 F.C.C. 2d 826, 852 (1975).

125. 516 F.2d 526 (2d Cir. 1975).

126. *Id.* at 536–37.

127. Fox Broadcasting Co., 67 R.R. 2d 1086 (1990).

128. 47 U.S.C. § 326.

129. 319 U.S. 190.

130. *Id.* at 215–16.

131. *E.g.,* Action for Children's Television v. Federal Communications Commission 756 F.2d 741, 744 (D.C.Cir. 1987); National Black Media Coalition v. Federal Communications Commission, 589 F.2d 578, 581 (D.C.Cir. 1978).

132. Federal Communications Commission v. Pacifica Foundation, 438 U.S. 726, 749–51, (1978); New Indecency Enforcement Standards to be applied to All Broadcast and Amateur Licensees, 2 F.C.C. Rcd. 2726 (1987). Indecency controls are discussed in detail in Part Three.

133. *See* Public Service Responsibility of Broadcast Licensees, F.C.C. (1946). Public service responsibilities were set forth in what was commonly referred to as the Blue Book, discussed in Deregulation of Radio, 84 F.C.C.2d 960, 994–95 (1981).

134. The Primer on Ascertainment of Community Problems by Broadcast Applicants, 27 F.C.C.2d 650 (1971).

135. *Id.* at 651.

136. *See* Henry v. Federal Communications Commission, 302 F.2d 191 (D.C.Cir. 1962), *cert. denied,* 371 U.S. 821 (1962).

137. Deregulation of Radio, 84 F.C.C.2d 968 (1981).

138. Revision of Programming and Commercialization Policies, Ascertainment Requirements and Program Log Requirements for Commercial Television, 98 F.C.C.2d 1076 (1984).

139. 84 F.C.C.2d at 1014; 98 F.C.C.2d at 1114.

140. Title VII of the Civil Rights Act of 1964, 42 U.S.C. § 2000g *et seq.*

141. 47 C.F.R. § 73.2080.

142. Id.

143. *See* City of Richmond v. J.A. Croson Co., 109 S.Ct. at 727–29. Outside the employment context, and to the extent congressionally endorsed, race-conscious preferences have been upheld insofar as they served an important governmental interest. *See* Metro Broad-

casting, Inc. v. Federal Communications Commission, 110 S. Ct. 3009.

144. Race-conscious preferences found to promote broadcast diversity have been upheld in deference to an amalgam of congressional powers including authority under the Commerce Clause, Spending Clause, and Civil War Amendments and Congress's institutional competence as a national legislature. Metro Broadcasting, Inc. v. Federal Communications Commission, 110 S.Ct. at 3008.

145. Stone v. Federal Communications Commission, 466 F.2d 316, 329 (D.C.Cir. 1972).

146. Id. at 330.

147. Id. at 332.

148. Id.

149. Ashbacker Radio Corp. v. Federal Communications Commission, 326 U.S. 327, 333 (1945).

150. Policy Statement on Comparative Broadcast Hearings, 1 F.C.C. 2d 393, 393 (1963).

151. Id.

152. Although litigated and glossed, the central criteria for renewal remain largely intact.

153. I F.C.C.2d at 393.

154. Id. at 394.

155. Id. at 394–99.

156. Id. at 394.

157. Id.

158. *See, e.g.,* Application of Simon Geller, 102 F.C.C.2d 1443 (1985).

159. *See* TV 9, Inc. v. Federal Communications Commission, 495 F.2d 929, 936–38 (D.C.Cir. 1973).

160. Steele v. Federal Communications Commission, 770 F.2d 1192 (D.C.Cir. 1985).

161. Coursing of the proceedings is discussed in Metro Broadcasting, Inc. v. Federal Communications Commission, 110 S. Ct. at 3006 n. 8.

162. Pub. L. 100–202, 101 Stat. 1329–31.

163. 110 S. Ct. 2997.

164. The Court refrained from assessing the constitutionality of gender preferences. Id. at 3005 n. 7.

165. *See* Central Florida Enterprises, Inc., v. Federal Communications Commission, 683 F.2d 503, 510 (D.C.Cir.) *cert. denied,* 460 U.S. 1084 (1983).

166. 15 F.C.C.2d 1149 (1951).

167. Id. at 1175, 1177–79.

168. Id. at 1176–78.

169. Id. at 1178–79.

170. Id. at 1175.

171. Id.

172. 444 F.2d 841 (D.C.Cir. 1970), *cert. denied,* 403 U.S. 923 (1971).

173. Id. at 863.

174. Id. at 844–46.

175. Id.

176. Id. at 845.

177. Id.

178. Id. at 854.

179. *See* Citizens Communications Center v. Federal Communications Commission, 447 F.2d 1201, 1211 (D.C.Cir. 1971).

180. 447 F.2d 1201.

181. Id. at 1210–11.

182. Id. at 1211–12.

183. Id. at 1213.

184. 598 F.2d 37 (D.C.Cir. 1978).

185. Id. at 51.

186. Cowles Broadcasting, Inc., 86 F.C.C.2d 993, 1009–10 (1981).

187. Id. at 1004–6.

188. Id. at 1015.

189. Id. at 1017.

190. 683 F.2d 503 (D.C.Cir. 1982).

191. Id. at 506.

192. Id., *quoting*, 86 F.C.C.2d at 1012.

193. Id.

194. Id. at 510.

195. Id.

196. Id. at 507.

197. Id. at 510.

198. 102 F.C.C.2d 1443 (1985).

199. Id.

200. Committee for Community Access v. Federal Communications Commission, 737 F.2d 74, 78 (D.C.Cir. 1984).

201. Central Florida Enterprises, Inc., v. Federal Communications Commission, 683 F.2d at 510.

202. Id.

203. *See* Bison City Television 49 Ltd. Partnership, 93 F.C.C.2d 4, 5 (1983).

204. *See* id.

205. 47 U.S.C. § 311 (c) (1).

206. Broadcast Renewal Applicants, 66 R.R. 2d 708 (1989).

207. Hearst Radio, Inc. (WBAL), 15 F.C.C.2d at 1178.

208. *See* 47 U.S.C. § 326.

209. Development of Policy Re: Changes in the Entertainment Format of Broadcast Stations, 60 F.C.C.2d 858, 863 (1976).

210. WNCN Listeners Guild v. Federal Communications Commission, 610 F.2d 838, 842 (D.C.Cir. 1979).

211. Citizens Committee to Save WEFM v. Federal Communications Commission, 506 F. 2d 246, 268 (D.C. Cir. 1974) (en banc).

212. 450 U.S. 582.

213. Id. at 604.

214. Id. at 593.

215. Id. at 595.

216. Id. at 589–90.

217. Id. at 590.

218. Id. at 601.

219. Id.

220. Id. at 603, *quoting* Red Lion Broadcasting Co. v. Federal Communications Commission, 395 U.S. at 390.

221. Id. at 604.

222. Id. The reluctance of the FCC and Court to intrude into program format is viewed approvingly in Spitzer, *Radio Formats by Administrative Choice*, 47 U. CHI. L.REV. 647 (1980).

223. 450 U.S. at 609 (Marshall, J., dissenting).

224. Id. at 614–17 (Marshall, J., dissenting).

225. Marshall suggested, for instance, taking account of extensive and genuine audience protest as evidence that the programming at issue uniquely serves the public interest. Id. at 619 n.36 (Marshall, J., dissenting).

226. *See* WEAM v. Federal Communications Commission, 808 F.2d 113, 117 (D.C.Cir. 1986).

227. 47 U.S.C. § 310(d).

228. Id.

229. *See* Applications for Voluntary Assignments or Transfer of Control, 32 F.C.C. 689, 690 (1962).

230. Id. at 690.

231. *See* Applications for Voluntary Assignments or Transfer of Control, 52 R.R.2d 1081 (1982).

232. Statement of Policy on Minority Ownership of Broadcast Facilities, 68 F.C.C.2d 979, 983 (1978).

233. Id.

234. Statement of Policy on Minority Ownership of Broadcast Facilities, 69 F.C.C.2d 1591, 1593 n.9 (1979).

235. 110 S. Ct. 2997.

236. *Id.*

237. 47 C.F.R. § 73.3555(c).

238. *Id.,* § 73.3555(d).

239. The statutory category of "other," as it is specifically identified among the basic qualifications concerning "citizenship, character, financial, technical and *other*" considerations, may be interpreted to include any factor relevant to the public interest (emphasis supplied).

240. A license may be revoked:

(1) for false statements knowingly made either in the application or in any statement of fact which may be required pursuant to section 308 of this title;
(2) because of conditions coming to the attention of the Commission which would warrant it in refusing to grant a license or permit on an original application;
(3) for willful or repeated failure to operate substantially as set forth in the license;
(4) for willful or repeated violation of, or willful or repeated failure to observe any provision of this chapter or any rule or regulation of the Commission

authorized by this chapter or by a treaty ratified by the United States;

(5) for violation of or failure to observe any final cease and desist order issued by the Commission under this section;

(6) for violation of section 1304, 1343, or 1464 of title 18; or

(7) for willful or repeated failure to allow reasonable access to or to permit purchase of reasonable amounts of time for the use of a broadcasting station by a legally qualified candidate for Federal elective office on behalf of his candidacy.

47 U.S.C. § 312(a). The FCC also has determined that licensees convicted of drug trafficking will be subject to Commission action including license revocation. Drug Trafficking Policy, 66 R.R. 2d 1617 (1989).

241. 47 U.S.C. § 307(c).

242. Fines are referred to by statute as forfeitures. 47 U.S.C. § 503 (b).

243. *Id.* at 503(b) (2).

244. *See* Weiss, Ostroff & Clift, *Station License Revocations and Denials of Renewal,* 1970–1978, 24 J. BROADCASTING 69, 69 (1980). The number approached the total revocations in the commission's entire history prior to 1970. *Id.*

245. *Id.* at 77. Intentional misrepresentations, even if relatively minor, are taken seriously because they cast doubt upon future reliability and integrity. *See* Federal Communications Commission v. WOKO, Inc., 329 U.S. 223, 229 (1946); Faulkner Radio, Inc., 61 F.C.C.2d 23, 24 (1976). For a critical evaluation of FCC standards applying to misrepresentations by licensees, *see* Murchison, *Misrepresentation and the FCC,* 37 FED. COM. L.J. 403 (1985).

246. *E.g.,* WLLE, Inc., 65 F.C.C.2d 774, 777 (1977).

247. *E.g., id.* (fraudulent billing practices); Monroe Broadcasters, Inc., 60 F.C.C.2d 792 (1976) (false advertising rate information).

248. Elimination of Unnecessary Broadcast Regulation, 59 R.R.2d 1500 (1986).

249. 47 U.S.C. § 326.

250. *E.g.,* Brandywine-Main Line Radio, Inc. v. Federal Communications Commission, 473 F.2d 16, 62 (D.C.Cir. 1972), *cert. denied,* 412 U.S. 922 (1973); United Broadcasting Co. v. Federal Communications Commission, 565 F.2d 699 (D.C.Cir. 1977). Such an option, however, merely may obscure constitutionally dubious content based regulatory impulses. *See generally* Columbia Broadcasting System, Inc. v. Democratic National Committee, 412 U.S. 94, 157–58 (1973) (Douglas, J., dissenting).

251. *See* New Indecency Enforcement Standards to be Applied to All Broadcast and Amateur Radio Licensees, 2 F.C.C. Rcd. at 2726.

252. Alabama Educational Television, 50 F.C.C.2d 461, 477 (1975).

253. Office of Communication, United Church of Christ v. Federal Communications Commission, 425 F.2d 543, 547–50 (D.C.Cir. 1969).

254. *Id.* at 547–48.

255. Anti-Defamation League of B'nai B'rith v. Federal Communications Commission, 403 F.2d 169, 170 (D.C.Cir. 1968), *cert. denied,* 394 U.S. 930 (1969).

256. *See* Syracuse Peace Council, 2 F.C.C. Rcd. at 5052–55.

257. 47 U.S.C. § 309(i) (1)–(2).

258. *Id.,* § 309 (i) (3).

Chapter 6

THE CABLE INDUSTRY

Cable television originated essentially as an auxiliary of broadcasting, but it has evolved into an independent medium which penetrates half of the nation's households.[1] The FCC generally describes cable as "(a) non-broadcast facility consisting of a set of closed transmission paths and associated signal generation, reception, and central equipment that is designed to provide cable service which includes video programming and which is provided to multiple subscribers within a community."[2] Although both cable and broadcast services transmit electronic signals generating sound and pictures on a television screen, the methodology for propagation is different. Broadcast signals travel over air; cable signals move along coaxial cable or fiber optic lines.

Problems with the effective transmission of broadcast signals are what originally led to the development of cable service. Given the limited range of broadcast emissions, and their susceptibility to interference from any obstacle between transmitting and receiving antennaes, cable emerged as a means for delivering television service of a high technical quality to areas that otherwise would be unserved. The first cable systems thus were constructed in areas which, because of remoteness or topographical impairment, essentially had no television. Cable service at the outset, therefore, consisted simply of a community antenna erected on high ground which picked up broadcast signals and retransmitted them by wire to subscribers.

1. REGULATORY HISTORY

A. INFERRED REGULATORY AUTHORITY

The Communications Act of 1934, as originally drawn, made no reference to cable. From cable television's emergence until Congress enacted legislation establishing a bifurcated scheme of federal and state regulation,[3] considerable debate existed over whether the Federal Communications Commission (FCC) had the authority to regulate the new medium. Initially, the commission itself declined jurisdiction on the grounds that it was not specifically delegated responsibility[4] and did not have adequate resources.[5] Although empowered to regulate common carriers and television, the FCC decided against including cable within the purview of the former[6] and concluded that cable did not affect broadcasting sufficiently to reach it concomitant with the duty to regulate it as a function of the public interest.[7]

After a decade of relative disinterest, the FCC began to take more seriously the impact of cable upon the broadcasting industry. It thus denied a common carrier's application to provide microwave service to a cable company because economic harm to a local broadcaster would adversely affect the public interest.[8] Given the FCC's statutory mandate to maximize the benefits of broadcasting service to the public and to guard the public interest,[9] the court of appeals in *Carter Mountain Transmission Corporation v. Federal Communications Commission*[10] concluded that the agency's concern for the economic viability of its licensees was appropriate.[11] A predicate thus began to evolve, which would operate until FCC jurisdiction was codified, which enabled the commission to regulate cable to the extent that it might impact broadcasting in a negative fashion.[12] That concern soon became the underpinning for the commission's formulation of a broad regulatory scheme. In 1966, the FCC assumed jurisdiction over all cable systems on the grounds that regulation of the new medium was critical to effectuation of its obligation to ensure efficient broadcast service.[13] Among other things, the commission expressed concern that cable's ability to import distant signals fragmented the audience of local broadcasters, diminished their revenue base, and thus impaired their service and viability.[14] Its particular worry was that ultrahigh frequency (UHF) service, which was relatively underdeveloped and not on a sound economic footing, was especially vulnerable.[15] Consequently, it adopted rules prohibiting the importation of signals into the hundred largest television markets unless the public interest would be served.[16]

1. The Reasonably Ancillary Jurisdictional Standard

The Supreme Court delineated federal jurisdiction over cable, at least until Congress charted it by statute when, in *United States v. Southwestern Cable Co.*,[17] it upheld the FCC's prohibition against importation of distant signals.[18] Finding "no need . . . to determine in detail the limits of the Commission's authority to regulate cable," the Court emphasized:

> that the authority which we recognize today under § 152(a) is restricted to that reasonably ancillary to the effective performance of the Commission's various responsibilities for the regulation of television broadcasting. The Commission may, for these purposes, issue "such rules and regulations and prescribe such restrictions and conditions, not inconsistent with law," as "public convenience, interest, or necessity requires." 47 U.S.C. § 303(r). We express no views as to the Commission's authority, if any, to regulate CATV under any other circumstances or for any other purposes.[19]

The Court recognized that the consequences of an unregulated cable industry could not be accurately forecast.[20] It found that the FCC's concerns with audience fragmentation and consequent revenue erosion in the broadcasting industry were legitimate and reasonable.[21] Given the commission's "broad responsibilities for the orderly development of an appropriate system of local television broadcasting,"[22] the Court considered it reasonable for the FCC to have concluded that "performance of these duties demand prompt and efficacious regulation of [cable] systems."[23]

Following the *Southwestern Cable Co.* decision, the FCC embarked on a regulatory course that engendered a panoply of rules governing cable systems. Premised upon its recognized ancillary jurisdiction, the commission promulgated regulations that affected both the industry's structure and programming content.[24] Protection of the "system of local broadcasting" has been blamed for stunting cable's growth during the 1970s and into the early 1980s.[25] The FCC's role attracted extensive criticism to the effect that it was "more concerned with protecting the economic interests of conventional broadcasters than with fully exploiting the resources of cable technology."[26] Regulation, especially to the extent that it governed content, raised First Amendment questions. In reviewing the various rules, however, the courts generally refrained from constitutional evaluation. Such analysis in part reflected a preference for assessments of whether the FCC had exceeded the authority which was inferred from its statutory obligations. Equally if not more significant to the course of review was uncertainty over cable's nature and its First Amendment status. The Supreme Court's references to community antenna television systems, in its early opinions,[27] intimated that cable at least then was being conceptualized largely as an auxiliary broadcast methodology rather than as an independent medium. Not until the mid–1980s would the Court declare in certain albeit unexplicated terms that cable was entitled to First Amendment protection.[28] To the extent that cable regulation has been directly confronted on content-related grounds, the pertinent issues are discussed in Chapter 10.

As FCC control of the cable industry became more aggressive and sweeping, the Court soon warned that the commission was pushing the limits of its jurisdiction. In *United States v. Midwest Video Corp.*,[29] the Court upheld origination rules that obligated cable systems with at least 3,500 subscribers to establish facilities for local production and program presentation.[30] The gist of the regulation was to make cable casters originate their own programming if they wanted to retransmit broadcast sig-

nals.[31] Without adverting to any constitutional issues concerning the invasion of editorial discretion,[32] the Court defined the critical question as "whether the Commission has reasonably determined that its origination rule will further the achievement of long-established regulatory goals in the field of television broadcasting by increasing the number of outlets for community self-expression and augmenting the public's choice of programs and types of services."[33] In finding that the requirement advanced those aims, the Court broadened the predicate for the FCC's jurisdiction. It observed that "the Commission's legitimate concern in the regulation of [cable] is not limited to controlling the competitive impact [cable] may have on broadcast services."[34] Rather:

> *Southwestern* refers to the Commission's "various responsibilities for the regulation of television broadcasting." These are considerably more numerous than simply assuring that broadcast stations operating in the public interest do not go out of business. Moreover, we must agree with the Commission that its "concern with CATV carriage of broadcast signals is not just a matter of avoidance of adverse effects, but extends also to requiring CATV affirmatively to further statutory policies." ... Since the avoidance of adverse effects is itself the furtherance of statutory policies, no sensible distinction even in theory can be drawn along those lines. More important, CATV systems, no less than broadcast stations, see, e.g., *Federal Radio Comm'n v. Nelson Bros. Co.*, 289 U.S. 266 (1933) (deletion of a station), may enhance as well as impair the appropriate provision of broadcast services. Consequently, to define the Commission's power in terms of the protection, as opposed to the advancement, of broadcasting objectives would artificially constrict the Commission in the achievement of its statutory purposes and be inconsistent with our recognition in *Southwestern* "that it was precisely because Congress wished 'to maintain, through appropriate administrative control, a grip on the dynamic aspects of radio trans-

mission,'...that it conferred upon the Commission a 'unified jurisdiction' and 'broad authority.' "[35]

The origination rule directly interested the FCC in the transmission of signals that did not primarily implicate the broadcast spectrum. Nonetheless, the Court concluded that:

the regulation is not the less, for that reason, reasonably ancillary to the Commission's jurisdiction over broadcast services. The effect of the regulation, after all, is to assure that in the retransmission of broadcast signals viewers are provided suitably diversified programming—the same objective underlying regulations sustained in *National Broadcasting Co. v. United States,*...as well as the local-carriage rule reviewed in *Southwestern* and subsequently upheld.... In essence the regulation is no different from Commission rules governing the technological quality of CATV broadcast carriage. In the one case, of course, the concern is with strength of the picture and voice received by the subscriber, while in the other it is with the content of the programming offered. But in both cases the rules serve the policies of §§ 1 and 303(g) of the Communications Act on which the cablecasting regulation is specifically premised,...and also, in the Commission's words, "facilitate the more effective performance of [its] duty to provide a fair, efficient, and equitable distribution of television service to each of the several States and communities" under § 307(b). In sum, the regulation preserves and enhances the integrity of broadcast signals and therefore is "reasonably ancillary to the effective performance of the Commission's various responsibilities for the regulation of television broadcasting."[36]

Chief Justice Burger, warning that the FCC had "strain[ed] the outer limits of... [its] jurisdiction,"[37] presaged an increasingly diminished role based upon ancillary authority. The FCC itself abandoned the cable origination rules in 1974.[38] It adopted regulations, however, that obligated most cable

systems to set aside channels for public, educational, leased, and local government access.[39] A few years earlier, it had rejected as a breach of the First Amendment a right of access in broadcasting,[40] which it also has referred to as the least constitutionally protected medium.[41] Avoiding any First Amendment issues,[42] the Court in *FCC v. Midwest Video Corp.*[43] determined that the access rules effectively had "relegated cable systems, *pro tanto,* to common-carrier status."[44] Although acknowledging the FCC's interest in maximizing opportunities for local expression and diversifying programming,[45] the Court found that the commission was precluded by statute from "treat[ing] persons engaged in broadcasting as common carriers."[46] Oddly, it observed that the access rules more seriously abrogated editorial control over program composition than the origination rules.[47] In another setting, the Court had depicted a mandatory publication rule as a patent invasion of editorial discretion.[48] The outer limits of jurisdiction reasonably ancillary to effectuate regulatory responsibilities in broadcasting, and which were pushed in the first *Midwest Video* case, thereby were exceeded in the second *Midwest Video* case.[49]

Shortly before invalidation of the access rules, the court of appeals, in *Home Box Office, Inc. v. Federal Communications Commission,*[50] had struck down regulations prohibiting the exhibition of certain feature films, major sporting events, and series programs on cable and subscription television.[51] The rules also barred commercial advertising and limited the total amount of program time that could be devoted to sports and feature films.[52] Such antisiphoning controls were designed to prevent the movement of popular fare from its established place on free television to pay services as a result of competitive bidding.[53] The court of appeals criticized the FCC for mouthing rationales in support of its action that recited acknowledged regulatory grounds but established no nexus between means and ends.[54] Noting that the rules prevented cable from competing for the subject programming, it could not see "(h)ow such an effect furthers any goal of the Communications Act."[55] The court of appeals noted for future reference that "the Commission, in developing its cable television regulations, [must] demonstrate that the objectives to be achieved by regulating cable television are also objectives for which the Commission could legitimately regulate the broadcast media."[56] As matters evolved, the FCC chose not to reintroduce the antisiphoning rules despite the court's observation that the commission might "after remand, be able to satisfy the jurisdictional prerequisites."[57] Instead, the FCC moved in the direction of deregulation. In 1980, the commission abandoned the distant importation rules[58] originally upheld in *Southwestern Cable*. It also eliminated the exclusivity rules which authorized local television stations, holding sole market rights to a syndicated program, to require cable operators to delete such shows when carried in from another market.[59] The court of appeals, characterizing the commission's action as "a major reversal of . . . regulatory policy,"[60] nonetheless concluded that repeal of the rules "reflects the 'rational weighing of competing policies' Congress intended to be exercised by the agency and to be sustained by a reviewing court."[61]

The FCC's sense, after approximately a decade of detailed regulation of the cable industry, was that the public interest would be promoted and served more effectively by increasing the exposure of both the broadcasting and cable industries to marketplace forces.[62] Surviving until recently from the initial outpouring of regulation governing the cable industry were must carry rules, which obligated cable systems to carry the signals of local stations.[63] Even those controls have been invalidated pursuant to the court

of appeals' decision in *Century Communications Corp. v. Federal Communications Commission*.[64] Reflecting cable's evolution from an auxiliary into an independent medium, the decision confronted constitutional questions and struck down the rules on First Amendment grounds.[65] Details of the issue thus are reserved for Chapter 10. Further indicative of cable's significance, however, was congressional enactment of a comprehensive scheme for regulating cable.

B. THE CABLE COMMUNICATIONS POLICY ACT OF 1984

Exactly half a century after Congress enacted a comprehensive regulatory scheme for broadcasting, it did likewise for cable. Unlike other provisions of the Communications Act of 1934, the Cable Communications Policy Act of 1984[66] divides regulatory authority between federal and state government. The Cable Act is the product of competing and converging interests of federal, state, and local authorities and the cable industry itself. Prior to its enactment, regulation largely was an extension of federal power asserted ancillary to governance of broadcasting in the public interest.[67] To the distress of state and local governments, the FCC had adopted a stance to the effect that its rules and regulations largely preempted their role. In *Capital Cities Cable, Inc. v. Crisp*,[68] the Supreme Court appeared to endorse the FCC's position that it had exclusive jurisdiction over the operational aspects of cable.[69] The cable industry itself tended to favor a minimum role for state and local governments, which made competing and what operators regarded as unrealistic demands upon potential franchisees. A special point of concern for cable operators was that, even if they received a franchise and invested the substantial amount of capital necessary to commence service, no assurance existed that the grant would be renewed.

The Cable Act thus emerged from negotiations among federal, state, and local government and the industry for the purpose of "establish[ing] a national policy concerning cable communications."[70] Among its other aims are to:

(2) establish franchise procedures and standards which encourage the growth and development of cable systems and which assure that cable systems are responsive to the needs and interests of the local community;
(3) establish guidelines for the exercise of Federal, State, and local authority with respect to the regulation of cable systems;
(4) assure and encourage that cable communications provide and are encouraged to provide the widest possible diversity of information sources and services to the public;
(5) establish an orderly process for franchise renewal which protects cable operators against unfair denials of renewal where the operator's past performance and proposal for future performance meet the standards established by this title; and
(6) promote competition in cable communications and minimize unnecessary regulation that would impose an undue economic burden on cable systems.[71]

Courts have identified:

two predominant objectives of the Cable Act: 1) to make the local franchising process the primary means of cable television regulation, and 2) to insure that the public receives the widest possible diversity of information services, in a manner which is responsive to the needs and interests of the local communities.[72]

Jurisdiction over cable thus is partially vested in the FCC, which sets policy concerning pole attachments,[73] access,[74] cross-ownership,[75] rates,[76] technical standards,[77] and employment policy.[78] Primary franchising authority is conferred upon state and local government.[79]

The Cable Act specifies that "(n)othing in

this title shall be construed to affect any authority of any State, political subdivision, or agency thereof, or franchising authority, regarding matters of public health, safety and welfare consistent with the express provision of this title."[80] While expressly acknowledging the pertinence of state and local police powers, such language makes it clear that they may not be used contrary to the terms or implications of the Cable Act. Litigation already has demonstrated that the lines between federal and state or local responsibility are less than clear. Although express statutory commands make it certain that states may not adopt conflicting cross-ownership rules,[81] regulate rates,[82] or treat cable operators as common carriers,[83] disputes seem likely to arise or already have emerged in other areas where the lines of authority are less clear. Such questions, which almost invariably center upon whether states can impose higher standards than the federal government, have arisen with respect to technical rules.[84] The Supreme Court, in *City of New York v. Federal Communications Commission*,[85] sided with federal regulators in determining that commission standards governing technical quality preempted stricter local criteria.[86] Since the FCC explicitly had stated its intent to preempt state and local regulation,[87] the outcome turned upon whether it was acting within the purview of its authority.[88] Although franchising authorities under the Cable Act "could regulate 'services, facilities, and equipment' in certain respects,"[89] the Court found dispositive a specific charge for the FCC to govern technical standards.[90] That legislative command, the Court determined, preserved the regulatory state of affairs preceding the Cable Act.[91] Nothing in the act itself or history, moreover, "indicated[d] that Congress explicitly had disapproved of the Commission's preemption of local technical standards."[92]

City of New York v. Federal Communications Commission, 108 S.Ct. 637 (1988)

Justice White delivered the opinion of the Court.

The Federal Communications Commission has adopted regulations that establish technical standards to govern the quality of cable television signals and that forbid local authorities from imposing more stringent technical standards. The issue is whether in doing so the Commission has exceeded its statutory authority.

I

This case deals with yet another development in the ongoing efforts of federal, state, and local authorities to regulate different aspects of cable television over the past three decades. See *Capital Cities Cable, Inc. v. Crisp,* 467 U.S. 691, 700–705 (1984); *United States v. Southwestern Cable Co.,* 392 U.S. 157, 161–178, 88 S.Ct. 1994, 1996–2005, 20 L.Ed.2d 1001 (1968). With the incipient development of cable television in the 1950s and 1960s from what had been more generally known as community antenna television systems, the Federal Communications Commission began to assert regulatory authority in this area. See *CATV Second Report and Order,* 2 F.C.C.2d 725 (1966). In 1972, the Commission first asserted authority over technical aspects of cable television and devised technical standards to govern the transmission of broadcast signals by cable, though without pre-empting regulation of similar matters by state or local franchising authorities. *Cable Television Report and Order,* 36 F.C.C.2d 143, on reconsideration, 36 F.C.C.2d 326 (1972), aff'd *sub nom. American Civil Liberties Union v. FCC,* 523 F.2d 1344 (CA9 1975). Within two years, however, the Commission became convinced from its experience with conflicting federal and local technical standards that there is "a compelling need for national uniformity in cable television technical standards" which would require it to pre-empt the field of signal-quality regulation in order to meet the "necessity to rationalize, interrelate, and bring into uniformity the myriad standards now being developed by numerous jurisdictions." *Cable Television Report and Order,* 49 F.C.C.2d 470,

477, 480 (1974). The Commission explained that a multiplicity of mandatory and nonuniform technical requirements undermined "the ultimate workability of the over-all system," could have "a deleterious effect on the development of new cable services," and could "seriously imped[e]" the "development and marketing of signal source, transmission, and terminal equipment." *Id.* at 478–479.

In 1984, the Court approved the pre-emptive authority that the Commission had asserted over the regulation of cable television systems. We held that in the Communications Act of 1934, Congress authorized the Commission "to regulate all aspects of interstate communication by wire or radio," including the subsequently developed medium of cable television, and that the Commission's authority "extends to all regulatory actions 'necessary to ensure the achievement of the Commission's statutory responsibilities.' " *Crisp, supra,* 467 U.S. at 700, 104 S.Ct. at 2701, quoting *FCC v. Midwest Video Corp.,* 440 U.S. 689, 706 (1979). Although the state law that was invalidated in *Crisp* regulated commercial advertising on cable television, rather than the technical quality of cable television signals, the Court recognized that for 10 years the Commission had "retained exclusive jurisdiction over all operational aspects of cable communication, including signal carriage and technical standards." *Crisp, supra,* 467 U.S. at 702.

A few months after the Court's decision in *Crisp,* Congress enacted the Cable Communications Policy Act of 1984 (Cable Act or Act), 98 Stat. 2780, 47 U.S.C. §§ 521–559 (1982 ed., Supp. III). Among its objectives in passing the Cable Act, Congress purported to "establish a national policy concerning cable communications" and to "minimize unnecessary regulation that would impose an undue economic burden on cable systems." 47 U.S.C. §§ 521(1), (6). The Act was also intended to establish guidelines for the exercise of Federal, State, and local authority with respect to the regulation of cable systems" through procedures and standards that "encourage the growth and development of cable systems and which assure that cable systems are responsive to the needs and interests of the local community." §§ 521(3), (2).

The Cable Act left franchising to state or local

authorities; those authorities were also empowered to specify the facilities and equipment that franchisees were to use, provided such requirements were "consistent with this title." Cable Act, §§ 624(a), (b), 47 U.S.C. § 544(a), (b) (1982 ed., Supp. III). Section 624(e) of the Cable Act provided that "[t]he Commission may establish technical standards relating to the facilities and equipment of cable systems which a franchising authority may require in the franchise." 47 U.S.C. § 544(e).

In 1985, the Commission promulgated regulations that would establish technical standards governing signal quality for one of four different classes of cable television channels and that would forbid local cable franchising authorities from imposing their own standards on any of the four classes of channels. 50 Fed.Reg. 7801, 7802 (1985). The Commission eventually adopted a modified version of these regulations, which reaffirmed the Commission's established policy of pre-empting local regulation of technical signal quality standards for cable television. *Id.*, at 52462, 52464–52465. The Commission found its statutory authority to adopt the regulations in § 624(e) of the Cable Act, 47 U.S.C. 544(e) (1982 ed., Supp. III), and in 47 U.S.C. §§ 154(i) and 303(r). 50 Fed.Reg., at 52466. Petitioners (the cities of New York, Miami, and Wheaton, and the National League of Cities) sought review of the regulations in federal court, where they contested the scope of the pre-emptive authority claimed by the Commission and insisted that franchising authorities could impose stricter technical standards than those specified by the Commission. . . .

III

A

In this case, there is no room for doubting that the Commission intended to pre-empt state technical standards governing the quality of cable television signals. In adopting the regulations at issue here, the Commission said:

> Technical standards that vary from community to community create potentially serious negative consequences for cable system operators and cable consumers in terms of the cost of service and the ability

of the industry to respond to technological changes. To address this problem, we proposed in the *Notice* to retain technical standards guidelines at the federal level which could be used, but could not be exceeded, in state and local technical quality regulations. . . .

> After a review of the record in this proceeding, we continue to believe that the policy adopted in 1974 was effective, should remain in force, and is entirely consistent with both the specific provisions and the general policy objectives underlying the 1984 Cable Act. This preemption policy has constrained state and local regulation of cable technical performance to Class I channels and has prohibited performance standards more restrictive than those contained in the Commission's rules. The reasons that caused the adoption of this policy appear to be as valid today as they were when the policy was first adopted. 50 Fed. Reg., at 52464.

As noted above, the policy adopted by the Commission in 1974, which was continued in effect by the 1985 regulations, was a pre-emptive policy applying in the area of technical standards governing signal quality. 49 F.C.C.2d, at 477–481. Since the Commission has explicitly stated its intent to exercise exclusive authority in this area and to pre-empt state and local regulation, this case does not turn on whether there is an actual conflict between federal and state law here, or whether compliance with both federal and state standards would be physically impossible. *De la Cuesta, supra,* 458 U.S., at 153, 102 S.Ct., at 3022.

B

The second part of the inquiry is whether the Commission is legally authorized to pre-empt state and local regulation that would establish complementary or additional technical standards, where it clearly is possible for a cable operator to comply with these standards in addition to the federal standards. We have identified at least two reasons why this part of the inquiry is crucial to our determination of the pre-emption issue. "First, an agency literally has no power to act, let alone pre-empt the validly enacted legislation of a sovereign State, unless and until Congress confers power upon it. Second, the best way of determining whether Congress intended the regulations of an administrative agency to displace state law is to examine the nature and scope of the authority granted by Congress to the agency." *Louisiana Public Service Comm'n, supra,* 476 U.S., at 374. The second reason was particularly relevant in *Louisiana Public Service Comm'n* because there we were obliged to assess the import of a statutory section in which Congress appeared to have explicitly limited the Commission's jurisdiction, so as to forbid it from preempting state laws concerning the manner in which telephone companies could depreciate certain plant and equipment. *Id.,* at 369–376, 379, construing 47 U.S.C. § 152(b).

We conclude here that the Commission acted within the statutory authority conferred by Congress when it pre-empted state and local technical standards governing the quality of cable television signals. When Congress enacted the Cable Act in 1984, it acted against a background of federal pre-emption on this particular issue. For the preceding 10 years, the Commission had pre-empted such state and local technical standards under its broad delegation of authority to "[m]ake such rules and regulations and prescribe such restrictions and conditions, not inconsistent with law, as may be necessary to carry out the provisions of this chapter [the communications laws, Title 47 of the U.S. Code, Chapter 5]," as a means of implementing its legitimate discretionary power to determine what the "public convenience, interest, or necessity requires" in this field. 47 U.S.C. §§ 303 and 303(r); see also 49 F.C.C.2d, at 481; 47 U.S.C. § 154(i). The Court's decision in *Crisp,* which was handed down during the time Congress was considering the legislation that within a few months became the Cable Act, broadly upheld the Commission's pre-emptive authority in very similar respects. 467 U.S., at 701–705, 104 S.Ct., at 2701–2703.

In the Cable Act, Congress sanctioned in relevant respects the regulatory scheme that the Commission had been following since 1974. In § 624 of the Cable Act, Congress specified that the local franchising authority could regulate "services, facilities, and equipment" in certain respects, and could enforce those requirements, but § 624(e) of the Act grants the Commission the power to "establish technical standards relating to the facilities and equipment of cable systems which a franchising authority may require in the franchise." 47 U.S.C. §§ 544(a)-(e) (1982 ed.,

Supp. III). This mirrors the state of the regulatory law before the Cable Act was passed, which permitted the local franchising authorities to regulate many aspects of cable services, facilities, and equipment but not to impose technical standards governing cable signal quality, since the Commission had explicitly reserved this power to the Federal Government.

It is also quite significant that nothing in the Cable Act or its legislative history indicates that Congress explicitly disapproved of the Commission's pre-emption of local technical standards. Given the difficulties the Commission had experienced in this area, which had caused it to reverse its ground in 1974 after two years of unhappy experience with the practical consequences of inconsistent technical standards imposed by various localities, we doubt that Congress intended to overturn the Commission's decade-old policy without discussion or even any suggestion that it was doing so. To the contrary, the House Report which discusses this section of the Act portrays it as nothing more than a straightforward endorsement of current law:

> Subsection (e) allows the Commission to set technical standards related to facilities and equipment required by a franchising authority pursuant to a franchising agreement. This provision does not affect the authority of a franchising authority to establish standards regarding facilities and equipment in the franchise pursuant to section 624(b) which are not inconsistent with standards established by the FCC under this subsection. H.R. Rep. No. 98–934, p. 70 (1984), U.S. Code Cong. & Admin. News, 1984, pp. 4655, 4707.

This passage from the House Report makes clear that the Act was not intended to work any significant change in the law in the respects relevant to this case. By noting that § 624(e) authorizes "the Commission to set technical standards related to facilities and equipment" and that it "does not affect the authority of a franchising authority to establish standards regarding facilities and equipment" that are not inconsistent with Commission standards, the House Report indicates both that Congress did not intend to remove from the Commission its longstanding power to establish pre-emptive technical standards, and that Congress did not intend to "affect the authority of a franchising authority" to set standards in these and similar matters regarding cable facilities and equipment. In particular, Congress did not manifest any intent to "affect the authority" of local franchising authorities by giving them the power to supplement the technical standards set by the Commission with respect to the quality of cable signals, a power which they generally had not been permitted to exercise for the last 10 years and which, according to the Commission's consistent view, disserves the public interest. Petitioners insist that under § 624, as evidenced by the passage from the House Report quoted above, a franchising authority may specify any technical standards that do not conflict with Commission standards and hence may set stricter standards for signal quality. But this disregards the Commission's own power to pre-empt, an authority that we do not believe Congress intended to take away in the Cable Act. And it also disregards the Commission's explicit findings, based on considerable experience in this area, that complementary or additional technical standards set by state and local authorities do conflict with the basic objectives of federal policy with respect to cable television—findings that the Commission first articulated in 1974 and then reiterated in 1986. See 49 F.C.C.2d, at 478–479; 50 Fed.Reg., at 52464–52465.

In sum, we find nothing in the Cable Act which leads us to believe that the Commission's decision to pre-empt local technical standards governing the quality of cable signals "is not one that Congress would have sanctioned." *Shimer,* 367 U.S., at 383. We therefore affirm the judgment of the Court of Appeals.

Despite narrowly construing the state's power to regulate service, facilities, and equipment in the *City of New York* case, and consistently endorsing a preemptive federal role in the controversies presented to it so far,[93] the potential for a mixed federal and state role with varying standards remains in other areas. Federal law governing cable employment practices,[94] for instance, might not preempt a state equal employment opportunity law that sets higher standards or imposes redundant or stiffer reporting requirements. Such variances between fed-eral and state law exist and are countenanced in the broader marketplace.

Arguments that a state may not prohibit a cable company from collecting monetary contributions from certain residents to finance construction in sparsely populated parts of a franchise area have been couched in terms of preemption.[95] Characterizing the construction contributions as rates, one cable company asserted that they were the exclusive concern of the FCC.[96] The district court in *Housatonic Cable Vision Co. v. Department of Public Utility Control,*[97] however, determined that such contributions were not rates for the purposes of the Cable Act.[98] It further concluded that provisions prohibiting "discrimination among customers of basic cable service"[99] and ensuring service to all potential groups of subscribers regardless of income supported the state's regulatory action.[100] The short history of the Cable Act thus demonstrates that lines of regulatory authority are to be influenced as much by litigation as by legislation.

1. Franchising

A franchise for a cable operator in many ways is the functional equivalent of a license for a broadcaster. Both enable the grantee to provide service for a fixed period of time. Unlike a broadcast license, which is awarded by the FCC, franchises are the responsibility of state and local government.[101] The Cable Act provides that a franchising authority, bounded by the terms of the statute, "may award . . . one or more franchises within its jurisdiction."[102] The terms of empowerment include a provision obligating the franchising authority to "assure that access to cable service is not denied to any group of potential cable subscribers because of the income of the residents of the local area in which such group resides."[103] A district court has cited that statutory charge in precluding a cable operator from effectively imposing higher charges on residents in a less profitable part of its franchise area as the condition for extending service to them.[104] The Cable Act also provides for modification[105] and renewal[106] of a franchise.

A. INITIAL FRANCHISE DECISION

Award of an exclusive cable franchise by a city may constitute an antitrust violation.[107] In *Community Communications Co., Inc. v. City of Boulder, Colorado*,[108] the Supreme Court determined that a home rule municipality did not qualify for state action immunity from federal antitrust laws unless it was effectuating a clear and overt state policy.[109] Although cable television franchises as a consequence tend to be nonexclusive in their terms, in reality they amount to a de facto monopoly. That consequence is a function of investment considerations. Because front end costs of wiring a community are so substantial, it generally is assumed that divided subscriptions would destroy profitability.

Given the practical status of cable in most instances as a monopoly, the franchising process has witnessed enormous competition and abuse. Local government has an interest in receiving the best possible service, which may induce unrealistic promises and bids by cable operators or unreasonable demands by officials. Often, overpromises which led to a franchise have been followed by efforts to renegotiate terms when it became clear that profitability would be dubious. Under such circumstances, franchising authorities have a choice of either acceding to scaled-down service or pursuing costly litigation that will delay the advent of cable in the community. A seamy appearance to the whole process was compounded by the tactics of applicants who, for instance, would award shares in the local cable company to prominent citizens. Since it was obvious that the value of the stock would soar if their company received the franchise, it was assumed that the individuals would exert whatever influence they might possess upon the selection process.

The assumption that cable is a natural monopoly is not a point of universal subscription. A court of appeals has observed "that the City's cable television market is currently a natural monopoly which, under present technology, offers room for only one operator at a time."[110] Another court, however, has found award of an exclusive franchise inimical to First Amendment interests.[111] In so doing, it demanded proof of a substantial government interest beyond mere recitation of the notion that a service area will economically support only one cable operator.[112] The following article, apart from depicting some of the less attractive aspects of the franchising process, asserts that cable and competition are not mutually exclusive.

Barnes, "The Cable Conspiracy," *The Washington Monthly*, June 1989, at 12.*

In 1982, Sacramento, Calif., became one of the last major metropolitan areas to decide to wire its residents for cable television. Assuming that cable was a "natural monopoly," similar to a public utility, Sacramento saw little reason not to copy the 5,000 other cities and counties across America and announce that it was accepting bids for a cable television "franchise." The lucky winner would have the right to provide cable service within the city and country of Sacramento in exchange for paying a "franchise fee" (which, as in most places, ran about 5 percent of revenues). Such franchise rights, in turn, would leave the company in control of a market that would generate revenues of about $60-million a year. That, at least, was the plan until a revolutionary new idea in cable economics—competition—rudely forced its way onto the Sacramento stage. This intrusion has left the nation's cable monopolists

---

*Reprinted with permission from The Washington Monthly. Copyright by the Washington Monthly Company, 1611 Connecticut Ave., N.W., Washington, D.C. 20009.

ill at ease and lent a bit of hope to the nation's cable consumers, who have been courted, then fleeced, from coast to coast. That's right, consumers—remember them?

Until the early 1960s, cable was little more than what it had been at its inception in the late 1940s: a way of bringing clear signals to poor reception areas, such as those in Pennsylvania's coal country. As cable operators began to add signals from distant viewing areas, however, broadcasters started to worry that their "exclusive" television licenses were being infringed upon. The Federal Communications Commission (FCC), which up to this point had pretty much ignored cable television, suddenly spewed forth regulations. Cable companies could carry only two stations in addition to local broadcasting stations. If a network affiliate in a top 50 market bought the rights to, say, *Hogan's Heroes*, the cable company could not import a signal from another station that also showed *Hogan's Heroes.* Cable stations could not show movies that were less than three years old or more than 10. They could not produce their own programing. And on and on.

The federal barriers to cable operation began to erode with a series of court and FCC decisions in the 1970s, and by the early '80s most of these regulatory inanities had been removed. Once the feds were out of the way, however, and cable was ready to show what it could do, another gatekeeper appeared: local government.

When the average American politician spies the chance to regulate a public franchise, his soul begins to sing, because life's experience has shown that such power easily leads to enrichment, either through new campaign contributions from those anxious for his favor or from the more direct solicitations known as graft. This has been the case with everything from liquor licenses to race tracks, and so it was with cable. The local politicians quickly set out to rationalize their role.

The normal law of economics, that competition between suppliers keeps prices low and the level of service high, simply did not apply to cable television, they argued. Powerful economies of scale made cable a "natural monopoly." Cable companies had to dig up city streets and make their way into people's homes; flat-out competition for something this large and intrusive was simply uneconomical. Moreover, the politicians argued, left

to their own devices the cable operators would bypass poorer neighborhoods. It was therefore incumbent upon local politicians to choose one supplier that would offer the best deal for consumers.

While cities could offer licenses to operate, there's one thing they couldn't do: regulate prices. A 1984 federal deregulation act stripped them of that right. This left consumers with the worst of both worlds. Having set up effective monopolies in what is now a $14.5-billion industry, city governments were powerless to control the resulting prices. For the cable companies it became a situation of gouge-as-gouge-can. Nationally, the price for cable service rose about 32 percent from 1984 to 1988. In Washington, D.C., families with young children now have to pay $33 a month for full service—or risk leaving their kids with a complex from being the only ones on the block without the Disney channel. As prices skyrocketed, city councils were forced to resort to impotent resolutions of protest. But they could harrumph all they liked as far as the cable operators were concerned; if a cable monopoly wasn't exactly a license to print money, it was the next best thing.

Congress is scheduled to hold hearings this summer to investigate the charge of price-gouging, and legislators have begun to wonder whether the 1984 deregulation should be reversed. That means that government may again muck things up. The problem isn't that there's been too much deregulation but that there hasn't been enough. And the answer isn't government price-setting, it's competition.

HERE A BRIBE, THERE A BRIBE

Cynics may suspect that the politicians who concocted the current system had more than the public interest in mind. The benefits to the politicians? They could shake down potential cable operators for hefty campaign contributions. Their stretched city budgets could be replenished with "franchise fees." Community groups could demand that franchises build elaborate "public access" studios for local programing, often starring—surprise!—the groups and the politicians themselves.

It's not just politicians who benefit from the

monopolies but the politicians' well-connected friends too. The properly connected found themselves being offered cable stock by bidders in exchange for the right words whispered in the right ears. In Denver in 1982, one city council member said that the only person she knew who didn't own cable stock was the coach of her son's Little League team. Then again, he didn't live in Denver.

Investigations by the FBI and local district attorneys have revealed widespread corruption in the cable industry, from its beginning to the present. In the mid–1970s Irving Kahn, head of Teleprompter, a pioneer in the cable industry, went to federal prison for trying to bribe the mayor of Johnstown, Pa. Allegations of cable corruption were part of the problem for Donald Manes, the Queens borough president who killed himself while under investigation. A recent *Wall Street Journal* editorial, quoting court papers, drew this portrait of a 1982 meeting between Manes and a cable executive: "Fearing the room was bugged, Manes tried unsuccessfully to communicate through hand gestures and lip movements his desire for a bribe." (Areas of America still without cable might try this pantomime as a parlor game, *Name that Bribe*.) In Sacramento, the man who chaired the Metropolitan Cable Commission when the monopoly contract was awarded, William M. Bryan, is himself now on trial in federal court for bribery. Prosecutors say Bryan attempted to steer a contract to a cable businessman in exchange for a $150,000 line of credit. In sentencing a Washington lawyer to jail in 1985, Federal District Judge Susan Getzendanner commented, "I think it was a bribe, and apparently what goes on in the cable industry all the time."

A JURY SHAKES THE SYSTEM

Back now to Sacramento, and the unraveling of this seamy system:

After much lobbying, the franchise contract first went to the United Tribune Cable Co. in 1982. Though the company had seemed eager to promise the world in exchange for the franchise, subsequently it balked at some of its extravagant pledges, such as planting 20,000 trees in the area.

United Tribune dropped out. The bidding was reopened.

One of the bidders was River City Cable Company, formed by a group of 73 local investors—whom the press later dubbed the "Gang of 73"—each making $2,000 investments. None of the people involved with River City had the least experience is running a cable television company, and $146,000 in working capital isn't much for starting one. But they had something more important: clout. The Gang of 73 was a Who's Who of Sacramento's politically powerful and well-connected, including Michael Deaver and a sitting federal district judge. Each investor was told by the organizers of the venture that they stood to realize a profit of as much as $120,000 or more by the mid–1990s, according to subsequent trial testimony. To actually run the system, the shell that called itself River City Cable teamed up with Scripps-Howard Broadcasting to form Sacramento Cable Television; the Gang of 73 owned 5 percent of this corporation. The combination of clout and capability worked. In 1983, Sacramento Cable was selected over four other bidders by the Sacramento Metropolitan Cable Commission to run the local system. All seemed smooth sailing.

One man who wasn't satisfied, however, was Rod Hansen, president of Pacific West Cable and one of the unsuccessful bidders. All he had was a cable company—no Gang of 73. He decided to apply to operate a second cable system in the city. "(The cable commission) told me that I was wasting my time," Hansen says. "When I persisted, they said I would have to put up a $40,000 nonrefundable deposit and all this other stuff. And even if I did that, they still told me my chances were nonexistent."

Had Hansen accepted that answer, that's where things would have ended. Instead, he got in touch with Harold Farrow, a noted First Amendment lawyer in Oakland. Hansen filed suit in 1983 charging that the city and county of Sacramento had violated his First Amendment rights of free speech by awarding what amounted to a monopoly to one company. Farrow argued that the process of granting cable franchises was akin to "the business of licensing the press that we thought we were done with a couple of hundred years ago."

It took four years for the case to come to trial in federal district court, but when the jury ruled, the whole cable television industry sat up and took notice. The judge asked the jury for certain findings of fact. The answers shocked the defendants.

Question: "Was the 'natural monopoly' argument a sham by defendants (city and council) to obtain increased campaign contributions for local elected officials?"

Answer: "Yes."

Question: "Were defendants motivated to provide such benefits (public access channels and other community grants) by either a desire to obtain increased political influence for elected or appointed local officials or a desire to favor local officials' political supporters?"

Answer: "Yes."

Jurors later told local press that it was the "influence peddling" by the Gang of 73 that had obtained the franchise for Sacramento Cable. "We felt the way the whole thing was written up was to exclude competition and it had to do with this Gang of 73," juror Judith Mosier told the *Sacramento Bee.*

COMPETITION ARISES, RATES FALL

This unexpected defeat was so total that the city and county did not even bother to appeal the jury verdict. Instead, the cable commission immediately rewrote its ordinance to allow free competition, requiring applicants only to obtain a license and bond from the government before tearing up the streets. Subsequently *two* other companies entered the fray—Hansen's Pacific West and Cable AmeriCal, which Sacramento Cable eventually bought out for $11-million.

One of the most frequently repeated arguments in favor of franchising is that without the guaranteed profits that come with a monopoly, no cable company would provide service to the poorest neighborhoods. Fewer poor people would buy the service, and they would default more often than their more prosperous neighbors—or so the theory went. Sacramento Cable set out to make this a self-fulfilling prophecy when, upon losing its monopoly status, it announced it was dropping plans to wire the low-income neighborhood of Oak Park. But a storm of public protest caused Sacramento Cable to reverse its decision. At the same time, Pacific West applied for a license to wire Oak Park, too. So it is supremely ironic that one of the city's lowest-income sections is likely to be one of the first in the area with competing cable systems.

The poor-will-suffer theory of cable monopoly was flawed anyway—poor people tend to watch television more avidly than others, making poor neighborhoods ripe markets. And the bunching of homes close together makes them cheaper to wire. In fact it's the poor who often subsidize service to affluent suburbs, which pay the same rates even though the distance between homes makes them more expensive to reach.

Competition brought another boon to Sacramento consumers: cheaper prices. As part of the settlement of a lawsuit by the city against Sacramento Cable for various non-payments, the company won the right to charge different rates in different neighborhoods, something the franchise agreement had prohibited. A few months after raising its rates to $16.50 for basic service, Sacramento Cable turned around and waived installation fees, offered several months of free viewing, and matched Pacific West's price of $13.50—but only, of course, in those areas where Pacific West had begun stringing cable. None of this solicitous behavior was on display in neighborhoods where Sacramento Cable still had its monopoly.

PROMISE NOW, AMEND LATER

Citizens seem to accept the "natural monopoly" argument with surprising alacrity. If cable is such a "natural monopoly," then why would city and state governments—not to mention companies with a franchise—go to such extraordinary lengths to enforce this supposed law of economics? As Rod Hansen and Pacific West were making progress in the Sacramento lawsuit, other cable operators made a beeline for the state capitol. They got legislation passed in both chambers to give local officials the authority to bar competitors on the grounds of—what else?—"the public interest." Gov. George Deukmejian vetoed the bill.

The same kind of lobbying to bolster this "natural monopoly" with unnatural help has occurred across the country. The city of New York spent years trying (unsuccessfully, as it turned out) to prevent an independent satellite cable provider from operating in Co-op City, the world's largest private apartment complex. Similarly, Dallas tried unsuccessfully to prevent a satellite provider from competing with its local franchised cable firm. Don Barden, who holds the Detroit franchise, includes a clause in his contracts that forbids his customers from contracting with any other operator, including satellite reception services or so-called "wireless cable".

But doesn't a contract with a franchise provide guarantees that consumers wouldn't have if they simply took their chances on whoever came in? This is one of the first arguments employed by the monopolists. It is also one of the most bogus. Before the contracts are signed, there is precious little a cable operator won't promise. They pledge gargantuan systems of 120 channels (less than half of which are generally used). Sacramento had its infamous 20,000 trees. Miami forced its franchise holder to finance a drug rehabilitation program. One of the favorite scams is the so-called "public access" channels. These are meant to appeal to a democratic dream—local studios providing talk shows and other programing on local issues. In reality, they typically become flatulence forums for windbag politicians, attracting little viewer interest.

Where cable operators have managed to keep their monopolistic grip, consumers have paid the price. Thomas Hazlett, a professor of economics at the University of California at Davis who has testified as an expert witness in numerous anti-franchising lawsuits, estimates that all the "bells and whistles" promised in order to win the franchise probably add 20 to 30 percent to the average customer's bill. "If a typical cable consumer pays $25 a month for basic service and a premium channel," he says, "at least $5 to $7 of that results from politically imposed costs, most of which is pure waste . . . (a) dollar so the mayor and his friends can have their own talk shows that nobody watches, and on and on."

Promise-the-moon is the m.o. only until the ink dries. The next step is equally predictable: once the franchise is awarded, the lucky winner shuffles sheepishly back to the city and admits that many of the promises were, financially speaking, quite unrealistic. The "giveback" negotiations then get under way. In a study of the 30 largest markets in the country, Hazlett found that 21 of them had acceded to givebacks. In eight of those instances, the givebacks occurred before a single home was wired.

Speedy hookups, anyone? Washington, D.C. began its franchising process in 1982, and the city is still less than half wired. Meanwhile, suburbs of San Diego, Phoenix, and parts of Fairfax, Va.—some of the few areas of the country that did not bother with franchising—got their MTV faster than their neighbors, who enjoyed the "protection" of the monopoly system.

TIME TO STOP PLAYING CABLE MONOPOLY

In contrast to the sordid record left by cable monopolists are a few examples of communities willing to allow competition. Their experience shows how well it works. From 1971 to 1984, the residents of Bryan and College Station, Texas, enjoyed direct competition for viewers, and customers saw their cable rates drop to the lowest in the state. In March 1986, the city of Huntsville gave a company called Cable Alabama, which had been operating in surrounding Madison County, permission to compete with Group W, the franchise holder. Residents had frequently complained about Group W's service and price— $10.45 a month for 12 channels. Cable Alabama offered 50 channels for $8.95 a month—more than four times as many channels for less money.

UA/Columbia and Cablevision of New Jersey have been the competitors in Hillsdale and Paramus, N.J., for a decade now. Borough Clerk Elizabeth Roter says the situation results in high awareness among the residents of cable rates between the two companies. A recent promotion campaign had both companies reducing charges to $9.95 a month, and both often offer reduced installation charges.

Probably the best known competition success story is Allentown, Pa., which has about 150,000 subscribers. Two companies, Service Electric and Twin County Cable, have provided state-of-the-art service to the residents since the early 1960s. Joe Rosenfeld, Allentown's cable administrator, says the two companies are keen competitors.

Complaints are few, he says, and if people are dissatisfied, they usually just switch companies.

Even if competition doesn't actually take place, or eventually comes to an end, the mere prospect of it can have remarkable effects. The residents of Presque Isle, Maine, complained about their small (12 channel) cable service for a long time. The city government finally announced plans to bring in a competitor. The franchise holder almost immediately upgraded to a 54 channel system.

Instead of allowing cities and counties to regulate cable rates, Congress should simply forbid franchising. There is no reason a cable operator cannot be treated under the law in exactly the same way as any developer who wants to build a house or an office building. He applies for a right of way to use the necessary public property and posts a bond to cover any damages incurred while ripping up streets or stringing wire along telephone poles.

Decades of Cable Monopoly have put franchise holders on Park Place, sent local officials directly to jail, and left hapless consumers with Virginia Avenue service. Time for a new game: Free Enterprise.[113]

B. Franchise Modification

The Cable Act sets forth conditions under which a cable operator may have its franchise modified.[114] By its terms, it does not necessarily operate as a deterrent to overpromising as a means of obtaining a franchise. A not uncommon demand upon applicants, as the condition of receiving a franchise, has been the setting aside of access channels along with the construction of facilities and provisions of equipment for access programming. Federal law provides, however, that:

> [d]uring the period a franchise is in effect, the cable operator may obtain from the franchising authority modification of . . . requirements for facilities or equipment, including public, educational, or governmental access facilities, or equipment, if the cable operator demonstrates that (i) it is commercially impracticable for the operator to comply with the require-

ment, and (ii) the proposal by the cable operator for modification of such requirement is appropriate because of commercial impracticability.[115]

Since the touchstone for modifying terms and conditions of access is "commercial impracticability," authorities have to assume responsibility that promises made are realistic or assume the risk that the cable operator is entitled to relief after the franchise is awarded.[116] Not surprisingly, many of the extravagant promises which preceded a franchise decision have been reduced or abandoned pursuant to a showing that they were "commercially impracticable." Service requirements also are subject to modification "if the cable operator demonstrates that the mix, quality and level of services required by the franchise at the time it was granted will be maintained after such modification."[117] Among other things, the letter provision takes into account problems that may arise with product design and supplies. Once a request for a modification is filed, the franchising authority must render a decision within 120 days unless the time is extended by mutual assent.[118] In the event of denial, the cable operator may obtain review in a federal court which may grant relief if it finds commercial impracticability.

The statutory provision for modification has been depicted as reflecting congressional

> recogni[tion] that cable operators compete in a changing marketplace. . . . [Congress] was sufficiently concerned with the plight of some cable operators, particularly urban franchisees committed to state-of-the-art systems, to create a federally protected right to modification of commercially impractical agreements.[119]

The court of appeals, in *Tribune–United Cable of Montgomery County v. Montgomery County, Maryland,*[120] thus precluded local authorities from commencing franchise revocation proceedings or enforcing penalty provisions of the franchise agreement until it acted upon a modification request.[121] The cable company had encountered problems in the nature of construction and equipment delays, operational failures, and softer than anticipated consumer demand.[122] It thus sought modification of terms including access and origination, equipment type, and construction schedule.[123] Emphasizing Congress' protective aim, the appeals court concluded that the right to modify "would mean very little if local franchising authorities were able to burden it by enforcing massive penalties during the pendency of the modification proceedings."[124]

Tribune–United Cable of Montgomery County v. Montgomery County, Maryland, 784 F. 2d 1227 (4th Cir. 1986)

Sprouse, Circuit Judge:

In 1981, Montgomery County solicited proposals for the construction of a cable television system. Following an evaluation of several proposals, the County awarded the franchise to Tribune-United. After lengthy negotiations, the parties executed a franchise agreement in May 1983. The more than two hundred page document granted Tribune-United a nonexclusive franchise to operate a cable system in Montgomery County. It covered the relationship between the parties, as well as all significant aspects of the construction and operation of the cable system; essentially, it called for a state-of-the-art cable system.

Tribune-United experienced difficulties, including serious construction problems, in complying with the franchise agreement within a few months after work on the system began. Instead of using conventional equipment, Tribune-United had elected to install the TRACS signal distribution system, which employed new technology. The sole supplier for the TRACS system was experiencing both financial and quality control problems, and its equipment deliveries were often late. These equipment difficulties resulted in construction delays and operational failures in

the Montgomery County cable system. Tribune-United did not meet its construction deadlines, and cable subscribers experienced numerous service problems. In addition, consumer demand for various services was far below predicted levels. The franchise agreement required construction of an Institutional Network (I-Net) for use by Montgomery County businesses. The lack of customer enthusiasm for the I-Net's design and the possibility of unanticipated regulation by the state public utility commission threatened the financial feasibility of developing the I-Net. Consequently, Tribune-United decided not to construct the I-Net system. . . .

On November 8, 1985, Tribune-United formally requested modification of the franchise agreement pursuant to section 545 of the Cable Communications Policy Act of 1984. 47 U.S.C. § 521 *et seq.* (Supp. 1985). Citing commercial impracticability, the company requested modification of the franchise agreement with regard to many of the same franchise provisions detailed in the default letters, including: the I-Net requirement; access and origination support requirements; the dual cable capacity requirement; and the construction schedule. Three days later, the County announced that it was commencing proceedings to revoke Tribune-United's franchise but that it would simultaneously consider the modification request. The County also announced that it had taken steps to draw down a five million dollar letter of credit held by Continental as well as a related security deposit and would assess nine thousand dollars a day in liquidated damages for construction delays.

The next day, November 13, 1985, Tribune-United brought this action for declaratory and injunctive relief to prevent the County and Continental from carrying out the penalty provisions of the franchise agreement until the County had acted on the pending modification request. The district court immediately issued a temporary restraining order in favor of Tribune-United. The following day, Montgomery County moved for reconsideration of the order. The district court held a hearing and, on November 19, 1985, issued a memorandum and order vacating the temporary restraining order. The next day, it denied Tribune-United's motion for a preliminary injunction. Tribune-United appeals from that judgment.

There is little save the language of the statute to guide us on this question. It would make little sense, however, for Congress to subordinate the County's enforcement power to the Act's modification procedures but at the same time to permit the County to enforce the very obligations sought to be modified. By making a local government's enforcement power "subject to section 545," Congress provided the cable operator an opportunity to show that certain aspects of the franchise agreement are commercially impractical, and, if it is successful in demonstrating that, it will be relieved entirely from the adverse aspects of those portions of the agreement.

The County accurately asserts that the language of the Act does not explicitly require that the imposition of penalties be stayed or enjoined pending the consideration of a modification request. The purposes and thrust of the Act, however, evince a congressional desire that franchise agreements be applied and modified so as to obtain a realistic and flexible regulatory framework recognizing the needs of both local governments and cable operators, but primarily concerned with providing viable cable systems responsive to the needs and interests of the local communities they serve.

Congress, by including section 545 in the Act, recognized that cable operators compete in a changing marketplace. H.R.Rep. No. 934, 98th Cong., 2d Sess. 70, *reprinted in* 1984 U.S.Code Cong. & Ad.News 4655, 4707. It was sufficiently concerned with the plight of some cable operators, particularly urban franchisees committed to state-of-the-art systems, to create a federally protected right to modification of commercially impractical agreements. That right would mean very little if local franchising authorities were able to burden it by enforcing massive penalties during the pendency of the modification proceedings.

Severely penalizing an embryonic cable operation which may be stymied by commercial impracticabilities before it has had an opportunity to take advantage of the federally mandated right to modification does not strike us as promoting the objectives of the Act. Short of a bad faith or frivolous application for modification, we hold

that such application automatically stays any action on the part of the franchising authority to enforce the penalty provisions of the franchise agreement until its decision has been finalized.

c. FRANCHISE RENEWAL

The Cable Act addresses perhaps the cable industry's paramount interest in uniform regulation of a national order by identifying the criteria for renewal.[125] Prior to congressional action, cable operators were subject to state and local standards which at best were vague and at worst nonexistent. Having invested substantial capital for the purposes of establishing a system, cable operators were concerned that they would lose their franchise at the whim of public officials or be subject to constant pressure for expensive alterations and improvements.

The FCC has accounted for similar concerns of broadcasters by creating a renewal expectancy for licensees that provide a certain quality of service.[126] The Cable Act accomplishes a similar aim by requiring a franchise renewal proceeding, at the request of the cable operator or upon the regulating authority's own initiative, to assess past performance and the community's future needs. A renewal decision must be tied to consideration of whether the franchisee has (1) substantially complied with material terms of the franchise and relevant law; (2) provided quality of service in a technical and business sense which is reasonable in light of community needs; (3) sufficient financial, legal, and technical ability to provide proposed future service; and (4) offered a proposal that is reasonable to meet future cable-related community needs and interests.[127] Denial of a franchise renewal must be based upon an identified deficiency in one of those four categories.[128]

d. FRANCHISE FEES

Congress has expressly provided that an annual franchise fee may not exceed 5 percent of a cable operator's gross revenues.[129] For purposes of the Cable Act, a franchise fee is "any tax, fee, or assessment of any kind imposed by a franchising authority or other government entity on a cable operator or cable subscriber, or both, solely because of their status as such."[130] Taxes or assessments of general applicability are not considered franchise fees unless they are "unduly discriminatory."[131] In *Group W Cable, Inc. v. City of Santa Cruz,*[132] a federal district court cited the federal fee controls in determining that a municipality's easement and right-of-way charges were subject to limitation.[133]

> The best available approximation of the fair market value of the use of the easements to provide cable service is the value to a cable operator of access to the Santa Cruz market. Cable operators will presumably pay a fee for use of the easements and rights of way that will enable them to serve the Santa Cruz market while earning a reasonable return on their investment. The First Amendment does not necessarily preclude allowing the market place to control the allocation of communication resources.... In theory, this leaves Santa Cruz free to fix a fee higher than Group W is willing to pay, but, in reality, Santa Cruz is restrained in two-ways: (1) California Government Code § 53066 and the Cable Communications Policy Act, 47 U.S.C. § 542 (b), limit any fee to not more than five percent of the gross revenue derived from cable operations in Santa Cruz, and, (2) Santa Cruz's interest in gaining cable service for its residents will also limit the fee it charges Group W, since it is not free to charge any other operator either less or more. Within the range from zero to five percent, Santa Cruz must set a content-neutral, nondiscriminatory fee; it cannot use the fee as a vehicle for selecting a preferred operator. Any fee set must be the same for any cable operator regardless of the nature of the service offered or any other consideration or distinction.[134]

Following enactment of the Cable Act, the FCC abandoned its preexisting regulations on franchise fees and "its past practice of adjudicating disputes over ... what constituted a franchise fee."[135] Respectively, the commission's rationales were that Congress had eliminated the need for the previous fee ceiling and that all fee controversies were best resolved in court.[136] Following a challenge to its policy against adjudicating disputes,[137] the FCC modified its position to the effect that it no longer had an interest in most franchise fee controversies.[138] Disclaiming any expertise in local taxation matters it considered best left to local courts, the commission limited exercise of its jurisdiction to concerns directly affecting national cable communications policy and implicating its special area of knowledge.[139] Absent a specific contrary directive from Congress, the court of appeals concluded that the FCC's forbearance policy was neither irrational nor contrary to statute.[140] It noted, however, that its affirmance was "based on our assessment that the Commission has *not totally abdicated its ultimate responsibility* for enforcing the franchise fee provision."[141] The decision thus reminds that the franchise fee section, like other parts of the Cable Act, must be viewed in context with Congress' broader purpose of "establish[ing] a 'national policy' concerning cable communications."[142]

2. Rates

Disputes over the regulation of rates predate the Cable Act. Several years before its enactment, the state of New York attempted to check rising rates for cable service. Upon review, the court of appeals determined that rate governance was within the FCC's ancillary jurisdiction so had been preempted.[143] Soon thereafter, the commission verified its policy to the effect that its intent was to preempt any local and state regulation in the field.[144]

The Cable Act generally prohibits federal or state authorities from regulating rates for cable service.[145] The only exception is (1) with respect to basic service, but (2) only if the cable system is not subject to effective competition.[146] In determining whether "effective competition" exists, the FCC has determined that the proper reference point is not a natural monopoly but cable's presence within a larger media universe. To the extent a service area received at least three broadcast signals, therefore, the commission determined that effective competition existed.[147]

The policy, although contested, largely has been upheld. In *American Civil Liberties Union v. Federal Communications Commission*,[148] the rules were challenged as arbitrary and irrational insofar as they used the single criterion of available broadcast signals to define effective competition and defined availability in terms of theoretical accessibility.[149] The appeals court found the commission's determination reasonable, given the broad latitude it had for defining effective competition[150] but also identified provisions that could not stand.[151] First, the court determined that Congress had defined "basic cable service" and that the FCC could not substitute its own meaning.[152] Second, the court found that the FCC exceeded its authority by allowing cable systems automatically to pass through any readily identifiable cost increase or decrease attributable to the provision of basic service.[153] Examples of what would have qualified for automatic pass-through included price changes in programming or altered copyright fees.[154] The court determined that Congress' provision for annual automatic five percent increases at the cable operator's discretion accounted for the gap that the FCC unnecessarily filled.[155] Given the identity of purpose, the court concluded that the augmentative rule "simply removed the five-percent cap that Congress placed on automatic increases."[156] Finally, the appeals court required the commission in determining "effective competition" to figure signal availability upon a more

meaningful basis than its counting of every signal that covers "*any* portion of the cable community."[157] Thus, "it was incumbent upon the FCC to craft the standard more carefully, to ensure that a signal is at least theoretically available over the entire cable community or at least some significant portion of it."[158]

American Civil Liberties Union v. Federal Communications Commission, 823 F.2d 1554 (D.C. Cir. 1987)

I. BACKGROUND
C. The Commission's Rules

Shortly after passage of the Cable Act, the FCC initiated a rulemaking to implement the Act's various provisions. After receiving comments from over 140 parties, including cable companies and their trade associations, municipalities, public interest groups and the Antitrust Division of the Department of Justice, the Commission issued its Report and Order in *Implementation of the Provisions of the Cable Communications Policy Act of 1984 ("Report and Order")*, 50 Fed.Reg. 18,637 (1985).

The primary focus of the rulemaking was to identify the circumstances and conditions under which franchising authorities would be permitted to regulate the rates charged by cable operators for "basic cable service." Because section 623 of the Act expressly instructed the FCC to permit local rate regulation in those circumstances where cable systems did not face "effective competition," the critical question before the FCC was how to measure the existence of "effective competition." Based on the comments submitted by the various parties, an internal staff study and materials drawn from the economic literature, the Commission concluded that effective competition would be deemed to exist where any three "off-the-air" broadcast signals were "available" in the cable community. *See Report and Order*, 50 Fed.Reg. at 18,648–50. The Commission ruled that a broadcast signal would be deemed "available" in either of the following circumstances: (1) the signal placed a predicted Grade B contour over *any* portion of the cable community;[a] or (2) the signal was "significantly viewed" in the community.[b] *See id.* at 18,650–51. Franchising authorities, however, would be permitted to submit "showings and engineering studies" indicating that a signal was not "in fact" available "anywhere" within the cable community. *Id.* at 18,651.

Having settled on a definition of "effective competition," the FCC went on to prescribe "standards" of rate regulation for those franchising authorities (few in number, as the FCC concedes) that would retain the authority to regulate "basic cable" rates under the Commission's rules. Three of those "standards" are pertinent here. First, the FCC adopted a definition of the term "basic cable service." Although the Act itself contains a definition of this phrase,[c] the Commission found that the Act's legislative history authorized it—for the purpose of adopting rate regulation "standards"—to fashion an alternative definition. The Commission exercised this purported authority by defining "basic cable service" as *"the* tier of service regularly provided to all subscribers that includes the retransmission of all must-carry broadcast television signals." *Report and Order,* 50 Fed.Reg. at 18,653 (emphasis added).

———————

a. A "predicted Grade B contour" is a measurement of the anticipated strength of a broadcast signal. Use of the Grade B contour enables the FCC to predict the "approximate extent" to which a signal is viewable in the community covered by the contour. See 47 C.F.R. § 73. 683(a) (1985).

b. A signal is considered to be "significantly viewed" if it is watched by a certain percentage of viewers in a community. The percentage share that a signal must attain to be considered significantly viewed varies depending on whether the television station is a network affiliate or an independent. 47 C.F.R. § 76.54 (1985) references a list of broadcast signals that the FCC currently considers to be significantly viewed. The FCC has established waiver procedures, however, by which franchising authorities may demonstrate that signals listed as significantly viewed should no longer qualify for that status. See *In re KCST-TV, Inc.,* 59 Rad.Reg.2d (P & F) 1270, 1274 (1986). The Commission is in the process of revising its rules to formalize these procedures.

c. The Act defines "basic cable service" as *"any* service tier which includes the retransmission of local television broadcast signals." Section 602(2), 47 U.S.C. § 522(2) (emphasis added).

Second, the FCC permitted cable operators to pass through to their subscribers certain "identifiable" costs incurred in the provision of basic service. These costs, the Commission found, could *automatically* be incorporated in the operator's rates without franchising authority approval. *Id.* at 18, 654–55. Third, the FCC granted a one-year exemption from rate regulation to those cable operators who become subject to regulation by virtue of changed circumstances. This one-year exemption, the Commission reasoned, would give a cable operator sufficient time to make the transition from an unregulated to a regulated entity. . . .

II. ANALYSIS

A. Rate Regulation

The FCC's rate regulation rules—which will effectively prohibit the regulation of cable rates in the overwhelming majority of local communities—are challenged by several individual municipalities, the National League of Cities and other interested parties. The petitioners launch a broad assault on virtually every argument cited by the FCC in support of its rules, and every component of the rules themselves. Thus, the petitioners assert that the FCC acted arbitrarily and irrationally in defining "effective competition" in terms of a *single* criterion (the availability of broadcast signals), in selecting "three" as the number of signals expected to offer sufficient competition to the myriad of services offered by cable systems, and in defining the availability of signals in terms of their *theoretical* viewability in the cable community. The petitioners also assail the rate regulation "standards" adopted by the FCC, arguing that they are arbitrary and inconsistent with the express terms of the Cable Act.

[1] Upon careful consideration of the arguments raised by the petitioners, and applying familiar principles of judicial review, we conclude that the FCC's rate regulation rules are, for the most part, neither arbitrary, capricious nor otherwise contrary to law. With certain exceptions enumerated below, the FCC addressed the significant comments made in the rulemaking proceeding, articulated the basis for its conclusions, and adopted rules that are at a minimum "reasonable." It is irrelevant, of course, that we might

have defined "effective competition" differently had we been presented in the first instance with the facts before the Commission. Having satisfied ourselves that the Commission carefully considered proposed alternatives, explained the reasons underlying its decision, and reached a rational conclusion, our role under the Administrative Procedure Act is largely at an end. Guided by these well-established principles of judicial review, we hold that the FCC's rate regulation rules are affirmed in all respects except to the extent specifically delineated below....

While the Commission's actions in general are not arbitrary, capricious, or otherwise contrary to law, we conclude that in several respects the Commission has gone astray. Specifically, three aspects of the Commission's rules cannot stand: (1) the redefinition of "basic cable service"; (2) the automatic pass through; and (3) the signal availability standard. We consider each in turn.

1. Redefinition of "Basic Cable Service"

Section 602(2) of the Cable Act defines the term "basic cable service" as follows:

> [T]he term "basic cable service" means any service tier which includes the retransmission of local television broadcast signals.

47 U.S.C. § 522(2). However, in performing its statutory task of "establish[ing] standards for... rate regulation," *id.* § 543(b)(2)(B), the Commission crafted a definition of "basic cable service" that departs materially from that set forth in the statute:

> Basic cable service is the tier of service regularly provided to all subscribers that includes the retransmission of all must-carry broadcast signals... and the public educational and governmental channels, if required by a franchising authority....

Report and Order, 50 Fed.Reg. at 18,653.

There is an important distinction between these two definitions with respect to the treatment of cable systems configured so as to include broadcast signals on every tier. As Congress has defined the term, "basic cable service" would encompass these multiple tiers of cable service, since the statutory definition refers to "any service tier." Under this system, any tier that includes the "retransmission of local television broadcast signals," even if this encompassed every tier offered

by a cable operator, would be considered "basic cable service." *Cf.* House Report at 40 (recognizing statutory definition could involve labeling multiple tiers to be "basic cable service"), *reprinted in* 1984 U.S.Code Cong. & AdNews at 4677.

Under the Commission's system, on the other hand, only one service tier of a particular cable system can be labeled "basic cable service," regardless of whether that cable operator configures its system so that each tier includes local broadcast signals. The Commission's stated justification for its departure from the statutory language is the Cable Act's legislative history, a portion of which suggests that the FCC has discretion to announce a new definition. Specifically, the FCC rests on the following language from the House Report:

> The Committee wishes to stress that it intends to give the Commission flexibility in promulgating these regulations. The definition in Sec. 602 [47 U.S.C. § 522(2)] of basic cable service is intended primarily for use in determining the extent of regulation that will be permitted during the... transition period. The regulations of the Commission under [subsection 623(b), 47 U.S.C. § 543(b)] serve a different purpose—defining the circumstances and extent of regulation that may occur beyond the transition period. As such, the Commission may fashion a definition of basic cable services most appropriate to achieve the purpose of the regulations, consistent with the provisions of Title VI.

Id. at 66, *reprinted in* 1984 U.S. Code Cong.& Admin. News at 4703; see also FCC Brief at 11–12 (invoking House Report language); *Report and Order,* 50 Fed.Reg. at 18,652 (same). With this go-ahead from the legislative history, the Commission invokes what it perceives to be the general deregulatory focus of the Act, *Report and Order,* 50 Fed.Reg. at 18,652–53, as well as prior "longstanding" Commission precedents, *id.* at 18,653, both of which, in the Commission's view, counsel in favor of a narrower definition of basic cable service than that set forth in the statute.

Also featured prominently in the FCC's explication is the argument that application of the statutory definition would lead to anomalous results. See FCC Brief at 19–20; *Report and Order,* 50 Fed.Reg. at 18,653 & n. 81. Specifically, use of the section 602(2) definition could lead to two different cable companies offering identical services having a different number of service tiers being considered "basic cable service"; this critical difference would thus be based solely on the way these two hypothetical cable operators chose to market their services.[d] In the Commission's view, applying the statutory definition and reaching different results for two such companies would represent a triumph of form over substance. Such a result, the FCC argues, is "clearly not intended by the statute." *Report and Order,* 50 Fed. Reg. at 18,653 n. 81; see also FCC Brief at 20 (labeling every tier of cable service as basic cable service "would clearly contravene the legislative intent and the statutory definition of basic cable service was therefore rejected by the Commission"). But *cf.* House Report at 40 ("The Committee recognizes that . . . [i]n some franchises this [definition] will mean that basic cable service includes mul-

---

d. This can be seen by considering hypothetical cable operators *X* and *Y,* each of which offer three service tiers. Operator *X* markets its services as follows: (1) Tier *A,* consisting of local broadcast signals and a weather channel, for $10 per month; (2) Tier *B,* consisting of the satellite services ESPN and CNN, for $5 per month; and (3) Tier *C,* consisting of Home Box Office and the Disney Channel, for $10 per month. Operator *X* requires that subscribers purchase Tier *A* in order to purchase Tier *B,* and to purchase Tiers *A* and *B* in order to purchase Tier *C.* Operator *Y,* in contrast, markets its services in this way: (1) Tier 1, consisting of local broadcast signals and a weather channel, for $10 per month; (2) Tier 2, consisting of local broadcast signals, a weather channel, ESPN, and CNN, for $15 per month; and (3) Tier 3, consisting of local broadcast signals, a weather channel, ESPN, CNN, Home Box Office, and the Disney Channel, for $25 per month. A subscriber purchasing Tiers *A, B,* and *C* from cable operator *X* is obviously receiving the same services, at the same price, as a subscriber purchasing Tier 3 from operator *Y.* Yet, because cable operator *Y* employs a cumulative, rather than an incremental, marketing and pricing approach, it faces the prospect of having Tiers 1, 2, and 3 all subject to rate regulation if the statutory definition were used. Operator *X,* on the other hand, has only one service tier, Tier *A,* potentially subject to rate regulation if the statutory definition were employed. In contrast, under the Commission's definition only one tier would be potentially subject to rate regulation in each cable system—in Operator's *X*'s system, Tier *A,* and in operator *Y*'s system, Tier 1.

tiple service tiers."), *reprinted in* 1984 U.S. Code Cong. & Admin. News at 4677.

This rather technical, definitional dispute is significant because under the Cable Act only "basic cable service" is potentially subject to rate regulation by local franchising authorities. See 47 U.S.C. § 543(b). Thus, the definition of "basic cable service" sets the parameters of the respective jurisdictions of local franchising authorities and the Commission. The fact that construction of the statutory term directly impacts such jurisdictional determinations should, in our view, be factored into a proper analysis of the statutory issue we face. *Cf. Board of Governors v. Dimension Financial Corp.,* 474 U.S. 361 (1986). That issue may be simply stated: Does the FCC enjoy discretion to adopt, as part of its regulations implementing the Cable Act, a definition of a particular term that is at odds with a definition of that very term contained in the Act itself? The question, we believe, answers itself. The Commission, however, answers yes.

Our task "in assessing a claim that an agency action contravenes its governing statute," *FAIC Securities, Inc. v. United States,* 768 F.2d 352, 361 (D.C.Cir.1985), has been marked out by the Supreme Court in *Chevron, USA v. NRDC,* 467 U.S. 837, 842–43 (1984). We are instructed to first determine

> whether Congress has directly spoken to the precise question at issue. If the intent of Congress is clear, that is the end of the matter; for the court, as well as the agency, must give effect to the unambiguously expressed intent of Congress.

Id. at 842–43. It is only if Congress' intent is "silent or ambiguous" that we consider, and grant deference to, the agency's construction. *Id.* at 843.

In making this determination of whether "Congress had an intention on the precise question at issue," the *Chevron* Court indicated that we were to employ "traditional tools of statutory construction." *Id.* at 843 n. 9, 104 S.Ct. at 2782 n. 9. The Commission employs a tool of statutory analysis, focusing solely on one passage from the House Report accompanying the Cable Act. As mentioned above, that passage indicates that the statutory definition was to apply "primarily" during the two-year transition period, and that after this period the Commission could fashion its own definition consistent with the provisions of the Act. See *Report and Order*, 50 Fed.Reg. at 18,652 (quoting House Report at 66, *reprinted in* 1984 U.S. Code Cong. & Admin. News at 4703). But the Commission's argument has overlooked an important component of a proper statutory analysis. While legislative history is undoubtedly one of the "traditional tools" of which *Chevron* speaks, it is beyond cavil that the first step in any statutory analysis, and our primary interpretive tool, is the language of the statute itself. See, e.g., *Landreth Timber Co. v. Landreth*, 471 U.S. 681, 685 (1985) ("It is axiomatic that '[t]he starting point in every case involving construction of a statute is the language itself.' ") (quoting *Blue Chip Stamps v. Manor Drug Stores*, 421 U.S. 723, 756 (1975) (Powell, J., concurring)); *Greyhound Corp. v. Mt. Hood Stages, Inc.*, 437 U.S. 322, 330 (1978) (same, citing other cases). This case poignantly illustrates the wisdom of this principle, for in leapfrogging ahead to the legislative history without carefully dwelling on the statute itself, the Commission has fallen into interpretive error.

Turning to the language of the language of the statute, we find that on the issue of defining "basic cable service," the statute speaks with crystalline clarity. It provides a precise definition in section 602(2) for the exact term the Commission now seeks to redefine. The statute in no wise indicates that the 602(2) definition is only transitory. From the face of the statute then, we are left with no ambiguity and thus no need to resort to legislative history for clarification. As this court has stated, "[o]nly where [the statutory] expression is genuinely ambiguous," *FAIC Securities*, 768 F.2d at 362, is legislative history useful or necessary. *Id.;* see also *Burlington N.R.R. v. Oklahoma Tax Comm'n*, ____U.S. ____, 107 S.St. 1855, 1859–60 (1987); *Maine v. Thiboutot*, 448 U.S. 1, 6 n. 4, (1980) ("Where the plain language . . . is as strong as it is here, ordinarily 'it is not *necessary* to look beyond the words of the statute.' ") (quoting *TVA v. Hill*, 437 U.S. 153, 184 n. 29 (1978) (emphasis in original)); *United States v. Oregon*, 366 U.S. 643, 648 (1961) ("Having concluded that [the statutory provisions] are clear and unequivocal on their face, we find no need to resort to the legislative history of the Act.").

The Supreme Court recently followed such an interpretive approach in an analogous setting in *Board of Governors v. Dimension Financial Corp.*, 474 U.S. 361 (1986). *Dimension Financial* presented the Court with two Federal Reserve Board regulatory definitions which conflicted with statutory provisions. In considering one such regulatory provision—the Board's definition of "demand deposit"—the Court looked only to the statutory language, which it found conclusive. The Court did not even cite any legislative history in this phase of its analysis, despite the fact that the Tenth Circuit had considered the statute's legislative history. See 744 F.2d 1402, 1407–08 (10th Cir.1984).

Following the Supreme Court's lead, we similarly decline to give overmuch weight to the measure's legislative history inasmuch as we find the pertinent part of the statute clear and unambiguous. The general interpretive principle—a reluctance to rely upon legislative history in construing an *unambiguous* statute—is of especial force where, as here, resort to legislative history is sought to support a result *contrary* to the statute's express terms. Whatever the limitations of the "plain meaning" rule in the run-of-the-mine case, "[w]e find no mandate in logic or in case law for reliance on legislative history to reach a result *contrary* to the plain meaning of a statute." *United Air Lines, Inc. v. CAB*, 569 F.2d 640, 647 (D.C.Cir.1977) (emphasis in original); see also *IBEW, Local No. 474 v. NLRB*, 814 F.2d 697, 712 (D.C.Cir.1987); *Universal City Studios v. Sony Corp.*, 659 F.2d 963, 968–69 (9th Cir. 1981); *Beacon Looms, Inc. v. S. Lichtenberg & Co.*, 552 F. Supp. 1305, 1310 (S.D.N.Y.1982) (It is "clear that a plain reading of an unambiguous statute cannot be eschewed in favor of a contrary reading, suggested only by the legislative history and not by the text itself."); *cf. United States v. American College of Physicians*, 475 U.S. 834 (1986) ("[D]espite the [Committee] Report's seeming endorsement of a *per se* rule, we are hesitant to rely on that inconclusive legislative history either to supply a provision *not* enacted by Congress . . . or to define a statutory term enacted by a prior Congress. . . . We agree, therefore, with . . . [the] rejection of the . . . argument that . . . Congress intended to establish a *per se* rule.") (citations omitted).

This is precisely the temptation to which the

FCC would have us succumb. The Commission asks us to disregard clear statutory language and embrace contraindications found in a committee report, but which are not without ambiguity themselves. Even if the pertinent passage from the House Report is seen as speaking with complete clarity, the fact remains that committee reports, even authoritative committee reports, are not law. *General Motors Corp. v. Ruckelshaus,* 742 F.2d 1561, 1570 n. 13 (D.C.Cir.1984), *cert. denied,* 471 U.S. 1074 (1985). Accordingly, we decline the Commission's invitation. We will not permit a committee report to trump clear and unambiguous statutory language. Rather, because there is no ambiguity on the face of the statute, we believe that the definition of "basic cable service" established by Congress in section 602(2) should apply in all circumstances.

In our view, application of the statutory definition will not lead to unreasonable results. *Cf. United Air Lines,* 569 F.2d at 647. As noted above, see pp. 1566–67, *supra,* the FCC complains that the statutory definition, by sanctioning the labeling of multiple service tiers as "basic cable service," will lead to different treatment of cable operators based solely on marketing differences. This type of "form over substance" result may indeed be the upshot of the statutory definition. But such a result is hardly absurd. *Cf. Commissioner v. Brown,* 380 U.S. 563, 571 (1965) ("Unquestionably the courts, in interpreting a statute, have some 'scope for adopting a restricted rather than a literal or usual meaning of its words where acceptance of that meaning would lead to absurd results.' ") (quoting *Helvering v. Hammel,* 311 U.S. 504, 510–11 (1941)); *In re Trans Alaska Pipeline Rate Cases,* 436 U.S. 631, 643 (1978) (same; quoting *Commissioner v. Brown*). Under the Cable Act, cable operators generally have the freedom to structure their service tiers in whatever way they wish. 47 U.S.C. § 545(d). While application of the statutory definition may lead them to choose one structure over another, this is hardly unreasonable. In any event, we discern no difficulties with application of the statutory definition that would lead us to reject it as irrational, unreasonable, or absurd.

In sum, applying the "traditional tools of statutory construction," *Chevron,* 467 U.S. at 843 n. 9, we are persuaded that Congress did indeed have an intent on the "precise question at issue." *Id.* at 842. This is not a situation where Congress has left gaps for the agency to fill. *Cf. id.* at 843–44. Rather, Congress has spoken directly and specifically by providing a definition of the exact term the Commission now seeks to redefine. And as noted above, Congress intended its definition of "basic cable service" to be just that—a comprehensive definition of the term. We are instructed by *Chevron* that "that is the end of the matter" and directed to "give effect to the unambiguously expressed intent of Congress." *Id.* at 842–43. We do so and hold that the Commission's redefinition of "basic cable service" is contrary to law; the Commission must apply the section 602(2) definition.

2. *Automatic Pass Through*

In addition to directing the FCC to develop regulations defining the circumstances in which effective competition exists (and rate regulation is therefore permissible), section 623 of the Act instructs the Commission to "establish standards for such rate regulation." 47 U.S.C. § 543(b)(2)(B). In its *Notice of Proposed Rulemaking,* the Commission described this task as "not only specifying what services can be regulated but also in what manner." 49 Fed. Reg. at 48,771.

After noting that it was provided "no specific guidance regarding the establishment of a rate regulation standard," the FCC offered its "tentative view" as to what administrative procedures should be used by franchising authorities in setting rates. *Id.* Then, "[w]ith respect to the substance of the rate making decision," *id.,* the Commission discussed its preference for a "zone of reasonableness" approach, and "[a]ccordingly . . . propose[d] that franchise authorities may prescribe rates that are within 10 percent, either above or below, of the average rate of the comparable cable system." *Id.*

In its *Report and Order,* the Commission reported that in their comments on these proposed rate regulation standards a number of cable interests had recommended that automatic "pass-throughs" be permitted. The FCC agreed:

Accordingly, our rules will permit cable systems to automatically pass through any readily identifiable increase (or decrease) in cost which is entirely attributable to the provision of basic service, e.g., the price of programming appearing on the basic service tier and copyright fees for retransmission of distant broadcast signals appearing on the basic service tier. These rate increases may be taken in addition to the 5% automatic annual increase to which most cable systems are entitled.

Report and Order, 50 Fed.Reg. at 18,655. The only rationale the FCC offered for this ruling is avoidance of what would be *pro forma* administrative proceedings, by virtue of the fact that the requested rate increase in such circumstances is due solely to increased cost. See *id.* ("value of automatic pass through...is the avoidance of *pro forma* administrative proceedings").

As noted above, the FCC promulgated this pass-through rule in the course of establishing "standards for rate regulation," thereby purporting to rely on section 623, or more precisely subsection 623(b)(2)(B), as authority. We conclude, however, that erecting this pass-through mechanism exceeded the Commission's authority under section 623. That provision begins with the admonition that "[a]ny federal agency...may not regulate...rates except to the extent provided under this section." 47 U.S.C. § 623(a). Given that delimiting provision, the FCC would seem to be impermissibly stretching the bounds of its lawful power when it uses a general direction to establish "standards for rate regulation" to justify direct regulation of the permissible amount of a rate increase.

But that is not all. In establishing the automatic pass through, the Commission has done more than potentially exceed the authority granted to it in subsection 623(b)(2)(B). The Commission has sought to employ this general power to fill a gap, as it were, by permitting automatic pass throughs. The problem is that no gap exists. The pass-through rule addresses a subject matter comprehensively treated by Congress in the Cable Act; indeed, this very subject is covered in other subsections of section 623.

Subsection (e)(1) of section 623 by its terms permits an automatic five percent per year increase "at the discretion of the cable operator." 47 U.S.C. § 543(e)(1). This increase is to be "[i]n addition to any other rate increase which is subject to the approval of a franchising authority." *Id.* Moreover, a different subsection of section

623, subsection (d), permits a cable operator to treat as granted any request for a rate increase on which the franchising authority does not act within 180 days. *Id.* § 543(d).

Taken together, these provisions create an elaborate scheme for automatic rate increases. By sanctioning such automatic increases, Congress was addressing concerns similar to those animating the FCC's development of its automatic pass through. Indeed, it would seem that the concerns were identical. The House Report indicates that the subsection (e)(1) automatic increase was intended to "allow the [cable] operator to adjust for inflation without being subject to city approval." House Report at 25, *reprinted in* 1984 U.S. Code Cong. & Admin. News at 4662. The FCC's rule is designed to account for increases in costs faced by the cable operator, such as "the price of programming...and copyright fees." *Report and Order,* 50 Fed. Reg. at 18,655. It seems reasonable to believe that these increased costs will be due to inflation.

But regardless of whether the motivations underlying the two rules are identical, it is unquestionable that they serve the same purpose. Functionally, therefore, the FCC has simply removed the five-percent cap that Congress placed on automatic increases. Far from justifying its actions in light of a specific statutory provision covering the same subject, the Commission's only reference to section 623(e)(1) is to say that under the Commission's automatic pass-through provision "rate increases may be taken in addition to the 5% automatic annual increase to which most cable systems are entitled." *Id.*

In our view, the Commission's establishment of the automatic pass through was contrary to law. Indeed, counsel for the FCC conceded as much at oral argument. Congress had already addressed the question; it conferred no power upon—and left no room for—the FCC to weigh in with an automatic increase of its own. This act of gratuitous administrative largesse cannot stand.

As noted earlier, see notes a & b *supra,* the measures of signal availability chosen by the Commission are highly imperfect—the fact that a particular house falls within the Grade B contour of a station does not mean that that station can in reality be picked up on a television set in that house. Moreover, while the Commission candidly admits that its selected measures are only theoretical indicators and will lead to errors in practical application, *Report and Order,* 50 Fed.Reg. at 18,651, it cannot be gainsaid that *no* measure of signal availability is an error-free indicator of actual signal reception. *Cf.* FCC Brief at 17. Thus, use of the Grade B contour and "significantly viewed" measures is not in itself problematic, much less arbitrary and capricious; the problem lies in the manner in which the Commission has incorporated these measures into its signal availability standard.

Because the Commission knew it was dealing with the theoretical and appreciated the practical flaws inherent in its chosen measures, it was incumbent upon the FCC to craft the standard more carefully, to ensure that a signal is at least theoretically available over the entire cable community or at least some significant portion of the cable community. The failure to do so could predictably lead, under the FCC's current rules, to irrational results—that is, a cable system could be labeled as subject to effective competition due to the presence of three broadcast signals even though at no point within the cable community are all three signals even theoretically available.

The FCC's response to these admitted difficulties with its approach—which is, after all, central to the entire determination of whether effective competition exists—is essentially to throw up its hands. The Commission emphasizes the truism that no standard is perfect and that the agency has included a waiver provision to address problems such as those we have identified. See FCC Brief at 39. As discussed above, we accept the proposition that no reasonable measure of signal availability is foolproof. We also agree that, to a point, a waiver procedure is adequate to address inherent difficulties with whatever standard is chosen. For example, a waiver proceeding would be appropriate to address a claim that while three Grade B contours theoretically covered the entire cable community, in reality only two off-the-air signals were available. What we cannot accept is the FCC's enormous margin of error created by its decision to "count" *every* signal that covers "*any* portion of the cable community." *Report and Order,*

50 Fed. Reg. at 18,651 (emphasis added). This remarkable standard is nowhere explained in the *Report and Order,* nor does the *Report and Order* reflect any awareness of the practical ramifications of this decision. What is more, the *Report and Order* fails to discuss why the "any portion" standard was selected over a more refined geographical qualification, such as "a significant portion of the cable community," or "over 75 percent of the cable community." This type of undifferentiated rulemaking is fundamentally flawed.

Accordingly, we are persuaded that the FCC's signal availability standard is arbitrary and capricious; we therefore remand that issue to the agency for a reasoned explanation of its chosen standard or the development of a new standard.

The commission on remand redefined "effective competition" to include a minimum of three broadcast signals, although not necessarily the same ones, throughout the cable service area.[159] Availability now is presumed when minimum criteria for signal coverage are satisfied, or it is "significantly viewed" in the service area.[160]

Cable systems functioning under a franchise awarded prior to the Cable Act were subject to rate regulation by state and local authorities for two years after its effective date.[161] Since rates have been largely deregulated, considerable consternation has been evidenced over rising cable rates. During the two years immediately after decontrol, rates for basic service jumped from an average of $11.23 to $14.48—a 29-percent increase.[162] Although the upward price movement was four times the rate of inflation,[163] the cable industry claims it is justified because service is improving and earlier regulated prices were artificially low.[164] Nonetheless, some state and local officials have urged Congress to push for significant regulation of cable service rates.[165] As a consequence, legislation is being considered that would redefine "effective competition" and enable franchising authorities to exercise more control over rates.

3. Concentration

The Cable Act incorporates diversification polices akin to those which restrict ownership of broadcast stations. Unlike the rules which bar cross-ownership of colocated broadcasting stations and newspapers,[166] cross-ownership of cable systems and television stations in the same community is proscribed by statute rather than by agency rule.[167] The provision further authorizes the FCC to "prescribe rules with respect to the ownership or control of cable systems by persons who own or control other media of mass communications which serve the same community served by a cable system."[168] Although seemingly authorized to reach media other than television, FCC rules go no further than the statute except to proscribe altogether cable ownership by broadcasting networks.[169]

Prior to the Cable Act, the FCC had adopted a cross-ownership rule that exempted cable systems owned in 1970.[170] The rule was challenged on the grounds that (1) the commission did not have the authority to promulgate it prior to receiving jurisdiction under the act and (2) a right of first refusal obtained in 1968 constituted an ownership interest.[171] In *Marsh Media, Ltd. v. Federal Communications Commission*,[172] the court of appeals noted the commission's well-established authority under the reasonably ancillary test.[173] It also noted that a right of first refusal did not qualify as an ownership interest under the agency rules.[174] Finally, it determined that any First Amendment claim was "foreclosed by the Supreme Court's decision in *Federal Communications Commission v. National Citizens Committee for Broadcasting* upholding . . . [the] rule . . . restricting cross-ownership of co-located daily newspapers and television stations."[175] The *Marsh Media* case is a useful reminder that, despite the

enactment of the Cable Act, its freshness means that some issues still may arise that will require assessment under preexisting standards.

4. Exclusivity

The FCC, in 1988, reinstated syndicated exclusivity rules[176] that had been abandoned several years earlier. In repealing such regulation in 1980, the Commission had determined that viewer interest in seeing programs when desired outweighed local broadcaster exclusivity interests.[177] Following an inquiry into the consequences of such deregulation, the FCC reintroduced syndicated exclusivity rules[178] pursuant to its sense that broadcasters otherwise were at a competitive disadvantage "with other media for products from which the programming producers can receive full value."[179] As a consequence, local broadcasters with exclusive rights to syndicated programming may prohibit cable operators from importing it from a distant station.[180]

In *United Video, Inc. v. Federal Communications Commission*,[181] the court of appeals upheld the rules. It found substantial evidence that regulation was necessary to prevent diversion of "a substantial portion of the broadcast audience to cable"[182] and consequent diminution of "the value of the programming [from] low[ered] advertising revenues."[183] The court also found the FCC's discernment of a "link between lack of program diversity and lowered broadcast revenues due to lack of exclusivity . . . sufficiently in accord with accepted economic theory."[184] Although acknowledging that the exclusivity requirement would "affect the content of cable programming," the court concluded that "it is content neutral."[185] It thus found the rules unaffected by a Cable Communication Policy Act of 1984 provision forbidding imposition of any content requirement.[186] Finally, the Court rejected a constitutional challenge which it characterized as a "desire to make commercial use of the copyrighted works of others [for which] [t]here is no First Amendment right."[187]

NOTES

1. STATISTICAL ABSTRACT OF THE UNITED STATES 1989, No. 900, at 544.

2. 47 C.F.R. § 76.5(a). Excluded from the definition are facilities that retransmit signals of only one broadcast station or serve only subscribers in a commonly owned multiple dwelling, common carriers, and facilities used only to operate an electric utility system. *Id.*

3. Cable Communications Policy Act of 1984, 47 U.S.C. § 521 *et seq.*

4. *See* CATV and TV Repeater Services, 26 F.C.C. 403, 427–28 (1952).

5. *Id.*

6. *See* Frontier Broadcasting Co. v. Collier, 16 R.R. 1005 (1958).

7. *See* In the Matter of Inquiry into the Impact of Community Antenna Systems, TV Translators, TV Satellites and TV Repeaters on the Orderly Development of Broadcasting, 18 R.R. 1573 (1959).

8. Carter Mountain Transmission Corp. v. Federal Communications Commission, 321 F.2d 359, 365–66 (D.C. Cir. 1963).

9. *Id.* at 362–63.

10. 321 F.2d 359.

11. *Id.* at 365–66.

12. *See* United States v. Southwestern Cable Co., 392 U.S. 157 (1968) (recognizing FCC power to issue cable regulations "reasonably ancillary" to its authority to govern broadcasting).

13. Second Report and Order, 6 R.R. 1717 (1966).

14. *See* United States v. Southwestern Cable Co., 392 U.S. at 175–77.

15. *See id.* at 175–76.

16. *See id.* at 166–67.

17. 392 U.S. 157.

18. *Id.* at 178.

19. *Id.*

20. *Id.* at 176–77.

21. *Id.* at 177.

22. *Id.*

23. *Id.* For an appraisal of the Court's analysis, as a creative but necessary form of problem solving in the absence of congressional guidance, *see* Mallamud, *Courts, Statutes and Administrative Agency Jurisdiction: A Consideration of Limits on Judicial Creativity,* 35 S.C. L. REV. 191 (1984).

24. The regulations are discussed in cases that follow.

25. *See* H.R. Rep. No. 98–934, 98th Cong., 2d Sess. 22 (1984).

26. *See* Bollinger, *Freedom of the Press and Public Access: Toward a Theory of Partial Regulation of the Mass Media,* 75 MICH. L. REV. 1, 40 (1976).

27. *See, e.g.,* United States v. Midwest Video Corp., 406 U.S. 649 (1972); United States v. Southwestern Cable Co., 392 U.S. 157.

28. City of Los Angeles v. Preferred Communications, Inc. 476 U.S. 488, 494 (1986).

29. 406 U.S. 649.

30. *Id.* at 653, 670–73.

31. *Id.* at 653–54.

32. The Court premised its decision on grounds the disputed rules were within the FCC's regulatory authority and supported by substantial evidence that they served the public interest. *Id.* at 670–73.

33. *Id.* at 667–68.

34. *Id.* at 664.

35. *Id.* at 664–65.

36. *Id.* at 669–70.

37. *Id.* at 676.

38. Amendment of Part 76, Subpart G of the Commission's Rules and Regulations Relative to Program Origination of Cable Television Systems; and Inquiry Into the Development of Cablecasting Service to Formulate Regulatory Policy and Rulemaking, 49 F.C.C.2d 1090, 1106 (1974).

39. *See* Federal Communications Commission v. Midwest Video Corp., 440 U.S. 689, 691 (1979).

40. *See* Columbia Broadcasting System, Inc. v. Democratic National Committee, 412 U.S. 94 (1973).

41. Federal Communications Commission v. Pacifica Foundation, 438 U.S. 726, 748 (1978).

42. It intimated, however, that cable casters might have public interest duties, including fairness obligations, akin to broadcasters. Federal Communications Commission v. Midwest Video Corp., 440 U.S. at 709.

43. 440 U.S. 689.

44. *Id.* at 700–1.

45. *Id.* at 699–700.

46. *Id.* at 702.

47. *Id.* at 700–2.

48. *See* Miami Herald Publishing Co. v. Tornillo, 418 U.S. 241, 258 (1974).

49. 440 U.S. at 709. The court observed that the "authority to compel cable operators to provide common carriage of public-originated transmissions must come specifically from Congress." *Id.* The Cable Communication Policy Act of 1984 responds to that notation by providing for access as part of a franchising agreement. 47 U.S.C. § 531.

50. 567 F.2d 9 (D.C. Cir.), *cert. denied,* 434 U.S. 839 (1977).

51. *See id.* at 18–19.

52. *See id.* at 19.

53. *See id.* at 28.

54. *Id.* at 36–40.

55. *Id.* at 28.

56. *Id.* at 34.

57. *Id.*

58. Report and Order in Docket Nos. 20988 and 21284, 79 F.C.C. 2d 663 (1980).

59. *Id.*

60. Malrite T.V. of New York v. Federal Communications Commission, 652 F.2d 1140 (2d Cir. 1981), *cert. denied,* 454 U.S. 1143 (1982).

61. *Id.* at 1152.

62. *See id.* at 1146.

63. *See* Century Communications Corp. v. Federal Communications Commission, 835 F.2d 292 (D.C.Cir. 1987), *cert. denied,* 108 S.Ct. 2015 (1988).

64. 835 F.2d 292.

65. *Id.* at 304–5.

66. 47 U.S.C. § 521 *et seq.*

67. *See* United States v. Southwestern Cable Company, 392 U.S. 157.

68. 467 U.S. 691 (1984).

69. *Id.* at 700.

70. 47 U.S.C. § 521 (1).

71. *Id.,* § 521 (2)-(6).

72. Rollins Cablevue, Inc. v. Saienni Enterprises, 637 F.Supp. 1315, 1318 (D.Del. 1986), *citing* Housatonic Cable Vision Co. v. Department of Public Utility Control, 622 F.Supp. 798, 811 (D.Conn. 1985).

73. 47 U.S.C. § 224.

74. *Id.,* § 532.

75. *Id.,* § 533.

76. *Id.,* § 543 (b) and (h).

77. *Id.,* § 544(e).

78. *Id.,* § 554.

79. *Id.,* § 541.

80. *Id.,* § 556(a).

81. *Id.,* § 533(d).

82. *Id.,* § 543(a) (b).

83. *Id.,* § 541(c).

84. *See* City of New York v. Federal Communications Commission, 108 S.Ct. 1637 (1988).

85. 108 S.Ct. 1637.

86. *Id.* at 1642.

87. *Id.* at 1643.

88. *Id.* at 1643.

89. *Id.* at 1644, *quoting* 47 U.S.C. § 544(a).

90. *Id.* at 1644.

91. *Id.*

92. *Id.*

93. *See* Capital Cities Cable, Inc. v. Crisp, 467 U.S. 691 (1984).

94. 47 U.S.C. § 554.

95. *See* Housatonic Cable Vision Co. v. Department of Public Utility Control, 622 F.Supp. 798.

96. *See id.* at 808.

97. 622 F.Supp 798.

98. *Id.* at 808.

99. *Id., quoting* 47 U.S.C. § 543(e) and (f).

100. *Id.* at 806.

101. 47 U.S.C. §§ 522(9), 541.

102. *Id.,* § 541(a) (1).

103. *Id.,* § 541(a) (3).

104. Housatonic Cable Vision Co. v. Department of Public Utility Control, 622 F.Supp. at 808.

105. 47 U.S.C. § 545.

106. *Id..* § 546.

107. *See* Community Communications Co., Inc. v. City of Boulder, Colorado, 445 U.S. 40 (1982).

108. 445 U.S. 40.

109. *Id.* at 51.

110. Central Telecommunications, Inc. v. TCI Cablevision, Inc. 800 F.2d 711, 717 (8th Cir. 1986).

111. Century Federal, Inc. v. City of Palo Alto, California, 648 F.Supp. 1465, 1476–77 D.Cal. 1986).

112. *Id.*

113. Barnes, *The Cable Conspiracy,* The Washington Monthly, June, 1989, at 12.

114. *See* 47 U.S.C. § 545.

115. *Id.,* § 545(a) (1) (A).

116. *Id.*

117. *Id.,* § 545(a) (1) (B).

118. *Id.,* § 545(a) (1) (B) (2).

119. Tribune-United Cable of Montgomery County v. Montgomery County, Maryland, 784 F.2d 1227, 1231 (4th Cir. 1986).

120. 784 F.2d 1227.

121. *Id.* at 1231.

122. *Id.* at 1228–29.

123. *Id.* at 1229.

124. *Id.* at 1231.

125. *See* 47 U.S.C. § 546(c) (1) (A)-(D).

126. *See* Chapter 5 of this book.

127. 47 U.S.C. § 546(c) (1) (A)-(D).

128. *Id.,* § 546(d).

129. 47 U.S.C. § 542(b).

130. *Id.,* § 542(g) (1).

131. *Id.,* § 542(g) (2) (A).

132. 679 F.Supp. 977 (N.D.Cal. 1984).

133. *Id.* at 980.

134. *Id.*

135. *See* American Civil Liberties Union v. Federal Communications Commission, 823 F. 2d 1554, 1562 (D.C.Cir. 1987).

136. *See id.*

137. *See* Yakima Valley Cablevision, Inc. v. Federal Communications Commission, 794 F.2d 737 (D.C.Cir. 1986).

138. *See* American Civil Liberties Union v. Federal Communications Commission, 823 F.2d at 1562–63.

139. *See id.*

140. *Id.* at 1574.

141. *Id.* (emphasis in original).

142. 47 U.S.C. § 521(1).

143. Brookhaven Cable TV, Inc. v. Kelly, 573 U.S. 765 (2d Cir. 1978), *cert. denied,* 441 U.S. 904 (1979).

144. Community Cable TV, Inc., 95 F.C.C.2d 1204, 1216 (1983).

145. 47 U.S.C. § 543 (a).

146. *Id.,* § 543 (b) (1).

147. *See* American Civil Liberties Union v. FCC, 823 F.2d at 1563.

148. 823 F.2d 1554.

149. *Id.* at 1563.

150. *Id.* at 1564.

151. *Id.* at 1565.

152. *Id.* at 1568–70. Congress defined "basic cable service" as "any service tier which includes the retransmission of local broadcast signals" 47 U.S.C. § 522 (2). The Commission characterized it as "the tier of service provided to all subscribers that includes the retransmission of all must-carry broadcast signals." American Civil Liberties Union v. FCC, 823 F.2d at 1565. Given subsequent invalidation of the must-carry rules, the Commission's definition of basic service would have been useless anyway. *See* Century Communications Corporation v. Federal Communications Commission, 835 F.2d 292 (D.C.Cir. 1987), *cert. denied,* 108 S.Ct. 2015 (1988).

153. American Civil Liberties Union v. Federal Communications Commission, 823 F.2d at 1570–71.

154. *Id.* at 1570.

155. *Id.* at 1571.

156. *Id.*

157. *Id.* at 1573 (emphasis in original).

158. *Id.* at 1572.

159. Cable Communications Policy Act Rules (Signal Availability Standard), 3 F.C.C. Rcd. 2617 (1988).

160. *Id.*

161. 47 U.S.C. § 543(c).

162. *See* Brotman, *Time to Pull the Cable?* NAT. L.J. 13, 14 (Dec. 18, 1989).

163. *See id.*

164. *See id.*

165. *See id.*

166. *See* Chapter 5 of this book.

167. 47 U.S.C. § 533 (a). The statute also prohibits common carriers from operating a cable system in their service areas. *Id.,* § 533 (b). Cross-ownership rules affecting common carriers are discussed in the next section of this chapter.

168. *Id.,* § 533 (c).

169. 47 C.F.R. § 76.501.

170. *See* Marsh Media, Ltd. v. Federal Communications Commission, 798 F.2d 772 (5th Cir. 1986).

171. *See id.* at 775.

172. 798 F.2d 772.

173. *Id.* at 775.

174. *Id.* at 776.

175. *Id.* at 776. The National Citizens Committee for Broadcasting decision is discussed in Chapter 5 of this book.

176. Syndicated exclusivity protects programming marketed by a supplier other than a network to a local television station.

177. *See Malrite TV of New York v. Federal Communications Commission,* 652 F. 2d 1140.

178. Amendment of Parts 73 and 76 of the Commission's Rules Relating to Program Exclusivity in the Cable and Broadcast Industries, 3 F.C.C. Rcd. 5299 (1988), *on rehearing,* 4 F.C.C. Rcd. 2711 (1989).

179. Amendment of Parts 73 and 76 of the Commission's Rules Relating to Program Exclusivity in the Cable and Broadcast Industries, 2 F.C.C. Rcd. 2393 (1987).

180. 3 F.C.C. Rcd. 5229.

181. 890 F. 2d 1173 (D.C. Cir. 1989).

182. *Id.* at 1178.

183. *Id.* at 1179.

184. *Id.* at 1180.

185. 47 U.S.C. §544 (f) (1) (prohibiting federal, state or local authority from "impos[ing] requirements regarding the provision or content of cable services").

186. 890 F.2d at 1189.

187. *Id.* at 1191.

Chapter 7

COMMON CARRIERS

I. THE NATURE AND REGULATION OF COMMON CARRIERS

Common carriers have characteristics associated with other media insofar as they are a means of propagation. Unlike print, broadcasting, and cable, common carriers generally do not make editorial decisions regarding content. Telephone lines or transmissions actually may be the passageway for signals that ultimately are converted into a print, broadcast, cable, or other format. The key distinguishing characteristic of a common carrier thus is a duty "by wire or radio to furnish . . . communication service upon reasonable request therefore."[1] Given the special role performed by common carriers, regulation of their traditional function has raised few real First Amendment questions.[2]

The Communications Act of 1934 defines a common carrier as "any person engaged as a common carrier for hire, in interstate or foreign radio transmission of energy."[3] Even before enactment of the Communications Act, the basic duties of common carriers were well established. Telegraph operators thus had "the duty of fairness and equality in the treatment of [their] customers and [were obligated to] serve them at reasonable rates and without unjust discrimination."[4] Requirements of equal access and nondiscrimination govern "like communication service."[5] What constitutes like service is left for the Federal Communications Commission (FCC) to determine on a case-by-case basis.[6]

What a common carrier is in some ways may be clarified by understanding what it is not. When cable was in its infancy, the FCC specifically considered whether it was a common carrier.[7] Because subscribers had no control over the particular information they received, the commission determined that cable did not so qualify.[8] The Supreme Court, in *United States v. Southwestern Cable Co.*,[9] essentially embraced the FCC's view in noting that cable for purposes of the Communications Act was not a common carrier.[10] In the mid–1970s, however, the FCC adopted access rules that effectively imposed upon cable operators the common carrier obligations of equal access and nondiscrimination.[11] The Supreme Court, in *Federal Communications Commission v. Midwest Video Corp.*,[12] invalidated the access rules and identified the differing nature and status of cable and common carriers.

With its access rules...the Commission has transferred control of the content of access cable channels from cable operators to members of the public who wish to communicate by the cable medium. Effectively, the Commission has relegated cable systems, *pro tanto,* to common-carrier status.[a] A common-carrier service in the communications context[b] is one that "makes a public offering to provide [communications facilities] whereby all members of the public who choose to employ such facilities may communicate or transmit intelligence of their own design and choosing...." *Report and Order, Industrial Radiolocation Service, Docket No. 16106,* 5 F. C. C. 2d 197, 202 (1966); see *National Association of Regulatory Utility Comm'rs v. FCC,* 173 U.S. App. D.C. 413, 424, 525 F. 2d 630, 641, cert. denied, 425 U.S. 992 (1976); *Multipoint Distribution Service,* 45 F. C. C. 2d 616, 618 (1974). A common carrier does not "make individualized decisions, in particular cases, whether and on what terms to deal." *National Association of Regulatory Utility Comm'rs v. FCC, supra,* at 424, 525 F. 2d, at 641.

The access rules plainly impose common-carrier obligations on cable operators.[c] Under

---

a. A cable system may operate as a common carrier with respect to a portion of its service only. See *National Association of Regulatory Utility Comm'rs v. FCC,* 174 U.S. App. D.C. 374, 381, 533 F. 2d 601, 608 (1976) (opinion of Wilkey, J.) ("Since it is clearly possible for a given entity to carry on many types of activities, it is at least logical to conclude that one can be a common carrier with regard to some activities but not others"); *First Report and Order in Docket No. 18397,* 20 F.C.C. 2d 201, 207 (1969).

b. Section 3(h) defines "common carrier" as "any person engaged as a common carrier for hire, in interstate or foreign communication by wire or radio or interstate or foreign radio transmission of energy...." Due to the circularity of the definition, resort must be had to court and agency pronouncements to ascertain the term's meaning. See *National Association of Regulatory Utility Comm'rs v. FCC,* 173 U.S. App. D.C. 413, 423, 525 F. 2d 630, 640, cert. denied, 425 U.S. 992 (1976); *Frontier Broadcasting Co. v. Collier,* 24 F.C.C. 251, 254 (1958); H.R. Conf. Rep. No. 1918, 73d Cong., 2d Sess., 46 (1934).

c. As we have noted, and as the Commission has held, cable systems otherwise "are not common carriers within the meaning of the Act." *United States v. South-*

the rules, cable systems are required to hold out dedicated channels on a first-come, non-discriminatory basis. 47 CFR §§ 76.254 (a), 76.256 (d) (1977). Operators are prohibited from determining or influencing the content of access programming. § 76.256 (b). And the rules delimit what operators may charge for access and use of equipment. § 76.256 (c).

II. THE RESTRUCTURING OF THE TELEPHONE INDUSTRY

Defined most broadly, a common carrier includes air and ground carriers, telegraph companies, and other methodologies for movement of goods or data. The most prominent contemporary concern in the field of communications, given the importance of the industry and the attention it has received, is with telephone service. The dominance and influence of the American Telephone and Telegraph Company (AT&T), which through its subsidiaries effectively monopolized local and long-distance telephone communications until recently, have been enduring concerns of federal regulation.

In 1956, the Department of Justice and AT&T negotiated an antitrust settlement incorporated into a final judgment that, for the next quarter of a century, defined the Bell System's scope of operations.[14] Terms of the decree required AT&T's manufacturing subsidiary, Western Electric Company, to refrain from producing any common carrier equipment of a type not sold or leased to Bell System companies.[15] AT&T itself largely was barred from engaging in any business other than the furnishing of common carrier services.[16] Such structural controls reflected a sense that AT&T's resources, technological expertise, and leverage if unrestrained would be a threat

---

western Cable Co., 392 U.S. at 169 n. 29; see *Frontier Broadcasting Co. v. Collier, supra.*

rather than an advantage to national economic interests.

United States v. Western Electric Co., Inc., 1956 Trade Reg. Rpts., § 68,246, at 71,134 (D.N.J.)

Thomas F. Meaney, District Judge.

[Discontinuance of Types of Businesses]

(A) The defendants are each enjoined and restrained from commencing, and after three (3) years from the date of this Final Judgment from continuing, directly or indirectly, to manufacture for sale or lease any equipment which is of a type not sold or leased or intended to be sold or leased to Companies of the Bell System, for use in furnishing common carrier communications services, except equipment used in the manufacture or installation of equipment which is of a type so sold or leased or intended to be so sold or leased; provided, however, that this Section shall not apply to the artificial larynx, by-products of reclamation of scrap, or equipment manufactured for the plaintiff, or for plaintiff's prime or subcontractors for the performance of contracts with plaintiff or subcontracts thereunder.

(B) After three (3) years from the date of this Final Judgment, the defendant Western is enjoined and restrained from engaging, either directly or indirectly, in any business not of a character or type engaged in by Western or its subsidiaries for companies of the Bell System, other than (1) businesses in which defendant AT&T may engage under Section V hereof, (2) businesses in which Western is required to engage under this Final Judgment, and (3) any business engaged in for the plaintiff or any agency thereof....

[AT&T's Line of Business]

The defendant AT&T is enjoined and restrained from engaging, either directly, or indirectly through its subsidiaries other than Western and Western's subsidiaries, in any business other than the furnishing of common carrier communications services; provided, however, that this Section V shall not apply to (a) furnishing services or facilities for the plaintiff or any agency thereof, (b) experiments for the purpose of testing or developing new common carrier communications services, (c) furnishing circuits to other communications common carriers, (d) for a period of five (5) years from the date of this Final Judgment, leasing and maintaining facilities for private communications systems, the charges for which are not subject to public regulation, to persons who are lessees from defendants or their subsidiaries of such systems forty-five (45) days after the date of this Final Judgment, (e) directory advertising, (f) advice or assistance to other communications common carriers, or (g) businesses or services incidental to the furnishing by AT&T or such subsidiaries of common carrier communications services.

[Jurisdiction Retained]

Jurisdiction is retained for the purpose of enabling any of the parties to this Final Judgment to apply to this Court at any time for such further orders and directions as may be necessary or appropriate for the construction or carrying out of this Final Judgment, or the modification or termination of any of the provisions thereof or for the enforcement of compliance therewith or for the punishment of violations thereof. Upon any such application by the plaintiff, the plaintiff shall be deemed to have made a sufficient showing of a change in circumstances warranting appropriate modification of this Final Judgment if it shall show elimination hereafter, in a substantial number of states, of public regulation of charges for common carrier communication services.

In entering the final judgment, the court retained jurisdiction "for the purpose of enabling any of the parties for this Final Judgment to apply to this Court at any time for such further orders and directions as may be necessary or appropriate."[17]

"[A]ny time" arrived more than two decades later when AT&T and the federal government filed a stipulation in *United States v. American Telephone & Telegraph Co.*[18] consenting to the entry of a "Modification of Final Judgment." The modified final judgment was the result of a Justice Department action alleging antitrust violations and originally seeking divestiture from AT&T of its Bell operating companies and the dissolution of Western Electric.[19] The modified final judgment reflected a settlement between the parties which essentially required AT&T to divest itself of the operating companies and thereby abandon its role as a supplier of local telephone service.[20] Geographic service zones, denominated as "exchange areas," defined the new service regions of the spin-off companies.[21] Such areas were conceived "to comprehend contiguous areas having common social and economic characteristics but not so large as to defeat the intent of the decree to separate the provision of intercity service from the provision of local exchange service."[22] Central to the new order, therefore, was that the new companies (sometimes referred to as Baby Bells) would "provide telephone service from one point in an exchange area to other points in the same exchange area—'exchange telecommunications'—and they would originate and terminate calls from one exchange area to another exchange area—'exchange access.' The interexchange portion of calls would ... however, be carried by AT&T" or its new competitors in the long-distance business.[23] The relationships between AT&T and its manufacturing arm, Western Electric, and its research arm, Bell Laboratories, were preserved.[24] All were obligated, however, to provide various types of support for the operating companies to ensure their viability and compliance with the decree.[25]

A prerequisite for divestiture, which proved to be the heart of the modified final judgment, was a determination that it served "the public interest."[26] The court found the standard satisfied, despite AT&T's claim that its depressed local rates were a function of FCC policy that required national rate averaging and thus were reasonable under federal law.[27] The court noted that FCC policy had changed in recent years but that AT&T's anticompetitive practices of using long-distance service to subsidize local rates

had not.[28] In addition, it was found that AT&T, again contrary to the public interest, had prohibited attachment of competitors' equipment to its network and had forced its operating companies to purchase equipment from Western Electric even when superior products were available from other sources.[29]

Apart from such specific identified acts, the court concluded that antitrust relief was justified by "AT&T's substantial domination of the telecommunications industry in general."[30] It referred to general antitrust policy which favors decentralization rather than aggregations or concentrations of industrial power.[31] Those concerns were magnified, in the court's view, by the crucial role of the telecommunications industry and the reality that "[t]he only pervasive two-way communication system is the telephone network."[32] Noting that past Bell System officials mostly "have been careful not to take advantage of [their] central position in American economic life, ... [it nonetheless observed] [t]here is no guarantee ... that future managers will be equally careful."[33] The court thus regarded the decree as a means not only of halting objectionable practices but also of ensuring that others did not occur.

Terms of the consent decree, although requiring AT&T to divest its operating companies,[34] lifted all restrictions imposed by the 1956 decree and left it "free to compete in all facets of the marketplace."[35] Although freed thereby to enter the computer and information services market,[36] a significant exception bars AT&T from entering into electronic publishing.[37] The restriction raises First Amendment questions and thus is considered in Chapter 11 of this volume. Constraints upon the divested operating companies preclude them from furnishing interexchange and information services[38] and manufacturing telecommunication equipment.[39] Such restrictions reflect concern with marketplace competition,[40] but restraints upon marketing customer premises equipment or publishing directories were rejected as contrary to the public interest.[41] Finally, because "a substantial AT&T bias has been designed into the integrated telecommunications network,"[42] the decree obligated the operating companies to provide all long-distance carriers with equal access to "interexchange and information services."[43]

United States v. American Telephone and Telegraph Co., 552 F.Supp. 131 (D.D.C. 1982), *aff'd*, 460 U.S. 1001 (1983)

OPINION

Harold H. Greene, District Judge.

These actions are before the Court for a determination whether a consent decree proposed by the parties is in the "public interest" and should therefore be entered as the Court's judgment. Over six hundred comments from interested persons, many of them objecting to various aspects of the proposal, have been received, and the Court has considered briefs submitted by the parties and others, and it has heard extensive oral argument. This opinion discusses the principal questions raised by these interested persons, and it embodies the Court's decision on the appropriateness of the proposed decree under the Tunney Act's public interest standard.

I

Preliminary Considerations

A. History of the Litigation

On January 14, 1949, the government filed an action in the District Court for the District of New Jersey against the Western Electric Company, Inc. and the American Telephone and Telegraph Company, Inc. (Civil Action No. 17–49). The complaint alleged that the defendants had monopolized and conspired to restrain trade in the manufacture, distribution, sale, and installation of telephones, telephone apparatus, equipment, materials, and supplies, in violation of sections 1, 2, and 3 of the Sherman Act, 15 U.S.C. §§ 1, 2, and 3. The relief sought included the divestiture by AT&T of its stock ownership in Western Elec-

tric; termination of exclusive relationships between AT&T and Western Electric; divestiture by Western Electric of its fifty percent interest in Bell Telephone Laboratories; separation of telephone manufacturing from the provision of telephone service; and the compulsory licensing of patents owned by AT&T on a non-discriminatory basis.

Periodic negotiations between AT&T and the government continued through 1954 and 1955, and by early December, 1955, the government and AT&T had reached an agreement.

The consent decree which was the product of this process included neither the divestiture of Western Electric nor any of the other structural relief originally requested by the government. Instead, an injunction was issued which precluded AT&T from engaging in any business other than the provision of common carrier communications services; precluded Western Electric from manufacturing equipment other than that used by the Bell System; and required the defendants to license their patents to all applicants upon the payment of appropriate royalties.

Despite the substantial differences between the structural relief requested in the government's 1949 complaint and the relief actually provided by the proposed decree, the District Court for the District of New Jersey accepted the proposal on January 24, 1956, after a brief hearing, stating:

> I feel that I can unhesitatingly accept the recommendation of the Attorney General, that this judgment is in the public interest, and that it is a satisfactory adjustment of this very, very vexatious problem; and I am therefore happy to go along with the recommendation made by the Attorney General and shall forthwith sign this judgment.

After the decree was approved, no major developments occurred in the case for the next several years. Until 1981, the entries in the court record concern primarily the patent licensing provisions.

This was the status of the *Western Electric* suit when the government filed a separate antitrust action on November 20, 1974, in this Court against AT&T, Western Electric, and Bell Telephone Laboratories, Inc. (Civil Action No. 74–1698). The complaint in the new action alleged monopolization by the defendants with respect to a broad variety of telecommunications services and equipment in violation of section 2 of the Sherman Act. In this lawsuit, the government initially sought the divestiture from AT&T of the Bell Operating Companies (hereinafter generally referred to as Operating Companies or BOCs) as well as the divestiture and dissolution of Western Electric. While the action was pending, the government changed its relief requests several times asking, at various times or in various alternatives, for the divestiture from AT&T of Western Electric and portions of the Bell Laboratories....

B. The Proposed Decree

On January 8, 1982, the parties to these two actions filed.... a stipulation consenting to the entry by the Court of the "Modification of Final Judgment" filed therewith. On the same day, they attempted to file in this Court a dismissal of the *AT&T* action pursuant to Rule 41(a)(1)(ii), Federal Rules of Civil Procedure. This Court ordered that the dismissal be lodged, not filed, and, in accordance with that order and the provisions of the Tunney Act, the dismissal has not yet been effected. See note 52 *infra*.

In their settlement proposal, the parties proposed that the Court enter the following judgment with respect to both lawsuits.

Section I of the proposed decree would provide for significant structural changes in AT&T. In essence, it would remove from the Bell System the function of supplying local telephone service by requiring AT&T to divest itself of the portions of its twenty-two Operating Companies which perform that function.

The geographic area for which these Operating Companies would provide local telephone service is defined in the proposed decree by a new unit, the "exchange area." According to the Justice Department, an exchange area "will be large enough to comprehend contiguous areas having common social and economic characteristics but not so large as to defeat the intent of the decree to separate the provision of intercity services from the provision of local exchange service." Court approval would be required for the inclusion in an exchange area of more than one standard metropolitan area or the territory of more than one State.

The Operating Companies would provide telephone service from one point in an exchange area to other points in the same exchange area—"exchange telecommunications"—and they would originate and terminate calls from one exchange area to another exchange area—"exchange access." The interexchange portion of calls from one exchange area to another exchange area would, however, be carried by AT&T and the other interexchange carriers, such as MCI and Southern Pacific Co.

The proposed decree sets forth general principles governing the configuration of the Operating Companies which AT&T would be required to divest. Under the proposal, AT&T would be required to endow the companies with sufficient personnel, facilities, systems, and rights to technical information to enable them to provide exchange telecommunications and exchange access services. These personnel, systems, facilities, and rights would be drawn from the Operating Companies and from AT&T and its other affiliates. AT&T would be permitted to choose to transfer some of these elements directly to the new Operating Companies and to place others in a central entity jointly owned by them.

AT&T would be required by the proposed decree to formulate a plan of reorganization which complied with these principles, and to submit the plan to the Department of Justice within six months after the Court approved the decree. The plan would not be effective without the Department's approval.

After divestiture, the new Operating Companies would be required to provide, through a centralized body, a single point of contact for national security and emergency preparedness. They would be permitted to use this or a similar central body to provide those services, such as administration and engineering, which "can most efficiently be provided on a centralized basis." In addition, until September 1987, AT&T, Western Electric, and Bell Laboratories would have to provide on a priority basis, all research, development, manufacturing, and other support services necessary to enable the Operating Companies to fulfill the requirements of the proposed decree.

Section II of the proposed decree would complement these structural changes by various restrictions which are said to be designed (1) to prevent the divested Operating Companies from discriminating against AT&T's competitors, and (2) to avoid a recurrence of the type of discrimination and cross-subsidization that were the basis of the *AT&T* lawsuit.

II

Power of the Court in this Public Interest Proceeding

Under the Tunney Act, the Court may approve the decree proposed by the parties only if it first determines that such approval is "in the public interest...."

IV

The Divestiture

A key feature of the proposed decree is the divestiture of the Operating Companies from the remainder of AT&T. In order to determine whether that divestiture is in the public interest, the Court must decide first whether it is a remedy that is likely to eliminate anticompetitive conditions within the telecommunications industry. In addition, the Court must assess the efficacy of alternative remedies and it must weigh the effect of the divestiture on the public interest generally, particularly on the level of charges for local telephone service.

A. Conditions Necessitating Antitrust Relief

1. Evidence of Anticompetitive Actions by AT&T

In its complaint and in documents filed thereafter (i.e., the several Statements of Contentions and Proof), the government asserted that AT&T monopolized the intercity telecommunications market and the telecommunications product market in a variety of ways in violation of the Sherman Act.

The evidence that was produced during the *AT&T* trial indicates that, at least with respect to several of the government's claims, this charge may be well taken. It would be inappropriate for the Court at this juncture to draw definitive conclusions with regard either to the sufficiency of the evidence to sustain a finding of liability or to the validity of AT&T's various legal and factual defenses. The Court is not called upon, in this public interest proceeding, to render a final judgment on this case; indeed, not all the evidence

that may bear on the issues has yet been adduced. It is not improper, however, for the Court to consider whether the state of proof at trial was such as to sustain this divestiture as being in the public interest. See 15 U.S.C. §§ 16(b)(2), (e).

In its intercity case, the government alleged that AT&T used its control over its local monopoly to preclude competition in the intercity market. The government proved *inter alia* that after 1968 AT&T included a "customer premises" provision in its interconnection tariff which deterred potential competitors from entering that market; that it refused to provide FX and CCSA services to specialized common carriers and domestic satellite carriers until 1974 when the FCC specifically ordered it to do so; and that it attempted to prevent competitors from offering metered long distance service that would compete with AT&T's own regular long distance service.

AT&T's basic rationale for these policies was that it was attempting to prevent competitors from "creamskimming." As viewed by AT&T, it would have been able successfully to combat creamskimming if it had priced each of its routes on the basis of the costs for operating that route. However, it concluded that the FCC had rejected this approach when it endorsed national rate averaging in the interest of promoting the goal of universal service. Accordingly, AT&T argued that, since rate averaging is inconsistent with competition, and since the basic rate averaging policy had been required by the FCC as being in the public interest, it was acting reasonably under the Communications Act in preventing competition as best and as long as it could.

What this line of reasoning fails to consider is that, at least by the mid–1970s, the FCC had clearly begun to promote competition in telecommunications. The government contended during the trial—correctly, in the Court's view—that AT&T had an obligation to follow the more recent FCC policy rather than the Commission's previous policies which may have suited it better, particularly since there was never a direct FCC rule against de-averaging. Moreover, even if, because of the lack of definite guidance from the FCC, AT&T's actions were to be regarded as reasonable under the Communications Act standards, it does not at all follow that these same actions were immunized under the standards of the Sherman Act.

What is significant about these events is that AT&T was able to adopt the policies described above in large part because of its control over the local exchange facilities. For example, it was because of its ownership and control of the local Operating Companies—whose facilities were and are needed for interconnection purposes by AT&T's competitors—that AT&T was able to prevent these competitors from offering FX and CCSA services. Similarly, AT&T was able to deter competition by manipulating prices for access to the Operating Company networks.

AT&T's control over the local Operating Companies was central also to the anticompetitive behavior alleged with respect to the second facet of the government's case, that involving customer-provided terminal equipment.

The government proved that AT&T prohibited the attachment of competitors' equipment to the network except through a protective connecting arrangement (PCA). There was evidence that some experts (including a panel of the National Academy of Sciences) believed that such a PCA was necessary if the nationwide telephone network was to be protected from a variety of harms. On the other hand, the government's evidence indicated that AT&T required PCAs for equipment that in all probability could not harm the network; that there were delays in providing PCAs; that the PCAs were over-designed and over-engineered, and, thus, over-priced; that PCAs were required for competitive equipment while identical equipment sold by AT&T did not require their use; and that PCAs could not guard against all four potential harms to the network.

Additionally, the alternative option of certification was available but never seriously pursued by Bell. Moreover, when ultimately certification was directly mandated by the FCC as a substitute for the protective connecting arrangement, the telephone network—AT&T's predictions to the contrary notwithstanding—did not cease to function in its customary fashion. Indeed, AT&T was unable during the trial to prove *any* actual harm to the network from the elimination of the PCAs.

In its procurement part of the case, the government alleged, and there was proof, that AT&T used its control over the local Operating Companies to force them to buy products from Western Electric even though other equipment manufacturers produced better products or products of identical quality at lower prices. Here, too, AT&T's control of the Operating Companies was central to the allegedly anticompetitive behavior.

Without making definitive findings on any or all of the issues, it is certainly clear that—to the extent that the proposed decree is offered by the government on the premise that it will destroy the basis of past anticompetitive behavior—the Court would not be justified in rejecting it as constituting a remedy for non-existent anticompetitive acts.

2. Concentration of Power in the Telecommunications Industry

There is an additional reason, largely independent of the factors discussed above, which supports some type of antitrust relief in this case: AT&T's substantial domination of the telecommunications industry in general.

The antitrust laws are most often viewed as only a means for ensuring free competition in order to achieve the most efficient allocation of society's resources. See pp. 149–150 *supra*. However, Congress and the courts have repeatedly declared that these laws also embody "a desire to put an end to great aggregations of capital because of the helplessness of the individual before them." *United States v. Aluminum Company of America,* 148 F.2d 416, 428 (2d Cir.1945) (footnote omitted). See also *Standard Oil Co. v. United States,* 221 U.S. 1, 50, 31 S.Ct. 502, 511, 55 L.Ed. 619 (1911); *United States v. Trans-Missouri Freight Ass'n,* 166 U.S. 290, 323–24 (1897).

The legislators who enacted the Sherman Act voiced concerns beyond the effects of anticompetitive activities on the economy: they also greatly feared the impact of the large trusts, which then dominated the business world, on the nation's political system, and they regarded the power of these trusts as an evil to be eradicated. Thus, Senator Sherman stated:

> If the concentrated powers of [a] combination are intrusted to a single man, it is a kingly prerogative, inconsistent with our form of government, and should be subject to the strong resistance of the State and national authorities. If anything is wrong, this is wrong. If we will not endure a king as a political

power we should not endure a king over the production, transportation, and sale of any of the necessaries of life.

21 Cong.Rec. 2457 (1890).

These views have been repeatedly echoed since that time, as, for example, during the congressional debates at the time of the enactment of the 1950 amendments to the Clayton Act. See 96 Cong.Rec. 16450 (1950) (Remarks of Sen. Kefauver); 95 Cong.Rec. 11494 (1950) (Remarks of Rep. Bryson); 95 Cong.Rec. 11486 (1949) (Remarks of Rep. Celler). See also *Brown Shoe Co. v. United States*, 370 U.S. 294, 344 (1962). As Justice Douglas stated in his dissenting opinion in *United States v. Columbia Steel Co.*, 334 U.S. 495, 536 (1948):

> Power that controls the economy should be in the hands of elected representatives of the people, not in the hands of an industrial oligarchy. Industrial power should be decentralized. It should be scattered into many hands so that the fortunes of the people will not be dependent on the whim or caprice, the political prejudices, the emotional stability of a few self-appointed men. The fact that they are not vicious men but respectable and social-minded is irrelevant. That is the philosophy and the command of the Sherman Act. It is founded on a theory of hostility to the concentration in private hands of power so great that only a government of the people should have it.

Our political system is designed so that the power of one group may be checked by the power of another. The antitrust laws require this same approach in the economic sphere. Obviously, if one company controlled an essential part of the economy, it would be in a position to gain an undue influence over economic decisions and, as a result, most likely over political decisions. Thus, the antitrust laws seek to diffuse economic power in order to promote the proper functioning of both our economic and our political systems. See generally, A.D. Neale, *The Antitrust Laws of the United States of America*, 422–23 (1962); Blake & Jones, *Antitrust Dialogue: Defense*, 65 Colum. L.Rev. 337, 384 (1965).

The significance of these concepts is accentuated by the context in which the Court must consider the public interest in these cases. The telecommunications industry plays a key role in modern economic, social, and political life. Indeed, many commentators have asserted that we are entering an age in which information will be the keystone of the economy as steel was when Justice Douglas wrote in the *Columbia Steel Co.* case.

The only pervasive two-way communications system is the telephone network. It is crucial in business affairs, in providing information to the citizenry, and in the simple conduct of daily life. In its present form, AT&T has a commanding position in that industry. The men and women who have guided the Bell System appear by and large to have been careful not to take advantage of its central position in America's economic life. There is no guarantee, however, that future managers will be equally careful. In any event, it is antithetical to our political and economic system for this key industry to be within the control of one company.

For these reasons, the Court concludes that the loosening of AT&T's control over telecommunications through the divestiture of the Operating Companies will entail benefits which transcend those which flow from the narrowest reading of the purpose of the antitrust laws.

B. Effect of the Divestiture

The remedy in an antitrust action—whether imposed by a court or agreed upon between the parties—is measured both by how well it halts the objectionable practices and by its prospects for minimizing the likelihood that such practices will occur in the future. See Part II *supra*. Where, as here, the Court has heard substantially all of the evidence, it is appropriate that it weigh the proposed remedy against the evidence in that context.

As indicated in Part IV(A) *supra*, the ability of AT&T to engage in anticompetitive conduct stems largely from its control of the local Operating Companies. Absent such control, AT&T will not have the ability to disadvantage competitors in the interexchange and equipment markets.

For example, with the divestiture of the Operating Companies AT&T will not be able to discriminate against intercity competitors, either by subsidizing its own intercity services with revenues from the monopoly local exchange services, or by obstructing its competitors' access to the local exchange network. The local Operating Companies will not be providing interexchange services, and they will therefore have no incentive to discriminate. Moreover, AT&T's competitors will be guaranteed access that is equal to that provided to AT&T, and intercity carriers therefore will no longer be presented with the problems that confronted them in that area. See Part VIII, *infra*.

V

Absence of Restrictions on AT&T

Under the terms of the proposed decree, the line of business restrictions and the licensing requirements imposed by the 1956 consent decree in the *Western Electric* case would be removed and AT&T would be free to compete in all facets of the marketplace. Some of the opponents of the proposed decree argue that several of the restrictions contained in the 1956 decree should not be eliminated, and others contend that the Court should also impose additional restrictions, not present in the 1956 decree. For the reasons explained in this part of the opinion and Part VI below, the Court finds that, with one exception (see Part VI(B) *infra*), the imposition of restrictions on AT&T would not be in the public interest.

The antitrust laws do not require that a company be prohibited from competing in a market unless it can be demonstrated that its participation in that market will have anticompetitive effects. Past restrictions on AT&T were justified primarily because of its control over the local Operating Companies. With the divestiture of these local exchange monopolies, continued restrictions are not required unless justified by some other rationale.

As defined by the Supreme Court, monopoly power is "the power to control prices or exclude competition." *United States v. Grinnell Corp., supra*, 384 U.S. at 571 (1966); *United States v. duPont & Co.*, 351 U.S. 377, 391 (1956). Although monopoly power may be inferred from a firm's predominant share of the market, size alone is not synonymous with market power, particularly where entry barriers are not substantial. *United States v. Grinnell, supra*, 384 U.S. at 571; *United States v. AT&T, supra*, 524 F.Supp. at 1347; Pos-

ner, *Market Power in Antitrust Cases*, 94 Harv.L.Rev. 937, 947–51 (1981).

Both the Department of Justice and AT&T contend that competition in the interexchange market is growing and that this increase in competition demonstrates an absence of monopoly power. There is some validity to this claim. The interexchange market is now being served not only by relatively young businesses but also by subsidiaries of such well established firms as ITT, Southern Pacific, and IBM.

That is not to say, however, that competition has flourished without impediment or that it would soar if the Bell System were not broken up. There is substantial merit to the suggestion that, absent divestiture, AT&T would still possess significant monopoly power, and that whatever competition developed in the past did so despite anticompetitive conditions. See Part IV *supra*. But the overriding fact is that the principal means by which AT&T has maintained monopoly power in telecommunications has been its control of the Operating Companies with their strategic bottleneck position. The divestiture required by the proposed decree will thus remove the two main barriers that previously deterred firms from entering or competing effectively in the interexchange market.

First. AT&T will no longer have the opportunity to provide discriminatory interconnection to competitors. The Operating Companies will own the local exchange facilities. Since these companies will not be providing interexchange services, they will lack AT&T's incentive to discriminate. Moreover, they will be required to provide all interexchange carriers with exchange access that is "equal in type, quality, and price to that provided to AT&T and its affiliates." Proposed Decree, Section II. See Part VIII *infra*.

Second. Once AT&T is divested of the local Operating Companies, it will be unable either to subsidize the prices of its interexchange service with revenues from local exchange services or to shift costs from competitive interexchange services.

With the removal by the decree of all these burdens on competition, the number of firms entering the interexchange market is thus likely to increase. This development should be further assisted by the reduction of other barriers to entry.

For example, although the cost of entering the telecommunications business is still substantial, the size of the required capital investment is not as great as it once was. In addition, as more competitors begin to offer more services that are comparable to those offered by AT&T, entrenched customer preferences in favor of AT&T will decrease.

With the removal of these barriers to competition, AT&T should be unable to engage in monopoly pricing in any market. To be sure, there are a number of routes for which AT&T is the sole interexchange carrier. However, several of these routes serve sparsely populated areas and appear to be only marginally profitable. On the other hand, should it turn out that these routes are in fact lucrative and that AT&T is nevertheless charging monopoly prices, then, following divestiture, market forces should fairly rapidly remedy the situation: because of the elimination of entry barriers, new entrants will be attracted to these markets, and prices, in turn, will fall to their competitive levels.

For these reasons, it appears that after divestiture, AT&T will largely lack the monopoly power that the opponents of the decree suggest, and the trend of increasing competition may therefore be expected to continue....

There is no merit to the claim that after divestiture AT&T will possess monopoly power in the area of equipment manufacturing. In reviewing the proof on anticompetitive behavior in the equipment market—even before divestiture—the Court found that the government's evidence on that aspect of the case was less convincing than, for example, on that involving intercity services. As explained in Part IV *supra,* where the government was able to show that AT&T's market share was high, it was generally unable to demonstrate significant anticompetitive behavior; where evidence of behavior was more damning, it had difficulty establishing market power. Thus, at a minimum the factual predicate for drastic restrictions in the equipment area is not as apparent as it might be with respect to other subjects.

After divestiture, AT&T's position in the equipment market will be further diminished, and that market is certain to become more competitive. To the extent that prior to divestiture AT&T was able to engage in anticompetitive con-

duct in the equipment market, that ability stemmed basically from its control of the Operating Companies. Once these local companies are divested, Western Electric will lose its captive customers. Not only does the proposed decree eliminate the Operating Companies' intra-enterprise incentive to purchase Western Electric equipment, but it also includes specific provisions that prohibit these companies from discriminating in the procurement of equipment. One of these provisions requires that within six months after the reorganization of AT&T, each Operating Company must submit to the Department of Justice compliance procedures explaining how that company plans to carry out its equipment procurement obligations. Proposed Decree, Sections II(B) and (C). If an Operating Company discriminates in procuring equipment, that act will constitute a violation of the decree, and an enforcement action may be brought against it.

There is likewise no merit to the argument that Western Electric will have an anticompetitive edge in the production of new equipment because its affiliation with Bell Laboratories and Long Lines will give it early access to technical information and network standards. This claim ignores the fact that after divestiture, the Operating Companies, not AT&T, will control the information necessary for local exchange and exchange access services. Thus, if equipment manufacturers need information about interconnecting their equipment to the local exchange network, it will be provided by companies that are not engaged in the manufacturing of equipment.

There is no competitive basis, therefore, for imposing any of the proposed restrictions on AT&T in the area of equipment manufacturing and marketing....

VI

The 1956 Decree and Line of Business Restrictions

The basic agreement embodied in the 1956 consent decree in the *Western Electric* case was that AT&T would not be required to divest itself of Western Electric, provided that AT&T would restrict its operations to the provision of common carrier communications services and that Western Electric would manufacture only the types of equipment used by the Bell System.

The decree which has now been submitted by the parties would eliminate all of the restrictions of the 1956 consent judgment. If that decree is entered by the Court, AT&T would be free to enter the computer market as well as to provide the full range of so-called information services.

There has been no serious opposition to the entry of AT&T into manufacturing and marketing of computers and other electronic equipment, and there is no question that this development would be in the public interest. It will accordingly be approved. By contrast, others who have submitted comments object to AT&T's entry into the information services market.

"Information services" are defined in the proposed decree at Section IV(J) as:

> the offering of a capability for generating, acquiring, storing, transforming, processing, retrieving, utilizing or making available information which may be conveyed via telecommunications....

Two distinctly different types of information services fall within this general category: services which would involve no control by AT&T over the content of the information other than for transmission purposes (such as the traditional data processing services), and services in which AT&T would control both the transmission of the information and its content (such as news or entertainment). Because these two types of services raise different concerns, they will be addressed separately.

A. Data Processing and Other Computer-Related Services

As technology has advanced, the line between communications and data processing has become blurred. Advances in communications technology, for example, now allow otherwise incompatible computers to converse with each other. New sophisticated telephone equipment located on a customer's premises not only performs switching and call routing functions but it also retrieves information much as does a traditional computer. Even ordinary telephones may be capable of performing functions that formerly required the support of a separate computer.

Providers of data processing services—like oth-

ers who have commented on the decree in other contexts—contend that AT&T should be prohibited from entering these fields because of its market power in the area of interexchange services. Shaping the argument to support their particular interests, these persons contend that AT&T will use the monopoly profits from its interexchange services to subsidize its computer-related services, and that it will use its control over the interexchange network to discriminate against other data processing competitors in providing access to that network.

As explained in Part V *supra*, there is little possibility that AT&T will be able to use its revenues from the interexchange market to subsidize its prices for computer services. That being true, AT&T would not possess any anticompetitive advantages over competitors on this basis, and the possibility of cross subsidization as a basis for rejecting this portion of the proposed decree may therefore be completely discounted.

The discrimination argument is slightly more serious. Since AT&T will be offering its own computer-related services, it may well have an incentive to discriminate in transmitting competitors' services. But what defeats the objections is that AT&T's actual ability to discriminate is quite remote. This segment of the information services industry is already well established, comprised of some of the nation's leading corporate giants, as well as of many smaller concerns. The FCC has found that "[t]here are literally thousands of unregulated computer service vendors offering competing services connected to the interstate telecommunications network." *Computer II, supra,* 77 F.C.C.2d at 426. These strongly competitive conditions will limit AT&T's ability to practice discrimination in two ways. First, AT&T's competitors will have the economic resources necessary to combat any attempt at discrimination. Second, the growing demand for information services will necessarily increase the demand for transmission facilities for these services. Such an increase in demand is likely to stimulate AT&T's interexchange competitors to offer satisfactory alternatives to the AT&T network, and any attempt by AT&T to discriminate would only further enhance this eventuality.

This fairly limited possibility of discrimination clearly does not outweigh the substantial advantages to the public that would be gained by allowing AT&T to develop this new technology. AT&T's entry into these technologically sophisticated fields will stimulate competition, and it is therefore likely to produce further technological advances, new products, and better services—all of which are likely to benefit the American consumer, American foreign trade, and national defense.

Since AT&T's participation in these areas will foster the traditional objectives of the Sherman Act and is not likely to lead to anticompetitive practices, the Court will not sustain the objections to this aspect of the proposed decree.

VII

Restrictions on the Divested Operating Companies

The proposed decree limits the Operating Companies, upon their divestiture, to the business of supplying local telephone service. In addition to a general prohibition against the provision of "any product or service that is not a natural monopoly service actually regulated by tariff," there are more specific restrictions in Section II(D) which deny the Operating Companies the opportunity to engage in the following activities: (1) the provision of interexchange services; (2) the provision of information services; (3) the manufacture of telecommunications products and customer premises equipment; (4) the marketing of such equipment and (5) directory advertising, including the production of the "Yellow Pages" directories.

The restrictions are based upon the assumption that the Operating Companies, were they allowed to enter the forbidden markets, would use their monopoly power in an anticompetitive manner. It is accordingly necessary for the Court first to determine whether these companies will actually have the incentive and opportunity to act anticompetitively. Second, the restrictions are, at least in one sense, directly anticompetitive because they prevent a potential competitor from entering the market. The Court must accordingly also consider the extent to which the participation of the Operating Companies would contribute to the creation of a competitive market.

A. Interexchange Services

The proposed decree prohibits the divested Operating Companies from providing interexchange services. This restriction is clearly necessary to preserve free competition in the interexchange market....

B. Information Services

The proposed decree prohibits the Operating Companies from providing information services, an umbrella description of a variety of services including electronic publishing and other enhanced uses of telecommunications. This prohibition is necessary for reasons similar to those justifying the restriction on interexchange services, as well as for additional reasons not relevant to the interexchange problem....

C. Manufacture of Equipment

The provision in the proposed decree which prohibits the Operating Companies from manufacturing telecommunications equipment and customer premises equipment (CPE) is also an outgrowth of the government's case in the *AT&T* action. The basic rationale of the procurement portion of that case was that

> a combination of vertical integration and rate-of-return regulation ... tended to generate decisions by the Operating Companies to purchase equipment produced by Western [Electric] that is more expensive or of less quality than that manufactured by the general trade.

United States v. AT&T, supra, 524 F.Supp. at 1373. The government presented evidence to support this theory, which tended to show that AT&T headquarters and the service components of the Bell System—the Bell Operating Companies and the Long Lines Department—engaged in systematic efforts to disadvantage outside suppliers. *Id.* at 1371–74. See also Part IV *supra*. That theory and that evidence directly support the proposed prohibition on the manufacture of equipment by the Operating Companies....

D. Marketing of Customer Premises Equipment

The proposed decree would also prohibit the Operating Companies from selling or leasing customer premises equipment. While the Department of Justice's comments and briefs tend to blur the distinction between manufacturing and marketing, in fact the restrictions on the two activities present wholly different considerations. Based upon a realistic assessment, marketing of CPE presents little potential for anticompetitive behavior by the Operating Companies. While the Operating Companies would have the theoretical ability to engage in the types of anticompetitive activities which support the prohibition on manufacturing of CPE, their incentives and their practical ability to do so would be minimal....

E. Directory Advertising

Each Bell Operating Company presently publishes Yellow Pages directories for its service area. The proposed decree would bar the divested Operating Companies from all activities related to directory advertising, including the production of the so-called Yellow Pages. This restriction lacks an appropriate basis and is not in the public interest.

Neither of the reasons underlying the other restrictions on the Operating Companies—the need to prevent cross subsidization and the importance of preventing competitor discrimination—has any relevance to the printed directory market.

All parties concede that the Yellow Pages currently earn supra-competitive profits. See, e.g., the Department of Justice Response to Comments at 71. There is no warrant therefore for proceeding on the premise that the advertising prices charged by the Operating Companies are artificially low as the result of a subsidy from local exchange service. Similarly, there is no possibility of improper discrimination by the Operating Companies against competing directory manufacturers since access to the local exchange network is not required for production of a printed directory. In short, the Operating Companies would have little or no ability to discriminate against competitors in the printed directory market, and this restriction thus has no procompetitive justification whatever.

To the contrary, the prohibition on directory production by the Operating Companies is distinctly anticompetitive in its effects, for at least two reasons. In the first place, the production of the Yellow Pages will be transferred from a number of smaller entities to one nationwide com-

pany—AT&T. This type of concentration is itself anathema to the antitrust laws. Furthermore, possession of the franchise for the printed directories will give AT&T a substantial advantage over its competitors in providing electronic directory advertising—a market in which the Operating Companies will not be engaged.

In addition to these factors directly related to competition, there are other reasons why the prohibition on publication of the Yellow Pages by the Operating Companies is not in the public interest. All those who have commented on or have studied the issue agree that the Yellow Pages provide a significant subsidy to local telephone rates. This subsidy would most likely continue if the Operating Companies were permitted to continue to publish the Yellow Pages.

The loss of this large subsidy would have important consequences for the rates for local telephone service. For example, the State of California claims that a two dollar increase in the rates for monthly telephone service would be necessary to offset the loss of revenues from directory advertising. Other states assert that increases of a similar magnitude would be required. Evidence submitted during the *AT&T* trial indicates that large rate increases of this type will reduce the number of households with telephones and increase the disparity, in terms of the availability of telephone service, between low income and well-off citizens. This result is clearly contrary to the goal of providing affordable telephone service for all Americans....

F. Removal of the Restrictions

It is probable that, over time, the Operating Companies will lose the ability to leverage their monopoly power into the competitive markets from which they must now be barred. This change could occur as a result of technological developments which eliminate the Operating Companies' local exchange monopoly or from changes in the structures of the competitive markets. In either event, the need for the restrictions upheld in Subparts A through C will disappear, and the decree should therefore contain a mechanism by which they may be removed.

Recognizing this fact, the Department of Justice has undertaken to report to the Court every three years concerning the continuing need for the restrictions imposed by the decree. Response to Comments at 62. In addition, both parties have agreed that the restrictions may be removed over the opposition of a party to the decree when the Court finds that "the rationale for [the restriction] is outmoded by technical developments." Department of Justice Brief at 32–33; AT&T Brief at 18.

VIII

Equal Exchange Access

One of the government's principal contentions in the *AT&T* case was that the Operating Companies provided interconnections to AT&T's intercity competitors which were inferior in many respects to those granted to AT&T's own Long Lines Department. There was ample evidence to sustain these contentions. See Part IV *supra*.

Although after divestiture the Operating Companies will no longer have the same incentive to favor AT&T, a substantial AT&T bias has been designed into the integrated telecommunications network, and the network, of course, remains in that condition. It is imperative that any disparities in interconnection be eliminated so that all interexchange and information service providers will be able to compete on an equal basis.

The Court has examined the equal access provisions of the decree and it is satisfied that, with limited exceptions, they meet the public interest standard.

B. Exceptions to Equality

The proposed decree contains some exceptions to the broad mandate of equality. These exceptions must be closely scrutinized to determine whether they will give AT&T an unjustified advantage over other carriers and thus obstruct the development of free competition.

First. Long distance calls may presently be placed over the AT&T network by dialing ten or eleven digits while twenty-two or twenty-three digits are necessary to use the facilities of the other interexchange carriers. This substantial disparity in dialing convenience has had a significant negative impact on competition. Under the proposed decree, this disparity will be drastically reduced, but some difference in the number of digits will remain: fourteen digits will be needed

for the use of the facilities of a competing carrier while ten or eleven will be required for calls placed over the AT&T network.

This conclusion is buttressed by the requirement in the proposed decree that the divested Operating Companies provide a service which will permit a subscriber to route his calls automatically to a single interexchange carrier other than AT&T. Appendix B(A)(2)(ii). By means of this service, the subscriber will be able to use that carrier's network by dialing only the same ten or eleven digits that are required of an AT&T subscriber. . . .

XII

Conclusion

The proposed reorganization of the Bell System raises issues of vast complexity. Because of their importance, not only to the parties but also to the telecommunications industry and to the public, the Court has discussed the various problems in substantial detail. It is appropriate to summarize briefly the major issues and the Court's decisions which are central to the proceeding.

A. The American telecommunications industry is presently dominated by one company—AT&T. It provides local and long-distance telephone service; it manufactures and markets the equipment used by telephone subscribers as well as that used in the telecommunications network; and it controls one of the leading communications research and development facilities in the world. According to credible evidence, this integrated structure has enabled AT&T for many years to undermine the efforts of competitors seeking to enter the telecommunications market.

The key to the Bell System's power to impede competition has been its control of local telephone service. The local telephone network functions as the gateway to individual telephone subscribers. It must be used by long-distance carriers seeking to connect one caller to another. Customers will only purchase equipment which can readily be connected to the local network through the telephone outlets in their homes and offices. The enormous cost of the wires, cables, switches, and other transmission facilities which comprise that network has completely insulated it from competition. Thus, access to AT&T's local network is crucial if long distance carriers and equipment manufacturers are to be viable competitors.

AT&T has allegedly used its control of this local monopoly to disadvantage these competitors in two principal ways. First, it has attempted to prevent competing long distance carriers and competing equipment manufacturers from gaining access to the local network, or to delay that access, thus placing them in an inferior position vis-a-vis AT&T's own services. Second, it has supposedly used profits earned from the monopoly local telephone operations to subsidize its long distance and equipment businesses in which it was competing with others.

For a great many years, the Federal Communications Commission has struggled, largely without success, to stop practices of this type through the regulatory tools at its command. A lawsuit the Department of Justice brought in 1949 to curb similar practices ended in an ineffectual consent decree. Some other remedy is plainly required; hence the divestiture of the local Operating Companies from the Bell System. This divestiture will sever the relationship between this local monopoly and the other, competitive segments of AT&T, and it will thus ensure—certainly better than could any other type of relief—that the practices which allegedly have lain heavy on the telecommunications industry will not recur.

B. With the loss of control over the local network, AT&T will be unable to disadvantage its competitors, and the restrictions imposed on AT&T after the government's first antitrust suit—which limited AT&T to the provision of telecommunications services—will no longer be necessary. The proposed decree accordingly removes these restrictions.

The decree will thus allow AT&T to become a vigorous competitor in the growing computer, computer-related, and information markets. Other large and experienced firms are presently operating in these markets, and there is therefore no reason to believe that AT&T will be able to achieve monopoly dominance in these industries as it did in telecommunications. At the same time, by use of its formidable scientific, engineering, and management resources, including particularly the capabilities of Bell Laboratories, AT&T should be able to make significant contributions

to these fields, which are at the forefront of innovation and technology, to the benefit of American consumers, national defense, and the position of American industry vis-a-vis foreign competition.

All of these developments are plainly in the public interest, and the Court will therefore approve this aspect of the proposed decree, with one exception. Electronic publishing, which is still in its infancy, holds promise to become an important provider of information—such as news, entertainment, and advertising—in competition with the traditional print, television, and radio media; indeed, it has the potential, in time, for actually replacing some of these methods of disseminating information.

Traditionally, the Bell System has simply distributed information provided by others; it has not been involved in the business of generating its own information. The proposed decree would, for the first time, allow AT&T to do both, and it would do so at a time when the electronic publishing industry is still in a fragile state of experimentation and growth and when electronic information can still most efficiently and most economically be distributed over AT&T's long distance network. If, under these circumstances, AT&T were permitted to engage both in the transmission and the generation of information, there would be a substantial risk not only that it would stifle the efforts of other electronic publishers but that it would acquire a substantial monopoly over the generation of news in the more general sense. Such a development would strike at a principle which lies at the heart of the First Amendment: that the American people are entitled to a diversity of sources of information. In order to prevent this from occurring, the Court will require, as a condition of its approval of the proposed decree, that it be modified to preclude AT&T from entering the field of electronic publishing until the risk of its domination of that field has abated.

C. After the divestiture, the Operating Companies will possess a monopoly over local telephone service. According to the Department of Justice, the Operating Companies must be barred from entering all competitive markets to ensure that they will not misuse their monopoly power. The Court will not impose restrictions simply for the sake of theoretical consistency. Restrictions must be based on an assessment of the realistic circumstances of the relevant markets, including the Operating Companies' ability to engage in anticompetitive behavior, their potential contribution to the market as an added competitor for AT&T, as well as upon the effects of the restrictions on the rates for local telephone service.

This standard requires that the Operating Companies be prohibited from providing long distance services and information services, and from manufacturing equipment used in the telecommunications industry. Participation in these fields carries with it a substantial risk that the Operating Companies will use the same anticompetitive techniques used by AT&T in order to thwart the growth of their own competitors. Moreover, contrary to the assumptions made by some, Operating Company involvement in these areas could not legitimately generate subsidies for local rates. Such involvement could produce substantial profits only if the local companies used their monopoly position to dislodge competitors or to provide subsidy for their competitive services or products—the very behavior the decree seeks to prevent.

Different considerations apply, however, to the marketing of customer premises equipment—the telephone and other devices used in subscribers' homes and offices—and the production of the Yellow Pages advertising directories. For a variety of reasons, there is little likelihood that these companies will be able to use their monopoly position to disadvantage competitors in these areas. In addition, their marketing of equipment will provide needed competition for AT&T, and the elimination of the restriction on their production of the Yellow Pages will generate a substantial subsidy for local telephone rates. The Court will therefore require that the proposed decree be modified to remove the restrictions on these two types of activities....

VII

Retention of Jurisdiction

Jurisdiction is retained by this Court for the purpose of enabling any of the parties to this Modification of Final Judgment, or, after the reorganization specified in section I, a BOC to apply to this Court at any time for such further orders or directions as may be necessary or appropriate for the construction or carrying out of this Modification of Final Judgment, for the modification of any of the provisions hereof, for the enforcement of compliance herewith, and for the punishment of any violation hereof.

The district court has retained jurisdiction enabling the parties and operating companies, after reorganization, to apply for further orders, direction, or modification.[44] The Department of Justice has undertaken to report to the court every three years on the continuing need for line of business restrictions. Divested companies interested in expanding their entrepreneurial horizons soon filed for waivers of the restrictions.[45] Expressing concern that the companies would divert resources away from furnishing effective telephone service or engage in anticompetitive practices, the court determined that waivers would not be considered until they had lost their monopoly status and substantial competition existed at the local level.[46]

United States v. Western Electric Co., Inc. 592 F.Supp. 846 (D.D.C. 1984)

Regional holding companies created by consent decree reorganizing major telecommunications company and divesting it of operating telephone companies requested a waiver of the "line of business" restrictions imposed by the decree so that they could pursue ventures other than providing local telephone service....

OPINION

Harold H. Greene, District Judge.

The Regional Holding Companies, have requested the Court to waive the "line of business" restrictions in section II(D) of the decree so that they may pursue ventures other than the provision of local telephone service. These motions raise the question whether and the extent to which these companies shall be permitted to engage in new business enterprises—perhaps the most important issue to have arisen since the AT&T Plan of Reorganization was approved last year.

Section II(D) of the decree mandates that

After completion of the reorganization . . . , no [Operating Company] shall, directly or through any affiliated enterprise:

1. provide interexchange telecommunications services or information services;

2. manufacture or provide telecommunications products or customer premises equipment (except for provision of customer premises equipment for emergency services); or

3. provide any other product or service, except exchange telecommunications and exchange access service, that is not a natural monopoly service actually regulated by tariff.

Section VIII(C) provides for the removal of these restrictions under certain circumstances. Motions filed by the Regional Holding Companies or their affiliated Operating Companies request permission to engage in enterprises ranging from real estate investments to foreign business ventures, and the Court is advised that additional motions, for further diversification, will follow. Some of the proposed enterprises are related and some are unrelated to the telecommunications business.[a]

---

a. The following waiver requests have been filed thus far: (1) Bell Atlantic's motion of January 26, 1984 to enter the equipment leasing market; (2) BellSouth's motion of January 27, 1984 to provide certain software programs and related services; (3) Pacific and Nevada Bell's motion of February 8, 1984 to enter into foreign business ventures; (4) Nynex's motion of February 15, 1984 to provide office equipment and related services; (5) BellSouth's motion of February 24, 1984 to bid on a request for proposal issued by NASA to provide communications services and equipment; (6) US West's motion of March 20, 1984, to provide real estate services and to engage in real estate transactions and investments; (7) Ameritech's motion of March 23, 1984 to provide computers and computer-based services to developers and tenants as part of shared-services arrangements for multi-tenant buildings; (8) Ameritech's motion of April 26, 1984 to provide consulting services to foreign telecommunications systems; and (9) NewVector's motion of April 20, 1984 to construct and operate a cellular radio system in the Gulf of Mexico (NewVector is a wholly-owned subsidiary of US West).

The key remedy adopted in the decree for the elimination of anticompetitive conditions within the telecommunications industry was the divestiture of the Operating Companies from AT&T. As a regulated monopoly, AT&T had both the incentive and ability—through cross subsidization and various discriminatory actions related to interconnection—to use its control over the local exchange facilities to foreclose or impede competition in the several competitive or potentially competitive markets. The functional separation of the Operating Companies from AT&T was designed to eliminate the potential for such anticompetitive behavior.

After examining the restrictions set forth in section II(D) of the proposed decree in light of that standard, the Court rejected two of these restrictions—that on marketing of customer premises equipment and that on the publication of the Yellow Pages—and it approved the remainder of the restrictions. . . . On that basis, the Department of Justice was required to report to the Court every three years concerning the continuing need for the retention of the restrictions.

It is in light of this history that the issues now before the Court must be analyzed. . . . Contrary to the claims of some of the Regional Holding Companies, the inclusion of section VIII(C) in the decree is not evidence of a general policy in favor of their diversification. That provision was included so that these companies could, at some later time, engage in nonregulated activities on a carefully controlled basis. No one connected with the negotiation, the drafting, or the modification of the decree envisioned that the Regional Holding Companies would seek to enter new competitive markets on a broad scale within a few months, let alone a few weeks, after divestiture—before the implementation of equal access and before the companies' commitment to an efficient and economical telephone operation could be tested. . . .

The line of business restrictions—like the remainder of the decree—became effective on January 1, 1984. Those restrictions were necessarily based upon the premise that, as of that time, they constituted an essential ingredient of the decree. Yet none of the requests for waivers is accompanied by a showing or even an allegation of changed circumstances that would justify a departure from the restrictions. The factual assumptions and the rationale underlying the Court's findings that these restrictions are in the public interest therefore remain sound....

Moreover, there are substantial reasons for concluding that a wholesale departure from the status quo at this time would *not* be in the public interest or consistent with the intended purposes of the decree.

A principal problem is that the diversion of capital and managerial resources in the pursuit of outside ventures may impede the implementation of equal access, and that this development, in turn, will hinder competition in the interexchange market. On that basis, some parties (e.g., MCI) urge that the Regional Holding Companies be prohibited from entering new lines of business altogether until they have fully fulfilled their equal access obligations under the decree. The Department of Justice likewise emphasizes that these companies have an incentive to use available financial resources to enter new markets rather than to meet their equal access obligations and that, given such an incentive, they may implement equal access with substantially less vigor and speed....

The Court would be derelict in its duties if it did not consider the possible effect the Regional Holding Companies' entry into unrelated lines of business will have on other provisions of the decree—one of which requires the prompt implementation of equal access. It was precisely this type of situation that the Court envisioned when it retained the power to ensure that the parties comply in full with the principles mandated by the decree, both in formulating the plan of reorganization and in their conduct after divestiture.

As evidenced both by the pending waiver requests and by reports of their intentions, the Regional Holding Companies are expending significant managerial and other resources to discover and analyze new business opportunities. Moreover, some of these companies candidly state that they regard the telephone business as of limited interest to them and the fate of the rate-payers as of little significance in the context of the decree. Thus, US West proclaims that the "Operating Companies owned by US West are in the telephone business rather than US West" and

that "US West does not itself intend to be a telephone company." Ameritech similarly asserts that, "[w]hile protecting ratepayers may be a worthy goal in the abstract, it is one that should be left to the regulators and the legislators to pursue as they see fit." And Bell Atlantic argues that its waiver requests must be granted even if diversification into new business will raise the company's cost of capital and divert the attention of its management from providing telephone service, because in its view the effect of diversification on the ratepayers "is extraneous to the Decree" and is therefore not a legitimate criterion for adjudging applications under section VIII(C).

The more the Regional Holding Companies diversify, the less central their telecommunications functions will obviously become to their corporate existence. To the extent that these companies perceive their new, unregulated businesses as more exciting, or more profitable than the provision of local telephone service to the American public—as they obviously do—it is inevitable that, should they be permitted to embark upon such business enterprises on a significant scale, their managerial talent and financial resources will be diverted from the business of providing such service. As a consequence, both the quality and the price of that service are bound to suffer. See also, note 122 *infra*.... The Regional Holding Companies assert that all these problems and fears are outweighed by the benefits they would derive from diversification, i.e., their ability to attract more capital and to increase revenue. In each of the waiver requests, the moving company argues that diversification will enhance its financial viability by reducing its overall risks. Diversified growth companies, it is said, are more attractive to securities investors and for that reason they are able to sell their stock at a higher price-earnings ratio, lowering their cost of equity capital. It follows, according to that line of reasoning, that a Regional Holding Company which is successful in diversifying could pass on its savings from lower capital costs to the ratepayers. These arguments are erroneous in every respect.

First. While the cost of capital depends on many different factors, some tangible and others intangible, there is no evidence that the Regional Holding Companies' cost of capital would decrease as a result of diversification. Because regulators are required by law to permit utilities to set rates which recover their cost of service—including the cost of capital—utilities have traditionally been less risky as investments than competitive ventures and their cost of capital from some sources has therefore tended to be lower. Thus, to the extent that a Regional Holding Company raises funds jointly for both its competitive ventures and its regulated services, the cost of capital may be lower for the competitive venture (because it will be averaged with the lower capital costs of the regulated monopoly) but higher for the regulated telephone service. The ratepayers will then, in effect, be subsidizing the activities of the competitive venture by assuming, through higher interest rates, part of its cost. It follows that, if diversification of the Regional Holding Companies into new competitive ventures enhances their financial viability at all, the beneficiaries will more likely than not be these holding companies, their managers, and their unregulated affiliates, not the Operating Companies which provide local telephone service....

Third. It may confidently be predicted that, even if the Regional Holding Companies could, somehow, reap significant profits from their outside ventures, they would not use them to benefit their regulated telephone affiliates. In fact, the opposite appears to be true.

Those predictions are also supported by recent experience. When the Court required AT&T to turn over its Yellow Pages operations to the Operating Companies, it assumed that the revenues from directory advertising would continue to be included in the rate base of the Operating Companies, providing a subsidy to local rates. Yet, the Regional Holding Companies, or some of them, have breached that understanding. Instead of funnelling Yellow Pages revenues to the Operating Companies, they have created separate subsidiaries to handle their directory publishing operations which do *not* feed the revenues from these operations into the rate base.

In short, it is likely that the competitive ventures of the Regional Holding Companies, which rely in a number of ways on the funds generated by the ratepayers, will not share the profits from these ventures with the ratepayers.

In further support of their argument that diversification is in the public interest, the Regional Holding Companies contend that an enterprise which is narrowly limited in scope cannot attract the executive and other talent required for quality performance. Thus, Ameritech states that if it is limited to the provision of local telephone service, it will lose its "efficiency and dynamism" and become stagnant and inefficient. Bell-South asserts that, if it is unable to respond to the technological changes and evolving market demands of exchange service, it may not only lose potential revenue but it may also forfeit its base of large customers. And Pacific Bell has informed the Court that the line of business restrictions are holding back its imagination and "flood of ideas."

There is no reason why the "efficiency and dynamism" of Ameritech, Pacific Bell's "flood of ideas," and the energies of the other Regional Holding Companies could not be directed toward improving local telephone service rather than pursuing extraneous ventures. Much can and should be done through the application of new technology, administrative efficiency, and marketing techniques to reduce the cost of telephone service, to improve its quality, and to make new features available to the public. If the Regional Holding Companies were determined to bring about such developments, they might well reap substantial benefits, and continue to attract the talent they seek.

One needs only to contemplate the advances made in the customer premises equipment market and the variety of telephone equipment now available on store shelves in the wake of divestiture and hence of competition to realize that, where there is a will, there are ample opportunities for technological and other advances in the telecommunications markets themselves. The Regional Holding Companies are only limited in the services they can provide; they are not limited to any particular technology in providing those services.

The principal substantive purpose of the divestiture was to promote competition and hence to create conditions which will reduce the cost and improve the quality and reliability of the telephone service. For the reasons stated, the diversion of energy, talent, capital, and other resources by the Regional Holding Companies to pursue outside ventures on a substantial scale at this early stage has the potential for threatening that basic objective of the decree. The Court will therefore carefully scrutinize requests for waivers in accordance with the guidelines discussed below, to ensure that, if approved, they will not frustrate the implementation of the decree, the plan of reorganization, or the principles underlying the divestiture.

This does not mean that the Court will not allow the Regional Holding Companies to engage in other activities, particularly if such activities would tend to increase competition. However, if there is to be a "second phase" restructuring of the telecommunications industry (see note 2 *supra*), it will evolve only in a deliberate, cautious manner, with every step tailored to ensure that the public's telephone service does not suffer, but improves in quality and price....

Considerable concern has been expressed by a number of parties that the Regional Holding Companies plan to enter the interexchange market....

To approve these plans and applications would be to contravene the decree's prohibitions in the most direct and obvious way. Indeed, even to leave open the possibility of Regional Holding Company entry into this market would have negative implications, for if the companies perceive themselves as future long distance competitors they will have incentives to spend ratepayer funds for long-distance network construction and to position themselves for successful entry by discriminating against other carriers in interconnection and by delaying their achievement of equal access.

It is therefore important that the Court state its position clearly. The Court will not even consider the substantive merits of a waiver request seeking permission to provide interexchange services until such time as the Regional Holding Companies lose their bottleneck monopolies and there is substantial competition in local telecommunications service. That is not now. The BellSouth motion for a waiver with respect to the NASA contract is therefore denied.

Similar considerations govern the appropriateness of entry of the Regional Holding Companies into the information services and equipment manufacturing markets. No significant technological or structural changes have occurred in these markets to justify a relaxation of these line

of business restrictions, and no requests for waivers in these markets will be considered unless and until such changes have taken place....

The Court [announced the following standards pursuant to which any waiver request would be assessed].

First. It is generally agreed that if the Regional Holding Companies conducted competitive activities through separate subsidiaries, intracompany transactions would become more apparent and thus cross subsidization and other anticompetitive conduct could more easily be prevented or rectified. The Regional Holding Companies themselves appear to acknowledge that such structural measures are a necessary safeguard. Accordingly, while, as a general matter, the Court is not eager to require the establishment of separate subsidiaries, that measure is warranted in this situation, and it will be required.

The decree was entered under the Sherman Act to eliminate anticompetitive conditions in the telecommunications industry. Within that legal framework, the bedrock purpose of the decree is to create conditions that will reduce the cost and improve the quality of telecommunications products and services. Under the decree, the Regional Holding Companies play an essential role—they are to provide efficient, economical, and, if possible, technologically advanced local telephone service. Their role is not to provide a source of ratepayer funds, credit, and other assets to finance competitive ventures, nor were they meant to be vast conglomerates in which telephone service is relegated to a subordinate place. Yet that is what is threatened by the broad diversification efforts presently under way. This conclusion is reinforced by the lack of restraint some of the Regional Holding Companies have shown in their desire to transform themselves rapidly from local telecommunications organizations into seven diversified "Bell Systems."

The decree contemplates that AT&T, as a company now engaged in competitive business, could enter various new fields as it sees fit; it did not contemplate such entry for the Regional Holding Companies except on a limited and slowly-evolving basis. The reason is simple: these companies, unlike AT&T, retain what is in law and in reality a monopoly over a critical aspect of the nation's telephone service.

The Court embraced diversification as it applies to AT&T, reasoning that, should that company squander its resources on unprofitable non-telecommunications ventures, raise its rates, or fail to render quality service, its customers could easily take their business to one of its long distance or equipment competitors. That is not so, however, with respect to the customers of the Operating Companies. These companies are at present the only entities with the license and the capacity to provide local telephone service to the general public. Thus, if they neglect their responsibilities in that regard in order to pursue what they may consider more interesting ventures, or if they are diverted from those responsibilities by unrelated or speculative business objectives, the public, unable to go elsewhere, will suffer in higher rates, deteriorating service, or both. Such a result would be entirely inconsistent with the basic purposes of the decree, and the Court will not approve requests which would help to bring it about.

Beyond these considerations, there is the overriding principle that the Court is obligated under the decree to make certain that the Regional Holding Companies do not impede competition in the non-telecommunications markets they seek to enter. Here again, wide diversification presents a serious threat in terms of cross subsidization and other anticompetitive practices.

The decree assumes, as does the Court, that the Regional Holding Companies may diversify on a significant scale only as they demonstrate the centrality to their corporate life of the responsibilities imposed upon them by the decree, their firm commitment to low-cost, high-quality telephone service, and the improbability of their involvement in anticompetitive conduct based upon their monopoly status. The rules established herein are designed to achieve these objectives while also permitting the Regional Holding Companies to enter into new business ventures to the extent that this will not be a threat to the fundamental purposes of the decree.

Following the Justice Department's first triennial review, the district court lifted restrictions that had barred the diverted companies from participating in nontelecommunications business, modified the prohibition against entering the information services market and left intact interexchange and manufacturing restrictions.[47] Upon review, the court of appeals remanded the case for purposes of determining whether the information services restriction should be lifted entirely.[48] The appeals court instructed that the decision on whether "generation of information" would be anticompetitive should be made according to "*present* market conditions."[49] Reference points for reconsidering the information services waiver were whether a company had the ability to raise prices or restrict output in the relevant market, which was defined as "the market to be entered."[50]

The court of appeals also noted that waivers should be granted so long as not inconsistent with the public interest which, it advised, should be construed flexibly not in terms of what "will *best* serve society" but what "is within the *reaches* of the public interest."[51] Finally, the appeals court asserted that construction of the consent decree was subject to "*de novo* appellate review."[52] Waivers from line of business restrictions have been granted also with respect to equipment leasing, computer sales, foreign operations, cellular telephone systems, office equipment, and real estate investment.[53]

The breakup of AT&T has engendered extensive commentary. The following articles speak to the purpose of the modified final judgment and critically assess it.

Lavey and Carlton, "Economic Goals and Remedies of the AT&T Modified Final Judgment," 71 Geo. L.J. 1947 (1983)*

The MFJ reflects concerns about four types of abuses of monopoly power. This section discusses

---

*Reprinted with the permission of the publisher, © 1983 The Georgetown Law Journal Association.

these abuses and examines the MFJ's response to them.

1. INTEREXCHANGE SERVICES

The MFJ clearly regards the BOCs as present monopolists in local telecommunications, even though there is currently some bypass of the BOCs' exchange facilities and bypass technologies are becoming increasingly attractive. The MFJ further assumes that the use of the BOCs' exchange (local) facilities is essential to competitors providing interexchange (toll) services, raising a concern that the BOCs could confer a competitive advantage on AT&T's interexchange services over the services of its competitors by denying exchange access to other common carriers, providing them with inferior exchange access, or charging them a higher price than what AT&T pays for equal exchange access.

The MFJ is not directed at eliminating the BOCs' monopoly control of local facilities. Rather, it seeks to prevent the abuse of this power to impair interexchange services. Thus, the MFJ does not prevent the BOCs from providing exchange services and exchange access by cable, optical fiber, cellular radio, or other new technologies, all of which could compete with their present exchange facilities. Instead, the MFJ attempts to constrain the BOCs' ability to use their monopoly position to engage in leverage.

The MFJ tries to achieve this objective by requiring that the BOCs not discriminate in providing current and future facilities to other interexchange carriers. Under the MFJ, the BOCs must provide to all interexchange carriers exchange access on an unbundled, tariffed basis that is equal in type, quality, and price to that provided to AT&T. The BOCs also may not discriminate in establishing and disseminating interconnection standards and in planning for new exchange-access facilities. These requirements of nondiscrimination are fortified by the ordered divestiture of the BOCs from AT&T and the elimination of joint ownership of facilities. Such actions are intended to decrease the likelihood that the BOCs will have an incentive to favor AT&T. In addition, the BOCs cannot provide interexchange telecommunications services on their own.

By fostering interexchange competition, these provisions aim at decreasing the prices and increasing the quantity, quality, and diversity of services available to consumers making interexchange calls. Unfortunately, it is possible that the combination of nondiscrimination requirements and divestiture will go beyond preventing abuses of monopoly power, to the detriment of competition and consumers' welfare. Divestiture alone would eliminate any incentive for the BOCs to favor one provider of interexchange services. The BOCs will have the incentive to make utilization of their facilities attractive to interexchange carriers and to potential users of interexchange services.

The BOCs may require flexibility in developing interconnection arrangements and prices. The MFJ's restrictions on the BOCs' prices, terms of offering services, and planning activities for interconnections may force the BOCs to justify differences in arrangements and prices as nondiscriminatory. The costs of proving nondiscrimination may be substantial, possibly increasing exchange access charges. In addition, fear of possible liability for discrimination may lead the BOCs to offer only a few interconnection arrangements and prices. Such a limited range of options may be suboptimal in terms of innovation, competition among interexchange carriers, and consumers' welfare.

2. INFORMATION SERVICES

The MFJ treats the use of the BOCs' exchange facilities as essential to providers of information services. The concern arises as to the treatment of rival information-service providers by the BOCs in terms of design of, access to, and charges for use of the BOCs' facilities. That is, how can the BOCs be prevented from abusing their monopoly power in exchange telecommunications to exclude competition in information services?

Under the MFJ, the BOCs can expand the quantity, quality, and range of exchange facilities that they offer to providers of information services, but cannot discriminate among such providers or provide information services themselves. The BOCs must charge equal access fees to all providers of information services making equal use of the BOCs' facilities. Before the MFJ, the vertical integration of the BOCs with AT&T could have provided the incentive for the BOCs to favor AT&T if AT&T competed against other suppliers of information services. The divestiture of the BOCs from AT&T and the requirement that the BOCs provide equal access to exchange facilities to all information services are aimed at eliminating the BOCs' ability and incentives to impair development of the information-services industry as a competitive, efficient market.

A related question addressed by the MFJ deals with the ability of AT&T itself to provide information services. The MFJ, as modified by Judge Greene, prohibits AT&T from engaging in electronic publishing over its own transmission facilities. This prohibition reflects concerns that these facilities are essential to providers of information services, that AT&T is a monopolist in interexchange services and that, if AT&T entered into electronic publishing, it would abuse its power to exclude competition. Judge Greene viewed electronic publishing as an infant industry populated by a small number of firms unable to fend for themselves in competition with AT&T if confronted by discriminatory actions undertaken by AT&T. The prohibition on AT&T providing electronic publishing removes the economic incentives for AT&T to discriminate against providers of these services.

In contrast, AT&T is not prohibited from engaging in remote-access data processing services, based on the view that other large corporations are already established in this field, making it unlikely that AT&T would or could exclude competition through discrimination. Judge Greene treated AT&T's entry into this field as likely to stimulate competition. He viewed the facilities of AT&T as less essential than those of the BOCs to providers of data processing services. Supposedly, if AT&T tried to cripple well-established competitors in remote-access data processing by discriminating against them in the price and quality of interexchange services, these competitors would have sufficient alternate transmission facilities available, such as microwave and satellite common carriers or private networks, to survive. Yet, anomalously, these alternatives are basically the same as those available to providers of information services, which are assumed in the MFJ to be subject to AT&T's monopoly power.

Under the 1980 decision of the Federal Communications Commission (FCC) in *Second Computer Inquiry*, AT&T, through a separate subsidiary, is not prohibited from providing any "enhanced service," including both electronic publishing and remote-access data processing, on an unregulated basis. The FCC found that the market for enhanced services is "truly competitive" and believed that market forces would protect the public interest in reasonable rates and availability of efficient enhanced services. Judge Greene, and to a lesser extent the DOJ, showed more concern than did the FCC about abuses of monopoly power by the BOCs and AT&T affecting competition in enhanced services and about the inability of regulators to prevent discrimination. The MFJ's more restrictive requirements on AT&T will limit the range of its activities that are not prohibited under the FCC's order in *Second Computer Inquiry*.

3. TERMINAL EQUIPMENT

Competition in the manufacturing and distribution of terminal equipment is a third concern of the MFJ. Before the MFJ, the BOCs distributed and installed terminal equipment manufactured largely by its corporate affiliate, Western Electric. A BOC also could exclude competing manufacturers or distributors of terminal equipment from selling in its franchise area if it denied, delayed, or charged a higher price for interconnection of terminal equipment made or distributed by its rivals. The vertical integration of the BOCs with Western Electric could have provided the BOCs with the incentive to favor Western Electric in their purchases and installation practices.

Three provisions of the MFJ affect this possible abuse of the BOCs' monopoly power. First, the MFJ prohibits discrimination by the BOCs among suppliers and products in interconnection with, use of, and charges for the BOCs' services and facilities. The obligation of nondiscrimination extends to the establishment and dissemination of interconnection standards. Next, the corporate affiliation between the BOCs and Western Electric is severed. Finally, the BOCs may not engage in the manufacture of telecommunications equipment. These provisions are aimed at lowering the prices and raising the quality of terminal equipment available to consumers.

The MFJ, however, was revised by Judge Greene to allow the BOCs to distribute new terminal equipment. This revision supposedly would aid manufacturers of terminal equipment by expanding sales if the BOCs become efficient distribution channels. Moreover, the end of the BOCs' affiliation with Western Electric suggests that the BOCs would lose the incentive to discriminate in their choices of which manufacturers' equipment to distribute. Yet, allowing the BOCs to distribute terminal equipment may give them the incentive to discriminate against rival distributors. This revision means that the MFJ's prohibition of discrimination by the BOCs will be relied upon to prevent the BOCs from abusing their market power to exclude competition in the distribution of terminal equipment.

Under this revision, BOCs are allowed to distribute, but not manufacture, terminal equipment. The explanation for this treatment does not lie in a difference in the possibility of anticompetitive discrimination. It does not seem that rival distributors could fend for themselves against discriminatory interconnecting by BOCs much better than rival manufacturers could, that consumers would be harmed less by discrimination against distributors, or that the rewards to the BOCs would be less when such conduct is directed against distributors. Instead, the court's reasoning is that distribution is an existing business of the BOCs, and continued participation by the BOCs may promote competition in distribution. Conversely, manufacturing is not an existing business of the BOCs and, supposedly, participation by the BOCs in manufacturing would create a greater risk of loss to consumers via anticompetitive leveraging than the likelihood that consumers would benefit from the BOCs as the most efficient suppliers.

4. SWITCHING AND TRANSMISSION EQUIPMENT

Procurements by the BOCs represent a large portion of total sales of switching and transmission equipment in the United States. Assuming that the corporate affiliation between Western Electric and the BOCs lessened the degree to which price and quality considerations formed the basis for the BOCs' procurement practices or the ability of other manufacturers to make equipment satisfying the BOCs' needs, the BOCs' procurement practices would have foreclosed competition in manufacturing switching and transmission equipment.

The MFJ provides that the BOCs must make nondiscriminatory procurements, nondiscriminatorily establish and disseminate technical information, sever their affiliation with Western Electric, and neither manufacture nor provide any switching or transmission equipment. These provisions seek to promote consumers' welfare by increasing competition in manufacturing such equipment and lessening incentives for inefficient purchases.

5. SUMMARY

The preceding discussion of the goals and remedies of the MFJ indicates the skepticism of the DOJ and the court about the effectiveness of state and federal regulators in limiting the ability of the BOCs and AT&T to abuse their market power. The MFJ assumes that the procompetitive policies set forth in the antitrust laws have not been and, without the MFJ's remedies, would not be implemented effectively by regulators. Underlying the MFJ is the supposition that AT&T is not immune from the antitrust laws by reason of pervasive regulation. According to the MFJ, drastic structural remedies, limitations on the scope of firms' activities, and clear prohibitions against discrimination are necessary to prevent future exclusionary conduct by these regulated firms.

Worthington, "If It Ain't Broke, Don't Fix It," 9 *Comm/ent L.J.* 583 (1987)*

The line-of-business restrictions take the BOCs' incentive to use control of their local telephone monopolies to compete unfairly in related markets that they seek to enter. As long as the BOCs

---

retain control of the local bottlenecks and competitors in related markets must depend on the BOCs to reach their customers, the line-of-business restrictions, enforced by the federal courts, will be the only effective means to preserve fair competition. Regulatory prohibitions against discrimination and cross-subsidy cannot contain the BOCs' virtually unlimited opportunity for bottleneck abuse. None of the factors that required imposition of the line-of-business restrictions in 1982 have changed. For the same reasons that the district court approved those restrictions as in the public interest, and that the Supreme Court affirmed its decision, they remain an "essential ingredient of the decree" necessary to "prevent recurrence of precisely the same structural and economic incentives that divestiture was designed to eliminate."

I

THE DECREE'S SUCCESSES

When the MFJ was proposed, many complained that divestiture would destroy the best telephone system in the world. The rallying cry was, "If it ain't broke, don't fix it." Divestiture-driven events have since proved that our telephone system was indeed broken and in need of fixing. The elimination of the Bell System's domination of virtually all aspects of telecommunications has permitted an ever-widening array of new services and products to become available to American consumers at steadily declining prices. Notwithstanding predictions that AT&T had garnered for itself the most profitable portions of the System's business and condemned the divested BOCs to the dregs, the BOCs have succeeded, probably beyond their own expectations, and AT&T has yet to achieve the pre-divestiture financial targets that it set for itself.

Although the Department and the BOCs are calling for further monumental change, there is no need to fix a telephone system that, by any measure, is generally performing well, with excellent prospects for continuing improvement. The Department's triennial report points with pride to the many examples of the MFJ's success: tremendous strides in implementing equal access; the unprecedented growth of competition in the

interexchange, information services, and equipment markets; and a promised redesign of BOC "local networks to accommodate the maximum number of information service providers." It is ironic that the DOJ and the BOCs are citing the MFJ's successes as justification for its repeal.

III

CONTINUED CONDITIONS REQUIRING THE RESTRICTIONS

Since the court entered the judgment, nothing has occurred which would diminish the BOCs' ability or incentive to use their local bottleneck power to cripple competition in telecommunications markets where they are permitted to compete. The BOCs' stranglehold on virtually all domestic and international telecommunications remains intact. The Department concedes that local exchange networks carry 99.9 percent of all interexchange traffic and 99.999 percent rely on them. Those networks—millions of miles of copper wire strung on poles, buried in conduits and tied together by BOC switches—still provide the only practical means of making and completing virtually every telephone call.

Nor has there been any change in the inability of regulators to prevent the abuses that inevitably accompany BOC competition in markets dependent on fair access to the local exchange. "At the heart of the government's case in *United States v. AT&T* was the failure of regulation to safeguard competition in the face of powerful incentives and abilities of a firm engaged in the provision of both regulated monopoly and competitive services." This failure of regulatory protection continues. . . .

Even if there was a sound theoretical framework for the illusory goal of cost allocation, the FCC cannot put theory into practice without the resources to audit the Bell Companies' accounting submissions. As the Department recognizes, "[t]he failure to devote sufficient resources to the audit process will reduce any prophylactic program, no matter how sound in theory or principle, to a sham that deceives rather than protects ratepayers and state regulators." The FCC's resources are inadequate to the task: "the Commission currently employs only 24 auditors, and they have very limited funds for travel;" the FCC's recent budget request cut one of its audit teams; the FCC admits that its current resources do not permit it to "monitor, audit and investigate cost allocations [among carriers' deregulated and regulated businesses] on an item-by-item basis;" and the FCC Chairman just characterized its funding in recent years as "inadequate." In 1982 the court accurately noted "the problems of supervision by a relatively poorly-financed, poorly-staffed government agency" over a gigantic corporation "with almost unlimited resources in funds and gifted personnel are no more likely to be overcome in the future than they were in the past." Nothing has happened in the last four years to change that conclusion.

McKenna and Slyter, "MFJ: Judicial Overkill—Further Perspective and Response," 9 *Comm/ent LJ.* 565 (1987)*

The Department's Report reached two fundamental conclusions: first, that technological developments are rapidly dispersing electronic network intelligence in a manner which is eroding the bottleneck power the BOCs have because of their control of local exchange networks; and second, that the welfare-enhancing role of regulation in the evolving telecommunications network is not performed (or served) by entry prohibitions, but rather by promotion of entry at all levels, ensuring the widespread availability of interconnection to essential facilities. In the context of today's telecommunications marketplace, both of these conclusions appear to be unassailable.

II

A BRIEF REJOINDER TO MR. WORTHINGTON

In his article for the Symposium, John Worthington sets forth a view of divestiture from the perspective of MCI Communications Corpora-

---

tion (MCI). MCI was, and remains, a key player in the development of the competitive telecommunications marketplace, and Mr. Worthington's views deserve consideration and respect. While advocating the position of MCI with considerable eloquence, Mr. Worthington nevertheless reaches several conclusions which are significantly flawed. Essentially, Mr. Worthington contends that all of the MFJ's line-of-business restrictions should be continued. For the most part, his argument is predicated on the historical ability of the integrated Bell System to exercise enormous market power, and not on the realities of the post-divestiture world. Mr. Worthington makes two major arguments: 1) FCC regulation has always been and will continue to be ineffective in controlling anticompetitive conduct by the BOCs; and 2) Congress is without power to remedy the current MFJ situation through targeted legislation. In this section, the authors briefly address each of these points and, in addition, comment briefly on an internal contradiction in Mr. Worthington's article which has marked much of the analysis of the MFJ since 1982.

A. The Efficacy of Regulation

Mr. Worthington contends at some length that FCC regulation will not provide a sufficient check on BOC market power, and that the line-of-business restrictions should, accordingly, be retained in their current form. Most of Mr. Worthington's arguments are directly addressed in our previous article. The collateral assertion set forth by Mr. Worthington, that the FCC is incompetent or biased, would not be a proper basis upon which to retain an anticompetitive injunction even if it were true. The point does not merit analysis. However, Mr. Worthington's implication that the FCC itself has conceded that it cannot effectively regulate the divested BOCs does deserve additional comment. In this context, the FCC's actual position on the effectiveness of its own regulatory regime becomes relevant.

First, even if the Commission's purported inability to regulate the unified Bell System were relevant to its post-divestiture regulatory abilities, the Commission has never stated that it was incapable of fulfilling its statutory mandate under the Communications Act. To the contrary, the Commission has been protective of its jurisdiction in dealing with the MFJ court from the beginning of the case. For example, on December 30, 1975, the FCC filed a *Memorandum As Amicus Curiae* with the MFJ court in which it elaborated on the interplay between its regulatory jurisdiction under the Communications Act, *vis-a-vis* the court's jurisdiction under the antitrust laws. While advising the court that FCC regulation had not totally preempted court jurisdiction, the Commission nevertheless advised the court that "[i]nsofar as the specific allegations of conduct are concerned . . . the Commission regards virtually all of them as within its own regulatory jurisdiction." The Commission in this *Memorandum* listed a series of regulatory actions which would be beyond the court's jurisdiction.

Similarly, in the Tunney Act proceeding prior to entry of the MFJ in 1982, the Commission again appeared and explained the function and scope of its regulatory powers. In recommending that the line-of-business restrictions be eliminated entirely, the Commission made repeated reference to the vitality of its own regulatory structure, and in fact noted that even the MFJ's equal access provisions generally duplicated the existing and contemplated regulatory scheme.

The Commission again reiterated its position in its recent comments to the court on the DOJ Report, in which the Commission unequivocally stated:

> However, the Commission has developed regulatory mechanisms more precisely tailored to the new marketplace conditions that should permit the Court to conclude that there is no substantial possibility that a BOC could use any market power it may possess to impede competition. Through several extensive proceedings, this Commission has developed safeguards that will ensure fair, unimpeded competition if the RBOCs are relieved of the decree's absolute entry restrictions.

Given this consistent position by the FCC on the scope of its own competence, the following statement in Mr. Worthington's article seems to raise a direct conflict: "The evidentiary record in *AT&T* includes testimony of FCC officials to the effect that the Commission was fundamentally unable to regulate an integrated Bell System." Thus, it is important to examine the source of this testimony. Mr. Worthington cites testimony of Walter Hinchman and William Melody as

proof of this ostensibly damning admission by the FCC. While testifying to this effect in a variety of proceedings prior to the AT&T divestiture, including the AT&T case itself, neither Mr. Hinchman nor Dr. Melody had any authority to speak for the FCC on this issue. In fact, not only did their testimony not reflect the position of the FCC itself, but the validity of their opinion can be seriously questioned. . . .

C. Cross-Subsidization

Mr. Worthington's article reflects a typical preoccupation with the issue of "cross-subsidization," pricing competitive services below cost and recovering the losses from regulated rates. This perceived danger to competition permeates much of the court's and the Department's analysis as well. However, elsewhere in his article, Mr. Worthington chides the BOCs for not engaging in the very cross-subsidization practices which he so roundly condemns. This inconsistency merits some brief comments.

Specifically, Mr. Worthington expresses dismay that the BOCs have not utilized revenues from competitive ventures "to hold down local rates." In the case of competitive Yellow Pages revenues, for example, Mr. Worthington claims that "the BOCs broke faith with Congress and the court, and chose to divert their Yellow Pages revenue away from the support of local telephone service." As a reason for maintaining the MFJ's provisions that preclude BOC entry into most businesses, Mr. Worthington quotes with approval the opinion of the court that it is likely that the BOCs "will not share the profits from these [competitive] ventures with the ratepayers." In essence, Mr. Worthington complains that BOCs have committed a moral, if not a legal, wrong by declining to cross-subsidize their local services with revenues from other businesses.

The mischief inherent in this position is readily apparent. It is difficult, if not impossible, to sustain a competitive venture in the long term while requiring that venture to subsidize another business. Thus, Mr. Worthington's subsidy plan makes little practical sense. But perhaps more significantly, if Mr. Worthington's proposal could be sustained, the end result would be to stifle exchange competition through below-cost pricing, precisely the evil about which MCI has complained so bitterly over the past decade.

We point out this inconsistency because it typifies the logic so often put forth in support of continuing the MFJ's line-of-business restrictions. As we noted in our previous article, the MFJ's most fundamental premise was that the BOCs would provide natural monopoly exchange services—and nothing else. Yet this premise was palpably false by the time the MFJ was implemented, both by virtue of the fact that exchange competition already existed and by virtue of the fact that the BOCs were in competitive interexchange, terminal equipment and directory publishing businesses. The Huber Report further confirms that the provision of local exchange service is not a natural monopoly. Yet the fact of exchange competition is conveniently ignored by parties whose rhetoric seems to indicate a hope that, if wishes are only sincere enough, the comfortable world envisioned in the MFJ might still come to pass. Mr. Worthington's position on cross-subsidizing local exchange service is an example of such a wish.

III. CONCENTRATION

Concern with aggregated power in the economic marketplace and its influence upon the information marketplace have accounted for cross-ownership restrictions upon telephone companies akin to those governing broadcasters and cable casters. The Cable Communications Policy Act of 1984 essentially codified a preexisting FCC rule barring cross-ownership of cable and telephone systems in the same service area.[54] Exceptions are provided for service of rural regions[55] or when "a cable system [otherwise] demonstrably could not exist."[56] Pursuant to any waiver it secures from the FCC, a telephone company also must obtain a franchise from the pertinent state or local authority.[57] Operating companies, created pursuant to the reorganization of AT&T, also are barred by terms of the modified final judgment from entering the cable business.[58]

The cross-ownership restraints in recent years have been subject to outside challenge and internal review. In *Northwestern Indiana Telephone Co. v. Federal Communications Commission*[59] the restraints were contested at first on somewhat technical grounds concerning the specific type of business relationships prohibited.[60] After remand, the court of appeals deferred to the commission's interpretation of its rules as applied to cover an array of relationships including loan and financial guarantees, consulting fees, leased office and pole space, subleased property, and signal facility construction and maintenance.[61] Intervening parties, in the meantime, asserted that the cross-ownership rules had been rendered inoperable by the Cable Act and in any event breached the First Amendment.[62] Because those issues had not been raised in the initial proceeding, however, the court refused to address them.[63]

While continuing to enforce the cross-ownership rules, the FCC itself actually has concluded that they perform a disservice. A 1981 report favored retention of the rules until cable operators could compete more effectively against telephone companies or the restrictions began to hinder development of new technologies.[64] In 1987, the commission commenced an inquiry to determine whether the restraints still were justified. Its conclusion was that the cable industry, which itself is now dominated by major corporations, no longer is a fledgling industry requiring protection.[65] Furthermore, it found that the rules were not promoting desired competition among cable operators, so new services were not evolving as anticipated.[66] The FCC thus concluded that the restrictions should be lifted and telephone companies allowed to compete with cable operators.[67] Despite its findings and deregulatory stance, the controls remain in place as congressional action ultimately is required to alter the terms of competition.

Modern peculiarities aside, dispute over the cross-ownership rules in some ways is reminiscent of the rivalry between broadcasters and cable casters during the 1960s and 1970s. Cable as a new technology offered benefits in terms of signal clarity and program choice which presented a threat to broadcasters and contributed to regulation that slowed the new industry's growth.[68] The benefits of coaxial cable now in place may be surpassed by the offerings of fiber optic lines. The transmission of light impulses, along channels of glass or plastic, present advantages over coaxial cable because the lines are smaller, lighter, easier to store and transport, and, because more efficient, able to transmit over greater distances. Most significantly, they have enormous signal carriage capacity which creates a potential for a single-line home or office hookup providing telephone, cable, computer, and information services.

The basic position of the telephone companies is that the public interest is served by such service consolidation and efficiencies.[69] Cross-ownership rules thus are regarded as a means for impeding progress and protecting an industry that has outgrown the need for nurturing.[70] The telephone companies further assert that their presence in the marketplace would provide a competitive prod which would help cable maximize its diversification potential and lower rates in the process.[71]

The cable industry has maintained that the telephone companies have wrapped themselves in the cloth of the public interest which hides their real self-interest. It alleges that the telephone companies regard entry into the cable television business as a way of updating their depreciated facilities with fiber optic technology.[72] Given high conversion costs and the speculative nature of the investment, the argument is that the public interest may be disserved by the loss of inexpensive telephone service.[73] Because fiber optic networks already can be constructed, and cross-ownership rules essentially prohibit program retailing, the cable industry's position seems to be that decontrol would benefit only the telephone companies at a considerable risk to the public.[74] The competing arguments seem destined to influence the saga of common carrier and cable cross-ownership restrictions as maintained or revised by Congress or the judiciary.

NOTES

1. 47 U.S.C. § 201(a).
2. Official restrictions upon a common carrier's other activities, such as a court order prohibiting AT&T from engaging in electronic publishing, present a First Amendment issue. *See* United States v. American Telephone and Telegraph Co., 552 F.Supp. 131, 180–186 (D.D.C. 1982), *aff'd,* 460 U.S. 1001 (1983). Similarly, cross-ownership rules concerning telephone companies have been challenged on constitutional grounds. *See* Northwestern Indiana Telephone Co. v. Federal Communications Commission, 872 F.2d 465 (D.C.Cir. 1989). Constitutional implications of such restrictions are discussed in Chapter 11 of this book.
3. 47 U.S.C. § 153(h).
4. Postal Telegraph-Cable Co. v. Associated Press, 228 N.Y. 370, 127 N.E. 256, 257 (1920).
5. 47 U.S.C. § 202(a).
6. *See* American Broadcasting Companies, Inc. v. Federal Communications Commission, 663 F.2d 133, 138 (D.C.Cir. 1980).
7. *See* CATV and TV Repeater Services, 26 F.C.C. 403 (1959).
8. *Id.* at 427–28.
9. 392 U.S. 157 (1968).
10. *Id.* at 172.
11. *See* Federal Communications Commission v. Midwest Video Corp., 440 U.S. 689, 700–01 (1979).
12. 440 U.S. 689.
13. *Id.* at 700–702.
14. *See* United States v. Western Electric Co., Inc., 1956 Trade Cases., § 68,246, at 71,134 (D.N.J. 1956).
15. *Id.* at 71, 137–38.
16. *Id.* at 71, 138.
17. *Id.* at 71, 143.
18. 552 F.Supp. 131.
19. *Id.* at 135–36.
20. *Id.* at 141–42.
21. *Id.* at 141.
22. *Id.*
23. *Id.*

24. *Id.* at 166–67.

25. *Id.* at 142.

26. *Id.* at 144.

27. *Id.* at 161.

28. *Id.*

29. *Id.* at 162–63.

30. *Id.* at 163.

31. *Id.* at 163–65.

32. *Id.* at 165.

33. *Id.*

34. *Id.*

35. *Id.* at 170.

36. *Id.* at 179–80.

37. *Id.* at 180–86.

38. *Id.* at 188–90.

39. *Id.* at 190–93.

40. *Id.* at 186–88.

41. *Id.* at 192–94. For a detailed examination of how structural change in the telephone industry has affected competitiveness, *see* Botein and Pearce, *The Competitiveness of the United States Telecommunications Industry: A New York Case Study,* 6 CARDOZO ARTS & ENT. L.J. 233 (1988).

42. United States v. American Telephone and Telegraph Company, 552 F. Supp. at 195.

43. *Id.* at 195.

44. *Id.* at 231.

45. *See* United States v. Western Electric Co., Inc., 592 F.Supp. 846 (D.D.C. 1984).

46. *Id.* at 868.

47. United States v. Western Electric Co., Inc., 673 F. Supp. 525 (D.D.C. 1987).

48. United States v. Western Electric Co., Inc., 900 F. 2d 283, 309 (D.C.Cir. 1990).

49. *Id.*

50. *Id.* at 296.

51. *Id.* at 309.

52. *Id.* at 293.

53. United States v. Western Electric Co., Inc., 604 F. Supp. 256 (D.D.C. 1984).

54. 47 U.S.C. § 533(b).

55. *Id.,* § 533(b) (3).

56. *Id.,* § 533(b) (4).

57. *Id.,* § 541(b) (1).

58. United States v. American Telephone & Telegraph Company, 552 F.Supp. at 189.

59. 824 F.2d 1205 (D.C.Cir. 1987).

60. *Id.* at 1208.

61. Northwestern Indiana Telephone Company v. FCC, 872 F.2d at 469.

62. *Id.* at 470–71.

63. *Id.* at 470–72.

64. *See* Telephone Company-Cable Television (Notice of Inquiry), 2 F.C.C. Rcd. 5092 (1987).

65. Telephone Company-Cable Television (Cross-Ownership Rules) (Further Notice of Inquiry and Notice of Proposed Rule-Making), 3 F.C.C. Rcd. 5852, 5853–54 (1988).

66. *Id.* at 5857–58.

67. *Id.* at 5866.

68. *See* Chapter 6 of this book.

69. *See* Sodolski, *Elimination of the Cross-Ownership Rules Would Serve the Public Interest and Benefit the Consumer,* 7 COMM. L. 1, 22 (1989).

70. *Id.*

71. *Id.*

72. *See* Mooney, *Cross-Ownership Restrictions—The Cable View,* 7 COMM. L. 20 (1989).

73. *Id.* at 20–21.

74. *Id.*

Part Three

CONTENT REGULATION OF THE MEDIA

Regulation even if structurally calibrated invariably may touch editorial freedom. Identifying the point at which the First Amendment[1] becomes implicated is not unlike pinpointing proximate cause for purposes of determining tort liability. Just as the consequences of negligence are not limitless, the First Amendment does not become activated by all official action conceivably or remotely affecting editorial discretion. As noted in previous chapters, the constitution does not afford comprehensive immunity that would blunt the operation of general economic regulation or even licensing requirements of a media-specific nature. Although the line at which First Amendment interests are actuated may be imprecise, constitutional issues are inescapable when government directly concerns itself with content.

Terms of the First Amendment have remained fixed since its enshrinement in 1791.[2] The universe which it governs and societal attitudes toward the media, however, have mutated significantly. Two centuries ago, the press essentially comprised an assortment of partisan publications pushing competing political agendas.[3] Given the technology of the time, information dissem-

inated by the press traveled in weeks and months rather than immediately.[4] Consistent with a singular service of commencing and maintaining political debate, discrete audiences identified with particular publishers and tended to be forgiving of distortion and imbalance.[5] The freedom of the press clause did not enter substantively into constitutional jurisprudence for 140 years after its ratification.[6] By that time, new media never contemplated by the framers had emerged and acquired a presence that almost certainly would have exceeded their imagination.

By its terms, freedom of the press is concerned with editorial freedom. Modern concepts, which have attempted to account for perceived consequences of an expanded and concentrated media industry, are more complex. Contemporary First Amendment protection has become a function of both the nature of the medium and the variant of expression being propagated. The Court essentially has created dual hierarchies within which media and speech types are ranked for First Amendment purposes. Consistent with the prevalent media at the time of the constitution's framing, and the press' most prominent concern, the print media[7] and political expression,[8] respectively, are afforded maximum First Amendment status. Nonpolitical expression, regardless of the medium in which it appears, may be less safeguarded or entirely unprotected.[9] The parallel construction of a media hierarchy might seem paradoxical. When the First Amendment was drafted, the print media represented the dominant, indeed only, facet of the press. Although broadcasting is the most pervasive medium of modern times,[10] it is afforded the least constitutional protection.[11] Even if terms of security for the print media have remained constant, therefore, it may be argued that the ambit of freedom for the press in a practical sense has been narrowed.[12]

Contemporary regulation largely has responded to economic and social forces which have altered the information marketplace and prompted concern for consequences of rather than just freedom of the press. Given movement toward a concentrated media industry, a particular concern over the course of this century has been ensuring diversity and balance. Since meaningful individual input into the information marketplace has been confounded by evolution toward a centralized media industry, concepts have emerged which would compensate by means of official mandate.[13] A prominent debate thus continues with respect to whether insistence upon a fair and responsible press is reconcilable with the notion of a fair press.

A second but equally significant concern is with the actual influence of modern media upon society. As the media have become an omnipresent force, concerned with matters not confined to raw politics, worries over the press' reach and effect have worked their way into regulatory initiatives. Louis Brandeis, as noted in Chapter 1, expressed alarm nearly a century ago over the power, direction, and photojournalistic capacity of the print media. Brandeis' distress with a medium that catered to "prurient taste," "occup[ied] the indolent," and concerned itself not with matters of "real interest" but "idle gossip,"[14] is essentially indistinguishable from contemporary reaction to television as "a vast wasteland."[15] A sense that the press should focus upon "matters of real interest to the community"[16] emblemizes some of the same concerns which have helped shape a public interest standard and fairness responsibilities in broadcasting.[17]

Radio and television in particular have engendered anxiety tied to perceptions reminiscent of reactions that delayed First Amendment recognition of motion pictures[18] on the grounds that they were a dangerous influence.[19] The constitutional status of broadcasting has been encumbered not only because of concern with its allegedly negative influences but because it is an entrepreneurial and editorial opportunity available only to a relative few.[20] The consequence for all media as they have evolved, but especially the newer electronic methodologies, has been incessant controversy over the practical meaning of the First Amendment, the glossing of the constitution to afford the public a right to receive diverse information in some contexts, and freedom of the press analysis that has moved beyond singular concern with editorial autonomy to factor in the consequences of press freedom.

NOTES

1. U.S. CONST., amend. I.
2. Despite Justice Black's insistence that the constitution's architects had performed all the balancing of competing interests required, Konigsberg v. State Board of California, 366 U.S. 36, 61 (1961) (Black, J., dissenting), First Amendment jurisprudence regularly has considered whether regulatory interests of perceived importance justify encroachment upon expressive freedom. *Id.* at 49–51.
3. *See* E. EMERY, THE PRESS AND AMERICA 68–69 (1962).
4. *See id.* at 54.

5. *See id.* at 73.

6. Freedom of the press surfaced within the Court's purview in 1931 when a state law authorizing suppression of "malicious, scandalous, and defamatory" publication was invalidated as an unconstitutional prior restraint. Near v. Minnesota, 283 U.S. 697 (1931). The *Near* decision is discussed in Chapter 1 of this book.

7. Print media generally comprise the most traditional forms of the press and include newspapers, magazines, pamphlets and books. Insofar as they can be disseminated and reproduced electronically, however, the distinction between long-established and newer media is increasingly clouded.

8. Political expression generally refers to speech that is relevant to informed self-government. Although the outer limits of what might qualify for that categorization may be debatable, political speech receives maximum constitutional protection. Central Hudson Gas & Electric Co., Inc. v. Public Service Commission of New York, 447 U.S. 561–63 (1980); *id.* at 579–83 (Stevens, J., concurring), *id.* at 595–99 (Rehnquist, J., dissenting).

9. Commercial, defamatory and indecent expression have proved more susceptible to official regulation. *E.g.,* Posadas de Puerto Rico Associates v. Tourism Co. of Puerto Rico, 478 U.S. 328 (1986) (commercial expression); Gertz v. Robert Welch, Inc., 418 U.S. 323 (1973) (defamation); FCC v. Pacifica Foundation, 438 U.S. 726 (1978) (indecency). Obscene expression and fighting words exist entirely outside the First Amendment's purview. *See* Roth v. United States, 354 U.S. 476 (1957); Chaplinsky v. New Hampshire, 315 U.S. 568 (1942).

10. Radio and television service is nearly universal in American households. *See* STATISTICAL ABSTRACT OF THE UNITED STATES 1989, no. 900, at 544 (radio and television receivers in 99 percent and 98 percent of American households respectively). Broadcasting also is the primary source of information for the public. CBS, Inc. v. Federal Communications Commission, 629 F.2d 1, 10 (D.C. Cir. 1982) (about 60 percent of population obtains information on current affairs from network news).

11. Federal Communications Commission v. Pacifica Foundation, 438 U.S. at 749–50.

12. *See* I. POOL, TECHNOLOGIES OF FREEDOM 326 (1983).

13. The fairness doctrine, for instance, obligated broadcasters to present controversial public issues and ensure that their coverage of such matters was balanced. *See* In the Matter of Handling of Public Interest Standards of the Communication Act, 48 F.C.C. 2d 1, 7 (1974) (hereafter cited as Fairness Report).

14. Brandeis and Warren, *The Right to Privacy,* 4 HARV. L. REV. 193, 195–96 (1890).

15. Minow, Address to the National Association of Broadcasters, May 9, 1961.

16. Brandeis and Warren, *The Right to Privacy,* 4 HARV. L.REV. at 195–96.

17. *See* Red Lion Broadcasting Co. v. Federal Communications Commission, 395 U.S. 367 (1969) (expounding upon status of broadcasters as public trustees and duty to serve public interest).

18. *See* Mutual Film Corp. v. Industrial Commission of Ohio, 236 U.S. 230 (1915), *overruled,* Joseph Burstyn, Inc., v. Wilson, 343 U.S. 495 (1952).

19. Modern and seminal jurisprudence concerning the press share concern with the media's effect especially upon children. Federal Communications Commission v. Pacifica Foundation, 438 U.S. at 748–50. Mutual Film Corp. v. Industrial Commission of Ohio, 236 U.S. at 242. *See also* National Association of Broadcasters v. Federal Communications Commission, 740 F.2d 1190, 1202 (D.C.Cir. 1984) (quoting legislative history to the effect that media are "fraught with possibilities for service of good or evil," 67 CONG. REC. 5557, 5558 (1926) (statement of Rep. Johnson).

20. *See* Red Lion Broadcasting Co. v. Federal Communications Commission, 395 U.S. at 388–90.

Chapter 8

THE PRINT MEDIA

The First Amendment, despite its unqualified terms, has a relative rather than absolute meaning.[1] Although undifferentiating too in its field of coverage, freedom of the press as interpreted has acquired maximum significance for the print media. The ordering of constituent elements of the press, apart from constitutional concerns associated with it, is a source of increasing and significant practical difficulty. Media-specific analysis and resultant variances in First Amendment status and security originate from the premise that "[e]ach [medium] tends to present its own peculiar problems"[2] and thus engenders "a law unto itself."[3]

Because modern media possess palpably distinct structural characteristics, the identification of unique attributes is not a daunting task. Print traditionally has enabled the reader to be exposed to information at an individualized rate and may lend itself to more depth and detail. Electronic mass media project visual and aural imagery that may etch indelible impressions or escape perception because they are fleeting or bypass an unfocused mind. Even those distinctions are imperfect, however, due to the consequences of computer recording and storage technologies. Research has yielded mixed results with respect to the influence of broadcasting upon behavior.[4]

Within the electronic media itself, significant differences exist beyond those that are structurally obvious. Broadcasting and cable casting, for instance, offer different programming menus attributable to divergent economic realities. Television profits are maximized by appealing to and maximizing a single mass audience.[5] Given its multichannel capacity, cable serves a variety of audiences.[6] While television as a consequence tends to invest in programming calculated to attract the most viewers and offend the least, it is more sensible as a matter of economics for cable to diversify service in a way that compounds multiple discrete audiences.[7] Radio, television, cable, and motion pictures, unlike traditional print media, do not have a strict literacy prerequisite.

Despite discernible differences among media, advertence to them for purposes of constitutional standing may be problematical insofar as characterizations fail to accommodate further evolution or to discount universal rather than distinctive features. Scarcity as a characteristic justifying special regulation of the broadcast media has proved at least as discernible with respect to newspapers.[8] The point has been made, however, that all resources including media are scarce,[9] and barriers to entry ultimately are a function more of capital requirements than any medium-peculiar constraint.[10] The process of fashioning constitutional distinctions has become further compounded by increasingly merging capabilities of modern media which, whether denominated as publishing, broadcasting, or cable, to some extent may utilize the atmosphere, transmit electronically, and generate imagery upon a television screen.[11] Even if a medium may be structured better for purposes of maximizing diversity, moreover, potential may outreach actual performance. Risks of medium-specific analysis, therefore, may include generalizing too little and too much.

Even if it is easy to identify differences among the media, jurisprudence has demonstrated how difficult it may be to explain the reason for such an exercise. The vexing nature of the exercise was evidenced by two decisions in which the Court upheld and invalidated regulations that imposed fairness obligations respectively upon broadcasters[12] and publishers.[13] Despite a scarcity argument in the latter and later instance, the Court's decision avoided any reference whatsoever to its previous holding acceding to such concern.

I. PROMOTION OF CONTENT DIVERSITY AND BALANCE

The central issue, in *Miami Herald Publishing Co. v. Tornillo,*[14] was "whether a state statute granting a political candidate a right to equal space to reply to criticism and attacks on his record by a newspaper violates the guarantees of a free press."[15] In assessing the constitutionality of the law, which presented an undeniable challenge to editorial autonomy, the Court recounted how the newspaper industry increasingly had become characterized by diminished intramural competition, and ownership and control had become ever more concentrated.[16] The consequences of those trends, as the Court observed, has been "to place in a few hands the power to inform the American people and shape public opinion."[17] Because much editorial product is the work of centralized and "homogen[ized] . . . editorial opinion, commentary, and analysis,"[18] the claim was advanced that "the public has lost any ability to respond to or contribute in a meaningful way to the debate on issues."[19] Further triggering official concern was a sense that reportorial bias and manipulation was the function "of the vast accumulations of unreviewable power in the modern media empires."[20]

The Court at least implicitly acknowledged that "(t)he right of free public expression . . . has lost its earlier reality."[21] Citing economic factors that have made entry into the modern publishing business "almost impossible,"[22] it noted that the solution of increased competition which was "available . . . when entry into publishing was relatively inexpensive" no longer was feasible.[23] Despite the altered circumstances in which the First Amendment operates, the Court refused to brook any premise or implication that official action was appropriate to ensure "fairness and accuracy [or] to provide for some accountability" by publishers.[24] Notwithstanding earlier references to the effect that the First Amendment does not immunize the press from certain responsibilities,[25] and betokens "a profound national commitment to the principle that debate on public issues should be uninhibited, robust, and wide-open,"[26] it dismissed their pertinence as a possible predicate for a legislated right of access.[27] Rather, the Court emphasized that it consistently had been alert to and intolerant of any official, as opposed to private, inhibition upon editorial autonomy.[28] Even if the notion of "a responsible press" might be a "desirable goal," it could not be "mandated by the Constitution and like many other virtues... cannot be legislated."[29]

The Court in sum found the core issue to be whether government may compel "editors or publishers to publish that which 'reason tells them should not be published.' "[30] The access provision thereby was denominated as a functional prior restraint insofar as it required dedication of "space that could be devoted to other material the newspaper may have preferred to print."[31] Apart from violating editorial freedom, the measure was derogated for undermining First Amendment values. The Court observed that publishers, confronted with the possibility of penalties, might steer a safe course that avoided controversy to the detriment of the information marketplace and the public.[32] Even without such consequences, the statute was found to be fatally defective "because of its intrusion into the function of editors."[33] The composition of a newspaper represents "the exercise of editorial control and judgment."[34] The Court concluded, therefore, that "(i)t has yet to be demonstrated how governmental regulation of this crucial process can be exercised consistent with First Amendment guarantees of a free press as they have evolved to this time."[35]

Miami Herald Publishing Co. v. Tornillo, 418 U.S. 241 (1974)

Mr. Chief Justice Burger delivered the opinion of the Court.

The issue in this case is whether a state statute granting a political candidate a right to equal space to reply to criticism and attacks on his record by a newspaper violates the guarantees of a free press.

The elimination of competing newspapers in most of our large cities, and the concentration of media that results from the only newspaper's being owned by the same interests which own a television station and a radio station, are important components of this trend toward concentration of control of outlets to inform the public.

The result of these vast changes has been to place in a few hands the power to inform the American people and shape public opinion. Much of the editorial opinion and commentary that is printed is that of syndicated columnists distributed nationwide and, as a result, we are told, on national and world issues there tends to be a homogeneity of editorial opinion, commentary, and interpretive analysis. The abuses of bias and manipulative reportage are, likewise, said to be the result of the vast accumulations of unreviewable power in the modern media empires. In effect, it is claimed, the public has lost any ability to respond or to contribute in a meaningful way to the debate on issues. The monopoly of the means of communication allows for little or no critical analysis of the media except in professional journals of very limited readership.

> This concentration of nationwide news organizations—like other large institutions—has grown increasingly remote from and unresponsive to the popular constituencies on which they depend and which depend on them. Report of the Task Force in Twentieth Century Fund Task Force Report for a National News Council, A Free and Responsive Press 4 (1973).

Appellee cites the report of the Commission on Freedom of the Press, chaired by Robert M. Hutchins, in which it was stated, as long ago as 1947, that "[t]he right of free public expression has... lost its earlier reality." Commission on Freedom of the Press, A Free and Responsible Press 15 (1947).

The obvious solution, which was available to dissidents at an earlier time when entry into publishing was relatively inexpensive, today would be to have additional newspapers. But the same economic factors which have caused the disappearance of vast numbers of metropolitan newspapers, have made entry into the marketplace of ideas served by the print media almost impossible. It is urged that the claim of newspapers to be "surrogates for the public" carries with it a concomitant fiduciary obligation to account for that stewardship. From this premise it is reasoned that the only effective way to insure fairness and accuracy and to provide for some accountability is for government to take affirmative action. The First Amendment interest of the public in being informed is said to be in peril because the "marketplace of ideas" is today a monopoly controlled by the owners of the market.

Proponents of enforced access to the press take comfort from language in several of this Court's decisions which suggests that the First Amendment acts as a sword as well as a shield, that it imposes obligations on the owners of the press in addition to protecting the press from government regulation. In *Associated Press v. United States,* 326 U.S. 1, 20 (1945), the Court, in rejecting the argument that the press is immune from the antitrust laws by virtue of the First Amendment, stated:

> The First Amendment, far from providing an argument against application of the Sherman Act, here provides powerful reasons to the contrary. That Amendment rests on the assumption that the widest possible dissemination of information from diverse and antagonistic sources is essential to the welfare of the public, that a free press is a condition of a free society. Surely a command that the government itself shall not impede the free flow of ideas does not afford non-governmental combinations a refuge if they impose restraints upon that constitutionally guaranteed freedom. Freedom to publish means freedom for all and not for some. Freedom to publish is guaranteed by the Constitution, but freedom to combine to keep others from publishing is not. Freedom of the press from governmental interference under the First Amendment does not sanction repression of that freedom by private interests. (Footnote omitted.)

In *New York Times Co. v. Sullivan,* 376 U.S. 254, 270 (1964), the Court spoke of "a profound national commitment to the principle that debate on public issues should be uninhibited, robust, and wide-open." It is argued that the "uninhibited, robust" debate is not "wide-open" but open only to a monopoly in control of the press. Appellee cites the plurality opinion in *Rosenbloom v. Metromedia, Inc.,* 403 U.S. 29, 47, and n. 15 (1971), which he suggests seemed to invite experimentation by the States in right-to-access regulation of the press. . . .

However much validity may be found in these arguments, at each point the implementation of a remedy such as an enforceable right of access necessarily calls for some mechanism, either governmental or consensual. If it is governmental coercion, this at once brings about a confrontation with the express provisions of the First Amendment and the judicial gloss on that Amendment developed over the years.

The Court foresaw the problems relating to government-enforced access as early as its decision in *Associated Press v. United States, supra.* There it carefully contrasted the private "compulsion to print" called for by the Association's bylaws with the provisions of the District Court decree against appellants which "does not compel AP or its members to permit publication of anything which their 'reason' tells them should not be published." 326 U.S., at 20 n. 18. In *Branzburg v. Hayes,* 408 U.S. 665, 681 (1972), we emphasized that the cases then before us "involve no intrusions upon speech or assembly, no prior restraint or restriction on what the press may publish, and no express or implied command that the press publish what it prefers to withhold." In *Columbia Broadcasting System, Inc. v. Democratic National Committee,* 412 U.S. 94, 117 (1973), the plurality opinion as to Part III noted:

> The power of a privately owned newspaper to advance its own political, social, and economic views is bounded by only two factors: first, the acceptance of a sufficient number of readers—and hence advertisers—to assure financial success; and, second, the journalistic integrity of its editors and publishers.

An attitude strongly adverse to any attempt to extend a right of access to newspapers was echoed by other Members of this Court in their separate opinions in that case. *Id.,* at 145 (Stewart, J., concurring); *id.,* at 182 n. 12 (Brennan, J., joined by Marshall, J., dissenting). Recently, while approving a bar against employment advertising specifying "male" or "female" preference, the Court's opinion in *Pittsburgh Press Co. v. Human Relations Comm'n,* 413 U.S. 376, 391 (1973), took pains to limit its holding within narrow bounds:

> Nor, *a fortiori,* does our decision authorize any restriction whatever, whether of content or layout, on stories or commentary originated by Pittsburgh Press, its columnists, or its contributors. On the contrary, we reaffirm unequivocally the protection af-

forded to editorial judgment and to the free expression of views on these and other issues, however controversial.

Dissenting in *Pittsburgh Press,* Mr. Justice Stewart, joined by Mr. Justice Douglas, expressed the view that no "government agency—local, state, or federal—can tell a newspaper in advance what it can print and what it cannot." *Id.,* at 400. See *Associates & Aldrich Co. v. Times Mirror Co.,* 440 F. 2d 133, 135 (CA9 1971).

We see that beginning with *Associated Press, supra,* the Court has expressed sensitivity as to whether a restriction or requirement constituted the compulsion exerted by government on a newspaper to print that which it would not otherwise print. The clear implication has been that any such a compulsion to publish that which " 'reason' tells them should not be published" is unconstitutional. A responsible press is an undoubtedly desirable goal, but press responsibility is not mandated by the Constitution and like many other virtues it cannot be legislated.

Appellee's argument that the Florida statute does not amount to a restriction of appellant's right to speak because "the statute in question here has not prevented the *Miami Herald* from saying anything it wished" begs the core question. Compelling editors or publishers to publish that which " 'reason' tells them should not be published" is what is at issue in this case. The Florida statute operates as a command in the same sense as a statute or regulation forbidding appellant to publish specified matter. Governmental restraint on publishing need not fall into familiar or traditional patterns to be subject to constitutional limitations on governmental powers. *Grosjean v. American Press, Co.,* 297 U.S. 233, 244–245 (1936). The Florida statute exacts a penalty on the basis of the content of a newspaper. The first phase of the penalty resulting from the compelled printing of a reply is exacted in terms of the cost in printing and composing time and materials and in taking up space that could be devoted to other material the newspaper may have preferred to print. It is correct, as appellee contends, that a newspaper is not subject to the finite technological limitations of time that confront a broadcaster but it is not correct to say that, as an economic reality, a newspaper can proceed to infinite expansion of its column space to accommodate the replies that a government agency determines or a statute commands the readers should have available.

Faced with the penalties that would accrue to any newspaper that published news or commentary arguably within the reach of the right-of-access statute, editors might well conclude that the safe course is to avoid controversy. Therefore, under the operation of the Florida statute, political and electoral coverage would be blunted or reduced. Government-enforced right of access inescapably "dampens the vigor and limits the variety of public debate," *New York Times Co. v. Sullivan,* 376 U.S., at 279. The Court, in *Mills v. Alabama,* 384 U.S. 214, 218 (1966), stated:

[T]here is practically universal agreement that a major purpose of [the First] Amendment was to protect the free discussion of governmental affairs. This of course includes discussions of candidates.

Even if a newspaper would face no additional costs to comply with a compulsory access law and would not be forced to forgo publication of news or opinion by the inclusion of a reply, the Florida statute fails to clear the barriers of the First Amendment because of its intrusion into the function of editors. A newspaper is more than a passive receptacle or conduit for news, comment, and advertising. The choice of material to go into a newspaper, and the decisions made as to limitations on the size and content of the paper, and treatment of public issues and public officials—whether fair or unfair—constitute the exercise of editorial control and judgment. It has yet to be demonstrated how governmental regulation of this crucial process can be exercised consistent with First Amendment guarantees of a free press as they have evolved to this time. Accordingly, the judgment of the Supreme Court of Florida is reversed.

II. CONTENT RESTRICTION

Although the print media generally have been afforded maximum First Amendment protection, even that security is relative rather than absolute. Editorial autonomy, like any other cognizable constitutional interest, may be eclipsed by what is perceived as an overarching regulatory concern. Reflective of the consequent balancing process, which at times may favor official over constitutional interests, was the Court's validation of an ordinance which prohibited employment discrimination on the basis of gender and thus barred classified advertising of job opportunities designated in terms of sex.[36] Justice Stewart, in *Pittsburgh Press Co. v. Pittsburgh Commission on Human Relations*,[37] characterized the law as an obvious prior restraint which unconstitutionally dictated to "a newspaper in advance what it can print and what it cannot."[38] The Court nonetheless concluded that the ordinance did not cross freedom of the press.[39] In so doing, it acknowledged that the regulation impaired editorial discretion.[40] Such infringement was justified, and First Amendment interests were discounted because of the illegal nature of the underlying activity.[41]

Pittsburgh Press Co. v. Pittsburgh Commission on Human Relations, 413 U.S. 376 (1973)

Mr. Justice Powell delivered the opinion of the Court.

The Human Relations Ordinance of the City of Pittsburgh (the Ordinance) has been construed below by the courts of Pennsylvania as forbidding newspapers to carry "help-wanted" advertisements in sex-designated columns except where the employer or advertiser is free to make hiring or employment referral decisions on the basis of sex. We are called upon to decide whether the Ordinance as so construed violates the freedoms of speech and of the press guaranteed by the First and Fourteenth Amendments. This issue is a sensitive one, and a full understanding of the context in which it arises is critical to its resolution....

The present proceedings were initiated on October 9, 1969, when the National Organization for Women, Inc. (NOW) filed a complaint with the Pittsburgh Commission on Human Relations (the Commission), which is charged with implementing the Ordinance. The complaint alleged that the Pittsburgh Press Co. (Pittsburgh Press) was violating § 8(j) of the Ordinance by "allowing employers to place advertisements in the male or female columns, when the jobs advertised obviously do not have bona fide occupational qualifications or exceptions...." Finding probable cause to believe that Pittsburgh Press was violating the Ordinance, the Commission held a hearing, at which it received evidence and heard argument from the parties and from other interested organizations. Among the exhibits introduced at the hearing were clippings from the help-wanted advertisements carried in the January 4, 1970, edition of the Sunday Pittsburgh Press, arranged by column. In many cases, the advertisements consisted simply of the job title, the salary, and the employment agency carrying the listing, while others included somewhat more extensive job descriptions.

On July 23, 1970, the Commission issued a Decision and Order. It found that during 1969 Pittsburgh Press carried a total of 248,000 help-wanted advertisements; that its practice before October 1969 was to use columns captioned "Male Help Wanted," "Female Help Wanted," and "Male-Female Help Wanted"; that it thereafter used the captions "Jobs—Male Interest," "Jobs—Female Interest," and "Male-Female"; and that the advertisements were placed in the respective columns according to the advertiser's wishes, either volunteered by the advertiser or offered in response to inquiry by Pittsburgh Press. The Commission first concluded that § 8(e) of the Ordinance forbade employers, employment agencies, and labor organizations to submit advertisements for placement in sex-designated columns. It then held that Pittsburgh Press, in violation of § 8(j), aided the advertisers by maintaining a sex-designated classification system. After specifically considering and rejecting the argument that the Ordinance violated the First Amendment, the Commission ordered Pittsburgh Press to cease and desist such violations and to utilize a classification system with no reference to sex....

II

There is little need to reiterate that the freedoms of speech and of the press rank among our most cherished liberties. As Mr. Justice Black put it: "In the First Amendment the Founding Fathers gave the free press the protection it must have to fulfill its essential role in our democracy." *New York Times Co. v. United States,* 403 U.S. 713, 717 (1971) (concurring opinion). The durability of our system of self-government hinges upon the preservation of these freedoms.

> [S]ince informed public opinion is the most potent of all restraints upon misgovernment, the suppression or abridgement of the publicity afforded by a free press cannot be regarded otherwise than with grave concern.... A free press stands as one of the great interpreters between the government and the people. To allow it to be fettered is to fetter ourselves. *Grosjean v. American Press Co.,* 297 U.S. 233, 250 (1936).

The repeated emphasis accorded this theme in the decisions of this Court serves to underline the narrowness of the recognized exceptions to the principle that the press may not be regulated by the Government. Our inquiry must therefore be whether the challenged order falls within any of these exceptions.

At the outset, however, it is important to identify with some care the nature of the alleged abridgment. This is not a case in which the challenged law arguably disables the press by undermining its institutional viability. As the press has evolved from an assortment of small printers into a diverse aggregation including large publishing empires as well, the parallel growth and complexity of the economy have led to extensive regulatory legislation from which "[t]he publisher of a newspaper has no special immunity." *Associated Press v. NLRB,* 301 U.S. 103, 132 (1937). Accordingly, this Court has upheld application to the press of the National Labor Relations Act, *ibid.;* the Fair Labor Standards Act, *Mabee v. White Plains Publishing Co.,* 327 U.S. 178 (1946); *Oklahoma Press Publishing Co. v. Walling,* 327 U.S. 186 (1946); and the Sherman Antitrust Act, *Associated Press v. United States,* 326 U.S. 1 (1945); *Citizen Publishing Co. v. United States,* 394 U.S. 131 (1969). See also *Branzburg v. Hayes,* 408 U.S. 665 (1972). Yet the Court has recognized on several occasions the special institutional needs of a vigorous press by striking down laws taxing the advertising revenue of newspapers with circulations in excess of 20,000, *Grosjean v. American Press Co., supra;* re-

quiring a license for the distribution of printed matter, *Lovell v. Griffin,* 303 U.S. 444 (1938); and prohibiting the door-to-door distribution of leaflets, *Martin v. Struthers,* 319 U.S. 141 (1943).

But no suggestion is made in this case that the Ordinance was passed with any purpose of muzzling or curbing the press. Nor does Pittsburgh Press argue that the Ordinance threatens its financial viability or impairs in any significant way its ability to publish and distribute its newspaper. In any event, such a contention would not be supported by the record.

III

In a limited way, however, the Ordinance as construed does affect the makeup of the help-wanted section of the newspaper. Under the modified order, Pittsburgh Press will be required to abandon its present policy of providing sex-designated columns and allowing advertisers to select the columns in which their help-wanted advertisements will be placed. In addition, the order does not allow Pittsburgh Press to substitute a policy under which it would make an independent decision regarding placement in sex-designated columns....

Under some circumstances, at least, a newspaper's editorial judgments in connection with an advertisement take on the character of the advertisement and, in those cases, the scope of the newspaper's First Amendment protection may be affected by the content of the advertisement. In the context of a libelous advertisement, for example, this Court has held that the First Amendment does not shield a newspaper from punishment for libel when with actual malice it publishes a falsely defamatory advertisement. *New York Times Co. v. Sullivan, supra,* at 279–280. Assuming the requisite state of mind, then, nothing in a newspaper's editorial decision to accept an advertisement changes the character of the falsely defamatory statements. The newspaper may not defend a libel suit on the ground that the falsely defamatory statements are not its own.

Similarly, a commercial advertisement remains commercial in the hands of the media, at least under some circumstances. In *Capital Broadcasting Co. v. Acting Attorney General,* 405 U.S. 1000

(1972), aff'g 333 F. Supp. 582 (DC 1971), this Court summarily affirmed a district court decision sustaining the constitutionality of 15 U.S.C. § 1335, which prohibits the electronic media from carrying cigarette advertisements. The District Court there found that the advertising should be treated as commercial speech, even though the First Amendment challenge was mounted by radio broadcasters rather than by advertisers. Because of the peculiar characteristics of the electronic media, *National Broadcasting Co. v. United States*, 319 U.S. 190, 226–227 (1943), *Capital Broadcasting* is not dispositive here on the ultimate question of the constitutionality of the Ordinance. Its significance lies, rather, in its recognition that the exercise of this kind of editorial judgment does not necessarily strip commercial advertising of its commercial character.

As for the present case, we are not persuaded that either the decision to accept a commercial advertisement which the advertiser directs to be placed in a sex-designated column or the actual placement there lifts the newspaper's actions from the category of commercial speech. By implication at least, an advertiser whose want ad appears in the "Jobs—Male Interest" column is likely to discriminate against women in his hiring decisions. Nothing in a sex-designated column heading sufficiently dissociates the designation from the want ads placed beneath it to make the placement severable for First Amendment purposes from the want ads themselves. The combination, which conveys essentially the same message as an overtly discriminatory want ad, is in practical effect an integrated commercial statement.... Discrimination in employment is not only commercial activity, it is *illegal* commercial activity under the Ordinance. We have no doubt that a newspaper constitutionally could be forbidden to publish a want ad proposing a sale of narcotics or soliciting prostitutes. Nor would the result be different if the nature of the transaction were indicated by placement under columns captioned "Narcotics for Sale" and "Prostitutes Wanted" rather than stated within the four corners of the advertisement.

The illegality in this case may be less overt, but we see no difference in principle here. Sex discrimination in nonexempt employment has been declared illegal under § 8(a) of the Ordinance, a provision not challenged here. And § 8(e) of the Ordinance forbids any employer, employment agency, or labor union to publish or cause to be published any advertisement "indicating" sex discrimination. This, too, is unchallenged. Moreover, the Commission specifically concluded that it is an unlawful employment practice for an advertiser to cause an employment advertisement to be published in a sex-designated column.

Section 8(j) of the Ordinance, the only provision which Pittsburgh Press was found to have violated and the only provision under attack here, makes it unlawful for "any person ... to aid ... in the doing of any act declared to be an unlawful employment practice by this ordinance." The Commission and the courts below concluded that the practice of placing want ads for nonexempt employment in sex-designated columns did indeed "aid" employers to indicate illegal sex preferences. The advertisements, as embroidered by their placement, signaled that the advertisers were likely to show an illegal sex preference in their hiring decisions. Any First Amendment interest which might be served by advertising an ordinary commercial proposal and which might arguably outweigh the governmental interest supporting the regulation is altogether absent when the commercial activity itself is illegal and the restriction on advertising is incidental to a valid limitation on economic activity.

IV

It is suggested, in the brief of an *amicus curiae*, that apart from other considerations, the Commission's order should be condemned as a prior restraint on expression. As described by Blackstone, the protection against prior restraint at common law barred only a system of administrative censorship:

> To subject the press to the restrictive power of a licenser, as was formerly done, both before and since the revolution, ... is to subject all freedom of sentiment to the prejudices of one man, and make him the arbitrary and infallible judge of all controverted points in learning, religion, and government. 4 W. Blackstone, Commentaries 152.

While the Court boldly stepped beyond this narrow doctrine in *Near v. Minnesota,* 283 U.S. 697 (1931), in striking down an injunction against further publication of a newspaper found to be a public nuisance, it has never held that all injunctions are impermissible. See *Lorain Journal Co. v. United States,* 342 U.S. 143 (1951). The special vice of a prior restraint is that communication will be suppressed, either directly or by inducing excessive caution in the speaker, before an adequate determination that it is unprotected by the First Amendment.

The present order does not endanger arguably protected speech. Because the order is based on a continuing course of repetitive conduct, this is not a case in which the Court is asked to speculate as to the effect of publication. Cf. *New York Times Co. v. United States,* 403 U.S. 713 (1971). Moreover, the order is clear and sweeps no more broadly than necessary. And because no interim relief was granted, the order will not have gone into effect before our final determination that the actions of Pittsburgh Press were unprotected.

V

We emphasize that nothing in our holding allows government at any level to forbid Pittsburgh Press to publish and distribute advertisements commenting on the Ordinance, the enforcement practices of the Commission, or the propriety of sex preferences in employment. Nor, *a fortiori,* does our decision authorize any restriction whatever, whether of content or layout, on stories or commentary originated by Pittsburgh Press, its columnists, or its contributors. On the contrary, we reaffirm unequivocally the protection afforded to editorial judgment and to the free expression of views on these and other issues, however controversial. We hold only that the Commission's modified order, narrowly drawn to prohibit placement in sex-designated columns of advertisements for nonexempt job opportunities, does not infringe the First Amendment rights of Pittsburgh Press.

Affirmed.

Mr. Chief Justice Burger, dissenting.

To my way of thinking, Pittsburgh Press has clearly acted within its protected journalistic discretion in adopting this arrangement of its classified advertisements. Especially in light of the newspaper's "Notice to Job Seekers," it is unrealistic for the Court to say, as it does, that the sex-designated column headings are not "sufficiently dissociate[d]" from the "want ads placed beneath [them] to make the placement severable for First Amendment purposes from the want ads themselves." *Ante,* at 388. In any event, I believe the First Amendment freedom of press includes the right of a newspaper to arrange the content of its paper, whether it be news items, editorials, or advertising, as it sees fit. In the final analysis, the readers are the ultimate "controllers" no matter what excesses are indulged in by even a flamboyant or venal press; that it often takes a long time for these influences to bear fruit is inherent in our system.

The Court's conclusion that the Commission's cease-and-desist order does not constitute a prior restrain gives me little reassurance. That conclusion is assertedly based on the view that the order affects only a "continuing course of repetitive conduct." *Ante,* at 390. Even if that were correct, I would still disagree since the Commission's order appears to be in effect an outstanding *injunction* against certain publications—the essence of a prior restraint....

In practical effect, therefore, the Commission's order in this area may have the same inhibiting effect as the injunction in *Near v. Minnesota,* 283 U.S. 697 (1931), which permanently enjoined the publishers of a newspaper from printing a "malicious, scandalous or defamatory newspaper, as defined by law." *Id.,* at 706. We struck down the injunction in *Near* as a prior restraint. In 1971, we reaffirmed the principle of presumptive unconstitutionality of prior restraint in *Organization for a Better Austin v. Keefe,* 402 U.S. 415 (1971). Indeed, in *New York Times Co. v. United States,* 403 U.S. 713 (1971), every member of the Court, tacitly or explicitly, accepted the *Near* and *Keefe* condemnation of prior restraint as presumptively unconstitutional. In this case, the respondents have, in my view, failed to carry their burden. I would therefore hold the Commission's order to be impermissible prior restraint. At the very least, we ought to make clear that a newspaper may not be subject to summary punishment for contempt for having made an "unlucky" legal guess on a particular advertisement or for having failed to secure advance Commission approval of a decision to run an advertisement under a sex-designated column.

Mr. Justice Douglas, dissenting.

While I join the dissent of Mr. Justice Stewart, I add a few words. As he says, the press, like any other business, can be regulated on business and economic matters. Our leading case on that score is *Associated Press v. United States,* 326 U.S. 1, which holds that a news-gathering agency may be made accountable for violations of the antitrust laws. By like token, a newspaper, periodical, or TV or radio broadcaster may be subjected to labor relations laws. And that regulation could constitutionally extend to the imposition of penalties or other sanctions if any unit of the press violated laws that barred discrimination in employment based on race or religion or sex.

Pennsylvania has a regulatory regime designed to eliminate discrimination in employment based on sex; and the commission in charge of that program issues cease-and-desist orders against violators. There is no doubt that Pittsburgh Press would have no constitutional defense against such a cease-and-desist order issued against it for discriminatory employment practices.

But I believe that Pittsburgh Press by reason of the First Amendment may publish what it pleases about any law without censorship or restraint by Government. The First Amendment does not require the press to reflect any ideological or political creed reflecting the dominant philosophy, whether transient or fixed. It may use its pages and facilities to denounce a law and urge its repeal or, at the other extreme, denounce those who do not respect its letter and spirit.

Commercial matter, as distinguished from news, was held in *Valentine v. Chrestensen,* 316 U.S. 52, not to be subject to First Amendment protection. My views on that issue have changed since 1942, the year *Valentine* was decided. As I have stated on earlier occasions, I believe that commercial materials also have First Amendment protection. If Empire Industries Ltd., doing business in Pennsylvania, wanted to run full-page advertisements denouncing or criticizing this Pennsylvania law, I see no way in which Pittsburgh Press could be censored or punished for running the ad, any more than a person could be punished for uttering the contents of the ad in a public address in Independence Hall. The *pros* and *cons* of legislative enactments are clearly discussion or dialogue that is highly honored in our First Amendment traditions.

The want ads which gave rise to the present litigation express the preference of one employer for the kind of help he needs. If he carried through to hiring and firing employees on the basis of those preferences, the state commission might issue a remedial order against him, if discrimination in employment was shown. Yet he could denounce that action with impunity and Pittsburgh Press could publish his denunciation or write an editorial taking his side also with impunity.

Where there is a valid law, the Government can enforce it. But there can be no valid law censoring the press or punishing it for publishing its views or the views of subscribers or customers who express their ideas in letters to the editor or in want ads or other commercial space. There comes a time, of course, when speech and action are so closely brigaded that they are really one. Falsely shouting "fire" in a theater the example given by Mr. Justice Holmes, *Schenck v. United States,* 249 U.S. 47, 52, is one example. *Giboney v. Empire Storage Co.,* 336 U.S. 490, written by Mr. Justice Black, is another. There are here, however, no such unusual circumstances.

As Mr. Justice Stewart says, we have witnessed a growing tendency to cut down the literal requirements of First Amendment freedoms so that those in power can squelch someone out of step. Historically, the miscreant has usually been an unpopular minority. Today it is a newspaper that does not bow to the spreading bureaucracy that promises to engulf us. It may be that we have become so stereotyped as to have earned that fate. But the First Amendment presupposes free-wheeling, independent people whose vagaries include ideas spread across the entire spectrum of thoughts and beliefs. I would let any expression in that broad spectrum flourish, unrestrained by Government, unless it was an integral part of action—the only point which in the Jeffersonian philosophy marks the permissible point of governmental intrusion.

I therefore dissent from affirmance of this judgment.

Mr. Justice Stewart, with whom Mr. Justice Douglas joins, dissenting.

I have no doubt that it is within the police power of the city of Pittsburgh to prohibit discrimination in private employment on the basis of race, color, religion, ancestry, national origin, place of birth, or sex. I do not doubt, either, that in enforcing such a policy the city may prohibit employers from indicating any such discrimination when they make known the availability of employment opportunities. But neither of those propositions resolves the question before us in this case.

That question, to put it simply, is whether any government agency—local, state, or federal—can tell a newspaper in advance what it can print and what it cannot. Under the First and Fourteenth Amendments I think no government agency in this Nation has any such power.

It is true, of course, as the Court points out, that the publisher of a newspaper is amenable to civil and criminal laws of general applicability. For example, a newspaper publisher is subject to nondiscriminatory general taxation, and to restrictions imposed by the National Labor Relations Act, the Fair Labor Standards Act, and the Sherman Act. In short, as businessman or employer, a newspaper publisher is not exempt from laws affecting businessmen and employers generally. Accordingly, I assume that the Pittsburgh Press Co., as an employer, can be and is completely within the coverage of the Human Relations Ordinance of the city of Pittsburgh.

But what the Court approves today is wholly different. It approves a government order dictating to a publisher in advance how he must arrange the layout of pages in his newspaper....

So far as I know, this is the first case in this or any other American court that permits a government agency to enter a composing room of a newspaper and dictate to the publisher the layout and makeup of the newspaper's pages. This is the first such case, but I fear it may not be the last. The camel's nose is in the tent. "It may be that it

is the obnoxious thing in its mildest and least repulsive form; but illegitimate and unconstitutional practices get their first footing in that way. . . ." *Boyd v. United States,* 116 U.S. 616, 635.

So long as Members of this Court view the First Amendment as no more than a set of "values" to be balanced against other "values," that Amendment will remain in grave jeopardy. See *Paris Adult Theatre I v. Slaton, ante,* p. 49 (First and Fourteenth Amendment protections outweighed by public interest in "quality of life," "total community environment," "tone of commerce," "public safety"); *Branzburg v. Hayes,* 408 U.S. 665 (First Amendment claim asserted by newsman to maintain confidential relationship with his sources outweighed by obligation to give information to grand jury); *New York Times Co. v. United States,* 403 U.S. 713, 748 (Burger, C. J., dissenting) (First Amendment outweighed by judicial problems caused by "unseemly haste"); *Columbia Broadcasting System, Inc. v. Democratic National Committee,* 412 U.S. 94, 199 (Brennan, J., dissenting) (balancing of "the competing First Amendment interests").

It is said that the goal of the Pittsburgh ordinance is a laudable one, and so indeed it is. But, in the words of Mr. Justice Brandeis, "Experience should teach us to be most on our guard to protect liberty when the Government's purposes are beneficent. Men born to freedom are naturally alert to repel invasion of their liberty by evil-minded rulers. The greatest dangers to liberty lurk in insidious encroachment by men of zeal, well-meaning but without understanding." *Olmstead v. United States,* 277 U.S. 438, 479 (dissenting opinion). And, as Mr. Justice Black once pointed out, "The motives behind the state law may have been to do good. But . . . [h]istory indicates that urges to do good have led to the burning of books and even to the burning of 'witches.' " *Beauharnais v. Illinois,* 343 U.S. 250, 274 (dissenting opinion).

The Court today holds that a government agency can force a newspaper publisher to print his classified advertising pages in a certain way in order to carry out governmental policy. After this decision, I see no reason why government cannot force a newspaper publisher to conform in the same way in order to achieve other goals thought socially desirable. And if government can dictate the layout of a newspaper's classified advertising pages today, what is there to prevent it from dictating the layout of the news pages tomorrow?

Those who think the First Amendment can and should be subordinated to other socially desirable interests will hail today's decision. But I find it frightening. For I believe the constitutional guarantee of a free press is more than precatory. I believe it is a clear command that government must never be allowed to lay its heavy editorial hand on any newspaper in this country.

The *Pittsburgh Press* decision adverted in part to the then constitutionally unprotected status of commercial speech.[42] Notwithstanding jurisprudential recontouring of the First Amendment to shelter such expression,[43] subsequent doctrine still allows government to prohibit advertisement of illegal activities.[44] Although the decision was influenced by the presence of commercial speech, the result thus would be identical pursuant to modern analysis. The episode demonstrates nicely how First Amendment protection may be influenced not only by the nature of the medium but also by the type of expression at issue. It reveals also a fundamental truth concerning constitutional rights and liberties including editorial freedom. The First Amendment by its terms and as explicated in the *Tornillo* decision may appear to be cast in unequivocal terms. The *Pittsburgh Press* decision exemplifies how "broad statements of principle . . . are sometimes qualified by contrary decision before the absolute limit of the stated principle is reached."[45]

NOTES

1. *See* Konigsberg v. State Bar of California, 366 U.S. 36, 49–51 (1961).

2. Joseph Burstyn, Inc. v. Wilson, 343 U.S. 495, 503 (1952).

3. Kovacs v. Cooper, 336 U.S. 77, 97 (1949) (Jackson, J., concurring).

4. *See Videoculture,* CHRISTIAN SCIENCE MONITOR, Aug. 25, 1985, at 25.

5. *See* Columbia Broadcasting System, Inc. v. Democratic National Committee, 412 U.S. 94, 187–88 (1973)

(Brennan, J., dissenting); Bazelon, *FCC Regulation of the Telecommunications Press,* 1975 DUKE L.J. 213, 230.

6. *See* Capital Cities Cable, Inc. v. Crisp, 467 U.S. 691, 700–01 (1984); Quincy Cable TV, Inc. v. Federal Communications Commission, 768 F.2d 1434, 1438–39 (D.C. Cir. 1985), *cert. denied,* 476 U.S. 1169 (1986).

7. *See id.*

8. Even at the time that spectrum scarcity was subscribed to as the predicate for fairness regulation of broadcasters, the number of radio and television stations exceeded the sum of daily newspapers. In 1970, therefore, a total of 1,748 daily newspapers were publishing contrasted with 862 television and 6,519 radio stations. STATISTICAL ABSTRACT OF THE UNITED STATES 1989, No. 900, at 544, No. 914, at 549.

9. *See* Telecommunications Research and Action Center v. Federal Communications Commission, 801 F.2d 501, 508 (D.C. Cir. 1986), *cert. denied,* 482 U.S. 919 (1987).

10. Because operation of any mass medium requires enormous financial resources, and because broadcast licenses are transferable in the marketplace, most citizens are disqualified on economic grounds from owning and operating an instrument of the press.

11. Publishers use satellite transmissions to communicate from editorial to printing plants and to disseminate and vend their product on public right of ways, and they may propagate content electronically so that it is received on a television screen. Cable draws some of its signals from broadcast emissions and requires easements to a wire service area. Broadcasting also uses a public resource by transmitting via airwaves. No medium thus seems to be unaffected by electronics or the need to use public resources.

12. Red Lion Broadcasting Co. v. Federal Communications Commission, 395 U.S. 367 (1969).

13. Miami Herald Publishing Co. v. Tornillo, 418 U.S. 241 (1974).

14. *Id.*

15. *Id.* at 243.

16. *Id.* at 248–52.

17. *Id.* at 250.

18. *Id.*

19. *Id.*

20. *Id.*

21. *Id.* at 250–51, *quoting* Commission on Freedom of the Press, A Free and Responsible Press 15 (1947).

22. Miami Herald Publishing Co. v. Tornillo, 418 U.S. at 251.

23. *Id.*

24. *Id.*

25. *See id.* at 251–52, *citing* Associated Press v. United States, 326 U.S. 1, 20 (1945).

26. 418 U.S. at 252, *citing* New York Times Co. v. Sullivan, 376 U.S. 254, 270 (1964).

27. 418 U.S. at 254.

28. *Id.* at 254–55.

29. *Id.* at 256.

30. *Id.*

31. *Id.*

32. *Id.* at 257.

33. *Id.* at 258.

34. *Id.*

35. *Id.*

36. Pittsburgh Press Company v. Pittsburgh Commission on Human Relations, 413 U.S. 376, 391 (1973).

37. 413 U.S. 376.

38. *Id.* at 400 (Stewart, J., dissenting). Justices Douglas and Blackmun and Chief Justice Burger agreed that the ordinance amounted to an unconstitutional prior restraint.

39. *Id.* at 382–83, 389–91.

40. *Id.* at 386–87.

41. *Id.* at 388–89.

42. *Id.* at 384–89.

43. *See* Virginia State Board of Pharmacy v. Virginia Citizens Consumer Council, 425 U.S. 748 (1976).

44. Posadas de Puerto Rico Associates v. Tourism Co. of Puerto Rico, 478 U.S. 328, 345–46 (1986).

45. Young v. American Mini Theatres, Inc., 427 U.S. 50, 65 (1976).

Chapter 9

BROADCASTING

I. PROMOTION OF CONTENT DIVERSITY AND BALANCE

A constitutional regimen inhospitable toward the concepts of officially imposed responsibility for the print media has proved more tolerant of like notions as they pertain to newer electronic media. The sense that broadcasting might be subject to editorial oversight predates the Communications Act of 1934 and has evolved further over the course of time.[1] The regulatory predecessor of the Federal Communications Commission (FCC) thus observed that if broadcasters did not afford an opportunity "for every school of thought, religious, political, social, and economic, . . . a well-founded complaint will receive the careful consideration of the Commission in its future action with reference to the station complained of."[2] The Federal Radio Commission, despite being prohibited from engaging in censorship, was not reluctant to factor content into licensing decisions. Its decision to deny renewal of the license of a religious broadcaster, in *Trinity Methodist Church, South v. Federal Radio Commission*,[3] was upheld pursuant to a determination that no prior restraint operated and that the public interest was disserved by

the licensee's defamatory and one-sided commentary.[4]

Trinity Methodist Church, South v. Federal Radio Commission, 62 F.2d 850 (D.C. Cir. 1932), *cert. denied*, **288 U.S. 599 (1933)**

Groner, Associate Justice.

Appellant, Trinity Methodist Church, South, was the lessee and operator of a radio-broadcasting station at Los Angeles, Cal., known by the call letters KGEF. The station had been in operation for several years. The Commission, in its findings, shows that, though in the name of the church, the station was in fact owned by the Reverend Doctor Shuler and its operation dominated by him. Dr. Shuler is the minister in charge of Trinity Church. The station was operated for a total of 23¼ hours each week.

We need not stop to review the cases construing the depth and breadth of the first amendment. The subject in its more general outlook has been the source of much writing since Milton's Areopagitica, the emancipation of the English press by the withdrawal of the licensing act in the reign of William the Third, and the Letters of Junius. It is enough now to say that the universal trend of decisions has recognized the guaranty of the amendment to prevent previous restraints upon publications, as well as immunity of censorship, leaving to correction by subsequent punishment those utterances or publications contrary to the public welfare. In this aspect it is generally regarded that freedom of speech and press cannot be infringed by legislative, executive, or judicial action, and that the constitutional guaranty should be given liberal and comprehensive construction. It may therefore be set down as a fundamental principle that under these constitutional guaranties the citizen has in the first instance the right to utter or publish his sentiments, though, of course, upon condition that he is responsible for any abuse of that right. *Near v. Minnesota* ex rel. Olson, 283 U.S. 697, 51 S. Ct. 625, 75 L. Ed. 1357. "Every freeman has an undoubted right to lay what sentiments he pleases before the public; to forbid this is to destroy the freedom of the press; but if he publishes what is improper, mischievous, or illegal, he must take the consequences of his own temerity." 4th Bl. Com. 151, 152. But this does not mean that the government, through agencies established by Congress, may not refuse a renewal of license to one who has abused it to broadcast defamatory and untrue matter. In that case there is not a denial of the freedom of speech, but merely the application of the regulatory power of Congress in a field within the scope of its legislative authority. See *KFKB Broadcasting Ass'n v. Federal Radio Commission*, 60 App. D.C. 79, 47 F.(2d) 670. . . .

In the case under consideration, the evidence abundantly sustains the conclusion of the Commission that the continuance of the broadcasting programs of appellant is not in the public interest. In a proceeding for contempt against Dr. Shuler, on appeal to the Supreme Court of California, that court said (In re Shuler, 210 Cal. 377, 292 P. 481, 492) that the broadcast utterances of Dr. Shuler disclosed throughout the determination on his part to impose on the trial courts his own will and views with respect to certain causes then pending or on trial, and amounted to contempt of court. Appellant, not satisfied with attacking the judges of the courts in cases then pending before them, attacked the bar association for its activities in recommending judges, charging it with ulterior and sinister purposes. With no more justification, he charged particular judges with sundry immoral acts. He made defamatory statements against the board of health. He charged that the labor

temple in Los Angeles was a bootlegging and gambling joint. In none of these matters, when called on to explain or justify his statements, was he able to do more than declare that the statements expressed his own sentiments. On one occasion he announced over the radio that he had certain damaging information against a prominent unnamed man which, unless a contribution (presumably to the church) of a hundred dollars was forthcoming, he would disclose. As a result, he received contributions from several persons. He freely spoke of "pimps" and prostitutes. He alluded slightingly to the Jews as a race, and made frequent and bitter attacks on the Roman Catholic religion and its relations to government. However inspired Dr. Shuler may have been by what he regarded as patriotic zeal, however sincere in denouncing conditions he did not approve, it is manifest, we think, that it is not narrowing the ordinary conception of "public interest" in declaring his broadcasts—without facts to sustain or to justify them—not within that term, and, since that is the test the Commission is required to apply, we think it was its duty in considering the application for renewal to take notice of appellant's conduct in his previous use of the permit, and, in the circumstances, the refusal, we think, was neither arbitrary nor capricious.

If it be considered that one in possession of a permit to broadcast in interstate commerce may, without let or hindrance from any source, use these facilities, reaching out, as they do, from one corner of the country to the other, to obstruct the administration of justice, offend the religious susceptibilities of thousands, inspire political distrust and civic discord, or offend youth and innocence by the free use of words suggestive of sexual immorality, and be answerable for slander only at the instance of the one offended, then this great science, instead of a boon, will become a scourge, and the nation a theater for the display of individual passions and the collision of personal interests. This is neither censorship nor previous restraint, nor is it a whittling away of the rights guaranteed by the First Amendment, or an impairment of their free exercise. Appellant may continue to indulge his strictures upon the characters of men in public office. He may just as freely as ever criticize religious practices of which he does not approve. He may even indulge private malice or personal slander—subject, of course, to be required to answer for the abuse thereof—but he may not, as we think, demand, of right, the continued use of an instrumentality of commerce for such purposes, or any other, except in subordination to all reasonable rules and regulations Congress, acting through the Commission, may prescribe.

Official intervention into broadcast content received an early constitutional boost when the Supreme Court, in *National Broadcasting Co. v. United States*,[5] determined that the FCC was more than a "traffic officer, policing the engineering and technical aspects of broadcasting."[6] Another quarter of a century would pass before the Court directly considered the First Amendment issues raised by fairness regulation and concluded, pursuant to the notion of spectrum scarcity, that "Government is permitted to put restraints on licensees in favor of others whose views should be expressed on this unique medium."[7] In the interim, Congress and the FCC, respectively, had codified and promulgated requirements intended to facilitate comprehensive and balanced coverage of public issues.

A. FAIRNESS REGULATION

Fairness regulation in its broadcast sense breaks down into statutory and administrative mandates that provide access for viewpoints and, in some instances, for individuals. The fairness doctrine exemplifies facilitation of viewpoint access in the sense that the licensee retains discretion to present competing perspectives and to decide who will do so.[8] Such a concept is distinguishable from access in the event of a personal attack and access or equal opportunity provisions for political candidates,[9] which afford designated individuals the opportunity to present ideas or information under certain circumstances.

1. Viewpoint Access

The fairness doctrine itself began to take formal shape in 1949 when the FCC authored a report that delineated a two-part responsibility for broadcasters. Essentially, licensees were obligated to "[1] devote a reasonable percentage of their broadcast time to the . . . consideration and discussion of public issues [and] . . . [2] make sufficient time available for full discussion thereof."[10] Balance of a presentation implicating fairness responsibilities was the responsibility of the licensee, who had the option to designate another person to offer a competing view, and was to be effectuated at the licensee's expense if no sponsorship was available.[11] Congress, in 1959, amended Section 315 of the Communications Act of 1934[12] in a way that later was construed as approving the fairness doctrine.[13] The inference is drawn from modification of the equal time provision for political candidates[14] to make clear it exempted licensees "from the obligation imposed upon them under this Act to operate in the public interest and to afford reasonable opportunity for their discussion of conflicting views on issues of public importance."[15] In 1967, the FCC promulgated rules affording access rights to individuals whose honesty, character, integrity, or other personal quality was attacked in the course of a broadcast[16] and to candidates whose opponents have been endorsed in a licensee's political editorial.[17] The basic fairness doctrine, and related personal attack and political editorial rules, soon were contested on the grounds that they abrogated freedom of the press.

The challenge arose after a licensee had refused to provide free reply time to an individual claiming that a religious broadcast, which portrayed him as sympathetic to communism and as antipatriotic, had constituted a personal attack upon him.[18] In *Red Lion Broadcasting Co. v. Federal Communications Commission*,[19] the Court upheld the commission's finding that the broadcast constituted a personal attack and that the licensee must provide free reply time.[20] It also provided a lengthy discourse in support of fairness regulation and held that such control did not exceed the commission's authority and "enhanced[d] rather than abridge[d] the freedoms of speech and press protected by the First Amendment."[21] Adverting to the chaotic circumstances that preceded government control of what it characterized as a "scarce resource," the Court emphasized how experience had demonstrated that use of "broadcast frequencies...could be regulated and rationalized only by the Government."[22] Minus such control, it observed, "the medium would be of little use because of the cacophony of competing voices, none of which could be clearly and predictably heard."[23]

The FCC's authority to promulgate the regulations at issue was derived from its general obligation to regulate in the public interest.[24] Apart from finding that the fairness doctrine paralleled statutory provisions relating to political candidates and was supported by legislative history,[25] the Court observed that "the 'public interest' in broadcasting clearly encompasses the presentation of controversial issues of importance and concern to the public."[26] Responding to the contention that the constitution safeguarded the exercise of editorial discretion by broadcasters to use and exclude from their frequencies whomever they chose,[27] the Court acknowledged that broadcasting was "a medium affected by a First Amendment interest."[28] Consistent with freedom of the press analysis for newer media, however, it emphasized that "differences in the characteristics of new media justify differences in the First Amendment standards applied to them."[29] From the Court's perspective, the crucial characteristic of broadcasting was spectrum scarcity. As the Court put it, "(w)here there are substantially more indi-

viduals who want to broadcast than there are frequencies to allocate, it is idle to posit an unabridgeable First Amendment right to broadcast comparable to the right of every individual to speak, write, or publish."[30]

The First Amendment status of broadcasters thus was set consciously and explicitly at a different level than that of publishers. The variance was premised upon circumstances which required licensing of broadcasters but did not thereby confer a "right ...to monopolize a radio frequency."[31] Given the unique nature of broadcasting, the Court found "nothing in the First Amendment which prevents the Government from requiring a licensee to share his frequency with others and to conduct himself as a proxy or fiduciary with obligations to present those views and voices which are representative of [the] community and which would otherwise, by necessity, be barred from the airwaves."[32] Scarcity thus was the premise for recognizing a right of the public "to have the medium function consistently with the ends and purposes of the First Amendment" and elevating it above the constitutional rights of broadcasters.[33] What later would become referred to as an "unusual ordering" of constitutional interests essentially prioritized First Amendment values over traditional concepts of editorial freedom. It became "the right of the public to receive suitable access to social, political, esthetic, moral, and other ideas and experiences which [was] crucial here."[34]

Arguments that fairness demands would deter rather than enhance coverage of controversial issues, because broadcasters would avoid presentations that would obligate them to provide free air time, proved unavailing. The Court observed that such a possibility was unlikely in view of the industry's past performance and lack of evidence that broadcasters intended to avoid controversy.[35] It pointed out, however, that "if present licensees should prove timorous, the

Commission is not powerless to insist that they give adequate and fair attention to public issues."[36] The Court thus spoke approvingly of conditioning the award or retention of a license upon compliance with fairness duties.[37]

Also rejected were arguments that technological progress was increasingly diminishing the significance of spectrum scarcity. Because competition for frequencies persisted, very high frequency (VHF) spectrum space was mostly occupied, ultrahigh frequency (UHF) operation only recently had showed possibilities of commercial viability, and radio had become so crowded that new applications at times had been suspended, the Court determined that "(s)carcity is not entirely a thing of the past."[38] It concluded that, because of spectrum scarcity, the government's role in allocating frequencies, and diminished viewpoint diversity absent official control, fairness regulation was "authorized by statute and constitutional."[39]

Red Lion Broadcasting Co. v. Federal Communications Commission, 395 U.S. 367 (1969)

Mr. Justice White delivered the opinion of the Court.

The Federal Communications Commission has for many years imposed on radio and television broadcasters the requirement that discussion of public issues be presented on broadcast stations, and that each side of those issues must be given fair coverage. This is known as the fairness doctrine, which originated very early in the history of broadcasting and has maintained its present outlines for some time. It is an obligation whose content has been defined in a long series of FCC rulings in particular cases, and which is distinct from the statutory requirement of § 315 of the Communications Act that equal time be allotted all qualified candidates for public office. Two aspects of the fairness doctrine, relating to personal attacks in the context of controversial public issues

and to political editorializing, were codified more precisely in the form of FCC regulations in 1967. The two cases before us now, which were decided separately below, challenge the constitutional and statutory bases of the doctrine and component rules. *Red Lion* involves the application of the fairness doctrine to a particular broadcast, and *RTNDA* arises as an action to review the FCC's 1967 promulgation of the personal attack and political editorializing regulations, which were laid down after the *Red Lion* litigation had begun.

I

A

The Red Lion Broadcasting Company is licensed to operate a Pennsylvania radio station, WGCB. On November 27, 1964, WGCB carried a 15-minute broadcast by the Reverend Billy James Hargis as part of a "Christian Crusade" series. A book by Fred J. Cook entitled "Goldwater—Extremist on the Right" was discussed by Hargis, who said that Cook had been fired by a newspaper for making false charges against city officials; that Cook had then worked for a Communist-affiliated publication; that he had defended Alger Hiss and attacked J. Edgar Hoover and the Central Intelligence Agency; and that he had now written a "book to smear and destroy Barry Goldwater." When Cook heard of the broadcast he concluded that he had been personally attacked and demanded free reply time, which the station refused. After an exchange of letters among Cook, Red Lion, and the FCC, the FCC declared that the Hargis broadcast constituted a personal attack on Cook; that Red Lion had failed to meet its obligation under the fairness doctrine as expressed in *Times-Mirror Broadcasting Co.,* 24 P & F Radio Reg. 404 (1962), to send a tape, transcript, or summary of the broadcast to Cook and offer him reply time; and that the station must provide reply time whether or not Cook would pay for it. On review in the Court of Appeals for the District of Columbia Circuit, the FCC's position was upheld as constitutional and otherwise proper. 127 U.S. App. D.C. 129, 381 F. 2d 908 (1967)....

Believing that the specific application of the fairness doctrine in *Red Lion,* and the promulgation of the regulations in *RTNDA*, are both authorized by Congress and enhance rather than abridge the freedoms of speech and press protected by the First Amendment, we hold them valid and constitutional, reversing the judgment below in *RTNDA* and affirming the judgment below in *Red Lion*.

II

The history of the emergence of the fairness doctrine and of the related legislation shows that the Commission's action in the *Red Lion* case did not exceed its authority, and that in adopting the new regulations the Commission was implementing congressional policy rather than embarking on a frolic of its own.

A

Before 1927, the allocation of frequencies was left entirely to the private sector, and the result was chaos. It quickly became apparent that broadcast frequencies constituted a scarce resource whose use could be regulated and rationalized only by the Government. Without government control, the medium would be of little use because of the cacaphony of competing voices, none of which could be clearly and predictably heard. Consequently, the Federal Radio Commission was established to allocate frequencies among competing applicants in a manner responsive to the public "convenience, interest, or necessity."

Very shortly thereafter the Commission expressed its view that the "public interest requires ample play for the free and fair competition of opposing views, and the commission believes that the principle applies . . . to all discussions of issues of importance to the public." *Great Lakes Broadcasting Co.,* 3 F.R.C. Ann. Rep. 32, 33 (1929), rev'd on other grounds, 59 App. D.C. 197, 37 F. 2d 993, cert. dismissed, 281 U.S. 706 (1930). This doctrine was applied through denial of license renewals or construction permits, both by the FRC, *Trinity Methodist Church, South v. FRC,* 61 App. D.C. 311, 62 F. 2d 850 (1932), cert. denied, 288 U.S. 599 (1933), and its successor FCC, *Young People's Association for the Propagation of the Gospel,* 6 F.C.C. 178 (1938). After an extended period during which the licensee was obliged not only

to cover and to cover fairly the views of others, but also to refrain from expressing his own personal views, *Mayflower Broadcasting Corp.,* 8 F.C.C. 333 (1940), the latter limitation on the licensee was abandoned and the doctrine developed into its present form.

There is a twofold duty laid down by the FCC's decisions and described by the 1949 Report on Editorializing by Broadcast Licensees, 13 F.C.C. 1246 (1949). The broadcaster must give adequate coverage to public issues, *United Broadcasting Co.,* 10 F.C.C. 515 (1945), and coverage must be fair in that it accurately reflects the opposing views. *New Broadcasting Co.,* 6 P & F Radio Reg. 258 (1950). This must be done at the broadcaster's own expense if sponsorship is unavailable. *Cullman Broadcasting Co.,* 25 P & F Radio Reg. 895 (1963). Moreover, the duty must be met by programming obtained at the licensee's own initiative if available from no other source. *John J. Dempsey,* 6 P & F Radio Reg. 615 (1950); see *Metropolitan Broadcasting Corp.,* 19 P & F Radio Reg. 602 (1960); *The Evening News Assn.,* 6 P & F Radio Reg. 283 (1950). The Federal Radio Commission had imposed these two basic duties on broadcasters since the outset, *Great Lakes Broadcasting Co.,* 3 F.R.C. Ann. Rep. 32 (1929), rev'd on other grounds, 59 App. D.C. 197, 37 F. 2d 993, cert. dismissed, 281 U.S. 706 (1930); *Chicago Federation of Labor v. FRC,* 3 F.R.C. Ann. Rep. 36 (1929), aff'd, 59 App. D.C. 333, 41 F. 2d 422 (1930); *KFKB Broadcasting Assn. v. FRC,* 60 App. D.C. 79, 47 F. 2d 670 (1931), and in particular respects the personal attack rules and regulations at issue here have spelled them out in greater detail.

When a personal attack has been made on a figure involved in a public issue, both the doctrine of cases such as *Red Lion* and *Times-Mirror Broadcasting Co.,* 24 P & F Radio Reg. 404 (1962), and also the 1967 regulations at issue in *RTNDA* require that the individual attacked himself be offered an opportunity to respond. Likewise, where one candidate is endorsed in a political editorial, the other candidates must themselves be offered reply time to use personally or through a spokesman. These obligations differ from the general fairness requirement that issues be presented, and presented with coverage of competing views, in that the broadcaster does not have the option of presenting the attacked party's side himself or choosing a third party to represent that side. But insofar as there is an obligation of the broadcaster to see that both sides are presented, and insofar as that is an affirmative obligation, the personal attack doctrine and regulations do not differ from the preceding fairness doctrine. The simple fact that the attacked men or unendorsed candidates may respond themselves or through agents is not a critical distinction, and indeed, it is not unreasonable for the FCC to conclude that the objective of adequate presentation of all sides may best be served by allowing those most closely affected to make the response, rather than leaving the response in the hands of the station which has attacked their candidacies, endorsed their opponents, or carried a personal attack upon them.

B

The statutory authority of the FCC to promulgate these regulations derives from the mandate to the "Commission from time to time, as public convenience, interest, or necessity requires" to promulgate "such rules and regulations and prescribe such restrictions and conditions... as may be necessary to carry out the provisions of this chapter...." 47 U.S.C. § 303 and § 303(r). The Commission is specifically directed to consider the demands of the public interest in the course of granting licenses, 47 U.S.C. §§ 307(a), 309(a); renewing them, 47 U.S.C. § 307; and modifying them. *Ibid.* Moreover, the FCC has included among the conditions of the Red Lion license itself the requirement that operation of the station be carried out in the public interest, 47 U.S.C. § 309(h). This mandate to the FCC to assure that broadcasters operate in the public interest is a broad one, a power "not niggardly but expansive," *National Broadcasting Co. v. United States,* 319 U.S. 190, 219 (1943), whose validity we have long upheld. *FCC v. Pottsville Broadcasting Co.,* 309 U.S. 134, 138 (1940); *FCC v. RCA Communications, Inc.,* 346 U.S. 86, 90 (1953); *FRC v. Nelson Bros. Bond & Mortgage Co.,* 289 U.S. 266, 285 (1933). It is broad enough to encompass these regulations.

The fairness doctrine finds specific recognition in statutory form, is in part modeled on explicit statutory provisions relating to political candidates, and is approvingly reflected in legislative history.

In 1959 the Congress amended the statutory requirement of § 315 that equal time be accorded each political candidate to except certain appearances on news programs, but added that this constituted no exception "*from the obligation imposed upon them under this Act to operate in the public interest and to afford reasonable opportunity for the discussion of conflicting views on issues of public importance.*" Act of September 14, 1959, § 1, 73 Stat. 557, amending 47 U.S.C. § 315(a) (emphasis added). This language makes it very plain that Congress, in 1959, announced that the phrase "public interest," which had been in the Act since 1927, imposed a duty on broadcasters to discuss both sides of controversial public issues. In other words, the amendment vindicated the FCC's general view that the fairness doctrine inhered in the public interest standard. Subsequent legislation declaring the intent of an earlier statute is entitled to great weight in statutory construction. And here this principle is given special force by the equally venerable principle that the construction of a statute by those charged with its execution should be followed unless there are compelling indications that it is wrong, especially when Congress has refused to alter the administrative construction. Here, the Congress has not just kept its silence by refusing to overturn the administrative construction, but has ratified it with positive legislation. Thirty years of consistent administrative construction left undisturbed by Congress until 1959, when that construction was expressly accepted, reinforce the natural conclusion that the public interest language of the Act authorized the Commission to require licensees to use their stations for discussion of public issues, and that the FCC is free to implement this requirement by reasonable rules and regulations which fall short of abridgment of the freedom of speech and press, and of the censorship proscribed by § 326 of the Act.

The objectives of § 315 themselves could readily be circumvented but for the complementary fairness doctrine ratified by § 315. The section applies only to campaign appearances by candidates, and not by family, friends, campaign managers, or other supporters. Without the fairness doctrine, then, a licensee could ban all campaign appearances by candidates themselves from the air and proceed to deliver over his station entirely to the supporters of one slate of candidates, to the exclusion of all others. In this way the broadcaster could have a far greater impact on the favored candidacy than he could by simply allowing a spot appearance by the candidate himself. It is the fairness doctrine as an aspect of the obligation to operate in the public interest, rather than § 315, which prohibits the broadcaster from taking such a step.

The legislative history reinforces this view of the effect of the 1959 amendment. Even before the language relevant here was added, the Senate report on amending § 315 noted that "broadcast frequencies are limited and, therefore, they have been necessarily considered a public trust. Every licensee who is fortunate in obtaining a license is mandated to operate in the public interest and has assumed the obligation of presenting important public questions fairly and without bias." S. Rep. No. 562, 86th Cong., 1st Sess., 8–9 (1959). See also, specifically adverting to Federal Communications Commission doctrine, *id.,* at 13.

Rather than leave this approval solely in the legislative history, Senator Proxmire suggested an amendment to make it part of the Act. 105 Cong. Rec. 14457. This amendment, which Senator Pastore, a manager of the bill and a ranking member of the Senate Committee, considered "rather surplusage," 105 Cong. Rec. 14462, constituted a positive statement of doctrine[a] and was altered to the present merely approving language in the conference committee. In explaining the language to the Senate after the committee changes, Senator Pastore said: "We insisted that that provision remain in the bill, to be a continuing reminder and admonition to the Federal Communications Commission and to the broad-

casters alike, that we were not abandoning the philosophy that gave birth to section 315, in giving the people the right to have a full and complete disclosure of conflicting views on news of interest to the people of the country." 105 Cong. Rec. 17830. Senator Scott, another Senate manager, added that: "It is intended to encompass all legitimate areas of public importance which are controversial," not just politics. 105 Cong. Rec. 17831....

In light of the fact that the "public interest" in broadcasting clearly encompasses the presentation of vigorous debate of controversial issues of importance and concern to the public; the fact that the FCC has rested upon that language from its very inception a doctrine that these issues must be discussed, and fairly; and the fact that Congress has acknowledged that the analogous provisions of § 315 are not preclusive in this area, and knowingly preserved the FCC's complementary efforts, we think the fairness doctrine and its component personal attack and political editorializing regulations are a legitimate exercise of congressionally delegated authority. The Communications Act is not notable for the precision of its substantive standards and in this respect the explicit provisions of § 315, and the doctrine and rules at issue here which are closely modeled upon that section, are far more explicit than the generalized "public interest" standard in which the Commission ordinarily finds its sole guidance, and which we have held a broad but adequate standard before. *FCC v. RCA Communications, Inc.,* 346 U.S. 86, 90 (1953); *National Broadcasting Co. v. United States,* 319 U.S. 190, 216–217 (1943); *FCC v. Pottsville Broadcasting Co.,* 309 U.S. 134, 138 (1940); *FRC v. Nelson Bros. Bond & Mortgage Co.,* 289 U.S. 266, 285 (1933). We cannot say that the FCC's declaratory ruling in *Red Lion,* or the regulations at issue in *RTNDA,* are beyond the scope of the congressionally conferred power to assure that stations are operated by those whose possession of a license serves "the public interest."

III

The broadcasters challenge the fairness doctrine and its specific manifestations in the personal attack and political editorial rules on conventional First Amendment grounds, alleging

---

a. The Proxmire amendment read: "[B]ut nothing in this sentence shall be construed as changing the basic intent of Congress with respect to the provisions of this act, which recognizes that television and radio frequencies are in the public domain, that the license to operate in such frequencies requires operation in the public interest, and that in newscasts, news interviews, news documentaries, on-the-spot coverage of news events, and panel discussions, all sides of public controversies shall be given as equal an opportunity to be heard as is practically possible." 105 Cong. Rec. 14457.

that the rules abridge their freedom of speech and press. Their contention is that the First Amendment protects their desire to use their allotted frequencies continuously to broadcast whatever they choose, and to exclude whomever they choose from ever using that frequency. No man may be prevented from saying or publishing what he thinks, or from refusing in his speech or other utterances to give equal weight to the views of his opponents. This right, they say, applies equally to broadcasters.

A

Although broadcasting is clearly a medium affected by a First Amendment interest, *United States v. Paramount Pictures, Inc.*, 334 U.S. 131, 166 (1948), differences in the characteristics of new media justify differences in the First Amendment standards applied to them. *Joseph Burstyn, Inc. v. Wilson*, 343 U.S. 495, 503 (1952). For example, the ability of new technology to produce sounds more raucous than those of the human voice justifies restrictions on the sound level, and on the hours and places of use, of sound trucks so long as the restrictions are reasonable and applied without discrimination. *Kovacs v. Cooper*, 336 U.S. 77 (1949).

Just as the Government may limit the use of sound-amplifying equipment potentially so noisy that it drowns out civilized private speech, so may the Government limit the use of broadcast equipment. The right of free speech of a broadcaster, the user of a sound truck, or any other individual does not embrace a right to snuff out the free speech of others. *Associated Press v. United States*, 326 U.S. 1, 20 (1945).

When two people converse face to face, both should not speak at once if either is to be clearly understood. But the range of the human voice is so limited that there could be meaningful communications if half the people in the United States were talking and the other half listening. Just as clearly, half the people might publish and the other half read. But the reach of radio signals is incomparably greater than the range of the human voice and the problem of interference is a massive reality. The lack of know-how and equipment may keep many from the air, but only a tiny fraction of those with resources and intel-

ligence can hope to communicate by radio at the same time if intelligible communication is to be had, even if the entire radio spectrum is utilized in the present state of commercially acceptable technology.

It was this fact, and the chaos which ensued from permitting anyone to use any frequency at whatever power level he wished, which made necessary the enactment of the Radio Act of 1927 and the Communications Act of 1934, as the Court has noted at length before. *National Broadcasting Co. v. United States*, 319 U.S. 190, 210–214 (1943). It was this reality which at the very least necessitated first the division of the radio spectrum into portions reserved respectively for public broadcasting and for other important radio uses such as amateur operation, aircraft, police, defense, and navigation; and then the subdivision of each portion, and assignment of specific frequencies to individual users or groups of users. Beyond this, however, because the frequencies reserved for public broadcasting were limited in number, it was essential for the Government to tell some applicants that they could not broadcast at all because there was room for only a few.

Where there are substantially more individuals who want to broadcast than there are frequencies to allocate, it is idle to posit an unabridgeable First Amendment right to broadcast comparable to the right of every individual to speak, write, or publish. If 100 persons want broadcast licenses but there are only 10 frequencies to allocate, all of them may have the same "right" to a license; but if there is to be any effective communication by radio, only a few can be licensed and the rest must be barred from the airwaves. It would be strange if the First Amendment, aimed at protecting and furthering communications, prevented the Government from making radio communication possible by requiring licenses to broadcast and by limiting the number of licenses so as not to overcrowd the spectrum.

This has been the consistent view of the Court. Congress unquestionably has the power to grant and deny licenses and to eliminate existing stations. *FRC v. Nelson Bros. Bond & Mortgage Co.*, 289 U.S. 266 (1933). No one has a First Amendment right to a license or to monopolize a radio frequency; to deny a station license because "the public interest" requires it "is not a denial of free speech." *National Broadcasting Co. v. United States,* 319 U.S. 190, 227 (1943).

By the same token, as far as the First Amendment is concerned those who are licensed stand no better than those to whom licenses are refused. A license permits broadcasting, but the licensee has no constitutional right to be the one who holds the license or to monopolize a radio frequency to the exclusion of his fellow citizens. There is nothing in the First Amendment which prevents the Government from requiring a licensee to share his frequency with others and to conduct himself as a proxy or fiduciary with obligations to present those views and voices which are representative of his community and which would otherwise, by necessity, be barred from the airwaves.

This is not to say that the First Amendment is irrelevant to public broadcasting. On the contrary, it has a major role to play as the Congress itself recognized in § 326, which forbids FCC interference with "the right of free speech by means of radio communication." Because of the scarcity of radio frequencies, the Government is permitted to put restraints on licensees in favor of others whose views should be expressed on this unique medium. But the people as a whole retain their interest in free speech by radio and their collective right to have the medium function consistently with the ends and purposes of the First Amendment. It is the right of the viewers and listeners, not the right of the broadcasters, which is paramount. See *FCC v. Sanders Bros. Radio Station,* 309 U.S. 470, 475 (1940); *FCC v. Allentown Broadcasting Corp.,* 349 U.S. 358, 361–362 (1955); 2 Z. Chafee, Government and Mass Communications 546 (1947). It is the purpose of the First Amendment to preserve an uninhibited marketplace of ideas in which truth will ultimately prevail, rather than to countenance monopolization of that market, whether it be by the Government itself or a private licensee. *Associated Press v. United States,* 326 U.S. 1, 20 (1945); *New York Times Co. v. Sullivan,* 376 U.S. 254, 270 (1964); *Abrams v. United States,* 250 U.S. 616, 630 (1919) (Holmes, J., dissenting). "[S]peech concerning public affairs is more than self-expression; it is the essence of self-government." *Garrison v. Louisiana,* 379 U.S. 64, 74–75 (1964). See Brennan, The Supreme Court and the Meiklejohn Interpretation

of the First Amendment, 79 Harv. L. Rev. 1 (1965). It is the right of the public to receive suitable access to social, political, esthetic, moral, and other ideas and experiences which is crucial here. That right may not constitutionally be abridged either by Congress or by the FCC.

B

Rather than confer frequency monopolies on a relatively small number of licensees, in a Nation of 200,000,000, the Government could surely have decreed that each frequency should be shared among all or some of those who wish to use it, each being assigned a portion of the broadcast day or the broadcast week. The ruling and regulations at issue here do not go quite so far. They assert that under specified circumstances, a licensee must offer to make available a reasonable amount of broadcast time to those who have a view different from that which has already been expressed on his station. The expression of a political endorsement, or of a personal attack while dealing with a controversial public issue, simply triggers this time sharing. As we have said, the First Amendment confers no right on licensees to prevent others from broadcasting on "their" frequencies and no right to an unconditional monopoly of a scarce resource which the Government has denied others the right to use.

In terms of constitutional principle, and as enforced sharing of a scarce resource, the personal attack and political editorial rules are indistinguishable from the equal-time provision of § 315, a specific enactment of Congress requiring stations to set aside reply time under specified circumstances and to which the fairness doctrine and these constituent regulations are important complements. That provision, which has been part of the law since 1927, Radio Act of 1927, § 18, 44 Stat. 1170, has been held valid by this Court as an obligation of the licensee relieving him of any power in any way to prevent or censor the broadcast, and thus insulating him from liability for defamation. The constitutionality of the statute under the First Amendment was unquestioned. *Farmers Educ. & Coop. Union v. WDAY,* 360 U.S. 525 (1959).

Nor can we say that it is inconsistent with the First Amendment goal of producing an informed public capable of conducting its own affairs to require a broadcaster to permit answers to personal attacks occurring in the course of discussing controversial issues, or to require that the political opponents of those endorsed by the station be given a chance to communicate with the public. Otherwise, station owners and a few networks would have unfettered power to make time available only to the highest bidders, to communicate only their own views on public issues, people and candidates, and to permit on the air only those with whom they agreed. There is no sanctuary in the First Amendment for unlimited private censorship operating in a medium not open to all. "Freedom of the press from governmental interference under the First Amendment does not sanction repression of that freedom by private interests," *Associated Press v. United States,* 326 U.S. 1, 20 (1945).

C

It is strenuously argued, however, that if political editorials or personal attacks will trigger an obligation in broadcasters to afford the opportunity for expression to speakers who need not pay for time and whose views are unpalatable to the licensees, then broadcasters will be irresistibly forced to self-censorship and their coverage of controversial public issues will be eliminated or at least rendered wholly ineffective. Such a result would indeed be a serious matter, for should licensees actually eliminate their coverage of controversial issues, the purposes of the doctrine would be stifled.

At this point, however, as the Federal Communications Commission has indicated, that possibility is at best speculative. The communications industry, and in particular the networks, have taken pains to present controversial issues in the past, and even now they do not assert that they intend to abandon their efforts in this regard. It would be better if the FCC's encouragement were never necessary to induce the broadcasters to meet their responsibility. And if experience with the administration of these doctrines indicates that they have the net effect of reducing rather than enhancing the volume and quality of coverage, there will be time enough to reconsider

the constitutional implications. The fairness doctrine in the past has had no such overall effect.

That this will occur now seems unlikely, however, since if present licensees should suddenly prove timorous, the Commission is not powerless to insist that they give adequate and fair attention to public issues. It does not violate the First Amendment to treat licensees given the privilege of using scarce radio frequencies as proxies for the entire community, obligated to give suitable time and attention to matters of great public concern. To condition the granting or renewal of licenses on a willingness to present representative community views on controversial issues is consistent with the ends and purposes of those constitutional provisions forbidding the abridgment of freedom of speech and freedom of the press. Congress need not stand idly by and permit those with licenses to ignore the problems which beset the people or to exclude from the airways anything but their own views of fundamental questions. The statute, long administrative practice, and cases are to this effect.

Licenses to broadcast do not confer ownership of designated frequencies, but only the temporary privilege of using them. 47 U.S.C. § 301. Unless renewed, they expire within three years. 47 U.S.C. § 307(d). The statute mandates the issuance of licenses if the "public convenience, interest, or necessity will be served thereby." 47 U.S.C. § 307(a). In applying this standard the Commission for 40 years has been choosing licensees based in part on their program proposals.... The Court upheld the regulations, unequivocally recognizing that the Commission was more than a traffic policeman concerned with the technical aspects of broadcasting and that it neither exceeded its powers under the statute nor transgressed the First Amendment in interesting itself in general program format and the kinds of programs broadcast by licensees. *National Broadcasting Co. v. United States,* 319 U.S. 190 (1943).

D

The litigants embellish their First Amendment arguments with the contention that the regulations are so vague that their duties are impossible to discern. Of this point it is enough to say that, judging the validity of the regulations on their face as they are presented here, we cannot conclude that the FCC has been left a free hand to vindicate its own idiosyncratic conception of the public interest or of the requirements of free speech....

It is argued that even if at one time the lack of available frequencies for all who wished to use them justified the Government's choice of those who would best serve the public interest by acting as proxy for those who would present differing views, or by giving the latter access directly to broadcast facilities, this condition no longer prevails so that continuing control is not justified. To this there are several answers.

Scarcity is not entirely a thing of the past. Advances in technology, such as microwave transmission, have led to more efficient utilization of the frequency spectrum, but uses for that spectrum have also grown apace. Portions of the spectrum must be reserved for vital uses unconnected with human communication, such as radio-navigational aids used by aircraft and vessels. Conflicts have even emerged between such vital functions as defense preparedness and experimentation in methods of averting midair collisions through radio warning devices. "Land mobile services" such as police, ambulance, fire department, public utility, and other communications systems have been occupying an increasingly crowded portion of the frequency spectrum and there are, apart from licensed amateur radio operators' equipment, 5,000,000 transmitters operated on the "citizens' band" which is also increasingly congested. Among the various uses for radio frequency space, including marine, aviation, amateur, military, and common carrier users, there are easily enough claimants to permit use of the whole with an even smaller allocation to broadcast radio and television uses than now exists.

Comparative hearings between competing applicants for broadcast spectrum space are by no means a thing of the past. The radio spectrum has become so congested that at times it has been necessary to suspend new applications. The very high frequency television spectrum is, in the country's major markets, almost entirely occupied, although space reserved for ultra high frequency television transmission, which is a relatively recent development as a commercially viable alternative, has not yet been completely filled.

The rapidity with which technological advances succeed one another to create more efficient use of spectrum space on the one hand, and to create new uses for that space by ever growing numbers of people on the other, makes it unwise to speculate on the future allocation of that space. It is enough to say that the resource is one of considerable and growing importance whose scarcity impelled its regulation by an agency authorized by Congress. Nothing in this record, or in our own researches, convinces us that the resource is no longer one for which there are more immediate and potential uses than can be accommodated, and for which wise planning is essential. This does not mean, of course, that every possible wavelength must be occupied at every hour by some vital use in order to sustain the congressional judgment. The substantial capital investment required for many uses, in addition to the potentiality for confusion and interference inherent in any scheme for continuous kaleidoscopic reallocation of all available space may make this unfeasible. The allocation need not be made at such a breakneck pace that the objectives of the allocation are themselves imperiled.

Even where there are gaps in spectrum utilization, the fact remains that existing broadcasters have often attained their present position because of their initial government selection in competition with others before new technological advances opened new opportunities for further uses. Long experience in broadcasting, confirmed habits of listeners and viewers, network affiliation, and other advantages in program procurement give existing broadcasters a substantial advantage over new entrants, even where new entry is technologically possible. These advantages are the fruit of a preferred position conferred by the Government. Some present possibility for new entry by competing stations is not enough, in itself, to render unconstitutional the Government's effort to assure that a broadcaster's programming ranges widely enough to serve the public interest.

In view of the scarcity of broadcast frequencies, the Government's role in allocating those frequencies, and the legitimate claims of those unable without governmental assistance to gain access to those frequencies for expression of their views, we hold the regulations and ruling at issue here are both authorized by statute and constitutional. The judgment of the Court of Appeals in *Red Lion* is affirmed and that in *RTNDA* reversed and the causes remanded for proceedings consistent with this opinion.

The fairness doctrine in the years since *Red Lion* has been a prominent subject of controversy and criticism.[40] Despite the FCC's eventual abandonment of it in 1987,[41] congressional pressure exists to reinstitute it.[42] Especially since the future of fairness regulation remains uncertain, an accounting of its practical nature and problems and attendant constitutional issues remains pertinent.

The FCC in 1974 issued a report that detailed extensively the reasons for and obligations of licensees bound by the fairness doctrine. It essentially reaffirmed the dual responsibilities consisting of (1) an affirmative obligation to provide reasonable amounts of time for coverage of public issues and (2) a companion duty to ensure opportunities for contrasting views.[43] The report, in terms largely redundant with the *Red Lion* decision, also recited the fairness doctrine's compatibility with First Amendment interests and values.[44] More important, it defined what constituted a controversial issue of public importance and a reasonable opportunity for opposing viewpoints, and it discussed the fairness doctrine's operation in a variety of programming contexts.

The Handling of Public Issues under the Fairness Doctrine and the Public Interest Standards of the Communications Act, 48 F.C.C.2d (1974)

FAIRNESS REPORT

. . .

II. THE FAIRNESS DOCTRINE GENERALLY

C. The Specifics of the Fairness Doctrine

21. In developing and implementing the fairness doctrine it has never been our intention to force licenses to conform to any single, preconceived notion of what constitutes the "ideal" in broadcast journalism. Our purpose has merely been to establish general guidelines concerning *minimal* standards of fairness. We firmly believe that the public's need to be informed can best be served through a system in which the individual broadcasters exercise wide journalistic discretion, and in which government's role is limited to a determination of whether the licensee has acted reasonably and in good faith. *Fairness Doctrine Primer*, 40 FCC 598, 599 (1964). In this regard, we are still convinced that "there can be no one all embracing formula which licensees can hope to apply to insure the fair and balanced presentation of all public issues. Different issues will inevitably require different techniques of presentation and production. The licensee will in each instance be called upon to exercise his best judgment and good sense in determining what subjects should be considered, the particular format of the programs to be devoted to each subject, the different shades of opinion to be presented, and the spokesmen for each point of view." *Report on Editorializing*, 13 FCC 1246, 1251 (1949).

22. It is obvious that under this method of handling fairness, many questionable decisions by broadcast editors may go uncorrected. But, in our judgment, this approach represents the most appropriate way to achieve "robust, wide open debate" on the one hand, while avoiding "the dangers of censorship and pervasive supervision" by the government on the other. *Banzhaf v. FCC*, 405 F.2d 1082, 1095 (D.C. Cir. 1968), *cert. denied sub nom. Tobacco Institute v. FCC*, 396 U.S. 842 (1969). In this respect, we are not unmindful of the dangers alluded to by the Court in *BEM:*

> Congress appears to have concluded...that of these two choices—private or official censorship—Government censorship would be the most pervasive, the most self-serving, the most difficult to restrain and hence the one most to be avoided. 412 U.S. 94 at 105.

We therefore recognize that reaching a determination as to what particular policies will best serve the public's right to be informed is a task of "great delicacy and difficulty," and that the Commission must continually walk a "tightrope" between saying too much and saying too little. *Id.* at 102, 117. However, we also believe that this

Commission has a clear responsibility and obligation to assume this task.

1. Adequate Time for the Discussion of Public Issues

23. The first, and most basic, requirement of the fairness doctrine is that it establishes an "affirmative responsibility on the part of broadcast licensees to provide a reasonable amount of time for the presentation over their facilities of programs devoted to the discussion and consideration of public issues.... " *Report on Editorializing,* 13 FCC at 1249. Determining what constitutes a "reasonable amount of time" is—like so many other programming questions—a responsibility of the individual broadcast licensee. It is the individual broadcaster who, after evaluating the needs of his particular community, "must determine what percentage of the limited broadcast day should appropriately be devoted to news and discussion or consideration of public issues, rather than to other legitimate services of radio broadcasting.... " *Id.* at 1247.

24. In reviewing the adequacy of the amount of a licensee's public issue programming, we will, of course, limit our inquiry to a determination of its reasonableness. We wish to make it plain, however, that we have allocated a very large share of the electromagnetic spectrum to broadcasting chiefly because of our belief that this medium can make a great contribution to an informed public opinion. See *Democratic National Committee,* 25 FCC 2d 216, 222 (1970). We are not prepared to allow this purpose to be frustrated by broadcasters who consistently ignore their public interest responsibilities. Indeed, "we regard strict adherence to the fairness doctrine"—including the affirmative obligation to provide coverage of issues of public importance—"as the single most important requirement of operation in the public interest—the '*sine qua non*' for grant of a renewal of license." *Committee for the Fair Broadcasting of Controversial Issues,* 25 FCC 2d 283, 292 (1970).

25. The individual broadcaster is also the person "who must select or be responsible for the selection of the particular news items to be reported or the particular local, state, national or international issues or questions of public interest to be considered.... " *Report on Editorializing,* 13 FCC at 1247. We have, in the past, indicated that some issues are so critical or of such great public importance that it would be unreasonable for a licensee to ignore them completely. See *Gary Soucie* (Friends of the Earth), 24 FCC 2d 743, 750–51 (1970). But such statements on our part are the rare exception, not the rule, and we have no intention of becoming involved in the selection of issues to be discussed, nor do we expect a broadcaster to cover each and every important issue which may arise in his community.

26. We wish to emphasize that the responsibility for the selection of program material is that of the individual licensee. That responsibility "can neither be delegated by the licensee to any network or other person or group, or be unduly fettered by contractual arrangements restricting the licensee in his free exercise of his independent judgments." *Report on Editorializing,* 13 FCC at 1248. We believe that stations, in carrying out this responsibility, should be alert to the opportunity to complement network offerings with local programming on these issues, or with syndicated programming.

2. A Reasonable Opportunity for Opposing Viewpoints

27. The usual fairness complaint does not involve an allegation that the licensee has not devoted sufficient time to the discussion of public issues. Rather, it concerns a claim that the licensee has presented one viewpoint on a "controversial issue of public importance" and has failed to afford a "reasonable opportunity for the presentation of contrasting viewpoints."

28. It has frequently been suggested that individual stations should not be expected to present opposing points of view and that it should be sufficient for the licensee to demonstrate that the opposing viewpoint has been adequately presented on another station in the market or in the print media. See *WSOC Broadcasting Co.,* 17 P & F Radio Reg. 548, 550 (1958). While we recognize that citizens receive information on public issues from a variety of sources, other considerations require the rejection of this suggestion. First, in amending section 315(a) of the Communications Act in 1959, Congress gave statutory approval to the fairness doctrine, including the requirement that broadcasters themselves provide an opportunity for opposing viewpoints. See *BEM,* 412 U.S. at 110, note 8. Second, it would be an ad-

ministrative nightmare for this Commission to attempt to review the overall coverage of an issue in all of the broadcast stations and publications in a given market. Third, and perhaps most importantly, we believe that the requirement that *each* station provide for contrasting views greatly increases the likelihood that individual members of the public will be exposed to varying points of view. The fairness doctrine will not insure perfect balance in debate and each station is not required to provide an "equal" opportunity for opposing views. Furthermore, since the fairness doctrine does not require balance in individual programs or series of programs, but only in a station's overall programming, there is no assurance that a listener who hears an initial presentation will also hear a rebuttal. Compare 47 U.S.C. 396(g) (1) (A). However, if all stations presenting programming relating to a controversial issue of public importance make an effort to round out their coverage with contrasting viewpoints, these various points of view will receive a much wider public dissemination. This requirement, of course, in no way prevents a station from presenting its own opinions in the strongest terms possible.

a. What is a *"controversial issue of public importance"*?

29. It has frequently been suggested that the Commission set forth comprehensive guidelines to aid interested parties in recognizing whether an issue is "controversial" and of "public importance." However, given the limitless number of potential controversial issues and the varying circumstances in which they might arise, we have not been able to develop detailed criteria which would be appropriate in all cases. For this very practical reason, and for the reason that our role must and should be limited to one of review, we will continue to rely heavily on the reasonable, good faith judgments of our licensees in this area.

30. Some general observations, however, are in order. First of all, it is obvious that an issue is not necessarily a matter of significant "public importance" merely because it has received broadcast or newspaper coverage. "Our daily papers and television broadcasts alike are filled with news items which good journalistic judgment would classify as newsworthy, but which the same editors would not characterize as containing impor-

tant controversial public issues." *Healey v. FCC*, 460 F.2d 917, 922 (D.C. Cir. 1972). Nevertheless, the degree of media coverage is one factor which clearly should be taken into account in determining an issue's importance. It is also appropriate to consider the degree of attention the issue has received from government officials and other community leaders. The principal test of public importance, however, is not the extent of media or governmental attention, but rather a subjective evaluation of the impact that the issue is likely to have on the community at large. If the issue involves a social or political choice, the licensee might well ask himself whether the outcome of that choice will have a significant impact on society or its institutions. It appears to us that these judgments can be made only on a case-by-case basis.

31. The question of whether an issue is "controversial" may be determined in a somewhat more objective manner. Here, it is highly relevant to measure the degree of attention paid to an issue by government officials, community leaders, and the media. The licensee should be able to tell, with a reasonable degree of objectivity, whether an issue is the subject of vigorous debate with substantial elements of the community in opposition to one another. It is possible, of course, that "programs initiated with no thought on the part of the licensee of their possible controversial nature will subsequently arouse controversy and opposition of a substantial nature which will merit presentation of opposing views." *Report on Editorializing*, 13 FCC at 1251. In such circumstances, it would be appropriate to make provision for opposing views when the opposition becomes manifest.

b. What specific issue has been raised?

32. One of the most difficult problems involved in the administration of the fairness doctrine is the determination of the *specific* issue or issues raised by a particular program. This would seem to be a simple task, but in many cases it is not. Frequently, resolution of this problem can be of decisional importance. See, e.g., *David C. Green*, 24 FCC 2d 171 (1970); *WCBS-TV*, 9 FCC 2d 921, 938 (1967).

33. This determination is complicated by the fact that it is frequently made without the benefit

of a transcript or tape of the program giving rise to the complaint. Hence, it is necessary in such cases to rely on the recollections of station employees and listeners. While the availability of an accurate transcript would facilitate the determination of the issue or issues raised, it would not in many cases clearly point up those issues. This is true because a broadcast may avoid explicit mention of the ultimate matter in controversy and focus instead on assertions or arguments which support one side or the other on that ultimate issue. This problem may be illustrated by reference to a hypothetical broadcast which takes place during the course of a heated community debate over a school bond issue. The broadcast presents a spokesman who forcefully asserts that new school construction is urgently needed and that there is also a need for substantial increases in teachers' salaries, both principal arguments advanced by proponents of the bond issue. The spokesman, however, does not explicitly mention or advocate passage of the bond issue. In this case, the licensee would be faced with a need to determine whether the spokesman had raised the issue of whether the school bonds should be authorized (which is controversial), or whether he had merely raised the question of whether present school facilities and teacher salaries are adequate (which might not be at all controversial).

34. In answering this question, we would expect a licensee to exercise his good faith judgment as to whether the spokesman had in an obvious and meaningful fashion presented a position on the ultimate controversial issue of whether the school bond issue should be approved. The licensee's inquiry should focus not on whether the statement bears some tangential relevance to the school bond question, but rather on whether that statement, in the context of the ongoing community debate, is so obviously and substantially related to the school bond issue as to amount to advocacy of a position on that question. If, for example, the arguments and views expressed over the air closely parallel the major arguments advanced by partisans on one side or the other of the public debate it might be reasonable to conclude that there had been a presentation on one side of the ultimate issue, i.e., authorization of the school bonds. Obviously, licensees in specific cases may differ in their answers to this inquiry. If a licensee's determination is *reasonable* and arrived at in good faith, however, we will not disturb it. *Cf., Media Access Project* (Georgia Power), 44 FCC 2d 755 (1973).

35. Before leaving this subject, we wish to make it clear that a fairness response is not required as a result of offhand or insubstantial statements. As we have stated in the past, "[a] policy of requiring fairness, statement by statement or inference by inference, with constant Governmental intervention to try to implement the policy, would simply be inconsistent with the profound national commitment to the principle that debate on public issues should be 'uninhibited, robust, wide-open' (*New York Times Co. v. Sullivan*, 376 U.S. 254, 270)." *National Broadcasting Co.* (AOPA complaint), 25 FCC 2d 735, 736–37 (1970).

c. What is a "reasonable opportunity" for contrasting viewpoints?

36. As noted above, the Commission's first task in handling a typical fairness complaint is to review the licensee's determination as to whether the issue specified in the complaint or the Commission's inquiry has actually been raised in the licensee's programming. Secondly, we must review the licensee's determination of whether that issue is "controversial" and of "public importance." If these questions are answered in the affirmative, either by admission of the licensee or by our determination upon review, we must then determine whether the licensee has afforded a "reasonable opportunity" in his overall programming for the presentation of contrasting points of view.

37. The first point to be made with regard to the obligation to present contrasting views is that it cannot be met "merely through the adoption of a general policy of not refusing to broadcast opposing views where a demand is made of the station for broadcast time." *Report on Editorializing*, 13 FCC at 1251. The licensee has a duty to play a conscious and positive role in encouraging the presentation of opposing viewpoints.[a] We do

---

a. This duty includes the obligation defined in *Cullman Broadcasting Co.*, 40 FCC 576, 577 (1963): "where the licensee has chosen to broadcast a sponsored program which for the first time presents one side of a controversial issue, has not presented (or does not plan

not believe, however, that it is necessary for the Commission to establish a formula for all broadcasters to follow in their efforts to find a spokesman for an opposing viewpoint. As we stated in *Mid-Florida Television Corp.*, 40 FCC 620 (1964):

> The mechanics of achieving fairness will necessarily vary with the circumstances, and it is within the discretion of each licensee, acting in good faith, to choose an appropriate method of implementing the policy to aid and encourage expression of contrasting viewpoints. Our experience indicates that licensees have chosen a variety of methods, and often combinations of various methods. Thus, some licensees, where they know or have reason to believe that a responsible individual or group within the community holds a contrasting viewpoint with respect to a controversial issue presented or to be presented, communicate to such an individual or group a specific offer of the use of their facilities for the expression of contrasting opinion, and send a copy or summary of material broadcast on the issue. Other licensees consult with community leaders as to who might be an appropriate individual or group for such a purpose. Still others announce at the beginning or ending (or both) of programs presenting opinions on controversial issues that opportunity will be made available for the expression of contrasting views upon request by responsible representatives of such views. *Id.* at 621.

If a licensee fails to present an opposing viewpoint on the ground that no appropriate spokesman is available, he should be prepared to demonstrate that he has made a diligent, good-faith effort to communicate to such potential spokesmen his willingness to present their views

___

to present) contrasting viewpoints in other programming, and has been unable to obtain paid sponsorship for the appropriate presentation of the opposing viewpoint or viewpoints, he cannot reject a presentation otherwise suitable to the licensee—and *thus leave the public uninformed*—on the ground that he cannot obtain paid sponsorship for that presentation." (emphasis in original).

We do not believe that the passage of time since *Cullman* was decided has in any way diminished the importance and necessity of this principle. If the public's right to be informed of the contrasting views on controversial issues is to be truly honored, broadcasters must provide the forum for the expression of those viewpoints at their own expense if paid sponsorship is unavailable.

on the issue or issues presented. *Columbia Broadcasting System Inc.*, 34 FCC 2d 773 (1972). There may well be occasions, particularly in cases involving major issues discussed in depth, where such a showing should include specific offers of response time to appropriate individuals in addition to general over-the-air announcements.

38. In making provision for the airing of contrasting viewpoints, the broadcasting should be alert to the possibility that a particular issue may involve more than two opposing viewpoints. Indeed, there may be several important viewpoints or shades of opinion which warrant broadcast coverage.

39. In deciding which viewpoints or shades of opinion are to be presented, licensees should employ a standard similar to that used to decide which political parties or candidates represent a viewpoint of sufficient importance to deserve coverage. As we stated in *Lawrence M. C. Smith*, 40 FCC 549 (1963), the broadcaster (in programs not covered by the "equal time" requirement of 47 U.S.C. Section 315) is not expected to present the views of all political parties no matter how small or insignificant, but rather:

> the licensee would be called upon to make a good faith judgment as to whether there can reasonably be said to be a need or interest in the community calling for some provision of announcement time to these other parties or candidates and, if so, to determine the extent of that interest or need and the appropriate way to meet it. 40 FCC at 550.

In evaluating a "spectrum" of contrasting viewpoints on an issue, the licensee should make a good faith effort to identify the *major* viewpoints and shades of opinion being debated in the community, and to make a provision for their presentation. In many, or perhaps most, cases it may be possible to find that only two viewpoints are significant enough to warrant broadcast coverage.[b] However, other issues may involve a range of markedly different and important policy alternatives. In such circumstances, the broadcaster must make a determination as to which shades of

___

b. This is not to say that a broadcaster is barred from presenting the views of small minorities, but only that the government will not *require* the coverage of every possible viewpoint or shade of opinion regardless of its significance.

opinion are of sufficient public importance to warrant coverage, and also the extent and nature of that coverage.

40. The question of the *reasonableness* of the opportunity for opposing viewpoints goes considerably deeper, however, than a mere finding that *some* provision has been made for the opposing viewpoints. Indeed, it has frequently been suggested that the wide discretion afforded the licensee in selecting a reply spokesman and format may undermine any possibility that treatment of the opposition view will be either reasonable or fair. Accordingly, it has been argued that the Commission should promulgate regulations establishing standards for the selection of an appropriate reply spokesman and format. We believe, however, that it should be adequate to remind licensees that they have a duty not " 'to stack the cards' by a deliberate selection of spokesmen for opposing points of view to favor one viewpoint at the expense of the other...." *Report on Editorializing*, 13 FCC at 1253. In the final analysis, fairness must be achieved, "not by the exclusion of particular views because of...the forcefulness with which the view is expressed, but by making the microphone available, for the presentation of contrary views *without deliberate restrictions designed to impede equally forceful presentation.*" *Id.* at 1253–54. (emphasis supplied); see also *Brandywine-Maine Line Radio, Inc.*, 24 FCC 2d 18, 23–24 (1970).

41. In providing for the coverage of opposing points of view, we believe that the licensee must make a reasonable allowance for presentations by genuine partisans who actually believe in what they are saying. The fairness doctrine does not permit the broadcaster "to preside over a 'paternalistic' regime," *BEM*, 412 U.S. at 130, and it would clearly not be acceptable for the licensee to adopt a "policy of excluding partisan voices and always itself presenting views in a bland, inoffensive manner...." *Democratic National Committee*, 25 FCC 2d 216, 222 (1970). Indeed, this point has received considerable emphasis from the Supreme Court:

> [N]or is it enough that he should hear the arguments of adversaries from his own teachers, presented as they state them, and accompanied by what they offer as refutations. That is not the way to do justice to the arguments, or bring them into real

contact with his own mind. He must be able to hear them from persons who actually believe them; who defend them in earnest, and do their very utmost for them. *Red Lion Broadcasting Co. v. FCC*, 395 U.S. at 392, n. 18, quoting J. S. Mill, *On Liberty* 32 (R. McCallum ed. 1947).

42. This does not mean, however, that the Commission intends to dictate the selection of a particular spokesman or a particular format, or indeed that partisan spokesmen must be presented in every instance. We do not believe that it is either appropriate or feasible for a governmental agency to make decisions as to what is desirable in each situation. In cases involving personal attacks and political campaigns, the natural opposing spokesmen are relatively easy to identify. This is not the case, however, with the majority of public controversies. Ordinarily, there are a variety of spokesman and formats which could reasonably be deemed to be appropriate. We believe that the public is best served by a system which allows individual broadcasters considerable discretion in selecting the manner of coverage, the appropriate spokesmen, and the techniques of production and presentation.

43. Frequently, the question of the reasonableness of the opportunity provided for contrasting viewpoints comes down to weighing the *time* allocated to each side. Aside from the field of political broadcasting, the licensee is not required to provide equal time for the various opposing points of view. Indeed, we have long felt that the basic goal of creating an informed citizenry would be frustrated if for every controversial item or presentation on a newscast or other broadcast the licensee had to offer equal time to the other side. Our reasons for granting the licensee broad discretion with respect to the amount or nature of time to be afforded can be summarized as follows:

> In our judgment, based on decades of experience in this field, this is the only sound way to proceed as a general policy. A contrary approach of equal opportunities, applying to controversial issues generally the specific equal opportunities requirements for political candidates would in practice not be workable. It would inhibit, rather than promote, the discussion and presentation of controversial issues in the various broadcast program formats (e.g., newscasts, interviews, documentaries). For it is just not practicable to require equality with respect to the large number of issues dealt with in a great variety

of programs on a daily and continuing basis. Further, it would involve this Commission much too deeply in broadcast journalism: we would indeed become virtually a part of the broadcasting "fourth estate" overseeing thousands of complaints that some issue had not been given "equal treatment". We do not believe that the profound national commitment to the principle that debate on public issue should be "uninhibited, robust, wide-open" (*New York Times v. Sullivan*, 376 U.S. 254, 270) would be promoted by a general policy of requiring equal treatment on all such issues, with governmental intervention to insure such mathematical equality. *Committee for the Fair Broadcasting of Controversial Issues*, 25 FCC 2d 283, 292 (1970).

Similarly, we do not believe that it would be appropriate for this Commission to establish any other mathematical ratio, such as 3 to 1 or 4 to 1, to be applied in all cases. We believe that such an approach is much too mechanical in nature and that in many cases our pre-conceived ratios would prove to be far from reasonable. In the case of a 10-second personal attack, for example, fairness may dictate that more time be afforded to answer the attack than was given the attack itself. Moreover, were we to adopt a ratio for fairness programming, the "floor" thereby established might well become the "ceiling" for the treatment of issues by many stations, and such a ratio might also lead to preoccupation with a mathematical formula to the detriment of the substance of the debate. It appears to us, therefore, that no precise mathematical formula would be appropriate for all cases, and the licensee must exercise good faith and reasonableness in considering the particular facts and circumstances of each case.

44. While the road to predicting Commission decisions in this area is not fully and completely marked, there are, nevertheless, a number of signposts which should be recognizable to all concerned parties. We have made it clear, for example, that "it is patently unreasonable for a licensee consistently to present one side in prime time and to relegate the contrasting viewpoint to periods outside prime time. Similarly, there can be an imbalance from the sheer weight on one side as against the other." *Committee for the Fair Broadcasting of Controversial Issues*, 25 FCC 2d at 293. This imbalance might be a reflection of the total *amount of time* afforded to each side, of the

frequency with which each side is presented, of the size of the listening *audience* during the various broadcasts, or of a combination of factors. It is incumbent upon a complainant to bring to the Commission's attention any specific factors which he believes point to a finding that fairness has not been achieved. From the standpoint of the licensee, however, the most important protection against arbitrary Commission rulings is the fact that we will not substitute our judgment for his. Our rulings are not based on a determination of whether we believe that the licensee has acted wisely or whether we would have proceeded as he did. Rather, we limit our inquiry to a determination of whether, in the light of all of the facts and circumstances presented, it is apparent that the licensee has acted in an arbitrary or unreasonable fashion.

45. The danger of an unwise Commission decision in this area is considerably reduced by the fact that no sanction is imposed on the broadcaster for isolated fairness violations during the course of the license term. The licensee is simply asked to make an additional provision for the opposing point of view, and this is certainly not too much to ask of a licensee who has been found to be negligent in meeting his fairness obligations. Indeed, it is to the benefit of both the licensee and his listening audience if broadcasters are informed of their fairness duties and given an opportunity to fulfill them on a timely basis.

D. The Complaint Procedure

46. It has sometimes been suggested that fairness complaints should not be considered at the time they are presented to the Commission, but with few exceptions should simply be placed in the station's license file to be reviewed in connection with its renewal application. This review would focus on the station's overall performance for the license period, and not on the specific facts of individual fairness violations. Some have argued that this approach would have two major advantages over present procedures. First, it might considerably reduce the Commission's administrative workload, since complaints would not be given any consideration unless there were a number of complaints against a single station which indicated a serious

pattern of violations. Secondly, it has been suggested that by avoiding a detailed review of individual complaints the Commission would be able to insure that it did not become too deeply involved in the day-to-day operations of broadcast journalism.

47. After giving careful consideration to this proposal, we believe that our present procedure of reviewing complaints on an ongoing basis is preferable. First, we do not believe it would be possible to make an "overall" assessment of license performance at renewal time without considering the specifics of individual complaints. It simply would not be possible to look at the bare complaints on file and make any knowledgable assessment of licensee performance. Secondly, we view consideration of fairness compliance only at renewal time as an inadequate safeguard of the public's paramount right to be informed and believe that we should continue our ongoing effort (through the complaint process) to advance the public's interests in receiving timely information on public issues. This, we believe, will provide an opportunity to remedy violations before a flagrant pattern of abuse develops. In addition to the benefits which flow to the listening public, this procedure aids the broadcaster by helping to head off practices which could (if left uncorrected) place his license in jeopardy. For this reason, we believe that most licensees welcome the opportunity to receive guidance on specific fairness matters on a timely basis.

48. Finally, a review only at renewal time would remove a major incentive for interested citizens to file fairness complaints—that is, the chance to have an opposing view aired over the station before the issue has become stale with the passage of time. At present, citizen complaints provide the principal means of insuring compliance with the fairness doctrine. If we were to remove the possibility that these complaints might result in broadcast time for a neglected point of view, we might well have to rely on government monitoring to carry out our investigative role. Such monitoring, of course, would represent an unfortunate step in the direction of deeper government involvement in the day-to-day operation of broadcast journalism. . . .

E. *Fairness and Accurate News Reporting*

58. In our 1949 *Report on Editorializing*, we alluded to a licensee's obligation to present the news in an accurate manner:

> It must be recognized, however, that the licensee's opportunity to express his own views . . . does not justify or empower any licensee to exercise his authority over the selection of program material to distort or suppress the basic factual information upon which any truly fair and free discussion of public issues must necessarily depend. . . . A licensee would be abusing his position as public trustee of these important means of mass communication were he to withhold from expression over his facilities relevant news or facts concerning a controversy or to slant or distort the presentation of such news. No discussion of the issues involved in any controversy can be fair or in the public interest where such discussion must take place in a climate of false or misleading information concerning the basic facts of the controversy, 13 FCC at 1254–55.

It is a matter of critical importance to the public that the basic facts or elements of a controversy should not be deliberately suppressed or misstated by a licensee. But, we must recognize that such distortions are "so continually done in perfect good faith, by persons who are not considered . . . ignorant or incompetent, that it is rarely possible, on adequate grounds, conscientiously to stamp the misrepresentations as morally culpable. . . ." J. S. Mill, *On Liberty* 31 (People's ed. 1921). Accordingly, we do not believe that it would be either useful or appropriate for us to investigate charges of news misrepresentations in the absence of substantial extrinsic evidence or documents that on their face reflect deliberate distortion. See *The Selling of the Pentagon*, 30 FCC 2d 150 (1971).

III. APPLICATION OF THE FAIRNESS DOCTRINE TO THE BROADCAST OF PAID ANNOUNCEMENTS

59. We turn now to the fairness doctrine problems which stem from the broadcast of paid announcements. For the purpose of this discussion, we will consider three general categories of such announcements: (1) advertisements which may properly be classified as "editorial" in nature; (2)

advertisements for commercial products or services; and (3) advertisements included in the Federal Trade Commission's so-called "counter-commercial" proposal.

The role of advertising in broadcasting and its relationship to the licensee's responsibility to broadcast in the public interest was considered by the Federal Radio Commission in 1929. 3 F.R.C. Ann. Rep. 32 (1929). It seems to us that the Commission at that time placed advertising in its proper context and perspective. It first noted that broadcasters are licensed to serve the public and not the private or selfish interests of individuals or groups. The Commission then stated that "[t]he only exception that can be made to this rule has to do with advertising; the exception, however, is only apparent because advertising furnishes the economic support for the service and thus makes it possible." *Id.* "The Commission . . . must recognize that, without advertising, broadcasting would not exist, and must confine itself to limiting this advertising in amount and in character so as to preserve the largest possible amount of service for the public." *Id.* at 35. Accordingly, we believe that any consideration of the applicability of the fairness doctrine to broadcast advertising must proceed with caution so as to ensure that the policies and standards which are formulated in this area will serve the genuine purposes of the doctrine without undermining the economic base of the system.

A. Editorial Advertising

60. Some "commercials" actually consist of direct and substantial commentary on important public issues. For the purpose of the fairness doctrine, these announcements should be recognized for what they are—editorials paid for by the sponsor. We can see no reason why the fairness doctrine should not apply to these "editorial advertisements" in the same manner that it applies to the commentary of a station announcer. At present, editorial advertising represents only a small percentage of total commercial time, and we cannot believe that an application of fairness here would have any serious effect on station revenues.

61. An example of an overt editorial advertisement would be a thirty- or sixty-second an-nouncement prepared and sponsored by an organization opposed to abortion which urges a constitutional amendment to override a decision of the Supreme Court legalizing abortion under certain circumstances. While the brevity of such announcements might make it difficult to develop the issue in great detail, they could, nevertheless, make a meaningful contribution to the public debate, and we believe that the fairness doctrine should be fully applicable to them.

62. Editorial advertisements may be difficult to identify if they are sponsored by groups which are not normally considered to be engaged in debate on controversial issues. This problem is most likely to arise in the context of promotional or institutional advertising; that is, advertising designed to present a favorable public image of a particular corporation or industry rather than to sell a product. Such advertising is, of course, a legitimate commercial practice and ordinarily does not involve debate on public issues. See, e.g., *Anthony R. Martin-Trigona,* 19 FCC 2d 620 (1969). In some cases, however, the advertiser may seek to play an obvious and meaningful role in public debate. In such instances, the fairness doctrine—including the obligation to provide free time in the circumstances described in the *Cullman* decision—applies.

63. In the past, we have wrestled with the application of the fairness doctrine to institutional advertisements which appeared to have discussed public issues, but which did not *explicitly* address the ultimate matter in controversy. An example of this problem may be found in the so-called "*ESSO*" case. *National Broadcasting Co.,* 30 FCC 2d 643 (1971). Here, the Commission found that certain commercials for Standard Oil Company constituted a discussion of one side of a controversial issue involving construction of the Alaskan pipeline. These advertisements did not explicitly mention that pipeline, but they did present what could be termed arguments in support of its construction. Specifically, we found that the advertisements argued that the Nation's urgent need for oil necessitated a rapid development of reserves on Alaska's North Slope. *Id.* at 643. The commercials also referred to the ability of an ESSO affiliate to build a pipeline in the far north, and yet "preserve the ecology." *Ibid.* As we noted

on rehearing, the problem involved here "is indeed a difficult one ... because the pipeline controversy is not specifically referred to...." *Wilderness Society*, 31 FCC 2d 729, 733, *reconsideration denied* 32 FCC 2d 714 (1971).

64. In the face of such difficulties, what guidance can the Commission give to its licensees and to the public? Professor Louis Jaffe has offered the following suggestion:

> [I]t is not easy to formulate a fully satisfactory rule for applying the fairness doctrine to advertising. Its application is most obvious where the advertisement is explicitly controversial. But the advertiser may avoid the explicit precisely to foreclose a claim of rebuttal, or because he believes the subliminal is more effective. It should suffice to trigger the doctrine that by implication he intends to speak to a current, publicly-acknowledged controversy. Jaffe, *The Editorial Responsibility of the Broadcaster: Reflections on Fairness and Access*, 85 *Harv. L. Rev.* 768, 777–78 (1972).

We believe that this suggestion comes close to the mark, but what we are really concerned with is an obvious participation in public debate and not a subjective judgment as to the advertiser's actual intentions. Accordingly, we expect our licensees to do nothing more than to make a reasonable, common sense judgment as to whether the "advertisement" presents a meaningful statement which obviously addresses, and advocates a point of view on, a controversial issue of public importance. This determination cannot be made in a vacuum; in addition to his review of the text of the ad, the licensee must take into account his general knowledge of the issues and arguments in the ongoing public debate. Indeed, this relationship of the ad to the debate being carried on in the community is critical. If the ad bears only a tenuous relationship to that debate, or one drawn by unnecessary inference, the fairness doctrine would clearly not be applicable.

65. The situation would be different, however, if that relationship could be shown to be both substantial and obvious. For example, if the arguments and views expressed in the ad closely parallel the major arguments advanced by partisans on one side or the other of a public debate, it might be reasonable to conclude that one side of the issue involved had been presented thereby raising fairness doctrine obligations. See, e.g.,

Media Access Project (Georgia Power), 44 FCC 2d 755, 761 (1973). We fully appreciate that, in many cases, this judgment may prove to be a difficult one and individual licensees may well reach differing conclusions concerning the same advertisement. We will, of course, review these judgments only to determine their reasonableness and good faith under the particular facts and circumstances presented and will not rule against the licensee unless the facts are so clear that the only reasonable conclusion would be to view the "advertisement" as a presentation on one side of a specific public issue.

B. Advertisements for Commercial Products or Services

66. Many advertisements which do not look or sound like editorials are, nevertheless, the subject of fairness complaints because the business, product, or service advertised is itself controversial. This may be true even though the advertisement does not mention any aspect of a controversy. Commercial announcements of precisely this type led to the current debate over fairness and advertising. This debate began in 1967 with our decision to extend the fairness doctrine to advertisements for cigarettes. *WCBS-TV*, 8 FCC 2d 381, *stay and reconsideration denied* 9 FCC 2d 921 (1967). These advertisements, like many others, addressed themselves solely to the desirability of the product. They tended to portray "the use of the particular cigarette as attractive and enjoyable ..." but avoided any mention of the then raging smoking-health controversy. 8 FCC 2d at 382. At the time, broadcasters argued that, in the absence of an affirmative discussion of the health issue, the commercials could not realistically be viewed as part of a public debate. 9 FCC 2d at 938. We rejected this argument and insisted that the issue should be defined in terms of the desirability of smoking. *Id.* With the issue defined in this fashion, it was a simple mechanical procedure to "trigger" the fairness doctrine and treat all cigarette advertisements—regardless of what they actually said—as being presentations on one side of a controversial issue. It seemed to be clear enough that *all* cigarette advertisements suggested that the use of the product was desirable.

67. In retrospect, we believe that this mechanical approach to the fairness doctrine represented a serious departure from the doctrine's central

purpose which, of course, is to facilitate "the development of an *informed* public opinion." *Report on Editorializing*, 13 FCC 1246, 1249 (1949) (emphasis supplied). We believe that standard product commercials, such as the old cigarette ads, make no meaningful contribution toward informing the public on any side of any issue. Indeed, as the D.C. Circuit Court of Appeals succinctly stated:

> Promoting the sale of a product is not ordinarily associated with any of the interests the First Amendment seeks to protect. As a rule, it does not affect the political process, does not contribute to the exchange of ideas, does not provide information on matters of public importance, and is not, except perhaps for the ad-men, a form of individual self-expression.... Accordingly, even if ... [such] commercials are protected speech, we think they are at best a negligible part of any exposition of ideas, and are of ... slight social value as a step to truth.... *Banzhaf v. FCC*, 405 F. 2d 1082, 1101–02 (D.C. Cir. 1968), quoting *Chaplinsky v. New Hampshire*, 315 U.S. 568, 572 (1942).

In this light, it seems to us to make little practical sense to view advertisements such as these as presenting a meaningful discussion of a controversial issue of public importance.

68. In our view, an application of the fairness doctrine to normal product commercials would, at best, provide the public with only one side of a public controversy. In the cigarette case, for example, the ads run by the industry did not provide the listening public with any information or arguments relevant to the underlying issue of smoking and health. At the time of our ruling, Commissioner Loevinger suggested that we were not really encouraging a balanced debate but, rather, were simply imposing our view that discouraging smoking was in the public interest. 9 FCC 2d at 953. While such an approach may have represented good policy from the standpoint of the public health, the precedent is not at all in keeping with the basic purposes of the fairness doctrine.

69. This precedent would not have been particularly troublesome if it had been limited to cigarette advertising as the Commission originally intended. In 1971, however, the D.C. Circuit ruled that the cigarette precedent could not logically be limited to cigarette advertising alone.

Friends of the Earth v. FCC, 449 F. 2d 1164 (D.C. Cir. 1971). In this decision, it was suggested that high-powered cars pollute the atmosphere more than low-powered cars. It was then determined that the fairness doctrine was triggered by the advertisements there involved because they extolled the virtues of high-powered cars and thus glorified product attributes aggravating an existing health hazard, namely air pollution. The commercials, of course, made no attempt at all to discuss the product in the context of the air pollution controversy. If these advertisements presented one point of view on the issue, then, by the same reasoning, the "contrasting" viewpoint must have been similarly presented in ads for low-powered cars. The problem with this kind of logic is that it engages both broadcasters and the Commission in the trivial task of "balancing" two sets of commercials which contribute nothing to public understanding of the underlying issue of how to deal with the problem of air pollution.

70. We do not believe that the underlying purposes of the fairness doctrine would be well served by permitting the cigarette case to stand as a fairness doctrine precedent. In the absence of some meaningful or substantive discussion, such as that found in the "editorial advertisements" referred to above, we do not believe that the usual product commercial can realistically be said to inform the public on any side of a controversial issue of public importance. It would be a great mistake to consider standard advertisements, such as those involved in the *Banzhaf* and *Friends of the Earth*, as though they made a meaningful contribution to public debate. It is a mistake, furthermore, which tends only to divert the attention of broadcasters from their public trustee responsibilities in aiding the development of an informed public opinion. Accordingly, in the future, we will apply the fairness doctrine only to those "commercials" which are devoted in an obvious and meaningful way to the discussion of public issues.

VI. CONCLUSION

90. It is hoped that this inquiry and report will provide a needed restatement and clarification of the essential principles and policies of the fairness doctrine—both in terms of its theoretical foun-

dations and its practical application. While we have here reaffirmed the basic validity and soundness of these principles and policies in ensuring that the medium of broadcasting will continue to function consistently with the ends and purposes of the First Amendment and the public interest, the Commission fully recognizes that their specific application in particular cases can involve questions and determinations of considerable complexity and difficulty. For this reason, the administration of the doctrine must proceed, within the framework of general policies set forth herein, on a case-by-case basis according to the particular facts and circumstances presented. We do wish to emphasize that in the final analysis, the fairness doctrine can fulfill its purpose and function only to the extent that *all* the parties involved—the broadcasters, the Commission, and individual members of the public—participate with a sense of reasonableness and good faith. . . .

Most litigation concerning the fairness doctrine has centered upon the duty to present balancing viewpoints. A West Virginia radio station's failure to air a tape furnished by a congresswoman, responding to a program favoring strip mining, led to a rare violation of the fairness doctrine's issue-raising component.[45] The FCC, noting that strip mining was an issue of central importance to residents of the state, concluded that the broadcaster's decision was "unreasonable."[46] It emphasized, however, that the circumstances were "exceptional . . . and would not counter our intention to stay out of decisions concerning the selection of specific programming matter."[47] For fairness responsibilities to be triggered, the issue in a given instance must be discernible in terms that are neither too narrow nor too broad. A matter of interest only to a discrete few may fail to qualify as an issue of "public importance."

The concept of "national security," in contrast, may be too wide-ranging to afford an effective reference point for assessing balance. A fairness claim tied to a study alleging imbalance in a network's coverage of affairs concerning national security thus failed because the issue was too amorphous.[48] Pursuant to a detailed analysis of news accounts over a year's time, concerning "[1] United States military and foreign affairs; [2] Soviet Union military and foreign affairs; [3] China military and foreign affairs; [4] Vietnam affairs," it was argued that national security threats had been reportorially discounted more than half of the time.[49] The court of appeals, in *American Security Council Educational Foundation v. Federal Communications Commission*,[50] upheld the commission's rejection of the fairness claim.[51] In so doing, it observed that "the indirect relationships among the issues aggregated . . . under the umbrella of 'national security' do not provide a basis for determining whether the public received a reasonable balance of conflicting views."[52]

The review of licensee responses to fairness requests largely has been deferential. In opposing the continuing operation of the fairness doctrine, one commissioner noted that in 1973 and 1974 only 19 out of 4,280 fairness complaints led to findings against the licensee.[53] A prominent exception, in which the FCC found a network documentary pension to be biased and subject to fairness requirements, was reversed by an appeals court.[54] The reviewing court, in *National Broadcasting Co., Inc. v. Federal Communications Commission*,[55] emphasized that it was the network's responsibility to determine program content and that the commission was limited to determining whether a licensee's judgment was reasonable and in good faith.[56] Although the decision was dismissed as moot, pending reconsideration, deference to licensee discretion has proved to be the norm in fairness analysis.[57]

Implementation of the fairness doctrine in connection with commercial advertising was curtailed after some experimentation. The FCC originally required licensees to balance cigarette advertisements with programming identifying the hazards of smoking.[58] Soon thereafter, it rejected a fairness claim by environmentalists who sought to balance commercials implicating ecological concerns.[59] The court of appeals determined that the cigarette and environmental issues were alike for fairness purposes and that the commission must apply a consistent rule.[60] Subsequently, the FCC determined that only advertisements "which obviously address[], and advocate[] a point of view on, a controversial issue of public importance" would be subject to fairness requirements.[61] The change was challenged, but an appeals court determined that the Commission was free to alter policy absent constitutional or statutory impediment.[62]

2. Personal Access

The fairness doctrine is framed in terms of viewpoint access, but construction of a paramount First Amendment right on the part of the viewers and listeners has engendered concepts of personal access rights. Jurisprudence has evolved in a direction that has precluded any notion of a general right of access but has acknowledged and upheld access rights of a discrete nature.[63]

A. GENERAL ACCESS

The FCC rejected the notion of a general right of access, but an appeals court found it to be a logical extension of the public's paramount rights recognized in *Red Lion*.[64] In *Columbia Broadcasting System, Inc. v. Democratic National Committee*,[65] the Supreme Court rejected the idea of an unqualified right of public access.[66] At the same time, it reiterated the status of licensees as public trustees and their duty to comply with fairness standards.[67]

The case arose out of a failed effort by an antiwar group to obtain time to air its views on a Washington, D.C., radio station.[68] Although reciting the same history of broadcasting that prompted it to endorse the fairness doctrine,[69] the Court found "clear that Congress intended to permit private broadcasting to develop with the widest journalistic freedom consistent with its public obligation."[70] It regarded access as a right that would enlarge government's role contrary to the First Amendment and statute.[71] Unlike the fairness doctrine, access would require the FCC "to oversee far more of the day-to-day operations of broadcasters' conduct deciding such questions as whether a particular individual or group has had sufficient opportunity to present its viewpoint and whether a particular viewpoint has been sufficiently aired."[72] Apart from the need for what it considered excessively detailed oversight, the Court found access objectionable on the grounds that the information marketplace would be "heavily weighted in favor of the financially affluent, or those with access wealth."[73] A further concern was "that the time alotted for editorial advertising could be monopolized by those of one political persuasion."[74]

The Court disparaged the notion of access on the grounds that it not only eroded journalistic discretion but also subordinated the public's paramount constitutional interests to private whim.[75] Dismissing the court of appeals' view that individual speakers are " 'the best judge' of what the listening public ought to hear," it found journalistic experience had proved the contrary.[76] Adding that "(f)or better or worse, editing is what editors are for," the Court concluded that even abuse of editorial power did not justify cramping or undercutting editorial discretion.[77] Although acknowledging the First Amendment value of "robust and wide open" debate on public issues, the Court determined that it did not justify trading " 'public trustee' broadcasting, with all its limitations, for a system of self-appointed editorial commentators."[78] The Court recognized that the fairness doctrine was imperfect but also that any "remedy does not lie in diluting licensee responsibility."[79] In closing, it observed that "some kind of limited right of access that is both practicable and desirable" might be devised in the future and that other media, such as cable, might enhance opportunities for discussion of public issues.[80]

Justice Douglas concurred in the judgment but would have predicated it on grounds that broadcasting should have the same First Amendment status as publishing.[81] He furthermore asserted that fairness controls were a major mistake and an encroachment upon the First Amendment.[82] Noting that scarcity is a characteristic of the print media too, Douglas found it inadequate as a reason for revamping the First Amendment's basic nature.[83] Even a scheme designed to promote First Amendment values, from his perspective, cut "against the grain of the First Amendment" insofar as they entailed "censorship or editing or screening by Government."[84]

In a dissenting opinion, Justice Brennan expressed sympathy for a right of access as a means for remediating circumstances that had blunted the original meaning of press freedom.[85] Brennan's support of access was based in large part upon his sense that the fairness doctrine underserved First Amendment interests. He thus observed that, given profit maximization aims of broadcasters, it was naive to expect them to offer meaningful controversy and thereby risk alienating sponsors and audience.[86] Instead of journalistic discretion as the exclusive determinant for apprising the public of competing views, Brennan considered it "imperative that citizens be permitted at least *some* opportunity to speak directly for themselves as genuine advocates on issues that concern them."[87] For Brennan, therefore, access was attractive as a methodology accounting not just for public viewing and listening interests but also for input opportunities largely foreclosed by the evolution of mass media.[88] Fur-

ther appealing to him was a means for facilitating presentation of views and voices that were truly "novel, unorthodox or unrepresentative of mainstream opinion" rather than merely representative of established or mainstream controversy.

Columbia Broadcasting System, Inc. v. Democratic National Committee, 412 U.S. 94 (1973)

Mr. Chief Justice Burger delivered the opinion of the Court (Parts I, II, and IV) together with an opinion (Part III), in which Mr. Justice Stewart and Mr. Justice Rehnquist joined.

We granted the writs of certiorari in these cases to consider whether a broadcast licensee's general policy of not selling advertising time to individuals or groups wishing to speak out on issues they consider important violates the Federal Communications Act of 1934, 48 Stat. 1064, as amended, 47 U.S.C. § 151 *et seq.*, or the First Amendment.

In two orders announced the same day, the Federal Communications Commission ruled that a broadcaster who meets his public obligation to provide full and fair coverage of public issues is not required to accept editorial advertisements. *Democratic National Committee,* 25 F.C.C. 2d 216; *Business Executives' Move for Vietnam Peace,* 25 F.C.C. 2d 242. A divided Court of Appeals reversed the Commission, holding that a broadcaster's fixed policy of refusing editorial advertisements violates the First Amendment; the court remanded the cases to the Commission to develop procedures and guidelines for administering a First Amendment right of access. *Business Executives' Move for Vietnam Peace v. FCC,* 146 U.S. App. D.C. 181, 450 F. 2d 642 (1971).

The complainants in these actions are the Democratic National Committee (DNC) and the Business Executives' Move for Vietnam Peace (BEM), a national organization of businessmen opposed to United States involvement in the Vietnam conflict. In January 1970, BEM filed a complaint with the Commission charging that radio station WTOP in Washington, D.C., had refused to sell it time to broadcast a series of one-minute spot announcements expressing BEM views on Vietnam. WTOP, in common with many, but not all, broadcasters, followed a policy of refusing to sell time for spot announcements to individuals and groups who wished to expound their views on controversial issues. WTOP took the position that since it presented full and fair coverage of important public questions, including the Vietnam conflict, it was justified in refusing to accept editorial advertisements. WTOP also submitted evidence showing that the station had aired the views of critics of our Vietnam policy on numerous occasions. BEM challenged the fairness of WTOP's coverage of criticism of that policy, but it presented no evidence in support of that claim....

In two separate opinions, the Commission rejected respondents' claims that "responsible" individuals and groups have a right to purchase advertising time to comment on public issues without regard to whether the broadcaster has complied with the Fairness Doctrine. The Commission viewed the issue as one of major significance in administering the regulatory scheme relating to the electronic media, one going "to the heart of the system of broadcasting which has developed in this country...." 25 F.C.C. 2d, at 221....

The Commission also rejected BEM's claim that WTOP had violated the Fairness Doctrine by failing to air views such as those held by members of BEM; the Commission pointed out that BEM had made only a "general allegation" of unfairness in WTOP's coverage of the Vietnam conflict and that the station had adequately rebutted the charge by affidavit....

A majority of the Court of Appeals reversed the Commission, holding that "a flat ban on paid public issue announcements is in violation of the First Amendment, at least when other sorts of paid announcements are accepted." 146 U.S. App. D.C., at 185, 450 F. 2d, at 646. Recognizing that the broadcast frequencies are a scarce resource inherently unavailable to all, the court nevertheless concluded that the First Amendment mandated an "abridgeable" right to present editorial advertisements. The court reasoned that a broadcaster's policy of airing commercial advertisements but not editorial advertisements constitutes unconstitutional discrimination. The court did not, however, order that either BEM's

or DNC's proposed announcements must be accepted by the broadcasters; rather, it remanded the cases to the Commission to develop "reasonable procedures and regulations determining which and how many 'editorial advertisements' will be put on the air." *Ibid.* ...

Mr. Justice White's opinion for the Court in *Red Lion Broadcasting Co. v. FCC*, 395 U.S. 367 (1969), makes clear that the broadcast media pose unique and special problems not present in the traditional free speech case. Unlike other media, broadcasting is subject to an inherent physical limitation. Broadcast frequencies are a scarce resource; they must be portioned out among applicants. All who possess the financial resources and the desire to communicate by television or radio cannot be satisfactorily accommodated. The Court spoke to this reality when, in *Red Lion*, we said "it is idle to posit an unabridgeable First Amendment right to broadcast comparable to the right of every individual to speak, write, or publish." *Id.*, at 388.

Because the broadcast media utilize a valuable and limited public resource, there is also present an unusual order of First Amendment values. *Red Lion* discussed at length the application of the First Amendment to the broadcast media. In analyzing the broadcasters' claim that the Fairness Doctrine and two of its component rules violated their freedom of expression, we held that "[n]o one has a First Amendment right to a license or to monopolize a radio frequency; to deny a station license because 'the public interest' requires it 'is not a denial of free speech.'" *Id.*, at 389. Although the broadcaster is not without protection under the First Amendment, *United States v. Paramount Pictures, Inc.*, 334 U.S. 131, 166 (1948), "[i]t is the right of the viewers and listeners, not the right of the broadcasters, which is paramount.... It is the right of the public to receive suitable access to social, political, esthetic, moral, and other ideas and experiences which is crucial here. That right may not constitutionally be abridged either by Congress or by the FCC." *Red Lion, supra,* at 390.

Balancing the various First Amendment interests involved in the broadcast media and determining what best serves the public's right to be informed is a task of a great delicacy and difficulty. The process must necessarily be undertaken within the framework of the regulatory scheme that has evolved over the course of the past half century. For, during that time, Congress and its chosen regulatory agency have established a delicately balanced system of regulation intended to serve the interests of all concerned. The problems of regulation are rendered more difficult because the broadcast industry is dynamic in terms of technological change; solutions adequate a decade ago are not necessarily so now, and those acceptable today may well be outmoded 10 years hence.

Thus, in evaluating the First Amendment claims of respondents, we must afford great weight to the decisions of Congress and the experience of the Commission. . . .

[After examining the history of broadcast regulation and legislative emphasis upon public obligations for licensees, the Court found it] clear that Congress intended to permit private broadcasting to develop with the widest journalistic freedom consistent with its public obligations. Only when the interests of the public are found to outweigh the private journalistic interests of the broadcasters will government power be asserted within the framework of the Act. License renewal proceedings, in which the listening public can be heard, are a principal means of such regulation. See *Office of Communication of United Church of Christ v. FCC,* 123 U.S. App. D.C. 328, 359 F. 2d 994 (1966), and 138 U.S. App. D.C. 112, 425 F. 2d 543 (1969).

Subsequent developments in broadcast regulation illustrate how this regulatory scheme has evolved. Of particular importance, in light of Congress' flat refusal to impose a "common carrier" right of access for all persons wishing to speak out on public issues, is the Commission's "Fairness Doctrine," which evolved gradually over the years spanning federal regulation of the broadcast media. Formulated under the Commission's power to issue regulations consistent with the "public interest," the doctrine imposes two affirmative responsibilities on the broadcaster: coverage of issues of public importance must be adequate and must fairly reflect differing viewpoints. See *Red Lion,* 395 U.S., at 377. In fulfilling the Fairness Doctrine obligations, the broadcaster must provide free time for the pre-

sentation of opposing views if a paid sponsor is unavailable, *Cullman Broadcasting Co.,* 25 P & F Radio Reg. 895 (1963), and must initiate programming on public issues if no one else seeks to do so. See *John J. Dempsey,* 6 P & F Radio Reg. 615 (1950); *Red Lion, supra,* at 378.

Since it is physically impossible to provide time for all viewpoints, however, the right to exercise editorial judgment was granted to the broadcaster. The broadcaster, therefore, is allowed significant journalistic discretion in deciding how best to fulfill the Fairness Doctrine obligations, although that discretion is bounded by rules designed to assure that the public interest in fairness is furthered. . . .

By minimizing the difficult problems involved in implementing such a right of access, the Court of Appeals failed to come to grips with another problem of critical importance to broadcast regulation and the First Amendment—the risk of an enlargement of Government control over the content of broadcast discussion of public issues. See, e.g., *Fowler v. Rhode Island,* 345 U.S. 67 (1953); *Niemotko v. Maryland,* 340 U.S. 268 (1951). This risk is inherent in the Court of Appeals' remand requiring regulations and procedures to sort out requests to be heard—a process involving the very editing that licensees now perform as to regular programming. Although the use of a public resource by the broadcast media permits a limited degree of Government surveillance, as is not true with respect to private media, see *National Broadcasting Co. v. United States,* 319 U.S., at 216–219, the Government's power over licensees, as we have noted, is by no means absolute and is carefully circumscribed by the Act itself.

Under a constitutionally commanded and Government supervised right-of-access system urged by respondents and mandated by the Court of Appeals, the Commission would be required to oversee far more of the day-to-day operations of broadcasters' conduct, deciding such questions as whether a particular individual or group has had sufficient opportunity to present its viewpoint and whether a particular viewpoint has already been sufficiently aired. Regimenting broadcasters is too radical a therapy for the ailment respondents complain of.

Under the Fairness Doctrine the Commission's

responsibility is to judge whether a licensee's overall performance indicates a sustained good-faith effort to meet the public interest in being fully and fairly informed. The Commission's responsibilities under a right-of-access system would tend to draw it into a continuing case-by-case determination of who should be heard and when. Indeed, the likelihood of Government involvement is so great that it has been suggested that the accepted constitutional principles against control of speech content would need to be relaxed with respect to editorial advertisements. To sacrifice First Amendment protections for so speculative a gain is not warranted, and it was well within the Commission's discretion to construe the Act so as to avoid such a result....

Thus, under the Fairness Doctrine broadcasters are responsible for providing the listening and viewing public with access to a balanced presentation of information on issues of public importance. The basic principle underlying that responsibility is "the right of the public to be informed, rather than any right on the part of the Government, any broadcast licensee or any individual member of the public to broadcast his own particular views on any matter...." Report on Editorializing by Broadcast Licensees, 13 F.C.C. 1246, 1249 (1949).

Consistent with that philosophy, the Commission on several occasions has ruled that no private individual or group has a right to command the use of broadcast facilities. See, e.g., *Dowie A. Crittenden,* 18 F.C.C. 2d 499 (1969); *Margaret Z. Scherbina,* 21 F.C.C. 2d 141 (1969); *Boalt Hall Student Assn.,* 20 F.C.C. 2d 612 (1969); *Madalyn Murray,* 40 F.C.C. 647 (1965); *Democratic State Central Committee of California,* 19 F.C.C. 2d 833 (1968); *U.S. Broadcasting Corp.,* 2 F.C.C. 208 (1935). Congress has not yet seen fit to alter that policy, although since 1934 it has amended the Act on several occasions....

The Commission was justified in concluding that the public interest in providing access to the marketplace of "ideas and experiences" would scarcely be served by a system so heavily weighted in favor of the financially affluent, or those with access to wealth. Cf. *Red Lion, supra,* at 392. Even under a first-come-first-served system, proposed by the dissenting Commissioner in these cases, the views of the affluent could well prevail over those of others, since they would have it within their power to purchase time more frequently. Moreover, there is the substantial danger, as the Court of Appeals acknowledged, 146 U.S. App. D.C., at 203, 450 F. 2d, at 664, that the time allotted for editorial advertising could be monopolized by those of one political persuasion.

These problems would not necessarily be solved by applying the Fairness Doctrine, including the *Cullman* doctrine, to editorial advertising. If broadcasters were required to provide time, free when necessary, for the discussion of the various shades of opinion on the issue discussed in the advertisement, the affluent could still determine in large part the issues to be discussed. Thus, the very premise of the Court of Appeals' holding—that a right of access is necessary to allow individuals and groups the opportunity for self-initiated speech—would have little meaning to those who could not afford to purchase time in the first instance.

If the Fairness Doctrine were applied to editorial advertising, there is also the substantial danger that the effective operation of that doctrine would be jeopardized. To minimize financial hardship and to comply fully with its public responsibilities a broadcaster might well be forced to make regular programming time available to those holding a view different from that expressed in an editorial advertisement; indeed, BEM has suggested as much in its brief. The result would be a further erosion of the journalistic discretion of broadcasters in the coverage of public issues, and a transfer of control over the treatment of public issues from the licensees who are accountable for broadcast performance to private individuals who are not. The public interest would no longer be "paramount" but, rather, subordinate to private whim especially since, under the Court of Appeals' decision, a broadcaster would be largely precluded from rejecting editorial advertisements that dealt with matters trivial or insignificant or already fairly covered by the broadcaster. 146 U.S. App. D.C., at 196 n. 36, 197, 450 F. 2d, at 657 n. 36, 658. If the Fairness Doctrine and the *Cullman* doctrine were suspended to alleviate these problems, as respondents suggest might be appropriate, the question arises whether we would have abandoned more than we have gained. Under such a regime the congressional objective of balanced coverage of public issues would be seriously threatened.

Nor can we accept the Court of Appeals' view that every potential speaker is "the best judge" of what the listening public ought to hear or indeed the best judge of the merits of his or her views. All journalistic tradition and experience is to the contrary. For better or worse, editing is what editors are for; and editing is selection and choice of material. That editors—newspaper or broadcast—can and do abuse this power is beyond doubt, but that is no reason to deny the discretion Congress provided. Calculated risks of abuse are taken in order to preserve higher values. The presence of these risks is nothing new; the authors of the Bill of Rights accepted the reality that these risks were evils for which there was no acceptable remedy other than a spirit of moderation and a sense of responsibility—and civility—on the part of those who exercise the guaranteed freedoms of expression.

It was reasonable for Congress to conclude that the public interest in being informed requires periodic accountability on the part of those who are entrusted with the use of broadcast frequencies, scarce as they are. In the delicate balancing historically followed in the regulation of broadcasting Congress and the Commission could appropriately conclude that the allocation of journalistic priorities should be concentrated in the licensee rather than diffused among many. This policy gives the public some assurance that the broadcaster will be answerable if he fails to meet its legitimate needs. No such accountability attaches to the private individual, whose only qualifications for using the broadcast facility may be abundant funds and a point of view. To agree that debate on public issues should be "robust, and wide-open" does not mean that we should exchange "public trustee" broadcasting, with all its limitations, for a system of self-appointed editorial commentators....

We reject the suggestion that the Fairness Doctrine permits broadcasters to preside over a "paternalistic" regime. See *Red Lion*, 395 U.S., at 390. That doctrine admittedly has not always brought to the public perfect or, indeed, even consistently high-quality treatment of all public events and issues; but the remedy does not lie in diluting licensee responsibility. The Commission stressed that, while the licensee has discretion in fulfilling its obligations under the Fairness Doctrine, it is required to "present representative community views and voices on controversial issues which are of importance to [its] listeners," and it is prohibited from "excluding partisan voices and always itself presenting views in a bland, inoffensive manner...." 25 F.C.C. 2d, at 222. A broadcaster neglects that obligation only at the risk of losing his license.

Conceivably at some future date Congress or the Commission—or the broadcasters—may devise some kind of limited right of access that is both practicable and desirable. Indeed, the Commission noted in these proceedings that the advent of cable television will afford increased opportunities for the discussion of public issues. . . .

Mr. Justice Douglas, concurring in the judgment.

While I join the Court in reversing the judgment below, I do so for quite different reasons.

My conclusion is that TV and radio stand in the same protected position under the First Amendment as do newspapers and magazines. The philosophy of the First Amendment requires that result, for the fear that Madison and Jefferson had of government intrusion is perhaps even more relevant to TV and radio than it is to newspapers and other like publications. That fear was founded not only on the spectre of a lawless government but of government under the control of a faction that desired to foist its views of the common good on the people. In popular terms that view has been expressed as follows:

> The ground rules of our democracy, as it has grown, require a free press, not necessarily a responsible or a temperate one. There aren't any halfway stages. As Aristophanes saw, democracy means that power is generally conferred on second-raters by third-raters, whereupon everyone else, from first-raters to fourth-raters, moves with great glee to try to dislodge them. It's messy but most politicians understand that it can't very well be otherwise and still be a democracy. Stewart, reviewing Epstein, News from Nowhere: Television and the News (1972), Book World, Washington Post, March 25, 1973, pp. 4–5.

If a broadcast licensee is not engaged in governmental action for purposes of the First Amendment, I fail to see how constitutionally we can treat TV and radio differently than we treat newspapers. It would come as a surprise to the public as well as to publishers and editors of newspapers to be informed that a newly created federal bureau would hereafter provide "guidelines" for newspapers or promulgate rules that would give a federal agency power to ride herd on the publishing business to make sure that fair comment on all current issues was made. In 1970 Congressman Farbstein introduced a bill, never reported out of the Committee, which provided that any newspaper of general circulation published in a city with a population greater than 25,000 and in which only one separately owned newspaper of general circulation is published "shall provide a reasonable opportunity for a balanced presentation of conflicting views on issues of public importance" and giving the Federal Communications Commission power to enforce the requirement.

Thomas I. Emerson, our leading First Amendment scholar, has stated that:

[A]ny effort to solve the broader problems of a monopoly press by forcing newspapers to cover all 'newsworthy' events and print all viewpoints, under the watchful eyes of petty public officials, is likely to undermine such independence as the press now shows without achieving any real diversity. The System of Freedom of Expression 671 (1970).

The sturdy people who fashioned the First Amendment would be shocked at that intrusion of Government into a field which in this Nation has been reserved for individuals, whatever part of the spectrum of opinion they represent. Benjamin Franklin, one of the Founders who was in the newspaper business, wrote in simple and graphic form what I had always assumed was the basic American newspaper tradition that became implicit in the First Amendment. In our early history one view was that the publisher must open his columns

to any and all controversialists, especially if paid for it. Franklin disagreed, declaring that his newspaper was not a stagecoach, with seats for everyone; he offered to print pamphlets for private distribution, but refused to fill his paper with private altercations. F. Mott, American Journalism 55 (3d ed. 1962).

It is said that TV and radio have become so powerful and exert such an influence on the public mind that they must be controlled by Government. Some newspapers in our history have exerted a powerful—and some have thought—a harmful interest on the public mind. But even Thomas Jefferson, who knew how base and obnoxious the press could be, never dreamed of interfering. For he thought that government control of newspapers would be the greater of two evils.

I deplore . . . the putrid state into which our newspapers have passed, and the malignity, the vulgarity, and mendacious spirit of those who write them. . . . These ordures are rapidly depraving the public taste.

It is however an evil for which there is no remedy, our liberty depends on the freedom of the press, and that cannot be limited without being lost.

Of course there is private censorship in the newspaper field. But for one publisher who may suppress a fact, there are many who will print it. But if the Government is the censor, administrative *fiat*, not freedom of choice, carries the day. . . .

Red Lion Broadcasting Co. v. FCC, 395 U.S. 367, in a carefully written opinion that was built upon predecessor cases, put TV and radio under a different regime. I did not participate in that decision and, with all respect, would not support it. The Fairness Doctrine has no place in our First Amendment regime. It puts the head of the camel inside the tent and enables administration after administration to toy with TV or radio in order to serve its sordid or its benevolent ends. In 1973—as in other years—there is clamoring to make TV and radio emit the messages that console certain groups. There are charges that these mass media are too slanted, too partisan, too hostile in their approach to candidates and the issues.

The same cry of protest has gone up against the newspapers and magazines. When Senator Joseph McCarthy was at his prime, holding in his hand papers containing the names of 205 "Communists" in the State Department (R. Feuerlicht, Joe McCarthy and McCarthyism 54 (1972)), there were scarcely a dozen papers in this Nation that stood firm for the citizen's right to due process and to First Amendment protection. That, however, was no reason to put the saddle of the federal bureaucracy on the backs of publishers. Under our Bill of Rights people are entitled to have extreme ideas, silly ideas, partisan ideas.

The same is true, I believe, of TV and radio. At times they have a nauseating mediocrity. At other times they show the dazzling brilliance of a Leonard Bernstein; and they very often bring humanistic influences of faraway people into every home.

Both TV and radio news broadcasts frequently tip the news one direction or another and even try to turn a public figure into a character of disrepute. Yet so do the newspapers and the magazines and other segments of the press. The standards of TV, radio, newspapers, or magazines—whether of excellence or mediocrity—are beyond the reach of Government. Government—acting through courts—disciplines lawyers. Government makes criminal some acts of doctors and of engineers. But the First Amendment puts beyond the reach of Government federal regulation of news agencies save only business or financial practices which do not involve First Amendment rights. . . .

We have . . . witnessed a slow encroachment by Government over that segment of the press that is represented by TV and radio licensees. Licensing is necessary for engineering reasons; the spectrum is limited and wavelengths must be assigned to avoid stations interfering with each other. *Red Lion Broadcasting Co. v. FCC,* 395 U.S., at 388. The Commission has a duty to encourage a multitude of voices but only in a limited way, *viz.,* by preventing monopolistic practices and by promoting technological developments that will open up new channels. But censorship or editing or the screening by Government of what licensees may broadcast goes against the grain of the First Amendment.

The Court in *National Broadcasting Co. v. United States,* 319 U.S. 190, 226, said, "Unlike other modes of expression, radio inherently is not available to all. That is its unique characteristic, and that is why, unlike other modes of expression, it is subject to governmental regulation."

That uniqueness is due to engineering and technical problems. But the press in a realistic sense is likewise not available to all. Small or "underground" papers appear and disappear; and

the weekly is an established institution. But the daily papers now established are unique in the sense that it would be virtually impossible for a competitor to enter the field due to the financial exigencies of this era. The result is that in practical terms the newspapers and magazines, like TV and radio, are available only to a select few. Who at this time would have the folly to think he could combat the *New York Times* or *Denver Post* by building a new plant and becoming a competitor? That may argue for a redefinition of the responsibilities of the press in First Amendment terms. But I do not think it gives us carte blanche to design systems of supervision and control or empower Congress to read the mandate in the First Amendment that "Congress shall make no law . . . abridging the freedom . . . of the press" to mean that Congress may, acting directly or through any of its agencies such as the FCC make "some" laws "abridging" freedom of the press.

Powerful arguments, summarized and appraised in T. Emerson, The System of Freedom of Expression, cc. XVII and XVIII (1970), can be made for revamping or reconditioning the system. The present one may be largely aligned on the side of the status quo. The problem implicates our educational efforts which are bland and conformist and the pressures on the press, from political and from financial sources, to foist boilerplate points of view on our people rather than to display the diversities of ideologies and culture in a world which, as Buckminster Fuller said, has been "communized" by the radio.

What kind of First Amendment would best serve our needs as we approach the 21st century may be an open question. But the old-fashioned First Amendment that we have is the Court's only guideline; and one hard and fast principle which it announces is that Government shall keep its hands off the press. That principle has served us through days of calm and eras of strife and I would abide by it until a new First Amendment is adopted. That means, as I view it, that TV and radio, as well as the more conventional methods for disseminating news, are all included in the concept of "press" as used in the First Amendment and therefore are entitled to live under the laissez-faire regime which the First Amendment sanctions.

The issues presented in these cases are momentous ones. TV and radio broadcasters have mined millions by selling merchandise, not in selling ideas across the broad spectrum of the First Amendment. But some newspapers have done precisely the same, loading their pages with advertisements; they publish, not discussions of critical issues confronting our society, but stories about murders, scandal, and slanderous matter touching the lives of public servants who have no recourse due to *New York Times Co. v. Sullivan,* 376 U.S. 254. Commissioner Johnson of the FCC wrote in the present case a powerful dissent. He said:

> Although the First Amendment would clearly ban governmental censorship of speech content, government must be concerned about the procedural rules that control the public forums for discussion. If someone—a moderator, or radio-television licensee—applies rules that give one speaker, or viewpoint, less time (or none at all) to present a position, then a censorship exists as invidious as outright thought control. There is little doubt in my mind that for any given forum of speech the First Amendment *demands* rules permitting as many to speak and be heard as possible. And if this Commission does not enact them, then the courts must require them. 25 F.C.C. 2d 216, 232. . . .

But the prospect of putting Government in a position of control over publishers is to me an appalling one, even to the extent of the Fairness Doctrine. The struggle for liberty has been a struggle against Government. The essential scheme of our Constitution and Bill of Rights was to take Government off the backs of people. Separation of powers was one device. An independent judiciary was another device. The Bill of Rights was still another. And it is anathema to the First Amendment to allow Government any role of censorship over newspapers, magazines, books, art, music, TV, radio, or any other aspect of the press. There is unhappiness in some circles at the impotence of Government. But if there is to be a change, let it come by constitutional amendment. The Commission has an important role to play in curbing monopolistic practices, in keeping channels free from interference, in opening up new channels as technology develops. But it has no power of censorship.

It is said, of course, that Government can control the broadcasters because their channels are in the public domain in the sense that they use the airspace that is the common heritage of all the people. But parks are also in the public domain. Yet people who speak there do not come under Government censorship. *Lovell v. Griffin,* 303 U.S. 444, 450–453; *Hague v. CIO,* 307 U.S. 496, 515–516. It is the tradition of Hyde Park, not the tradition of the censor, that is reflected in the First Amendment. TV and radio broadcasters are a vital part of the press; and since the First Amendment allows no Government control over it, I would leave this segment of the press to its devices. . . .

The Court in today's decision by endorsing the Fairness Doctrine sanctions a federal saddle on broadcast licensees that is agreeable to the traditions of nations that never have known freedom of press and that is tolerable in countries that do not have a written constitution containing prohibitions as absolute as those in the First Amendment. Indeed after these cases were argued the FCC instituted a "non-public" inquiry to determine whether any broadcaster or cablecaster has broadcast " 'obscene, indecent or profane language' in violation of" 18 U.S.C. § 1464. . . .

We ourselves have, of course, made great inroads on the First Amendment of which obscenity is only one of the many examples. So perhaps we are inching slowly toward a controlled press. But the regime of federal supervision under the Fairness Doctrine is contrary to our constitutional mandate and makes the broadcast licensee an easy victim of political pressures and reduces him to a timid and submissive segment of the press whose measure of the public interest will now be echoes of the dominant political voice that emerges after every election. The affair with freedom of which we have been proud will now bear only a faint likeness of our former robust days.

I said that it would come as a surprise to the public as well as to publishers and editors of newspapers to learn that they were under a newly created federal bureau. Perhaps I should have said that such an event *should* come as a surprise. In fact it might not in view of the retrogressive steps we have witnessed.

We have allowed ominous inroads to be made on the historic freedom of the newspapers. The effort to suppress the publication of the Pentagon Papers failed only by a narrow margin and actually succeeded for a brief spell in imposing prior restraint on our press for the first time in our history. See *New York Times Co. v. United States,* 403 U.S. 713.

In recent years the admonition of Mr. Justice Black that the First Amendment gave the press freedom so that it might "serve the governed, not the governors" (*id.,* at 717) has been disregarded.

"The Government's power to censor the press was abolished so that the press would remain forever free to censure the Government. The press was protected so that it could bare the secrets of government and inform the people. Only a free and unrestrained press can effectively expose deception in government. And paramount among the responsibilities of a free press is the duty to prevent any part of the government from deceiving the people and sending them off to distant lands to die of foreign fevers and foreign shot and shell." *Ibid.*

The right of the people to know has been greatly undermined by our decisions requiring, under pain of contempt, a reporter to disclose the sources of the information he comes across in investigative reporting. *Branzburg v. Hayes,* 408 U.S. 665.

The *Boston Globe* reports:

> In the last two years at least 20 Federal Grand Juries have been used to investigate radical or antiwar dissent. With the power of subpoena, the proceedings secret, and not bound by the rules of evidence required in open court, they have a lot more leverage than, for example, the old House Un-American Activities Committee.

Many reporters have been put in jail, a powerful weapon against investigative reporting. As the *Boston Globe* states, "in reality what is being undermined here is press freedom itself."

In the same direction is the easy use of the stamp "secret" or "top secret" which the Court recently approved in *Environmental Protection Agency v. Mink,* 410 U.S. 73. That decision makes a shambles of the Freedom of Information Act. In tune with the other restraints on the press are provisions of the new proposed Rules of Evidence which the Court recently sent to Congress. Proposed Rule 509 (b) provides:

> The government has a privilege to refuse to give evidence and to prevent any person from giving evidence upon a showing of reasonable likelihood of danger that the evidence will disclose a secret of state or official information, as defined in this rule.

Under the statute if Congress does not act, this new regime of secrecy will be imposed on the Nation and the right of people to know will be further curtailed. The proposed code sedulously protects the Government; it does not protect newsmen. It indeed pointedly omits any mention of the privilege of newsmen to protect their confidential sources.

These growing restraints on newspapers have the same ominous message that the overtones of the present opinion have on TV and radio licensees.

The growing specter of governmental control and surveillance over all activities of people makes ominous the threat to liberty by those who hold the executive power. Over and over again, attempts have been made to use the Commission as a political weapon against the opposition, whether to the left or to the right.

Experience has shown that unrestrained power cannot be trusted to serve the public weal even though it be in governmental hands. The fate of the First Amendment should not be so jeopardized. The constitutional mandate that the Government shall make "no law" abridging freedom of speech and the press is clear; the orders and rulings of the Commission are covered by that ban; and it must be carefully confined lest broadcasting—now our most powerful media—be used to subdue the minorities or help produce a Nation of people who walk submissively to the executive's notions of the public good....

What Walter Lippman wrote about President Coolidge's criticism of the press has present relevancy. Coolidge, he said, had

> declared for peace, good-will, understanding moderation; disapproved of conquest, aggression, exploitation; pleaded for a patriotic press, for a free press; denounced a narrow and bigoted nationalism, and announced that he stood for law, order, protection of life, property, respect for sovereignty and principle of international law. Mr. Coolidge's catalog of the virtues was complete except for one virtue. ...That is the humble realization that God has not endowed Calvin Coolidge with an infallible power to determine in each concrete case exactly what is right, what is just, what is patriotic....Did he rec-

ognize this possibility he would not continue to lecture the press in such a way as to make it appear that when newspapers oppose him they are unpatriotic, and that when they support him they do so not because they think his case is good but because they blindly support him. Mr. Coolidge's notion... would if it were accepted by the American press reduce it to utter triviality. J. Luskin, Lippman, Liberty, and the Press 60 (1972).

Brennan, J., dissenting.

Radio and television have long been recognized as forms of communication "affected by a First Amendment interest" and, indeed, it can hardly be doubted that broadcast licensees are themselves protected by that Amendment. *Red Lion Broadcasting Co. v. FCC*, 395 U.S., at 386. *See United States v. Paramount Pictures, Inc.*, 334 U.S. 131, 166 (1948); Z. Chafee, Free Speech in the United States 545–546 (1941). Recognition of this fact does not end our inquiry, however, for it is equally clear that the protection of the First Amendment in this context is not limited solely to broadcasters. On the contrary, at least one set of competing claims to the protection of that Amendment derives from the fact that, because of the limited number of broadcast frequencies available and the potentially pervasive impact of the electronic media, "the people as a whole retain their interest in free speech by radio and their collective right to have the medium function consistently with the ends and purposes of the First Amendment." *Red Lion Broadcasting Co. v. FCC, supra*, at 390.

Over 50 years ago, Mr. Justice Holmes sounded what has since become a dominant theme in applying the First Amendment to the changing problems of our Nation. "[T]he ultimate good," he declared, "is better reached by free trade in ideas," and "the best test of truth is the power of the thought to get itself accepted in the competition of the market...." *Abrams v. United States*, 250 U.S. 616, 630 (1919) (dissenting opinion); see also *Whitney v. California*, 274 U.S. 357, 375–376 (1927) (Brandeis, J., concurring); *Gitlow v. New York*, 268 U.S. 652, 672–673 (1925) (Holmes, J., dissenting). Indeed, the First Amendment itself testifies to our "profound national commitment to the principle that debate on public issues should be uninhibited, robust, and wide-open," and the Amendment "rests on the assumption

that the widest possible dissemination of information from diverse and antagonistic sources is essential to the welfare of the public...." *Associated Press v. United States*, 326 U.S. 1, 20 (1945). For "it is only through free debate and free exchange of ideas that government remains responsive to the will of the people and peaceful change is effected." *Terminiello v. Chicago*, 337 U.S. 1, 4 (1949); see also *Thornhill v. Alabama*, 310 U.S. 88, 102 (1940); *Palko v. Connecticut*, 302 U.S. 319, 326–327 (1937).

With considerations such as these in mind, we have specifically declared that, in the context of radio and television broadcasting, the First Amendment protects "the right of the public to receive suitable access to social, political, esthetic, moral, and other ideas and experiences...." *Red Lion Broadcasting Co. v. FCC, supra*, at 390. And, because "[i]t is the purpose of the First Amendment to preserve an uninhibited marketplace of ideas in which truth will ultimately prevail, rather than to countenance monopolization of that market, whether it be by the Government itself or a private licensee," "[i]t is the right of the viewers and listeners, not the right of the broadcasters, which is paramount." *Ibid.*

Thus, we have explicitly recognized that, in light of the unique nature of the electronic media, the public have strong First Amendment interests in the reception of a full spectrum of views—presented in a vigorous and uninhibited manner—on controversial issues of public importance. And, as we have seen, it has traditionally been thought that the most effective way to insure this "uninhibited, robust, and wide-open" debate is by fostering a "free trade in ideas" by making our forums of communication readily available to all persons wishing to express their views. Although apparently conceding the legitimacy of these principles, the Court nevertheless upholds the absolute ban on editorial advertising because, in its view, the Commission's Fairness Doctrine, in and of itself, is sufficient to satisfy the First Amendment interests of the public. I cannot agree....

In fulfilling their obligations under the Fairness Doctrine, however, broadcast licensees have virtually complete discretion, subject only to the Commission's general requirement that licensees act "reasonably and in good faith," "to determine what issues should be covered, how much time should be allocated, which spokesmen should appear, and in what format." Thus, the Fairness Doctrine does not in any sense require broadcasters to allow "non-broadcaster" speakers to use the airwaves to express their own views on controversial issues of public importance. On the contrary, broadcasters may meet their fairness responsibilities through presentation of carefully edited news programs, panel discussions, interviews, and documentaries. As a result, broadcasters retain almost exclusive control over the selection of issues and viewpoints to be covered, the manner of presentation, and, perhaps most important, who shall speak. Given this doctrinal framework, I can only conclude that the Fairness Doctrine, standing alone, is insufficient—in theory as well as in practice—to provide the kind of "uninhibited, robust, and wide-open" exchange of views to which the public is constitutionally entitled.

As a practical matter, the Court's reliance on the Fairness Doctrine as an "adequate" alternative to editorial advertising seriously overestimates the ability—or willingness—of broadcasters to expose the public to the "widest possible dissemination of information from diverse and antagonistic sources." As Professor Jaffe has noted, "there is considerable possibility the broadcaster will exercise a large amount of self-censorship and try to avoid as much controversy as he safely can." Indeed, in light of the strong interest of broadcasters in maximizing their audience, and therefore their profits, it seems almost naive to expect the majority of broadcasters to produce the variety and controversiality of material necessary to reflect a full spectrum of viewpoints. Stated simply, angry customers are not good customers and, in the commercial world of mass communications, it is simply "bad business" to espouse—or even to allow others to espouse—the heterodox or the controversial. As a result, even under the Fairness Doctrine, broadcasters generally tend to permit only established—or at least moderated—views to enter the broadcast world's "marketplace of ideas."

Moreover, the Court's reliance on the Fairness Doctrine as the *sole* means of informing the public seriously misconceives and underestimates the public's interest in receiving ideas and informa-

tion directly from the advocates of those ideas without the interposition of journalistic middlemen. Under the Fairness Doctrine, broadcasters decide what issues are "important," how "fully" to cover them, and what format, time, and style of coverage are "appropriate." The retention of such *absolute* control in the hands of a few Government licensees is inimical to the First Amendment, for vigorous, free debate can be attained only when members of the public have at least *some* opportunity to take the initiative and editorial control into their own hands.

Our legal system reflects a belief that truth is best illuminated by a collision of genuine advocates. Under the Fairness Doctrine, however, accompanied by an absolute ban on editorial advertising, the public is compelled to rely *exclusively* on the "journalistic discretion" of broadcasters, who serve in theory as surrogate spokesmen for all sides of all issues. This separation of the advocate from the expression of his views can serve only to diminish the effectiveness of that expression. Indeed, we emphasized this fact in *Red Lion:*

> Nor is it enough that he should hear the arguments of adversaries from his own teachers, presented as they state them, and accompanied by what they offer as refutations. That is not the way to do justice to the arguments, or bring them into real contact with his own mind. He must be able to hear them from persons who actually believe them; who defend them in earnest, and do their very utmost for them.

Thus, if the public is to be honestly and forthrightly apprised of opposing views on controversial issues, it is imperative that citizens be permitted at least *some* opportunity to speak directly for themselves as genuine advocates on issues that concern them.

Moreover, to the extent that broadcasters actually permit citizens to appear on "their" airwaves under the Fairness Doctrine, such appearances are subject to extensive editorial control. Yet it is clear that the effectiveness of an individual's expression of his views is as dependent on the style and format of presentation as it is on the content itself. And the relegation of an individual's views to such tightly controlled formats as the news, documentaries, edited interviews, or panel discussions may tend to minimize, rather than maximize the effectiveness of speech. Under a limited scheme of editorial advertising, however, the crucial editorial controls are in the speaker's own hands.

Nor are these cases concerned solely with the adequacy of coverage of those views and issues which generally are recognized as "newsworthy." For also at stake is the right of the public to receive suitable access to new and generally unperceived ideas and opinions. Under the Fairness Doctrine, the broadcaster is required to present only "*representative* community views and voices on controversial issues" of public importance. Thus, by definition, the Fairness Doctrine tends to perpetuate coverage of those "views and voices" that are already established, while failing to provide for exposure of the public to those "views and voices" that are novel, unorthodox, or unrepresentative of prevailing opinion.

Finally, it should be noted that the Fairness Doctrine permits, indeed *requires,* broadcasters to determine for themselves which views and issues are sufficiently "important" to warrant discussion. The briefs of the broadcaster-petitioners in this case illustrate the type of "journalistic discretion" licensees now exercise in this regard. Thus, ABC suggests that it would refuse to air those views which *it* considers "scandalous" or "crackpot," while CBS would exclude those issues or opinions that are "insignificant" or "trivial." Similarly, NBC would bar speech that strays "beyond the bounds of normally accepted taste," and WTOP would protect the public from subjects that are "slight, parochial or inappropriate."

The genius of the First Amendment, however, is that it has always defined what the public ought to hear by permitting speakers to say what they wish. As the Court of Appeals recognized, "[i]t has traditionally been thought that the best judge of the importance of a particular viewpoint or issue is the individual or group holding the viewpoint and wishing to communicate it to others." 146 U.S. App. D.C., at 195, 450 F. 2d, at 656. Indeed, "supervised and ordained discussion" is directly contrary to the underlying purposes of the First Amendment, for that Amendment "presupposes that right conclusions are more likely to be gathered out of a multitude of tongues, than through any kind of authoritative selection." Thus, in a related context, we have explicitly recognized that editorial advertisements constitute "an important outlet for the promulgation of information and ideas by persons who do not themselves have access to [media] facilities," and the unavailability of such editorial advertising can serve only "to shackle the First Amendment in its attempt to secure 'the widest possible dissemination of information from diverse and antagonistic sources.' " *New York Times Co. v. Sullivan,* 376 U.S., at 266.

The Fairness Doctrine's requirement of full and fair coverage of controversial issues is, beyond doubt, a commendable and, indeed, essential tool for effective regulation of the broadcast industry. But, standing alone, it simply cannot eliminate the need for a further, complementary airing of controversial views through the limited availability of editorial advertising. Indeed, the availability of at least *some* opportunity for editorial advertising is imperative if we are ever to attain the " 'free and general discussion of public matters [that] seems absolutely essential to prepare the people for an intelligent exercise of their rights as citizens.' " *Grosjean v. American Press Co.,* 297 U.S. 233, 250 (1936)....

Here, of course, there can be no doubt that the broadcast frequencies allotted to the various radio and television licensees constitute appropriate "forums" for the discussion of controversial issues of public importance. Indeed, unlike the streets, parks, public libraries, and other "forums" that we have held to be appropriate for the exercise of First Amendment rights, the broadcast media are dedicated *specifically* to communication. And, since the expression of ideas—whether political, commercial, musical, or otherwise—is the exclusive purpose of the broadcast spectrum, it seems clear that the adoption of a limited scheme of editorial advertising would in no sense divert that spectrum from its intended use. Cf. *Lloyd Corp., Ltd. v. Tanner, supra,* at 563; *Amalgamated Food Employees Union v. Logan Valley Plaza, supra,* at 320.

Moreover, it is equally clear that, with the assistance of the Federal Government, the broadcast industry has become what is potentially the most efficient and effective "marketplace of ideas" ever devised. Indeed, the electronic media are today "the public's prime source of information," and we have ourselves recognized that broadcast "technology . . . supplants atomized, relatively informal communication with mass media as a prime source of national cohesion and news...." *Red Lion Broadcasting Co. v. FCC,* 395 U.S., at 386 n. 15. Thus, although "full and free discussion" of ideas may have been a reality in the heyday of political pamphleteering, modern technological developments in the field of communications have made the soapbox orator and the leafleteer virtually obsolete. And, in light of the current dominance of the electronic media as the most effective means of reaching the public, any policy that *absolutely* denies citizens access to the airwaves necessarily renders even the concept of "full and free discussion" practically meaningless.

Regrettably, it is precisely such a policy that the Court upholds today. And, since effectuation of the individual's right to speak through a limited scheme of editorial advertising can serve only to further, rather than to inhibit, the public's interest in receiving suitable exposure to "uninhibited, robust, and wide-open" debate on controversial issues, the challenged ban can be upheld only if it is determined that such editorial advertising would unjustifiably impair the broadcaster's assertedly overriding interest in exercising *absolute* control over "his" frequency. Such an analysis, however, hardly reflects the delicate balancing of interests that this sensitive question demands. Indeed, this "absolutist" approach wholly disregards the competing First Amendment rights of all "non-broadcaster" citizens, ignores the teachings of our recent decision in *Red Lion Broadcasting Co. v. FCC, supra,* and is not supported by the historical purposes underlying broadcast regulation in this Nation....

Although the overriding need to avoid overcrowding of the airwaves clearly justifies the imposition of a ceiling on the number of individuals who will be permitted to operate broadcast stations and, indeed, renders it "idle to posit an unabridgeable First Amendment right to broadcast comparable to the right of every individual to speak, write, or publish," it does not in any sense dictate that the continuing First Amendment rights of all nonlicensees be brushed aside entirely. Under the existing system, broadcast licensees are granted a preferred status with respect to the airwaves, not because they have competed successfully in the free market but, rather, "because of their initial government selection...." *Red Lion Broadcasting Co. v. FCC, supra,* at 400. And, in return for that "preferred status," licensees must respect the competing First Amendment rights of others. Thus, although the broadcaster has a clear First Amendment right to be free from Government censorship in the expression of his own views and, indeed, has a significant interest in exercising reasonable journalistic control over the use of his facilities, *"[t]he right of free speech of a broadcaster . . . does not embrace a right to snuff out the free speech of others." Id.,* at 387 (emphasis added). Indeed, after careful consideration of the nature of broadcast regulation in this country, we have specifically declared that

> as far as the First Amendment is concerned those who are licensed stand no better than those to whom licenses are refused. A license permits broadcasting, but the licensee has no constitutional right to . . . monopolize a radio frequency to the exclusion of his fellow citizens. *Id.,* at 389.

Viewed in this context, the *absolute* ban on editorial advertising seems particularly offensive because, although broadcasters refuse to sell any air time whatever to groups or individuals wishing to speak out on controversial issues of public importance, they make such air time readily available to those "commercial" advertisers who seek to peddle their goods and services to the public. Thus, as the system now operates, any person wishing to market a particular brand of beer, soap, toothpaste, or deodorant has direct, personal, and instantaneous access to the electronic media. He can present his own message, in his own words, in any format he selects, and at a time of his own choosing. Yet a similar individual seeking to discuss war, peace, pollution, or the suffering of the poor is denied this right to speak. Instead, he is compelled to rely on the beneficence of a corporate "trustee" appointed by the Government to argue his case for him.

It has long been recognized, however, that although access to public forums may be subjected to reasonable "time, place, and manner" regulations, "[s]elective exclusions from a public forum may not be based on *content* alone...." *Police Dept. of Chicago v. Mosley,* 408 U.S., at 96 (emphasis added); see e.g., *Shuttlesworth v. City of Birmingham,* 394 U.S. 147 (1969); *Edwards v. South*

Carolina, 372 U.S. 229 (1963); *Fowler v. Rhode Island,* 345 U.S. 67 (1953); *Niemotko v. Maryland,* 340 U.S. 268 (1951); *Saia v. New York,* 334 U.S. 558 (1948). Here, of course, the differential treatment accorded "commercial" and "controversial" speech clearly violates that principle. Moreover, and not without some irony, the favored treatment given "commercial" speech under the existing scheme clearly reverses traditional First Amendment priorities. For it has generally been understood that "commercial" speech enjoys *less* First Amendment protection than speech directed at the discussion of controversial issues of public importance. See, e.g., *Breard v. Alexandria,* 341 U.S. 622 (1951); *Valentine v. Chrestensen,* 316 U.S. 52 (1942).

The First Amendment values of individual self-fulfillment through expression and individual participation in public debate are central to our concept of liberty. If these values are to survive in the age of technology, it is essential that individuals be permitted at least *some* opportunity to express their views on public issues over the electronic media. Balancing those interests against the limited interest of broadcasters in exercising "journalistic supervision" over the mere allocation of *advertising* time that is already made available to some members of the public, I simply cannot conclude that the interest of broadcasters must prevail.

Specifically, the Court hypothesizes three potential sources of difficulty: (1) the availability of editorial advertising might, in the absence of adjustments in the system, tend to favor the wealthy; (2) application of the Fairness Doctrine to editorial advertising might adversely affect the operation of that doctrine; and (3) regulation of editorial advertising might lead to an enlargement of Government control over the content of broadcast discussion. These are, of course, legitimate and, indeed, important concerns. But, at the present time, they are concerns—not realities. We simply have no sure way of knowing whether, and to what extent, if any, these potential difficulties will actually materialize. The Court's bare assumption that these hypothetical problems are both inevitable and insurmountable indicates an utter lack of confidence in the ability of the Commission and licensees to adjust to the changing conditions of a dynamic medium. This sudden

lack of confidence is, of course, strikingly inconsistent with the general propositions underlying all other aspects of the Court's approach to this case....

For the present, however, and until such time, if ever, as these assertedly "overriding" administrative difficulties actually materialize, I must agree with the conclusion of the Court of Appeals that although "it may unsettle some of us to see an antiwar message or a political party message in the accustomed place of a soap or beer commerical ... we must not equate what is habitual with what is right—or what is constitutional. A society already so saturated with commercialism can well afford another outlet for speech on public issues. All that we may lose is some of our apathy."

The Court's observation that a "limited right of access might be devised in the future"[89] prompted two proposals that were rejected by the commission.[90] One suggestion would have afforded licensees the option of operating under the fairness doctrine or be deemed in compliance with it if they set aside one hour per week for a minimum number of access spots of varying length.[91] The proposal responded to the concern expressed in the *Democratic National Committee* decision that unconditional access would favor the wealthy or be monopolized by a single viewpoint[92] by allocating time on a first demand and representative spokesperson basis.[93] Another suggestion would have obligated licensees to identify annually the ten controversial issues it had covered most heavily in the prior year, the offers it had made for responses, and the representative programming presented on each issue.[94]

In *National Citizens Committee for Broadcasting v. Federal Communications Commission,*[95] the court of appeals determined that the commission had failed "to consider carefully" the suggestions and thus remanded them for further examination.[96] In subsequently detailing its reasons for rejecting the "access as fairness" proposal, the FCC asserted that the "emphasis upon speakers rather than ideas is at cross-purposes to that of the Fairness Doctrine."[97] Because the presentation of balanced viewpoints is designed "to inform the public," the commission noted that any substitute principle must do likewise, and the access proposal failed on that count.[98] With respect to the listing and reporting suggestion, the commission found it redundant with then existing ascertainment obligations[99] and at odds with the review of fairness complaints on a particularized basis rather than at renewal time.[100] To date the FCC has not found a general access proposal consistent with its essential requirements:

> ... that [1] licensee discretion be preserved ... [2] no right of access accrue to particular persons or groups ... [3] the access system ... not ... allow important issues to escape timely discussion ... [and] [4] the system not draw the government into the role of deciding who should be allowed on the air and when.[101]

Although the final criterion was denominated the "[m]ost important," a continuing implication of the fairness doctrine was the power of government to decide *what* "should be allowed on the air."

B. LIMITED ACCESS

Notwithstanding rejection of broadly conceived access rights, Congress and the commission have devised access rights of a limited nature. Other than a right of reasonable access for political candidates,[102] the opportunities are contingent upon triggering events rather than affirmative in nature.

1) *Personal Attack Rule.* The personal attack rule[103] has been regarded as a component of the fairness doctrine even though it creates a conditional right of access. In essence, the rule provides that an individual, whose honesty, character, integrity, or like personal quality is attacked in the course of coverage of a controversial issue of public importance, has a right to respond in person.[104] Upon the occurrence of such an attack, the licensee has affirmative duties to notify the victim of the time, date, and nature of the broadcast, to provide a script or a tape of the incident, and to offer a reasonable opportunity to respond.[105] The rule does not operate with respect to personal attacks on foreign groups or foreign public figures, by legally qualified candidates for public office or their proxies, or in the event of bona fide news reporting.[106]

The right of access, in the event of a personal attack, is subject to significant constraints and deference to licensee judgment. If the attack does not occur in the course of a discussion of a controversial issue of public importance, the rule does not operate, and a claimant must seek more traditional relief in the nature of a defamation or privacy action.[107] A commission determination, that a particular comment related back to earlier discussion of a public controversy so was subject to the rule, was vacated upon appeal.[108] The reviewing court determined that, instead of substituting its own judgment regarding the continuity of the controversy, the FCC must assess "the objective reasonableness" of the licensee's judgment that debate had ceased.[109] Appraisal of a broadcaster's decision, consistent with general fairness standards, has been subject to standards of unreasonableness or bad faith.[110]

2) *Political Editorials.* In the event a licensee endorses or opposes a legally qualified candidate for public office, an opportunity exists for other candidates or their spokesperson or the opposing candidate or spokesperson to respond.[111] As with the personal attack rule, affirmative obligations exist for the licensee to furnish within twenty-four hours the date and time of the editorial, a script or tape, and a reasonable opportunity to respond.[112] If the editorial is broadcast within seventy-two hours of the election, the licensee must ensure that notice and oppor-

tunity are afforded in a way that ensures a reasonable chance to reply.[113] Editorializing on ballot issues rather than candidates does not trigger operation of the political editorial rule.[114]

3) *Equal Opportunity for Political Candidates.* Section 315 of the Communications Act provides in general terms that "(i)f any licensee shall permit any person who is a legally qualified candidate for any public office to use a broadcast station, he shall afford equal opportunities to all other such candidates for that office in the event of such broadcast."[115] A "legally qualified candidate" has been defined as a person who (1) has publicly announced an intention to run for office, (2) is qualified by pertinent law to hold the office being sought, or (3) has made a substantial showing of being a bona fide candidate by having participated in campaign activities such as making speeches, distributing literature or press releases, operating a campaign committee, or establishing a campaign headquarters.[116]

a) *Use.* The concept of "use," for purposes of Section 315, is defined in terms of an appearance by the actual candidate.[117] "Use [of] a broadcast station" has to be significant enough to activate the equal opportunity obligation. Appearances of a few seconds have been dismissed as inconsequential and not implicating the terms of the statute.[118] Use has been construed to include a comedian's satirical campaign for public office, despite claims it deprived him of his livelihood.[119] The broadcast of old movies starring Ronald Reagan, at the time he was running for the presidency, also proved to be a use for purposes of Section 315.[120]

Identifiable on-air talent, even if appearing in a routine role such as a newscaster that is unrelated to candidacy, is also subject to equal opportunity requirements.[121] Because equal opportunity obligations arise in connection with each appearance by a candidate, broadcast personnel may be compelled to leave their employment in the event they choose to run for public office. A challenge to Section 315 because it allegedly (1) deprived a journalist of the right to seek public office and (2) invaded First Amendment guarantees was rejected on both grounds.[122] In *Branch v. Federal Communications Commission,*[123] the court of appeals held that the law did not extinguish or unreasonably burden the claimant's right to run for public office.[124] Given the diminished First Amendment status of broadcasters, the appeals court concluded that a licensee's editorial discretion was not wrongfully diluted.[125] It thereby declined an invitation to find that the scarcity rationale was obsolete and that Section 315 was no longer constitutionally congruent.[126]

Branch v. Federal Communications Commission, 824 F.2d 37 (D.C. Cir. 1987)

Bork, Circuit Judge:

I

The petitioner, William Branch, is a television reporter who covers general assignments for station KOVR in Sacramento, California. He appears on the air in newscasts, on average, about three minutes per day, reporting stories assigned to him by the station. Branch lives in nearby Loomis, California, a small community of about 4,000 people. Beginning late in 1982, he participated in a successful effort to incorporate Loomis as a town. In 1984 Branch decided to seek election to the new Loomis town council.

Branch was aware that a federal statute—47 U.S.C. § 315(a) (1982)—imposes certain "equal time" burdens on broadcasters. He therefore consulted with station management for advice before commencing his campaign. The KOVR news editors calculated that the station would be required to provide thirty-three hours—or about one and a half broadcast days—of response time to Branch's opponents if he continued to work there during his campaign. They told Branch that KOVR was unwilling to provide that amount of time to his opponents, and that if he wished to maintain his candidacy he must take an unpaid leave of absence during the campaign, with no guarantee that he would be able to resume his duties after the election.

Branch immediately sought judicial and administrative determination of his rights, but was unable to get a ruling before the 1984 election. Put to a choice, he continued his work at KOVR and dropped out of the town council race. Upon terminating his candidacy, however, he filed a petition for a declaratory ruling from the Commission on the effect of the "equal opportunities" requirement in 47 U.S.C. § 315(a) on newscaster candidates. Branch sought a ruling that would enable him to run for the Loomis town council in a future election without requiring his employer to offer equal time to his opponents. He specifically asked the Commission to rule on two issues: whether the statute required broadcast stations to provide equal time to the opponents of newscaster candidates; and whether the statute was constitutional as so applied.

The Commission denied the petition. After reviewing the language and purposes of the statute, as well as its legislative history, the Commission concluded that newscaster candidates do not come within any special exemption from a station's statutory obligation to provide equal time to other candidates. . . .

III

Branch initially contends that the statute's "equal time" provisions do not apply to him because the statute exempts the television appearances of a newscaster candidate from their coverage. In matters of statutory construction, we "employ[] traditional tools of statutory construction," and "[i]f the intent of Congress is clear, that is the end of the matter." *Chevron U.S.A. Inc. v. Natural Resources Defense Council, Inc.,* 467 U.S. 837, 843–44 & n. 9 (1984). The statutory language at issue reads in full:

> If any licensee shall permit any person who is a legally qualified candidate for any public office to use a broadcasting station, he shall afford equal opportunities to all other candidates for the office in the use of such broadcasting station: *Provided,* That

such licensee shall have no power of censorship over the material broadcast under the provision of this section. No obligation is hereby imposed under this subsection upon any licensee to allow the use of its station by any such candidate. Appearance by a legally qualified candidate on any—

> (1) bona fide newscast,
>
> (2) bona fide news interview,
>
> (3) bona fide news documentary (if the appearance of the candidate is incidental to the presentation of the subject or subjects covered by the news documentary), or
>
> (4) on-the-spot coverage of bona fide news events (including but not limited to political conventions and activities incidental thereto),

shall not be deemed to be use of a broadcasting station within the meaning of this subsection. Nothing in the foregoing sentence shall be construed as relieving broadcasters, in connection with the presentation of newscasts, news interviews, news documentaries, and on-the-spot coverage of news events, from the obligation imposed upon them under this chapter to operate in the public interest and to afford reasonable opportunity for the discussion of conflicting views on issues of public importance.

47 U.S.C. § 315(a) (1982). Branch reads the statutory language to mean: the "equal opportunities" requirement applies only when there is a "use" of a broadcasting station; a candidate's appearance on a bona fide newscast does not constitute such a "use"; thus Branch's appearances on KOVR's bona fide news broadcasts are not subject to the "equal opportunities."

The legislative history of the 1959 amendments conclusively establishes three critical and overlapping points. First, Congress' central concern in taking action was to overrule the Commission's *Lar Daly* decision. E.g., S.Rep. No. 562, 86th Cong., 1st Sess. 2–10 (1959) U.S.Code Cong. & Admin.News 2564, 2565–2572; *id.* at 14 (additional views of Sen. Hartke) ("All of us agree on the importance of reporting a bill to reverse the *Lar Daly* decision."); H.R.Rep. No. 802, 86th Cong., 1st Sess. 2–4 (1959); *id.* at 18 (supplemental views of Reps. Mack & Hemphill) ("This legislation is a result of the clamor which followed that decision."). This concern was so important and so immediate that Congress was unwilling even to wait for that decision to be considered by the courts on appeal. See, e.g., H.R.Rep. No. 802, *supra,* at 4; 105 Cong.Rec. 16,230 (1959) (Reps. Harris & Pucinski); *id.* at 16,236 (Rep. Flynt).

Second, the purpose of overruling *Lar Daly* was to restore the understanding of the law that had prevailed previously. E.g., S.Rep. No. 562, *supra*, at 2–6, 17–19 U.S.Code Cong. & Admin.News at 2565–2570, 2579–2581; H.R.Rep. No. 802, *supra*, at 2–3. That understanding, as we have noted, required "equal opportunities" whenever any candidate appeared on the air, unless the candidate was the subject of "a routine news broadcast." ...

Third, Congress objected to the imposition of "equal opportunities" obligations on any station that carried news coverage of a candidate, because it deterred the broadcast media from providing the public with full coverage of political news events, and many other news events as well. E.g., S.Rep. No. 562, *supra*, at 9–10, 13, 14 U.S. Code Cong. & Admin.News at 2571–2573, 2575–2577; H.R.Rep. No. 802, *supra*, at 4–5. To the extent that Congress may have done more than reverse *Lar Daly*, by exempting broadcast coverage of news interviews and news documentaries in addition to newscasts and on-the-spot coverage of news events, it did so to protect a station's ability to exercise broad discretion in choosing which *newsworthy events* to present to the public.

Thus Congress' intent in enacting the amended section 315 is readily discernible. "Appearance by a legally qualified candidate," which is not "deemed to be use of a broadcasting station," is coverage of the candidate that is presented to the public as news. The "appearance" of the candidate is itself expected to be the newsworthy item that activates the exemption. "By modifying all four categories not deemed to be 'use' with the phrase 'bona fide,' Congress plainly emphasized its reliance on newsworthiness as the basis for an exemption." *Office of Communication of the United Church of Christ v. FCC*, 590 F.2d 1062, 1065 (D.C.Cir.1978).

The thrust of the language is brought out further in the third and fourth specific exemptions. The "news documentary" exemption applies only "if the appearance of the candidate is incidental to *the presentation of the subject or subjects covered by the news documentary*." 47 U.S.C. § 315(a)(3) (1982) (emphasis added). This passage relates the candidate's appearance to the subjects covered in the program. If the candidate's appearance has nothing to do with the subjects that are being covered

as news—whether because the candidate is a regular employee on all such programs or, to take another example, because the candidate is being offered a gratuitous appearance that realistically is unrelated to the news content of the program—then the exemption does not apply. Similarly, the fourth exemption for "on-the-spot coverage" of news applies only to "coverage of bona fide news events." *Id.* § 315(a)(4). Here again the focus is on a news *event* that is being covered, with the candidate's appearance expected to occur as part of the event *being covered.*

When a broadcaster's employees are sent out to cover a news story involving other persons, therefore, the "bona fide news event" is the activity engaged in by those other persons, not the work done by the employees covering the event. The work done by the broadcaster's employees is not a part of the event, for the event would occur without them and they serve only to communicate it to the public. For example, when a broadcaster's employees are sent out to cover a fire, the fire is the "bona fide news" event and the reporter does not become a part of that event merely by reporting it. There is nothing at all "newsworthy" about the work being done by the broadcaster's own employees, regardless of whether any of those employees happens also to be a candidate for public office.

This reading of the statute as not exempting newscasters is also compelled by the weight of the legislative history. As we have said, Congress' intent in the 1959 amendments was to return the industry to the situation that had prevailed before *Lar Daly*. The status quo before *Lar Daly* allowed a candidate to appear on the air as the *subject* of "routine" news coverage without triggering the "equal opportunities" rule, see *Blondy*, 40 F.C.C. at 285, but did not exempt appearances by a candidate who is "regularly employed as a station announcer." See 23 Fed.Reg. at 7818; *In re Kenneth E. Spengler*, 14 Rad.Reg. (P & F) 1226b (1957). Nowhere in the legislative history is there the slightest indication that Congress intended, for the first time, to sweep the latter class of appearances within the scope of the exemption.

Moreover, Congress' objection to *Lar Daly* was that it discouraged wide broadcast coverage of political news events by restricting a station's ability to determine which news *events* to present to the public. Congress solved this problem by exempting any on-air appearance by a candidate who is the *subject* of news coverage. It is irrelevant to that problem whether a station has broad discretion to determine which of its employees will actually present the news on the air. That issue may raise very different problems, which we will consider later, but it did not arise at all in Congress' debates on the 1959 amendments. On the contrary, considerable concern was voted about the possibility that "sham" news events—events that are not bona fide news but are staged by the candidate—might be seen as exempt from the "equal opportunities" rule. See, e.g., H.R. Rep. No. 802, *supra*, at 6; 105 Cong.Rec. 14,462 (1959) (Sen. Long) (the amendments apply to a candidate "when he was making news"); *id.* at 16,236 (Rep. MacDonald) ("staged events . . . should not be viewed as news"). This possibility was eventually foreclosed, however, by the wording of the fourth exemption. In denying any exemption for candidate appearances through "sham" news events, Congress once again expressed its view that exemption should be made only for on-air appearances that are intrinsically newsworthy. At all times, the focus was not on preserving anyone's "right" to appear on the air, but on preserving broadcasters' ability to present to the public certain kinds of news programs and news events.

In opposition to that consistent approach, Branch asks this court to read the phrase "[a]ppearance by a legally qualified candidate on any [news program]" as exempting from the "equal opportunities" rule all on air work done by newscaster candidates. We cannot do so. As we have already noted, such a reading would be at odds with the law before *Lar Daly*, which Congress explicitly sought to restore through the 1959 amendments. In addition, this reading would raise a station's news employees to an elevated status not shared by any of its other employees: although the work done on the air by any other employee on any other program would not be exempt, see, e.g., *Paulsen v. FCC*, 491 F.2d 887 (9th Cir.1974), the work done on the air by news employees would be. Yet this novel division was never endorsed, or even discussed, by Congress.

IV

We have determined that section 315 does not exempt newscaster candidates from the strictures of the "equal opportunities" rule. Branch challenges the statute, as so interpreted, on several constitutional grounds. . . .

A

Branch's first objection is that the statute extinguishes his right to seek political office. That he has such a right is undeniable, though the Constitution and the Supreme Court's cases in the area do not pinpoint the precise grounds on which it rests. See, e.g., *Jenness v. Fortson*, 403 U.S. 431, 438–40 (1971); *Lubin v. Panish*, 415 U.S. 709, 716 (1974); *Bullock v. Carter*, 405 U.S. 134, 142–43 (1972); *cf. Williams v. Rhodes*, 393 U.S. 23, 30–31 (1968). But whatever its source, the right is not implicated in this case. "In approaching candidate restrictions, it is essential to examine in a realistic light the extent and nature of their impact on voters." *Bullock*, 405 U.S. at 143. Here that impact is slight. The "equal opportunities" rule does not extinguish anyone's right to run for office. It simply provides that certain uses of a broadcast station by a candidate entitle other candidates for the same office to equal time. That the rule will affect some candidates favorably and others unfavorably is obvious. It may cause certain candidates to receive less time on the air than if the statute did not exist. But the Supreme Court has held that no individual has any right of access to the broadcast media. *Columbia Broadcasting System, Inc. v. Democratic Nat'l Comm.*, 412 U.S. 94 (1973). "It is the right of the viewers and listeners, not the right of the broadcasters, which is paramount." *Red Lion Broadcasting Co. v. FCC*, 395 U.S. 367, 390 (1969).

The core of Branch's challenge on this point is that the statute imposes an undue burden on his ability to run for office because he cannot, during the time he is a candidate, do his normal work of reporting news on the air for station KOVR. But nobody has ever thought that a candidate has a right to run for office and at the same time to avoid all personal sacrifice. See *United States Civil Serv. Comm'n v. National Ass'n of Letter Carriers*, 413 U.S. 548, 567 (1973) ("Neither the right to associate nor the right to pratcipate in political activities is absolute in any event.") Even if the practicalities of campaigning for office are put to one side, many people find it necessary to choose between their jobs and their candidacies. The Hatch Act requires government employees to resign from work if they wish to run for certain political offices, see 5 U.S.C. §§ 7324–7327 (1982), and involves many more intrusive restrictions as well, yet the Supreme Court has upheld it against constitutional challenge. See *Letter Carriers,* 413 U.S. 548; *United Public Workers v. Mitchell,* 330 U.S. 75 (1947). More recently, the Court upheld a Texas law that required certain public officials to resign from office if they wished to become candidates for certain other offices. *Clements v. Fashing,* 457 U.S. 957 (1982).

Indeed, the burdens Branch complains of are borne by all other radio and television personalities under section 315, though the exception he seeks would apply only to newscasters. In *Paulsen v. FCC,* 491 F.2d 887 (9th Cir.1974), those burdens were upheld against essentially the same objection made here. The petitioner, a television performer who had announced his candidacy for President, contended that section 315 "forces him to give up his means of livelihood as a television performer in order to run for office." *Id.* at 891–92. In *Paulsen* the challenge was clothed in an equal protection guise, and perhaps at bottom Branch's challenge is also one of equal protection. However that may be, the argument is the same, and so is the result.

B

Branch's second constitutional objection to section 315 is that the "equal opportunities" rule violates the first amendment. He cites *Miami Herald Publishing Co. v. Tornillo,* 418 U.S. 241 (1974), where the Supreme Court unanimously struck down a Florida law that gave political candidates a right to reply to criticisms and attacks published in newspapers. The Court held that the law compelled editors or publishers to publish material against their will, thus exacting an unconstitutional "penalty on the basis of the content of a newspaper." *Id.* at 256. The Court broadly declared that a "[g]overnment-enforced right of ac-

cess inescapably 'dampens the vigor and limits the variety of public debate.' " *Id.* at 257 (quoting *New York Times Co. v. Sullivan,* 376 U.S. 254, 279 (1964)). The "equal opportunities" rule, in Branch's view, is identical to a right-of-reply statute in its impact.

The Supreme Court has expressly held, however, that the first amendment's protections for the press do not apply as powerfully to the broadcast media. In *Red Lion Broadcasting Co. v. FCC,* 395 U.S. 367 (1969), the Court upheld the government's authority "to put restraints on licensees in favor of others whose views should be expressed on this unique medium." *Id.* at 390. What makes the broadcast medium unique, in the Court's view, is the scarcity of broadcast frequencies. *Id.* at 389–90.

While doubts have been expressed that the scarcity rationale is adequate to support differing degrees of first amendment protection for the print and electronic media, see, e.g., *Telecommunications Research & Action Center v. FCC,* 801 F.2d 501, 506–09 (D.C.Cir.), *reh'g denied,* 806 F.2d 1115 (1986); *Meredith Corp. v. FCC,* 809 F.2d 863, 866–67 (D.C.Cir.1987), it remains true, nonetheless, that Branch's first amendment challenge is squarely foreclosed by *Red Lion.* In *Red Lion,* the Supreme Court upheld as constitutional the Commission's authority to enforce the fairness doctrine, which requires broadcast stations to give fair coverage to each side of a public issue, and in particular upheld "its specific manifestations in the personal attack and political editorial rules." 395 U.S. at 386. In the course of its opinion, the Court held that the statutory "equal opportunities" rule in section 315 and the Commission's own fairness doctrine rested on the same constitutional basis of the government's power to regulate "a scarce resource which the Government has denied others the right to use." . . .

C

Branch's final constitutional challenge to section 315 is that it impermissibly limits the discretion of broadcast stations to select the particular people who will present news on the air to the public. Branch thus attempts to press the third-party rights of broadcasters who are not themselves parties to this case. Although the general rule is that a party "must assert his own legal rights and interests, and cannot rest his claim to relief on the legal rights or interests of third parties," *Warth v. Seldin,* 422 U.S. 490, 499 (1975), the Supreme Court has also stated that "[w]ithin the context of the First Amendment, the Court has enunciated...concerns that justify a lessening of prudential limitations on standing."

Here the "activity sought to be protected is at the heart of the business relationship between" Branch and KOVR, and Branch's "interests in challenging the statute are completely consistent with the First Amendment interests of the [broadcasters he] represents" It makes no difference that a broadcaster could bring this challenge in a separate suit.

Nonetheless, the third-party challenge Branch advances is rebutted by *Red Lion.* A burden on the ability to present a particular broadcaster on the air, which applies to all broadcasters irrespective of the content of the news they present, is a much less significant burden than rules requiring the transmission of replies to personal attacks and political editorials, which were upheld in *Red Lion.* The latter provisions apply directly to political speech, and weigh more heavily on some messages than on others, depending on the precise content of the message conveyed. In contrast, the burdens on broadcasters that Branch asserts here do not "impair the discretion of broadcasters to present their views on any issue or to carry any particular type of programming." *Columbia Broadcasting System, Inc. v. FCC,* 453 U.S. 367, 396–97 (1981). Moreover, we note again that there is no right of any particular individual to appear on television. See, e.g., *Columbia Broadcasting System, Inc. v. Democratic Nat'l Comm.,* 412 U.S. 94, 113 (1973).

The petition for review is, therefore,

Denied.

b) *Exemptions.* Even if its basic prerequisites are met, the contingent right of equal opportunity is not available in the event that a candidate's appearance is in the course of bona fide news coverage or a documentary. Section 315 imposes no affirmative duty to provide time, and a candidate's appearance in a:

(1) Bona fide newscast,

(2) Bona fide news interview,

(3) Bona fide news documentary (if the appearance of the candidate is incidental to the presentation of the subject or subjects covered by the news documentary), or

(4) On-the-spot coverage of bona fide news events (included but not limited to political conventions and activities incidental thereto), shall not be deemed to be use of a broadcasting station within the meaning of this subsection. Nothing in the foregoing sentence shall be construed as relieving broadcasters, in connection with the presentation of newscasts, news interviews, news documentaries and on-the-spot coverage of news events, from the obligation imposed upon them under this Act to operate in the public interest and to afford reasonable opportunity for the discussion of conflicting views on issues of public importance.[127]

The exemptions reflect congressional response to FCC rulings requiring equal opportunity for rivals of incumbents whose activities had been the subject of routine news reporting.[128] Section 315, as amended, attempts to strike a balance between general interests in an informed public and more particularized concern with the accrual of special advantage or influence in the course of a political campaign.

The question of what constitutes exempt programming has proved to be perhaps the thorniest issue under Section 315. Congress itself suspended the equal opportunity provision in 1960 to enable Democratic and Republican presidential candidates to debate without creating an obligation to provide time to other contestants. During the course of the 1964 campaign, the FCC rendered a decision that proved problematical to the coverage of news in the course of a political campaign. Specifically it determined that news conferences by an incumbent and primary rival were not exempt as "bona fide news events."[129] The ruling contrasted with a nearly simultaneous finding that the provision of network time to President Johnson, for discussion of two major foreign policy events several weeks before the election, qualified as "on the spot coverage of a bona fide news event."[130] Both rulings essentially reflected the commission's determination that the subjective judgment of the licensee alone should not determine the availability of the exemption. Later in 1972, the FCC determined that a regularly scheduled Sunday interview program, which was expanded from its normal length to feature a joint appearance by the two main candidates for the Democratic nomination, constituted a "bona fide news interview."[131] Upon review, the commission's ruling was reversed on the grounds that the departure from the normal format transformed the interview into a debate.[132] As a consequence, the FCC was compelled to order the award of free time to a candidate who had been excluded from the program.[133]

The operation of Section 315 thus proved to be troublesome insofar as free time obligations deterred coverage of news events and confounded any broadcast debates. Regulation designed to facilitate informed self-government was operating at cross-purposes with that goal. Since the mid–1970s, the commission has steered a course of review that is more deferential to a licensee's subjective judgment regarding the availability of an exemption. The FCC, moreover, initiated affirmative steps to ensure that political news reporting would not be chilled and that debates would not be impaired. News conferences or debates thus could be covered without incurring equal time obligations pursuant to a licensee's good faith determination that it was newsworthy.[134] The ruling reflected the

commission's growing sense that the risk of political favoritism was less than the danger of inadequate coverage of the issues central to self-government.[135]

The substantial deference now accorded licensee judgment was evinced in 1980 when President Carter held a news conference that was carried by all networks in prime time and contained several comments critical of his main rival for the Democratic nomination.[136] Despite any advantage that incumbency affords a candidate, the FCC refused to second-guess licensee determinations in the particular instance and asserted that it would not do so "absent strong evidence" that bona fide news judgment was not being exercised.[137]

c) *Lowest unit charge.* Congress has structured Section 315 in a way that prevents broadcasters from reaping windfall profits from the imperative of political campaigning. Rates for political candidates generally are not to exceed "charges made for comparable use of such stations by other users thereof."[138] That provision subjects candidates to general marketplace forces. During the forty-five-day period preceding a primary election or the sixty-day period preceding a federal election, however, rates for candidates may not exceed "the lowest unit charge of the station for the same class and amount of time for the same period."[139] The provision essentially obligates licensees to provide bulk discounts that would be afforded to their heaviest advertisers even if the candidate purchases time but once. Broadcasters are not required to eliminate rate classes based on the time of day or to extend the lowest unit rate to representatives of a candidate.[140]

d) *Censorship and liability.* A licensee is expressly prohibited from censoring any "material broadcast under the provisions of" Section 315.[141] Absent special protection, a liability problem would arise in the event a candidate beyond a licensee's control uttered actionable statements. The Supreme Court thus conferred upon broadcasters immunity from liability for any defamatory comments made by a candidate in the course of a Section 315 appearance.[142] In so doing, it also exempted such remarks altogether from actionability in the form of a traditional defamation action.[143] Such a determination was considered to be essential to a full effectuation of the legislation's underlying purpose.[144]

Farmers Educational and Cooperative Union of America v. WDAY, Inc., 360 U.S. 525 (1959)

Mr. Justice Black delivered the opinion of the Court.

We must decide whether § 315 of the Federal Communications Act of 1934 bars a broadcasting station from removing defamatory statements contained in speeches broadcast by legally qualified candidates for public office, and if so, whether that section grants the station a federal immunity from liability for libelous statements so broadcast. Section 315 reads:

> (a) If any licensee shall permit any person who is a legally qualified candidate for any public office to use a broadcasting station, he shall afford equal opportunities to all other such candidates for that office in the use of such broadcasting station: *Provided,* That such licensee shall have no power of censorship over the material broadcast under the provisions of this section. No obligation is imposed upon any licensee to allow the use of its station by any such candidate.

This suit for libel arose as a result of a speech made over the radio and television facilities of respondent, WDAY, Inc., by A. C. Townley—a legally qualified candidate in the 1956 United States senatorial race in North Dakota. Because it felt compelled to do so by the requirements of § 315, WDAY permitted Townley to broadcast

his speech, uncensored in any respect, as a reply to previous speeches made over WDAY by two other senatorial candidates. Townley's speech, in substance, accused his opponents, together with petitioner, Farmers Educational and Cooperative Union of America, of conspiring to "establish a Communist Farmers Union Soviet right here in North Dakota." Farmers Union then sued Townley and WDAY for libel in a North Dakota State District Court. That court dismissed the complaint against WDAY on the ground that § 315 rendered the station immune from liability for the defamation alleged. . . .

Petitioner alternatively argues that § 315 does not grant a station immunity from liability for defamatory statements made during a political broadcast even though the section prohibits the station from censoring allegedly libelous matter. Again, we cannot agree. For under this interpretation, unless a licensee refuses to permit any candidate to talk at all, the section would sanction the unconscionable result of permitting civil and perhaps criminal liability to be imposed for the very conduct the statute demands of the licensee. Accordingly, judicial interpretations reaching the issue have found an immunity implicit in the section. And in all those cases concluding that a licensee had no immunity, § 315 had been construed—improperly as we hold—to permit a station to censor potentially actionable material. In no case has a court even implied that the licensee would not be rendered immune were it denied the power to censor libelous material.

We are aware that causes of action for libel are widely recognized throughout the States. But we have not hesitated to abrogate state law where satisfied that its enforcement would stand "as an obstacle to the accomplishment and execution of the full purposes and objectives of Congress." Here, petitioner is asking us to attribute to § 315 a meaning which would either frustrate the underlying purposes for which it was enacted, or alternatively impose unreasonable burdens on the parties governed by that legislation. In the absence of clear expression by Congress we will not assume that it desired such a result. Agreeing with the state courts of North Dakota that § 315 grants a licensee an immunity from liability for

libelous material it broadcasts, we merely read §
315 in accordance with what we believe to be its
underlying purpose.

4) *Reasonable access for political candidates.*
Unlike rules governing political editorials,
personal attacks, and equal opportunity,
Section 312(a) (7) of the Communications
Act[145] affords political candidates a right of
reasonable access that is affirmative rather
than contingent in nature. Without such a
right, it is conceivable that a licensee could
avoid equal opportunity obligations altogether by denying time to any candidate. By
its terms, Section 312(a) (7) authorizes the
FCC to revoke a license "for willful or repeated failure to allow reasonable access
to or to permit purchase of reasonable
amounts of time for the use of a broadcasting station by a legally qualified candidate for Federal elective office on behalf
of his candidacy."[146] In operation, the law
has been read as "creat[ing] an affirmative,
promptly enforceable right of reasonable access to the use of broadcast stations for individual candidates seeking federal elective
office."[147]

The access right was formally recognized,
in *CBS, Inc. v. Federal Communications Commission,*[148] after three networks responded
negatively to requests by President Carter's
reelection committee to purchase half an
hour of air time.[149] The Court found generally "that the statutory rights of access . . .
properly balances the First Amendment
rights of federal candidates, the public, and
broadcasters."[150] It distinguished the limited
access right from a general right of access,[151]
rejected several years earlier,[152] and found
the former permissible because it did not
significantly cramp editorial discretion.[153]
Moreover, the Court found the right of reasonable access promotive of the First
Amendment interests not only of candidates
in presenting but of the public in receiving

"information necessary for the operation of
the democratic process."[154]

CBS, Inc. v. Federal Communications Commission, 453 U.S. 367 (1981)

Chief Justice Burger delivered the opinion of the
Court.

We granted certiorari to consider whether the
Federal Communications Commission properly
construed 47 U.S.C. § 312(a)(7) and determined
that petitioners failed to provide "reasonable access to . . . the use of a broadcasting station" as
required by the statute. 449 U.S. 950 (1980).

I

A

On October 11, 1979, Gerald M. Rafshoon,
President of the Carter-Mondale Presidential
Committee, requested each of the three major
television networks to provide time for a 30-
minute program between 8 p.m. and 10:30 p.m.
on either the 4th, 5th, 6th, or 7th of December
1979. The Committee intended to present, in
conjunction with President Carter's formal announcement of his candidacy, a documentary
outlining the record of his administration.

The networks declined to make the requested
time available. Petitioner CBS emphasized the
large number of candidates for the Republican
and Democratic Presidential nominations and
the potential disruption of regular programming
to accommodate requests for equal treatment,
but it offered to sell two 5-minute segments to
the Committee, one at 10:55 p.m. on December
8 and one in the daytime. Petitioner American
Broadcasting Cos. replied that it had not yet
decided when it would begin selling political
time for the 1980 Presidential campaign, but
subsequently indicated that it would allow such
sales in January 1980. App. 58. Petitioner National Broadcasting Co., noting the number of
potential requests for time from Presidential
candidates, stated that it was not prepared to

sell time for political programs as early as December 1979.

On October 29, 1979, the Carter-Mondale Presidential Committee filed a complaint with the Federal Communications Commission, charging that the networks had violated their obligation to provide "reasonable access" under § 312(a)(7) of the Communications Act of 1934, as amended. Title 47 U.S.C. § 312(a)(7), as added to the Act, 86 Stat. 4, states:

> The Commission may revoke any station license or construction permit—
>
> . . . . .
>
> (7) for willful or repeated failure to allow reasonable access to or to permit purchase of reasonable amounts of time for the use of a broadcasting station by a legally qualified candidate for Federal elective office on behalf on his candidacy....

Perhaps the most telling evidence of congressional intent, ... is the contemporaneous amendment of § 315(a) of the Communications Act. That amendment was described by the Conference Committee as a "conforming amendment" necessitated by the enactment of § 312(a)(7). S. Conf. Rep. No. 92–580, *supra,* at 22; H. Conf. Rep. No. 92–752, *supra,* at 22. Prior to the "conforming amendment," the second sentence of 47 U.S.C. § 315(a) (1970 ed.) read: "No obligation is imposed upon any licensee to allow the use of its station by any such candidate." This language made clear that broadcasters were not common carriers as to affirmative, rather than responsive, requests for access. As a result of the amendment, the second sentence now contains an important qualification: "No obligation is imposed *under this subsection* upon any licensee to allow the use of its station by any such candidate." 47 U.S.C. § 315(a) (emphasis added). Congress retreated from its statement that "no obligation" exists to afford individual access presumably because § 312(a)(7) compels such access in the context of federal elections. If § 312(a)(7) simply reaffirmed the pre-existing public interest requirement with the added sanction of license revocation, no conforming amendment to § 315(a) would have been needed.

Thus, the legislative history supports the plain meaning of the statute that individual candidates for federal elective office have a right of reasonable access to the use of stations for paid political broadcasts on behalf of their candidacies, without reference to whether an opponent has secured time....

In support of their narrow reading of § 312(a)(7) as simply a restatement of the public interest obligation, petitioners cite our decision in *Columbia Broadcasting System, Inc. v. Democratic National Committee,* 412 U.S. 94 (1973), which held that neither the First Amendment nor the Communications Act requires broadcasters to accept paid editorial advertisements from citizens at large. The Court in *Democratic National Committee* observed that "the Commission on several occasions has ruled that no private individual or group has a right to command the use of broadcast facilities," and that Congress has not altered that policy even though it has amended the Communications Act several times. *Id.,* at 113. In a footnote, on which petitioners here rely, we referred to the then recently enacted § 312(a)(7) as one such amendment, stating that it had "essentially codified the Commission's prior interpretation of § 315(a) as requiring broadcasters to make time available to political candidates." *Id.,* at 113–114, n. 12.

However, "the language of an opinion is not always to be parsed as though we were dealing with language of a statute." *Reiter v. Sonotone Corp.,* 442 U.S., at 341. The qualified observation that § 312(a)(7) "essentially codified" existing Commission practice was not a conclusion that the statute was in all respects coextensive with that practice and imposed no additional duties on broadcasters. In *Democratic National Committee,* we did not purport to rule on the precise contours of the responsibilities created by § 312(a) (7) since that issue was not before us. Like the general public interest standard and the equal opportunities provision of § 315(a), § 312(a)(7) reflects the importance attached to the use of the public airwaves by political candidates. Yet we now hold that § 312(a)(7) expanded on those predecessor requirements and granted a new right of access to persons seeking election to federal office.

Although Congress provided in § 312(a) (7) for greater use of broadcasting stations by federal candidates, it did not give guidance on how the Commission should implement the statute's access requirement. Essentially, Congress adopted a "rule of reason" and charged the Commission with its enforcement. Pursuant to 47 U.S.C. § 303(r), which empowers the Commission to "[m]ake such rules and regulations and prescribe such restrictions and conditions, not inconsistent with law, as may be necessary to carry out the provisions of [the Communications Act]," the agency has developed standards to effectuate the guarantees of § 312(a)(7). See also 47 U.S.C. § 154(i). The Commission has issued some general interpretative statements, but its standards implementing § 312(a)(7) have evolved principally on a case-by-case basis and are not embodied in formalized rules. The relevant criteria broadcasters must employ in evaluating access requests under the statute can be summarized from the Commission's 1978 Report and Order and the memorandum opinions and orders in these cases.

Broadcasters are free to deny the sale of air time prior to the commencement of a campaign, but once a campaign has begun, they must give reasonable and good-faith attention to access requests from "legally qualified" candidates for federal elective office. Such requests must be considered on an individualized basis, and broadcasters are required to tailor their responses to accommodate, as much as reasonably possible, a candidate's stated purposes in seeking air time. In responding to access requests, however, broadcasters may also give weight to such factors as the amount of time previously sold to the candidate, the disruptive impact on regular programming, and the likelihood of requests for time by rival candidates under the equal opportunities provision of § 315(a). These considerations may not be invoked as pretexts for denying access; to justify a negative response, broadcasters must cite a realistic danger of substantial program disruption—perhaps caused by insufficient notice to allow adjustments in the schedule—or of an excessive number of equal time requests. Further, in order to facilitate review by the Commission, broadcasters must explain their reasons for refusing time or making a more limited counteroffer. If broadcasters take the appropriate factors into account and act reasonably and in good faith, their decisions will be entitled to deference even if the Commission's analysis would have differed in the first instance. But if broadcasters adopt "across-the-board policies" and do not attempt to respond to the individualized situation of a particular candidate, the Commission is not compelled to sustain their denial of access. . . .

The Commission has concluded that, as a threshold matter, it will independently determine whether a campaign has begun and the obligations imposed by § 312(a)(7) have attached. 74 F.C.C 2d, at 665–666. Petitioners assert that, in undertaking such a task, the Commission becomes improperly involved in the electoral process and seriously impairs broadcaster discretion.

However, petitioners fail to recognize that the Commission does not set the starting date for a campaign. Rather, on review of a complaint alleging denial of "reasonable access," it examines objective evidence to find whether the campaign has already commenced, "taking into account the position of the candidate *and the networks* as well as other factors." *Id.*, at 665 (emphasis added). As the Court of Appeals noted, the "determination of when the statutory obligations attach does not control the electoral process, . . . the determination is controlled by the process." 202 U.S. App. D.C., at 384, 629 F. 2d, at 16. Such a decision is not, and cannot be, purely one of editorial judgment.

Moreover, the Commission's approach serves to narrow § 312(a) (7), which might be read as vesting access rights in an individual candidate as soon as he becomes "legally qualified" without regard to the status of the campaign. See n. 11, *supra.* By confining the applicability of the statute to the period after a campaign commences, the Commission has limited its impact on broadcasters and given substance to its command of *reasonable* access.

Just prior to the *CBS, Inc.* decision, an appeals court determined that "broadcasters may fulfill their obligation [under Section 312(a) (7)] either by allotting free time to a candidate *or* by selling the candidate time at the rates prescribed by Section 315(b)."[155] In *Kennedy for President Committee v. Federal Communications Commission*,[156] the court of appeals denied a candidate's request for free time under Section 312(a)(7) to respond to a rival's critical remarks.[157] It concluded that the provision did not create a right to use a licensee's "facilities without charge."[158] The court further observed that a contingent right to reply for free would undercut the exemptions for bona fide news reporting and documentaries created by Section 315(a).[159] A legitimate claim under Section 312(a)(7) would have been presented, therefore, only if the candidate had been denied an opportunity to purchase time.[160]

3. Fairness Regulation Reconsidered

The existence of fairness regulation and the operation of the fairness doctrine in particular have provoked extensive controversy especially after the Supreme Court constitutionalized the concept in 1969.[161] Criticism has been couched in both practical and First Amendment terms. Although consistently dismissed by the FCC for more than a decade, arguments against the fairness doctrine ultimately were subscribed to by the FCC itself in abandoning it.[162]

In respectively formulating and validating the fairness doctrine, the FCC and the Court originally assumed that it would ensure comprehensive and balanced coverage of controversial public issues.[163] Detractors maintained that instead of facilitating robust debate, the fairness doctrine miscomprehended marketplace forces and thus deterred it.[164] Because profit optimization is a function of audience maximization, television programming strategies cater to mainstream tastes.[165] Such commentary echoed Justice Brennan's sense that orthodox rather than provocative controversy was the result of licensee concerns with potential alienation of audience and sponsors who might be offended by radical or unpopular views.[166] Also identified as a factor contributing to "safe controversy" was a broadcaster's desire to minimize the risk of a fairness complaint.[167] Presaging fairness deregulation was the following article which was co-authored by a critic soon before being appointed FCC chairman.

Fowler and Brenner, A Marketplace Approach to Broadcast Regulation, 60 Tex. L.Rev. 207 (1982)

...

D. THE FLAWED RATIONALES SUPPORTING THE MODEL

1. Defects of the Scarcity Rationale.—Spectrum scarcity always has been the cornerstone of the justification for abandoning the marketplace approach and reducing first amendment protection for broadcasters. The Supreme Court pointed to spectrum scarcity in its ratification of the trusteeship model in *NBC,* and the Court has cited scarcity in some of its other, although not in all, pronouncements supporting Commission content regulation. But the use of spectrum scarcity to justify "public interest" determinations over licensees is fraught with serious logical and empirical infirmities.

First, virtually all goods in society are scarce. In most sectors of the economy, the interplay of supply and demand regulates the distribution of goods. If a good becomes especially scarce, its price is bid up. Ideally the highest bidder will make the best use of the resource. The application of the trusteeship model to broadcasting is a substantial deviation from the ordinary allocation of scarce goods and services in society.

One might argue, however, that deviations from the market should occur with regard to communications media. For instance, in wartime the government might be justified in regulating the amount of newsprint any one paper received. The supply of newsprint could be reduced for newspapers intending to print only comics or other purely entertainment features. But no factors remotely comparable exist in broadcasting today. Yet the trusteeship model results in broadcast regulation that resembles this hypothetical.

Apart from this basic misunderstanding of scarcity, other factors should lead to a rejection of the belief that a condition of true scarcity prevails in broadcasting. Scarcity is a relative concept even when applied to the limited spectrum earmarked for broadcast use. Additional channels can be added, without increasing the portion reserved for broadcast, by decreasing the bandwidth of each channel. Technology is an independent variable that makes scarcity a relative concept. At some point, quality becomes so reduced or costs so great that new channels should not be added. But until that point is reached, saturation of the spectrum has not occurred. The continued evolution of spectrum efficiency techniques makes it difficult to say with certainty that saturation of channels will ever be permanent in any market.

Channels can also be added by revising the interference rules. The Commission has traditionally shied away from this solution because of concerns about the risk of degrading signal quality. Under the present allocation scheme, the Commission assigns frequencies for television and FM radio to localities throughout the United States. The Commission created a master "table of allocations" to accomplish this purpose. New assignments are added to the tables quite frequently in FM and occasionally in television. In addition, less than full strength service, such as low-power television, which radiates in an area as small as one-tenth of the typical television service area, can be added to the existing allocation scheme without creating destructive interference.

The Commission's approach to AM radio has been to allow new stations to "shoe-horn" in, based on predicted levels of interference with existing stations. By allowing this expansion of AM service, the Commission has acknowledged that new outlets can be brought to the market without the need for finite limits. The stream of new AM stations is proof of the dubiety of scarcity in that band. Indeed, the Commission is considering a similar demand-based approach to the FM band. In short, the theoretically scarce airwaves continue to absorb more and more new channels and could accommodate additional channels. The only major factor limiting expansion—other than unacceptable levels of interference—is the cost of accommodating those new channels.

The scarcity rationale focuses on the wrong scarce resource, megahertz, instead of advertising dollars. Even in the indirect marketplace of over-the-air commercial broadcasting, the number of stations depends on the amount of advertising dollars or on other funding sources in the community. Except in the largest cities, where the Commission's allocation policies have limited the number of outlets, advertising support or subscriber dollars restrict broadcast opportunities more than does the number of channels.

In addition, scarcity is not the only reason behind the present limited number of VHF television stations (channels 2–13), which are the most profitable outlets. The Commission's allocation of only three VHF commercial outlets in most communities is hardly an unavoidable product of the limited ether; rather, it derives from the Commission's landmark allocation scheme for television, the *Sixth Report and Order*. The goal of the *Sixth Report* was to ensure as far as possible that most communities in the United States would have at least one local television channel, preferably VHF. The arrangement, however, has resulted in a national distribution system in which at most only three VHF commercial outlets prevail in most markets. As Commission studies have found, this "three to a market" approach of the *Sixth Report* assures the dominant position of the commercial television networks. At the very least, one can hardly explain the availability of only the three VHF television outlets carrying the three commercial networks as a force of nature caused by a limited spectrum. It should serve instead as a basis for authorizing more outlets, not for regulating those that already exist.

The scarcity upon which the trusteeship model relies exists only in some, not all, markets. Even under the current allocation scheme, which assigns fewer channels than could be accommodated on the available spectrum, channels outside larger cities go wanting for lack of a taker. This situation is especially true for allocations in the UHF band, where some channels have remained unclaimed for decades. It is capricious to justify regulation of broadcasters in nonsaturated markets by claiming that their operation employs a scarce resource unavailable to potential entrants in other markets.

Scarcity does exist in the sense that there is no more room for additional full-power VHF stations in the largest markets under current levels of permitted interference. Yet one can always buy an existing station, just as one may be likelier to consider buying an existing newspaper operation than trying to launch a new one. Furthermore, the current complement of VHF stations exceeds the number of daily newspapers in large cities, and the total number of broadcast outlets far exceeds the number of daily circulated newspapers. So a relatively low number of outlets in one medium should not lead to content-based rules in another.[a]

Finally, the scarcity notion also fails to recognize the substitutes for over-the-air distribution. In audio service, cassette and phono disc recordings vie with AM and FM channels and their subcarrier services like Muzak. Cable television, low-power television, multipoint distribution service, cassette and disc, and, in the future, direct broadcast satellites provides substitutes for over-the-air video service in many markets. A five-meter backyard satellite dish can, for those who can afford them, bring in more channels "off the air" than a television antenna picks up in a city with the greatest number of stations on the air.

Nonspectrum-utilizing distribution modes like cable and video cassette provide virtually limitless diversity of scheduling and content. Where new high-capacity cable systems are in place, no scarcity exists with respect to the television spectrum. What may inhibit the number of cable channels, is again, a scarcity of dollars to support advertiserbased or subscription channels. Similarly, choice in video cassette programming is completely determined by what the consumer is willing to spend for software.[b] Thus, the scarcity

rationale, as used to justify the regulation of broadcasting in a different manner than other media, misperceives what scarcity is in a free economy. Moreover, it ignores the practical realities that go a long way toward explaining the limited number of channels in some markets.

Even if one assumes that the absence of more television channel space in the largest markets justifies a licensing policy in those markets, this assumption establishes nothing about the form the regulations should take. The trusteeship model endorsed the giant leap from scarcity to the current panoply of federal regulation over all broadcasters, not just those in saturated markets. Logic, however, does not support the assumption that the trusteeship scheme is more likely to maximize consumer welfare, even in markets without available outlets, than would a system relying on the judgment of marketplace players.

The fairness doctrine also proved troubling because of the potential it created for a meddlesome official role. The possibility of such treachery, enabling "administration after administration to toy with radio or TV in order to serve . . . sordid or . . . benevolent ends,"[168] was adverted to by Chief Judge Bazelon in the following article.

Bazelon, FCC Regulation of the Telecommunications Press, 1975 DUKE L.J. 213*

> The main, main thing is The Post is going to have damnable, damnable problems out of this one. They have a television station. . . . And they're going to have to get it renewed.
>
> Taped Statement of Richard Nixon to H. R. Haldeman and John Dean, Sept. 15, 1972.

This statement is indicative, albeit an unusual example, of the First Amendment problems raised

---

a. Professor Emerson argues that the significant comparison among media is the number of printing presses versus the number of persons who wish to use broadcast facilities, not the number of newspapers versus the number of stations. T. Emerson, The System of Freedom of Expression 662 (1970). Because the number of printing presses or copying machines is not limited by spectrum slots, television is the "scarcer" medium. But this distinction fails to distinguish between a medium of individual communication and a medium of mass communication. The distribution available by mimeograph and paper pales next to the circulation of a major daily paper; it is not an adequate substitute for the reach of a daily. Just because anyone has access to a copier does not mean that he can start a successful daily paper. The limiting factor in broadcasting is the same as in print: economic support.

b. In evaluating the "scarcity" of outlets for information, it is important to consider all information providers, from broadcast outlets and newspapers to magazines, paperback books, direct mail fliers, billboards, posters, handbills, sound trucks, and tee shirts.

All of these provide some form of expression and each undercuts the significance of broadcast stations as necessary outlets for expression.

*Copyright 1975. Duke University School of Law.

by a comprehensive system for the licensing of speakers. Individuals who must obtain permission to engage in activity protected by the First Amendment are vulnerable to the various sub silentio pressures that prior approval permits and which Richard Nixon threatens in the statement quoted above. They may, therefore, find it easier to tailor their views to the wishes of the licensor rather than risk its displeasure. The manner in which the licensor conveys its wishes or exercises pressure on the speaker under a comprehensive licensing scheme often is disguised in an apparently noncoercive action, which might seem innocuous to others not subject to the licensing scheme. Control of these pressures is thus particularly difficult. The motivation for communicating pressure may involve the rather crass political concerns voiced by Richard Nixon in the statement quoted above. The motivation may range from racial discrimination to a laudable desire to upgrade the quality of the particular speech involved. But under the First Amendment, the licensor's motivation should be irrelevant: the exercise of power over speech leads the government knee-deep into regulation of expression. And that, we have always assumed, is forbidden by the First Amendment. The Supreme Court has so held, time and again.

But traditional assumptions do not apply to the regulation of telecommunications speech. The licensing scheme mandated by the Federal Communications Act permits a wide-ranging and largely uncontrolled administrative discretion in the review of telecommunications programming. That discretion has been used, as we might expect and as traditional First Amendment doctrine presumes, to apply sub silentio pressure against speech in the following instances: to discourage broadcast of song lyrics that allegedly promote the use of drugs, to halt radio talk shows that deal explicitly with sex, to discourage specialized or highly opinionated programming, to force networks to schedule "adult" programming after 9:00 p.m., and to restrict, through Executive Office pressure, adverse commentary on presidential speeches. The methods of communicating these pressures are by now familiar to FCC practitioners: the prominent speech by a Commissioner, the issuance of a notice of inquiry, an official statement of licensee responsibility

couched in general terms but directed against specific programming, setting the licensee down for a hearing on "misrepresentations," forwarding listener complaints with requests for a formal response to the FCC, calling network executives to "meetings" in the office of the Chairman of the FCC or of some other Executive Branch officials, compelled disclosure of future programming on forms with already delineated categories and imposing specific regulatory action on a particularly visible offender against this background. All these actions assume their *in terrorem* effect because of the FCC power to deny renewal of broadcast licenses or to order a hearing on the renewal application. Recently, there have been indications that the threat of antitrust or Internal Revenue Service actions has served to buttress certain "raised eyebrow" suggestions. I do not mean by recitation of these examples to alert you to a great danger or to engage in any sort of journalistic effort to inform the public. This has been fully accomplished by persons more able than myself. My only concern is with the legal implications of these examples in the context of our traditional constitutional order.

I should perhaps admit that, in at least one incident, appellate judges also have engaged in such "raised eyebrow" tactics. I speak of a speech I gave to the Federal Communications Bar on the Fortieth Anniversary of the FCC. There, as in part I do here, I criticized the performance of the broadcast media and suggested in general terms that the media devote more attention to the public interest, as they themselves know the public interest. It is certainly easy to criticize the broadcast media, and I am sure many readers of this Article have experienced the desire to "chill" the media into adopting one policy or another. I criticize not the seductiveness of this enterprise— because, after all, that is free speech too—but rather the background against which the criticism echoes and which makes the criticism, at least when made by the FCC, much more potent than its persuasiveness would require. I am aware that unless we are willing to do away with the entire system of program regulation, the line between permissible regulatory activity and impermissible "raised eyebrow" harassment of vulnerable licensees will be exceedingly vague. The fact remains, however, that the use of "raised eyebrow" tactics presents serious issues which should at least engage our undivided attention as we review communications policy and the Constitution.

Beyond these various forms of "raised eyebrow" regulation, the Federal Communications Act permits more overt forms of speech regulation: these include the Fairness Doctrine (encompassing also the equal time and editorial reply rules) and review of programming at license renewal and at assignment to determine whether past and proposed future programming meets the FCC's criteria of balance.

I think it is beyond cavil that we would not tolerate this sort of regulation in any context other than telecommunications; the First Amendment would forbid it. But somehow telecommunications speech is different and permits, many think, a different First Amendment regime.

By imposing fairness responsibilities upon broadcasters, the FCC reserved for itself significant content-related and editorial responsibility. In deference to traditional notions of freedom of the press, however, the commission in reviewing fairness complaints almost invariably presumed and deferred to good faith licensee judgment.[169] An actual fairness violation proved to be the rare exception in a system affording licensees broad leeway "in selecting the manner of coverage, the appropriate spokesmen, and the technique of production and presentation."[170] Such deference to constitutional imperatives, however, fueled objections that the fairness doctrine offered little utility in exchange for potentially profound First Amendment treachery.

The fairness doctrine thus had become subject to comprehensive reproach for deviating from traditional First Amendment norms that protected editorial autonomy, actually disserving the public's paramount right to receive program diversity and endangering First Amendment values generally. By the mid–1980s, concerns and distress that previously had been confined to dissenting opinion[171] or critical commentary began surfacing in mainstream jurisprudence and the FCC's own reassessments. In *Federal Communications Commission v. League of Women Voters of California,*[172] the Supreme Court effectively invited Congress or the FCC to notify it if the time had come to discard the fairness doctrine's scarcity rationale as an obsolete notion.[173] Although it did not directly review the fairness requirement itself, the Court in two significant footnotes acknowledged the pertinence of forces that might have undercut the viability of scarcity.[174] It also made clear that the commission was welcome to demonstrate that the fairness doctrine undermined rather than advanced First Amendment interests.[175]

Federal Communications Commission v. League of Women Voters of California, 468 U.S. 364 (1984)

Justice Brennan delivered the opinion of the Court.

The fundamental principles that guide our evaluation of broadcast regulation are by now well established. First, we have long recognized that Congress, acting pursuant to the Commerce Clause, has power to regulate the use of this scarce and valuable national resource. The distinctive feature of Congress' efforts in this area has been to ensure through the regulatory oversight of the FCC that only those who satisfy the "public interest, convenience, and necessity" are granted a license to use radio and television broadcast frequencies. 47 U.S.C. § 309(a).[a]

---

a. See *FCC v. National Citizens Committee for Broadcasting,* 436 U.S. 775, 799–800 (1978); *Columbia Broadcasting System, Inc. v. Democratic National Committee,* 412 U.S. 94, 101–102 (1973); *Red Lion Broadcasting Co. v. FCC,* 395 U.S. 367, 387–390 (1969); *National Broadcasting Co. v. United States,* 319 U.S. 190, 216 (1943); *Federal Radio Comm'n v. Nelson Bros. Bond & Mortgage Co.,* 289 U.S. 266, 282 (1933).

The prevailing rationale for broadcast regulation

Second, Congress may, in the exercise of this power, seek to assure that the public receives through this medium a balanced presentation of information on issues of public importance that otherwise might not be addressed if control of the medium were left entirely in the hands of those who own and operate broadcasting stations. Although such governmental regulation has never been allowed with respect to the print media, *Miami Herald Publishing Co. v. Tornillo*, 418 U.S. 241 (1974), we have recognized that "differences in the characteristics of new media justify differences in the First Amendment standards applied to them." *Red Lion Broadcasting Co. v. FCC*, 395 U.S. 367, 386 (1969). The fundamental distinguishing characteristic of the new medium of broadcasting that, in our view, has required some adjustment in First Amendment analysis is that "[b]roadcast frequencies are a scarce resource [that] must be portioned out among applicants." *Columbia Broadcasting System, Inc. v. Democratic National Committee*, 412 U.S. 94, 101 (1973). Thus, our cases have taught that, given spectrum scarcity, those who are granted a license to broadcast must serve in a sense as fiduciaries for the public by presenting "those views and voices which are representative of [their] community and which would otherwise, by necessity, be barred from the airwaves." *Red Lion, supra*, at 389. As we observed in that case, because "[i]t is the purpose of the First Amendment to preserve an uninhibited marketplace of ideas in which truth will ultimately prevail, . . . the right of the public to receive suitable access to social, political, esthetic, moral, and other ideas and experiences [through the medium of broadcasting] is crucial here [and it] may not consti-

tutionally be abridged either by Congress or by the FCC." 395 U.S., at 390.

Finally, although the Government's interest in ensuring balanced coverage of public issues is plainly both important and substantial, we have, at the same time, made clear that broadcasters are engaged in a vital and independent form of communicative activity. As a result, the First Amendment must inform and give shape to the manner in which Congress exercises its regulatory power in this area. Unlike common carriers, broadcasters are "entitled under the First Amendment to exercise 'the widest journalistic freedom consistent with their public [duties].' " *CBS, Inc. v. FCC*, 453 U.S. 367, 395 (1981) (quoting *Columbia Broadcasting System, Inc. v. Democratic National Committee, supra*, at 110). See also *FCC v. Midwest Video Corp.*, 440 U.S. 689, 703 (1979). Indeed, if the public's interest in receiving a balanced presentation of views is to be fully served, we must necessarily rely in large part upon the editorial initiative and judgment of the broadcasters who bear the public trust. See *Columbia Broadcasting System, Inc. v. Democratic National Committee, supra*, at 124–127.

Our prior cases illustrate these principles. In *Red Lion*, for example, we upheld the FCC's "fairness doctrine"—which requires broadcasters to provide adequate coverage of public issues and to ensure that this coverage fairly and accurately reflects the opposing views—because the doctrine advanced the substantial governmental interest in ensuring balanced presentations of views in this limited medium and yet posed no threat that a "broadcaster [would be denied permission] to carry a particular program or to publish his own views." 395 U.S., at 396.[b] Similarly, in *CBS, Inc.*

---

based on spectrum scarcity has come under increasing criticism in recent years. Critics, including the incumbent Chairman of the FCC, charge that with the advent of cable and satellite television technology, communities now have access to such a wide variety of stations that the scarcity doctrine is obsolete. See, e.g., Fowler & Brenner, A Marketplace Approach to Broadcast Regulation, 60 *Texas L. Rev.* 207, 221–226 (1982). We are not prepared, however, to reconsider our longstanding approach without some signal from Congress or the FCC that technological developments have advanced so far that some revision of the system of broadcast regulation may be required.

b. We note that the FCC, observing that "[i]f any substantial possibility exists that the [fairness doctrine] rules have impeded, rather than furthered, First Amendment objectives, repeal may be warranted on that ground alone," has tentatively concluded that the rules, by effectively chilling speech, do not serve the public interest, and has therefore proposed to repeal them. Notice of Proposed Rulemaking In re Repeal or Modification of the Personal Attack and Political Editorial Rules, 48 Fed. Reg. 28298, 28301 (1983). Of course, the Commission may, in the exercise of its discretion, decide to modify or abandon these rules, and we express no view on the legality of either course. As *v. FCC, supra,* the Court upheld the right of access for federal candidates imposed by § 312(a)(7) of the Communications Act both because that provision "makes a significant contribution to freedom of expression by enhancing the ability of candidates to present, and the public to receive, information necessary for the effective operation of the democratic process," *id.,* at 396, and because it defined a sufficiently *"limited* right of 'reasonable' access" so that "the discretion of broadcasters to present their views on any issue or to carry any particular type of programming" was not impaired. *Id.,* at 396–397 (emphasis in original). Finally, in *Columbia Broadcasting System, Inc. v. Democratic National Committee, supra,* the Court affirmed the FCC's refusal to require broadcast licensees to accept all paid political advertisements. Although it was argued that such a requirement would serve the public's First Amendment interest in receiving additional views on public issues, the Court rejected this approach, finding that such a requirement would tend to transform broadcasters into common carriers and would intrude unnecessarily upon the editorial discretion of broadcasters. *Id.,* at 123–125. The FCC's ruling, therefore, helped to advance the important purposes of the Communications Act, grounded in the First Amendment, of preserving the right of broadcasters to exercise "the widest journalistic freedom consistent with [their] public obligations," and of guarding against "the risk of an enlargement of Government control over the content of broadcast discussion of public issues." *Id.,* at 110, 126.

Thus, although the broadcasting industry plainly operates under restraints not imposed upon other media, the thrust of these restrictions has generally been to secure the public's First Amendment interest in receiving a balanced presentation of views on diverse matters of public concern. As a result of these restrictions, of course, the absolute freedom to advocate one's own positions without also presenting opposing

viewpoints—a freedom, enjoyed, for example, by newspaper publishers and soapbox orators—is denied to broadcasters. But, as our cases attest, these restrictions have been upheld only when we were satisfied that the restriction is narrowly tailored to further a substantial governmental interest, such as ensuring adequate and balanced coverage of public issues, e.g., *Red Lion,* 395 U.S., at 377. See also *CBS, Inc. v. FCC, supra,* at 396–397; *Columbia Broadcasting System, Inc. v. Democratic National Committee,* 412 U.S., at 110–111; *Red Lion, supra,* at 396. Making that judgment requires a critical examination of the interests of the public and broadcasters in light of the particular circumstances of each case. E.g., *FCC v. Pacifica Foundation,* 438 U.S. 726 (1978).

The FCC's refusal to extend the fairness doctrine to another medium led to its further destablization. In *Telecommunications Research and Action Center v. Federal Communications Commission,*[176] the court of appeals upheld the commission's determination that teletext resembled the print media more than broadcasting and thus should not be governed by the implications of scarcity including fairness obligations.[177] In so doing, the appeals court sharply attacked the scarcity rationale as a selective concept creating an indefensible constitutional dichotomy for print and other media.[178] It expressed the hope, moreover, that "the Supreme Court will one day revisit this area of the law and either eliminate the distinction . . . , or announce a constitutional distinction that is more usable than the present one."[179]

Telecommunications Research and Action Center v. Federal Communications Commission, 801 F.2d 501 (D.C. Cir. 1986), *cert. denied,* 107 S.Ct. 3196 (1987)

Bork, Circuit Judge:

Petitioners challenge the Federal Communications Commission's decision not to apply three forms of political broadcast regulation to a new

---

we recognized in *Red Lion,* however, were it to be shown by the Commission that the fairness doctrine "[has] the net effect of reducing rather than enhancing" speech, we would then be forced to reconsider the constitutional basis of our decision in that case. 395 U.S., at 393.

technology, teletext. Teletext provides a means of transmitting textual and graphic material to the television screens of home viewers.

The Communications Act of 1934, 47 U.S.C. § 312(a)(7) (1982), requires broadcast licensees to "allow reasonable access . . . for the use of a broadcasting station by a legally qualified candidate for Federal elective office on behalf of his candidacy." In addition, under 47 U.S.C. § 315(a) (1982), if the licensee "permit[s] any person who is a legally qualified candidate for any public office to use a broadcasting station," he or she incurs the additional obligation of "afford[ing] equal opportunities to all other such candidates for that office." Complementing these statutory provisions, there exists a form of political broadcast regulation that the Commission created early in its history in the name of its mandate to ensure the use of the airwaves in the "public 'convenience, interest, or necessity.' " See *Red Lion Broadcasting v. FCC*, 395 U.S. 367, 376–77 (1969). The "fairness doctrine," as this policy is known, "provides that broadcasters have certain obligations to afford reasonable opportunity for the discussion of conflicting views on issues of public importance." 47 C.F.R. § 73.1910 (1985).

The case before us presents the question whether the Commission erred in determining that these three political broadcast provisions do not apply to teletext. Because we find that the Commission acted reasonably with respect to section 312(a)(7) and the fairness doctrine, but erroneously held section 315 not to apply to teletext, we affirm in part and reverse in part, and remand to the Commission for further proceedings. . . .

II

In the Commission's view the regulation of teletext's "unique blend of the print medium with radio technology" raises first amendment problems not associated with the regulation of traditional broadcasting. Thus, the argument goes, existing Supreme Court precedent upholding political content regulation of traditional broadcasting does not necessarily justify the application of such regulation to the new medium of teletext. While not concluding that this application to a "print medium" like teletext would violate the first amendment, the Commission suggested that its application of that regulation would be sufficiently suspect to justify not imputing to Congress an intent to apply "section 315 and similar statutory provisions, and . . . associated rules and policies, to the teletext medium." 101 F.C.C.2d at 834. To appreciate the Commission's argument, a brief discussion of the case law will be useful.

In *Red Lion Broadcasting Co. v. FCC*, 395 U.S. 367 (1969), the Supreme Court rejected a first amendment challenge to the fairness doctrine and related rules governing personal attacks and political editorials by licensees. In reasoning that applies generally to political broadcasting regulation, the Court found justification for limiting first amendment protection of broadcasting in the "scarcity doctrine." Given the fact of a limited number of broadcast frequencies and the "massive" problem of broadcast interference, the Court remarked that "only a tiny fraction of those with resources and intelligence can hope to communicate by radio at the same time if intelligible communication is to be had, even if the entire radio spectrum is utilized in the present state of commercially acceptable technology." *Id.* at 388. The Court observed that this necessitated the division of the radio spectrum into usable portions, the assignment of subdivisions of the frequency to individual users, and regulation under which the "Government . . . tell[s] some applicants that they [cannot] . . . broadcast at all because there [is] room for only a few." *Id.* Therefore, the Court asserted, because "there are substantially more individuals who want to broadcast than there are frequencies to allocate, it is idle to posit an unabridgeable First Amendment right to broadcast comparable to the right of every individual to speak, write or publish." *Id.*

Observing that licenses and those who can obtain no license have identical first amendment rights, the Court in *Red Lion* further concluded that

> [t]here is nothing in the First Amendment which prevents the Government from requiring a licensee to share his frequency with others and to conduct himself as a proxy or fiduciary with obligations to present those views and voices which are representative of his community and which would otherwise, by necessity, be barred from the airwaves.

395 U.S. at 389. The Court then enunciated the classic formulation of the scarcity doctrine:

> Because of the scarcity of radio frequencies, the Government is permitted to put restraints on licensees in favor of others whose views should be expressed on this unique medium. But the people as a whole retain their interest in free speech by radio and their collective right to have the medium function consistently with the ends and purposes of the First Amendment. It is the right of the viewers and listeners, not the right of the broadcasters, which is paramount.

Id. at 390. It was on this principle that the Court found no first amendment infirmity in political broadcast regulation.

The Commission believes, however, that the regulation of teletext falls not within the permissive approach of *Red Lion,* but rather within the strict first amendment rule applied to content regulation of the print media. In *Miami Herald Publishing Co. v. Tornillo,* 418 U.S. 241 (1974), the Court struck down an editorial right-of-reply statute that applied to newspapers. The content regulation in *Tornillo* bore a strong resemblance to that upheld in *Red Lion.* In *Tornillo* the Court held that such regulation impermissibly interfered with the newspapers' "editorial control and judgment." *Id.* at 258. The Court made the broad assertion that "[i]t has yet to be demonstrated how governmental regulation of this crucial [editorial] process can be exercised consistent with the First Amendment guarantees of a free press." *Id.* If the Commission's view is correct, and *Tornillo* rather than *Red Lion* applies to teletext, that service is entitled to greater first amendment protections than ordinary broadcasting and it would be proper, at a minimum, to construe political broadcasting provisions narrowly to avoid constitutionally suspect results.

The Commission has offered two grounds for its view that *Tornillo* rather than *Red Lion* is pertinent. Both reasons relate to the textual nature of teletext services. First the Commission read an "immediacy" component into the scarcity doctrine:

> Implicit in the "scarcity" rationale . . . is an assumption that broadcasters, through their access to the radio spectrum, possess a power to communicate ideas through sound and visual images in a manner that is significantly different from traditional avenues of communication because of the immediacy of the medium.

53 Rad.Reg.2d (P & F) at 1324. Second, the Commission held that the print nature of teletext "more closely resembles, and will largely compete with, other print communication media such as newspapers and magazines." *Id.* Under this analysis, scarcity of alternative first amendment resources does not exist with respect to teletext. We address these points in turn.

With respect to the first argument, the deficiencies of the scarcity rationale as a basis for depriving broadcasting of full first amendment protection, have led some to think that it is the immediacy and the power of broadcasting that causes its differential treatment. Whether or not that is true, we are unwilling to endorse an argument that makes the very effectiveness of speech the justification for according it less first amendment protection. More important, the Supreme Court's articulation of the scarcity doctrine contains no hint of any immediacy rationale. The Court based its reasoning entirely on the physical scarcity of broadcasting frequencies, which, it thought, permitted attaching fiduciary duties to the receipt of a license to use a frequency. This "immediacy" distinction cannot, therefore, be employed to affect the ability of the Commission to regulate public affairs broadcasting on teletext to ensure "the right of the public to receive suitable access to social, political, esthetic, moral, and other ideas and experiences." *Red Lion,* 395 U.S. at 390.

The Commission's second distinction—that a textual medium is not scarce insofar as it competes with other "print media"—also fails to dislodge the hold of *Red Lion.* The dispositive fact is that teletext is transmitted over broadcast frequencies that the Supreme Court has ruled scarce and this makes teletext's content regulable. We can understand, however, why the Commission thought it could reason in this fashion. The basic difficulty in this entire area is that the line drawn between the print media and the broadcast media, resting as it does on the physical scarcity of the latter, is a distinction without a difference. Employing the scarcity concept as an analytic tool, particularly with respect to new and unforeseen technologies, inevitably leads to strained reasoning and artificial results.

It is certainly true that broadcast frequencies are scarce but it is unclear why that fact justifies content regulation of broadcasting in a way that would be intolerable if applied to the editorial process of the print media. All economic goods are scarce, not least the newsprint, ink, delivery trucks, computers, and other resources that go into the production and dissemination of print journalism. Not everyone who wishes to publish a newspaper, or even a pamphlet, may do so. Since scarcity is a universal fact, it can hardly explain regulation in one context and not another. The attempt to use a universal fact as a distinguishing principle necessarily leads to analytical confusion.

Neither is content regulation explained by the fact that broadcasters face the problem of interference, so that the government must define useable frequencies and protect those frequencies from encroachment. This governmental definition of frequencies is another instance of a universal fact that does not offer an explanatory principle for differing treatment. A publisher can deliver his newspapers only because government provides streets and regulates traffic on the streets by allocating rights of way. Yet no one would contend that the necessity for these governmental functions, which are certainly analogous to the government's function in allocating broadcast frequencies, could justify regulation of the content of a newspaper to ensure that it serves the needs of the citizens.

There may be ways to reconcile *Red Lion* and *Tornillo* but the "scarcity" of broadcast frequencies does not appear capable of doing so. Perhaps the Supreme Court will one day revisit this area of the law and either eliminate the distinction between print and broadcast media, surely by pronouncing *Tornillo* applicable to both, or announce a constitutional distinction that is more usable than the present one. In the meantime, neither we nor the Commission are free to seek new rationales to remedy the inadequacy of the doctrine in this area. The attempt to do that has led the Commission to find "implicit" considerations in the law that are not really there. The Supreme Court has drawn a first amendment distinction between broadcast and print media on a premise of the physical scarcity of broadcast frequencies. Teletext, whatever its similarities to print media, uses broadcast frequencies, and that, given *Red Lion,* would seem to be that. . . .

V

The fairness doctrine "provides that broadcasters have certain obligations to afford reasonable opportunity for the discussion of conflicting views on issues of public importance." 47 C.F.R. § 73.1910 (1985). The doctrine arose "under the Commission's power to issue regulations consistent with the 'public interest,' . . . [and] imposes two affirmative obligations on the broadcaster: coverage of issues of public importance must be adequate and must fairly reflect differing viewpoints." *Columbia Broadcasting System, Inc. v. Democratic National Committee,* 412 U.S. 94, 110–11 (1973). The basic purpose of the fairness doctrine is to ensure that the American public not be left uninformed. *Green v. FCC,* 447 F.2d 323, 329 (D.C.Cir. 1971). In serving this interest, the Commission has emphasized that "the public's need to be informed can best be served through a system in which the individual broadcasters exercise wide journalistic discretion, and in which government's role is limited to a determination of whether the licensee has acted reasonably and in good faith." *Fairness Report,* 48 F.C.C.2d 1, 9 (1974). . . .

The FCC in the teletext docket decided to exempt that service entirely from the requirements of the fairness doctrine. The Commission premised its decision on the fact that Congress never actually codified the Commission's fairness doctrine, and that the Commission, therefore, had no obligation to extend its own policy to new services like teletext. Petitioners dispute this interpretation, arguing that the fairness doctrine "is a statutory obligation that requires *all* broadcasting services to provide reasonable opportunities for the presentation of contrasting viewpoints on controversial matters of public importance." Brief for TRAC/MAP at 34–35 (emphasis in original). Because teletext constitutes broadcasting under the terms of the statute, petitioners argue that the fairness doctrine must be applied. . . .

We begin our analysis by reciting the classic formulation of the fairness doctrine:

> The Commission has . . . recognized the necessity for licensees to devote a reasonable percentage of their

broadcast time to the presentation of news and programs devoted to the consideration and discussion of public issues of interest in the community served by the particular station. And we have recognized, with respect to such programs, the paramount right of the public in a free society to be informed and to have presented to it for acceptance or rejection the different attitudes and viewpoints concerning these vital and often controversial issues which are held by the various groups which make up the community.

Editorializing by Broadcast Licensees, 13 F.C.C. 1246, 1249 (1949). Thus, the fairness doctrine imposes obligations on "licensees" in the use of their "broadcast time." Teletext is broadcast time operated by Commission licensees or by lessees under the control of licensees. We find it clear, therefore, that the fairness doctrine by its terms applies to teletext; no extension is necessary. Indeed, it appears an affirmative departure from precedent for the Commission to say that a licensee's fairness obligations apply only to a part of its broadcast time. Thus, we must examine whether the doctrine amounts to a statutory obligation preclusive of the Commission's making such a departure, and, if not, whether the Commission adequately explained its change in policy.

The dispute about whether the fairness doctrine is a statutory obligation or a Commission policy centers around a 1959 amendment to section 315 of the Communications Act of 1934. Congress amended section 315(a) explicitly to exclude from the definition of "use of a broadcasting station" such programming as bona fide newscasts, bona fide news interviews, bona fide news documentaries, and on-the-spot coverage of bona fide news events. See Pub.L. No. 86–274, 73 Stat. 557 (1959). Alongside the insertion of this change in the statute, Congress also added the following language to section 315(a):

> Nothing in the foregoing sentence shall be construed as relieving broadcasters, in connection with the presentation of newscasts, news interviews, news documentaries, and on-the-spot coverage of news events, from the obligation imposed on them under this Act to operate in the public interest and to afford reasonable opportunity for the presentation of conflicting views on issues of public importance.

47 U.S.C. § 315(a) (1982). See also Pub.L. No. 86–274, 73 Stat. 557 (1959). Petitioners suggest

that we must treat this passage as a codification of the fairness doctrine as applied at the time of the 1959 amendment and that the Commission, therefore, may not alter the fairness obligation, even if it believes such a change to be required in the public interest. We disagree.

We do not believe that language adopted in 1959 made the fairness doctrine a binding statutory obligation; rather, it ratified the Commission's longstanding position that the public interest standard authorizes the fairness doctrine. The language, by its plain import, neither creates nor imposes any obligation, but seeks to make it clear that the statutory amendment does not affect the fairness doctrine obligation as the Commission had previously applied it. The words employed by Congress also demonstrate that the obligation recognized and preserved was an administrative construction, not a binding statutory directive. Congress described the obligation to which it addressed its admonition as one "imposed . . . *under the Act*," 47 U.S.C. § 315(a) (1982) (emphasis added), not by the Act. This suggests that Congress viewed the doctrine as an obligation promulgated pursuant to authority conferred under the Act, specifically, the public interest mandate, and not as a fixed requirement frozen in place by the Act. Thus, by its 1959 amendment, "Congress . . . expressly accepted . . . that the public interest language of the Act authorized the Commission to require licensees to use their stations for discussion of public issues, and that the FCC is free to implement this requirement by reasonable rules and regulations." *Red Lion,* 395 U.S. at 382. "In other words, the amendment vindicated the FCC's general view that the Fairness Doctrine inhered in the public interest standard." *Id.* at 380.

Because the fairness doctrine derives from the mandate to serve the public interest, the Commission is not bound to adhere to a view of the fairness doctrine that covers teletext. "An agency's view of what is in the public interest may change, either with or without a change in circumstances." *Greater Boston Corp. v. FCC,* 444 F.2d 841, 852 (D.C.Cir. 1970) (footnote omitted), *cert. denied,* 403 U.S. 923 (1971). To the extent that the Commission's exemption of teletext amounts to a change in its view of what the public interest requires, however, the Commission has an obligation to acknowledge and justify that change in order to satisfy the demands of reasoned decisionmaking.

The influence of critical ferment also had become evident in the FCC's own review of the fairness doctrine. In 1985, it asserted that "the multiplicity of voices in the marketplace today" had erased the problem of spectrum scarcity, so the regulation no longer was a "necessary . . . or appropriate means by which to effectuate this interest."[180] Despite evidence it cited in support of the fairness doctrine's deficiencies,[181] and articulated judicial misgivings about the principle,[182] the FCC deferred steps that would negate the principle pending legislative action.[183] Although Congress voted to incorporate the fairness doctrine into statute,[184] the president vetoed it.[185] In the meantime, the FCC was under increasing pressure to correlate policies and actions with its new sense that the fairness doctrine subverted First Amendment interests.[186] A direct constitutional challenge to the doctrine's constitutionality was dismissed on jurisdictional grounds,[187] although a companion claim regarding the commission's failure to commence a rule making to eliminate or modify it was found reviewable.[188] The matter subsequently was vacated[189] following the resolution of *Meredith Corp. v. Federal Communications Commission.*[190] The court of appeals ordered the FCC, which had found a fairness violation, to consider the licensee's contention that the fairness doctrine was unconstitutional.[191] Consistent with an approving cue from the *Telecommunication Research and Action Committee* decision,[192] to the effect that the fairness doctrine had not been implicitly codified by congressional action,[193] the commission abandoned the fairness doctrine for virtually all of the reasons sounded over the years by critics.[194]

Without reaching the constitutional issues,

the court of appeals upheld the FCC's decision in *Syracuse Peace Council v. Federal Communications Commission*[195] as a legitimate rendition under the "public interest" standard.[196] Finding that the fairness doctrine was not absolutely compelled by the constitution or by statute,[197] the appeals court deferred to the FCC's determination that it chilled coverage of important issues, subjected the editorial process to official second-guessing and potential abuse, and no longer was necessary owing to the expanded availability of broadcasting outlets.[198]

Syracuse Peace Council, 2 F.C.C. Rcd. 5043 (1987)

. . .

1. Based upon compelling evidence of record, the Commission, in its *1985 Fairness Report*, concluded that the fairness doctrine disserved the public interest. Evaluating the explosive growth in the number and types of information sources available in the marketplace, the Commission found that the public has "access to a multitude of viewpoints without the need or danger of regulatory intervention." The Commission also determined that the fairness doctrine "chills" speech, finding that "in stark contravention of its purpose, [the doctrine] operates as a pervasive and significant impediment to the broadcasting of controversial issues of public importance." In addition, the agency found that its enforcement of the doctrine acts to inhibit the expression of unpopular opinion; it places the government in the intrusive role of scrutinizing program content; it creates the opportunity for abuse for partisan political purposes; and it imposes unnecessary costs upon both broadcasters and the Commission. . . .

(a) Chilling Effect of the Doctrine

42. In the *1985 Fairness Report*, the Commission evaluated the efficacy of the fairness doctrine in achieving its regulatory objective. Based upon the compelling evidence of record, the Commission determined that the fairness doctrine, in operation, thwarts the purpose that it is designed

to promote. Instead of enhancing the discussion of controversial issues of public importance, the Commission found that the fairness doctrine, in operation, "chills" speech.

43. The Commission documented that the fairness doctrine provides broadcasters with a powerful incentive not to air controversial issue programming above that minimal amount required by the first part of the doctrine. Each time a broadcaster presents what may be construed as a controversial issue of public importance, it runs the risk of a complaint being filed, resulting in litigation and penalties, including loss of license. This risk still exists even if a broadcaster has met its obligations by airing contrasting viewpoints, because the process necessarily involves a vague standard, the application and meaning of which is hard to predict. Therefore, by limiting the amount of controversial issue programming to that required by the first prong (i.e., its obligation to cover controversial issues of vital importance to the community), a licensee is able to lessen the substantial burdens associated with the second prong of the doctrine (i.e., its obligation to present contrasting viewpoints) while conforming to the strict letter of its regulatory obligations. The licensee, consistent with its fairness doctrine obligations, may forego coverage of other issues that, although important, do not rise to the level of being vital.

44. As the Commission demonstrated, the incentives involved in limiting the amount of controversial issue programming are substantial. A broadcaster may seek to lessen the possibility that an opponent may challenge the method in which it provided "balance" in a renewal proceeding. If it provides one side of a controversial issue, it may wish to avoid either a formal Commission determination that it violated agency policy or the financial costs of providing responsive programming. More important, however, even if it intends to or believes that it has presented balanced coverage of a controversial issue, it may be inhibited by the expenses of being second-guessed by the government in defending a fairness doctrine complaint at the Commission, and if the case is litigated in court, the costs of an appeal. Further, in view of its dependence upon the goodwill of its audience, a licensee may seek to avoid the possible tarnish to its reputation that even an al-

legation that it violated the governmental policy of "balanced" programming could entail.

45. Furthermore, the Commission determined that the doctrine inherently provides incentives that are more favorable to the expression of orthodox and well-established opinion with respect to controversial issues than to less established viewpoints. The Commission pointed out that a number of broadcasters who were denied or threatened with the denial of renewal of their licenses on fairness grounds had provided controversial issue programming far in excess of the typical broadcaster. Yet these broadcasters espoused provocative opinions that many found to be abhorrent and extreme, thereby increasing the probability that these broadcasters would be subject to fairness doctrine challenges. The Commission consequently expressed concern that the doctrine, in operation, may have penalized or impeded the expression of unorthodox or unpopular opinion, depriving the public of debates on issues of public opinion that are "uninhibited, robust, and wide-open." The doctrine's encouragement to cover only major or significant viewpoints, with which much of the public will be familiar, inhibits First Amendment goals of ensuring that the public has access to innovative and less popular viewpoints.

46. As noted above, these various incentives are not merely speculative. The record compiled in the fairness inquiry revealed over 60 reported instances in which the fairness doctrine inhibited broadcasters' coverage of controversial issues. Although some have sought to disparage or discount the significance of some of the specific examples cited, we have carefully reviewed these criticisms and continue to believe that those specific instances of broadcasters' conduct were broadly illustrative of a prevalent reaction to the doctrine and that the record from the inquiry overwhelmingly demonstrated that broadcasters act upon those incentives and limit the amount of controversial issue programming presented on the airwaves.

47. The Commission demonstrated in the *1985 Fairness Report* that broadcasters—from network television anchors to those in the smallest radio stations—recounted that the fear of governmental sanction resulting from the doctrine creates a climate of timidity and fear, which de-

ters the coverage of controversial issue programming. The record contained numerous instances in which the broadcasters decided that it was "safer" to avoid broadcasting specific controversial issue programming, such as series prepared for local news programs, than to incur the potentially burdensome administrative, legal, personnel, and reputational costs of either complying with the doctrine or defending their editorial decisions to governmental authorities. Indeed, in the *1985 Fairness Report,* the Commission gave specific examples of instances in which broadcasters declined to air programming on such important controversial issues such as the nuclear arms race, religious cults, municipal salaries, and other significant matters of public concern. In each instance, the broadcaster identified the fairness doctrine as the cause for its decision.

48. The record in the fairness inquiry demonstrated that this self-censorship is not limited to individual programs. In order to avoid fairness doctrine burdens, the Commission found that stations have adopted company "policies" which have the direct effect of diminishing the amount of controversial material that is presented to the public on broadcast stations. For example, some stations refuse to present editorials; other stations will not accept political advertisements; still others decline to air public issue (or editorial) advertising; and others have policies to decline acceptance of nationally produced programming that discusses controversial subjects or to have their news staffs avoid controversial issues as a matter of routine. The Commission concluded, therefore, that the doctrine "inhibits the presentation of controversial issues of public importance to the detriment of the public and in degradation of the editorial prerogatives of broadcast journalists."

49. Further, we believe that enforcement actions such as the one in this proceeding provide substantial disincentives to broadcasters to cover controversial issues of importance in their community. As a direct result of the Commission second-guessing the editorial discretion of Meredith's station WTVH in its coverage of an important, controversial issue, Station WTVH became embroiled in a burdensome, regulatory quagmire. Even though it has, under today's decision, ultimately prevailed in this adjudication,

the station has incurred substantial litigation expenses associated with the initial adjudication, the reconsideration proceeding, the case on appeal and the subsequent remand. Its reputation has been tarnished for nearly three years by a formal adjudication by this Commission that it was unfair in its programming and somehow did not live up to professional journalistic standards. In addition, its editorial judgment as a broadcast journalist has been subject to question by government authorities. Based upon this experience, we believe that, if we were to continue to impose the doctrine, some broadcasters would continue to seek to avoid the substantial burdens associated with the doctrine by limiting their coverage of controversial issues of public importance.

50. Several commenters in this adjudication challenge the Commission's determination in 1985 that the fairness doctrine in operation inhibits the expression of controversial issues of public importance. The arguments presented by these parties, however, are the same contentions which already have been carefully considered and rejected by the Commission in its *1985 Fairness Report.* Therefore, for the reasons set forth in that *Report,* we do not find them persuasive, and we reaffirm the fundamental determinations contained in the *1985 Fairness Report.*

51. Fisher Broadcasting Inc. was the sole broadcaster in this proceeding to assert to us that the fairness doctrine has not inhibited its stations' coverage of controversial issues of public importance. In the 1985 inquiry, Westinghouse Broadcasting & Cable Co. was the sole broadcaster to make a similar claim. We do not believe, however, that statements by these or other licensees demonstrate generally an absence of a "chilling effect" in the broadcasting industry. As we stated in the *1985 Fairness Report:*

> [W]e do not believe that the isolated representations of some broadcasters to the effect that the doctrine does not have any effect on the type, frequency or duration of the controversial viewpoints they air are probative of an absence of chilling effect within the industry as a whole; the fact that some broadcasters may not be inhibited in the presentation of controversial issues of public importance does not prove that broadcasters in general are similarly uninhibited.

The record in that *Report* demonstrates that many broadcasters are in fact inhibited by fairness doctrine burdens from covering controversial issues of public importance. No broadcaster indicated to us that its coverage of controversial issues has increased as a result of the fairness doctrine, and absent such evidence to offset the numerous instances of chill that we have identified, we can only conclude that the overall net effect of the doctrine is to reduce the coverage of controversial issues of public importance, in contravention of the standard announced in *Red Lion.*

(b) The Extent and Necessity of Government Intervention into Editorial Discretion

52. As explained above, the Supreme Court has held that restrictions on the content of broadcasters' speech must be narrowly tailored to achieve a substantial government interest in order to pass constitutional muster. As part of an analysis of such a requirement, we look to the *1985 Fairness Report,* in which the Commission examined the appropriate role of government in regulating the expression of opinion. Historically, the Commission has taken the position that the agency had an affirmative obligation, derived from the First Amendment, to oversee the content of programming through enforcement of the fairness doctrine in order to ensure the availability of diverse viewpoints to the public. After careful reflection, however, the Commission, with respect to the fairness doctrine, repudiated the notion that it was proper for a governmental agency to intervene actively in the marketplace of ideas. The Commission found that the enforcement of the doctrine requires the "minute and subjective scrutiny of program content," which perilously treads upon the editorial prerogatives of broadcast journalists. The Commission further found that in administering the doctrine it is forced to undertake the dangerous task of evaluating particular viewpoints. The fairness doctrine thus indisputably represents an intrusion into a broadcaster's editorial discretion, both in its enforcement and in the threat of enforcement. It requires the government to second-guess broadcasters' judgment on the issues they cover, as well as on the manner and balance of

coverage. The penalties for noncompliance range from being required to provide free air time, under some circumstances, to providing contrasting viewpoints, in others, to loss of license, in extreme cases. Even though an individual violation might not lead to license revocation, the court in *Meredith* noted that the mere finding of a violation "has its own coercive impact."

53. In this regard, the Commission noted that, under the fairness doctrine, a broadcaster is only required to air "*major* viewpoints and shades of opinion" to fulfill its balanced programming obligation under the second part of the doctrine. In administering the fairness doctrine, therefore, the Commission is obliged to differentiate between "significant" viewpoints which warrant presentation to fulfill the balanced programming obligation and those viewpoints that are not deemed "major" and thus need not be presented. The doctrine forces the government to make subjective and vague value judgments among various opinions on controversial issues to determine whether a licensee has complied with its regulatory obligations.

54. In addition, the Commission expressed concern that the fairness doctrine provides a dangerous vehicle—which had been exercised in the past by unscrupulous officials—for the intimidation of broadcasters who criticize governmental policy. It concluded that the inherently subjective evaluation of program content by the Commission in administering the doctrine contravenes fundamental First Amendment principles. We reaffirm these determinations and find that enforcement of the fairness doctrine necessarily injects the government into the editorial process of broadcast journalists.

55. In further analyzing whether the fairness doctrine is narrowly tailored to achieve a substantial government interest, we look again to our evaluation in the *1985 Fairness Report* of whether this type of government regulation is in fact necessary to ensure the availability of diverse sources of information and viewpoints to the public. In that *Report,* the Commission undertook a comprehensive review of the information outlets currently available to the public. This review, as discussed in more detail below, revealed an explosive growth in both the number and types of

such outlets in every market since the 1969 *Red Lion* decision. And this trend has continued unabated since 1985. For example, 96% of the public now has access to five or more television stations. Currently, listeners in the top 25 markets have access to an average of 59 radio stations, while those in even the smallest markets have access to an average of six radio stations. In contrast to that, only 125 cities have two or more daily newspapers published locally. Nationwide, there are 1315 television and 10,128 radio stations, while recent evidence indicates that there are 1657 daily newspapers. The number of television stations represents a 54% increase since the *Red Lion* decision, while the number of radio stations represents a 57% increase. Not only has the number of television and radio stations increased the public's access to a multiplicity of media outlets since 1969, but the advent and increased availability of such other technologies as cable and satellite television services have dramatically enhanced that access. As a result of its 1985 review, the Commission determined that "the interest of the public in viewpoint diversity is fully served by the multiplicity of voices in the marketplace today" and that the growth in both radio and television broadcasting alone provided "a reasonable assurance that a sufficient diversity of opinion on controversial issues of public importance [would] be provided in each broadcast market." It concluded, therefore, and we continue to believe, that government regulation such as the fairness doctrine is not necessary to ensure that the public has access to the marketplace of ideas.

56. None of the commenters in this proceeding has challenged the underlying data contained in the *1985 Fairness Report* demonstrating the significant increase in the number and types of information services. In its Comments, however, the ACLU attempts to discount the importance of the Commission's findings. For example, disputing the significance of the substantial growth in the number of television stations, the ACLU argues that most of this increase has been in UHF independent stations which, it speculates, may not contribute to the diversity of viewpoints. We disagree. The ACLU has provided no meaningful basis for us to reconsider our conclusion that independent stations can contribute—and do

contribute—significantly to the marketplace of ideas. Therefore, we continue to believe that the contributions of UHF stations must be considered in any meaningful assessment of the information services marketplace.

57. In its Comments, the ACLU also attempts to downplay the importance of our finding that the number of signals received by individual television viewers has increased substantially. In making its argument, the ACLU does not question the existence of the substantial growth in the number of signals available to individual television households. Rather, it argues that not all of the signals of these stations originate in the viewers' community of license. However, as we stated in our *1985 Fairness Report,* in assessing viewpoint diversity in the context of the fairness doctrine, "the relevant inquiry is not what stations are licensed to a community, but rather what broadcast signals [an individual] can actually receive." Viewers can obtain information on controversial issues of public importance from stations which they can receive whether or not the signal happens to originate in their community. Similarly, citing the *1985 Fairness Report,* the ACLU acknowledges that the number of radio stations has increased dramatically. It speculates, however, that "despite the dramatic growth of radio over the past three decades, viewpoint diversity on controversial issues of public importance *may* not have changed. ..." Specifically, it argues that most of the increase is in FM stations which, in its view, carry less controversial issue programming than their AM counterparts, and that public affairs programming on radio generally has decreased. We are not persuaded by these speculative contentions. To the contrary, we remain convinced that the dramatic growth in the number of both radio stations and television stations has in fact increased the amount of information, as well as the diversity of viewpoints, available to the public in both large and small broadcast markets. We therefore reaffirm our determination in the *1985 Fairness Report* that the fairness doctrine is not necessary in any market to ensure that the public has access to diverse viewpoints from today's media outlets. Its intrusive means of interfering with broadcasters' editorial discretion, therefore, can

no longer be characterized as narrowly tailored to meet a substantial government interest.

(c) Conclusion

58. As noted above, under the standard of review set forth in *Red Lion,* a governmental regulation such as the fairness doctrine is constitutional if it furthers the paramount interest of the public in receiving diverse and antagonistic sources of information. Under *Red Lion,* however, the constitutionality of the fairness doctrine becomes questionable if the chilling effect resulting from the doctrine thwarts its intended purpose. Applying this precedent, we conclude that the doctrine can no longer be sustained.

59. In the *1985 Fairness Report,* we evaluated whether the fairness doctrine achieved its purpose of promoting access to diverse viewpoints. After compiling a comprehensive record, we concluded that, in operation, the fairness doctrine actually thwarts the purpose which it is designed to achieve. We found that the doctrine inhibits broadcasters, on balance, from covering controversial issues of public importance. As a result, instead of promoting access to diverse opinions on controversial issues of public importance, the actual effect of the doctrine is to "overall lessen [] the flow of diverse viewpoints to the public." Because the net effect of the fairness doctrine is to reduce rather than enhance the public's access to viewpoint diversity, it affirmatively disserves the First Amendment interests of the public. This fact alone demonstrates that the fairness doctrine is unconstitutional under the standard of review established in *Red Lion.*

60. Furthermore, almost two decades of Commission experience in enforcing the fairness doctrine since *Red Lion* convince us that the doctrine is also constitutionally infirm because it is not narrowly tailored to achieve a substantial government interest. Because the fairness doctrine imposes substantial burdens upon the editorial discretion of broadcast journalists and, because technological developments have rendered the doctrine unnecessary to ensure the public's access to viewpoint diversity, it is no longer narrowly tailored to meet a substantial government interest and therefore violates the standard set forth in *League of Women Voters.* The doctrine requires the government to second-guess broadcasters' judg-

ment on such sensitive and subjective matters as the "controversiality" and "public importance" of a particular issue, whether a particular viewpoint is "major," and the "balance" of a particular presentation. The resultant overbreadth of the government's inquiry into these matters is demonstrated by the chill in speech that we have identified. The doctrine exacts a penalty, both from broadcasters and, ultimately, from the public, for the expression of opinion in the electronic press. As a result, broadcasters are denied the editorial discretion accorded to other journalists, and the public is deprived of a more vigorous marketplace of ideas, unencumbered by governmental regulation.

61. In sum, the fairness doctrine in operation disserves both the public's right to diverse sources of information and the broadcaster's interest in free expression. Its chilling effect thwarts its intended purpose, and it results in excessive and unnecessary government intervention into the editorial processes of broadcast journalists. We hold, therefore, that under the constitutional standard established by *Red Lion* and its progeny, the fairness doctrine contravenes the First Amendment and its enforcement is no longer in the public interest.

C. PREFERRED CONSTITUTIONAL APPROACH

62. Our review of the Supreme Court precedent in the application of First Amendment principles to the electronic media leads to an inescapable conclusion: throughout the development of these principles, the Supreme Court has repeatedly emphasized that its constitutional determinations in this area of the law are closely related to the technological changes in the telecommunications marketplace. For example, in the *Red Lion* decision itself, the Court indicated that advances in technology could have an effect on its analysis of the constitutional principles applicable to the electronic media. The Court of Appeals noted this in *Meredith v. FCC,* when it said that the *Red Lion* decision "was expressly premised on the scarcity of broadcast frequencies 'in the present state of commercially available technology' as of 1969." And in *Columbia Broad-*

casting System, Inc. v. Democratic National Committee, the Supreme Court stated that:

> Balancing the various First Amendment interests involved in the broadcast media and determining what best serves the public's right to be informed is a task of great delicacy and difficulty.... The problems of regulation are rendered more difficult because the broadcast industry is dynamic in terms of technological change; solutions adequate a decade ago are not necessarily so now, and those acceptable today may well be outmoded ten years hence.

63. The Court's most recent statement on this issue came in its decision in *FCC v. League of Women Voters of California.* Acknowledging that certain persons, including former Chairman Mark Fowler, "charge that with the advent of cable and satellite television technology, communities now have access to such a wide variety of stations that the scarcity doctrine is obsolete," the Court indicated that it may be willing to reassess its traditional reliance upon spectrum scarcity upon a "signal" from the Congress or this Commission "that technological developments have advanced so far that some revision of the system of broadcast regulation may be required."

64. That principles applicable to the government's regulation of a rapidly changing industry such as telecommunications should be revisited and revised in light of technological advances is not an unusual proposition. Indeed, the Commission, in its task of managing an everchanging technological and economic marketplace, has the responsibility to consider new developments in reviewing existing, and in applying new, rationales in that marketplace. With respect to the fairness doctrine itself, a policy that the Commission defended before the Supreme Court in 1969, our comprehensive study of the telecommunications market in the *1985 Fairness Report* has convinced us that a rationale that supported the doctrine in years past is no longer sustainable in the vastly transformed, diverse market that exists today. Consequently, we find ourselves today compelled to reach a conclusion regarding the constitutionality of the fairness doctrine that is very different from the one we reached in 1969.

65. We believe that the *1985 Fairness Report,* as reaffirmed and further elaborated on in today's action, provides the Supreme Court with the signal referred to in *League of Women Voters.* It also

provides the basis on which to reconsider its application of constitutional principles that were developed for a telecommunications market that is markedly different from today's market. We further believe that the scarcity rationale developed in the *Red Lion* decision and successive cases no longer justifies a different standard of First Amendment review for the electronic press. Therefore, in response to the question raised by the Supreme Court in *League of Women Voters,* we believe that the standard applied in *Red Lion* should be reconsidered and that the constitutional principles applicable to the printed press should be equally applicable to the electronic press.

1. Basis for Reconsidering Red Lion

66. In the *1985 Fairness Report,* the Commission examined, in a comprehensive manner, the number and types of outlets currently providing information to the public, including the traditional broadcast services, the new electronic sources, and the print media. The Commission found in recent years that there had been an explosive growth in both the number and types of outlets providing information to the public. Hence, the Supreme Court's apparent concern that listeners and viewers have access to diverse sources of information has now been allayed.

67. With respect to the number of radio stations, the Commission demonstrated that in 1985 there were 9,766 radio stations nationwide, a 48 percent increase in radio stations overall since the date of the Supreme Court's decision in *Red Lion* and a 30 percent increase in the number of radio stations since the *1974 Fairness Report.* As stated above, that number now stands at 10,128 a 54% increase since the 1969 *Red Lion* decision. The Commission also concluded in the *1985 Fairness Report* that the growth in FM stations, in particular, had been dramatic. Specifically, the Commission found that this service had increased by 113 percent since the *Red Lion* decision and by 60 percent since the *1974 Fairness Report.* Further, the Commission found "of particular significance" the fact that the number of radio voices in each local market had grown. With continuing technological advances in spectrum efficiency, the Commission predicted that the number of radio outlets would continue to increase.

68. With respect to television stations, the Commission documented that in 1985 the number of television stations overall was 1,208, an increase of 44.3 percent since the *Red Lion* decision and 28 percent since *1974 Fairness Report*. And that number has increased to 1315 today, a 57% increase since the 1969 *Red Lion* decision. The Commission also found in the *1985 Fairness Report* the growth in UHF stations in particular to have been even more dramatic than the overall growth in television stations: the number of UHF stations increased by 113 percent since the *Red Lion* decision and 66.4 percent since the *1974 Fairness Report*. The Commission found further that the growth in television broadcasting has directly resulted in a significant increase in the number of signals available to individual viewers in both the larger and smaller markets. Specifically, without the enhancing capability of cable television, the Commission determined that 96 percent of the television households receive five or more television signals. In 1964, only 59 percent of these households were able to receive five or more stations. With the growth of UHF television, the increase in the importance of independent television and the development of new program distribution systems among group owners, the Commission also found that the structure of the medium had become more competitive.

69. Although the Commission found that the number of radio and television outlets alone ensured that the public had access to diverse sources of information in each broadcast market (large and small), it also found that cable television, which had increased exponentially during the period from 1969 to 1985, had enhanced significantly the amount of information available to the public. Since the *1974 Fairness Report,* the Commission demonstrated that the number of persons subscribing to cable television had increased by 345 percent and the number of cable systems had increased by 111 percent. Based upon its assessment of the marketplace, the Commission predicted that cable television would continue to expand in the future. It determined further that there had been a significant change in the nature of cable service, as the number of channels available to individual subscribers had increased dramatically. For example, in 1969 only 1 percent of all cable systems had the capability of carrying

more than 12 channels; by 1987 69 percent of all cable systems (and 92% of cable subscribers) had this capacity. Thus, in addition to the substantial increases in the absolute number of cable systems and in the percentage of cable subscribers, the Commission concluded that the amount of information available to an individual viewer on a single cable system had increased. The statistical data contained in ACLU's comments actually support a reaffirmation of this determination. Characterizing cable as "the most dynamic video medium today," the ACLU states that "[a]pproximately 71 million television households—74.7 percent of all television households—have access to cable television service." It also notes that 47 percent of all television households are actual subscribers of that service. It asserts further that both the availability and number of subscribers to cable television will continue to increase. Specifically, in three years it predicts that almost 90 percent of television households will have access to cable and that 54 percent will subscribe to it.

70. In addition, the Commission evaluated the contributions of a number of new electronic technologies unavailable at the time of the *Red Lion* decision, including low power television, MMDS, video cassette recorders (VCRs), and satellite master antenna systems (SMATV). It found that each of these new services also were contributing significantly to the diversity of information available to the public. Noting the development of a number of additional information technologies, the Commission determined that there were a number of other electronic services, such as direct home to satellite services, satellite news gathering, subscription television, FM radio subcarriers, teletext, videotext and home computers "have the potential of becoming substitute information sources in the marketplace of ideas." Some of these technologies, such as teletext and videotext, are beginning to merge characteristics of the electronic media with those of the print media, further complicating the choice of an appropriate constitutional standard to be applied to their regulation.

71. As noted above, none of the commenters in this proceeding has challenged the underlying data contained in the *1985 Fairness Report* with respect to the dramatic increase in the number and types of alternative technologies available to

the public. For instance, ACLU's own data demonstrate the soundness of our determination that the number of broadcast outlets has exploded and that cable television has evolved into a significant information source. In its Comments, the ACLU also asserts that in the short period of time since the *1985 Fairness Report,* the number of low power television stations has increased by 12 percent from 341 stations to 383 stations.

72. We believe that the dramatic changes in the electronic media, together with the unacceptable chilling effect resulting from the implementation of such regulations as the fairness doctrine, form a compelling and convincing basis on which to reconsider First Amendment principles that were developed for another market. Today's telecommunications market offers individuals a plethora of information outlets to which they have access on a daily basis. Indeed, this market is strikingly different from even that offered by the daily print media. While there are 11,443 broadcast stations nationwide, recent evidence indicates that there are only 1657 daily newspapers overall. On a local level, 96% of the public has access to five or more television stations, while only 125 cities have two or more local newspapers. The one-newspaper town is becoming an increasing phenomenon. Our review of the Supreme Court's statements on the relationship between constitutional principles and technological developments leads us to conclude that it would now be appropriate for the Supreme Court to reassess its *Red Lion* decision.

2. The Scarcity Rationale

73. Certain parties, taking the position that the basis underlying the scarcity rationale in *Red Lion* is either illogical or anachronistic, assert that the appropriate constitutional test to assess content-based regulations of the electronic media is the one enunciated for the print media. These commenters point to the explosive growth in the number and types of information sources in support of their assertion that the scarcity doctrine is no longer viable. Other commenters, in contrast, state that the general standards of First Amendment jurisprudence applied by the Court in cases not involving broadcast regulation are irrelevant in determining whether the fairness doctrine and other content-based regulations are

constitutional. They assert that the increase in the number and types of information sources has nothing to do with the existence of scarcity in the constitutional sense, and emphasize that the appropriate standard of review is that applied by the Court in *Red Lion* and its progeny specifically relating to broadcast regulation. These parties describe two different notions of scarcity—numerical scarcity and spectrum (or allocational) scarcity. We do not believe that any scarcity rationale justifies differential First Amendment treatment of the print and broadcast media.

74. As stated above, we no longer believe that there is scarcity in the number of broadcast outlets available to the public. Regardless of this conclusion, however, we fail to see how the constitutional rights of broadcasters—and indeed the rights of the public to receive information unencumbered by government intrusion—can depend on the number of information outlets in particular markets. Surely, a requirement of multiple media outlets could not have formed the basis for the framers of the First Amendment to proscribe government interference with the editorial process. At the time the First Amendment was adopted, there were only eight daily newspapers, seventy weekly newspapers, ten semi-weekly newspapers and three tri-weekly newspapers published in America.

75. Because there is no longer a scarcity in the number of broadcast outlets, proponents of a scarcity rationale for the justification of diminished First Amendment rights applicable to the broadcast medium must rely on the concept of spectrum (or allocational) scarcity. This concept is based upon the physical limitations of the electromagnetic spectrum. Because only a limited number of persons can utilize broadcast frequencies at any particular point in time, spectrum scarcity is said to be present when the number of persons desiring to disseminate information on broadcast frequencies exceeds the number of available frequencies. Consequently, these frequencies, like all scarce resources, must be allocated among those who wish to use them.

76. In fact, spectrum scarcity was one of the bases articulated by the Court in *Red Lion* for the disparate treatment of the broadcast and the print media. Reliance on spectrum scarcity, however, "has come under increasing criticism in re-

cent years." For example, the Court of Appeals has recently questioned the rationality of spectrum scarcity as the basis for differentiating between the print and broadcast media. In *TRAC v. FCC*, the Court asserted that:

> [T]he line drawn between the print media and the broadcast media, resting as it does on the physical scarcity of the latter, is a distinction without a difference. Employing the scarcity concept as an analytic[al] tool . . . inevitably leads to strained reasoning and artificial results.
>
> It is certainly true that broadcast frequencies are scarce but it is unclear why that fact justifies content regulation of broadcasting in a way that would be intolerable if applied to the editorial process of the print media. All economic goods are scarce, not least the newsprint, ink, delivery trucks, computers, and other resources that go into the production and dissemination of print journalism. . . . Since scarcity is a universal fact, it can hardly explain regulation in one context and not another. The attempt to use a universal fact as a distinguishing principle necessarily leads to analytical confusion.

We agree with the court's analysis of the spectrum scarcity rationale, and we believe that it would be desirable for the Supreme Court to reconsider its use of a constitutional standard based upon spectrum scarcity in evaluating the intrusive type of content-based regulation at issue in this proceeding.

77. At the outset, we note that the limits on the number of persons who can use frequencies at any given time is not absolute, but is, in part, economic: greater expenditures on equipment and/or advances in technology could make it possible to utilize the spectrum more efficiently in order to permit a greater number of licensees. So the number of outlets in a market is potentially expandable, like the quantities of most other resources.

78. Nevertheless, we recognize that technological advancements and the transformation of the telecommunications market described above have not eliminated spectrum scarcity. All goods, however, are ultimately scarce, and there must be a system through which to allocate their use. Although a free enterprise system relies heavily on a system of property rights and voluntary exchange to allocate most of these goods, other methods of allocation, including first-come-first-

served, administrative hearings, lotteries, and auctions, are or have been relied on for certain other goods. Whatever the method of allocation, there is not any logical connection between the method of allocation for a particular good and the level of constitutional protection afforded to the uses of that good.

79. In the allocation of broadcast frequencies, the government has relied, for the most part, on a licensing scheme based on administrative hearings to promote the most effective use of this resource. Congress has also authorized the allocation of frequencies through the use of lotteries. Moreover, although the government allocates broadcast frequencies to particular broadcast speakers in the initial licensing stage, approximately 71% of today's radio stations and 54% of today's television stations have been acquired by the current licensees on the open market. Hence, in the vast majority of cases, broadcast frequencies are "allocated"—as are the resources necessary to disseminate printed speech—through a functioning economic market. Therefore, after initial licensing, the only relevant barrier to acquiring a broadcast station is not governmental, but—like the acquisition of a newspaper—is economic.

80. Additionally, there is nothing inherent in the utilization of the licensing method of allocation that justifies the government acting in a manner that would be proscribed under a traditional First Amendment analysis. In contexts other than broadcasting, for example, the courts have indicated that, where licensing is permissible, the First Amendment proscribes the government from regulating the content of fully protected speech. There are those who argue that the acceptance by broadcasters of government's ability to regulate the content of their speech is simply a fair exchange for their ability to use the airwaves free of charge. To the extent, however, that such an exchange allows the government to engage in activity that would be proscribed by a traditional First Amendment analysis, we reject that argument. It is well-established that government may not condition the receipt of a public benefit on the relinquishment of a constitutional right. The evil of government intervention into the editorial process of the press (whether print or electronic) and the right of individuals to receive political

viewpoints unfettered by government interference are not changed because the electromagnetic spectrum (or any other resource necessary to convey expression) is scarce or because the government (in conjunction with the marketplace) allocates that scarce resource. Indeed, the fact that government is involved in licensing is all the more reason why the First Amendment protects against government control of content.

81. On the other hand, the fact that government may not impose unconstitutional conditions on the receipt of a public benefit does not preclude the Commission's ability, and obligation, to license broadcasters in the public interest, convenience and necessity. The Commission may still impose certain conditions on licensees in furtherance of this public interest obligation. Nothing in this decision, therefore, is intended to call into question the validity of the public interest standard under the Communications Act.

82. Rather, we simply believe that, in analyzing the appropriate First Amendment standard to be applied to the electronic press, the concept of scarcity—be it spectrum or numerical—is irrelevant. As Judge Bork stated in *TRAC v. FCC,* "Since scarcity is a universal fact, it can hardly explain regulation in one context and not another. The attempt to use a universal fact as a distinguishing principle necessarily leads to analytical confusion." Consequently, we believe that an evaluation of First Amendment standards should not focus on the *physical differences* between the electronic press and the printed press, but on the *functional similarities* between these two media and upon the underlying values and goals of the First Amendment. We believe that the function of the electronic press in a free society is identical to that of the printed press and that, therefore, the constitutional analysis of government control of content should be no different. With this in mind, we return to the *Red Lion* decision and consider its divergence from traditional First Amendment precepts protecting the role of the press in a democratic society.

3. Divergence of Red Lion from Traditional First Amendment Precepts

83. We believe that the articulation of lesser First Amendment rights for broadcasters on the basis of the existence of scarcity, the licensing of broadcasters, and the paramount rights of listeners departs from traditional First Amendment jurisprudence in a number of respects. Specifically, the Court's decision that the listeners' rights justifies government intrusion appears to conflict with several fundamental principles underlying the constitutional guarantee of free speech.

84. First, this line of decisions diverges from Supreme Court pronouncements that "the First Amendment 'was fashioned to assure *unfettered* interchange of ideas for the bringing about of political and social changes desired by the people.' " The framers of that Amendment determined that the best means by which to protect the free exchange of ideas is to prohibit any governmental regulation which "abridg[es] the freedom of speech or of the press." They believed that the marketplace of ideas is too delicate and too fragile to be entrusted to governmental authorities.

85. In this regard, Justice Potter Stewart once stated that "[t]hose who wrote our First Amendment put their faith in the proposition that a free press is indispensable to a free society. They believed that 'fairness' was far too fragile to be left for a government bureaucracy to accomplish." In the same vein, Justice Byron White has stated that:

> Of course, the press is not always accurate, or even responsible, and may not present full and fair debate on important public issues. But the balance struck by the First Amendment with respect to the press is that society must take the risk that occasionally debate on vital matters will not be comprehensive and that all viewpoints may not be expressed.... Any other accommodation—any other system that would supplant private control of the press with the heavy hand of government intrusion—would make the government the censor of what the people may read and know.

Indeed, the Supreme Court has often emphasized that:

> The freedom of speech and of the press guaranteed by the Constitution embraces at the least the liberty to discuss publicly and truthfully all matters of public concern without previous restraint *or fear of subsequent punishment.*

Consequently, a cardinal tenet of the First Amendment is that governmental intervention in the marketplace of ideas of the sort involved in the enforcement of the fairness doctrine is not acceptable and should not be tolerated.

86. The fairness doctrine is at odds with this fundamental constitutional precept. While the objective underlying the fairness doctrine is that of the First Amendment itself—the promotion of debate on important controversial issues—the means employed to achieve this objective, government coercion, is the very one which the First Amendment is designed to prevent. As the Supreme Court has noted, "By protecting those who wish to enter the marketplace of ideas from governmental attack, the First Amendment protects the public's interest in receiving information." Yet the fairness doctrine *uses* government intervention in order to foster diversity of viewpoints, while the scheme established by the framers of our Constitution *forbids* government intervention for fear that it will stifle robust debate. In this sense, the underlying rationale of the fairness doctrine turns the First Amendment on its head.

87. Indeed, even when approving the doctrine in the *1974 Fairness Report,* the Commission recognized the anomaly of a policy which purports to further First Amendment values by the very mechanism proscribed by that constitutional provision. In that *Report,* the Commission explained that:

> th[e] [doctrine's] affirmative use of government power to expand broadcast debate would seem to raise a striking paradox, for freedom of speech has traditionally implied an absence of governmental supervision or control. Throughout most of our history, the principal function of the First Amendment has been to protect the free marketplace of ideas by precluding governmental intrusion.

88. The *Red Lion* decision also is at odds with the well-established precept that First Amendment protections are especially elevated for speech relating to matters of public concern, such as political speech and other matters of public importance. Indeed, the Supreme Court, in the context of broadcast regulation, recently stated that the expression of opinion on matters of public concern is "entitled to the most exacting degree of First Amendment protection." The Court has recognized that this type of speech is "indispensible to decisionmaking in a democracy." As the Court has stated, "speech concerning public affairs is more than self-expression, it is the es-

sence of self-government." Because it is the people in a democratic system who "are entrusted with the responsibility for judging and evaluating the relative merits of conflicting arguments," the "[g]overnment is forbidden to assume the task of ultimate judgment, lest the people lose their ability to govern themselves."

89. The type of speech regulated by the fairness doctrine involves opinions on controversial issues of public importance. This type of expression is "precisely that . . . which the Framers of the Bill of Rights were most anxious to protect—speech that is 'indispensible to the discovery and spread of political truth'. . . . " Yet, instead of safeguarding this type of speech from regulatory intervention, the doctrine anomalously singles it out for governmental scrutiny.

90. Further, the *Red Lion* decision cannot be reconciled with well-established constitutional precedent that governmental regulations directly affecting the content of speech are subjected to particularly strict scrutiny. The Supreme Court has emphasized that "[i]f the marketplace of ideas is to remain free and open, governments must not be allowed to choose 'which issues are worth discussing or debating. . . .' " As noted above, enforcement of the fairness doctrine not only forces the government to decide whether an issue is of "public importance," but also whether the broadcaster has presented "significant" contrasting viewpoints. Unorthodox minority viewpoints do not receive favored treatment as do their "significant" counterparts. As the Court recently asserted, "[r]egulations which permit the Government to discriminate on the basis of the content of the message cannot be tolerated under the First Amendment."

91. The difference in the *Red Lion* approach becomes apparent when considering the validity of the fairness doctrine. The fairness doctrine indisputably regulates the content of speech. Like the statute invalidated in *FCC v. League of Women Voters of California,* "enforcement authorities must necessarily examine the content of the message that is conveyed to determine whether the views expressed concern 'controversial issues of public importance.' " Yet even in the *League* case, the Court applied a standard that the regulation be narrowly tailored to achieve a substantial government interest, a standard traditionally reserved

for content-neutral regulations. In contrast, a traditional First Amendment analysis would require a content-based regulation, such as the fairness doctrine, to be a "precisely drawn means of serving a compelling state interest." Even under a traditional approach, therefore, content-based regulations are not necessarily invalid, but they are subject to a much higher standard of review than the one applicable to the broadcast media.

92. Because the dissemination of a particular viewpoint by a broadcaster can trigger the burdens associated with broadcasting responsive programming, the doctrine directly penalizes—through the prospect or reality of government intrusion—the speaker for expressing his or her opinion on a matter of public concern. For even if the broadcaster has, in fact, presented contrasting viewpoints, the government, at the request of a complainant, may nevertheless question the broadcaster's presentation, which in and of itself is a penalty for simply covering an issue of public importance.

93. In this regard, we note that sound journalistic practice already encourages broadcasters to cover contrasting viewpoints on a topic of controversy. The problem is not with the goal of the fairness doctrine, it is with the use of government intrusion as the means to achieve that goal. With the existence of a fairness doctrine, broadcasters who intend to, and who do in fact, present contrasting viewpoints on controversial issues of public importance are nevertheless exposed to potential entanglement with the government over the exercise of their editorial discretion. Consequently, these broadcasters may shy away from extensive coverage of these issues. We believe that, in the absence of the doctrine, broadcasters will more readily cover controversial issues, which, when combined with sound journalistic practices, will result in more coverage and more diversity of viewpoint in the electronic media; that is, the goals of the First Amendment will be enhanced by employing the very means of the First Amendment: government restraint.

94. Finally, we believe that under the First Amendment, the right of viewers and listeners to receive diverse viewpoints is achieved by guaranteeing them the right to receive speech unencumbered by government intervention. The *Red Lion* decision, however, apparently views the no-

tion that broadcasters should come within the free press and free speech protections of the First Amendment as antagonistic to the interest of the public in obtaining access to the marketplace of ideas. As a result, it is squarely at odds with the general philosophy underlying the First Amendment, i.e., that the individual's interest in free expression and the societal interest in access to viewpoint diversity are both furthered by proscribing governmental regulation of speech. The special broadcast standard applied by the Court in *Red Lion*, which sanctions restrictions on speakers in order to promote the interest of the viewers and listeners, contradicts this fundamental constitutional principle.

4. First Amendment Standard Applicable to the Press

95. Under a traditional First Amendment analysis, the type of governmental intrusion inherent in the fairness doctrine would not be tolerated if it were applied to the print media. Indeed, in *Miami Herald Publishing Co. v. Tornillo*, the Supreme Court struck down, on First Amendment grounds, a Florida statute that compelled a newspaper to print the response of a political candidate that it had criticized. Invoking a purpose strikingly similar to the fairness doctrine, the state had attempted to justify the statute on the grounds that the "government has an obligation to ensure that a wide variety of views reach the public." The Court reasoned that the mechanism employed by the state in implementing this objective, however, was "governmental coercion," and thus contravened "the express provisions of the First Amendment and the judicial gloss on that Amendment developed over the years." The Court also found that a governmentally imposed right of reply impermissibly "intrud[ed] into the function of editors." In addition, the Court stated that the inevitable result of compelling the press "to print that which it would not otherwise print" would be to reduce the amount of debate on governmental affairs:

> Faced with the penalties that would accrue to any newspaper that published news or commentary arguably within the reach of the right-of-access statute, editors might well conclude that the safe course is to avoid controversy. Therefore, under the operation of the Florida statute, political and electoral coverage would be blunted or reduced. Govern-

ment-enforced right of access inescapably " 'dampens the vigor and limits the variety of public debate.' "

Also, the fact that a newspaper could simply add to its length did not dissuade the Court from concluding that the access requirement would improperly intrude into the editorial discretion of the newspaper.

96. Relying on *Tornillo,* the Court, in *Pacific Gas & Electric Co. v. Public Utilities Commission of California,* recently determined that a state administrative order requiring a utility to place the newsletter of its opponents in its billing envelopes contravened the First Amendment. "[B]ecause access was awarded only to those who disagreed with [the utility's] views and who are hostile to [the utility's] interests," Justice Lewis Powell, in the plurality opinion, expressed concern that "whenever [the utility] speaks out on a given issue, it may be forced . . . to help disseminate hostile views." As a consequence, the regulation had the effect of reducing the free flow of information and ideas that the First Amendment seeks to promote. In evaluating the utility's First Amendment rights to be free from governmentally-coerced speech, the plurality expressly stated that it was irrelevant that the ratepayers, rather than the utility, owned the extra space in the billing envelopes. It asserted that the "forced association with potentially hostile views burdens the expression of views . . . and risks forcing [the utility] to speak where it would prefer to remain silent" irrespective of who is deemed to own this extra space.

97. We believe that the role of the electronic press in our society is the same as that of the printed press. Both are sources of information and viewpoint. Accordingly, the reasons for proscribing government intrusion into the editorial discretion of print journalists provide the same basis for proscribing such interference into the editorial discretion of broadcast journalists. The First Amendment was adopted to protect the people *not from journalists, but from government.* It gives the people the right to receive ideas that are unfettered by government interference. We fail to see how that right changes when individuals choose to receive ideas from the electronic media instead of the print media. There is no doubt that the electronic media is powerful and that broad-

casters can abuse their freedom of speech. But the framers of the Constitution believed that the potential for abuse of private freedoms posed far less a threat to democracy than the potential for abuse by a government given the power to control the press. We concur. We therefore believe that full First Amendment protections against content regulation should apply equally to the electronic and the printed press. . . .

99. We further believe, as the Supreme Court indicated in *FCC v. League of Women Voters of California,* that the dramatic transformation in the telecommunications marketplace provides a basis for the Court to reconsider its application of diminished First Amendment protection to the electronic media. Despite the physical differences between the electronic and print media, their roles in our society are identical, and we believe that the same First Amendment principles should be equally applicable to both. This is the method set forth in our Constitution for maximizing the public interest; and furthering the public interest is likewise our mandate under the Communications Act. It is, therefore, to advance the public interest that we advocate these rights for broadcasters.

The FCC's abandonment of the fairness doctrine suggests the possibility that the related personal attack rule likewise must fall. The agency's general counsel at least has acknowledged the logic.[199] The ultimate fate of the fairness doctrine, however, remains in doubt. Legislative response has included the sense that the commission's action constituted a defiance of Congress's will.[200] Fairness advocates continue to regard the principle as a critical methodology for ensuring coverage of pluralistic views, especially minority sentiments,[201] and emphasize notable accomplishments of vigorous fairness enforcement.[202] Because congressional support for statutory enactment of the fairness doctrine remains widespread,[203] its resurrection with the support of a more sympathetic president remains possible. It even is conceivable that the scarcity premise may survive judicial challenge, as evidenced by fresh jurisprudential reference to it as a basis for upholding other broadcast diversification policies.[204] Since the judiciary has the final word in the charting of constitutional perimeters,[205] the question of whether broadcasters will operate on the same First Amendment level as publishers for fairness or any other purpose ultimately may be influenced less by legislative or administrative action than by future case law.

II. CONTENT RESTRICTION

A. INDECENCY

Notwithstanding the FCC's determination that broadcasters should be accorded constitutional parity with publishers,[206] distinctions continue to be made resulting in identifiable variances in status.[207] Regardless of media context, obscenity is constitutionally unprotected expression and may be entirely proscribed. Sexually explicit material falling short of an obscenity definition, and depicted in terms of indecency, may be subject to constraint even though constitutionally protected. The distribution of adult literature or exhibition of adult motion pictures, for instance, is subject to a reasonable time, place, and manner requirement.[208] As a consequence, zoning ordinances mandating the concentration or dispersal of adult bookstores or movie houses have been upheld.[209] Similarly, restrictions have been imposed upon the airing of what is officially classified as indecent programming.[210] Unlike quality of life interests, which have justified regulations limiting the availability of published indecency,[211] control of sexually explicit broadcasting is referenced to purportedly unique characteristics of radio and television. Restrictions thus are a function of merged concern with broadcasting's pervasive nature, interference with privacy, and accessibility to children.[212] Although time channeling and

zoning restrictions have been presented as comparable concepts, the scope of broadcast material subject to the former requirement appears to be more sweeping than expression governed by zoning requirements.

The regulation of indecent broadcasting results from tension between two statutes. The Communications Act specifically prohibits the FCC from exercising "the power of censorship."[213] A general criminal statute, however, subjects "(w)hoever utters any obscene, indecent, or profane language by means of radio communication [to being] fined not more than $10,000 or imprisoned not more than two years, or both."[214] Not until the late 1970s, in *Federal Communications Commission v. Pacifica Foundation*,[215] did the Supreme Court speak authoritatively on the subject. Even before then, extensive programming that was "on its face . . . coarse, vulgar, suggestive and indecent [and] . . . by any standards . . . flagrantly and patently offensive in the context of the broadcast field" contributed to an FCC determination that the public interest had been disserved and license renewal was denied.[216] Since *Pacifica*, the commission has adopted a sterner demeanor and has formulated criteria for purposes of defining and curtailing indecent programming.[217] Although long warning of the potential for serious penalties,[218] the FCC only recently has begun to impose significant sanctions on a widespread basis.[219]

1. Pre-Pacifica Regulation

The commission's first major statement concerning indecent programming arose in the course of reviewing license renewal applications of stations owned by the Pacifica Foundation. The frequent implication of Pacifica in the context of indecency controversies illustrates the conflict that exists between diversity goals and concerns with offensive programming. Pacifica stations tend to provide precisely the heterodox programming that critics have found lacking in a broadcasting industry catering to mainstream tastes. Its capacity for unsettling majoritarian conventions or dominant tastes, however, has regularly pitted it and diversity values against content concerns.

The first complaint against a Pacifica station related to readings of poems and a novel by their respective authors and a discussion among several homosexuals regarding their concerns and attitudes.[220] With the exception of one poetry reading, all of the programs were presented late at night.[221] Distinguishing the content from programs that were "patently offensive," the commission upheld the licensee's judgment that they served "the needs and interests of its listening public."[222] Seemingly influential was the perception of the dramatic works as serious and their authorship by "eminent" or "notable" writers and playwrights.[223] The licensee, moreover, demonstrated that passages not meeting its "broadcast standards of good taste" were edited out.[224] Although recognizing that provocative programming "as shown by the complaints here, . . . may offend some listeners,"[225] the FCC concluded that "those offended [did not] have the right, through the Commission's licensing power, to rule such programming off the airwaves."[226] A contrary result would allow "only the wholly inoffensive, the bland, [to] gain access to the radio microphone or TV camera."[227] In sum, the FCC expressed reluctance to take action unless "the facts of the particular case, established in a hearing record, flagrantly call for" it.[228]

Pacifica Foundation, 36 F.C.C. 147 (1964)

MEMORANDUM OPINION AND ORDER

. . .

2. *The programing issues.*—The principal complaints are concerned with five programs: (i) a December 12, 1959, broadcast over KPFA, at 10 p.m., of certain poems by Lawrence Ferlinghetti

(read by the poet himself); (ii) "The Zoo Story," a recording of the Edward Albee play broadcast over KPFK at 11 p.m., January 13, 1963; (iii) "Live and Let Live," a program broadcast over KPFK at 10:15 p.m. on January 15, 1963, in which eight homosexuals discussed their attitudes and problems; (iv) a program broadcast over KPFA at 7:15 p.m. on January 28, 1963, in which the poem, "Ballad of the Despairing Husband," was read by the author Robert Creeley; and (v) "The Kid," a program broadcast at 11 p.m. on January 8, 1963, over KPFA, which consisted of readings by Edward Pomerantz from his unfinished novel of the same name. The complaints charge that these programs were offensive or "filthy" in nature, thus raising the type of issue we recently considered in *Palmetto Bctg. Co.*, 33 FCC 483; 34 FCC 101. We shall consider the above five matters in determining whether, on an overall basis, the licensee's programing met the public-interest standard laid down in the Communications Act. *Report and Statement of Policy re: Commission En Banc Programing Inquiry,* 20 Pike & Fischer R.R. 1901. . . .

4. There is, we think, no question but that the broadcasts of the programs, "The Zoo Story," "Live and Let Live," and "The Kid," lay well within the licensee's judgment under the public-interest standard. The situation here stands on an entirely different footing than *Palmetto, supra,* where the licensee had devoted a substantial period of his broadcast day to material which we found to be patently offensive—however much we weighted that standard in the licensee's favor—and as to which programing the licensee himself never asserted that it was not offensive or vulgar, *or that it served the needs of his area or had any redeeming features.* In this case, Pacifica has stated its judgment that the three above-cited programs served the public interests and specifically, the needs and interests of its listening public. Thus, it has pointed out that in its judgment, "The Zoo Story" is a "serious work of drama" by an eminent and "provocative playwright"—that it is "an honest and courageous play" which Americans "who do not live near Broadway ought to have the opportunity to hear and experience. . . ." Similarly, as to "The Kid," Pacifica states, with supporting authority, that Mr. Pomerantz is an author who has obtained notable recognition

for his writings and whose readings from his unfinished novel were fully in the public interest as a serious work meriting the attention of its listeners; Pacifica further states that prior to broadcast, the tape was auditioned by one of its employees who edited out two phrases because they did not meet Pacifica's broadcast standards of good taste; and that while "certain minor swear words are used, . . . these fit well within the context of the material being read and conform to the standards of acceptability of reasonably intelligent listeners." Finally, as to the program, "Live and Let Live," Pacifica states that "so long as the program is handled in good taste, there is no reason why subjects like homosexuality should not be discussed on the air"; and that it "conscientiously believes that the American people will be better off as a result of hearing a constructive discussion of the problem rather than leaving the subject to ignorance and silence."

5. We recognize that as shown by the complaints here, such provocative programming as here involved may offend some listeners. But this does not mean that those offended have the right, through the Commission's licensing power, to rule such programing off the airwaves. Were this the case, only the wholly inoffensive, the bland, could gain access to the radio microphone or TV camera. No such drastic curtailment can be countenanced under the Constitution, the Communications Act, or the Commission's policy, which has consistently sought to insure "the maintenance of radio and television as a medium of freedom of speech and freedom of expression for the people of the Nation as a whole" (*Editorializing Report*, 13 FCC 1246, 1248). In saying this, we do not mean to indicate that those who have complained about the foregoing programs are in the wrong as to the worth of these programs and should listen to them. This is a matter solely for determination by the individual listeners. Our function, we stress, is not to pass on the merits of the program—to commend or to frown. Rather, as we stated (par. 3), it is the very limited one of assaying, at the time of renewal, whether the licensee's programming, on an overall basis, has been in the public interest and, in the context of this issue, whether he has made programing judgments reasonably related to the public interest. This does not pose a close question in the case: Pacifica's judgments as to the above programs clearly fall within the very great discretion which the act wisely vests in the licensee. In this connection, we also note that Pacifica took into account the nature of the broadcast medium when it scheduled such programing for the late evening hours (after 10 p.m., when the number of children in the listening audience is at a minimum).

6. As to the Ferlinghetti and Creeley programs, the licensee asserts that in both instances, some passages did not measure up to "Pacifica's own standards of good taste." Thus, it states that it did not carefully screen the Ferlinghetti tape to see if it met its standards, "because it relied upon Mr. Ferlinghetti's national reputation and also upon the fact that the tape came to it from a reputable FM station." It acknowledges that this was a mistake in its procedures and states that "in the future, Pacifica will make its own review of all broadcasts. . . ." With respect to the Creeley passage (i.e., the poem, "Ballad of a Despairing Husband"), Pacifica again states that in its judgment it should not have been broadcast. It "does not excuse the broadcast of the poem in question," but it does explain how the poem "slipped by" KPFA's drama and literature editor who auditioned the tape. It points out that prior to the offending poem, Mr. Creeley, who "has a rather flat, monotonous voice," read 18 other perfectly acceptable poems—and that the station's editor was so lulled thereby that he did not catch the few offensive words on the 19th poem. It also points out that each of the nine poems which followed was again perfectly acceptable, and that before rebroadcasting the poem on its Los Angeles station, it deleted the objectionable verse.

7. In view of the foregoing, we find no impediment to renewal on this score. We are dealing with two isolated errors in the licensee's application of its own standards—one in 1959 and the other in 1963. The explanations given for these two errors are credible. Therefore, even assuming, arguendo, that the broadcasts were inconsistent with the public-interest standard, it is clear that no unfavorable action upon the renewal applications is called for. The standard of public interest is not so rigid that an honest mistake or error on the part of a licensee results in drastic action against him where his overall record dem-

onstrates a reasonable effort to serve the needs and interests of his community. (See note 2, supra). Here again, this case contrasts sharply with *Palmetto,* where instead of two isolated instances, years apart, we found that the patently offensive material was broadcast for a substantial period of the station's broadcast day for many years. (See par. 3, supra.)

8. We find, therefore, that the programing matters raised with respect to the Pacifica renewals pose no bar to a grant of renewal. Our holding, as is true of all such holdings in this sensitive area, is necessarily based on, and limited to, the facts of the particular case. But we have tried to stress here, as in *Palmetto,* an underlying policy— that the licensee's judgment in this freedom-of-speech area is entitled to very great weight and that the Commission, under the public-interest standard, will take action against the licensee at the time of renewal only where the facts of the particular case, established in a hearing record, flagrantly call for such action. We have done so because we are charged under the act with "promoting the larger and more effective use of radio in the public interest" (sec. 303(g)), and obviously, in the discharge of that responsibility, must take every precaution to avoid inhibiting broadcast licensees' efforts at experimenting or diversifying their programing. Such diversity of programing has been the goal of many Commission policies (e.g., multiple ownership, development of UHF, the fairness doctrine). Clearly, the Commission must remain faithful to that goal in discharging its functions in the actual area of programing itself.

Although the commission had intimated that undue official concern with indecency might undermine "diversity of programming" aims,[229] a subsequent decision presaged a trend toward increased content concern.[230] In *Eastern Educational Radio (WUHY-FM),*[231] the FCC considered a counterculture musician's use of "patently offensive" speech in the course of a taped interview.[232] Although routine use of expletives is common to many people's conversations and in particular cultural settings,[233]

the commission found an indecency violation and imposed a $100 forfeiture.[234]

The conflict between diversity and indecency concerns became more palpable when the FCC determined that a radio call-in program concerning sexual topics was not merely indecent but obscene.[235] Acknowledging a licensee's right to present provocative programming that may offend some,[236] and asserting it did not intend to prohibit all discussion of sex,[237] the FCC nonetheless determined that "we are not dealing with works of dramatic or literary art."[238]

The commission's action prompted a challenge by citizens groups alleging that they "were being deprived of listening alternatives in violation of their First Amendment rights."[239] In reaffirming its order, the FCC maintained that its decision was predicated upon the presence of children in the audience and more importantly upon "the pervasive, intrusive nature of radio."[240] In *Illinois Citizens Committee v. Federal Communications Commission,*[241] the court of appeals agreed that the subject matter constituted "commercial exploitation of interests in titillation [as] the broadcaster's sole end."[242] Consequently, it was denominated under standards of obscenity governing expression which, even if inoffensive in part, panders to prurient interests.[243]

Illinois Citizens Committee for Broadcasting v. Federal Communications Commission, 515 F.2d 397 (D.C. Cir. 1974)

Leventhal, Circuit Judge:

I. STATEMENT OF FACTS

In response to increasing complaints from listeners, the Commission, in January of 1973, asked its staff to tape certain radio call-in programs that focused on sexual topics. The staff taped 61 hours of programs, 22 minutes of which were culled for presentation to the Commissioners on March 21. The Commissioners also heard an 11-minute segment that included an on-the-air complaint from a listener.

On March 27, the Commission released a Notice of "Inquiry into alleged broadcasts and cablecasts of obscene, indecent or profane material by licensees, permittees or cable systems." The inquiry was to be a nonpublic fact-finding proceeding to determine whether certain television, cable, and radio licensees had broadcast material in violation of 18 U.S.C. § 1464 (1970).

After listening to the taped excerpts on March 21, 1973, the FCC instructed its staff to prepare a Notice of Apparent Liability under sections 503(b)(1)(E) and 503(b)(2) of the Communications Act of 1934, as amended, against Sonderling Broadcasting Corporation (Sonderling) for violations of § 1464. The Notice specifically cited Sonderling's "Femme Forum," a call-in show that ran Monday through Friday, from 10 a.m. to 3 p.m. on WGLD-FM, Oak Park, Illinois. The Commission focused on two programs that had been excerpted in the tapes—one, on February 23, 1973, was on the topic of oral sex;[a] the other, on February 21, 1973, discussed "How do you keep your sex life alive?" and included specific descriptions of the techniques of oral sex. The Notice "concluded" that these broadcasts called for the imposition of a forfeiture of $2,000 against Sonderling because they contained "obscene or indecent matter." It also informed Sonderling of a licensee's statutory right to refuse to pay the forfeiture voluntarily and thus to require the FCC to seek to recover it in a trial *de novo*

---

a. One exchange cited by the FCC from this program is as follows:

Female Listener: . . . of course I had a few hangups at first about—in regard to this, but you know what we did—I have a craving for peanut butter all that [sic] time so I used to spread this on my husband's privates and after a while, I mean, I didn't even need the peanut butter anymore.

Announcer: (Laughs) Peanut butter, huh?

Listener: Right. Oh, we can try anything—you know—any, any of these women that have called and they have, you know, hangups about this, I mean they should try their favorite—you know like—uh . . .

Announcer: Whipped cream, marshmallow, . . .

(J.A. 31–32). Other segments concerned aversions to swallowing the semen at climax, overcoming fears as to having the penis bitten off, and so forth. (J.A. 32).

before a court. Despite its belief that the Commission's action was illegal, Sonderling decided to pay the fine because of "the tremendous financial burden involved."

Asserting that the public had an interest in seeking review of the FCC action despite Sonderling's acquiescence, Petitioners filed an Application for Remission of Forfeiture and a Petition for Reconsideration. They allege that their members and contributors include many numbers of the Chicago area who are being deprived of listening alternatives in violation of their rights under the First Amendment. . . .

V. THE FCC's DETERMINATION THAT THE BROADCAST IS OBSCENE

In its Memorandum Order and Opinion the Commission asserted that Sonderling's broadcast was a clear-cut violation of the law, "well within the constitutional boundaries [for obscenity] established by the Supreme Court," and therefore not entitled to protection under the First Amendment. (J.A. 104, 106)

The excerpts cited by the Commission contain repeated and explicit descriptions of the techniques of oral sex. And these are presented, not for educational and scientific purposes, but in a context that was fairly described by the FCC as "titillating and pandering." (J.A. 38) The principles of *Ginzburg v. United States*, 383 U.S. 463, 86 S.Ct. 942, 16 L.Ed.2d 31 (1966), are applicable, for commercial exploitation of interests in titillation is the broadcaster's sole end. It is not a material difference that here the tone is set by the continuity provided by the announcer rather than, as in *Ginzburg*, by the presentation of the material in advertising and sale to solicit an audience. We cannot ignore what the Commission took into account—that the announcer's response to a complaint by an offended listener and his presentation of advertising for auto insurance are suffused with leering innuendo. Moreover, and significantly, "Femme Forum" is broadcast from 10 a.m. to 3 p.m. during daytime hours when the radio audience may include children—perhaps home from school for lunch, or because of staggered school hours or illness. Given this combination of factors, we do not think that the FCC's evaluation of this material infringes upon rights protected by the First Amendment.

The FCC found Sonderling's broadcasts obscene under the standards of *Roth v. United States,* 354 U.S. 476, 77 S.Ct. 1304, 1 L.Ed.2d 1498 (1957), and *Memoirs v. Massachusetts,* 383 U.S. 413, 86 S.Ct. 975, 16 L.Ed.2d 1 (1966). The Supreme Court subsequently reformulated those standards in *Miller v. California,* 413 U.S. 15, 93 S.Ct. 2607, 37 L.Ed.2d 419 (1973), which sets out the following "basic guidelines for the trier of fact":

> (a) whether "the average person, applying contemporary community standards" would find that the work, taken as a whole, appeals to the prurient interest . . . (b) whether the work depicts or describes, in a patently offensive way, sexual conduct specifically defined by the applicable state law, and (c) whether the work, taken as a whole, lacks serious literary, artistic, political, or scientific value.

413 U.S. at 24, 93 S.Ct. at 2615. In *Huffman v. United States,* 163 U.S.App. D.C. 417, 502 F.2d 419 (1974), we analyzed how the *Miller* standards deviate from those previously enunciated. *Miller* rejected the *Memoirs* rule that material was condemnable only if "utterly without redeeming social value" and substituted a rule that permits prohibition if the material lacks "serious literary, artistic, political, or scientific value." 413 U.S. at 24–25, 93 S.Ct. at 2615. In this respect, *Miller* expanded the range of material that can be found obscene. However, it also contracted the definition of obscenity by limiting it to encompass only materials that "depict or describe patently offensive 'hardcore' sexual conduct specifically defined by the regulating state law." 413 U.S. at 27, 93 S.Ct. at 2616. *Accord Jenkins v. Georgia,* 418 U.S. 153, 94 S.Ct. 2750, 41 L.Ed.2d 640 (1974); *Hamling v. United States,* 418 U.S. 87, 94 S.Ct. 2887, 41 L.Ed.2d 590 (1974). The material broadcast by Sonderling, say Petitioners, is not "utterly without redeeming social value" and thus is not obscene under the *Memoirs* standards applied by the Commission. The licensee may have had a right to less demanding treatment under *Memoirs* had he refused to pay the forfeiture. However, he accepted the fine and waived his right to a jury trial at a time when *Memoirs* prevailed, and that matter should not be reopened now. The public is in a somewhat different position. They seek through this case, to define what they will be entitled to hear in the future. (Reply Br. 26–27) For that purpose, of future entitlement, we think it appropriate to apply the *Miller* standard concerning the purpose of the regulated material, and the *Miller* standard does not rescue the material in these broadcasts, which make no literary, artistic, political, or scientific contribution.

The Commission reasonably concluded that the dominant theme of the material broadcast by Sonderling was addressed to the prurient interest and was therefore condemnable under that element of the *Memoirs* test. (J.A. 38) *Miller,* however, requires that the material depict or describe "in a patently offensive way, sexual conduct specifically defined by the applicable . . . law." 413 U.S. at 24, 93 S.Ct. at 2615. Although Petitioners filed a reply brief after the Court's decision in *Miller,* they did not challenge the possible lack of the requisite statutory specificity. Rather, they assert that *Miller* retained the first two tests of *Memoirs* and that these tests were misapplied by the Commission. (Reply Br. 14) We see no point in pursuing in the abstract the question whether the finding of obscenity here survives the narrowing of the second test that was accomplished in *Miller,* especially since we have the additional elements of titillation and probable exposure to children, which even some of the dissenting Justices in *Miller* thought sufficient to permit condemnation. *Paris Adult Theatre I v. Slaton,* 413 U.S. 49, 114, 93 S.Ct. 2628, 37 L.Ed.2d 446 (1973) (Brennan, J., dissenting). Moreover, *Miller's* specificity requirement is designed to "provide fair notice to a dealer," 413 U.S. at 27, 93 S.Ct. at 2616, and it is not clear whether it is a requirement that may be insisted upon by the public when waived by the licensee. Petitioners' goal is to determine what *material* is withdrawn from censorship on grounds of obscenity because of the protections of the First Amendment, and that turns primarily on the nature of the social purpose that may redeem material that otherwise stands condemned. In this respect *Miller* narrows the protection afforded by *Memoirs* in a manner that undercuts the most important feature of Petitioners' claim. . . .

Petitioners object that the Commission's determination was based on a brief condensation of offensive material and did not take into account the broadcast as a whole, as would seem to be required by certain elements of both the *Memoirs* and the *Miller* tests. The Commission's approach is not inappropriate in evaluating a broadcasting program that is episodic in nature—a cluster of individual and typically disconnected commentaries, rather than an integrated presentation. It is commonplace for members of the radio audience to listen only to short snatches of a broadcast, and programs like "Femme Forum" are designed to attract such listeners. Moreover, the pervasive pandering approach here makes the broadcast pornographic even though some of its elements may be unoffensive. *Ginzburg v. United States, supra,* 383 U.S. at 471, 86 S.Ct. 942. If the licensee or the public representatives have reason to believe that an assessment of the impact of an offensive segment would be substantially affected by consideration of the program as a whole, they should be given an opportunity to offer such evidence. There was no such proffer in this case.

We conclude that, where a radio call-in show during daytime hours broadcasts explicit discussions of ultimate sexual acts in a titillating context, the Commission does not unconstitutionally infringe upon the public's right to listening alternatives when it determines that the broadcast is obscene.

2. The Pacifica Decision

The premise of the *Sonderling* decision, combined with the special characteristics of the medium adverted to by the commission, suggested the possibility of an obscenity standard that would vary by medium. Eventually, the Supreme Court was drawn into the controversy of reconciling interests of diversity and taste. At issue for the Court was the broadcast of a satirists's twelve-minute monologue, recorded in a live performance, containing repeated references to "words you couldn't say on the public . . . airwaves."[244] The presentation included detailed renditions of the terms' meanings, implications, and use of them in a variety of contexts that evoked consistent laughter from the audience. The entire monologue was reproduced in the appendix to the Court's opinion.[245]

Appendix to Opinion of the Court in Federal Communications Commission v. Pacifica Foundation

The following is a verbatim transcript of "Filthy Words" prepared by the Federal Communications Commission.

Aruba-du, ruba-tu, ruba-tu. I was thinking about the curse words and the swear words, the cuss words and the words that you can't say, that you're not supposed to say all the time, [']cause words or people into words want to hear your words. Some guys like to record your words and sell them back to you if they can, (laughter) listen in on the telephone, write down what words you say. A guy who used to be in Washington knew that his phone was tapped, used to answer, Fuck Hoover, yes, go ahead. (laughter) Okay, I was thinking one night about the words you couldn't say on the public, ah, airwaves, um, the ones you definitely wouldn't say, ever, [']cause I heard a lady say bitch one night on television, and it was cool like she was talking about, you know, ah, well, the bitch is the first one to notice that in the litter Johnie right (murmur) Right. And, uh, bastard you can say, and hell and damn so I have to figure out which ones you couldn't and ever and it came down to seven but the list is open to amendment, and in fact, has been changed, uh, by now, ha, a lot of people pointed things out to me, and I noticed some myself. The original seven words were, shit, piss, fuck, cunt, cocksucker, motherfucker, and tits. Those are the ones that will curve your spine, grow hair on your hands and (laughter) maybe, even bring us, God help us, peace without honor (laughter) um, and a bourbon. (laughter). And now the first thing that we noticed was that word fuck was really repeated in there because the word motherfucker is a compound word and it's another form of the word fuck. (laughter) You want to be a purist it doesn't really—it can't be on the list of basic words. Also, cocksucker is a compound word and neither half of that is really dirty. The word— the half sucker that's merely suggestive (laughter) and the word cock is a half-way dirty word, 50% dirty—dirty half the time, depending on what you mean by it. (laughter) Uh, remember when you first heard it, like in 6th grade, you used to giggle. And the cock crowed three times, heh (laughter) the cock—three times. It's in the Bible, cock in the Bible. (laughter) And the first time you heard about a cock-fight, remember—What? Huh? naw. It ain't that, are you stupid? man. (laughter, clapping) It's chickens, you know, (laughter) Then you have the four letter words from the old Anglo-Saxon fame. Uh, shit and fuck. The word shit, uh, is an interesting kind of word in that the middle class has never really accepted it and approved it. They use it like, crazy but it's not really okay. It's still a rude, dirty, old kind of gushy word. (laughter) They don't like that, but they say it, like, they say it like, a lady now in a middle-class home, you'll hear most of the time she says it as an expletive, you know, it's out of her mouth before she knows. She says, Oh shit oh shit, (laughter) oh shit. If she drops something, Oh, the shit hurt the broccoli. Shit. Thank you. (footsteps fading away) (papers ruffling)

Read it! (from audience)

Shit! (laughter) I won the Grammy, man, for the comedy album. Isn't that groovy? (clapping, whistling) (murmur) That's true. Thank you. Thank you man. Yeah. (murmur) (continuous clapping) Thank you man. Thank you. Thank you very much, man. Thank, no, (end of continuous clapping) for that and for the Grammy, man, [']cause (laughter) that's based on people liking it man, yeh, that's ah, that's okay man. (laughter) Let's let that go, man. I got my Grammy. I can let my hair hang down now, shit. (laughter) Ha! So! Now the word shit is okay for the man. At work you can say it like crazy. Mostly figuratively, Get that shit out of here, will ya? I don't want to see that shit anymore. I can't *cut* that shit, buddy. I've had that shit up to here. I think you're full of shit myself. (laughter) He don't know shit from Shinola. (laughter) you know that? (laughter) Always wondered how the Shinola people felt about that (laughter) Hi, I'm the new man from Shinola. (laughter) Hi, how are ya? Nice to see ya. (laughter) How are ya? (laughter) Boy, I don't know whether to shit or wind my watch. (laughter) Guess, I'll shit on my watch. (laughter) Oh, *the* shit is going to hit *de* fan. (laughter) Built like a brick shit-house. (laughter) Up, he's up shit's creek. (laughter) He's had it. (laughter) He hit me, I'm sorry. (laughter)

Hot shit, holy shit, tough shit, eat shit, (laughter) shit-eating grin. Uh, whoever thought of that was ill. (murmur laughter) He had a shit-eating grin! He had a what? (laughter) Shit on a stick. (laughter) Shit in a handbag. I always like that. He ain't worth shit in a handbag. (laughter) Shitty. He acted real shitty. (laughter) You know what I mean? (laughter) I got the money back, but a real shitty attitude. Heh, he had a shit-fit. (laughter) Wow! Shit-fit. Whew! Glad I wasn't there. (murmur, laughter) All the animals—Bull shit, horse shit, cow shit, rat shit, bat shit. (laughter) First time I heard bat shit, I really came apart. A guy in Oklahoma, Boggs, said it, man. Aw! Bat shit. (laughter) Vera reminded me of that last night, ah (murmur). Snake shit, slicker than owl shit. (laughter) Get your shit together. Shit or get off the pot. (laughter) I got a shit-load full of them. (laughter) I got a shit-pot full, all right. Shit-head, shit-heel, shit in your heart, shit for brains, (laughter) shit-face, heh (laughter) I always try to think how that could have originated; the first guy that said that. Somebody got drunk and fell in some shit, you know. (laughter) Hey, I'm shit-face. (laughter) Shit-face, *today*. (laughter) Anyway, enough of that shit. (laughter) The big one, the word fuck that's the one that hangs them up the most. [']Cause in a lot of cases that's the very act that hangs them up the most. So, it's natural that the word would, uh, have the same effect. It's a great word, fuck, nice word, easy word, cute word, kind of. Easy word to say. One syllable, short u. (laughter) Fuck. (Murmur) You know, it's easy. Starts with a nice soft sound fuh ends with a *kuh*. Right? (laughter) A little something for everyone. Fuck (laughter) Good word. Kind of a proud word, too. Who are you? I am *FUCK*. (laughter) *FUCK OF THE MOUNTAIN*. (laughter) Tune in again next week to FUCK OF THE MOUNTAIN. (laughter) It's an interesting word too, [']cause it's got a double kind of a life—personality—dual, you know, whatever the right phrase is. It leads a double life, the word fuck. First of all, it means, sometimes, most of the time, fuck. What does it mean? It means to make love. Right? We're going to make love, yeh, we're going to fuck, yeh, we're going to fuck, yeh, we're going to make love. (laughter) we're really going to fuck, yeh, we're going to make love. Right? And it also means the beginning of life, it's the act that begins life, so there's the word hanging around with words like love, and life, and yet on the other hand, it's also a word that we really use to hurt each other with, man. It's a heavy. It's one that you have toward the end of the argument. (laughter) Right? (laughter) You finally can't make out. Oh, fuck you man. I said, fuck you. (laughter, murmur) Stupid fuck. (laughter) Fuck you and everybody that looks like you. (laughter) man. It would be nice to change the movies that we already have and substitute the word fuck for the word kill, wherever we could, and some of those movies cliches would change a little bit. Madfuckers still on the loose. Stop me before I fuck again. Fuck the ump, fuck the ump, fuck the ump, fuck the ump, fuck the ump. Easy on the clutch Bill, you'll fuck that engine again. (laughter) The other shit one was, I don't give a shit. Like it's worth something, you know? (laughter) I don't give a shit. Hey, well, I don't take no shit, (laughter) you know what I mean? You know why I don't take no shit? (laughter) [']Cause I don't give a shit. (laughter) If I give a shit, I would have to pack shit. (laughter) But I don't pack no shit cause I don't give a shit. (laughter) You wouldn't shit me, would you? (laughter) That's a joke when you're a kid with a worm looking out the bird's ass. You wouldn't shit me, would you? (laughter) It's an eight-year-old joke but a good one. (laughter) The additions to the list. I found three more words that had to be put on the list of words you could never say on television, and they were fart, turd and twat, those three. (laughter) Fart, we talked about, it's harmless. It's like tits, it's a cutie word, no problem. Turd, you can't say but who wants to, you know? (laughter) The subject never comes up on the panel so I'm not worried about that one. Now the word twat is an interesting word. Twat! Yeh, right in the twat. (laughter) Twat is an interesting word because it's the only one I know of, the only slang word applying to the, a part of the sexual anatomy that doesn't have another meaning to it. Like, ah, snatch, box and pussy all have other meanings, man. Even in a Walt Disney movie, you can say, We're going to snatch that pussy and put him in a box and bring him on the airplane. (murmur, laughter) Everybody loves it. The twat stands alone, man, as it should. And two-way words. Ah, ass is okay providing you're riding into town on a religious feast day. (laughter) You can't say, up your *ass*. (laughter) You can say, stuff it! (murmur) There are certain things you can say its weird but you can just come so close. Before I cut, I, uh, want to, ah, thank you for listening to my words, man, fellow, uh space travelers. Thank you man for tonight and thank you also. (clapping whistling)

The monologue, when aired by a New York Pacifica station in the middle of a weekday afternoon, was preceded by warnings that it might offend some listeners.[246] It elicited a single complaint, however, from a man who did not hear the warning while driving with his young son.[247] Despite Pacifica's argument that the humorist, George Carlin, was a "significant social satirist who 'like Twain and Sahl before him' examines the language of ordinary people," the commission found the broadcast subject to administrative sanction.[248] Choosing not to impose a formal penalty, the order was filed for reference in the event of future complaints.[249] The FCC asserted as grounds for special regulatory consideration for broadcasting: (1) the medium's accessibility by unsupervised children, (2) special privacy interests of the home, (3) the possibility of unconsenting adults being exposed to offensive language without warning, and (4) spectrum scarcity requiring government to license in the public interest.[250]

Although the court of appeals reversed the commission's determination,[251] the Supreme Court in *Federal Communications Commission v. Pacifica Foundation*[252] held that the commission had not breached statutory curbs upon censorship, had properly found the broadcast indecent, and had crossed no First Amendment interest. With respect to an alleged violation of the statutory prohibition of censorship, the Court determined that Section 326 essentially translated into a bar against advance meddling or excision.[253] It then found that the provision "has never been construed to deny the Commission the power to review the content of completed broadcasts in the performance of its regulatory duties."[254] Responding to the other statutory question, that the material did not appeal to prurient interests,[255] the Court found that the concept of indecency was not coextensive with but more encompassing than obscenity.[256] Dismissing as unrealistic the contention "that Congress intended to impose precisely the same limitations on the dissemination of patently offensive matter by different" media, it found the absence of prurient appeal non-determinative of whether a broadcast might be indecent.[257]

Pursuant to the notion "that each medium presents special First Amendment problems,"[258] the Court identified two of the four rationales advanced by the FCC as having "relevance to the present case."[259] It thus observed "(f)irst, the broadcast media have established a uniquely pervasive presence in the lives of all Americans."[260] Because an individual's privacy interests were implicated by exposure to unwanted expression in public and at home, and because warnings might not be effective in all cases,[261] the Court concluded that private remediation in the form of tuning out was insufficient.[262] "Second, [the Court found that] broadcasting is uniquely accessible to children, even those too young to read."[263] Easy availability, coupled with "government's interest in the 'well being of its youth' and in supporting" parental authority, "amply justify special treatment of indecent broadcasting."[264]

In noting the perimeters of its holding, the Court emphasized that the case did "not involve a two-way radio conversation between a cab driver and a dispatcher, or a telecast of an Elizabethan comedy."[265] Nor had it subjected to sanction "an occasional expletive in either setting" or determined that a criminal prosecution in the case at hand was appropriate.[266] Given an analysis analogous to nuisance theory, the Court noted that "context is all-important."[267] Rel-

evant variables included time of day, program content, and audience composition.[268] Adverting to the adage that a "nuisance may be merely a right thing in the wrong place—like a pig in the parlor instead of the barnyard,"[269] the Court closed by noting "that when the Commission finds that a pig has entered the parlor, the exercise of its regulatory power does not depend on proof that the pig is obscene."[270]

Justice Stevens, who authored the Court's opinion, included a section commanding the support of Chief Justice Burger and Justice Rehnquist. Although not representing the views of a majority, the plurality maintained that indecent expression even if constitutionally protected "surely lies at the periphery of First Amendment concern."[271] A majority of the Court has yet to coalesce formally in support of the notion that protected albeit indecent expression should be afforded less constitutional regard.[272] Justice Powell, in a concurring opinion, disagreed with the notion that the Court could decide on the basis of content what "speech protected by the First Amendment is most 'valuable' and hence deserving of the most protection."[273] He joined in upholding the FCC's action, however, based upon interests in protecting children and unconsenting adults from the expression at issue.[274] Powell also expressed doubt whether the decision would prevent any adult wanting "to receive Carlin's message in Carlin's words from doing so."[275]

Justice Brennan, in a sharp dissent, maintained that the Court had misconceived the privacy interests of persons who voluntarily had allowed radio into their presence[276] and wrongly derogated the concerns of those who would be willing participants in discourse offensive to some.[277] He criticized the Court for denying minors "access to materials that are not obscene, and are therefore protected"[278] and undercutting parental autonomy to decide the subjects to which children are exposed.[279] Unlike zoning ordinances governing the location of adult expression, Brennan found no purpose in the FCC's action but to control content.[280] He found in such regulation:

> a depressing inability to appreciate that in our land of cultural pluralism, there are many who think, act, and talk differently from the Members of this Court, and who do not share their fragile sensibilities. It is only an acute ethnocentric myopia that enables the Court to approve the censorship of communications solely because of the words they contain.[281]

In closing, Brennan observed that the decision would affect most those broadcasters and audiences who do not subscribe to "majoritarian conventions, [and] express themselves using words that may be regarded as offensive by those from different socioeconomic backgrounds."[282] The *Pacifica* opinions thus exhibit the collision of diversification ideals and forces of dominant taste.

Federal Communications Commission v. Pacifica Foundation, 438 U.S. 726 (1978)

Mr. Justice Stevens delivered the opinion of the Court (Parts I, II, III, and IV-C) and an opinion in which the Chief Justice and Mr. Justice Rehnquist joined (Parts IV-A and IV-B).

This case requires that we decide whether the Federal Communications Commission has any power to regulate a radio broadcast that is indecent but not obscene.

A satiric humorist named George Carlin recorded a 12-minute monologue entitled "Filthy Words" before a live audience in a California theater. He began by referring to his thoughts about "the words you couldn't say on the public, ah, airwaves, um, the ones you definitely wouldn't say, ever." He proceeded to list those words and repeat them over and over again in a variety of colloquialisms. The transcript of the recording, which is appended to this opinion, indicates frequent laughter from the audience.

At about 2 o'clock in the afternoon on Tuesday, October 30, 1973, a New York radio station, owned by respondent Pacifica Foundation, broadcast the "Filthy Words" monologue. A few weeks later a man, who stated that he had heard the broadcast while driving with his young son, wrote a letter complaining to the Commission. He stated that, although he could perhaps understand the "record's being sold for private use, I certainly cannot understand the broadcast of same over the air that, supposedly, you control."

The complaint was forwarded to the station for comment. In its response, Pacifica explained that the monologue had been played during a program about contemporary society's attitude toward language and that, immediately before its broadcast, listeners had been advised that it included "sensitive language which might be regarded as offensive to some." Pacifica characterized George Carlin as "a significant social satirist" who "like Twain and Sahl before him, examines the language of ordinary people.... Carlin is not mouthing obscenities, he is merely using words to satirize as harmless and essentially silly our attitudes towards those words." Pacifica stated that it was not aware of any other complaints about the broadcast.

On February 21, 1975, the Commission issued a declaratory order granting the complaint and holding that Pacifica "could have been the subject of administrative sanctions." 56 F.C.C. 2d 94, 99. The Commission did not impose formal sanctions, but it did state that the order would be "associated with the station's license file, and in the event that subsequent complaints are received, the Commission will then decide whether it should utilize any of the available sanctions it has been granted by Congress."

In its memorandum opinion the Commission stated that it intended to "clarify the standards which will be utilized in considering" the growing number of complaints about indecent speech on the airwaves. *Id.*, at 94. Advancing several reasons for treating broadcast speech differently from other forms of expression,[a] the Commission

---

a. "Broadcasting requires special treatment because of our important considerations: (1) children have access to radios and in many cases are unsupervised by parents; (2) radio receivers are in the home, a place where people's privacy interest is entitled to extra deference, see *Rowan v. Post Office Dept.*, 397 U.S. 728

found a power to regulate indecent broadcasting in two statutes: 18 U.S.C. § 1464 (1976 ed.), which forbids the use of "any obscene, indecent, or profane language by means of radio communications," and 47 U.S.C. § 303 (g), which requires the Commission to "encourage the larger and more effective use of radio in the public interest."

The Commission characterized the language used in the Carlin monologue as "patently offensive," though not necessarily obscene, and expressed the opinion that it should be regulated by principles analogous to those found in the law of nuisance where the "law generally speaks to *channeling* behavior more than actually prohibiting it.... [T]he concept of 'indecent' is intimately connected with the exposure of children to language that describes, in terms patently offensive as measured by contemporary community standards for the broadcast medium, sexual or excretory activities and organs, at times of the day when there is a reasonable risk that children may be in the audience." 56 F.C.C. 2d, at 98.

Applying these considerations to the language used in the monologue as broadcast by respondent, the Commission concluded that certain words depicted sexual and excretory activities in a patently offensive manner, noted that they "were broadcast at a time when children were undoubtedly in the audience (i.e., in the early afternoon)," and that the prerecorded language, with these offensive words "repeated over and over," was "deliberately broadcast." *Id.,* at 99. In summary, the Commission stated: "We therefore hold that the language as broadcast was indecent and prohibited by 18 U.S.C. [§] 1464." *Ibid.*

After the order issued, the Commission was asked to clarify its opinion by ruling that the broadcast of indecent words as part of a live newscast would not be prohibited. The Commission issued another opinion in which it pointed out that it "never intended to place an absolute pro-

hibition on the broadcast of this type of language, but rather sought to channel it to times of day when children most likely would not be exposed to it." 59 F.C.C. 2d 892 (1976). The Commission noted that its "declaratory order was issued in a specific factual context," and declined to comment on various hypothetical situations presented by the petition. *Id.,* at 893. It relied on its "long standing policy of refusing to issue interpretive rulings or advisory opinions when the critical facts are not explicitly stated or there is a possibility that subsequent events will alter them." *Ibid.*

The United States Court of Appeals for the District of Columbia Circuit reversed, with each of the three judges on the panel writing separately. 181 U.S. App. D.C. 132, 556 F. 2d 9. Judge Tamm concluded that the order represented censorship and was expressly prohibited by § 326 of the Communications Act. Alternatively, Judge Tamm read the Commission opinion as the functional equivalent of a rule and concluded that it was "overbroad." 181 U.S. App. D.C., at 141, 556 F. 2d, at 18. Chief Judge Bazelon's concurrence rested on the Constitution. He was persuaded that § 326's prohibition against censorship is inapplicable to broadcasts forbidden by § 1464. However, he concluded that § 1464 must be narrowly construed to cover only language that is obscene or otherwise unprotected by the First Amendment. 181 U.S. App. D.C., at 140–153, 556 F. 2d, at 24–30. Judge Leventhal, in dissent, stated that the only issue was whether the Commission could regulate the language "*as broadcast.*" *Id.,* at 154, 556 F. 2d, at 31. Emphasizing the interest in protecting children, not only from exposure to indecent language, but also from exposure to the idea that such language has official approval, *id.,* at 160, and n. 18, 556 F. 2d, at 37, and n. 18, he concluded that the Commission had correctly condemned the daytime broadcast as indecent.

Having granted the Commission's petition for certiorari, 434 U.S. 1008, we must decide: (1) whether the scope of judicial review encompasses more than the Commission's determination that the monologue was indecent "as broadcast"; (2) whether the Commission's order was a form of censorship forbidden by § 326; (3) whether the broadcast was indecent within the meaning of §

(1970); (3) unconsenting adults may tune in a station without any warning that offensive language is being or will be broadcast; and (4) there is a scarcity of spectrum space, the use of which the government must therefore license in the public interest. Of special concern to the Commission as well as parents is the first point regarding the use of radio by children." *Id.,* at 97.

1464; and (4) whether the order violates the First Amendment of the United States Constitution.

The relevant statutory questions are whether the Commission's action is forbidden "censorship" within the meaning of 47 U.S.C. § 326 and whether speech that concededly is not obscene may be restricted as "indecent" under the authority of 18 U.S.C. § 1464 (1976 ed.). The questions are not unrelated, for the two statutory provisions have a common origin. Nevertheless, we analyze them separately.

Section 29 of the Radio Act of 1927 provided:

> Nothing in this Act shall be understood or construed to give the licensing authority the power of censorship over the radio communications or signals transmitted by any radio station, and no regulation or condition shall be promulgated or fixed by the licensing authority which shall interfere with the right of free speech by means of radio communications. No person within the jurisdiction of the United States shall utter any obscene, indecent, or profane language by means of radio communication. 44 Stat. 1172.

The prohibition against censorship unequivocally denies the Commission any power to edit proposed broadcasts in advance and to excise material considered inappropriate for the airwaves. The prohibition, however, has never been construed to deny the Commission the power to review the content of completed broadcasts in the performance of its regulatory duties.

Entirely apart from the fact that the subsequent review of program content is not the sort of censorship at which the statute was directed, its history makes it perfectly clear that it was not intended to limit the Commission's power to regulate the broadcast of obscene, indecent, or profane language. A single section of the 1927 Act is the source of both the anticensorship provision and the Commission's authority to impose sanctions for the broadcast of indecent or obscene language. Quite plainly, Congress intended to give meaning to both provisions. Respect for that intent requires that the censorship language be read as inapplicable to the prohibition on broadcasting obscene, indecent, or profane language.

There is nothing in the legislative history to contradict this conclusion. The provision was discussed only in generalities when it was first enacted. In 1934, the anticensorship provision and the prohibition against indecent broadcasts were re-enacted in the same section, just as in the 1927 Act. In 1948, when the Criminal Code was revised to include provisions that had previously been located in other Titles of the United States Code, the prohibition against obscene, indecent, and profane broadcasts was removed from the Communications Act and re-enacted as § 1464 of Title 18. 62 Stat. 769 and 866. That rearrangement of the Code cannot reasonably be interpreted as having been intended to change the meaning of the anticensorship provision. H. R. Rep. No. 304, 80th Cong., 1st Sess., A106 (1947). Cf. *Tidewater Oil Co. v. United States,* 409 U.S. 151, 162.

We conclude, therefore, that § 326 does not limit the Commission's authority to impose sanctions on licensees who engage in obscene, indecent, or profane broadcasting.

III

The only other statutory question presented by this case is whether the afternoon broadcast of the "Filthy Words" monologue was indecent within the meaning of § 1464. Even that question is narrowly confined by the arguments of the parties.

The Commission identified several words that referred to excretory or sexual activities or organs, stated that the repetitive, deliberate use of those words in an afternoon broadcast when children are in the audience was patently offensive, and held that the broadcast was indecent. Pacifica takes issue with the Commission's definition of indecency, but does not dispute the Commission's preliminary determination that each of the components of its definition was present. Specifically, Pacifica does not quarrel with the conclusion that this afternoon broadcast was patently offensive. Pacifica's claim that the broadcast was not indecent within the meaning of the statute rests entirely on the absence of prurient appeal.

The plain language of the statute does not support Pacifica's argument. The words "obscene, indecent, or profane" are written in the disjunctive, implying that each has a separate meaning. Prurient appeal is an element of the obscene, but the normal definition of "indecent" merely refers to nonconformance with accepted standards of morality. . . .

Because neither our prior decisions nor the language or history of § 1464 supports the conclusion that prurient appeal is an essential component of indecent language, we reject Pacifica's construction of the statute. When that construction is put to one side, there is no basis for disagreeing with the Commission's conclusion that indecent language was used in this broadcast.

IV

Pacifica makes two constitutional attacks on the Commission's order. First, it argues that the Commission's construction of the statutory language broadly encompasses so much constitutionally protected speech that reversal is required even if Pacifica's broadcast of the "Filthy Words" monologue is not itself protected by the First Amendment. Second, Pacifica argues that inasmuch as the recording is not obscene, the Constitution forbids any abridgment of the right to broadcast it on the radio.

A

The first argument fails because our review is limited to the question whether the Commission has the authority to proscribe this particular broadcast. As the Commission itself emphasized, its order was "issued in a specific factual context." 59 F.C.C. 2d, at 893. That approach is appropriate for courts as well as the Commission when regulation of indecency is at stake, for indecency is largely a function of context—it cannot be adequately judged in the abstract. . . .

It is true that the Commission's order may lead some broadcasters to censor themselves. At most, however, the Commission's definition of indecency will deter only the broadcasting of patently offensive references to excretory and sexual organs and activities. While some of these references may be protected, they surely lie at the periphery of First Amendment concern. Cf. *Bates v. State Bar of Arizona*, 433 U.S. 350, 380–381. *Young v. American Mini Theatres, Inc.*, 427 U.S. 50, 61. The danger dismissed so summarily in *Red Lion*, in contrast, was that broadcasters would respond to the vagueness of the regulations by refusing to present programs dealing with important social and political controversies.

Invalidating any rule on the basis of its hypothetical application to situations not before the Court is "strong medicine" to be applied "sparingly and only as a last resort." *Broadrick v. Oklahoma*, 413 U.S. 601, 613. We decline to administer that medicine to preserve the vigor of patently offensive sexual and excretory speech.

B

When the issue is narrowed to the facts of this case, the question is whether the First Amendment denies government any power to restrict the public broadcast of indecent language in any circumstances. For if the government has any such power, this was an appropriate occasion for its exercise.

The words of the Carlin monologue are unquestionably "speech" within the meaning of the First Amendment. It is equally clear that the Commission's objections to the broadcast were based in part on its content. The order must therefore fall if, as Pacifica argues, the First Amendment prohibits all governmental regulation that depends on the content of speech. Our past cases demonstrate, however, that no such absolute rule is mandated by the Constitution. . . .

The question in this case is whether a broadcast of patently offensive words dealing with sex and excretion may be regulated because of its content. Obscene materials have been denied the protection of the First Amendment because their content is so offensive to contemporary moral standards. *Roth v. United States*, 354 U.S. 476. But the fact that society may find speech offensive is not a sufficient reason for suppressing it. Indeed, if it is the speaker's opinion that gives offense, that consequence is a reason for according it constitutional protection. For it is a central tenet of the First Amendment that the government must remain neutral in the marketplace of ideas. If there were any reason to believe that the Commission's characterization of the Carlin monologue as offensive could be traced to its political content—or even to the fact that it satirized contemporary attitudes about four-letter words— First Amendment protection might be required. But that is simply not this case. These words offend for the same reasons that obscenity offends. Their place in the hierarchy of First Amendment values was aptly sketched by Mr. Justice Murphy when he said: "[S]uch utterances are no essential part of any exposition of ideas, and are of such slight social value as a step to truth that any benefit that may be derived from them is clearly outweighed by the social interest in order and morality." *Chaplinsky v. New Hampshire,* 315 U.S., at 572.

Although these words ordinarily lack literary, political, or scientific value, they are not entirely outside the protection of the First Amendment. Some uses of even the most offensive words are unquestionably protected. See, e.g., *Hess v. Indiana,* 414 U.S. 105. Indeed, we may assume, *arguendo,* that this monologue would be protected in other contexts. Nonetheless, the constitutional protection accorded to a communication containing such patently offensive sexual and excretory language need not be the same in every context. It is a characteristic of speech such as this that both its capacity to offend and its "social value," to use Mr. Justice Murphy's term, vary with the circumstances. Words that are commonplace in one setting are shocking in another. To paraphrase Mr. Justice Harlan, one occasion's lyric is another's vulgarity. Cf. *Cohen v. California,* 403 U.S. 15, 25.

In this case it is undisputed that the content of Pacifica's broadcast was "vulgar," "offensive," and "shocking." Because content of that character is not entitled to absolute constitutional protection under all circumstances, we must consider its context in order to determine whether the Commission's action was constitutionally permissible.

C

We have long recognized that each medium of expression presents special First Amendment problems. *Joseph Burstyn, Inc. v. Wilson,* 343 U.S. 495, 502–503. And of all forms of communication, it is broadcasting that has received the most limited First Amendment protection. Thus, although other speakers cannot be licensed except under laws that carefully define and narrow official discretion, a broadcaster may be deprived of his license and his forum if the Commission decides that such an action would serve "the public interest, convenience, and necessity." Similarly, although the First Amendment protects

newspaper publishers from being required to print the replies of those whom they criticize, *Miami Herald Publishing Co. v. Tornillo,* 418 U.S. 241, it affords no such protection to broadcasters; on the contrary, they must give free time to the victims of their criticism. *Red Lion Broadcasting Co. v. FCC,* 395 U.S. 367.

The reasons for these distinctions are complex, but two have relevance to the present case. First, the broadcast media have established a uniquely pervasive presence in the lives of all Americans. Patently offensive, indecent material presented over the airwaves confronts the citizen, not only in public, but also in the privacy of the home, where the individual's right to be left alone plainly outweighs the First Amendment rights of an intruder. *Rowan v. Post Office Dept.,* 397 U.S. 728. Because the broadcast audience is constantly tuning in and out, prior warnings cannot completely protect the listener or viewer from unexpected program content. To say that one may avoid further offense by turning off the radio when he hears indecent language is like saying that the remedy for an assault is to run away after the first blow. One may hang up on an indecent phone call, but that option does not give the caller a constitutional immunity or avoid a harm that has already taken place.

Second, broadcasting is uniquely accessible to children, even those too young to read. Although Cohen's written message might have been incomprehensible to a first grader, Pacifica's broadcast could have enlarged a child's vocabulary in an instant. Other forms of offensive expression may be withheld from the young without restricting the expression at its source. Bookstores and motion picture theaters, for example, may be prohibited from making indecent material available to children. We held in *Ginsberg v. New York,* 390 U.S. 629, that the government's interest in the "well-being of its youth" and in supporting "parents' claim to authority in their own household" justified the regulation of otherwise protected expression. *Id.,* at 640 and 639. The ease with which children may obtain access to broadcast material, coupled with the concerns recognized in *Ginsberg,* amply justify special treatment of indecent broadcasting.

It is appropriate, in conclusion, to emphasize the narrowness of our holding. This case does not involve a two-way radio conversation between a cab driver and a dispatcher, or a telecast of an Elizabethan comedy. We have not decided that an occasional expletive in either setting would justify any sanction or, indeed, that this broadcast would justify a criminal prosecution. The Commission's decision rested entirely on a nuisance rationale under which context is all-important. The concept requires consideration of a host of variables. The time of day was emphasized by the Commission. The content of the program in which the language is used will also affect the composition of the audience, and differences between radio, television, and perhaps closed-circuit transmissions, may also be relevant. As Mr. Justice Sutherland wrote, a "nuisance may be merely a right thing in the wrong place,—like a pig in the parlor instead of the barnyard." *Euclid v. Ambler Realty Co.,* 272 U.S. 365, 388. We simply hold that when the Commission finds that a pig has entered the parlor, the exercise of its regulatory power does not depend on proof that the pig is obscene.

The judgment of the Court of Appeals is reversed.

Mr. Justice Powell, with whom Mr. Justice Blackmun joins, concurring in part and concurring in the judgment.

I join Parts I, II, III, and IV-C of Mr. Justice Stevens' opinion....

It is conceded that the monologue at issue here is not obscene in the constitutional sense. See 56 F.C.C. 2d 94, 98 (1975); Brief for Petitioner 18. Nor, in this context, does its language constitute "fighting words" within the meaning of *Chaplinsky v. New Hampshire,* 315 U.S. 568 (1942). Some of the words used have been held protected by the First Amendment in other cases and contexts. E.g., *Lewis v. New Orleans,* 415 U.S. 130 (1974); *Hess v. Indiana,* 414 U.S. 105 (1973); *Papish v. University of Missouri Curators,* 410 U.S. 667 (1973); *Cohen v. California,* 403 U.S. 15 (1971); see also *Eaton v. Tulsa,* 415 U.S. 697 (1974). I do not think Carlin, consistently with the First Amendment, could be punished for delivering the same monologue to a live audience composed of adults who, knowing what to expect, chose to attend his performance. See *Brown v. Oklahoma,* 408 U.S. 914 (1972) (Powell, J., concurring in

result). And I would assume that an adult could not constitutionally be prohibited from purchasing a recording or transcript of the monologue and playing or reading it in the privacy of his own home. Cf. *Stanley v. Georgia,* 394 U.S. 557 (1969).

But it also is true that the language employed is, to most people, vulgar and offensive. It was chosen specifically for this quality, and it was repeated over and over as a sort of verbal shock treatment. The Commission did not err in characterizing the narrow category of language used here as "patently offensive" to most people regardless of age.

The issue, however, is whether the Commission may impose civil sanctions on a licensee radio station for broadcasting the monologue at two o'clock in the afternoon. The Commission's primary concern was to prevent the broadcast from reaching the ears of unsupervised children who were likely to be in the audience at that hour. In essence, the Commission sought to "channel" the monologue to hours when the fewest unsupervised children would be exposed to it. See 56 F.C.C. 2d, at 98. In my view, this consideration provides strong support for the Commission's holding.

The Court has recognized society's right to "adopt more stringent controls on communicative materials available to youths than on those available to adults." *Erznoznik v. Jacksonville,* 422 U.S. 205, 212 (1975); see also, e.g., *Miller v. California,* 413 U.S. 15, 36 n. 17 (1973); *Ginsberg v. New York,* 390 U.S. 629, 636–641 (1968); *Jacobellis v. Ohio,* 378 U.S. 184, 195 (1964) (opinion of Brennan, J.). This recognition stems in large part from the fact that "a child . . . is not possessed of that full capacity for individual choice which is the presupposition of First Amendment guarantees." *Ginsberg v. New York, supra,* at 649–650 (Stewart, J., concurring in result). Thus, children may not be able to protect themselves from speech which, although shocking to most adults, generally may be avoided by the unwilling through the exercise of choice. At the same time, such speech may have a deeper and more lasting negative effect on a child than on an adult....

In most instances, the dissemination of this kind of speech to children may be limited without also limiting willing adults' access to it. Sellers of printed and recorded matter and exhibitors of motion pictures and live performances may be required to shut their doors to children, but such a requirement has no effect on adults' access. See *id.*, at 634–635. The difficulty is that such a physical separation of the audience cannot be accomplished in the broadcast media. During most of the broadcast hours, both adults and unsupervised children are likely to be in the broadcast audience, and the broadcaster cannot reach willing adults without also reaching children. This, as the Court emphasizes, is one of the distinctions between the broadcast and other media to which we often have adverted as justifying a different treatment of the broadcast media for First Amendment purposes. See *Bates v. State Bar of Arizona,* 433 U.S. 350, 384 (1977); *Columbia Broadcasting System, Inc. v. Democratic National Committee,* 412 U.S. 94, 101 (1973); *Red Lion Broadcasting Co. v. FCC,* 395 U.S. 367, 386–387 (1969); *Capital Broadcasting Co. v. Mitchell,* 333 F. Supp. 582 (DC 1971), aff'd *sub nom, Capital Broadcasting Co. v. Acting Attorney General,* 405 U.S. 1000 (1972); see generally *Joseph Burstyn, Inc. v. Wilson,* 343 U.S. 495, 502–503 (1952). In my view, the Commission was entitled to give substantial weight to this difference in reaching its decision in this case.

A second difference, not without relevance, is that broadcasting—unlike most other forms of communication comes directly into the home, the one place where people ordinarily have the right not to be assaulted by uninvited and offensive sights and sounds. *Erznoznik v. Jacksonville, supra,* at 209; *Cohen v. California,* 403 U.S., at 21; *Rowan v. Post Office Dept.,* 397 U.S. 728 (1970). Although the First Amendment may require unwilling adults to absorb the first blow of offensive but protected speech when they are in public before they turn away, see, e.g., *Erznoznik, supra,* at 210–211, but cf. *Rosenfeld v. New Jersey,* 408 U.S. 901, 903–909 (1972) (Powell, J., dissenting), a different order of values obtains in the home. "That we are often 'captives' outside the sanctuary of the home and subject to objectionable speech and other sound does not mean we must be captives everywhere." *Rowan v. Post Office Dept., supra,* at 738. The Commission also was entitled to give this factor appropriate weight in the circumstances of the instant case. This is not to say, however, that the Commission has an unrestricted license

to decide what speech, protected in other media, may be banned from the airwaves in order to protect unwilling adults from momentary exposure to it in their homes. Making the sensitive judgments required in these cases is not easy. But this responsibility has been reposed initially in the Commission, and its judgment is entitled to respect.

It is argued that despite society's right to protect its children from this kind of speech, and despite everyone's interest is not being assaulted by offensive speech in the home, the Commission's holding in this case is impermissible because it prevents willing adults from listening to Carlin's monologue over the radio in the early afternoon hours. It is said that this ruling will have the effect of "reduc[ing] the adult population . . . to [hearing] only what is fit for children." *Butler v. Michigan,* 352 U.S. 380, 383 (1957). This argument is not without force. The Commission certainly should consider it as it develops standards in this area. But it is not sufficiently strong to leave the Commission powerless to act in circumstances such as those in this case.

The Commission's holding does not prevent willing adults from purchasing Carlin's record, from attending his performances, or, indeed, from reading the transcript reprinted as an appendix to the Court's opinion. On its face, it does not prevent respondent Pacifica Foundation from broadcasting the monologue during late evening hours when fewer children are likely to be in the audience, nor from broadcasting discussions of the contemporary use of language at any time during the day. The Commission's holding, and certainly the Court's holding today, does not speak to cases involving the isolated use of a potentially offensive word in the course of a radio broadcast, as distinguished from the verbal shock treatment administered by respondent here. In short, I agree that on the facts of this case, the Commission's order did not violate respondent's First Amendment rights.

II

As the foregoing demonstrates, my views are generally in accord with what is said in Part IV-C of Mr. Justice Stevens' opinion. See *ante,* at 748–750. I therefore join that portion of his opinion.

I do not join Part IV-B, however, because I do not subscribe to the theory that the Justices of this Court are free generally to decide on the basis of its content which speech protected by the First Amendment is most "valuable" and hence deserving of the most protection, and which is less "valuable" and hence deserving of less protection. Compare *ante,* at 744–748; *Young v. American Mini Theatres, Inc.,* 427 U.S. 50, 63–73 (1976) (opinion of Stevens, J.), with *id.,* at 73 n. 1 (Powell, J., concurring). In my view, the result in this case does not turn on whether Carlin's monologue, viewed as a whole, or the words that constitute it, have more or less "value" than a candidate's campaign speech. This is a judgment for each person to make, not one for the judges to impose upon him.

The result turns instead on the unique characteristics of the broadcast media, combined with society's right to protect its children from speech generally agreed to be inappropriate for their years, and with the interest of unwilling adults in not being assaulted by such offensive speech in their homes. Moreover, I doubt whether today's decision will prevent any adult who wishes to receive Carlin's message in Carlin's own words from doing so, and from making for himself a value judgment as to the merit of the message and words. Cf. *id.,* at 77–79 (Powell, J., concurring). These are the grounds upon which I join the judgment of the Court as to Part IV.

Mr. Justice Brennan, with whom Mr. Justice Marshall joins, dissenting.

For the second time in two years, see *Young v. American Mini Theatres, Inc.,* 427 U.S. 50 (1976), the Court refuses to embrace the notion, completely antithetical to basic First Amendment values, that the degree of protection the First Amendment affords protected speech varies with the social value ascribed to that speech by five Members of this Court. See opinion of Mr. Justice Powell, *ante,* at 761–762. Moreover, as do all parties, all Members of the Court agree that the Carlin monologue aired by Station WBAI does not fall within one of the categories of speech, such as "fighting words." *Chaplinsky v. New Hampshire,* 315 U.S. 568 (1942), or obscenity, *Roth v. United States,* 354 U.S. 476 (1957), that is totally without First Amendment protection. This conclusion, of course, is compelled by our cases expressly holding that communications containing some of the words found condemnable here are fully protected by the First Amendment in other contexts. See *Eaton v. Tulsa,* 415 U.S. 697 (1974); *Papish v. University of Missouri Curators,* 410 U.S. 667 (1973); *Brown v. Oklahoma,* 408 U.S. 914 (1972); *Lewis v. New Orleans,* 408 U.S. 913 (1972); *Rosenfeld v. New Jersey,* 408 U.S. 901 (1972); *Cohen v. California,* 403 U.S. 15 (1971). Yet despite the Court's refusal to create a sliding scale of First Amendment protection calibrated to this Court's perception of the worth of a communication's content, and despite our unanimous agreement that the Carlin monologue is protected speech, a majority of the Court nevertheless finds that, on the facts of this case, the FCC is not constitutionally barred from imposing sanctions on Pacifica for its airing of the Carlin monologue. This majority apparently believes that the FCC's disapproval of Pacifica's afternoon broadcast of Carlin's "Dirty Words" recording is a permissible time, place, and manner regulation. *Kovacs v. Cooper,* 336 U.S. 77 (1949). Both the opinion of my Brother Stevens and the opinion of my Brother Powell rely principally on two factors in reaching this conclusion: (1) the capacity of a radio broadcast to intrude into the unwilling listener's home, and (2) the presence of children in the listening audience. Dispassionate analysis, removed from individual notions as to what is proper and what is not, starkly reveals that these justifications, whether individually or together, simply do not support even the professedly moderate degree of governmental homogenization of radio communications—if, indeed, such homogenization can ever be moderate given the preeminent status of the right of free speech in our constitutional scheme—that the Court today permits.

A

Without question, the privacy interests of an individual in his home are substantial and deserving of significant protection. In finding these interests sufficient to justify the content regulation of protected speech, however, the Court commits two errors. First, it misconceives the nature of the privacy interests involved where an individual voluntarily chooses to admit radio communications into his home. Second, it ignores the constitutionally protected interests of both those who wish to transmit and those who desire to receive broadcasts that many—including the FCC and this Court—might find offensive.

"The ability of government, consonant with the Constitution, to shut off discourse solely to protect others from hearing it is . . . dependent upon a showing that substantial privacy interests are being invaded in an essentially intolerable manner. Any broader view of this authority would effectively empower a majority to silence dissidents simply as a matter of personal predilections." *Cohen v. California, supra,* at 21. I am in wholehearted agreement with my Brethren that an individual's right "to be let alone" when engaged in private activity within the confines of his own home is encompassed within the "substantial privacy interests" to which Mr. Justice Harlan referred in *Cohen,* and is entitled to the greatest solicitude. *Stanley v. Georgia,* 394 U.S. 557 (1969). However, I believe that an individual's actions in switching on and listening to communications transmitted over the public airways and directed to the public at large do not implicate fundamental privacy interests, even when engaged in within the home. Instead, because the radio is undeniably a public medium, these actions are more properly viewed as a decision to take part, if only as a listener, in an ongoing public discourse. See Note, Filthy Words, the FCC, and the First Amendment: Regulating Broadcast Obscenity, 61 Va. L. Rev. 579, 618 (1975). Although an individual's decision to allow public radio communications into his home undoubtedly does not abrogate all of his privacy interests, the residual privacy interests he retains vis-à-vis the communication he voluntarily admits into his home are surely no greater than those of the people present in the corridor of the Los Angeles courthouse in *Cohen* who bore witness to the words "Fuck the Draft" emblazoned across Cohen's jacket. Their privacy interests were held insufficient to justify punishing Cohen for his offensive communication.

Even if an individual who voluntarily opens his home to radio communications retains privacy interests of sufficient moment to justify a ban on protected speech if those interests are "invaded in an essentially intolerable manner," *Cohen v. California, supra,* at 21, the very fact that those interests are threatened only by a radio broadcast precludes any intolerable invasion of privacy; for unlike other intrusive modes of communication, such as sound trucks, "[t]he radio can be turned off," *Lehman v. Shaker Heights,* 418 U.S. 298, 302 (1974)—and with a minimum of effort. As Chief Judge Bazelon aptly observed below, "having elected to receive public air waves, the scanner who stumbles onto an offensive program is in the same position as the unsuspecting passers-by in *Cohen* and *Erznoznik* [*v. Jacksonville,* 422 U.S. 205 (1975)]; he can avert his attention by changing channels or turning off the set." 181 U.S. App. D.C. 132, 149, 556 F. 2d 9, 26 (1977). Whatever the minimal discomfort suffered by a listener who inadvertently tunes into a program he finds offensive during the brief interval before he can simply extend his arm and switch stations or flick the "off" button, it is surely worth the candle to preserve the broadcaster's right to send, and the right of those interested to receive, a message entitled to full First Amendment protection. To reach a contrary balance, as does the Court, is clearly to follow Mr. Justice Stevens' reliance on animal metaphors, *ante,* at 750–751, "to burn the house to roast the pig." *Butler v. Michigan,* 352 U.S. 380, 383 (1957).

The Court's balance, of necessity, fails to accord proper weight to the interests of listeners who wish to hear broadcasts the FCC deems offensive. It permits majoritarian tastes completely to preclude a protected message from entering the homes of a receptive, unoffended minority. No decision of this Court supports such a result. Where the individuals constituting the offended majority may freely choose to reject the material being offered, we have never found their privacy interests of such moment to warrant the suppression of speech on privacy grounds. . . .

Most parents will undoubtedly find understandable as well as commendable the Court's sympathy with the FCC's desire to prevent offensive broadcasts from reaching the ears of unsupervised children. Unfortunately, the facial appeal of this justification for radio censorship masks its constitutional insufficiency. . . .

Because the Carlin monologue is obviously not an erotic appeal to the prurient interests of children, the Court, for the first time, allows the government to prevent minors from gaining access to materials that are not obscene, and are therefore protected, as to them. It thus ignores our recent admonition that "[s]peech that is neither obscene as to youths nor subject to some other legitimate proscription cannot be suppressed solely to protect the young from ideas or images that a legislative body thinks unsuitable for them." 422 U.S., at 213–214. The Court's refusal to follow its own pronouncements is especially lamentable since it has the anomalous subsidiary effect, at least in the radio context at issue here, of making completely unavailable to adults material which may not constitutionally be kept even from children. This result violates in spades the principle of *Butler v. Michigan, supra. Butler* involved a challenge to a Michigan statute that forbade the publication, sale, or distribution of printed material "tending to incite minors to violent or depraved or immoral acts, manifestly tending to the corruption of the morals of youth." 352 U.S., at 381. Although *Roth v. United States, supra,* had not yet been decided, it is at least arguable that the material the statute in *Butler* was designed to suppress could have been constitutionally denied to children. Nevertheless, this Court found the statute unconstitutional. Speaking for the Court, Mr. Justice Frankfurter reasoned:

> The incidence of this enactment is to reduce the adult population of Michigan to reading only what is fit for children. It thereby arbitrarily curtails one of those liberties of the individual, now enshrined in the Due Process Clause of the Fourteenth Amendment, that history has attested as the indispensable conditions for the maintenance and progress of a free society. 352 U.S., at 383–384.

Where, as here, the government may not prevent the exposure of minors to the suppressed material, the principle of *Butler* applies *a fortiori.* The opinion of my Brother Powell acknowledges that there lurks in today's decision a potential for " 'reduc[ing] the adult population . . . to [hearing] only what is fit for children,' " *ante,* at 760, but expresses faith that the FCC will vigilantly prevent this potential from ever becoming a reality. I am far less certain than my Brother Powell that such faith in the Commission is warranted, see *Illinois Citizens Committee for Broadcasting v. FCC,*

169 U.S. App. D.C. 166, 187–190, 515 F. 2d 397, 418–421 (1975) (statement of Bazelon, C. J., as to why he voted to grant rehearing en banc); and even if I shared it, I could not so easily shirk the responsibility assumed by each Member of this Court jealously to guard against encroachments on First Amendment freedoms.

In concluding that the presence of children in the listening audience provides an adequate basis for the FCC to impose sanctions for Pacifica's broadcast of the Carlin monologue, the opinions of my Brother Powell, *ante,* at 757–758, and my Brother Stevens, *ante,* at 749–750, both stress the time-honored right of a parent to raise his child as he sees fit—a right this Court has consistently been vigilant to protect. See *Wisconsin v. Yoder,* 406 U.S. 205 (1972); *Pierce v. Society of Sisters,* 268 U.S. 510 (1925). Yet this principle supports a result directly contrary to that reached by the Court. *Yoder* and *Pierce* hold that parents, *not* the government, have the right to make certain decisions regarding the upbringing of their children. As surprising as it may be to individual Members of this Court, some parents may actually find Mr. Carlin's unabashed attitude towards the seven "dirty words" healthy, and deem it desirable to expose their children to the manner in which Mr. Carlin defuses the taboo surrounding the words. Such parents may constitute a minority of the American public, but the absence of great numbers willing to exercise the right to raise their children in this fashion does not alter the right's nature or its existence. Only the Court's regrettable decision does that.

C

As demonstrated above, neither of the factors relied on by both the opinion of my Brother Powell and the opinion of my Brother Stevens—the intrusive nature of radio and the presence of children in the listening audience—can, when taken on its own terms, support the FCC's disapproval of the Carlin monologue. These two asserted justifications are further plagued by a common failing: the lack of principled limits on their use as a basis for FCC censorship. No such limits come readily to mind, and neither of the opinions constituting the Court serve to clarify the extent to which the FCC may assert the privacy and children-in-the-audience rationales as justification for expunging from the airways protected communications the Commission finds offensive. Taken to their logical extreme these rationales would support the cleansing of public radio of any "four-letter words" whatsoever, regardless of their context. The rationales could justify the banning from radio of a myriad of literary works, novels, poems, and plays by the likes of Shakespeare, Joyce, Hemingway, Ben Jonson, Henry Fielding, Robert Burns, and Chaucer; they could support the suppression of a good deal of political speech, such as the Nixon tapes; and they could even provide the basis for imposing sanctions for the broadcast of certain portions of the Bible.

In order to dispel the specter of the possibility of so unpalatable a degree of censorship, and to defuse Pacifica's overbreadth challenge, the FCC insists that it desires only the authority to reprimand a broadcaster on facts analogous to those present in this case, which it describes as involving "broadcasting for nearly twelve minutes a record which repeated over and over words which depict sexual or excretory activities and organs in a manner patently offensive by its community's contemporary standards in the early afternoon when children were in the audience." Brief for Petitioner 45. The opinions of both my Brother Powell and my Brother Stevens take the FCC at its word, and consequently do no more than permit the Commission to censor the afternoon broadcast of the "sort of verbal shock treatment," opinion of Mr. Justice Powell, *ante*, at 757, involved here.... For my own part, even accepting that this case is limited to its facts, I would place the responsibility and the right to weed worthless and offensive communications from the public airways where it belongs and where, until today, it resided: in a public free to choose those communications worthy of its attention from a marketplace unsullied by the censor's hand.

II

The absence of any hesitancy in the opinions of my Brothers Powell and Stevens to approve the FCC's censorship of the Carlin monologue on the basis of two demonstrably inadequate grounds is a function of their perception that the decision will result in little, if any, curtailment of communicative exchanges protected by the First Amendment. Although the extent to which the Court stands ready to countenance FCC censorship of protected speech is unclear from today's decision, I find the reasoning by which my Brethren conclude that the FCC censorship they approve will not significantly infringe on First Amendment values both disingenuous as to reality and wrong as a matter of law.

My Brother Stevens, in reaching a result apologetically described as narrow, *ante*, at 750, takes comfort in his observation that "[a] requirement that indecent language be avoided will have its primary effect on the form, rather than the content, of serious communication," *ante*, at 743 n. 18, and finds solace in his conviction that "[t]here are few, if any, thoughts that cannot be expressed by the use of less offensive language." *Ibid.* The idea that the content of a message and its potential impact on any who might receive it can be divorced from the words that are the vehicle for its expression is transparently fallacious. A given word may have a unique capacity to capsule an idea, evoke an emotion, or conjure up an image. Indeed, for those of us who place an appropriately high value on our cherished First Amendment rights, the word "censor" is such a word. Mr. Justice Harlan, speaking for the Court, recognized the truism that a speaker's choice of words cannot surgically be separated from the ideas he desires to express when he warned that "we cannot indulge the facile assumption that one can forbid particular words without also running a substantial risk of suppressing ideas in the process." *Cohen v. California*, 403 U.S., at 26. Moreover, even if an alternative phrasing may communicate a speaker's abstract ideas as effectively as those words he is forbidden to use, it is doubtful that the sterilized message will convey the emotion that is an essential part of so many communications. This, too, was apparent to Mr. Justice Harlan and the Court in *Cohen*.

> [W]e cannot overlook the fact, because it is well illustrated by the episode involved here, that much linguistic expression serves a dual communicative function: it conveys not only ideas capable of relatively precise, detached explication, but otherwise inexpressible emotions as well. In fact, words are often chosen as much for their emotive as their cognitive force. We cannot sanction the view that the

436 Content Regulation of the Media

Constitution, while solicitous of the cognitive content of individual speech, has little or no regard for that emotive function which, practically speaking, may often be the more important element of the overall message sought to be communicated. *Id.,* at 25–26.

My Brother Stevens also finds relevant to his First Amendment analysis the fact that "[a]dults who feel the need may purchase tapes and records or go to theaters and nightclubs to hear [the tabooed] words." *Ante,* at 750 n. 28. My Brother Powell agrees: "The Commission's holding does not prevent willing adults from purchasing Carlin's record, from attending his performances, or, indeed, from reading the transcript reprinted as an appendix to the Court's opinion." *Ante,* at 760. The opinions of my Brethren display both a sad insensitivity to the fact that these alternatives involve the expenditure of money, time, and effort that many of those wishing to hear Mr. Carlin's message may not be able to afford, and a naive innocence of the reality that in many cases, the medium may well be the message. . . .

III

It is quite evident that I find the Court's attempt to unstitch the warp and woof of First Amendment law in an effort to reshape its fabric to cover the patently wrong result the Court reaches in this case dangerous as well as lamentable. Yet there runs throughout the opinions of my Brothers Powell and Stevens another vein I find equally disturbing: a depressing inability to appreciate that in our land of cultural pluralism, there are many who think, act, and talk differently from the Members of this Court, and who do not share their fragile sensibilities. It is only an acute ethnocentric myopia that enables the Court to approve the censorship of communications solely because of the words they contain.

"A word is not a crystal, transparent and unchanged, it is the skin of a living thought and may vary greatly in color and content according to the circumstances and the time in which it is used." *Towne v. Eisner,* 245 U.S. 418, 425 (1918) (Holmes, J.). The words that the Court and the Commission find so unpalatable may be the stuff of everyday conversations in some, if not many,

of the innumerable subcultures that compose this Nation. Academic research indicates that this is indeed the case. See B. Jackson, "Get Your Ass in the Water and Swim Like Me" (1974); J. Dillard, Black English (1972); W. Labov, Language in the Inner City: Studies in the Black English Vernacular (1972). As one researcher concluded, "[w]ords generally considered obscene like 'bullshit' and 'fuck' are considered neither obscene nor derogatory in the [black] vernacular except in particular contextual situations and when used with certain intonations." C. Bins, "Toward an Ethnography of Contemporary African American Oral Poetry," Language and Linguistics Working Papers No. 5, p. 82 (Georgetown Univ. Press 1972). Cf. *Keefe v. Geanakos,* 418 F. 2d 359, 361 (CA1 1969) (finding the use of the word "motherfucker" commonplace among young radicals and protesters).

Today's decision will thus have its greatest impact on broadcasters desiring to reach, and listening audiences composed of, persons who do not share the Court's view as to which words or expressions are acceptable and who, for a variety of reasons, including a conscious desire to flout majoritarian conventions, express themselves using words that may be regarded as offensive by those from different socio-economic backgrounds. In this context, the Court's decision may be seen for what, in the broader perspective, it really is: another of the dominant culture's inevitable efforts to force those groups who do not share its mores to conform to its way of thinking, acting, and speaking. See *Moore v. East Cleveland,* 431 U.S. 494, 506–511 (1977) (Brennan, J., concurring).

Pacifica, in response to an FCC inquiry about its broadcast of Carlin's satire on " 'the words you couldn't say on the public . . . airways,' " explained that "Carlin is not mouthing obscenities, he is merely using words to satirize as harmless and essentially silly our attitudes towards those words." 56 F.C.C. 2d, at 95, 96. In confirming Carlin's prescience as a social commentator by the result it reaches today, the Court evinces an attitude toward the "seven dirty words" that many others besides Mr. Carlin and Pacifica might describe as "silly." Whether today's decision will similarly prove "harmless" remains to be seen. One can only hope that it will.

3. Post-Pacifica Regulation

Twice emphasizing an "inten[t] strictly to observe the narrowness of the *Pacifica* holding,"[283] the commission (1) renewed a license despite an organized morality group's objection that a public television station's broadcast of "Masterpiece Theatre," "Monty Python's Flying Circus," and other programs "consistently [propagated] offensive, vulgar ... material"[284] and (2) denied a request to prohibit the use of the word "nigger," which had been uttered on the air by a political candidate.[285] In the second instance, the agency further noted that its concern with indecency was limited to references of a sexual or excretory nature.[286] Even prior to the Court's decision in *Pacifica,* the commission had issued a clarification to the effect that it was not concerned with offensive speech arising in the course of news coverage, at least when no opportunity existed for editing. The limiting principles, however, did not deter critical evaluation of the FCC's regulatory pitch and of the *Pacifica* decision itself.

The rationales for regulating indecent expression are both new and old. Concern with the medium's pervasive or intrusive nature and its accessibility to children represented a departure point for content control of the least protected component of the press.[287] The regulatory predicates, however, borrow from rationales that were constructed near the turn of the century in response to the development and emergence of other mass media.[288] Unlike the scarcity premise, which has operated as a platform from which diversity aims were pursued, even if unsatisfactorily, the predicate of *Pacifica* is candidly conceived to inhibit expression and to define permissible bounds of diversity.

The unique characteristics attributed to broadcasting and its consequently diminished First Amendment status help explain why the Court employed what appeared to be a less exacting standard of review than it would in another setting. A city ordinance that barred exhibition of nudity on drive-in theater screens, for instance, was invalidated.[289] Despite arguments in support of the need to protect children, the Court in *Erznoznik v. Jacksonville,*[290] found the measure overbroad to the extent that it reached non-obscene expression.[291] With respect to privacy interests, it noted that offended persons could "avoid further bombardment of [their] sensibilities by averting [their] eyes."[292]

Also "pitting the First Amendment rights of speakers against the privacy rights of those who may be unwilling viewers or auditors,"[293] and raising questions related to the presence of children, was the case of an individual wearing a jacket with the words "Fuck the Draft" on it. Although maybe no less difficult to avert one's gaze under such circumstances than to switch channels, and conceivable that a child might focus for a prolonged time upon the message, the Court found such expression comfortably within a First Amendment ambit that presumed judicial inability to make principled distinctions based upon taste.[294] Moreover, in *Cohen v. California,*[295] it lectured that

> (s)urely the State has no right to cleanse public debts to the point where it is grammatically palatable to the most squeamish of us. Yet no readily ascertainable general principle exists for stopping short of that result were we to affirm the [conviction for offensive conduct]. For, while the four-letter word being litigated here is perhaps more distasteful than most others of its genre, it is nevertheless often true that one man's vulgarity is another's lyric. Indeed, we think it is largely because governmental officials cannot make principled

decisions in this area that the Constitution leaves matters of taste and style so largely to the individual.[296]

Upon examination, the rationales enabling the Court to "avert its eyes" from the instruction of *Cohen* seem to raise as many questions as they answer. Concern that children have ready access or are peculiarly vulnerable to the influence of radio and television has yet to translate into conclusive findings of profoundly adverse effects.[297] If access and exposure are relative realities and lend themselves to variable context-based standards, it is unclear why equally if not more stringent controls do not operate against adult-oriented publications and offensive street or playground epithets. Finally, the Court has long recognized parental autonomy as a constitutionally protected interest[298] and adverted to it in facilitating other First Amendment guarantees[299] and even in curtailing a competing fundamental right.[300] Despite the availability of inexpensive technology that enables parents to control the television viewing of a child even when they are not present[301] and thereby exercise more effective control than exists against chance encounters in public, its pertinence as discussed later in this chapter has been largely discounted.

Privacy concerns, although adverted to in support of content regulation, arguably cut in the opposite direction. Constitutional concepts of privacy pertain not only to intrusion into a protected sphere but also to personal autonomy. Insofar as a constitutional violation requires state action,[302] it is the latter notion of privacy that would seem to be implicated in a constitutional sense by indecent or offensive broadcasting. Traditional First Amendment notions favoring autonomous over authoritative selection[303] also might favor further an emphasis upon personal rather than individual control. Pursuant to

a focus upon personal autonomy rather than official protection of sensitivity, self-help remedies akin to asking an unwanted house guest to leave might figure more prominently. Such questions were avoided, however, given a diminished standard of review for a less protected medium.

One court has suggested that the real worry about broadcasting, especially its pervasiveness, is the sense that "it is the immediacy and power of broadcasting that [warrant] different treatment."[304] If so, such a premise would deviate too from constitutional norms insofar as they disfavor official control tied to degree of influence.[305] The *Pacifica* decision in sum has been subject to criticism for departing from the concept of the First Amendment as guaranteeing diverse expressive opportunities and individualizing responsibility for selection.

> The first amendment, in theory, trusts the public to make sound decisions and assumes the risk that it will not. A system of official control designed to curb expression that may offend or affront has the potential for reaching views that merely are unpopular or unorthodox. The transfer of responsibility for content evaluation thus has more profoundly subversive potential than any harmful tendencies of indecent or offensive expression.
>
> In a constitutional value system that supposedly favors pluralism and autonomous over authoritative selection, adverse consequences of expression may be addressed or remedied by preemptive or reactive personal action. Official catering to the tastes of some to dictate what information is available to others represents inverted thinking. Individuals wanting to see or hear what may not be broadcast, it is true, have alternative means of obtaining access to such material. The burden and cost of practical private regulation that would effectively screen out unwanted expression, however, would be incurred only once and consequently be less imposing than the tariff on multiple diversity-motivated purchases. Despite the disparity of costs, which

seem to favor first amendment concerns, the Court essentially has favored the taxing of pluralism rather than intolerance.[306]

Competing against criticism that the FCC had reached too deeply into a constitutionally protected sphere was the claim that it had not gone far enough.[307] A decade after *Pacifica,* the commission revisited the question of indecency in response to complaints concerning sexually explicit programming.[308] In a series of orders against three broadcast stations[309] and an amateur radio operator,[310] and accompanying announcement of new enforcement standards,[311] the FCC attempted "to clarify when it will exercise its enforcement authority... in the future."[312] In so doing, the commission expressly observed that, instead of concerning itself merely with the seven words at issue in *Pacifica,* it would "apply the generic definition of broadcast indecency advanced in *Pacifica,* which is: '(1)anguage or material that depicts or describes, in terms patently offensive as measured by contemporary community standards for the broadcast medium, sexual or excretory activities or organs.' "[313]

Unlike the previous indecency actions, which had concerned programming directed toward small, discrete audiences,[314] one of the complaints concerned a "shock radio" format which drew a large audience in a major market.[315] Rejecting characterizations of the speech at issue as "incidental use of sexually-oriented language, sexual innuendo and double entendre,"[316] the FCC in *Infinity Broadcasting Corp. of Pennsylvania*[317] found "explicit references to masturbation, ejaculation, breast size, penis size, sexual intercourse, nudity, urination, oral-genital contact, erections, sodomy, bestiality, menstruation, and testicles."[318] Although finding none of the subjects *"per se* beyond the realm of acceptable broadcast discussion,"[319] the commission determined

that particular references were "patently offensive, and their sexual and excretory import...clear."[320] It noted that presentation consisted not of an "occasional off-color reference or expletive but a dwelling on matters sexual and excretory, in a pandering and titillating fashion."[321] Context thus "aggravate[d] rather then dilute[d] or ameliorate[d] the patent offensiveness of what [was] said."[322]

Infinity Broadcasting Corp. of Pennsylvania, 2 F.C.C. Rcd. 2705 (1987)

Memorandum Opinion and Order

1. The Commission has before it three complaints with respect to certain programming, broadcast on Station WYSP(FM), Philadelphia, Pennsylvania, which allegedly violated Title 18, United States Code, Section 1464. Under Section 503(b)(1)(D) of the Communications Act of 1934, as amended, the Commission has authority to impose a forfeiture or other sanction upon a licensee who has violated Section 1464. At issue is whether the broadcasts in question constitute a violation of Section 1464 and, if so, what penalties, if any, should be imposed upon Infinity Broadcasting Corporation of Pennsylvania ("Infinity"), licensee of WYSP(FM)....

7. Under the prevailing test, indecent speech is "language that describes, in terms patently offensive as measured by contemporary community standards for the broadcast medium, sexual or excretory activities and organs." Such indecent speech is actionable at times of the day when there is a reasonable risk that children may be in the audience. *Pacifica Foundation,* 56 FCC 2d 94, 98 (1975). Speech that is indecent must involve more than the isolated use of an offensive word. See, e.g., *FCC v. Pacifica Foundation,* 438 U.S. 726, 750 (1978). Further, what is indecent "is largely a function of context" and cannot adequately be judged in the abstract. *Id.* at 742. The crux of Infinity's argument appears to be that only concentrated and repeated use of the specific offensive words at issue in the *Pacifica* case would support a finding that programming contravenes

18 U.S.C. §1464. Infinity distinguishes that type of speech, which it asserts Mr. Stern has not used, from what it characterizes as his incidental use of sexually-oriented language, sexual innuendo and double entendre.

8. We do not accept Infinity's interpretation of the test governing indecency. We take this occasion, however, to clarify prior Commission statements regarding indecency. As an initial matter, analysis of whether particular speech is indecent cannot turn on a mechanistic classification of language, e.g., as double entendre, innuendo or expletives. Rather, in each case the words broadcast and the context in which they were broadcast must be considered in order to decide whether the indecency test, as articulated by the Commission and upheld by the Supreme Court, has been met. For example, despite any characterization of the words in the George Carlin monologue at issue in *Pacifica,* the dispositive factor was that those words were used in a context that was found to be patently offensive. In addition, the words were broadcast at a time of day when there was a reasonable risk that children may have been in the audience. In this regard, we find untenable the view that the holding in *Pacifica* limits a finding of indecency to use of the seven offensive words contained in the Carlin monologue.

9. Likewise, the mere assertion that sexually-oriented programming involves innuendo or double entendre cannot serve to exempt it from the coverage of the statute. Instead, the broadcast must be examined in context to determine whether its meaning can reasonably be considered to contain patently offensive references to sexual or excretory activities and organs. Words that in one context may be innuendo or double entendre may be rendered explicit in other contexts when they are intermingled with explicit references that make the meaning of the entire discussion clear or capable only of one meaning. The latter may constitute actionable indecency. As such determinations are difficult, we shall approach this issue cautiously. Finally, while in the *Pacifica* case the 12-minute long Carlin monologue, consisting of a repetitious barrage of seven particular words, was characterized as "verbal shock treatment," repetitive use of specific sexual or excretory words or phrases is not an absolute requirement for a finding of indecency.

10. With these principles in mind, we turn to an examination of the material providing the basis for the complaints in this case. Based on our review of tape recordings, it is plain that references to sexual and excretory activities and organs are a staple of the Howard Stern Show. We agree that much of the material is properly characterized by Infinity as innuendo and double entendre and hence is not actionable indecency. Nevertheless, it is clear that, in other instances, the context of the references in question rendered them explicit. Although not involving the specific words used in the *Pacifica* case, the recordings do contain explicit references to masturbation, ejaculation, breast size, penis size, sexual intercourse, nudity, urination, oral-genital contact, erections, sodomy, bestiality, menstruation and testicles. None of these subjects is *per se* beyond the realm of acceptable broadcast discussion.

11. Examined in context, however, we find that certain references in this programming are patently offensive, and their sexual and excretory import are clear. The context of this material is one in which there is not merely an occasional off-color reference or expletive but a dwelling on matters sexual and excretory, in a pandering and titillating fashion. And, having established the sexual and excretory premise of the programming, the context tends to aggravate rather than dilute or ameliorate the patent offensiveness of what is said. In order to address the complaints before us, the tape recordings were considered in their entirety. The following excerpts illustrate the nature of the programming involved:

> Howard Stern: "God, my testicles are like down to the floor. Boy, Susan, you could really have a party with these. I'm telling you honey."
> Ray: "Use them like Bocci balls."

Excerpt 2

> Howard Stern: "Let me tell you something, honey. Those homos you are with are all limp."
> Ray: "Yeah. You've never even had a real man."
> Howard Stern: "You've probably never been with a man with a full erection."

Excerpt 3

> Susan: "No, I was in a park in New Rochelle. N.Y."
> Howard Stern: "In a park in New Rochelle? On your knees?"
> Susan: "No, no."
> Ray: "And squeezing someone's testicles, probably."

Excerpt 4
Talking to a caller

> Howard Stern: "I'd ask your penis size and stuff like that, but I really don't care."

Excerpt 5
As part of a discussion of lesbians

> Howard Stern: "I mean to go around porking other girls with vibrating rubber products and they want the whole world to come to a standstill."

Excerpt 6

> Howard Stern: "Have you ever had sex with an animal?"
> Caller: "No."
> Howard Stern: "Well, don't knock it. I was sodomized by Lambchop, you know that puppet Sherri Lewis holds?"
> Howard Stern: "Baaaaah. That's where I was thinking that Sherri Lewis, instead of like sodomizing all the people at the Academy to get that shot on the Emmys she could've had Lambchop do it."

12. Having reviewed fully the material at issue, we believe it makes repeated references to sexual and excretory organs and activities in a manner that is patently offensive as measured by contemporary community standards for the broadcasting medium. It was broadcast at a time of day during which there was a reasonable risk that children may have been in the audience. It would, thus, be actionable indecency under the clarified standards set forth in this case. We are mindful, however, that there may have been some uncertainty as to the precise reach of the *Pacifica* decision and that prior rulings, including some addressing complaints about this very licensee, may have suggested that the Commission had a different view of what would be considered indecent. Thus, we are limiting our action to a warning to Infinity and other broadcast licensees that this material would be actionable under the indecency standard as clarified today.

Citing again the notion of indecency as "largely a function of context,"[323] and noting that indecency is actionable when "a reasonable risk [exists] that children may be in the audience," the FCC in the *Regents of the University of California*[324] found lyrics in recorded music played on a university radio station to be indecent.[325] Specifically, it found "several clearly discernible references to sexual organs and activities . . . [that were] patently offensive by contemporary community standards for the broadcast medium."[326] The observation suggested the possibility that standards for discerning indecency, unlike the determination of obscenity pursuant to local or state community criteria,[327] are national.[328] Later, the FCC would confirm that the standard was of "an average broadcast viewer" based not "on a local standard, but . . . on a broader standard for broadcasting generally."[329] The *Regents of the University of California* case also introduced a significant modification with respect to the timing of indecent programming. Although previously "indicat[ing] that it might be permissible to air programs containing indecent material after 10 p.m. when accompanied by a warning,"[330] the FCC asserted that "no such arbitrary time of day will govern hereafter."[331] Instead it would examine "(d)ata concerning audience composition . . . to assess the risk that children may be present."[332] Pursuant to such an assessment, the commission found "a significant number of children remain in the . . . area radio audience during the time here in question."[333]

In the third broadcasting case, *Pacifica Foundation, Inc.*,[334] the FCC found that the presentation of excerpts from a play appearing in Los Angeles and an interview with its directors and actors constituted actionable indecency.[335] The director had characterized the play, focusing upon two homosexuals dying of AIDS, as "blazingly erotic."[336] In finding extensive use of patently offensive language referring to sexual and excretory organs or functions, the FCC cited the following examples.

> 20.... In the first of the three vignettes presented, the words "shit" and "fucking" were used repetitively.
>
> 22. As the presentation moved to the second vignette, the scene shifted to one character's description of an anonymous sexual encounter in which he had participated. He was told by the listening character to "make it hot" and to keep in mind that he would be "playing with" himself while being told the story.[337]

Rejecting claims that the presentation should be considered in light of the play's broader message, the commission concluded that its patently offensive nature was aggravated rather than diminished by context.[338] It also dismissed arguments that the station's audience rarely consisted of children and "point[ed] out that the test of indecency focuses on the *risk* of the presence of children in the audience."[339]

Because prior actions had suggested the possibility that the commission might be concerned with indecency to the extent it implicated the specific words at issue in *Pacifica*[340] and broadcasts after 10 p.m.,[341] the FCC imposed no actual sanctions. Rather, it issued warnings in the individual cases and to all broadcasters that the material at issue would be actionable under newly clarified indecency standards.[342] From its rulings, the commission extracted and abstracted a general statement of principle.

New Indecency Enforcement Standards to be Applied to All Broadcast and Amateur Radio Licensees, 2 F.C.C. Rcd. 2726 (1987)

The Commission, by this public notice, puts all broadcast and amateur radio licensees on notice to new standards that the Commission will apply in enforcing the prohibition against obscene and indecent transmissions.

Reaffirming its authority to regulate the broadcast and amateur radio transmission of indecent or obscene material, the Commission took action on April 16, 1987, against four licensees and articulated standards to clarify when it will exercise its enforcement authority over such situations in the future. The actions reflect the Commission's intent to apply the definition of indecent transmissions set forth in the *Pacifica* case, which was affirmed by the Supreme Court in 1978. *Pacifica Foundation*, 56 FCC 2d 94 (1975), *aff'd, FCC v. Pacifica Foundation*, 438 U.S. 726 (1978). Prior to the Commission's April 16 actions, the Commission had limited its enforcement efforts to the specific material involved in *Pacifica*, that is, to seven particular words that were broadcast in a George Carlin monologue.

On April 16, however, the Commission determined that it is more appropriate to apply the *generic* definition of broadcast indecency advanced in *Pacifica*, which is:

> language or material that depicts or describes, in terms patently offensive as measured by contemporary community standards for the broadcast medium, sexual or excretory activities or organs.

The Commission specifically ruled that such indecency will be actionable if broadcast or transmitted at a time of day when there is a "reasonable risk that children may be in the audience," a standard also upheld by the Supreme Court in the *Pacifica* case. Section 1464 of the Criminal Code, 18 U.S.C. Section 1464, prohibits the broadcast of obscene or indecent material; and the Communications Act of 1934 empowers the Commission to impose a range of civil sanctions when a violation of Section 1464 occurs, including the issuance of warnings, the imposition of fines and, in severe cases, the revocation of licenses. See 47 U.S.C. Sections 312(a)(6), 503(b)(1)(D).

With respect to indecent speech, the Commission stated that repetitive use of specific sexual or excretory words or phrases is not the only material that can constitute indecency. It further stated, however, that if a broadcast consists solely of the use of expletives, then deliberate and repetitive use of such expletives in a patently offensive manner would be a requisite to a finding of indecency. If a broadcast goes beyond the use of expletives, the Commission noted, then the context in which the allegedly indecent language is broadcast will serve as an important factor in determining whether it is, in fact, indecent.

The Commission reaffirmed the *Pacifica* test that indecency will be actionable when there is a reasonable risk that children may be in the audience, but found that this benchmark is not susceptible to a uniform standard. The Commission addressed the risk of children in the audience during the time frame and with regard to the market before it in each case.

The Commission found that, despite prior assumptions that children were not in the broadcasting audience at 10:00 p.m., recent evidence for the markets involved indicates that there is still a reasonable risk that children may be in the listening audience at the hours during which the relevant broadcasts were made. The Commission further stated that indecent broadcasts could be made at times when there is not a reasonable risk that children may be in the audience and that, when such broadcasts were made, advance warnings would continue to be required.

In reaffirming its authority to regulate indecent broadcasts and amateur transmissions, the Commission specifically rejected the rationale that scarcity of the airwaves gives it the requisite authority to regulate indecency. The Commission also explained that it was not diminishing the First Amendment rights of broadcasters. Rather, the Commission pointed out that the regulation of indecency by channeling it to hours when there is not a reasonable risk that children may be in the audience is consistent with the First Amendment rights afforded newspapers and magazines.

The Commission relied on the nuisance rationale propounded in *Pacifica,* which generally speaks to channeling behavior rather than prohibiting it. Furthermore, the Commission found its action consistent with the principle established by the Supreme Court in *Young v. American Mini-Theatres,* 427 U.S. 50 (1976), and reaffirmed in *Renton v. Playtime Theatres, Inc.,* 106 S.Ct. 925 (1986), that reasonable time, place and manner restrictions may be imposed on the dissemination of indecent material consistent with the First Amendment. The Commission concluded that, in order to limit children's access to such material on radio and television, time channeling is a reasonable time, place and manner restriction. The Commission noted that the owner of a movie theater is able to separate adults from children and can be forced to refuse children admission to certain films, and, likewise, the owner of a book store is able to separate adults from children and can be required not to sell certain publications to children. For the broadcast medium, however, the Commission reasoned that the only practicable means for separating adults from children in the broadcast audience is to impose time restrictions.

In applying the newly articulated standards to the three broadcast cases and the amateur radio case before it, the Commission determined that each of the licensees in question had broadcast or transmitted material that would constitute actionable indecency. The Commission also acknowledged, however, that prior rulings may have indicated to licensees that only repetitive use of the specific words at issue in the 1978 *Pacifica* case would be actionable if broadcast prior to 10:00 p.m. Accordingly, the FCC limited its sanctions in the broadcast cases to issuing a warning to each licensee. The Commission stated however, that violations by these licensees occurring after their receipt of their respective warnings would render them liable to more severe sanctions. The Commission hereby notifies all other broadcasters and amateur radio licensees that violations of the Commission's new standards occurring after the publication of this Public Notice will subject them to the full range of sanctions available to the Commission.

The broadcast of obscene material, by contrast, is prohibited at all times. To be obscene, material must meet a three-prong test: (1) an average person, applying contemporary community standards, must find that the material, as a whole, appeals to the prurient interest; (2) the material must depict or describe, in a patently offensive way, sexual conduct specifically defined by the applicable state law; and (3) the material, taken as a whole, must lack serious literary, artistic, political, or scientific value. See *Miller v. California,* 413 U.S. 15 (1973).

In each of the cases before it, the Commission noted that, although it was addressing the particular facts therein, the decisions will have a precedential effect on all broadcast and amateur licensees. The Commission also noted that there have been questions as to the Commission's enforcement policy in this complicated area of the law and, through its authority to issue declaratory rulings in order to remove uncertainty, see 5 U.S.C. Section 554(e), it has sought to resolve those questions in these proceedings.

The new standards were particularly significant to the extent that they broadened the concept of indecency and assigned to licensees responsibility for determining whether children might be in the audience and figuring out what if any time was appropriate for programming that might offend some persons. Concern with identifying proper perimeters was particularly acute insofar as the Supreme Court's decision in *Pacifica* related back to a single complaint over a program aired at a time when it might have been reasonable to assume that children were in school. Concern that an organized minority with narrow standards of tolerance may dictate what is fit for consumption in the marketplace of ideas has been accentuated by the fact that complaints appear to be emanating primarily from so-called prodecency groups.[343] Responding to requests for further clarification, the FCC constructed a partial safe harbor for indecent programs. Although announcing that it would defer to parental control for programs after midnight,[344] the commission did not indicate at what time in the morning its interest would renew. The commission also declined to explicate further the meaning of "patently offensive"[345] or to accept the contention that a work's "merit" alone would make it *per se* not indecent."[346] It correlated the "contemporary community standards" used to measure patent offensiveness, however, to "broadcasting generally" rather than the state or locality.[347]

The FCC's indecency policy interested not only broadcasters but also organized groups which urged broader application of its indecency standards.[348] Resisting arguments to prohibit some sexually explicit material altogether, the commission maintained that it could impose only reasonable time, place, and manner restrictions and that parents would have responsibility for supervising children after midnight.[349]

Infinity Broadcasting Corp. of Pennsylvania, 3 F.C.C. Rcd. 930 (1989) (Reconsideration Order)

By the Commission.

I. BACKGROUND

1. The Commission has before it for consideration petitions and comments pertaining to three rulings adopted on April 16, 1987, involving the prohibition contained in 18 U.S.C. § 1464 against the broadcast or transmission of indecent material. See *Pacifica Foundation, Inc.*, 2 FCC Rcd 2698 (1987) (*KPFK-FM*); *The Regents of the University of California*, 2 FCC Rcd 2703 (1987) (*KCSB-FM*); *Infinity Broadcasting Corp. of Pa.*, 2 FCC Rcd 2705 (1987) (*WYSP (FM)*).

2. The Communications Act of 1934, as amended, empowers the Commission to impose administrative sanctions for violations of Section 1464, including warnings, imposition of fines and, in severe cases, the revocation of licenses. In 1975, the Commission ruled that a 12-minute monologue by comedian George Carlin entitled "Filthy Words" broadcast by Station WBAI(FM), New York, New York, at 2:00 p.m. in the afternoon was indecent within the meaning of Section 1464. In so ruling, the Commission defined indecency as "language that describes, in terms patently offensive as measured by contemporary community standards for the broadcast medium, sexual or excretory activities or organs, when there is a reasonable risk that children may be in the audience." The Commission said that the concept of indecency is intimately connected with the exposure of children to material that most parents regard as inappropriate for them to hear. Analogizing to the law of nuisance, the Commis-

sion said such material is inappropriate for broadcast when there is a reasonable risk that children may be in the audience. The Commission suggested that this risk might not exist during late evening hours and that indecent programs could conceivably be broadcast at such times, if accompanied by appropriate warnings.

3. The Supreme Court upheld the Commission. The Court observed that the ease with which children may obtain access to broadcast material, coupled with the government's interest in protecting the well-being of its youth, and parents claim to authority in their homes, amply justify the channeling of indecent broadcasts. Thus, stressing the Commission's nuisance theory, the Court concluded that the FCC may, consistent with the first amendment, require broadcasters to channel indecent speech to times of day when there is not a reasonable risk that children may be in the audience.

4. In cases decided subsequent to the Supreme Court's ruling, the Commission took a very limited approach to enforcing the prohibition against indecent broadcasts. Unstated, but widely assumed, and implemented for the most part through staff rulings, was the belief that only material that closely resembled the George Carlin monologue would satisfy the indecency test articulated by the FCC in 1975. Thus, no action was taken unless material involved the repeated use, for shock value, of words similar or identical to those satirized in the Carlin "Filthy Words" monologue. Also widely shared was the view that such broadcasts would be actionable only if aired before 10:00 p.m. As a result, the Commission, since the time of its ruling in 1975, has taken no action against any broadcast licensee for violating the prohibition against indecent broadcasts.

5. Our April 1987 rulings in the three cases required us to readdress the subject thoroughly at the full Commission level for the first time since the Supreme Court's 1978 decision. On close analysis, we found that the highly restricted enforcement standard employed after the 1975 *Pacifica* decision was unduly narrow as a matter of law and inconsistent with our enforcement responsibilities under Section 1464. Essentially, we concluded that, although enforcement was clearly easier under the former standard, it could lead to anamolous results that could not be jus-

tified. Under that standard, material that portrayed sexual or excretory activities or organs in as patently offensive a manner as the earlier Carlin monologue—and, consequently, of concern with respect to its exposure to children—would have been permissible to broadcast simply because it avoided certain words. That approach, in essence, ignored an entire category of speech by focusing exclusively on specific words rather than the generic definition of indecency. This made neither legal nor policy sense. Accordingly, we concluded that we must take the more difficult approach to enforcing Section 1464. Therefore, each of our rulings advised broadcasters that in judging indecency complaints, we shall use the generic definition of indecency articulated by the Commission in 1975 and approved by the Supreme Court in 1978 as applied to the Carlin monologue. In applying that definition to the three cases before us in April, we recognized the importance of context to indecency determinations, noting that such determinations cannot be made in the abstract. Instead, we determined, based on the facts of each case, that the broadcasts at issue—or certain portions thereof—were indecent. We also found that, at least with respect to the particular markets involved, available evidence suggested there were still significant numbers of children in the audience at 10:00 p.m. We therefore advised that broadcasters should no longer assume that 10:00 p.m. is automatically the time after which indecent broadcasts may safely be aired. Rather, we indicated that indecent material would be actionable (that is, would be held in violation of 18 U.S.C. § 1464), if broadcast when there is a reasonable risk that children may be in the audience, a determination that was to be based on ratings data on a market-by-market basis.

6. In sum, in each of the cases before us, we found that the licensee had broadcast indecent material on the particular programs in question, at a time when there was a reasonable risk of children in the audience. We declined to take enforcement action, however, because each broadcaster had proffered a reasonable basis for believing it was permissible to air the subject material under the circumstances involved. Therefore, we limited ourselves to warning the licensees that the broadcasts would be actionable under the

revised enforcement standards made clear in our decisions.

II. THE PLEADINGS

7. Petitioner NAB asks the Commission to clarify, and petitioner ACT asks us to reconsider, not our rulings themselves, but the rulings as characterized in the public notice summarizing the cases. Petitioners do not challenge the Commission's authority to channel indecent broadcasts to late night hours. Instead, they maintain that our construction of Section 1464 is unconstitutionally vague and overbroad. To remedy these asserted constitutional failings, petitioners ask us to adopt several revisions. Collectively, they urge us to: (1) provide more precise guidance as to the elements pertinent to whether material is "patently offensive" and violates "contemporary community standards for the broadcast medium"; (2) consider the literary, artistic, political and scientific value of programming in judging whether it is patently offensive and, thus, indecent; (3) exempt news and informational programming from a finding of indecency; (4) defer to reasonable good faith judgments made by licensees applying the requirements set forth by the Commission; (5) apply rulings prospectively, not sanctioning licensees until they have notice that particular material has been judged to be indecent; and (6) adopt a fixed time of day after which non-obscene, adult oriented programming may be aired, or articulate a similar "bright line" test.

8. In contrast, MIM argues in its comments that the Commission has not gone far enough in its regulation of indecency. MIM asserts that indecent material cannot be aired by a broadcaster at any time because the prohibition set out in 18 U.S.C. § 1464 is, on its face, absolute and unqualified. MIM also suggests that the present definition of indecency be expanded to encompass a wide range of material, including that which is "more than indelicate and less than immodest." MIM generally urges the Commission to reject the positions advanced by petitioners.

III. DISCUSSION

9. As the Supreme Court has stressed, pronouncements about broadcast indecency should be confined to specific factual settings because of the crucial role of context to the issue. For this reason, we decline to address at length the generalized contentions of the parties. To dispel apparent uncertainty about the scope and effect of our recent rulings, however, we will briefly review the applicable standards and the points raised to the extent they bear on the three cases before us.

10. As a threshold matter, we acknowledge the difficulty and the sensitivity of the task at hand. Provocative programming will inevitably offend some listeners or viewers, but we must always be mindful of the first amendment limitations on the government's ability to regulate the content of speech. The consistent and long-held policy under the Communications Act has been to preserve radio and television as media of free speech and free expression. By law, however, the Commission is duty-bound to enforce the restrictions on indecent radio transmissions. And, of course, we must do so consistent with constitutional requirements. Our task is to harmonize these responsibilities with due regard for the competing interests involved.

11. We begin our consideration of petitioners requests as we began our 1975 *Pacifica* ruling, by stating: "In order to avoid the error of overbreadth, it is important to make it explicit whom we are protecting and from what." In exercising its authority to enforce the prohibition against indecency expressed in Section 1464, the Commission is advancing the government interest in safeguarding children from patently offensive descriptions or depictions of sexual or excretory activities or organs, so as to enable parents to decide effectively what material of this kind their children will see or hear. The United States Court of Appeals for the Second Circuit has held that this "interest in protecting children from salacious material is no doubt quite compelling."

12. MIM urges us to apply Section 1464 in a manner that would prohibit at all times of the day the broadcast of certain sexually explicit, yet non-obscene material. When the Supreme Court affirmed the Commission's *Pacifica* ruling in 1978, however, it made plain that our authority under Section 1464 is limited to the imposition of reasonable time, place and manner restrictions on the broadcast of indecent material in order to advance the government's interest in protecting

children and in enabling parents to determine when and how their children are to be exposed to this material. It is clear that our application of Section 1464 must be consistent with the constitutional principles derived from the *Pacifica* decision. Thus, under Section 1464, we may only do that which is necessary to restrict children's access to indecent broadcasts; we may not go further so as to preclude access by adults who are interested in seeing or hearing such material. The unqualified reading of Section 1464 pressed by MIM, under which the broadcast of indecent material would be prohibited altogether would, we believe, run afoul of this constitutional premise. With this brief preface, we turn to petitioners§ arguments, which we evaluate in the context of our three rulings in April.

Patent Offensiveness and the Role of Merit

13. Petitioners seek further clarification of the term "patently offensive," as that term is used in the definition of indecency. Specifically, petitioners inquire as to the relevance of a work's serious literary, artistic, political or scientific value (i.e., serious merit) in determining whether particular material is patently offensive and, thereby, indecent.

14. "Patently offensive" is a phrase that must, of necessity, be construed with reference to specific facts. We cannot and will not attempt to provide petitioners with a comprehensive index or thesaurus of indecent words or pictoral depictions that will be considered patently offensive. There is no way to construct a definitive list that would be both comprehensive and not over-inclusive in the abstract, without reference to the specific context. All we hold here, therefore, is that, in the three cases before us, we properly found the material identified as indecent to be patently offensive.

15. Our approach here is consistent with that of the courts, which have likewise never attempted to identify with the degree of certainty requested by petitioners the complete and definitive range of material that fall within the generic, legal definitions of certain categories of speech. We note, for example, that the phrase "patently offensive" is also used in the obscenity context and that the courts insist on construing that phrase with reference to specific facts, thereby developing its meaning on a case-by-case basis. The fact that its meaning can only be given greater specificity on a case-by-case basis does not make the term "patently offensive" unconstitutionally vague in the indecency context any more than it does in the obscenity context. Broadcasters, when judging whether certain material is legally indecent, must exercise the same kind of judgment that they are obligated to exercise when judging whether certain material is legally obscene. They must apply a generic definition with reference to the guidance provided by existing case law on the matter. Broadcasters may not reasonably expect to relieve themselves of this legal obligation by demanding that we exercise their editorial judgment for them.

16. As we stated in our April rulings, and as we re-emphasize today, the question of whether material is patently offensive requires careful consideration of context. The Supreme Court has said that the term "context" encompasses a "host of variables." These variables, whose interplay will vary depending on the facts presented, include, as the Court noted, an examination of the actual words or depictions in context to see if they are, for example, "vulgar" or "shocking," a review of the manner in which the language or depictions are portrayed, an analysis of whether allegedly offensive material is isolated or fleeting, a consideration of the ability of the medium of expression to separate adults from children, and a determination of the presence of children in the audience.

17. The merit of a work is also one of the many variables that make up a work's "context," as the Court implicitly recognized in *Pacifica* when it contrasted the Carlin monologue to Elizabethan comedies and works of Chaucer. But merit is simply one of many variables, and it would give this particular variable undue importance if we were to single it out for greater weight or attention than we give other variables. We decline to do so in deciding the three cases before us. We must, therefore, reject an approach that would hold that if a work has merit, it is *per se* not indecent. At the same time, we must reject the notion that a work's "context" can be reviewed in a manner that artificially excludes merit from the host of variables that ordinarily comprise context. The ultimate determinative factor in our analysis,

however, is whether the material, when examined in context, is patently offensive. In the three cases before us, we reaffirm our prior rulings answering this question in the affirmative.

Contemporary Community Standards for the Broadcast Medium

24. Petitioners also ask for clarification of the phrase "contemporary community standards for the broadcast medium," as that term is used in the indecency definition and was used in each of our three April rulings. We clarify that the Commission used the term "contemporary community standards" in a manner analogous to the definition set forth in the Supreme Court's decision in *Hamling v. United States.* In that case, the Court explained that the purpose of "contemporary community standards was to ensure that material is judged neither on the basis of a decisionmaker's personal opinion, nor by its effect on a particularly sensitive or insensitive person or group. Rather, decisionmakers are to draw on their views of the average person in the community. The Court also noted that, by referring to contemporary community standards in *Miller,* it did not intend to require, as a constitutional matter, the use of any precise geographic area in evaluating material. Hence, in a Commission proceeding for indecency, in which the Commission applies a concept of "contemporary community standards for the broadcast medium," indecency will be judged by the standard of an average broadcast viewer or listener. Thus, we determined in each of the three cases before us that an average listener would find material patently offensive. In making the required determination of indecency, Commissioners draw on their knowledge of the views of the average viewer or listener, as well as their general expertise in broadcast matters. The determination reached is thus not one based on a local standard, but one based on a broader standard for broadcasting generally.

The Role of Reasonable Licensee Judgments

25. Petitioner ACT urges us to defer to reasonable, good faith judgments of licensees in deciding whether a licensee has violated Section 1464. In this way, ACT contends, we will help to avoid inhibiting programming decisions and intruding into the broadcast editorial process. In a related vein, petitioner NAB advocates a policy under which Commission rulings would have prospective effect only. Under this approach, the Commission would refine its standards of what is indecent on a case-by-case basis, but would not penalize a licensee for a broadcast unless the licensee had specific notice that the Commission or a court had previously found that broadcast to be indecent. Absent a ruling squarely on point, a licensee's decision to air programming would be considered reasonable and automatically beyond the reach of Section 1464 under this scenario.

26. ACT does not contend that deference to reasonable licensee judgments in interpreting Section 1464 is required as a matter of law, and we find no basis on the record before us to allow such judgments to preclude a finding that a licensee has violated its statutory duties. Indeed, given the variety of programming aired by licensees, such a policy would largely read the prohibition against indecent transmissions out of Section 1464. Congress cannot have intended such a result, and we find no basis for reading such a provision into the statute. Although we acknowledge that the statute requires a broadcaster to make judgments as to whether certain material would violate the statute, the fact that the decision may not always be an easy one cannot excuse the broadcaster from having to exercise its judgment, any more than it can excuse the Commission from exercising its enforcement responsibilities. We note, however, that it is standard procedure for the Commission, in deciding whether to impose a sanction for violation of the law and, if so, what those sanctions should be, to give weight to the reasonable determinations of licensees endeavoring to comply with the law. Because licensees demonstrating reasonable judgment have no cause to fear the imposition of unjustified sanctions, we reject the petitioners§ contentions that the editorial decisions of broadcasters will be inappropriately chilled by continuation of this approach. . . .

III. CONCLUSION

28. Nothing said herein changes the outcome in any of the decisions in question. The Commission, therefore, reaffirms each of the above-

captioned rulings. In each case, we reviewed a tape recording of the programming involved to determine whether the context was such that the licensee had aired sexual or excretory material in a manner that was patently offensive as measured by contemporary community standards for the broadcast medium. Because we found that each had aired such material in a manner that was patently offensive according to contemporary community standards for the broadcast medium, we determined that each had broadcast indecent material. We emphasize the narrowness of our holdings in that they are limited to the specific broadcasts at issue. We hold simply that the broadcasts here...meet the definition of indecency affirmed by the Supreme Court in *Pacifica*.

29. Furthermore, these indecent broadcasts were aired when there was a reasonable risk that children may have been in the audience. Accordingly, they were broadcast in violation of Section 1464. We also reaffirm our conclusion in April that prior rulings could have led the licensees reasonably to conclude that the broadcasts were permissible. Thus, while we warned these and other licensees that the programs were, in fact, indecent and must be channeled, and even then preceded and accompanied by appropriate warnings, we did not and do not impose any sanctions upon these licensees.

Congress in 1988 enacted legislation requiring the FCC to enforce its indecency standards at all hours rather than by time channeling.[350] Although the commission complied with the legislative directive, action in that regard was stayed by a court order.[351] In the meantime, the FCC's new indecency policy had been upheld in large part upon appeal.

In *Action for Children's Television v. Federal Communications Commission*,[352] the court of appeals found that the commission's redirected focus upon a "generic definition of indecency" rather than designated words was not unreasonable or unconstitutionally vague.[353] Vagueness, the appeals court observed, resulted not from the absence of reasoned analysis but was inherent in the

subject matter.[354] Because the regulatory focus was upon indecent rather than obscene material, the court concluded that the refusal to immunize material with "serious merit" from regulatory review did not constitute an overbreadth problem.[355] It found, however, that "in view of the curtailment of broadcaster freedom and adult listener choice that [time] channeling entails,"[356] the FCC was obligated to construct more precise standards regarding permissible hours for broadcasting indecent material.[357] It thus vacated part of the order under review and remanded two of the cases[358] for reassessment of the times at which such programming might be offered.[359]

Action for Children's Television v. Federal Communications Commission, 852 F.2d 1332 (D.C. Cir. 1988)

Ruth Bader Ginsburg, Circuit Judge:

I

Petitioners in this case are commercial broadcasting networks, public broadcasting entities, licensed broadcasters, associations of broadcasters and journalists, program suppliers, and public interest groups; they seek review of a December 1987 FCC order which affirmed, on reconsideration, three April 1987 rulings, and announced a new gauge for administering the restraint, imposed by 18 U.S.C. § 1464 (1982), on the use of indecent language in radio communications. The Commission also warned broadcasters that "10:00 p.m. can no longer be considered the hour after which indecent programming may be aired"; instead, 12:00 midnight is the FCC's "current thinking" on "a reasonable delineation point." *In re Infinity Broadcasting Corp. of Pennsylvania*, 64 Rad.Reg.2d (P & F) 211, 219 n. 47 (1987) (*Reconsideration Order*).

Petitioners maintain that the FCC's broadened indecency enforcement standard is facially invalid because unconstitutionally vague. Intervenors American Civil Liberties Union Foundation (ACLU), et al. present a second facial challenge:

the FCC's mode of stamping material indecent, they contend, is substantially overbroad. Petitioners also urge that the Commission's action is arbitrary and capricious because the change in regulatory course was not accompanied by the requisite "reasoned analysis."

Adhering to the view that broadcast material that is indecent but not obscene may be channeled to certain times of day, but not proscribed entirely, the FCC indicated in its *Reconsideration Order* that 12:00 midnight to 6:00 a.m. would be "safe harbor" hours for such material. 64 Rad.Reg.2d at 217, 219 n. 47. Petitioners, joined by intervenors ACLU et al., contend that this time restraint, stretching to all but the hours most listeners are asleep, lacks record support and, in violation of the first amendment, effectively denies adults access to constitutionally-protected material.

We hold that the FCC adequately explained why it decided to change its enforcement standard. Consideration of petitioners' vagueness challenge, we conclude, is not open to lower courts, in view of the Supreme Court's 1978 *Pacifica* decision. Intervenors' overbreadth plea, we rule, is not effective argument to the extent that it attacks the FCC's generic definition of indecent material.

We further hold, however, that the FCC failed to adduce evidence or cause, particularly in view of the first amendment interest involved, sufficient to support its hours restraint; consequently, we vacate two of the FCC's declaratory orders and remand for reconsideration of the times at which programs containing indecent material may be broadcast.

IV

The FCC acknowledges a change of regulatory course: The Commission now measures broadcast material against the generic definition of indecency, while formerly "no action was taken unless material involved the repeated use, for shock value, of words similar or identical to those satirized in the Carlin 'Filthy Words' monologue." *Reconsideration Order,* 64 Rad.Reg.2d at 213 para. 4. Petitioners charge that the Commission has failed to supply an adequate explanation for the change. See *Motor Vehicle Mfrs. Ass'n v. State Farm*

Mut. Auto. Ins. Co., 463 U.S. 29, 42 (1983); *Action for Children's Television v. FCC,* 821 F.2d 741, 745 (D.C.Cir.1987). Specifically, petitioners say that the Commission, directly after *Pacifica,* had tailored the standard to make it reasonably certain and to afford broadcasters ample breathing space. Brief of Petitioners at 39. The new standard, they contend, is "inherently vague" and was installed without any evidence of a problem justifying a thickened regulatory response. *Id.*

The explanation offered by the Commission, in its *Reconsideration Order,* is that it found the deliberately-repeated-use-of-dirty-words policy "unduly narrow as a matter of law" and inconsistent with its obligation responsibly to enforce section 1464. 64 Rad.Reg.2d at 214 para. 5. The former approach permitted the unregulated broadcast of any material that did not contain Carlin's "filthy words," no matter how the material might affect children exposed to it. It made no legal or policy sense, the FCC said, to regulate the Carlin monologue but not "material that portrayed sexual or excretory activities or organs in as patently offensive a manner . . . simply because it avoided certain words." *Id.*

We find the FCC's explanation adequate. Short of the thesis that *only* the seven dirty words are properly designated indecent—an argument petitioners disavow—some more expansive definition must be attempted. The FCC rationally determined that its former policy could yield anomalous, even arbitrary, results. No reasonable formulation tighter than the one the Commission has announced has been suggested in this review proceeding. The difficulty, or "abiding discomfort," we conclude, is not the absence of "reasoned analysis" on the Commission's part, but the "[v]agueness . . . inherent in the subject matter." *Pacifica Foundation v. FCC,* 556 F.2d at 35 (Leventhal, J., dissenting). We turn next to that issue.

V

Petitioners charge that the term "indecent" is inherently unclear, and that the FCC's generic definition of indecency adds nothing significant in the way of clarification. The Commission's definition, petitioners therefore contend, provides broadcasters no meaningful guide identifying the category of material subject to regulation; accordingly, petitioners urge, the definition should be ruled unconstitutionally vague. In our view the Supreme Court's disposition of *Pacifica* stops "what the Constitution calls an 'inferior court' " from addressing this question on the merits. Cf. *Pacifica Foundation v. FCC,* 556 F.2d at 37 (Leventhal, J., dissenting) (referring to duty of "inferior court" to apply Supreme Court decisions endeavoring "to resolve the 'intractable' question of obscenity").

The generic definition of indecency now employed by the FCC is virtually the same definition the Commission articulated in the order reviewed by the Supreme Court in the *Pacifica* case. However, the Court did not address, specifically, whether the FCC's definition was on its face unconstitutionally vague. The Court did hold the Carlin monologue indecent within the meaning of section 1464. 438 U.S. at 741, 98 S.Ct. at 3036. We infer from this holding that the Court did not regard the term "indecent" as so vague that persons "of common intelligence must necessarily guess at its meaning and differ as to its application." *Connally v. General Constr. Co.,* 269 U.S. 385, 391 (1926). The Court referred to the "normal definition of 'indecent,'" quoted a dictionary definition, and noted that the Commission's definition uses "indecency" to indicate "patent offensiveness." 438 U.S. at 740 & nn. 14, 15.

Moreover, while observing that the Pacifica Foundation took issue with the FCC's definition of indecency, the Court quoted elements of the definition with seeming approval: "The Commission identified several words that referred to excretory or sexual activities or organs, stated that the repetitive, deliberate use of those words in an afternoon broadcast when children are in the audience was patently offensive, and held that the broadcast was indecent." 438 U.S. at 739. The Court ultimately declared: "When [Pacifica's] construction [that prurient appeal is an essential component of indecent language] is put to one side, there is no basis for disagreeing with the Commission's conclusion that indecent language was used in this broadcast." *Id.* at 741. In sum, if acceptance of the FCC's generic definition of "indecent" as capable of surviving a

vagueness challenge is not implicit in *Pacifica,* we have misunderstood Higher Authority and welcome correction.

VI

Intervenors ACLU et al. argue that the FCC's generic definition of indecency is substantially overbroad. As we read *Pacifica,* only two members of the five-member majority thought it in order to rule on overbreadth, so we proceed to address that issue on the merits. The ACLU's challenge is predicated on the absence of redemption from indecency status for material that has "serious merit." We hold that "serious merit" need not, in every instance, immunize indecent material from FCC channeling authority.

Indecent but not obscene material, we reiterate, qualifies for first amendment protection whether or not it has serious merit. Children's access to indecent material, however, may be regulated, because "even where there is an invasion of protected freedoms 'the power of the state to control the conduct of children reaches beyond the scope of its authority over adults. . . .' " *Ginsberg v. New York,* 390 U.S. 629, 638 (1968) (quoting *Prince v. Massachusetts,* 321 U.S. 158, 170, (1944)). Channeling is designed to protect unsupervised children. See *infra* pp. 1343–1344. Some material that has significant social value may contain language and descriptions as offensive, from the perspective of parental control over children's exposure, as material lacking such value. Since the overall value of a work will not necessarily alter the impact of certain words or phrases on children, the FCC's approach is permissible under controlling case law: merit is properly treated as a factor in determining whether material is patently offensive, but it does not render such material per se not indecent. See *Reconsideration Order,* 64 Rad.Reg.2d at 216–17 para. 17. The FCC's definition, therefore, is not vulnerable to the charge that it is substantially overbroad.

VII

We have upheld the FCC's generic definition of indecency in light of the sole purpose of that definition: to permit the channeling of indecent material, in order to shelter children from exposure to words and phrases their parents regard as inappropriate for them to hear. See *Reconsideration Order,* 64 Rad.Reg. at 213 para. 2. Petitioners press two linked objections to the FCC's "current thinking" that 12:00 midnight is the hour after which indecent material may be broadcast without sanctions. The FCC's channeling decision is arbitrary and capricious, petitioners contend, because it is not based on an adequate factual or analytic foundation. *State Farm,* 463 U.S. at 43, 103 S.Ct. at 2867. Tied to and coloring that contention, petitioners charge that the Commission's action regarding channeling violates the first amendment because it reduces adults to seeing and hearing material fit only for children. See *Butler v. Michigan,* 352 U.S. 380, 383 (1957).

We agree that, in view of the curtailment of broadcaster freedom and adult listener choice that channeling entails, the Commission failed to consider fairly and fully what time lines should be drawn. We therefore vacate, in the *Pacifica Foundation* and *Regents of U.C.* cases, the FCC's ruling that the broadcast under review was actionable, and we remand those cases to the agency for thoroughgoing reconsideration of the times at which indecent material may be aired.

We are impelled by the Supreme Court's *Pacifica* decision, however, to affirm the declaratory ruling in *Infinity.* The FCC in that case held actionable portions of a talk show that airs 6:00–10:00 a.m. Monday through Friday. In *Pacifica,* the Court affirmed a similar declaratory order regarding material broadcast 2:00 p.m. on a Tuesday. No principle has been suggested to us under which we might rationally command different treatment of the *Infinity* early morning program and the *Pacifica* early afternoon broadcast, viewing those broadcasts in the context of the parent-child concerns underpinning the FCC's indecent speech regulation. Having upheld the Commission's standard for "indecent material," we conclude that the FCC's adjudication in *Infinity* must remain in place just as the Supreme Court ordered with respect to the Commission's adjudication in *Pacifica.* The FCC itself, however, would be acting with utmost fidelity to the first amendment

were it to reexamine, and invite comment on, its daytime, as well as evening, channeling prescriptions. Cf. *infra* note 21.

Each of the April 29, 1987 rulings reported an FCC finding that the broadcast occurred at a time of day when there was a reasonable risk that children may have been in the audience. In *Pacifica Foundation,* involving a 10:00–11:00 p.m. broadcast, the Commission relied on ratings data indicating that "approximately 112,200 children aged 12–17 are in the Los Angeles metro survey area radio audience per average quarter hour between 7 p.m. and midnight on Sunday night." 2 FCC Rcd at 2699. In *Regents of U.C.,* involving a program aired after 10:00 p.m., available data indicated that

> approximately 1,200 children between 12 and 17 years of age are still in the radio audience per average quarter hour in the Santa Barbara area between 7 p.m. and midnight on Saturday evenings. There are approximately 4,900 children within this age group within the City of Santa Barbara itself and 27,800 in the county.

2 FCC Rcd at 2704 n. 10.

Even were we to treat each of the two rulings solely as an ad hoc adjudication, we would regard the evidence on which the Commission rested its channeling decisions as insubstantial, and its findings more ritual than real. It is familiar law that an agency treads an arbitrary course when it fails to "articulate any rational connection between the facts found and the choice made" (citations omitted). We conclude that the Commission followed such a course here.

In each instance under inspection the cited population figures appear to estimate the number of teens in the *total* radio audience. There is no indication of the size of the predicted audience for the specific radio stations in question. Cf. *Reconsideration Order,* 64 Rad.Reg.2d at 217 para. 18.

More troubling, the FCC ventures no explanation why it takes teens aged 12–17 to be the relevant age group for channeling purposes. In the Commission's 1976 legislative proposal, cited to the Supreme Court in the FCC's *Pacifica* brief, the Commission would have required broadcasters to minimize the risk of exposing to indecent material children *under* age 12. The FCC reasoned: "Age 12 was selected since it is the accepted upper limit for children's programming in the industry and at the Commission. The Commission considered using the generally recognized age of majority—18—but concluded that it would be virtually impossible for a broadcaster to minimize the risk of exposure to 18-year-olds." 122 Cong.Rec. at 33,367 n. 119. The FCC further referred to the distinction between obscene and merely indecent material in observing that "a reduced age seemed in order." *Id.* We cannot tell from the record before us whether the Commission is now spreading the focus of its concern to children over 12. See Brief for Respondents at 44 n. 46. If it is thus widening its sights, that apparent change in policy warrants explanation. If, on the other hand, the FCC continues to consider children under 12 as the age group of concern, it should either supply information on the listening habits of children in that age range, or explain how it extrapolates relevant data for that population from the available ratings information.

Furthermore, we note that in the Los Angeles case there is no basis for comparison between the number of teens estimated to be in the radio audience and the total number of teens in the listening area. In Santa Barbara, for which comparative data are available, the figure attracting the FCC's concern amounts to, at most, 4.3 percent of the age group population. The Commission published no reason why it determined that the potential exposure of four percent of all children amounts to a "reasonable risk" for channeling purposes.

We do not, however, remand solely for reconsideration of the individual rulings. In the *Reconsideration Order* the FCC offered some advice to broadcasters:

> [W]hereas previously we indicated that 10:00 p.m. was a reasonable delineation point, we now indicate that 12:00 midnight is our current thinking as to when it is reasonable to expect that it is late enough to ensure that the risk of children in the audience is minimized and to rely on parents to exercise increased supervision over whatever children remain in the viewing and listening audience.

64 Rad.Reg.2d at 219 n. 47. The Commission next listed several competing interests, see *infra* p. 1343, and said that its approach accommodated them. As noted by Commissioner Dennis,

however, "the arguments the majority gives in support of midnight as the critical hour may well be equally true if applied to an earlier hour." *Id.* at 220 (Dennis, Comm'r, concurring). We agree that the FCC's midnight advice, indeed its entire position on channeling, was not adequately thought through.

At oral argument of this case on June 1, 1988, General Counsel for the FCC suggested that if this court found the midnight safe harbor problematic, we could disregard it and permit the Commission to make future channeling decisions on a case-by-case basis. However, the FCC itself has recognized that "the effect of that approach may well be to cause broadcasters to forego the broadcast of certain protected speech altogether, rather than to channel it to late night hours." *Id.* at 219 n. 47. In common with the Commission, we are constrained to agree with that assessment. Facing the uncertainty generated by a less than precise definition of indecency *plus* the lack of a safe harbor for the broadcast of (possibly) indecent material, broadcasters surely would be more likely to avoid such programming altogether than would be the case were one area of uncertainty eliminated. We conclude that, in view of the constitutionally protected expression interests at stake, the FCC must afford broadcasters clear notice of reasonably determined times at which indecent material safely may be aired.[a]

---

a. In the 1987 *Pacifica Foundation* order the FCC suggested that channeling can be viewed as a valid time, place, and manner restriction on speech. 2 FCC Rcd at 2699 para. 14 & n. 3; cf. *Reconsideration Order,* 64 Rad.Reg.2d at 215 para. 12. We disagree. Time, place, and manner regulations must be content-neutral. *Pacific Gas & Elec. v. Public Utils. Comm'n of Cal.,* 475 U.S. 1, 20 (1986). Channeling, however, is a content-based regulation of speech. See *Boos v. Barry,* ___ U.S. ___ , 108 S.Ct. 1157, 1163 (1988) (plurality opinion of O'Connor, J.): "Regulations that focus on the direct impact of speech on its audience [are not content-neutral]. To take an example factually close to *Renton [v. Playtime Theatres, Inc.,* 475 U.S. 41 (1986) (ordinance regulating adult-movie theaters)], if the ordinance there was justified by the city's desire to prevent the psychological damage it felt was associated with viewing

It is not within our authority to instruct the FCC to establish a safe harbor by means of a rulemaking proceeding (citation omitted). We call attention, however, to the clear statement made by one Commissioner: "The fact is the Commission has no scientific body of information that conclusively establishes one time as more appropriate than another as the critical hour after which to permit broadcast of indecent speech. What is necessary is a notice of proposed rulemaking to establish a record." *Reconsideration Order,* 64 Rad.Reg.2d at 220 (Dennis, Comm'r, concurring). The inadequate record relevant to channeling made in the cases the Commission adjudicated lends support to that Commissioner's view.

The FCC noted that a channeling decision must accommodate these competing interests:

> (1) the government, which has a compelling interest in protecting children from indecent material; (2) parents, who are entitled to decide whether their children are exposed to such material if it is aired; (3) broadcasters, who are entitled to air such material at times of day when there is not a reasonable risk that children may be in the audience; and (4) adult listeners, who have a right to see and hear programming that is inappropriate for children but not obscene.

---

adult movies, then analysis of the measure as a content-based statute would have been appropriate." See also *id.* at 1171 (Brennan, J., concurring): "[A]ny restriction on speech, the application of which turns on the content of the speech, is a content-based restriction regardless of the motivation that lies behind it."

Content-based restrictions ordinarily "may be sustained only if the government can show that the regulation is a precisely drawn means of serving a compelling state interest." *Consolidated Edison Co. v. Public Serv. Comm'n,* 447 U.S. 530, 540, 100 S.Ct. 2326, 2334 (1980). The Supreme Court has recognized a government's interest in "safeguarding the physical and psychological well-being of a minor" as "compelling." *New York v. Ferber,* 458 U.S. 747, 756–57 (1982), quoting *Globe Newspaper Co. v. Superior Court,* 457 U.S. 596, 607 (1982). But that interest, in the context of speech control, may be served only by carefully-tailored regulation. Here, the precision necessary to allow scope for the first amendment shielded freedom and choice of broadcasters and their audiences cannot be accomplished, we believe, unless the FCC adopts a reasonable safe harbor rule.

Id. at 219 n. 47. At the June 1, 1988 oral argument, the FCC's General Counsel, in response to the court's inquiry, clarified the government's interest: it is the interest in protecting unsupervised children from exposure to indecent material; the government does not propose to act *in loco parentis* to deny children's access *contrary* to parents' wishes. Therefore the first two interests identified by the FCC coalesce; the government's role is to facilitate parental supervision of children's listening. "[T]he Commission is advancing the government interest in safeguarding children from patently offensive [material], so as to enable parents to decide effectively what material of this kind their children will see or hear." *Id.* at 215 para. 11. Thus, the FCC must endeavor to determine what channeling rule will most effectively promote parental—as distinguished from government—control.

A securely-grounded channeling rule would give effect to the government's interest in promoting parental supervision of children's listening, without intruding excessively upon the licensee's range of discretion or the fare available for mature audiences and even children whose parents do not wish them sheltered from indecent speech. Such a rule would present a clearly-stated position enabling broadcasters to comprehend what is expected of them and to conform their conduct to the legal requirement.

Following the Supreme Court's determination that a congressional ban on telephone dial-a-porn services was unconstitutional to the extent it proscribed non-obscene expression[360] as discussed in Chapter 11, the FCC readjusted its regulatory bearing. After having the case concerning the congressionally directed 24 hour a day ban remanded to it, the FCC in 1990 abandoned time channeling notions in favor of comprehensive proscription.[361] Critical to the Commission's revised policy was its sense that, unlike in the dial-a-porn context, techology did not afford a less restrictive regulatory alternative.[362] Because children are part of the audience at all hours, the FCC concluded that a total ban was the least restrictive means of accounting for a compelling regulatory interest.[363]

B. Children's Programming

Concern with the presence of youth in the audience and their well-being also has engendered proposals for officially influencing the general nature and availability of children's programming. The FCC's response to such initiatives, however, has been more consonant with the deference to licensee discretion characterizing fairness regulation than its more assertive posture with respect to indecency. Interest in promoting the number and variety of programs directed at children implicates issues of editorial discretion. Concern with actual content, on the grounds that it might have an adverse impact on children, must compete against constitutional principles that militate against "reducing the adult population . . . to [receiving] only what is fit for children."[364]

1. Quantitative Concerns

The FCC at times has flirted with but nonetheless refrained from adopting quantitative standards for children's programming. In 1974 it issued a policy statement that essentially requested licensees to make reasonable efforts to increase programming on weekdays and weekends that would educate and inform rather than just entertain children.[365] The proposal had no appreciable effect upon the amount of such programming provided by broadcasters.[366] The commission concluded that the size of the particular audience and the limited interest of advertisers in it combined to create a disincentive for commercial programming aimed at children.[367] In 1979, therefore, the FCC initiated a rule making to consider various options ranging from whether to establish quantitative standards to whether it should consider programming from sources other than commercial broadcasting.[368]

Children's Television Programming and Advertising Practices, 75 F.C.C.2d 138 (1979)

NOTICE OF PROPOSED RULEMAKING

4. In 1971 we established this proceeding with a *First Notice of Inquiry* to explore and define the fundamental issues in children's television. In 1974 we issued our *Children's Television Report and Policy Statement,* which established policies and guidelines for children's programming and advertising and left to industry self-regulation the manner of coming into compliance. In 1978 we re-established our *Children's Television Task Force* and issued a *Second Notice of Inquiry* to determine what changes had taken place since 1974. The Task Force staff was asked to evaluate the effectiveness of broadcast industry self-regulation in improving children's programming and advertising practices, and, in addition, to investigate the overall effect of new technologies and alternative sources of programming on the availability of children's programming. . . .

6. Commercial television licensees have been on notice since the issuance of our *Policy Statement* in 1974 that they have a duty as public trustees "to develop and present programming which will serve the unique needs of the child audience." The Task Force report concluded that industry self-regulation during the last five years has not been effective in fully achieving the changes in amount, scheduling, and age specificity of commercial television's children's programming we stated that we expected to follow from our 1974 *Policy Statement.* Further, the report concluded that, under the existing market structure, the economic incentives facing commercial television broadcasters make it unlikely that they will voluntarily meet the policy guidelines without quantifying the Commission's expectations. The staff report proposed a range of policy options avail-

able to us and recommended certain of these options. . . .

14. The 1974 *Policy Statement* asked licensees to do the following: 1) "make a meaningful effort" in the area of overall amount of programming for children; 2) air "a reasonable amount" of programming for children designed to educate and inform, and not simply to entertain; 3) air informational programming separately targeted for both preschool children and school-age children; and 4) air programming for children scheduled during weekdays as well as on weekends.

The following is a summary of the staff's findings on commercial licensee compliance with the programming guidelines of the 1974 *Policy Statement,* based on detailed studies of changes in the amount and scheduling of various kinds of programming between 1973–74 and 1977–78. While we are aware that many licensees have made efforts to provide higher-quality programming for children during this time period, the staff report does not examine the quality of programming. The Task Force's report considered solely compliance with the 1974 *Policy Statement,* which addressed the amount, scheduling, and type of children's programming available.

15. *Overall Amount of Children's Programming.* Our staff's report found that the average amount of time devoted to children's programs, both entertainment and non-entertainment, on a per-station basis increased from 10.5 hours per week in 1973–74 to 11.3 hours per week in 1977–78—an increase of less than one hour per week. This change was entirely accounted for by a significant increase in children's programming on independent stations (14.3 hours in 1977–78 as compared with 10.6 hours in 1973–74). No increase occurred in the amount of time devoted to children's programs by network affiliates (10.4 hours per network affiliate in 1973–74 as compared with 10.4 hours in 1977–78).

16. *Programming Designed to Educate and Inform Children.* Our staff's report found that no significant increase has occurred in the number of educational and instructional programs for children aired during the composite weeks (network-originated: 1973–74, 3, 1977–78, 3; syndicated: 1973–74, 11; 1977–78, 12). The average amount of time devoted to educational children's pro-

grams on a per-station basis remained essentially the same for the 1977–78 broadcast season compared with the 1973–74 broadcast season (network-originated: 1973–74, 2.77 hours; 1977–78, 2.76 hours; syndicated: 1973–74, 1.42 hours; 1977–78, 1.14 hours).

17. *Age-Specific Programming.* The 1974 *Policy Statement* stated that commercial television licensees have a responsibility to air more programming directed toward both the preschool and school-age audiences. Despite our statement that licensees should make a "meaningful effort" to air age-specific programs, the staff found that few licensees have made a greater effort to do so. Parties filing comments indicated a general absence of preschool programming on network-affiliated stations, with the exception of those carrying CBS' *Captain Kangaroo.* Essentially the same number of programs was broadcast for the preschool audience by network affiliates during 1977–78 as was broadcast at the time of the 1974 *Policy Statement.* Some independent stations in the top 50 markets, however, did increase their preschool programming.

18. *Scheduling of Children's Programs.* The *Policy Statement* addressed scheduling of children's programs because at that time programs for children were shown primarily on weekends. Our staff found that the proportion of children's programs scheduled on the weekend decreased somewhat between 1973–74 and 1977–78, from 53.7 percent to 47.3 percent, but nearly half of children's programs are still shown on weekends, when only 8 percent of children's television viewing occurs.

19. The staff found that in 1977–78, 60 percent of children's programs on network affiliates were shown on weekends. Network affiliates continue to air over 50 percent of their children's programs on Saturdays alone. In many markets there are still no independent commercial television outlets. Consequently, in those markets viewers depend solely on network affiliates, who air the majority of their children's programming on weekends. . . .

21. The staff's report also analysed broadcasters' compliance with our programming guidelines in the context of children's cognitive abilities, the market for children's television programming, and recent technological developments.

22. *Benefits to Children.* The *Report* found that television has an opportunity to provide considerable educational benefits to children. Most children watch many hours of television a day. In addition children have been shown to acquire attitudes and behavior, as well as cognitive skills, from watching television. Thus, both cultural and informational programming may have a large influence on children. Preschool children in particular may benefit from educational programming since, unlike adults and older children, they do not read and have access to relatively few alternative sources of information.

23. The Task Force reported that several features both of children themselves and of the television industry cause commercial television broadcasters to serve children differently and less well than any other significant audience group. Based on differences in cognitive development, children form at least two distinct audiences, preschoolers (ages two to five) and school-age children (ages six to twelve). These groups have sufficiently different educational needs that nonentertainment programming for children must be directed at one group or the other to be fully effective.

24. *The Market for Children's Programs.* In the advertiser-supported broadcasting system programming is paid for not by viewers but by advertisers, who desire the largest possible audience of potential buyers for their advertised products. The report asserts that children, particularly younger children, have an influence on decisions to buy only relatively few advertised products. Purchases of products advertised to children fall into a very few categories and constitute only a small portion of household budgets. Thus, though many firms do advertise to children, the amount of money spent on children's advertising appears to be small relative to the amount spend advertising to adults. Broadcasters have little incentive to present programming designed to attract children and even less incentive to program for specific subcategories of children.

25. In markets with few television outlets broadcasters will attempt to maximize their audience by presenting programming appealing to the largest number of people. In markets with many television outlets, some stations will find it more profitable to program for the tastes of smaller groups, including children, than to compete for and further divide the broad general audience. Thus television broadcasters are likely to present more programming, and perhaps more diverse programming, for children in markets with many outlets than in markets with few outlets. Independent stations, which often program for audiences not served by network affiliates, are likely to present more children's programming than network affiliates.

26. Our staff has concluded based on the above analysis that the small numbers of children and their limited appeal to advertisers, combined with the small number of outlets in most markets, create incentives for the commercial television system to neglect the specific needs of the child audience. The report asserts that, as a consequence of the incentives facing television broadcasters, the amount of children's programming on advertiser-supported stations will be less than the amount of programming that would be presented for an adult audience of similar size and viewing habits. The children's programming that is broadcast will be designed to attract the largest child audience rather than specific age subgroups. Because programming designed for specific age groups will probably attract relatively small numbers of children, programming of that type is likely to be kept to a minimum. In addition, children's programming usually will be scheduled for time periods in which no other audience groups are available in large numbers. Even when located in these marginal time periods, children's programs will be subject to preemption by programming that attracts larger general audiences, such as sports events. Broadcasters will also be less willing to spend money to produce children's programming than adult programming.

27. *New Technologies and Children's Programming.* The staff report suggests that parents appear to desire more television programming for their children, and in particular more educational programming, than is available on advertiser-supported television stations. Cable and subscription television also provide evidence that parents desire children's educational programming strongly enough to pay for it, either directly or indirectly, when it is available. Cable television suppliers offer three different program packages

for children, one of which is a full-time channel of children's programming. The material offered on cable has a higher educational content than that presented by advertiser-supported broadcasters. In addition, four of the six operating subscription television (STV) stations offer programming for children. This evidence from cable and STV suggests that children's programming provided by advertiser-supported stations falls far short of viewer demand. We invite comment on the staff's interpretation of the evidence concerning demand for children's programming.

28. *Overall Compliance.* On the basis of the staff's analysis it appears that, whether the FCC definition of children's programs or a broader industry categorization of children's programs is used, the commercial television industry as a whole has not, after five years of notice under our *Policy Statement,* complied fully with our existing programming guidelines. The availability of programming for other audiences that also attracts children does not satisfy the Commission's requirement that television licensees provide educational and age-specific programming specifically designed for children, scheduled throughout the broadcast week. On this basis alone, we may consider taking further action, assuming the accuracy of the staff's analysis.

29. The staff's conclusion is reinforced by its analysis that the market incentives under the current structure of commercial broadcasting appear to run counter to the programming policies and guidelines created in the *Policy Statement.* The Task Force report suggests that without formal regulations or processing guidelines only increases in the number of television stations or other video programming outlets in a market will foster any further increases in the amount or diversity of children's programming. The Commission invites comment on the staff's analysis and conclusions concerning broadcaster compliance with the *Policy Statement* and the staff's overall analysis of the market's behavior and its effect on the availability of children's television.

V. Policy Options

30. This section sets forth a range of options for FCC action with regard to television programming for children. We propose to adopt one of these options or other options submitted by parties after consideration of the complete record submitted in response to this *Notice.* Accordingly, we encourage comments on the options presented below. We do not, however, foreclose the possibility that other equally viable options will emerge from public comments, and if so, we will fully consider them.

31. *Option 1. Rescind the Policy Statement and rely on other program sources for children's programming.* If the staff analysis is correct, the economic incentives of the advertiser-supported broadcasting system do not encourage the provision of specialized programming for children. We may, therefore, choose to rescind the *Policy Statement* and find that commercial television broadcasters no longer have any specific obligation to serve the child audience. Instead we would rely on other program sources, such as public broadcasting, federally-funded children's programs, cable television, subscription television, or any combination of other program sources to meet the demand for more age-specific educational programming for children. We recognize, however, that public broadcasting has been hampered by the disadvantages that UHF stations have faced in the past, and that cable and subscription television are not available in all communities. These alternatives offer a potential solution only in the long run. We invite comment on whether we should rescind the *Policy Statement* and rely solely on other program sources to meet the demand for educational programming.

32. *Option 2. Maintain or Modify the Policy Statement.* The staff report has concluded that five years of experience with broadcaster self-regulation under the *Policy Statement* indicates that very few changes in children's programming practices have occurred. In view of our concerns about the constitutional limits to our authority we could still conclude that a reaffirmed FCC *Policy Statement* remains the only viable policy option, in spite of the staff's analysis of the economic incentives of commercial broadcasters.

33. If we choose to maintain our *Policy Statement,* we might, in addition, modify the television license renewal form in order to obtain more comprehensive and precise information about licensee programming practices for children. For example, we could ask television licensees to provide a complete listing of programming that

meets our definition of children's programs as part of their annual programming report. We could also require that television licensees classify this programming according to intended audience (preschool or school-age), and report the amount of time devoted to children's programs and the scheduling of these programs. We invite comments on the appropriateness of maintaining the *Policy Statement* with or without the alternative of requiring licensees to provide additional information about the type, amount, and scheduling of their children's programs.

34. Alternatively, the staff's analysis that television broadcasters have little incentive to produce educational programs for children may lead us to reevaluate our *Policy Statement*. We could, for example, reaffirm the obligation of television broadcasters to provide more programs for children but rescind our policies requiring educational and age-specific programming. We could also maintain the existing standards of the *Policy Statement* but apply these standards to the availability of programming in the market rather than maintain an individual licensee obligation. We solicit comment on these alternatives.

35. *Option 3. Mandatory Programming Rules.* The staff has recommended that the Commission consider adopting an interim rule concerning the amount, scheduling, and type of programming for children. The rule suggested by the Task Force would require that all commercial television broadcasters provide 5 hours per week of educational programming for preschool children (ages two to five) and 2 ½ hours per week of educational programming for school-age children (ages six to twelve). The rule would further require that this programming be scheduled between 8:00 a.m. and 8:00 p.m., Monday through Friday. The Commission invites comment on this proposal as well as suggestions for alternatives and reasons for proposing them.

36. We have always recognized that educational programming can also be entertaining. Nonetheless, the question of how broadly we define educational programming is an essential element of this discussion. In our *Policy Statement* we broadly characterize educational programming:

> There are many imaginative and exciting ways in which the medium can be used to further a child's understanding of a wide range of areas: history,

science, literature, the environment, drama, music, fine arts, human relations, other cultures and languages, and basic skills such as reading and mathematics which are crucial to a child's development.

It is our intent to continue to define educational programming in a broad manner and to give deference to licensees' own classifications of their children's programs. We invite comment on the appropriateness of our definition.

37. We realize that television as a mass medium always has the potential to reach broad audiences. Nonetheless, we stated in 1974 that we believe that programming can be designed for specific age groups of children. If this rule option were adopted, we would propose to continue to define preschool programming as programming originally produced and broadcast primarily for a child audience ages two to five. We would propose to continue to define school-age programming as programming originally produced and broadcast primarily for a child audience ages six to twelve. We invite comment on the appropriateness of these definitions.

38. The proposed rule might apply to all licensees equally or only to some classes of licensees, such as network affiliates or VHF stations. We solicit comment on the appropriateness of treating various classes of licensees differently, and on the reasonableness of different programming standards for network affiliates and independents or for VHF and UHF stations.

39. The staff report asserts that with a large number of video outlets in each market sufficient diversity in programming would occur to make it likely that educational programming for children be provided without FCC intervention. Accordingly, we intend that, if adopted, the mandatory programming rule would be an interim measure and that the rule would contain a "sunset" clause setting forth conditions under which it would be rescinded. Criteria for rescinding the rule might include the expiration of a given time period or some structural condition such as national cable penetration reaching some specified level. Alternatively, the criteria might be applied on a market-by-market basis and might include the number of over-the-air stations in the market, cable penetration in the market, percentage of homes in the market passed by cable, or some combination of these. Widespread

and low-cost availability of videocassette and videodisc equipment and programming might also make mandatory advertiser-supported broadcasting of children's programs unnecessary. We invite comments on the appropriateness of a "sunset" provision for rescinding the rule and the criteria for determining when this provision should take effect.

40. *Option 4. Children's Programming License Renewal Processing Guidelines.* The Commission could also achieve the objectives outlined in the staff report through the adoption of a processing guideline. Currently, the FCC staff is given delegated authority to process license renewals routinely and to make findings that they serve the public interest only where certain specific standards for local, informational, and non-entertainment programs are met by the broadcast licensee during the past license term....

41. A possible processing guideline for children's programming could incorporate the same provisions as the proposed rule (see Option 3 *supra*) or different standards. Under a processing guideline, the staff would review each television license renewal application to determine whether it conforms to the standards established for educational children's programming.

42. If a television licensee proposed programming for the next three-year license term that fell below the Commission's guidelines, the staff would send the renewal application to the Commission for full review to determine if the renewal should be granted. If the television licensee aired, during the last license period, programming that fell below the Commission's guidelines, the staff could grant the renewal if the licensee submitted a satisfactory explanation. If the staff determined that the explanation was unsatisfactory, the staff would send the application to the Commission for full review.

43. An additional standard for investigation of renewal applications in our local or news and public affairs processing guidelines is "promise v. performance". If a licensee promised more than the FCC's minimum guidelines and has, during the past license period, substantially deviated from these program percentages, the staff may request justification or additional information on an applicant's programming proposal be-

fore granting the renewal. We invite comment on whether this standard should be applied to an applicant's past children's programming proposals.

44. The staff defers to licensee discretion in categorization of programming. If, however, a petition-to-deny is filed, the staff must determine whether the licensee has met the program guidelines. We invite comment on how the staff should determine whether the licensee has met the age-specific and educational standards of a processing guideline if a petition-to-deny challenging a licensee's programming during the last renewal term is filed.

45. A processing guideline would allow the Commission more flexibility in special cases than a mandatory rule. This option might be used in conjunction with a reaffirmed *Policy Statement* and modified license renewal form (see Option 2 *supra*).

46. *Option 5. Increasing the Number of Video Outlets.* Our staff's report concluded that in the long run increases in the number of advertiser-supported video outlets per market and more television programming paid for by viewers would provide the most promising means of increasing the amount and diversity of programming serving children. In addition, the fact that more broadcast outlets are competing for the same audience may affect broadcasters' programming strategies, making it more profitable to present specialized programming strongly preferred by a relatively small audience than to try to compete for the mass audience. While the staff believes that increasing the number of outlets per market should result in a better match of programming with viewers' preferences, it provides no guarantee that any specific type of programming, such as educational programming for preschoolers, will be provided.

47. Before considering specific options for increasing the number of outlets, the Commission invites comment on the staff's proposition that increasing the number of outlets per market will improve the availability of educational programming for children. We also request suggestions and opinions on a general strategy that the Commission might undertake to achieve structural changes that increase the number of outlets per

market, if it were to accept the staff's premise. One approach might take the form of a new policy statement or doctrine directed to promoting structural alternatives to advertiser-supported television rather than to maintaining our 1974 *Policy Statement,* which promotes educational children's programming on commercial television stations.

48. Increasing the number of advertiser-supported outlets could most easily be accomplished by making UHF stations more comparable with VHF stations. Congress has required the Commission to "devise a plan for UHF stations to reach comparability with VHF in as short a time as practicable." We solicit opinion concerning the likely effect of an increase in the number of UHF stations on children's programming.

49. Wider introduction of the various pay television options would not only increase the number of outlets but would allow viewers to express their preferences by purchasing the kind of programming they want. Possible increases in the availability of pay television options may come from expanded cable and subscription television services, more widespread use of new technologies such as videocassette and videodisc, and possibly direct satellite-to-home broadcasting.

50. Cable television, over-the-air subscription television (STV), and direct satellite-to-home broadcasting may offer, in the long run, a greater likelihood than advertiser-supported broadcasting of meeting consumer preferences because consumers have the option of paying for the kind of programming they want. In addition, cable television overcomes the problem of channel scarcity by offering, in newer systems, 30 or more channels.

51. Although these for-pay programming services are increasing in availability, in the short term they will not be available to the majority of television households. Even in the long term it is likely that only advertiser-supported over-the-air broadcasting will be available to all television households. We invite comment on the desirability of depending upon technologies that may not be available to all households to provide programming for children. We also invite comment on the extent to which reductions in the cost of cable, STV, or possibly direct satellite-to-home broadcasting may affect the availability of children's programming.

52. With videocassettes and videodiscs viewers may eventually be able to buy almost any kind of programming they want and to view whenever they want. Cassette and disc libraries equipped with viewing equipment may make this programming widely available to the public at large. The Commission invites comment on whether videocassettes and videodiscs by themselves or in combination with other forms of pay television are practical alternatives to over-the-air broadcasting, and whether the availability of these alternative sources of programming should affect our policies for advertiser supported broadcasting....

55. We believe that television programming has an enormous potential for enriching the lives of children. This potential is still largely unrealized. We expect that, acting within the limits of our authority, we can adopt one or more policies that will result in better service for children.

Four years later, the FCC determined that licensees had an obligation to consider the needs and interests of all segments of the communities they serviced.[369] The commission rejected, however, the concept of mandatory quotas on the grounds that they would invade constitutionally protected editorial interests[370] and discourage innovation and experimentation.[371] Critical to its decision was a broadened focus upon sources other than broadcasting which led to the conclusion, contrary to previous intimation, that an extensive and diverse menu of children's programming existed.[372] In *Action For Children's Television v. FCC,*[373] the court of appeals upheld official focus upon the media universe rather than the specific medium.[374] Although noting that alternatives such as public broadcasting and cable did not relieve broadcasters of their obligation to serve the public interest, the court allowed that the FCC was not obligated to regulate in disregard of the fact that specific needs were met by other sources.[375]

Action for Children's Television v. Federal Communications Commission, 756 F.2d 899 (D.C. Cir. 1985)

Petitioner Action for Children's Television and supporting intervenors ("petitioners") challenge Federal Communications Commission's January 4, 1984 Report and Order defining the obligations of television broadcast licensees to their child audiences. See *In re Children's Television Programming and Advertising Practices,* 96 F.C.C.2d 634 (1984) ("1984 Order"). There the Commission found that the video market, considered as a whole, does not exhibit a clear failure to serve the needs and interests of the child audience, and that mandatory programming rules (including flexible processing guidelines for license renewal applications) raise serious problems of law and policy; and accordingly elected simply to reaffirm "the general licensee obligations emphasized by the Commission in its [*Children's Television Report and Policy Statement,* 50 F.C.C.2d 1 (1974) ("1974 Statement"), *aff'd sub nom., Action for Children's Television v. FCC,* 564 F.2d 458 (D.C.Cir.1977)] and . . . the general requirement that stations provide programming responsive to the needs and interests of the communities they serve." 96 F.C.C.2d at 655 (footnote omitted). Petitioners assert that the agency improperly considered the children's programming available from *all* video sources in finding no market failure warranting more intensive regulation of commercial broadcasting; that it gave insufficient consideration to flexible processing guidelines; that it arbitrarily and without explanation dropped the 1974 Statement's requirement that licensees make a reasonable effort to provide age-specific, informational, and educational children's programming; and that it ignored relevant evidence.

[1] After carefully considering petitioners' arguments, we conclude that the Commission's decision was within the broad scope of its discretion and was adequately explained by the 1984 Order. See *FCC v. WNCN Listeners Guild,* 450 U.S. 582, 593–96 (1981); *NAACP v. FCC,* 682 F.2d 993, 998 (D.C.Cir.1982). The differences between the 1984 Order and the 1974 Statement are attributable to changes in the Commission's judgment about how best to serve the public interest, convenience and necessity, and the reasons for these changes are stated in the Order with sufficient clarity to withstand judicial scrutiny. See *Motor Vehicle Manufacturers Ass'n, Inc. v. State Farm Mutual Automobile Insurance Co.,* 463 U.S. 29, 42–43 (1983). . . .

Only two issues raised by petitioners require brief discussion. First, petitioners assert that it was improper for the Commission, in making its determination of public needs for children's programming, to take into account such programming available on cable television or on noncommercial television broadcasting stations. We think not. As to cable: While that medium is not available in all areas or to all segments of the viewing community, it has a sufficiently broad and increasing presence that the Commission may appropriately consider its offerings in determining the necessity for such nationwide rules as petitioners favored. This does not mean, and we do not interpret the Commission to suggest, that in a particular service area where cable penetration is insubstantial or nonexistent that medium can have any effect upon the broadcaster's assessment of the most significant needs of his community; or that the broadcaster in any community can disregard the needs of those not served by cable. We also see no need for the Commission to blind itself to the contribution of noncommercial television. To be sure, Congress did not intend noncommercial broadcasting to "relieve commercial broadcasters of their responsibilities to present public affairs and public service programs, and in general to program their stations in the public interest," S.Rep. No. 222, 90th Cong., 1st Sess. 6, reprinted in 1967 U.S. Code Cong. & Ad. News 1772, 1777. But that does not mean that the Commission must require commercial broadcasters to pursue those responsibilities in disregard of the fact that some gaps in the public interest may have been filled by that source while other needs remain entirely unmet.

The second issue relates to age-specific programming. The 1974 Statement set forth the Commission's expectation that broadcast licensees would henceforth make a reasonable effort "to present programming designed to meet the needs of three specific age groups: (1) pre-school children, (2) primary school aged children, and (3) elementary school aged children." 50 F.C.C.2d at 7. Petitioners express the fear that the 1984 Order, which does not explicitly discuss age-specific programming, will relieve licensees of that obligation, echoing concerns voiced by Commissioner Rivera in his dissent from the Order. See 96 F.C.C.2d at 660 n. 11. We do not read the 1984 Order that way—nor, based on their representations at oral argument, do the broadcasters or the Commission. While it imposes no detailed age-specific requirements on licensees, and expresses doubts about a number of the programming categories relied on by the 1974 Statement (e.g., "informational" and "educational"), it explicitly affirms that "there is a continuing duty, under the public interest standard, on each licensee to examine the program needs of the child part of the audience and to be ready to demonstrate at renewal time its attention to those needs." 96 F.C.C.2d at 656. It is absurd to believe that "the program needs of the child part of the audience" were thought to be uniform, from pre-school through elementary school. It seems clear to us that under the 1984 Order broadcasters faced with renewal challenges based on the adequacy of their children's programming can be called upon to explain why they chose to focus on the needs and interests of certain age groups or other segments of the child audience, or why they emphasized emotional rather than cognitive needs. Licensees can expect the Commission to defer to reasonable programming decisions in this field, but that is a far cry from the wholesale abolition of licensee responsibility perceived by petitioners.

While the FCC's decision not to impose quantitative standards was under review, a challenge arose in the course of a license renewal proceeding based upon a broadcaster's failure to provide any regularly scheduled weekday children's programming.[376] The petitioning group, in *Washington Association for Television and Children v. Federal Communications Commission*,[377] claimed that such neglect violated the commission's policy on children's program-

ming.[378] The court of appeals, however, found no requirement for regularly scheduled programming explicit or implicit in the commission's policy.[379] It noted the anomaly that would result, moreover, if a broadcaster providing regularly scheduled cartoons were found in compliance and a licensee offering educational specials were found in violation.[380]

Washington Association for Television and Children v. Federal Communications Commission, 712 F.2d 677 (D.C. Cir. 1983)

Wald, Circuit Judge:

Petitioner Washington Association for Television and Children (WATCH) filed petitions with Federal Communications Commission (FCC or Commission) opposing the license renewals of three television stations in Washington, D.C. on the grounds that the stations had failed to provide any regularly scheduled weekday children's programs, in contravention of Commission policy. The Commission granted the license renewals without holding a hearing, explaining that although licensees had a duty to provide weekday children's programming, they had no duty to provide it on a *regularly scheduled basis*. *Evening News Association,* 89 F.C.C.2d 911 (1982). WATCH appeals the Commission's refusal to hold a hearing. We conclude that the Commission reasonably interpreted its prior policy statement as not imposing a flat requirement that all television stations provide regularly scheduled weekday children's programs.

I. BACKGROUND

A.   The   Commission's   Policy   on   Children's   Programming

In 1974, the FCC, after a lengthy rulemaking, issued a *Children's Television Report and Policy Statement* ("*Children's Policy Statement*") in which it outlined broadcasters' duty to provide children's programming. 50 F.C.C.2d 1 (1974), *reconsid. denied,* 55 F.C.C.2d 691 (1975).

The FCC found that "broadcasters have a special obligation to serve children," 50 F.C.C.2d at 5, but declined to establish numerical requirements for what quantity of children's programming would satisfy that obligation. The Commission decided instead to consider "on an ad hoc basis" whether TV stations were devoting enough time to children's shows. *Id.* at 6 (footnote omitted). The Commission emphasized, however, that:

> [W]e do expect stations to make a meaningful effort in this area. . . . [A] few stations present no programs at all for children. We trust that this *Report* will make it clear that such performance will not be acceptable. . . .

The Commission also expressed concern over the "tendency on the part of many stations to confine all or most of their children's programming to Saturday and Sunday mornings" and the "relative absence" of weekday programming. *Id.* at 8. While it again declined to adopt a "specific scheduling rule," the Commission explained that:

> [I]t is [not] a reasonable scheduling practice to relegate all [children's] programming . . . to one or two days . . . [and] we do expect to see considerable improvement in scheduling practices in the future.

Id. In short, the Commission expected television stations to provide weekday children's programming, but did not specify how much or what kind.

We turn, then, to the only issue properly before us: whether a station that offers no regularly scheduled weekday children's programming cannot satisfy the dictates of the *Children's Policy Statement* under any circumstances. We find no such requirement in the *Policy Statement*.

As WATCH concedes, nothing in the *Policy Statement* explicitly requires regularly scheduled children's programming. We also do not find such a requirement to be implicit in the *Policy Statement*. Certainly regularly scheduled programming is an important component of programming. But in the *Children's Policy Statement*, the FCC declined to set hard and fast rules in favor of giving the broadcasting industry "flexibility" in meeting its obligation to children. 50 F.C.C.2d at 18; See *Action for Children's Television v. FCC,* 564 F.2d 458, 479, 481 (D.C.Cir.1977) (upholding the Commission's decision "not to adopt specific regulations governing . . . programming practices for children's television" and

to instead rely on industry "self-regulatory efforts"). The few flat statements to be found in the *Policy Statement* merely prohibit TV stations from making grossly inadequate efforts—e.g., presenting "no programs at all for children," 50 F.C.C.2d at 6, or relegating "all" children's programming to the weekends, *id.* at 8.

Nor would WATCH's position make sense from a policy standpoint. Its argument implies that a station that broadcasts a regularly scheduled half-hour of cartoons once a week (and sufficient other children's programming) could comply with the *Children's Policy Statement,* but that the station would violate the *Policy Statement* if it replaced the cartoons with, say, three hours per week of educational specials. We fail to see the logic of such a requirement.

Finally, this court gives "great deference" to an agency's interpretation of its own regulations. *Udall v. Tallman,* 380 U.S. 1, 16 (1965); see *Red Lion Broadcasting Co. v. FCC,* 395 U.S. 367, 381 (1969) (deference to FCC's statutory interpretation); *Federal Election Commission v. Democratic Senatorial Campaign Committee,* 454 U.S. 27, 39 (1981) (agency's statutory construction must be upheld if it is "sufficiently reasonable," even if it is not "the only reasonable one or even the reading the court would have reached" on its own). Here, deference is enhanced because the Commission has consistently interpreted the *Policy Statement,* albeit implicitly, not to require regularly scheduled weekday children's programming. See *License Renewal Applications of Certain California Television Stations,* 68 F.C.C.2d 1074, 1075 (1978) (approving license renewals over objection that "the licensees do not provide age-specific programs for both school age and pre-school children on a regular weekday basis"); cf. *Notice of Proposed Rulemaking,* 75 F.C.C.2d 138, 143 (1979) (discussing scheduling of children's shows without distinguishing between regularly scheduled and non-regularly scheduled programs); *Channel 20, Inc.,* 70 F.C.C.2d 1770, 1773 (noting with approval that the licensee has "aired its children's programming throughout the broadcast week" without distinguishing between regularly scheduled and non-regularly scheduled programs), *reconsid. denied,* 73 F.C.C.2d 648 (1979).

In sum, we cannot say that the Commission acted unreasonably in interpreting its own policy statement as not imposing a flat requirement that stations must offer regularly scheduled weekday children's programming. The Commission's decision to grant the three challenged license renewals is *affirmed*.

2. Qualitative Concerns

Concern with the actual content of broadcasting has engendered official response not only with respect to indecency but also in regard to violence and advertising. Although generally deferential in its posture, the FCC has acted at least unofficially to account for concerns with excessive violence.

A. VIOLENCE

The FCC has refrained from taking action to control directly programming of a violent nature. Following a request that the commission respond to televised violence in the same way it did to cigarette advertisements, the FCC explicated its reasons for exercising restraint.[381] Despite determinations by the surgeon general that violent programs like cigarettes might have undesirable individual and societal results,[382] the FCC concluded that programming of a general nature did not present a controversial issue of public importance.[383] It thus refused to invoke the fairness doctrine or to require broadcast warnings that subject matter might be hazardous to a child's "mental health and well being."[384] A dissenting commissioner found the presence of violence in general programming an even stronger reason for intervention.[385]

Complaint by George D. Corey, 37 F.C.C. 2d 641 (1972)

Dear Mr. Corey: This is in reference to your letter dated March 27, 1972, concerning three Boston television stations, namely, WBZ-TV, WNAC-TV and WSBK-TV.

In your letter you state that these stations have continued to carry programming directed at chil-

dren which contains an inappropriate amount of violence. You also state that such operation is not in the public interest in that there is a casual relationship between the viewing of televised violence and children's anti-social behavior.

Therefore, you request the Commission to take one of several alternative courses of action. First, you request the Commission to conduct a complete investigation into the extent of children's programs containing violence on these stations and, once having ascertained the results of such a study, to require the stations to either (1) eliminate such programming, (2) substantially reduce such programming, or (3) broadcast such programming only after 9:00 p.m. as is done in Great Britain....

Alternatively, you request the Commission to either withhold renewing the licenses for these stations or grant them only probationary licenses until the Commission decides what action it will take in regard to the broadcasting of violence in children's programs. Finally, you request the Commission to require the licensees of WBZ-TV, WNAC-TV and WSBK-TV to comply with the fairness doctrine by broadcasting the following public service notice or its equivalent: *Warning:* Viewing of violent television programming by children can be hazardous to their mental health and well being....

The issues raised in your letter regarding violence in television programming, particularly as it relates to children's programming, apply to the television industry as a whole. As such, we do not believe that it would be appropriate at this time to make an *ad hoc* determination whether the presentation of such programming by one, two or three, licensees may have a detrimental effect on children. Instead, we believe that it is more appropriate to consider such industry wide problems through the Commission's rule making forum. See, for example, *Hale v. F.C.C.,* 425 F.2d 556 (1970)....

We also believe the questions raised concerning violent episodes in children's programming are distinguishable from our holding in the cigarette advertising matter.

The Commission's ruling *in* the *Banzhaf* case, *In the Matter of Television Station WCBS,* 8 FCC 2d 381 (1967), *recons. denied,* 9 FCC 2d 921, *affirmed sub. nom. Banzhaf v. F.C.C.,* 405 F.2d 1082

(C.A.D.C. 1968), *cert. denied,* 396 U.S. 842 (1969), held that the fairness doctrine is applicable to cigarette advertising. The Commission took note of the 1964 *Report of the Advisory Committee to the Surgeon General of the Public Health Service* and other studies which found a link between smoking and various diseases. In that case the Commission was presented with evidence that cigarette advertisements promoted smoking as attractive and enjoyable. The Commission concluded, therefore, that "...a station which presents such advertisements has the duty of informing its audience of the other side of this controversial issue of public importance—that, however, enjoyable, such smoking may be a hazard to the smoker's health."

However, it could not reasonably or logically be concluded that the mere viewing of a person smoking a cigarette during a movie being broadcast on television constitutes a discussion of a controversial issue of public importance thus raising a fairness doctrine obligation. Similarly, we cannot agree that the broadcast of violent episodes during entertainment programs necessarily constitutes the presentation of one side of a controversial issue of public importance. It is simply not an appropriate application of the fairness doctrine to say that an entertainment program—whether it be Shakespeare or an action-adventure show—raises a controversial issue if it contains a violent scene and has a significant audience of children. Were we to adopt your construction that the depiction of a violent scene is a discussion of one side of a controversial issue of public importance, the number of controversial issues presented on entertainment shows would be virtually endless (e.g., a scene with a high-powered car; or one showing a person taking an alcoholic drink or cigarette; depicting women in a soft feminine or light romantic role). Finally, we note that there are marked differences in the conclusiveness of the hazard established in this area as against cigarette smoking. See the *Surgeon General's Report on the Impact of Televised Violence,* pp. 11–12....

DISSENTING OPINION OF COMMISSIONER NICHOLAS JOHNSON

The Commission today gives incredibly short shrift to one of children's television's most pressing problems: violence....

The majority attempts, rather disingenuously, to distinguish *Banzhaf* on the grounds 1) that the Surgeon General has not found a close link between violence on children's television and a child's anti-social behavior and 2) that broadcasting violence does not promote such violence in the same way that a cigarette advertisement promotes smoking.

Yet the majority itself notes that the Surgeon General has determined that "televised violence may lead to increased aggressive behavior in certain sub groups of children." *Television and Growing Up: Report on the Impact of Televised Violence* (1971) at 7. And that report goes on to reveal the more general conclusion that "a modest relationship exists between the viewing of violence and aggressive behavior." *Id.* at 9. The multivolume staff backup uses much stronger language. In any event, the existence of this casual link is surely close enough to warrant considerable concern.

Further, the fact that violence on children's television is not promoted through advertising, but simply exists as a substantial component of children's television fare, is not only irrelevant but actually cuts the other way. Not only would it be rather bizarre if advertisers attempted to promote the "goodness" of violence in the same manner they promote cigarettes, but, to the child, the fact of continuous violent programming is, in itself, a promotion of the idea. What made *Banzhaf* a break through was the application of the fairness doctrine to advertising in such a forceful manner. Thus, the absence of advertising in this case makes it a stronger one than *Banzhaf,* not weaker.

To assert that violence on children's television does not raise a controversial issue of public importance is, then, to close one's eyes to a very real problem. Indeed, by refusing to require that licensees at least warn parents of the potential dangers inherent in current children's programming, the majority has, in my judgment, left our licensees wide open to possible tort liability. For, if the television set manufacturer is legally liable for the physical damage done by radiation from the set, why should the network be free of responsibility for the psychic harm done by what *it* radiates from the set? (See *How To Talk Back To Your Television Set* 172 (Bantam, 1970)).

One of the reasons the cigarette manufacturers *wanted* the warning ("Caution: Cigarette smoking may be hazardous to your health") printed on the cigarette packs is that, without such a warning to the user, they were taking a substantial risk of hundreds of millions of dollars of tort liability to the survivors of the 300,000 people they helped kill every year. Now that the evidence of the relation of violent programming to violent behavior (and other psychic harm to children) is so clear, it is only a matter of time before the networks' tort liability will also begin to grow. One would think that they would *want* such warnings broadcast to avoid it. The FCC, in its eagerness to serve the industry's profits, may actually be handing it a loss from which it will be a long time in recovering.

While recourse to the courts is certainly one means of dealing with this problem, and whatever the industry's best interest may be, this Commission also has a responsibility to the public as well as the broadcasters, a responsibility which it completely ignores by today's decision. The majority has, once again, passed the buck to the courts. I dissent.

In a subsequent *Report on the Broadcast of Violent, Indecent, and Obscene Material*,[386] the FCC observed that, with respect to "sexually-oriented or violent material which might be inappropriate for [children], industry self-regulation [was] preferable to the adoption of rigid governmental standards."[387] Its preference for private control was premised upon the grounds that government regulation would intrude "too deeply in[to] programming content, raising serious constitutional questions" and necessitate judgments that were too subjective.[388] The report also documented the commission's efforts to encourage broadcasters to police themselves.[389] What resulted was the family viewing hour which, as a function of licensee practice rather than official mandate, was designed to eliminate violent or sexually oriented programming from early prime-time viewing hours.[390]

Report on the Broadcast of Violent, Indecent, and Obscene Material, 51 F.C.C. 2d 418 (1975)

In response to Congressional directives, the Federal Communications Commission submits its report of actions with respect to televised violence and obscenity. This report addresses "specific positive action taken and planned by the Commission to protect children from excessive programming of violence and obscenity."

Congressional concern over the effects of television upon young people has been longstanding. The Senate Judiciary Committee's Subcommittee on Juvenile Delinquency under Senators Kefauver and later Dodd conducted investigations into this area in 1954, 1955, 1961–62 and 1964. In 1969, the National Commission on the Causes and Prevention of Violence, chaired by Dr. Milton Eisenhower, reported that:

> It is reasonable to conclude that a constant diet of violent behavior on television has an adverse effect on human character and attitudes. Violence on television encourages violent forms of behavior, and fosters moral and social values about violence in daily life which are unacceptable in a civilized society.

Subsequent to this finding, the Senate Commerce Committee's Communications Subcommittee, under Senator John O. Pastore, requested the Department of Health, Education and Welfare to initiate an inquiry into "the present scientific knowledge about the effect of entertainment television on children's behavior."

Results of that one-year study by the Surgeon General's Scientific Advisory Committee on Television and Social Behavior, added support to the view that a steady stream of violence on television may have an adverse effect upon our society— and particularly on children. Continuing studies funded by the Department of Health, Education and Welfare during 1972–1974, as reported in the April 3–5, 1974 hearings before Senator Pastore's Subcommittee, gave further evidence of the harmful effects of televised violence on children. Research continues in this area, but the existing evidence is sufficient to justify consideration of changes in industry practices.

The Federal Communications Commission has received substantial evidence that parents, the Congress, and others are deeply concerned. In 1972, the Commission received over 2,000 complaints about violent or sexually-oriented programs. In 1974, that volume had increased to nearly 25,000. Further, the Commission has received petitions to deny broadcast license renewals and petitions for rulemaking expressing the desire that the Commission take action with respect to televised violence, particularly as it affects children. Mindful of the public interest questions raised by the Report to the Surgeon General, subsequent research findings, and the continuing concerns of Congress and the general public, the Commission undertook a study of specific solutions to the problems of televised violence and sexually-oriented material in mid–1974.

Staff discussion and study focused upon two questions: (1) what steps might be taken to prohibit the broadcasting of obscene or indecent material and (2) what steps might be taken to protect children from other sexually-oriented or violent material which might be inappropriate for them. With respect to questions of obscene and indecent material, direct governmental action is required by statute, and the Commission intends to meet its responsibilities in this area. With respect to the broader question of what is *appropriate* for viewing by children, the Commission is of the view that industry self-regulation is preferable to the adoption of rigid governmental standards. We believe that this is the case for two principal reasons: (1) the adoption of rules might involve the government too deeply in programming content, raising serious constitutional questions, and (2) judgments concerning the suitability of particular types of programs for children are highly subjective. As a practical matter, it would be difficult to construct rules which would take into account all of the subjective considerations involved in making such judgments. We are concerned that an attempt at drafting such rules could lead to extreme results which would be unacceptable to the American public.

SEXUAL OR VIOLENT MATERIAL WHICH IS INAPPROPRIATE FOR CHILDREN

Administrative actions regulating violent and sexual material must be reconciled with consti-tutional and statutory limitations on the Commission's authority to regulate program content. Although the unique characteristics of broadcasting may justify greater governmental supervision than would be constitutionally permissible in other media, it is clear that broadcasting is entitled to First Amendment protection. *Columbia Broadcasting System v. Democratic National Committee,* 412 U.S. 94 (1973); *Red Lion Broadcasting Co. v. FCC,* 395 U.S. 367 (1968); *United States v. Paramount Pictures,* 334 U.S. 131 (1948). Congress expressed its concern that the Commission exercise restraint in the area of program regulation by enacting section 326 of the Communications Act which specifically prohibits "censorship" by this agency.

On the other hand, the Communications Act requires the Commission to insure that broadcast licensees operate in a manner consistent with the "public interest." In the *Red Lion* decision, the Supreme Court affirmed the view that broadcasters are "public trustees" with fiduciary responsibilities to their communities. The Commission has long maintained the policy that program service in the public interest is an essential part of a licensee's obligation. *Programming Policy Statement,* 20 P&F R.R. 1901 (1960). We have also made it clear that broadcasters have particular responsibilities to serve the special needs of children. *Children's Television Report and Policy Statement,* 39 F.R. 39396 (November 6, 1974).

In light of the constraints placed on the Commission by the Constitution and section 326 of the Communications Act, the Commission "walks a tightrope between saying too much and saying too little" when applying the public interest standard to programming. *Banzhaf v. FCC,* 405 F.2d 1082, 1095 (D.C. Cir. 1967); *Columbia Broadcasting System v. Democratic National Committee, supra.* For this reason, the Commission has historically exercised caution in the area of program regulation.

Regulatory action to limit violent and sexually-oriented programming which is neither obscene nor indecent is less desirable than effective self-regulation, since government-imposed limitations raise sensitive First Amendment problems. In addition, any rule making in these areas would require finding an appropriate balance between the need to protect children from harmful material and the adult audience's interest in diverse programming. Government rules could create the risk of improper governmental interference in sensitive, subjective decisions about programming, could tend to freeze present standards and could also discourage creative developments in the medium.

With these considerations in mind, Chairman Wiley initiated the first of a series of discussions with the executives of the three major television networks on November 22, 1974. In suggesting such meetings, the Chairman sought to serve as a catalyst for the achievement of meaningful self-regulatory reform. He suggested the following specific proposals for the networks to consider:

(1) *New Commitment*—There should be a new commitment to reduce the level and intensity of violent and sexually-oriented material.

(2) *Scheduling*—Programs which are considered to be inappropriate for viewing by young children should not be broadcast prior to 9 p.m. local time.

(3) *Warnings*—At times when such programs are broadcast, they should include audio and video warning at the outset of the program (and at the first "break"), in addition, similar to the practice in France, a small white dot might be placed in the corner of the screen during the course of a program to warn those viewers who tune in while the program is in progress that it may not be appropriate for viewing by young children.

(4) *Advance Notice*—Affiliates should be provided warnings in advance to be included in local TV Guide and newspaper program listings and promotional materials.

In addition, the Chairman raised the possibility of adoption of a rating system similar to that used in the motion picture industry. In making these suggestions, it was understood that the decision as to which programs are so excessively violent or explicitly sexually-oriented as to be inappropriate for young children would remain in the broadcaster's sound discretion. Also, it was recognized that non-entertainment programming, such as news, public affairs, documentaries and instructional programs would be exempt from the scheduling rule. . . .

At the time of the November 22nd meeting, no commitments were sought from the networks and none were offered. The meeting provided an opportunity for a free and candid exploration of a mutually recognized problem affecting broadcast service. Arrangements were made at that time for a continuation of discussions at the staff level and for a later meeting with top network executives. Staff members of the Commission met separately with representatives of each network in New York on December 10–11, 1974.

Not all of the proposals advanced by the Commission were found to be acceptable by the networks. However, each of the networks developed a set of guidelines which it believed should govern its programming, and policy statements incorporating these guidelines were released to the public. A common element of the three statements is that they provide that the first hour of network entertainment programming in prime time will be suitable for viewing by the entire family.

A second meeting between the Commission's Chairman and the network officials was held in Washington on January 10, 1975. At this meeting, representatives of the National Association of Broadcasters were present. During the course of this meeting, each of the networks made it clear that programs presented during this "Family Viewing" period would be appropriate for young children. Also discussed at that meeting were proposals that reforms be incorporated in the NAB Code.

On February 4, 1975, the NAB Television Code Review Board adopted a proposed amendment to the NAB Television Code similar to the guidelines adopted by the three networks but which would expand the "Family Viewing" period to include "the hour immediately preceding" the first hour of network programming in prime time. The new proposal would go into effect in September 1975, but must first be approved by the NAB Television Board, which meets in early April in Las Vegas, Nevada. The Commission has no reason to expect that the Television Board will reject the proposal of the Television Code Review Board.

Taken together, the three network statements and the NAB proposed policy would establish the following guidelines for the Fall 1975 television season:

(1) *Scheduling*—"The first hour of network entertainment programming in prime time" and "the immediately preceding hour," is to be designated as a "Family Viewing" period. In effect, this would in-

clude the period between 7 p.m. and 9 p.m. Eastern Time during the first six days of the week. On Sunday, network programming typically begins at a different time; the guidelines would therefore provide that the "Family Viewing" period will begin and end a half-hour earlier.

(2) *Warnings*—"Viewer advisories" will be broadcast in audio and video form "in the occasional case when an entertainment program" broadcast during the "Family Viewing" period contains material which may be unsuitable for viewing by younger family members. In addition, "viewer advisories" will be used in later evening hours for programs, which contain material that might be disturbing to significant portions of the viewing audience.

(3) *Advance Notice*—Broadcasters will attempt to notify publishers of television program listings as to programs which will contain "advisories." Responsible use of "advisories" in promotional material is also advised.

Thus, the network and NAB proposals are designed to give parents general notice that after the evening news, and for the duration of the designated period, the broadcaster will make every effort to assure that programming presented (including series and movies) will be appropriate for the entire family. After that time, parents themselves will have to exercise greater caution to be confident that particular programs are suitable for their children. Warnings would continue to be broadcast in later hours to notify viewers of those programs that might be disturbing to significant portions of the audiences.

The Commission believes that the recent actions taken by the three networks and the National Association of Broadcasters Television Code Review Board are commendable and go a long way toward establishing appropriate protections for children from violent and sexually-oriented material. This new commitment suggests that the broadcast industry is prepared to regulate itself in a fashion that will obviate any need for governmental regulation in this sensitive area.

It is inevitable that there will be some disagreements over particular programs and the question of their suitability for children. Interpretation of which programs are appropriate for family viewing remains, as it should, the responsibility of the broadcaster. The success of this program will depend upon whether that respon-

sibility is exercised both with good faith and common sense judgment. Thus, meaningful evaluation by Congress and the public of the efficacy of these self-regulatory measures must await observation of how they are interpreted and applied by the broadcasters.

The industry proposal represents an effort to strike a balance between two conflicting objectives. On the other hand, it is imperative that licensees act to assist parents in protecting their children from objectionable programming. On the other hand, broadcasters believe that if the medium is to achieve its full maturity, it must continue to present sensitive and controversial themes which are appropriate, and of interest, to adult audiences.

Parents, in our view, have—and should retain—the primary responsibility for their children's well-being. This traditional and revered principle, like other examples which could be cited has been adversely affected by the corrosive processes of technological and social change in twentieth-century American life. Nevertheless, we believe that it deserves continuing affirmation.

Television, as a guest in the American home, also has some responsibilities in this area. In providing a forum for the discussion of excessive violence and sexual material on television, the Commission has sought to remind broadcasters of their responsibility to provide some measure of support to concerned parents.

It is obvious that the reforms proposed by the industry will not provide absolute assurance that children or particularly sensitive adults will be insulated from objectionable material. However, no reform short of a wholesale proscription of all violent and sexually-oriented material would have that effect. Surveys have indicated that some children will be viewing television during all hours of the broadcast day, and not just during the hours now designated for "Family Viewing". Some, who are not properly supervised, may be exposed to programming which a responsible adult would consider inappropriate for them. We believe, however, that the industry plan provides a reasonable accommodation of parental and industry responsibilities.

It should be stressed that the networks do not view the post 9 p.m. viewing period as a time to be filled with blood, gore and explicit sexual depictions. The presidents of all three networks have assured the Commission that there will continue to be restraint in the selection and presentation of program material later in the evening.

We recognize that there will be some disagreements with specific aspects of these industry self-regulatory measures. As we have already indicated, the "Family Viewing" period will be presented at different hours in different time zones. This special period would ordinarily end at 9:00 p.m. in New York and Los Angeles, at 8:00 p.m. in the Midwest, and as early as 7:00 p.m. in portions of the Mountain Time Zone. In addition, the fact that the "Family Viewing" period may be presented at a different time on Sunday may create some confusion.

The success of the entire "Family Viewing" principle depends upon the good-faith and responsibility of the networks and other broadcasters. It is important that the "program advisories" and advance notices not be used in a titillating fashion so as to commercially exploit the presentation of violent or sexually-oriented material. Also, the new guidelines will not gain the acceptance of the American people if broadcasters prove to be unreasonably expansive in deciding which programs are appropriate for family viewing.

Despite these considerations, we believe the new guidelines represent a major accomplishment for industry self-regulation, and we are optimistic that these principles will be applied in a responsible manner which will be acceptable to the American people.

The family viewing hour accurately may be depicted as an example of regulation by raised eyebrow.[391] In fact, the action was challenged as a product of official coercion.[392] Although the court of appeals remanded various claims to the commission, the issues were never formally resolved in court. Nor is the family viewing hour now an enforced policy.

B. ADVERTISING

Consistent with its general deregulatory posture and consequent disinclination to set quantitative standards for children's programming, the FCC refused to ban or limit advertising on children's programs.[393] Its determination "that the general deregulation of television commercialization extends to children's television" was found to be without a "reasoned basis," especially given the commission's long-standing premise that "the television marketplace *does not* function adequately when children make up the audience."[394] The FCC has implemented qualitative standards requiring a clear distinction between programming and advertising on children's programs.[395] The commission has determined that programs based upon products marketed for children,[396] however, did not constitute a commercial.[397] Congress, however, has directed the agency to pursue an inquiry into commercial guidelines for children's television that would focus upon programs developed around such products.[398]

Congress in 1988 enacted legislation, directing the FCC to set standards for children-oriented advertising and prescribing quantitative standards, but the president vetoed it.[399] Two years later, the Children's Television Act of 1990 was passed.[400] The law limits advertising aimed at children to 12 minutes per hour on weekdays and 10.5 minutes per hour on weekends.[401]

C. DRUGS

Prompted in part by its concern with children is the FCC's response to programming that may cast illegal drug use in a favorable light. The FCC had placed broadcasters on notice that they were required "to have knowledge of the content of their programming and on the basis of this knowledge to evaluate the desirability of broadcasting music dealing with drug use."[402] Licensees may fulfill their obligation to obtain specific knowledge pursuant to prescreening by a responsible station employee, monitoring selections as they are played, or evaluating public complaints.[403]

A First Amendment challenge, in *Yale Broadcasting Co. v. Federal Communications Commission,*[404] analogized to the principle that a bookseller cannot be required to examine every book in the store to ensure none is obscene.[405] The court of appeals distinguished the circumstances of broadcasting from bookselling, however, on the grounds that fewer works had to be evaluated and the knowledge could be obtained without prescreening.[406] It also minimized the possibility of any serious sanctions in the event a licensee misinterpreted or failed to identify what are often incoherent or obscure lyrics. Reminiscent of the *Pacifica* decision,[407] the court observed that "[a]t some point along the scale of human intelligibility the sounds produced may slide over from characteristics of free speech, which should be protected, to those of noise pollution, which the Commission has ample authority to debate."[408]

Chief Judge Bazelon, in dissent, maintained that the "responsibility" requirement in practice could translate into "prohibition."[409] Even conceding the significance of the regulatory interest, he suggested that the court had neglected pertinent constitutional considerations including whether the expression was protected or actually harmful and, if so, whether alternative remedies would have been more appropriate.[410] Serious First Amendment concerns also were expressed in Justice Douglas' dissent from the Supreme Court's refusal to review the case.[411]

Yale Broadcasting Co. v. Federal Communications Commission, 478 F.2d 594 (D.C. Cir.), *cert. denied,* **414 U.S. 914 (1973)**

Wilkey, Circuit Judge:

The source of this controversy is a Notice issued by the Federal Communications Commis-

sion regarding "drug oriented" music allegedly played by some radio stations. This Notice and a subsequent Order, the stated purposes of which were to remind broadcasters of a pre-existing duty, required licensees to have knowledge of the content of their programming and on the basis of this knowledge to evaluate the desirability of broadcasting music dealing with drug use.

I. SUBSTANCE OF THE FIRST AND SECOND NOTICES

In the late 1960's and early 1970's the FCC began receiving complaints from the public regarding alleged "drug oriented" songs played by certain radio broadcasters. In response to these complaints the Commission issued a Notice, the stated purpose of which was to remind broadcasters of their duty to broadcast in the public interest. To fulfill this obligation licensees were told that they must make "reasonable efforts" to determine before broadcast the meaning of music containing drug oriented lyrics. The Notice specified that this knowledge must be in the possession of a management level executive of the station, who must then make a judgment regarding the wisdom of playing music containing references to drugs or the drug culture.

This initial Notice led to substantial confusion within the broadcast industry and among the public. Confusion centered around the meaning of phrases such as "knowing the content of the lyrics," "ascertain before broadcast," and "reasonable efforts."

In order to clarify these ambiguities, the FCC issued a second Memorandum and Order clarifying and modifying certain parts of the original Notice. The thrust of this Order was that (1) the Commission was not prohibiting the playing of "drug oriented" records, (2) no reprisals would be taken against stations that played "drug oriented" music, but (3) it was still necessary for a station to "know" the content of records played and make a "judgment" regarding the wisdom of playing such records. . . .

III. AN UNCONSTITUTIONAL BURDEN ON FREEDOM OF SPEECH

Appellant's first argument is that the Commission's action imposes an unconstitutional burden on a broadcaster's freedom of speech. . . .

Here the goal is to assure the broadcaster has adequate knowledge. Knowledge is required in order that the broadcaster can make a judgment about the wisdom of its programming. It is beyond dispute that the Commission requires stations to broadcast in the public interest. In order for a broadcaster to determine whether it is acting in the public interest, knowledge of its own programming is required. The Order issued by the Commission has merely reminded the industry of this fundamental metaphysical observation—in order to make a judgment about the value of programming one must have knowledge of that programming.

We say that the licensee must have *knowledge* of what it is broadcasting; the precise *understanding* which may be required of the licensee is only that which is reasonable. No radio licensee faces any realistic possibility of a penalty for misinterpreting the lyrics it has chosen or permitted to be broadcast. If the lyrics are completely obscure, the station is not put on notice that it is in fact broadcasting material which would encourage drug abuse. If the lyrics are meaningless, incoherent, the same conclusion follows. The argument of the appellant licensee, that so many of these lyrics are obscure and ambiguous, really is a circumstance available to some degree in his defense for permitting their broadcast, at least until their meaning is clarified. Some lyrics or sounds are virtually unintelligible. To the extent they are completely meaningless gibberish and approach the equivalent of machinery operating or the din of traffic, they, of course, do not communicate with respect to drugs or anything else, and are not within the ambit of the Commission's order. Speech is an expression of sound or visual symbols which is intelligible to some other human beings. At some point along the scale of human intelligibility the sounds produced may slide over from characteristics of free speech, which should be protected, to those of noise pollution, which the Commission has ample authority to abate.

We not only think appellant's argument invalid, we express our astonishment that the licensee would argue that before the broadcast it has no knowledge, and cannot be required to have any knowledge, of material it puts out over the airwaves. We can understand that the individual radio licensees would not be expected to know in advance the content or the quality of a network program, or a free flowing panel discussion of public issues, or other audience participation program, and certainly not a political broadcast. But with reference to the broadcast of that which is frequently termed "canned music," we think the Commission may require that the purveyors of this to the public make a reasonable effort to know what is in the "can." No producer of pork and beans is allowed to put out on a grocery shelf a can without knowing what is in it and standing back of both its content and quality. The Commission is not required to allow radio licensees, being freely granted the use of limited air channels, to spew out to the listening public canned music, whose content and quality before broadcast is totally unknown.

Supposedly a radio licensee is performing a public service—that is the raison d'etre of the license. If the licensee does not have specific knowledge of what it is broadcasting, how can it claim to be operating in the public interest? Far from constituting any threat to freedom of speech of the licensee, we conclude that for the Commission to have been less insistent on licensees discharging their obligations would have verged on an evasion of the Commission's own responsibilities.

By the expression of the above views we have no desire whatsoever to express a value judgment on different types of music, poetry, sound, instrumentation, etc., which may appeal to different classes of our most diverse public. "De gustibus non est disputandum." But what we are saying is that whatever the style, whatever the expression put out over the air by the radio station, for the licensee to claim that it has no responsibility to evaluate its product is for the radio station to abnegate completely what we had always considered its responsibility as a licensee. All in all, and quite unintentionally, the appellant-licensee in its free speech argument here has told us a great deal about quality in this particular medium of our culture.

Bazelon, Chief Judge:

The panel opinion found that the language of the Commission's directives does not purport to censor popular songs. But that language can only be understood in the light of the Commission's course of conduct.

The Commission's initial statement in the area

of "drug-oriented" songs was a "Public Notice" issued on March 5, 1971. The Notice, entitled "Licensee Responsibility to Review Records Before Their Broadcast," did not specifically prohibit the playing of particular songs. But broadcasters might well have read it as a prohibition. For one thing, two members of the Commission, including the member reported to be the originator of the Notice, appended to it a formal statement explaining that their goal was to "discourage, if not eliminate, the playing of records which tend to promote and/or glorify the use of illegal drugs." Five weeks after the Notice was issued, the Commission's Bureau of Complaints and Compliance provided broadcasters the names of 22 songs which had come to its attention as "so-called drug-oriented song lyrics."

The Commission's action was reported by responsible organs of the press as an act of censorship. It appears that radio stations moved quickly to ban certain songs. In some cases stations stopped playing, regardless of subject or lyric, all the works of particular artists whose views might lift the Commission's eyebrow. Broadcasters circulated the list of 22 songs throughout the industry as a "do not play" list.

The Commission's subsequent "Memorandum Opinion and Order", issued on April 16, 1971, and designated by the Commission as its "definitive statement" on the subject, appeared to backtrack somewhat. The Order repudiated the list of 22 songs. It stated that the evaluation of which records to play "is one solely for the licensee," and that "[t]he Commission cannot make or review such individual licensee judgment."

But the Commission's order went further. Instead of rescinding the Public Notice, the Order restated its basic threat: "the broadcaster could jeopardize his license by failing to exercise licensee responsibility in this area." As we have recognized, "licensee responsibility" is a nebulous concept. It could be taken to mean—as the panel opinion takes it—only that "a broadcaster must 'know' what it is broadcasting." On the other hand, in light of the earlier Notice, and in light of the renewed warnings in the Order about the dangers of "drug-oriented" popular songs, broadcasters might have concluded that "responsibility" meant "prohibition".

The Commissioners themselves were unclear

on the matter. The Order expressed full adherence to the policy of the prior Notice. But two Commissioners issued concurring statements indicating that the Order restored the status quo prior to the March 5 Notice. A third Commissioner issued a dissenting statement indicating that the Order did not restore the status quo. A fourth Commissioner issued a rather enigmatic statement indicating his agreement with both the Notice and the Order but observing that they established an "impossible assignment." The confusion was crystallized later in 1971 in Congressional testimony by FCC Chairman Burch. At one point, the Chairman offered this assurance:

> Chairman Burch:...[C]ontrary to Commissioner Johnson's statement that we banned drug lyrics, we did not ban drug lyrics....

Moments later, however, the following ensued:

> Senator Nelson: All I am asking is: If somebody calls to the FCC's attention that a particular station is playing songs that, in fact, do promote the use of drugs in the unanimous judgment of the Commission, if you came to that conclusion, what would you do?
>
> Chairman Burch: I know what I would do, I probably would vote to take the license away....

Yale Broadcasting Co. v. Federal Communications Commission, 414 U.S. 914 (1973) (denial of certiorari)

Mr. Justice Douglas, dissenting.

In March 1971, the FCC issued a public notice, Licensee Responsibility to Review Records Before Their Broadcast, 28 F.C.C. 2d 409, which was interpreted in many quarters as a prohibition on the playing of "drug related" songs by licensees. That belief was strengthened five weeks later when the Commission's Bureau of Complaints and Compliance provided broadcasters with the names of 22 songs labeled "drug oriented" on the basis of their lyrics. The industry widely viewed this as a list of banned songs, and many licensees quickly acted to remove other songs from the air as well. Some announcers were fired for playing suspect songs.

In April the Commission denied a petition for reconsideration, but attempted to "clarify" its previous order. 31 F.C.C. 2d 377. But although it repudiated the list of banned songs, it reiterated the basic threat by noting that "the broadcaster could jeopardize his license by failing to exercise licensee responsibility in this area." The nature of that responsibility was unclear. The new statement indicated reaffirmation of the prior decision, yet two concurring commissioners indicated that it restored the status quo to the March notice. It seems clear, however, that the Commission majority intended to coerce broadcasters into refusing to play songs that in the Commission's judgment were somehow "drug related." The April order suggested the prescreening of songs as one method of compliance. And in subsequent testimony before Congress, the Chairman of the Commission stated that if a licensee was playing songs that in the Commission's judgment "promote the use of hard drugs," "I know what I would do, I would probably vote to take the license away."

Still unsure of its responsibilities, but desiring to avoid distorting its artistic judgments by superimposing the Commission's vague sociological ones, petitioner Yale Broadcasting Company drafted its own station policy and submitted it to the Commission, asking for a declaratory ruling on whether it complied with the Commission's orders. The station proposed to fulfill its duties in this area by public service and news programming rather than by censoring its music. It elaborated its policy in a six-page statement. The Commission, finding the proposed policy too "abstract," declined to issue any declaratory ruling. The petitioners then brought this action, challenging the Commission's actions on First Amendment grounds, and arguing that the regulations were impermissibly vague. Petitioners also argued that they should have been the subject of formal rule-making procedures.

In *Columbia Broadcasting System, Inc. v. Democratic National Committee,* 412 U.S. 94, 148 (1973) (concurring in judgment), I indicated my view that TV and radio stand in the same protected position under the First Amendment as do newspapers and magazines. I had not participated in

the earlier opinion in *Red Lion Broadcasting Co. v. FCC,* 395 U.S. 367 (1969), which placed broadcasters under a different regime, authorizing governmental regulation to ensure "fairness" of presentation. I explained in *Columbia Broadcasting, supra,* the inevitable danger resulting from placing such powers in governmental hands—a danger appreciated by the Framers of the First Amendment. "The Fairness Doctrine has no place in our First Amendment regime. It puts the head of the camel inside the tent and enables administration after administration to toy with TV or radio in order to serve its sordid or its benevolent ends." 412 U.S., at 154. The instant case well illustrates those dangers.

I doubt that anyone would seriously entertain the notion that consistent with the First Amendment the Government could force a newspaper out of business if its news stories betrayed too much sympathy with those arrested on marihuana charges, or because it published articles by drug advocates such as Timothy Leary. The proposition is so clear that rarely has the Government ever tried such a thing. See *Near v. Minnesota,* 283 U.S. 697 (1931). If the Government set up a new bureau with the job of reviewing newspaper stories for such "dangerous" tendencies, and with the power to put out of business those publications which failed to conform to the bureau's standards, the publisher would not have to wait until his newspaper had been destroyed to challenge the bureau's authority. The threat of governmental action alone would impose a prohibited restraint upon the press. "[I]nhibition as well as prohibition against the exercise of precious First Amendment rights is a power denied to government." *Lamont v. Postmaster General,* 381 U.S. 301, 309 (1965) (Brennan, J., concurring). Cf. *Bantam Books, Inc. v. Sullivan,* 372 U.S. 58 (1963); *Dombrowski v. Pfister,* 380 U.S. 479 (1965).

Yet this is precisely the course taken here by the FCC. The Commission imposes on the licensees a responsibility to analyze the meaning of each song's lyrics and make a judgment as to the social value of the message. The message may be clear or obscure, and careful scrutiny would seem required. This task is to be carried out under the Commission's watchful eye and with the knowledge that repeated errors will be punished by revocation of the license. For now the regulation is applied to song lyrics; next year it may apply to comedy programs, and the following year to news broadcasts.

In *New York Times Co. v. Sullivan*, 376 U.S. 254, 279 (1964), we said that the State could not impose on newspapers the burden, under penalty of civil liability, of checking out every controversial statement for "truth." "Under such a rule, would-be critics of official conduct may be deterred from voicing their criticism, even though it is believed to be true and even though it is in fact true, because of doubt whether it can be proved in court or fear of the expense of having to do so. They tend to make only statements which 'steer far wider of the unlawful zone.' . . . The rule thus dampens the vigor and limits the variety of public debate. It is inconsistent with the First and Fourteenth Amendments." *Ibid.* Songs play no less a role in public debate, whether they eulogize the John Brown of the abolitionist movement, or the Joe Hill of the union movement, provide a rallying cry such as "We Shall Overcome," or express in music the values of the youthful "counterculture." The Government cannot, consistent with the First Amendment, require a broadcaster to censor its music any more than it can require a newspaper to censor the stories of its reporters. Under our system the Government is not to decide what messages, spoken or in music, are of the proper "social value" to reach the people.

I dissent.

D. COMMERCIALS

Advertising is a form of commercial expression which, as discussed previously,[412] until recently was entirely beyond the First Amendment's pale and even now has diminished constitutional status. Consistent with its inclination during the 1980s to rely upon marketplace forces, the FCC eliminated all quantitative commercial guidelines for television.[413] Notwithstanding policy trends, First Amendment principles remain subject to dilution given broadcasting's bottom rank in the constitutional hierarchy of the press. Broadcast advertising in sum is subject to all conditions governing commercial speech generally plus other constraints that are medium specific.

Typifying the unique status of and standards for radio and television advertising is the prohibition of commercials promoting the use of tobacco.[414] An FCC determination that "radio and television stations which carry cigarette advertising [must] devote a significant amount of broadcast time to presenting the case against cigarette smoking"[415] was upheld in *Banzhaf v. Federal Communications Commission.*[416] Soon afterward, as noted previously,[417] the commission aborted the use of the fairness doctrine as a means for promoting a balanced coverage of the issues raised by commercials. Meanwhile after *Banzhaf*, fairness obligations prompted by cigarette advertisements were displaced by a total ban of such commercials "on any medium of electronic communication subject to the jurisdiction of the FCC."[418] Although the law was challenged by broadcasters as an invasion of their First Amendment freedom, a district court in *Capital Broadcasting Co. v. Mitchell*[419] upheld the prohibition.[420] The court premised its decision both upon the unprotected status of commercial speech at the time and the diminished constitutional status of broadcasting.[421] A dissenting opinion by Judge Wright suggested that both regulatory and constitutional goals were served better by reliance on the fairness doctrine rather than on proscription.[422] He noted that antismoking commercials had such "a devastating effect on cigarette consumption" that tobacco companies actually considered the ban preferable to public debate.[423] Wright thus asserted that the congressional act constituted misguided paternalism insofar as it cut off controversial speech and thereby deprecated First Amendment interests and undermined public health aims.[424]

Capital Broadcasting Co. v. Mitchell, 333 F.Supp. 582 (D.C.C. 1971), aff'd, 415 U.S. 1000 (1972)

Gasch, District Judge.

In 1965, in an attempt to alert the general public to the documented dangers of cigarette smoking, Congress enacted legislation requiring a health warning to be placed on all cigarette packages. By 1969 it was evident that more stringent controls would be required and that both the FCC and the FTC were considering independent action. Under such circumstances Congress enacted the Public Health Cigarette Smoking Act of 1969, (hereafter referred to as the Act) which, as pertinent hereto, provides:

> Sec. 6. After January 1, 1971, it shall be unlawful to advertise cigarettes on any medium of electronic communication subject to the jurisdiction of the Federal Communications Commission.

Petitioners allege that the ban on advertising imposed by Section 6 prohibits the "dissemination of information with respect to a lawfully sold product..." in violation of the First Amendment. It is established that product advertising is less vigorously protected than other forms of speech. *Breard v. City of Alexandria*, 341 U.S. 622, 642 (1951) *Murdock v. Com. of Pennsylvania*, 319 U.S. 105, 110–111 (1943); *Valentine v. Chrestensen*, 316 U.S. 52, 54 (1942); *Banzhaf v. Federal Communications Commission*, 132 U.S.App. D.C. 14, 405 F.2d 1082, 1101 (1968) cert. denied, 396 U.S. 842 (1969). The unique characteristics of electronic communication make it especially subject to regulation in the public interest. *National Broadcasting Co. v. United States*, 319 U.S. 190, 226–227 (1943); *Office of Communication of United Church of Christ v. Federal Communications Commission*, 123 U.S.App. D.C. 328, 359 F.2d 994, 1003 (1966). Whether the Act is viewed as an exercise of the Congress' supervisory role over the federal regulatory agencies or as an exercise of its power to regulate interstate commerce, Congress has the power to prohibit the advertising of cigarettes in any media. The validity of other, similar advertising regulations concerning the federal regulatory agencies has been repeatedly upheld

whether the agency be the FCC, the FTC, or the SEC. Petitioners do not dispute the existence of such regulatory power, but urge that its exercise in context of the Act is unconstitutional. In that regard it is dispositive that the Act has no substantial effect on the exercise of petitioners' First Amendment rights. Even assuming that loss of revenue from cigarette advertisements affects petitioners with sufficient First Amendment interest, petitioners, themselves, have lost no right to speak—they have only lost an ability to collect revenue from others for broadcasting their commercial messages. See, *Business Executives' Move for Vietnam Peace v. F.C.C.*, 450 F.2d 642 at 654 (D.C.Cir. 1971). Finding nothing in the Act or its legislative history which precludes a broadcast licensee from airing its own point of view on any aspect of the cigarette smoking question, it is clear that petitioners' speech is not at issue. Thus, contrary to the assertions made by petitioners, Section 6 does not prohibit them from disseminating information about cigarettes, and, therefore, does not conflict with the exercise of their First Amendment rights....

J. Skelly Wright, Circuit Judge (dissenting):

Cigarette smoking and the danger to health which it poses are among the most controversial and important issues before the American public today. Yet Congress, in passing the Public Health Cigarette Smoking Act of 1969, has suppressed the ventilation of these issues on the country's most pervasive communication vehicle—the electronic media. Under the circumstances, in my judgment, no amount of attempted balancing of alleged compelling state interests against freedom of the press can save this Act from constitutional condemnation under the First Amendment. The heavy hand of government has destroyed the scales.

It would be difficult to argue that there are many who mourn for the Marlboro Man or miss the ungrammatical Winston jingles. Most television viewers no doubt agree that cigarette advertising represents the carping hucksterism of Madison Avenue at its very worst. Moreover, overwhelming scientific evidence makes plain that the Salem girl was in fact a seductive merchant of death—that the real "Marlboro Country" is the graveyard. But the First Amendment does not protect only speech that is healthy or harmless. The Court of Appeals in this circuit has approved the view that "cigarette advertising implicitly states a position on a matter of public controversy." *Banzhaf v. F.C.C.*, 132 U.S.App. D.C. 14, 34, 405 F.2d 1082, 1102 (1968), cert. denied, 396 U.S. 842 (1969). For me, that finding is enough to place such advertising within the core protection of the First Amendment.

I

The *Banzhaf* case, decided three years ago, upheld an FCC determination that, since cigarette advertising was controversial speech on a public issue, the so-called "fairness doctrine" applied to it. Stations carrying cigarette advertising were therefore required to "tell both sides of the story" and present a fair number of anti-smoking messages.

The history of cigarette advertising since *Banzhaf* has been a sad tale of well meaning but misguided paternalism, cynical bargaining and lost opportunity. In the immediate wake of *Banzhaf,* the broadcast media were flooded with exceedingly effective anti-smoking commercials. For the first time in years, the statistics began to show a sustained trend toward lesser cigarette consumption. The *Banzhaf* advertising not only cost the cigarette companies customers, present and potential; it also put the industry in a delicate, paradoxical position. While cigarette advertising is apparently quite effective in inducing brand loyalty, it seems to have little impact on whether people in fact smoke. And after *Banzhaf,* these advertisements triggered the anti-smoking messages which were having a devastating effect on cigarette consumption. Thus the individual tobacco companies could not stop advertising for fear of losing their competitive position; yet for every dollar they spent to advance their product, they forced the airing of more anti-smoking advertisements and hence lost more customers.

It was against this backdrop that the Consumer Subcommittee of the Senate Committee on Commerce met to consider new cigarette legislation. The legislative prohibition against requiring health warnings in cigarette advertisements had just expired, and the Federal Trade Commission

had indicated that it might soon require such warnings if not again stopped by Congress. In addition, the FCC was moving toward rule making which would have removed cigarette advertising from the electronic media. Thus Congress had to decide whether to extend the ban on FTC action and institute a similar restraint against the FCC or, alternatively, to allow the regulatory agencies to move forcefully against cigarette advertisements.

The context in which this decision had to be made shifted dramatically when a representative of the cigarette industry suggested that the Subcommittee draft legislation permitting the companies to remove their advertisements from the air. In retrospect, it is hard to see why this announcement was thought surprising. The *Banzhaf* ruling had clearly made electronic media advertising a losing proposition for the industry, and a voluntary withdrawal would have saved the companies approximately $250,000,000 in advertising costs, relieved political pressure for FTC action, and removed most anti-smoking messages from the air.

At the time, however, the suggestion of voluntary withdrawal was taken by some as a long delayed demonstration of industry altruism. Congress quickly complied with the industry's suggestion by banning the airing of television and radio cigarette commercials. Moreover, the new legislation provided additional rewards for the industry's "altruism" including a delay in pending FTC action against cigarette advertising and a prohibition against stricter state regulation of cigarette advertising and packaging. The result of the legislation was that as both the cigarette advertisements and most anti-smoking messages left the air, the tobacco companies transferred their advertising budgets to other forms of advertising such as newspapers and magazines where there was no fairness doctrine to require a response.

The passage of the Public Health Cigarette Smoking Act of 1969 marked a dramatic legislative *coup* for the tobacco industry. With the cigarette smoking controversy removed from the air, the decline in cigarette smoking was abruptly halted and cigarette consumption almost immediately turned upward again. Thus whereas the *Banzhaf* ruling, which required that both sides of the controversy by aired, significantly depressed cigarette sales, the 1969 legislation which effectively banned the controversy from the air, had the reverse effect. Whereas the *Banzhaf* decision had increased the flow of information by air so that the American people could make an informed judgment on the hazards of cigarette smoking, the 1969 Act cut off the flow of information altogether.

Of course, the fact that the legislation in question may be a product of skillful lobbying or of pressures brought by narrow private interests, or may have been passed by Congress to favor a particular industry, does not necessarily affect its constitutionality. Cf. *United States v. O'Brien,* 391 U.S. 367, 383–385 (1968); *Arizona v. California,* 283 U.S. 423, 455 (1931). But when the "inevitable effect" of the legislation is the production of an unconstitutional result, the statute cannot be allowed to stand. See *Gomillion v. Lightfoot,* 364 U.S. 339, 342, 81 S.Ct. 125, 5 L.Ed.2d 110 (1960). The legislative history related above shows that the effect of this legislation was to cut off debate on the value of cigarettes just when *Banzhaf* had made such a debate a real possibility. The theory of free speech is grounded on the belief that people will make the right choice if presented with all points of view on a controversial issue. See Emerson, Toward a General Theory of the First Amendment, 72 Yale L.J. 877, 881 (1963); A. Meiklejohn, Political Freedom 26–28 (1960). When *Banzhaf* opened the electronic media to different points of view on the desirability of cigarette smoking, this theory was dramatically vindicated. Once viewers saw both sides of the story, they began to stop or cut down on smoking in ever increasing numbers. Indeed, it was presumably the very success of the *Banzhaf* doctrine in allowing people to make an informed choice that frightened the cigarette industry into calling on Congress to silence the debate....

Indeed, the desirability of cigarette smoking has become still more controversial since *Banzhaf* was decided. Issues such as whether Congress should end price supports for tobacco, require stricter health warnings, or even outlaw the sale of cigarettes altogether are matters of widespread public debate. The Surgeon General has stated and reiterated his official position that the health hazards of cigarette smoking make it an undesirable habit. The Government is, of course, entitled to take that position and to attempt to persuade the American people of its validity. But the Government is emphatically not entitled to monopolize the debate or to suppress the expression of opposing points of view on the electronic media by making such expression a criminal offense.

Of course, it is true that the courts have on occasion recognized a narrow exception to these general First Amendment principles. Where otherwise protected speech can be shown to present a "clear and present danger" of a severe evil which the state has a right to prevent, suppression of that speech has on occasion been permitted. The argument is made here that the state has an overwhelming interest in the preservation of the health of its citizens and that cigarette advertising poses a clear and present danger to this interest.

Although this argument is superficially attractive, it cannot withstand close scrutiny. The clear and present danger test has always been more or less confined to cases where the state has asserted an overriding interest in its own preservation or in the maintenance of public order. While it cannot be denied that public health is also a vital area of state concern, it is different from the state interest in security in one crucial respect. Whereas there are always innocent victims in riots and revolutions, the only person directly harmed by smoking cigarettes is the person who decides to smoke them. The state can stop speech in order to protect the innocent bystander, but it cannot impose silence merely because it fears that people will be convinced by what they hear and thereby harm themselves. As cases like *Stanley v. Georgia* and *Griswold v. Connecticut* make clear, the state has no interest at all in what people read, see, hear or think in the privacy of their own home or in front of their own television set. At the very core of the First Amendment is the notion that people are capable of making up their own minds about what is good for them and that they can think their own thoughts so long as they do not in some manner interfere with the rights of others.

III

This opinion is not intended as a Magna Carta for Madison Avenue. In my view, Congress retains broad power to deal with the evils of cigarette advertising. It can force the removal of deceptive claims, require manufacturers to couple their advertisements with a clear statement of the hazardous nature of their product, and provide for reply time to be awarded to anti-cigarette groups. But the one thing which Congress may not do is cut off debate altogether.

The only interest which might conceivably justify such a total ban is the state's interest in preventing people from being convinced by what they hear—the very sort of paternalistic interest which the First Amendment precludes the state from asserting. Even if this interest were sufficient in the purely commercial context, the *Banzhaf* decision makes clear that cigarette messages are not ordinary product advertising but rather speech on a controversial issue of public importance—*viz.*, the desirability of cigarette smoking. The Government simply cannot have it both ways. Either this is controversial speech in the public arena or it is not. If it is such speech, then Section 6 of the Public Health Cigarette Smoking Act is unconstitutional; if it is not, then *Banzhaf* was wrongly decided. Although I respect the opinion of my colleagues in this case, my own view is that the *Banzhaf* decision was correct and that this law is unconstitutional. I come to that position not only because *stare decisis* dictates it, but also because I think that when people are given both sides of the cigarette controversy, they will make the correct decision. That, after all, is what the First Amendment is all about. And our too brief experience with the *Banzhaf* doctrine shows that the theory works in practice.

I respectfully dissent.

Although rendered prior to the emergence of commercial expression as a constitutionally protected form of speech, the twists of modern commercial speech doctrine suggest the *Capital Broadcasting* decision retains not only vitality but possible potential for expansion. The Court's recent determination, that government may ban expression concerning an activity it has the power to make illegal even if the authority is not actually exercised,[425] suggests the possibility that a ban on cigarette advertising irrespective of medium might be permissible. A like implication follows for any product or service which, even if not unlawful, could be declared illegal.

NOTES _____

1. *See* Red Lion Broadcasting Co. v. Federal Communications Commission, 395 U.S. 367, 375–77 (1969) (citing early applications of fairness principles dating back to 1930).

2. Great Lakes Broadcasting Co., 3 F.R.C. Ann. Rep. 32 (1929), *aff'd in part, rev'd in part,* 37 F.2d 993 (D.C.Cir.), *cert. denied,* 281 U.S. 706 (1930).

3. 62 F.2d 850 (D.C.Cir. 1932), *cert. denied,* 288 U.S. 599 (1933).

4. *Id.* at 851–53. The *Trinity* case is an early example of FCC action that implicates First Amendment expressive interests. For an argument that licensing of religious broadcasters implicates the First Amendment's establishment clause, *see* Lacey, *The Electric Church: An FCC "Established" Institution?* 31 FED. COM. L.J. 235 (1979).

5. 319 U.S. 190 (1943).

6. *Id.* at 217–18.

7. Red Lion Broadcasting Co. v. Federal Communications Commission, 395 U.S. at 390.

8. The Handling of Public Issues under the Fairness Doctrine and the Public Interest Standards of the Communications Act, 48 F.C.C.2d 1, 8 (1974) (hereafter cited as "Fairness Report").

9. *See infra* II.A.2.b. in this chapter.

10. Report on Editorializing by Broadcast Licensees, 13 F.C.C. 1246, 1249 (1949). The fairness doctrine thus evolved into a requirement for broadcasters to (1) set aside reasonable amounts of air time for the coverage of controversial issues of public importance, and (2) provide opportunities for contrasting points of view. Fairness Report, 48 F.C.C.2d at 7.

11. 13 F.C.C. at 1252.

12. 47 U.S.C. § 315.

13. Red Lion Broadcasting Co. v. Federal Communications Commission, 395 U.S. at 380–82.

14. *See infra* II.A.2.b in this chapter.

15. 47 U.S.C. § 315 (a) (4).

16. The rule is codified in 47 C.F.R. § 73.1920.

17. The rule is codified in 47 C.F.R. § 73.1930.

18. *See* Red Lion Broadcasting Co. v. Federal Communications Commission, 395 U.S. at 371–72.

19. 395 U.S. 367.

20. *Id.* at 375.

21. *Id.*

22. *Id.* at 376.

23. *Id.*

24. *Id.* at 379–80.
25. *Id.* at 378.
26. *Id.* at 385.
27. *Id.* at 386.
28. *Id.*
29. *Id.*
30. *Id.* at 388.
31. *Id.* at 389.
32. *Id.*
33. *Id.* at 390.
34. *Id.*
35. *Id.* at 393.
36. *Id.* at 393.
37. *Id.* at 394.
38. *Id.* at 396.
39. *Id.* at 401.
40. *E.g.*, Price, *Taming Red Lion: The First Amendment and Structural Approaches to Media Regulation,* 31 FED. COM. L.J. 215 (1979); Van Alstyne, *The Mobius Strip of the First Amendment: Perspectives on Red Lion,* 29 S.C.L. Rev. 539 (1978).
41. Syracuse Peace Council, 2 F.C.C. Rcd. 5043 (1987), *aff'd,* Syracuse Peace Council v. Federal Communications Commission, 867 F.2d 654 (D.C.Cir. 1989).
42. Shortly before the FCC abandoned the fairness doctrine, Congress had voted to codify it as a statute only to have the president veto the measure. *See* New York Times, Aug. 25, 1987, at C26, col. 6; *id.,* June 21, 1987, at 1, cols. 4–5.
43. Fairness Report, 48 F.C.C.2d at 7.
44. *Id.* at 5–6.
45. Rep. Patsy Mink, 59 F.C.C.2d 987–88 (1976).
46. *Id.* at 994.
47. *Id.*
48. American Security Council Educational Foundation v. Federal Communications Commission, 607 F.2d 438 (D.C.Cir. 1979).
49. *Id.* at 442.
50. 607 F.2d 438.
51. *Id.* at 452.
52. *Id.*
53. Public Issues under the Fairness Doctrine and the Public Interest Standards of the Communications Act, 58 F.C.C.2d 691, 709 (1976) (Cm'r Robinson dissenting) (hereafter cited as Reconsideration of the Fairness Report).
54. National Broadcasting Co., Inc. v. Federal Communications Commission, 516 F.2d 1101 (D.C.Cir. 1974), *dismissed as moot,* (1975), *cert. denied,* 424 U.S. 910 (1976). The program at issue concerned alleged deficiencies in private pension plans.
55. 516 F.2d 1101.
56. *Id.* at 1115.
57. *But see* Council on Religion and the Homosexual, 68 F.C.C.2d 1500 (1978) (broadcaster's determination, that coverage of anti-gay rights controversy in another community did not require balance, found "unreasonable" given impact on local public).
58. WCBS-TV, 8 F.C.C.2d 381 (1967), *aff'd,* Banzhaf v. Federal Communications Commission, 405 F.2d 1082 (D.C.Cir. 1968).
59. *See e.g.,* Media Access Project (Georgia Power), 44 F.C.C.2d 755 (1973); Wilderness Society, 31 F.C.C.2d 729 (1971).
60. Friends of the Earth v. Federal Communications Commission, 449 F.2d 1164 (D.C.Cir. 1971).
61. Fairness Report, 48 F.C.C.2d at 23.
62. Public Interest Research Group v. Federal Communications Commission, 522 F.2d 1060 (1st Cir. 1975), *cert. denied,* 424 U.S. 965 (1976).
63. *See* CBS, Inc. v. Federal Communications Commission, 453 U.S. 367 (1981) (upholding reasonable right of access for federal candidates); Columbia Broadcasting System, Inc. v. Democratic National Committee, 412 U.S. 94 (1973) (denying general right of access for public).
64. Business Executives Move for Vietnam Peace v. Federal Communications Commission, 450 F.2d 642, 654–58 (D.C.Cir. 1971), *rev'd,* 412 U.S. 94 (1973).
65. 412 U.S. 94.
66. *Id.* at 110–11.
67. *Id.* at 111–13.
68. *Id.* at 98.
69. *Id.* at 103–10.
70. *Id.* at 110.
71. *Id.* at 126–27.
72. *Id.*
73. *Id.* at 123.
74. *Id.*
75. *Id.* at 124–25.
76. *Id.* at 124.
77. *Id.* at 124–25.
78. *Id.* at 125.
79. *Id.* at 131.
80. *Id.*
81. *Id.* at 148 (Douglas, J., concurring).
82. *Id.* at 162–63 (Douglas, J., concurring).
83. *Id.* at 159–60 (Douglas, J., concurring).
84. *Id.* at 158 (Douglas, J., concurring).
85. *Id.* at 195–96 (Brennan, J., dissenting).
86. *Id.* at 187–88 (Brennan, J., dissenting).
87. *Id.* at 189–90 (Brennan, J., dissenting) (emphasis in original).
88. *Id.* at 195–96 (Brennan, J., dissenting).
89. *Id.* at 131.
90. Reconsideration of the Fairness Report, 58 F.C.C.2d 691, 699 (1976), *aff'd in part, remanded in part,* National Citizens Committee For Broadcasting v. Federal Communications Commission, 567 F.2d 1095

(D.C.Cir. 1977). Conflict between First Amendment mythology and reality, with respect to the actual functioning of the information marketplace and scarcity of attractive options, is discussed in Weinberg, *Questioning Broadcast Regulation,* 86 MICH. L.REV. 1269, 1285–89 (1988).

91. *See* 567 F.2d at 1112.

92. Columbia Broadcasting System, Inc. v. Democratic National Committee, 412 U.S. at 123.

93. *See* National Citizens Committee for Broadcasting v. Federal Communications Commission, 567 F.2d at 1112.

94. *See id.* at 1115.

95. 567 F.2d 1095.

96. *Id.* at 1110.

97. Handling of Public Issues under the Fairness Doctrine and the Public Interest Standards of the Communications Act, 74 F.C.C.2d 163 (1979).

98. *Id.* at 171–72.

99. *Id.* at 179.

100. *Id.* at 179–80.

101. National Citizens Committee for Broadcasting v. Federal Communications Commission, 567 F.2d at 1113, *citing* Reconsideration of the Fairness Report, 58 F.C.C.2d at 699.

102. 47 U.S.C. § 312(a) (7).

103. 47 C.F.R. § 73.1920.

§ 73.1920 Personal attacks

(a) When, during the presentation of views on a controversial issue of public importance, an attack is made upon the honesty, character, integrity or like personal qualities of an identified person or group, the licensee shall, within a reasonable time and in no event later than one week after the attack, transmit to the persons or group attacked:

(1) Notification of the date, time and identification of the broadcast;

(2) A script or tape (or an accurate summary if a script or tape is not available) of the attack; and

(3) An offer of a reasonable opportunity to respond over the licensee's facilities.

(b) The provisions of paragraph (a) of this section shall not apply to broadcast material which falls within one or more of the following categories:

(1) Personal attacks on foreign groups or foreign public figures;

(2) Personal attacks occurring during uses by legally qualified candidates.

(3) Personal attacks made during broadcasts not included in paragraph (b) (2) of this section and made by legally qualified candidates, their authorized spokespersons, or those associated with them in the campaign, on other such candidates, their authorized spokespersons or persons associated with the candidates in the campaign; and

(4) Bona fide newscasts, bona fide news interviews, and on-the-spot coverage of bona fide news events, including commentary or analysis contained in the foregoing programs.

104. *Id.,* § 73.1920(a).

105. *Id.,* § 73.1920(a) (1)–(3).

106. *Id.,* § 73.1920(b) (1)–(4).

107. *See* Straus Communications, Inc. v. Federal Communications Commission, 530 F.2d 1001 (D.C.Cir. 1976).

108. *Id.* at 1010–11.

109. *Id.* at 1011.

100. *See* Polish American Congress v. Federal Communications Commission, 520 F.2d 1248 (7th Cir. 1975), *cert. denied,* 424 U.S. 927 (1976).

111. 47 C.F.R. § 73.1930.

§ 73.1930 Political editorials.

(a) Where a licensee, in an editorial,

(1) Endorses or,

(2) Opposes a legally qualified candidate or candidates, the licensee shall, within 24 hours after the editorial, transmit to, respectively,

(i) The other qualified candidate or candidates for the same office or,

(ii) The candidate opposed in the editorial,

(A) Notification of the date and the time of the editorial,

(B) A script or tape of the editorial and

(C) An offer of reasonable opportunity for the candidate or a spokesman of the candidate to respond over the licensee's facilities. Where such editorials are broadcast on the day of the election or within 72 hours prior to the day of the election, the licensee shall comply with the provisions of this paragraph sufficiently far in advance of the broadcast to enable the candidate or candidates to have a reasonable opportunity to prepare a response and to present it in a timely fashion.

112. *Id.* § 73.1930 (a) (2) (i) (ii) (A) and (B).

113. *Id.,* § 73.1930 (a) (2) (i) (ii) (C).

114. *Id.*

115. 47 U.S.C. § 315(a).

116. 47 C.F.R. § 1940 (a).

117. When a representative of or spokesperson appears to promote a candidate, however, the fairness doctrine may apply. *See* Letter to Nicholas Zapple, 23 F.C.C.2d 707 (1970). Given "presentation of one side of a controversial issue of public importance" under such circumstances, the FCC observed that "barring

unusual circumstances, it would not be reasonable for a licensee to refuse to sell time to" rival supporters or representatives. *Id.* at 708. The licensee, however, is not obligated to provide such response time for free. *Id.* Even if an appearance includes criticism of an opposing candidate, the same fairness principles operate at least insofar as "mere criticism [does] not constitute a personal attack within the meaning of [agency] rules." *Id.* at 709.

118. Time, Inc., 55 R.R.2d 581 (1984).

119. Pat Paulsen, 33 F.C.C.2d 297, *aff'd,* 491 F.2d 887 (9th Cir. 1974).

120. Adrian Weiss, 58 F.C.C.2d 342 (1976).

121. Branch v. Federal Communications Commission, 824 F.2d 37 (D.C.Cir.), *cert. denied,* 108 S.Ct. 1220 (1987).

122. *Id.* at 47–50.

123. 824 F.2d 37.

124. *Id.* at 47–49.

125. *Id.* at 50.

126. *Id.* at 49–50.

127. 47 U.S.C. § 315 (a) (1)–(4).

128. *See, e.g.,* Columbia Broadcasting System, Inc. (Lar Daley), 26 F.C.C.2d 715 (1959).

129. Columbia Broadcasting System, 3 R.R.2d 623 (1964).

130. Republican National Committee, 3 R.R.2d 647 (1974).

131. Hon. Shirley Chisholm, 35 F.C.C.2d 572 (1972).

132. Chisholm v. FCC, No. 72–1505 (D.C. Cir. 1972).

133. Hon. Shirley Chisholm, 35 F.C.C.2d 579, 581 (1972).

134. Chisholm v. Federal Communications Commission, 538 F.2d 349 (D.C. Cir.), *cert. denied,* 429 U.S. 890 (1976). The Commission later ruled a broadcaster may sponsor a debate so long as it does not favor a particular candidacy. Henry Geller, 95 F.C.C.2d 1236 (1983), *aff'd,* League of Women Voters Education Fund v. Federal Communications Commission 731 F.2d 995 (D.C. Cir. 1984). The decision rested upon the premise that the public interest was advanced coextensively with multiplied opportunities for debates. 95 F.C.C.2d at 1244.

135. Henry Geller, 95 F.C.C.2d at 1244.

136. Kennedy for President Committee v. Federal Communications Commission, 636 F.2d 417 (D.C. Cir. 1980).

137. *Id.* at 427.

138. 47 U.S.C. § 315 (b) (2).

139. *Id.,* § 315 (b) (1).

140. *See* Political Primer, 100 F.C.C.2d 1476 (1984).

141. 47 U.S.C. § 315 (a).

142. Farmers Educational & Cooperative Union of America v. WDAY, Inc., 360 U.S. 525 (1959).

143. *Id.* at 535.

144. *Id.* at 535–36.

145. 47 U.S.C. § 312 (a) (7).

146. *Id.*.

147. CBS, Inc. v. Federal Communications Commission, 453 U.S. at 377.

148. 453 U.S. 367.

149. *See id.* at 371–73.

150. *Id.* at 397.

151. *Id.* at 396.

152. *See* Columbia Broadcasting System, Inc. v. Democratic National Committee, 412 U.S. 94.

153. CBS, Inc. v. Federal Communications Commission, 453 U.S. at 395–97.

154. *Id.* at 396.

155. Kennedy for President Committee v. Federal Communications Commission, 636 F.2d 433, 444 (D.C. Cir. 1980).

156. 636 F.2d 432.

157. *Id.* at 449.

158. *Id.*

159. *Id.*

160. *Id.* at 450.

161. *See* Red Lion Broadcasting Company v. FCC, 395 U.S. 367. For an argument to the effect that media-specific governance imposing special regulations on some but not all elements of the press is both defensible and desirable, *see* Bollinger, *Freedom of the Press and Public Access: Toward a Theory of Partial Regulation of the Mass Media,* 75 MICH. L. REV. (1976). The premise is directly challenged in L. POWE, JR., AMERICAN BROADCASTING AND THE FIRST AMENDMENT (1987).

162. *See* Syracuse Peace Council, 2 F.C.C. Rcd. 5043 (1987), *aff'd,* Syracuse Peace Council v. Federal Communications Commission, 867 F.2d 654.

163. Red Lion Broadcasting Co. v. Federal Communications Commission, 395 U.S. at 377–80, 385; Fairness Report, 48 F.C.C.2d at 7.

164. *See, e.g.,* Fowler & Brenner, *A Marketplace Approach to Broadcast Regulation,* 60 TEX. L. REV. 207, 229 (1982); Bazelon, *FCC Regulation of the Telecommunications Press,* 1975 DUKE L.J. 213, 231–32.

165. *Id.*

166. As Brennan observed, broadcasters assume "angry customers are not good customers and . . . it is simply 'bad business' to espouse—or even to allow others to espouse—the heterodox or the controversial." Columbia Broadcasting System, Inc. v. Democratic National Committee, 412 U.S. at 187 (Brennan, J., dissenting).

167. *See* Inquiry into § 73.1910 of the Commission's Rules and Regulations Concerning the General Fairness Doctrine Obligation of Broadcasting Licensees, 102 F.C.C.2d 145, 157–69 (1985) (hereafter cited as Fairness Inquiry).

168. S. SIMMONS, THE FAIRNESS DOCTRINE AND THE MEDIA 219–20 (1978). *See also* Fairness Inquiry, 102 F.C.C.2d at 192–94.

169. Fairness Report, 48 F.C.C.2d at 8, 23.

170. *Id.* at 16.

171. *E.g.,* Columbia Broadcasting System, Inc. v. Democratic National Committee, 412 U.S. at 148–70 (Douglas, J., concurring).

172. 468 U.S. 364 (1984).

173. *Id.* at 376–79, nn. 11–12.

174. *Id.* at 376–77, n. 11.

175. *Id.* at 378–79, n. 12.

176. 801 F.2d 501 (D.C. Cir. 1986), *cert. denied,* 482 U.S. 919 (1987).

177. *Id.* at 508.

178. *Id.* at 508–09.

179. *Id.* at 509.

180. Fairness Inquiry, 102 F.C.C.2d at 147.

181. *Id.* at 169 (chills expression), 188–90 (impedes expression of unpopular opinion) 190–92 (invades editorial discretion), 194–96 (invites partisan political abuse), 195–96 (imposes unnecessary costs on broadcasters and FCC).

182. Federal Communications Commission v. League of Women Voters of California, 468 U.S. 364; Telecommunications Research and Action Committee v. Federal Communications Commission, 801 F.2d 501.

183. Fairness Inquiry, 102 F.C.C.2d at 148.

184. *See* N.Y. Times, June 21, 1987, at 1, cols. 4–5.

185. *See id.*

186. Fairness Inquiry, 102 F.C.C.2d at 155.

187. Radio-Television News Directors Association v. Federal Communications Commission, 809 F.2d 860, 863 (D.C.Cir.), *vacated* 831 F.2d 1148 (1987).

188. *Id.*

189. Radio-Television News Directors Association v. Federal Communications Commission, 831 F.2d at 1148 (D.C. Cir. 1987).

190. 809 F.2d 863 (D.C. Cir. 1987).

191. *Id.* at 872–74.

192. 801 F.2d 501.

193. *Id.* at 504.

194. Syracuse Peace Council, 2 F.C.C. Rcd. 5043 (1987).

195. 867 F.2d 654 (D.C. Cir. 1989).

196. *Id.* at 650–52.

197. *Id.*

198. *Id.* at 660–62.

199. *See* New York Times, Aug. 5, 1987, at C26, col. 6.

200. *Id.*

201. *Id.*

202. The determination that tobacco advertising had to be balanced by competing expression engendered highly effective anti-smoking messages. *See* Banzhaf v. Federal Communications Commission, 405 F.2d 1082. Counterspeech has been credited for discouraging so many persons from smoking that the tobacco lobby favored a total ban on broadcast cigarette advertising as an alternative. *See* Capital Broadcasting Co. v. Mitchell, 333 F. Supp. 582, 587 (D.D.C. 1971) (Wright, J., dissenting), *aff'd,* 405 U.S. 1000 (1972).

203. *See* N.Y. Times, Aug. 5, 1987, at C26, col. 6.

204. In upholding minority ownership policies discussed in Chapter 5 of this book, the Court noted that it has "long recognized" that spectrum scarcity justifies special restraints upon broadcasters. Metro Broadcasting, Inc. v. Federal Communications Commission, 110 S.Ct.2997, 3010 (1990).

205. Marbury v. Madison, U.S. (1 Cranch) 137, 177 (1803).

206. Syracuse Peace Council, 2 F.C.C. Rcd. at 5055–57.

207. Apart from indecency standards discussed below, broadcasters remain subject to the special structural considerations and controls discussed in Chapter 5 of this book.

208. *See* Young v. American Mini Theatres, Inc., 427 U.S. 50, 63 (1976).

209. *E.g., id.* (ordinance requiring dispersal); Schad v. Borough of Mt. Ephraim, 452 U.S. 61 (1981) (ordinance requiring clustering).

210. *See* Infinity Broadcasting Corp. of Pennsylvania, 3 F.C.C. Rcd. 930, 931 (1987) (Reconsideration Order); New Indecency Enforcement Standards to be Applied to all Broadcast and Amateur Radio Licensees, 2 F.C.C. Rcd. at 2726 (1987) (hereafter cited as Indecency Standards). A reviewing court pointed out a critical distinction insofar as it determined that the FCC's standards were not content neutral. *See* Action for Children's Television v. Federal Communications Commission, 852 F.2d 1332, 1343 (D.C. Cir. 1988), *citing* Boos v. Barry, 108 S.Ct. 1157, 1163 (1988). While zoning restrictions designed to improve neighborhood quality may have a secondary impact on a particular category of expression, the FCC's direct regulatory concern is with the nature and consequence of the speech itself. 852 F.2d at 1343.

211. *See* City of Renton v. Playtime Theatres, Inc., 475 U.S. 41, 48 (1986); Young v. American Mini Theatres, Inc. 457 U.S. at 71–72.

212. FCC v. Pacifica Foundation, 438 U.S. 726, 748–50 (1978).

213. 47 U.S.C. § 326.

214. 18 U.S.C. § 1464.

215. 438 U.S. 726.

216. Palmetto Broadcasting Co., 33 F.C.C. 250, 257–58 (1962); *aff'd,* Robinson v. Federal Communications Commission, 334 F.2d 534 (D.C. Cir.), *cert. denied,* 379 U.S. 843 (1964). Indecent programming and character

deficiencies were considered so serious that the action deprived the community of its only local radio licensee at the time, 33 F.C.C. at 258–59.

217. *See* Infinity Broadcasting Corp. of Pennsylvania, 3 F.C.C. Rcd. 930; Indecency Standards, 2 F.C.C. Rcd. 2726.

218. Potential sanctions include license revocation, 47 U.S.C. 312(a), short term renewal, *id.*, § 307(c); and forfeiture, *id.*, § 502. A licensee's renewal application also might be denied.

219. Since April 1987, the FCC has issued 12 letters of inquiry and levied seven fines in response to programming complaints. *See* Radio Static, Detroit *Free Press*, Jan. 30, 1990, § E, at 1, 4.

220. Pacifica Foundation, 36 F.C.C. 147 (1964).

221. *Id.*

222. *Id.* at 148–49.

223. *Id.* at 149.

224. *Id.*

225. *Id.*

226. *Id.*

227. *Id.*

228. *Id.* at 151.

229. *Id.*

230. At issue was language which, several years later, would become the focal point of content control. *See* Eastern Educational Radio (WUHY-FM), 24 F.C.C.2d 408 (1970). Word usage was the focal point of Federal Communications Commission v. Pacifica Foundation, 438 U.S. 726.

231. 24 F.C.C.2d 408.

232. *Id.* at 409–10.

233. *Id.* at 410.

234. *Id.* at 415.

235. Sonderling Broadcasting Corp., WGLD-FM, 41 F.C.C.2d 777, 784 (1973), *aff'd* Illinois Citizens Committee for Broadcasting v. Federal Communications Commission, 515 F.2d 397 (D.C. Cir. 1974).

236. *Id.*

237. *Id.*

238. *Id.*

239. Illinois Citizens for Broadcasting v. Federal Communications Commission, 515 F.2d at 401.

240. *Id.* at 420.

241. 515 F.2d 397.

242. *Id.* at 404.

243. *Id.* at 406.

244. FCC v. Pacifica Foundation, 438 U.S. at 729.

245. *Id.* at 751–55.

246. *Id.* at 730.

247. *Id.*

248. *Id.*

249. *Id.*

250. *Id.* at 731 n.2.

251. 556 F.2d 9 (D.C. Cir. 1971), *rev'd,* 438 U.S. 726 (1978).

252. 438 U.S. 726.

253. *Id.* at 735.

254. *Id.*

255. *Id.* at 739–40.

256. *Id.* at 741.

257. *Id.*

258. *Id.* at 748.

259. *Id.*

260. *Id.*

261. *Id.*

262. *Id.* at 748–49.

263. *Id.* at 749.

264. *Id.* at 749–50.

265. *Id.* at 750.

266. *Id.*

267. *Id.*

268. *Id.*

269. *Id., citing* Euclid v. Ambler Realty Co., 272 U.S. 365, 388 (1926).

270. *Id.* at 750–51.

271. *Id.* at 743 (plurality opinion).

272. *Id.* at 761 (Powell, J., concurring); *id.* at 762–63 (Brennan, J., dissenting).

273. *Id.* at 761 (Powell, J., concurring).

274. *Id.* at 762 (Powell, J., concurring).

275. *Id.* (Powell, J., concurring).

276. *Id.* at 764 (Brennan, J., dissenting).

277. *Id.* at 766 (Brennan, J., dissenting).

278. *Id.* at 767 (Brennan, J., dissenting).

279. *Id.* at 768–70 (Brennan, J., dissenting).

280. *Id.* at 774–75 (Brennan, J., dissenting).

281. *Id.* at 775 (Brennan, J., dissenting).

282. *Id.* at 776 (Brennan, J., dissenting).

283. WGBH Educational Foundation, 69 F.C.C.2d 1250, 1254 (1978); Julian Bond, 69 F.C.C.2d 943, 944 (Broadcast Bureau 1978).

284. WGBH Educational Foundation, 69 F.C.C.2d at 1250–51.

285. Julian Bond, 69 F.C.C.2d at 944–45.

286. *Id.* at 944.

287. Federal Communications Commission v. Pacifica Foundation, 438 U.S. at 748.

288. *See* Mutual Film Corp. v. Industrial Commission of Ohio, 236 U.S. 230, 242 (1915) (concern with impact of motion pictures upon audience especially children); Brandeis and Warren, The Right to Privacy, 4 HARV. L.REV. 193, 195 (1890) ("(i)nstantaneous photographs and newspaper enterprise have invaded the sacred precincts of private and domestic life").

289. Erznoznik v. Jacksonville, 422 U.S. 205, 217–18 (1975).

290. 422 U.S. 205.

291. *Id.* at 213–14.

292. *Id.* at 211, *quoting* Cohen v. California, 403 U.S. 5, 21 (1971).

293. Erznoznik v. Jacksonville, 422 U.S. at 208.

294. Cohen v. California, 403 U.S. at 23.

295. 403 U.S. 15.

296. *Id.* at 25. For criticism of the *Cohen* decision *see* A. COX, THE ROLE OF THE SUPREME COURT IN AMERICAN GOVERNMENT 47–48 (1976) (state has interest in quality of public discourse); A. BICKEL, THE MORALITY OF CONSENT 72 (1975) (expression constituted an assault and may create environment in which actions previously not possible become possible).

297. *See Videoculture,* CHRISTIAN SCIENCE MONITOR, Aug. 25, 1985, at 25.

298. Pierce v. Society of Sisters, 268 U.S. 510, 534–35 (1925) (parental liberty in directing upbringing and education of children).

299. Wisconsin v. Yoder, 406 U.S. 205, 213–14 (1972) (parental discretion in accommodating child's education to free exercise of religion).

300. H.L. v. Matheson, 450 U.S. 398, 413 (1981) (upholding parental notification requirement which conditions child's liberty to elect an abortion).

301. Devices enabling parents to block out channels at certain times on a given day are available at relatively inexpensive cost. Although affording control to parents, their utility requires detailed study and awareness of forthcoming programming.

302. *See, e.g.,* Jackson v. Metropolitan Edison Co., 419 U.S. 345, 349 (1974).

303. United States v. Associated Press, 52 F. Supp. 362, 372 (1943), *aff'd,* 326 U.S. 1 (1945).

304. Telecommunication Research and Action Center v. Federal Communications Commission, 801 F.2d at 508.

305. *See* First National Bank of Boston v. Bellotti, 435 U.S. 765, 790–91 (1978); Buckley v. Valeo, 424 U.S. 1, 48–49 (1976).

306. Lively, *Deregulatory Illusions and Broadcasting: The First Amendment's Enduring Forked Tongue,* 66 N.C. L.REV. 963, 974 (1988).

307. Two of three complaints received by the FCC, with respect to a popular Philadelphia radio program, came from the National Federation for Decency in Tupelo, Mississippi. Infinity Broadcasting Corp. of Pennsylvania, 2 F.C.C. Rcd. 2705, 2707 n.1. (1987).

308. *See* 2 F.C.C. Rcd. 2705; Regents of the University of California, 2 F.C.C. Rcd. 2703 (1987); Pacifica Foundation, Inc., 2 F.C.C. Rcd. 2698 (1987).

309. *See* id.

310. David Hildebrand, 2 F.C.C. Rcd. 2708 (1987).

311. Indecency Standards, 2 F.C.C. Rcd. 2726.

312. *Id.* at 2726.

313. *Id.*

314. The *Pacifica* decision itself had concerned a station programming towards the interests of a generally discrete, educated and devoted audience.

315. Infinity Broadcasting Corp. of Pennsylvania, 2 F.C.C. Rcd. at 2705.

316. *Id.*

317. 2 F.C.C. Rcd. 2705.

318. *Id.* at 2706.

319. *Id.* at 2706.

320. *Id.*

321. *Id.*

322. *Id.*

323. Regents of the University of California, 2 F.C.C. Rcd. at 2704.

324. 2 F.C.C. Rcd. 2703.

325. *Id.*

326. *Id.*

327. *See* Miller v. California, 413 U.S. 15, 30–31 (1973).

328. 2 F.C.C. Rcd. at 2703. *See* Miller v. California, 413 U.S. 15, 30–34 (1973).

329. Infinity Broadcasting Corp. of Pennsylvania, 3 F.C.C. Rcd. at 933.

330. Regents of the University of California, 2 F.C.C. at 2704.

331. *Id. Accord* Pacifica Foundation, Inc., 2 F.C.C. Rcd. at 2699.

332. Regents of the University of California, 2 F.C.C. Rcd. at 2704.

333. *Id.*

334. 2 F.C.C. Rcd. 2698.

335. *Id.* at 2700–01.

336. *Id.* at 2700.

337. *Id.*

338. *Id.*

339. *Id.* at 2701.

340. *See* Infinity Broadcasting Corp. of Pennsylvania, 2 F.C.C. Rcd. at 2705.

341. *See* Regents of the University of California, 2 F.C.C. Rcd. at 2704.

342. *See* Indecency Standards, 2 F.C.C. Rcd. 2726.

343. *See, e.g.,* Infinity Broadcasting Corp. of Pennsylvania, 2 F.C.C. Rcd. at 2705 n.1. *See also* Radio Static, Detroit *Free Press,* Jan. 30, 1990, § E, at 1, 4.

344. Infinity Broadcasting Corp. of Pennsylvania, 3 F.C.C. Rcd. at 937 n.47.

345. *Id.* at 931–32.

346. *Id.* at 932.

347. *Id.* at 933.

348. *Id.* at 931.

349. *Id.*

350. P.L. No. 100–459 (1988).

351. The appeals court, however, subsequently remanded the case to the FCC for an inquiry into the ban. Action for Children's Television v. Federal Com-

munications Commission, Med. L.Rptr. (D.C.Cir. 1989).

352. 852 F.2d 1332 (D.C.Cir. 1988).

353. *Id.* at 1338–39.

354. *Id.* at 1338.

355. *Id.* at 1339–40.

356. *Id.* at 1341.

357. *Id.*

358. *Id.* The remanded cases were Regents of the University of California, 2 F.C.C. Rcd. 2703; Pacifica Foundation, Inc., 2 F.C.C. Rcd. 2698.

359. 852 F.2d at 1341.

360. *See* Sable Communications of California, Inc. v. Federal Communications Commission, 109 S. Ct. 2829 (1989).

361. Enforcement of Prohibitions Against Broadcast Indecency in 18 U.S.C. § 1464, 5 F.C.C. Rcd. 5297 (1990).

362. *Id.*

363. *Id.*

364. Butler v. Michigan, 352 U.S. 380, 383 (1957).

365. *See* Children's Television Report and Policy Statement, 50 F.C.C.2d 1 (1974). The report followed an inquiry into children's programming and associated advertising practices. *Id.* at 1, *citing* First Notice of Inquiry, 28 F.C.C.2d 368 (1971). Problems with respect to mandatory programming for any identifiable subgroup of the citizenry are discussed in Powe, *American Voodoo: If Television Doesn't Show It, Maybe It Won't Exist,* 59 TEX. L.REV. 879 (1981).

366. *See* Children's Television Programming and Advertising Practices, 75 F.C.C.2d 138, 143 (1979).

367. *Id.* at 145.

368. *Id.* at 146–52.

369. *See* Children's Television Programming, 96 F.C.C.2d 634, 655 (1984).

370. *Id.* at 652–53.

371. *Id.* at 654.

372. *Id.* at 646.

373. 756 F.2d 899 (D.C.Cir. 1985).

374. *Id.* at 900–01.

375. *Id.* at 901.

376. *See* Washington Association for Television and Children v. Federal Communications Commission, 712 F.2d 677, 679 (D.C.Cir. 1983).

377. 712 F.2d 677.

378. *Id.* at 679.

379. *Id.* at 684–85.

380. *Id.*

381. Complaint by George D. Corey, 37 F.C.C.2d 641 (1975).

382. *Id.* at 641.

383. *Id.* at 643.

384. *Id.* at 641, 643–44.

385. *Id.* at 645 (Cmr. Johnson dissenting).

386. 51 F.C.C.2d 418.

387. *Id.* at 419. A comprehensive examination of televised violence and its effects, and argument that First Amendment interests should not be crossed lightly, is contained in Krattenmaker & Powe, *Televised Violence: First Amendment Principles and Social Science Theory,* 64 VA. L. REV. 1123 (1978). For a competing argument that the First Amendment presents no serious barrier to indecency controls, *see* Albert, *Constitutional Regulation of Televised Violence,* 64 VA. L. REV. 1299 (1978).

388. 51 F.C.C.2d at 419.

389. *Id.* at 421–22.

390. *Id.* at 422.

391. Regulation by raised eyebrow is a form of administrative browbeating, which reflects an official expression of concern in an informal fashion rather than by adjudicative proceeding or rulemaking. *See* Robinson, *The FCC and the First Amendment: Observations on 40 Years of Radio and Television Regulation,* 52 MINN. L.REV. 67, 119–20 (1967). The implied threat of adverse action, in the event official concerns are not addressed, may be especially effective when an individual's or entity's livelihood or enterprise depends on remaining in the good graces of the agency that makes licensing decisions.

392. Writers Guild of America, West, Inc. v. American Broadcasting Co., Inc, 609 F.2d 355 (9th Cir. 1979), *cert. denied,* 449 U.S. 824 (1980).

393. *See* Memorandum Opinion and Order on Reconsideration of the Report, 104 F.C.C.2d 358 (1986), *remanded,* Action for Children's Television v. Federal Communications Commission, 821 F.2d 741 (D.C.Cir. 1987). The FCC previously, however, had banned product endorsements by program hosts and had required clear separation between programs and commercials. *See* Action for Children's Television v. Federal Communications Commission, 564 F.2d 458 (D.C.Cir. 1977).

394. *See* Action for Children's Television v. Federal Communications Commission, 821 F.2d 741, 745–46 (D.C. Cir.1981).

395. Action for Children's Television, 58 R.R.2d 61 (1985).

396. *Id.*

397. *Id.*

398. Bill curtailing kid's TV ads becomes law, Chicago *Tribune,* Oct. 18, 1990, at 2.

399. *See* Reagan Kills children's TV bill, *Broadcasting,* Nov. 14, 1988, at 68.

400. Children's Television Act of 1990.

401. *Id.*

402. Yale Broadcasting Co. v. Federal Communications Commission, 478 F.2d 594, 595 (D.C.Cir.), *cert. denied,* 414 U.S. 914 (1973). *See* Licensee Responsibility

to Review Records before Their Broadcast, 31 F.C.C.2d 377 (1971); 28 F.C.C.2d 409 (1971).

403. *Id.* at 597.

404. 478 F.2d 594.

405. *Id.* at 597–98.

406. *Id.* at 598.

407. 438 U.S. 726.

408. *Id.* at 599.

409. *Id.* at 604 (Bazelon, C.J., dissenting).

410. *Id.* at 606 (Bazelon, C.J., dissenting).

411. 414 U.S. 914–18 (Douglas, J., dissenting).

412. *See* Chapter 2 of this book.

413. Revision of Programming and Commercialization Policies, Ascertainment Requirements, and Program Log Requirements for Commercial Television, 94 F.C.C.2d 678 (1983). As noted earlier in this chapter, inclusion of children's advertising in general decontrol of broadcast commercials was remanded for further consideration. Action for Children's Television v. Federal Communications Commission, 821 F.2d 741.

414. *See* 15 U.S.C. § 1335.

415. *See* Banzhaf v. Federal Communications Commission, 405 F.2d 1082.

416. 405 F.2d 1082.

417. *See supra,* II.A.1 in this chapter.

418. 15 U.S.C. § 1335.

419. 333 F.Supp. 52 (D.D.C. 1971); *aff'd without opinion,* 415 U.S. 1000 (1972).

420. *Id.* at 584, 586.

421. *Id.*

422. *Id.* at 589–94 (Wright, J., dissenting).

423. *Id.* at 588. (Wright, J., dissenting).

424. *Id.* at 587–94 (Wright, J., dissenting).

425. *See* Posadas de Puerto Rico Associates v. Tourism Co. of Puerto Rico, 478 U.S. 328, 345–46 (1986).

Chapter 10

CABLE

Cable television as a relatively new medium remains in the early phase of having its First Amendment status resolved. Being an even newer medium than broadcasting, it is conceivable that many of the lessons learned from the constitutional appraisal of broadcasting could lead to a more efficient appraisal of cable. Insofar as official sense tends toward a media-general rather than a medium-specific approach, it would be likely that cable more quickly would approach First Amendment parity with the more traditional media.

I. EVOLVING CONSTITUTIONAL STANDARDS

During cable's early developmental period, the industry was subjected to an array of controls that would have seemed to implicate obvious First Amendment questions. Distant importation, origination, access, and antisiphoning rules directly impinged on editorial discretion.[1] The Federal Communications Commission's (FCC's) access requirements, in particular, imposed upon cable casters a demand that the commission and the Supreme Court had concluded was constitu-

tionally impermissible when applied to broadcasting[2]—the least protected of all media.[3] Eventually, in *Federal Communications Commission v. Midwest Video Corp.*,[4] access rules were invalidated on the grounds that they effectively converted cable into a common carrier.[5] Avoidance of the constitutional question reflected uncertainty with respect to what if any First Amendment status cable should have. Implicit in the determination that cable could not be equated with a common carrier, however, was the sense that cable casters possessed some degree of editorial discretion of a constitutional order.

Not until 1984 did the Supreme Court speak directly to the First Amendment interests of cable. Even then, the references were general and glancing. In *City of Los Angeles v. Preferred Communications, Inc.*,[6] the Court considered a lower court ruling dismissing a cable company's complaints contesting franchising regulations that prevented it from competing against another operator.[7] The company had been unsuccessful in obtaining a franchise from the city and subsequently was turned down by a local utility when, in seeking to bypass the municipality's denial, it sought pole space anyway.[8] Although the city did not deny that excess physical capacity existed to accommodate additional cable service, it justified its action in terms of the physical scarcity of pole space, the limited economic demand for cable, "and the practical and esthetic disruptive effect that installing and maintaining a cable system has on the public right-of-way."[9]

The Court's response was that "[w]e . . . think that the activities in which [the cable company] allegedly seeks to engage plainly implicate First Amendment interests."[10] The extent to which constitutional concerns were touched, or the status of cable casters, however, was left underdeveloped. The Court noted that cable "partakes of some of the aspects of speech and the communication of ideas as do the traditional enterprises of newspaper and book publishers, public speakers, and pamphleteers."[11] Offsetting any intimation that cable is on a constitutional par with publishing, however, is the observation that the medium also "would seem to implicate First Amendment interests as do the activities of wireless broadcasters, which were found to fall within the ambit of the First Amendment in *Red Lion*."[12] The *Red Lion* decision, as discussed previously,[13] probably is more notable for its emphasis upon permissible controls rather than its deference to the editorial discretion of broadcasters.

Although acknowledging a First Amendment presence, left largely unamplified, the Court noted that identification of such an interest did "not end the inquiry."[14] It observed that even protected speech is subject to reasonable time and place restrictions.[15] Furthermore, "where speech and conduct are joined in a single course of action, the First Amendment values must be balanced against competing societal interests."[16] Such a limiting principle, speaking in terms of speech and conduct, intimated a legitimate regulatory interest in consequences unre-

lated to content.[17] Never directly addressed, therefore, was the precise status of cable as an element of the press. Given the undeveloped nature of the litigation, the Court chose not to pursue further its constitutional inquiry other than to observe that "[w]here a law is subjected to a colorable First Amendment challenge, the rule of rationality which will sustain legislation against other constitutional challenges typically does not have the same controlling force."[18]

In a concurring opinion, Justice Blackmun spoke in terms of the medium's First Amendment status. He thus adverted to the traditional and fundamental notion that "[d]ifferent communications media are treated differently for First Amendment purposes."[19] To be discerned from that premise, according to Blackmun, was "whether the characteristics of cable television make it sufficiently analogous to another medium to warrant application of an already existing standard or whether those characteristics require a new analysis."[20]

City of Los Angeles v. Preferred Communications, Inc., 476 U.S. 488 (1984)

Justice Rehnquist delivered the opinion of the Court.

Respondent Preferred Communications, Inc., sued petitioners City of Los Angeles (City) and the Department of Water and Power (DWP) in the United States District Court for the Central District of California. The complaint alleged a violation of respondent's rights under the First and Fourteenth Amendments, and under §§ 1 and 2 of the Sherman Act, by reason of the City's refusal to grant respondent a cable television franchise and of DWP's refusal to grant access to DWP's poles or underground conduits used for power lines. The District Court dismissed the complaint for failure to state a claim upon which relief could be granted. See Fed. Rule Civ. Proc. 12(b)(6). The Court of Appeals for the Ninth Circuit affirmed with respect to the Sherman Act, but reversed as to the First Amendment claim. 754 F.2d 1396 (1985). We granted certiorari with respect to the latter issue, 474 U.S. 979 (1985)....

The complaint further alleged that cable operators are First Amendment speakers, *id.*, at 3a, that there is sufficient excess physical capacity and economic demand in the south central area of Los Angeles to accommodate more than one cable company, *id.*, at 4a, and that the City's auction process allowed it to discriminate among franchise applicants based on which one it deemed to be the "best." *Id.*, at 6a. Based on these and other factual allegations, the complaint alleged that the City and DWP had violated the Free Speech Clause of the First Amendment, as made applicable to the States by the Fourteenth Amendment, §§ 1 and 2 of the Sherman Act, the California Constitution, and certain provisions of state law. *Id.*, at 11a–19a.

The City did not deny that there was excess physical capacity to accommodate more than one cable television system. But it argued that the physical scarcity of available space on public utility structures, the limits of economic demand for the cable medium, and the practical and esthetic disruptive effect that installing and maintaining a cable system has on the public right-of-way justified its decision to restrict access to its facilities to a single cable television company.... 754 F.2d, at 1401.

We do think that the activities in which respondent allegedly seeks to engage plainly implicate First Amendment interests. Respondent alleges:

> The business of cable television, like that of newspapers and magazines, is to provide its subscribers with a mixture of news, information and entertainment. As do newspapers, cable television companies use a portion of their available space to reprint (or retransmit) the communications of others, while at the same time providing some original content. App. 3a.

Thus, through original programming or by exercising editorial discretion over which stations or programs to include in its repertoire, respondent seeks to communicate messages on a wide variety of topics and in a wide variety of formats. We recently noted that cable operators exercise "a significant amount of editorial discretion re-

garding what their programming will include." *FCC v. Midwest Video Corp.*, 440 U.S. 689, 707 (1979). Cable television partakes of some of the aspects of speech and the communication of ideas as do the traditional enterprises of newspaper and book publishers, public speakers, and pamphleteers. Respondent's proposed activities would seem to implicate First Amendment interests as do the activities of wireless broadcasters, which were found to fall within the ambit of the First Amendment in *Red Lion Broadcasting Co. v. FCC, supra*, at 386, even though the free speech aspects of the wireless broadcasters' claim were found to be outweighed by the Government interests in regulating by reason of the scarcity of available frequencies.

Of course, the conclusion that respondent's factual allegations implicate protected speech does not end the inquiry. "Even protected speech is not equally permissible in all places and at all times." *Cornelius v. NAACP Legal Defense & Educational Fund, Inc.*, 473 U.S. 788, 799 (1985). Moreover, where speech and conduct are joined in a single course of action, the First Amendment values must be balanced against competing societal interests. See, e.g., *Members of City Council v. Taxpayers for Vincent, supra*, at 805–807; *United States v. O'Brien*, 391 U.S. 367, 376–377 (1968). We do not think, however, that it is desirable to express any more detailed views on the proper resolution of the First Amendment question raised by respondent's complaint and the City's responses to it without a fuller development of the disputed issues in the case. We think that we may know more than we know now about how the constitutional issues should be resolved when we know more about the present uses of the public utility poles and rights-of-way and how respondent proposes to install and maintain its facilities on them....

... Where a law is subjected to a colorable First Amendment challenge, the rule of rationality which will sustain legislation against other constitutional challenges typically does not have the same controlling force. But cf. *Ohralik v. Ohio State Bar Assn.*, 436 U.S. 477, 459 (1978). This Court "may not simply assume that the ordinance will always advance the asserted state interests sufficiently to justify its abridgment of expressive activity." *Taxpayers for Vincent*, 466 U.S., at 803, n.

22; *Landmark Communications, Inc v. Virginia,* 435 U.S. 829, 843–844 (1978).

Justice Blackmun, with whom Justice Marshall and Justice O'Connor join, concurring.

I join the Court's opinion on the understanding that it leaves open the question of the proper standard for judging First Amendment challenges to a municipality's restriction of access to cable facilities. Different communications media are treated differently for First Amendment purposes. Compare, e.g., *Miami Herald Publishing Co. v. Tornillo,* 418 U.S. 241 (1974), with *FCC v. League of Women Voters of California,* 468 U.S. 364, 380 (1984). In assessing First Amendment claims concerning cable access, the Court must determine whether the characteristics of cable television make it sufficiently analogous to another medium to warrant application of an already existing standard or whether those characteristics require a new analysis. As this case arises out of a motion to dismiss, we lack factual information about the nature of cable television. Recognizing these considerations, *ante,* at 493–494, the Court does not attempt to choose or justify any particular standard. It simply concludes that, in challenging Los Angeles' policy of exclusivity in cable franchising, respondent alleges a cognizable First Amendment claim.

Lower courts have taken signals from both the majority and concurring opinions in the *Preferred* decision. In *Quincy Cable TV, Inc. v. Federal Communications Commission,*[21] the court of appeals considered whether must carry rules, obligating cable operators to carry the signals of local broadcasters, were "fundamentally at odds with the First Amendment."[22] Determining whether rules purportedly aimed at activity unrelated to speech have an acceptable secondary impact upon expression depends upon the presence of a substantial state interest and the breadth of the regulatory sweep.[23] The court of appeals invalidated the must carry rules on the grounds that their justification, to prevent "the destruction of free, local television," was fanciful rather than substan-

tial.[24] It also found them fatally overbroad insofar as they "indiscriminately protected every local broadcaster, regardless of whether it was in fact threatened, and regardless of the quantity of local service in the community and the degree to which the cable operator in question already carried local outlets."[25]

The *Quincy* court also examined the nature of cable to determine what medium it was most akin to and thus what status it should possess within the constitutional hierarchy of media.[26] It noted that even if "cable and broadcast television appear virtually indistinguishable" to viewers, they differ in at least one critical respect.[27] Key to the appeals court's conclusion that cable was more akin to publishing than broadcasting, therefore, was its perception that cable was not affected by the scarcity problems associated with radio and television.[28] Nor could it "discern other attributes of cable television that would justify a standard of review analogous to the more forgiving First Amendment analysis applied to the broadcast media."[29] It rejected the notion that "use of a public right of way" supported less exacting constitutional review.[30] Although recognizing the community disruption and inconvenience inherent in the process of constructing a cable system, the court of appeals found no connection between that reality and an interest in controlling the program content.[31] Nor did it find any natural monopoly characteristic of cable comparable "to the physical constraints imposed by the limited size of the electromagnetic spectrum."[32] To the contrary, it noted that any economic constraint was analogous to those characteristics of the print media previously rejected as a basis for content control.[33] Finally, the appeals court was sufficiently impressed with "cable's virtually unlimited channel capacity" to dispense entirely with suggestions that broadcasting was the appropriate reference point for assessing cable.[34]

Quincy Cable TV, Inc. v. Federal Communications Commission, 768 F.2d 1434 (1985), cert. denied, 476 U.S. 1169 (1986)

J. Skelly Wright, Circuit Judge.

... It has become something of a truism to observe that "differences in the characteristics of news media justify differences in the First Amendment standards applied to them." *Red Lion Broadcasting Co. v. FCC, supra*, 395 U.S. at 386 See also *FCC v. Pacifica Foundation*, 438 U.S. 726, 748 (1978); *Joseph Burstyn, Inc. v. Wilson*, 343 U.S. 495, 503 (1952); *Tele-Communications of Key West, Inc. v. United States, supra*, 757 F.2d at 1338–39. The suggestion is not that traditional First Amendment doctrine falls by the wayside when evaluating the protection due novel modes of communication. For the core values of the First Amendment clearly transcend the particular details of the various vehicles through which messages are conveyed. Rather, the objective is to recognize that those values are best served by paying close attention to the distinctive features that differentiate the increasingly diverse mechanisms through which a speaker may express his view.

This sensitivity to the uniqueness of each medium precludes facile adoption of the First Amendment jurisprudence that has developed around challenges to FCC regulation of broadcast television and radio. From the prespective of the viewer, no doubt, cable and broadcast television appear virtually indistinguishable. For purposes of First Amendment analysis, however, they differ in at least one critical respect. Unlike ordinary broadcast television, which transmits the video image over airwaves capable of bearing only a limited number of signals, cable reaches the home over a coaxial cable with the technological capacity to carry 200 or more channels.

The distinction is of fundamental significance in light of the Supreme Court's oft-repeated suggestion that the First Amendment tolerates far more intrusive regulation of broadcasters than of other media precisely because of the inescapable physical limitations on the number of voices that can simultaneously be carried over the electro-

magnetic spectrum. See, e.g., *FCC v. League of Women Voters of California, supra*, 104 S.Ct. at 3116; see also *Preferred Communications, Inc. v. City of Los Angeles, supra*, 754 F.2d at 1403. These limitations, the Supreme Court observed early on, engender a peculiar irony of the broadcast medium: limited regulation, by converting aural and visual chaos into channels of effective communication, furthers rather than impedes the First Amendment's mission. "With everybody on the air," wrote Justice Frankfurter, "nobody could be heard.... [T]he radio spectrum is simply not large enough to accommodate everybody." *National Broadcasting Co. v. United States*, 319 U.S. 190, 212–13 (1943). Without the imposition of some governmental control, "the cacophony of competing voices" would drown each other out. *Red Lion Broadcasting Co. v. FCC, supra*, 395 U.S. at 376. Moreover, quite independent of the objective of bringing communicative order to the otherwise chaotic airwaves, the First Amendment tolerates a modest degree of government oversight of broadcast radio and television because such regulation assures that broadcasters, privileged occupants of a physically scarce resource, act in a manner consistent with their status as fiduciaries of the public's interest in responsible use of the spectrum. *Id.* at 389.

As this and other courts have recognized, the "scarcity rationale" has no place in evaluating government regulation of cable television.

The First Amendment theory espoused in *National Broadcasting Co.* and reaffirmed in *Red Lion Broadcasting Co.* cannot be directly applied to cable television since an essential precondition of that theory—physical interference and scarcity requiring an umpiring role for government—is absent ... *Home Box Office, Inc. v. FCC, supra*, 567 F.2d at 45. See also *Preferred Communications, Inc. v. City of Los Angeles, supra*, 754 F.2d at 1404; *Omega Satellite Products Co. v. City of Indianapolis*, 694 F.2d 119, 127 (7th Cir.1982); Note, *Cable Television and the First Amendment*, 71 Colum.L.Rev. 1008 (1971).

Nor do we discern other attributes of cable television that would justify a standard of review analogous to the more forgiving First Amendment analysis traditionally applied to the broadcast media. We cannot agree, for example, that the mere fact that cable operators require use of a public right of way—typically utility poles—somehow justifies lesser First Amendment scrutiny. See *Omega Satellite Products Co. v. City of Indianapolis, supra,* 694 F.2d at 127. The potential for disruption inherent in stringing coaxial cables above city streets may well warrant some governmental regulation of the process of installing and maintaining the cable system. But hardly does it follow that such regulation could extend to controlling the nature of the programming that is conveyed over that system. No doubt a municipality has some power to control the placement of newspaper vending machines. But any effort to use that power as the basis for dictating what must be placed in such machines would surely be invalid.

Nor, on this record, can we concur in the suggestion that the "natural monopoly characteristics" of cable create economic constraints on competition comparable to the physical constraints imposed by the limited size of the electromagnetic spectrum. *Omega Satellite Products Co. v. City of Indianapolis, supra,* 694 F.2d at 127; see also *Berkshire Cablevision of Rhode Island, Inc. v. Burke,* 571 F.Supp 976, 985–988 (D.R.I.1983). At the outset, the "economic scarcity" argument rests on the entirely unproven—and indeed doubtful—assumption that cable operators are in a position to exact monopolistic charges. See G. Shapiro, P. Kurland and J. Mercurio, Cable Speech: The Case for First Amendment Protection 9–11 (1983). Moreover, the tendency toward monopoly, if present at all, may well be attributable more to governmental action—particularly the municipal franchising process—than to any "natural" economic phenomenon. See R. Posner, Cable Television: The Problem of Local Monopoly 4 (Ford Foundation Memorandum RM–6309-FF 1970). In any case, whatever the outcome of the debate over the monopolistic characteristics of cable, the Supreme Court has categorically rejected the suggestion that purely economic constraints on the number of voices available in a given community justify otherwise unwarranted intrusions into First Amendment rights. *Miami Herald Publishing Co. v. Tornillo,* 418 U.S. 241, 247–256 (1974). While *Miami Herald* involved the conventional press, as this court has had prior occasion to observe, there is no meaningful "distinction between cable television and

newspapers on this point." *Home Box Office, Inc. v. FCC, supra,* 567 F.2d at 46.

Indeed, once one has cleared the conceptual hurdle of recognizing that all forms of television need not be treated as a generic unity for purposes of the First Amendment, the analogy to more traditional media is compelling. Two influential commissions have in fact reached precisely that conclusion. In the words of the Cabinet Committee on Cable Communications, "[C]able development has the potential of creating an electronic medium of communications more diverse, more pluralistic and more open, more like the print and film media than like our present broadcast system." Cabinet Committee on Cable Communications, Cable: Report to the President, Ch. I, p. 14 (1974). See also Sloan Commission on Cable Communications, On the Cable 92 (1971) ("Cable television, by freeing television from the limitations of radiated electro-magnetic waves, creates . . . a situation more nearly analogous to that of the [print] press.").

In sum, beyond the obvious parallel that both cable and broadcast television impinge on the senses via a video receiver, the two media differ in constitutionally significant ways. In light of cable's virtually unlimited channel capacity, the standard of First Amendment review reserved for occupants of the physically scarce airwaves is plainly inapplicable. Accordingly, we must look elsewhere to determine the appropriate yardstick against which to measure the constitutionality of the must-carry rules.

Prior to the *Preferred* and *Quincy* decisions, a competing judicial view had equated cable with broadcasting for First Amendment purposes. In *Berkshire Cablevision of Rhode Island, Inc., v. Burke,*[35] the district court examined the constitutionality of public access requirements and concluded that cable and newspapers "are constitutionally distinguishable."[36] The court noted that newspapers unlike cable traditionally have operated free from any form of official content control[37]—a point subject to criticism on the grounds that it merely identifies a custom instead of examining the validity of its limits.

It further observed that wholesale comparisons to economic scarcity were misplaced insofar as the franchising process accounts for scarcity akin to that in broadcasting.[38] Presuming that an individual denied an opportunity to present an opinion in a newspaper could publish by means of a competing leaflet, pamphlet, or other inexpensive print vehicle, but could not do the electronic equivalent if denied access to cable, the court concluded that economic scarcity had special meaning for cable.[39] Observing that "scarcity is scarcity [regardless of] its particular source,"[40] it concluded that broadcasting represented the proper First Amendment model for cable.[41]

Berkshire Cablevision of Rhode Island, Inc. v. Burke, 571 F. Supp. 976 (D.R.I. 1983), *vacated on other grounds,* **773 F.2d 382 (1st Cir. 1985)**

...Newspapers and cable television cannot be equated. More to the point, the two media are constitutionally distinguishable. Although a cable operator's selection of its programming is similar to the editorial function of a newspaper publisher or a television broadcaster, this similarity does not mean that each medium is entitled to the same measure of First Amendment protection. "Each method of communicating ideas is a 'law unto itself' and that law must reflect the 'differing natures, values, abuses and dangers of each method.'" *Metromedia, Inc. v. City of San Diego,* 453 U.S. 490, 501 (1981) (quoting *Kovacs v. Cooper,* 336 U.S. 77, 97 (1949)).

CATV and newspapers first differ in that only the latter have historically operated virtually free from any form of government control over their content. As Justice White noted in his concurrence in *Miami Herald Publishing Co. v. Tornillo:* "According to our accepted jurisprudence, the First Amendment erects a virtually insurmountable barrier between government and the print media so far as government tampering, in advance of publication, with news and editorial content is concerned." 418 U.S. at 259 (White, J.,

concurring) (citations omitted). It was in this historical setting that the *Tornillo* court struck down the Florida right-of-access law.

Cable television does not have a similar history of freedom from government regulation over either its operations or the content of its programming. See *Community Communications v. City of Boulder, Colorado,* 660 F.2d 1370, 1378 n. 9, 1379 (10th Cir. 1981), *petition for cert. dismissed,* 456 U.S. 1001 (1982). Indeed, government franchising of the cable television industry is virtually indispensable. For example, since constructing a cable television system requires use of the public streets or telephone poles, the government has a substantial interest in limiting the number of cable operators who build cable systems. See *Omega Satellite Products v. City of Indianapolis, supra,* 694 F.2d at 127; *Community Communications, supra,* 660 F.2d at 1377–78.

Of course, the flip side to government franchising is that it insulates cable operators from unnecessary competition. The award of a franchise serves as a rational way of choosing which cable operator will provide cable television service within a particular service area. Cable operators often compete for a cable franchise but very rarely develop competing cable systems for the same service area. Such a franchising system recognizes the economic realities of the cable industry, which, as a practical matter, create a "natural monopoly" for the first cable operator to construct a cable system in a given service area. Testimony in this case established that to construct the Newport County cable system would cost approximately seven million dollars. Because of these start-up costs and the nature of the cable television market, see Meyerson, the First Amendment and the Cable Television Operator, 4 Comm/ent L.J. 1, 4–6 (19—), cable systems have operated largely free from competition. See *Omega Satellite Products v. City of Indianapolis, supra,* 694 F.2d at 127–28; Cabinet Committee on Cable Communications, Report to the President, Cable at 10 (1974); *First Report and Order,* 20 F.C.C.2d 201, 222 n. 27 (1969).

Despite these fundamental differences between cable television and newspapers (CATV's use of the public right-of-way and its ease of monopolization), on the basis of the Supreme Court's *Tornillo* decision both the D.C. Circuit in *Home*

Box Office and the Eighth Circuit in *Midwest Video II,* as explained above, rejected "scarcity which is the result solely of economic conditions" as a rationale for content regulation of CATV systems. However, the Tenth Circuit's more recent opinion in *Community Communications, supra,* reflects an unwillingness to incorporate *Tornillo* wholesale into the cable television context. As that opinion stated, the "cable broadcasting medium presents very different circumstances" from those before the Supreme Court in *Tornillo. Community Communications,* 660 F.2d at 1379. In *Community Communications* the appellant City of Boulder had argued that because a cable operator has a natural monopoly for his franchise area, "the cable broadcasting medium [is] 'scarce' in much the same way that the finiteness of the electromagnetic spectrum makes wireless broadcasting a medium of essentially limited access." *Id.* at 1378. Although not explicitly adopting the City's reasoning, the court did agree that "natural monopoly *is* a constitutionally permissible justification for some degree of regulation of cable operators," although the court warned that this conclusion did "not mean that the full panoply of principles governing the regulation of wireless broadcasters necessarily applies to cable operators." *Id.* at 1379 (emphasis added).

Clearly, then, one basic issue in the instant case is whether or not economic "scarcity" is a constitutionally sufficient rationale for the regulation of cable television. It is the opinion of this court that the Tenth Circuit has developed the more sensible approach to the question. While it is true that the Supreme Court has rejected economic scarcity as a basis for the regulation of newspapers, the lack of any access requirement for newspapers simply does not prevent a member of the general public from expressing his opinions *in that same medium,* which in such a case is print, of course. Any person may distribute a written message in the form of a leaflet, pamphlet, or other relatively inexpensive form of "publication." In contrast, a resident of Newport County who does not have seven million dollars to develop his own cable system is shut out of that medium with no way to express his ideas with the widely acknowledged power of the small screen. Quite frankly, I am unwilling to say that the Supreme Court would ignore this distinction were the issue to come before it.

The result is that *Red Lion,* the seminal case of contemporary communications law, retains its vitality in the high-tech world of cable television. To be sure, the scarcity rationale for governmental regulation here takes a somewhat different form, but the goal remains the same as in 1969: to *promote* the First Amendment by making a powerful communications medium available to as many of our citizens as is reasonably possible. For this court, at least, scarcity is scarcity—its particular source, whether "physical" or "economic," does not matter if its effect is to remove from all but a small group an important means of expressing ideas.

A subsequent district court decision, affirmed without opinion by the Supreme Court,[42] sided with the analysis expounded by the *Quincy* court to the extent that it rejected analogies to broadcasting. In *Community Television of Utah, Inc. v. Wilkinson,*[43] the district court concluded that "even if the cable medium is 'economically' scarce, this rationale does not justify content regulation like that in the broadcast medium."[44] Because "cable is not limited to a finite number of channels the way broadcasting is" and "demand for cable services determines the number of cable channels," which at least technically "is subject to extensive expansion," the court found no problem of interference and no need for official traffic or content control.[45] Consequently, it determined that "[a]s long as the material carried on cable channels is protected by the Constitution, licensing authorities need not police the content of those channels."[46]

Community Television of Utah, Inc. v. Wilkinson, 611 F.Supp. 1099 (D. Utah), *aff'd,* **800 F.2d 989 (10th Cir. 1986),** *aff'd,* **107 S.Ct. 1559 (1987)**

The physical scarcity of broadcast spectrum space justifies governmental regulation of the use of that space. "There is a fixed natural limitation upon the number of stations that can operate without interfering with one another." *National*

Broadcasting Co., Inc. v. United States, 319 U.S. 190, 213 (1943). The regulation of the broadcast medium is vital as a "traffic control" device. Licensing is required to avoid interference between stations; without governmental rationing of broadcast frequencies, chaos would result. See *id.*

It has long been established that the FCC's role as a "traffic controller" has included a duty to insure that broadcast licenses are used in the public interest. Broadcast frequencies are scarce public resources; this physical scarcity justifies allocation according to the public interest. *Pacifica* 438 U.S. at 731 n. 2. The FCC's duties to protect the public interest justify limited program content regulation in the broadcast medium to insure the best programming for the most people. To promote this interest, the FCC has always had the power to review the content of completed broadcasts in deciding whether to renew licenses. See *id.* at 735. The FCC's action in *Pacifica* was an exercise of this power. The limited regulation validated in *Pacifica* is therefore merely an extension of the long tradition of indirect content regulation accomplished through the license renewal process. *Pacifica* upheld a type of regulation appropriate to the unique characteristics of the broadcast medium.

Because of its special characteristics, broadcasting is the form of communication that has received the most limited first amendment protection. *Id.* at 748. In the cable medium, the physical scarcity that justifies content regulation in broadcasting is not present. The Court in *Pacifica* deliberately limited its discussion to the broadcast medium.

Amicus Morality in Media, Inc. argues that *Pacifica* applies to the present case because both broadcast and cable are "scarce media." Seizing on scarcity as the justification for broadcast regulation, *amicus* tries to prove that cable is a scarce medium. Because each locality generally only has one cable franchise, it is argued that cable television is "economically" scarce. *Amicus* claims that this "economical" scarcity, like the "physical" scarcity characteristic of the broadcast medium, justifies content regulation.

It is not clear from the record before the court whether the cable medium truly is scarce in the "economic" sense discussed above. Under the new Policy Act, states may allow as many or as few cable franchises as they choose. Policy Act §

621(a)(1). Yet even if the cable medium is "economically" scarce, this scarcity does not justify content regulation like that in the broadcast medium. See, e.g., *Home Box Office, Inc. v. FCC,* 567 F.2d 9, 44–45 (D.C.Cir.1977). This is true because cable is not limited to a finite number of channels the way broadcasting is. The demand for cable services determines the number of cable channels. The number of additional channels, in a technical sense, is subject to extensive expansion. See, e.g., *Home Box Office, Inc. v. Wilkinson,* 531 F.Supp. 987, 1002 (D.Utah 1982). As a result, there is no danger of interference between channels. The government therefore need not "control traffic" by rationing channels. As long as the material carried on cable channels is protected by the Constitution, licensing authorities need not police the content of those channels in the public interest, because no physically scarce public resource is involved. The supply and demand of the market place will determine the type of programming that will be successful. The public interest in receiving diverse information, an interest which the market might not adequately respect, is protected by the new Policy Act. The "special access" channels established by the Policy Act guarantee a variety of programs.

The determination that broadcasting is not an apt model for setting standards governing cable does not ensure status on a par with the print media. Although affirming the result,[47] the Supreme Court is free at a later date to introduce a superseding rationale. Equally important, the district court's seemingly approving reference to the Cable Act's access rules suggests countenance of a regulation that is constitutionally intolerable for both print and broadcasting.[48] The possibility remains, therefore, that cable will be governed by an entirely new, rather than an existing, set of criteria and be a "law unto itself."[49]

II. PROMOTION OF CONTENT DIVERSITY AND BALANCE

Concerns with First Amendment values of diversity and a balanced marketplace of ideas have been as profoundly sounded in connection with cable as with other mass media. Federal access requirements were invalidated in *Federal Communications Commission v. Midwest Video Corp.,*[50] as discussed in chapter 6, by avoiding any First Amendment issues. Although expressing no view on the constitutional question, the Court "acknowledge[d] that it [was] not frivolous."[51] The FCC has subjected cable operators to the entire panoply of fairness regulation, including the fairness doctrine, personal attack and political editorials rules, and equal opportunity provisions, which govern broadcasting.[52] The pertinence of the Court's observation and future operation of those rules may depend not only upon the eventual constitutional status afforded cable but also future vitality of the fairness doctrine for broadcasting.

The Cable Communications Policy Act of 1984[53] introduced the possibility of access as a permissible franchise condition rather than a constitutional right. Specifically, it provides that "(a) franchising authority may establish requirements in a franchise with respect to the designated use of channel capacity for public, educational, or governmental use."[54] The Cable Act also authorizes franchising authorities to set terms for other use if access channels are not being utilized for their designated purpose.[55] A separate provision requires cable systems with at least thirty-six channels to set aside capacity for commercial access[56] and subjects smaller operators to a like requirement if obligated by franchise terms.[57] Cable operators are prohibited from "exercis[ing] any editorial control over any" access channels.[58] However, they are free to set rates and terms of access for commercial channels and consider program content to assure usage will not adversely affect cable system operation or market development.[59]

First Amendment challenges to mandatory access so far have proved unsuccessful.[60] Similarly unavailing was a constitutional challenge to a franchise requirement obligating a cable company to originate four and one half hours per week of local programming. In *Chicago Cable Communications v. Chicago Cable Commission*[61] the court of appeals determined that the differences between cable and other media justified its stricter regulations.[62] It found that the origination requirement was supputed by "the important or substantial interest" of "localism," and because "the minimal requirements [did] not divest [cable operators] of discretion" over what to transmit, the provision's incidental impact upon First Amendment interests was not excessive.[63]

First Amendment considerations aside, the question exists whether access ever will be a meaningful concept in a practical sense. Experience even in service areas with large audiences and significant funding so far has demonstrated underuse as the norm rather than the exception.[64] To the extent that reality holds true, access may be a theory well linked to First Amendment theory but an actual methodology that is marginally relevant to both the speaking and the viewing or listening interests of the public.

III. CONTENT RESTRICTION

Official restrictions upon the content of cable programming present in a different context many of the same problems examined in connection with other media. Must carry rules requiring cable casters to retransmit local broadcast signals impose upon cable operators the functional equivalent of requiring a publisher to print "that which 'reason' tells them should not be published."[65] Restrictions upon indecent programming raise questions that, in the context of broadcasting, were answered by allowing such constraints to operate.[66] Past analytical experience with respect to other media has proved relevant in assessing modern problems of cable content regulation.

A. MUST CARRY RULES

The requirement that cable operators must carry the signals of local broadcasters relates back to the array of rules that emerged in the 1960s when the FCC regulated cable under jurisdiction that was "reasonably ancillary" to its governance of broadcasting.[67] Must carriage reflects the sense that exclusion of local signals from a cable system would subject local broadcasting to audience erosion and diminished advertising revenue and thus undermine its viability.[68] Although the rules were invalidated in *Quincy Cable TV, Inc. v. Federal Communications Commission*,[69] the court of appeals left open the possibility that a more narrowly tailored variant of must carriage might be permissible.[70] The commission subsequently adopted new must carry rules which would operate for a fixed period ending after five years.[71] Its rationale for the narrower requirement was that viewers needed time to become familiar with the devices, enabling them to switch between cable and broadcast service, that it was requiring cable systems to provide.[72] The number of must carry signals also varied in accordance with a cable system's channel capacity.[73]

In *Century Communications Corp. v. Federal Communications Commission*,[74] the court of appeals found the revised must carry rules to be incompatible with the First Amendment. As in *Quincy Cable TV, Inc.*, the appeals court determined that the government interest was not substantial enough to justify their operation.[75] It determined that the commission's assertions, that consumers were ignorant of the differences between broadcast and cable technology and needed five years to become educated, were based upon con-

jecture rather than on evidence.[76] The court found, based upon actual experience pursuant to the *Quincy Cable TV, Inc.* decision and other government studies, "that the absence of must carry would not harm local broadcasting."[77] Missing from its perspective, therefore, was evidence of "a substantial governmental interest . . . outweigh[ing] the incidental burden on first amendment interests conceded by all parties here."[78]

The court of appeals further determined that even the scaled-down must carry rules were not tailored narrowly enough.[79] That conclusion too was premised upon a failure of proof. Thus, the court noted that "(i)t is wholly unclear to us why it should take five years to inform consumers that with the installation of [the] switch and a television antenna they can view more local channels."[80] In sum, the reincarnated must carry rules fell because the FCC had "failed 'to put itself in a position to know' whether the problem that its regulations seek to solve 'is a real or fanciful threat.' "[81] Even so, the court of appeals pointed out that it did "not suggest that must carry rules are *per se* unconstitutional [or] mean to intimate that the FCC may not regulate the cable industry so as to advance substantial governmental interests."[82]

Century Communications Corp. v. Federal Communications Commission, 835 F.2d 292 (D.C. Cir. 1987), *cert. denied* 108 S.Ct. 2018 (1988)

Wald, Chief Judge:

I. FACTS

Since the mid–1960's, when the nascent cable television industry began to loom as a threat to ordinary broadcast television, the Federal Communications Commission has labored to protect the local broadcast media through regulation of the cable industry. The Commission's objective in these endeavors was not merely to protect an established industry from the encroachment of an upstart young competitor, although such a result was clearly the by-product of the regulatory posture that developed. Rather, the Commission took the position that without the power to regulate cable it could not discharge its statutory obligation to provide for "fair, efficient, and equitable" distribution of service among "the several States and communities." If permitted to grow unfettered, the Commission feared, cable might well supplant ordinary broadcast television. A necessary consequence of such displacement would be to undermine the FCC's mandate to allocate the broadcast spectrum in a manner that best served the public interest. In particular, if an unregulated, unlicensed cable industry were to threaten the economic viability of broadcast television, the Commission would be powerless to effect what it saw (and continues to see) as one of its cardinal objectives: the development of a "system of [free] local broadcasting stations, such that 'all communities of appreciable size [will] have at least one television station as an outlet for local self-expression.' "

Quincy Cable TV, 768 F.2d at 1439 (citations and footnote omitted). See also *United States v. Southwestern Cable Co.*, 392 U.S. 157, 88 S.Ct. 1994, 20 L.Ed.2d 1001 (1968) (approving FCC regulation of cable as within the agency's authority so long as its actions are "reasonably ancillary" to its regulation of broadcast television); *Amendment of Part 76 of the Commission's Rules Concerning Carriage of Television Broadcast Signals by Cable Television Systems*, 1 F.C.C. Rcd 864 (1986) (hereinafter "*Report and Order*"), *reconsid. denied*, 2 F.C.C. Rcd 3593 (hereinafter, "*Recon. Order*"), at ¶¶ 1–29 (tracing history of cable regulation).

Must-carry rules in various forms have been major tools in this campaign to protect local broadcasting from cable....

In the aftermath of *Quincy Cable TV*, the FCC immediately suspended enforcement of the must-carry rules. Four months later, it announced its intention to undertake rulemaking proceedings, see *Notice of Inquiry and Notice of Proposed Rulemaking*, 50 Fed.Reg. 48232 (1985), and eventually, in November 1986, 16 months after *Quincy Cable TV* had been handed down, the agency released a new, more limited set of must-carry rules designed to accommodate *Quincy Cable TV's* concerns. See *Report & Order*. In the decision to promulgate these new rules, the Commission

took note of the many comments, submitted primarily but not exclusively by broadcasting interests, arguing that some form of FCC intervention remained necessary to protect local broadcasting. See *Report & Order* at ¶¶ 36–51; see also *id.* at ¶¶ 52–57 (describing comments, primarily from cable operators, arguing that the reinstitution of must-carry was unnecessary and undesirable).

The most salient feature of the new rules was that the Commission substantially altered its stated justification for imposing must-carry rules at all. No longer did the Commission argue, as it had prior to the *Quincy Cable TV* decision, that the rules were needed for the indefinite future to ensure viewer access to local broadcast stations. Rather, the Commission now argued that must-carry rules were needed to guarantee such access during a shorter-term transition period during which viewers could become accustomed to an existing and inexpensive but largely unknown piece of equipment known as the "input-selector device."

Such devices, if hooked up to a television, allow viewers at any given time to select, simply by flicking a switch, between shows offered by their cable system and broadcast television shows offered off-the-air. These devices, the most common of which is known in the cable industry as an "A/B switch," are about the size of a standard light-switch, and work by being hooked up to a roof-top, attic or television-top antenna. According to a study cited by the Commission in its report explaining the new must-carry rules, the cost of buying such a switch is approximately $7.50, and the cost of buying an outdoor antenna to go with it is approximately $50. See Joint Appendix ("J.A.") at 240–42 (cited at *Report & Order* at ¶ 124). Outdoor antennas are generally the more expensive of the three types of antennas.

The Commission estimated that it would take approximately five years for the public to become acclimated to the existence of these switches, and accordingly, its interim rules should be in place for that same five years. See 47 C.F.R. § 76.64 (stating that rules remain in force until January 15, 1992); see also *Report & Order* at ¶ 138. At that point, the need for ongoing must-carry rules to ensure viewer access to local broadcast stations would be obviated. See *Report & Order* at ¶ 163 ("once cable subscribers become accustomed to using off-the-air reception on an equal basis with cable service, then cable systems no longer will have an artificial ability to limit their subscribers' access to over-the-air broadcast signals"); see also *id.* at ¶ 138 ("While we have found that short-term must carry regulations are necessary in order to ensure that broadcasting remains a competitive alternative source of programming in the interim period, the record clearly supports no more extensive regulatory program than that which we are adopting".)

Because the Commission envisioned these switches as guaranteeing effective viewer choice between local and cable shows, it ultimately added to the new must-carry regime the requirement that cable systems offer subscribers, for pay, input-selector devices that could be hooked up to their TVs. See 47 C.F.R. § 76.66; see also *Report & Order* at ¶ 140; *Recon. Order* at ¶¶ 80–94 (sketching input-selector requirements and amending earlier regulations so as not to require cable operators to install such devices for free or at cost). It did so over the reservations of some broadcasting concerns, who viewed the input-selector devices as less protective than must-carry rules. See *Report & Order* at ¶¶ 45–47 (noting that "broadcasting interests" did not regard the A/B switch as an efficacious way of protecting local broadcasting). The Commission, observing that relatively few consumers knew about the switch-and-antenna mechanism and noting that the long history of must-carry rules had created a public "misperception" that "broadcast signals will always be available as part of their basic cable service," see *Report & Order* at ¶¶ 121–22, also promised to require cable operators to educate the viewing public about the availability of the switch-and-antenna mechanism. See, e.g., *Report & Order* at ¶¶ 1, 136.

In addition to thus offering a new and more limited justification for must-carry rules, the Commission also substantially limited the sweep of the new rules in a number of respects. It set forth limits on how many channels a cable carrier must devote to must-carry: carriers with 20 channels or less were not required to carry any must-carry stations; carriers with between 21 and 26 stations could be required to carry up to 7 channels of must-carry signals; and carriers with 27 or more channels could be required to devote up to 25% of their system to must-carry signals. See 47 C.F.R. § 76.56; see also *Report & Order* at ¶¶ 150–52. It also limited the pool of potential must-carry channels to those satisfying a "viewing standard" generally demonstrating a minimum viewership of the channel in question. See 47 C.F.R. § 76.5(d)1(ii); 47 C.F.R. § 76.55 (stating that a broadcast station qualifies for inclusion in must-carry pool if it demonstrates that it attains at least an average share of total viewing hours of at least 2 percent and a net weekly circulation of 5 percent in noncable households in the county where the cable system is located); see also *Report & Order* at ¶¶ 145–46. The Commission also authorized cable operators to refuse to carry more than one station affiliated with the same commercial network. See *Report & Order* at ¶ 153. Finally, the Commission limited the number of noncommercial stations required to be carried, stating that when the cable system had fewer than 54 channels and an eligible noncommercial station or translater existed, the cable operator must devote at least one channel to a noncommercial station; and that when the cable system had 54 or more stations, it must devote two must-carry channels to such endeavors. See 47 C.F.R. § 76.56.

Constitutional and statutory challenges to these new must-carry rules were lodged shortly after their promulgation by an array of cable operators and public interest group. . . .

B. An O'Brien-*Test Analysis of the New Regulations*

In *United States v. O'Brien,* the Supreme Court stated:

> [W]e think it clear that a government regulation is sufficiently justified if it is within the constitutional power of the Government; if it furthers an important or substantial governmental interest; if the governmental interest is unrelated to the suppression of free expression; and if the incidental restriction on alleged First Amendment freedoms is no greater than is essential to the furtherance of that interest.

391 U.S. at 377. . . .

We stress at the outset that both the justification offered by the FCC for its new regulations and the scope of those new initiatives differ rather markedly from the justification for and scope of the initial must-carry rules struck down in *Quincy Cable TV.* We therefore do not by any means accept petitioners' characterization, see Brief for Joint Petitioners at 1, of the new must-carry rules as mere imitations of those invalidated in *Quincy Cable TV* and thus deserving of a hasty execution. Although *Quincy Cable TV* supplies the structural framework for our analysis, the new must-carry rules are to be evaluated on their own terms: they should not suffer by dint of their association with the previous must-carry regime.

Our reservations about the new must-carry rules do, however, implicate both the substantiality of the governmental interest advanced and the narrowness of their design.

1. The Substantiality of the Governmental Interest

It may well be that upon a suitable record showing, the justification offered by the FCC, that interim regulations are needed to keep local broadcasts accessible to viewers while the new switch-and-antenna technology takes hold, would satisfy the *O'Brien* standard. See e.g., *FCC v. WNCN Listeners Guild,* 450 U.S. 582, 594 (1981) (deeming "the policy of promoting the widest possible dissemination of information from diverse sources to be consistent with both the [Commission's] public interest standard and the First Amendment"); cf. *FCC v. National Citizens Committee for Broadcasting,* 436 U.S. 775, 795 (1978) (noting first amendment value of achieving " 'widest possible dissemination of information from diverse and antagonistic sources' ") (citations omitted). The difficulty is that here, as in *Quincy Cable TV,* the FCC's judgment that transitional rules are needed is predicated not upon substantial evidence but rather upon several highly dubious assertions of the FCC, from which we conclude that the need for a new saga of must-carry rules is more speculative than real. See e.g., *Home Box Office, Inc. v. FCC,* 567 F.2d 9, 50 (D.C.Cir.), *cert. denied,* 434 U.S. 829 (1977) (requiring agencies to present "a record that convincingly shows a problem to exist" in order to satisfy the "substantial interest" prong of the *O'Brien* test); see also *Quincy Cable TV,* 768 F.2d at 1455 n. 44 (noting Supreme Court cases requiring "more than an unsubstantiated assertion of the importance of the governmental interest"). Such speculative fears alone have never been held sufficient to justify trenching on first amendment liberties.

The agency's first questionable contention is that consumers are not now aware and cannot be expected to become aware in fewer than five years that the installation of an A/B switch could preserve their choice of programs:

> [T]he perception [exists] that cable systems may be able to preclude access by their subscribers to off-the-air broadcast signals. This perception derives not from any inherent characteristic of cable service, but rather from cable subscribers' current expectation that broadcast signals will always be available as part of their basic cable service. This expectation is a direct result of the former must-carry rules, which, in fact, required cable systems to carry all available off-the-air broadcast television signals. The expectation that local broadcast signals will be carried by their cable system has caused many subscribers to perceive that there is no need to install or maintain the capability to receive broadcast signals off-the-air.
>
> . . . . .
>
> If we did not adopt interim must-carry rules now, until our long-term regulatory plan to educate consumers on the need for independent access to off-the-air signals and to make input selector switches available takes hold, harm to the public interest would ensue.

See *Report & Order* at ¶¶ 121, 126.

The FCC, however, adduces scant evidence for its judgment of a widespread "misperception" among cable subscribers that the only means of access to off-the-air signals is through cable service. It puts forth no attitudinal surveys, or polls, suggesting the likely pace of consumer adaptation to the A/B switch technology. Nor does it offer analogies illustrating how swiftly consumers have incorporated previous electronic innovations. Such evidence might have shown what the FCC simply assumes here: that upon the disappearance of must-carry regulations, consumers would collectively fail to install with any dispatch the switches and antennas necessary to gain access to local broadcast stations, conceivably imperiling the survival of these stations and thereby depriving viewers of diverse broadcasting offerings....

In appraising the FCC's argument that the indelibility of consumer ignorance justifies the reimposition of must-carry rules, we are thus left to ask whether the FCC's contention is so obvious or commonsensical that it needs no empirical support to stand up. We conclude that it is not. For one thing, the FCC's own report elsewhere belies the agency's fears of viewer lethargy. The Commission notes:

> There is evidence that video consumers are now becoming accustomed to switching between alternate program input sources. We observe that many cable systems now offer services through dual cables in order to provide greater channel capacity. Such systems employ switching devices to select between the two cables and often mark the switch positions with "A" and "B" designations. *Cable subscribers apparently have accepted this switching arrangement and do not find it inconvenient.*

See *Report & Order* at ¶ 164 (emphasis added).

More generally, we simply cannot accept, without evidence to the contrary, the sluggish profile of the American consumer that the Commission's argument necessarily presupposes. In a culture in which even costly items like the video-cassette recorder, the cordless telephone, the compact disc-player and the home computer have spread like wildfire, it begs incredulity to simply assume that consumers are so unresponsive that within the span of five years they would not manage to purchase an inexpensive hardware-store switch upon learning that it could provide access to a considerable storehouse of new television stations and shows.

Even were we to accept, however, the Commission's view that consumer ignorance cannot be readily eradicated, we have a second fundamental problem with the Commission's judgment that its interim must-carry rules are needed to advance a substantial governmental interest sufficient to support burdening cable operators' first amendment rights. The Commission relies heavily on its assumption that in the absence of must-carry rules, cable companies would drop local broadcasts. Experience belies that assertion. As cable operators reported to the Commission during rulemaking proceedings, see *Report & Order* at ¶ 53, during the 16 months that elapsed between *Quincy Cable TV* and the reimposition of the modified must-carry rules, cable companies generally did not drop the local broadcast signals that they had been carrying prior to *Quincy Cable TV.*

The FCC responds that this constitutes "only limited direct evidence," and that in any event some cable companies did drop individual broadcast stations, see *Report & Order* at ¶ 131. One might also speculate on behalf of the FCC that the inaction of cable companies after *Quincy Cable TV* may have partially resulted from their expectation that some new must-carry rules would inevitably emerge. Nevertheless, given *Quincy Cable TV's* vigorous denunciation of the breadth of the old must-carry rules, one can hardly assume that cable companies expected the FCC to reintroduce anything like the old sweeping must-carry requirements. Also undercutting the FCC's fearful assumption is the fact that both the Federal Trade Commission and the Department of Justice have concluded, in separate reports, that the absence of must-carry would not harm local broadcasting. See *Report & Order* at ¶ 54 (noting Federal Trade Commission study, submitted in FCC rulemaking, that an analysis of 24 satellite television stations showed that "absent must-carry rules, cable systems can be expected to carry many or most local broadcast stations"); *id.* at ¶ 55 (noting that Department of Justice also concludes that must-carry rules are not needed to foster localism); *id.* at ¶ 114 (FCC acknowledges during post-*Quincy Cable TV* hiatus that "many cable systems are now providing locally originated programming services").

For these reasons, we conclude that the FCC has not demonstrated that the new must-carry rules further a substantial governmental interest, as the rules must to outweigh the incidental burden on first amendment interests conceded by all parties here. As we stated in *Quincy Cable TV*, "[a]t least in those instances in which both the existence of the problem and the beneficial effects of the agency's response to that problem are concededly susceptible of some empirical demonstration, the agency must do something more than merely posit the existence of the disease sought to be cured." 768 F.2d at 1455. The FCC error in this case was its failure to go that extra step here.

2. The Congruence between Means and Ends

The second prong of the *O'Brien* test focuses on the congruence between the means chosen by the agency and the end it seeks to achieve. In this case, even were we convinced that the interest in whose name the FCC purports to act was more than a "fanciful threat," see *Home Box Office, Inc.*

v. FCC, 567 F.2d 9, 50 (D.C. Cir.), *cert. denied*, 434 U.S. 829 (1977), the new must-carry regulations, because of their lengthy duration, are too broad to pass muster even under the *O'Brien* test.

If any interim period of must-carry rules is, in fact, necessary, the FCC adduces literally no evidence that this period must last for fully five years. Such a period is strikingly long in an industry that the FCC itself characterizes as "rapidly evolving." See *Report & Order* at ¶ 133. In the absence of any empirical support for the new must-carry rules, the FCC falls back on what it terms a "sound predictive judgment," see *Recon. Order* at ¶ 62, that it will take about five years for consumers to learn about the switch-and-antenna mechanism, and thus that a five-year transition period is needed during which the agency will provide consumer education.

We are, however, unpersuaded. In large part our reluctance to countenance reimposing must-carry rules for five years based on a "sound predictive judgment" that is never explained reflects our perceptions about consumer aptitude stated earlier. Such a guess about consumer instincts hardly presents the sort of issue where, "if complete factual support . . . for the Commission's judgment or prediction is not possible," we should defer to the Commission's expert judgment. See *FCC v. National Citizens Committee for Broadcasting*, 436 U.S. at 814. It is wholly unclear to us why it should take five years to inform consumers that with the installation of a $7.50 switch and a television antenna they can view more local channels. The FCC report does nothing to shed light on this matter.

Additionally, we are skeptical—and the FCC's report says nothing to relieve this skepticism—that any consumer education campaign will have much impact so long as viewers can continue to rely on must-carry to get their fix of local broadcasts. It is entirely likely that not until the waning few months of the five-year must-carry regime would the FCC's admonitions about the need for switches and antennas begin to sink in, much as the existence of switches and antennas has largely gone unnoticed in a consumer population already accessed to local television as a result of must-carry in recent years. Opting for a five-year interim period therefore merely delays the inevitable, but almost certainly brief, period during

which TV owners will learn of, purchase, and install the requisite equipment. We therefore find it difficult to defer blindly to the Commission's unproven belief that half a decade is necessary.

III. CONCLUSION

Our decision today is a narrow one. We hold simply that, in the absence of record evidence in support of its policy, the FCC's reimposition of must-carry rules on a five-year basis neither clearly furthers a substantial governmental interest nor is of brief enough duration to be considered narrowly tailored so as to satisfy the *O'Brien* test for incidental restrictions on speech. We do not suggest that must-carry rules are *per se* unconstitutional, and we certainly do not mean to intimate that the FCC may not regulate the cable industry so as to advance substantial governmental interests. But when trenching on first amendment interests, even incidentally, the government must be able to adduce either empirical support or at least sound reasoning on behalf of its measures. As in *Quincy Cable TV*, we reluctantly conclude that the FCC has not done so in this case, but instead has failed to " 'put itself in a position to know' " whether the problem that its regulations seek to solve " 'is a real or fanciful threat.' " *Quincy Cable TV*, 768 F.2d at 1457–59 (quoting *Home Box Office, Inc. v. FCC*, 567 F.2d 9, 50 (D.C.Cir.), *cert. denied*, 434 U.S. 829 (1977)). Accordingly, we have no choice but to strike down this latest embodiment of must-carry.

So Ordered.

Studies pursuant to the *Century Communications Corp.* case indicate that cable systems have not excluded local signals to any significant extent.[83] Pursuant to a statutorily prescribed inquiry into the cable industry, the FCC has recommended congressional enactment of a must carriage requirement. Must carriage has been proposed, absent elimination of compulsory copyright licensing for local programming, to ensure that the competitive relationship between the cable and broadcasting is not "drastically changed [so as] to upset the balance of the market."[84]

B. Indecency

The Cable Act compounds the general criminal statute against obscenity by providing that anyone transmitting "over any cable system any matter which is obscene or otherwise unprotected by the Constitution of the United States shall be fined not more than $10,000 or imprisoned not more than two years."[85] Indecency, although more vulnerable to regulation in medium-specific contexts,[86] remains constitutionally protected speech[87] and thus should be unaffected by the statute.

The power of states to regulate cable indecency was the central issue of *Community Television of Utah, Inc. v. Wilkinson*.[88] The Cable Act provides for "the criminal or civil liability of cable programmers or cable operators pursuant to the Federal, State, or local law of libel, slander, obscenity, incitement, invasions of privacy, false or misleading advertising, or other similar laws."[89] State law, at issue in the *Wilkinson* case, subjected indecent programming as defined by statute to fines up to $10,000.[90] Because the prohibited expression was not obscene and thus was constitutionally protected, the district court found that the state law was fatally overbroad.[91] It refused to find persuasive, moreover, the contention that the Supreme Court's approval of broadcast indecency controls[92] justified validation of the state's enactment.[93] The district court noted a significant factual difference between the state's chilling monetary penalties and "very mild" sanction in *Pacifica*.[94] Significantly, the court, adverting to a brief filed by the FCC, distinguished cable from broadcasting in terms of the rationale for indecency regulation. Dismissing or discounting concerns with pervasiveness, privacy, and accessibility by children, it noted that (1) cable service requires the affirmative act of subscribing and the payment of fees on a regular basis, (2) viewers receive guides providing notice of the nature and content of programs, and (3) lockboxes are available to prevent exposure to unwanted programming.[95]

Community Television of Utah, Inc. v. Wilkinson, 611 F.Supp. 1099 (D. Utah), aff'd, 800 F.2d 989 (10th Cir. 1986), aff'd, 107 S.Ct. 1559 (1987)

Aldon J. Anderson, Senior District Judge.

INTRODUCTION

On April 20, 1983, the Utah State Legislature passed the Cable Television Programming Decency Act ("Cable Decency Act"). Utah Code Ann. §§ 76–10–1701 to –1708 (Supp.1983). The Act gives certain state officials authority to bring nuisance actions against anyone who continuously and "knowingly distributes indecent material within this state over any cable television system or pay-for-viewing television programming." *Id.* § 76–10–1703. The Act defines "indecent material" as follows:

> a visual or verbal depiction, display, representation, dissemination, or verbal description of:
>   (a) A human sexual or excretory organ or function; or
>   (b) A state of undress so as to expose the human male or female genitals, pubic area, or buttocks, with less than a fully opaque covering, or showing of the female breast with less than a fully opaque covering of any portion below the top of the nipple; or
>   (c) An ultimate sexual act, normal or perverted, actual or simulated; or
>   (d) Masturbation
> which the average person applying contemporary community standards for cable television or pay-for-viewing television programming would find is presented in a patently offensive way for the time, place, manner and context in which the material is presented.

Id. § 76–10–1702(4).

On April 21, 1983, the plaintiffs Community Television of Utah, Inc., Community Cable of Utah, Inc., Utah Satellite, Inc., and Wasatch Community TV, Inc. filed this action. Claiming that the Act infringes upon their first amendment rights, these cable operator plaintiffs sought declaratory and injunctive relief....

B. The Cable Communications Policy Act of 1984

The Cable Communications Policy Act of 1984 is the first federal statute to establish a comprehensive regulatory scheme for the cable industry. The provisions of the Policy Act relevant to this case concern the allocation of federal, state and local regulatory power. In the Policy Act, Congress refined the general presumption, announced in *Capital Cities,* that states have no power to regulate program content. In the section of the Policy Act entitled "Coordination of Federal, State and Local Authority" it states that any state or local act or regulation which is inconsistent with the provisions of the Policy Act is pre-empted and superseded. Cable Communications Policy Act § 636(c). The Policy Act retains exclusive federal regulatory power over program content in all but a few limited areas....

2. State Power to Regulate Programs Carried on All Other Channels

Section 638 of the Policy Act delineates the scope of state power to regulate programs carried on all other channels. It is therefore the last section of the Policy Act that might arguably authorize the enforcement of the Utah law. Section 638 preserves certain federal, state and local government powers to regulate the content of cable television programs:

> Nothing in this title shall be deemed to affect the criminal or civil liability of cable programmers or cable operators pursuant to the Federal, State or local law of libel, slander, obscenity, incitement, invasions of privacy, false or misleading advertising, or other similar laws, except that cable operators shall not incur any such liability for any program carried on any channel designated for public, educational, governmental use [under § 611] or on any other channel obtained under section 612 or under similar arrangements.

Id. § 638.

Hence, § 638 explicitly preserves state power to regulate obscenity. As both sides of this case agree, Utah's Cable Decency Act extends beyond "obscene" materials to regulate those termed "indecent." "Indecency" and "obscenity" are legal terms of art which have different definitions and different constitutional implications. See *infra* Part II of this opinion. The obscenity provision of § 638 therefore does not, by its terms, allow enforcement of Utah's Cable Decency Act, which regulates "indecency." The question here is whether the Cable Decency Act is one of the "other similar laws" which § 638 permits states to enact and enforce.

The list in § 638 is a classic collection of laws regulating expression which the Supreme Court has deemed unprotected by the first amendment. See *New York Times Co. v. Sullivan,* 376 U.S. 254 (1964) (libel and slander); *Roth v. United States,* 354 U.S. 476 (1957) (obscenity); *Brandenburg v. Ohio,* 395 U.S. 444 (1969) (incitement); *Time, Inc. v. Hill,* 385 U.S. 374 (1967) (invasion of privacy); *Virginia Pharmacy Board v. Virginia Consumer Counsel,* 425 U.S. 748 (1976) (false or misleading advertising). The plain purpose of § 638 is to preserve federal, state and local regulation of unprotected expression in the areas noted.

Upon examination, Utah's Cable Decency Act does not appear to fit within § 638 because "indecent" expression is not wholly unprotected speech. The very distinction between obscenity and indecency rests to a great extent upon the different levels of constitutional protection extended to both classes of expression. Indecency, which has been found subject to limited regulation under extremely limited circumstances, see Part II of this opinion, is conspicuously absent from the list of wholly unprotected expression contained in § 638.

II. FIRST AMENDMENT CONSIDERATIONS

A. The Overbreadth Doctrine

The free speech clause of the first amendment to the Constitution of the United States provides "the indispensable condition of nearly every other form of freedom": "Congress shall make no law...abridging the freedom of speech." U.S. Const. amend. I. The United States Supreme Court has the responsibility of defining the scope of this clause. Therefore, this court must be guided by Supreme Court precedent in resolving the issues presented.

The plaintiffs allege that Utah's Cable Decency Act violates the first amendment. They challenge the Cable Decency Act on its face, claiming that it is overbroad. In a democratic society which relies upon elected officials for most policy decisions, it is "strong medicine" for a court to invalidate a statute on its face. See *Broadrick v. Oklahoma*, 413 U.S. 601 (1973). It is therefore important for the court to explain the general circumstances under which facial invalidation for overbreadth is appropriate.

A law is overbroad "if it 'does not aim specifically at evils within the allowable area of (government) control, but... sweeps within its ambit other activities that constitute an exercise' of protected expressive or associational rights." L. Tribe, American Constitutional Law § 12–24, at 710 (1978) (quoting *Thornhill v. Alabama*, 310 U.S. 88, 97 (1940)). An overbroad law is void on its face; it need not be challenged "as applied" to the particular facts of a case. *Id.*

Overbroad laws, for which facial invalidation is appropriate, have two characteristics. First, the overbreadth is substantial; protected activity must be a significant part of the law's "target." *Id.* at 711. The literal scope of many laws encompasses some protected expression. Yet unless the "target area" of these laws contains significant protected expression, they are not overbroad; they can only be challenged "as applied" to particular cases. *Id.*

Second, the unconstitutional applications of an overbroad law cannot be satisfactorily excised. *Id.* If a court can adopt a limiting construction which will omit unconstitutional applications, the law is not overbroad. In addition, a law is not overbroad if its constitutionally infirm sections may be struck down without "rewriting" it. *Id.* at 714, 717.

Facial invalidation is the appropriate cure for the "chilling effect" created by overbroad laws. By definition, an overbroad law addresses significant protected expression; protected activity is therefore deterred within the law's "target area." This deterrence injures first amendment rights even if a well intentioned prosecutor enforces the law only against unprotected activity. See Note, "The First Amendment Overbreadth Doctrine," 83 Harv. L.Rev. 853 (1970).

If Utah's Cable Decency Act is overbroad, facial invalidation is therefore the appropriate remedy. This is true even though it may be difficult for courts to judge whether particular materials are indecent without a factual context. See *FCC v. Pacifica Foundation*, 438 U.S. 726, 742 (1978). The question whether particular materials are indecent is not before the court in this case. Regardless

of the particular applications of the law, the court may strike it down on its face if its "target area" is too broad; a division of this court has already used this remedy twice to invalidate overbroad cable TV laws. See *Home Box Office, Inc. v. Wilkinson*, 531 F.Supp. 987 (D. Utah 1982); *Community Television of Utah, Inc. v. Roy City*, 555 F.Supp. 1164 (D.Utah 1982).

With the foregoing guidelines in mind, the court must now proceed to determine whether the Utah law is overbroad and void on its face....

C. The Miller Test

The overbreadth doctrine evidences the United States Supreme Court's grave concern for the protection of first amendment rights. In *Roth v. United States*, 354 U.S. 476 (1957), the Court held that obscenity is not protected by the first amendment. However, the difficulty came in articulating precisely what obscenity is. Although some thought that they knew obscenity when they saw it, a comprehensive "definition" of obscenity did not emerge until 1973 in the case of *Miller v. California*, 413 U.S. (1973).

In *Miller* the Court noted that "in the area of freedom of speech and press the courts must always remain sensitive to any infringement on genuinely serious literary, artistic, political, or scientific expression. This is an area in which there are few eternal verities." *Id.* at 22–23. The *Miller* Court required that state statutes be "carefully limited" so as not to intrude upon legitimate expression. *Id.* at 23–24. Thus, the Court set forth a comprehensive three part test for obscenity:

> The basic guidelines for the trier of fact must be: (a) whether "the average person, applying contemporary community standards" would find that the work, taken as a whole, appeals to the prurient interest [citations omitted]; (b) whether the work depicts or describes, in a patently offensive way, sexual conduct specifically defined by the applicable state law; and (c) whether the work, taken as a whole, lacks serious literary, artistic, political, or scientific value.

Id. at 24.

In order to be found obscene, the material challenged must meet all three of the prongs of the *Miller* test. Material that does not do so is by definition not obscene and therefore protected from obscenity laws. Utah already has an obscenity statute which comports with the requirements of *Miller.* See Utah Code Ann. § 76–10–1201 to 1228 (1978 & Supp. 1983); *State v. Piepenburg,* 602 P.2d 702 (Utah 1979); *Piepenburg v. Cutler,* 649 F.2d 783 (10th Cir.1981). Yet the Cable Decency Act is broader. The statute regulates "indecent" material and does not limit itself to material that is legally obscene. It is evident that the Cable Decency Act does not equate indecency with obscenity.

In view of the perspective given by *Miller,* the statute is overbroad for two reasons. First, the law does not address either prong (a) or prong (c) of the *Miller* test. The Decency Act does not require, as prong (a) does, that the material appeal to the "prurient interest." Further, the law does not require that the material, taken as whole, "lack serious literary, artistic, political, or scientific value," which prong (c) demands.

Second, some of the Utah statutory definitions fail to comply adequately with prong (b) of the *Miller* test. To fall within prong (b), material must depict or describe sexual conduct in a patently offensive way. Under the Utah statute material is indecent if it is patently offensive for the time, place, manner and context shown, whether or not the material depicts or describes sexual conduct. Cable Decency Act § 1702(4).

These are results that the *Miller* Court sought to avoid. The *Miller* Court balanced the interest of freedom of expression and the legitimate interest of the state in regulating materials that depict sexual conduct. *Miller,* 413 U.S. at 23–25, 27. But the failure of the legislature to incorporate adequately all three prongs of the *Miller* test means that protected speech may be prohibited. This is because cable TV operators would be subject to civil penalties plus costs and attorney's fees for distributing material that, taken as a whole, does not appeal to the prurient interest. These penalties would also chill distribution of material that may have serious literary, artistic, political, or scientific value. The first amendment seeks to protect these critical and substantial values. The Cable Television Programming Decency Act fails to incorporate these values and is therefore an unconstitutional regulation of cable television.

In addition, the statute's separability clause cannot save it from overbreadth. The Act as a whole fails to satisfy the *Miller* requirements. This Court cannot rewrite the statute to add in the *Miller* requirements for the legislature. The separability doctrine cannot save a statute which in significant respect fails to incorporate constitutionally mandated protections.

D. The Scope and Application of FCC v. Pacifica Foundation

Defendants urge upon the court that *FCC v. Pacifica Foundation,* 438 U.S. 726 (1978), modifies *Miller*'s constitutional mandate. They argue that *Pacifica* expands the legitimate scope of state regulatory powers beyond the limits articulated in *Miller.* Defendants further contend that *Pacifica* established guidelines that the Utah Act follows.

a. *The Factual Limitations of Pacifica.*—The holding in *Pacifica* is narrow. The Court merely agreed that the FCC had the statutory authority to take note of past program content when deciding whether to renew a broadcast license. Although the FCC has no statutory power to "censor" broadcasts by excising indecent material before it is broadcast, it may impose sanctions by refusing to renew the license of stations who broadcast such material. *Id.* at 735–738. The Court itself stressed the factual limitations of its holding:

> It is appropriate, in conclusion, to emphasize the narrowness of our holding. This case does not involve a two-way radio conversation between a cab driver and a dispatcher, or a telecast of Elizabethan comedy. We have not decided that an occasional expletive in either setting would justify any sanction or, indeed, that this broadcast would justify a criminal prosecution. The Commission's decision rested entirely on a nuisance rationale under which *context* is all important. The concept requires consideration of a host of variables. The time of day was emphasized by the Commission. The content of program in which the language is used will also affect the composition of the audience, and differences between radio, television, and perhaps closed-circuit transmissions, may also be relevant.

Id. at 750, 98 S.Ct. at 3041 (emphasis added and footnote omitted).

Moreover, the concurring opinion viewed the holding even more narrowly. Justice Powell felt that "the Commission's order was limited to the facts of this case." *Id.* at 761 n. 4. This view is supported by what the Court allowed. The Court deferred to the FCC and relied on its expertise in regulating station licenses.

Because the factual basis of its holding is very narrow, *Pacifica* does not validate the Decency Act. Stressing that the material at issue was broadcast in the mid afternoon, see *id.* at 750, the Court did not approve regulation at all times of day. The Utah statute, under the circumstances stated therein, imposes a fine upon cable operators who distribute material outlawed by the statute at *any* time. The attorney general's guidelines purport to allow adult material to be presented from midnight to 7:00 a.m. These guidelines do not cure the constitutional infirmity. See discussion *infra* at 1114–1115.

Furthermore, the Court only approved a very mild penalty. The FCC did not immediately revoke the station's license, issue a cease and desist order, impose a fine, deny license renewal or impose a short term renewal. The penalty imposed was only a notation of the complaint in the station's license file. This penalty may have had no impact on the station's day to day operation, other than to cause the station to broadcast the monologue in the evening. *Id.* at 760 (concurring opinion).

The Utah Act subjects the cable operators to a potential fine of $1,000 for the first offense and escalates to $10,000 for a second offense as well as reasonable costs and attorney's fees for distributing material outlawed by the statute. Although the cause of action is not technically criminal, it does establish an increased penalty for repeated showings and is manifestly intended to deter distribution of indecent material. The sanction in *Pacifica* was far less punitive and chilling. The Commission's action caused Justice Powell to write: "since the Commission may be expected to proceed cautiously, as it has in the past, [citation omitted] I do not foresee an undue 'chilling' effect on broadcasters' exercise of their rights." *Id.* at 761–62 n. 4. The *Pacifica* Court was closely divided, with four Justices dissenting and two concurring. If the penalty had been greater the result in the case may have been different. *Pacifica* cannot be read to allow all state and local governments to regulate cable content in accord with their respective views of indecency by imposing civil fines. . . .

2. *The Application of Pacifica's Rationale to the Present Case*

Defendants attempt to show that *Pacifica*'s rationale applies to cable television. The Court's reasoning in *Pacifica* was two-fold. First, broadcasting has a pervasive presence which might intrude into the home and violate an individual's right to be left alone. Second, children may easily obtain access to indecent broadcast material, undermining both the "government's interest in the 'well-being of its youth'" and parents' authority over their children. *Id.* 438 U.S. at 748–50.

a. *Interference with the Right of Privacy.*—Defendants argue that cable television is more pervasive than the FM radio broadcasting at issue in *Pacifica.* Therefore, defendants claim, indecency on cable television can be regulated through civil sanctions. This analysis oversimplifies the *Pacifica* Court's decision. The Court did not say that pervasiveness by itself establishes a right to regulate protected expression. According to the Court, pervasiveness which *results* in an unwarranted intrusion upon one's right to be left alone justifies regulation of FM broadcasts. That is, the right to be left alone in one's own home outweighs the first amendment rights of those who wish to intrude into that home. *Id.* at 748.

The practical and critical distinction between *Pacifica* and the present case is apparent: cable television is not an uninvited intruder. As the FCC observed in its *amicus curiae* brief submitted to this court:

> First, cable is a subscriber medium, generally only available if the person who views it has affirmatively contacted the cable system and asked that a wire be brought into his home and attached to his television set. Without that voluntary act, there is no cable programming. Second, as to certain interstate-transmitted services, particularly as to entertainment channels such as HBO, Showtime, and the Movie Channel, a subscriber must usually pay a premium in addition to its subscriber fee in order to receive service. Otherwise, the signal is scrambled both aurally and visually, precluding reception in the home. Third, a subscriber may, if it so chooses, acquire a "lock box" which prevents reception of any particular cable programming without his authorization. [Fourth], television guides, providing

advance notice of the nature of upcoming program offerings, are almost always available.

Memorandum for the Federal Communications Commission as *Amicus Curiae* at 5–6.

The distinction that the FCC and plaintiffs urge is that cable TV is not an intruder but an invitee whose invitation can be carefully circumscribed. See *Pacifica* at 748–49. Because a subscriber must initiate the service, there is no uninvited intrusion into the privacy interest that the Court articulated in *Pacifica*. The individual who complained about Carlin's monologue never subscribed to radio programs. In addition, the complainant did not pay an additional fee to be able to listen to Carlin's monologue, as a subscriber to HBO, Showtime or the Movie Channel must. No lock box device even existed. In addition, it does not appear that a radio program guide provided any information in advance to warn potential listeners of the content of Carlin's monologue.

b. *The Interests of Children.*—Defendants argue alternatively that the state's interest in protecting children justifies regulation of indecency. In *Pacifica* the Court wrote that the "ease with which children may obtain access to broadcast material, coupled with the concerns recognized in *Ginsberg,* amply justify special treatment of indecent broadcasting." *Id.* at 750. In *Ginsberg v. New York,* 390 U.S. 629 (1968), the Court upheld a New York law that prohibited the sale of "harmful" indecent material, not legally obscene, to persons under 17 years of age. The concerns emphasized in *Ginsberg v. New York* consisted of two separate interests that justified a different constitutional standard for minors. First, the state has an interest in the well-being of its youth. Second, parents have an interest in exercising authority over their children.

(1) *The State's Interest in the Well-Being of its Youth.* In *Ginsberg* the governmental and parental interests listed above both gave support to the same conclusion that the law was valid. In contrast, defendants set parental and governmental interests at odds with each other. Defendants allege that "not all parents will exercise [the] necessary degree of control. Many parents may be indifferent to this material or ignorant of its harmful effect." Defendants' Amended Memorandum in Opposition to Plaintiffs' Joint Motion for Sum-

mary Judgment at 26 (filed Mar. 22, 1984). In so arguing, defendants make a fundamental departure from *Pacifica.* According to the defendants, since not all parents will do their job in limiting their children's access to indecent material, the state must step in.

In drafting the Decency Act, the legislature addressed the admirable goal of protecting children from deleterious material. In the intent statement of the Decency Act, the legislators wrote that "children have access to cable television and, in many cases, are unsupervised by parents." *Id.* at 2. Thus, the legislators sought to assist parents in their supervisory role.

The language of the statute provides that civil fines apply only to material that "is presented in a patently offensive way for the time, place, manner and context in which the material is presented." Utah Code Ann. § 76–10–1702(4) (Supp.1983). This language, defendants argue, indicates that the legislature intended to prohibit presentation of "indecent" material only during the daytime. Defendants claim that *Pacifica* allows the state to channel indecent material to the early morning hours (12:00 a.m. to 7:00 a.m.) because of the interests of children.

Although protecting children is a very desirable and legitimate goal, the Act itself does not mention children anywhere. It does not provide any systematic procedure for protecting children. Section –1702(4) provides no limiting principle consistent with applicable constitutional standards. Even assuming *arguendo* that *Pacifica* validates a prohibition limited to the daytime, the statutory language does not channel indecency to specific viewing hours. The legal infirmities of the statute are so great that this court could not so limit the statute even through purposive construction without engaging in improper judicial legislation. Thus, the scope of the language is so uncertain as to chill legitimate expression in a way that the overbreadth doctrine forbids.

Even though the language in section –1702 is constitutionally insufficient, the Attorney General argues that he has promulgated rules which cure any defect. These rules provide for nonenforcement during the "adult viewing hours" (midnight to 7:00 a.m.). The statute does not provide for any such rulemaking authority. In addition, if a subsequent attorney general decides to rescind the guidelines, protected speech will be threatened. This analysis assumes, without deciding, that such guidelines would be sufficient to cure any constitutional infirmity.

Moreover, localities possess an independent right to enforce the Decency Act. *Id.* § 76–10–1704(2). In addition, the statute provides that this "act does not preclude the . . . right of cities, counties, or other political subdivision from further regulating the distribution of indecent material over any cable television system or pay-for-viewing television programming." *Id.* § 76–10–1707. The Attorney General can neither prevent local government from enforcing the law to its fullest extent nor avert local enactment of other similarly inhibitory laws.

A further fact that must be taken into account is that the Act does not consider the rights of consenting adults under *Miller* to view nonobscene material. In *Pacifica* Justice Powell's concurrence emphasized the importance of protecting the rights of adults while at the same time insulating children from indecency. Justice Powell feared that the *Pacifica* ruling might "have the effect of 'reduc(ing) the adult population . . . to (hearing) only what is fit for children.' [citation omitted] This argument is not without force." *Pacifica*, 438 U.S. at 760. Justice Powell concluded that the holding of the Court "does not prevent respondent Pacifica Foundation from broadcasting the monologue during late evening hours when fewer children are likely to be in the audience." *Id.* at 760. Thus, *Pacifica* seems to preserve the right of adults to listen to Carlin's monologue on the radio. Utah's cable television law would prevent adults from exercising their rights in a manner consistent with the rationale of *Pacifica*.

(2) *The Parental Interest in Supervising Children*— Restrictions in the Utah Act may well be inconsistent with the right of parental control articulated in *Pacifica* and *Ginsberg*. The enforcement of the Act could result in a ban of certain defined materials that may have serious literary, artistic, political or scientific value and that some parents want to show their children. Under Utah's law they could not do so, even though rulings of the Supreme Court allow parents to provide materials for their children that the children themselves cannot purchase: "the prohibition against

sales to minors does not bar parents who so desire from purchasing the magazines for their children." *Ginsberg v. New York,* 390 U.S. at 630.

Thus, the distinctions between *Pacifica* and the present case are manifest. *Pacifica* does not authorize the regulation attempted by the Utah Legislature. At best *Pacifica* stands for the proposition that a federal regulatory agency can monitor consumer complaints directed at broadcasters who operate in the public domain. The differences between radio and cable make *Pacifica* easily distinguishable and contradict defendants' argument.

E. The Utah Law as a Time, Place and Manner Restriction

Defendants argue that the Act, limited by the attorney general's guidelines, operates as a legitimate time, place and manner restriction and can be upheld on that basis. The phrase "time, place, and manner" is a legal term of art. The Supreme Court has sustained such restrictions when they regulate without regard to content, serve a significant governmental interest, and leave open ample alternative channels for communication. *Metromedia, Inc. v. City of San Diego,* 453 U.S. 490, 515–17 (1981).

Although the Decency Act purports to regulate cable material according to "the time, place, and context in which the material is presented," the Act cannot qualify as valid time, place, or manner restriction. This is because the Utah law and the attorney general's guidelines regulate according to content. The statute regulates according to content because it provides that fines will only be imposed when the material distributed violates the specific standards set forth in section – 1702. The Attorney General states that "I do not plan to enforce the Act *based on any program containing indecency* which begins after midnight or which ends by seven o'clock in the morning." Cable Television Programming Decency Act of 1983, Op.Att'y Gen. No. 83–001, p. 10 (October 17, 1983) (emphasis added). Thus, the Attorney General distinguishes between permissible and impermissible cable material by reference to its content. See *Metromedia,* 453 U.S. at 516. Therefore, the Act cannot be sustained as a valid time, place or manner restriction.

III. CONCLUSION

Cable television is a powerful form of communication. Used properly, it can edify and inspire as well as entertain. Used improperly, it can seriously damage the quality of life that we have and reduce public tastes to their lowest common denominator. Following Supreme Court precedent, today's ruling delineates an area in which private individuals, particularly parents, must assume an important responsibility for maintaining a decent society. The first amendment puts "the decision as to what views shall be voiced largely into the hands of each of us, in the hope that the use of such freedom will ultimately produce a more capable citizenry and more perfect polity and in the belief that no other approach would comport with the premise of individual dignity and choice upon which our political system rests." *Cohen v. California,* 403 U.S. 15 (1971).

Upon review, the court of appeals affirmed the decision for the reasons stated in the district court opinion.[96] The Supreme Court affirmed without opinion.[97] Although distinguishing cable from broadcasting, for purposes of indecency control, the points of distinction illustrate the inherent treacheries of medium-specific analysis. Like receipt of cable, broadcast viewing or listening requires the affirmative acts of purchasing the necessary equipment, installation activation, and selection. Program guides and blocking devices also are available for broadcast service. At most, therefore, the distinguishing factors rest not upon different characteristics but shades of relativity. Left for consideration is whether those somewhat fine distinctions will or should continue to outweigh the broad functional similarities of media.

NOTES

1. As noted in Chapter 6, such rules were examined without reaching constitutional questions.
2. Columbia Broadcasting System v. Democratic National Committee, 412 U.S. 94 (1973).
3. Federal Communications Commission v. Pacifica Foundation, 438 U.S. 726, 748 (1978).
4. 440 U.S. 689 (1989).
5. *Id.* at 700–02.
6. 476 U.S. 488 (1986).
7. *Id.* at 490.
8. *Id.*
9. *Id.* at 492.
10. *Id.* at 494.
11. *Id.*
12. *Id.* at 494–95.
13. *See* Chapters 1, 9 of this book.
14. City of Los Angeles v. Preferred Communications, Inc., 476 U.S. at 495.
15. *Id.*
16. *Id.*
17. *Id.*
18. *Id.*
19. *Id.* at 496 (Blackmun, J., concurring).
20. *Id.* (Blackmun, J., concurring).
21. 768 F.2d 1434 (D.C.Cir. 1985), *cert. denied,* 476 U.S. 1169 (1986).
22. *Id.* at 1438.
23. *Id.* at 1444–45, *citing* United States v. O'Brien, 391 U.S. 367, 377 (1968).
24. *Id.* at 1455–56.
25. *Id.* at 1460. Revised must carry rules would resurface and be invalidated again in Century Communications Corp. v. Federal Communications Commission, 835 F.2d 292 (D.C. Cir. 1987), *cert. denied,* 108 S.Ct. 2015 (1988).
26. Quincy Cable TV, Inc., v. Federal Communications Commission, 768 F.2d at 1438, 1447–50.
27. *Id.* at 1448.
28. *Id.* at 1450.
29. *Id.* at 1449.
30. *Id.*
31. *Id.*
32. *Id.* at 1449–50.
33. *Id.* at 1450, *citing* Miami Herald Publishing Co. v. Tornillo, 418 U.S. 241 (1974).
34. *Id.*
35. 571 F.Supp. 976 (D.R.I. 1983), *vacated as moot,* 773 F.2d 382 (1st Cir. 1985).
36. *Id.* at 985.
37. *Id.*
38. *Id.* at 985–86.
39. *Id.* at 986.
40. *Id.*
41. *Id.* at 986–87.
42. Community Television of Utah, Inc. v. Wilkinson, 611 F.Supp. 1099 (D. Utah 1985), *aff'd,* 800 F.2d 989 (10th Cir. 1986), *aff'd,* 107 S.Ct. 1559 (1987).
43. 611 F.Supp. 1099.
44. *Id.* at 1112.
45. *Id.* at 1113.
46. *Id.*

47. 107 S.Ct. 1559.

48. *See* Miami Herald Publishing Co. v. Tornillo, 418 U.S. 241; Columbia Broadcasting System v. Democratic National Committee, 412 U.S. 94.

49. Kovacs v. Cooper, 336 U.S. 77, 97 (1949) (Jackson, J., concurring).

50. 440 U.S. 689.

51. *Id.* at 709 n.19.

52. *See* 47 C.F.R. §§ 76.205, 76.209.

53. 47 U.S.C. § 521 *et seq.*

54. *Id.,* § 531(a).

55. *Id.,* § 531(d).

56. *Id.,* § 532(b) (1) (A).

57. *Id.,* § 532(b) (1) (B).

58. *Id.,* § 531(e), § 532(c) (2).

59. *Id.,* § 531(c) (1).

60. *See* Erie Telecommunications, Inc. v. City of Erie, 659 F. Supp. 580 (W.D. Pa. 1987), *aff'd,* 853 F.2d 1084 (3d Cir. 1988).

61. 879 F.2d 1540 (7th Cir. 1989), *cert. denied.*

62. *Id.* at 1548.

63. *Id.* at 1549–51.

64. *See* B. SCHMIDT, FREEDOM OF THE PRESS VERSUS PUBLIC ACCESS 208–09 (1976).

65. Miami Herald Publishing Co. v. Tornillo, 418 U.S. at 254.

66. See Chapter 9 of this book.

67. *See* Chapter 6 of this book.

68. *See* Quincy Cable TV, Inc. v. Federal Communications Commission, 768 F.2d at 1441–42.

69. 768 F.2d 1434.

70. *Id.* at 1463.

71. *See* Century Communications Corp. v. Federal Communications Commission, 835 F.2d 292.

72. *See id.* at 296.

73. *See id.*

74. 835 F.2d 292.

75. *Id.* at 304.

76. *Id.*

77. *Id.* at 303.

78. *Id.*

79. *Id.* at 303–04.

80. *Id.*

81. *Id.* at 304–05.

82. *Id.* at 304.

83. *See Broadcasting,* Sept. 26, 1989, at 80.

84. In the matter of Competition, Rate Deregulation and the Commission's Policies Relating to the Provision of Cable Television Service, 85 F.C.C. Rcd. (1990).

85. 47 U.S.C. § 559.

86. FCC v. Pacifica Foundation, 438 U.S. at 746–48.

87. *Id.* at 746; *id.* at 761 (Powell, J., concurring); *id.* at 762–63 (Brennan, J., dissenting).

88. 611 F.Supp. 1099.

89. 47 U.S.C. § 558.

90. Community Television of Utah, Inc., v. Wilkinson, 611 F. Supp. at 1110.

91. *Id.* at 1108–09.

92. *See* Federal Communications Commission v. Pacifica Foundation, 438 U.S. 726.

93. Community Television of Utah, Inc. v. Wilkinson, 611 F.Supp. at 1109–11.

94. *Id.* at 1110.

95. *Id.* at 1113–14.

96. 800 F.2d 989.

97. 107 S.Ct. 1559.

Chapter 11

COMMON CARRIERS

Given the nature of common carriers, and the responsibility to provide equal access to their facilities on a nondiscriminatory basis, First Amendment issues have been less frequent than with other media. In response to the dominant telecommunication carrier's interest in expanding into more traditional media services, content diversification policies have justified what essentially amounts to a prior restraint.[1] The telephone industry too has been subject to content controls governing use of their facilities for the dissemination of obscene or indecent messages.[2]

I. PROMOTION OF CONTENT DIVERSIFICATION

Terms of the modified final judgment discussed in chapter 7, enabling American Telephone and Telegraph Company (AT&T) to commence new business activities, contain a significant restriction. Pursuant to concern with "potential dangers to competition and to First Amendment values,"[3] the company was prohibited from engaging in electronic publishing.[4] Given AT&T's existing interexchange network, the district court worried that the company could discriminate against competing electronic publishers by giving priority to its own traffic and obtaining proprietary information concerning its rivals.[5] Because "[t]he electronic publishing industry is still in its infancy," but has the potential to become "a very significant part of the American communications system," it determined that AT&T's "resources would dwarf any efforts of its competitors" and "mere presence . . . would be likely to deter other potential competitors from ever entering the market."[6]

Beyond mere competitive concerns, the district court tied its decision to First Amendment values.[7] Although a constitutional claim of freedom of the press was not present, the court chose to emphasize "the goal of the First Amendment . . . to achieve 'the widest possible dissemination of information from diverse and antagonistic sources.'"[8] What essentially constituted a prior restraint thus was implemented on the premise that the "risks to the public interest" otherwise were too profound.[9]

United States v. American Telephone and Telegraph Co., 552 F.Supp. 131 (D.D.C. 1982), Aff'd, 460 U.S. 1001 (1983)

B. Electronic Publishing Services

The second type of information service which AT&T would be permitted to provide under the proposed decree are those services in which it would control, or have a financial interest in, the content of the information being transmitted. Those services are generally referred to as electronic publishing or information publishing services.

A number of organizations have objected to entry of the proposed decree unless it is modified to include a ban on electronic publishing. However, the decree itself does not specifically refer to the concept of electronic publishing, let alone provide a suitable definition. In order to conduct a meaningful discussion of the relevant issues, therefore, electronic publishing must first be defined. After drawing on various sources the Court has concluded that, for purposes of this opinion, electronic publishing will be regarded as:

> the provision of any information which a provider or publisher has, or has caused to be originated, authored, compiled, collected, or edited, or in which he has a direct or indirect financial or proprietary interest, and which is disseminated to an unaffiliated person through some electronic means.

A number of persons have argued that because of potential dangers to competition and to First Amendment values, AT&T should be prohibited from engaging in such activities. For the reasons stated below, the Court agrees.

The threat to competition that is claimed to be posed by AT&T in this industry is that, through the use of cross-subsidization and customer discrimination, it will use its power in the interexchange market to disadvantage competing electronic publishers. While the possibility of cross-subsidization is as remote here as it is with respect to other subjects considered herein, there is a real danger that AT&T will use its control of the interexchange network to undermine competing publishing ventures.

AT&T could discriminate against competing electronic publishers in a variety of ways. It could, for example, use its control over the network to give priority to traffic from its own publishing operations over that of competitors. A second concern is that, inasmuch as AT&T has access to signalling and traffic data, it might gain proprietary information about its competitors' publishing services. Furthermore, it appears that AT&T

would have both the incentive and the opportunity to develop technology, facilities, and services that favor its own publishing operations and the areas served by these operations rather than the operations of the publishing industry at large. Similarly, AT&T could discriminate in interconnecting competitors to the network and in providing needed maintenance on competitors' lines. Finally, AT&T might submit tariffs that would have the effect of favoring AT&T's publishing operations to the disadvantage of competing concerns.

AT&T and the Department of Justice provide the same response to these arguments that they make in other contexts: that market forces will curtail AT&T's ability effectively to engage in these practices. In the absence of special problems and concerns relating only to the electronic publishing industry, the Court probably would, as it has in other instances, accept that response. However, in the view of the Court a different conclusion is appropriate here, for the peculiar characteristics of the electronic publishing market would both render anticompetitive acts more damaging to AT&T's competitors in that market and insulate such acts from correction by market forces.

The electronic publishing industry is still in its infancy. Although this business may some day be a very significant part of the American communications system, at present, and most likely for the next several years, a small number of relatively small firms will be experimenting with new technology to provide services to an American public that is, for the most part, still almost totally unfamiliar with them. There can be no doubt that, if AT&T entered this market, the combination of its financial, technological, manufacturing, and marketing resources would dwarf any efforts of its competitors. In fact, AT&T's mere presence in the electronic publishing area would be likely to deter other potential competitors from even entering the market.

It is also readily apparent that competitors in the electronic publishing industry—far more so than competitors in any other industry—could easily be crushed were AT&T to engage in the types of anticompetitive behavior described above. Unlike most products and services, information in general and news in particular are by definition especially sensitive to even small impediments or delays. Information is only valuable if it is timely; by and large it is virtually worthless if its dissemination is delayed. This quality is especially important in electronic publishing because up-to-date information and constant availability are the features likely to be sought by subscribers.

The trial record in the *AT&T* case reveals many instances when AT&T was slow to respond to the needs of competitors, both in providing essential products or parts and in servicing these products and parts. Any delays of that kind, were they to occur in the context of the transmission of electronic publishing information, would quickly cause subscribers to desert their unreliable publishers and thus cripple AT&T's competitors in that business.

Finally, electronic publishers remain more dependent upon the AT&T network than others in the telecommunications business. In some areas, AT&T is the sole provider of intercity services. Elsewhere, where competition does exist, the other common carriers—although capable of handling voice transmissions—frequently lack the sophisticated facilities necessary to meet the needs of the electronic publishers. Systems that are specifically designed to transmit data do not provide a satisfactory solution; most of these systems lease part, if not all, their facilities from AT&T. Nor are satellites the answer, for at least for the present they do not appear to present a realistic alternative, given their restricted availability, potential transmission problems, and high costs.

Thus, even if AT&T should engage in anticompetitive activity, publishers would have no realistic alternative transmission system by which to reach their subscribers. The low level of demand for these services that exists at present makes it unlikely that competing interexchange carriers would construct transmission systems to be used solely for the delivery of electronic publishing services, and publishers would therefore be forced to accept the inferior services provided by AT&T.

Based on competitive considerations alone, therefore, the Court might well be justified in barring AT&T from electronic publishing industry. Beyond that, AT&T's entry into the electronic publishing market poses a substantial danger to First Amendment values.

The goal of the First Amendment is to achieve "the widest possible dissemination of information from diverse and antagonistic sources." *Associated Press v. United States*, 326 U.S. 1, 20 65 S.Ct. 1416, 1424, 89 L.Ed. 2013 (1945). See also *FCC v. National Citizens Committee for Broadcasting*, 436 U.S. 775, 795, 98 S.Ct. 2096, 2112, 56 L.Ed.2d 697 (1978). This interest in diversity has been recognized time and again by various courts. In *Red Lion Broadcasting v. FCC*, 395 U.S. 367, 390, 89 S.Ct. 1794, 1806, 23 L.Ed.2d 371 (1969), for example, the Supreme Court observed that

> [I]t is the purpose of the First Amendment to preserve an uninhibited marketplace of ideas in which truth will ultimately prevail, rather than to countenance monopolization of that market.

See also *New York Times Co. v. Sullivan*, 376 U.S. 254, 270, 84 S.Ct. 710, 720, 11 L.Ed.2d 686 (1964). Judge Learned Hand, speaking for the Court of Appeals for the Second Circuit, similarly noted that the media serve "one of the most vital of all general interests: the dissemination of news from as many different sources, and with as many different facets and colors as possible." *United States v. Associated Press*, 52 F.Supp. 362, 372 (S.D.N.Y. 1943), *aff'd*, 321 U.S. 1, 64 S.Ct 397, 88 L.Ed. 497 (1945).

The striving for diversity in sources of information has found expression not merely in the traditional and constitutional prohibition on control of news by government but also in some private contexts, notably in regard to the broadcast media. The Federal Communications Commission is charged by the Communications Act with granting broadcast licenses in the "public interest, convenience and necessity." 47 U.S.C. §§ 301, 303, 307, 309. Pursuant to that public interest standard, the Commission has time and again adopted rules designed to promote diversity among the broadcast media[a] These rules, and the

---

a. FCC policies prohibit formation or transfer of co-located newspaper-broadcast combinations (*FCC v. National Citizens Committee for Broadcasting, supra,* 436 U.S.

policies underlying them, have repeatedly been sustained by the Supreme Court and the Court of Appeals for this Circuit.

For example, in *United States v. Storer Broadcasting Co.*, 351 U.S. 192, 201–04, 76 S.Ct. 763, 769–771, 100 L.Ed. 1081 (1956), the Supreme Court, recognizing the importance of diversity and the authority of the FCC to determine the public interest, upheld rules placing limitations on the total number of broadcast stations a person may own or control. See also, *National Broadcasting Co. v. United States*, 319 U.S. 190, 63 S.Ct. 997, 87 L.Ed. 1344 (1943). Likewise, in *FCC v. National Citizens Committee for Broadcasting*, 436 U.S. 775, 98 S.Ct. 2096, 56 L.Ed.2d 697 (1978), the Court sustained regulations which banned the award or transfer of a broadcast license where there was a common ownership of a broadcast station and a daily newspaper located in the same locality, stating (436 U.S. at 801–02, 98 S.Ct. at 2115),

> ... the Commission has acted 'to enhance the diversity of information heard by the public....' The regulations are a reasonable means of promoting the public interest in diversified mass communications.

Certainly, the Court does not here sit to decide on the allocation of broadcast licenses. Yet, like the FCC, it is called upon to make a judgment with respect to the public interest and, like the FCC, it must make that decision with respect to a regulated industry and a regulated company.

In determining whether the proposed decree is in the public interest, the Court must take into account the decree's effects on other public policies, such as the First Amendment principle of diversity in dissemination of information to the American public. See Part II *supra*. Consideration of this policy is especially appropriate because, as the Supreme Court has recognized, in promoting diversity in sources of information, the values underlying the First Amendment coincide with the policy of the antitrust laws. *FCC v. National Citi-*

775, 98 S.Ct. 2096, 56 L.Ed.2d 697; common ownership of more than one broadcast station in the same area (47 C.F.R. §§ 73.35, 73.240, 73.636); operation of cable systems by a telephone company (47 C.F.R. § 63.54); and ownership of cable systems by a television network (47 C.F.R. § 74.1131).

zens Committee for Broadcasting, supra, 436 U.S. at 800, n. 18, 98 S.Ct. at 2114, n. 18.

Applying this diversity principle to the issue here under discussion, it is clear that permitting AT&T to become an electronic publisher will not further the public interest.

During the last thirty years, there has been an unremitting trend toward concentration in the ownership and control of the media. Diversity has disappeared in many areas; newspapers have gone out of business; others have merged; and much of the flow of news and editorial opinion appears more and more to be controlled and shaped by the three television networks and a handful of news magazines and metropolitan newspapers.

This concentration presents obvious dangers even today. Unless care is taken, both the concentration and the attendant dangers will be significantly increased by the new technologies. Indeed, it is not at all inconceivable that electronic publishing, with its speed and convenience will eventually overshadow the more traditional news media, and that a single electronic publisher would acquire substantial control over the provision of news in large parts of the United States. See also Part IV(A) *supra*.

The concentration that now exists in the media has presumably been brought about by impersonal economic and technological forces, and it is obviously beyond the concern of this or any other court. But the particular concentration that may emerge from the proposed decree is subject to the Court's jurisdiction in this antitrust case as part of the instant proceeding. Not only is AT&T a regulated company, and not only does the proceeding stem directly from serious charges of anticompetitive conduct, but the Court has been mandated not to approve the proposed decree unless it finds it to be in the public interest. AT&T's ability, described above, to use its control of the interexchange network to reduce or eliminate competition in the electronic publishing industry is the source of this threat to the First Amendment principle of diversity.

In sum, for a variety of reasons, the entry of AT&T into electronic publishing involves risks to the public interest that are greater than those which would be involved by that company's entry into other markets. Since under the Sherman Act, it is appropriate to bar a company from a market if the restriction is necessary to permit the development of competition in that market (*Ford Motor Co. v. United States, supra,* 405 U.S. at 577–78, 92 S.Ct. at 1151–52), and since First Amendment values, too, support a ban on electronic publishing by AT&T, the Court will require that the company be prohibited from entering that market.

At the same time, a prohibition on electronic publishing does not impose an undue burden on AT&T. The company is free to enter all the other computer, computer-related, and information services markets; and it will simply be barred from the creation or control of the information to be transmitted. AT&T may thus fulfill its traditional function of providing a delivery system for information which others wish to transmit, and it may also manufacture and market equipment for the electronic publishing industry and provide transmission services for other electronic publishers.

The restriction on electronic publishing—like any limitation on competition—should only remain in effect for the period necessary to establish conditions conducive to free and fair competition. Since it is not likely that the factors enumerated above which militate against AT&T's immediate entry into the electronic publishing market will continue to exist indefinitely, the Court will place a time limit on its prohibition. See *Ford Motor Co. v. United States, supra,* 405 U.S. at pp. 562, 575 n. 10, 92 S.Ct. at pp. 1142, 1150 n. 10, where the Court upheld an antitrust decree that prohibited Ford from entering the spark plug manufacturing business but limited that prohibition to a period of ten years.

Section VII of the proposed decree allows modifications to be made in its provisions upon the application of a party or an Operating Company. It is the intention of the Court to remove the prohibition on electronic publishing at the end of seven years from the entry of the decree should application for such removal be made pursuant to Section VII. That seven-year period should be sufficient for the development of electronic publishing as a viable industry, for the acquisition of sufficient strength by individual publishers adequate to permit them to compete, and for the development of means other than the AT&T network for the transmission of the messages of electronic publishers. During that same period, the new AT&T will also have acquired a track record with respect to behavior toward its competitors in other areas of the telecommunications business.

II. CONTENT RESTRICTION

Congress in 1988 enacted legislation that entirely prohibited obscene and indecent telephone transmissions.[10] The measure responded to "sexually-oriented pre-recorded messages (popularly known as 'dial-a-porn')" which were provided on special lines leased from the telephone company.[11] Although finding no constitutional barrier to the prohibition of obscene communications, since they are beyond the First Amendment's concern, the Supreme Court in *Sable Communications of California, Inc. v. Federal Communications Commission,* concluded that the indecency ban was unconstitutional.[12] In so doing, the Court distinguished private telephone communications from what it referred to as the uniquely pervasive nature of broadcasting, justifying indecency controls in that medium.[13] It also dismissed a suggested captive audience rationale and noted the affirmative acts required to obtain access to the service.[14] With respect to concerns about accessibility by children, the Court noted that FCC rules required use of credit cards, access codes, and scrambling devices.[15] Absent evidence of the effectiveness of that "technological approach," the Court concluded that the law represented "another case of 'burn[ing] up the house to roast the pig.' "[16] Justice Scalia, in a concurring opinion, noted that the constitution may foreclose the ban on indecent speech but does not "require[] public utilities to carry it."[17] Justice Brennan, for reasons stated in earlier decisions,[18] would have invalidated the prohibition with respect to obscene communications as well.

Sable Communications of California, Inc. v. Federal Communications Commission, 109 S.Ct. 2829 (1989)

Justice White delivered the opinion of the Court.

The issue before us is the constitutionality of § 223(b) of the Communications Act of 1934. 47 U.S.C. § 223(b). The statute, as amended in 1988, imposes an outright ban on indecent as well as obscene interstate commercial telephone messages. The District Court upheld the prohibition against obscene interstate telephone communications for commercial purposes, but enjoined the enforcement of the statute insofar as it applied to indecent messages. We affirm the District Court in both respects.

I

In 1983, Sable Communications, Inc., a Los Angeles-based affiliate of Carlin Communications, Inc., began offering sexually-oriented prerecorded telephone messages (popularly known as "dial-a-porn") through the Pacific Bell telephone network. In order to provide the messages, Sable arranged with Pacific Bell to use special telephone lines, designed to handle large volumes of calls simultaneously. Those who called the adult message number were charged a special fee. The fee was collected by Pacific Bell and divided between the phone company and the message provider. Callers outside the Los Angeles metropolitan area could reach the number by means of a long-distance toll call to the Los Angeles area code.

In 1988, Sable brought suit in District Court seeking declaratory and injunctive relief against enforcement of the recently amended § 223(b). The 1988 amendments to the statute imposed a blanket prohibition on indecent as well as obscene interstate commercial telephone messages. Sable brought this action to enjoin the FCC and the Justice Department from initiating any criminal investigation or prosecution, civil action or administrative proceeding under the statute. Sable also sought a declaratory judgment, challenging the indecency and the obscenity provisions of the amended § 223(b) as unconstitutional, chiefly under the First and Fourteenth Amendments to the Constitution....

...[I]n April 1988, Congress amended § 223(b) of the Communications Act to prohibit indecent as well as obscene interstate commercial telephone communications directed to any person regardless of age. The amended statute, which took effect on July 1, 1988, also eliminated the requirement that the FCC promulgate regulations for restricting access to minors since a total ban was imposed on dial-a-porn, making it illegal for adults, as well as children, to have access to the sexually explicit messages, Pub. L. 100–297, 102 Stat. 424. It was this version of the statute that was in effect when Sable commenced this action.

III

In the ruling at issue in No. 88–515, the District Court upheld § 223(b)'s prohibition of obscene telephone messages as constitutional. We agree with that judgment. In contrast to the prohibition on indecent communications, there is no constitutional barrier to the ban on obscene dial-a-porn recordings. We have repeatedly held that the protection of the First Amendment does not extend to obscene speech. See, e.g., *Paris Adult Theatre I v. Slaton*, 413 U.S. 49, 69 (1973). The case before us today does not require us to decide what is obscene or what is indecent but rather to determine whether Congress is empowered to prohibit transmission of obscene telephonic communications.

In its facial challenge to the statute, Sable argues that the legislation creates an impermissible national standard of obscenity, and that it places message senders in a "double bind" by compelling them to tailor all their messages to the least tolerant community.

We do not read § 223(b) as contravening the "contemporary community standards" requirement of *Miller v. California*, 413 U.S. 15 (1973). Section 223(b) no more establishes a "national standard" of obscenity than do federal statutes prohibiting the mailing of obscene materials, 18 U.S.C. § 1461, see *Hamling v. United States*, 418 U.S. 87 (1974) or the broadcasting of obscene messages, 18 U.S.C. § 1464. In *United States v. Reidel*, 402 U.S. 351 (1971), we said that Congress could prohibit the use of the mails for commercial distribution of materials properly classifiable as obscene, even though those materials were being distributed to willing adults who stated that they were adults. Similarly, we hold today that there is no constitutional stricture against Congress' prohibiting the interstate transmission of obscene commercial telephone recordings.

We stated in *United States v. 12 200-ft. Reels of Film*, 413 U.S. 123 (1973), that the *Miller* standards, including the "contemporary community standards" formulation, apply to federal legislation. As we have said before, the fact that "distributors of allegedly obscene materials may be subjected to varying community standards in the various federal judicial districts into which they transmit the materials does not render a federal statute unconstitutional because of the failure of application of uniform national standards of obscenity." *Hamling v. United States, supra,* at 106.

Furthermore, Sable is free to tailor its messages, on a selective basis, if it so chooses, to the communities it chooses to serve. While Sable may be forced to incur some costs in developing and implementing a system for screening the locale of incoming calls, there is no constitutional impediment to enacting a law which may impose such costs on a medium electing to provide these messages. Whether Sable chooses to hire operators to determine the source of the calls or engages with the telephone company to arrange for the screening and blocking of out-of-area calls or finds another means for providing messages compatible with community standards is a decision for the message provider to make. There is no constitutional barrier under *Miller* to prohibiting communications that are obscene in some communities under local standards even though they are not obscene in others. If Sable's audience is comprised of different communities with different local standards, Sable ultimately bears the burden of complying with the prohibition on obscene messages.

IV

In No. 88–525, the District Court concluded that while the government has a legitimate interest in protecting children from exposure to indecent dial-a-porn messages, § 223(b) was not sufficiently narrowly drawn to serve that purpose and thus violated the First Amendment. We agree....

Sexual expression which is indecent but not obscene is protected by the First Amendment; and the government does not submit that the sale of such materials to adults could be criminalized solely because they are indecent. The government may, however, regulate the content of constitutionally protected speech in order to promote a compelling interest if it chooses the least restrictive means to further the articulated interest. We have recognized that there is a compelling interest in protecting the physical and psychological well-being of minors. This interest extends to shielding minors from the influence of literature that is not obscene by adult standards. *Ginsberg v. New York*, 390 U.S. 629, 639–640 (1968); *New York v. Ferber*, 458 U.S. 747, 756–757 (1982). The government may serve this legitimate interest, but to withstand constitutional scrutiny, "it must do so by narrowly drawn regulations designed to serve those interests witout unnecessarily interfering with First Amendment freedoms. *Hynes v. Mayor of Oradello*, 425 U.S., at 620; *First National Bank of Boston v. Bellotti*, 435 U.S. 765, 786 (1978)." *Schaumberg v. Citizens for a Better Environment*, 444 U.S 620, 637 (1980). It is not enough to show that the government's ends arc compelling; the means must be carefully tailored to achieve those ends.

In *Butler v. Michigan*, 352 U.S. 380 (1957), a unanimous Court reversed a conviction under a statute which made it an offense to make available to the general public materials found to have a potentially harmful influence on minors. The Court found the law to be insufficiently tailored since it denied adults their free speech rights by allowing them to read only what was acceptable for children. As Justice Frankfurter said in that case, "Surely this is to burn the house to roast the pig." *Id.*, at 383. In our judgment, this case, like *Butler*, presents us with "legislation not reasonably restricted to the evil with which it is said to deal." *Ibid.*

In attempting to justify the complete ban and criminalization of the indecent commercial telephone communications with adults as well as minors, the government relies on *FCC v. Pacifica Foundation*, 438 U.S. 726 (1978), a case in which the Court considered whether the FCC has the power to regulate a radio broadcast that is indecent but not obscene. In an emphatically narrow holding, the *Pacifica* Court concluded that special treatment of indecent broadcasting was justified.

Pacifica is readily distinguishable from this case, most obviously because it did not involve a total ban on broadcasting indecent material. The FCC rule was not " 'intended to place an absolute prohibition on the broadcast of this type of language, but rather sought to channel it to times of day when children most likely would not be exposed to it.' " *Pacifica, supra,* at 733, quoting *Pacifica Foundation,* 59 F.C.C. 2d 892 (1976). The issue of a total ban was not before the Court. 438 U.S., at 750, n. 28.

The *Pacifica* opinion also relied on the "unique" attributes of broadcasting, noting that broadcasting is "uniquely pervasive," can intrude on the privacy of the home without prior warning as to program content, and is "uniquely accessible to children, even those too young to read." *Id.,* at 748–749. The private commercial telephone communications at issue here are substantially different from the public radio broadcast at issue in *Pacifica.* In contrast to public displays, unsolicited mailings and other means of expression which the recipient has no meaningful opportunity to avoid, the dial-it medium requires the listener to take affirmative steps to receive the communication. There is no "captive audience" problem here; callers will generally not be unwilling listeners. The context of dial-in services, where a caller seeks and is willing to pay for the communication, is manifestly different from a situation in which a listener does not want the received message. Placing a telephone call is not the same as turning on a radio and being taken by surprise by an indecent message. Unlike an unexpected outburst on a radio broadcast, the message received by one who places a call to a dial-a-porn service is not so invasive or surprising that it prevents an unwilling listener from avoiding exposure to it.

The Court in *Pacifica* was careful "to emphasize the narrowness of [its] holding." *Id.,* at 750. As we did in *Bolger v. Youngs Drug Products Corp.,* 463 U.S. 60 (1983), we distinguish *Pacifica* from the case before us and reiterate that "the government

may not 'reduce the adult population...to... only what is fit for children.' " 463 U.S., at 73, quoting *Butler v. Michigan, supra,* at 383.

The Government nevertheless argues that the total ban on indecent commercial telephone communications is justified because nothing less could prevent children from gaining access to such messages. We find the argument quite unpersuasive. The FCC, after lengthy proceedings, determined that its credit card, access code, and scrambling rules were a satisfactory solution to the problem of keeping indecent dial-a-porn messages out of the reach of minors. The Court of Appeals, after careful consideration, agreed that these rules represented a "feasible and effective" way to serve the Government's compelling interest in protecting children. 837 F. 2d, at 555.

The Government now insists that the rules would not be effective enough—that enterprising youngsters could and would evade the rules and gain access to communications from which they should be shielded. There is no evidence in the record before us to that effect, nor could there be since the FCC's implementation of § 223(b) prior to its 1988 amendment has never been tested over time. In this respect, the Government asserts that in amending § 223(b) in 1988, Congress expressed its view that there was not a sufficiently effective way to protect minors short of the total ban that it enacted. The Government claims that we must give deference to that judgment.

To the extent that the Government suggests that we should defer to Congress' conclusion about an issue of constitutional law, our answer is that while we do not ignore it, it is our task in the end to decide whether Congress has violated the Constitution. This is particularly true where the legislature has concluded that its product does not violate the First Amendment. "Deference to a legislative finding cannot limit judicial inquiry when First Amendment rights are at stake." *Landmark Communications, Inc. v. Virginia,* 435 U.S. 829, 843 (1978). The Government, however, also urges us to defer to the factual findings by Congress relevant to resolving the constitutional issue; it relies on *Walters v. National Association of Radiation Survivors,* 473 U.S. 305, 331 n. 12 (1985), and *Rostker v. Goldberg,* 453 U.S. 57, 72–73 (1981). Beyond the fact that whatever deference is due legislative findings would not foreclose our independent judgment of the facts bearing on an issue of constitutional law, our answer is that the congressional record contains no legislative findings that would justify us in concluding that there is no constitutionally acceptable less restrictive means, short of a total ban, to achieve the Government's interest in protecting minors.

There is no doubt Congress enacted a total ban on both obscene and indecent telephone communications. But aside from conclusory statements during the debates by proponents of the bill, as well as similar assertions in hearings on a substantially identical bill the year before, H.R. 1786, that under the FCC regulations minors could still have access to dial-a-porn messages, the Congressional record presented to us contains no evidence as to *how* effective or ineffective the FCC's most recent regulations were or might prove to be. It may well be that there is no fail-safe method of guaranteeing that never will a minor be able to access the dial-a-porn system. The bill that was enacted, however, was introduced on the floor; nor was there a committee report on the bill from which the language of the enacted bill was taken. No Congressman or Senator purported to present a considered judgment with respect to how often or to what extent minors could or would circumvent the rules and have access to dial-a-porn messages. On the other hand, in the hearings on H.R. 1786, the committee heard testimony from the FCC and other witnesses that the FCC rules would be effective and should be tried out in practice. Furthermore, at the conclusion of the hearing, the chairman of the subcommittee suggested consultation looking toward "drafting a piece of legislation that will pass constitutional muster, while at the same time providing for the practical relief which families and groups are looking for." Hearings, at 235. The bill never emerged from Committee.

For all we know from this record, the FCC's technological approach to restricting dial-a-porn messages to adults who seek them would be extremely effective, and only a few of the most enterprising and disobedient young people will manage to secure access to such messages. If this is the case, it seems to us that § 223(b) is not a narrowly tailored effort to serve the compelling interest of preventing minors from being exposed to indecent telephone messages. Under our precedents, § 223(b), in its present form, has the invalid effect of limiting the content of adult telephone conversations to that which is suitable for children to hear. It is another case of "burn[ing] up the house to roast the pig." *Butler v. Michigan*, 352 U.S., at 383.

Because the statute's denial of adult access to telephone messages which are indecent but not obscene far exceeds that which is necessary to limit the access of minors to such messages, we hold that the ban does not survive constitutional scrutiny.

Justice Scalia, concurring.

I note that while we hold the Constitution prevents Congress from banning indecent speech in this fashion, we do not hold that the Constitution requires public utilities to carry it.

Justice Brennan, with whom Justice Marshall and Justice Stevens join, concurring in part and dissenting in part.

I agree that a statute imposing criminal penalties for making, or for allowing others to use a telephone under one's control to make, any indecent telephonic communication for a commercial purpose is patently unconstitutional. I therefore join Parts I, II, and IV of the Court's opinion.

In my view, however, § 223(b)(1)(A)'s parallel criminal prohibition with regard to obscene commercial communications likewise violates the First Amendment. I have long been convinced that the exaction of criminal penalties for the distribution of obscene materials to consenting adults is constitutionally intolerable. In my judgment, "the concept of 'obscenity' cannot be defined with sufficient specificity and clarity to provide fair notice to persons who create and distribute sexually oriented materials, to prevent substantial erosion of protected speech as a byproduct of the attempt to suppress unprotected speech, and to avoid very costly institutional harms." *Paris Adult Theatre I v. Slaton*, 413 U.S. 49, 103 (1973) (Brennan, J., dissenting). To be sure, the Government has a strong interest in protecting children against exposure to pornographic material that might be harmful to them. *New York v. Ferber*, 458 U.S. 747,

775–777 (1982) (Brennan, J., concurring in judgment); *Ginsberg v. New York,* 390 U.S. 629 (1968). But a complete criminal ban on obscene telephonic messages for profit is "unconstitutionally overbroad, and therefore invalid on its face," as a means for achieving this end. *Miller v. California,* 413 U.S. 15, 47 (1973) (Brennan, J., dissenting).

The very evidence the Court adduces to show that denying adults access to all indecent commercial messages "far exceeds that which is necessary to limit the access of minors to such messages," *ante,* at 15, also demonstrates that forbidding the transmission of all obscene messages is unduly heavy-handed. After painstaking scrutiny, both the FCC and the Second Circuit found that "a scheme involving access codes, scrambling, and credit card payment is a feasible and effective way to serve this compelling state interest" in safeguarding children. *Carlin Communications, Inc. v. FCC,* 837 F.2d 546, 555, cert. denied, 488 U.S. ___ (1988). And during the 1987 Hearings on H.R. 1786, a United States Attorney speaking on behalf of the Justice Department described the FCC's proposed regulations as "very effective," because they would "dramatically reduc[e] the number of calls from minors in the United States, almost eliminating them." Telephone Decency Act of 1987; Hearings on H.R. 1786 before the Subcommittee on Telecommunications and Finance of the House Committee on Energy and Commerce, 100th Cong., 1st Sess., 231 (1987). In addition, as the Court notes, *ante,* at 13–14, no contrary evidence was before Congress when it voted to impose a total prohibition on obscene telephonic messages for profit. Hence, the Government cannot plausibly claim that its legitimate interest in protecting children warrants this draconian restriction on the First Amendment rights of adults who seek to hear the messages that Sable and others provide.

Section 223(b)(1)(A) unambiguously proscribes all obscene commercial messages, and thus admits of no construction that would render it constitutionally permissible. Because this criminal statute curtails freedom of speech far more radically than the Government's interest in preventing harm to minors could possibly license on the record before us, I would reverse the District Court's decision in No. 88–515 and strike down the statute on its face. Accordingly, I dissent from Part III of the Court's opinion.

If viewed strictly as a medium-focused decision, the consequent irony would be the elevation of editorial discretion for a medium with no pertinent First Amendment interest to a level higher than that afforded some constitutionally protected media. The result is understandable, however, on the grounds that it is the protected nature of the speech rather than the medium disseminating it which is dispositive. What is effectively demonstrated nonetheless is the interaction between speech and media that must be accounted for in factoring actual First Amendment guarantees.

NOTES _____

1. *See* United States v. American Telephone and Telegraph Co., 552 F.Supp. 131, 183–86 (D.D.C. 1982), *aff'd,* 460 U.S. 1001 (1983).

2. *See* Sable Communications of California, Inc. v. Federal Communications Commission, 109 S.Ct. 2829 (1989).

3. United States v. American Telephone and Telegraph Co. 552 F.Supp. at 181.

4. *Id.*

5. *Id.*

6. *Id.* at 182.

7. *Id.* at 183.

8. *Id. quoting* Associated Press v. United States, 326 U.S. 1, 20 (1945).

9. 552 F.Supp. at 185.

10. 47 U.S.C. § 223.

11. Sable Communications of California, Inc. v. Federal Communications Commission, 109 S.Ct. at 2832.

12. *Id.* at 2839.

13. *Id.* at 2837.

14. *Id.*

15. *Id.*

16. *Id.* at 2839, *quoting* Butler v. Michigan, 352 U.S. 380, 383 (1957).

17. *Id.* at 2840 (Scalia, J., concurring).

18. *Id.* at 2840–41 (Brennan, J., concurring). Justice Brennan's position, that obscenity is regulable only when the interests of unconsenting adults or children are present, is amplified in Chapter 2 of this book.

APPENDIXES

Appendix A

NEW TECHNOLOGIES

Broadcasting and cable are the dominant electronic media of their time. Although newer communications methodologies have emerged, their potentiality so far exceeds their actuality. This appendix identifies those media that have evolved at least to the point of capturing regulatory attention. Also noted are technologies which, although not independent means for disseminating information, enhance the process in one way or another.

I. SATELLITE MASTER ANTENNA SYSTEMS

The basic principle of satellite master antenna systems (SMATVs) is not unlike that of the early community antenna systems. An SMATV essentially is a mini-cable system which sets up a satellite receiving station in an office or residential complex and carries signals by wire to subscribers. The methodology differs from the larger cable systems only insofar as no public easements or rights of way are used. Although it functions side-by-side with locally franchised cable systems, SMATV has escaped comparable state and local regulation. Efforts to assert local control have been preempted by the FCC,

which "based its authority over SMATV upon the federal interest in 'the unfettered development of interstate transmission of satellite signals.' "[1] The commission itself has refused to impose restrictions upon the medium on the grounds "that open entry policies in the satellite field would create a more diverse and competitive telecommunications environment."[2] The FCC's preemption order was upheld by the court of appeals in *New York State Commission on Cable Television v. Federal Communications Commission.*[3]

II. HOME SATELLITE DISHES

Private reception of satellite signals is less a traditional medium than a way of intercepting signals for personal use. The FCC, in 1979, determined that the Communications Act did not mandate licensing of receive-only satellite dishes.[4] At that time, the devices were in use primarily in rural areas that were unserved or underserved by broadcasting or cable. Soon after the deregulatory order, however, the cost of the technology began to drop to the point that receive-only dishes became widely affordable. Their accessibility proved distressing to broadcasters and cable casters alike, who saw a segment of their respective audiences obtaining new programming minus commercials or a monthly fee. Responding to those concerns, the Cable Communications Policy Act of 1984 prohibits unauthorized reception of encrypted signals to the extent that they are marketed to the public.[5] The industry thus has commenced scrambling many of its signals to prevent unauthorized reception. The FCC's position is that, because encryption protects copyright and other economic concerns of programmers, it also serves the public interest.[6] Despite arguments that the cable industry has used its influence to make program services for home satellite dish owners artificially high, the FCC has concluded that no specific evidence of such practices exists and has recommended against regulation of home satellite program prices.[7]

III. MULTIPOINT DISTRIBUTION SERVICE

Multipoint distribution service (MDS) provides service especially in those areas that have yet to receive cable and sometimes where broadcasting is underdeveloped or inaccessible. MDS essentially transmits microwave signals that, upon being received, are converted to a lower television frequency and carried by wire to an empty VHF channel. Traditionally, MDS operators have been licensed as common carriers. When it began to expand service from general data transmission to program distribution, however, MDS attracted increasing interest from potential regulators. The FCC, with judicial approval, has preempted state and local regulation.[8] More recently, the commission altered MDS' status as a common carrier insofar as the actual nature of service provided may determine how the medium will be regarded.[9] Multichannel multipoint distribution service offers program diversification at a much lower start-up cost than and without

the lengthy construction process of cable. Although MDS cannot compete with cable in terms of the total number of channels offered, if has been touted as a needed source of competition for cable.

IV. DIRECT BROADCAST SATELLITES

Direct broadcast satellites (DBS) constitute communications technology that so far has failed to meet expectations. The concept of transmitting programming directly from studio to home is simple and attractive. The service would cover large geographical areas and reach areas that would be unprofitable for cable. In the early 1980s, the FCC set up a licensing process for DBS operators, required compliance with international standards, and for the most part governed the service under the broadcast provisions of the Communications Act of 1934.[10] Soon thereafter, international proceedings set aside a band for DBS, and specific assignments were made. So far, however, DBS has proved in large part economically infeasible because of the cost of launching satellites, the relatively lower price of cable service, and the inadequate subscriber base in areas that cable is unlikely to penetrate.[11]

NOTES

1. New York State Commission on Cable Television v. FCC, 749 F.2d 804, 808 (D.C.Cir. 1984), *citing* Earth Satellite Communications, Inc., 55 R.R.2d 1427, 1432 (1983).

2. 749 F.2d at 808, *citing* 55 R.R.2d at 1433.

3. 749 F.2d at 810.

4. Regulation of Domestic Receive-Only Satellite Earth Stations, 74 F.C.C.2d 205, 217–18 (1979). The conclusion, and consequent elimination of mandatory licensing, was premised upon statutory authority being limited to transmission. *Id., citing,* 47 U.S.C. §§ 153(cc), 153(d), and 301.

5. 47 U.S.C. § 605(a) and (b)

6. Scrambling of Satellite Television Signals, 2 F.C.C. Rcd. 1669, 1701 (1987).

7. Inquiry into the Scrambling of Satellite Televi-

sion Signals and Access to Those Signals by Owners of Home Satellite Dish Antennas, 3 F.C.C. Rcd. 1202, 1211 (1988).

8. New York State Commission on Cable Television v. Federal Communications Commission, 669 F.2d 58, 65–66 (2d Cir. 1982).

9. 47 C.F.R. § 21.900–908.

10. Inquiry into the Development of Regulatory Policy in Regard to Direct Broadcast Satellites for the Pe-

riod Following the 1983 Regulatory Administrative Radio Conference, 90 F.C.C. 2d 676, 709 (1982), *aff'd,* National Association of Broadcasters v. Federal Communications Commission, 740 F.2d 1190 (D.C.Cir. 1984).

11. Problems with respect to satellite development and usage within a world community are discussed in Wiessner, *The Public Order of the Geostationary Orbit,* 9 YALE J. WORLD PUB. ORDER 217 (1983).

Appendix B

COMMUNICATIONS ACT OF 1934

TITLE I—GENERAL PROVISIONS

§ 151. Purposes of chapter; Federal Communications Commission created

For the purpose of regulating interstate and foreign commerce in communication by wire and radio so as to make available, so far as possible, to all the people of the United States a rapid, efficient, Nation-wide, and world-wide wire and radio communication service with adequate facilities at reasonable charges, for the purpose of the national defense, for the purpose of promoting safety of life and property through the use of wire and radio communications, and for the purpose of securing a more effective execution of this policy by centralizing authority heretofore granted by law to several agencies and by granting additional authority with respect to interstate and foreign commerce in wire and radio communication, there is created a commission to be known as the "Federal Communications Commission," which shall be constituted as hereinafter provided, and which shall execute and enforce the provisions of this chapter....

§ 152. Application of chapter

(a) The provisions of this chapter shall apply to all interstate and foreign communication by wire or radio and all interstate and foreign transmission of energy by radio, which originates and/or is received within the United States, and to all persons engaged within the United States in such communication or such transmission of energy by radio, and to the licensing and regulating of all radio stations as hereinafter provided; but it shall not apply to persons engaged in wire or radio communication or transmission in the Canal Zone, or to wire or radio communication or transmission wholly within the Canal Zone. The provisions of this chapter shall apply with respect to cable service, to all persons engaged within the United States in providing such service, and to the facilities of cable operators which relate to such service, as provided in subchapter V-A of this chapter....

§ 154. Federal Communications Commission

(a) Number of commissioners; appointment; chairman

The Federal Communications Commission (in this chapter referred to as the "Commission") shall be composed of five commissioners appointed by the President, by and with the advice and consent of the Senate, one of whom the President shall designate as chairman....

(i) Duties and powers

The Commission may perform any and all acts, make such rules and regulations, and issue such orders, not inconsistent with this chapter, as may be necessary in the execution of its functions....

TITLE II—COMMON CARRIERS

§ 201.   *Service and charges*

(a) It shall be the duty of every common carrier engaged in interstate or foreign communication by wire or radio to furnish such communication service upon reasonable request therefor; and, in accordance with the orders of the Commission, in cases where the Commission, after opportunity for hearing, finds such action necessary or desirable in the public interest, to establish physical connections with other carriers, to establish through routes and charges applicable thereto and the divisions of such charges, and to establish and provide facilities and regulations for operating such through routes.

(b) All charges, practices, classifications, and regulations for and in connection with such communication service, shall be just and reasonable, and any such charge, practice, classification, or regulation that is unjust or unreasonable is declared to be unlawful: *Provided,* That communications by wire or radio subject to this chapter may be classified into day, night, repeated, unrepeated, letter, commercial, press, Government, and such other classes as the Commission may decide to be just and reasonable, and different charges may be made for the different classes of communications: *Provided further,* That nothing in this chapter or in any other provision of law shall be construed to prevent a common carrier subject to this chapter from entering into or operating under any contract with any common carrier not subject to this chapter, for the exchange of their services, if the Commission is of the opinion that such contract is not contrary to the public interest: *Provided further,* That nothing in this chapter or in any other provision of law shall prevent a common carrier subject to this chapter from furnishing reports of positions of ships at sea to newspapers of general circulation, either at a nominal charge or without charge, provided the name of such common carrier is displayed along with such ship position reports. The Commission may prescribe such rules and regulations as may be necessary in the public interest to carry out the provisions of this chapter.

§ 202.   *Discriminations and preferences*

(a) *Charges, services, etc.*

It shall be unlawful for any common carrier to make any unjust or unreasonable discrimination in charges, practices, classifications, regulations, facilities, or services for or in connection with like communication service, directly or indirectly, by any means or device, or to make or give any undue or unreasonable preference or advantage to any particular person, class of persons, or locality, or to subject any particular person, class of persons, or locality to any undue or unreasonable prejudice or disadvantage.

(b) *Charges or services included*

Charges or services, whenever referred to in this chapter, include charges for, or services in connection with, the use of common carrier lines of communication, whether derived from wire or radio facilities, in chain broadcasting or incidental to radio communication of any kind.

(c) *Penalty*

Any carrier who knowingly violates the provisions of this section shall forfeit to the United States the sum of $6,000 for each such offense and $300 for each and every day of the continuance of such offense....

§ 223.   *Obscene or harassing telephone calls in the District of Columbia or in interstate or foreign communications*

(a) Whoever—

(1) in the District of Columbia or in interstate or foreign communication by means of telephone—

(A) makes any comment, request, suggestion or proposal which is obscene, lewd, lascivious, filthy, or indecent;

(B) makes a telephone call, whether or not conversation ensues, without disclosing his identity and with intent to annoy, abuse, threaten, or harass any person at the called number;

(C) makes or causes the telephone of another repeatedly or continuously to ring, with intent to harass any person at the called number; or

(D) makes repeated telephone calls, during which conversation ensues, solely to harass any person at the called number; or

(2) knowingly permits any telephone facility under his control to be used for any purpose prohibited by this section,

shall be fined not more than $50,000 or imprisoned not more than six months, or both.

(b)(1) Whoever knowingly—

(A) in the District of Columbia or in interstate or foreign communication, by means of telephone, makes (directly or by recording device) any obscene communication for commercial purposes to any person, regardless of whether the maker of such communication placed the call; or

(B) permits any telephone facility under such person's control to be used for an activity prohibited by clause (i),

shall be fined in accordance with Title 18, or imprisoned not more than two years, or both.

(2) Whoever knowingly—

(A) in the District of Columbia or in interstate or foreign communication, by means of telephone, makes (directly or by recording device) any indecent communication for commercial purposes to any person, regardless of whether the maker of such communication placed the call; or

(B) permits any telephone facility under such person's control to be used for an activity prohibited by subparagraph a, shall be fined not more than $50,000 or imprisoned not more than six months, or both.

§ 224. *Pole attachments*

(a) *Definitions*

As used in this section:

(1) The term "utility" means any person whose rates or charges are regulated by the Federal Government or a State and who owns or controls poles, ducts, conduits, or rights-of-way used, in whole or in part, for wire communication. Such term does not include any railroad, any person who is cooperatively organized, or any person owned by the Federal Government or any State.

(2) The term "Federal Government" means the Government of the United States or any agency or instrumentality thereof.

(3) The term "State" means any State, territory, or possession of the United States, the District of Columbia, or any political subdivision, agency, or instrumentality thereof.

(4) The term "pole attachment" means any attachment by a cable television system to a pole, duct, conduit, or right-of-way owned or controlled by a utility.

(b) *Authority of Commission to regulate rates, terms, and conditions; enforcement powers; promulgation of regulations*

(1) Subject to the provisions of subsection (c) of this section, the Commission shall regulate the rates, terms, and conditions for pole attachments to provide that such rates, terms, and conditions are just and reasonable, and shall adopt procedures necessary and appropriate to hear and resolve complaints concerning such rates, terms, and conditions. For purposes of enforcing any determinations resulting from complaint procedures established pursuant to this subsection, the Commission shall take such action as it deems appropriate and necessary, including issuing cease and desist orders, as authorized by section 312(b) of this title.

(2) Within 180 days from February 21, 1978, the Commission shall prescribe by rule regulations to carry out the provisions of this section.

(c) *State regulatory authority over rates, terms, and conditions; preemption; certification; circumstances constituting State regulation*

(1) Nothing in this section shall be construed to apply to, or to give the Commission jurisdiction with respect to rates, terms, and conditions for pole attachments in any case where such matters are regulated by a State.

(2) Each State which regulates the rates, terms, and conditions for pole attachments shall certify to the Commission that—

(A) it regulates such rates, terms, and conditions; and

(B) in so regulating such rates, terms, and conditions, the State has the authority to consider and does consider the interests of the subscribers of cable television services, as well as the interests of the consumers of the utility services.

(3) For purposes of this subsection, a State shall not be considered to regulate the rates, terms, and conditions for pole attachments—

(A) unless the State has issued and made effective rules and regulations implementing the State's regulatory authority over pole attachments; and

(B) with respect to any individual matter, unless the State takes final action on a complaint regarding such matter—

(i) within 180 days after the complaint is filed with the State, or

(ii) within the applicable period prescribed for such final action in such rules and regulations of the State, if the prescribed period does not extend beyond 360 days after the filing of such complaint.

(d) Determination of just and reasonable rates; definition

(1) For purposes of subsection (b) of this section, a rate is just and reasonable if it assures a utility the recovery of not less than the additional costs of providing pole attachments, nor more than an amount determined by multiplying the percentage of the total usable space, or the percentage of the total duct or conduit capacity, which is occupied by the pole attachment by the sum of the operating expenses and actual capital costs of the utility attributable to the entire pole, duct, conduit, or right-of-way.

(2) As used in this subsection, the term "usable space" means the space above the minimum grade level which can be used for the attachment of wires, cables, and associated equipment.

TITLE III—PROVISIONS RELATING TO RADIO

§ 301. License for radio communication or transmission of energy

It is the purpose of this chapter, among other things, to maintain the control of the United States over all the channels of radio transmission; and to provide for the use of such channels, but not the ownership thereof, by persons for limited periods of time, under licenses granted by Federal authority, and no such license shall be construed to create any right, beyond the terms, conditions, and periods of the license. No person shall use or operate any apparatus for the transmission of energy or communications or signals by radio (a) from one place in any State, Territory, or possession of the United States or in the District of Columbia to another place in the same State, Territory, possession, or District; or (b) from any State, Territory, or possession of the United States, or from the District of Columbia to any other State, Territory, or possession of the United States; or (c) from any place in any State, Territory, or possession of the United States, or in the District of Columbia, to any place in any foreign country or to any vessel; or (d) within any State when the effects of such use extend beyond the borders of said State, or when interference is caused by such use or operation with the transmission of such energy, communications, or signals from within said State to any place beyond its borders, or from any place beyond its borders to any place within said State, or with the transmission or reception of such energy, communications or signals from and/or to places beyond the borders of said State; or (e) upon any vessel or aircraft of the United States (except as provided in section 303(t) of this title); or (f) upon any other mobile stations within the jurisdiction of the United States, except under and in accordance with this chapter and with a license in that behalf granted under the provisions of this chapter. . . .

§ 303. Powers and duties of Commission

Except as otherwise provided in this chapter, the Commission from time to time, as public convenience, interest, or necessity requires, shall—

(a) Classify radio stations;

(b) Prescribe the nature of the service to be rendered by each class of licensed stations and each station within any class;

(c) Assign bands of frequencies to the various classes of stations, and assign frequencies for each individual station and determine the power which each station shall use and the time during which it may operate;

(d) Determine the location of classes of stations or individual stations;

(e) Regulate the kind of apparatus to be used with respect to its external effects and the purity and sharpness of the emissions from each station and from the apparatus therein;

(f) Make such regulations not inconsistent with law as it may deem necessary to prevent interference between stations and to carry out the provisions of this chapter: *Provided, however,* That changes in the frequencies, authorized power, or in the times of operation of any station, shall not be made without the consent of the station licensee unless, after a public hearing, the Commission shall determine that such changes will promote public convenience or interest or will serve public necessity, or the provisions of this chapter will be more fully complied with;

(g) Study new uses for radio, provide for experimental uses of frequencies, and generally encourage the larger and more effective use of radio in the public interest;

(h) Have authority to establish areas or zones to be served by any station;

(i) Have authority to make special regulations applicable to radio stations engaged in chain broadcasting;

(j) Have authority to make general rules and regulations requiring stations to keep such records of programs, transmissions of energy, communications, or signals as it may deem desirable: ...

(m)(1) Have authority to suspend the license of any operator upon proof sufficient to satisfy the Commission that the licensee—

(A) has violated, or caused, aided, or abetted the violation of, any provision of any Act, treaty, or convention binding on the United States, which the Commission is authorized to administer, or any regulation made by the Commission under any such Act, treaty, or convention; or ...

(D) has transmitted superfluous radio communications or signals or communications containing profane or obscene words, language, or meaning, or has knowingly transmitted—

(1) false or deceptive signals or communications, or

(2) a call signal or letter which has not been assigned by proper authority to the station he is operating: or

(E) has willfully or maliciously interfered with any other radio communications or signals; or

(F) has obtained or attempted to obtain, or has assisted another to obtain or attempt to obtain, an operator's license by fraudulent means ...

(r) Make such rules and regulations and prescribe such restrictions and conditions, not inconsistent with law, as may be necessary to carry out the provisions of this chapter, or any international radio or wire communications treaty or convention, or regulations annexed thereto, including any treaty or convention insofar as it relates to the use of radio, to which the United States is or may hereafter become a party.

(s) Have authority to require that apparatus designed to receive television pictures broadcast simultaneously with sound be capable of adequately receiving all frequencies allocated by the Commission to television broadcasting when such appartus is shipped in interstate commerce; or is imported from any foreign country into the United States, for sale or resale to the public ...

§ 307. Licenses

(a) Grant

The Commission, if public convenience, interest, or necessity will be served thereby, subject to the limitations of this chapter, shall grant to any applicant therefor a station license provided for by this chapter.

(b) Allocation of facilities

In considering applications for licenses, and modifications and renewals thereof, when and insofar as there is demand for the same, the Commission shall make such distribution of licenses, frequencies, hours of operation, and of power among the several States and communities as to provide a fair, efficient, and equitable distribution of radio service to each of the same.

(c) Terms

No license granted for the operation of a television broadcasting station shall be for a longer term than five years and no license so granted for any other class of station (other than a radio broadcasting station) shall be for a longer term than ten years, and any license granted may be revoked as hereinafter provided. Each license granted for the operation of a radio broadcasting station shall be for a term of not to exceed seven years. The term of any license for the operation of any auxiliary broadcast station or equipment which can be used only in conjunction with a primary radio, television, or translator station shall be concurrent with the term of the license for such primary radio, television, or translator station. Upon the expiration of any license, upon application therefor, a renewal of such license may be granted from time to time for a term of not to exceed five years in the case of television broadcasting licenses, for a term of not to exceed seven years in the case of radio broadcasting station licenses, and for a term of not to exceed ten years in the case of other licenses, if the Commission finds that public interest, convenience, and necessity would be served thereby. In order to expedite action on applications for renewal of broadcasting station licenses and in order to avoid needless expense to applicants for such renewals, the Commission shall not require any such applicant to file any information which previously has been furnished to the Commission or which is not directly material to the considerations that affect the granting or denial of such application, but the Commission may require any new or additional facts it deems necessary to make its findings. Pending any hearing and final decision on such an application and the disposition of any petition for rehearing pursuant to section 405 of this title, the Commission shall continue such license in effect. Consistently with the foregoing provisions of this subsection, the Commission may by rule prescribe the period or periods for which licenses shall be granted and renewed for particular classes of stations, but the Commission may not adopt or follow any rule which would preclude it, in any case involving a station of a particular class, from granting or renewing a license for a shorter period than that prescribed for stations of such class if, in its judgment, public interest, convenience, or necessity would be served by such action.

§ 308. *Requirements for license...*

(b) Conditions

All applications for station licenses, or modifications or renewals thereof, shall set forth such facts as the Commission by regulation may prescribe as to the citizenship, character, and financial, technical, and other qualifications of the applicant to operate the station; the ownership and location of the proposed station and of the stations, if any, with which it is proposed to communicate; the frequencies and the power desired to be used; the hours of the day or other periods of time during which it is proposed to operate the station; the purposes for which the station is to be used; and such other information as it may require. The Commission, at any time after the filing of such original application and during the term of any such license, may require from an applicant or licensee further written statements of fact to enable it to determine whether such original application should be granted or denied or such license revoked. Such application and/or such statement of fact shall be signed by the applicant and/or licensee....

§ 309. *Application for license*

(a) Considerations in granting application

Subject to the provisions of this section, the Commission shall determine, in the case of each application filed with it to which section 308 of this title applies, whether the public interest, convenience, and necessity will be served by the granting of such application, and, if the Commission, upon examination of such application and upon consideration of such other matters as the Commission may officially notice, shall find that public interest, convenience, and necessity would be served by the granting thereof, it shall grant such application....

(d) Petition to deny application; time; contents; reply; findings

(1) Any party in interest may file with the Commission a petition to deny any application (whether as originally filed or as amended) to

which subsection (b) of this section applies at any time prior to the day of Commission grant thereof without hearing or the day of formal designation thereof for hearing; except that with respect to any classification of applications, the Commission from time to time by rule may specify a shorter period (no less than thirty days following the issuance of public notice by the Commission of the acceptance for filing of such application or of any substantial amendment thereof), which shorter period shall be reasonably related to the time when the applications would normally be reached for processing. The petitioner shall serve a copy of such petition on the applicant. The petition shall contain specific allegations of fact sufficient to show that the petitioner is a party in interest and that a grant of the application would be prima facie inconsistent with subsection (a) of this section. Such allegations of fact shall, except for those of which official notice may be taken, be supported by affidavit of a person or persons with personal knowledge thereof. The applicant shall be given the opportunity to file a reply in which allegations of fact or denials thereof shall similarly be supported by affidavit.

(2) If the Commission finds on the basis of the application, the pleadings filed, or other matters which it may officially notice that there are no substantial and material questions of fact and that a grant of the application would be consistent with subsection (a) of this section, it shall make the grant, deny the petition, and issue a concise statement of the reasons for denying the petition, which statement shall dispose of all substantial issues raised by the petition. If a substantial and material question of fact is presented or if the Commission for any reason is unable to find that grant of the application would be consistent with subsection (a) of this section, it shall proceed as provided in subsection (e) of this section.

(e) Hearings; intervention; evidence; burden of proof

If, in the case of any application to which subsection (a) of this section applies, a substantial and material question of fact is presented or the Commission for any reason is unable to make the finding specified in such subsection, it shall formally designate the application for hearing on the ground or reasons then obtaining and shall forth-

with notify the applicant and all other known parties in interest of such action and the grounds and reasons therefor, specifying with particularity the matters and things in issue but not including issues or requirements phrased generally. When the Commission has so designated an application for hearing, the parties in interest, if any, who are not notified by the Commission of such action may acquire the status of a party to the proceeding thereon by filing a petition for intervention showing the basis for their interest not more than thirty days after publication of the hearing issues or any substantial amendment thereto in the Federal Register. Any hearing subsequently held upon such application shall be a full hearing in which the applicant and all other parties in interest shall be permitted to participate. The burden of proceeding with the introduction of evidence and the burden of proof shall be upon the applicant, except that with respect to any issue presented by a petition to deny or a petition to enlarge the issues, such burdens shall be as determined by the Commission.

(h) Form and conditions of station licenses

Such station licenses as the Commission may grant shall be in such general form as it may prescribe, but each license shall contain, in addition to other provisions, a statement of the following conditions to which such license shall be subject: (1) The station license shall not vest in the licensee any right to operate the station nor any right in the use of the frequencies designated in the license beyond the term thereof nor in any other manner than authorized therein; (2) neither the license nor the right granted thereunder shall be assigned or otherwise transferred in violation of this chapter; (3) every license issued under this chapter shall be subject in terms to the right of use or control conferred by section 606 of this title.

(i) Certain initial licenses and permits; random selection procedure; significant preferences; rules

(1) If there is more than one application for any initial license or construction permit which will involve any use of the electromagnetic spectrum, then the Commission, after determining that each such application is acceptable for filing,

shall have authority to grant such license or permit to a qualified applicant through the use of a system of random selection.

(2) No license or construction permit shall be granted to an applicant selected pursuant to paragraph (1) unless the Commission determines the qualifications of such applicant pursuant to subsection (a) of this section and section 308(b) of this title. When substantial and material questions of fact exist concerning such qualifications, the Commission shall conduct a hearing in order to make such determinations. For the purpose of making such determinations, the Commission may, by rule, and notwithstanding any other provision of law—

(A) adopt procedures for the submission of all or part of the evidence in written form;

(B) delegate the function of presiding at the taking of written evidence to Commission employees other than administrative law judges; and

(C) omit the determination required by subsection (a) of this section with respect to any application other than the one selected pursuant to paragraph (1).

(3)(A) The Commission shall establish rules and procedures to ensure that, in the administration of any system of random selection under this subsection used for granting licenses or construction permits for any media of mass communications, significant preferences will be granted to applicants or groups of applicants, the grant to which of the license or permit would increase the diversification of ownership of the media of mass communications. To further diversify the ownership of the media of mass communications, an additional significant preference shall be granted to any applicant controlled by a member or members of a minority group.

(B) The Commission shall have authority to amend such rules from time to time to the extent necessary to carry out the provisions of this subsection. Any such amendment shall be made after notice and opportunity for hearing.

(C) For purposes of this paragraph:

(i) The term "media of mass communications" includes television, radio, cable television, multipoint distribution service, direct broadcast satellite service, and other services, the licensed facilities of which may be substantially devoted toward providing programming or other information services within the editorial control of the licensee.

(ii) The term "minority group" includes Blacks, Hispanics, American Indians, Alaska Natives, Asians and Pacific Islanders.

(4)(A) The Commission, not later than 180 days after September 13, 1982, shall, after notice and opportunity for hearing, prescribe rules establishing a system of random selection for use by the Commission under this subsection in any instance in which the Commission, in its discretion determines that such use is appropriate for the granting of any license or permit in accordance with paragraph (1).

(B) The Commission shall have authority to amend such rules from time to time to the extent necessary to carry out the provisions of this subsection. Any such amendment shall be made after notice and opportunity for hearing.

§ 310. *License ownership restrictions*

(a) *Grant to or holding by foreign government or representative*

The station license required under this chapter shall not be granted to or held by any foreign government or the representative thereof.

(b) *Grant to or holding by alien or representative, foreign corporation, etc.*

No broadcast or common carrier or aeronautical en route or aeronautical fixed radio station license shall be granted to or held by—

(1) any alien or the representative of any alien;

(2) any corporation organized under the laws of any foreign government;

(3) any corporation of which any officer or director is an alien or of which more than one-fifth of the capital stock is owned of record or voted by aliens or their representatives or by a foreign government or representative thereof or by any corporation organized under the laws of a foreign country;

(4) any corporation directly or indirectly controlled by any other corporation of which

any officer or more than one-fourth of the directors are aliens, or of which more than one-fourth of the capital stock is owned of record or voted by aliens, their representatives, or by a foreign government or representative thereof, or by any corporation organized under the laws of a foreign country, if the Commission finds that the public interest will be served by the refusal or revocation of such license. . . .

(d) Assignment and transfer of construction permit or station license

No construction permit or station license, or any rights thereunder, shall be transferred, assigned, or disposed of in any manner, voluntarily or involuntarily, directly or indirectly, or by transfer of control of any corporation holding such permit or license, to any person except upon application to the Commission and upon finding by the Commission that the public interest, convenience, and necessity will be served thereby. Any such application shall be disposed of as if the proposed transferee or assignee were making application under section 308 of this title for the permit or license in question; but in acting thereon the Commission may not consider whether the public interest, convenience, and necessity might be served by the transfer, assignment, or disposal of the permit or license to a person other than the proposed transferee or assignee.

§ 311. Requirements as to certain applications in the broadcasting service

(a) Notices of filing and hearing; form and contents

When there is filed with the Commission any application to which section 309(b)(1) of this title applies, for an instrument of authorization for a station in the broadcasting service, the applicant—

(1) shall give notice of such filing in the principal area which is served or is to be served by the station; and

(2) if the application is formally designated for hearing in accordance with section 309 of this title, shall give notice of such hearing in such area at least ten days before commencement of such hearing.

The Commission shall by rule prescribe the form and content of the notices to be given in compliance with this subsection, and the manner and frequency with which such notices shall be given. . . .

(c) Agreement between two or more applicants; approval of Commission; pendency of application

(1) If there are pending before the Commission two or more applications for a permit for construction of a broadcasting station, only one of which can be granted, it shall be unlawful, without approval of the Commission, for the applicants or any of them to effectuate an agreement whereby one or more of such applicants withdraws his or their applications or applications.

(2) The request for Commission approval in any such case shall be made in writing jointly by all the parties to the agreement. Such request shall contain or be accompanied by full information with respect to the agreement, set forth in such detail, form, and manner as the Commission shall require.

(3) The Commission shall approve the agreement only if it determines that (A) the agreement is consistent with the public interest, convenience, or necessity; and (B) no party to the agreement filed its application for the purpose of reaching or carrying out such agreement.

§ 311. Requirements as to certain applications in the broadcasting service . . .

(c) Agreement between two or more applicants; approval of Commission; pendency of application

(1) If there are pending before the Commission two or more applications for a permit for construction of a broadcasting station, only one of which can be granted, it shall be unlawful, without approval of the Commission, for the applicants or any of them to effectuate an agreement whereby one or more of such applicants withdraws his or their applications or applications.

(2) The request for Commission approval in any such case shall be made in writing jointly by all the parties to the agreement. Such request shall contain or be accompanied by full information with respect to the agreement, set forth in such detail, form, and manner as the Commission shall by rule require.

(3) The Commission shall approve the agreement only if it determines that (A) the agreement is consistent with the public interest, convenience, or necessity; and (B) no party to the agreement filed its application for the purpose of reaching or carrying out such agreement....

§ 312. *Administrative sanctions*

(a) *Revocation of station license or construction permit*

The Commission may revoke any station license or construction permit—

(1) for false statements knowingly made either in the application or in any statement of fact which may be required pursuant to section 308 of this title;

(2) because of conditions coming to the attention of the Commission which would warrant it in refusing to grant a license or permit on an original application;

(3) for willful or repeated failure to operate substantially as set forth in the license;

(4) for willful or repeated violation of, or willful or repeated failure to observe any provision of this chapter or any rule or regulation of the Commission authorized by this chapter or by a treaty ratified by the United States;

(5) for violation of or failure to observe any final cease and desist order issued by the Commission under this section;

(6) for violation of section 1304, 1343, or 1464 of Title 18; or

(7) for willful or repeated failure to allow reasonable access to or to permit purchase of reasonable amounts of time for the use of a broadcasting station by a legally qualified candidate for Federal elective office on behalf of his candidacy.

(b) *Cease and desist orders*

Where any person (1) has failed to operate substantially as set forth in a license, (2) has violated or failed to observe any of the provisions of this chapter, or section 1304, 1343, or 1464 of title 18, or (3) has violated or failed to observe any rule or regulation of the Commission authorized by this chapter or by a treaty ratified by the United States, the Commission may order such person to cease and desist from such action.

(c) *Order to show cause*

Before revoking a license or permit pursuant to subsection (a) of this section, or issuing a cease and desist order pursuant to subsection (b) of this section, the Commission shall serve upon the licensee, permittee, or person involved an order to show cause why an order of revocation or a cease and desist order should not be issued. Any such order to show cause shall contain a statement of the matters with respect to which the Commission is inquiring and shall call upon said licensee, permittee, or person to appear before the Commission at a time and place stated in the order, but in no event less than thirty days after the receipt of such order, and give evidence upon the matter specified therein; except that where safety of life or property is involved, the Commission may provide in the order for a shorter period. If after hearing, or a waiver thereof, the Commission determines that an order of revocation or a cease and desist order should issue, it shall issue such order, which shall include a statement of the findings of the Commission and the grounds and reasons therefor and specify the effective date of the order, and shall cause the same to be served on said licensee, permittee, or person....

(e) *Procedure for issuance of cease and desist order*

The provisions of section 558(c) of title 5 which apply with respect to the institution of any proceeding for the revocation of a license or permit shall apply also with respect to the institution, under this section, of any proceeding for the issuance of a cease and desist order.

(f) *Willful or repeated violations*

For purposes of this section:

(1) The term "willful", when used with reference to the commission or omission of any act, means the conscious and deliberate commission or omission of such act, irrespective of any intent to violate any provision of this chapter or any rule or regulation of the Commission authorized by this chapter or by a treaty ratified by the United States.

(2) The term "repeated", when used with reference to the commission or omission of any act, means the commission or omission of such act more than once or, if such commission or omission is continuous, for more than one day.

§ 313. *Application of antitrust laws to manufacture, sale, and trade in radio apparatus*

(a) *Revocation of licenses*

All laws of the United States relating to unlawful restraints and monopolies and to combinations, contracts, or agreements in restraint of trade are declared to be applicable to the manufacture and sale of and to trade in radio apparatus and devices entering into or affecting interstate or foreign commerce and to interstate or foreign radio communications. Whenever in any suit, action, or proceeding, civil or criminal, brought under the provisions of any of said laws or in any proceedings brought to enforce or to review findings and orders of the Federal Trade Commission or other governmental agency in respect of any matters as to which said Commission or other governmental agency is by law authorized to act, any licensee shall be found guilty of the violation of the provisions of such laws or any of them, the court, in addition to the penalties imposed by said laws, may adjudge, order and/or decree that the license of such licensee shall, as of the date the decree or judgment becomes finally effective or as of such other date as the said decree shall fix, be revoked and that all rights under such license shall thereupon cease: *Provided, however,* That such licensee shall have the same right of appeal or review as is provided by law in respect of other decrees and judgments of said court.

(b) *Refusal of licenses and permits*

The Commission is hereby directed to refuse a station license and/or the permit hereinafter required for the construction of a station to any person (or to any person directly or indirectly controlled by such person) whose license has been revoked by a court under this section.

§ 315. *Candidates for public office*

(a) *Equal opportunities requirement; censorship prohibition; allowance of station use; news appearances exception; public interest; public issues discussion opportunities*

If any licensee shall permit any person who is a legally qualified candidate for any public office to use a broadcasting station, he shall afford equal opportunities to all other such candidates for that office in the use of such broadcasting station: *Pro-vided,* That such licensee shall have no power of censorship over the material broadcast under the provisions of this section. No obligation is imposed under this subsection upon any licensee to allow the use of its station by any such candidate. Appearance by a legally qualified candidate on any—

(1) bona fide newscast,

(2) bona fide news interview,

(3) bona fide news documentary (if the appearance of the candidate is incidental to the presentation of the subject or subjects covered by the news documentary), or

(4) on-the-spot coverage of bona fide news events (including but not limited to political conventions and activities incidental thereto),

shall not be deemed to be use of a broadcasting station within the meaning of this subsection. Nothing in the foregoing sentence shall be construed as relieving broadcasters, in connection with the presentation of newscasts, news interviews, news documentaries, and on-the-spot coverage of news events, from the obligation imposed upon them under this chapter to operate in the public interest and to afford reasonable opportunity for the discussion of conflicting views on issues of public importance.

(b) *Broadcast media rates*

The charges made for the use of any broadcasting station by any person who is a legally qualified candidate for any public office in connection with his campaign for nomination for election, or election to such office shall not exceed—

(1) during the forty-five days preceding the date of a primary or primary runoff election and during the sixty days preceding the date of a general or special election in which such person is a candidate, the lowest unit charge of the station for the same class and amount of time for the same period; and

(2) at any other time, the charges made for comparable use of such station by other users thereof.

(c) *Definitions*

For purposes of this section—

(1) the term "broadcasting station" includes a community antenna television system; and

(2) the terms "licensee" and "station licensee" when used with respect to a community

antenna television system mean the operator of such system.

(d) Rules and regulations

The Commission shall prescribe appropriate rules and regulations to carry out the provisions of this section....

§ 317. *Announcement of payment for broadcast*

(a) Disclosure of person furnishing

(1) All matter broadcast by any radio station for which any money, service or other valuable consideration is directly or indirectly paid, or promised to or charged or accepted by, the station so broadcasting, from any person, shall, at the time the same is so broadcast, be announced as paid for or furnished, as the case may be, by such person: *Provided,* That "service or other valuable consideration" shall not include any service or property furnished without charge or at a nominal charge for use on, or in connection with, a broadcast unless it is so furnished in consideration for an identification in a broadcast of any person, product, service, trademark, or brand name beyond an identification which is reasonably related to the use of such service or property on the broadcast....

§ 325. *False, fraudulent, or unauthorized transmissions*

(a) False distress signals; rebroadcasting programs

No person within the jurisdiction of the United States shall knowingly utter or transmit, or cause to be uttered or transmitted, any false or fraudulent signal of distress, or communication relating thereto, nor shall any broadcasting station rebroadcast the program or any part thereof of another broadcasting station without the express authority of the originating station....

§ 326. *Censorship*

Nothing in this chapter shall be understood or construed to give the Commission the power of censorship over the radio communications or signals transmitted by any radio station, and no regulation or condition shall be promulgated or fixed by the Commission which shall interfere with the right of free speech by means of radio communication.

TITLE V—PENAL PROVISIONS— FORFEITURES

§ 501. *General penalty*

Any person who willfully and knowingly does or causes or suffers to be done any act, matter, or thing, in this chapter prohibited or declared to be unlawful, or who willfully and knowingly omits or fails to do any act, matter, or thing in this chapter required to be done, or willfully and knowingly causes or suffers such omission or failure, shall, upon conviction thereof, be punished for such offense, for which no penalty (other than a forfeiture) is provided in this chapter, by a fine of not more than $10,000 or by imprisonment for a term not exceeding one year, or both; except that any person, having been once convicted of an offense punishable under this section, who is subsequently convicted of violating any provision of this chapter punishable under this section, shall be punished by a fine of not more than $10,000 or by imprisonment for a term not exceeding two years, or both.

§ 502. *Violation of rules, regulations, etc.*

Any person who willfully and knowingly violates any rule, regulation, restriction, or condition made or imposed by the Commission under authority of this chapter, or any rule, regulation, restriction, or condition made or imposed by any international radio or wire communications treaty or convention, or regulations annexed thereto, to which the United States is or may hereafter become a party, shall, in addition to any other penalties provided by law, be punished, upon conviction thereof, by a fine of not more than $500 for each and every day during which such offense occurs.

§ 503. *Forfeitures*

(b) Activities constituting violations authorizing imposition of forfeiture penalty; amount of penalty; procedures applicable; persons subject to penalty; liability exemption period

(1) Any person who is determined by the Commission, in accordance with paragraph (3) or (4) of this subsection, to have—

    (A) willfully or repeatedly failed to comply substantially with the terms and conditions of any license, permit, certificate, or other instrument or authorization issued by the Commission;

(B) willfully or repeatedly failed to comply with any of the provisions of this chapter or of any rule, regulation, or order issued by the Commission under this chapter or under any treaty, convention, or other agreement to which the United States is a party and which is binding upon the United States;

(C) violated any provision of section 317(c) or 509(a) of this title; or

(D) violated any provision of section 1304, 1343, or 1464 of Title 18;

shall be liable to the United States for a forfeiture penalty. A forfeiture penalty under this subsection shall be in addition to any other penalty provided for by this chapter; except that this subsection shall not apply to any conduct which is subject to forfeiture under subchapter II of this chapter, part II or III of subchapter III of this chapter, or section 507 of this title.

(2)(A) If the violator is (i) a broadcast station licensee or permittee, (ii) a cable television operator, or (iii) an applicant for any broadcast or cable television operator license, permit, certificate, or other instrument or authorization issued by the Commission, the amount of any forfeiture penalty determined under this section shall not exceed $25,000 for each violation or each day of a continuing violation, except that the amount assessed for any continuing violation shall not exceed a total of $250,000 for any single act or failure to act described in paragraph (1) of this subsection.

(B) If the violator is a common carrier subject to the provisions of this chapter or an applicant for any common carrier license, permit, certificate, or other instrument of authorization issued by the Commission, the amount of any forfeiture penalty determined under this subection shall not exceed $100,000 for each violation or each day of a continuing violation, except that the amount assessed for any continuing violation shall not exceed a total of $1,000,000 for any single act or failure to act described in paragraph (1) of this subsection.

(C) In any case not covered in subparagraph (A) or (B), the amount of any forfeiture penalty determined under this subsection shall not exceed $10,000 for each violation or each day of a continuing violation, except that the amount assessed for any continuing violation shall not exceed a total of $75,000 for any single act or failure to act described in paragraph (1) of this subsection.

(D) The amount of such forfeiture penalty shall be assessed by the Commission, or its designee, by written notice. In determining the amount of such a forfeiture penalty, the Commission or its designee shall take into account the nature, circumstances, extent, and gravity of the violation and, with respect to the violator, the degree of culpability, any history of prior offenses, ability to pay, and such other matters as justice may require....

§ 509. *Prohibited practices in contests of knowledge, skill, or chance*

(a) *Influencing, prearranging, or predetermining outcome*

It shall be unlawful for any person, with intent to deceive the listening or viewing public—

(1) To supply to any contestant in a purportedly bona fide contest of intellectual knowledge or intellectual skill any special and secret assistance whereby the outcome of such contest will be in whole or in part prearranged or predetermined.

(2) By means of persuasion, bribery, intimidation, or otherwise, to induce or cause any contestant in a purportedly bona fide contest of intellectual knowledge or intellectual skill to refrain in any manner from using or displaying his knowledge or skill in such contest, whereby the outcome thereof will be in whole or in part prearranged or predetermined.

(3) To engage in any artifice or scheme for the purpose of prearranging or predetermining in whole or in part the outcome of a purportedly bona fide contest of intellectual knowledge, intellectual skill, or chance.

(4) To produce or participate in the production for broadcasting of, to broadcast or participate in the broadcasting of, to offer to a licensee for broadcasting, or to sponsor, any radio program, knowing or having reasonable ground for believing that, in connection with a purportedly bona fide contest of intellectual knowledge, intellectual skill, or chance constituting any part of such program, any person

has done or is going to do any act or thing referred to in paragraph (1), (2), or (3) of this subsection. . . .

TITLE VI—CABLE COMMUNICATIONS

§ 521. *Purposes*

The purposes of this subchapter are to—

(1) establish a national policy concerning cable communications;

(2) establish franchise procedures and standards which encourage the growth and development of cable systems and which assure that cable systems are responsive to the needs and interests of the local community;

(3) establish guidelines for the exercise of Federal, State, and local authority with respect to the regulation of cable systems;

(4) assure that cable communications provide and are encouraged to provide the widest possible diversity of information sources and services to the public;

(5) establish an orderly process for franchise renewal which protects cable operators against unfair denials of renewal where the operator's past performance and proposal for future performance meet the standards established by this subchapter; and

(6) promote competition in cable communications and minimize unnecessary regulation that would impose an undue economic burden on cable systems. . . .

§ 531. *Cable channels for public, educational, or governmental use*

(a) *Authority to establish requirements with respect to designation or use of channel capacity*

A franchising authority may establish requirements in a franchise with respect to the designation or use of channel capacity for public, educational, or governmental use only to the extent provided in this section.

(b) *Authority to require designation for public, educational, or governmental use*

A franchising authority may in its request for proposals require as part of a franchise, and may require as part of a cable operator's proposal for a franchise renewal, subject to section 546 of this title, that channel capacity be designated for public, educational, or governmental use, and channel capacity on institutional networks be designated for educational or governmental use, and may require rules and procedures for the use of the channel capacity designated pursuant to this section.

(c) *Enforcement authority*

A franchising authority may enforce any requirement in any franchise regarding the providing or use of such channel capacity. Such enforcement authority includes the authority to enforce any provisions of the franchise for services, facilities, or equipment proposed by the cable operator which relate to public, educational, or governmental use of channel capacity, whether or not required by the franchising authority pursuant to subsection (b) of this section.

(d) *Promulgation of rules and procedures*

In the case of any franchise under which channel capacity is designated under subsection (b) of this section, the franchising authority shall prescribe—

(1) rules and procedures under which the cable operator is permitted to use such channel capacity for the provision of other services if such channel capacity is not being used for the purposes designated, and

(2) rules and procedures under which such permitted use shall cease.

(e) *Editorial control by cable operator*

Subject to section 544(d) of this title, a cable operator shall not exercise any editorial control over any public, educational, or governmental use of channel capacity provided pursuant to this section. . . .

§ 532. *Cable channels for commercial use*

(a) *Purpose*

The purpose of this section is to assure that the widest possible diversity of information sources are made available to the public from cable systems in a manner consistent with growth and development of cable systems.

(b) Designation of channel capacity for commercial use

(1) A cable operator shall designate channel capacity for commercial use by persons unaffiliated with the operator in accordance with the following requirements:

(A) An operator of any cable system with 36 or more (but not more than 54) activated channels shall designate 10 percent of such channels which are not otherwise required for use (or the use of which is not prohibited) by Federal law or regulation.

(B) An operator of any cable system with 55 or more (but not more than 100) activated channels shall designate 15 percent of such channels which are not otherwise required for use (or the use of which is not prohibited) by Federal law or regulation.

(C) An operator of any cable system with more than 100 activated channels shall designate 15 percent of all such channels.

(D) An operator of any cable system with fewer than 36 activated channels shall not be required to designate channel capacity for commercial use by persons unaffiliated with the operator, unless the cable system is required to provide such channel capacity under the terms of a franchise in effect on October 30, 1984.

(E) An operator of any cable system in operation on October 30, 1984, shall not be required to remove any service actually being provided on July 1, 1984, in order to comply with this section, but shall make channel capacity available for commercial use as such capacity becomes available until such time as the cable operator is in full compliance with this section.

(c) Use of channel capacity by unaffiliated persons; editorial control; restriction on service

(1) If a person unaffiliated with the cable operator seeks to use channel capacity designated pursuant to subsection (b) of this section for commercial use, the cable operator shall establish, consistent with the purpose of this section, the price, terms and conditions of such use which are at least sufficient to assure that such use will not adversely affect the operation, financial condition, or market development of the cable system.

(2) A cable operator shall not exercise any editorial control over any video programming provided pursuant to this section, or in any other way consider the content of such programming, except that an operator may consider such content to the minimum extent necessary to establish a reasonable price for the commercial use of designated channel capacity by an unaffiliated person.

(3) Any cable system channel designated in accordance with this section shall not be used to provide a cable service that is being provided over such system on October 30, 1984, if the provision of such programming is intended to avoid the purpose of this section.

(d) Right of action in district court; relief; factors not to be considered by court

Any person aggrieved by the failure or refusal of a cable operator to make channel capacity available for use pursuant to this section may bring an action in the district court of the United States for the judicial district in which the cable system is located to compel that such capacity be made available. If the court finds that the channel capacity sought by such person has not been made available in accordance with this section, or finds that the price, terms, or conditions established by the cable operator are unreasonable, the court may order such system to make available to such person the channel capacity sought, and further determine the appropriate price, terms, or conditions for such use consistent with subsection (c) of this section, and may award actual damages if it deems such relief appropriate. In any such action, the court shall not consider any price, term, or condition established between an operator and an affiliate for comparable services.

(e) Petition to Commission; relief

(1) Any person aggrieved by the failure or refusal of a cable operator to make channel capacity available pursuant to this section may petition the Commission for relief under this subsection upon a showing of prior adjudicated violations of this section. Records of previous adjudications resulting in a court determination that the operator has violated this section shall be considered as

sufficient for the showing necessary under this subsection. If the Commission finds that the channel capacity sought by such person has not been made available in accordance with this section, or that the price, terms, or conditions established by such system are unreasonable under subsection (c) of this section, the Commission shall, by rule or order, require such operator to make available such channel capacity under price, terms, and conditions consistent with subsection (c) of this section.

(2) In any case in which the Commission finds that the prior adjudicated violations of this section constitute a pattern or practice of violations by an operator, the Commission may also establish any further rule or order necessary to assure that the operator provides the diversity of information sources required by this section.

(3) In any case in which the Commission finds that the prior adjudicated violations of this section constitute a pattern or practice of violations by any person who is an operator of more than one cable system, the Commission may also establish any further rule or order necessary to assure that such person provides the diversity of information sources required by this section.

(f) Presumption of reasonableness and good faith

In any action brought under this section in any Federal district court or before the Commission, there shall be a presumption that the price, terms, and conditions for use of channel capacity designated pursuant to subsection (b) of this section are reasonable and in good faith unless shown by clear and convincing evidence to the contrary....

(h) Cable service obscene, lewd, etc., or otherwise unprotected by Constitution

Any cable service offered pursuant to this section shall not be provided, or shall be provided subject to conditions, if such cable service in the judgment of the franchising authority is obscene, or is in conflict with community standards in that it is lewd, lascivious, filthy, or indecent or is otherwise unprotected by the Constitution of the United States.

§ 533. Ownership restrictions

(a) Persons owning or controlling television station licensees

It shall be unlawful for any person to be a cable operator if such person, directly or through 1 or more affiliates, owns or controls, the licensee of a television broadcast station and the predicted grade B contour of such station covers any portion of the community served by such operator's cable system.

(b) Common carriers; provision of direct video programming; exception; waiver

(1) It shall be unlawful for any common carrier, subject in whole or in part to subchapter II of this chapter, to provide video programming directly to subscribers in its telephone service area, either directly or indirectly through an affiliate owned by, operated by, controlled by, or under common control with the common carrier.

(2) It shall be unlawful for any common carrier, subject in whole or in part to subchapter II of this chapter, to provide channels of communications or pole line conduit space, or other rental arrangements, to any entity which is directly or indirectly owned by, operated by, controlled by, or under common control with such common carrier, if such facilities or arrangements are to be used for, or in connection with, the provision of video programming directly to subscribers in the telephone service area of the common carrier.

(3) This subsection shall not apply to any common carrier to the extent such carrier provides telephone exchange service in any rural area (as defined by the Commission).

(4) In those areas where the provision of video programming directly to subscribers through a cable system demonstrably could not exist except through a cable system owned by, operated by, controlled by, or affiliated with the common carrier involved, or upon other showing of good cause, the Commission may, on petition for waiver, waive the applicability of paragraphs (1) and (2) of this subsection. Any such waiver shall be made in accordance with section 63.56 of title 47, Code of Federal Regulations (as in effect September 20, 1984) and shall be granted by the Commission upon a finding that the issuance of

such waiver is justified by the particular circumstances demonstrated by the petitioner, taking into account the policy of this subsection.

(c) Promulgation of rules

The Commission may prescribe rules with respect to the ownership or control of cable systems by persons who own or control other media of mass communications which serve the same community served by a cable system.

(d) Regulation of ownership by States or franchising authorities

Any State or franchising authority may not prohibit the ownership or control of a cable system by any person because of such person's ownership or control of any media of mass communications or other media interests.

(e) Holding of ownership interests or exercise of editorial control by States or franchising authorities

(1) Subject to paragraph (2), a State or franchising authority may hold any ownership interest in any cable system.

(2) Any State or franchising authority shall not exercise any editorial control regarding the content of any cable service on a cable system in which such governmental entity holds ownership interest (other than programming on any channel designated for educational or governmental use), unless such control is exercised through an entity separate from the franchising authority....

§ *541. General franchise requirements*

(a) Authority to award franchises; construction of cable systems over rights-of-way and through easements; conditions for use of easements; equal access to service

(1) A franchising authority may award, in accordance with the provisions of this subchapter 1 or more franchises within its jurisdiction.

(2) Any franchise shall be construed to authorize the construction of a cable system over public rights-of-way, and through easements, which is within the area to be served by the cable system and which have been dedicated for compatible uses, except that in using such easements the cable operator shall ensure—

(A) that the safety, functioning, and appearance of the property and the convenience and safety of other persons not be adversely affected by the installation or construction of facilities necessary for a cable system;

(B) that the cost of the installation, construction, operation, or removal of such facilities be borne by the cable operator or subscriber, or a combination of both; and

(C) that the owner of the property be justly compensated by the cable operator for any damages caused by the installation, construction, operation, or removal of such facilities by the cable operator.

(3) In awarding a franchise or franchises, a franchising authority shall assure that access to cable service is not denied to any group of potential residential cable subscribers because of the income of the residents of the local area in which such group resides....

(c) Status of cable system as common carrier or utility

Any cable system shall not be subject to regulation as a common carrier or utility by reason of providing any cable service....

(e) State regulation of facilities serving subscribers in multiple dwelling units

Nothing in this subchapter shall be construed to affect the authority of any State to license or otherwise regulate any facility or combination of facilities which serves only subscribers in one or more multiple unit dwellings under common ownership, control, or management and which does not use any public right-of-way.

§ *542. Franchise fees*

(a) Payment under terms of franchise

Subject to the limitation of subsection (b) of this section, any cable operator may be required under the terms of any franchise to pay a franchise fee.

(b) Amount of fees per annum

For any twelve-month period, the franchise fees paid by a cable operator with respect to any cable system shall not exceed 5 percent of such cable operator's gross revenues derived in such period from the operation of the cable system. For purposes of this section, the 12-month period shall be the 12-month period applicable under the franchise for accounting purposes. Nothing in this subsection shall prohibit a franchising authority and a cable operator from agreeing that franchise fees which lawfully could be collected for any such 12-month period shall be paid on a prepaid or deferred basis; except that the sum of the fees paid during the term of the franchise may not exceed the amount, including the time value of money, which would have lawfully been collected if such fees had been paid per annum.

(c) Increases passed through to subscribers

A cable operator may pass through to subscribers the amount of any increase in a franchise fee, unless the franchising authority demonstrates that the rate structure specified in the franchise reflects all costs of franchise fees and so notifies the cable operator in writing....

(e) Decreases passed through to subscribers

Any cable operator shall pass through to subscribers the amount of any decrease in a franchise fee....

(g) "Franchise fee" defined

For the purposes of this section—

(1) the term "franchise fee" includes any tax, fee, or assessment of any kind imposed by a franchising authority or other governmental entity on a cable operator or cable subscriber, or both, solely because of their status as such;

(2) the term "franchise fee" does not include—

(A) any tax, fee, or assessment of general applicability (including any such tax, fee, or assessment imposed on both utilities and cable operators or their services but not including a tax, fee, or assessment which is unduly discriminatory against cable operators or cable subscribers);

(B) in the case of any franchise in effect on October 30, 1984, payments which are required by the franchise to be made by the cable operator during the term of such franchise for, or in support of the use of,

public, educational, or governmental access facilities;

(C) in the case of any franchise granted after October 30, 1984, capital costs which are required by the franchise to be incurred by the cable operator for public, educational, or governmental access facilities;

(D) requirements or charges incidental to the awarding or enforcing of the franchise, including payments for bonds, security funds, letters of credit, insurance, indemnification, penalties, or liquidated damages; or

(E) any fee imposed under Title 17.

(h) Uncompensated services; taxes, fees and other assessments; limitation on fees

(1) Nothing in this chapter shall be construed to limit any authority of a franchising authority to impose a tax, fee, or other assessment of any kind on any person (other than a cable operator) with respect to cable service or other communications service provided by such person over a cable system for which charges are assessed to subscribers but not received by the cable operator.

(2) For any 12-month period, the fees paid by such person with respect to any such cable service or other communications service shall not exceed 5 percent of such person's gross revenues derived in such period from the provision of such service over the cable system.

(i) Regulatory authority of Federal agencies

Any Federal agency may not regulate the amount of the franchise fees paid by a cable operator, or regulate the use of funds derived from such fees, except as provided in this section.

§ 543. Regulation of rates

(a) Limitation on regulatory power of Federal agencies, States, or franchising authorities

Any Federal agency or State may not regulate the rates for the provision of cable service except to the extent provided under this section. Any franchising authority may regulate the rates for the provision of cable service, or any other communications service provided over a cable system to cable subscribers, but only to the extent provided under this section.

(b) Promulgation of regulations; scope; contents; periodic review and amendment

(1) Within 180 days after October 30, 1984, the Commission shall prescribe and make effective regulations which authorize a franchising authority to regulate rates for the provision of basic cable service in circumstances in which a cable system is not subject to effective competition. Such regulations may apply to any franchise granted after the effective date of such regulations. Such regulations shall not apply to any rate while such rate is subject to the provisions of subsection (c) of this section.

(2) For purposes of rate regulation under this subsection, such regulations shall—

　(A) define the circumstances in which a cable system is not subject to effective competition; and

　(B) establish standards for such rate regulation.

(3) The Commission shall periodically review such regulations, taking into account developments in technology, and may amend such regulations, consistent with paragraphs (1) and (2), to the extent the Commission determines necessary.

(c) Regulation by franchising authority during initial two-year period

In the case of any cable system for which a franchise has been granted on or before the effective date of this subchapter, until the end of the 2-year period beginning on such effective date, the franchising authority may, to the extent provided in a franchise—

　(1) regulate the rates for the provision of basic cable service, including multiple tiers of basic cable service;

　(2) require the provision of any service tier provided without charge (disregarding any installation or rental charge for equipment necessary for receipt of such tier); or

　(3) regulate rates for the initial installation or the rental of 1 set of the minimum equipment which is necessary for the subscriber's receipt of basic cable service....

(e) Additional increases; reduction by amount of increase under franchise provisions

(1) In addition to any other rate increase which is subject to the approval of a franchising authority, any rate subject to regulation pursuant to this section may be increased after the effective date of this subchapter at the discretion of the cable operator by an amount not to exceed 5 percent per year if the franchise (as in effect on the effective date of this subchapter) does not specify a fixed rate or rates for basic cable service for a specified period or periods which would be exceeded if such increase took effect.

(2) Nothing in this section shall be construed to limit provisions of a franchise which permits a cable operator to increase any rate at the operator's discretion; however, the aggregate increases per year allowed under paragraph (1) shall be reduced by the amount of any increase taken such year under such franchise provisions.

Nothing in this subchapter shall be construed as prohibiting any Federal agency, State, or a franchising authority, from—

　(1) prohibiting discrimination among customers of basic cable service, or

　(2) requiring and regulating the installation or rental of equipment which facilitates the reception of basic cable service by hearing impaired individuals.

(f) Nondiscrimination; facilitation of reception by hearing-impaired individuals

Nothing in this title shall be construed as prohibiting any Federal agency, State, or a franchising authority, from—

　(1) prohibiting discrimination among customers of basic cable service, or

　(2) requiring and regulating the installation or rental of equipment which facilitates the reception of basic cable service by hearing impaired individuals....

§ 544. Regulation of services, facilities, and equipment

(a) Regulation by franchising authority

Any franchising authority may not regulate the services, facilities, and equipment provided by a cable operator except to the extent consistent with this subchapter.

(b)   Requests for proposals, establishment and enforcement of requirements

In the case of any franchise granted after the effective date of this subchapter the franchising authority, to the extent related to the establishment or operation of a cable system—

(1) in its request for proposals for a franchise (including requests for renewal proposals, subject to section 546 of this title), may establish requirements for facilities and equipment, but may not establish requirements for video programming or other information services; and

(2) subject to section 545 of this title, may enforce any requirements contained within the franchise—

(A) for facilities and equipment; and

(B) for broad categories of video programming or other services.

(c)   Enforcement authority respecting franchise effective under prior law

In the case of any franchise in effect on the effective date of this subchapter, the franchising authority may, subject to section 545 of this title, enforce requirements contained within the franchise for the provision of services, facilities, and equipment, whether or not related to the establishment or operation of a cable system.

(d)   Cable service obscene, indecent or otherwise unprotected by Constitution

(1) Nothing in this subchapter shall be construed as prohibiting a franchising authority and a cable operator from specifying, in a franchise or renewal thereof, that certain cable services shall not be provided or shall be provided subject to conditions, if such cable services are obscene or are otherwise unprotected by the Constitution of the United States.

(2)(A) In order to restrict the viewing of programming which is obscene or indecent, upon the request of a subscriber, a cable operator shall provide (by sale or lease) a device by which the subscriber can prohibit viewing of a particular cable service during periods selected by that subscriber....

(e)   Technical standards

The Commission may establish technical standards relating to the facilities and equipment of cable systems which a franchising authority may require in the franchise.

(f)   Limitation on regulatory powers of Federal agencies, States, or franchising authorities; exceptions

(1) Any Federal agency, State, or franchising authority may not impose requirements regarding the provision or content of cable services, except as expressly provided in this subchapter....

§ 545.   Modification of franchise obligations

(a)   Grounds for modification by franchising authority; public proceeding; time of decision

(1) During the period a franchise is in effect, the cable operator may obtain from the franchising authority modifications of the requirements in such franchise—

(A) in the case of any such requirement for facilities or equipment, including public, educational, or governmental access facilities or equipment, if the cable operator demonstrates that (i) it is commercially impracticable for the operator to comply with such requirement, and (ii) the proposal by the cable operator for modification of such requirement is appropriate because of commercial impracticability; or

(B) in the case of any such requirement for services, if the cable operator demonstrates that the mix, quality, and level of services required by the franchise at the time it was granted will be maintained after such modification.

(2) Any final decision by a franchising authority under this subsection shall be made in a public proceeding. Such decision shall be made within 120 days after receipt of such request by the franchising authority, unless such 120 day period is extended by mutual agreement of the cable operator and the franchising authority.

(b) Judicial proceedings; grounds for modification by court

(1) Any cable operator whose request for modification under subsection (a) of this section has been denied by a final decision of a franchising authority may obtain modification of such franchise requirements pursuant to the provisions of section 555 of this title.

(2) In the case of any proposed modification of a requirement for facilities or equipment, the court shall grant such modification only if the cable operator demonstrates to the court that—

(A) it is commercially impracticable for the operator to comply with such requirement; and

(B) the terms of the modification requested are appropriate because of commercial impracticability.

(3) In the case of any proposed modification of a requirement for services, the court shall grant such modification only if the cable operator demonstrates to the court that the mix, quality, and level of services required by the franchise at the time it was granted will be maintained after such modification.

(c) Rearrangement, replacement or removal of service

Notwithstanding subsections (a) and (b) of this section, a cable operator may, upon 30 days' advance notice to the franchising authority, rearrange, replace, or remove a particular cable service required by the franchise if—

(1) such service is no longer available to the operator, or

(2) such service is available to the operator only upon the payment of a royalty required under section 801(b)(2) of Title 17 which the cable operator can document

(A) is substantially in excess of the amount of such payment required on the date of the operator's offer to provide such service, and

(B) has not been specifically compensated for through a rate increase or other adjustment.

(d) Rearrangement of particular services from one service tier to another or other offering of service

Notwithstanding subsections (a) and (b) of this section, a cable operator may take such actions to rearrange a particular service from one service tier to another, or otherwise offer the service, if the rates for all of the service tiers involved in such actions are not subject to regulation under section 543 of this title.

(e) Requirements for services relating to public, educational, or governmental access

A cable operator may not obtain modification under this section of any requirement for services relating to public, educational, or governmental access.

(f) "Commercially impracticable" defined

For purposes of this section, the term "commercially impracticable" means, with respect to any requirement applicable to a cable operator, that it is commercially impracticable for the operator to comply with such requirement as a result of a change in conditions which is beyond the control of the operator and the nonoccurrence of which was a basic assumption on which the requirement was based.

§ 546. Renewal

(a) Commencement of proceedings; time; public notice and participation; purpose

During the 6-month period which begins with the 36th month before the franchise expiration, the franchising authority may on its own initiative, and shall at the request of the cable operator, commence proceedings which afford the public in the franchise area appropriate notice and participation for the purpose of—

(1) identifying the future cable-related community needs and interests; and

(2) reviewing the performance of the cable operator under the franchise during the then current franchise term.

(b) Submission of renewal proposals; contents; time

(1) Upon completion of a proceeding under subsection (a) of this section, a cable operator seeking renewal of a franchise may, on its own initiative or at the request of a franchising authority, submit a proposal for renewal.

(2) Subject to section 544 of this title, any such proposal shall contain such material as the franchising authority may require, including proposals for an upgrade of the cable system.

(3) The franchising authority may establish a date by which such proposal shall be submitted.

(c) Notice of proposal; renewal; preliminary assessment of nonrenewal; administrative review; issues; notice and opportunity for hearing; transcript; written decision

(1) Upon submittal by a cable operator of a proposal to the franchising authority for the renewal of a franchise, the franchising authority shall provide prompt public notice of such pro-

posal and, during the 4-month period which begins on the completion of any proceedings under subsection (a) of this section, renew the franchise or, issue a preliminary assessment that the franchise should not be renewed and, at the request of the operator or on its own initiative, commence an administrative proceeding, after providing prompt public notice of such proceeding, in accordance with paragraph (2) to consider whether—

(A) the cable operator has substantially complied with the material terms of the existing franchise and with applicable law;

(B) the quality of the operator's service, including signal quality, response to consumer complaints, and billing practices, but without regard to the mix, quality, or level of cable services or other services provided over the system, has been reasonable in light of community needs;

(C) the operator has the financial, legal, and technical ability to provide the services, facilities, and equipment as set forth in the operator's proposal; and

(D) the operator's proposal is reasonable to meet the future cable-related community needs and interests, taking into account the cost of meeting such needs and interests.

(2) In any proceeding under paragraph (1), the cable operator shall be afforded adequate notice and the cable operator and the franchise authority, or its designee, shall be afforded fair opportunity for full participation, including the right to introduce evidence (including evidence related to issues raised in the proceeding under subsection (a) of this section), to require the production of evidence, and to question witnesses. A transcript shall be made of any such proceeding.

(3) At the completion of a proceeding under this subsection, the franchising authority shall issue a written decision granting or denying the proposal for renewal based upon the record of such proceeding, and transmit a copy of such decision to the cable operator. Such decision shall state the reasons therefor.

(d) Basis for denial

Any denial of a proposal for renewal shall be based on one or more adverse findings made with respect to the factors described in subparagraphs (A) through (D) of subsection (c)(1) of this section, pursuant to the record of the proceeding under subsection (c) of this section. A franchising authority may not base a denial of renewal on a failure to substantially comply with the material terms of the franchise under subsection (c)(1)(A) of this section or on events considered under subsection (c)(1)(B) of this section in any case in which a violation of the franchise or the events considered under subsection (c)(1)(B) of this section occur after the effective date of this subchapter unless the franchising authority has provided the operator with notice and the opportunity to cure, or in any case in which it is documented that the franchising authority has waived its right to object, or has effectively acquiesced.

(e) Judicial review; grounds for relief

(1) Any cable operator whose proposal for renewal has been denied by a final decision of a franchising authority made pursuant to this section, or has been adversely affected by a failure of the franchising authority to act in accordance with the procedural requirements of this section, may appeal such final decision or failure pursuant to the provisions of section 555 of this title. . . .

§ 553.   Unauthorized reception of cable service

(a) Unauthorized interception or receipt or assistance in intercepting or receiving service; definition

(1) No person shall intercept or receive or assist in intercepting or receiving any communications service offered over a cable system, unless specifically authorized to do so by a cable operator or as may otherwise be specifically authorized by law.

(2) For the purpose of this section, the term "assist in intercepting or receiving" shall include the manufacture or distribution of equipment intended by the manufacturer or distributor (as the case may be) for unauthorized reception of any communications service offered over a cable system in violation of subparagraph (1).

(b) Penalties for willful violation

(1) Any person who willfully violates subsection (a)(1) of this section shall be fined not more than

$1,000 or imprisoned for not more than 6 months, or both.

(2) Any person who violates subsection (a)(1) of this section willfully and for purposes of commercial advantage or private financial gain shall be fined not more than $25,000 or imprisoned for not more than 1 year, or both, for the first such offense and shall be fined not more than $50,000 or imprisoned for not more than 2 years, or both, for any subsequent offense....

§ 555. *Judicial proceedings*

(a) Any cable operator adversely affected by any final determination made by a franchising authority under section 545 or 546 of this title may commence an action within 120 days after receiving notice of such determination, which may be brought in—

(1) the district court of the United States for any judicial district in which the cable system is located; or

(2) in any State court of general jurisdiction having jurisdiction over the parties.

(b) The court may award any appropriate relief consistent with the provisions of the relevant section described in subsection (a) of this section.

§ 556. *Coordination of Federal, State, and local authority*

(a) *Regulation by States, political subdivisions, State and local agencies, and franchising authorities*

Nothing in this subchapter shall be construed to affect any authority of any State, political subdivision, or agency thereof, or franchising authority, regarding matters of public health, safety, and welfare, to the extent consistent with the express provisions of this subchapter.

(b) *State jurisdiction with regard to cable services*

Nothing in this chapter shall be construed to restrict a State from exercising jurisdiction with regard to cable services consistent with this subchapter.

(c) *Preemption*

Except as provided in section 557 of this title, any provision of law of any State, political subdivision, or agency thereof, or franchising authority, or any provision of any franchise granted by such authority, which is inconsistent with this chapter shall be deemed to be preempted and superseded....

§ 558. *Criminal and civil liability*

Nothing in this subchapter shall be deemed to affect the criminal or civil liability of cable programmers or cable operators pursuant to the Federal, State, or local law of libel, slander, obscenity, incitement, invasions of privacy, false or misleading advertising, or other similar laws, except that cable operators shall not incur any such liability for any program carried on any channel designated for public, educational, governmental use or on any other channel obtained under section 532 of this title or under similar arrangements.

§ 559. *Obscene programming*

Whoever transmits over any cable system any matter which is obscene or otherwise unprotected by the Constitution of the United States shall be fined not more than $10,000 or imprisoned not more than 2 years, or both....

§ 605. *Unauthorized publication or use of communications*

(a) *Practices prohibited*

Except as authorized by chapter 119, Title 18, no person receiving, assisting in receiving, transmitting, or assisting in transmitting, any interstate or foreign communication by wire or radio shall divulge or publish the existence, contents, substance, purport, effect, or meaning thereof, except through authorized channels of transmission or reception, (1) to any person other than the addressee, his agent, or attorney, (2) to a person employed or authorized to forward such communication to its destination, (3) to proper accounting or distributing officers of the various communicating centers over which the communication may be passed, (4) to the master of a ship under whom he is serving, (5) in response to a subpena issued by a court of competent jurisdiction, or (6) on demand of other lawful authority. No person not being authorized by the sender shall intercept any radio communication and divulge or publish the existence, contents, substance, purport, effect, or meaning of such intercepted communication to any person. No person not being entitled thereto shall receive or assist in receiving any interstate or foreign communication by radio and use such communication (or any information therein contained) for his own benefit or for the benefit of another not entitled thereto. No person having received any intercepted radio communication or having become acquainted with the contents, substance, purport, effect, or meaning of such communication (or any part thereof) knowing that such communication was intercepted, shall divulge or publish the existence, contents, substance, purport, effect, or meaning of such communication (or any part thereof) or use such communication (or any information therein contained) for his own benefit or for the benefit of another not entitled thereto. This section shall not apply to the receiving, divulging, publishing, or utilizing the contents of any radio communication which is transmitted by any station for the use of the general public, which relates to ships, aircraft, vehicles, or persons in distress, or which is transmitted by an amateur radio station operator or by a citizens band radio operator.

(b) Exceptions

The provisions of subsection (a) of this section shall not apply to the interception or receipt by any individual, or the assisting (including the manufacture or sale) of such interception or receipt, of any satellite cable programming for private viewing if—

(1) the programming involved is not encrypted; and

(2)(A) a marketing system is not established under which—

(i) an agent or agents have been lawfully designated for the purpose of authorizing private viewing by individuals, and

(ii) such authorization is available to the individual involved from the appropriate agent or agents; or

(B) a marketing system described in subparagraph (A) is established and the individuals receiving such programming has obtained authorization for private viewing under that system.

(c) Scrambling of Public Broadcasting Service programming

No person shall encrypt or continue to encrypt satellite delivered programs included in the National Program Service of the Public Broadcasting Service and intended for public viewing by retransmission by television broadcast stations; except that as long as at least one unencrypted satellite transmission of any program subject to this subsection is provided, this subsection shall not prohibit additional encrypted satellite transmissions of the same program.

(d) Definitions

For purposes of this section—

(1) the term "satellite cable programming" means video programming which is transmitted via satellite and which is primarily intended for the direct receipt by cable operators for their retransmission to cable subscribers;

(2) the term "agent", with respect to any person, includes an employee of such person;

(3) the term "encrypt", when used with respect to satellite cable programming, means to transmit such programming in a form whereby the aural and visual characteristics (or both) are modified or altered for the purpose of preventing the unauthorized receipt of such programming by persons without authorized equipment which is designed to eliminate the effects of such modification or alteration;

(4) the term "private viewing" means the viewing for private use in an individual's dwelling unit by means of equipment, owned or operated by such individual, capable of receiving satellite cable programming directly from a satellite;

(5) the term "private financial gain" shall not include the gain resulting to any individual for the private use in such individual's dwelling unit of any programming for which the individual has not obtained authorization for that use; and

(6) the term "any person aggrieved" shall include any person with proprietary rights in the intercepted communication by wire or radio, including wholesale or retail distributors

of satellite cable programming, and, in the case of a violation of paragraph (4) of subsection (d) of this section shall also include any person engaged in the lawful manufacture, distribution, or sale of equipment necessary to authorize or receive satellite cable programming.

(e) Penalties; civil actions; remedies; attorney's fees and costs; computation of damages; regulation by State and local authorities

(1) Any person who willfully violates subsection (a) of this section shall be fined not more then $2,000 or imprisoned for not more than 6 months, or both.

(2) Any person who violates subsection (a) of this section willfully and for purposes of direct or indirect commercial advantage or private financial gain shall be fined not more than $50,000 or imprisoned for not more than 2 years, or both, for the first such conviction and shall be fined not more than $100,000 or imprisoned for not more than 5 years, or both, for any subsequent conviction.

(3)(A) Any person aggrieved by any violation of subsection (a) of this section or paragraph (4) of subsection (e) of this section may bring a civil action in a United States district court or in any other court of competent jurisdiction.

(B) The court—

(i) may grant temporary and final injunctions on such terms as it may deem reasonable to prevent or restrain violations of subsection (a) of this section;

(ii) may award damages as described in subparagraph (C); and

(iii) shall direct the recovery of full costs, including awarding reasonable attorneys' fees to an aggrieved party who prevails....

(f) Universal encryption standard

Within 6 months after November 16, 1988, the Federal Communications Commission shall initiate an inquiry concerning the need for a universal encryption standard that permits decryption of satellite cable programming intended for private viewing. In conducting such inquiry, the Commission shall take into account—

(1) consumer costs and benefits of any such standard, including consumer investment in equipment in operation;

(2) incorporation of technological enhancements, including advanced television formats;

(3) whether any such standard would effectively prevent present and future unauthorized decryption of satellite cable programming;

(4) the costs and benefits of any such standard on other authorized users of encrypted satellite cable programming, including cable systems and satellite master antenna television systems;

(5) the effect of any such standard on competition in the manufacture of decryption equipment; and

(6) the impact of the time delay associated with the Commission procedures necessary for establishment of such standards.

(g) Rulemaking for encryption standard

If the Commission finds, based on the information gathered from the inquiry required by subsection (f) of this section, that a universal encryption standard is necessary and in the public interest, the Commission shall initiate a rulemaking to establish such a standard.

TABLE OF CASES

TABLE OF AUTHORITIES

Articles excerpted in the text are indicated by italics.

Albert, Constitutional Regulation of Televised Violence, 64 Va. L. Rev. 1299 (1978), 487n.

Aman, SEC v. Lowe: Professional Regulation and the First Amendment, 1985 Sup. Ct. Rev. 93 (1985), 178n.

Ashdown, Gertz and Firestone: A Study in Constitutional Policy-Making, 61 Minn. L. Rev. 645 (1977), 163n.

Bagdikian, The Media Monopoly (1983), 183–85.

Barnes, The Cable Conspiracy, The Washington Monthly 12 (June 1983), 267–72, 286n.

Barnett, From New Technology to Moral Rights: Passive Carriers, Teletext, and Deletion as a Copyright Infringement, 31 *J. Copyright Soc'y.* 427 (1984), 168n.

Bazelon, FCC Regulation of the Telecommunications Press, 1975 Duke L. J. 213 (1975), 336n., 392–94, 483n.

Beard, The Sale, Rental, and Reproduction of Motion Picture Videocassettes: Piracy or Privilege? 15 N. Eng. L. Rev. 435 (1979 & 1980), 167n.

Berney, When Academic Freedom and Freedom of Speech Confront Holocaust Denial and Group Libel, 8 Cardozo L. Rev. 559 (1987), 162n.

Bickel, The Morality of Consent (1975), 486n.

Blackstone, Commentaries on the Laws of England (1872), 51n.

Blasi, Toward a Theory of Prior Restraint: The Central Linkage, 66 Minn. L. Rev. 11 (1981), 52n.

Bollinger, Freedom of the Press and Public Access: Toward a Theory of Partial Regulation of the Mass Media, 75 Mich. L. Rev. 1 (1976), 285n., 483n.

Botein and Pearce, A New York Case Study: The Competitiveness of the United States Telecommunications Industry, 6 Cardozo Arts & Ent. L. J. (1988), 318n.

Brandeis and Warren, The Right to Privacy, 4 Harv. L. Rev. 193 (1890), 49n., 164n., 323n., 485n.

Brennan, Address, 32 Rutgers L. Rev. (1979), 48n.

Brotman, Time to Pull the Cable?, Nat. L. J. 13 (December 18, 1989), 286n.

Caldwell, The Standard of Public Interest, Convenience or Necessity as Used in the Radio Act of 1927, 1 Air L. Rev. 295 (1930), 252n.

Cass, Commercial Speech, Constitutionalism, Collective Choice, 56 U. Cin. L. Rev. 1317 (1988), 167n.

Collins, The Local Service Concept in Broadcasting: An Evaluation and Recommendation

Mooney, Cross-Ownership Restrictions—The Cable View, 7 Comm. L. 20 (1989), 319n.

Murchison, Misrepresentation and the FCC, 37 Fed. Com. L. J. 403 (1985), 252n.

Nimmer, Introduction—Is Freedom of the Press a Redundancy? What Does It Add to Freedom of Speech? 26 Hastings L. J. 639 (1975), 49n.

Owen, Economics and Freedom of Expression (1975), 178n.

Pool, Technologies of Freedom, (1983), 323n.

Posner, The Federal Trade Commission, 37 U. Chicago L. Rev. 47 (1969), 51n.

Powe, American Broadcasting and the First Amendment (1987), 483n.

Powe, American Voodoo: If Television Doesn't Show It, Maybe It Won't Exist, 59 Tex. L. Rev. 879 (1981), 486n.

Price, Taming Red Lion: The First Amendment and Structural Approaches to Media Regulation, 31 Fed. Com. L. J. 215 (1979), 481n.

Prosser & Keeton on the Law of Torts (Stet 5th ed. 1985), 164nn.

Report of the Attorney General's Commission on Pornography (1986), 165n.

Report of the U.S. Commission on Obscenity and Pornography (1970), 165n.

Robinson, The FCC and the First Amendment: Observations on 40 Years of Radio and Television Regulation, 52 Minn. L. Rev. 67 (1967), 487n.

Schmidt, Freedom of the Press versus Public Access (1976), 513n.

Simmons, The Fairness Doctrine and the Media (1978), 484n.

Sims, Right of Publicity: Survivability Reconsidered, 49 Fordham L. Rev. 453 (1981), 164n.

Sodolski, Elimination of the Cross-Ownership Rules Would Serve the Public Interest and Benefit the Consumer, 7 Comm. L. 1 (1989), 319n.

Spitzer, Radio Formats by Administrative Choice, 47 U. Chi. L. Rev. 647 (1980), 255n.

Stewart, Or of the Press, 26 Hastings L. J. 631 (1975), 48n.

Sylvester, How the States Govern the News Media—A Survey of Selected Jurisdictions, 16 Sw. U.L. Rev. 723 (1986), 163n.

de Tocqueville, Democracy in America (1956) 49n.

Van Alstyne, The Mobius Strip of the First Amendment: Perspectives on Red Lion, 29 S.C. L. Rev. 539 (1978), 481n.

Watkins, Gertz and the Common Law of Defamation: Of Fault, Nonmedia Defendants and Conditional Privileges, 15 Tex. Tech. L. Rev. 823 (1984), 163n.

Weinberg, Questioning Broadcast Regulation, 86 Mich. L. Rev. 1269 (1988), 482n.

Weiss, Ostroff & Clift, Station License Revocations and Denials of Renewal, 1970–78, 24 J. Broadcasting 69 (1980), 256n.

Wiessner, The Public Order of the Geostationary Orbit: Blueprints for the Future, 9 *Yale J. World Pub. Ord.* 217 (1983), 529n.

Worthington, If It Ain't Broke, Don't Fix It, 9 Comm/ent L.J. 583 (1987), 314–15

Yudof, When Governments Speak: Toward a Theory of Government Expression and the First Amendment, 57 Tex. L. Rev. 563 (1979), 50n.

INDEX

About the Author

DONALD E. LIVELY is Visiting Professor of Law at St. Thomas University in Miami where he teaches and writes extensively on communications law. Professor Lively has published in many law reviews and journals and is recognized in particular for his contributions to First Amendment literature concerning the media.